PSYCHOLOGY

Sixth Edition

PSYCHOLOGY
THE SCIENCE OF BEHAVIOR

Neil R. Carlson
The University of Massachusetts

C. Donald Heth
The University of Alberta

Harold Miller
Brigham Young University

John W. Donahoe
The University of Massachusetts

William Buskist
Auburn University

G. Neil Martin
Middlesex University, UK

PEARSON
A and B

Boston   New York   San Francisco
Mexico City   Montreal   Toronto   London   Madrid   Munich   Paris
Hong Kong   Singapore   Tokyo   Cape Town   Sydney

Editor in Chief: Susan Hartman
Editorial Assistant: Deb Hanlon
Senior Development Editor: Sharon Geary
Executive Marketing Manager: Pamela Laskey
Senior Production Administrator: Donna Simons
Cover Administrator and Designer: Kristina Mose-Libon
Composition Buyer: Linda Cox
Manufacturing Buyer: Megan Cochran
Editorial Production Service: Kathy Smith, Nesbitt Graphics, Inc.
Electronic Composition: Nesbitt Graphics, Inc.
Interior Designer: Jerilyn Bockorick, Nesbitt Graphics, Inc.
Photo Researcher: Laurie Frankenthaler
Copy Editor: Jay Howland
Illustrator: Jay Alexander

For related titles and support materials, visit our online catalog at
www.ablongman.com

Between the time website information is gathered and then published, it is not unusual for some sites to have closed. Also, the transcription of URLs can result in typographical errors. The publisher would appreciate notification where these errors occur so that they may be corrected in subsequent editions.

Cataloging-in-Publication Data is on file at the Library of Congress

ISBN 0-205-47289-3

The photo credits appear on page 667, which constitutes an extension of the copyright page.

Printed in the United States of America

10   9   8   7   6   5   4   3   2   Q-WC-V   10   09   08   07   06

Dedications

From Neil R. Carlson

Dedicated to my wife, Mary.

From C. Donald Heth

Dedicated to Shannon and to Glenn, for the joy of our travels together.

From Harold Miller

Dedicated to Bill Buskist—prized student, prize-winning teacher,
and beneficent coauthor and friend.

From John W. Donahoe

Dedicated to my wife, Millie, and to our children, Kirk, Lisa, and Grant.

From William Buskist

Dedicated to the memory of my grandmother, Marion E. Short,
and my uncle, Dr. Kenneth Trout.

About the Authors

Neil R. Carlson, The University of Massachusetts

Neil Carlson is Professor Emeritus at the University of Massachusetts, Amherst. His research focused on the role of the limbic system in learning and species-typical behavior. He received his undergraduate degree and Ph.D. from the University of Illinois, Urbana. In addition to writing *Psychology: The Science of Behavior,* Dr. Carlson is also the author of two best-selling behavioral neuroscience textbooks—*Physiology of Behavior* (currently in its ninth edition) and *Foundations of Physiological Psychology* (currently in its sixth edition).

C. Donald Heth, The University of Alberta

Don Heth received his undergraduate degree at New College in Sarasota, Florida and his Ph.D. degree at Yale University. At the University of Alberta, Dr. Heth teaches introductory psychology courses and a fourth-year seminar to students in the honors program. He is an active researcher in the areas of human wayfinding and navigation, comparative spatial cognition, and models of eating disorders. Recently he has been involved with projects to describe lost person behavior and to develop computerized tools to manage this information in operational settings.

Harold Miller, Brigham Young University

Hal Miller has been a professor of psychology at BYU since 1985. He served as Dean of General and Honors Education from 1988 to 1993 and is a Karl G. Maeser General Education Professor. Dr. Miller's research interests include behavioral economics, evolutionary psychology, and educational reform. He is an associate editor of the *Journal of the Experimental Analysis of Behavior.* Dr. Miller received his Bachelor of Science degree from Arizona State University and his Ph.D. from Harvard University.

John W. Donahoe, The University of Massachusetts

John Donahoe is an Emeritus Professor in the Department of Psychology at the University of Massachusetts at Amherst. Dr. Donahoe is an active researcher in the area of learning and cognition and a long-time teacher of the introductory psychology course. He is an author of *Learning and Complex Behavior* (http://www.lcb-online.org) and *Neural-Network Models of Cognition: Biobehavioral Foundations.* Dr. Donahoe received a Ph.D. in experimental psychology with a subspecialty in neurophysiology from the Thomas Hunt Morgan School of Biological Sciences at the University of Kentucky.

William Buskist, Auburn University

William Buskist is the Distinguished Professor in the Teaching of Psychology at Auburn University and a Faculty Fellow at Auburn's Biggio Center for the Enhancement of Teaching and Learning. He has taught introductory psychology at Auburn for over 20 years. His primary research interests center on the behaviors and qualities of effective teachers, and he has published a large number of articles and books in the general area of the teaching of psychology. He is currently president-elect of the Society for the Teaching of Psychology (Division Two of the American Psychological Association) and will serve as president in 2007. He graduated with both his bachelor's and doctoral degrees from Brigham Young University.

G. Neil Martin, Middlesex University, UK

G. Neil Martin is Principal Lecturer in Psychology at Middlesex University, UK, and a Fellow of the Royal Society of Arts. He was educated in Wales, Scotland, and England, graduating with a first-class Masters of Arts degree in psychology from the University of Aberdeen, Scotland. He earned his Ph.D. in the psychophysiology of human olfactory perception at the University of Warwick. Dr. Martin wrote *Human Neuropsychology,* the first European textbook in the area, now in its second edition (Pearson Education, 2006), as well as *Essential Biological Psychology* (Hodder Arnold, 2003) and *Study Guide—Psychology* (Pearson Education, 2005) with Dr. Nicola Brunswick. With Dr. Brunswick, he was author of the first European on-line course in introductory psychology (Pearson Education, 2001, 2003), now in its third edition. He is the author of over 150 articles on psychology, serves on several editorial boards, and acts as consultant to industry, business, and the media on the psychology of olfaction and humor. Dr. Martin is lead author on the European edition of Carlson's *Psychology: The Science of Behavior.*

Brief Contents

Contents

3 Evolution, Heredity, and Behavior   54

4 Biology of Behavior   82

5 Learning and Behavior   122

6 Sensation   154

13 Motivation and Emotion 400

14 Personality 436

16 Lifestyles, Stress, and Health   508

17 The Nature and Causes of Mental Disorders   542

Preface

In this sixth edition of *Psychology: The Science of Behavior*, we have combined our talents, experience, and psychological perspectives to provide a more global perspective on the field of psychology than most introductory textbooks. We believe that this unique view offers students a more contemporary, balanced, and exciting overview of psychology than ever before.

Originally published 22 years ago, *Psychology: The Science of Behavior* has continued to evolve and improve, experiencing success with five U.S. editions, three adapted Canadian editions, two adapted European editions, as well as editions in Australia and New Zealand. The book continues to be published in many countries where English is a second language. The foundations of the text's strength and the reasons for the text's longevity, we believe, are the clarity of writing; the quality of coverage; and the distinctive behavioral, biological, and evolutionary approaches we take in introducing and explaining topics to the student.

As authors we all share a basic philosophy about the goals of psychology as an experimental and natural science, and we have challenged one another to sharpen and refine our thinking as well as our writing. In this text we have attempted to convey our own fascination with the pursuit of knowledge. We have tried to explain how psychologists go about discovering the causes of behavior and to point out the connections between behavior and its biological underpinnings. We have provided integrated findings across different subdisciplines to show the student that all of what we do as psychologists is related, even though different psychologists concern themselves with different phenomena or with different levels of analysis of these phenomena. One of the text's major themes is that behavior can best be understood in the context of its adaptive significance; our exploration of this theme effectively leads students through the discovery process and enables them to think critically about contemporary issues and their own experiences. The text continues to combine a scholarly survey of research with real-world applications of research results to problems that confront us today. Using the discovery method to take students inside the research process, we foster a critical understanding of the logic and significance of empirical findings. This approach is featured prominently in special Evaluating Scientific Issues sections.

A Word from Author Neil Carlson

"I have long believed that one of the most important approaches to the study of behavior is biological psychology.

After all, the brain is the organ responsible for all the phenomena that psychologists study—for example, perception, learning and memory, thinking and cognition, language, and emotion. And mental disorders are more than ever being understood as malfunctions of systems in the brain, caused by interactions between hereditary and environmental factors. Our knowledge of human brain functions has been expanding enormously as a result of studies using functional imaging, which permit us to see moment-to-moment activation of brain structures as volunteers perform various tasks. Advances in molecular genetics make it possible to investigate the role that genes play in the normal and abnormal development of brain mechanisms.

My coauthors and I made it our goal to show psychology as a lively and developing science. Basing the text on biology and behavior, we sought not only to describe the basic principles, but also to depict the process of research discovery in a way that was both scholarly and personally engaging.

Functional brain imaging, large-scale computer modeling, artificial resequencing of genetic material, and the other tools developed since the early 1980s have all extended the frontiers of psychology. But these developments only serve to remind us that we must understand the deeper implications of our discipline's discoveries. What does it mean to decode the brain's signals underlying intention and movement? Will the Human Genome Project provide a catalog of psychological traits with the same detail it gives for physical characteristics? Questions like these face us with much more immediacy than they did when this text first appeared. We hope we have provided a foundation for students to tackle these and other issues that they face in their study of psychology and in their lives."

Pedagogical Aids

After six editions, we believe that we have evolved a practical and efficient set of pedagogical features for an upper-level text. In this edition we have concentrated on increasing the effectiveness of the features rather than spinning off new elements that might distract the reader from the central material. Each chapter begins with a *preview* that gives students a survey of what the chapter discusses. These previews are designed both to engage students' interest and to present the scope of the chapter. The chapter preview is followed by an *opening vignette,* a lively narrative that illustrates phenomena covered in the chapter. As in previous editions, we have provided summaries where they will do the most good: immediately following a sizable chunk of material. Each chapter contains several of these *interim summaries,* found at the end of each major section. The summaries provide students with a chance to relax a bit and review what they have just read. Taken together, they provide a much longer summary than students would tolerate at the end of a chapter and will, we believe, serve them better. *Questions to consider,* designed to entice students to apply what they have learned to everyday issues, follow each interim summary. *Key terms* are highlighted and defined in the text and are listed alphabetically, with page references, at the end of each chapter so that a student can see at a glance what new vocabulary is being introduced and can quickly scan the terms to review for an exam. New to this edition is a complete *glossary* at the end of the book giving the definitions of all key terms. *Figure and table references* also are highlighted in the text to let students easily find their place after examining any given figure or table.

Each chapter of this edition contains two special features: a critical-thinking section called *Evaluating Scientific Issues* and a section called *Biology and Culture.* Examples of issues covered in Evaluating Scientific Issues include subliminal self-help media, hypnosis and criminal investigation, the existence of a language-acquisition device in the brain, "physiological" versus "psychological" drug addiction, the cancer-prone personality, and clinical versus actuarial diagnosis. The Biology and Culture sections highlight the interaction of biology (evolution, genetics, and physiology) and culture (learning, experience, and socialization) with examples from cross-cultural research. Examples of topics include ethnocentrism, the Deaf community, cultural contexts for remembering, and cultural differences in the definition of intelligence.

In addition, the *visual program* of the text has been revised to better highlight our biological and anatomical emphasis. We have again tapped the talents of Jay Alexander, the medical illustrator responsible for the successful art program in Carlson's *Physiology of Behavior* textbook. Jay has reviewed and updated the art program throughout this edition, creating a more vibrant, diverse, and contemporary presentation.

We hope you will find these study and review aids as well as the special features helpful to you as you study psychology.

Instructor Supplements

New! Instructor's Classroom Kit and CD-ROM, Volumes I and II

Our unparalleled Classroom Kit includes every instructional aid an introductory psychology professor needs to manage his or her course. We have made our resources even easier to use by placing all of our print supplements in two convenient volumes. Organized by chapter, each volume contains an Instructor's Manual, Test Bank, Grade Study Guide, and slides from the *Psychology: The Science of Behavior,* Sixth Edition, PowerPoint™ presentation. Electronic versions of the Instructor's Manual, Test Bank, Grade Aid Study Guide, PowerPoint™ presentations, images from the text, and video clips—all searchable by key terms—are made easily accessible to instructors on the accompanying Classroom Kit CD-ROMs.

Resources in the Instructor's Classroom Kit:

- *Instructor's Manual* Written for this edition by Jeffrey Green of Virginia Commonwealth University and Angelina MacKewn of University of Tennessee, Martin, this robust teaching resource can be used by first-time or experienced instructors. Included are at-a-glance organizational grids, handouts, detailed chapter outlines, lecture material, suggested reading and video sources, teaching objectives, and classroom activities and demonstrations.

- *Test Bank* Featuring more than 100 questions per chapter, the Test Bank includes multiple-choice, true/false, short answer, and essay questions, each coded with difficulty rating, page references, and answer justifications. The Test Bank was written for this edition by textbook coauthor Hal Miller of Brigham Young University. The Test Bank is also available in TestGen 5.5 computerized version, for use in personalizing tests.

- *Grade Aid Study Guide with Practice Tests* To help instructors integrate the Grade Aid Study Guide into their courses, we've included the study guide in the Classroom Kit. Developed by Hal Miller of Brigham Young University, one of the textbook authors, this comprehensive and interactive study guide encourages active reading and helps students engage with their textbook. Each chapter includes: "Before You Read," with a brief chapter summary and chapter learning objectives; "As You Read," a collection of demonstrations, activities, and exercises; "After You Read," containing three short practice quizzes and one comprehensive practice test; and "When You Have Finished," containing Web links for further information and crossword puzzles using key terms from the text. An appendix includes answers to all practice tests and crossword puzzles. This study guide is available as a stand-alone product for students as well.

- *PowerPoint™ Presentation* An exciting interactive tool for use in the classroom, the PowerPoint™ Presentation for *Psychology: The Science of Behavior* includes images from and key topics covered in the textbook. The PowerPoint™ is included on the Instructor's Classroom Kit CD-ROM; it can also be downloaded from our Instructor Resource Center at *www.ablongman.com.*

MyPsychLab

This interactive and instructive multimedia resource can be used to supplement a traditional lecture course or to administer a course entirely online. It is an all-inclusive tool: a text-specific e-book plus multimedia tutorials, audio, video, simulations, animations, and controlled assessment to completely engage students and reinforce learning. Fully customizable and easy to use, MyPsychLab meets the individual teaching and learning needs of every instructor and every student. Visit our site at *www.mypsychlab.com.*

Allyn & Bacon Introduction to Psychology Transparency Package, © 2007

The Transparency Kit includes approximately 230 full-color acetates to enhance classroom lecture and discussion—including images from all of Allyn & Bacon's Introduction to Psychology texts.

Allyn & Bacon Digital Media Archive for Introduction to Psychology, © 2007

New Publication! This comprehensive source includes still images from all of our Introduction to Psychology textbooks, Web links, and animations.

Insights into Psychology Video or DVD, Vol. I–IV

These video programs include two or three short clips per topic, covering such topics as animal research, parapsychology, language acquisition, Alzheimer's disease, bilingual education, genetics and IQ, and much more. A Video Guide containing critical-thinking questions accompanies each video. Also available on DVD.

The Blockbuster Approach: A Guide to Teaching Introductory Psychology with Video

The Blockbuster Approach is a unique print resource for instructors who enjoy enhancing their classroom presentations with film. With heavy coverage of general, abnormal, social, and developmental psychology, this guide suggests a wide range of films to use in class, and provides questions for reflection and other pedagogical tools to make the use of film more effective in the classroom.

New! Interactive Lecture Questions for Clickers

These lecture questions will jump-start exciting classroom discussions.

Course Management

Use these preloaded, customizable content and assessment items to teach your online courses. Available in CourseCompass, Blackboard, and WebCT formats.

Student Supplements

MyPsychLab—Student Version

This interactive and instructive multimedia resource is an all-inclusive tool: a text-specific e-book plus multimedia tutorials, audio, video, simulations, animations, and controlled assessment to completely engage students and reinforce learning. Easy to use, MyPsychLab meets the individual learning needs of every student. Visit our site at *www.mypsychlab.com.*

Grade Aid Study Guide with Practice Tests
Now included in MyPsychLab or available for separate purchase

Developed by coauthor Hal Miller of Brigham Young University, this comprehensive and interactive study guide includes for each chapter: "Before You Read," with a brief chapter summary and chapter learning objectives; "As You Read," a collection of demonstrations, activities, and exercises; "After You Read," containing three short practice quizzes and one comprehensive practice test; and "When You Have Finished," containing Web links for further information and crossword puzzles using key terms from the text. An appendix includes answers to all practice tests and crossword puzzles.

Tutor Center One-on-One Tutoring!
Now included in MyPsychLab or available for separate purchase

www.ablongman.com/tutorcenter/psych
A support service that's available when the instructor is not! Every copy of *Psychology: The Science of Behavior,* Sixth Edition, is packaged with access to the Tutor Center, providing free, high-quality one-on-one tutoring to students. Qualified tutors will answer questions students have about material in the text. The Tutor Center is open during peak study hours—in the late afternoon and evenings, 5:00 p.m. to midnight (Eastern Time), Sunday through Thursday during the academic year.

Research Navigator™
Now included in MyPsychLab or available for separate purchase

www.ablongman.com/researchnavigator
The easiest way for students to start a research assignment or research paper. Research Navigator™ helps students quickly and efficiently make the most of their research time and write better papers. The program provides extensive help with the research process and includes three exclusive databases of credible and reliable source material: EBSCO's ContentSelect Academic Journal Database, *The New York Times* Search by Subject Archive, and our own "Best of the Web" Link Library. The accompanying Research Navigator Guide (with access code) helps point students in the right direction as they explore the tremendous array of information on psychology available on the Internet.

Acknowledgments

We are delighted to present *Psychology: The Science of Behavior* and to have had the opportunity to collaborate with one another on this sixth edition. We hope that this textbook will spark further interest in the discipline of psychology and pave the way to greater understanding of human behavior.

This book has been the product of teamwork from its very beginning. Writing this edition has been an immensely pleasurable experience because of the help we have received from others.

We are especially pleased to acknowledge the remarkable team at Allyn & Bacon, which has consistently and strongly supported the concept of a sixth edition of the Carlson text. We thank Karon Bowers for her encouragement at the start of this edition and Susan Hartman, Editor in Chief, for her guidance through its later stages. Sharon Geary, Senior Development Editor, has supported us throughout the entire project with patience and humor. We would also like to thank Senior Production Administrator, Donna Simons, who skillfully ensured the quality, accuracy, and unique look of the text, and Kathy Smith, who guided us through the myriad requirements of production. And we thank Pamela Laskey for her marketing expertise in launching this edition.

Professors who write do so with an invisible audience listening to their words—the audience of previous classes and former students. We've had the good fortune to teach many fine students who, through their questions and observations, have shaped our teaching.

We've also had generous colleagues who reviewed our chapters and offered their advice. They are listed at the right. We offer great thanks to these dedicated instructors, who took time to review the text, provided helpful feedback, and allowed us to share in their classroom experiences and those of their students. Their contributions have improved the text, and we are indebted to each of them.

Deborah Wearing provided helpful reflections on the Chapter 1 vignette, and we gratefully acknowledge her input.

We end these comments by expressing the deepest appreciation to our spouses and our families. To our loved ones, who have tolerated the disruptions produced by our work and who have supported us during this project, goes our fondest acknowledgment.

Neil R. Carlson
C. Donald Heth
Harold Miller
John W. Donahoe
William Buskist
G. Neil Martin

Reviewers of the Sixth Edition

Ted A. Barker
Okaloosa Walton College

Daniel Barrett
Western Connecticut State University

Brian Carpenter
Washington University, St. Louis

Patrick J. Carroll
University of Texas at Austin

Philip Dunwoody
Juniata College

Rebecca Foushee
Fontbonne University

Gabriel Frommer
Indiana University

Peter J. Green
Barton College

Timothy Jay
Massachusetts College of Liberal Arts

Dr. Alan Lambert
Washington University

Lisa Lewen
Georgia Institute of Technology

Gregory Manley
University of Texas, San Antonio

David W. Martin
North Carolina State University

David G. McDonald
University of Missouri

Don Morgan
North Country Community College

LeShawndra N. Price
George Washington University

Joshua S. Redford
University of Buffalo

C. R. Snyder
University of Kansas

Al Witkofsky
Salisbury University

Nancy Woolf
University of California, Los Angeles

Nikki Yonts
Lyon College

Diana Younger
University of Texas–Permian Basin

To the Reader

This is a book about something that belongs to you. That's true in an obvious sense, given that this textbook describes the mechanisms of behavior that we, as humans, all share. You have inherited, through the intricate machinery of your ancestors' genes, a brain that once contemplated the African savannah and that now can comprehend the information age. You have also acquired, through your life's experiences, a tremendous store of knowledge and memories that affect your thoughts and emotions in ways distinctive just to you. Your psychology, in that sense, belongs to you.

But there is something else about this book that also belongs to you. Psychology is an international discipline, built by scholars around the world. It is part of the scientific knowledge of our civilization that you inherit.

There are some things you should know about the book before you start reading. Each chapter begins with a chapter outline and a brief overview of the material to be discussed. This overview tells you what to expect when you read the chapter and helps you keep track of your progress.

Because every discipline has its own vocabulary—and psychology is no exception—important terms are specially marked in the text. Each one is highlighted where its definition or description is given. These key terms are listed alphabetically at the end of each chapter, and succinct definitions are provided in the Glossary at the end of the book.

The book contains tables, figures (graphs, diagrams, and drawings), and photographs. They are there to illustrate important points, and in some cases to say something that cannot be said with words alone. To help you quickly find your place again once you've looked at them, figure and table references are highlighted like this: (See **Figure 5•10**).

Rather than presenting a long summary at the end of each chapter, we have provided interim summaries—reviews of the information that has just been presented. These summaries divide chapters into more easily managed chunks. When you reach an interim summary in your reading, take the opportunity to relax and think about what you have read. You might even want to take a five-minute break after reading the interim summary, then read it once again to remind yourself of what you just read, then go on to the next section. If you read the material this way, you will learn it with much less effort than you would otherwise have to expend.

The Grade Aid Study Guide that accompanies this text is an excellent aid to actively learning the material in the book. By thinking about and answering the study questions, you will be sure not to miss important points. In addition, each chapter in the study guide includes self-tests so you can assess your comprehension of the material.

Although this book has six authors and is a collaborative effort, each of us is ultimately responsible for his own chapters. You will see that we speak in the first person; we write "I" and "me" rather than "we" and "us." Each of us has illustrated points with examples from our own lives or from the lives of people we know, and these narratives demand personal pronouns. If you want to know which of us wrote a particular chapter, write to us and we will be happy to tell you.

We have not met you, but we feel as if we have been talking to you while working on this book. Writing is an "unsocial" activity in the sense that it is done alone. It can even be an antisocial activity when the writer must say, "No, I'm too busy writing to talk with you now." So as we wrote the book, we consoled ourselves by imagining that you were listening to us. You will get to meet us, at least vicariously, through our words as you read this book. If you then want to make the conversation two-way, please write or e-mail us: Neil Carlson, Department of Psychology, Tobin Hall, University of Massachusetts, Amherst, MA 01003, nrc@psych.umass.edu; Don Heth, Department of Psychology, University of Alberta, Edmonton, Alberta T6G 2E9, dheth@ualberta.ca; or Hal Miller, Department of Psychology, Brigham Young University, Provo, UT 84602, harold_miller@byu.edu. We hope to hear from you.

1

THE SCIENCE OF PSYCHOLOGY

What Is Psychology?

Explaining Behavior • The Goals of Psychological Research • Fields of Psychology

Psychology is the science of behavior, and psychologists try to explain behavior by discovering its causes. In addition, some psychologists try to apply the discoveries of psychological research to practical problems. Scientific psychology consists of many subfields, each investigating different types of behavior or searching for different types of causes.

The Rise of Psychology as a Science

Philosophical Roots of Psychology • Biological Roots of Psychology

The science of psychology is rooted in philosophy and biology. Philosophers developed the principles of materialism and empiricism, which made it possible to conceive of studying the human mind and, eventually, behavior. Biologists developed experimental methods that enabled us to study the brain and discover its role in the control of behavior.

Major Trends in the Development of Psychology

Structuralism • Functionalism • Freud's Psychodynamic Theory • Psychology in Transition • Behaviorism • Humanistic Psychology • Reaction against Behaviorism: The Cognitive Revolution • The Biological Revolution

The first laboratory of experimental psychology was established by Wilhelm Wundt in Germany in 1879. Wundt's structuralism was soon abandoned, but other laboratories developed new methods to study the causes of behavior. Charles Darwin's principle of natural selection led to the development of functionalism, which in turn inspired the development of behaviorism, a movement in psychology that insisted that only observable behavior could be studied scientifically. Sigmund Freud's psychodynamic theory and humanistic psychologists have had wide appeal with the general public. More recently, cognitive psychologists have restored an emphasis on the study of mental processes. New developments in the research methods of neurobiology have strengthened the biological emphasis in psychological research.

I like to begin my introductory psychology course with a discussion of the big issues behind the topics of the term. Several years ago, I decided to use a television documentary about Clive Wearing, a noted expert on Renaissance and contemporary music. At the peak of his career, Wearing suffered a brain infection that left him unable to remember anything new or recall any episodes from his past. The film is a powerful demonstration of the role of memory in our lives and what happens when crucial areas of our brain are damaged. It would, I thought, be a good introduction to the term.

The documentary follows Wearing's wife Deborah as she visits him. As she enters his hospital room, Wearing joyfully rushes to greet her and tells her he loves her. And then, most startlingly, he claims never to have seen her since his illness. It is, Deborah tells the camera, a symptom of his brain's damage. Wearing feels, all the time, as if he has woken up just that minute from unconsciousness and is truly awake for the first time since his illness. He relives this experience every waking moment when his thoughts are not elsewhere. The film chronicles the impact of this extremely dense amnesia on Wearing's life. For example, he knows that he was a conductor but cannot recall conducting any specific concert; yet, when asked to conduct his choir for the documentary, he read the music, recognizing it as a piece familiar to him and directed the singers with professional ease.

In the documentary, Wearing's condition seems to make him very angry and frustrated. He did not remember anything about Deborah's life, but he hugs her every time she enters his room.

I had intended to use this film as a way of talking about what makes us human. As you will see as you read the chapters that follow, our behaviors reveal complexities of language, decision making, learning, memory, and the like. Are we, I planned to ask my class when the film finished, any less human when these capacities fail? Clive Wearing's case makes this question all the more poignant.

But as the film screened in class, something Deborah said arrested me: "The most important thing in his life . . . is his love for me." I realized then, as I hadn't when I had previewed the documentary, that the story is just as much Deborah's as it is Clive's: how she interprets his greetings, his moods, and his constant denials that he has recently met her.

Clive Wearing and his wife, Deborah, on their wedding day in 1983.

We were going to discuss that day in class how psychology has developed as a science. I had intended to trace how writers and scientists had thought about the human mind over four centuries of speculation. They had pointed to issues of philosophy and natural history and had related psychology to them. My lesson plan for that day had been to show how these different interpretations fit together and provide us with a concept of human nature. But Deborah Wearing's observation struck me with the straightforward yet profound questions it added to my earlier ones: With his memory and span of consciousness so affected, what is the source of Clive's feelings toward Deborah? And what enables her to recognize these in return?

The film finished and I decided to change my opening question. I turned to the class and asked them: Is Wearing the same person he was when he married Deborah?

Here are two facts about the world you live in:

- There is a man whose otherwise normal life is disturbed at night, when he will suddenly leap from his bed and prowl around his bedroom growling like a lion, his fingers curled into claws. In the morning he remembers nothing of these episodes.

- When atoms are placed in a strong magnetic field, the axes around which their electrons spin become aligned with that magnetic field. If a radio pulse is directed at the atoms, they will wobble like spinning tops and then return to their alignment. It takes different amounts of time for atoms of different elements to realign.

When you entered college, you undoubtedly expected to learn about such facts and to understand how they relate to other, similar facts. But when you entered a course in psychology, you may not have expected to encounter facts as different as these two in the same textbook. Nevertheless, both of these facts are of interest to psychologists.

What does it mean to be a psychologist? If you asked your fellow students this question, you would receive several different answers. In fact, if you asked this question of several psychologists, you would still receive more than one answer. Psychologists are probably the most diverse group of people in our society to share the same title. The Bureau of Labor Statistics estimated that psychologists held about 106,000 jobs in 2004, with about 30,000 more employed as professors at colleges and universities across the United States (Bureau of Labor Statistics, 2004). Psychologists engage in research, teaching, counseling, and psychotherapy; they advise industry and governmental agencies about personnel matters, the design of products, advertising and marketing, and legislation; they devise and administer tests of personality, achievement, and ability. Psychologists study a wide variety of phenomena, including physiological processes within the nervous system, genetics, environmental events, personality characteristics, mental abilities, and social interactions. And yet psychology is a new discipline; the first person who ever

▲ *The research interests of psychologists vary widely. One researcher might be interested in the origins of aggression; another might be interested in childhood memory. Psychologists seek answers to innumerable research questions through the study of behavior.*

called himself a "psychologist" was still alive in 1920, and professors he trained lived into the 1960s and 1970s.

To my coauthors and me, psychology is exciting partly because it is so diverse and is changing so rapidly. But these aspects of the field may sometimes be confusing to you, a student faced with understanding this large and complex discipline. So this first chapter will give you an overview of what it means to be a psychologist. The chapter will describe the nature of psychology, its goals, and its history.

What Is Psychology?

In this book we will study the science of **psychology**—a science with a special focus on behavior. The primary emphasis is on discovering and explaining the causes of behavior; for example, Clive Wearing's behavior is the means by which his doctors can understand the physical damage his brain has suffered. Of course, the book will describe the applications of these discoveries to the treatment of mental disorders and the improvement of society—but the focus will be on the way psychologists discover the facts that make these applications

possible. This is an important guide to understanding psychology as a science. As you read this book, you should concentrate on how this process of discovery works.

To help you, I should make a key distinction. The word *psychology* comes from two Greek words, *psukhe,* meaning "breath" or "soul," and *logos,* meaning "word" or "reason." The modern meaning of *psycho-* is "mind" and the modern meaning of *-logy* is "science"; thus, the word *psychology* literally means "the science of the mind." But this is a little bit misleading. As the title of this book indicates, and as I just stated, psychology is the science of *behavior.* The difference can be traced to the way psychologists have thought about the mind. Early in the development of psychology, people conceived of the mind as an independent, free-floating spirit. Later, they described it as a characteristic of a functioning brain whose ultimate role was to control behavior. Thus, the focus turned from the mind, which cannot be directly observed, to behavior, which can. And because the brain is the organ that both contains the mind and controls behavior, psychology very soon incorporated the study of the brain. (It is this recognition, by the way, that relates the two facts I cited at the start of this chapter. You will see how this is so in later chapters.)

Explaining Behavior

The ultimate goal of research in psychology is to understand human behavior: to explain why people do what they do. Different kinds of psychologists are interested in different kinds of behavior and in different levels of explanation. Not all psychologists study humans; some conduct research using laboratory animals or study the behavior of wild animals in their natural habitats. Research using animals has provided many insights into the factors that affect human behavior.

How do we, as psychologists, provide an "explanation" of behavior? First, we must describe it. We must become familiar with the things that people (or other animals) do. We must learn how to categorize and measure behavior so that we can be sure that different psychologists in different places are observing the same phenomena. Next, we must discover the causes of the behavior we observe—the events responsible for a behavior's occurrence. If we can discover the events that caused the behavior, we have "explained" it. Events that cause other events (including behavior) to occur are called **causal events.**

Different psychologists are interested in different behavior. For example, one psychologist might be interested in how vision is coordinated with movement; another might be interested in courtship. Even when they are interested in the same behavior, different psychologists may study different categories of causal events—what I referred to earlier as different "levels of explanation." Some look inside the organism in a literal sense, seeking physiological causes such as the activity of nerve cells or the secretions of glands. Others look inside the organism in a metaphorical sense, explaining behavior in terms of hypothetical mental states such as anger, fear, curiosity, or love. Still others look only for events in the environment (including things that other people do) that cause behavior to occur. The word "levels" does not mean that one approach is superior or is more fundamental than another. It refers to a common choice of causes to study and methods of research to use. The use of different levels of explanation is one reason why psychology is such a diverse discipline.

The Goals of Psychological Research

What is the purpose of this quest for explanations? Intellectual curiosity is one answer. An essential part of human nature seems to be a need to understand what makes things work—and what could be more interesting than trying to understand our fellow human beings? But psychological research is more than an idle endeavor of curious scientists; it holds the promise of showing us how to solve our most important and pressing problems.

Human behavior is at the root of most of the world's problems: poverty, crime, overpopulation, drug addiction, bigotry, pollution, terrorism, and war. If global warming adversely affects our planet, or if forests and lakes die because of acid rain, it will be because of our behavior: It is we who produce the polluting chemicals and spew them into the atmosphere. Numerous health-related problems—such as cardiovascular disease, some forms of cancer, and a large number of stress-related illnesses—are caused (or at least aggravated) by individuals' behavior. Heavy smoking, obesity, lack of exercise, poor diet, unsanitary personal habits, and stressful lifestyles are responsible for illnesses found around the world. Inappropriate agricultural practices, inefficient distribution of food, and wars and tribal conflicts—which you will note are the products of human behavior—are responsible for much of the hunger and starvation that exists in the world today. If people's behavior could be changed, people's living conditions could be drastically improved.

Psychological research has not yet provided us with the solutions to these problems. We hope that while reading this book and learning what psychologists have discovered about human behavior, you will think about what can be done. Sometimes discoveries that originate from different sciences still need knowledge of psychology to facilitate their implementation. For example, when the celebrated British explorer James Cook experimented with the use of sauerkraut to prevent scurvy, he realized that his sailors would probably resist having something new in their diet. Cook did what any parent would think of doing: He increased the status of sauerkraut by ordering his officers to eat it (Berwick, 2003). Within a short while, ordinary seamen were demanding this "privilege" too. Cook had few problems with scurvy afterwards.

Fields of Psychology

Psychologists sometimes identify themselves in terms of their activities. Some of us are scientists, trying to discover the causes of behavior. Some of us are practitioners of. *applied psychology,* applying what our scientific colleagues have learned to the solution of problems in the world outside the laboratory. And, of course, some psychologists perform both roles. This section describes the various fields of psychological research and the areas of applied psychology.

Areas of Psychological Research Most research psychologists work in colleges or universities or are employed by private or governmental research laboratories. Research psychologists differ from one another in two principal ways: in the *types of behavior* they investigate and in the *causal events* they analyze. That is, they explain different types of behavior, and they explain them in terms of different types of causes. For example, two psychologists might both be interested in memory, but they might attempt to explain memory in terms of different causal events—one may focus on physiological events, whereas the other may focus on environmental events.

To explore the areas of psychological research, let's look at an important behavioral problem: drug abuse. As you know, drug abuse is one of the most serious problems society faces. It cuts across both culture and geography. Alcohol abuse can lead to divorce, loss of employment, automobile accidents, birth defects, and cirrhosis of the liver. Heroin addiction can lead to fatal overdoses. Addicts who take drugs intravenously run a serious risk of contracting and spreading AIDS. Why do people use these drugs and subject themselves to these dangers? What can psychological research tell us about the causes of—and possible solutions to—the problem of drug abuse?

Physiological psychology examines the physiology of behavior. The organism's physiology, especially its nervous system, is considered to be the appropriate level of explanation. Physiological psychologists study almost all behavioral phenomena that can be observed in nonhuman animals, including learning, memory, sensory processes, emotional behavior, motivation, sexual behavior, and sleep. The phenomenon in nonhuman animals is considered a model that can help us understand the causal events in human behavior.

Much about drug abuse can certainly be explained in terms of human physiology. Physiological psychologists have discovered that all drugs having the potential for addiction act on a particular system in the brain that is involved in our reactions to pleasurable stimuli such as food, warmth, and sexual contact. Some drugs artificially activate this system, providing effects on behavior similar to those that pleasurable events naturally produce. Understanding how these drugs affect the brain may help us develop medications to help addicts break their habits.

Comparative psychology is the study of the behavior of members of a variety of species in an attempt to explain behavior in terms of evolutionary adaptation to the environment. Comparative psychologists study behavioral phenomena similar to those studied by physiological psychologists. They are likely to study inherited behavioral patterns, such as courting and mating, predation and aggression, defensive behavior, and parental behavior.

Comparative studies of the effects of drugs have shown that all species of mammals tested so far react to addictive drugs the same way humans do. That is, if laboratory animals are allowed to control the amount of drug injected into a vein, they will become addicted to this drug.

Behavior analysis is the branch of psychology that studies the effect of environmental events on behavior. Behavior analysts are primarily interested in learning and motivation. They believe that an important cause of a specific behavior is the relationship between the behavior and some consequent event. Behaviors that produce pleasant outcomes tend to be repeated, whereas those that produce unpleasant consequences (or no consequences at all) are less likely to be repeated. Behavior analysts do their research in the laboratory or in applied settings such as schools, homes, or businesses. Their findings have been applied to teaching, business management, and psychotherapy.

Behavior analysts have contributed much to the study of drug addiction. They have developed methods for studying the way that pleasurable events (including the effects of drugs) lead people to repeat certain behaviors. They have discovered that some of the negative effects of addictive drugs, including withdrawal symptoms, are learned. They have developed methods that can indicate the abuse potential of newly developed medications before they are tried on people. Applied psychologists have used the discoveries of behavior analysts in treating people with drug addictions.

Behavior genetics is the branch of psychology that studies the role of genetics in behavior. The genes we inherit from our parents include a blueprint for the construction of a human brain. Each blueprint is a little different, which means that no two brains are exactly alike. Therefore, no two people will act exactly alike, even in identical situations. Behavior geneticists study the role of genetics in behavior by examining similarities in physical and behavioral characteristics of blood relatives, whose genes are more similar than those of unrelated individuals. They also perform breeding experiments with laboratory animals to see what aspects of behavior can be transmitted to an animal's offspring. Using new techniques of molecular genetics, behavior geneticists can even alter parts of the gene during these experiments to determine how differences in the genetic code relate to behavioral differences among animals.

One of the major contributions of behavior genetics to the study of drug abuse has been the development of strains of laboratory animals that are especially susceptible to the effects of drugs. Comparisons of these animals with others that tend not to become addicted may help us understand the physiological mechanisms involved in drug dependence.

Cognitive psychology is the study of mental processes and complex behaviors such as perception, attention, learning and memory, verbal behavior, concept formation, and problem solving. To cognitive psychologists, the events that cause behavior consist of functions of the human brain that occur in response to environmental events. Cognitive researchers' explanations involve characteristics of inferred mental processes, such as imagery, attention, and mechanisms of language. Most cognitive psychologists do not study physiological mechanisms, but recently some have begun collaborating with neurologists and other professionals involved in brain scanning. The study of the biology of cognition has been greatly aided by the development of harmless brain-scanning methods that permit us to measure the activity of various parts of the human brain.

The primary contribution of cognitive psychology to the study of drug addiction has been the development of therapeutic methods that have proved useful in the treatment of addictive behavior. Cognitive–behavioral therapists have discovered that teaching people coping strategies can enable them to better resist the temptations of addictive drugs.

Cognitive neuroscience is closely allied with both cognitive psychology and physiological psychology. Researchers in this branch of psychology are generally interested in the same phenomena studied by cognitive psychologists, but they attempt to discover the particular brain mechanisms responsible for cognitive processes. One of the principal research techniques in cognitive neuroscience is to study the behavior of people whose brains have been damaged by natural causes such as diseases, strokes, or tumors.

Cognitive neuroscientists have developed many tests that are useful in assessing behavioral and cognitive deficits caused by abnormal brain functions. For example, they have developed tests that show how the intake of alcohol, nicotine, and other drugs by pregnant women can affect the development of their babies.

Developmental psychology is the study of physical, cognitive, emotional, and social development, especially of children. Some developmental psychologists study phenomena of adolescence or adulthood—in particular, the effects of aging. The causal events they study are as comprehensive as all of psychology: physiological processes, cognitive processes, and social influences.

Developmental psychologists have helped us understand how drug-taking behavior can change over the course of an individual's life. In addition, their research on infant development has made it possible to describe the age by which any given cognitive ability (such as memory) is normally present. This knowledge provides a baseline that scientists can use to develop tests to assess behavioral and cognitive deficits caused by the brain damage associated with addictive drugs.

Social psychology is the study of the effects of people on people. Social psychologists explore phenomena such as perception (of oneself as well as of others); cause-and-effect relations in human interactions; attitudes and opinions; interpersonal relationships; group dynamics; and emotional behavior, including aggression and sexual behavior.

Drug addiction is not affected by physiological factors alone: It also has causes in the phenomena that social psychologists study. For example, children who begin smoking do not do so because their first cigarette gives them pleasure—this experience is usually unpleasant. Instead, young people smoke because their peers do, and because smoking is portrayed so attractively in advertisements and the media. Social influences also are involved in addictions to alcohol and illegal drugs. If we want to try to do something about these influences, we must first understand them.

Personality psychology is the study of individual differences in temperament and patterns of behavior. Personality psychologists look for causal events in a person's history, both genetic and environmental. Some personality psychologists are closely allied with social psychologists; others work on problems related to adjustment to society and hence study problems of interest to applied psychologists.

Personality differences certainly play a role in a person's susceptibility to drug addiction. One of the major contributions of personality psychologists to our understanding of drug addiction has been the development of tests of personality that can be used to study the factors involved in susceptibility to drug abuse.

Evolutionary psychology seeks to explain cognitive, social, and personality aspects of psychology by looking at their adaptive significance during the evolution of modern species. Clearly, the discoveries of comparative psychologists and behavioral geneticists are of interest to evolutionary psychologists. However, evolutionary psychologists use the theory of evolution by means of natural selection as a guiding principle. Our species presumably evolved as it did because certain traits (such as the ability to walk upright) gave us a competitive advantage over species without those traits. The task of the evolutionary psychologist is to trace the development of such differences and to explore how their adaptive advantages might explain the behavior of modern humans.

On the surface, drug addiction might appear to be a real conundrum for evolutionary psychology. Why would a species like ours, which is capable of foresight and planning, fall prey to substances that are so harmful? Evolutionary psychologists attempt to unravel such puzzles by looking at possible side effects of drug use. Perhaps addictions are caused by processes that normally work to our benefit but interact harmfully with certain substances that were not originally part of the environment of early humans.

Cross-cultural psychology is the study of the impact of culture on behavior. Because the ancestors of people of different racial and ethnic groups lived in different environments that presented different problems and opportunities, different cultures developed different strategies for adapting to their environments. Today these strategies show themselves in laws, customs, myths, religious beliefs, and ethical principles. The importance of cross-cultural research and the interaction between biological and cultural factors on people's behavior are explored in the special Biology and Culture feature you will find in each of the rest of the chapters of this book.

Undoubtedly, cross-cultural research can teach us much about drug addiction. Some cultures have traditions of drug use that generally do not lead to drug abuse; members of other cultures have more problems when they encounter these drugs. Although some differences may be genetic (for example, differences in individuals' ability to metabolize alcohol or in the sensitivity of nerve cells to particular drugs), many of the differences can best be understood if we study the customs and habits surrounding drug use. In some societies, for example, drugs are associated with sacred rituals. It may be that by restricting drug use to these rituals, a society regulates the frequency and amount of drugs used by its members.

Clinical psychology is the study of mental disorders and problems of adjustment. Most clinical psychologists are practitioners who try to help people solve their problems, whatever the causes. The rest are scientists who look for a wide variety of causal events, including genetic and physiological factors as well as environmental factors such as parental upbringing, interactions with siblings, and other social stimuli. They also do research to evaluate and improve methods of psychotherapy.

Clinical psychologists (and other mental health professionals, such as psychiatrists) are the people we call on to apply to individuals what we have learned about the causes of a disorder. Their contribution to addressing the problem of drug addiction has been an important one: the development of therapeutic methods used to prevent and treat drug abuse.

You will have undoubtedly noted that some of the fields I have described take contrasting views of the way behavior should be explained. Behavior analysts, for example, focus on the environment as a source of differences among individuals; in contrast, behavior geneticists look at genetic variation. Similarly, cultural psychologists and evolutionary psychologists might point to different explanations for cultural practices. These contrasting views provide the field of psychology with a large part of its vitality. You will undoubtedly develop your own opinion of the worth of specific approaches as my coauthors and I discuss them throughout this book. Be alert, however, to the possible value of viewpoints opposed to your own. And remember, too, that psychologists may be working with different levels of explanation and that for any given behavior there is more than one cause.

Fields of Applied Psychology
Although discovering the causes of behavior is important, not all psychologists are involved in research. In fact, *most* psychologists work outside the laboratory, applying the findings of research psychologists to problems related to people's behavior. This section describes some of the most important fields of applied psychology. As we saw in the previous subsection, some clinical psychologists perform research devoted to discovering the causes of mental disorders and problems of adjustment. But most clinical psychologists are applied psychologists, dedicated to improving human functioning, especially that of individuals

in distress. They are primarily engaged in psychological assessment and psychotherapy. Clinical psychologists work in private practice (on their own or as part of a joint practice), in hospitals and mental health clinics, as part of government services, in work organizations, and sometimes as professors.

Clinical neuropsychologists specialize in the identification and treatment of the behavioral consequences of nervous system disorders and injuries. They typically work in hospitals in close association with neurologists (physicians who specialize in diseases of the nervous system), although some teach or have private practices.

Health psychologists use their skills to promote behavior and lifestyles that maintain health and prevent illness. Health psychologists are employed in hospitals, government agencies, universities, and private practice.

School psychologists were among the first applied psychologists. School psychology is related to clinical psychology. As the name implies, school psychologists try to help solve the behavioral problems of students at school. The school psychologist deals with all aspects of school life—learning, social relations, testing, violence, substance abuse, and neglect.

Consumer psychologists help organizations that manufacture products or that buy products or services. Consumer psychologists study the motivation, perception, learning, cognition, and purchasing behavior of individuals in the marketplace and their use of products at home. Some consumer psychologists take a marketer's perspective; some take a consumer's perspective; and some adopt a more or less neutral perspective.

Community psychologists are concerned with the welfare of individuals in the social system—usually, disadvantaged persons. In general, the community psychologist favors modifying and improving "the system" rather than treating the individual person as a problem.

Organizational psychologists, members of one of the largest and oldest fields of applied psychology, deal with the workplace. Their predecessors concentrated on industrial work processes (such as the most efficient way to shovel coal), but organizational psychologists now spend more effort analyzing modern plants and offices. Most are employed by large companies and organizations.

Engineering psychologists (sometimes called ergonomists or human factors psychologists) mainly focus on the ways that people and machines work together. They study machines ranging from cockpits to computers, from robots to MP3 players, from telephones to transportation vehicles for disabled persons. Engineering psychologists use knowledge of behavior and its causes to help designers and engineers design better machines.

Forensic psychologists advise members of the legal and justice systems with respect to psychological knowledge. Many legal issues depend on principles of human behavior. For example, criminal law in the United States recognizes that a severe mental disorder or defect can impair a person's ability to understand the wrongfulness of an action, and the code allows such a claim as a defense against a criminal charge. Some individual states extend this doctrine to the ability to control unlawful behavior. A forensic psychologist may be called upon to provide expert testimony on these and other legal matters.

Interim Summary

What Is Psychology?

Psychology is the science of behavior, and psychologists study a large variety of behaviors in humans and other animals. They attempt to explain these behaviors by studying the events that cause them. Different psychologists are interested in different behaviors and in different categories of causes.

This section identified 12 different approaches to understanding the causes of behavior. Physiological psychologists study the role of the brain in behavior. Comparative psychologists study the evolution of behavior by comparing the behavioral capacities of various species of animals. Behavior analysts study the relation of the environment to behavior—in particular, the effects of the consequences of behavior. Behavior geneticists study the role of genetics in behavior. Cognitive psychologists study complex human behaviors such as cognition, memory, and attention. Cognitive neuroscientists study the brain mechanisms responsible for cognition. Developmental psychologists study the development of behavior throughout the life span. Social psychologists study the effects of people on the behavior of other people. Personality psychologists study individual differences in temperament and patterns of behavior. Evolutionary psychologists study the influence of natural selection on behavior. Cross-cultural psychologists study the impact of culture on behavior. Clinical psychologists study the causes and treatment of mental disorders and problems of adjustment.

In addition to thinking of psychology as a scientific discipline, we can also consider it as a profession, in which psychologists apply their knowledge of behavior to the solution of certain kinds of problems. Clinical psychologists help people with their mental and behavior problems. Clinical neuropsychologists help people with the behavioral effects of nervous system disorders. Health psychologists promote healthy behavior and lifestyles. School psychologists work with students. Consumer psychologists advise organizations that buy or sell goods and services. Community psychologists work to change the social system in ways that improve people's welfare. Organizational psychologists help organizations become more efficient and effective. Engineering psychologists help design machines that are safer and easier to operate. Forensic psychologists advise members of the legal and justice systems with respect to psychological factors they may face.

1. Before you read this section, how would you have answered the question "What is psychology?" Would your answer be different now?
2. What problems would you like psychologists to work on? If you wanted to be a psychologist, which field do you think you would be most interested in? What questions might you want to answer?

The Rise of Psychology as a Science

As mentioned at the start of this chapter, psychology is a young science; it started in the late 1800s in Germany. However, humans have certainly been curious about psychological issues for much longer than that. To understand how psychology as a science came into being, we must first trace its roots back through philosophy and the natural sciences, because these disciplines provided the methods we now use to study human behavior. These roots took many centuries to develop. Let's examine them and see how they set the stage for the emergence of the science of psychology in the late nineteenth century.

Philosophical Roots of Psychology

Perhaps the most notable part of our mental experience is that each of us is conscious of our own existence. Furthermore, we are aware of this consciousness and tend to relate it to our own behavior. That is, although we may sometimes find ourselves engaged in things we had not planned to do, we generally have the impression that our conscious mind controls our behavior. We consider alternatives, make plans, and then act. We get our bodies moving; we engage in behavior.

It is ironic that, although consciousness is a private experience, we give it such importance in our public lives. Even though we can experience only our own consciousness directly, we assume that our fellow human beings also are conscious; and, to at least some extent, we attribute consciousness to other animals as well. To the degree that our behavior is similar to that of others, we tend to assume that our mental states, too, resemble one another. Much earlier in the history of our species, it was common to attribute a life-giving *animus,* or spirit, to anything that seemed to move or grow independently. Because they believed that the movements of their own bodies were controlled by their minds or spirits, early people inferred that the sun, moon, wind, and tides were similarly animated. This primitive philosophy is called **animism** (from the Latin *animare,* "to quicken, enliven, endow with breath or soul"). Even gravity was explained in animistic terms: Rocks fell to the ground because the spirits within them wanted to be reunited with the earth.

Obviously, our interest in animism is historical. Scientific understanding of our natural world requires that we reject such notions as the idea that rocks fall because they "want to." Rather, we refer to the existence of natural forces inherent in physical matter, even if these forces are not completely understood. But note that different interpretations can be placed on the same events. And we are prone to subjective (albeit more sophisticated) interpretations of natural phenomena, just as our ancestors were. In fact, when we try to explain why people do what they do, we tend to attribute at least some of their behavior to the action of a motivating spirit—namely, a will. In our daily lives, this explanation of behavior may often suit our needs. On a scientific level, however, we need to base our explanations on phenomena that can be observed and measured. We cannot objectively and directly observe "will."

Psychology as a science must be based on the assumption that behavior is strictly subject to physical laws, just as any other natural phenomenon is. This assumption allows us to discover these laws objectively, using the scientific method (to be described in Chapter 2). The rules of scientific research impose discipline on humans, whose natural inclinations might lead them to incorrect conclusions. It seemed natural for our ancestors to believe that rocks had spirits, just as it seems natural for people nowadays to believe that behavior can be affected by a person's will. In contrast, the idea that feelings, emotions, imagination, and other private experiences are the products of physical laws of nature did not come easily; it was developed by thinkers and scholars through many centuries.

▲ *Animism attempts to explain natural phenomena by supernatural means. This painting, from the tomb of Ramses VI, depicts the ancient Egyptian belief that the sun was a god, borne across the heavens on a special boat, to be swallowed each evening by Nut, the goddess of the sky.*

▲ *René Descartes (1596–1650).*

back upon itself"). Energy coming from the outside source would be reflected back through the nervous system to the muscles, which would contract (see **Figure 1•1**). The term *reflex* is still in use today, though of course we now explain the phenomenon differently.

What set humans apart from the rest of the world, according to Descartes, was their possession of a mind. The mind was not part of the natural world, and therefore it obeyed different laws. Thus, Descartes was a proponent of **dualism,** the belief that all reality can be divided into two distinct entities: mind and matter. He distinguished between "extended things," or physical bodies, and "thinking things," or minds. Physical bodies, he believed, do not think; so minds could not be made of ordinary matter. Although Descartes was not the first to propose dualism, his thinking differed from that of his predecessors in one important way: He suggested that a causal link existed between the mind and its physical housing.

Although later philosophers pointed out that this theoretical link actually contradicted the belief in dualism, the proposal of causal interaction between mind and matter was absolutely vital to the development of a psychological science. Descartes reasoned that the mind controlled the movements of the body and that the body, through its sense organs, supplied the mind with information about what was happening in the environment. Descartes hypothesized that this interaction between mind and body took place in the

Although the history of Western philosophy properly begins with the ancient Greeks, we will begin here with René Descartes (1596–1650), a seventeenth-century French philosopher and mathematician. Descartes has been called the father not only of modern philosophy but also of a biological tradition that led to modern physiological psychology. He advocated a rationalistic approach—the sober, impersonal investigation of natural phenomena by means of sensory experience and human reasoning. He assumed that the world was a purely mechanical entity that, having once been set in motion by God, ran its course without divine interference. To understand the world, people had only to understand how it was constructed. This stance challenged the established authority of the Roman Catholic Church, which believed that the purpose of philosophy was to reconcile human experiences with the truth of God's revelations.

To Descartes, animals were creatures of the natural world only; accordingly, their behavior was controlled by natural causes and could be understood by the methods of science. His view of the human body was much the same: It was a machine affected by natural causes and producing natural effects. For example, the application of a hot object to a finger would cause an almost immediate withdrawal of the arm from the source of stimulation. Reactions like this did not require participation of the mind; they occurred automatically. Descartes called these actions **reflexes** (from the Latin *reflectere,* "to bend

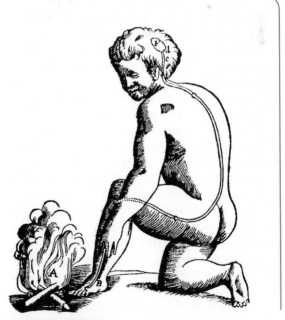

FIGURE 1•1 Descartes's diagram of a withdrawal reflex. The energy from the fire would be transmitted physically to the brain, where it would release a type of fluid that would inflate the muscles and cause movement.

(Stock Montage)

pineal body, a small organ situated on top of the brain stem, buried beneath the large cerebral hemispheres of the brain. When the mind decided to perform an action, it tilted the pineal body in a particular direction, causing fluid to flow from the brain into the proper set of nerves. This flow of fluid caused the appropriate muscles to inflate and move.

How did Descartes come up with this mechanical concept of the body's movements? Western Europe in the seventeenth century was the scene of great advances in the sciences. It was not just the practical application of science that impressed Europeans; it was the beauty, imagination, and fun of it as well. Craftsmen constructed many elaborate mechanical toys and devices during this period. The young René Descartes was greatly impressed by the moving statues in the French royal gardens at Saint-Germain-en-Laye (Jaynes, 1970). These devices served as models for Descartes as he theorized about how the body worked. He conceived of the muscles as balloons. They became inflated when a fluid passed through the nerves that connected them to the brain and spinal cord, just as water flowed through pipes to activate the statues. This inflation was the basis of the muscular contraction that causes us to move.

Descartes's explanation was one of the first to use a technological device as a model of the nervous system. In science, a **model** is a relatively simple system that works on known principles and is able to do at least some of the things that a more complex system can do. For example, after scientists discovered that elements of the nervous system communicate by means of electrical impulses, researchers developed models of the brain based on telephone switchboards and later on computers. Abstract models, which are completely mathematical in their properties, also have been developed.

Although Descartes's model of the human body was mechanical, it was controlled, as we have seen, by a nonmechanical (in fact, nonphysical) mind. Thus, humans were born with a special capability that made them greater than simply the sum of their physical parts. Their knowledge was more than merely a physical phenomenon. Perhaps because of the Catholic culture in which he lived, Descartes refused to deny a spiritual basis to human actions.

It was an English philosopher, John Locke (1632–1704), who took this analysis one step farther. Locke did not exempt the mind from the laws of the material universe. In place of Descartes's rationalism (pursuit of truth through reason), Locke advocated **empiricism**—the pursuit of truth through observation and experience. Locke rejected the belief, prevalent in the seventeenth century, that ideas were innately present in an infant's mind. Instead, he proposed that all knowledge must come through experience; it is empirically derived. (In Greek, *empeiria* means "experience.") His model of the mind was the *tabula rasa* or "cleaned slate"—the ancient method of writing on waxed tablets that were scraped clean before use. Locke meant to imply that at birth our minds were empty and ready to accept the writings of experience.

Some of our knowledge is undoubtedly more than simple snippets of experiences. Locke believed that knowledge developed through linkages of simple, primary sensations: simple ideas combined to form complex ones. Amending this notion somewhat, the Irish bishop, philosopher, and mathematician George Berkeley (1685–1753) suggested that our knowledge of events in the world also required inferences based on the accumulation of past experiences. For example, our visual perception of depth involves several elementary sensations, such as observing the relative movements of objects as we move our heads and the convergence of our eyes (turning inward toward each other or away) as we focus on near or distant objects. Although our knowledge of visual depth seems to be immediate and direct, it is actually a secondary, complex response constructed from a number of simple elements. Our perceptions of the world can also involve integrating the activity of different sense organs, such as when we see, hear, feel, and smell the same object.

As philosophers, Locke and Berkeley were speculating on the origins of knowledge and dealing with the concept of learning. (In fact, modern psychologists are still concerned with the issues that Berkeley raised.) But although they rejected Descartes's version of the mind, they still were trying to fit a nonquantifiable variable—reason—into the equation.

With the work of the Scottish philosopher James Mill (1773–1836), speculation about the mind completed an intellectual swing from animism (physical matter animated by spirits) to *materialism*—mind composed entirely of matter. **Materialism** is the belief that reality can be known only through an understanding of the physical world, of which the mind is a part. Mill did not invent materialism, but he developed it into a complete system for looking at human nature. He worked on the assumption that humans were fundamentally the same as other animals. Like other species, humans were thoroughly physical in their makeup and were completely subject to the physical laws of the universe. Essentially, Mill agreed with Descartes's approach to understanding the human body but rejected the concept of an immaterial mind. Mind, to Mill, was as passive as the body. It responded to the environment in precisely the same way. The mind, no less than the body, was a machine.

Biological Roots of Psychology

René Descartes and his model of muscular physiology provide a good beginning for a discussion of the biological roots of psychology. You may have noted from the dates that Descartes lived at the same time as Galileo, when the latter was exploring the use of simple models of inclined planks to investigate the physical laws of motion. Like Galileo's models of gravitational motion, Descartes's concept was based on an actual working model (the moving statue) whose movements seemed similar to those of human beings. Unlike Galileo, however, Descartes relied on simple similarity as "proof" of his theory; he did not have the means to offer a scientific proof. But technological development soon made experimentation and manipulation possible in the biological realm as well. For example, Descartes's hydraulic model of muscular movement was shown to be incorrect by Luigi Galvani (1737–1798), an Italian physiologist who discovered that he could make muscles contract by applying an electrical current directly to them or to the nerves attached to them. The muscles themselves contained the energy needed to contract; they did not have to be inflated by pressurized fluid. Indeed, a Dutch physiologist made the same assertion even more pointedly when he demonstrated, by flexing his arm in a barrel of water, that his muscles did not increase in volume as Descartes's theory would have predicted.

The work of the German physiologist Johannes Müller (1801–1858) clearly shows the way emerging biological knowledge shaped the evolution of psychology. Müller was a forceful advocate of applying experimental procedures to the study of physiology. He recommended that biologists should do more than observe and classify; they should remove or isolate animals' organs, test their responses to chemicals, and manipulate other conditions to see how the organism worked. His most important contribution to what would become the science of psychology was his **doctrine of specific nerve energies.** Müller noted that the basic message sent along all nerves was the same—an electrical impulse—regardless of whether the message concerned, for example, a visual perception or an auditory sensation. What, then, accounts for the brain's ability to distinguish different kinds of sensory information? Why do we see what our eyes detect, hear what our ears detect, and so on? After all, the optic nerves and the auditory nerves both send the same kind of message to the brain.

Müller's answer was that the messages are sent over different channels. Because the optic nerves are attached to the eyes, the brain interprets impulses received from these nerves as visual sensations. You have probably noticed that rubbing your eyes causes sensations of flashes of light. When you rub your eyes, the pressure against them stimulates visual receptors located inside. As a result of this stimulation, messages are sent through the optic nerves to the brain. The brain interprets these messages as sensations of light.

▲ *Johannes Müller (1801–1858).*

Müller's doctrine had important implications. If the brain recognizes the nature of a particular sensory input by means of the particular nerve that brings the message, then perhaps the brain is similarly specialized, with different parts having different functions. In other words, if different nerves convey messages about different kinds of information, then those regions of the brain that receive these messages must have different functions.

Pierre Flourens (1774–1867), a French physiologist, provided experimental evidence for the implications of Müller's doctrine of specific nerve energies. Flourens operated on animals, removing various parts of the nervous system. He found that the resulting effects depended on which parts were removed. He observed what the animal could no longer do and concluded that the missing capacity must have been the function of the part removed. For example, if an animal could not move its leg after part of its brain was removed, then that region must normally control leg movements. This method of removal of part of the brain, called **experimental ablation** (from the Latin *ablatus*, "carried away"), was soon adopted by neurologists, and it is still used by scientists on animals today. Through experimental ablation Flourens claimed to have discovered the regions of the brain that control heart rate and breathing, purposeful movements, and visual and auditory reflexes.

Paul Broca (1824–1880) applied Müller's logic, although not his method, to humans. In 1861 Broca, a French surgeon, performed an autopsy on the brain of a man who had had a stroke several years previously. The stroke (damage to the brain caused in this case by a blood clot) had robbed the man of the ability to speak. Broca discovered that the stroke had damaged part of the cerebral cortex on the left side of the man's brain. He suggested that this region of the brain is a center for speech.

Although subsequent research has found that speech is not controlled by a single "center" in the brain, the area that Broca identified (now known as Broca's area) is indeed necessary for speech production. The comparison of postmortem anatomical findings with patients' behavioral and intellectual deficits has become an important means of studying the functions of the brain. Psychologists can operate on the brains of laboratory animals, but they obviously cannot operate on the brains of humans. Instead, they must study the effects of brain damage that occurs from accidental or natural causes.

In 1870 the German physiologists Gustav Fritsch and Eduard Hitzig introduced the use of electrical stimulation as a tool for mapping the functions of the brain. The results of this method complemented those produced by the experimental destruction of nervous tissue and provided some answers that experimental ablation could not. For example, Fritsch and Hitzig discovered that applying a small electrical shock to different parts of the cerebral cortex caused movements of different parts of the body. In fact, the body appeared to be "mapped" on the surface of the brain

FIGURE 1•2 Cortical motor map. Stimulation of various parts of the motor cortex causes contraction of muscles in various parts of the body.

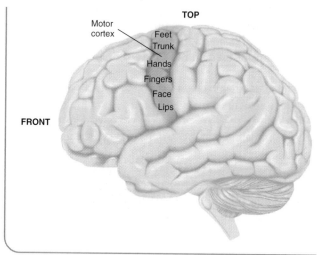

(see **Figure 1•2**). Decades later, when techniques of human brain surgery had advanced to the point where painless surgery could be performed on conscious patients, the Canadian neurosurgeon Wilder Penfield would be able to show that highly specific sensory experiences and even memories could be mapped in a similar way.

The work of the German physicist and physiologist Hermann von Helmholtz (1821–1894) did much to demonstrate that mental phenomena could be explained by physiological means. This extremely productive scientist made contributions to both physics and physiology. He actively disassociated himself from natural philosophy, from which many assumptions about the nature of the mind had been derived. Müller, under whom Helmholtz had conducted his first research, believed that human organs were endowed with a vi-

▲ *Hermann von Helmholtz (1821–1894).*

tal immaterial force that coordinated physiological behavior, a force that was not subject to experimental investigation. Helmholtz would allow no such assumptions about unproved (and unprovable) phenomena. He advocated a purely scientific approach that would base conclusions on objective investigation and precise measurement.

Before Helmholtz's work, the transmission of impulses through nerves was thought to be as fast as the speed of electricity in wires; under this assumption, transmission would be virtually instantaneous, considering the small distances that impulses have to travel within the human body. Helmholtz successfully measured the speed of the nerve impulse and found that it was only about 90 feet per second, which is considerably slower than the speed of electricity in wires. This finding suggested to later researchers that the nerve impulse is more complex than a simple electrical current passing through a wire, which is indeed true.

Having shown that neural conduction was not instantaneous, Helmholtz next sought to measure the speed of a person's reaction to a physical stimulus. Here, however, he encountered a difficulty that no amount of careful measurement could solve: He discovered that there was too much variability from person to person to make the kind of scientific laws that were common in physics. This variability interested scientists who followed him and who tried to explain individual differences in behavior. Because both the velocity of nerve impulses and individuals' reactions to stimuli could be measured, researchers theorized that mental events themselves could be the subject of scientific investigation. Possibly, if the proper techniques could be developed, it would be possible to investigate what went on within the human brain. Thus, Helmholtz's research was very important in setting the stage for the science of psychology.

In Germany, a contemporary of Helmholtz's, Ernst Weber (1795–1878), began work that led to the development of a method for measuring the magnitude of human sensations. Weber, an anatomist and physiologist, found that people's ability to distinguish between two similar stimuli—such as the brightness of two lights, the heaviness of two objects, or the loudness of two tones—followed orderly laws. This regularity suggested to Weber and his followers that perceptual phenomena could be studied as scientifically as physics or biology. In Chapter 6 we will consider the study of the relation between the physical characteristics of a stimulus and the perceptions produced, a field called **psychophysics.**

Interim Summary

The Rise of Psychology as a Science

By the mid-nineteenth century, philosophy had embraced two concepts that would lead to the objective investigation of the human mind: the principles of materialism and empiricism. Materialism maintained that the mind was made of matter.

Thus, all natural phenomena, including human behavior, could be explained in terms of physical entities: the interaction of matter and energy. Empiricism emphasized that all knowledge was acquired by means of sensory experience; no knowledge was innate. By directing attention to the tangible, sensory components of human activity, these concepts laid the foundation for a scientific approach in psychology. At this time, the divisions between science and philosophy were still blurred. Subsequent developments in the natural sciences, especially in biology and physiology, provided the necessary ingredients that, united with the critical, analytical components of philosophy, formed the scientific discipline of psychology. These ingredients were experimentation and verification.

QUESTIONS TO CONSIDER

1. Explaining things, whether scientifically or through myths and legends, seems to be a human need. It seems that people would rather invent a myth to explain a phenomenon than simply say, "I don't know." Can you think of a possible explanation for this need?
2. Which of the philosophers and scientists described in this section appeal to you the most? Would you like to know more about any of them and their times? What questions would you like to ask these men if it were possible to meet them?

Major Trends in the Development of Psychology

Psychology as a science, as distinct from philosophy and biology, began in Germany in the late nineteenth century with Wilhelm Wundt (1832–1920). Wundt was the first person to call himself a psychologist. He shared the conviction of other German scientists that all aspects of nature, including the human mind, could be studied scientifically. His book *Principles of Physiological Psychology* was the first textbook of psychology; and Wundt is generally considered to have started, in 1879, the first laboratory devoted to the study of psychological phenomena.

You may have already noted the high preponderance of German scholars in our survey of early influences on psychology. The fact that Germany was the birthplace of psychology had as much to do with social, political, and economic influences as with the abilities of the nation's scientists and scholars. The German university system was well established, and professors were highly respected members of society. The academic tradition in Germany emphasized a scientific approach to a large number of subject areas, such as history, phonetics, archaeology, aesthetics, and literature. Thus, in contrast to

▲ *Wilhelm Wundt (1832–1920).*

French and British scholars, who adopted the more traditional, philosophical approach to the study of the human mind, German scholars were open to the possibility that the human mind could be studied scientifically. German science also emphasized the importance of classification. We will see the significance of this to psychology shortly. Experimental physiology, one of the most important roots of experimental psychology, was well established in Germany. A more mundane and practical factor that favored Germany as the birthplace of psychology was that its universities were well financed; there was money to support researchers who wanted to expand scientific investigation into new fields. It was in this climate that Müller, Helmholtz, and Wundt conducted their research.

Structuralism

Wundt defined psychology as the "science of immediate experience." This approach was labeled **structuralism** by one of his students. Its subject matter was the *structure* of the mind, a structure built from the elements of consciousness, such as ideas and sensations. The raw material of structuralism was supplied by trained observers who described their own experiences. The observers were taught to engage in **introspection** (literally, "looking within"); they observed stimuli and described their experiences. Wundt and his associates made inferences about the nature of mental processes by seeing how changes in the stimuli caused changes in trained observers' verbal reports.

Like George Berkeley, Wundt was particularly interested in the way basic sensory information gave rise to complex perceptions. His trained observers attempted to ignore complex perceptions and to report only the elementary data. For example, the sensation of seeing a patch of red is immediate and elementary, whereas the perception of an apple is complex.

Wundt was an ambitious and prolific scientist who wrote many books and trained many other scientists in his laboratory. Many of these brought the new conception of psychology to North America, where it created quite a sensation. For example, in 1889, one of Wundt's protégés, James Mark Baldwin (1861–1934), was appointed professor of psychology at the University of Toronto. His appointment was quite controversial: Students and prominent faculty members petitioned against him, a newspaper denounced his psychological training in an editorial, and the matter almost caused a political scandal (Hoff, 1992). Baldwin survived this controversy, however, and later joined the faculty of Princeton University. There he helped start a journal, *Psychological Review,* that today is one of the premier journals in psychology. Other psychologists trained by Wundt, such as Edward Bradford Titchener, also became leaders of American psychology. However, Wundt's method did not survive the test of time; structuralism died out in the early twentieth century. The major problem with his approach was the difficulty of reporting the raw data of sensation, unmodified by experience. Also, the emphasis of psychological investigation shifted from the study of the mind to the study of behavior. More recently, psychologists have resumed the study of the human mind, but better methods are now available for studying it. Although structuralism has been supplanted, Wundt's contribution must be acknowledged. He established psychology as an experimental science, independent of philosophy. He trained many psychologists, a number of whom established their own laboratories and continued to advance the new discipline.

Functionalism

The next major trend in psychology was known as functionalism. This approach was in large part a reaction against the structuralism of Wundt. Structuralists were interested in what they called the components of consciousness (ideas and sensations); functionalists focused on the processes of conscious activity (perceiving and learning). **Functionalism** grew from the new perspective on nature supplied by Charles Darwin and his followers. Proponents stressed the biological significance (the purpose, or *function*) of natural processes, including behavior. The emphasis was on overt, observable behavior, not on private mental events.

Charles Darwin (1809–1882) proposed the theory of evolution in his book *On the Origin of Species by Means of Natural Selection,* published in 1859. As you may know, his work, more than that of any other person, revolutionized biology. According to the concept of *natural selection,* the consequences of an animal's characteristics affect its ability to survive. Instead of simply identifying, describing, and naming species, biologists now began to look at the adaptive significance of the ways in which species differed.

Darwin's theory was important to psychology because it suggested that scientists could best explain behavior, like other biological characteristics, by understanding its role in the adaptation of an organism to its environment. Thus, behavior has a biological context. Darwin assembled evidence that behavior, like body parts, could be inherited. In *The Expression of the Emotions in Man and Animals,* published in 1872, he proposed that the facial gestures animals make in expressing emotions were descended from movements that previously had other functions. New areas of exploration were opened for psychologists by the ideas that an evolutionary continuity existed among various animal species and that behaviors, like parts of the body, had evolutionary histories.

The most important psychologist to embrace functionalism was the American scholar William James (1842–1910). As James said, "My thinking is first, last, and always for the sake of my doing." That is, thinking was not an end in itself; its function was to produce useful behavior. Although James was a champion of experimental psychology, he did not appear to enjoy research, instead spending most of his time reading, thinking, teaching, and writing. Although James did not produce any important experimental research during his tenure as professor of philosophy (later, professor of psychology) at Harvard University, his teaching and writing influenced those who followed him. His theory of emotion is one of the most famous and durable psychological theories. It is still quoted in modern textbooks. (Yes, you will read about it later in Chapter 13 of this book.) Psychologists still find it worthwhile to read James's writings; he supplied ideas for experiments that continue to sound fresh and new today.

Unlike structuralism, functionalism was not supplanted. Functionalist textbooks were widely used in departments of psychology during their early years, and the tenets of functionalism strongly influenced the development of psychological explanations. One of the last functionalists, James Angell (1869–1949), described its basic principles:

1. Functional psychology is the study of mental operations, not of mental structures. (For example, the mind remembers; it does not contain a memory.) It is not enough to compile a catalogue of what the mind does; we must try to understand what the mind accomplishes by this doing.

2. Mental processes must be studied not as isolated and independent events but as part of the biological activity of the organism. These processes are aspects of the organism's adaptation to the environment and are a product of its evolutionary history. For example, the fact that we are conscious implies that consciousness has adaptive value for our species.

3. Functional psychology studies the relation between the environment and the response of the organism to the environment. There is no meaningful distinction between mind and body; they are part of the same entity.

Consider these points when you read the section on behaviorism.

Freud's Psychodynamic Theory

When psychology was developing as a fledgling science, an important figure, Sigmund Freud (1856–1939), was formulating a theory of human behavior that would greatly affect psychology and psychiatry and radically influence intellectuals of all kinds. Freud began his career as a neurologist, so his work was firmly rooted in biology. He soon became interested in behavioral and emotional problems and began formulating his psychodynamic theory of personality, which would evolve over his long career. Although Freud's approach was based on observation of patients and not on scientific experiments, he remained convinced that the biological basis of his theory would eventually be established.

Freud's theory will be detailed in Chapter 14; I'll discuss him here only to mark his place in the history of psychology. His theory of the mind included structures, but his structuralism was quite different from Wundt's. Freud devised his concepts of ego, superego, id, and other mental structures through talking with his patients, not through laboratory experiments. His hypothetical mental operations included many that were unconscious and hence not available to introspection. And unlike Wundt, Freud emphasized function; his mental structures served biological drives and instincts and reflected our animal nature.

Psychology in Transition

Psychology as a science was to take a radical turn in the early decades of the twentieth century. Before we consider this change, it might help you to see how the different intellectual contributions of the structuralists and the functionalists had shaped the way psychology was practiced at universities in North America.

The controversy over James Mark Baldwin's appointment at Toronto quickly died down, helped in part when

▲ *Mary Whiton Calkins (1867–1930).*

▲ *James Mark Baldwin (1861–1934).*

Baldwin's rival for the job was appointed to a similar position. Baldwin was given a rather handsome budget of $1,550 for equipment, which he promptly used to create one of the first psychological laboratories in North America (Baldwin, 1892). Like the laboratories of Wundt in Germany and of James at Harvard University, the Toronto facility was designed for the experimental investigation of the mind, with attention to the control of noise and light. Baldwin went immediately to work in his new environment, even publishing a paper on handedness based on observations of his infant daughter.

The new emphasis on experiment and observations was becoming prominent in the classroom as well. Mary Whiton Calkins (1867–1930), for example, wrote a lengthy description of the psychology course she taught to seniors at Wellesley College (Calkins, 1892). Her students studied the anatomy of the brain and received laboratory exercises in the dissection of lamb brains, the measurement of sensation, and the comparison of associations to simple words. Calkins reported that the experiments on taste "were so unpopular that I should never repeat them in a general class of students who are not specializing in the subject." This leads the modern reader to wonder just what it was that she asked her students to taste.

Through the efforts of both researchers and instructors, psychology became part of university curricula throughout the United States. Professors of psychology joined academic societies and became recognized as members of an emerging scientific discipline.

Meanwhile, textbooks of psychology began to reflect the prominence of physiological observation and the measurement of human reactivity. Shortly after setting up his laboratory, Baldwin finished a major handbook of current psychological knowledge. In it he incorporated not only the work of Mill and Wundt but also that of Darwin and other natural historians. He formulated a special principle (nowadays called "the Baldwin Effect") that, he thought, could explain the evolution of mental phenomena. And he speculated on the relationship between consciousness and muscular movement (Richards, 1987). Wundt had founded the science of psychology on the assumption that it should describe the contents of the mind. By the beginning of the twentieth century, however, psychologists like James and Baldwin had returned to the problem that vexed Descartes: How do we understand the actions that the mind supposedly determines?

Behaviorism

The next major trend that we will consider, behaviorism, likewise reflected this concern with action. Behaviorists went farther than James or Baldwin, however, by rejecting the special nature of mental events and by denying that unobservable and unverifiable mental events were properly the subject matter of psychology. Behaviorists believe that because psychology is the study of observable behavior, mental events, which cannot be observed, are outside the realm of psychology. **Behaviorism** is thus the study of the relation between people's environments and their behavior, without appeal to hypothetical events occurring within their heads.

One of the first behaviorists was Edward Thorndike (1874–1949), an American psychologist who, as a student at Harvard, studied the behavior of animals. (Interestingly, Thorndike conducted his initial tests of animal intelligence in the basement of the house of William James, the functionalist.) Thorndike noticed that some events, usually those that one would expect to be pleasant, seemed to "stamp in" a response that had just occurred, thereby making it more likely to occur again. Noxious events seemed to "stamp out" the response, or make it less likely to occur. (Nowadays, we call these processes *reinforcement* and *punishment;* they are described in more detail in Chapter 5.) Thorndike defined the **law of effect** as follows:

> Any act which in a given situation produces satisfaction becomes associated with that situation, so that when the situation recurs the act is more likely than before to recur also. Conversely, any act which in a given situation produces discomfort becomes disassociated from that situation, so that when the situation recurs the act is less likely than before to recur. (Thorndike, 1905, p. 203)

The law of effect is certainly in the functionalist tradition. It asserts that the consequences of a behavior act back upon the organism, affecting the likelihood that the behavior will occur again. This process is very similar to the principle of natural selection. Just as organisms that successfully adapt to their environments are more likely to survive and breed, so behaviors that cause useful outcomes become more likely to recur.

Despite Thorndike's insistence that the subject matter of psychology was behavior, his explanations contained mentalistic terms. For example, in his law of effect he spoke of "satisfaction," which is certainly not a phenomenon that can be directly observed. Later behaviorists recognized this contradiction and replaced terms such as *satisfaction* and *discomfort* with more objective concepts that reflected only the behavior.

Another major figure in the development of the behavioristic trend was not a psychologist at all but a physiologist: Ivan Pavlov (1849–1936), a Russian who studied the physiology of digestion (for which work he later received a Nobel Prize). In the course of studying the stimuli that produce salivation, Pavlov discovered that hungry dogs would salivate at the sight of the attendant who brought in their dishes of food. Although first labeling this phenomenon a "psychic reflex," Pavlov soon traced it to the experience the dog had received. Pavlov found that a dog would salivate at a completely arbitrary stimulus, such as the sound of a bell, if the stimulus was quickly followed by the delivery of a bit of food into the animal's mouth.

Pavlov's discovery had profound significance for psychology. He showed that through experience an animal could learn to make a response to a stimulus that had never caused this response before. This ability might explain how organisms learn cause-and-effect relations in the environment. In contrast, Thorndike's law of effect suggested an explanation for the adaptability of an individual's behavior to its particular environment. So from Thorndike's and Pavlov's studies two important behavioral principles had been discovered.

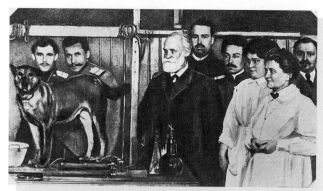

▲ *Ivan Pavlov (1849–1936) in his laboratory with some of his collaborators. His research revealed valuable information about the principles of learning.*

▲ *John B. Watson (1878–1958).*

▲ *Margaret Floy Washburn (1871–1939).*

Behaviorism as a formal school of psychology began with the publication of a book by John B. Watson (1878–1958), *Psychology from the Standpoint of a Behaviorist.* Watson, a professor of psychology at Johns Hopkins University, was a popular teacher and writer and a very convincing advocate of the behavioral perspective. Even after leaving Johns Hopkins for a highly successful career in advertising, he continued to lecture and write magazine articles about psychology.

According to Watson, psychology was a natural science whose domain was restricted to observable events: the behavior of organisms. Watson believed that the elements of consciousness studied by the structuralists were too subjective to lend themselves to scientific investigation. He defined psychology as the objective study of stimuli and the behavior they produced. He reduced even thinking to a form of behavior—"talking to ourselves":

> Now what can we observe? We can observe behavior— *what the organism does or says.* And let us point out at once: that saying is doing—that is, behaving. Speaking overtly or to ourselves (thinking) is just as objective a type of behavior as baseball. (Watson, 1930, p. 6)

Behaviorism is still very much in evidence today in psychology. Its renowned advocates have included B. F. Skinner (1904–1990), one of the most influential psychologists of the twentieth century. But psychologists, including modern behaviorists, have moved away from the strict behaviorism of Watson; mental processes such as imagery and attention are again considered to be proper subject matter for scientific investigation.

In this sense, modern psychologists have moved more toward a view expressed by Margaret Floy Washburn (1871–1939) early in the debate over behavior. Washburn (1922), although advocating her own version of structuralism, suggested to behaviorists that they regard introspection itself as a form of behavior that could help them understand the inaccessible processes of mental life. Today, as Washburn

would have wished, Watson's emphasis on objectivity in psychological research remains. Even those modern psychologists who most vehemently protest against what they see as the narrowness of behaviorism use the same principles of objectivity to guide their research. As research scientists, they must uphold the principles of objectivity that evolved from empiricism to functionalism to behaviorism. A psychologist who studies private mental events realizes that these events can be studied only indirectly, by means of behavior—verbal reports of inner experiences. Unlike Wundt, present-day psychologists realize that these reports are not pure reflections of these mental events; like other behaviors, these responses can be affected by many factors. Consequently, they strive to maintain an objective stance to ensure that their research findings will be valid and capable of being verified.

Humanistic Psychology

For many years philosophers and other intellectuals have been concerned with what they see as the special attributes of humanity—with free will and spontaneity, with creativity and consciousness. As the science of psychology developed, these phenomena received less attention than others, because researchers could not agree on objective ways to study them. Humanistic psychology developed during the

1950s and 1960s as a reaction against both behaviorism and the psychodynamic approach of Freud. Although psychodynamic theory certainly dealt with mental phenomena that could not be objectively measured, it saw people as products of their environment and of innate, unconscious forces. Humanistic psychologists insist that human nature goes beyond environmental influences, and they argue that psychologists should study conscious processes, not unconscious drives. In addition, they note that psychoanalytical theory seems preoccupied with disturbed people, ignoring positive phenomena such as happiness, satisfaction, love, and kindness.

Humanistic psychology is an approach to the study of human behavior that emphasizes human experience, choice and creativity, self-realization, and positive growth. Humanistic psychologists emphasize the positive sides of human nature and the potential we all share for personal growth. In general, humanistic psychologists do not believe that we will understand human consciousness and behavior through scientific research. Thus, the humanistic approach has not had a significant influence on psychology as a science. Its greatest impact has been on the development of methods of psychotherapy that are based on a positive and optimistic view of human potential.

Reaction against Behaviorism: The Cognitive Revolution

Proponents of behaviorism restricted the subject matter of psychology to observable behavior. And, despite their differences from the structuralists, they also tended to analyze behavior by dividing it into smaller elements. Even as behaviorism became the dominant trend in psychology, a contrasting school of thought began to emphasize how unobservable factors influence larger patterns of human consciousness.

This movement began when a German psychologist, Max Wertheimer (1880–1943), bought a toy that presented a series of pictures in rapid succession. Each picture was slightly different from the preceding one, resulting in the impression of continuous motion—like a movie. Wertheimer and his colleagues suggested that psychological processes provided the continuity. They therefore attempted to discover the *organization* of cognitive processes, not their elements. They called their approach **Gestalt psychology.** *Gestalt* is a German word that roughly translates into "unified form." Gestalt psychologists insisted that perceptions resulted from patterns of interactions among many elements, in the same way we recognize a song by the relations between the notes rather than by the individual notes themselves.

Although the Gestalt school of psychology no longer exists, its insistence that the elements of an experience are organized into larger units was very influential. These organizational processes are not directly observable, yet they still

determine behavior. Since the 1960s, many psychologists likewise have begun to reject the restrictions of behaviorism and have turned to the study of consciousness, feelings, imagery, and other private events.

Much of *cognitive psychology* (described in the first section of this chapter) analyzes mental activities in terms of **information processing.** According to this approach information received through the senses is "processed" by various systems of neurons in the brain. Some systems store the information in the form of memory; other systems control behavior. Some systems operate automatically and unconsciously, whereas others are conscious and require effort. Because the information processing approach was first devised to describe the operations of complex physical systems such as computers, the modern model of the human brain is, for most cognitive psychologists, the computer. As you will learn in Chapter 7, however, another model—the artificial neural network—is beginning to replace the computer.

Although cognitive psychologists now study mental structures and operations, they have not gone back to the introspective methods that structuralists such as Wundt employed. They use objective research methods, just as behaviorists do. For example, several modern psychologists have studied the phenomenon of imagery. If you close your eyes and imagine what the open pages of this book look like, you are viewing a mental image of what you have previously seen. This image exists only within your brain, and it can be experienced by you and no one else. I have no way of knowing whether your images are like mine any more than I know whether the color red looks the same to you as it does to me. The experience of imagery cannot be shared in a scientific sense.

But behaviors that are based on images can indeed be measured. For example, one researcher (Kosslyn, 1973, 1975) asked a group of people to memorize several drawings. Then he asked the participants to imagine one of the drawings, focusing their attention on a particular feature of the image. Next, he asked a question about a detail of the image that was either "near" the point they were focusing on or "far" from it. For example, if they were picturing a boat, he might ask them to imagine that they were looking at its stern (back). Then he might ask whether the boat had a rudder at the stern, or whether a rope was fastened to its bow (front).

Kosslyn found that people could very quickly answer a question about a feature of the boat that was near the place they were focusing on, but that they took longer to answer a question about a part that was farther away. It was as if they had to scan their mental image to get from one place to the other. (See **Figure 1•3.**)

Because we cannot observe what is happening within a person's head, the concept of imagery remains hypothetical. However, this hypothetical concept very nicely explains and organizes some concrete results—namely, the time it takes for a person to give an answer. Although the explanation for

FIGURE 1•3 A drawing used in the imagery study by Kosslyn.

(From Kosslyn, S. M. [1973]. *Perception and Psychophysics, 14,* 90–94. Reprinted with permission.)

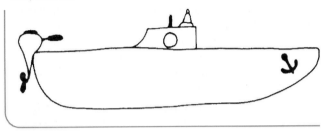

the results of this experiment is phrased in terms of private events (mental images), the behavioral data (how long it takes to answer the questions) are empirical and objective.

The Biological Revolution

Although the first scientific roots of psychology were in biology and physiology, the biological approach to behavior has become so prevalent since the early 1990s that it can properly be called a revolution. During the early and mid-twentieth century, the dominance of behaviorism led to a de-emphasis of biological factors in the study of behavior. At the time scientists had no way of studying what went on in the brain, but that did not prevent people from spinning elaborate theories of how the brain controlled behavior. Behaviorists rejected such speculation. They acknowledged that the brain controlled behavior but argued that because we could not see what was happening inside the brain, we should refrain from inventing physiological explanations that could not be verified.

One of the few dissenters from the prevailing behaviorist view of the time was a Canadian psychologist, Donald Hebb (1904–1985). Hebb had graduated from Dalhousie

▲ *Donald Hebb (1904–1985).*

University with aspirations of being a novelist. After a brief stint teaching in Quebec, he was admitted as a part-time student at McGill University. Although his initial academic record at McGill has been described as "dismal" (Ferguson, 1982), Hebb was inspired by the physiological approach to psychology then taught at McGill by a professor who had worked with Pavlov. After completing his graduate work in the United States, Hebb returned to McGill in 1947. Challenging the behaviorists, Hebb argued that behavioral and mental phenomena could be related directly to brain activity. In his most influential work, published soon after his return to McGill, he suggested several simple principles by which the nervous system organized itself into special "circuits" that could represent mental activity (Hebb, 1949).

Cognitive psychologists had inherited from early behaviorists a suspicion of the value of biology in explaining behavior. Thus, the cognitive revolution did not lead to a renewed interest in biology. But the extraordinary advances in neurobiology in the late twentieth century revolutionized psychology and vindicated Hebb's viewpoint (Klein, 1999). And many of Hebb's students and associates were at the forefront of subsequent developments in psychology (Adair, Paivio, & Ritchie, 1996).

Neurobiologists (biologists who study the nervous system) and scientists and engineers in allied fields have developed ways to study the brain that were unthinkable just a few decades ago. We can study fine details of nerve cells, discover their interconnections, analyze the chemicals they use to communicate with one another, produce drugs that block the action of these chemicals or mimic their effects, see the internal structure of a living human brain, and measure the activity of different parts of the brain—regions as small as a few cubic millimeters—while people are watching visual displays, listening to words, or performing various kinds of cognitive tasks. In addition, it seems as though every day we learn of new genes that play roles in particular behaviors, and drugs that are designed to duplicate or block the effects of these genes.

Interim Summary

Major Trends in the Development of Psychology

Psychology has come a long way in a relatively short time. The first laboratory of experimental psychology was established in 1879, only a century and a quarter ago. Wilhelm Wundt established psychology as a discipline that was independent of philosophy. Wundt's approach was based on the premise that, through introspection, the mind's contents could be described. Even though Wundt's structuralism did not last, interest in psychology continued to grow. The discipline took on added breadth and scope with the emergence of functionalism, which grew out of Darwin's theory of evolution and stressed the adaptive value of biological phenomena. Functionalism gave rise to the objectivity of behaviorism, and scientific objectivity still dominates the way we do research.

The cognitive revolution began because some psychologists believed that a strict emphasis on observable behavior missed the complexity of human cognition and behavior—an opinion that modern behaviorists contest. The biological revolution in psychology is manifested in the increased interest of psychologists in all fields—not just physiological psychology—in the role of biological factors in behavior.

QUESTIONS TO CONSIDER

1. Although the science of psychology began in Germany, it soon migrated to the United States, where it flourished. Can you think of any characteristics of American society that might explain why psychology developed faster here than elsewhere in the world?

2. As you have learned, psychologists study a wide variety of behaviors. Do you think that there are any behaviors that psychologists cannot explain (or should not try to explain)?

Suggestions for Further Reading

Wearing, D. (2005). *Forever today: A memoir of love and amnesia*. London: Transworld.

This book provides additional details on the case of Clive Wearing, the man at the center of the opening vignette. Written by his wife, Deborah, it also describes the impact of his condition on his family.

Butterfield, H. (1959). *The origins of modern science: 1300–1800*. New York: Macmillan.

Whitehead, A. N. (1925). *Science and the modern world*. New York: Macmillan.

These books by Butterfield and Whitehead describe the history of science in general. Whitehead's is old, but it is a classic.

Schultz, D. P., & Schultz, S. E. (1996). *A history of modern psychology* (6th ed.). Fort Worth, TX: Harcourt Brace.

Several books describe the history of psychology, including its philosophical and biological roots; you may wish to read one of them and then expand your reading to learn more. This book by Duane Schultz and Sydney Schultz is a standard text on the topic.

Key Terms

animism (p. 10)

behavior analysis (p. 7)

behavior genetics (p. 7)

behaviorism (p. 18)

causal event (p. 5)

clinical neuropsychologist (p. 9)

clinical psychology (p. 8)

cognitive neuroscience (p. 7)

cognitive psychology (p. 7)

community psychologist (p. 9)

comparative psychology (p. 6)

consumer psychologist (p. 9)

cross-cultural psychology (p. 8)

developmental psychology (p. 7)

doctrine of specific nerve energies (p. 13)

dualism (p. 11)

empiricism (p. 12)

engineering psychologist (p. 9)

evolutionary psychology (p. 8)

experimental ablation (p. 13)

forensic psychologist (p. 9)

functionalism (p. 16)

Gestalt psychology (p. 20)

health psychologist (p. 9)

humanistic psychology (p. 20)

information processing (p. 20)

introspection (p. 15)

law of effect (p. 18)

materialism (p. 12)

model (p. 12)

organizational psychologist (p. 9)

personality psychology (p. 8)

physiological psychology (p. 6)

psychology (p. 5)

psychophysics (p. 14)

reflex (p. 11)

school psychologist (p. 9)

social psychology (p. 7)

structuralism (p. 15)

2

THE WAYS AND MEANS OF PSYCHOLOGY

The Scientific Method in Psychology

Identifying the Problem: Getting an Idea for Research • Designing an Experiment • Performing an Experiment • Performing a Correlational Study • Reporting and Generalizing a Study • *Evaluating Scientific Issues: Format for Critical Thinking*

The scientific method is the most effective procedure for understanding natural phenomena and cause-and-effect relations. Starting with hypotheses—speculation about the way variables are related—researchers use experiments and observational studies to investigate phenomena. Researchers must use valid and reliable operational definitions of independent and dependent variables. They must avoid confounding variables if their results are to be clear and understandable. Finally, they hope to generalize the results of their research beyond the particular participants they have studied.

Ethics

Research with Human Participants • Research with Animals • *Biology and Culture: Cross-Cultural Research*

Psychologists must abide by the ethical principles established by governmental agencies and professional societies. They must obtain informed consent from human participants before enlisting them for a study. Participants' dignity must be respected and their well-being protected. Animals used in research must be housed properly and treated humanely.

Understanding Research Results

Descriptive Statistics: What Are the Results? • Inferential Statistics: Distinguishing Chance from Significance

After researchers have collected data from a study, they analyze the results. They first describe the data using descriptive statistics, such as measures of central tendency, variability, and correlation. Next, they use inferential statistics to determine whether the results are statistically significant. They estimate the likelihood that the results could have occurred by chance.

Justine's parents operate a small company that employs five people. The employees assemble custom testing devices used in the oil exploration industry. The summer after her first year of college, Justine decided to put her skills to work by trying to increase the company's productivity. She reasoned that if the employees could complete more of the testing devices per day, the company would be more profitable for her parents and the workers themselves would benefit through their profit-sharing plan.

One evening Justine stayed at the assembly laboratory to work on one of the devices herself. After a couple of hours, her neck was strained and her arms and hands tingled from maintaining a bent position over the bench at which she was working. Justine convinced her parents to invest in height-adjustable chairs to replace the existing stationary seats. When the new chairs arrived, she adjusted them so that each employee seemed to be at a comfortable position. Justine held an informal meeting with the employees and told them that she thought the new chairs would reduce discomfort and therefore permit them to be more productive. She said that she would keep track of how many units they finished over the next several days and would let them know if the chairs had helped. At the end of the week, the employees eagerly asked Justine how they had done. Justine proudly announced that they had completed 20 percent more of the testing units than they had during the same amount of time before the chairs arrived. The workers congratulated her for her insight and help.

Over the next week Justine continued to check in with the employees and to collect data. She then got together with her friend Lawrence, who had recently taken a statistics course. Lawrence helped her conduct a formal statistical test to compare the production figures for the seven workdays before Justine introduced the new chairs and the seven workdays afterward. They found that productivity had increased significantly more than would be expected by chance. Her intervention had worked, or so it appeared. Justine stopped her daily visits with the employees.

Is it a change in the type of chair that can improve productivity, or the prospect of any change?

A few weeks later, though, Justine happened to look at the employees' production figures and was disappointed to find that productivity had fallen to the same level as before the new chairs arrived. Justine decided to start over with the old chairs, monitor the employees' output, and then reintroduce the adjustable chairs to see what would happen. After a week with the old chairs, productivity inexplicably increased 20 percent again. Justine was understandably perplexed. Increased productivity with the old chairs? Justine gave up on her project. What had happened? Justine was sure that she had diligently applied the scientific method and that her intervention should have had clear-cut results.

The overarching goal of psychology as a science is the explanation of behavior. As scientists, the vast majority of quantitative psychologists believe that behavior, like other natural phenomena, can be studied objectively. The scientific method permits us to discover the nature and causes of behavior. This approach has become the predominant method of investigation among quantitative psychologists for a very practical reason: The results obtained by following the scientific method are likely to turn out to be correct.

This chapter will show you how the scientific method is used in psychological research. What you learn here will help you understand the research described in the rest of the book. But even more than that, what you learn here can be applied to everyday life. Knowing how a psychologist can be misled by the results of improperly conducted research can help us all avoid being misled by more casual observations. Understanding the scientific method can also help us, as consumers of information, distinguish worthwhile from flawed research reported in the mass media.

Does using the scientific method guarantee that the results of research will be important? No, it does not. The results of some properly performed studies may have no current relevance to what goes on in everyday life. The scientific method guarantees only that the particular question being asked will be answered. When a scientist asks a trivial question, nature returns a trivial answer.

Popular depictions of science focus on white lab coats and elaborate equipment. But "scientific" does not mean "technical." Psychologists do not necessarily need a formal laboratory or special equipment to use the scientific method. Depending on the question being asked, a psychologist might need no more than a pad of paper, a pencil, and some natural phenomenon—such as another person's behavior—to observe. It is also the case that no area of psychological investigation is inherently more "scientific" than any other. For example, the physiological analysis of hunger is not inherently more scientific than the study of social factors affecting people's willingness to help victims of accidents.

The Scientific Method in Psychology

The goal of scientific psychological research is to discover the causes of behavior. To do so we need to describe behaviors and the events that are responsible for their occurrence in a language that is both precise enough to be understood by others and general enough to apply to a wide variety of situations. As we saw in Chapter 1, this language takes the form of explanations, which are general statements about the events that cause phenomena to occur.

Scientists, including quantitative psychologists, use an agreed-upon approach to discovery and explanation—the scientific method. The **scientific method** consists of a set of rules that dictate the general procedure a scientist must follow in his or her research. These rules are not arbitrary; as we will see, they are based on logic and common sense. The rules were originally devised by philosophers who were attempting to determine how we could understand reality. By nature, we are all intuitive psychologists, trying to understand why others do what they do—so it is important to realize how easily we can be fooled about the actual causes of behavior. Thus, everyone, not just professional psychologists, should know the basic steps of the scientific method.

Psychologists conduct three major types of scientific research. These classes of research are common across many of the sciences. The first type includes **naturalistic observation** and **clinical observation**—observation of people or animals in their natural environment or while they are undergoing treatment or diagnosis for a psychological condition. These methods are the least formal and are constrained by the fewest rules. Naturalistic observations provide the foundations of the biological and social sciences. For example, Charles Darwin's observation and classification of animals, plants, and fossils during his voyage around the world provided him with the raw material for his theory of evolution. Paul Broca's observation of the man who lost his ability to speak suggested to him that language was located in a specific region of the brain. As these two examples illustrate, a researcher might perceive new facts following careful observation.

Second, **correlational studies** are observational in nature, but they involve more formal measurement—of environmental events, of individuals' physical and social characteristics, and of their behavior. Researchers examine the relations of these measurements in an attempt to explain the observed behaviors. At the conclusion of a correlational study, a researcher might conclude that some of the phenomena measured are related in a particular way.

Finally, **experiments** go beyond mere measurement. A psychologist performing an experiment makes things happen and observes the results. As you will see, following a properly designed experiment, a researcher can positively identify the causal relations among events.

Let's consider how we might use the scientific method to gain an understanding of a psychological experience you may have encountered. You've undoubtedly seen those multicolored posters that, when you cross your eyes just the right amount, reveal a three-dimensional image of an object or a scene. (See **Figure 2•1**.) In the classroom, when I discuss the way we visually perceive the world around us (material you'll find in Chapter 7), I sometimes show students samples of these images, which go by the long-winded label of *single-image random dot stereograms* or *SIRD stereograms*. Invariably, some students can see the hidden object quickly, whereas others fail to see it after long minutes of straining. Given that our individual visual systems are generally alike, what explains this difference? Would giving the students a picture of the hidden image help them find it in the stereogram?

The three classes of research often occur in a progressive sequence, with each stage providing increasingly more compelling evidence. For example, naturalistic observations of yourself or your friends in front of one of these images could provide the context of the problem. You likely would observe that some people take much longer than others identifying the hidden objects in the SIRD stereogram. Observational evidence would identify the phenomenon and might indicate something about its magnitude. Correlational evidence would arise when you started to observe relations between observations. For example, you might note that you and your friends seem to bring the three-dimensional image into focus much faster when a small two-dimensional picture of the

FIGURE 2•1 A version of a SIRD stereogram. Hold the image 5 to 10 inches in front of you. As you look at the image, imagine that it is really much farther away. Do not focus on the image itself, but rather on a spot three or four feet or so behind the image. The flat field of stones will start to develop layers of different distances. Seeing the three-dimensional image may take some time. If you cannot see it after a reasonable period of time, ask someone who can see it to give you a verbal clue, then try again.

(© Gary W. Priester)

object appears alongside the stereogram. Finally, systematic investigation of the phenomenon through experimentation could produce concrete evidence about the causal role that visual hints may play in helping people see the three-dimensional object.

Quantitative psychologists place great weight on results of experiments. Experiments provide evidence about the processes that affect behavior and in this sense provide general accounts of phenomena. For example, suppose we give some of the students, but not others, a visual hint—an idea of what the image looks like. If we found that those who had the hint were faster at finding the three-dimensional view, we would now have systematic evidence about the causal role of visual hints. Demonstrating the role of visual expectations in this situation might help us generalize the concept of expectation to other types of perception.

To understand the confidence that psychologists place in experiments, we must understand how experiments are conducted. The following five steps summarize the rules of the scientific method that apply to experiments—the form of scientific research that identifies cause-and-effect relations. As we will see later, many of these rules also apply to observational and correlational studies. Some new terms introduced here without definition will be described in detail later in this chapter.

1. *Identify the problem and formulate hypothetical cause-and-effect relations among variables.* This step involves identifying variables (particular behaviors and particular environmental and physiological events) and describing the relations among them in general terms. Consider the following hypothesis: Expectation of an image facilitates its detection in a SIRD stereogram. This statement describes a relation between two variables—expectation of an image and detection of that same image—and states that the first will increase the second.

2. *Design the experiment.* Experiments involve the manipulation of independent variables and the observation of dependent variables. For example, if we wanted to test the hypothesis about the relation between expectation and detection of an image, we would have to do something to produce an expectation (the independent variable) and see whether that experience altered the ability of a participant in the experiment to detect a hidden image (the dependent variable). Each variable must be *operationally defined;* and the independent variable must be controlled so that only it, and no other variable, is responsible for any changes in the dependent variable.

3. *Perform the experiment.* The researcher must organize the material needed to perform the experiment, train the people who will perform the research, recruit volunteers whose behavior will be observed, and randomly assign each of these volunteers to an experimental group or a control group. The experiment is performed and the observations are recorded.

4. *Evaluate the hypothesis by examining the data from the study.* Do the results support the hypothesis, or do they suggest that it is wrong? This step often involves special mathematical procedures used to determine whether an observed effect is *statistically significant.* These procedures will be discussed in the Understanding Research Results section later in this chapter.

5. *Communicate the results.* Once the experimenters have learned something about the causes of a behavior, they must tell others about their findings. In most cases psychologists write an article that includes a description of the experiment's procedure and results and a discussion of their significance. They send the article to one of the many journals that publish results of psychological research. Journal editors and expert reviewers determine which research is methodologically sound and important enough to publish. In addition, researchers often present their findings at conferences or professional conventions. As a result, other psychologists can incorporate the findings into their own thinking and hypothesizing.

Following these steps decreases the chances that we will be misled by our observations or form incorrect conclusions in our research. As we shall see in Chapter 11, we as humans have a tendency to accept some types of evidence even though the rules of logic indicate that we should not. This tendency sometimes serves us well in our daily lives, but it can lead us to make the wrong conclusions when we try to understand the true causes of natural phenomena, including our own behavior.

Identifying the Problem: Getting an Idea for Research

Like most professions, science is a very competitive enterprise. Most scientists want to be recognized for their work. They want to discover and explain interesting phenomena and to have other scientists acknowledge their importance. They may hope that the fruits of their research will affect the public at large.

Sometimes great science is created by great scientists. What makes a scientist great? Obviously, no one achieves greatness simply by following the rules. The scientific method is not difficult to understand or to master, and the laboratory methods required for even the most technical research can be mastered in only a few years of study. A great scientist certainly needs to be hardworking and dedicated—perhaps even obstinate and relentless. Most of all, a great scientist needs great ideas.

More often, though, great science results from the cumulative work of many excellent, though perhaps not great, scientists who have solid ideas. This implies that the accumulation of most scientific information occurs as the result of long-term research programs in which findings of individual researchers are part of a larger collective (and often international) endeavor.

▲ *Researchers communicate their results to other scientists through professional journals or conferences.*

Most research occurs in institutional settings such as universities, where scientists, students, and technicians all are involved in the effort. Long-term projects require financial support. Psychological research in the United States has historically been supported by major federal agencies such as the National Science Foundation and the National Institute of Mental Health. Before providing funding, these agencies rigorously review the merits of a proposed research program and its potential for long-term scientific value. They provide an independent evaluation of the worth of a scientific idea.

In this environment of competition and rigorous evaluation, a successful scientist needs to have *good ideas*. Where do they come from?

Hypotheses A hypothesis is the starting point of any study. It is an idea, phrased as a general statement, that a scientist

wishes to test through scientific research. In the original Greek, *hypothesis* means "suggestion," and the word still conveys the same meaning. When scientists form a hypothesis, they are suggesting that a relation exists among various phenomena (for example, between expectation of an image and a person's ability to detect it in a SIRD stereogram). Thus, a **hypothesis** is a tentative statement about a cause-and-effect relation between two or more events.

A common misconception is that research hypotheses occur spontaneously and mysteriously to scientists. Hypotheses do not spring out of thin air; they occur to scientists as a result of accumulated research and scholarship. Research breeds more research. That is, worthwhile research does not merely answer questions; it suggests new questions to be asked—new hypotheses to be tested. Productive and creative scientists formulate new hypotheses by thinking about the implications of studies that they have performed or that have been performed by others. The best scientists see ideas that others have missed and then translate these ideas into innovative programs of research.

Theories A **theory** is a set of statements that describes and explains known facts, proposes relations among variables, and makes new predictions. In a sense, then, a theory is an elaborate form of hypothesis. A scientific theory operates within the scientific method to organize a system of facts and related hypotheses to explain some larger aspect of nature. A good theory fuels the creation of new hypotheses. (More accurately, a good scientist, contemplating a good theory, thinks of more good hypotheses to test.) For example, Albert

▲ *Some of the earliest scientific theories involved the movements of celestial bodies, especially those of the planets.*

Einstein's theory of relativity states that time, matter, and energy are interdependent: Changes in any one component will produce changes in the others. The hypotheses suggested by this theory revolutionized science; the field of nuclear physics largely rests on experiments stimulated by Einstein's theory.

A good theory is one that generates *testable hypotheses*—hypotheses that can potentially be supported or proved wrong by scientific research. Some theories are so general or so abstract that they do not produce testable hypotheses and hence cannot be subjected to scientific rigor. For example, Sigmund Freud theorized that conflicts between mental structures such as the id and the superego were significant determinants of personality and behavior. Because there is no way to observe or measure these structures, there is no way to test the idea of conflict among them (although we will see that testable hypotheses can be generated from other aspects of Freud's theorizing).

The framework for any given psychological research endeavor is usually larger in scope than a hypothesis but smaller in scope than a full-fledged theory. For example, the frustration–aggression hypothesis suggests that people (and other animals) tend to become aggressive when they do not achieve a goal that they have been accustomed to achieving. This hypothesis explains behavior, proposes a link between behavior and events, and makes a prediction that might fit many different situations. Indeed, many experiments have been performed to test this hypothesis under different conditions. However, the hypothesis also presupposes the existence of other psychological constructs, such as goals. In this way it is more than a hypothesis: It could form the basis of a larger theory about how we identify goals and how we recognize whether we've attained them.

Even though the frameworks that most psychologists construct are not full-fledged theories, they serve a similar function by stimulating researchers to think about old problems in new ways and by showing how findings that did not appear to be related to each other can be explained by a single concept. There is even a scientific journal, *Psychological Review,* devoted to articles of this type. (*Psychological Review,* you may recall from Chapter 1, is the journal founded by James Mark Baldwin.)

Naturalistic and Clinical Observations as Sources of Hypotheses and Theories

Psychology is about behavior. To understand human behavior, or the behavior of other animals, we first have to know something about that behavior. Much of what we know about behavior comes from ordinary experience: from observing other people, listening to their stories, watching films, reading novels. In effect, we perform observations throughout our lives. But careful, systematic observations permit trained observers, already well informed about a particular topic, to discover subtly different categories of behavior and to develop hypotheses about their causes.

Naturalists are people who carefully observe animals in their natural environment, disturbing them as little as possible. Naturalistic observations, then, are what naturalists see and record. All sciences—physical, biological, and social—begin with simple observation. For example, people described mountains, volcanoes, canyons, plains, and the multitude of rocks and minerals found in these locations long before they attempted to understand their formation. Thus, observation and classification of the landscape and its contents began long before the development of the science of geology.

Psychologists who are also naturalists apply the procedures of naturalistic observation to questions of behavior. The important feature of naturalistic observations is that the observer remains in the background, trying not to interfere with the people (or animals) being observed. For example, suppose we are interested in studying the social behavior of preschoolers. We want to know under what conditions children share their toys or fight over them, how children react to newcomers to the group, and so on. The best way to begin to get some ideas is to watch groups of children. We would unobtrusively start taking notes, classifying behaviors into categories and seeing what events provoked them—and what the effects of these behaviors might be. These naturalistic observations would teach us how to categorize and measure the children's behavior and would help us develop hypotheses that could be tested in experiments or in correlational studies.

Clinical observations are somewhat different. One very important source of observational data is obtained by clinical psychologists. In the course of diagnosis or treatment, a psychologist can often observe important patterns of behavior. As with naturalistic observations, these patterns could form the basis of hypotheses about the causes of behavior. Clinical psychologists often report the results of their observations in detailed descriptions known as **case studies.** Unlike a naturalist, however, a clinical psychologist most likely does *not* remain in the background, because the object of therapy is to change the patient's behavior and to solve problems. Indeed, the psychologist is ethically constrained to engage in activities designed to benefit the patient; he or she cannot arbitrarily withhold some treatment or apply another just for the

▲ *Much can be learned through careful observation of animals in their natural environment. The results of such observations often suggest hypotheses to be tested by subsequent studies.*

▲ *An important feature of naturalistic observation is that the observer remains in the background.*

sake of new observations. So, like the naturalist, a clinician is bound by certain rules that limit the kinds of observations that can be made: The clinician cannot interfere with the treatment regime prescribed for the patient.

In some cases, psychologists *do* interfere with a situation in a natural or clinical setting. They may, for example, ask questions at job sites or on the street—places that we might regard as naturalistic settings. In one common procedure, a **survey study,** researchers may ask people specially designed and controlled questions, perhaps about their beliefs, opinions, or attitudes. Survey studies are designed to elicit a special kind of behavior—answers to the questions. The observations, then, are usually descriptions of the classes of responses to these questions. Many people may participate in a survey study, but they all are given the same, *standardized,* questions. As these questions become more specific and precise, they allow the same formal measurement of relations that underlies correlational studies.

A clinical psychologist, too, may manipulate the treatment given to a patient, with the desire of producing a more beneficial response. The psychologist may report the result in the manner of a case study, but such manipulation would make the process an experiment, not an observational study.

Designing an Experiment

Although naturalistic observations enable a psychologist to classify behaviors into categories and to offer hypothetical ex-

planations for these behaviors, only an experiment can determine whether these explanations are correct. Let us see how to design an experiment. We will examine experimental variables and their operational definition and control.

Variables The hypothesis proposed earlier—"Expectation of an image increases a person's ability to detect it in a SIRD stereogram"—describes a relation between expectation and the detection of an image. Scientists refer to these two components as **variables:** things that can vary in value. Thus, temperature is a variable, and so is happiness. Virtually anything that can differ in amount, degree, or presence versus absence is a variable.

Scientists either *manipulate* or *measure* the values of variables. **Manipulation** literally means "handling" (from *manus,* "hand"). Because of abuses in the history of human research (which I will describe later), the term *manipulation* is sometimes incorrectly understood to mean something that researchers do to participants. Psychologists use the word, however, to describe setting the values of a variable in order to examine that variable's effect on another variable. In the SIRD experiment, one value of the expectation variable would be set at "visual expectation present" and the other at "visual expectation absent." Measuring variables is what it sounds like. Just as we measure the variable of temperature with a thermometer, so psychologists devise instruments to measure psychological variables. The results of experimental manipulations and measurements of variables help us evaluate hypotheses.

To test the visual expectation hypothesis with an experiment, we would assemble two groups of volunteers to serve as participants. We would present participants in the **experimental group** with an experience that would give them an expectation about the nature of the image hidden in the SIRD stereogram. For example, we might show these participants an image somewhat similar to that in the SIRD. We would not give participants in the **control group** such an experience, and they therefore would have no expectation. We would then measure the ability of participants in both groups to detect the hidden image; we could then determine whether the outcomes in the two groups differed. Provided that we had randomly assigned the volunteers to make sure that our two groups were alike at the start of the experiment, we could attribute any differences in detection ability to the experimental manipulation of expectation. (See **Figure 2·2.**)

Our imaginary experiment examines the effect of one variable on another. The variable that we manipulate (expectation of the image) is called the **independent variable.** The variable that we measure (recognition of the image) is the **dependent variable.** An easy way to keep the names of these variables straight is to remember that a hypothesis describes how the value of a dependent variable *depends* on the value of an independent variable. Our hypothesis proposes that recognition of the hidden image depends to some extent on prior expectation of what it looks like. (See **Figure 2·3.**)

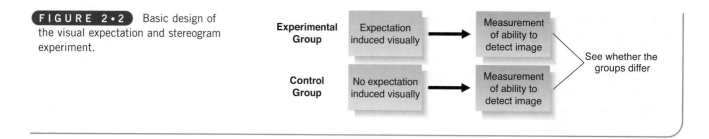

Scientists want to understand the causes of behavior in more than one specific situation. Thus, the variables that hypotheses deal with are expressed in general terms. Independent and dependent variables are *categories* into which various behaviors are classified. For example, we would probably classify hitting, kicking, and throwing objects at someone as included within the category of "interpersonal aggression." Presumably, these forms of aggression would have very similar causes. A psychologist must know enough about a particular type of behavior to be able to classify it correctly.

Even though one of the first steps in psychological research involves naming and classifying behaviors, however, we must be careful to avoid committing the nominal fallacy. The **nominal fallacy** is the erroneous belief that we have explained an event merely by naming it. (*Nomen* means "name.") Classifying a behavior does not explain it; classifying only prepares us to examine and discover events that cause a behavior.

For example, suppose that we see a man frown and shout at other people without provocation, criticize their work when it is really acceptable, and generally act unpleasantly toward everyone around him. Someone says, "Wow, he's really angry today!" Does this statement explain his behavior? No; it only *describes* the behavior. Instead of saying he is angry, we might better say that his behavior is hostile and aggressive. This statement does not claim to explain why he is acting the way he is. To say that he is angry suggests that an internal state is responsible for his behavior—that anger is causing his behavior. But all we have observed is his behavior, not his internal state. Even if he is experiencing feelings of anger, these feelings are not a full account of his behavior. What we really need to know is *what events made him act the way he did.* Perhaps he has a painful toothache. Perhaps he just learned that he failed to get a job he wanted. Perhaps he just read a book that promoted assertiveness. Events like these are causes of both behavior and feelings. Unless the underlying events are discovered and examined, we have not explained behavior in a scientifically meaningful way.

Yet identifying causes is not as simple as merely identifying preceding events. Many internal and external events may precede any behavior. Some of these events are causal, but some almost certainly will be completely unrelated to the observed behavior. For example, you get off your commuter train because your stop is announced, not because someone coughs or someone else turns the page of a newspaper, even though all of these events may happen just before you stand up and leave the train. The task of a psychologist is to determine which of the many events that occurred before a particular behavior caused that behavior to happen.

Operational Definitions Hypotheses are phrased in general terms, but when we design an experiment (step 2 of the scientific method) we need to decide what *particular* variables we will manipulate and measure. For example, to produce an expectation of what the hidden image looks like, we must arrange a particular situation that has this effect. Similarly, we must measure the participants' detection of the image. Both expectation and ability to detect must be translated into specific operations.

This translation of generalities into specific operations is called an **operational definition**: the definition of independent variables and dependent variables in terms of the operations a researcher performs in order to set their values or to measure them. In our proposed experiment, a rudimentary operational definition of the independent and dependent variables and the setting in which they were studied might be the following:

Setting: Participants of both groups were comfortably seated in front of a projection screen. Participants received 20 presentations of different SIRD stereograms and were asked to press a button when they had identified the hidden object on the screen. Before each presentation, participants heard a verbal "priming stimulus" naming the hidden object.

Independent variable: The experimenter created a visual expectation for each participant in the experimental group

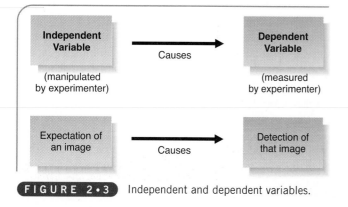

FIGURE 2•3 Independent and dependent variables.

by displaying for one second, during the verbal priming stimulus, a silhouette image of the target, of the same orientation and size as hidden in the stereogram. Participants in the control group received only the verbal priming stimulus and a random geometric shape not related to the hidden object.

Dependent variable: Detection of the image was measured by the time between the first appearance of the stereogram and the participant's pressing the response button. All participants were asked to be reasonably confident they had detected the object before pressing the button. (See **Figure 2•4**.)

If research results are to be understood, evaluated, and utilized by other people (step 5 of the scientific method), the investigator must provide others with a thorough and adequate description of the procedures used to manipulate the independent variable and to measure the dependent variable. For example, a complete definition of the dependent variable (detection of the SIRD stereogram image) would have to include a detailed description of each stereogram used.

Any general concept can be operationalized in many different ways. By selecting one particular operational definition, the researcher may or may not succeed in manipulating the independent variable or in measuring the dependent variable. For example, there is certainly no single definition of visual expectation. Another investigator, using a different set of operations to produce an expectation (such as a three-dimensional model of the object), might obtain results that are different from ours. Which operational definition is correct? Which set of results should we believe? To answer these questions, we need to address the issue of *validity.*

The **validity** of operational definitions has to do with how appropriate they are for testing the researcher's hypothesis—how accurately they represent the variables whose values have been manipulated or measured. Obviously, only experiments that use valid operational definitions of their variables can yield meaningful results. Let's consider this operational definition of detection: the length of the time interval between initial presentation of the stereogram and the pressing of the response button. How can we know that the participant has actually seen the hidden image? Even with the best of intentions, a person in an experiment like this might be reacting to his or her own imagination rather than actual visual perception. As one possible check, we could construct our stereograms so that the image appears in one of the four quadrants of the display screen. We could then ask participants to point to the quadrant in which they had seen the image. Using only those times that were associated with correct points would increase the validity of our measure.

Operational definitions are used to develop manipulations and measures of a vast array of psychological concepts. Some of these are quite abstract and seemingly removed from behavior, such as anger and self-esteem. Given enough research effort, the validity of an operational definition will emerge. If different investigators define the variables in slightly different ways but their experiments yield similar results, we become more confident that we are approaching a good explanation of the phenomenon we are studying.

Control of Independent Variables We have seen that a scientist performs an experiment by manipulating the value of the independent variable and then observing whether this change affects the dependent variable. If an effect is seen, the scientist can conclude that there is a cause-and-effect relation between the variables. That is, changes in the value of the independent variable cause changes in the value of the dependent variable.

When conducting an experiment, the researcher must manipulate the value of the independent variable—and *only* the independent variable. For example, if we want to determine whether ambient (background) environmental noise has an effect on people's reading speed, we must choose our source of noise carefully. If we used the sound track from a television show to supply the noise and found that it slowed people's reading speed, we could not conclude that the effect was caused purely by "noise." We might have selected an interesting show, thus distracting the participants' attention from the material they were reading because of the content of the TV program rather than because of "noise." If we want to do this experiment properly, we should use noise that is neutral and not a source of interest by itself—for instance, noise

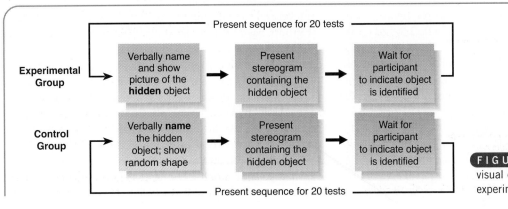

FIGURE 2•4 Details of the visual expectation and stereogram experiment.

like the *sssh* sound that is heard when an FM radio is tuned between stations.

If we used a TV program sound track as our manipulation of noise, we would inadvertently cause **confounding of variables**—we would introduce the effects of another variable besides noise on reading speed. One of the meanings of the word *confound* is "to fail to distinguish." If a researcher inadvertently introduces one or more extra, unwanted, independent variables that vary synchronously with the intended independent variable, he or she will not be able to distinguish the effects of any one of them on the dependent variable. That is, the effects of the variables will be confounded. In our example, the noise of the TV program would be mixed with the content of the program in the experimental condition, whereas in the control condition there would be neither noise nor content. You can see that any effect of the manipulation on reading could be due to either noise or content or even to their combination. It would be impossible to reach any conclusion about the experimental hypothesis.

There are many ways in which confounding of variables can occur. To understand the problems that can arise, let's examine some of the mistakes a researcher can make. I'll begin with a true story. When I was a graduate student, I accompanied several fellow students to hear a talk that was presented by a visitor to the zoology department. He described research he had conducted in a remote area of South America. He was interested in determining whether a particular species of bird could recognize a large bird that normally preys on it. He had constructed a set of cardboard models that bore varying degrees of resemblance to the predator: They ranged from a perfect representation, to two models of noncarnivorous birds, to a neutral stimulus (a triangle, I think). The researcher restrained each bird he was testing and suddenly presented it with each of the test stimuli, in decreasing order of similarity to the predator—that is, from predator to harmless birds to triangle. He observed a relation between the amount of alarm that the birds showed and the similarity that the model bore to the predator. The most predator-like model produced the greatest response. (See **Figure 2•5**.)

One of us pointed out—to the embarrassment of the speaker—that the study contained a fatal flaw that made it impossible to conclude whether a relation existed between the independent variable (similarity of the model to the predator) and the dependent variable (amount of alarm). It's a fairly subtle but important problem. Can you figure it out? Reread the previous paragraph, consult Figure 2.5, and think about the problem before you read on.

Now, the answer: When testing the birds' responses to the models, the investigator presented each model at a different time *but always in the same order.* Very likely, even if the birds had been shown the *same* model again and again, they would have exhibited less and less of a response. We very commonly observe this phenomenon, called *habituation,* when a stimulus is presented repeatedly. The last presentation produces a much smaller response than the first. Consequently, we do not

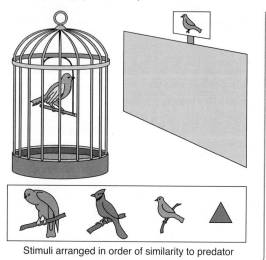

FIGURE 2•5 A schematic representation of the flawed predator experiment.

Stimuli arranged in order of similarity to predator

know whether the decrease in signs of alarm occurred because the stimuli looked less and less like the predator or simply because the birds became habituated to the stimuli.

Could the zoologist have carried out his experiment in a way that would have permitted him to infer a causal relation? Yes, and perhaps the solution has occurred to you already. Here is the answer: The researcher should have presented the stimuli in different orders to different birds. Some birds would see the predator first, others would see the triangle first, and so on. Then he could have calculated the average amount of alarm that the birds showed to each of the stimuli, without the results' being contaminated by habituation. This type of procedure is called **counterbalancing.** To *counterbalance* means to "weigh evenly," and counterbalancing would have been accomplished if the investigator had made sure that each of the models was presented equally often (to different participant birds, of course) as the first, second, third, or fourth stimulus. The effects of habituation would thus be spread equally among all the stimuli. (See **Figure 2•6**.)

Consider a second example of confounding. Let's suppose we believe that oil extracted from a tropical bean might reduce aggressiveness. We decide to test our hypothesis by feeding this oil to a group of rats. We mix the oil with some rat food and feed this mixture to members of the experimental group. Members of the control group receive the same food without the additive. (Oil versus no oil is the independent variable manipulation.) A month later, we test the aggressiveness of each rat from the experimental and control conditions. To do so, we take the rat's food away for several hours so that it will be hungry, then place it in a small cage with another hungry rat (which is from a separate group of rats used only for the purpose of providing a competitor during the test). The cage contains food (with no oil added, of course) in a dish so small that only one rat can eat from it at a time. Our

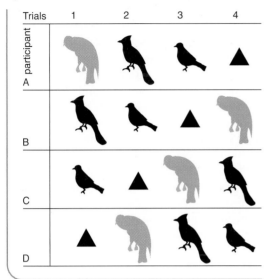

FIGURE 2·6 Counterbalancing in the predator experiment. The predator experiment could be improved by changing the order of presentation of the models.

dependent measure of aggressiveness is the amount of time each rat manages to monopolize the food.

Suppose we find that rats in the experimental group spend less time at the food dish than do rats in the control group. Can we conclude that the oil reduces aggressiveness? Not necessarily. If the results are to be valid, the only difference between the two groups of rats should be that the experimental rats ate some of the oil and the control rats did not. But suppose that the oil tastes bad. In this case the rats in the experimental group might eat less food. At the end of the month they might be so weakened by partial starvation that they cannot compete effectively with healthy rats that have been eating a normal diet. Or perhaps the oil tastes good—so good that the animals in the experimental group eat more than those in the control group. In this case they might be less hungry than their competitors during the test and hence less motivated to fight for the food.

To perform this experiment properly, we would have to prepare two diets that tasted the same and contained the same number of calories. We might have to add an ordinary oil (such as corn oil) to the control rats' food to match the total fat content of the experimental group's diet, and we might have to add a flavoring agent to both diets to mask any unpleasant (or particularly tasty) flavor of the special oil. And we would have to weigh the animals daily and measure how much they ate; if the groups differed on either measure we would have to adjust the diets and start again.

You can appreciate by now that it is often difficult to be sure that independent variables are not confounded. Scientists must be certain that when they manipulate an independent variable, that variable only, *and no other variable,* is affected.

Performing an Experiment

After designing a study with due regard for the dangers of confounds, we must decide how best to conduct it. We are now at step 3 of the scientific method: Perform the experiment. We must decide who will participate, what instructions to give, and what equipment and materials to use. We must ensure that the data collected will be accurate; otherwise, all effort will be in vain.

Reliability of Measurements

A procedure described by an operational definition that produces consistent results under consistent conditions is said to have high **reliability.** For example, measurements of people's height and weight are extremely reliable. Measurements of their academic aptitude (by means of standard commercial tests) also are reliable, but somewhat less so.

Suppose that we operationally define detection of a hidden image as the time it takes before the participant blinks. Eye-blink measurements can be made reliably and accurately, but it is problematic to consider this as a valid or true measure of image detection, because there are many reasons for a participant to blink other than having detected the hidden image. Achieving reliability is usually much easier than achieving validity. Reliability is mostly a result of care and diligence on the part of researchers in the planning and execution of their studies.

Let's look at an example of a factor that can decrease the reliability of an operationally defined variable. Suppose that in our study on the effects of visual expectation on detection of a hidden image, we select the stereograms to be presented to each participant by randomly drawing 20 images from a large collection of digital stereogram images. However, some of the collection of images were poorly scanned, so they are out of focus when projected. You can easily appreciate how this extraneous factor would affect our measurement of detection and would add to the differences we observe among the participants.

Careful researchers can identify and control most of the extraneous factors that might affect the reliability of their measurements. Conditions throughout the experiment should always be as consistent as possible. For example, the same instructions should be given to each person who participates in the experiment, all equipment should be in good working order, and all assistants hired by the researcher should be well trained in performing their tasks. Noise and other sources of distraction should be kept to a minimum.

The subjectivity of the experimenters who are taking a measurement is another factor that affects reliability. Our definition of inducing an expectation is *objective;* that is, even a non-expert could follow our procedure and obtain the same results. But researchers often attempt to study variables whose measurement is *subjective;* that is, it requires judgment and expertise. For example, suppose that a psychologist wants to count the number of friendly interactions that a child has with other children in a group. This measurement requires that someone watch the child and note each time a friendly interaction occurs. But it is difficult to be absolutely specific about what constitutes a friendly interaction and what does not. What if the child looks at another child and their gazes meet? One observer may say that the look conveyed interest in what the other child was doing and so should be scored as a friendly interaction. Another observer may disagree.

The solution in this case: First, in order to make the measurement as objective as possible, try to specify as precisely as possible the criteria to be used for defining an interaction as "friendly". Next, two or more people should watch the child's behavior and score it independently; that is, neither person should be aware of the other person's ratings. If the two observers' ratings agree, we can say that the scoring system has high **interrater reliability.** If they disagree, interrater reliability is low, and there is no point in continuing the study. Instead, the rating system should be refined, and the raters should be trained to apply it consistently. Any investigator who performs a study in which measuring the dependent variables requires some degree of skill and judgment must do what is necessary to produce high interrater reliability.

Selecting the Participants

Now let's turn to the participants in our experiment. How do we choose them? How do we assign them to the experimental or control group? These decisions must be carefully considered, because just as independent variables can be confounded, so can variables that are inherent in participants whose behavior is being observed.

Suppose a professor wants to determine which of two teaching methods works best. She teaches two courses in introductory psychology, one that meets at 8:00 a.m. and another that meets at 4:00 p.m. She considers using one teaching method for the morning class and the other for the afternoon class. She speculates that at the end of the term the final examination scores will be higher for her morning class. If her surmise proves correct, will she be able to conclude that the morning teaching method is superior to the method used in the afternoon? No; a good researcher would understand that the method considered here would produce a significant interpretation problem. There likely would be differences between the two groups of participants other than the teaching method they experienced. People who sign up for a class that meets at 8:00 a.m. are likely, for many reasons, to differ in some ways from those who sign up for a 4:00 p.m. class. Some people prefer to get up early; others prefer to sleep late. Perhaps the school schedules athletic practices in the late afternoon, which means that athletes will not be able to enroll in the 4:00 p.m. class. Therefore, the professor would not be able to conclude that any observed differences in final examination scores were caused solely by the differences in the teaching methods. Personal characteristics of the participant groups would be confounded with the two teaching methods.

The most common way to avoid confounding participant characteristics with the manipulated values of an independent variable is **random assignment.** Random assignment

means that each participant has an equal chance of being assigned to any of the conditions or groups of the experiment. One way to accomplish random assignment is to list the names of the available participants and then toss a coin for each one to determine the participant's assignment to one of two groups. (More typically, the assignment is made by computer or by consulting a list of random numbers.) We can expect people to have different abilities, personality traits, and other characteristics that may affect the outcome of the experiment. But if people are randomly assigned to the experimental conditions, these differences should be equally distributed across the groups. Randomly assigning students to two sections of a course meeting at the same time of day would help solve the problem faced by the professor who wants to study different teaching methods.

Even after researchers have designed an experiment and randomly assigned participants to the groups, they must remain alert to the problem of confounding participant characteristics with their independent variable manipulations. Some problems will not emerge until the investigation is actually performed. Suppose that we wish to learn whether anger decreases a person's ability to concentrate. We begin by acting very rudely toward the participants in the experimental group, which presumably makes them angry, but we treat the participants in the control group politely. After the rude or polite treatment, the participants watch a video that shows a constantly changing display of patterns of letters. Participants are instructed to press a button whenever a particular letter appears. This vigilance test is designed to reveal how carefully participants are paying attention to the letters.

The design of this experiment seems sound. Assuming that the participants in the experimental group are really angry and that our letter identification test is a good dependent measure of concentration, we should be able to draw conclusions about the effects of anger on concentration. However, the experiment, as performed under real conditions, may not work out the way we expect. Suppose that some of our "angry" participants simply walk away. All researchers must assure participants that their participation is voluntary and that they are free to leave at any time; some angry participants may well exercise this right and withdraw from the experiment. If they do, we will now be comparing the behavior of two groups of participants that have a different mix of personal characteristics—one group composed of people who are willing to submit to the researcher's rude behavior (because the objectors have withdrawn) and another group of randomly selected people, some of whom would have left had they been subjected to the rude treatment. Now the experimental group and the control group are no longer equivalent. (See **Figure 2•7.**)

The moral of this example is that a researcher must continue to attend to the possibility of confounded variables even after the experiment is under way. The solution in this case? There probably is none, given our chosen method of producing anger. Because we cannot force participants to continue in the experiment, there is a strong possibility that some of them will leave. Some psychological variables are by

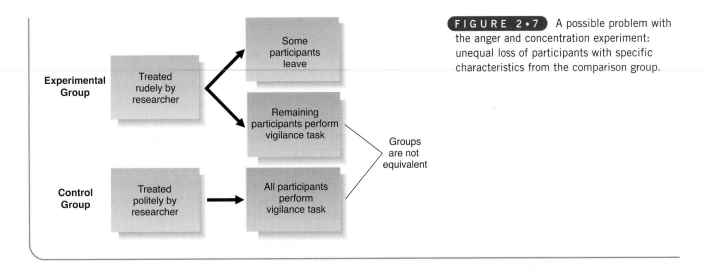

FIGURE 2·7 A possible problem with the anger and concentration experiment: unequal loss of participants with specific characteristics from the comparison group.

their very nature difficult to investigate. But difficult does not mean impossible. We must go back to the drawing board and devise a better experiment with which to test the hypothesis.

Expectancy Effects

Research participants are not passive beings whose behavior is controlled solely by the independent variables manipulated by the researcher. In the opening vignette, we saw that Justine learned this fact when she tried to improve production at her parents' company. Participants in experiments know that they are being observed, and this knowledge is certain to affect their behavior. This is a basic concept in the sciences: Observation can change that which you observe. The facts in Justine's case represent what is known as the *Hawthorne effect.* Back in the 1930s, the managers of the Hawthorne plant of the Western Electric company wondered whether increasing the level of lighting in the plant would increase productivity. It did, but the managers found that the increase in productivity was short-lived. They went on to do some more investigating and found that productivity actually went up when they subsequently lowered the level of lighting. The commonly accepted explanation of these findings is based on the fact that the workers knew that an experiment was being conducted and that they were being monitored. That knowledge may have made them work harder regardless of whether lighting levels were increased or decreased. The workers may even have been pleased—and motivated—by the fact that management was obviously trying to improve their work environment, and may have tried to return the favor. Of course, the effect would not last indefinitely, and eventually production returned to normal. Adair (1984) provides a detailed analysis of these original studies and the methods that have evolved in field experiments to counter the Hawthorne effect.

One way to think about the Hawthorne effect is that the participants were trying to help the researchers confirm their expectation that changes in lighting would improve produc-

tivity. There is compelling evidence that this type of cooperation with researchers can occur even in very sophisticated laboratory research: If research participants figure out the researcher's hypothesis, they will sometimes behave as if the hypothesis is true, even if it is not. The possibility that a researcher's expectations can be guessed by a participant is a dangerous state of affairs for good science. For this reason, researchers routinely keep the details of their hypotheses to themselves when dealing with participants, at least until after the independent variable is manipulated and the dependent variable measured. But the situation is more troublesome when participants manage to figure out not only the researcher's hypothesis but also the independent variable manipulations on their own. You may have heard that deception is sometimes used in psychological research. Overall, deception is relatively rare. When it is used, however, the sole reason is to disguise the nature of an independent variable manipulation (and perhaps the dependent measure). If researchers mislead participants about the reason for the experimental events, the intention is to prevent the participants from acting as if the hypothesis were true when it might in fact not be. When deception is used, researchers take great pains to disclose the truth to participants at the earliest possible moment and to reestablish a trusting relationship. Interestingly, people who actually have participated in deception experiments are generally quite accepting of the rationale for the use of this technique (Sharpe, Adair, & Roese, 1992). Let's turn now to other techniques that have been developed to reduce the likelihood that research participants will become aware of the investigator's expectations.

Single-Blind Experiments

Suppose that we want to study the effects of a stimulant drug on a person's ability to perform a task that requires fine manual dexterity. We will administer the drug to one group of participants and leave another group untreated. (Of course, the experiment will have to be supervised by a physician, who will prescribe the drug.) We will count how many times each participant can thread a needle in a 10-minute period (our operational definition of fine manual dexterity). We will then see whether taking the drug had any effect on the number of needle threadings.

But there is a problem in our design. For us to conclude that a cause-and-effect relation exists, the treatment of the two groups must be identical except for the single variable that is being manipulated. In this case the mere administration of a drug may have effects on behavior, independent of its pharmacological effects. The behavior of participants who know that they have just taken a stimulant drug is very likely to be affected by this knowledge as well as by the drug circulating in their bloodstreams.

To solve this problem we would give pills to the members of both groups. People in one group would receive the stimulant; those in the other group would receive an identical-looking pill that contained no active drug—a **placebo** pill. Participants would not be told which type of pill they were taking, but they would know that they had a 50–50 chance of receiving either the stimulant or the inactive substance. By using this improved experimental procedure, called a **single-blind study,** we could infer that any observed differences in needle-threading ability of the two groups were produced solely by the pharmacological effects of the stimulant drug.

Double-Blind Experiments In a single-blind experiment only the participants are kept unaware of their assignment to a particular experimental group; the researcher knows which treatment each participant receives. Now let us look at an example in which it is important to keep both the researchers and the participants in the dark. Suppose we believe that if patients with mental disorders take a particular drug, they will be more willing to engage in conversation. This would be an important outcome, because enhanced communicativeness could facilitate their therapy. So we give the real drug to some patients and administer a placebo to others. We talk with all the patients afterwards and rate the quality of the conversation. But "quality of conversation" is a difficult dependent variable to measure, and the rating is therefore likely to be subjective. The fact that we, the researchers, know who received the drug and who received the placebo leaves open the possibility that we may tend to give higher conversation quality ratings to those who took the drug. Of course, we would not intentionally cheat, but even honest people tend to perceive results in a way that favors their own preconceptions.

The solution to this problem is simple. Just as the participants should not know whether they are receiving a drug or a placebo, neither should the researchers. That is, we should use a **double-blind study.** Either another person should administer the pills, or the researchers should be given a set of identical-looking pills in coded containers so that both researchers and participants are unaware of the nature of the contents. Now the researchers' ratings of conversation quality cannot be affected by any preconceived ideas the researchers

may have. Keep in mind that someone who has no direct contact with the participants is keeping track of who gets which pills so that the effect of the independent variable manipulation can be tested.

The double-blind procedure does not apply only to experiments that use drugs as the independent variable. Suppose that the experiment just described attempted to evaluate the effects of a new form of psychotherapy, not a drug, on the willingness of a participant to talk. If the same person does both the psychotherapy and the rating, that person might tend to see the results in the light most favorable to his or her own expectations. In this case, then, one person should perform the psychotherapy and another person should evaluate the quality of conversation with the participants. The evaluator will not know whether a particular participant has just received the new psychotherapy or is a member of the control group that received the old standard therapy.

Scientists who conduct research with laboratory animals may also have to use single-blind or double-blind procedures. Let's consider a case that calls for a single-blind procedure. Suppose that we want to know whether a particular drug will affect an animal's ability to learn a particular task. Just before we train the animals in the experimental group, we give them the drug. But how do we administer the drug? Suppose we must put a pill into the animal's mouth and have the animal swallow it. Or suppose we administer the drug by injecting it. Either of these administration procedures may affect the animal's behavior in the learning task. To avoid this problem, we have to administer placebo pills or injections to animals in the control group as well.

Performing a Correlational Study

To be sure that a cause-and-effect relation exists between variables, we must perform an experiment in which we manipulate an independent variable and measure its effects on a dependent variable. But there are some variables—especially variables intrinsic to an individual—that a psychologist cannot manipulate. For example, a person's gender, genetic history, income, social class, family environment, and personality are obviously not under the researcher's control. Because these variables cannot be manipulated, they cannot be investigated in an experiment. Nevertheless, such variables are important and interesting, because they often affect people's behavior. A different method must therefore be used to study them: a **correlational study.**

The design and conduct of a correlational study is relatively simple: For each member of a group of people we measure two or more variables as they are found to exist, and we determine whether the variables are related by using a statistical procedure called *correlation.* Correlational studies often investigate the effects of personality variables on behavior. For example, we may ask whether shyness is related to daydreaming. Our hypothesis is that shy people tend to daydream more than do less shy people. We decide how to assess a person's shyness and the amount of daydreaming he or she engages in each day, and we then measure these two variables for a group of people. Some people will be very shy and some not shy at all. Some people will daydream a lot and others hardly at all. If we find that relatively shy people tend to daydream more (or less) than do relatively less shy people, we can conclude that the variables are related.

Suppose that we do, in fact, find that shy people spend more time daydreaming. Such a finding tells us that the variables are related—we say they are *correlated*—but it does not permit us to make any conclusions about cause and effect. Shyness may have caused the daydreaming, or daydreaming may have caused the shyness, or perhaps some other variable that we did not measure caused both shyness and an increase in daydreaming. In other words, *correlations do not necessarily indicate cause-and-effect relations.* (See **Figure 2•8**.) An experiment is necessary to prove a cause-and-effect relation.

A good illustration of this principle is provided by a correlational study that attempted to determine whether membership in the Boy Scouts would affect a person's subsequent participation in community affairs (Chapin, 1938). The investigator compared a group of men who had once been Boy Scouts with a group of men who had not. He found that the men who had been Boy Scouts tended to join more community affairs groups later in life.

The investigator concluded that the experience of being a Boy Scout increased a person's tendency to join community organizations. However, this conclusion was not warranted. All we can say is that people who join the Boy Scouts in their youth tend to join community organizations later in life. It could be that people who, for one reason or another, are "joiners" tend to join the Boy Scouts when they are young and community organizations when they are older. To determine cause and effect, we would have to perform an experiment. For example, we would make some boys join the Boy Scouts and prevent others from doing so, and then see how many organizations they voluntarily joined later in life. But because we cannot interfere in people's lives in such a way, we can never be certain that being a Boy Scout increases a person's tendency to join community organizations later.

The news media often report the results of correlational studies as if they implied causal relations. For example, one newspaper routinely points out the high incomes earned by its subscribers, implying that by subscribing you can cause your own income to rise. But correlation does not prove causation. It could be that having a high income causes you to buy the newspaper (perhaps for the specific news of your profession). You might think of this logic when you receive that seductive recruiting brochure from some business school showing that its graduates earn 40 percent more than those of other schools.

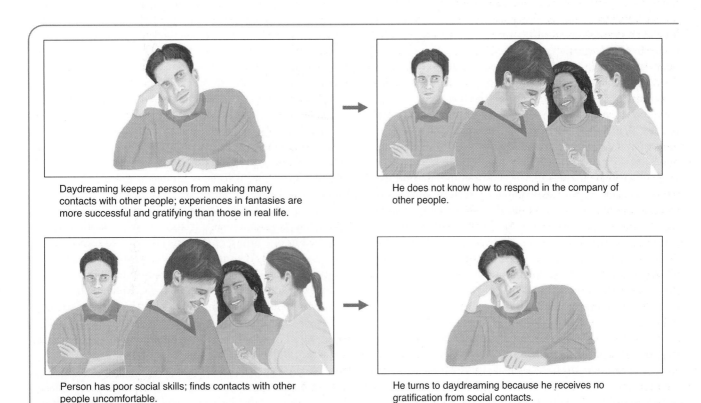

Daydreaming keeps a person from making many contacts with other people; experiences in fantasies are more successful and gratifying than those in real life.

He does not know how to respond in the company of other people.

Person has poor social skills; finds contacts with other people uncomfortable.

He turns to daydreaming because he receives no gratification from social contacts.

FIGURE 2•8   An example of a correlation. Correlations do not necessarily indicate cause-and-effect relations: Daydreaming could cause shyness, or shyness could cause daydreaming.

▲ *To study possible causes of daydreaming when we cannot manipulate variables, we could use a matching procedure.*

Can anything be done to reduce some of the uncertainty inherent in correlational studies? The answer is yes. When attempting to study the effects of a variable that cannot be altered (such as gender, age, socioeconomic status, or personality characteristics), we can use a procedure called **matching.** Rather than selecting participants randomly, we *match* the participants in each of the groups on all of the relevant variables except the one being studied. For instance, if we want to study the effects of shyness on daydreaming, we might select two groups of participants: one group composed of people who score very high on the shyness test and another group composed of people who score very low. We could then place further restrictions so that the effects of other variables are minimized. We could make sure that average age, intelligence, income, and personality characteristics (other than shyness) of people in the two groups are the same. If we find that, say, the shy group is, on average, younger than the non-shy group, we will replace some of the people in the shy group with older shy people until the average age is the same.

If, after following this matching procedure, we find that shyness is still related to daydreaming, we can be more confident that the differences between the two variables are not caused by a third variable. The limitation of the matching procedure is that we may not know all the variables that should be held constant. If, unbeknownst to us, the two groups are not matched on an important variable, the results will be misleading. In any case, even the matching procedure does not permit us to decide which variable is the cause and which is the effect; we still do not know whether shyness causes daydreaming or daydreaming causes shyness.

The strengths and limitations of correlational studies will become evident in subsequent chapters in this book. For example, almost all studies that attempt to discover the environmental factors that influence personality characteristics or the relation between these characteristics and people's behavior are correlational.

Reporting and Generalizing a Study

Scientists in all disciplines report the details of their research methods in professional publications known as *journals,* using sufficient detail that other investigators can repeat, or *replicate,* the research. The **replication** process is one of the great strengths of science; it ensures that erroneous results and incorrect conclusions are weeded out. When scientists publish a study, they know that if the findings are important enough, others will try to replicate their work to be sure that the results were not just a statistical fluke—or the result of errors in the design or execution of the original study. Statistical anomalies and incompetently conducted research usually will be uncovered through unsuccessful attempts to replicate. The insistence on replicability of research results also helps inhibit fraud in science, because the unreliability of falsified findings is likely to be discovered.

When we carry out an experiment or a correlational study, we probably assume that our participants are representative of the larger population. In fact, a representative group of participants is usually referred to as a **sample** of the larger population. For example, if we study the behavior of a group of five-year-old children, we want to make conclusions about five-year-olds in general. We want to be able to **generalize,** or extend, our specific results to the population as a whole—to conclude that the results tell us something about human nature in general, not simply about our particular participants.

Many researchers recruit their participants from introductory courses in psychology. The results of studies that use these students as participants can be best generalized to other groups of students who are similarly recruited. But in the strictest sense, the results cannot be generalized to students in other courses, to adults in general, or even to all students enrolled in introductory psychology—after all, students who volunteer to serve as participants may be different from those who do not. Even if we used truly random samples of all age groups of adults in our area, we could not generalize the results to people who live in other geographical regions. If our ability to generalize is really so limited, is it worthwhile to do psychological research?

The answer is that we are not so strictly limited. Most psychologists assume that a relation among variables that is observed in one group of humans also will be seen in other groups, as long as the sample of participants is not especially unusual. For example, we may expect data obtained from prisoners to have less generality than data obtained from university students. One feature of the scientific method we have discussed before helps achieve generalizability: replication. When results are replicated with different samples of people, we gain confidence in their generalizability.

The problems associated with generalizing occur in observational and correlational studies as often as in experiments. In the last hours of the 2004 presidential election, several web-based news organizations obtained access to the exit polling data collected by a consortium of opinion survey companies.

▲ *Exit polls, such as this one for an election in Azerbaijan, can be generalized only if the sample accurately reflects those who voted.*

On the basis of these data, some of these websites declared that the winner of the 2004 election would be . . . John Kerry.

What went wrong? The opinion polling group, Edison Media Research and Mitofsky International, later issued a report on the accuracy of their exit poll (Edison Media Research and Mitofsky International, 2005). Nationally, their poll had predicted that Kerry would win by a margin of 3 percent—an unprecedented degree of error, as he lost by 2.5 percent. The report suggested that the poll takers might have encountered a difference in the willingness of Kerry or Bush voters to be interviewed. Everyone has the right to refuse to answer a poll taker's questions. Perhaps Bush voters exercised this prerogative more. If more Kerry voters were interviewed because of this differential refusal rate, the exit poll would have described a sample of voters that did not represent the full electorate. An alternative explanation might be that, when questioned, voters gave different responses than their actual behavior in the voting booth.

The lesson from this incident is that generalization occurs in two ways. We attempt to generalize from the observations of our sample to a different group. And we generalize from one context, usually under our control, to a different context. The better our research design, control, and sampling, the better our chances of successful generalization.

Evaluating Scientific Issues

Format for Critical Thinking

In each of the subsequent chapters in this book, you will find a section called "Evaluating Scientific Issues." These sections present a controversial issue or an unanswered question and then examine the quality of the evidence concerning the issue. Each section begins with a description of the controversy. In most cases, this description includes an assertion that a certain state of affairs is true. For example, the section in Chapter 6 evaluates the assertion that subliminal messages can be used in teaching or advertising, and the section in Chapter 12 evaluates the assertion that television viewing impairs children's cognitive development.

After presenting the assertion, we will examine the evidence in favor of it. Next, we will look at the contrary evidence along with a critique of the evidence in favor of the assertion. The critiques refer back to the rules of the scientific method, described in this chapter. We will then accept or reject the assertion—or see that more evidence is needed before a decision can be made.

The point of these sections is to help you develop your ability to think critically—to learn to evaluate controversies by examining the nature and quality of the evidence and by drawing from the evidence only those conclusions that logically follow from it. Unfortunately, many people misuse or misinterpret research findings or misrepresent falsehoods as rigorous scientific truths in attempts to alter our attitudes and opinions or to sell us something. For example, advertisers will cite the opinions of scientific "experts." But there is no certified board of experts who are always right; we need to know the basis for the experts' opinions. That is, we need to know what the evidence is and understand how to evaluate it.

People who try to convince us of something often use nonscientific arguments. They may say something like "Everyone knows that . . ." or "Contrary to what so-called experts say, common sense tells us that. . . ." (The rule seems to be: If you cannot find an expert to quote, then condemn experts as "living in an ivory tower" or being "out of touch with reality.") People trying to convince us of something also will cite their personal experiences or will quote others' testimonials. If the cases they cite are rich with personal details, it is difficult not to be swayed by them.

Although some of you will eventually become psychologists, most of you will not. Nevertheless, we hope that by reading this book you will come to appreciate that being able to apply the scientific method to issues in psychological research will help you evaluate critically other issues that you will encounter in everyday life.

Interim Summary

The Scientific Method in Psychology

The scientific method allows us to determine the causes of phenomena. There are three basic forms of scientific research: naturalistic or clinical observations, correlational studies, and experiments. Only experiments permit us to be certain that a cause-and-effect relation exists. An experiment tests the truth of a hypothesis—a tentative statement about a relation between an independent variable and a dependent variable. Hypotheses come from information gathered through naturalistic observations, from previous experiments, or from formal theories.

To perform an experiment, a scientist manipulates the values of the independent variable and measures changes in the dependent variable. Because a hypothesis is stated in general terms, the scientist must specify the particular operations that he or she will perform to manipulate the independent variable and to measure the dependent variable. That is, the researcher must provide operational definitions, which may require some ingenuity and hard work. Operational definitions are a necessary part of the procedure of testing a hypothesis; they also can eliminate confusion by giving concrete form to the hypothesis, making its meaning absolutely clear to other scientists.

Validity is the degree to which an operational definition succeeds in producing a particular value of an independent variable or in measuring the value of a dependent variable. Reliability has to do with the consistency and precision of an operational definition. Researchers achieve high reliability by carefully controlling the conditions of their studies and by ensuring that procedures are followed correctly. Measurement involving subjectivity requires researchers to seek high interrater reliability.

When designing an experiment researchers must be sure to control extraneous variables that may confound their results. If an extra variable is inadvertently manipulated and if this extra variable has an effect on the dependent variable, then the results of the experiment will be invalid. Confounding of participant variables can be caused by improper assignment of participants to groups or by treatments that cause some participants to leave the experiment. Another problem involves participants' expectations. Most participants in psychological research try to figure out what the researcher is trying to accomplish, and their conclusions can affect their behavior. If knowledge of the experimental condition could alter the participants' behavior, one solution is to conduct the experiment with a single-blind procedure. Concealment or deception is sometimes a solution as well. If knowledge about the participants' condition might also alter the researcher's assessment of the participants' behavior, a double-blind procedure can be used.

Correlational studies involve assessing relations among variables that the researcher cannot readily manipulate, such as personality characteristics, age, and gender. The investigator attempts to hold these variables constant by matching members in each of the groups on all relevant variables except for the one being studied. The problem is that investigators may miss a variable that affects the outcome. And, of course, even a well-designed correlational study cannot determine which variable is the cause and which is the effect.

Researchers are almost never interested only in the particular participants they study; they want to be able to generalize their results to a larger population. The confidence that researchers can have in their generalizations depends on the nature of the variables being studied and on the composition of the sample group of participants. Replicability also supports generalization.

QUESTIONS TO CONSIDER

1. How might you apply the five steps of the scientific method to a question of your own—for example, the question of whether occasionally taking time out from studying for stretching and a little exercise affects a student's grades?
2. What is the relation between theories and hypotheses?
3. Suppose that you were interested in studying the effects of sleep deprivation on learning ability. Which of these two variables would be the independent variable and which would be the dependent variable? How might you operationally define these variables?
4. What is the difference between description and explanation in psychology?
5. In what ways might an operational definition be reliable yet not valid? Valid yet not reliable?

Ethics

Because psychologists must study living participants, they must respect ethical rules as well as scientific rules. Ethical conduct is mandatory in both human and animal research.

Research with Human Participants

Great care is needed in the treatment of human participants, because we can hurt people in very subtle ways. Title 42 of the United States Code requires that every institution receiving research support funds have an institutional review board (IRB) that will review the ethics of human research and ensure that researchers comply with ethical principles and guidelines. But in addition to this regulatory requirement, psychological researchers also subscribe to the Ethical Principles of Psychologists and Code of Conduct (American Psychological Association, 2002). As a code of conduct, these principles focus the attention of researchers on fundamental values and issues, because they and similar codes (e.g., Canadian Psychological Association, 2000) have developed from common social and cultural roots (see Adair, 2001; Hadjistavropoulos et al., 2002). Codes of research ethics make these shared values explicit.

Codes of human research ethics can be understood as widely accepted values about everyday interpersonal relations translated to the context of human research. In their everyday lives, most people believe that (1) it is wrong to hurt others needlessly; (2) it is good to help others; (3) it is usually wrong to make others do things contrary to their wishes and best interests; (4) it is usually wrong to lie to others; (5) we should respect others' privacy; (6) under most circumstances we should not break our promises to keep others' secrets; and (7) we should afford special protection to those who are relatively powerless or especially vulnerable to harm.

How are these interpersonal values translated to research relationships between researchers and participants? Codes of research ethics tell us that (1) we should minimize harm to participants, whether physical or mental; (2) we should maximize the benefits of research to participants in particular and society in general; (3) participants should be fully informed about the nature of the research in which they are invited to participate, including risks and benefits, and their **informed consent** to participate must be voluntary; (4) deception in research is generally unacceptable, although it may be tolerated under limited circumstances; (5) we should not intrude into the private lives of participants without their permission; (6) with certain exceptions, we should promise **confidentiality**—we should guarantee participants that information they provide will be kept anonymous or confidential unless they agree to make it public; and (7) vulnerable populations (e.g., children, prisoners, seriously ill patients, persons with compromised cognitive abilities) should be treated with special care.

Difficulties sometimes arise when researchers try to translate everyday values to research. Research procedures that represent good science are sometimes in conflict with respect for participants' dignity. The interesting problem that researchers set for themselves is to resolve these conflicts—to accomplish the best possible research while simultaneously ensuring that participants are treated properly. I have chosen my words carefully here. Sometimes researchers speak as though the values of scientific inquiry themselves are contrary to the value of respecting people. This is not the case. Effective research procedures, not the values of scientific inquiry, are sometimes in conflict with good treatment of participants. The goal is to identify and use research procedures that are both as ethical and as scientifically valid as possible.

You may have noticed that the list of research ethics values derived from interpersonal values includes exceptions to the general rules (as is the case for the interpersonal values themselves). For example, sometimes telling participants the full truth about the nature of the research will invalidate the research results. If I, as a researcher, tell you that I believe your enjoyment of your favorite activity will decline if I start to pay you for doing it, you may feel pressure to act as if I am correct, even if I am wrong. In this type of situation, the researcher may decide that concealing the hypothesis from you, or actively deceiving you about the nature of the hypothesis, would be good science. Yet there is a conflict with the interpersonal value of not telling lies. The result of ethical decision making and ethics review by IRBs is sometimes to identify an acceptable balance. The researcher may be permitted to use concealment or minor deception, but only if there is no foreseeable harm to participants and if the researcher can reestablish trust with participants by immediately disclosing the truth to them in a **debriefing** on completion of their participation. I think that it is interesting that this is also the nature of the corresponding values in interpersonal relations. Most of us believe that it is wrong to conceal important information from one another or to lie to one another. Yet many people at times do not strictly observe these interpersonal values, and still believe that they have acted properly. Good business practice, for example, sometimes involves concealing proprietary information from competitors to protect intellectual property rights. Neither opposing football teams nor chess players reveal their strategies. We may say to someone, "Thank you for the lovely sweater," even though our personal taste does not run to chartreuse. Sometimes telling the truth (e.g., revealing our dislike of the sweater) conflicts with our value of not harming others (e.g., not criticizing a friend's gift). Even so, we are likely to lie only if doing so does not undermine trust in the relationship—just as in the laboratory. The details of ethical conflicts in the laboratory and the living room differ, but the underlying problems and solutions are similar.

Another way to look at value conflicts is the old saying that "The exception proves the rule." In our daily lives most of us take seriously the confidences placed in us by others. Likewise, in our research we respect our promises of confidentiality. But the person in private life who promises to keep an as-yet-unstated secret and the researcher who makes the same promise can face a similar conflict of values if the secret turns out to pose a risk of harm to someone or to reveal ongoing harmful acts. A private citizen who learns that a neighbor is sexually abusing a child, or a researcher who learns that a participant is doing so, may feel compelled to intervene on the child's behalf and report the abuse. The conflicting value of protecting children from harm may justify breaking the promise of confidentiality. The shared basis for interpersonal and research values, as these examples illustrate, virtually guarantees that conflicts among values will arise in both contexts. The task then is to solve those problems in a sensitive and ethical manner.

Research with Animals

Although most psychologists study the behavior of their fellow humans, some study the behavior of other animals. Any time we use another species of animal for our own purposes,

▲ *Should animals be used in psychological research? Most psychologists and other researchers strongly believe that animal research, conducted humanely, is necessary and ethically justified.*

we should be sure that what we are doing is both humane and worthwhile. A good case can be made that such psychological research qualifies on both counts. Humane treatment is a matter of procedure. We know how to maintain laboratory animals in good health and in comfortable, sanitary conditions. For experiments that involve surgery, we know how to administer anesthetics and analgesics so that animals do not suffer. Most industrially developed societies have very strict regulations about the care of animals and require approval of the procedures that will be used in animal experiments. American psychologists who use animals in their research adhere to ethical guidelines developed by the American Psychological Association and regulations of various federal agencies such as the National Institutes of Health and the U.S. Department of Agriculture. Under these guidelines all projects involving animals, including teaching and research projects but excepting some purely observational studies, are reviewed by a committee that must include a veterinarian and a member of the public community not affiliated with the institution where the research is carried out. These committee members rigorously review the experimental procedures and have the authority to prevent or halt a project that does not adhere to ethical principles.

Because we, as humans, have the power to decide whether a research project is carried out, and other animals do not, it is important to ask whether research involving animals is a form of exploitation. We use animals for many purposes. We eat animals' meat and their eggs and drink their milk; we turn animals' hides into leather; we extract insulin and other hormones from animals' organs to treat people with diseases; we train animals to do useful work on farms or to entertain us. These are all forms of exploitation. Even having a pet can be considered a form of exploitation: It is we, not they, who decide that animals will live in our homes. The fact is, we have been using other animals throughout the history of our species.

Whether the use of animals in research is justified is a question that must be asked every time a study is proposed. One factor to consider is the nature of the controls placed on research activity as compared to the controls on some other uses of animals. For example, we know that, sadly, some pet owners cause much more suffering among animals than scientific research does. As Miller (1983) notes, pet owners are not required to receive permission to keep their pets from boards of experts that include veterinarians; nor are they subject to periodic inspections to ensure that their homes are clean and sanitary, that their pets have enough space to exercise properly, and that their diets are appropriate.

The core reality is that our species is beset by medical, mental, and behavioral problems, many of which can be solved only through research involving nonhuman animals. Research with laboratory animals has produced important discoveries about the possible causes or potential treatments of neurological and mental disorders, including Parkinson's disease, schizophrenia, bipolar disorder, anxiety disorders, obsessive-compulsive disorders, anorexia nervosa, obesity, and drug addictions. Although much progress has been made, these problems are still with us and cause much human suffering.

But, as a result of discoveries described in Chapter 4, we now have the ability to describe the inner workings of the human brain in healthy and alert people and to even produce motion pictures of the brain at work. This research has the promise of providing answers to the problems I mentioned, but only if we can understand the basic principles of neurology and behavior. Often, this understanding can only be gained by research that involves animals. Some people have suggested that instead of using laboratory animals in our research, we could use tissue cultures or computer simulations. Unfortunately, tissue cultures or computer simulations are seldom interchangeable substitutes for living organisms. We have no way to study behavioral problems such as addictions in tissue cultures, nor can we program a computer to simulate the workings of an animal's nervous system. If we could, we would already have all the answers.

Biology and Culture

Cross-Cultural Research

Although most psychologists study members of their own cultures, *cross-cultural psychologists* (see Chapter 1) are interested in the effects of cultures on behavior (Berry, Poortinga, Segall, & Dasen, 2002). The term *culture* traditionally referred to a group of people who live together in a common environment, who share customs and religious beliefs and practices, and who often resemble one another genetically. However, definitions of culture now vary widely.

▲ *Some cultures are small and relatively homogeneous, such as the culture of these Maori people living in New Zealand's North Island, who are shown dressed for a festival.*

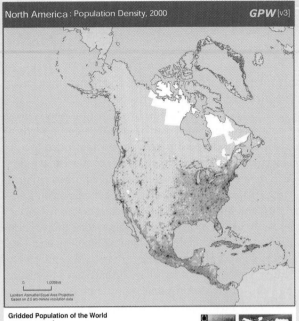

▲ *Population density, revealed by this population density map of North America, is an important ecological cultural variable.*

For example, "North American culture" includes people of diverse ethnic and religious backgrounds, political beliefs, and economic statuses, while "Fore people" includes a small, fairly homogeneous group of people living in the highlands of Papua New Guinea. Within a broadly defined culture, we can identify subcultures based on ethnicity, age, political beliefs, and other characteristics by which people define themselves. Keep in mind that "culture" is not synonymous with country or continent. Many cultures can exist within a single geographic zone.

Cross-cultural research lets psychologists test the generality of the results of a study performed with members of a particular culture. If similar studies performed with members of different cultures produce similar results, we can be more confident that we have discovered a general principle that applies broadly to members of our species. On the other hand, if the studies yield different results in different cultures, we need to carry out further research. Obviously, differences among cultures affect the variables we are interested in. We need to perform further cross-cultural research to identify these differences. The cross-cultural approach lends itself to questions of immense political and economic importance. For example, think of the many issues that arise when people migrate from one culture to another (Berry, 2001).

Cultures differ with respect to two major classes of variables: biological and ecological. Biological variables include such factors as diet, genetics, and endemic diseases. Ecological variables include such factors as geography, climate, political systems, population density, religion, cultural myths, and education. Behavioral differences among people of different cultures result from differences in both biological and ecological variables.

Identifying the cultural variables responsible for behavioral differences is a difficult process, for culture can be viewed as affecting behavior in different ways (Lonner & Adamopoulos, 1997). In cross-cultural research, culture is considered to be a treatment variable—something like an independent variable (Berry, Poortinga, Segall, & Dasen, 2002). But cultures, like people, differ in many ways, and people are born into their cultures, not assigned to them by psychologists performing experiments. Thus, cross-cultural comparisons are subject to the same limitations that affect other correlational studies.

Psychologists who do cross-cultural research have investigated social behaviors, personality differences, approaches to problem solving, intellectual abilities, perceptual abilities, and aesthetics. (Segall, Dasen, Berry, and Poortinga, 1999, provide an engaging overview.) This text examines the interplay between biology and culture, such as the role of the environment in brain development, the effects of cultural differences in child-rearing practices, cultural definitions of intelligence, cultural differences in emotional expressions, and expressions of mental disorders in different cultural contexts. In particular, the Biology and Culture features throughout the book should help you appreciate the effects of variables that people within a culture are rarely aware of because they are an implicit part of their own lives.

Interim Summary

Ethics

Because psychologists study living organisms, they must follow ethical principles in the treatment of these organisms. Federal law requires review by an institutional review board before any human research is undertaken in institutions receiving funding from agencies of the United States. Ethical principles for research are similar to those that guide people in their everyday lives and include minimizing harm to participants, ensuring informed consent, respecting confidentiality, and avoiding deception in most circumstances.

Research that involves the use of laboratory animals also is guided by ethical principles. It is incumbent on all scientists using these animals to see that they are housed comfortably and treated humanely, and laws have been enacted to ensure that they are. Research with animals has produced many benefits to humankind and promises to continue to do so.

QUESTIONS TO CONSIDER

1. In your opinion, should principles of ethical research be absolute, or should they be flexible? Suppose that a researcher proposed to perform an experiment whose results could have important and beneficial consequences for society, perhaps a real reduction in violent crime. However, the proposed study would violate ethical guidelines, because it would involve deception and a significant degree of psychological pain for the participants. Should the researcher be given permission to perform the experiment? Should an exception be made because of the potential benefits to society?

2. Why do you think some people apparently are more upset about using animals for research and teaching than about exploiting animals for other purposes?

Understanding Research Results

Our study is finished. We have a collection of data—numbers representing the measurements of behavior we have made. Now what do we do? How do we know what we found? Was our hypothesis supported? To answer these questions, we must analyze the data we have collected. We will use some statistical methods to do so.

Descriptive Statistics: What Are the Results?

In the examples of experimental research that we have considered so far, the behavior of participants assigned to groups (conditions) was observed and measured. Once a study is finished, we need some way to compare these measurements. To

do so, we will first use **descriptive statistics,** mathematical procedures that permit us to summarize sets of numbers. Using these procedures, we will calculate measures that summarize the performance of the participants in each group. Then we can compare these measures to see whether the groups of participants behaved differently (step 4 of the scientific method). We can also use these measures to describe the results of the experiment to others (step 5 of the scientific method). You are already familiar with some descriptive statistics. For example, you know how to calculate the average of a set of numbers; an average is a common *measure of central tendency.* You may be less familiar with *measures of variability,* which tell us how groups of numbers differ from one another, and with measures of *relations,* which tell us how closely related two sets of numbers are.

Measures of Central Tendency When we say that the average weight of an adult male in North America is 173 pounds or that the average salary of a female university graduate was $40,750 in 2004, we are using a **measure of central tendency,** a statistic that represents many observations. There are several different measures of central tendency, but the most common is the average, also called the **mean.** We calculate the mean of a set of observations by adding the individual values and dividing by the number of observations. The mean is the most frequently used measure of central tendency in reports of psychological experiments.

Although the mean is usually selected to measure central tendency, it is not the most precise measure, especially if a set of numbers contains a few extremely high or low values. The most representative measure of central tendency is the *median.* For this reason, we usually see the phrase "median family income" rather than "mean family income" in newspaper or magazine articles. To calculate the **median** of a set of numbers, we arrange them in numerical order and find the midpoint. For example, the median of the numbers 1, 2, and 6 is 2.

To understand why the median is the best representative of a set of numbers that contains some extreme values, consider a small town of 100 families. Ninety-nine of the families, all of whom work in the local lumber mill, make between $25,000 and $30,000 per year. However, the income of one family is $3 million per year (an extreme value, to be sure). This family consists of a popular novelist and her husband, who moved to the area because of its mild climate. The *mean* income for the town as a whole, considering the novelist as well as the mill workers, is $59,000 per year. In contrast, the *median* income for the town is $30,000 per year. Clearly, the median represents the typical family income of the town better than the mean does. Why, then, would we ever bother to use the mean rather than the median? As we will see later in this section, the mean is used to calculate other important statistics and has special mathematical properties that often make it more useful than the median.

Measures of Variability Many experiments produce two sets of numbers, one consisting of the experimental group's

TABLE 2•1	Two Sets of Numbers Having the Same Mean and Median but Different Ranges

Sample A	Sample B
8	0
9	5
10 Median	10 Median
11	15
12	20
Total: 50	Total: 50
Mean: 50/5 = 10	Mean: 50/5 = 10
Range: 12 – 8 = 4	Range: 20 – 0 = 20

scores and one of the control group's scores. If the mean scores of these two groups differ, the researcher can conclude that the independent variable had an effect. However, the researcher must decide whether the difference between the two groups is larger than what would probably occur by chance. To make this decision, the researcher calculates a **measure of variability**—a statistic that describes the degree to which scores in a set of numbers differ from one another. The psychologist then uses this measure as a basis for comparing the means of the two groups.

Two sets of numbers can have the same mean or median and still be very different in their overall character. For example, the mean and the median of both sets of numbers listed in **Table 2•1** are the same, but the sets of numbers are clearly different. The variability of the scores in Sample B is greater.

One way of stating the difference between the two sets of numbers in Table 2.1 is to say that the numbers in Sample A range from 8 to 12 and the numbers in Sample B range from 0 to 20. The **range** of a set of numbers is simply the largest number minus the smallest. Thus, the range of Sample A is 4 and the range of Sample B is 20.

The range is not used very often to describe the results of psychological experiments, however—because another measure of variability, the **standard deviation**, has more useful mathematical properties. As **Table 2•2** shows, to calculate the standard deviation of a set of numbers, you first calculate the mean and then find the difference between each number and the mean. These different scores are squared (that is, multiplied by themselves) and then summed. The mean calculated from this total is called the *variance;* the standard deviation is the square root of the variance. The more different the numbers are from one another, the larger the standard deviation will be.

Measurement of Relations

In correlational studies, the investigator measures the degree to which two variables are related. For example, suppose that we have developed a new aptitude test and hope to persuade a college administrator to use the test when evaluating applicants. We need to show a relation between scores on our test and measures of suc-

cess (such as grades) in the college's program. Assume that the college uses a letter grading system in which A designates the top grade and F designates a failure. (There is no grade E.) To analyze our test quantitatively, we need to convert these labels into numerical scores; we use the convention that an A is 4, an F is 0, and the letters in between have corresponding values.

We give the test to 10 students entering the college and later obtain their average grades. We will have two scores for each person, as shown in **Table 2•3**. We can examine the relation between these variables by plotting the scores on a graph. For example, student R. J. received a test score of 14 and earned an average grade of 3.0. We can represent this student's score as a point on the graph shown in **Figure 2•9**. The horizontal axis represents the test score, and the vertical axis represents the average grade. We put a point on the graph that corresponds to R. J.'s score on both of these measures.

We do this for each of the remaining students and then look at the graph, called a **scatterplot,** to determine whether the two variables are related. When we examine the scatterplot (refer to Figure 2.9), we see that the points tend to be located along a diagonal line that runs from the lower left to

TABLE 2•2	Calculation of the Variance and Standard Deviation of Two Sets of Numbers Having the Same Mean

Sample A

Score	Difference between Score and Mean	Difference Squared
8	10 – 8 = 2	4
9	10 – 9 = 1	1
10	10 – 10 = 0	0
11	11 – 10 = 1	1
12	12 – 10 = 2	4
Total: 50	Total:	10
Mean: 50/5 = 10	Mean (variance):	10/5 = 2
	Square root (standard deviation):	$\sqrt{2}$ = 1.41

Sample B

Score	Difference between Score and Mean	Difference Squared
0	10 – 0 = 10	100
5	10 – 5 = 5	25
10	10 – 10 = 0	0
15	15 – 10 = 5	25
20	20 – 10 = 10	100
Total: 50	Total:	250
Mean: 50/5 = 10	Mean (variance):	250/5 = 50
	Square root (standard deviation):	$\sqrt{50}$ = 7.07

TABLE 2•3	Test Score and Average Grades of Ten Students	
Student	Test Score	Average Grade[a]
A. C.	15	2.8
B. F.	12	3.2
C. G.	19	3.5
L. H.	8	2.2
R. J.	14	3.0
S. K.	11	2.6
P. R.	13	2.8
A. S.	7	1.5
J. S.	9	1.9
P. V.	18	3.8

[a]0 = F; 4 = A

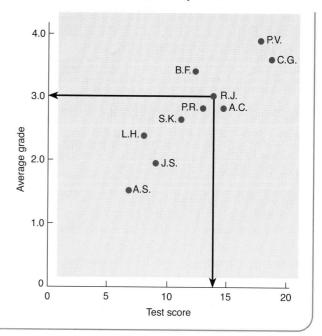

FIGURE 2•9 A scatterplot of the test scores and average grades of 10 students. An example of graphing one data point (student R. J.) is shown by the colored lines.

the upper right, indicating that a rather strong relation exists between students' test scores and their average grades. High scores are associated with good grades, low scores with poor grades.

Although scatterplots are useful, we need a more convenient way to communicate the results to others, so we calculate the **correlation coefficient,** a number that expresses the strength of a relation. Calculating this statistic for the two sets of scores gives a correlation of +0.9 between the two variables.

The size of a correlation coefficient can vary from 0 (no relation) to plus or minus 1.0 (a perfect relation). A perfect relation means that if we know the value of a person's score on one measure, then we can predict exactly what his or her score will be on the other. Thus, a correlation of +0.9 is very close to perfect; our hypothetical aptitude test is an excellent predictor of how well a student will do at the college. A *positive correlation* indicates that high values on one measure are associated with high values on the other and that low values on one are associated with low values on the other.

Correlations can be negative as well as positive. A *negative correlation* indicates that high values on one measure are associated with low values on the other, and vice versa. An example of a negative correlation is the relation between people's mathematical ability and the amount of time it takes them to solve a series of math problems. People with the highest level of abil-

ity will take the least time to solve the problems. For purposes of prediction, a negative correlation is just as good as a positive one. Examples of scatterplots illustrating high and low correlations, both positive and negative, are shown in **Figure 2•10**.

If the points in a scatterplot fall along a line, the relation is said to be *linear*. But many relations are nonlinear. For example, consider the relation between level of illumination and reading speed. Obviously, it is impossible to read in the dark. As the light level increases, people's reading speed will increase, but once an adequate amount of light falls on a page, further increases in light will have no effect. Finally, the light will become so bright and dazzling that people's reading speed will decline. (See **Figure 2•11**.) A correlation coefficient cannot accurately represent a nonlinear relation such as this, because the mathematics involved in calculating this measure assume that the relation is linear. Scientists who discover nonlinear relations in their research usually present them in graphs or express them as nonlinear mathematical formulas.

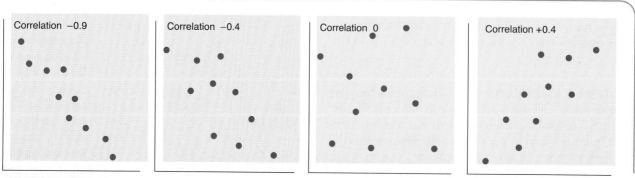

FIGURE 2•10 Scatterplots of variables having several different levels of correlation.

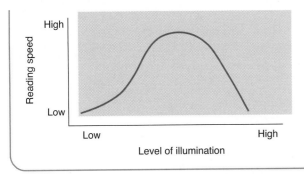

FIGURE 2·11 A nonlinear relation. Results of a hypothetical experiment investigating the relation between level of illumination and reading speed. A correlation coefficient cannot adequately represent this kind of relation.

Inferential Statistics: Distinguishing Chance from Significance

When we perform an experiment, we select a sample of participants from a larger population. In doing so, we hope that the results from the sample will be similar to those we might have obtained had we included the entire population in the experiment. We randomly assign the participants to groups in an unbiased manner, manipulate only the relevant independent variables, and measure the dependent variable using a valid and reliable method. After the experiment is completed, we must examine the results and decide whether a relation really exists between independent and dependent variables.

But what does it mean to conclude that a relation "really" exists? As a matter of common sense, we'd like to say that our results are not due to some rare fluke or chance accident. We must, then, measure how likely it is that our results might be due to chance. If we find it improbable that our results are accidental, then we can describe them as possessing **statistical significance**—as being probably not due to chance. As we saw, descriptive statistics enable us to summarize our data. **Inferential statistics** enable us to calculate the probability that our results are due to chance and thereby tell us whether the results are statistically significant.

The concept of statistical significance is not easy to grasp, so I want to make sure you understand the purpose of this discussion. Recall our experiment designed to test the hypothesis that a visual expectation of an image increases the rate of detection of the image in a SIRD stereogram. We show some participants but not others a silhouette of the image. Next, we show stereograms to participants in both groups and record how long it takes them to detect the image. To see whether viewing the silhouette has improved detection of the image, we calculate the mean response time for both groups. If the means are different, we can conclude that visual expectation *does* affect people's ability to recognize an image.

But how different is different? Suppose that we tested two groups of people, both treated exactly the same way. Would the mean scores of the two groups be precisely the same? Of course not. *By chance,* they would be at least slightly different. Suppose that we find that the mean score for the group that was shown the image is lower than the mean score for the control group. How much lower would it have to be before we could rightfully conclude that the difference between the groups was significant?

Assessment of Differences between Samples The obvious way to determine whether two group means differ significantly is to look at the size of the difference. If it is large, then we can be fairly confident that the independent variable had a significant effect. If it is small, then the difference may well be due to chance. What we need are guidelines to help us determine when a difference is large enough to be statistically significant.

The following example, based on a real classroom demonstration and results, will explain how these guidelines are constructed. A few years ago, I performed a simple correlational study to test the following hypothesis: In North America people whose first names end in vowels will, on average, be shorter than people whose first names end in consonants. (I'll reveal the rationale for this hypothesis later.)

First, I distributed a blank card to each student in a psychology class and asked each student to print his or her first name on the card together with his or her height. There were 76 students in the class, and I found that the mean height for all students was 67.2 inches. Next I divided the participants into two groups: those whose first names ended in vowels and those whose first names ended in consonants. **Table 2·4** contains a listing of these two groups. You can see that the means for the two groups differed by 4.1 inches.

A difference of 4.1 inches seems large, but how can we be sure that it is not due to chance? What we really need to know is how large a difference there would be if the means had been calculated from two groups that were randomly selected. For comparison, I divided the class into two random groups by shuffling the cards with the students' names on them and dealing them out into two piles, "A" and "B." Then I calculated the mean height of the people whose names were in each of the piles. Subtracting the "B" group mean from the "A" group showed me that the difference between the means was −0.7 inch. (See **Table 2·5**.)

I divided the cards into two random piles five more times, calculating the means and subtracting the "B" mean from the "A" mean each time. The differences for these five random divisions ranged from −0.3 to 0.7 inch. (See **Table 2·6**.) It began to look as if a mean difference of 4.1 inches was bigger than would be expected to occur by chance.

Next, I divided the cards into two random piles 1000 times. (I used my computer to do the chore.) *Not once* in 1000 times was the difference between the means greater than 3.0 inches. Therefore, I concluded that if the class is divided randomly into two groups, the chance that the means of their heights will differ by 4.1 inches is much less than one time in a thousand, or 0.1 percent. Thus, I can safely say that when I divided the students into two groups according to the last letters of their first names, I was dividing them in a way that was somehow related to their height. The division was

TABLE 2·4 Height (in Inches) of Selected Samples of Students

Name Ends in Consonant		Name Ends in Vowel
65	61	67
67	68	68
71	70	62
72	65	63
73	73	62
65	60	64
74	70	60
74	72	63
67	63	61
69	67	69
68	73	63
75	66	65
72	71	69
71	72	71
65	64	69
66	69	65
70	73	70
72	75	63
72	72	63
71	66	64
62	71	65
62	68	63
80	70	66
		75
Total:	3257	72
Mean:	3257/47 = 69.3	65
		66
		65
		65

Total: 1890
Mean: 1890/29 = 65.2
Difference between means: 69.3 – 65.2 = 4.1

TABLE 2·5 Height (in Inches) of Students Assigned Randomly to Two Groups

Group A		Group B	
65	71	63	62
72	63	62	63
72	74	70	65
70	72	70	75
61	71	65	71
69	65	64	80
66	71	75	71
70	67	63	68
66	72	70	71
65	66	75	73
66	72	67	62
65	73	65	72
64	63	68	65
72	69	63	72
63	62	69	66
65	60	67	73
62	70	68	65
67	68	60	73
	69		61
	64		74

Total: 2561   Total: 2586
Mean: 67.4   Mean: 68.1
Difference: –0.7

We can see that only 15 out of 1000 times (1.5 percent) is the difference between the means of the two groups as large as or larger than 2.2 inches: 11 + 4 = 15. (See Figure 2.12.) Therefore, if we had obtained a difference of 2.2 inches between the means of the groups and concluded that people whose first names end in vowels tend to be shorter than people whose first names end in consonants, *the likelihood of our being wrong would have been only 1.5 percent.* The calculations show that we will obtain a difference of at least 2.2 inches between the means purely by chance only 1.5 percent of the time. Because 1.5 percent is a small number, we are fairly safe in concluding that the relation is statistically significant.

TABLE 2·6 Mean Heights (in Inches) of Five Random Divisions of Students into Two Groups

Group A	Group B	Difference
67.6	67.9	–0.3
68.1	67.4	0.7
67.8	67.6	0.2
67.9	67.5	0.4
68.0	67.4	0.6

not equivalent to random selection; a person's height *really is* related to the last letter of his or her first name.

Figure 2·12 presents a frequency distribution of the differences between the means of the two groups for 1000 random divisions of the class. The height of a point on the graph represents the number of times (the frequency) that the difference between the means fell into that particular range. For example, the difference between the means fell between –0.2 and +0.2 inch 170 times.

Suppose that the difference between the means in my observational study had been smaller than 4.1 inches—say, 2.2 inches. Would we conclude that the difference represented a real relation, or would we decide that the difference was due to chance? A look at Figure 2.12 will help us decide.

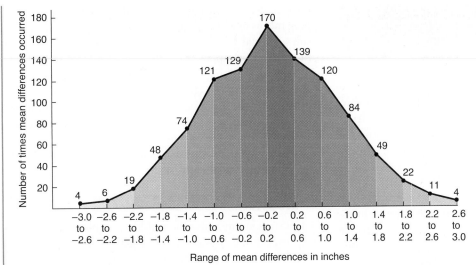

FIGURE 2·12 A frequency distribution. This distribution illustrates the number of occurrences of various ranges of mean differences in height. The group of 76 people was divided randomly into two sets of numbers 1000 times.

The method used to determine the statistical significance of my findings involves the same principles that researchers use to determine whether the results observed in an experiment represent a real difference or are merely due to chance. In this example we considered two possibilities: (1) that the difference between the means was due to chance, and (2) that the difference between the means occurred because the last letter of a person's first name is related to his or her height. Because a difference of 4.1 inches would be expected less than one time in a thousand, we rejected alternative 1 and concluded that alternative 2 was correct. The results supported my original hypothesis.

Ordinarily, psychologists who conduct experiments or correlational studies like this one do not use their computers to divide their participants' scores randomly 1000 times. Instead, they calculate the mean and standard deviation for each group and consult a table that statisticians have already prepared for them, available in a special software format. The table is based on special mathematical properties of the mean and standard deviation, and describes what is called a *normal distribution;* the shape of a normal distribution is similar to the frequency distribution depicted in Figure 2.12. Using a normal distribution as a guide, psychologists can tell how likely it is that their results could have been obtained by chance. For example, the table would tell us how likely it is that the last letter of a person's first name is *not really* related to his or her height. If the likelihood of a chance result is low enough, psychologists will conclude that their research results are statistically significant. Most psychologists consider a 5 percent probability of chance to be statistically significant but are much more comfortable with 1 percent or less.

Please note that statistical tests help us decide whether results are representative of the larger population, but not whether they are *important.* In general usage the word *significant* does mean "important," but *statistical* significance simply means that the results appear not to be caused by chance. For example, suppose a school board experiments with a new teaching method and finds that the test scores of students taught by the new method are higher than those of students taught the old way. Although the difference is statistically significant, it is very small. (A small difference can be statistically significant if the variability within the groups is low enough or if the groups are very large.) Because changing over to the new method would be extremely expensive, the school system would probably decide to continue with the old method.

Oh yes, why would I ever guess (hypothesize) that the last letter of a person's first name would be related to his or her height? The answer is that in English, feminine names are more likely than masculine names to end in a vowel (Paula, Tara, Marie, etc.). Because women tend to be shorter than men, I could expect that among a group of English-speaking students, a group of students whose first names ended in vowels would be shorter, on average, than those whose first names ended in consonants.

▲ *Although individuals vary widely in height, men are taller, on average, than women—and this explains the finding in my classroom observational study.*

Interim Summary

Understanding Research Results

Psychologists need ways to communicate their results to others accurately and concisely. They typically employ three kinds of descriptive statistics: measures of central tendency, variability, and relations. The most common examples of these measures are the mean, the median, the standard deviation, and the correlation coefficient.

If psychologists test a hypothesis by comparing the scores of two groups of participants, they must have some way of determining whether the observed difference in the mean scores is larger than what would be expected by chance. The first name–height example was a correlational study. However, the procedure employed was based on the same logic that a psychologist would use in assessing the significance of the results of an experiment.

Psychologists perform experiments by observing the performance of two or more groups of participants who have been exposed to different conditions, each representing different values of the independent variable. Next, they calculate the group means and standard deviations of the values of the dependent variable that were measured. Finally, they deter-mine the statistical significance of the results. To do so, they plug means and standard deviations into a formula and consult a special table that statisticians have devised. (This almost always happens via software.) The table indicates the likelihood of getting such results when the independent variable actually has no effect on the dependent variable. If the probability of obtaining these results by chance is sufficiently low, the psychologists will reject the possibility that the independent variable had *no effect* and will decide in favor of the alternative—that the independent variable really did have an effect on the dependent variable.

QUESTIONS TO CONSIDER

1. Can you think of some real-life variables that you would expect to be positively and negatively correlated?
2. What does it mean to say that a study produced statistically significant results? Why might the results of a study be statistically significant but nevertheless unimportant?
3. I hypothesized that people whose names ended in a vowel would be shorter than those whose names ended in a consonant. How would my analysis have differed if I had merely said that the two groups would be different?

Suggestions for Further Reading

Christensen, L. B. (2003). *Experimental methodology* (9th ed.). Boston: Allyn and Bacon.

Abelson, R. P. (1995). *Statistics as principled argument.* Hillsdale, NJ: Lawrence Erlbaum Associates.

Several standard textbooks discuss the scientific method in psychological research. The Christensen book covers ethical and practical issues as well as theoretical ones. Abelson's book explores the logic behind statistical tests.

Barber, T. X. (1976). *Pitfalls in human research.* New York: Pergamon Press.

McCain, G., & Segal, E. M. (1981). *The game of science* (4th ed.). Belmont, CA: Brooks/Cole.

Both of these books are rather entertaining accounts of the whys and wherefores of the scientific method. Most of us enjoy reading about oth-ers' mistakes, perhaps thinking that we could have done things better. Barber's book allows us to indulge in this activity; it discusses specific instances of studies that were flawed.

Bell, J. (1999). *Evaluating psychological information: Sharpening your critical thinking skills* (3rd ed.). Boston: Allyn and Bacon.

Bell's book provides what the title claims: an excellent way to sharpen your critical thinking skills. It is full of exercises to help you accomplish that goal.

Key Terms

case study (p. 30)

clinical observation (p. 27)

confidentiality (p. 43)

confounding of variables (p. 34)

control group (p. 31)

correlation coefficient (p. 48)

correlational studies (p. 27)

correlational study (p. 38)

counterbalancing (p. 34)

debriefing (p. 43)

dependent variable (p. 31)

descriptive statistics (p. 46)

double-blind study (p. 38)

experiment (p. 27)

experimental group (p. 31)

generalize (p. 40)

hypothesis (p. 29)

independent variable (p. 31)

inferential statistics (p. 49)

informed consent (p. 43)

interrater reliability (p. 36)

manipulation (p. 31)

matching (p. 40)

mean (p. 46)

measure of central tendency (p. 46)

measure of variability (p. 47)

median (p. 46)

naturalistic observation (p. 27)

nominal fallacy (p. 32)

operational definition (p. 32)

placebo (p. 38)

random assignment (p. 36)

range (p. 47)

reliability (p. 35)

replication (p. 40)

sample (p. 40)

scatterplot (p. 47)

scientific method (p. 27)

single-blind study (p. 38)

standard deviation (p. 47)

statistical significance (p. 49)

survey study (p. 31)

theory (p. 29)

validity (p. 33)

variable (p. 31)

3

EVOLUTION, HEREDITY, AND BEHAVIOR

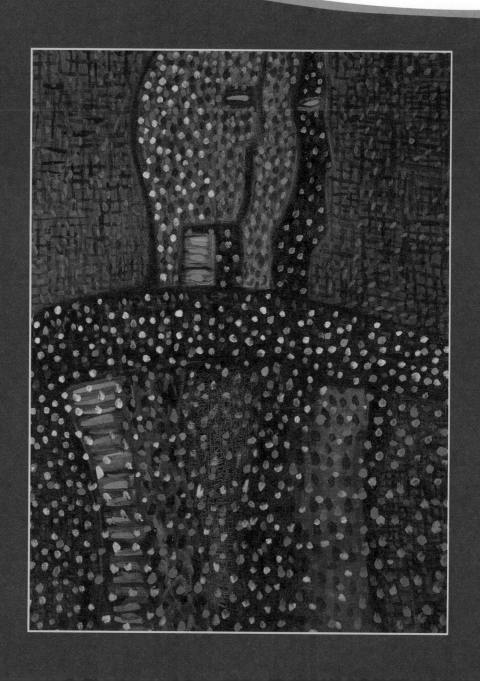

The Development of Evolutionary Science

The Voyage of the *Beagle* • The Origin of Species

Heredity and environment interact to influence our behavior. To understand these influences, many psychologists study evolution, genetics, and events in the immediate environment that affect behavior. Our understanding of biological evolution stems from Darwin's work on natural selection.

Natural Selection and Evolution

Natural Selection as a Three-Step Process: Variation, Selection, and Retention • Darwinian Principles of Natural Selection • Natural Selection in Human Evolution

Natural selection occurs because organisms vary physically, behaviorally, and genetically. Some physical and behavioral characteristics provide a competitive advantage for survival and reproduction. If these characteristics have a genetic basis, they are likely to increase in frequency in successive generations. In human evolution, natural selection has favored an upright posture and increases in brain size. These two factors contributed to the exploration and settling of new environments and, eventually, to culture.

Heredity and Genetics

Basic Principles of Genetics • The Importance of Genetic Diversity • Sex-Linked Characteristics • Mutations and Chromosomal Aberrations • Genetic Disorders • Heredity and Behavior • Studying Genetic Influences • *Evaluating Scientific Issues: The Genetics of Alcoholism*

Genes contain instructions for the synthesis of protein molecules. These molecules control bodily development and regulate physiological processes. Sexual reproduction provides for genetic diversity through the recombination of genes. Genetic diversity increases the chance that some members of a species may survive environmental changes. The expression of a gene depends on the interaction of the gene with other genes, the sex of the individual possessing the gene, and the environmental conditions under which that individual lives. Changes in genetic material caused by mutations or chromosomal aberrations produce changes in gene expression and play a primary role in the cause of genetic disorders. Artificial selection, concordance studies, and segregation analysis are the primary techniques that psychologists and other scientists use in studying the relation between genes and behavior. Research raises the question of whether genetic factors may be involved in alcoholism.

Sociobiology

Reproductive Strategies and the Biological Basis of Parenting • The Biological Basis of Altruism • Some Comments about Sociobiology • *Biology and Culture: Thinking Critically about Selection*

Sociobiology, the study of the biological basis of social behavior, extends Darwin's work to the explanation of complex human behavior. Sex differences in the resources that parents invest in procreation and in caring for their offspring have led to the evolution of four different patterns of selecting mates and rearing offspring. Altruism increases the reproductive success of others with whom an individual may have many genes in common. We are likely to engage in altruistic acts toward others who may later be in a position to return the favor to us or to our relatives. Sociobiologists have been criticized for neglecting the role of the environment in determining human behavior. When thinking critically about selection as a means of producing complex and diverse outcomes, we must avoid several common misconceptions. Behavior is due to the complex interaction of evolutionary, genetic, and environmental variables.

John Harold Johnson Jr. died at the young age of 25. He died from sickle-cell anemia, a disorder in which the red blood cells that carry oxygen to the body become curved and sticky instead of round and smooth. This change in shape causes the red blood cells to become stuck in the smaller blood vessels, a painful condition that leads to widespread damage to organs of the body. Sickle-cell anemia is known to run in families, but how could John have the disease when neither his parents nor his sister had it? Moreover, his entire family was long-lived. John's father, for whom he was named, died only recently at the age of 87; at this writing his mother and sibling are still alive. What's more, John Jr. came from an accomplished family. His father rose from a poor background to found *Ebony* magazine and several other companies as well. In fact, John Harold Johnson Sr. was the first African American included in the Forbes 400 list of the wealthiest Americans. John Jr.'s mother and his sister were also superior achievers. His mother suggested the name for the magazine, and his sister now runs the publishing company that the father founded. By virtue of both genetic endowment and life experience, John Jr. seemed truly to be a favored son.

John Harold Johnson Sr., founder of Ebony *magazine.*

If evolution favors "survival of the fittest," then how could it be that John Jr. would die so young? And, more generally, how could such a disease remain in the human family if its effects were so devastating? Why would a gene that causes death not be eliminated from the human population over the course of time? The answers to these questions, and many more besides, are provided by Darwin's principle of natural selection together with the biological mechanisms that implement it—genetics.

The Development of Evolutionary Science

"Survival," popular culture tells us, belongs to the "fittest," whether in business, sports, or art. So when we come across a story like that of John Harold Johnson Jr., we are puzzled. At first glance he seemed to have every advantage—genetic and environmental. Charles Darwin, too, was struck by similarly puzzling phenomena, and he searched for principles that might make sense of them. Later in life Darwin (1809–1882) reflected on his achievements as follows:

> From my early youth I have had the strongest desire to understand and explain whatever I observed—that is, to group all facts under some general laws. . . . With such moderate abilities as I possess, it is truly surpris-

ing that I should have influenced to a considerable extent the belief of scientific men on some important points. (Darwin, 1888/1950, pp. 67–71)

These words seem surprisingly modest coming as they do from a man who influenced the course of scientific thought more than any other since Isaac Newton. Charles Darwin argued that, over successive generations, organisms become adapted to their environments. Today, his concept of **biological evolution**—which accounts for the changes that take place in the characteristics of a population of organisms over time—stands as the primary explanation of the origin and diversity of life and as the unifying theme of all biology.

The scope of Darwin's work goes beyond biology and influences other natural sciences, especially psychology. Psychologists have become increasingly aware of the way in which the modern synthesis of Darwin's theory with discoveries in genetics helps us understand behavior. As we shall see in this chapter, many behavioral differences among individuals and species are associated with genetic and other biological differences. Understanding these differences and their evolution allows psychologists to appreciate the possible origins and **adaptive significance** of behavior that adjust to changing environmental conditions.

To better understand the nature of the process of adaptation, let us return to the fate of the otherwise favored son John Harold Johnson Jr. Sickle-cell anemia is caused by a gene that, when present in a single copy, does not produce the disease. Because each of John Jr.'s parents had only one copy of the gene, they did not express the disease. But by chance, John Jr. had received *two* sickle-cell genes—one from his father and one from his mother. Thus, knowledge of genetics lets us understand how John Jr. could have sickle-cell anemia although his parents and sibling were free of the disease. But how can we account for the persistence of the sickle-cell gene in the human population? Why has such a potentially lethal genetic disease continued to plague humanity? Here, knowledge of natural selection, not genetics, provides the answer. The sickle-cell gene is found primarily in people who trace their ancestry to populations that previously lived in Africa and around the Mediterranean. In this region human populations have long coexisted with an insect called the *Anopheles* mosquito. The mosquito gets the proteins it needs to produce its eggs from human blood—and in the process of biting humans, the mosquito injects them with a parasite that causes malaria. The parasite reproduces inside red blood cells and, from time to time, releases more parasites from the infected cells. In so doing it destroys the red blood cells. The destruction of these cells produces the symptoms of malaria—chills and anemia (due to insufficient oxygen)—and can cause death when blood vessels in the brain and other organs become clogged with the debris of the destroyed cells. Even today, almost 2 out of every 100 children under four years of age die of malarial infection in African countries such as Angola and Sierra Leone.

What does the prevalence of malaria in John Jr.'s ancestors have to do with the persistence of the sickle-cell gene? The sickle-cell gene was selected in this population of humans because one copy of the gene causes only those few red blood cells initially infected by the parasite to sickle. These few misshapen cells are then removed by the spleen and the parasite dies. Because parents with only one copy of the gene are more likely to live long enough to have children, and because on average only one out of every four of such parents' children will receive two copies of the gene, the *population* of humans in the malaria-infested region benefits from the persistence of the sickle-cell gene. On average, two out of every four children receive immunity from malaria, because they have only a single copy of the gene; one child remains susceptible to malaria, having no copy of the gene; and one child receives two copies and suffers sickle-cell anemia. Thus, on average, the sickle-cell gene benefits the survival of the population of individuals as a whole: Twice as many offspring benefit as lose from the continued existence of the gene. Individual offspring such as John Harold Johnson Jr. pay a heavy price for the legacy of that long-ago benefit. In the environment of the United States, infection by the malarial parasite is almost nonexistent, as the introduction of insecticides into the environment has eliminated the prior benefit of the sickle-cell gene. But the cost to the individual, as opposed to the population, remains. For the individual, in the words of Ecclesiastes, "the race is not to the swift, nor the battle to the strong, . . . nor favor to the men of skill; but time and chance happen to them all."

The consequences of natural selection and genetics for John Harold Johnson Jr. were expressed in the *structure* of his body—in particular, in his red blood cells. However, natural selection affects *function* (behavior) as well as structure. In fact, the effects of natural selection on structure and function are closely related: Unless a structure is used in a way that benefits survival of the population, the genes for that structure cannot be naturally selected by the environment. Consider the complex structure of the eye. If the eye did not provide information that guided behavior, the various components of that structure could not have been selected over time. In fact, natural selection has favored the formation of neural circuits that govern the movement of the eye. When an object enters the periphery of vision, the eye rapidly moves to focus on that object. (These movements are among the visual reflexes discussed in Chapter 6.) Over the evolution of the human species, individuals who immediately attended to moving objects were more likely to behave adaptively—to avoid predators, to dodge projectiles, to greet approaching members of the group, and so on. Individuals who behaved in these ways were more likely to survive to the age of reproduction and pass on their genes to their offspring. Among those genes were those that shaped both the structure and function of the eye.

In summary, the case of John Harold Johnson Jr. teaches us two general and important lessons about evolution through natural selection. First, the outcomes of natural selection are understandable on the level of *populations* of individuals, not on the level of the individual. Although it is individuals who live or die, who reproduce or not, it is the effect of their fate on the population as a whole that determines the course of natural selection. John Jr. died because he carried genes that had benefited the population of which his ancestors were members. The second lesson that John Jr. teaches us is that *past environments* determine the effects of natural selection on the individual. To the extent that present environments are like past environments, natural selection adapts us to the present. But when the present differs from the past—as in John Jr.'s case—the adaptiveness is lost. (We'll encounter this problem again when we look at obesity in Chapter 13.) Strictly speaking, natural selection "prepares" us to live in the past; it is only to the extent that past environments are like the present that we are adapted to the present.

By understanding how adaptive behavior developed through the long-term process of evolution, psychologists improve their understanding of how our behavior adjusts to changes in the present environment. To better understand the present, we must understand the past—the development of our species as well as the development of the individual. We behave as we do because we are members of the human species—an *ultimate cause*—and because we have learned to act in particular ways—a *proximate cause*. **Ultimate causes** (from the Latin *ultimus*, "farthest, final") are events and conditions that over successive generations slowly shaped the behavior of our species. **Proximate causes** (from the Latin *proximus*, "near") arise from the present environment. Both ancestral and present environments affect individual development.

Consideration of the role of evolutionary factors in behavior has led to a new subfield within psychology: *evolutionary psychology,* described in Chapter 1 (Daly & Wilson, 1999; Tooby & Cosmides, 1989). This area of psychology investigates how organisms' evolutionary history affects the development of behavior patterns and cognitive strategies, especially those related to reproduction and survival (Leger, 1991). As we shall see, evolutionary psychology has made a significant contribution to our understanding of behavior.

In addition to improving our understanding of individual behavior, evolutionary psychology provides a broader perspective from which to view the psychological adaptations of our species that gave rise to the development of culture. **Culture** is the sum of socially transmitted knowledge, customs, and behavior patterns that is common to a particular group of people. Thus culture is a means, in addition to the effects of natural selection on genes, by which the environment of one generation affects the behavior of the next generation. And, of course, the changes wrought by culture can occur much more rapidly than those by natural selection. No account of behavior can be complete without considering the role of both evolution (the legacy of past environments) and culture (the legacy of present environments). Although cultural influences are much more pronounced in humans than other species, some evidence of cultural transmission can be found in other social species. For example, if a chimpanzee acquires a skill (such as operating a device to secure food) while separated from its group, other individuals in that group rapidly acquire exactly the same skill when the trained chimp returns to the group (White, Horner, & de Waal, 2005). Without the cultural transmission of this skill, it might never have been acquired by the others.

This chapter will review the development of Darwin's theory of evolution and describe how evolution operates. We'll then explore the general principles of heredity and genetics, the means by which biological and behavioral characteristics are passed from one generation to the next. Finally, we'll examine sociobiology, a branch of biobehavioral science that attempts to understand evolutionary influences on social behavior.

The Voyage of the *Beagle*

Let's return to Charles Darwin and the work that laid the foundations for the present-day discipline of evolutionary psychology. As a young man, Darwin had relatively few scholarly interests. He was, however, interested in nature, and he spent much of his time hiking the English countryside, examining rock formations and shooting birds. Not certain what to do with his life, he entered into the study of theology at Christ's College, Cambridge, with the thought of becoming a country parson—a not uncommon occupation for upper-class Englishmen of uncertain interests. In 1831 Darwin chanced to meet Captain Robert Fitz Roy, who was looking for someone to serve as an unpaid naturalist and traveling companion during a five-year voyage on a naval vessel—the HMS *Beagle.* The *Beagle*'s mission was to explore and survey

▲ *Charles Darwin (1809–1882).*

the coast of South America and to make worldwide nautical observations that might benefit the British navy.

Darwin was eager to volunteer, although he needed to overcome his father's objections before he received his family's support for the voyage. Darwin was to learn later that Captain Fitz Roy nearly rejected him because of the shape of his nose! Fitz Roy believed that the nose indicated a person's character. He suspected that anyone having a nose like Darwin's would not "possess sufficient energy and determination for the voyage." In the end, though, Darwin's upper-class background and well-placed references persuaded Fitz Roy to accept him (Engel, 1962; Gould, 1977). Darwin later noted, "I think he was afterwards well satisfied that my nose had spoken falsely" (Darwin, 1888/1950, p. 36).

During the voyage Darwin observed the animals and plants of South America, Australia, South Africa, and the islands of the Pacific, South Atlantic, and Indian oceans. These included most notably the Galapagos Islands off the west coast of South America. Darwin spent most of his time doing what he enjoyed most—collecting specimens of animals (which he shot), plants, and objects of every sort. These specimens were sent back to England at various times during the trip and were later examined by naturalists throughout Europe.

Darwin did not form his theory of evolution while at sea. Although he was impressed by the tremendous diversity among seemingly related animals, his original theological training adhered to the doctrine of essentialism, a view that could be traced to the Greek philosopher Plato. For Plato, all living things belonged to fixed classes or "kinds," each class defined by unchanging characteristics that defined the essential quality of each species and separated one species from another (Mayr, 2001).

The Origin of Species

Darwin's voyage on the *Beagle* ended in 1836. He returned to England still marveling at the many ways that plants and animals varied as the environment changed. He sifted through his collections, comparing the similarities and differences among the creatures he had found. He carefully reviewed the work of earlier naturalists (including his own grandfather), who had speculated about the concept of evolution but had been unable to provide a convincing account of how these changes might occur. Darwin became interested in **artificial selection,** the procedure in which animal breeders mate animals to produce offspring with desirable characteristics. Using artificial selection, breeders selectively mate animals with characteristics such as heavy wool coats in sheep or high milk production in cows. In an example that was familiar in Darwin's day, a pigeon fancier who wanted to produce a pigeon with colorful plumage would examine the available stock and permit only the most colorful birds to mate with one another. When this process was repeated over generations, the population of birds in the colony became more colorful. Plumage color was, in some as yet unknown way, passed from one generation to the next. Darwin was intrigued with artificial selection and in fact had bred pigeons himself. (See **Figure 3•1.**) He speculated that if artificial selection produced such different varieties of pigeons, perhaps some process that occurred in nature could have a similar effect.

It would be another year and a half before Darwin's naturalistic observations and knowledge of artificial selection bore fruit. Darwin recalled the event in his autobiography:

> I happened to read for amusement Malthus on *Population,* and being well prepared to appreciate the struggle for existence which everywhere goes on from long continued observation of plants and animals, it at once struck me that under these circumstances favorable variations would tend to be preserved, and unfavorable ones to be destroyed. The result would be the formation of a new species. (Darwin, 1888/1950, p. 54)

What struck Darwin was the idea of **natural selection** as a consequence of differential rates of reproduction of organisms having different characteristics. An organism that possessed a characteristic that helped it to survive would be more likely to live longer and to produce more offspring than an organism that did not have this characteristic. Thus, within any given population, some members would produce more offspring than others. If these characteristics could pass from one generation to the next by inheritance, then natural selection would have an effect that was comparable to artificial selection.

Darwin came to this realization in September 1838, but he did not publish his ideas until 20 years later. Why did he wait so long? Among other things, he devoted considerable time to gathering supportive evidence. He took great pains to develop a clear and coherent case for his account. He examined and reexamined his specimens, carefully studied current research and theory in the natural sciences, conducted his own research on artificial selection, and continually tested his ideas with his closest scientific colleagues, whom he often met at a pub in London.

Darwin might have been even slower to publish his theory if another naturalist, Alfred Wallace, had not independently arrived at the same insight. In 1858 Wallace, while suffering from a bout of fever in the Spice Islands, read the same book by Thomas Robert Malthus that had inspired Darwin. Wallace also recognized that the natural environment, through its effect on differential reproduction, could be the source of new species. Unlike Darwin, Wallace quickly wrote up the idea and sent the paper to—of all people—Charles Darwin, who was already known for published work on

(a)

(b)

(c)

(d)

FIGURE 3•1 Varieties of pigeons that have been produced through artificial selection. (a) Wild rock pigeon. This type is believed to be the ancestor of each of the other breeds of pigeons shown here. (b) Blue grizzle frillback. (c) English pouter. (d) Indian fantail.

related subjects. Thus Wallace as well as Darwin had devised a principle by which the natural environment could accomplish the same result as artificial selection but without the intervention of a "selector."

What was Darwin to do? If he published his idea now, he might appear to have stolen it from Wallace. If he did not publish his idea, years of painstaking labor might be wasted. Darwin described his dilemma to his colleagues, who knew that he had come to this discovery some 20 years before. They suggested that Darwin and Wallace make a joint presentation of their separate works before a scientific society—the Linnaean Society—so that each might stake a claim to the principle of natural selection. This was done, and within only one year Darwin published the massive book on which he had been working for many years—a book that he described as an "abstract" of his ideas. Darwin's "abstract," which we know today as *On the Origin of Species* (1859), ran to 500 pages and established both his priority in developing the principle of natural selection and his careful accumulation of evidence to support that principle.

Interim Summary

The Development of Evolutionary Science

Understanding behavior requires psychologists to learn about both proximate causes of behavior (how animals adapt to environmental changes through learning) and ultimate causes (how historical events in the evolution of a species shaped behavior). Evolutionary psychology is a relatively new subfield of psychology that studies how evolutionary and genetic variables influence adaptive behavior. Darwin's voyage on the HMS *Beagle* and his subsequent observations and research in artificial selection led him to develop the idea of biological evolution through natural selection.

QUESTIONS TO CONSIDER

1. In what ways are psychology and biology related disciplines? How does understanding biological aspects of behavior contribute to understanding psychological aspects of behavior?
2. Does natural selection produce survival of the fittest *individual*? Explain your answer, using an example.
3. What might be the effects of reducing genetic variability in a population of organisms?

Natural Selection and Evolution

This section will begin with a general account of the process of evolution through natural selection. We'll then look at components of the process in somewhat greater detail; fi-

nally, we'll consider the implications of natural selection for human evolution.

Natural Selection as a Three-Step Process: Variation, Selection, and Retention

Evolution through natural selection is the result of repeated cycles of a three-step process that acts across the generations—variation, selection, and retention. *Variation,* as Darwin observed, causes each living organism to be unique: Each differs somewhat from every other, even others within the same species. Before Darwin, scientists had focused on the ways that members of the same species were alike—the essential features that all individuals presumably shared with the group. It was these common features that were thought to be important by earlier biologists. Individual differences were merely a nuisance that obscured the essential features of the group. After Darwin, individual differences moved to center stage; similarities among individuals were seen as abstractions that might be useful for some purposes (for example, in classification) but were not fundamental to the evolutionary process. We now understand that variation between individuals provides the raw material on which natural selection acts. Variation is the source of whatever novelty can arise from repeated cycles of the three-step process, because natural selection can act only on characteristics that already exist.

Variation itself is undirected, in the sense that the factors that affect variation are different from those that affect selection (Campbell, 1974). Selection by the environment, however, favors (or disfavors) some variants over others. *Selection* confers to the evolutionary process whatever direction it appears to display. But evolution is not directed toward any particular end. That is, the future does not draw the present toward itself; rather, the past pushes the present into the future. It is only to the extent that future environments share features in common with past environments that evolution through natural selection makes us well adapted—as we saw in the poignant case of John Harold Johnson Jr. A similar, and particularly alarming, example may be found with AIDS (acquired immune-deficiency syndrome). AIDS is the result of infection by a virus (HIV, or human immunodeficiency virus) that is ravaging some communities. It has been discovered that some populations of humans are relatively resistant to infection by the HIV virus. These are humans who trace their ancestry to northern European populations that were devastated during the Middle Ages by the bacterium that caused bubonic plague (the Black Death) (Galvani & Slatkin, 2003; cf. Kolata, 1998). During the fourteenth century and intermittently thereafter, roughly one-third of the population of Europe was killed by the Black Death. Those individuals who survived selection by the plague bacterium had immune reactions that were especially effective in combating the infection. It now appears that those same immune reactions resist infection by and progression of the AIDS virus. The plague bacterium and the HIV virus both attack the same group of white blood cells; thus, the gene that benefits the immune response to bubonic plague also benefits the immune response to HIV. More than 10 percent of the ancestors of today's northern Europeans have at least one copy of the gene, but only about 5 percent of Italians and essentially no Africans, American Indians, or Asians have the protective gene. Clearly, it was not the "purpose" of natural selection by the plague bacterium to make northern Europeans resistant to a viral infection that would not exist for 600 years! Natural selection is locked in a perpetual embrace with the environment, and the environment is always in the lead. The course of selection depends utterly on the environment. If the selecting environment is constant or changes gradually, the process of natural selection effectively adapts us to the environment. The process only appears to display foresight and purpose. This illusion is shattered when the selecting environment changes (Donahoe, 2003; Skinner, 1966; Sober, 1984).

The third step, *retention,* is necessary if evolution is to occur. That is, variation provides the raw material, and selection operates on random variations; but unless the selected variations are retained so that they can contribute to the pool of genetic variations on which subsequent selection operates, evolution cannot occur. **Figure 3•2** summarizes the three-step process of evolution through natural selection. It is important to note that Darwin was ignorant of how the effects of selection were retained through genes. Gregor Mendel's work on genetics was published in 1866—only seven years after Darwin's *On the Origin of Species*—but was not generally known until the early 1900s, well after Darwin's death in 1882. Because Darwin could not explain how the effects of selection were retained, even most biologists did not accept his account of evolution until the principle of natural selection was integrated with the burgeoning science of genetics in the 1930s. This integration of natural selection with genetics is now known as the Modern Synthesis in biology (e.g., Dobzhansky, 1937).

Darwinian Principles of Natural Selection

On the understanding that Darwin was ignorant of the genetic mechanism underlying retention, let's look at Darwin's ideas in more detail. Natural selection is the key to Darwin's account of biological evolution. The account is based on two premises (Eldredge, 1998): First, individuals within a population show variability in inherited behavioral and physical characteristics. Second, the capacity of any given environment to sustain a population of any species is limited, producing competition. Darwin and Wallace realized that these two factors meant that individuals whose characteristics enabled them to compete more effectively for resources were more likely to survive and reproduce. To the extent that these characteristics could be passed on to offspring, they would be more likely to appear in the population during the next generation. Darwin's careful naturalistic observations also convinced him that behavioral adaptations were especially important to survival and were therefore an important part of evolution. In fact, the biologist E. O. Wilson has described the ability of behavior to adapt as "the pacemaker of evolution" (Wilson, 1975).

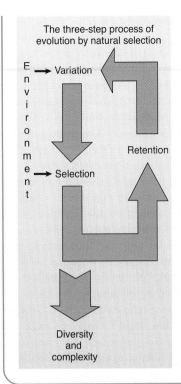

FIGURE 3•2

The three-step process of evolution by natural selection. Initial differences in characteristics provide the variation on which natural selection operates within a given environment. Individuals whose characteristics favor reproductive fitness in that environment are more likely to survive. The individual's genes are retained when they are passed to the next generation and contribute to the variation on which subsequent selections operate. Over repeated cycles of this process, diverse and complex species can emerge.

The ability of an individual to produce offspring constitutes **reproductive success**—defined as the number of viable offspring an individual produces relative to the number of viable offspring produced by other members of the same species. Contrary to popular interpretation, "survival of the fittest" does not necessarily mean survival of the strongest or most physically fit. The evolutionary bottom line is reproductive success. Physical strength is only one of many factors that may affect reproductive success. In humans, for example, intelligence and sociability are characteristics that play an important role in an individual's ability to provide for a family. These characteristics are therefore candidates for selection.

As stated earlier, variation and competition are the critical factors that Darwin realized would determine whether any particular animal and its offspring would enjoy reproductive success. Let's take a look at each of these factors beginning with variation.

Variation The term **variation** refers to the countless differences among members of the same species, including differences in physical characteristics such as size and strength and differences in behavioral characteristics such as intelligence and sociability. What is responsible for these differences? First, the genetic makeup of an individual organism, its **genotype,** differs from that of all other individuals (except in the case of identical twins). Second, the physical characteristics and behavior of an individual organism, which together make up its **phenotype,** also vary from those of every other individual.

It is important to recognize that every individual's phenotype is produced by the interaction of its genotype with the environment. The genotype partially determines how the environment influences an organism's development and behavior. Likewise, the environment partially determines how the genotype affects the organism's structure and function. For instance, identical twins have exactly the same genotype. If they are separated at birth and one twin has a better diet than the other, their phenotypes will be different: The better-fed twin is likely to be taller and stronger. However, despite the difference in diet between the two, one twin is unlikely to be exceptionally tall or muscular if the genotype shared with the other twin does not promote these characteristics. Likewise, neither twin will realize his or her full potential for tallness and muscularity if he or she does not have a nutritious diet. In this example, both the genotype (the genes related to tallness and muscularity) and a favorable environment (a nutritious diet) must be present for either twin to become tall and muscular.

The selection of particular phenotypes and their associated genotypes is determined by whatever advantage or disadvantage they confer in a particular environment. Consider, for example, Darwin's finches, the 13 species of finch that Darwin discovered on the Galapagos Islands. These birds showed striking physical differences in beak size. Some finches had a phenotype of a small, thin beak, whereas others had a large, thick beak. Birds with small, thin beaks fed on small seeds covered by weak shells; birds with large, thick beaks fed on large seeds covered by tough shells.

By studying the relationship between rainfall, food supply, and the size of the various finch populations on one island, Peter and Rosemary Grant (2002) discovered that the amount of rainfall and the size of the food supply differentially affected the death rates of finches with certain kinds of beaks. During droughts, small seeds became scarce, and finches with small, thin beaks died at a higher rate than finches with bigger, thicker beaks. During the next few years, the relative number of finches with bigger, thicker beaks increased—just as the principle of natural selection predicted. But when rain was plentiful, small seeds became abundant, and the number of finches with smaller, thinner beaks subsequently increased.

The Grants' study makes two important points. First, although evolution generally occurs over long periods of time, natural selection also can produce important changes in the space of only a few years (Eldredge & Gould, 1972). Second, phenotypic variation (here, differences in beak characteristics) can produce important selective advantages that affect survival. If all the Galapagos finches had had small, thin beaks most, if not all, would have died during periods of drought. None would have been left to reproduce; these finches would have become extinct. Fortunately, phenotypic variation in beak size occurred among the finches. And, because phenotypic variation is caused by genetic variation (different genotypes give rise to different phenotypes), some finches—those having large, thick beaks—had an advantage. Their food supply (the larger seeds) was relatively unaffected by the drought, and they outsurvived and outreproduced the finches with small, thin beaks.

You might think that all the finches should have developed large, thick beaks. However, when rain is plentiful and small seeds are abundant, feeding is easier for birds with small, thin beaks. Under such environmental conditions, these birds have a phenotypic (and genotypic) advantage. So from the standpoint of the species, diversity in genotype can be an advantage.

Selection Selection based on **competition** is the second factor underlying the process of natural selection. Because individuals of a given species share a common environment, competition within and between species for food, mates, and territory is inevitable. For example, every salmon captured and eaten by one bald eagle is a fish that cannot be captured and eaten by another bald eagle. And if one bald eagle finds a suitable mate, then there is one fewer potential mate for other bald eagles.

Competition also occurs between species when members of different species vie for similar ecological resources, such as food and territory. For example, yellow-headed blackbirds and red-winged blackbirds eat the same foods and occupy the same type of breeding territories; thus, they compete for these resources. Such competition does not involve competition for mates (yellow-headed blackbirds do not court red-winged blackbirds, or vice versa). But although these species do not compete for mates, they do compete for other resources that indirectly influence reproductive success. The ability to find and court a suitable mate depends on the ability to stake out and defend a territory that has an adequate food supply. So a yellow-headed blackbird's chances of finding a mate and successfully rearing a family depend not only on its success in competing against other yellow-headed blackbirds, but also on its success in competing against red-winged blackbirds.

A good example of competition at work has recently been found in the breeding behaviors of red squirrels in northern Canada. The average spring temperature in that region has increased by about 4 degrees Fahrenheit since 1975. This change has in turn increased the quantity of seeds available to red-squirrel mothers with newly born young to feed. Research has shown that the number of seed-containing pine cones that are stored by the squirrels in this region increased from the early 1990s to the early 2000s. Over the same decade the average date at which female squirrels gave birth advanced by more than two weeks (Réale, McAdam, Boutin, & Berteaux, 2003). The old adage about early birds and worms seems to apply to squirrels and nuts as well.

Natural selection works because the members of any species have different phenotypes. Because these phenotypes are caused, in part, by different genotypes, successful individuals pass on more of their genes to the next generation. Over time, competition for food and other resources allows only the best-adapted phenotypes (and their associated genotypes) to survive and reproduce, thereby producing evolutionary change. In the case of the red squirrel, the genotype of each new generation produced a birth date that was about one day earlier than that of the previous generation.

Natural Selection in Human Evolution

We have seen the importance of diversity in a species such as Darwin's finches on the Galapagos Islands. It is equally clear that diversity exists in our own species, *Homo sapiens* ("man who is wise"). However, you may be surprised to learn that the diversity in our species was once much greater than is apparent today. Archaeologists and evolutionary biologists who study the early history of hominids (the evolutionary line that predates our species) have shown that other human species existed during the course of evolution. Indeed, for several lengthy periods, different members of the hominid line inhabited the same geographical areas (Tattersall, 2000). But in the ancient environments of our ancestors, *Homo sapiens* outcompeted other hominids, with the result that our species is the only surviving descendant of that line.

Why has our particular evolutionary line been successful (at least, so far)? No single answer is possible, because human evolution has taken place over millions of years, across many environments, and under the impact of such events as ice ages and volcanic catastrophes. However, a short overview of our own evolutionary trajectory provides some clues to the characteristics that define us as a unique species.

The ancestral species that ultimately led to *Homo sapiens* appears to have diverged from the other great apes about 4.4 million years ago, in east Africa, with the early hominid *Ardipithecus ramidus* (Tattersall, 1997). The characteristics of this early hominid are inadequately known, but two later species from about 3.5 million years ago are better characterized. The fossilized remains of both of these species exhibit, as we do, bipedalism. **Bipedalism** is the habitual ability to walk upright on the hind legs and is a defining characteristic of hominids. These two later hominid species were *Australopithecus anamensis* and *Australopithecus afarensis*; *Australopithecus* designates a southern genus, and the species names designate the areas where the fossils were found. The fossilized remains of a female *afarensis* from about 3.8 to 3 million years ago revealed an intermediate body structure that still showed signs of an apelike ability to climb trees. Many theories attempt to explain why bipedalism evolved; two such explanations cite hominids' need to see greater distances across the savannah grasslands and the need to carry young in the arms.

Because fossil evidence of early humans is still very incomplete, though growing, differences remain in in1terpretations of our origins. A common view (Strait, Grine, & Moniz, 1997) is that over the period from 3 to 2 million years ago, the hominid line split into two branches. The African environment may have turned drier, causing changes in the readily available sources of food. One line of hominids evolved into a genus with powerful jaws that could crush and chew fibrous plants and nuts. As shown in **Figure 3.3**, this line comprised the genus *Paranthropus* and did not lead to *Homo sapiens*. The other line from *Australopithecus* ultimately led to early humans. About 2.5 to 1.8 million years ago, this second line branched into two new species, *Homo rudolfensis* and *Homo habilis*. Each was sufficiently different from their common

FIGURE 3·3 A reconstruction of the evolutionary history of hominid species. To construct a possible family tree, paleoarchaeologists examine fossil characteristics to identify similarities between species. Once a grouping of species is established, the age of the fossils can suggest a chronology. Reconstructions such as this are, however, speculative, because fossils are fragmentary and difficult to compare directly.

(From Tattersall, I. (2000, January). *Scientific American*, p. 60. Reprinted with permission from Patricia J. Wynne.)

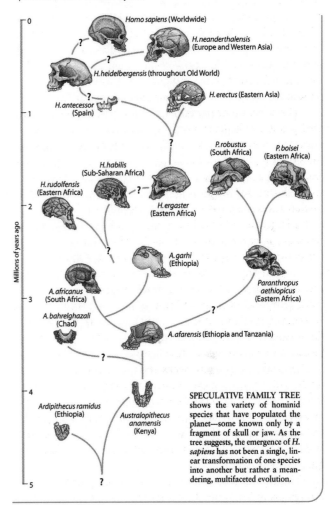

ancestor to be designated a new genus, *Homo*. The name *Homo habilis* means "handy man" and was chosen because this species is thought to have produced the many stone tools found at the sites where *habilis* fossils have been found. When hominids became bipedal, their forelimbs were freed from the demands of locomotion and could now be subject to natural selection that favored manual dexterity.

If stone tools were indeed fabricated by *Homo habilis*, these tools would have given *habilis* a marked advantage relative to its competitors. As shown in Figure 3.3, at about the time of the emergence of *habilis*, at least three other hominid species were living in East Africa. The ability to make and use tools would have benefited many behaviors, including obtaining food and—perhaps—fending off enemies. Hominid skull fossils from this period also show a marked increase in **encephalization;** that is, an increase in brain size. Increased manual dexterity required more complexly interconnected nerve cells to control the fine movements of the fingers and thumb; more nerve cells and neural connections required a bigger brain; a bigger brain required more energy to supply the increased number of cells; more energy required greater consumption of food; more consumption required better food-gathering techniques; and, to complete the circle, better techniques required increased manual dexterity (Aiello & Wheeler, 1995). The selecting factors that underlie evolution are complex and often interrelated.

Archaeologists are uncertain about how tool use might have altered hominid life (Mithen, 1996). Tool use may have been associated with specific campsites that were used by groups of early humans to share food and raise children. Thus, the use of tools may also have fostered the development of social behavior. Alternatively, early humans may have scavenged food opportunistically and carried their tools with them rather than using them communally.

Hominids began to spread out from their African home about 1.8 million years ago. One species, *Homo erectus,* has been discovered as far away as Java and China. Tool use was by this time highly developed, but it reflected a particular technology. *Homo erectus* fashioned tools by repeatedly chipping small flakes from a larger stone until the stone became suitable to use as a hand axe or other implement. By contrast, about 600,000 years ago in Africa, a new species, *Homo heidelbergensis,* developed a different approach. These human ancestors fabricated stone tools in a more systematic way—the core of the stone was prepared so that a single well-directed blow produced the finished tool.

The last two major hominid groups evolved from *heidelbergensis.* They were *Homo neanderthalensis,* the Neanderthals, and *Homo sapiens,* modern man. Current evidence indicates that the line leading to *Homo sapiens* originated in Africa some 150,000 to 200,000 years ago. Some of these human predecessors then migrated north and west. *Sapiens* shared a common environment with *neanderthalensis* in Europe and the Middle East for a considerable time, but Neanderthals finally became extinct about 50,000 years ago. Whether *sapiens* and *neanderthalensis* ever interbred is disputed, but most archaeologists believe that they did not—possibly because of vocal deficiencies in *neanderthalensis,* although this too is controversial (Boe, Heim, Abry, & Badin, 2004; Lieberman, 1992). What is certain is that *Homo sapiens* is now the most widely distributed species on the planet. What also is certain is that despite our wide distribution, we continue to show evidence of our origins on the African savannah: Our relatively hairless bodies and numerous sweat glands were adaptations to the heat of the savannah. These adaptations now require most of us to wear clothing, however. Both an Eskimo in furs in Alaska and an astronaut in a space suit on the moon are surrounding themselves with warm and humid microenvironments that duplicate the macroenvironment at the origin of our species.

As we have seen, two interrelated adaptations played a critical role in the evolution of our species—bipedalism and encephalization. Some of the immediate benefits of these adaptations are easy to see. Bipedalism freed the hands for grabbing, holding, and throwing objects. Encephalization, promoted by the greater neural demands of manual dexterity, facilitated tool making, food gathering, hunting, and escaping from predators. And, more generally, encephalization expanded the capacity for learning and remembering. Humans who could make tools and then recall how they were made improved their hunting and self-defense skills and thereby lived longer and reproduced more than their less able contemporaries.

The selective pressures that favored encephalization are particularly complex. For example, Dunbar (1993) has suggested that in our species the open environment of the savannah favored survival of groups over more solitary individuals. Large groups can function effectively only when individual members recognize and remember others in the group and can recall the nature of their past interactions with the others. Did we groom each other when we last met, or did we fight? Although one chimpanzee may look pretty much like any other chimpanzee to a human, that cannot be true for the chimpanzees themselves. Dunbar found that among our relatives in other primate species, encephalization increased as the size of the typical social group increased. If we extrapolate from his findings, we would conclude that modern humans function best in a group of about 148 individuals. Our ancestors may have competed more effectively than other hominids because our larger brains aided social coordination and thereby allowed us to meet environmental challenges collectively. For example, memorizing and recalling actions, such as hunting and tool production, and communicating these skills may have developed early, followed by the emergence of the capacity to manipulate symbols (Donald, 1993).

Another factor favoring encephalization was the advantage of planning—the capacity to anticipate future events and to take into account the effects that those events would have on an individual or group of individuals. Such planning would have been involved in the organization of hunts, the institution of social customs (such as funeral rituals), and the planting and harvesting of crops. The portion of the brain that is most important for planning—for acquiring and maintaining behavior whose consequences are delayed—is the frontal region, the portion of the human brain that has expanded most rapidly over evolutionary time.

Other factors also may have favored encephalization. The brain regions that control the precise finger movements underlying manual dexterity are adjacent to and intermingled with those that now control the intricate tongue and mouth movements of speech. The regions of the brain that control the dominant hand (most humans are right-handed) also are adjacent to the regions that control speech and further suggest an intimate relation between manual dexterity

▲ *Cultural evolution includes the development of specific kinds of tools designed to accomplish particular tasks, from cutting meat to producing steel to processing and storing complex information.*

and the articulatory movements of speech. Some evidence of the similar neural structures underlying manual and articulatory responses comes from studies in which subjects were asked to repeat a specified sequence of finger movements and articulatory movements. For example, the sequence of finger movements might be—little finger, ring finger, ring finger, index finger, middle finger, middle finger, little finger. The sequence of articulatory movements might produce the speech sounds—pah, dah, dah, gah, tah, tah, pah. Note that the repetitions and changes of movements occur at the same points within the two sequences. When the times between successive responses were examined, finger and articulatory responses were spaced similarly—for example, shorter times between repetitions than between changes (Rosenbaum, 2002).

Undoubtedly, the interaction between bipedalism and encephalization had effects that enabled humans to exploit new environments and to establish well-organized communities (Roth & Dicke, 2005). This trend contributed to the increased life span of humans and aided the gradual accumulation of knowledge as older members of early human communities began to share their experience with younger members through language. Although the fossil record cannot tell us when language first developed, we can be sure that early humans who were able to communicate with others had a distinct advantage over those who could not.

Language originated and subsequently evolved because of its immense adaptive significance. As Skinner (1986) noted, language provided not only a simple means of warning others of danger, but also a means of communicating important information to others, such as the location of a good hunting spot or instructions on the crafting of tools. But perhaps the most important advantage conferred by language was its ability to reinforce the already strong social tendencies of early humans. Dunbar (1993) has suggested that conversation ultimately replaced the typical grooming behavior of primates as a more efficient way to strengthen social bonds. If so, this ability to converse may have ultimately led to the development and transmission of cultural traditions. There is less evidence that our last major rivals, the Neanderthals, developed a substantial cultural tradition (Tattersall, 2000). Culture and its great facilitator, language—not physical en-

durance or strength—may have given our species the critical advantage over our near cousin the Neanderthal.

As cultures continued evolving, our species gained an increasing ability to control and modify the environment. The same intellectual resourcefulness that permitted early humans to discover and use fire and to invent useful tools prompted other advances—the agricultural revolution of 10,000 years ago, the industrial revolution of 150 years ago, and the silicon revolution that began only 50 years ago with the inventions of the transistor, the integrated circuit, and the computer. **Cultural evolution,** a culture's adaptive change in response to changes in the environment, is possible only because natural selection has favored the capacity for learning and language. Harris (1991) noted that our capacity for learning has evolved because it permits "a more flexible and rapid method of achieving reproductive success" and allows entire groups of people to "adjust or take advantage of novel opportunities in a single generation without having to wait for the appearance and spread of genetic mutations" (p. 27). As examples, advances in science have allowed us to control life-threatening diseases such as polio, smallpox, malaria, tetanus, typhoid fever, and diphtheria. Without science we might have required thousands of years to evolve immunities to these diseases.

Interim Summary

Natural Selection and Evolution

The central factor in biological evolution is natural selection, which is a three-step process consisting of trait variation, selection, and retention. Selection occurs when some members of a species produce more offspring than others. Members of a species vary in their genetic makeup. If any of the traits affected by those genes give an individual a competitive advantage over other members of the species—for example, a better ability to escape predators, find food, or attract mates—then that individual is also more likely to have greater reproductive success. Its offspring will then carry those genes into the next generation. Two important adaptations that occurred during earlier periods of human evolution were *bipedalism,* the ability to walk upright on two feet, and *encephalization,* an increase in brain size. The combination of these two factors allowed early humans to explore and settle new environments and led to advances in tool making, hunting, food gathering, and self-defense. Encephalization appears to have been associated with language development and cultural evolution.

QUESTIONS TO CONSIDER

1. How do ultimate and proximate causes of behavior influence human behavior today—for example, eating?
2. What argument might support the suggestion that the human species is no longer evolving via natural selection? Is this a valid argument? Explain.

Heredity and Genetics

Darwin's work identified the process of natural selection and opened up new frontiers for exploration and experimentation. However, as I noted previously, Darwin was not aware of Mendel's work on genetics and therefore did not suggest a biological mechanism that would implement selection.

Although Darwin built a strong case for natural selection, he could not explain a key assumption of his account—inheritance. His observations indicated that individual differences occurred within species and that these differences could be affected by selection. However, he did not know how these differences were passed from parent to offspring or why differences occurred among offspring of the same parents. Seven years after *On the Origin of Species,* Gregor Mendel (1822–1884), an Austrian monk, published experiments in which he had crossbred pea plants. Mendel demonstrated conclusively that the height, flower color, seed shape, and other traits of pea plants were transmitted from one generation to the next. And, most importantly, he demonstrated that these traits were transmitted in discrete form, the form that came to be called genes. Darwin, in contrast, had incorrectly guessed that the units of heredity—whatever they might be—varied continuously.

Genetics is the study of the structure and functions of genes and how they are transmitted from one population to the next over the generations (Suzuki, Griffiths, Miller, & Lewontin, 1989). Genetics also involves the study of how the **heredity** of an organism—its genetic makeup—influences its physical and behavioral characteristics.

Basic Principles of Genetics

Heredity is determined by genetic material called **DNA (deoxyribonucleic acid).** DNA consists of strands of sugar and phosphate that are connected by nucleotide molecules of adenine, thymine, guanine, and cytosine. The structure of DNA was discovered by James Watson and Francis Crick in 1953. Watson (1968) told the story of their discovery in his fascinating (and controversial) book *The Double Helix.*

DNA is configured like a twisted ladder. The sugar and phosphate form the sides of a ladder; the nucleotides form the rungs. (See **Figure 3•4.**) A particular sequence of nucleotides at a particular location along the DNA molecule is the **gene.** Some genes are made up of a short sequence of nucleotides,

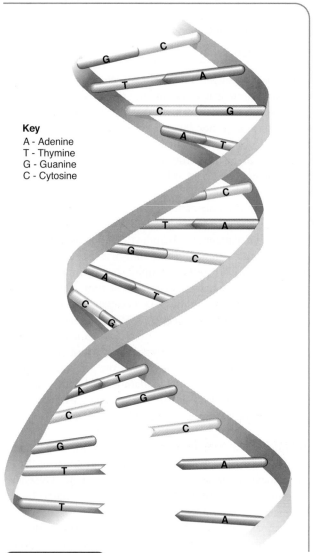

Key
A - Adenine
T - Thymine
G - Guanine
C - Cytosine

FIGURE 3•4 The structure and composition of DNA. DNA resembles a twisted ladder whose sides are composed of molecules of sugar and phosphate and whose rungs are made up of combinations of four nucleotide bases: adenine, thymine, guanine, and cytosine. Genes are segments of DNA that direct the synthesis of proteins and enzymes according to the particular sequences of nucleotide bases they contain. In essence, genes serve as "recipes" for the synthesis of these proteins and enzymes, which regulate the cellular and other physiological processes of the body, including those responsible for behavior.

(Based on Watson, J. D. (1976). *Molecular biology of the gene.* Menlo Park: Benjamin.)

whereas others contain very long sequences. Regardless of their length, the particular sequence of these nucleotides directs the synthesis of a protein molecule. These protein molecules regulate the biological and physical development of the body and its organs. The total set of genetic material in a species is known as the **genome.** The Human Genome Project has found that the 23 sets of DNA molecules in humans contain 30,000 to 40,000 genes. The researchers found the number of human genes surprisingly low—only about twice the number of genes in a common housefly (The Genome Sequencing Consortium, 2001).

Genes as "Recipes" for Protein Synthesis

Genes influence our physical and behavioral development in only one way—through protein synthesis. Proteins are strings of amino acids, arranged in a chain. The order of amino acids within the string is specified by the sequence of nucleotides in the DNA molecule. Each sequence of three nucleotides corresponds to a particular amino acid. Thus, genes are "recipes" for constructing proteins.

Strictly speaking, *there are no genes for behavior,* but only for the protein-based physical structures and physiological processes that affect behavior. For example, if we were interested in the genetic basis of learning, we would look for genes that affect the synthesis of proteins that influence learning. Evidence from behavioral and pharmacological studies indicates that learning is affected by a brain chemical called dopamine (Schultz, 2001). A gene that affects the synthesis of or receptivity to dopamine would act indirectly, but we might view it as a "learning" gene. Note, however, that we are really speaking of a gene that affects dopamine, not learning per se. That same gene might influence any behavior that is affected by dopamine.

Genes also specify proteins that govern the synthesis of other proteins. These are called **enzymes.** As we will see later, a faulty enzyme-specifying gene may produce serious physiological and behavioral problems.

Chromosomes and Meiosis

Genes are located in DNA molecules on *chromosomes.* (A few genes also are located in DNA of cellular structures called mitochondria. Mitochondria are important for energy production within the cell and are thought to have come from separate organisms that were originally incorporated into cells in a kind of symbiotic relation. Because mitochondrial DNA is passed along the maternal line primarily, such DNA has played an important role in research tracing human evolution, although controversy remains; Friderun & Cummins, 1996.) **Chromosomes** are threadlike structures of DNA that are found in the nucleus of every cell. Within the cell, chromosomes come in pairs. We inherit 23 individual chromosomes from each of our parents, making a total of 23 pairs. For 22 of these pairs of chromosomes, the DNA molecules are of corresponding types. That is, we have two genes for each protein, one from each pair of chromosomes. The chromosomes with corresponding genes are called **autosomes.** The remaining pair of chromosomes are the **sex chromosomes,** and they contain genes that affect the sex

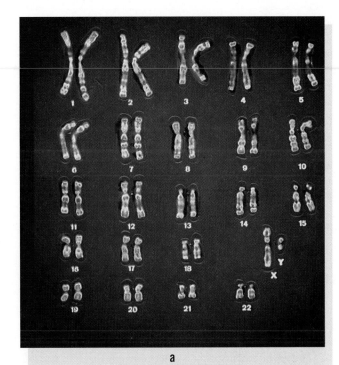

a

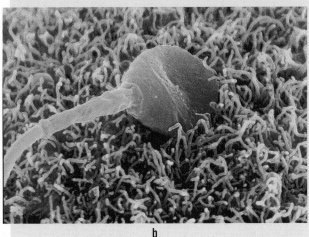

b

▲ *(a) Human chromosomes. The presence of a Y chromosome indicates that this sample came from a male. A sample from a female would include two X chromosomes. (b) Fertilization. A human sperm penetrates an egg.*

characteristics distinguishing males from females. In females, the two sex chromosomes have corresponding genes, and they are known as X chromosomes. In males, one of the chromosomes does not have corresponding genes and is called the Y chromosome. Thus the sex chromosomes for females are XX and for males XY.

Sexual reproduction occurs with the union of a sperm, which carries genes from the male, and an ovum (egg), which carries genes from the female. Sperm and ova differ from other cells in the body in two ways. First, the sperm and ovum, which are collectively known as **germ cells,** contain only one chromosome from each of the 23 pairs of chromosomes. All other cells of the body, known as somatic cells, contain 23 pairs of chromosomes. Sperm and ova are produced by a process known as **meiosis,** in which the 23 pairs of chromosomes in a cell separate into two groups, with only one member of each pair joining each group. The cell then divides into two germ cells, each containing 23 *individual* chromosomes. The assignment of a chromosome to a group is a random process. Thus, a single individual can produce 2^{23} (8,388,608) different germ cells.

Second, in the process of meiosis, corresponding portions of paired chromosomes may be interchanged, thereby producing a recombination of genes and adding still greater variation to the reproduction process. Because the union of a particular sperm with an ovum is also variable, the fertilized egg can produce 8,388,608 × 8,388,608, or 70,368,774,177,664 different possible offspring! Parenthood is a gamble, but a gamble that all species must accept if they are to endure.

Only identical twins are genetically identical. Identical twins occur when a fertilized ovum divides, giving rise to two identical fertilized eggs. Fraternal twins occur when a woman produces two ova, each of which is fertilized by different sperm. These individuals are no more alike than any other two siblings.

The sex of the offspring is determined by the 23rd pair of chromosomes. Female sex chromosomes consist of only X chromosomes. Each ovum contains an X chromosome in addition to 22 autosomes. Male sex chromosomes consist of an X and a Y chromosome. Each sperm cell contains either an X or a Y chromosome in addition to 22 autosomes. Thus, the sex of offspring is determined by the Y chromosome in the male sperm cell. (See **Figure 3•5.**)

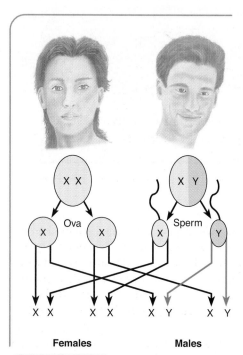

FIGURE 3•5 Determination of sex. The sex of human offspring depends on whether the sperm that fertilizes the ovum carries an X or a Y chromosome.

Dominant and Recessive Traits   Although each of the 22 pairs of autosomes contains corresponding pairs of genes, the members of the pair need not be identical. Genes can come in different forms called **alleles.** (*Allele,* like *alias,* comes from the Greek *allos,* "other.") Consider eye color. The pigment found in the iris of the eye is produced by a particular pair of genes. If corresponding genes from each parent are the same allele, the gene combination is called *homozygous* (from the Greek *homo,* "same," and *zygon,* "yolk"). However, if the parents contribute different alleles, the gene combination is said to be *heterozygous* (from the Greek *hetero,* "different"). The character or trait produced by the pair of genes depends on the particular gene combination. Some alleles are said to be **dominant genes.** For these alleles, the character that is expressed by the phenotype depends on the presence of only that allele. Thus, whether the gene is present on both chromosomes or on only one chromosome, that character is expressed. Other alleles are said to be **recessive genes.** For such alleles, *both* chromosomes must contain the allele for the character to be expressed. Remembering the case of John Harold Johnson Jr. and sickle-cell anemia, the sickle-cell allele is a recessive gene. It was not expressed in either parent, because each had only one allele. The fertilized egg that produced John Jr. unfortunately had two sickle-cell alleles. (For another example of dominant and recessive genes, see **Figure 3•6.**)

The genetic contributions to behavior usually are more complex than the simple dominant–recessive relation of sickle-cell anemia. First, characteristics often are influenced by multiple genes, not by a single pair. That is, they are under *polygenic* control. A second complication is that characteristics are affected not only by genes but also by the environments in which the genes are expressed. For example, genetic factors can produce high blood pressure (hypertension), but whether that character is expressed depends on environmental events such as the amount of salt in the diet (Barlassina & Taglietti, 2003) or the presence of stress (Rosmand, 2005).

The Importance of Genetic Diversity

As we have seen, no two individuals (except identical twins) are genetically identical. One benefit of sexual reproduction, in contrast to asexual reproduction as in fungi, is that sexual reproduction increases genetic diversity (see West-Eberhard, 2005). Offspring acquire genes from each parent and in so doing receive different combinations of genes than those of either parent. Genetically diverse species have a better chance of surviving in a changing environment, because when the environment changes, some offspring may have combinations of genes that allow them to live and reproduce in the new environment. Of course, some new combinations of genes may be unhelpful for a given individual even though the population as a whole benefits.

Many insects have survived environmental changes because of the advantages of diversity combined with the great number of their offspring. Also, because the life span of many insect species is very short, many generations are born

FIGURE 3•6 Patterns of inheritance for eye color. (a) If one parent is homozygous for the dominant eye-color gene (BB) and the other parent is homozygous for the recessive eye-color gene (bb), then all of their children will be heterozygous for eye color (Bb) and will have brown eyes. (b) If one parent is heterozygous (Bb) and the other parent is homozygous recessive (bb), then each child will have a 50 percent chance of being heterozygous (brown eyes) and a 50 percent chance of being homozygous recessive (eye colors other than brown). (c) If one parent is homozygous dominant (BB) and the other parent is heterozygous (Bb), then each child will have a 50 percent chance of being homozygous for the dominant eye color (BB) and a 50 percent chance of being heterozygous (Bb)—and in either case will have brown eyes.

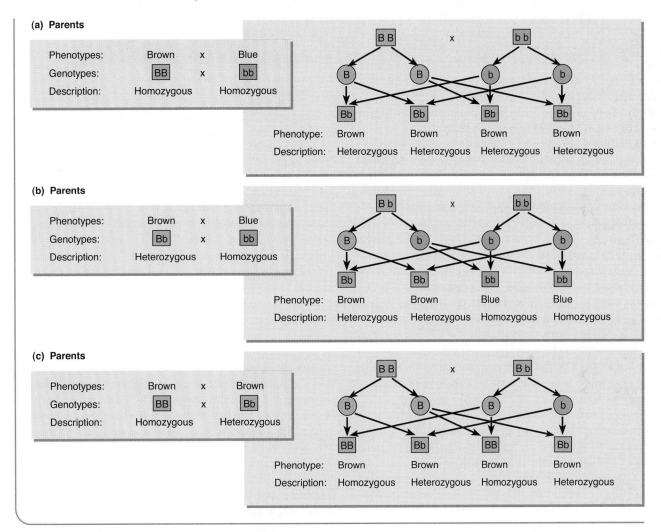

and die in a relatively short time. As an example, consider the peppered moth. (See photos on page 70.) Until the 1800s the most common wing color of these European moths was light. However, with the advent of the industrial revolution, the bark of many of the light-colored trees on which these moths came to rest turned dark with soot. Because a light-colored moth on a dark background is more visible to pre-dating birds, the lighter-colored moths were more likely to be eaten than their darker cousins. Over time the darker variety became the more numerous. The latent capacity of the peppered-moth genome to produce a darker wing color ensured that the species survived this change in environment

(Dawkins, 1996). Rapidly reproducing species can change their nature when nature changes. Similarly, sexually reproducing species are favored because of the adaptive value of genetic diversity. In the case of the peppered moth, interestingly, the lighter variety is again becoming more numerous as pollution controls are enacted (Grant & Wiseman, 2002).

Sex-Linked Characteristics

When a gene is located on a sex chromosome, the person's sex will affect the expression of the trait involved. For example, if a recessive allele on the X chromosome is not paired with a

▲ *The light and dark varieties of peppered moth are shown on trees with light-colored bark (left) and with dark-colored bark. Note the differences in the visibility of the two varieties on the different backgrounds.*

corresponding allele on the Y chromosome, the single recessive allele on the X chromosome can be expressed. Thus, males are more likely than females to express such recessive genes. The reason is that males have XY sex chromosomes, whereas females have sex XX chromosomes. Therefore, females have a chance that the dominant allele is located in the corresponding position on the other X chromosome. The gene for hemophilia, which is carried on the sex chromosomes, is an example of such a recessive allele. In hemophilia, clotting of the blood after an injury is delayed; even a minor cut or a bruise may take many minutes or even hours to clot. Because females have two X chromosomes, they can carry an allele for hemophilia but still have normal blood clotting if the dominant allele is present. Males, however, have only a single X chromosome. If they have the recessive gene on the X chromosome that they received from their mother, they have hemophilia. The gene for hemophilia is an example of a *sex-linked gene.*

Some sex-related genes express themselves in both sexes and are called *sex-influenced genes.* For example, male pattern baldness (thin hair across the top of the head) develops when males inherit one or both alleles for baldness, but is seldom seen in women in either case. This is because the expression of male pattern baldness is affected by male sex hormones, which occur at much lower levels in women.

Mutations and Chromosomal Aberrations

Changes in the genome can be produced by processes other than recombinations of segments of chromosomes that occur during meiosis. The other sources of genetic diversity are mutations or chromosomal aberrations. **Mutations** are chance alterations in the DNA sequence of nucleotides within a single gene. Although most mutations are harmful, some may produce genes that are beneficial in some environments. Mutations can occur either spontaneously during normal biological processes or can result from external causes such as high-energy radiation.

Hemophilia provides one of the most famous examples of mutation. Although hemophilia has appeared many times in human history, it had particularly far-reaching effects when a spontaneous mutation was passed among the royal families of nineteenth-century Europe. Through genealogical analysis, researchers have discovered that this particular mutant gene arose with Queen Victoria (1819–1901). She was the first in her family line to bear affected children—two female carriers and an afflicted son. The tradition calling for nobility to marry other nobility allowed the mutant gene to spread rapidly throughout the royal families of Europe, most notably to the royal family of Russia.

The second type of genetic change, **chromosomal aberration,** may involve a change in part of a chromosome (for example, deletion of a gene) or a change in the total number of chromosomes (for example, failure of paired chromosomes to separate during meiosis). An example of a disorder caused by a chromosomal aberration—in this case, a partial deletion of genetic material in chromosome 5—is the *cri-du-chat syndrome.* Infants who have this syndrome have gastrointestinal, cardiac, and mental problems and also make crying sounds that resemble a cat's mewing (hence the syndrome's name, "cry of the cat"). The severity of the syndrome appears to be related directly to the amount of genetic material that is missing. Early special training can lessen, though not eliminate, difficulties in self-care and communication for such individuals. Once again, this example demonstrates that behavior is the joint effect of both genetic and environmental factors: Even a behavior with a known genetic basis can be modified by experience to some extent.

Genetic Disorders

Some genes decrease an organism's ability to survive—its viability. These "killer genes" are more common than you might imagine, but they are almost always recessive. When a child inherits a healthy allele from one parent and a lethal allele from the other, the lethal gene is not expressed. A few lethal genetic disorders are dominant, however, and most often express themselves in spontaneous abortions and stillborn babies.

There are many human genetic disorders. Three well-known genetic disorders with intellectual and behavioral effects are Down syndrome, Huntington's disease, and phenylketonuria (PKU).

Down syndrome is named after the British physician John Langdon Down. In Down syndrome there is an extra 21st chromosome. When an ovum is formed during meiosis, the 21st pair of chromosomes fails to separate; then, when the ovum is fertilized, the sperm provides a third 21st chromosome. People with Down syndrome have various degrees of impaired physical, psychomotor, and cognitive development. The risk of Down syndrome increases with the age of the mother (Rischer & Easton, 1992). About 40 percent of all Down syndrome children are born to women over 40. To a lesser extent, the age of the father also increases the chances of Down syndrome. Down syndrome cannot be inherited.

Huntington's disease (sometimes called *Huntington's chorea*) is caused by a dominant lethal gene that is not expressed until the afflicted person is 30 to 40 years old. Before that time, functioning is normal; but with the onset of the disease, certain portions of the brain begin to degenerate, and corresponding progressive mental and physical deterioration set in. (The word *chorea* comes from the Greek for "dance" and refers to the uncoordinated movements that occur during the later stages of the disease.) Because the onset of Huntington's disease occurs after sexual maturity, this gene can be passed from parent to child. Perhaps the best known case of Huntington's disease is that of Woody Guthrie, the author of the folk song "This Land Is Your Land." There is now a test for the disease, but Woody Guthrie's son, the folk singer Arlo Guthrie, decided not to take it. Fortunately, Arlo did not receive the gene from his father.

Phenylketonuria (PKU) is caused by a recessive gene. Infants who are homozygous for the gene are unable to break down phenylalanine, an amino acid found in many high-protein foods. As a result, blood levels of phenylalanine increase and cause brain damage and impairment of intellectual functioning. A test for the disease is routinely given to newborns. Newborns testing homozygous for this recessive gene are placed on a low-phenylalanine diet shortly after birth. When the diet is carefully followed, brain development is normal. Again, environment and genes interact to produce the phenotype.

Heredity and Behavior

Even casual observation confirms that people differ from one another. However, it may surprise you to learn that humans are genetically much less diverse than other primates. For example, we show less genetic diversity than our closest relatives, the chimpanzee (Strachan & Read, 1999). Nevertheless, each of us possesses unique combinations of genes and lives in our own unique environment. Accordingly, we are diverse. We differ in size and shape, in personality and intelligence, and in artistic and athletic abilities, to name but a few traits. To what extent are human differences due to genetic differences or to environmental differences?

To answer this question experimentally would be difficult. First, if we want to determine whether a difference is due to one of two variables, we must hold the other variable constant. But we cannot vary the heredity of humans while holding their environments constant. Nor can we vary their environments while holding heredity constant. Thus, for humans, the experimental procedures normally used to determine the effect of a variable cannot be implemented—and even if experiments of this sort were possible, we would not want to conduct them for ethical reasons.

Second, because the effects of heredity and environment interact, if we were to manipulate the value of one variable while holding the other variable constant, the effect of the manipulated variable would depend on the specific value of the variable we held constant. If we had held the other variable constant at a different value, the manipulated variable might have had a different effect. For example, manipulating genes known to affect high blood pressure might have little effect if the environment was held constant at a value in which there was no salt. We might then incorrectly conclude that these genes had no effect on blood pressure.

Keeping these complications in mind, how can scientists assess the roles of genetic and environmental differences in behavior? First, statistical procedures can be applied to humans, because these procedures are observational and do not involve direct manipulation of variables. Darwin's cousin Francis Galton (1869) began the effort to apply correlational methods to the study of heredity in humans. A common measure of the degree to which genes affect behavior in a given environment is heritability. Heritability is a statistical correlational measure that estimates the proportion of the variability in a trait that is due to naturally occurring genetic differences among individuals in a population. Heritability varies from 0.0 (no effect of genetic differences on variability) to 1.0 (complete genetic determination of variability). The measure pertains to the variation of a trait in a specific *population*; it does not indicate the contribution of genetic factors to the characteristics of any one individual. A second, and complementary, approach is **behavior genetics.** Behavior genetics usually takes an experimental approach in which the researcher manipulates genetic variables and measures the effects of these manipulations on behavior. Clearly, behavior genetics is largely restricted to the study of nonhuman animals. The next section will look more closely at both experimental techniques (with nonhuman animals) and correlational approaches (with humans) in research on genes and behavior.

Studying Genetic Influences

Laboratory methods have been used to study the relation between heredity and behavior for only about 100 years. Experimental work began with Mendel's careful analysis of the effect of crossbreeding pea plants with different characteristics. Mendel crossed pea plants with one trait—for example, wrinkled peas—with plants with a different trait—for example, smooth peas. He was fortunate to have chosen a species in which discrete traits (wrinkled or smooth) were controlled by a single gene. Many traits vary continuously and are controlled by several genes. Traits that are discretely expressed by single genes are called **mendelian traits** and display the patterns of inheritance shown in Figure 3.6.

Most traits of interest to behavior genetics are not mendelian but are continuously varying characteristics that are controlled by more than one gene, and the genes may be located on different chromosomes. These polygenic traits are known as **nonmendelian traits.** Because nonmendelian traits are polygenic, their study requires methods different from those used by Mendel. Polygenic traits play an important role in human evolution (Carroll, 2003). Let's consider several methods for their study.

Experimental Procedures for Determining the Effects of Genes

As mentioned earlier in this chapter, artificial selection involves selective breeding within a population of organisms. Artificial selection can be used to study any inherited trait, including a nonmendelian one. By using artificial selection procedures with animals, researchers have demonstrated the heritability of many traits. These include aggression, docility, preference for alcohol, running speed, and mating behavior.

Perhaps the best known example of artificial selection is the classic study of maze learning in rats conducted by Robert Tryon (1940). Tryon began with an unselected group of rats and had them learn a maze. As you might imagine, some rats learned with few errors and some with many errors. Tryon then interbred the rats that learned with the fewest errors with their kind and interbred the rats that learned with the most errors with their kind. The offspring of this artificial selection procedure then learned the maze, and their offspring were in turn interbred in the same manner.

Tryon continued this artificial selection procedure over successive generations—having rats learn the maze and selectively breeding the best with the best and the worst with the

▲ *Tryon's selective breeding study showed that a rat's ability to learn how to navigate a maze was affected by genetic factors.*

worst. After seven generations the maze-learning performance of the two groups did not overlap to any extent. (See **Figure 3•7.**) It is important to note that the two groups did not differ on their first attempt at the maze, however: The difference emerged with training. Artificial selection had produced two groups of rats that learned at different rates.

It would be simplistic to conclude that the differences in maze performance indicated that this behavior was affected only by genetic differences. For example, Cooper and Zubek (1958) demonstrated that differences in maze performance were virtually eliminated when researchers stimulated "maze-bright" and "maze-dull" groups of rats by rearing them in enriched environments (cages containing geometric objects such as tunnels, ramps, and blocks). Differences also were eliminated when Tryon's rats were raised in impoverished environments (cages containing only food and water). Thus,

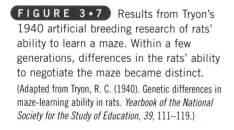

FIGURE 3•7 Results from Tryon's 1940 artificial breeding research of rats' ability to learn a maze. Within a few generations, differences in the rats' ability to negotiate the maze became distinct.
(Adapted from Tryon, R. C. (1940). Genetic differences in maze-learning ability in rats. *Yearbook of the National Society for the Study of Education, 39,* 111–119.)

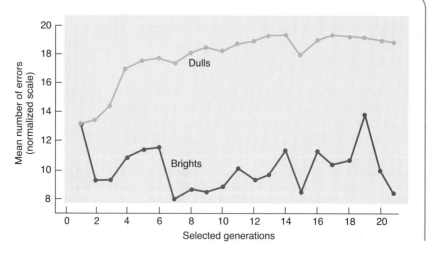

the effects of the genetic differences depended on the environments in which the genes were expressed. It also would be a mistake to conclude that Tryon's two groups differed in some more general respect such as "intelligence" or "ability to learn." For example, Tryon's "dull" rats learned a task that required escape from water faster than the "bright" rats (Searles, 1949; see McClearn, 1963 for a review). General effects of selection can be expected only if the selecting environments are diverse, such as the varying challenges that *Homo sapiens* and many other species have faced over evolutionary time.

A powerful research technique that can be used to directly manipulate genes and their expression is **molecular genetics**—the branch of genetics that studies genes at the level of DNA and then relates that information to the structure and function of the organism. This rapidly growing field has developed laboratory techniques to study genes. Its greatest accomplishment to date has been to determine essentially the complete sequence of nucleotides for the entire human genome. This was accomplished on April 14, 2003.

One of the laboratory techniques for studying the effects of genes at the molecular level involves causing **knockout mutations.** As discussed earlier, mutations are changes in the sequence of nucleotides within the DNA molecule. They usually occur because of factors in the environment, but molecular biologists have developed methods that directly affect gene expression by radiating a laboratory animal and damaging genes or by inserting nucleotides that prevent the expression of a gene. This method produces what is called a knockout mutation. In one such study with rats, scientists knocked out a gene that is expressed in a part of the brain known to be important for spatial learning in humans. When this gene was knocked out, the rats were impaired in their recall of the location of a platform where they could escape from a pool of water (Nakazawa, Sun, Rondi-Reig, Wilson, & Tanegawa, 2003). By examining the changes in an animal's performance after a gene has been knocked out, researchers can obtain clues about the function of that gene.

Investigators can combine the methods of molecular biology with those of artificial selection to study the effects of genes on behavior. For example, a biochemically detectable change can be produced in a genetically inactive portion of a chromosome. This change then becomes a **genetic marker** for the genes that are nearby on the chromosome. If artificial selection produces a change in behavior, as in maze performance in Tryon's experiment, the researchers can examine the genetic markers to see if the artificially selected subgroups differ in the frequency of the genetic marker. If the groups differ, then the genes that were responsible for the difference must lie nearby on the chromosome. By using multiple markers on different chromosomes, researchers can increase their chance of finding the locations of the relevant genes. As an example, this technique has been used to isolate the location of a gene that affects exploratory behavior in fruit-fly larvae (Osborne et al., 1997).

Correlational Procedures for Determining the Effects of Genes

With humans, as I pointed out earlier, most experimental procedures are precluded by ethical considerations. Human behavior cannot be subjected to artificial selection, and human genes cannot be knocked out or marked. Nevertheless, science has learned much about the effects of genes on human behavior through correlational procedures. In correlational procedures, behavior geneticists examine individuals with naturally occurring differences in behavior to determine if differences in genetic variables are related to (correlated with) the behavior. We cannot manipulate the genotype of humans, but we can observe their behavior (the behavioral phenotype) and, given their informed consent, analyze the sequences of nucleotides to see if they are correlated with the phenotype. Keep in mind that any conclusions must acknowledge that the effect of a gene can be modified by the particular environment in which the observations were made.

One correlational procedure is **concordance research,** or research on behavioral similarities in twins, which takes advantage of the fact that identical twins possess identical genes. Recall that identical twins, technically *monozygotic (MZ) twins,* arise from a single fertilized ovum, or zygote. The zygote divides into two genetically identical cells, and the twins develop independently thereafter. In contrast, fraternal twins, technically *dizygotic (DZ) twins,* arise from the fertilization of two different ova by two different sperm. As such, DZ twins are genetically no more alike than any other two siblings. If genes affect a given behavior, then MZ twins should be more alike with respect to that behavior than DZ twins or other siblings who are raised in similar environments.

Two individuals are said to be *concordant* for a trait if both express that same trait. If only one of the two individuals expresses the trait, then they are said to be *discordant* for the trait. In these terms, MZ twins should be concordant more often than other pairs of individuals who are less genetically similar. As shown in **Table 3•1,** MZ twins are indeed more often con-

▲ *Research with identical twins has provided psychologists with information about the role of heredity in behavioral traits.*

TABLE 3•1 Comparison of Concordance Rates between Monozygotic (MZ) and Dizygotic (DZ) Twins for Various Traits		
Concordance		
Trait	**MZ**	**DZ**
Blood type	100%	66%
Eye color	99	28
Mental retardation	97	37
Measles	95	87
Idiopathic epilepsy	72	15
Schizophrenia	69	10
Diabetes	65	18
Identical allergy	59	5
Tuberculosis	57	23

Source: Table 7.4, p. 161 from *Concepts of Genetics,* 2nd ed. by William S. Klug and Michael R. Cummings. Copyright © 1986 by Scott, Foresman and Company. Reprinted by permission of Pearson Education, Inc.

cordant for many traits. For example, blood type, which has a heritability of 1.0, is highly concordant in MZ twins. Conversely, when a trait shows little concordance in MZ twins, the effect of heredity on that trait is low. Environmental similarity also can affect concordance, of course. For example, consider the characteristic of religious belief. Here, a high concordance would likely reflect the fact that the two individuals acquired their belief from their common parents. Consistent with this expectation, the concordance rates for religious belief are essentially the same—and moderately high—for both MZ and DZ twins (Loehlin & Nichols, 1976). Thus, there is no evidence that religious beliefs are genetically based.

In research described in later chapters, studies comparing the performance of MZ and DZ twins show that genetic factors also affect cognitive skills such as scores on intelligence tests (Bouchard & McGue, 1981), language ability, personality traits such as extroversion (the tendency to be outgoing), personality development, and certain psychological disorders such as schizophrenia and mental retardation (Bouchard & Propping, 1993).

Segregation analysis is another correlational procedure that can help identify genetic contributions to human behavior. Although behavioral geneticists cannot insert a genetic marker, they can identify specific regions of chromosomes and correlate the presence or absence of these regions with a behavioral phenotype. The marked regions may be genes already identified through previous work or simply regions whose nucleotide sequences are relatively constant. Behavior geneticists use the information from concordances and kin relations to identify a trait that seems to reflect genetic influences. They then examine the chromosomes to see if any of the various markers are differentially associated—segregated—with the behavioral trait. If some markers are segregated between the behavioral phenotypes, then the critical genes must

lie near the markers. Additional work in molecular biology can then be directed toward those regions of the chromosome to identify the genes precisely.

The potential power of segregation analysis is illustrated by a study of a language deficit (Lai, Fisher, Hurst, Vargha-Khadem, & Monaco, 2001). Members of three generations of a family showed a pronounced language disorder that involved—among other characteristics—problems in the processing of word sounds and the use of grammar. One gene on the seventh chromosome, designated with the letters FOXP2, showed a mutation that was unique to those members of the family who had the language disorder. The mutation was not seen in a large sample of individuals unrelated to the family who did not show the language-disorder phenotype. The finding strongly suggested that a normally functioning FOXP2 gene may affect the fine articulatory movements that make normal speech possible (Pinker, 2001). An especially intriguing result arose as a by-product of this work. When the map of the human genome was compared to analogous genetic sequences in other primates, it was found that the FOXP2 gene had changed quite rapidly after humans diverged from the other great apes (Enard et al., 2002). Based on the rate at which mutations are thought to occur, the estimated date at which the modern human form of FOXP2 emerged was within the last 200,000 years of human evolution. As Figure 3.3 showed, this was around the time that *Homo sapiens* was in competition with its Neanderthal cousins.

Evaluating Scientific Issues

The Genetics of Alcoholism

Alcohol is the substance most commonly abused by humans, and alcohol abuse has very severe consequences (Helzer & Canino, 1992). Among these are increased risks of liver damage, loss of employment, marital discord, estrangement from family members and friends, and/or being injured or injuring others in an accident. Because of the pervasiveness of alcoholism, many researchers have investigated whether genetic factors play a role in the condition. Evidence from several lines of research is consistent with this possibility, including concordance rates in twin studies and artificial selection studies with animals (for a review see Begleiter & Kissin, 1995).

● **Alcoholism Concordance Studies with Twins**
Twin studies have consistently shown that concordance rates for alcoholism are higher for MZ twins than for DZ twins. For example, a study of nearly 4000 Australian twins found that MZ twins were more alike in alcohol consumption than DZ twins (Heath, Meyer, & Martin, 1990). Similarly, studies of twins from the United States showed that concordance rates were higher for MZ twins than DZ twins, *but only if*

the twins were males (McGue, Pickens, & Svikis, 1992; Pickens et al., 1991). The concordance rates for males were substantial for MZ twins (averaging 77 percent in the two studies) and noticeably smaller for male DZ twins (averaging 57 percent). Thus, the concordance rates were consistent with a genetic component in alcohol consumption. However, concordance rates were appreciable in DZ males and did not differ among females (averaging 36 percent across both MZ and DZ twins). This pattern of concordances suggests substantial environmental as well as genetic influence on drinking behavior.

● **Artificial Selection Studies on Alcoholism**

Findings from artificial selection studies also have indicated a genetic contribution to alcohol consumption. Strains of rats can be bred for their preference for alcohol. After several generations of interbreeding, one strain of rats will voluntarily drink alcohol, prefer alcohol to other liquids, learn new responses in order to obtain alcohol, and develop a tolerance for and physical dependence on alcohol. These rats also show symptoms of withdrawal when alcohol is no longer available. The other strain will show none of these characteristics (Lumeng, Murphy, McBride, & Li, 1995). Furthermore, examination of the brains of these two strains of rats shows distinct differences in the chemical composition of specific brain regions.

● **What Should We Conclude?**

Both twin studies and artificial selection studies have pointed in the same direction—toward a genetic influence on alcohol consumption. Convergent evidence is important in science, because it shows that different approaches arrive at the same conclusion. Thus, the finding is likely to be both reliable and valid. We are thus more likely to believe that a relationship between heredity and alcoholism really exists. Continuing efforts to examine the genetic role in alcoholism rely on converging evidence, particularly with the genetic techniques now available. However, none of the preliminary research evidence has yet demonstrated the existence or location of a particular gene or set of genes for alcoholism (Buck, 1998). Also, remember that it is not uncommon for preliminary research to identify a candidate for a gene that affects some behavioral phenotype but for later research to show the gene has other effects that are not specifically related to that phenotype (e.g., Blum, Noble, Montgomery, Sheridan, & Ritchie, 1990; Gerlernter, Goldman, & Risch, 1993).

Further, even if studies conclusively demonstrate that a particular gene is correlated with a particular behavioral phenotype (such as alcoholism), this does not necessarily eliminate a role for the environment in producing that phenotype. Remember that genes always require an environment for their expression and that different environments may affect genes in different ways. A person who has the gene (or set of genes) for alcoholism will not become an alcoholic if he or she does not first consume alcohol. Thus, an individual may carry the gene and have parents who are alcoholics, but the person will never become an alcoholic in an environment in which alcohol is not available. In the words of a researcher on the genetics of alcoholism, "It is unlikely that genes drive us to drink" (Plomin, 1990).

Interim Summary

Heredity and Genetics

The instructions for the synthesis of proteins, which oversee the structure of the body and all of its processes, are contained in genes. Genes are found on chromosomes, which consist of DNA and are found in every cell. We inherit 23 individual chromosomes, each of which contains thousands of genes, from each parent. This means that our genetic blueprint represents a recombination of the genetic instructions that our parents inherited from their parents. Such recombination makes for tremendous genetic diversity. Genetically diverse species have a better chance of adapting to a changing environment than do genetically nondiverse species. Diverse species are more likely to have genes that enable them to survive in the new environment.

The expression of a gene depends on several factors, including interactions with other genes (which produce polygenic traits), the sex of the individual carrying the particular gene, and the environmental conditions under which that individual lives. Changes in genetic material caused by mutations or chromosomal aberrations may change the expression of a gene. For example, hemophilia, which decreases the ability of blood to clot after even minor injuries, is the result of a mutation. Down syndrome, which involves impaired mental development, is the result of a chromosomal aberration.

Behavior genetics is the study of how genes influence behavior. Psychologists and other scientists use both experimental methods, such as artificial selection, and correlational methods, such as concordance rates in twin studies, to investigate the relation between genes and behavior. Alcoholism is one area of human behavior to which behavior genetics has been applied.

QUESTIONS TO CONSIDER

1. How would you explain the fact that a sister and brother may have blue eyes and brown eyes, respectively?
2. How might the gene related to the development of athletic ability interact with environmental variables to produce a specific phenotype (for example, a specific level of athletic ability in a specific individual)?
3. How would you design a study to assess the role of genes in human aggression? Could you use more than one approach to gathering this information? If so, what would these different approaches entail?

Sociobiology

Sociobiology is the study of the genetic bases of social behavior. Social behavior is any behavior involving interactions between members of the same species. Sociobiology integrates information from several fields of social science as well as from evolutionary psychology and behavior genetics. Typically, sociobiologists observe and perform experiments on the social behavior of nonhuman animals and then explore the implications of those findings for social behavior in humans.

Reproductive Strategies and the Biological Basis of Parenting

Because reproductive and parenting behavior are so obviously related to species survival, these behaviors have been a major focus of sociobiological research. Much of this work has concerned **reproductive strategies**—various systems of mating and rearing offspring.

Of the various human reproductive strategies, traditional Western cultures sanction only **monogamy:** the mating of one female and one male. If offspring result, the culture endorses parental sharing in the raising of the child. However, different reproductive strategies occur in different species—including our own (Barash, 1982). Three additional major classes of reproductive strategy are possible. (See **Figure 3•8.**) In **polygyny** one male mates with more than one female; in **polyandry** one female mates with more than one male; and in **polygynandry** several females mate with several males. (*Poly* refers to many, *gyn* to female, and *andry* to male.) This section will consider only monogamy and polygyny, because they are by far the predominant reproductive strategies in humans.

These four reproductive strategies evolved because of important sex differences in the resources that each parent invests in conceiving and rearing offspring (Trivers, 1972). **Parental investment** is the time, physical effort, and risks to life involved in procreation and in the feeding, nurturing, and protection of offspring. From an evolutionary perspec-

▲ *Large male elephant seals are more successful in competing for females than are smaller males. But is there a point at which larger size could become maladaptive?*

tive, individuals that make a greater investment in parenting should be more discriminating when choosing a mate and, in turn, should be more sought after as mates.

Competition for mates may lead to **sexual selection**—natural selection for traits that are characteristic of a sex, such as body size or particular behavior patterns. For example, in species such as herd animals (e.g., buffalo) or some birds, the larger and more aggressive males more successfully compete for and gain access to females and thereby enjoy greater reproductive success.

Among humans polygyny is by far the most common reproductive strategy. In fact, although many cultures do not officially sanction polygyny, most males in human societies engage in polygynous mating practices. Such behavior is especially common in males who have reproductively advantageous assets such as wealth or power (Badcock, 1991). Monogamy is the next most popular reproductive strategy, with about 15 percent of all cultures practicing as well as sanctioning this strategy. Let's now look more closely at polygyny and monogamy.

Polygyny: High Female and Low Male Parental Investment
For most mammals, including humans, the costs associated with reproduction are much higher for females than males. Females have fewer opportunities than males to reproduce, because they produce only one ovum or a few ova periodically, whereas males can produce numerous sperm at relatively brief intervals. A female can bear only a limited number of offspring in a lifetime, regardless of the number of males with whom she mates. In contrast, a male is limited in his reproductive success only by the number of females he can impregnate. Females also carry the fertilized ovum in their bodies during long gestation periods. This requires diverting a major portion of their own metabolic resources to nourishing the fetus. Because they carry the fertil-

	Male partner	
	One	Multiple
Female partner One	Monogamy	Polyandry
Female partner Multiple	Polygyny	Polygynandry

FIGURE 3•8 Reproductive strategies. Different numbers of males' mating with different numbers of females yield the four reproductive strategies of monogamy, polygyny, polyandry, and polygynandry.

ized ovum, females assume the risks that accompany pregnancy and childbirth, including discomfort and possible risks to health. The contributions of the male to reproduction can be minimal—sperm and time for intercourse. Once the offspring is born, females often continue to devote some of their metabolic resources to the infant by nursing it. They also usually devote more time and physical energy to caring for offspring than do males. This difference between the parental investments of males and females is dramatically illustrated by King Ismail of Morocco, who reportedly fathered 1056 children (Young, 1998)!

Because females in polygynous species invest so heavily in their offspring, they are usually quite selective in their mates, choosing to mate preferentially with males that possess specific attributes, such as physical size, strength, and aggressiveness. Such selectivity makes adaptive sense for both the female and her progeny. Bearing the offspring of such males means that her male offspring will tend to possess the same adaptively significant attributes as the father and thus be more likely to win their own quests for mating privileges. Also, her female offspring will be more likely to be attracted to the same male attributes. The net effect is that the genes of the mother may have greater representation in future generations than will genes of females who mate with males having less adaptive attributes.

Monogamy: Shared, but Not Always Equal, Parental Investment

Monogamy is common in species whose environments demand contributions from both parents to increase the survival and ultimately the reproductive success of their offspring. In these environments, sharing parental duties enhances fitness in comparison to the involvement of only one parent. For example, foxes provide food, milk, and protection for their offspring. A single female attempting to fulfill these responsibilities would put the pups at risk: Hunting would be difficult with the pups straggling along, but leaving the pups would risk predation. The reproductive strategy exhibited by foxes is that both parents hunt and protect the cubs. By committing themselves to the joint care of their pups, both male and female foxes enhance the chance that their offspring will survive and reproduce—that the parents' genes will be represented in the next generation.

Although both males and females in monogamous species share parenting responsibilities, females continue to have greater parental investment in the offspring. Many of the reasons for greater female investment endure—the limited opportunity for mating, the cost of pregnancy and lactation, and so on. As a result, very few monogamous species, including our own, are exclusively monogamous. In fact, there is a strong tendency in most monogamous species toward patterns of reproductive behavior and parental investment that resemble those in polygynous species. For example, in monogamous species females tend to be more careful than males in selecting a mate, and males tend to be more sexually promiscuous than females (Badcock, 1991). Unmarried women tend to seek long-term sexual relationships, whereas unmarried men tend to prefer more diversity and casualness in their sexual relationships (Tavris & Sadd, 1977).

Learning and culture, as well as the ancestral environment (via genes), affect reproductive behavior in humans. The advent of effective contraception for females has reduced the relation between mating and childbearing and, as a result, could affect human reproductive strategies in the future. Contemporary Western cultures do not measure reproductive success by the number of children but by the quality of the children's and the parents' lives. Most people have the biological capacity to produce a large number of children, but many choose not to do so.

The Biological Basis of Altruism

Altruistic behavior is another area of particular interest in sociobiology. **Altruism** is behavior that involves self-sacrifice. If individuals behave at what appear to be a cost to themselves but a benefit to others, then that behavior is said to be altruistic. But altruism appears to conflict with what is known about evolution through natural selection. If natural selection favors traits that benefit survival, how could behavior that reduces survival be selected? And yet abundant examples of altruism exist even among animals other than humans. Consider, for example, the honeybee that sacrifices its life on behalf of its hive mates by stinging an intruder, or the prairie dog that gives an alarm call that warns other prairie dogs of a predator but increases its own chances of being eaten. Examples of altruistic behavior abound in humans. In its most extreme form, human altruism is demonstrated when one person risks his or her life to save the life of another. How can such self-sacrifice be understood? How can there be an evolutionary account of such behavior?

Kin Selection

One evolutionary explanation of altruistic behavior flows from the realization that the survival of the *genes,* not the individual who carries those genes, is the cornerstone of evolution through natural selection. An individual's genes are held in common with those with whom the individual is genetically related. For example, a parent shares 50 percent of his or her genes with each offspring—half of each child's genes come from the father and half from the mother. Thus, a parent who disadvantages himself to benefit his children is to some extent benefiting his own genes! The geneticist William D. Hamilton (1964, 1970) realized that, strictly speaking, natural selection favors not reproductive success but **inclusive fitness**—the reproductive success of those individuals who share many of the same genes.

In confirmation of the implications of the concept of inclusive fitness, experiments have demonstrated that altruistic behavior is more apt to occur when the organism that benefits is genetically related to the organism that pays the cost. Bees and other social insects, such as termites, are among the most altruistic organisms, because their genetic relationship causes them to share a particularly high percentage of their genes in common. Birds make alarm calls on sighting a hawk if their relatives are near, but not otherwise (Wilson, 1975). In general, altruistic acts are aimed at close relatives such as parents, siblings, grandparents, and grandchildren. The closer the family relation, the more likely the genetic overlap among the individuals involved. Such biologic favoritism toward relatives is called **kin selection** (Mayr, 2001). Is kin selection a factor in human behavior when grandparents raise the children of their drug-addicted daughters? Could the fact that age may prevent the grandparents from propagating their genes by having more children also contribute to this behavior?

Reciprocal Altruism   Not all instances of altruistic behavior can be given an evolutionary explanation by an appeal to kin selection. What about altruism shown between unrelated individuals? Could this also be affected by genetic variables? Evolutionary biologists have identified an additional genetic source of altruistic behavior: **reciprocal altruism** (Trivers, 1971). Reciprocal altruism occurs when genetically unrelated persons engage in behavior that reduces fitness at the moment but enhances fitness in the longer term. For example, one individual may share his or her food now, and the other individual may, in turn, share food later. Thus, each individual has increased his or her fitness—the likelihood of passing genes on to the next generation.

Reciprocal altruism may be thought of as the biological version of the Golden Rule—"Do unto others as you would have them do unto you." However, the biological version is not as generously applicable as the Golden Rule. To aid fitness, altruistic behavior must carry a low risk to the altruist but a high benefit for the recipient. The lower the cost to the altruist, the more likely the altruistic act will benefit the altruist's fitness. There also must be a good chance that the situation will be reversed in the future. If the altruist is not likely ever to benefit from similar action on the part of the recipient, the fitness of the altruist is decreased. Finally, the recipient must be able to recognize the altruist, for otherwise the behavior cannot be reciprocated. Does this genetic analysis of the conditions required for reciprocal altruism help explain why people are more likely to be altruistic in small communities than in big cities? Again, cultural factors and individual experience undoubtedly play a role in this form of altruism as well, but the genetic analysis of reciprocal altruism contributes to the explanation.

An example of the effects of individual experience on altruism is provided by studies of emotional closeness between individuals. Emotional closeness is defined as enjoying a positive personal relationship with another person, being concerned with and caring for them. One study asked participants to rate how willing they would be to behave altruistically toward various relatives even when helping them would be at a cost to themselves (Korchmaros and Kenny, 2001). In addition, participants also indicated how emotionally close they were to these relatives. The researchers found that emo-

tional closeness had a significant effect on altruistic behavior. People were more likely to help those with whom they shared a close emotional relationship, over and above the closeness of their genetic relationship.

Some Comments about Sociobiology

Sociobiology has been controversial among some psychologists, social scientists, and the general public. Several types of objections have been raised by critics, most based on an incomplete understanding of sociobiology. One objection has been that human behavior is too complex to be understood by natural selection alone. However, no sociobiologist would ever make this claim. Social behavior—indeed all behavior—is the concerted effect of both the ancestral environment, as reflected in our genetic makeup, and our individual experience, as reflected in our nervous systems. To claim that evolution has *something* to say about social behavior is not to claim that evolution has *everything* to say about it. Another objection has been that sociobiology is based on simplistic analogies between the behaviors of nonhuman animals and of humans. It is true that experimental work in sociobiology has been largely restricted to nonhumans, but experimental work is similarly limited in any science that deals with human behavior. The highly controlled observations possible in the laboratory can rarely be achieved with humans and would not be acceptable for ethical reasons in any case. Care must always be taken when we apply findings from animal research to humans—or, for that matter, from any one species to any other.

We are encouraged to seek commonalities in the behavior of humans and other species by the fact of evolution—that all animal species are related to one another through branching descent—and the fact of selection—that all species have been subjected to selection by a partially common environment.

Biology and Culture

Thinking Critically about Selection

The criticisms of sociobiological accounts of human behavior are specific examples of the reservations that have been raised about natural selection as a basis for understanding the diversity and complexity of life. Before Darwin these phenomena seemed beyond the reach of a natural-science explanation. The origins and development of life were a mystery—what Darwin (1859) called "that mystery of mysteries." After Darwin the *possibility* of a natural-science explanation of life appeared. Repeated cycles of variation, selection, and retention held promise of an account that could be tested through the methods of science.

Today natural selection is the central unifying principle of biology from molecules to man. Moreover, Darwin's account of how selection processes produced the richness of life is seen as a general natural-science approach to the explanation of the emergence of order and complexity in many fields. The repeated actions of physical, chemical, and biological processes—each of which can be subjected to independent scrutiny in the laboratory—may be competent to yield complex outcomes as their emergent product. The evolution of the solar system of planets from an initial swirling mass of randomly moving particles is but one example, with selection provided by gravity and other physical processes. Science and technology also are putting the selectionist approach to practical use, as in the design of complex electronic circuits from an initial random assortment of components (e.g., Mead, 1989). (For more general treatments of selectionism, see Dennett, 1995; Donahoe, 2003; Mayr, 2000; Palmer & Donahoe, 1992; and Sober, 1984.) Darwin identified a means whereby complex phenomena in many fields might be explained as products of the repeated action of a three-step process that did not require external supervision.

One general criticism of selectionism as an explanation of the diversity and complexity of life is that not all of the steps of the evolutionary process are known. When complex electronic circuits are developed through a selection process, we can examine each step in the sequence and assure ourselves that the circuits came about through the cumulative effects of selection. When we examine naturally occurring processes, however, only glimpses of the entire sequence are visible. In the evolution of our species, for example, we see only a tooth here, a leg bone there. Darwin recognized the incompleteness of our knowledge of all of the steps in any natural process. Commenting on the meagerness of the fossil record, he remarked that "we are confessedly ignorant; nor do we know how ignorant we are" (Darwin, 1859). The fossil record is much fuller now than when Darwin made his comment, but our knowledge remains imperfect. Faced with imperfect knowledge, scientists seek to fill in the gaps rather than resigning themselves to concluding that "then a miracle occurs." Not all of the gaps may ever be filled, but none will be filled unless we continue to look.

A second general criticism of selectionism is that it undermines our uniqueness, and even our worth, as a species. Consider the sociobiological account of altruism. We prefer to think of ourselves as selfless individuals who help others from the goodness of our hearts. Sociobiology suggests that often altruism is, at least in part, a selfish act that we undertake because it promotes the survival of our genes. But is this not a kind of selflessness? It is our genes that benefit, not necessarily we as individuals. And, most importantly, knowledge of evolution through natural selection opens the possibility that we can remedy the effects of prior selections that once benefited populations as a whole but now exact a heavy price from the individual. Recall the effects of the sickle-cell gene on John Harold Johnson Jr. Through **genetic engineering** and other applications of knowledge of natural selection, we can implement what might be called "counterselections" to modify the untoward effects of selection. If we can apply our knowledge with care, is this not testimony to the uniqueness and worth of our species (Campbell, 1976)?

Interim Summary

Sociobiology

The study of the genetic contribution to social behavior is the primary goal of sociobiology. Sociobiology is augmented by evolutionary psychology, which attempts to explain behavior by the adaptiveness of psychological mechanisms. Sociobiologists have been especially interested in aspects of social behavior that are related to reproduction and the rearing of offspring, because these aspects are most clearly affected by natural selection. Different reproductive strategies have evolved because of sex differences in the resources that parents invest in procreative and child-rearing activities. These resources include the time, physical effort, and risks to life involved in procreation and in the feeding, nurturing, and protecting of offspring. Primarily because of greater female investment, polygynous and monogamous reproductive strategies are most common in humans.

Altruism also has been an important topic of study among sociobiologists, because it presents an intriguing scientific puzzle. On the surface, altruism would seem difficult to explain in terms of natural selection. After all, why would natural selection favor a behavior that lowers an organism's reproductive success while increasing the reproductive success of other organisms? Sociobiology provides two answers to this question: inclusive fitness, in which altruistic behavior benefits those with whom an organism shares many genes, and reciprocal altruism, in which altruistic behavior benefits the altruist at some later time when the beneficiary reciprocates the good deed.

Sociobiology has been criticized on the grounds that research on animal social behavior is not relevant to understanding human social behavior and that environmental factors play a greater role than genetic factors in shaping human behavior. Sociobiologists reply that natural selection has shaped and continues to shape the evolution of culture; that findings from animal research can be generalized to humans with appropriate caution; that genes and environment interact to determine behavior; and, finally, that sociobiology is an attempt to understand human social behavior, not to justify it.

QUESTION TO CONSIDER

Do you believe that human social behavior has a genetic component? Explain your rationale.

Suggestions for Further Reading

Darwin, C. (1859). *On the origin of species by means of natural selection.* London: Murray.

This book contains the full argument that Darwin marshaled in defense of evolution by natural selection. It is a must for serious students of evolutionary psychology.

Dawkins, R. (1996). *Climbing Mount Improbable.* New York: W. W. Norton.

An excellent discussion of the role of diversity in the natural world. Some beautiful graphics and illustrations supplement this readable text.

Dennett, D. (1995). *Darwin's dangerous idea.* New York: Simon and Schuster.

This is a literary and challenging look at the philosophical implications of natural selection, particularly with respect to human nature. Dennett takes issue with Stephen J. Gould, listed below, on the suitability of adaptation as an explanation in psychology and other biological sciences.

Gould, S. J. (1996). *Full house: The spread of excellence from Plato to Darwin.* New York: Harmony Books.

Until his death in 2002, Gould authored an extensive set of books on evolution, the history of biology, and genetic determinism. This book sets some of the principles of evolution in a wide context. Gould is a gifted and witty author; reading his work is a pleasure.

Russell, P. J. (1992). *Genetics.* New York: HarperCollins.

A very good introductory presentation of the basic principles of genetics.

Plomin, R. (1990). *Nature and nurture: An introduction to behavioral genetics.* Pacific Grove, CA: Brooks/Cole.

This very brief book (144 pages), authored by one of the field's preeminent scholars, is an excellent, simple-to-read introduction to the field of behavior genetics. The relevance of behavior genetics to our understanding of the origins of common behaviors and problems comes across especially clearly.

Plomin, R. and Colledge, E. (2001). Genetics and psychology: Beyond heritability. *European Psychologist, 6,* 4, 229–240.

Special issue, *The Psychologist.* 2001, 4, 3.

The Plomin and Colledge and the Special issue of *The Psychologist* describe the role of behavioral genetics in a very accessible way.

Wilson, E. O. (1975). *Sociobiology: The new synthesis.* Cambridge, MA: Harvard University Press.

This well-written and engaging graduate-level text represents the evolutionary argument for the biological basis of social behavior. The last chapter contains applications of the theory to humans.

Key Terms

adaptive significance (p. 56)

alleles (p. 68)

altruism (p. 77)

artificial selection (p. 59)

autosomes (p. 67)

behavior genetics (p. 71)

biological evolution (p. 56)

bipedalism (p. 63)

chromosomal aberration (p. 70)

chromosomes (p. 67)

competition (p. 62)

concordance research (p. 73)

culture (p. 58)

cultural evolution (p. 65)

DNA (deoxyribonucleic acid) (p. 66)

dominant gene (p. 68)

Down syndrome (p. 71)

encephalization (p. 64)

enzymes (p. 67)

genes (p. 66)

genetics (p. 66)

genetic engineering (p. 79)

genetic marker (p. 73)

genome (p. 67)

genotype (p. 61)

germ cells (p. 67)

heredity (p. 66)

Huntington's disease (p. 71)

inclusive fitness (p. 77)

kin selection (p. 78)

knockout mutation (p. 73)

meiosis (p. 67)

mendelian trait (p. 72)

molecular genetics (p. 73)

monogamy (p. 76)

mutations (p. 70)

natural selection (p. 59)

nonmendelian trait (p. 72)

parental investment (p. 76)

phenotype (p. 61)

phenylketonuria (PKU) (p. 71)

polyandry (p. 76)

polygynandry (p. 76)

polygyny (p. 76)

proximate causes (p. 57)

recessive gene (p. 68)

reciprocal altruism (p. 78)

reproductive strategies (p. 76)

reproductive success (p. 61)

segregation analysis (p. 74)

sex chromosomes (p. 67)

sexual selection (p. 76)

sociobiology (p. 76)

ultimate causes (p. 57)

variation (p. 61)

4

BIOLOGY OF
BEHAVIOR

The Brain and Its Components

Structure of the Nervous System • Cells of the Nervous System • The Excitable Axon: The Action Potential • Communication with Other Cells: Synapses • A Simple Neural Circuit

The central nervous system consists of the brain and the spinal cord. The peripheral nervous system consists of nerves that connect the central nervous system to sense organs, muscles, and glands. The primary functions of the brain are to control behavior, to process information about the environment, and to regulate the physiological processes of the body. The brain floats in cerebrospinal fluid, enclosed by the meninges, and is protected from many chemicals by the blood–brain barrier. The functions of the brain are accomplished by circuits of neurons (nerve cells), supported by glial cells. Neurons communicate with one another by releasing chemicals called neurotransmitters. The message transmitted from place to place—the action potential—is a change in the electrochemical properties of the neuron. Synapses, the junctions between neurons, are either excitatory or inhibitory: Excitatory synapses increase a neuron's activity, and inhibitory synapses decrease it.

Drugs and Behavior

Effects of Drugs on Synaptic Transmission • Neurotransmitters, Their Actions, and Drugs That Affect Them • *Evaluating Scientific Issues: "Physiological" versus "Psychological" Drug Addiction*

Drugs that affect behavior do so by facilitating or interfering with synaptic transmission. The most important neurotransmitters are glutamate, which has excitatory effects, and GABA, which has inhibitory effects. Other important categories of neurotransmitters include acetylcholine; the monoamines (dopamine, norepinephrine, and serotonin); the peptides; and the cannabinoids. Circuits of neurons that secrete particular neurotransmitters have different effects on behavior; this fact accounts for the effects of drugs that facilitate or interfere with them. Although the side effects of addictive drugs (tolerance and withdrawal symptoms) are important, they are not responsible for addiction. Addiction is caused by the effects of drugs on neurons in the brain that are involved in reinforcement (reward).

Study of the Brain

Experimental Ablation • Visualizing the Structure of the Brain • Measuring the Brain's Activity • Stimulating the Brain's Activity • Altering Genetics • *Biology and Culture: Environmental Effects on Brain Development*

Physiological psychologists study the biological processes of the brain using experimental ablation, electrical and chemical recording or stimulation, and genetic manipulation. The development of scanning devices has revolutionized the study of the living human brain. Research shows that the development of the nervous system is influenced by both genetic and environmental variables. Recent studies have found that new neurons can be produced even in adult brains.

Control of Behavior and the Body's Physiological Functions

Organization of the Cerebral Cortex • Lateralization of Function • Vision • Audition • Somatosensation and Spatial Perception • Planning and Moving • Episodic and Spatial Memory: Role of the Hippocampus • Emotions: Role of the Amygdala • Control of Internal Functions and Automatic Behavior

The cerebral cortex, the outer layer of the cerebral hemispheres, receives sensory information, controls perceptual and learning processes, and formulates plans and actions. The thalamus relays sensory information to the cerebral cortex. Some brain functions are lateralized—controlled primarily by one side of the brain. Each of the four lobes of the brain is involved with specific activities: The occipital lobe and the temporal lobe control seeing; the temporal lobe controls hearing; the parietal lobe controls perception of the body and the space around it; and the frontal lobe controls motor activities, planning, attention to emotionally related stimuli, spontaneous behavior, and speech. The cerebellum helps control rapid, skilled movements, and the basal ganglia help control automatic movements, especially slower ones. The hippocampus plays a critical role in episodic memory and spatial navigation. The amygdala is involved in emotions—especially negative ones. The brain stem and the hypothalamus control species-typical behaviors, such as those involved in eating, drinking, fighting, courting, mating, and caring for offspring. The hypothalamus also regulates internal functions through its control of the autonomic nervous system and the endocrine system. Endocrine glands secrete hormones, which affect physiological functions and behavior.

Miss S. was a 60-year-old woman who had a history of high blood pressure, which was not responding well to the medication she was taking. One evening she was sitting in her reclining chair reading the newspaper when the phone rang. She got out of her chair and walked to the phone. As she did, she began to feel giddy and stopped to hold on to the kitchen table. She had no memory of what happened after that.

The next morning a neighbor, who usually stopped by to have coffee with Miss S., found her lying on the floor, mumbling incoherently. The neighbor called an ambulance, which took Miss S. to a hospital.

Two days after her admission, the neurological resident in charge of her case told a group of us that she had had a stroke in the back part of the right side of the brain. He attached a CT scan to an illuminated viewer mounted on the wall and showed us a white spot caused by the accumulation of blood in a particular region of her brain. (You can look at the scan yourself; it is shown in Figure 4.21.)

We then went to see Miss S. in her hospital room. Miss S. was awake but seemed a little confused. The resident greeted her and asked how she was feeling. "Fine, I guess," she said. "I still don't know why I'm here."

"Can you see the other people in the room?"

"Why, sure."

"How many are there?"

She turned her head to the right and began counting. She stopped when she had counted the people at the foot of her bed. "Seven," she reported. "What about us?" asked a voice from the left of her bed. "What?" she said, looking at the people she had already counted. "Here, to your left. No, toward your left!" the voice repeated. Slowly, rather reluctantly, she began turning her head to the left. The voice kept insisting, and finally, she saw who was talking. "Oh," she said, "I guess there are more of you."

The resident approached the left side of her bed and touched her left arm. "What is this?" he asked. "Where?" she said. "Here," he answered, holding up her arm and moving it gently in front of her face.

"Oh, that's an arm."

"An arm? Whose arm?"

"I don't know." She paused. "I guess it must be yours."

"No, it's yours. Look, it's a part of you." He traced with his fingers from her arm to her shoulder.

"Well, if you say so," she said, sounding unconvinced.

When we returned to the residents' lounge, the chief of neurology said that we had seen a classic example of unilateral (one-sided) neglect, caused by damage to a particular part of the brain. "I've seen many cases like this," he explained. "People can still perceive sensations from the left side of their bodies, but they just don't pay attention to them. A woman will put makeup on only the right side of her face, and a man will shave only half of his beard. When these patients put on a shirt or a coat, they will use their left hand to slip it over their right arm and shoulder, but then they'll just forget about their left arm and let the garment hang from one shoulder. They also don't look at things located toward the left—or even at the left halves of things. Once I saw a man who had just finished eating breakfast. He was sitting in his bed, with a tray in front of him. There was half a pancake on his plate. 'Are you all done?' I asked. 'Sure,' he said. I turned the plate around so that the uneaten part was on his right. He gave a startled look and said, 'Where the hell did that come from?'"

The human brain is the most complex object that we know. As far as our species is concerned, it is the most important piece of living tissue in the world. It is also the only object capable of studying itself. (If it could not do so, this chapter could not exist.) Our perceptions, our thoughts, our memories, and our emotions are all products of our brains. If a surgeon transplants a heart, a liver, or a kidney—or even all three organs—we do not ask ourselves whether the identity of the recipient has been changed. But if a brain transplant were feasible (it isn't), we would undoubtedly say that the owner of the brain was getting a new body rather than the reverse.

The Brain and Its Components

The brain is the largest part of the nervous system. It contains anywhere between 10 billion and 100 billion nerve cells—no one has counted them all—and about as many helper cells, which take care of important support and housekeeping functions. For many decades neuroscientists have known that the brain contains many different types of nerve cells. These cells differ in shape, size, and the kinds of chemicals they produce, and they perform different functions.

To understand how the brain works, we need to understand how individual nerve cells work and how they communicate with one another. Let's look first at the basic structure of the nervous system and at the nature and functions of the cells that compose it.

Structure of the Nervous System

The brain has three major functions: Controlling behavior, processing and retaining the information we receive from the environment, and regulating the body's physiological processes. How does it accomplish these tasks?

The brain cannot act alone. It needs to receive information from the body's sense organs, and it must be connected with the muscles and glands of the body if it is to affect behavior and physiological processes. The nervous system consists of two divisions. The brain and the spinal cord make up the **central nervous system**. The **spinal cord** is a long, thin structure attached to the base of the brain and running the length of the spinal column. The central nervous system communicates with the rest of the body through the **peripheral nervous system,** which consists of **nerves**—bundles of fibers that transmit information to and from the central nervous system. Sensory information (information about what is happening in the environment or within the body) is conveyed from sensory organs to the brain and spinal cord. Information from the head and neck region (for example, from the eyes, ears, nose, and tongue) reaches the brain through the **cranial nerves.** Sensory information from the rest of the body reaches the spinal cord (and ultimately the brain) through the **spinal nerves.** The cranial nerves and spinal nerves also carry information away

TABLE 4•1	The Major Divisions of the Nervous System
Central Nervous System (CNS)	**Peripheral Nervous System (PNS)**
Brain	Nerves
Spinal cord	

from the central nervous system. The brain controls muscles, glands, and internal organs by sending messages to these structures through these nerves. (See **Table 4•1.**)

Figure 4•1 shows an overview of the nervous system. The man's back has been opened and the back part of the vertebral column has been removed so that we can see the spinal cord and the nerves attached to it. The skull has been opened, and a large opening has been cut in the *meninges,* the membranes that cover the central nervous system, so that we can see the surface of the brain.

The human brain consists of three major parts: the *brain stem,* the *cerebellum,* and the *cerebral hemispheres.* **Figure 4•2** shows a view of the left side of the brain. The lower portions of the cerebellum and brain stem extend beneath the left cerebral hemisphere; the upper portions are normally hidden. We also see the *thalamus,* a part of the brain described later in this chapter.

If the human brain is cut away from the spinal cord and removed from the skull, it looks as if it has a handle or stem. The **brain stem** is one of the most primitive regions of the brain, and its functions are correspondingly basic—primarily control of physiological functions and automatic behaviors. In fact, the brains of some animals, such as amphibians, consist primarily of a brain stem and a simple cerebellum.

The **cerebellum,** attached to the back of the brain stem, looks like a miniature version of the cerebral hemispheres. The primary function of the cerebellum is to control and coordinate movements; especially rapid, skilled movements. The pair of **cerebral hemispheres** (the two halves of the *cerebrum*) constitutes the largest part of the human brain. The cerebral hemispheres contain the parts of the brain that evolved most recently—and thus are involved in perceptions, memories, and behaviors of particular interest to psychologists. (Refer to Figure 4.2.)

Because the central nervous system is vital to an organism's survival, it is exceptionally well protected. The brain is encased in the skull, and the spinal cord runs through the middle of the spinal column—through a stack of hollow bones known as **vertebrae.** (See Inset C, Figure 4.1.) Both the brain and the spinal cord are enclosed by a three-layered set of membranes called the **meninges.** (*Meninges* is the plural of *meninx,* the Greek word for "membrane." You have probably heard of a disease called *meningitis,* which is an inflammation of the meninges.) The brain and spinal cord do not come into direct contact with the bones of the skull and

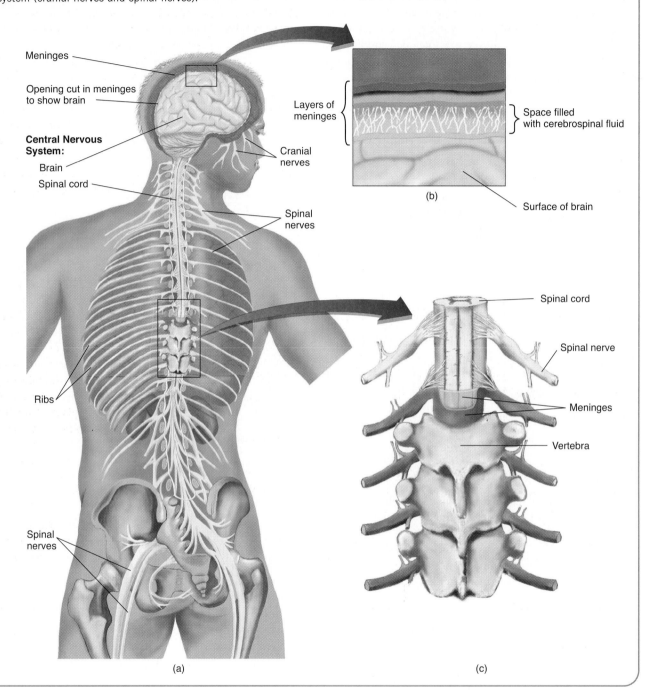

FIGURE 4•1 The central nervous system (brain and spinal cord) and the peripheral nervous system (cranial nerves and spinal nerves).

vertebrae. Instead, they float in a clear liquid called **cerebrospinal fluid (CSF).** This fluid fills the space between two of the meninges and provides a cushion surrounding the brain and spinal cord, protecting them from being bruised by the bones that encase them. CSF is produced in the **cerebral ventricles,** hollow, fluid-filled chambers located within the brain. (See Inset B, Figure 4.1.)

The brain is protected from chemical assault as well as physical shock. The cells of the body receive water and nutrients from the capillaries, the smallest of the blood vessels. In most of the body, the walls of the capillaries have small openings that let chemicals freely pass from the blood into the surrounding tissue. The brain is an exception: Its capillaries do not have these openings, so fewer substances can pass from the blood to the brain. This impediment to the exchange of chemicals is called the **blood–brain barrier.** Its major function is to diminish the likelihood that toxic chemicals found in what we eat or drink can find their way into the brain, where they might do damage to neurons. Of course, there are many poisons that can affect the brain, so this barrier is not foolproof.

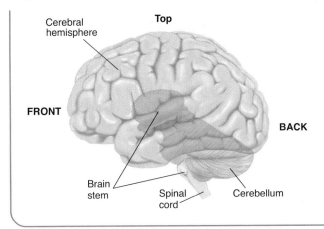

FIGURE 4·2 A view of the left side of the brain, showing its three major parts: brain stem, cerebellum, and cerebral hemisphere. The thalamus is attached to the upper end of the brain stem.

The surface of the cerebral hemispheres is covered by the **cerebral cortex.** (The word *cortex* means "bark" or "rind.") The cerebral cortex consists of a thin layer of tissue approximately 3 millimeters thick. It is often referred to as **gray matter** because of its appearance. It contains billions of nerve cells. (The structure and functions of nerve cells are described in the next section.) It is in the cerebral cortex that perceptions take place, memories are stored, and plans are formulated and executed. The nerve cells in the cerebral cortex are connected to other parts of the brain by bundles of nerve fibers called **white matter,** so named because of the shiny white appearance of the substance that coats and insulates these fibers. **Figure 4·3** shows a slice of the brain. As you can see, the gray matter and white matter are distinctly different.

The human cerebral cortex is very wrinkled; it is full of bulges separated by grooves. The bulges are called *gyri* (singular: *gyrus*), and the large grooves are called *fissures*. Fissures and gyri expand the amount of surface area of the cortex and greatly increase the number of nerve cells it can contain. Animals with the largest and most complex brains, including humans and the higher primates, have the most wrinkled brains and thus the largest cerebral cortexes.

As we saw, the peripheral nervous system consists of the cranial and spinal nerves that connect the central nervous system with sense organs, muscles, internal organs, and glands. Nerves are bundles of many thousands of individual fibers, all wrapped in a tough, protective membrane. Under a microscope, nerves look something like telephone cables, with their bundles of wires. Like the individual wires in a telephone cable, nerve fibers transmit messages through the nerve, from a sense organ to the brain or from the brain to a muscle or gland. (See **Figure 4·4**.)

Cells of the Nervous System

Neurons, or nerve cells, are the elements of the nervous system that bring sensory information to the brain, store memories, reach decisions, and control the activity of the muscles. They are assisted in their task by another kind of cell: the **glia.** Glia (or *glial cells*) get their name from the Greek word for glue. At one time scientists thought that glia simply held neurons—the important elements of the nervous system—in place. They do that, but they also do much more. During development of the brain, some types of glial cells form long fibers that guide developing neurons from their place of birth to their final resting place. Other types of glia manufacture chemicals that neurons need to perform their tasks and absorb chemicals that might impair neurons' functioning. Others form protective insulating sheaths around nerve fibers. Still others serve as the brain's immune system, protecting it from invading microorganisms.

But let's get back to neurons. Neurons are cells that can receive information from other neurons (or from cells in sense organs), process this information, and communicate

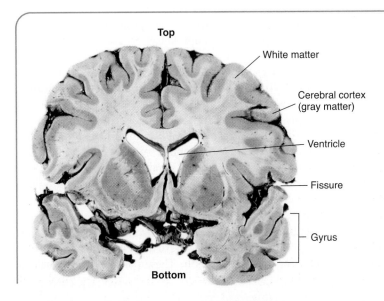

FIGURE 4·3 A photograph of a slice of a human brain showing fissures and gyri and the layer of cerebral cortex that follows these convolutions.
(Harvard Medical School/Betty G. Martindale)

FIGURE 4•4 A scanning electron micrograph of the cut end of a nerve, showing bundles of nerve fibers (also known as axons) and sheaths of connective tissue that encase them. BV = blood vessel; A = individual axons.

(From *Tissues and Organs: A Text-Atlas of Scanning Electron Microscopy*, by Richard G. Kessel and Randy H. Kardon. San Francisco: W. H. Freeman, 1979. Reprinted by permission of the authors and Visuals Unlimited.)

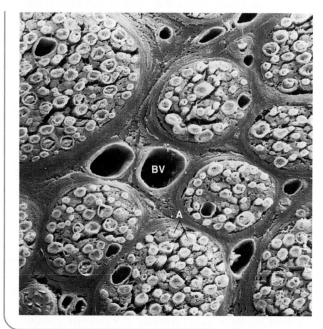

the processed information to other neurons (or to cells in muscles, glands, or internal organs). Thus, neurons contain structures specialized for receiving, processing, and transmitting information. These structures are shown in **Figure 4•5**.

Dendrites, treelike growths attached to the body of a nerve cell, function principally to receive messages from other neurons. (*Dendron* means "tree.") They transmit the information they receive down their "trunks" to the cell body. The dendrites of some neurons receive information from other neurons through **dendritic spines,** small protuberances on their surfaces. The **soma,** or cell body, is the largest part of the neuron and contains the mechanisms that control the metabolism and maintenance of the cell. In most neurons, the soma also receives messages from other neurons. The nerve fiber, or **axon,** carries messages away from the soma toward the cells with which the neuron communicates. These messages, called *action potentials,* consist of brief changes in the electrical charge of the axon.

Axons end in **terminal buttons,** which are located at the ends of the "twigs" that branch off their ends. Terminal buttons secrete a chemical called a **neurotransmitter** whenever an action potential is sent down the axon (that is, whenever the axon fires). The neurotransmitter affects the activity of the other cells with which the neuron communicates. Thus, the message is conveyed *chemically* from one neuron to another. Most drugs that affect the nervous system and hence alter a person's behavior do so by affecting the chemical transmission of messages between cells.

Many axons, especially long ones, are insulated with a substance called *myelin.* The white matter located beneath the cerebral cortex gets its color from the **myelin sheaths** around the axons that travel through these areas. Myelin, part protein and part fat, is produced by glial cells that wrap parts of themselves around segments of the axon, leaving small bare patches of the axon between them. (Refer to Figure 4.5.) The principal function of myelin is to insulate axons from one another and thus to prevent the scrambling of messages. Myelin also increases the speed of the action potential.

To appreciate how important the myelin sheath is, consider the symptoms of one neurological disease. In some disorders, people's immune systems begin to attack parts of their own bodies. One such disorder is *multiple sclerosis,* so named because an autopsy of the brain and spinal cord will show numerous patches of hardened, damaged tissue. (*Skleros* is Greek for "hard.") The immune systems of people who have multiple sclerosis attack a protein in the myelin sheath of axons in the central nervous system, stripping it away. Although most of the axons survive this assault, they can no longer function normally, and so—depending on where the damage occurs—people who have multiple sclerosis suffer from a variety of neurological symptoms.

Figure 4.5 is very schematic; it's designed to illustrate the important parts of neurons and the synaptic connections between them. **Figure 4•6** is a photograph made with a scanning electron microscope. It shows the actual appearance of a neuron and some terminal buttons that form synapses with it. The terminal buttons were broken off from their axons when the tissue was being prepared, but by comparing this photograph with Figure 4.5 you can begin to imagine some of the complexity of the nervous system.

The Excitable Axon: The Action Potential

The message carried by the axon—the action potential—involves an electrical current, but it does not travel down the axon the way electricity travels through a wire. Electricity travels through a wire at hundreds of millions of feet per second. But, as you learned in Chapter 1, Hermann von Helmholtz discovered that the axon transmits information at a much slower rate—about 90 feet per second.

The membrane of an axon is electrically charged. When the axon is resting (that is, when no action potential is occurring), the inside is charged at –70 millivolts (thousandths of a volt) with respect to the outside. An **action potential** is an abrupt, short-lived reversal in the electrical charge of an axon. This temporary reversal begins at the end of the axon that attaches to the soma and is transmitted to the end that divides into small branches capped with terminal buttons. For convenience, an action potential is usually referred to as the *firing* of an axon.

The electrical charge of an axon at rest—the **resting potential**—occurs because of an unequal distribution of positively and negatively charged particles inside the axon and in the fluid that surrounds it. These particles, called **ions,** are

FIGURE 4·5 The basic parts of a neuron and its connections with other neurons (synapses). The detail depicts the structure of a synapse.

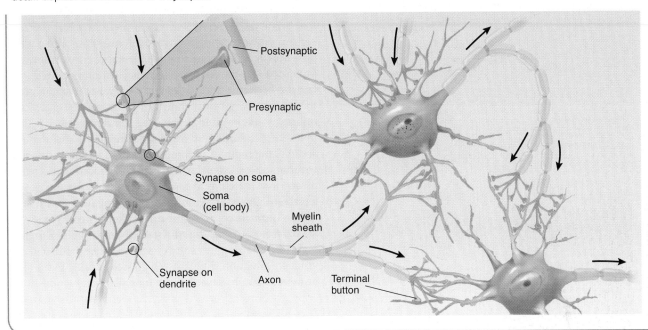

Postsynaptic

Presynaptic

Synapse on soma

Soma
(cell body)

Myelin
sheath

Synapse on
dendrite

Axon

Terminal
button

produced when various substances—including ordinary table salt—are dissolved in water. Molecules of table salt (sodium chloride) break down into positively charged sodium ions (Na⁺) and negatively charged chloride ions (Cl⁻). (In case you were wondering, sodium is abbreviated as *Na* because its original Latin name was *natrium*.) Normally, ions cannot penetrate the membrane that surrounds all cells. However, the membrane of axons contains special submicroscopic proteins that serve as ion channels or ion transporters. **Ion channels** can open or close; when they are open, a particular ion can enter

or leave the axon. As we will see, the membrane of the axon contains two types of ion channels: sodium channels and potassium channels. **Ion transporters** work like pumps. They use the energy resources of the cell to transport particular ions into or out of the axon. (See **Figure 4·7**.)

When the axon is resting, the outside of the membrane is positively charged (and the inside is negatively charged) because the fluid inside the axon contains more negatively charged ions and fewer positively charged ions. When the membrane of the axon is resting, its ion channels are closed, so ions cannot move in or out of the axon. An action potential is caused when the end of the axon attached to the soma becomes excited, which opens sodium ion channels located there. (I'll describe this excitation later.) The opening of these ion channels permits positively charged sodium ions (Na⁺) to enter; this reverses the membrane potential at that location. This reversal causes nearby ion channels to open, which produces another reversal at *that* point. The process continues all the way to the terminal buttons at the ends of the branches at the other end of the axon.

Note that an action potential is a *brief* reversal of the membrane's electrical charge. As soon as the charge reverses, the sodium ion channels close and potassium ion channels open for a short time, letting positively charged potassium ions (K⁺) flow out of the axon. This outflow of positive ions restores the normal electrical charge. Thus, an action potential resembles the "wave" that sports fans often make in a stadium during a game. People in one part of the stadium stand up, raise their arms over their heads, and sit down again. People seated next to them see that a wave is starting, so they do the same—and the wave travels around the stadium. Everyone remains at the same place, but the effect is that of something

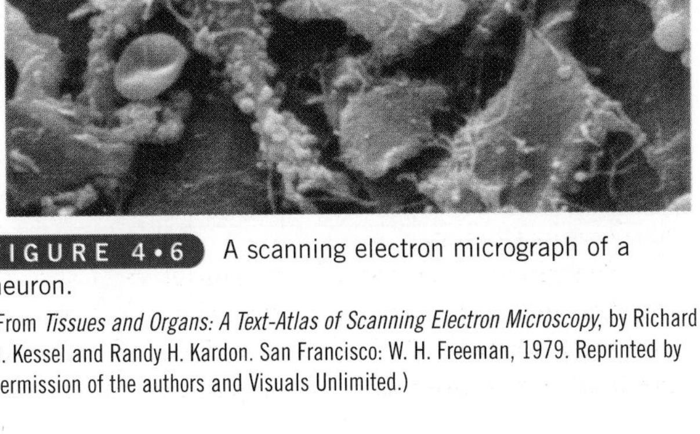

Neuron

Terminal buttons forming
synapses with neuron

FIGURE 4·6 A scanning electron micrograph of a neuron.

(From *Tissues and Organs: A Text-Atlas of Scanning Electron Microscopy*, by Richard G. Kessel and Randy H. Kardon. San Francisco: W. H. Freeman, 1979. Reprinted by permission of the authors and Visuals Unlimited.)

FIGURE 4•7 Ion channels and ion transporters. These structures regulate the numbers of ions found inside and outside the axon. An unequal distribution of positively and negatively charged ions is responsible for the axon's electrical charge.

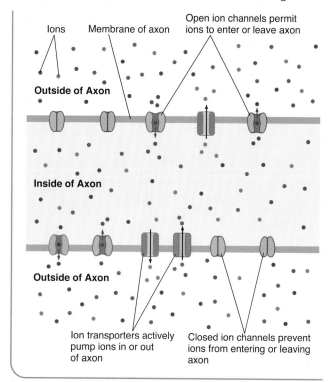

circling in the stands around the playing field. Similarly, electricity does not really travel down the length of an axon. Instead, the entry of positive ions in one location reverses the charge at that point and causes ion channels in the adjacent region to open, and so on. (See **Figure 4•8**.)

You may be wondering what happens to the sodium ions that enter the axon and the potassium ions that leave it. This is where the ion transporters come in. As diagrammed in Figure 4.8, after an action potential has moved along the axon, the ion transporters pump sodium ions out of the axon and pump potassium ions back in, restoring the normal balance.

An action potential is an all-or-none event—either it happens or it does not. Action potentials in a given axon are all the same size; there are no large or small action potentials. This fact has been stated as the **all-or-none law**. But if action potentials cannot vary in size, how can axons convey quantitative information? For example, how can **sensory neurons**—neurons that receive information from sense receptors—tell the brain about the strength of a stimulus? And how can **motor neurons**—neurons whose axons form synapses with a muscle—tell the muscle how forcefully to contract? The answer is simple: A single action potential is not the basic element of information; rather, quantitative information is represented by an axon's *rate of firing*. Strong stimuli (such as bright lights) trigger a high rate of firing in axons of sensory neurons that receive visual information. Similarly, a high rate of firing in the axons of motor neurons causes strong muscular contractions.

Communication with Other Cells: Synapses

Neurons communicate with other cells through synapses, by means of a process known as *synaptic transmission*. A **synapse** is the junction of a terminal button of one neuron and the membrane of another cell—another neuron or a cell in a muscle, a gland, or an internal organ. Let us first consider synapses between one neuron and another. The terminal button belongs to the **presynaptic neuron**—the neuron "before the synapse" that sends the message. As we saw, when terminal buttons become active, they release a chemical called a neurotransmitter. The neuron that receives the message (that detects the neurotransmitter) is called the **postsynaptic neuron**—the neuron "after the synapse." (Refer to detail, Figure 4.5.) A neuron receives messages from many terminal buttons, and in turn its terminal buttons form synapses with

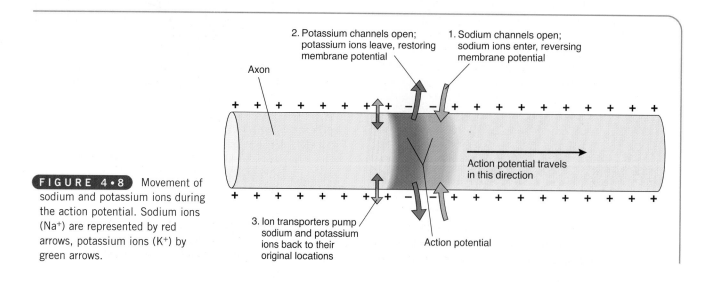

FIGURE 4•8 Movement of sodium and potassium ions during the action potential. Sodium ions (Na$^+$) are represented by red arrows, potassium ions (K$^+$) by green arrows.

many other neurons. The drawing in Figure 4.5 is much simplified; thousands of terminal buttons can form synapses with a single neuron.

There are two basic types of synapses: *excitatory synapses* and *inhibitory synapses*. Excitatory synapses do just what their name implies—when the axon fires, the terminal buttons release a neurotransmitter that excites the postsynaptic neurons with which they form synapses. The effect of this excitation is to increase the rate of firing of the axons of the postsynaptic neurons. Inhibitory synapses do just the opposite—when they are activated, they *lower* the rate at which these axons fire.

The rate at which a particular axon fires is determined by the activity of all the synapses on the dendrites and soma of the cell. If the excitatory synapses are more active, the axon will fire at a high rate. If the inhibitory synapses are more active, it will fire at a low rate or perhaps not at all. (See **Figure 4•9**.)

How do molecules of a neurotransmitter exert their excitatory or inhibitory effect on the postsynaptic neuron? When an action potential reaches a terminal button, it causes the terminal button to release a small amount of a neurotransmitter into the **synaptic cleft,** the fluid-filled space between the terminal button and the membrane of the postsynaptic neuron. (Note that the terminal button and the presynaptic membrane do not touch each other.) The neurotransmitter causes reactions in the postsynaptic neuron that either excite or inhibit it. These reactions are triggered by special submicroscopic protein molecules embedded in the postsynaptic membrane called **neurotransmitter receptors**. (See **Figure 4•10**.)

A molecule of a neurotransmitter binds with its receptor the way a particular key fits in a particular lock. After their release from a terminal button, molecules of a neurotransmitter diffuse across the synaptic cleft, bind with the receptors, and activate them. Once they are activated, the receptors produce excitatory or inhibitory effects on the postsynaptic neuron. They do so by opening ion channels. Most ion channels found at excitatory synapses permit sodium ions to enter the postsynaptic membrane; most of those found at inhibitory synapses permit potassium ions to leave. (See **Figure 4•11**.)

As I mentioned earlier, multiple sclerosis is caused by an autoimmune disorder that attacks a protein in the myelin sheaths of axons in the central nervous system. Another autoimmune disorder attacks a different protein—the neurotransmitter receptor that is found in the membrane of muscle fibers. Almost as fast as new receptors are produced, the immune system destroys them. The result of this attack is progressive *myasthenia gravis,* or "grave muscle weakness." Myasthenia gravis is not a very common disorder, but most experts believe that many mild cases go undiagnosed. I will have more to say about this disorder later in this chapter, in a section on drugs that affect synaptic transmission.

The excitation or inhibition produced by a synapse is short-lived; the effects soon pass away, usually in a fraction of a second. At most synapses the effects are terminated by a process called **reuptake**. Molecules of the neurotransmitter are released and are quickly taken up again by the terminal button, so the neurotransmitter has only a short time to stimulate

the postsynaptic receptors. (See **Figure 4•12**.) The rate at which the terminal button takes back the neurotransmitter determines how prolonged the effects of the chemical on the postsynaptic neuron will be. The faster the neurotransmitter is taken back, the shorter its effects will be on the postsynaptic neuron. As we will see, some drugs affect the nervous system by slowing down the rate of reuptake, thus prolonging the effects of the neurotransmitter.

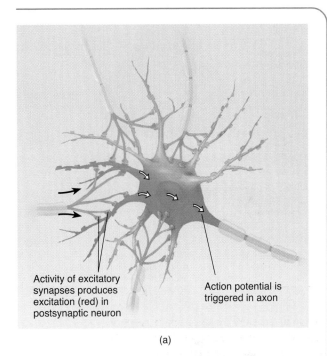

Activity of excitatory synapses produces excitation (red) in postsynaptic neuron

Action potential is triggered in axon

(a)

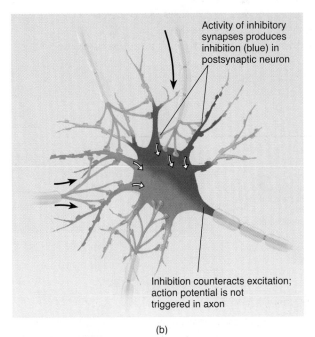

Activity of inhibitory synapses produces inhibition (blue) in postsynaptic neuron

Inhibition counteracts excitation; action potential is not triggered in axon

(b)

FIGURE 4•9 Interaction between the effects of excitatory and inhibitory synapses. Excitatory and inhibitory effects combine to determine the rate of firing of the neuron.

FIGURE 4•10 The release of a neurotransmitter from a terminal button. The drawing depicts the inset portion of Figure 4.5. *Top:* Before the arrival of an action potential. *Middle:* Just after the arrival of an action potential. Molecules of neurotransmitter have been released. *Bottom:* Activation of receptors. The molecules of neurotransmitter diffuse across the synaptic cleft and some of them activate receptors in the postsynaptic membrane.

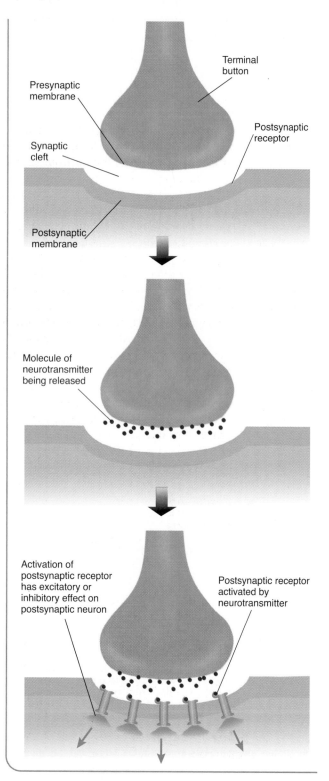

Terminal button

Presynaptic membrane

Postsynaptic receptor

Synaptic cleft

Postsynaptic membrane

Molecule of neurotransmitter being released

Activation of postsynaptic receptor has excitatory or inhibitory effect on postsynaptic neuron

Postsynaptic receptor activated by neurotransmitter

FIGURE 4•11 Postsynaptic receptors. An ion channel opens when a molecule of the neurotransmitter binds with the receptor. For purposes of clarity the drawing is schematic; molecules of neurotransmitter are actually much larger than individual ions.

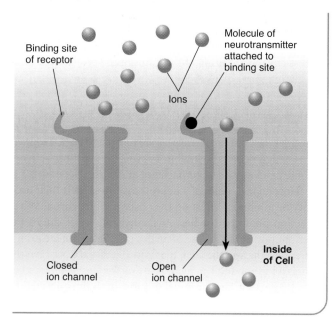

Binding site of receptor

Molecule of neurotransmitter attached to binding site

Ions

Closed ion channel

Open ion channel

Inside of Cell

A Simple Neural Circuit

Let's try to put together what we know about neurons, action potentials, and synapses by seeing how a simple neural circuit works. The trillions of interconnections of the billions of neurons in our central nervous system provide us with the capacities for perception, thinking, memory, and action. Although we do not yet know enough to draw a neural wiring diagram for such complex functions, we can in fact diagram some of the simpler reflexes that are triggered by certain kinds of sensory stimuli. For example, when your finger touches a painfully hot object, your hand withdraws. When your eye is touched, your eyes close and your head draws back. When a baby's cheek is touched, it turns its mouth toward the object, and if the object is of the appropriate size and texture, the baby begins to suck. All these activities occur quickly, without thought.

We begin by examining a simple assembly of three neurons and a muscle that control a withdrawal reflex. Suppose you think your iron is cold, but you touch it to be sure. In fact, it is hot, and the heat stimulates the dendrites of sensory neurons in your finger. As a result, messages are sent down the axon to terminal buttons located in the spinal cord. These terminal buttons release a neurotransmitter that excites an **interneuron,** a neuron located entirely within the central nervous system. The terminal buttons of the interneuron release a neurotransmitter that excites a motor neuron. The axon of the motor neuron joins a nerve and travels to a muscle. When the axon fires, the terminal buttons of the motor neuron

FIGURE 4•12 Reuptake of molecules of neurotransmitter.

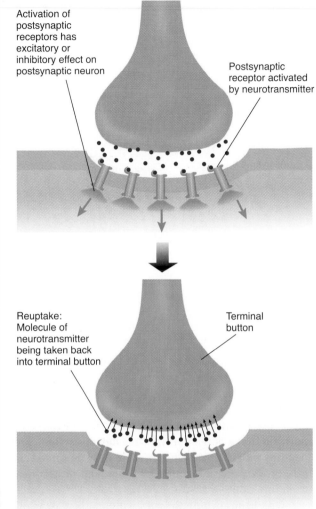

FIGURE 4•12 Reuptake of molecules of neurotransmitter.

Activation of postsynaptic receptors has excitatory or inhibitory effect on postsynaptic neuron

Postsynaptic receptor activated by neurotransmitter

Reuptake: Molecule of neurotransmitter being taken back into terminal button

Terminal button

release their neurotransmitter, causing the muscle cells to contract. As a result, your hand moves away from the hot iron. (See **Figure 4•13**.)

The next example adds a little complexity to the circuit. Suppose you have removed a hot casserole from the oven. As you walk to the table to put it down, the heat begins to penetrate the rather thin potholders you are using. The pain caused by the hot casserole triggers a withdrawal reflex that would tend to make you drop it. And yet you manage to keep hold of the casserole long enough to get to the table and put it down. What prevented your withdrawal reflex from making you drop the dish on the floor?

As we saw earlier, the rate at which a neuron fires depends on the relative activity of the excitatory and inhibitory synapses on it. The pain from the hot casserole increases the activity of excitatory synapses on the motor neurons, which tend to cause the hand to open. However, this excitation is counteracted by inhibition from another source—the brain. The brain contains neural circuits that recognize what a disaster it would be if you dropped the casserole on the floor. These neural circuits send information to the spinal cord that prevents the withdrawal reflex from making you drop the dish.

Figure 4•14 shows how this information reaches the spinal cord. As you can see, an axon from a neuron in the brain reaches the spinal cord, where it forms a synapse with an inhibitory interneuron. When the neuron in the brain becomes active, it excites this inhibitory interneuron. The interneuron releases an inhibitory neurotransmitter, which decreases the rate of firing of the motor neuron, preventing your hand from opening. This circuit provides an example of a contest between two competing tendencies: to drop the casserole and to hold on to it. Complex decisions about behavior are made within the brain by much more complicated circuits of neurons, but the basic principles remain the same.

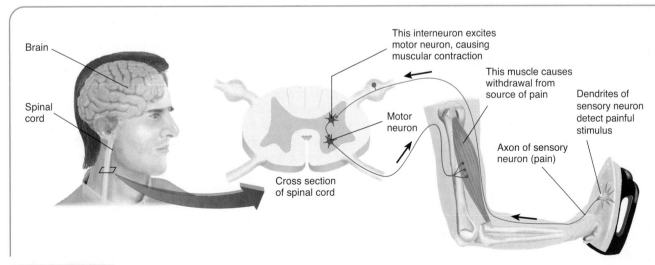

Brain

Spinal cord

This interneuron excites motor neuron, causing muscular contraction

This muscle causes withdrawal from source of pain

Dendrites of sensory neuron detect painful stimulus

Motor neuron

Axon of sensory neuron (pain)

Cross section of spinal cord

FIGURE 4•13 A schematic representation of the elements of a withdrawal reflex. Although this figure shows just one sensory neuron, one interneuron, and one motor neuron, in reality many thousands of each type of neuron would be involved.

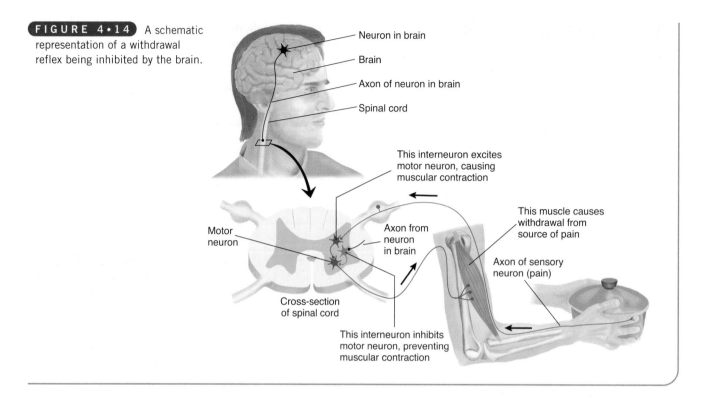

A schematic representation of a withdrawal reflex being inhibited by the brain.

Of course, reflexes are more complicated than this description, and the mechanisms that inhibit them are even more so. And thousands of neurons are involved in this process. The five neurons shown in Figure 4.14 represent many others: Dozens of sensory neurons detect the hot object, hundreds of interneurons are stimulated by their activity, hundreds of motor neurons produce the contraction—and thousands of neurons in the brain must become active if the reflex is to be inhibited. Yet this simple model provides an overview of the process by which decisions are made in the nervous system.

Interim Summary

The Brain and Its Components

The brain has three major functions: controlling behavior, processing and storing information about the environment, and regulating the body's physiological processes.

The central nervous system consists of the spinal cord and the three major divisions of the brain: the brain stem, the cerebellum, and the cerebral hemispheres. The central nervous system floats in a pool of cerebrospinal fluid, contained by the meninges, which protects it from physical shock. The blood–brain barrier protects the brain from toxic substances in the blood. The cerebral cortex, which covers the cerebral hemispheres, is wrinkled by fissures and gyri. The brain communicates with the rest of the body through the peripheral nervous system, which includes the spinal nerves and cranial nerves.

The basic element of the nervous system is the neuron, with its dendrites, soma, axon, and terminal buttons. Neurons are assisted in their tasks by glia, which provide physical support, aid in the development of the nervous system, provide neurons with chemicals they need, remove unwanted chemicals, provide myelin sheaths for axons, and protect neurons from infections.

One neuron communicates with another (or with cells of muscles, glands, or internal organs) through synapses. A synapse is the junction of the terminal button of the presynaptic neuron with the membrane of the postsynaptic cell. Synaptic communication is chemical; when an action potential travels down an axon (when the axon "fires"), it causes a neurotransmitter to be released by the terminal buttons. An action potential consists of a brief change in the electrical charge of the axon, produced by the brief entry of positively charged sodium ions into the axon followed by a brief exit of positively charged potassium ions. Ions enter the axon through ion channels, and ion transporters eventually restore the proper concentrations of ions inside and outside the cell.

Molecules of the neurotransmitter released by terminal buttons bind with neurotransmitter receptors in the postsynaptic membrane and either excite or inhibit the firing of the postsynaptic cell. The combined effects of excitatory and inhibitory synapses acting on a particular neuron determine the rate of firing of that neuron. The reflex is the simplest element of behavior, and it illustrates the contest between excitation and inhibition.

1. The brain is the seat of our perceptions, thoughts, memories, and feelings. Why, then, do we so often refer to our hearts as the location of our feelings and emotions? For example, why do you think we say, "He acted with his heart, not with his head"?

2. The blood–brain barrier keeps many chemicals in the blood out of the brain. There are a few places in the brain where this barrier does not exist, including the part of the brain stem that contains the neural circuits that trigger vomiting. Can you think of an explanation for the lack of a blood–brain barrier in this region?

Drugs and Behavior

Long ago, people discovered that the sap, fruit, leaves, bark, or roots of various plants could alter their perceptions and behavior, could be used to relieve pain or treat diseases, or could be used as poisons to kill animals for food. They also discovered that some substances affected people's moods in ways that they wanted to experience again and again.

Why do plants produce chemicals that have specific effects on the cells of our nervous system? They do so because the chemicals are toxic to animals—primarily insects—that eat them. Our neurons are also sensitive to these chemicals, so they affect us as well. Of course, some chemicals produced by plants have beneficial effects in humans, and have consequently been extracted or synthesized in the laboratory for use as therapeutic drugs. The therapeutic use of drugs are of obvious benefit to society, and the abuse of addictive drugs is responsible for much misery and unhappiness. But drugs are also important tools to help scientists discover how the brain works. For example, we know that certain drugs relieve anxiety and others reduce the symptoms of schizophrenia. Discovering how these drugs affect the brain can help our understanding of the causes of these disorders and can provide information we need to develop even better forms of treatments.

Effects of Drugs on Synaptic Transmission

Drugs that affect our thoughts, perceptions, emotions, and behavior do so by affecting the activity of neurons in the brain. As we saw, communication between neurons involves the release of neurotransmitters, which bind with receptors and either excite or inhibit the activity of the postsynaptic cell. Drugs can affect this process in may ways. They can stimulate or inhibit the release of neurotransmitters, mimic the effects of neurotransmitters on postsynaptic receptors, block these effects, or interfere with the reuptake of a neurotransmitter once it is released. Through these mechanisms (and others too complicated to describe here), a drug can alter the perceptions, thoughts, and behaviors controlled by particular neurotransmitters. Let's briefly examine some of these mechanisms. In the next section I will provide specific examples of drugs and the neurotransmitters they affect.

Stimulating or Inhibiting the Release of Neurotransmitters Some drugs stimulate certain terminal buttons to release their neurotransmitter continuously, even when the axon is not firing. Other drugs prevent certain terminal buttons from releasing their neurotransmitter when the axon fires. The effects of a particular drug are usually specific to one neurotransmitter. (See **Figure 4•15**.)

Stimulating or Blocking Postsynaptic Receptors Neurotransmitters produce their effects by stimulating postsynaptic receptors; this excites or inhibits postsynaptic neurons by open-

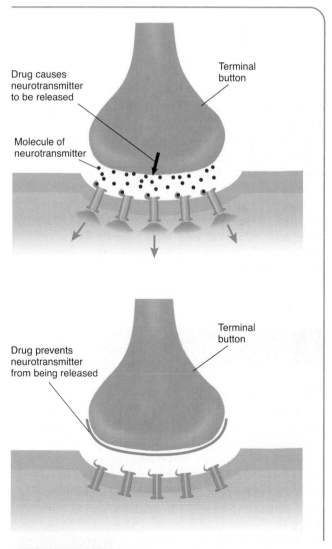

FIGURE 4•15 Effects of drugs on the release of a neurotransmitter. *Top:* Stimulation of release. *Bottom:* Inhibition of release.

ing ion channels and permitting ions to enter or leave the neurons. Some drugs mimic the effects of particular neurotransmitters by directly stimulating particular kinds of receptors. If we use the lock-and-key analogy to describe the effects of a neurotransmitter on a receptor, then a drug that stimulates receptors works like a master key, turning the receptors on even when the neurotransmitter is not present. (See **Figure 4•16**.)

Some drugs bind with receptors and do *not* stimulate them, This action blocks receptors, making them inaccessible to the neurotransmitter and thus inhibiting synaptic transmission. To continue the lock-and-key analogy, a drug that blocks receptors plugs up the lock so that the key will no longer fit into it.

Inhibiting Reuptake

The effects of most neurotransmitters are kept brief by the process of reuptake. Molecules of the neurotransmitter are released by a terminal button, stimulate the receptors in the postsynaptic membrane for a fraction of a second, and are then taken back into the terminal button. Some drugs inhibit the process of reuptake so that molecules of the neurotransmitter continue to stimulate the postsynaptic receptors for a long time. Therefore, inhibition of reuptake increases the effect of the neurotransmitter. (See **Figure 4•17**.)

Neurotransmitters, Their Actions, and Drugs That Affect Them

Now that we've seen the most important ways that drugs can affect synaptic transmission, let's look at the most important neurotransmitters and consider some examples of drugs that interact with them. Because neurotransmitters have two general effects on postsynaptic membranes—excitatory or inhibitory—you might expect that there would be two kinds of neurotransmitters. But in reality there are many different kinds—several dozen, at least.

In the brain most synaptic communication is accomplished by two neurotransmitters: **glutamate,** which has excitatory effects, and **GABA,** which has inhibitory effects. (If you really want to know, *GABA* stands for *gamma-amino butyric acid.*) Almost every neuron in the brain receives excitatory input from terminal buttons that secrete glutamate and inhibitory input from terminal buttons that secrete GABA. (Another inhibitory neurotransmitter, *glycine,* is found in the lower brain stem and the spinal cord, but I won't discuss this chemical here.)

What do all the other neurotransmitters do? In general, they have modulating effects rather than information-transmitting effects. That is, the release of neurotransmitters other than glutamate and GABA tends to activate or inhibit entire circuits of neurons that are involved in particular brain functions. These effects include facilitation of learning, control of wakefulness and vigilance, suppression of impulsive behaviors, and suppression or enhancement of anxiety. Thus, because particular drugs can selectively affect neurons that secrete particular neurotransmitters, these drugs can have specific effects on behavior.

Given the importance of glutamate and GABA, let's look at these two neurotransmitters first.

Glutamate   As I just mentioned, glutamate is the most important excitatory neurotransmitter in the brain. It is also the major excitatory neurotransmitter in the spinal cord. With the exception of neurons that detect painful stimuli, all sensory organs transmit information to the brain through axons whose terminals release glutamate.

One type of glutamate receptor (the *NMDA receptor*) plays a critical role in the effects of environmental stimulation on the developing brain and is also responsible for many of the changes in synaptic connections that are responsible for learning. This receptor is partially deactivated by alcohol, which accounts for the fact that binge drinkers often have no memory for what happened while they were drunk. In addition, researchers believe that the effect of alcohol on this receptor is responsible for the dangerous convulsions that

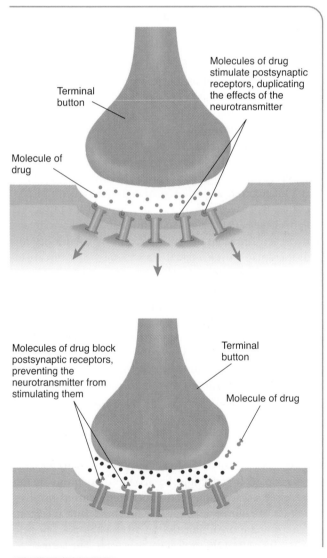

FIGURE 4•16   Effects of drugs on the postsynaptic receptors. *Top:* Stimulation of receptors, mimicking the effects of the neurotransmitter. *Bottom:* Blocking of receptors, preventing the neurotransmitter from binding with the receptors.

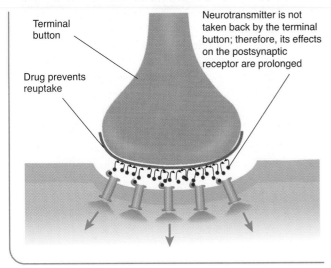

FIGURE 4·17 Reuptake inhibition. Drugs that block reuptake of the neurotransmitter strengthen and prolong the effects of the neurotransmitter on postsynaptic receptors.

Terminal button

Drug prevents reuptake

Neurotransmitter is not taken back by the terminal button; therefore, its effects on the postsynaptic receptor are prolonged

can be caused by sudden withdrawal from heavy, long-term alcohol abuse. When this receptor is suppressed for a long time, a compensatory mechanism makes it become more sensitive to glutamate. If the person suddenly stops taking alcohol, a rebound effect causes glutamate to have such a strong effect that the normal balance of excitation and inhibition in the brain is disrupted.

GABA Some drugs depress behavior, causing relaxation, sedation, or even loss of consciousness. Most of these drugs act on a particular type of GABA receptor (the GABA$_A$ receptor), increasing its sensitivity to the neurotransmitter. **Barbiturates** act this way. In low doses, barbiturates have a calming effect. In progressively higher doses, they produce difficulty in walking and talking, unconsciousness, coma, and death. Barbiturates are abused by people who want to achieve the relaxing, calming effect of the drugs, especially to counteract the anxiety and irritability that can be produced by stimulants. A dose of a barbiturate sufficient to cause relaxation is not much lower than a fatal dose; thus, these drugs do not have much of a safety factor. Physicians rarely prescribe barbiturates.

By far the most commonly used depressant drug is ethyl alcohol, the active ingredient in alcoholic beverages. This drug also acts on the GABA$_A$ receptor. The effects of alcohol and barbiturates are additive: A moderate dose of alcohol plus a moderate dose of barbiturates can be fatal.

Many **antianxiety drugs** are members of a family known as the **benzodiazepines,** which include the well-known tranquilizer Valium (diazepam). These drugs, too, act on GABA$_A$ receptors on neurons in various parts of the brain, including a region that is involved in fear and anxiety. Benzodiazepines are much safer than barbiturates—a lethal dose is more than a hundred times higher than a therapeutic dose. They are sometimes used to treat people who are afflicted by periodic attacks of severe anxiety. In addition, some benzodiazepines serve as sleep medications. These drugs also are used to treat the convulsions caused by sudden withdrawal from heavy, long-term alcohol abuse.

Acetylcholine Acetylcholine (ACh) is the primary neurotransmitter secreted by the axons of motor neurons, and it is also released by several groups of neurons in the brain. Because all muscular movement is accomplished by the release of acetylcholine, you will not be surprised to learn that the immune systems of people with myasthenia gravis (described in the previous section) attack acetylcholine receptors.

The axons and terminal buttons of acetylcholinergic neurons are distributed widely throughout the brain. Three systems have received the most attention from neuroscientists. One system controls most of the characteristics of REM sleep—the phase of sleep during which most dreaming occurs. Another system is involved in activating neurons in the cerebral cortex and facilitating learning, especially perceptual learning. A third system controls the functions of another part of the brain involved in learning: the hippocampus. (I will describe this structure later in this chapter.)

Two drugs, botulinum toxin and the venom of the black widow spider, affect the release of acetylcholine. **Botulinum toxin,** produced by a bacterium that can grow in improperly canned food, prevents the release of ACh. The drug is an extremely potent poison; someone once calculated that a teaspoonful of pure botulinum toxin could kill the world's entire human population. Extremely dilute solutions (they had better be!) of this drug, usually referred to as *botox,* can be injected into people's facial muscles to stop muscular contractions that are causing wrinkles. **Black widow spider venom** has the opposite effect: It stimulates the release of ACh. Although the effects of black widow spider venom can also be fatal to infants or frail, elderly people, the venom is much less toxic than botulinum toxin.

▲ *The venom of the black widow spider causes the release of acetylcholine, which can cause numbness, muscle pain and cramps, sweating, salivation, and difficulty breathing. Fortunately, a single bite is very rarely fatal for a healthy adult.*

Although the effects of most neurotransmitters on the postsynaptic membrane are terminated by reuptake, acetylcholine is an exception. After being released by the terminal button, ACh is deactivated by an enzyme that is present in the postsynaptic membrane. This enzyme, *AChE (acetylcholinesterase),* can be inactivated by various drugs. One of them, **neostigmine,** can help people with myasthenia gravis. The drug lets the patient regain some strength, because the acetylcholine that is released has a more prolonged effect on the few acetylcholine receptors that remain. (Fortunately, neostigmine cannot cross the blood–brain barrier, so it does not affect the AChE found in the central nervous system.)

The best known drug that affects acetylcholine receptors is **nicotine,** found in the leaves of the tobacco plant, *Nicotiniana tabacum.* Nicotine is a highly addictive drug; as evidence, consider the fact that after undergoing surgery for lung cancer, approximately 50 percent of patients continue to smoke. The addictive nature of nicotine indicates that acetylcholine plays a role in the reinforcement (reward) mechanisms of the brain. I'll have more to say about the nature of reinforcement later in this chapter and in Chapters 5 and 13.

Another drug, **curare,** blocks acetylcholine receptors. Because these are the receptors on muscles, curare, like botulinum toxin, causes paralysis. However, the effects of curare

▲ *This native of Peru is inserting a curare-tipped dart into his blowgun. Curare kills animals by blocking acetylcholine receptors, which paralyzes muscles and causes suffocation.*

are much faster. The drug is extracted from several species of plants found in South America, where it was discovered long ago by people who used it to coat the tips of arrows and darts. Within minutes of being struck by one of these points, an animal collapses, ceases breathing, and dies. Nowadays, curare (or any of various drugs with the same site of action) is used to paralyze patients who are to undergo surgery so that their muscles will relax completely and not contract when they are cut with a scalpel. An anesthetic also must be used, because a person who receives only curare will remain perfectly conscious and sensitive to pain, even though paralyzed. And, of course, a respirator must supply air to the lungs during the procedure.

Monoamines Dopamine, norepinephrine, and serotonin are three chemicals that belong to a family of compounds called **monoamines.** Because the molecular structures of these substances are similar, some drugs affect the activity of all of them to some degree. The monoamines are produced by several systems of neurons in the brain. Most of these systems consist of a relatively small number of cell bodies located in the brain stem, whose axons branch repeatedly and give rise to an enormous number of terminal buttons distributed throughout many regions of the brain. Monoaminergic neurons thus serve to modulate the function of widespread regions of the brain, increasing or decreasing the activities of particular brain functions.

Dopamine (DA) has been implicated in several important functions, including movement, attention, learning, and the reinforcing effects of drugs that people tend to abuse. A progressive degenerative disease that destroys one set of DA neurons causes **Parkinson's disease,** a movement disorder characterized by tremors, rigidity of the limbs, poor balance, and difficulty in initiating movements. People with Parkinson's disease are given a drug called L-DOPA. Once this chemical reaches the brain, it is taken up by the DA neurons that still

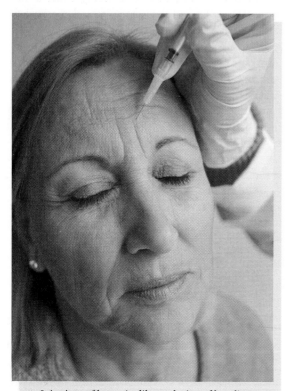

▲ *Injections of botox (a dilute solution of botulinum toxin) are used to smooth out wrinkles. The drug blocks the release of acetylcholine, which paralyzes muscles whose contraction causes the wrinkles.*

survive and is converted to dopamine. As a result, these neurons release more dopamine, which alleviates the patients' symptoms.

Several drugs inhibit the reuptake of dopamine, thus serving to prolong and strengthen its effects. The best known of these drugs are amphetamine and cocaine. The fact that people abuse these drugs indicates that dopamine plays an important role in reinforcement. (In fact, nicotine exerts its reinforcing effect by indirectly increasing the activity of terminal buttons that release dopamine.)

Dopamine has been implicated as a neurotransmitter that might be involved in schizophrenia, a serious mental disorder whose symptoms include hallucinations, delusions, and disruption of normal, logical thought processes. Drugs such as Thorazine (chlorpromazine) and Clozaril (clozapine) relieve the symptoms of this disorder, apparently by blocking particular types of dopamine receptors. The physiology of schizophrenia is discussed in Chapter 17.

Almost every region of the brain receives input from neurons that secrete the second monoamine, **norepinephrine (NE)**. Release of NE (also known as *noradrenaline)* appears to cause an increase in vigilance—attentiveness to events in the environment. Norepinephrine also plays a role in the control of REM sleep.

The third monoamine neurotransmitter, **serotonin,** has complex behavioral effects. Serotonin plays a role in the regulation of mood; in the control of eating, sleep, and arousal; and in the regulation of pain. A deficiency in the release of serotonin in the cerebral cortex is associated with alcoholism and antisocial behavior. Like NE neurons, serotonin-secreting neurons are involved in the control of REM sleep. Drugs such as Prozac (fluoxetine), which inhibit the reuptake of serotonin and thus strengthen and prolong its effects, are used to treat depression, anxiety disorder, and obsessive-compulsive disorder. A drug that causes the release of serotonin (fenfluramine) was used as an appetite suppressant in the 1990s, but adverse side effects took this drug off the market.

Several hallucinogenic drugs appear to produce their effects by interacting with serotonergic transmission. For example, **LSD** (lysergic acid diethylamide) produces distortions of visual perceptions that some people find awesome and fascinating but that simply frighten other people. This drug, which is effective in extremely small doses, stimulates one category of serotonin receptor.

Peptides As I have discussed, terminal buttons excite or inhibit postsynaptic neurons by releasing neurotransmitters. These chemicals travel a very short distance and affect receptors located on a small patch of the postsynaptic membrane. But some neurons release chemicals that get into the general circulation of the brain and stimulate receptors on many thousands of neurons, some located a considerable distance away. These chemicals are called **neuromodulators,** because they modulate the activity of the neurons they affect. We can think of neuromodulators as the brain's own drugs. As these chemicals diffuse through the brain, they can activate or

inhibit circuits of neurons that control a variety of functions; thus, they can modulate particular categories of behavior.

Most neuromodulators are peptides. (The most important exception to this rule is described in the next subsection.) **Peptides** are molecules that consist of two or more amino acids attached together by special chemical links called peptide bonds. One of the best known families of peptides is the **endogenous opioids.** *Endogenous* means "produced from within"; *opioid* means "like opium." Several years ago it became clear that opiates—drugs such as opium, morphine, and heroin—reduce pain because they have direct effects on the brain. (Please note that the term *opioid* refers to endogenous chemicals, and *opiate* refers to drugs.) The endogenous opioids stimulate special opioid receptors located on neurons in several parts of the brain. Their behavioral effects include decreased sensitivity to pain and a tendency to persist in ongoing behavior. Opioids are released while an animal is engaging in important species-typical behaviors, such as mating or fighting. The behavioral effects of opioids ensure that a mating animal or an animal fighting to defend itself is less likely to be deterred by pain; thus, conception is more likely to occur and a defense is more likely to be successful.

People abuse opiates not because opiates reduce pain, however, but because they cause the release of dopamine in the brain, which has a reinforcing effect on behavior. It is this reinforcing effect that normally encourages an animal performing a useful and important behavior to continue in that behavior. Unfortunately, the reinforcing effect is not specific to useful and important behaviors and can lead to addiction.

To help drug addicts pharmacologists have developed drugs that block opioid receptors. One of them, **naloxone,** is used clinically to reverse opiate intoxication. This drug has saved the lives of many drug abusers brought to the emergency room in heroin-induced comas. An injection of naloxone blocks the effects of the heroin, and the person quickly revives.

Various peptide neuromodulators other than the opioids play important roles in behaviors important to survival, such as control of eating and metabolism, drinking, mineral balance, mating, parental care, and social bonding. Some reduce anxiety; others increase it. Some promote eating; others curb the appetite. Research on the effects of these chemicals is discussed in later chapters.

Cannabinoids You have undoubtedly heard of *Cannabis sativa,* the plant that produces hemp and marijuana. You probably also know that the plant produces a resin that has physiological effects on the brain. The principal active ingredient in this resin is THC (tetrahydrocannibinol), which affects perception and behavior by activating receptors located on neurons in the brain. THC mimics the effects of **endogenous cannabinoids**—chemicals produced and released by neurons in the brain.

THC produces analgesia and sedation, stimulates appetite, reduces nausea caused by drugs used to treat cancer,

▲ *The effects of the endogenous cannabinoids, produced and released in the brain, are mimicked by THC, the active ingredient of* Cannabis sativa, *the marijuana plant.*

relieves asthma attacks, decreases pressure within the eyes in patients with glaucoma, and reduces the symptoms of certain motor disorders. On the other hand, THC interferes with concentration and memory, alters visual and auditory perception, and distorts perception of the passage of time (Iversen, 2003). Devane and colleagues (1992) discovered the first—and most important—endogenous cannabinoid, a lipidlike (fatlike) substance, which they named **anandamide,** from the Sanskrit word *ananda,* or "bliss."

Cannabinoid receptors are found on terminal buttons of neurons that secrete glutamate, GABA, acetylcholine, dopamine, norepinephrine, and serotonin. (That is, almost all of the neurotransmitters I've mentioned in this chapter.) Thus, the secretion of anandamide—or the smoking of marijuana—alters the release of these neurotransmitters, and this has widespread effects in the brain. Recent research indicates that the endogenous cannabinoids modulate the synaptic changes that appear to be responsible for learning, which accounts for the fact that THC disrupts short-term memory (Fegley et al., 2004). Cannabinoids also appear to play an essential role in the reinforcing effects of opiates: A genetically engineered mutation that prevents the production of cannabinoid receptors abolishes the reinforcing effects of morphine, but not of cocaine, amphetamine, or nicotine (Cossu et al., 2001).

Table 4•2 lists the neurotransmitters discussed in this section, summarizes their effects, and lists some drugs that interact with them.

Evaluating Scientific Issues

"Physiological" versus "Psychological" Drug Addiction

As we all know, some drugs have very potent reinforcing effects, which lead some people to abuse them or even to become addicted to them. Some people (psychologists, health professionals, and laypeople) believe that "true" addiction is caused by the unpleasant physiological effects that occur when an addict tries to stop taking the drug. For example, in the 1960s Eddy and colleagues (1965) defined *physical dependence* as "an adaptive state that manifests itself by intense physical disturbances when the administration of a drug is suspended" (p. 723). In contrast, they defined *psychic dependence* as a condition in which a drug produces "a feeling of satisfaction and a psychic drive that requires periodic or continuous administration of the drug to produce pleasure or to avoid discomfort" (p. 723). Many people regard the latter as less important than the former. But, as we shall see, the reverse is true.

● Evidence for Physiological Addiction

For many years, heroin addiction has been considered the prototype for all drug addictions. People who habitually take heroin (or other opiates) become physically dependent on the drug—that is, they show *tolerance* and *withdrawal symptoms*. **Tolerance** is the decreased sensitivity to a drug that comes from its continued use; drug users must take larger and larger amounts of the drug in order for it to be effective. Once people have taken an opiate regularly enough to develop tolerance, they will suffer withdrawal symptoms if they stop taking the drug. **Withdrawal symptoms** are primarily the opposite of the effects of the drug itself. For example, heroin produces euphoria; withdrawal from it produces *dysphoria*— a feeling of anxious misery. (*Euphoria* and *dysphoria* mean "easy to bear" and "hard to bear," respectively.) Heroin produces constipation; withdrawal from it produces nausea, cramping, and diarrhea. Heroin produces relaxation; withdrawal from it produces agitation. Most investigators believe that the withdrawal symptoms are produced by the body's attempt to compensate for the unusual condition of heroin intoxication. That is, most systems of the body, including those controlled by the brain, are regulated so that they stay at an optimal value. When a drug artificially changes these systems for a prolonged time, homeostatic mechanisms begin to produce the opposite reaction, which partially compensates for the disturbance from the optimal value. These compensatory mechanisms account for the fact that more and more heroin must be taken to achieve the effects that were produced when the person first started taking the drug. They also account for the symptoms of withdrawal: When the person stops taking the drug, the compensatory mechanisms make themselves felt, unopposed by the action of the drug.

● How Important Is Physiological Addiction?

Heroin addiction has provided such a striking example of drug dependence that some authorities have concluded that

TABLE 4·2 The Major Neurotransmitters, Their Primary Effects, and Drugs That Interact with Them

Neurotransmitter	Primary Effects	Drugs That Interact with Neurotransmitter	Effects of Drugs
Glutamate	Primary excitatory neurotransmitter in brain	Alcohol	Desensitization of NMDA receptor
GABA	Primary excitatory neurotransmitter in brain	Barbiturates Benzodiazepines ("tranquilizers") Alcohol	Desensitization of GABA$_A$ receptor
Acetylcholine (ACh)	Excites muscular contraction, activates cerebral cortex, controls REM sleep, controls hippocampus	Botulinum toxin Black widow spider venom Neostigmine Nicotine	Blocks release of ACh Stimulates release of ACh Blocks AChE; enhances effects of ACh Stimulates ACh receptors
Monoamines Dopamine (DA)	Facilitates movement, attention, learning, reinforcement	L-DOPA Amphetamine, cocaine Antipsychotic drugs	Increases synthesis of dopamine Inhibit reuptake of dopamine Block dopamine receptors
Norepinephrine (NE)	Increases vigilance, controls REM sleep		
Serotonin	Regulates mood; controls eating, sleep, arousal, regulation of pain; suppresses risky behaviors	Fluoxetine (Prozac) LSD	Inhibits reuptake of serotonin Stimulates certain serotonin receptors
Endogenous opioids	Reduce pain, reinforce ongoing behavior	Opiates (heroin, morphine, etc.) Naloxone	Stimulate opioid receptors Blocks opioid receptors
Anandamide (endogenous cannabinoid)	Analgesia, nausea reduction, decreased pressure in eyes, interference with short-term memory, increased appetite	THC	Stimulates cannabinoid receptors

"real" addiction does not occur unless a drug causes tolerance and withdrawal. Without doubt, withdrawal symptoms make it difficult for a person to stop taking heroin—they help keep the person hooked. But withdrawal symptoms do not explain why a person becomes a heroin addict in the first place; that fact is explained by the drug's reinforcing effect. Certainly, people do not start taking heroin so that they will become physically dependent on it and feel miserable when they go without it. Instead, they begin taking it because it makes them feel good.

Even though the withdrawal effects of heroin make it difficult to stop taking the drug, these effects alone are not sufficient to keep most people hooked. In fact, when the cost of their heroin habit gets too high, some addicts quit cold turkey. Doing so is not as painful as most people believe; withdrawal symptoms have been described as similar to a bad case of the flu—unpleasant, but survivable. After a week or two, when their nervous systems have adapted to the absence of the drug, these addicts may recommence their habit, which now costs less to sustain.

If the only reason for taking the drug were to avoid unpleasant withdrawal symptoms, addicts would be incapable of following this strategy. The reason that people take—and continue to take—drugs such as heroin is that the drugs give them a pleasurable "rush"; in other words, the drugs have a reinforcing effect on their behavior.

There are two other kinds of evidence that contradict the assertion that drug addiction is caused by physical dependence. First, some very potent drugs, including cocaine, do not produce physical dependency. That is, people who take the drug do not show tolerance; and if they stop, they do not show withdrawal symptoms. As a result, experts believed for many years that cocaine was a relatively innocuous drug, not in the same league as heroin. Obviously, they were wrong: Cocaine is even more addictive than heroin. As a matter of fact, laboratory animals that can press a lever and give themselves injections of cocaine are more likely to die than those who can give themselves injections of heroin. Second, some drugs produce physical dependence (tolerance and withdrawal symptoms) but are not abused (Jaffe, 1985).

The reason for this is that they do not have reinforcing effects on behavior—they are simply not fun to take.

● What Should We Conclude?

The most important lesson we can learn from the mistaken distinction between "physiological" and "psychological" addiction is that we should never underestimate the importance of "psychological" factors. After all, given that behavior is controlled by circuits of neurons in the brain, even "psychological" factors involve physiological mechanisms. People often pay more attention to physiological symptoms than psychological ones—they consider them more "real." But behavioral research has now shown that an exclusive preoccupation with physiology can hinder our understanding of the causes of addiction.

Interim Summary

Drugs and Behavior

Many chemicals found in nature have behavioral effects, and many more have been synthesized in the laboratory. Drugs can facilitate or interfere with synaptic activity. Facilitators include drugs that cause the release of a neurotransmitter (such as the venom of the black widow spider); drugs that directly stimulate postsynaptic receptors, thus duplicating the effects of the neurotransmitter itself (such as nicotine); and drugs that inhibit the reuptake of a neurotransmitter (such as amphetamine and cocaine). Drugs that interfere with synaptic activity include those that inhibit the release of a neurotransmitter (such as botulinum toxin) and those that block receptors (such as curare).

In the brain most synaptic communication is accomplished by two neurotransmitters: glutamate, which has excitatory effects, and GABA, which has inhibitory effects. Acetylcholine (ACh) controls muscular movements and is involved in control of REM sleep, activation of the cerebral cortex, and modulation of a brain structure involved in memory. Nicotine stimulates ACh receptors, and curare blocks them (and causes paralysis). Neostigmine, which is used to treat myasthenia gravis, suppresses the destruction of ACh by an enzyme. The monoamines also modulate important brain functions. Dopamine (DA) facilitates movements and plays a role in reinforcing behaviors. L-DOPA, which stimulates production of DA, is used to treat Parkinson's disease; and cocaine produces reinforcing effects on behavior by blocking the reuptake of dopamine. Drugs that block dopamine receptors are used to treat the symptoms of schizophrenia. The release of norepinephrine (NE) increases vigilance, and NE-secreting neurons play a role in the control of REM sleep. The release of serotonin helps suppress aggressive behavior and risk-taking behavior, and drugs that inhibit the

reuptake of serotonin are used to treat anxiety disorders, depression, and obsessive-compulsive disorder.

Most peptides serve as neuromodulators, which resemble neurotransmitters but travel farther and are dispersed more widely, where they can modulate the activity of many neurons. The best-known neuromodulators are the endogenous opioids, which are released when an animal is engaged in important behavior. They serve to reduce pain and reinforce the ongoing behavior. Anandamide, the most important of the endogenous cannabinoids, helps regulate the release of many neurotransmitters. THC, the active ingredient in marijuana, acts on cannabinoid receptors and mimics the effects of anandamide. Cannabinoids have some beneficial effects but also impair short-term memory.

Opiates produce tolerance and withdrawal symptoms, which make their habitual use increasingly expensive and make quitting more difficult. But the primary reason for addiction is the reinforcing effect, not the unpleasant symptoms produced when an addict tries to quit. Tolerance appears to be produced by homeostatic mechanisms that counteract the effects of the drug. The distinction between "physiological" addiction (complete with tolerance and withdrawal effects) and "psychological" addiction (lacking these effects) has obscured the true cause of addiction: the reinforcing effect of the drug. Cocaine was once thought to be relatively harmless because it does not produce "real" (that is, physiological) addiction; obviously, we now know better.

QUESTIONS TO CONSIDER

1. As we saw, opioids are useful neuromodulators because they encourage an animal to continue fighting or mating. Can you think of other behaviors that might be influenced by neuromodulators? Can you think of mental or behavioral problems that might be caused if too much or too little of these neuromodulators were secreted?

2. Suppose that someone takes a drug for anxiety. Suppose further that she is planning to go out for drinks with friends. Her husband advises her to enjoy an evening with her friends but not to have any drinks. Why is this a good suggestion?

3. Many useful drugs have been found in nature, and more are yet to be discovered. What are some of the consequences of deforestation, especially of tropical forests with unusually rich diversity of species? Who owns the resources and the drugs that are discovered—the indigenous people who live there? The governments of the countries where the resources are located? The pharmaceutical companies that extract and develop purified forms of the substances?

4. If you were in charge of the research department of a pharmaceutical company, what new behaviorally active drugs would you seek? Analgesics? Antianxiety drugs? Antiaggression drugs? Memory-improving drugs? Should behaviorally active drugs be taken only by people who clearly have afflictions such as schizophrenia, depression,

or obsessive-compulsive disorder? Or should we try to find drugs that help people who want to improve their intellectual performance or social adjustment or simply to feel happier?

Study of the Brain

As Chapter 1 explained, many scientists are interested in the brain, and many psychologists are involved in brain research with humans and laboratory animals. We now have at our disposal a range of research methods that would have been impossible to imagine just a few decades ago. We have ways to identify neurons that contain particular chemicals. We have ways to use special microscopes to observe particular ions entering living neurons when the appropriate ion channels open. We have ways to inactivate individual genes or to insert new genes in laboratory animals to see what happens to the animals' physiology and behavior. We have ways to view details of the structure of a living human brain and to study the activity of various brain regions while the person is performing various perceptual or behavioral tasks. In fact, just listing and briefly describing these methods would take up an entire chapter. In this section I will describe only the most important research methods, which will give you a taste of the research performed by physiological psychologists.

Experimental Ablation

The earliest research method of physiological psychology involved the study of brain damage. As Chapter 1 described, Pierre Flourens developed the method of experimental ablation in studies with laboratory animals, and Paul Broca applied this method when he studied a man whose brain damage had destroyed his language abilities.

To study the effect of experimental brain disruption on animal behavior, the investigator produces a **brain lesion**, an injury to a particular part of the brain, and then studies the effects of the lesion on the animal's behavior. Of course, researchers do not deliberately damage the brains of humans in order to study their functions. Instead, like Paul Broca, we study the behavior of people whose brains have been damaged by a stroke, by disease, or by head injury. If particular behaviors are disrupted, we can conclude that the damaged part of the brain must somehow be involved in those behaviors.

To produce a brain lesion in laboratory animals, the researcher must follow the ethical rules described in Chapter 2. The researcher first anaesthetizes an animal, prepares it for surgery, and drills a hole in its skull. In most cases the region under investigation is located deep within the brain. To reach this region, the investigator uses a special device called a **stereotaxic apparatus** to insert a fine wire (called an electrode) or a thin metal tube (called a cannula) into a particular location in the

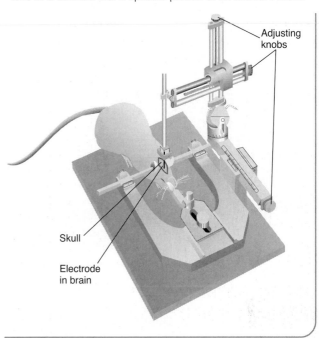

FIGURE 4·18 A stereotaxic apparatus, used to insert a wire or a cannula into a specific portion of an animal's brain.

Adjusting knobs

Skull

Electrode in brain

brain. (The term *stereotaxic* refers to the ability to manipulate an object in three-dimensional space. See **Figure 4·18**.)

Once the correct region is located, its function can be altered. Experimenters can produce *electrolytic lesions* by passing an electrical current through the electrode, which produces heat that destroys a small portion of the brain around the tip of the electrode. Alternatively, they may establish *excitotoxic lesions* by injecting a chemical through the cannula that overstimulates neurons in the region around the tip of the cannula, which kills the neurons. After a few days the animal recovers from the operation, and the researcher can assess its behavior. Later, the investigator can remove the animal's brain from the skull, slice it, and examine it under a microscope to determine the true extent of the lesion. (See **Figure 4·19**.)

Obviously, researchers studying the behavior of a person with brain damage cannot remove the brain and examine it (unless the person happens to die and the family consents to an autopsy for this purpose). This means that researchers seldom have the opportunity to examine the brains of patients they have studied. Fortunately, the development of brain scanners permits us to determine the location and extent of damage to a living brain.

Visualizing the Structure of the Brain

Brain scanning techniques were originally developed to permit physicians to determine the causes of patients' neurological symptoms by locating regions of brain damage, visualizing brain tumors, or revealing abnormalities in

FIGURE 4•19 A brain lesion made with the aid of a stereotaxic apparatus. The photograph shows a thin slice of a mouse brain, stained with a dye that shows the location of cell bodies.

(Courtesy of Neil Carlson)

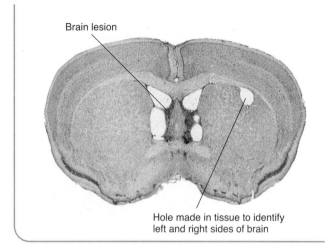

Brain lesion

Hole made in tissue to identify left and right sides of brain

brain structure caused by faulty development. But once researchers gained the ability to see the three-dimensional structure of the brain, they could correlate brain damage or abnormalities in brain development with the observations they had made of the behavior and abilities of patients they had studied.

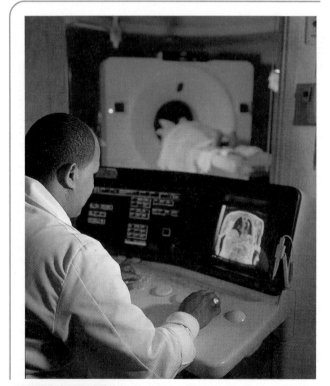

FIGURE 4•20 A patient whose brain is being scanned by a computerized tomography (CT) scanner.

(Photo © Casey McNamara/Index Stock Imagery, Inc.)

FIGURE 4•21 CT scans from a patient with a brain lesion caused by a damaged area (the white spot in the lower left corner of scan 2). Because left and right are traditionally reversed on CT scans, the damaged area is actually in the right hemisphere.

(Courtesy of Dr. J. McA. Jones, Good Samaritan Hospital, Portland, Oregon.)

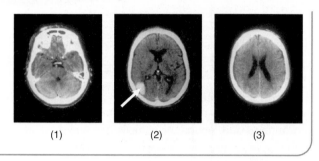

(1)   (2)   (3)

The first machine to reveal the three-dimensional structure of the brain was the **CT scanner** (see **Figure 4•20**). (CT stands for *computerized tomography. Tomos,* meaning "cut," describes the CT scanner's ability to produce a picture that looks like a slice of the brain. The device is often called a *CAT scanner*—the *A* is for *axial*—but the neurologists I've talked with use the term *CT.* They probably think that *CAT* sounds a little too cute.) The scanner sends a narrow beam of X-rays through a person's head. The beam is moved around the head, and a computer calculates the amount of radiation that passes through it at various points along each angle. The result is a two-dimensional image of a "slice" of the person's head, parallel to the top of the skull.

Figure 4•21 shows three CT scans of the brain of a patient with an injury—Miss S., whose case is described in this chapter's opening vignette. The scans are arranged from the bottom of the brain (scan 1) to the top (scan 3). You can easily see the damaged area, a white spot, in the lower left corner of scan 2.

A more recent brain-imaging technique is known as **magnetic resonance imaging (MRI)**. MRI scans are produced by placing a person's head within a strong magnetic field. This field causes the molecules within its influence to become aligned with the lines of magnetic force. A radio signal is then generated around the person, which has the effect of tilting these aligned atoms, just as you might nudge a spinning top and cause it to wobble. The scanner measures the time it takes the molecules to stop wobbling and recover to their aligned state. Because different molecules take different times to recover, an image can be constructed that distinguishes between different materials within the head, such as gray matter, white matter, and cerebrospinal fluid. MRI scanners can produce images of the brain with higher resolution than those produced by CT scanners (see **Figure 4•22**). However, CT scanners are still in use because they are cheaper and do not contain magnets; the magnetism exerted by an MRI scanner can interact with objects such as pacemakers or metal clips that have been placed in a patient's body.

FIGURE 4•22 An MRI scan of a human brain.
(Photo © ISM/Phototake, Inc.)

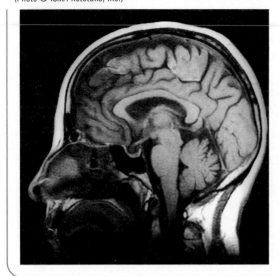

Measuring the Brain's Activity

Because the brain's physiology involves both electrical and chemical processes, measuring techniques have been developed for each. **Microelectrodes** are extremely thin wires that able to detect the electrical currents of individual neurons. With suitable amplification, microelectrodes can be used to measure the minute electrical changes of individual action potentials. Arrays of dozens of ultrathin wires can even enable a researcher to simultaneously record the activity of dozens of neurons. Other electrical recording techniques

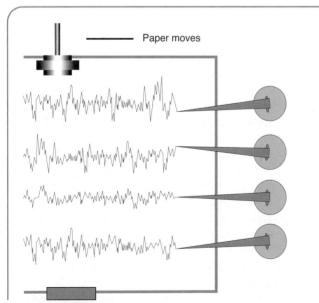

Paper moves

FIGURE 4•23 A record from an EEG machine. The pens trace changes in the electrical activity of the brain, recorded by electrodes placed on a person's scalp.

FIGURE 4•24 Magnetoencephalography. The recording apparatus enclosing a person's head is shown on the monitor to the left. The regions of increased electrical activity are shown in the inset in the lower right, superimposed on an image of the brain derived from an MRI scan.
(Photo courtesy of VSM MedTech Ltd.)

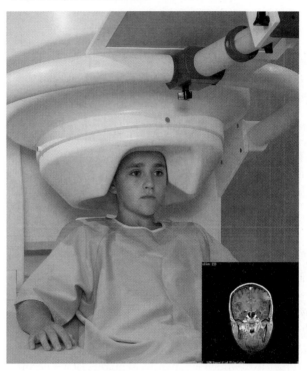

involve larger electrodes placed outside the skull. These electrodes can measure the electrical activity of large groups of neurons. For example, the **electroencephalogram (EEG)** makes a graph on a long sheet of paper of the brain's activity, recorded through metal disks attached to a person's skull (see **Figure 4•23**). The EEG can be used to diagnose seizure disorders (epilepsy) and to monitor the various stages of sleep (described in Chapter 9).

In another method, known as **magnetoencephalography (MEG),** a recording device detects the minute magnetic fields that are produced by the electrical activity of neurons in the cerebral cortex. These devices can be used clinically—for example, to find brain abnormalities that produce seizures so that they can be removed surgically. MEG can also be used in experiments to measure regional brain activity that accompanies the performance of various behaviors or cognitive tasks. (See **Figure 4•24**.)

The metabolic activity of specific brain regions can be measured by two special scanning methods: *PET scanning* and *functional MRI scanning*. **Positron emission tomography (PET)** takes advantage of the fact that when radioactive molecules decay, they emit subatomic particles called positrons. The first step in PET is to give a person an injection of a radioactive chemical that accumulates in the brain. (The chemical eventually breaks down and leaves the cells.

The dose given to humans is harmless.) The person's head is placed in the PET scanner, which detects the positrons. The computer determines which regions of the brain have taken up the radioactive chemical, and it produces a picture of a slice of the brain, showing which regions contain the highest concentrations of the chemical. Researchers can use a wide variety of chemicals. For example, they can use a chemical that accumulates in metabolically active cells, in which case the PET scan reveals the brain regions that are most active. They can also use chemicals that bind with particular receptors (for example, serotonin receptors) and determine which brain regions contain these receptors.

Figure 4•25 shows yet another use of PET. The scans were taken before and after dopamine-secreting neurons were surgically implanted into the brain of a person with Parkinson's disease. The scan shows an increase in the amount of dopamine in a region of the brain that controls movements, revealed by the presence of a radioactive chemical that becomes incorporated into molecules of dopamine.

The most recent development in brain imaging is **functional MRI (fMRI).** Biomedical engineers have devised modifications to existing MRI scanners that measure the rate of metabolism in regions of the brain by detecting levels of oxygen in the brain's blood vessels. Functional MRI scans have a higher resolution than PET scans, they can be acquired much more rapidly, and they do not require the production of radioactive chemicals with very short half-lives, which is expensive. Thus, fMRI has become

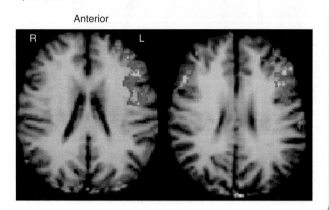

Anterior

R   L

the preferred method of measuring the activity of the human brain. (See **Figure 4•26.**)

Stimulating the Brain's Activity

So far, this section has discussed studying the brain by destroying parts of it (or observing the effects of such destruction when it occurs naturally), visualizing the brain's structure, and measuring the brain's activity. Another research method artificially activates neurons in particular parts of the brain to see what effects this stimulation has on behavior. For example, weak electrical stimulation of one part of a laboratory animal's brain, just sufficient to trigger action potentials in axons in that region, has a reinforcing (rewarding) effect on the animal's behavior. If the animal has the opportunity to press a lever that delivers a brief pulse of electricity through electrodes that have been surgically implanted in its brain, it will do so—up to thousands of times an hour. (See **Figure 4•27.**) The implication is that the brain has a system of neurons involved in reinforcement; and this hypothesis is confirmed by recording studies in both humans and laboratory animals, which indicate that the neurons activated by this stimulation also are activated by events that reinforce behavior, such as the administration of food, water, or addictive drugs. One functional MRI study of heterosexual male college students even found that the sight of a photograph of a beautiful woman activates this region (Aharon et al., 2001).

As we saw in the previous subsection, neural activity induces magnetic fields that can be detected by means of magnetoencephalography. Similarly, magnetic fields can be used to stimulate neurons by inducing electrical currents in brain tissue. **Transcranial magnetic stimulation (TMS)** uses a coil of wires, usually arranged in the shape of the numeral 8, to

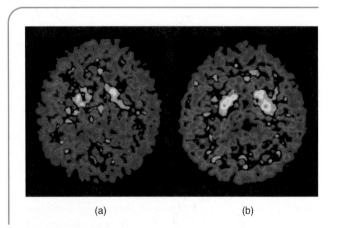

(a)   (b)

FIGURE 4•25 PET scans of a patient with Parkinson's disease showing accumulation of radioactive L-DOPA in a brain region involved in movement that receives input from terminal buttons that secrete dopamine. (a) Preoperative scan. (b) Scan taken 13 months after a transplant of dopamine-secreting cells. The increased uptake of L-DOPA indicates that the transplant was secreting dopamine.

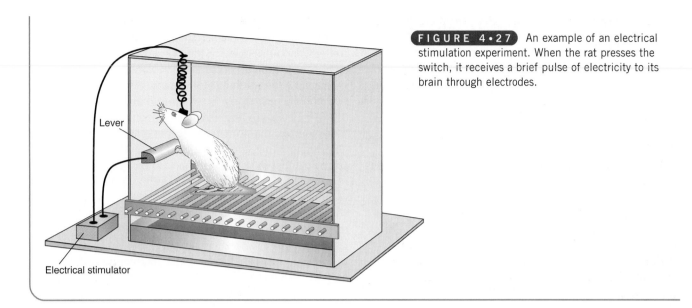

FIGURE 4·27 An example of an electrical stimulation experiment. When the rat presses the switch, it receives a brief pulse of electricity to its brain through electrodes.

stimulate neurons in the human cerebral cortex. The stimulating coil is placed on top of the skull so that the crossing point in the middle of the 8 is located immediately above the region to be stimulated. Pulses of electricity send magnetic fields that activate neurons in the cortex. Because the processing of information in the cerebral cortex involves intricate patterns of activity in particular circuits of neurons, the stimulation disrupts normal activity in that region of the brain. For example, stimulation of a particular region of the cerebral cortex will disrupt a person's ability to detect movements in visual stimuli. These findings confirm the results of recording and lesion studies with laboratory animals and studies of people with brain damage, which indicate that this region in involved in perception of visual movement. In addition, TMS has been used to treat the symptoms of mental disorders such as depression.

Figure 4·28 shows an electromagnetic coil used in transcranial magnetic stimulation and its placement on a person's head.

Altering Genetics

Thanks to the advances in genetics discussed in Chapter 3, neuroscientists can now manipulate genetic mechanisms that control the development of the nervous system. For example, a **targeted mutation** (a genetic "knockout") can be produced in mice. This procedure inactivates a gene—for example, the gene responsible for producing a particular neurotransmitter or a particular receptor. The effects of the knockout on the animals' behavior suggest what the normal role of the neurotransmitter might be. For example, a targeted mutation that prevents production of a particular peptide causes a hereditary sleep disorder known as narcolepsy, which, we now know, is caused by degeneration of the neurons that secrete this peptide (Chemelli et al., 1999).

Researchers also can insert genes into animals' DNA, which can alter the development of the brain or the functioning of particular types of neurons after the animals are born. For example, Tang and colleagues (1999) found that a genetic modification that increased the production of a particular type of receptor increased the animals' learning ability in a particular task. Along with the findings of other experiments, these results suggest that these receptors are involved in producing changes in synapses that are responsible for memory formation.

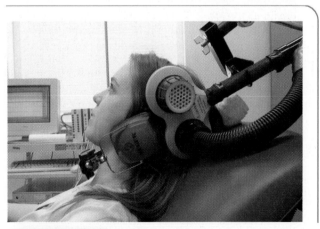

FIGURE 4·28 Transcranial magnetic stimulation. The coil applies electromagnetic stimulation of the brain, which interferes with the region of the cerebral cortex below the crossing point of the figure 8 of the coil.

(Photo by George Ruhe/The New York Times)

Biology and Culture

Environmental Effects on Brain Development

One of the oldest controversies in psychology concerns the respective roles of nature and nurture in human development. Normally, when people ask, "Is it caused by biological or social factors?" or "Is it innate or learned?" they are referring to the origins of a particular behavior, talent, or personality trait. Almost always, biology and innateness are placed on the "nature" side of the dichotomy; social factors and learning are placed on the "nurture" side. Historically, this was considered to be an appropriate division.

As you will see throughout this book, however, most modern psychologists consider the nature–nurture issue to be a relic of outdated thinking about behavior. That is, as we learn more about the ways in which behaviors, talents, and personality traits develop, we discover that both types of factors enter in: biological and social, hereditary and cultural. The task of the modern psychologist is not to find out which one of these factors is more important but to discover the particular roles played by each of them and to determine the ways in which they interact.

As you know, the body develops according to a program established by the genes. The only way the genes can influence our personalities and behavior is through their effect on physical development. Brain development obviously plays a critical role in this regard, but the endocrine system and the structure of other parts of our bodies have important effects, too. For example, having a male or female body certainly influences our behavior and affects the way we are treated by other people. Because these factors also may are so important, many people believe that heredity is the sole influence on normal development of the brain. Few consider the possibility that environmental factors also may have important influences on the normal development of the brain, and that this development may extend not just to the early months of infancy, but through to adulthood. Modern methods have begun to show us how the brain responds to experience.

● **Evidence for the Effects of Experience on Brain Development**

Can the environment affect brain development? In the 1960s Mark Rosenzweig and his colleagues began a research program designed to examine this question (Rosenzweig and Bennett, 1996). The researchers divided litters of rats and placed the animals into two kinds of environments: enriched and impoverished. The enriched environment contained such things as running wheels, ladders, slides, and toys that the rats could explore and manipulate. The researchers changed these objects every day to maximize the animals' experiences and to ensure that they would learn as much as possible. In contrast, the impoverished environments were plain cages in a dimly illuminated, quiet room.

Rosenzweig and his colleagues found many differences in the brains of the animals raised in the two environments.

The brains of rats raised in the enriched environment had a thicker cerebral cortex, a better blood supply, more protein content, and more acetylcholine (a neurotransmitter that appears to play an important role in learning). Subsequent studies have found changes on a microscopic level as well. Greenough and Volkmar (1973) found that the neurons of rats raised in the enriched environment had larger and more complex dendritic trees. Turner and Greenough (1985) found that synapses in their cerebral cortexes were larger and that more synapses were found on each of their neurons. And changes occur even in the adult brain: Sirevaag, Black, Shafron, and Greenough (1988) found that when rats were placed in an enriched environment between the ages of 30 and 60 days (young adulthood), the capillaries in their visual cortexes grew more branches and their surface areas increased, presumably to accommodate the growth that was stimulated by the experience.

Even the brains of adult humans can be modified by experience. If you've ever visited London, England, you probably found it to be a confusing city. Built around archaic footpaths and courtyards, its modern streets are a baffling maze, made all the worse by modern one-way traffic laws. To be a taxi driver in this environment and navigate this maze requires exceptional spatial skill. London taxi drivers spend years learning the street layout, and only after passing a demanding exam are they licensed to operate on the street. Learning takes place in the brain; the drivers' navigational ability must be a result of changes in the neural circuitry of their brain that occurred during their years of training. Using MRI technology, Maguire and colleagues (2000) found that these taxi drivers' brains were physically different from those of other Londoners—a portion of the hippocampus, a part of the brain known to be involved in learning, was enlarged. In fact, the size of this region of a cabby's hippocampus was positively correlated with his or her ability to navigate the London streets.

Although a reasonable explanation for the enlarged hippocampus of London cabbies is that their training induced growth in this structure, it is possible that some people are born with larger hippocampuses and that these are the people most likely to be able to successfully complete the training and pass the exam. (As you will recall from Chapter 2, correlation does not prove causation.) Let's examine some evidence to assess the plausibility of the hypothesis that learning can change the size of parts of the brain.

One possibility is that learning stimulates the growth of new synaptic connections, which would entail the growth of new dendrites and branches of axons. These alterations might then cause an expansion of the brain regions where the growth occurs. There is some evidence for this phenomenon. For example, the region of the brain that is devoted to the analysis of sensory information from the fingers of the left hand is larger in musicians who play stringed instruments. (These fingers are used to press the strings.) A similar phenomenon is seen in the brains of blind people who learn to read Braille (Elbert et al., 1995; Sadato et al., 1996).

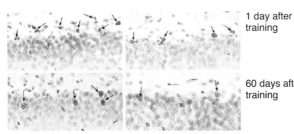

FIGURE 4•29 Effects of learning on neurogenesis, seen in sections through a part of the hippocampus of rats that received training on a learning task or were exposed to a control condition that did not lead to learning. Arrows indicate newly formed cells.

(From Leuner, B., Mendolia-Loffredo, S., Kozorovitskiy, Y., Samburg, D., Gould, E., and Shors, T. J. Learning enhances the survival of new neurons beyond the time when the hippocampus is required for memory. *Journal of Neuroscience,* 2004, *24,* 7477–7481. Copyright © 2004 by the Society of Neuroscience.)

1 day after training

60 days after training

Training task   Control condition

What about the possibility that learning can encourage the growth of new neurons? For many years researchers believed that *neurogenesis* (production of new neurons) cannot take place in the fully developed brain. However research has now shown this belief to be incorrect—the adult brain contains some **stem cells** that can divide and produce new neurons. (Stem cells are undifferentiated cells that can divide and produce any of a variety of differentiated cells.) Researchers can detect the presence of newly produced cells by administering a small amount of a radioactive form of one of the chemicals that stem cells use to produce the DNA needed for neurogenesis. The next day, the investigators remove the animals' brains, stain slices of the brain with a special dye, and examine them under a microscope. Such studies have found evidence for neurogenesis in just two parts of the adult brain: the hippocampus and the *olfactory bulb,* which is involved in the sense of smell (Doetsch and Hen, 2005). Evidence indicates that exposure to new odors can increase the survival rate of new neurons in the olfactory bulbs, and training on a learning task can enhance neurogenesis in the hippocampus. (See **Figure 4•29.**) So perhaps learning to navigate in London really does increase the size of a cabby's hippocampus. In addition, depression or exposure to stress can suppress neurogenesis in the hippocampus, and drugs that reduce stress and depression can reinstate neurogenesis.

Environmental stimulation does not begin at the time of birth. While in the uterus, fetuses feel the movements of their mothers' bodies and hear the sounds of their mothers' voices and sounds from the external environment that pass through the abdominal wall. After they are born, infants receive much environmental stimulation when they are nursed, when they are bathed, when their diapers are changed, and when they are simply held and cuddled. This stimulation clearly contributes to normal development. When infants are born prematurely and must be placed in isolators, they are deprived of the stimulation that occurs in the uterus and receive less handling than do normal full-term infants. Several studies have found that gentle stroking of premature infants can reduce the effects of this environmental deprivation; it increases their growth rates and rates of motor development (Solkoff, Yaffe, Weintraub, & Blase, 1969; Solkoff and Matuszak, 1975). According to evidence from experiments using infant rats reviewed by Schanberg and Field (1987), stroking and handling an infant may stimulate the release of hormones necessary for normal growth and development (including development of the brain).

● **Conclusions**

We've looked at only a few of the many effects of environment on physiological development that researchers have discovered so far. It is clear that the brain does not develop in a vacuum. Instead, its development is shaped and guided by interactions with the environment. One of the most exciting recent discoveries about the adult brain is that it is still capable of growing new neurons, and that growth and survival of these neurons can be affected by interactions with the environment. Consequently, development is not a process confined to the immature. Not only has the nature–nurture issue become a relic of the past; so has the assumption that physiology is solely a product of heredity. Interactions between genes and environment begin early in development and continue throughout life.

Interim Summary

Study of the Brain

The study of the brain, with all its complexity, requires a variety of research methods. Some methods alter the brains of laboratory animals. These methods may include selective destruction of parts of the brain, recording of the brain's electrical or chemical activity, electrical or chemical stimulation of specific brain regions, or modification of the parts of the genetic code that affect neural processes. Electroencephalography and magnetoencephalography reveal the electrical events in the human brain. Other methods, including CT scans, PET imaging, and structural and functional MRI scans, provide images of the structure and activity of the human brain.

The nature–nurture controversy was important in the past, when psychologists asked whether particular behaviors, talents, or personality traits were caused by hereditary factors ("nature") or by experience ("nurture"). This controversy is now over, because psychologists realize that almost all characteristics are affected by both factors. What is less generally recognized is that the normal development of the brain—often assumed to be programmed solely by hereditary factors—is also affected by the environment.

1. Would you like to have an electrode placed in your brain so that you could see what reinforcing (rewarding) brain stimulation feels like? Why or why not?

2. Suppose it were necessary to make an MRI scan of your brain. Would you want to see the scans afterwards?

3. Suppose you had an fMRI scanner and many volunteers. You could present various types of stimuli while scans were being taken, and you could have the volunteers perform various types of mental tasks and behaviors that did not involve their moving around. What kinds of experiments would you perform?

4. Although the basic program that controls brain development is contained in our chromosomes, environmental factors also can influence this process. Why do you think the process of development is not completely automatic and programmed? What is the evolutionary benefit of letting the environment influence it? Would humans be better off if development were simply automatic, or does such flexibility have some potential benefits?

Control of Behavior and the Body's Physiological Functions

As mentioned earlier, the brain has three major functions: controlling behavior, processing and retaining information about the environment, and regulating the physiological functions of the body. The first two roles look outward toward the environment, and the third looks inward. The outward-looking roles include several functions: perceiving events in the environment, learning about them, making plans, and acting. The inward-looking role requires the brain to measure and regulate internal characteristics such as body temperature, blood pressure, and nutrient levels. The outward-looking roles are, of course, of particular interest to psychology. This section will examine how the brain performs all three kinds of functions, beginning with the portions of the brain that control behavior and process information.

The cells of the brain are organized in *modules*—clusters of neurons that communicate with one another. Modules are connected to other modules, receiving information from some of them, processing this information, and sending the results on to others. Particular modules have particular functions, just as the transistors, resistors, and capacitors in a computer chip do. The task of psychologists interested in understanding the brain is to identify the modules, discover their functions, trace their interconnections, and understand the ways in which the activities of these complex assemblies give rise to our perceptions, memories, feelings, and actions. Despite the progress we have made so far, the end of this task is not even remotely in sight.

Organization of the Cerebral Cortex

If we want to understand the brain functions most important to the study of behavior—perceiving, learning, planning, and moving—we should start with the cerebral cortex. Because we will be discussing the various regions of the cerebral cortex, it will be good to start with the names used for them. The cerebral cortex contains a large groove, or fissure, called the **central fissure**. The central fissure provides an important dividing line between the anterior (front) part of the cerebral cortex and the posterior (back) regions. (See **Figure 4·30**.)

As Figure 4.30 shows, the cerebral cortex is divided into four areas, or *lobes*, named for the bones of the skull that cover them: the frontal lobe, parietal lobe, temporal lobe, and occipital lobe. Of course, the brain contains two of each lobe, one in each hemisphere, on each side of the brain. The **frontal lobe** (the "front") includes everything in front of the central fissure. The **parietal lobe** (the "wall") is located on the side of the cerebral hemisphere, just behind the central fissure, in back of the frontal lobe. The **temporal lobe** (the "temple") juts forward from the base of the brain, beneath the frontal and parietal lobes. The **occipital lobe** (*ob*, "against"; *caput*, "head") lies at the very back of the brain, behind the parietal and temporal lobes. The discussions that follow will look in detail at the functions of each of these lobes.

Regions of Primary Sensory and Motor Cortex We

become aware of events in our environment by means of the five major senses: vision, audition, olfaction (smell), gustation (taste), and the somatosenses (the "body" senses: touch, pain, and temperature). Three areas of the cerebral cortex receive information from the sensory organs. The **primary visual cortex,** which receives visual information, is located at the back of the brain, on the inner surfaces of the occipital lobe. The **primary auditory cortex,** which receives auditory information, is located within the temporal lobe on the inner surface of a deep fissure in the side of the brain. The **primary somatosensory cortex,** a vertical strip near the middle of the cerebral hemispheres on the parietal lobe, receives information from the body senses. As Figure 4.30 shows, different regions of the primary somatosensory cortex receive information from different regions of the body. In addition, the base of the somatosensory cortex receives gustatory information, and a portion of the frontal lobe, not visible from the side, receives olfactory information.

The three regions of primary sensory cortex in each hemisphere receive information from the opposite side of the body. Thus, the primary somatosensory cortex of the left hemisphere learns what the right hand is holding, the left primary visual cortex learns what is happening to the person's right, and so on. The connections between the sensory organs and the cerebral cortex are said to be **contralateral** (*contra*, "opposite"; *lateral*, "side"). However, the two most primitive forms of sensory information, smell and taste, are transmitted to the **ipsilateral** hemisphere. That is, the right side of the tongue and the right nostril send information to the right side of the brain.

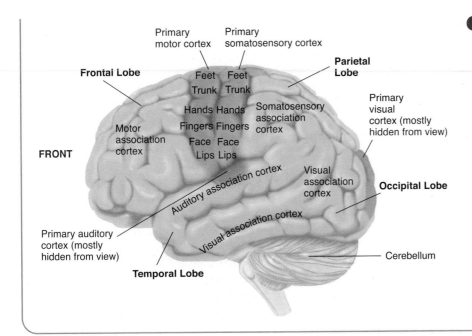

A side view of the human brain, showing the location of the four lobes of the cerebral cortex, the primary sensory and motor areas, and the regions of association cortex. The central fissure is the dividing line between the primary motor cortex and the primary somatosensory cortex.

The region of the cerebral cortex most directly involved in the control of movement is the **primary motor cortex** within the frontal lobe, located just in front of the primary somatosensory cortex. Neurons in different parts of the primary motor cortex are connected to muscles in different parts of the body. The connections, like those of the sensory regions of the cerebral cortex, are contralateral; the left primary motor cortex controls the right side of the body and vice versa. Thus, for example, if a neurosurgeon electrically stimulates the "hand" region of the left primary motor cortex, the patient's right hand will move. (Refer to Figure 4.30.) I like to think of the strip of primary motor cortex as the keyboard of a piano, with each key controlling a different movement. We will see shortly who the "player" of this piano is.

Association Cortex The regions of primary sensory and motor cortex occupy only a small part of the cerebral cortex. The rest of the cerebral cortex accomplishes what is done between sensation and action: perceiving, learning and remembering, planning, and moving. These processes take place in the *association areas* of the cerebral cortex. The anterior region is involved in movement-related activities, such as planning and executing behaviors. The posterior part is involved in perceiving and learning.

Each primary sensory area of the cerebral cortex sends information to adjacent regions, called the **sensory association cortex.** Circuits of neurons in the sensory association cortex analyze the information received from the primary sensory cortex; perception takes place there, and memories are stored there. The regions of the sensory association cortex located closest to the primary sensory areas receive information from only one sensory system. For example, the region closest to the primary visual cortex analyzes visual information and stores visual memories. Regions of the sensory association cortex located far from the primary sensory areas receive

information from more than one sensory system; thus, they are involved in several kinds of perceptions and memories. These regions make it possible to integrate information from more than one sensory system. For example, we can learn the connection between the sight of a particular face and the sound of a particular voice. (Refer again to Figure 4.30.)

Just as regions of the sensory association cortex of the posterior part of the brain are involved in perceiving and remembering, so the frontal association cortex is involved in the planning and execution of movements. The anterior part of the frontal lobe—known as the **prefrontal cortex**—contains the **motor association cortex.** The motor association cortex controls the primary motor cortex; thus, it directly controls behavior. If the primary motor cortex is the keyboard of the piano, then the motor association cortex is the piano player.

Obviously, we behave in response to events happening in the world around us. Therefore, the sensory association cortex of the posterior part of the brain sends information about the environment—and information about what we have learned from past experience—to the motor association cortex (prefrontal cortex), which translates the information into plans and actions. (See **Figure 4•31.**)

The Thalamus If you stripped away the cerebral cortex and the white matter that lies under it, you would find the **thalamus,** located in the heart of the cerebral hemispheres. (Thalamos is Greek for "inner chamber.") The thalamus is divided into two parts, one in each cerebral hemisphere. Each part looks rather like a football, with the long axis oriented from front to back. **Figure 4•32** shows the two halves of the thalamus, along with several other brain structures that will be described later in this chapter.

The thalamus performs two basic functions. The first—and most primitive—is similar to that of the cerebral cortex. Parts of the thalamus receive sensory information, other parts

FIGURE 4•31 The relation between the association cortex and the regions of primary sensory and motor cortex. Arrows refer to the flow of information.

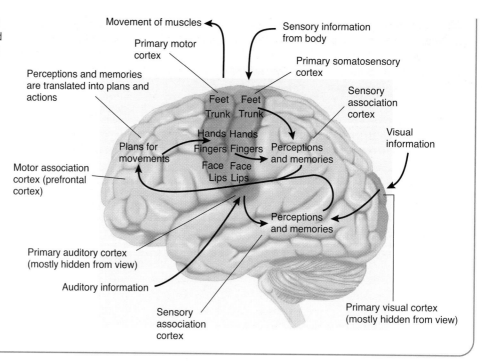

integrate the information, and still other parts assist in the control of movements through their influence on circuits of neurons in the brain stem. However, the second role of the thalamus—that of a relay station for the cortex—is even more important. As the cerebral hemispheres evolved, the cerebral cortex grew in size and its significance for behavioral functions increased. The thalamus took on the function of receiving sensory information from the sensory organs, performing some simple analyses, and passing the results on to the primary sensory cortex. Thus, all sensory information (except for olfaction, which is the most primitive of all sensory systems) is sent to the thalamus before it reaches the cerebral cortex.

Lateralization of Function

Although the two cerebral hemispheres cooperate with each other, they do not perform identical functions. Some functions are *lateralized*—performed by neural circuits located primarily on one side of the brain. In general, the left hemisphere participates in the *analysis* of information—the extraction of the elements that make up the whole of an experience. This ability makes the left hemisphere particularly good at recognizing *serial events*—events whose elements occur one after another. The left hemisphere also is involved in controlling serial behaviors. The serial functions performed by the left hemisphere include verbal activities, such as talking, understanding the speech of other people, reading, and writing. In general, damage to the various regions of the left hemisphere disrupts these abilities. (In a few people the functions of the left and right hemispheres are reversed.) We'll look at language and the brain in more detail in Chapters 9 and 10.

In contrast, the right hemisphere is specialized for *synthesis*; it is particularly good at putting isolated elements together to perceive things as a whole. For example, our ability to draw sketches (especially of three-dimensional objects), read maps, and construct complex objects out of smaller elements depends heavily on circuits of neurons located in the

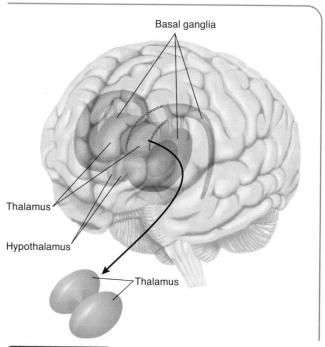

FIGURE 4•32 The location of the basal ganglia, thalamus, and hypothalamus, ghosted into a semitransparent brain.

right hemisphere. The right hemisphere is also especially involved in understanding the meaning of metaphorical statements such as "People who live in glass houses shouldn't throw stones" or the moral of stories such as the one about the race between the tortoise and the hare. Damage to the right hemisphere disrupts these abilities.

We are not aware of the fact that each hemisphere perceives the world differently. Although the two cerebral hemispheres perform somewhat different functions, our perceptions and our memories are unified. This unity is accomplished by the **corpus callosum,** a large band of axons that connects the two cerebral hemispheres. The corpus callosum connects corresponding parts of the left and right hemispheres: the left and right temporal lobes, the left and right parietal lobes, and so on. Because of the corpus callosum, each region of the association cortex knows what is happening in the corresponding region of the opposite side of the brain. **Figure 4·33** shows a photograph of a brain, viewed from above, that has been partially dissected. We see bundles of axons that pass through the corpus callosum, connecting groups of neurons in corresponding regions of the left and right hemispheres.

If the corpus callosum connects the two hemispheres and permits them to interchange information, what happens if the corpus callosum is cut? In fact, neurosurgeons sometimes deliberately cut the corpus callosum (in a procedure called the *split-brain operation*) to treat a certain type of epilepsy. As a result, the two hemispheres process information independently and sometimes even attempt to engage in competing behaviors. I'll describe the interesting effects of this operation on perceptions and consciousness in Chapter 9.

Vision

The primary business of the occipital lobe—and of the lower part of the temporal lobe—is seeing. Total damage to the primary visual cortex, located in the inner surface of the posterior occipital lobe, produces blindness. Because the visual field is "mapped" onto the surface of the primary visual cortex, a small lesion in the primary visual cortex produces a "hole" in a specific part of the field of vision.

The visual association cortex is located in the rest of the occipital lobe and in the lower portion of the temporal lobe. (Refer to Figure 4.30.) Damage to the visual association cortex will not cause blindness. In fact, visual acuity may be very good; people with such damage may be able to see small objects and may even be able to read. However, they will not be able to *recognize* objects by sight. For example, when looking at a drawing of a clock, these individuals may say that they see a circle, two short lines forming an angle in the center of the circle, and some dots spaced along the inside of the circle; but they will not be able to recognize what the picture shows. On the other hand, if handed a real clock, they will immediately recognize it by touch. This fact tells us that these people have not simply forgotten what clocks are. Similarly, people may fail to recognize their spouses by sight but will be able to do so

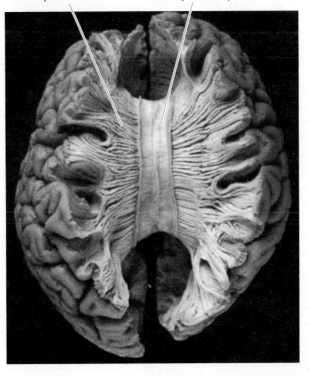

FIGURE 4·33 A photograph of a brain, viewed from above, that has been partially dissected, showing bundles of axons that pass through the corpus callosum.
(Photo from Terence H. Williams, Nedzad Gluhbegovic, Jean Y. Jew, *The Human Brain: Dissections of the Real Brain,* 2007.)

Bundles of axons in corpus callosum

Membrane that covers middle part of corpus callosum

from the sound of the spouses' voice. This deficit in visual perception is called **visual agnosia** (*a-*, "without"; *gnosis,* "knowledge"). We'll deal with this phenomenon further in Chapter 7.

Audition

The temporal lobe contains both the primary auditory cortex and the auditory association cortex. The primary auditory cortex is hidden from view on the inner surface of the upper temporal lobe. The auditory association cortex is located on the lateral surface of the upper temporal lobe. (Refer to Figure 4.30.) Damage to the primary auditory cortex leads to hearing losses, whereas damage to the auditory association cortex produces more complex deficits. Damage to the left auditory association cortex causes language deficits. People with such damage are no longer able to comprehend speech, presumably because they have lost the circuits of neurons that decode speech sounds. However, the deficit is more severe than that. They also lose the ability to produce meaningful speech; their speech becomes a jumble of words. We'll look again at language deficits produced by brain damage in Chapter 10.

Damage to the right auditory association cortex does not seriously affect speech perception or production, but it does affect people's ability to recognize nonspeech sounds, including patterns of tones and rhythms. The damage also can impair the ability to perceive the location of sounds in the environment. The right hemisphere is very important in the perception of space, and the contribution of the right temporal lobe to this function is to participate in perceiving the placement of sounds.

Somatosensation and Spatial Perception

The primary functions of the parietal lobe are perception of our own body and the location of objects in the world around us. (Refer to Figure 4.30.) Damage to parts of the parietal lobe that receive information from the visual system disrupts people's ability to perceive and remember the location of items in their environment. Damage to parts of the left parietal lobe can disrupt the ability to read or write without causing serious impairment in the ability to talk and understand the speech of other people. Damage to part of the right parietal lobe can interfere with people's ability to perceive designs and three-dimensional shapes. A person with such damage can analyze a picture into its parts but has trouble integrating these parts into a consistent whole. Thus, he or she has difficulty drawing a coherent picture. (See **Figure 4•34**.)

The right parietal lobe also plays a role in people's ability to pay attention to stimuli located toward the opposite (left) side of the body. As we saw in the opening vignette, Miss S. displayed a symptom called unilateral neglect. A CT scan of her brain (shown in Figure 4.21) reveals that her stroke damaged part of the association cortex of the right parietal lobe.

Most neuropsychologists believe that the left parietal lobe plays an important role in our ability to keep track of the location of the moving parts of our own body, whereas the

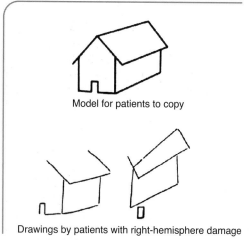

Model for patients to copy

Drawings by patients with right-hemisphere damage

FIGURE 4•34   Attempts to copy a drawing of a house by patients with damage to the right parietal lobes.

(Reproduced from Gainotti, G., and Tiacci, C. (1970). *Neuropsychologia*, 1970, *8*, 289–303, with permission from Elsevier.)

right parietal lobe helps us keep track of the space around us. People with right parietal lobe damage usually have difficulty with spatial tasks such as reading maps. People with left parietal lobe damage usually have difficulty identifying parts of their own bodies by name. For example, when asked to point to their elbows, they may actually point to their shoulders.

People with damage to the left parietal lobe often have difficulty performing arithmetic calculations. This deficit is probably related to other spatial functions of the parietal lobe. For example, try to multiply 55 by 12 without using pencil and paper. Close your eyes and work on the problem for a while. Then try to analyze how you did it. Most people report that they try to imagine the numbers arranged one above the other as they would be if they were using paper and pencil. In other words, they "write" the problem out mentally. Apparently, damage to the parietal lobes makes it impossible for people to keep the imaginary numbers in place and remember what they are.

Planning and Moving

As we have seen, a considerable amount of the brain is devoted to gathering and storing sensory information. Similarly, much of the brain is involved in the control of movement.

The Frontal Lobes   The frontal lobes occupy the largest portion of the cerebral cortex. Although the principal function of the frontal lobes is motor activity, they also are involved in planning strategies for action, evaluating them, and changing them if necessary. They also contain a region involved in the control of speech. (Refer to Figure 4.30.)

Damage to the primary motor cortex produces a very specific effect: paralysis of the side of the body opposite to the brain damage. If a portion of the region is damaged, then only the corresponding parts of the body will be paralyzed. However, damage to the prefrontal cortex (refer to Figure 4.31) produces more complex behavioral deficits.

People with damage to the frontal lobes show *perseveration*—they have difficulty adopting new strategies. One of the reasons for this tendency appears to be that these people have difficulty in evaluating the success of what they are doing. If given a task to solve, they may solve it readily; but if the problem is changed, they will fail to abandon the strategy and learn a new one. They have little insight into their own problems and are uncritical of their performance on various tasks.

In terms of daily living, the most important consequences of damage to the frontal lobes are probably lack of foresight and difficulty making plans. A person with frontal lobe damage might perform fairly well on a test of intelligence but be unable to hold a job. Presumably, planning is related to the general motor functions of the frontal lobes. Just as we can use the posterior regions of the brain to imagine something we have perceived, so we can use the frontal region to imagine something we might do. Perhaps we test various possible actions by imagining ourselves doing them and guessing what the consequences of these actions might be. When people's frontal lobes are damaged, they often do or say things that have unfavorable consequences because they have lost the ability to plan their actions.

As discussed in Chapter 1, Paul Broca discovered that damage to a particular region of the left frontal lobe disrupts speech. This region, which we now call Broca's area, lies at the base of the frontal lobe, just in front of the "face" region of the primary motor cortex. Thus, Broca's area controls the muscles used for talking. Circuits of neurons located in Broca's area appear to contain memories of the sequences of muscle movements that are needed to pronounce words. We'll discuss more on the effects of lesions in Broca's area in Chapter 10.

The Cerebellum The cerebellum ("little cerebrum") plays an important role in the control of movement. (Refer to Figure 4.30.) The cerebellum receives sensory information, especially about the position of body parts, so it knows what the parts of the body are doing. It also receives information from the cortex of the frontal lobes, so it knows what movements the frontal lobes intend to accomplish. The cerebellum is basically a computer that compares the location of body parts with the intended movements and assists the frontal lobes in executing these movements—especially rapid, skilled ones. Without the cerebellum, the frontal lobes would produce jerky, uncoordinated, inaccurate movements—which is exactly what happens when a person's cerebellum is damaged. Besides helping the frontal lobes accomplish their tasks, the cerebellum monitors information regarding posture and balance; it keeps us from falling down when we stand or walk, and it produces eye movements that compensate for changes in the position of the head.

Recently researchers have discovered that the cerebellum may also play a role in people's cognitive abilities. For a long time neurologists have known that cerebellar damage can interfere with people's ability to speak, but the deficit seemed to involve control of the speech muscles rather than the cognitive abilities involved in language. In the 1990s, however, researchers making PET scans of the brains of people working on various types of cognitive tasks discovered that parts of their cerebellums became active—even when the people were not moving. Many neuroscientists now believe that as we learn more about the cerebellum we will discover that its functions are not limited to motor tasks. By the way, the cerebellum contains about as many neurons as the cerebrum does.

The Basal Ganglia The **basal ganglia** are a collection of groups of neurons located in the depths of the cerebral hemispheres, adjacent to the thalamus. (Refer to Figure 4.32.) The basal ganglia are involved in the control of movements—particularly slow movements, and those that involve the large muscles of the body. For example, Parkinson's disease is caused by degeneration of dopamine-secreting neurons in the midbrain whose axons travel to parts of the basal ganglia. The release of dopamine in the basal ganglia helps facilitate movements. The symptoms of Parkinson's disease are weakness, tremors, rigidity of the limbs, poor balance, and difficulty in initiating movements.

Episodic and Spatial Memory: Role of the Hippocampus

The **limbic system,** a set of structures located in the cerebral hemispheres, plays an important role in learning and memory, and in the expression of emotion. The limbic system consists of several regions of the **limbic cortex**—the cerebral cortex located around the edge of the cerebral hemispheres where they join with the brain stem. (*Limbus* means "border"; hence the term *limbic* system.) Besides the limbic cortex, the most important components of the limbic system are the *hippocampus* and the *amygdala.* The hippocampus and the amygdala get their names from their shapes; *hippocampus* means "sea horse" and *amygdala* means "almond."

Figure 4•35 shows a view of the right hemisphere of the brain, rotated slightly and seen from the left. We can see the limbic cortex, located on the inner surface of the right cerebral hemisphere. The left hippocampus and amygdala, located in the middle of the temporal lobe, are shown projecting out into the place where the missing left hemisphere would be. We can also see the right hippocampus and amygdala, "ghosted in." We also see a structure that does not belong to the limbic system—the corpus callosum. As I mentioned earlier, the corpus callosum consists of a band of nerve fibers that enables the left and right cerebral hemispheres to communicate with each other.

We already encountered the **hippocampus** earlier in this chapter, when I discussed evidence that when London taxi drivers successfully learn to navigate around the city, part of

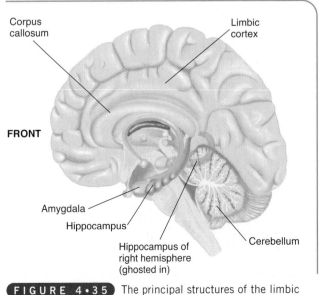

FIGURE 4•35 The principal structures of the limbic system.

their hippocampus increases in size. The hippocampus also is involved in *episodic memory*—that is, in our ability to learn and remember experience from our daily lives. As we will see in Chapter 8, when the hippocampus is destroyed, people can still remember events that occurred before their brains were damaged, but they lose the ability to learn anything new. For them, "yesterday" is always the time before their brain damage occurred. Everything after that slips away, just as the memory of a dream often slips away soon after a person awakens. In addition, although these people can find their way around places that were familiar to them before the damage occurred, they are unable to learn to navigate new neighborhoods—or even the interiors of buildings that are new to them.

Emotions: Role of the Amygdala

Damage to the **amygdala,** located in the middle of the temporal lobe, just in front of the hippocampus, affects emotional behavior—especially negative emotions, such as those caused by painful, threatening, or stressful events. In addition, the amygdala controls physiological reactions that help provide energy for short-term activities such as fighting or fleeing. If an animal's amygdala is destroyed, it no longer reacts to prevent events that normally produce stress and anxiety. We might think that an animal would be better off if it did not become "stressed out" by unpleasant or threatening situations, but research has shown that animals with damaged amygdalas do not survive in the wild. These animals fail to compete successfully for food and other resources, and they often act in ways that provoke attacks by other animals. Similarly, people with damage to the amygdala must live in institutions where they can be cared for so that they will not harm themselves or others. We'll look at the role of the amygdala in emotion and stress in Chapters 13 and 16.

Control of Internal Functions and Automatic Behavior

The brain stem and the hypothalamus are involved in homeostasis and control of species-typical behaviors. **Homeostasis** (from the root words *homoios,* "similar," and *stasis,* "standstill") refers to maintenance of a proper balance of physiological variables such as temperature, concentration of fluids, and the amount of nutrients stored within the body. **Species-typical behaviors** are the more or less automatic behaviors exhibited by most members of a species that are important to survival, such as eating, drinking, fighting, courting, mating, and caring for offspring.

The Brain Stem The brain stem contains three structures: the *medulla,* the *pons,* and the *midbrain.* **Figure 4•36** shows a view of the left side of the brain. The cerebral hemispheres are semitransparent so that the details of the brain stem can be seen. We also see the *hypothalamus* and the *pituitary gland,* which are discussed below.

The brain stem contains circuits of neurons that control functions vital to the survival of the organism in particular and the species in general. For example, circuits of neurons in the **medulla,** the part of the brain stem adjacent to the spinal cord, control heart rate, blood pressure, rate of respiration, and—especially in simpler animals—crawling or swimming motions. Circuits of neurons in the **pons,** the part of the brain stem just above the medulla, are involved in control of sleep and wakefulness. Circuits of neurons in the **midbrain,** the part of the brain stem just above the pons, control movements used in fighting and sexual behavior and decrease sensitivity to pain while a person is engaged in these activities.

The Hypothalamus *Hypo-* means "less than" or "beneath"; and, as its name suggests, the **hypothalamus** is located below the thalamus, at the base of the brain. (Refer to Figure 4.36.) The hypothalamus is a small region, consisting of less than 1 cubic centimeter of tissue (smaller than a grape). But relative importance far exceeds its size.

The hypothalamus, like the brain stem, participates in homeostasis and species-typical behaviors. It receives sensory information, including information from receptors inside the organs of the body; thus, it is informed about changes in the organism's physiological status. It also contains specialized sensors that monitor various characteristics of the blood that flows through the brain, such as temperature, nutrient content, and amount of dissolved salts. In turn, the hypothalamus controls the **pituitary gland,** an endocrine gland attached by a stalk to the base of the hypothalamus. (Refer to Figure 4.36.)

Hormones are chemicals produced by *endocrine glands* (from the Greek *endo-,* "within," and *krinein,* "to secrete"). (As

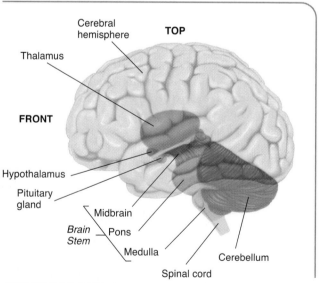

FIGURE 4•36 The divisions of the brain stem: the medulla, the pons, and the midbrain. The thalamus, hypothalamus, and pituitary gland are attached to the anterior end of the brain stem.

we will see in Chapter 13, hormones also are secreted by fat tissue and by special cells in the walls of the stomach and intestines.) **Endocrine glands** secrete hormones into the blood, which carries them to all parts of the body. **Hormones** are chemicals similar to neurotransmitters or neuromodulators, except that they act over much longer distances. Like neurotransmitters and neuromodulators, hormones produce their effects by stimulating receptors. These receptors are located on (or in) particular cells, which are known as **target cells**. When hormones bind with their receptors, they produce physiological reactions in these cells. Almost every cell of the body contains hormone receptors of one kind or another. This includes neurons, which means that hormones can affect behavior by altering the activity of particular groups of neurons in the brain. For example, sex hormones have important effects on behavior, which will be discussed in later chapters.

The pituitary gland has been called the "master gland," because the hormones it secretes act on target cells located in other endocrine glands; thus, the pituitary gland controls the activity of other endocrine glands. And because the hypothalamus controls the pituitary gland, the hypothalamus controls the endocrine system. The more important endocrine glands and the functions they regulate are shown in **Figure 4•37**.

The hypothalamus also controls much of the activity of the **autonomic nervous system (ANS),** a division of the peripheral nervous system that consists of nerves that control the functions of the glands and internal organs. The other division of the peripheral nervous system—the one that transmits information from sense organs to the central nervous system and from the central nervous system to the muscles, is called the **somatic nervous system.** Through the nerves of the autonomic ("self governing") nervous system, the hypothalamus controls activities such as sweating, shedding tears, salivating, secreting digestive juices, changing the size of blood vessels (which alters blood pressure), and the secretions of some endocrine glands. The autonomic nervous system has two branches. The **sympathetic branch** directs activities that involve the expenditure of energy. For example, activity of the sympathetic branch can increase the flow of blood to the muscles when we are about to fight someone or run away from a dangerous situation. In contrast, the **parasympathetic branch** controls quiet activities such as digestion of food. For example, activity of the parasympathetic branch stimulates the secretion of digestive enzymes and increases the flow of blood to the digestive system. (See **Table 4•3** and **Figure 4•38**.)

Psychophysiologists can monitor the activity of the autonomic nervous system and its relation to psychological phenomena such as emotion. For example, when people become angry, their heart rate and blood pressure rise. The lie detector, described in Chapter 13, works (or, more accurately, is

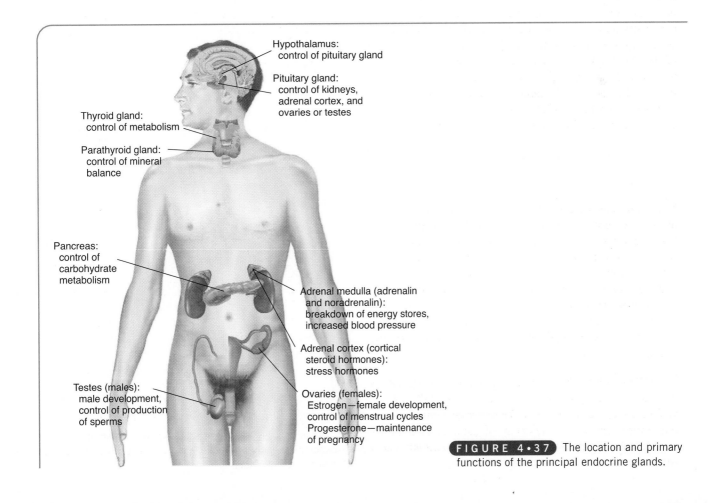

FIGURE 4•37 The location and primary functions of the principal endocrine glands.

TABLE 4·3	The Major Divisions of the Peripheral Nervous System
Division	**Function**
Somatic Nervous System	
Sensory nerves	Transmission of information from sense organs to central nervous system
Motor nerves	Control of skeletal muscles
Autonomic Nervous System	
Sympathetic branch	Support of activities that require the expenditure of energy (through increased blood flow to muscles, increased supply of nutrients of muscles)
Parasympathetic branch	Support of quiet activities that help restore energy supplies (through increased blood flow to digestive system, secretion of digestive enzymes)

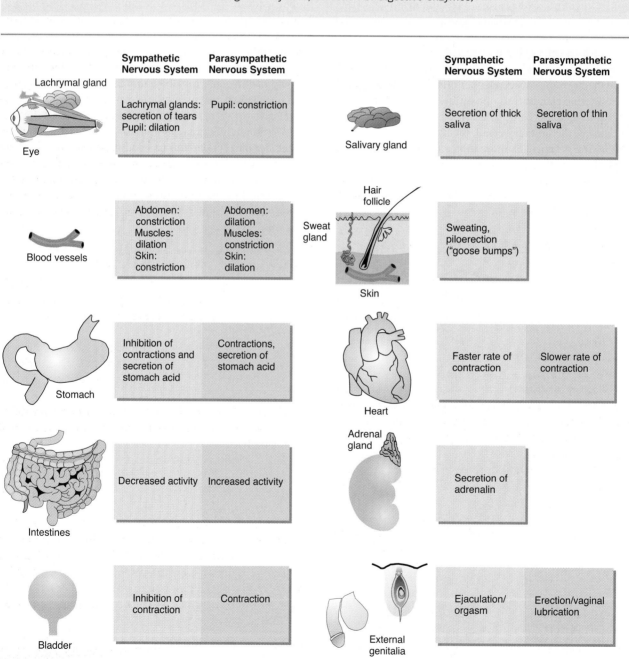

FIGURE 4·38 The organs controlled by the autonomic nervous system. The reciprocal actions of the sympathetic and parasympathetic branches are noted next to each organ.

said to work) by recording emotional responses controlled by the autonomic nervous system.

The homeostatic functions of the hypothalamus can involve either internal physiological changes or behavior. For example, the hypothalamus is involved in the control of body temperature. It can directly lower a person's body temperature by causing sweating to occur, or it can raise it by causing shivering to occur. If these measures are inadequate, the hypothalamus can send messages to the cerebral cortex that will cause the person to engage in a learned behavior, such as turning on an air conditioner or turning up the thermostat. Damage to the hypothalamus can cause impaired regulation of body temperature, changes in food intake, sterility, and stunting of growth.

Interim Summary

Control of Behavior and the Body's Physiological Functions

Anatomically, the cerebral cortex is divided into four lobes: frontal, parietal, occipital, and temporal. Functionally, the cerebral cortex is organized into the primary sensory cortex (with its visual, auditory, and somatosensory regions); the primary motor cortex; and the association cortex. The association cortex consists of sensory regions that are responsible for perceiving and learning and the motor regions that are responsible for planning and acting. Within the cerebral hemispheres, the thalamus relays sensory information to the cerebral cortex.

Some brain functions are lateralized; that is, the right and left hemispheres are involved with somewhat different functions. The left hemisphere is mostly concerned with analysis—with the extraction of information about details of perception, such as the series of sounds that constitute speech or the symbols that constitute writing. The right hemisphere is mostly concerned with synthesis—with putting together a perception of the general form and shape of things from smaller elements that are present at the same time. The two hemispheres share information through the corpus callosum, a large bundle of axons.

The three lobes behind the central fissure are generally concerned with perceiving, learning, and remembering: visual information in the occipital and lower temporal lobes, auditory information in the upper temporal lobe, and somatosensory information in the parietal lobe. The other functions of these lobes are related to these perceptual processes; for example, the parietal lobes are concerned with perception of space as well as knowledge about the body. The frontal lobes are concerned with motor functions, including the planning of strategies for action. A region of the left frontal cortex (Broca's area) is specialized for control of speech. The cerebellum and basal ganglia assist the frontal lobes with the details of executing movements.

The limbic system includes the limbic cortex as well as the hippocampus and the amygdala, both located within the temporal lobe. The hippocampus is involved in learning and memory; people with damage to this structure can recall old memories but are unable to learn anything new. The amygdala is involved in emotions and emotional behaviors, such as defense and aggression, and it plays an important role in physiological reactions that have beneficial effects in the short run.

The brain stem, which consists of the medulla, the pons, and the midbrain, contains neural circuits that control vital physiological functions and produce species-typical automatic movements such as those used in locomotion, fighting, and sexual behavior. The hypothalamus receives sensory information from sense receptors elsewhere in the body and also contains its own specialized receptors, such as those used to monitor body temperature. It controls the pituitary gland, which in turn controls most of the endocrine glands of the body; it also controls the internal organs through the autonomic nervous system. Hormones, secreted by endocrine glands, are chemicals that act on hormone receptors in target cells and produce physiological reactions in these cells. The hypothalamus can control homeostatic processes directly and automatically through its control of the pituitary gland and the autonomic nervous system, or it can cause neural circuits in the cerebral cortex to execute more complex, learned behavior.

QUESTIONS TO CONSIDER

1. If you were to have a stroke (and let's hope you don't), in which region of the cerebral cortex and in which hemisphere would you prefer the brain damage to be located? Why?
2. Damage to the corpus callosum produces different behavioral deficits depending on whether the anterior or the posterior corpus callosum is affected. Why do you think this is so?
3. Explain why a brain lesion that impairs a person's ability to speak often also affects movements of the right side of the body.
4. The cerebellum is one of the largest parts of the brain and contains billions of neurons. What does this fact suggest about the complexity of the task of coordinating movements of the body?
5. Suppose that you wanted to build a lie detector. You would monitor reactions that might indicate emotional responses produced by the act of lying. What behavioral and physiological functions would you want to record?
6. Tranquilizers reduce negative emotional reactions. In what part (or parts) of the brain do you think these drugs might act? Why?

Suggestions for Further Reading

Grilly, D. M. (2002). *Drugs and human behavior* (4th ed.). Boston: Allyn and Bacon.

Meyer, J. S., & Quenzer, L. F. (2005) *Psychopharmacology: Drugs, the brain, and behavior.* Sunderland, MA: Sinauer Associates.

If you are interested in learning more about the effects of drugs that are often abused, you may want to read these books, both of which contain much helpful information about the effects of popular drugs and their use and abuse in society.

Carlson, N. R. (2005). *Foundations of physiological psychology* (6th ed.). Boston: Allyn and Bacon.

My introductory textbook of physiological psychology discusses the topics presented in this chapter in more detail.

Key Terms

acetylcholine (ACh) (p. 97)

action potential (p. 88)

all-or-none law (p. 90)

amygdala (p. 116)

anandamide (p. 100)

antianxiety drug (p. 97)

autonomic nervous system (ANS) (p. 117)

axon (p. 88)

barbiturate (p. 97)

basal ganglia (p. 115)

benzodiazepine (p. 97)

black widow spider venom (p. 97)

blood–brain barrier (p. 86)

botulinum toxin (p. 97)

brain lesion (p. 103)

brain stem (p. 85)

central fissure (p. 110)

central nervous system (p. 85)

cerebellum (p. 85)

cerebral cortex (p. 87)

cerebral hemispheres (p. 85)

cerebral ventricle (p. 86)

cerebrospinal fluid (CSF) (p. 86)

contralateral (p. 110)

corpus callosum (p. 113)

cranial nerve (p. 85)

CT scanner (p. 104)

curare (p. 98)

dendrite (p. 88)

dendritic spine (p. 88)

dopamine (DA) (p. 98)

electroencephalogram (EEG) (p. 105)

endocrine gland (p. 117)

endogenous cannabinoid (p. 99)

endogenous opioid (p. 99)

frontal lobe (p. 110)

functional MRI (fMRI) (p. 106)

GABA (p. 96)

glia (p. 87)

glutamate (p. 96)

gray matter (p. 87)

hippocampus (p. 115)

homeostasis (p. 116)

hormone (p. 117)

hypothalamus (p.116)

interneuron (p. 92)

ion (p. 88)

ion channel (p. 89)

ion transporter (p. 89)

ipsilateral (p. 110)

limbic cortex (p. 115)

limbic system (p. 115)

LSD (p. 99)

magnetic resonance imaging (MRI) (p. 104)

magnetoencephalography (MEG) (p. 105)

medulla (p. 116)

meninges (p. 85)

microelectrode (p. 105)

midbrain (p. 116)

monoamine (p. 98)

motor association cortex (p. 111)

motor neuron (p. 90)

myelin sheath (p. 88)

naloxone (p. 99)

neostigmine (p. 98)

nerve (p. 85)

neuron (p. 87)

neuromodulator (p. 99)

neurotransmitter (p. 88)

neurotransmitter receptor (p. 91)

nicotine (p. 98)

norepinephrine (NE) (p. 99)

occipital lobe (p. 110)

parasympathetic branch (p. 117)

parietal lobe (p. 110)

Parkinson's disease (p. 98)

peptide (p. 99)

peripheral nervous system (p. 85)

pituitary gland (p. 116)

pons (p. 116)

positron emission tomography (PET) (p. 105)

postsynaptic neuron (p. 90)

prefrontal cortex (p. 111)

presynaptic neuron (p. 90)

primary auditory cortex (p. 110)

primary motor cortex (p. 111)

primary somatosensory cortex (p. 110)

primary visual cortex (p. 110)

resting potential (p. 88)

reuptake (p. 91)

sensory association cortex (p. 111)

sensory neuron (p. 90)

serotonin (p. 99)

soma (p. 88)

somatic nervous system (p. 117)

species-typical behavior (p. 116)

spinal cord (p. 85)

spinal nerve (p. 85)

stem cells (p. 109)

stereotaxic apparatus (p. 103)

sympathetic branch (p. 117)

synapse (p. 90)

synaptic cleft (p. 91)

target cell (p. 117)

targeted mutation (p. 107)

temporal lobe (p. 110)

terminal button (p. 88)

thalamus (p. 111)

transcranial magnetic stimulation (TMS) (p. 106)

tolerance (p. 100)

vertebra (p. 85)

visual agnosia (p. 113)

white matter (p. 87)

withdrawal symptom (p. 100)

LEARNING
AND BEHAVIOR

Procedures for the Study of Basic Learning Processes

Pavlov's Procedure • Thorndike's Procedure • Comparison between Pavlov's and Thorndike's Procedures for Studying Learning

Learning is an adaptive process in which behavior in a given environment changes with experience. The critical aspect of experience is the event that follows the behavior. Some subsequent events make the behavior more likely, and are called reinforcers. Other subsequent events make the behavior less likely, and are called punishers. However, not all changes in behavior are due to learning, and not all learning is immediately reflected in behavior. Two types of laboratory procedures are used to study fundamental learning process—Pavlov's classical procedure and Thorndike and Skinner's operant procedure. In the classical procedure an eliciting stimulus follows an environmental stimulus. In the operant procedure an eliciting stimulus follows a response. In either procedure some stimulus and some behavior unavoidably precede the eliciting stimulus, which functions as reinforcer.

Conditions Required for Learning

Temporal Contiguity • Behavioral Discrepancy • *Biology and Culture: Learning, Superstition, and Ritualistic Behavior*

Pavlov's and Thorndike's procedures indicate that two conditions are required for reinforcement—temporal contiguity and behavioral discrepancy. In order for an eliciting stimulus to function as a reinforcer, the stimulus that guides behavior and the behavior that is acquired must appear before or accompany the eliciting stimulus. In addition, the eliciting stimulus must evoke behavior that is not already occurring. As discussed in the section on Biology and Culture, the conditions required for learning may occasionally be met by chance sequences of events. These chance sequences contribute to the formation of superstitious behavior and cultural rituals.

The Outcomes of Learning

Acquisition • Extinction • Stimulus Generalization • Stimulus Discrimination • Punishment • *Evaluating Scientific Issues: What Is Insight?*

The fundamental learning process produces many important outcomes. Acquisition of behavior may be affected by habituation, orienting responses, and shaping as well as interactions with the effects of natural selection. Once acquisition has taken place in an environment, similar environments can guide the same behavior (stimulus generalization). Also, previously neutral stimuli from the learning environment can then strengthen any additional behavior that precedes them (conditioned reinforcement). The main neural systems responsible for reinforcement originate in midbrain nuclei that liberate the neuromodulator dopamine. Other stimuli can weaken the behavior that precedes them (punishment). If behavior has consequences in one environment but not in different environments, then the acquired behavior becomes restricted to the first environment (stimulus discrimination). If an acquired behavior no longer has consequences in that environment, then the behavior weakens (extinction). Over time, basic learning processes can produce a number of complex outcomes including automatic reinforcement, equivalence classes, and insight.

Cellular Mechanisms of Reinforcement

Long-Term Potentiation • Sensory Learning

Research is beginning to understand the critical events that take place between and within nerve cells during learning. The increased responsiveness of neurons to neurotransmitters is affected by neuromodulators released from midbrain nuclei. This effect is known as long-term potentiation. The combinations of environmental stimuli that guide complex behavior are dependent on the effect of a subcortical structure called the hippocampus on neurons in the sensory-association cortex. This effect is known as sensory learning.

Behavior in Experienced Learners

Instructional Control • Observational Learning • *Evaluating Scientific Issues: How Do Complex Outcomes Arise from Simple Processes?*

The behavior of experienced humans is typically not maintained by reinforcers that result from natural selection but from prior learning (conditioned reinforcers). The behavior of experienced learners is increasingly affected by stimuli that are dependent on prior learning. Very often these stimuli are verbal stimuli provided by other persons (instructional control) or other stimuli arising from their behavior (observational learning). Darwin discovered the way in which complex phenomena can be produced by simple selection processes. Darwin's approach—selectionism—enlightens our understanding of the emergence of complexity and diversity at many different levels of observation.

With the start of World War II, the official policy of the National Socialist German Workers' Party (the Nazi Party) shifted from discrimination to extermination of the Jews. Two of the millions of victims of this policy were a middle-class woman named Judith and her 12-year-old daughter, Natalie. They were sent to the Ravensbrück concentration camp for women in the winter of 1942. Their husband and father had been imprisoned at another camp some months earlier. The weather was very cold when they arrived at the camp. Nevertheless, the prisoners' clothing was confiscated and replaced by flimsy gowns that provided little protection from the elements. Those women who were able to work could avoid the gas chamber, but the combination of inadequate clothing and food began to take its toll—women began to die. When an inmate died, some of the women stripped the body and added the dead woman's gown to their own. In this way they warded off some of the effects of the cold. Judith refused to engage in this practice. Young Natalie, however, sought out the gowns of the dead and immediately donned them. Judith died at Ravensbrück. Natalie survived and was reunited with her father when the Allies liberated the camps at the end of the war.

What was responsible for the difference in the reactions of Natalie and Judith? They were exposed to the same conditions in the camp, but they responded very differently. In fact, the younger and less experienced daughter responded more adaptively than did the older and more experienced mother. Natalie's mother had to know even better than Natalie that exposure to the cold together with inadequate food was a deadly combination. Yet Judith refused to scavenge gowns from her fellow inmates. How can this be understood?

Understanding how experience changes, or fails to change, behavior is the subject of this chapter. The conditions that change behavior are conventionally studied under the heading of learning. **Learning** is an adaptive process by which individual experience produces long-lasting changes in the environmental guidance of behavior. Science began its search for answers to questions about behavioral change at the turn of the last century in the laboratories of Ivan Pavlov in Russia and Edward Thorndike in the United States. These researchers worked independently of each other, and their methods differed in important respects. However, the research programs that they initiated have converged on a common understanding of how experience changes behavior. In the first section of this chapter, we will see how Pavlov and Thorndike approached their common task. We'll then consider the conditions required for learning, the outcomes of learning, and the behavior of experienced learners.

Procedures for the Study of Basic Learning Processes

Both Ivan Pavlov (1849–1936) and Edward Thorndike (1874–1949) realized that learners—especially experienced learners—are capable of a wide range of possible responses in any given environment. Judith and Natalie, for example, had different individual experiences before entering the concentration camp, and these differences undoubtedly contributed to their different responses in the camp. In addition to individual experience, a second source of responding is natural selection by the ancestral environment. As we saw in Chapter 3, responses that are elicited by the environment as the result of natural selection are called reflexes. To identify the basic processes that produce learning, researchers must control these sources of variation. Experiments on learning cannot eliminate the effects of selection by the ancestral environment, but investigators can minimize individual differences by studying learning with organisms whose genetic variation is restricted and whose prior experience is controlled. In this way, investigators can attribute any changes in behavior that occur during the experiment to variables manipulated within the experiment and not to pre-experimental differences.

Pavlov and Thorndike appreciated the need for controlled observations. They began searching for the conditions that promote learning using nonhuman animals whose genetic and experiential histories could be specified. Indeed, almost all research that seeks to identify fundamental biobehavioral processes must be conducted with nonhuman animals, because of the greater control they permit. Principles based on research with nonhuman animals must then be evaluated with humans as far as possible. The principles of learning that are described in this chapter are consistent with later findings with humans, including human infants, whose prior experience is more limited than that of adults. The continuity of life envisioned by Darwin's principle of natural selection anticipates continuity in the principles that describe the behavior of all organisms. Indeed, both Pavlov and Thorndike explicitly viewed their work as following in Darwin's footsteps (Pavlov, 1927; Thorndike, 1903; see also Donahoe, 1999). That is, they sought a principle that described how the *individual* environment changed behavior and the neural mechanisms that underlie behavior, just as Darwin had previously sought a principle that described how the *ancestral* environment affected behavior and its underlying hereditary mechanisms. In short, Pavlov and Thorndike sought a principle of selection by the individual environment that complemented natural selection by the ancestral environment. The two principles would be complementary, because the processes that implement selection by the individual environment are themselves products of natural selection.

Pavlov's Procedure

Pavlov and Thorndike began their work on learning using nonhuman animals—dogs for Pavlov and chicks and cats for Thorndike. Both also began each experiment by introducing into an animal's environment a stimulus that already evoked behavior as a result of natural selection. This stimulus and the behavior it evoked provided a reference point from which the experimenters could detect any changes in behavior that were produced by their procedures. In Pavlov's case, a dog was lightly restrained in a harness and a bowl of food was presented after an environmental stimulus, such as the ticking sound of a metronome. (See **Figure 5•1**.) The presentation of the food caused the dog to look toward the bowl, to eat, and to salivate. The impetus for Pavlov's experiments had been prompted by an incidental observation that he had made during his prior work on digestion. Pavlov had noted that the dog began to salivate when it heard the sound of the approaching footsteps of the caretaker who normally fed it. Instead of dismissing this as merely an unwanted intrusion into his work on digestion (for which he was ultimately awarded a Nobel Prize), Pavlov realized that this learned behavior might provide a clue into how the learning process worked. This sensitivity to observations, especially unexpected observations, is one hallmark of good science.

Pavlov found that after several occurrences of the ticking sound before the presentation of food, the animal began to look toward the food bowl and to salivate when it heard the

FIGURE 5•1 Pavlov's original classical conditioning procedure. A stimulus is presented (for example, the sound of a metronome ticking), and then the experimenter provides access to a small amount of food in a bowl. Saliva flows into a tube.

sound. Pairing the sound with food and its elicited salivary response produced a change in the environmental guidance of behavior; that is, learning had occurred. The sound–salivation relation was a changed environment–behavior relation that had been selected during Pavlov's procedure. Such changes are clearly a part of everyday experience, as when we salivate on seeing an ice-cream cone or flinch on seeing an overinflated balloon about to explode. In our experience, seeing an ice-cream cone is often followed by eating the ice cream, and eating evokes salivation. Thus, seeing the ice cream becomes enough to evoke salivation. Similarly, the sight of an overinflated balloon often is followed by a loud bang, which evokes a startle response. So seeing a balloon being overinflated becomes enough to cause us to shrink away. (See **Figure 5•2.**)

Thorndike's Procedure

Thorndike's approach to the study of learning also involved the introduction of an eliciting stimulus—food—into the organism's environment. Unlike Pavlov, however, Thorndike introduced the food after a *response,* not a stimulus. If a chick ran to the end of a passageway, it received food; if a cat operated a latch that allowed it to exit a chamber, it received food. (See **Figure 5•3.**) Food was an eliciting stimulus that evoked approach and eating and presumably salivation, although salivation was not measured by Thorndike. Presenting food after the response (running or operating the latch, respectively) caused the response to increase in strength. When the chick was placed in the passageway, it ran instead of meandering about. When the cat was placed in the chamber, which Thorndike called a puzzle box, it operated the latch instead of trying to squeeze between the bars of the puzzle box. Once again, the introduction of a stimulus that already evoked behavior had changed the way that the environment guided behavior.

In summary, introducing a stimulus that evoked a response promoted learning in both Pavlov's and Thorndike's procedures. The sorts of changes produced by Thorndike's procedure are the stuff of daily life. For example, a child who has received a treat or has been praised after picking up his or her toys is more likely to pick them up in the future. The likelihood that the beginning learner engages in a given behavior in a given environment is affected by the eliciting stimuli that the learner has experienced in that environment.

Comparison between Pavlov's and Thorndike's Procedures for Studying Learning

The fundamental similarities and differences between Pavlov's and Thorndike's procedures are shown in **Figure 5•4.** Pavlov's procedure controlled the relation of an environmental stimulus to an eliciting stimulus, whereas Thorndike's procedure controlled the relation of a response to the eliciting stimulus. In Pavlov's procedure a specified environmental stimulus must occur before the eliciting stimulus. In Thorndike's procedure a specified response must occur before the eliciting stimulus. However, as shown in Figure 5.4, *some* environmental stimulus invariably precedes the eliciting stimulus in Thorndike's procedure, and *some* behavioral response invariably precedes the eliciting stimulus in Pavlov's procedure. Thus, the two procedures do not so much differ with respect to whether a stimulus or a response precedes the eliciting stimulus, but whether the relation of these events to the eliciting stimulus is reliable. At the moment when the eliciting stimulus is first presented, the organism cannot tell whether it is experiencing Pavlov's procedure or Thorndike's procedure. Pavlov's dog likely pricked up its ears on hearing the ticking of the metronome, and this response may have preceded the food. Thorndike's cat likely saw the ring that oper-

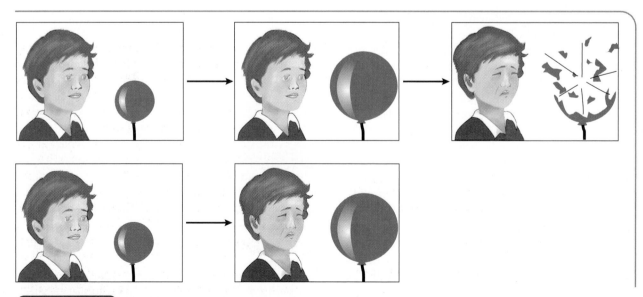

FIGURE 5•2 A classical conditioning procedure outside the laboratory. A boy watches a balloon expand until it bursts, causing the boy to grimace. Thereafter, when the boy sees a balloon being overinflated, he grimaces even before the balloon bursts.

FIGURE 5·3 Thorndike's original operant conditioning procedure. A cat placed in the puzzle box had to pull the ring of wire inside the box to operate the latch. The door would then open, and the cat could escape from the puzzle box and gain access to food. The graph shows the reduction in the time one cat needed to operate the latch over repeated trails.

(Adapted from Thorndike, E. L. (1898). Animal intelligence. *Psychological Review Monograph Supplement, 2* [whole No. 8].)

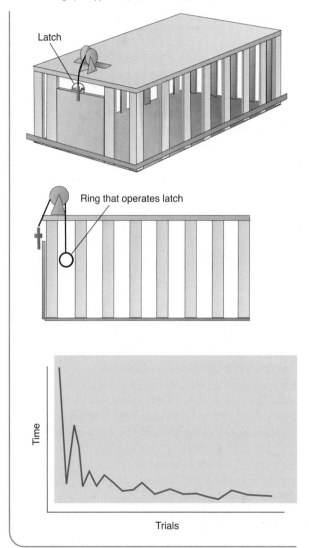

FIGURE 5·4 The similarities and differences between Pavlov's and Thorndike's procedures. In both procedures the environment may be viewed as a continuously changing sequence of stimuli (S) and behavior as a continuously changing sequence of responses (R). Into that stream of environmental and behavioral events, a stimulus is introduced that elicits a response. In Pavlov's procedure the eliciting stimulus is introduced after another stimulus—the ticking sound of a metronome. In Thorndike's procedure the eliciting stimulus is introduced after a response—operation of the latch. Note that some response inevitably occurs before the eliciting stimulus in Pavlov's procedure and some stimulus inevitably occurs before the response in Thorndike's procedure.

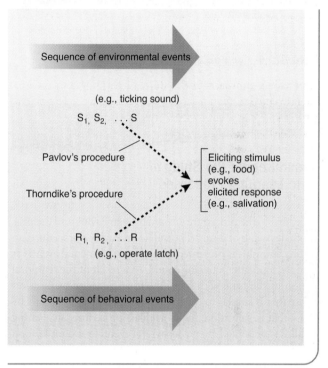

ated the latch before pulling it, and this stimulus may have preceded the food. Given that the two procedures differ only in the reliability with which environmental or behavioral events precede the eliciting stimulus, it is not surprising that findings from the two procedures lead to the same conclusions about the nature of the learning process—the process whereby experience changes the environmental guidance of behavior.

In spite of the fundamental similarities between Pavlov's and Thorndike's procedures, the difference between the relations that are manipulated in the procedures has important implications. As B. F. Skinner (1937) appreciated more keenly than others, Pavlov's procedure limits the behavior that may be brought under environmental control to those responses that can already be elicited by other stimuli. The dog learns to salivate to the ticking sound, but little else. However, Thorndike's procedure opens up the possibility of changing the environmental guidance of *any* behavior of which an organism is capable: Simply select a response and follow it by an eliciting stimulus. Thus, the full behavioral repertoire of the learner can potentially be modified by Thorndike's procedure. Because of the greater scope of Thorndike's procedure, it is more often used in "real-world" applications of learning principles. Thorndike himself largely left laboratory research and went on to apply his methods to the field of education, becoming the most extensively published psychologist in history (Jonçich, 1968). Pavlov lamented Thorndike's departure from the laboratory and toward the application of learning principles, commenting that it was evidence of "the practical bent of the American mind."

▲ *Students' raising of their hands in response to their teacher's questions is reinforced by the opportunity to speak and receive attention from their teacher.*

Interim Summary

Procedures for the Study of Basic Learning Processes

Researchers study learning in the laboratory using two basic procedures—the procedure devised by Ivan Pavlov and the procedure devised by Edward Thorndike. In Pavlov's procedure, an eliciting stimulus is presented after an environmental event; for example, food after a ticking sound. As a result of the temporal relation of the tone with food, the tone comes to evoke a response that is similar to the response originally evoked only by food—that is, salivation. In Thorndike's procedure, an eliciting stimulus is presented after a behavioral event; for example, food after the operation of a latch. As a result of the temporal relation of latch operation to food, latch operation (as well as salivation) becomes stronger in that environment. The learner is immersed in a continuous stream of environmental and behavioral events; as a consequence, some response necessarily occurs before the eliciting stimulus in Pavlov's procedure, and some environmental stimulus necessarily occurs before the eliciting stimulus in Thorndike's procedure. The procedures differ only with respect to which type of event *reliably* precedes the reinforcer—a particular stimulus in the Pavlov case and a particular response in the Thorndike case. Although the same learning process occurs in both procedures, Skinner appreciated that Thorndike's procedure is more important for understanding behavioral change, because *any* response of the learner can potentially be strengthened in that procedure, whereas only those responses that are already elicitable by some stimulus can be strengthened in Pavlov's procedure.

QUESTIONS TO CONSIDER

1. What is the basic procedural difference between Pavlov's and Thorndike's experiment? Given that difference, why does the text claim that the same basic learning process is studied with both procedures?

2. Do you believe that learning in humans can be based on the same learning processes as those that occur in other animals? Explain your answer.

Conditions Required for Learning

Using both Pavlov's and Thorndike's procedures, laboratory research has sought to identify the factors that are necessary for learning to occur. Two factors have been identified. Their technical names are *temporal contiguity* and *behavioral discrepancy*. Let's look at the experimental findings relating to each of these factors.

Temporal Contiguity

Pavlov's procedure allows the experimenter to manipulate the temporal (time) interval between the presentation of a relatively neutral stimulus (for example, a ticking sound) and the eliciting stimulus (for example, food). In contrast, Thorndike's procedure allows the experimenter to manipulate the temporal interval between the occurrence of a response (operating the latch) and the eliciting stimulus. What effect does **temporal contiguity,** or closeness in time, between these pairs of events have on the strength of the measured response—salivation in Pavlov's case and latch operation in Thorndike's?

Before we address this question, let me introduce some technical terms that are conventionally used to describe these procedures. Pavlov's procedure is called a *classical* or *respondent* procedure. It is called "classical" because it was the first procedure used to study learning systematically. It is called "respondent" to emphasize that the behavior that is acquired is a response to an eliciting stimulus. This text will refer to Pavlov's procedure as the **classical procedure**. Thorndike's procedure is called an *operant* or *instrumental* procedure. Thorndike's procedure is called "operant" to emphasize that the response *operates* on the environment to produce the eliciting stimulus. It is called "instrumental" to indicate that the response serves to produce the eliciting stimulus. I shall refer to Thorndike's procedure as the **operant procedure**. Every scientific field uses technical terms so that the meaning of its statements is unambiguous. Although technical terms are necessary, committing them to memory is always a chore.

In Pavlov's classical procedure, the stimulus (e.g., the ticking sound) that reliably precedes the eliciting stimulus is called the **conditioned stimulus (CS)**. It is so called because its ability to evoke the elicited response is *conditional* on (that is, dependent on) its being paired with the eliciting stimulus— the food. The eliciting stimulus is called the **unconditioned stimulus (US)** because its ability to evoke the elicited response is not conditional on anything that happens within the experiment. The organism comes into the experiment already capable of responding to the unconditioned stimulus. Conditioned and unconditioned stimuli are most commonly denoted by the acronyms *CS* and *US*, respectively. The response that is elicited by the US is called the **unconditioned response (UR)**. After several pairings of the CS with the US, the CS by itself comes to evoke a response that in the typical case resembles the UR. But because the response that is evoked by the CS is conditional on pairing the CS with the US, it is called the **conditioned response (CR)**. As applied to Pavlov's original experiment, the ticking sound was the CS, the food was the US, the salivation that was elicited by food was the UR, and the salivation that came to be evoked by the CS was the CR. The learning that occurs under the controlled conditions provided by the classical and operant procedures is called **conditioning** in both cases. It is learning that is conditional on the pairing of events in the two procedures.

Now let's return to the effect of temporal contiguity. As shown in **Figure 5•5,** the CS may be presented either before the US/UR, in which case the procedure is called a *forward* conditioning procedure, or after the US/UR, in which case it is called a *backward* procedure. Using the classical procedure, researchers can vary the time interval between the CS and the US for different learners to determine the effect of this variable on conditioning.

The effect of varying the time interval between the CS and the US/UR for different groups of subjects is shown in **Figure 5•6.** When the CS followed the US/UR (a backward procedure) or was simultaneous with the US/UR (0 ms), conditioning failed to occur. When the CS came before the US/UR (a forward procedure), the CS acquired control of the response. As Figure 5.6 shows, the strength of the response increased as the time interval lengthened to 225 ms and then

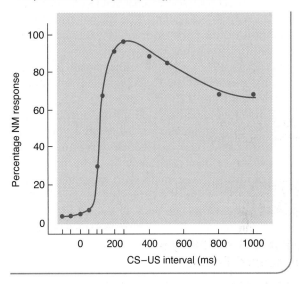

FIGURE 5•6 The effect of varying the time interval between the onset of the CS and onset of the US/UR. A CS–US interval below zero indicates conditioning procedure.

(Adapted from Smith, M. C., Coleman, S. P., & Gormezano, I. (1969). Classical conditioning of the rabbit's nictitating membrane response at backward, simultaneous, and forward CS–US intervals. *Journal of Comparative and Physiological Psychology, 69,* 226–231.)

declined if the interval lengthened further (Smith, Coleman, & Gormezano, 1969). The strength of the CR was measured by the percentage of CS-alone presentations that evoked a CR. The results graphed in Figure 5.6 were obtained with a CS of a tone and a US of a mild shock in the region of the eye of a rabbit. The UR and CR both were movements of the rabbit's nictitating membrane, a membrane that extends to partially cover the rabbit's eye. (The nictitating membrane is vestigial in humans; only the pink tissue in the inner corners of our eyes remains). The nictitating-membrane response allowed a better controlled experiment than Pavlov's salivary response. Rabbits very rarely move this membrane unless the eye is threatened, whereas dogs salivate intermittently at low levels in the absence of either the CS or US. With the nictitating-membrane response, the experimenter could be more confident that when responding occurred after the tone, the CS–US/UR relation, not some other variable, was responsible for the CR. Although the precise time interval at which conditioning is optimal varies slightly for different CSs and USs, the general finding has been confirmed: Conditioning in the classical procedure is best when the CS precedes the US/UR by a brief time interval. The critical temporal relation appears to be between the CS and the UR, because conditioning can occur even with a backward CS–US relation when the UR is of substantial duration. Longer-duration URs allow a backward CS to overlap the UR (Donahoe & Vegas, 2004). Longer-duration responses are common when responses are mediated by the autonomic nervous system, as in emotional responses elicited by strong aversive stimuli.

Temporal relations between events can also be investigated with the operant procedure—although using the operant

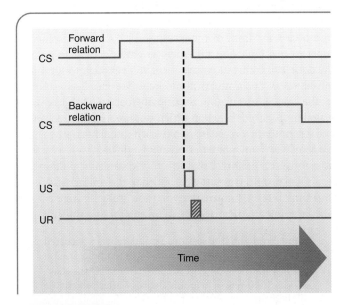

FIGURE 5•5 In classical conditioning procedures, two possible temporal relations may exist between the conditioned stimulus (CS) and the unconditioned stimulus (US) and the response it elicits (UR). A forward procedure exists when the CS occurs before the US/UR. A backward procedure exists when the CS follows the US/UR.

procedure is more difficult, because other responses can intervene between the operant response and the eliciting stimulus and complicate the interpretation of findings. In the operant procedure the experimenter manipulates the time interval between the operant response and the eliciting stimulus. For example, different rats can press a lever and then receive food at various time intervals after the press. Or different pigeons can peck a disk on the wall of a test chamber and receive food after various time intervals. The findings from operant experiments are also clear: As the time delay increases between the operant response and eliciting stimulus, the strength of the operant declines (e.g., Catania, 1971; Grice, 1948). The strength of the operant response increases if the eliciting stimulus follows the response by no more than a few seconds.

In sum, results from both classical and operant procedures indicate that an eliciting stimulus can change the environmental guidance of behavior only when it occurs very soon after the CS or the operant response, respectively. Thus, the fundamental learning process acts over only a short time interval. This conclusion has been confirmed with both infant and adult human learners using techniques such as air-puff-elicited eye blinks as the US and UR (Rovee-Collier & Gekowski, 1979; Spence, 1956). The finding that learning occurs only within a short time period surrounding the occurrence of an eliciting stimulus is summarized as the *temporal contiguity requirement.*

Effects of Temporal Contiguity with a Reinforcer on Human Behavior

When an eliciting stimulus strengthens the environmental control of behavior, whether in the classical or operant procedure, the eliciting stimulus is said to function as a **reinforcing stimulus,** or simply as a *reinforcer.* Eliciting stimuli that can function as reinforcers in operant procedures are appetitive stimuli; that is, they are stimuli that elicit approach behavior.

The relations of reinforcers to the behavior of humans are usually more complex than those manipulated in highly controlled classical and operant procedures. Nevertheless, there are some types of human behavior that we can understand, in large part, by considering only temporal contiguity of reinforcers with stimuli or responses. Consider phobias, which are unreasonable fears of certain stimuli—for example, harmless spiders, birds, and other objects. When we look closely at the life histories of persons with phobias, we often discover experiences in which the object of the phobia has been paired with an aversive stimulus (Merckelbach & Muris, 1997). Pairing an object with a stimulus that evokes pain or fear causes the object itself to be feared, even when the fear is irrational. Which stimuli become objects of phobias are influenced by natural selection as well as by experience. Studies show that objects that are often involved in phobias, such as spiders, become CSs more rapidly when paired with an aversive US than do neutral stimuli (Ohman, Fredrikson, Hugdahl, & Rimmo, 1976). Panic disorders (see Chapter 17) also are affected by the stimulus–reinforcer pairings of the classical procedure (e.g., Bouton, Mineka, & Barlow, 2001). Again, the life histories of those afflicted with panic disorders often include pairings of the feared situation with an aversive US (Acierno, Hersen, & Van Hasselt, 1993).

A particularly unfortunate effect of pairing a stimulus with a reinforcer occurs in drug addiction. When an addicting drug is taken by injection or other means, the stimuli that are present when the drug is taken become paired with the effects of the drug. The result: Stimuli from the general environment as well as the sight of drug paraphernalia or the prick of a needle can become CSs for the responses elicited by the drug. As we saw in Chapter 4, drugs of addiction introduce into the body compounds that the neurons of the brain normally produce; that is, neurotransmitters. When these neurons detect the increased level of the neurotransmitter, the neurons reduce their production of the transmitter. This reduced production is the UR to the US of drug ingestion. The reduced production of the neurotransmitter then becomes the CR to the CS and is responsible for withdrawal effects when the person is placed in an environment in which drugs were previously taken (Eikelboom & Stewart, 1982). Experiments with animals have confirmed these conditioned effects: If a rat is addicted to a drug by injection and the rat is then injected with a placebo (a compound that has no effect, such as a weak salt solution), then the rat promptly shows withdrawal symptoms (Higgins, Budney, & Bickel, 1994; Stewart, 2004). Withdrawal due to conditioned responses is a major reason why drug treatments often fail. Addicts may become drug-free during a rehabilitation program—but when they return to the environment in which they were previously addicted, conditioned withdrawal responses are evoked and relapse is likely.

Temporal contiguity of a response with a reinforcer—the operant procedure—can also produce changes in human behavior. This is one basis for superstitions (Skinner, 1948). Have you ever jiggled a key in a lock in a particular way and, if the door opened, continued to jiggle it in that same way thereafter? Have you ever pressed an elevator button repeatedly before the elevator came and then continued to press it many times on future occasions? Both of these responses could be considered superstitious. Only one movement might be enough to unlock the door; only one button press might be enough to summon the elevator. Such superstitious behavior has been studied in the laboratory. In one experiment college students were seated in front of a panel on which were mounted three levers and a counter that registered points. The students were told to try to get as many points as possible, but they were not told how to get the points. Unknown to the students, pulling the levers had no effect; points were added to the counter after various time intervals no matter what the students were doing. The experimenter reported the following for one student:

> About 5 min into the session, a point delivery occurred after she had stopped pulling the lever temporarily and had just put her hand on the lever frame. This behavior was followed by a point delivery after which she climbed on the table and put her right hand to the counter. Just as she did so a point was delivered. Thereafter, she began to touch many things in turn.... About 10 minutes later, a point was delivered just as she jumped to the floor, and touching was replaced by jumping. After five jumps, a point was delivered when she jumped and touched the ceiling with her shoe in

her hand. Jumping to touch the ceiling continued repeatedly . . . until she stopped about 25 min. into the session, perhaps because of fatigue. (Koichi, 1987)

Natural selection has produced a learning mechanism that is sensitive to temporal contiguity between events when an eliciting stimulus occurs—whether with the stimulus–reinforcer events of the classical procedure or the response–reinforcer events of the operant procedure. Usually it takes several co-occurrences of these events before the environmental control of behavior is changed, but phobias and superstitions illustrate that only a single pairing may sometimes be sufficient (see also Staddon & Simmelhag, 1971; Timberlake & Lucas, 1985). The temporal contiguity requirement is quite reasonable in terms of the neural mechanisms that underlie behavioral change; the underlying processes must occur at about the same time in interconnected neurons if the connectivity between the neurons is to change. However, the contiguity requirement also invites a question: How can we understand those instances of human behavior that appear sensitive to events that take place long after the response has occurred? For example, work done in the office on Monday may not produce a paycheck until the end of the week. How can behavior be acquired and maintained by a paycheck if the fundamental learning process requires temporal contiguity? We will return to this question later in the chapter, when we consider other conditioning phenomena and the neural mechanisms that underlie behavioral change.

For many years, temporal contiguity was thought to be the only factor required for learning: If the reinforcer occurred immediately after the CS in the classical procedure or immediately after the response in the operant procedure, then the environmental guidance of behavior changed. The CR became stronger during the CS, and the operant became stronger during the environment in which the reinforcer had occurred. However, in the late 1960s and the early 1970s it became evident that something in addition to contiguity was required.

Behavioral Discrepancy

The clearest demonstration that learning required a second factor was provided by a two-stage experimental design known as the **blocking design** (Kamin, 1969). The blocking design can be implemented in either classical or operant procedures. In its most basic form, a stimulus is paired with a reinforcer during the first phase until a response becomes conditioned to that stimulus. Then, in the second phase, the stimulus continues to be presented, but a second stimulus is introduced that overlaps the original stimulus; meanwhile, the reinforcer continues to be presented—now after both stimuli. As a specific example, a tone might be paired with food, which conditions salivation to the tone. Then a light is presented at the same time as the tone, and food is given as before. If temporal contiguity were all that was required for learning, then the light should also become an effective CS, because the light stands in the same temporal relation to the food as the tone did during the first stage. What the blocking-design experiments revealed, however, was that the light did *not* become an effective CS, even though its temporal relation to the reinforcer was favorable. When the tone was presented by itself, the CR occurred; but when the light was presented alone, the CR usually failed to occur. Conditioning of the CR to the light had been *blocked* by prior conditioning to the tone. (See **Figure 5•7** for a summary of the blocking design.) Blocking of conditioning was first demonstrated with the classical procedure, but the finding was soon replicated with the operant procedure (vom Saal & Jenkins, 1970).

The clearest interpretation of the results of the blocking design, and of many related findings, was provided by Robert Rescorla and Alan Wagner (1972): Stated in terms of behavior, an eliciting stimulus functions as a reinforcer only if it evokes a response that is not already occurring (Donahoe et al., 1982). Thus, when a CS or an operant response is followed by food, food acts as a reinforcer only if the learner is not already salivating when the CS appears or the operant response occurs. In the blocking design, only the CS presented during the first stage was paired with an eliciting stimulus that evoked a *change* in behavior. When the second stimulus was introduced during the second phase of the experiment, it occurred together with a CS that already evoked salivation because it had previously been paired with food. As a result, the presentation of food did not produce a sufficient change in ongoing behavior to permit the second stimulus to acquire the CR. Only a stimulus that evokes a **behavioral discrepancy**, or behavioral change, can function as a reinforcer. Note the great economy of the learning mechanism: Conditioning occurs only if the learner is not already behaving in ways that are called for in that environment. Note also that the same

	Experimental (blocking) group	Control group
Conditioning phase 1	CS1 (tone) ⟶ US (food)	CS3 (click) ⟶ US (food)
Conditioning phase 2	CS1 (tone) plus ⟶ US (food) CS2 (light)	CS1 (tone) plus ⟶ US (food) CS2 (light)
Test phase	CS1 (tone) presented alone — CR CS2 (light) presented alone — **no CR**	CS1 (tone) presented alone — CR CS2 (light) presented alone — CR

FIGURE 5•7 A blocking design. The experimental group is first conditioned to respond to CS1. Then, after CRs are acquired to CS1, CS2 is presented at the same times as CS1 and conditioning continues as before. Finally, CS1 and CS2 are presented separately. In the experimental group only CS1 then evoked a CR. In the control group, which received the same procedure except that CS2 was not accompanied by a stimulus that already evoked the CR, both CS1 and CS2 evoked CRs when they were presented separately.

eliciting stimulus will again function as a reinforcer if it is presented in another environment in which the elicited response is not already occurring.

It is difficult to directly test the importance of the behavioral discrepancy requirement with human behavior—humans have such a rich history of experience before entering any experiment that almost every stimulus already controls some behavior. In addition, important factors in human behavior, such as what a person thinks when a stimulus occurs, are not easily measurable. Nevertheless, the evidence from studies of human behavior is consistent with the conclusion from the better-controlled nonhuman experiments: Learning occurs only when the potential reinforcer produces a change in behavior (Gluck & Bower, 1988). Speaking nontechnically, an eliciting stimulus functions as a reinforcer only if the learner is "surprised" to receive the stimulus and to engage in the behavior it evokes. Gordon Bower, a prominent contributor to the literature on human learning, put it this way: "The learning mechanism seems to be 'switched on' mainly when environmental events do not confirm expectations" (Bower, 1970, p. 70). Perhaps this is why parents who lavish praise on their children independently of the child's behavior may find that their praise is ineffective as a reinforcer. Frequent and indiscriminate praise is not "surprising." Conversely, parents who dole out praise sparingly may find the same words quite effective reinforcers. The more restricted the learner's contact with a stimulus, the more vigorous the behavior evoked by that stimulus and the more effectively the stimulus functions as a reinforcer (cf. Premack, 1959; Timberlake & Allison, 1974).

Biology and Culture

Learning, Superstition, and Ritualistic Behavior

Are you a superstitious person? Do you have a lucky charm or an object of clothing that you feel brings you good luck? Do you have a special routine or ritual that you follow before an important event? Many people—in every culture—have these charms and rituals. Some rituals become codified into culturewide practices such as celebrations and ceremonies. How do superstitions and rituals arise? Why do they exist, and what functions do they serve?

● Learning and Genes

We discovered in Chapters 3 and 4 that behavior is shaped by continual interaction between an organism's genetic endowment and its environment. Genetic differences and environmental differences select particular patterns of behavior. In turn, these behavior patterns help to adapt a species to its environment. Species-typical patterns affect the processes by which individual organisms adapt to their environments. Shettleworth (1972) describes these patterns as "constraints on learning," because they can restrict learning to events that are evolutionarily important to the ecology of the organism.

Jenkins, Barrera, Ireland, and Woodside (1978) provide a good example. They observed dogs that they had conditioned using a lightbulb on the wall as a CS and food as the US. The dogs exhibited conditioned responses to the light that would normally occur to signals for food in the dog's natural ecology. For example, many of the dogs "pointed" to the light, just as they might point to prey in a natural setting. Others showed a "begging" response typical of the way dogs interact socially during feeding.

Ernst Mayr (1974), an evolutionary biologist, provided a useful framework describing how these two factors—genes and environment—interact to determine what organisms learn. He argued that the type of *genetic program*, the specific set of genetic instructions an organism inherits at birth, determines the extent to which the organism's behavior may be changed by environmental factors. Across species, the capacity to learn varies along a continuum. At one end are species having *closed genetic programs*, and at the other end are those having *open genetic programs*. Species having closed programs, such as insects and some amphibians and reptiles, generally have short life spans, mature quickly, and receive little or no care from their parents. At birth these animals are genetically predisposed to respond in certain ways in particular situations.

Consider the courtship ritual of a fish called the three-spined stickleback. The ritual is characterized by a "zigzag dance" in which the movements of the dance occur in response to stimuli associated with specific behaviors performed by each fish (see **Figure 5•8**). These fish do not learn to dance; they dance flawlessly at the first opportunity for mating. Keep in mind, though, that saying that a species possesses a closed genetic program does not mean that members of that species cannot learn. It simply means that in terms of what is learned and how learning is reflected in behavior, the species' learning capacity is restricted compared to that of other species. For instance, honeybees can learn to discriminate objects on the basis of color, but they cannot learn most of the sorts of things that you and I can—or even that the family cat or dog can.

Species that have relatively open genetic programs, which include mammals and birds, generally have longer life spans and extended periods of immaturity and parental care. For organisms with open genetic programs, learning is the primary means by which individuals adapt to their environments.

Humans, of course, possess an open genetic program. Courtship rituals vary from one culture to the next; they are not stereotyped, as is the zigzag dance of the stickleback. Consider the Sandalu bachelor ritual, practiced for centuries among unmarried males of the Laiapu Enga tribe of New Guinea (Schwab, 1995). The purpose of the ritual was twofold. First, the ritual was intended to restore the males' worthiness to marry by "purifying" them after they had seen female genitals, which males occasionally glimpsed beneath the grass skirts as the women danced. Second, the ritual was intended to increase the men's fertility for marriage.

The ritual unfolded over several days. The young men would seclude themselves near a creek; there they would bathe, chant and sing an incantation in praise of the Sandalu ritual, adopt new names, spit to rid themselves of the effects of bad language, and wash both eyes and eyelids with water

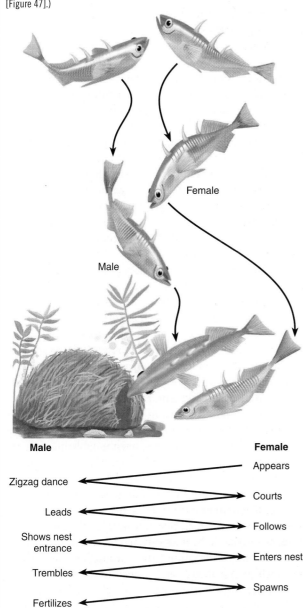

FIGURE 5•8 The zigzag courtship dance of the three-spined stickleback. Each part of the dance is triggered by a response made by the other fish.

(From Tinbergen, N. (1951). *The study of instinct.* Oxford University Press, p. 49 [Figure 47].)

Male | **Female**

Zigzag dance ← → Appears

Leads ← → Courts

Shows nest entrance ← → Follows

Trembles ← → Enters nest

Fertilizes ← → Spawns

while muttering a purifying incantation—for example, "I have seen the private parts of a woman. . . . Take this off my eyes; let it go down the river." Then they would participate in a ceremony intended to induce dreaming. Finally, when the women came dancing into the camp, a man would give his girlfriend a token that publicly announced their engagement.

Although the courtship rituals of the three-spined stickleback and the Laiapu Enga have similar purposes—procreation—the basis of the rituals is quite different. The zigzag dance is an expression of a genetic program that produced a nervous system that responds in a stereotyped manner to the presence of a receptive mate. The Sandalu

bachelor ritual (and most other human behavior) was the result of a genetic program that produces a malleable nervous system that individual experiences act upon. The greatest legacy of natural selection to humans is the inherited capacity of human behavior to undergo modification through interaction with the environment.

People in the United States learn the courtship rituals that are valued by their culture, just as the Laiapu Enga learned those that were valued by their culture. In fact, all cultural customs and rituals are maintained because they are reinforced by other persons in a given culture (Guerin, 1992, 1995). Social rituals, especially those surrounding courtship and reproductive behavior, arise and endure because of our inherited capacity for behavior to be affected by its consequences.

● **The Origins of Superstitious and Ritualistic Behavior**
How might particular cultural practices such as the Sandalu bachelor ritual arise—as well as practices of our own that the Laiapu Enga people might think equally peculiar? What are the origins of rituals, and what possible adaptive value might these practices have?

We have seen that whenever behavior is followed by a reinforcer, that behavior becomes more likely. Most often, the behavior operates on the environment to produce the reinforcer; there is a cause-and-effect relation between response and reinforcement. We learn to press the button on a drinking fountain because that response makes the water flow. But a response does not have to *cause* the reinforcer for the behavior to be affected.

Consider the following example, based on an experiment by Skinner (1948). We place a hungry pigeon inside an **operant chamber** and program the apparatus to dispense a bit of food every 15 seconds. After a few minutes, we look at the bird and discover that it is spinning around frantically, counterclockwise. We replace the first bird with another. This time, after a few minutes of occasional food presentations, we find the pigeon standing in the middle of the floor, bobbing its head up and down like a mechanical toy.

Skinner explained these behaviors in the following way: When a reinforcer is intermittently given to an animal independently of what the animal does, the animal seldom simply waits quietly for the next reinforcer. Instead, it tends to persist in what it was doing when the reinforcement occurred. Perhaps the first pigeon was turning around when the food dispenser was first activated. The pigeon heard the noise, turned toward its source, and saw the food. It ate, waited in the vicinity of the food dispenser, and finally turned to go. Just then, another bit of food was delivered, so the bird went back to eat it. The next time, the pigeon turned away a little sooner and made a couple of revolutions before some food was dispensed again. From then on, the pigeon began to spin around after each reinforcer. From the bird's point of view, spinning around was what produced the food. Under these conditions, the bird acquired **superstitious behavior**—behavior that appeared to bring food but in fact only happened to occur before the food appeared.

▲ *A superstitious behavior: Do you think that crossing her fingers will improve the remote chance of winning the lottery?*

Humans acquire some superstitious behavior in the same way. For example, if we do well on a test after studying while listening to the radio, the next time we study for a test we may again turn on the radio. Most baseball pitchers perform some ritual before throwing the ball to the batter—scuffing the ground with their shoes, rubbing the ball, tugging on their hats, turning the ball in the glove, and the like. A baseball pitcher performs a given ritual because, in his past, the behavior has preceded his throwing strikes. Note that superstitions can become self-fulfilling prophesies. That is, if the superstitious behavior produces stimuli that often precede throwing strikes, then those stimuli will acquire control of the pitching behavior. In this way, the superstitious behavior is maintained, because often it does in fact precede the reinforcer. Whether the behavior is relevant or irrelevant, if it precedes success it tends to be repeated.

Of course, we can only speculate about the kinds of environmental conditions that give rise to the superstitious behavior and rituals of all human cultures. Probably these behaviors were inadvertently reinforced sometime long ago and then taught to subsequent generations. The precise origins of the Sandalu ritual are unknown (Schwab, 1995). But for our purposes (and for the Laiapu Enga), the origins are not important. What is important is that this ritual, like any other, bound a community of people together. Although we may think the Sandalu ritual was strange, the ritual served as a centerpiece of the people's culture for hundreds of years. The Sandalu ritual was not the result of a genetic program, however. Through the influence of Western civilization, the Sandalu bachelor ritual has now been replaced by more "modern" courtship rituals—but rituals nevertheless. When the social environment of the Laiapu Enga changed, their behavior changed. The behavior of the Laiapu Enga was modified by Western cultural influences, a behavioral change that could occur because of the open genetic program in our species.

Interim Summary

Conditions Required for Learning

Studies using both classical and operant procedures have identified two conditions as necessary for learning—*temporal contiguity* and *behavioral discrepancy*. The temporal contiguity requirement means that the stimuli and responses that are affected by the reinforcer must occur close in time to the reinforcer. The behavioral discrepancy requirement means that an eliciting stimulus can function as a reinforcer only if it evokes a response that is not already occurring before its presentation. The importance of behavioral discrepancy is illustrated by the blocking design, in which a stimulus that is in temporal contiguity with an eliciting stimulus will not become a CS if the stimulus is accompanied by another stimulus that already evokes the CR. Nontechnically speaking, learning occurs only when the eliciting stimulus is "surprising."

Although real-life situations are generally more complex than the laboratory situations researchers use to study learning in simple classical and operant procedures, the fundamental learning processes revealed by these procedures clearly play an important role in life outside the laboratory—as illustrated in the formation of phobias and withdrawal from drug addiction. The effect of the individual environment on behavior is also affected by the legacy of the ancestral environment—the organism's genetic endowment. For some species, such as insects, the individual environment can change behavior within only a relatively restricted range. Such species have closed genetic programs. For other species, most notably humans, the individual environment can modify behavior within a much wider range. Such species have relatively open genetic programs. Neither selection by the individual environment nor the ancestral environment can guarantee that all behavior is optimally adapted. Sometimes noncausal sequences of environment and behavioral events are acquired because the environment, including the culture, provides sufficient reinforcers for them to persist. Rituals and superstitions can result from such arbitrary sequences of events.

QUESTIONS TO CONSIDER

1. Comment on the following in terms of what you know about fundamental learning processes: A teacher wishes to encourage her students, so she praises their work even when it may not be of good quality. She hopes that this will increase their self-esteem and improve their performance in the classroom.
2. How do you tell the difference between two events that just happen to occur together and two events that are causally related? Are the fundamental learning processes sensitive to this difference? Explain.

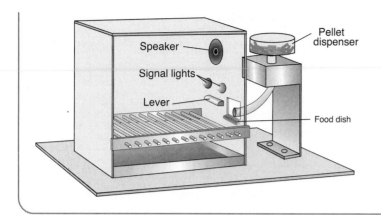

FIGURE 5•9 An operant chamber used for the conditioning of lever pressing in rats. When the rat presses the lever, a small pellet of food can be delivered.

Speaker

Signal lights

Lever

Pellet dispenser

Food dish

The Outcomes of Learning

All the forms of behavior discussed in later chapters of this book are affected by the basic learning processes described in this chapter. We learn to perceive the world, to remember what we perceive, to speak about what we remember, and so on. The basic learning processes enlighten our understanding of the more complex behavior that emerges with experience. In this section we'll look more closely at how **reinforcement,** or the process by which reinforcers exert their effects, changes the environmental guidance of behavior. We will consider the processes of acquisition and extinction of behaviors, the processes of stimulus generalization and discrimination, the functions of punishment, and the relation of basic learning processes to "insight" in problem solving.

Acquisition

The learning of a response, or **acquisition,** takes place when a response is followed by a reinforcer and the response becomes stronger in the environment in which that response occurred. In short, in acquisition reinforcers change the environmental guidance of behavior. When simple responses are acquired, as when a rat learns to press a lever, the procedure is straightforward. First the animal is placed in a test chamber and allowed to explore the environment. (See **Figure 5•9.**) Exploration permits the animal's response to various extraneous stimuli in the environment to habituate. **Habituation** is a simple form of learning that occurs when environmental stimuli evoke responses but those responses decrease when they produce no specific consequences. For example, a rat might see the ceiling of the chamber and rear up toward it. However, if rearing had no consequences (such as allowing the rat to escape the chamber), rearing would decline in strength. The decline in rearing is an example of habituation. Rearing was an **orienting response** to a stimulus from the ceiling—a response to a stimulus that facilitates its detection. For example, in Pavlov's procedure, an orienting response would occur if the dog turned toward the sound of the metronome.

In the second step of lever-press training, the experimenter permits the rat to receive a few presentations of food from a feeder before initiating the operant procedure. Habituation ensures that in the test environment the strengths of responses that might compete with lever pressing will be low. Feeder training ensures that food will be an effective elicitor of behavior—here, approach and eating.

Finally, the experimenter arranges an operant procedure in which lever pressing is followed immediately by food. Once habituation and feeder training have taken place, even a single instance of a lever press followed by food is often enough to produce measurable increases in the strength of lever pressing, as shown in **Figure 5•10** (Skinner, 1938).

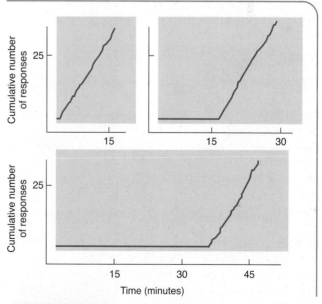

FIGURE 5•10 Lever pressing after the first press was followed by a food pellet for three different animals. Note that responding was immediately strengthened and continued as further presses were also followed by food.

(Adapted from Skinner, B. F. (1938). *Behavior of Organisms.* New York: Appleton-Century.)

Shaping Most behavior is not acquired in a highly controlled environment such as an operant chamber and is not as simple as lever pressing. Most learning takes place under more variable stimulus conditions and involves more complex responses. Because of this, acquisition often requires **shaping.** Shaping is a procedure in which a person (or a lab animal) acquires a complex target response through reinforcement of successively closer approximations to the target response. Under some circumstances, even simple lever pressing can involve shaping. Suppose that other responses to a rat's test environment had not been habituated and that these responses competed with the rat's learning to approach and touch the lever. To reduce the competition, the experimenter might begin by delivering food when the rat simply looked toward the lever, then when it walked toward the lever, and then when it touched the lever. After this shaping procedure, lever pressing would become more likely, and the presentation of food after the first press could increase its strength. Shaping is not restricted to interventions by the experimenter. For example, some ways of pressing the lever are more efficient than others—for example, pressing with a paw rather than the nose. Over time, the more efficient response will often be shaped by natural **contingencies,** or sequential temporal relations, without the intervention of a trainer.

▲ *Complex behaviors, such as riding a bicycle, are not learned all at once. Instead, they are shaped; that is, we first learn behaviors that only approximate the level of skill we will ultimately need to perform the behavior properly.*

Learning in real-world situations often involves shaping (McIlvane & Dube, 2003). For example, a teacher may first praise even poorly formed letters produced by a child who is just learning to write. As time goes on, only more accurately drawn letters will be followed by approval. **Response chaining,** a form of shaping, is very commonly used to train the behavior of children with developmental disabilities. Consider what seems to be a simple skill, such as tooth brushing. Actually, this skill consists of a series of responses, each under the control of somewhat different stimuli. Going to get the toothbrush in the bathroom is a response to finishing a meal. Opening the door of the bathroom cabinet is a response to entering the bathroom. Taking the toothbrush and the toothpaste from the cabinet are responses to looking into the open cabinet. Removing the cap from the toothpaste is a response to seeing the toothpaste tube, and so on. Teaching a developmentally disabled child to brush his or her teeth requires not simply reinforcing tooth brushing (the target response) but reinforcing each of the sequence of responses that ultimately lead to the target behavior; that is, shaping.

Natural Selection and Acquisition Reinforcement is the process by which individual experience changes the environmental guidance of behavior. It is well to remember, however, that sensitivity to reinforcement is itself a product of natural selection. That is, sensitivity to reinforcement must contribute to reproductive fitness if the biological mechanisms that implement reinforcement are to be selected. The adaptiveness of the ability to learn is obvious. Organisms that learn to avoid predators, to gather and hunt food, and so on are clearly more likely to survive and reproduce.

The contribution of learning to natural selection—fitness—can be demonstrated in the laboratory. Learned behavior affects both competition for mates and reproductive success. In classical lab procedure with male Siamese fighting fish, experimenters turned on a light immediately before allowing a male fish to see (but not contact) another male (Hollis, 1982). As a result the light became a CS for whatever behavioral, neural, and hormonal responses are elicited in a male fish by the sight of a possible competitor. Next, the experimenters turned on the light a few seconds before giving the male access to another male that had not had such experience. The male that received the warning light was more likely to win its fight with the untrained male and thus to gain access to any females that might appear. Similarly, a male fish that had previously received a light paired with a chance to see a female of its species mated sooner and produced more offspring than a male that did not have this experience (Hollis, 1997). In the natural environment, male fish that learn to respond to stimuli indicating the presence of another male or a female have a reproductive advantage over males that do not learn. Natural selection would clearly favor the biological mechanisms that permitted learning.

Taste aversions, or learned responses of nausea and withdrawal in reaction to certain tastes, provide a particularly interesting example of the interplay between natural selection and the acquisition of learned behavior (Garcia & Koelling,

1966). In a laboratory taste-aversion experiment, an animal ingests some food that has a distinctive taste, such as lemon, and is then injected with a substance that produces nausea and gastric distress, such as lithium chloride. Even when the distinctive taste is ingested hours before the injection of the nausea-inducing substance, the animal will avoid the taste in the future. The fact that the taste stimulus acquires control over nausea responses even when the elicited response is not temporally contiguous with the taste differentiates taste aversions from most forms of conditioning. In other respects, taste aversions are comparable to other instances of conditioning (LoLordo & Droungas, 1989). From an evolutionary perspective, taste (and smell) stimuli have a special relation to alimentary responses. The only way for substances to enter the stomach is through the mouth, where their entry necessarily stimulates taste and olfactory receptors. Because of the invariant relation over evolutionary time between these stimuli and the gastric consequences of ingestion, natural selection has favored neural pathways that facilitate taste-aversion learning relative to other environment–behavior relations. Taste aversions benefit survival. Animals in the wild typically take a small bite of a novel substance and wait to see if nausea develops before ingesting larger amounts of the substance.

Humans acquire conditioned taste aversions, too, and this can complicate the treatment of cancer with chemotherapy. The nausea induced by chemotherapy becomes conditioned to the taste of the food that was most recently consumed, and the patient avoids the food thereafter. This causes weight loss, which further harms the patient. To ward off chemotherapy-induced taste aversions, before receiving chemotherapy the patient may be asked to consume a distinctively flavored but nonpreferred food to which an aversion would not be harmful (Bernstein, 1991).

Conditioned Reinforcement

In laboratory studies of fundamental learning processes, as we've seen, experimenters use reinforcers that evoke easily measurable responses. In the classical procedure, for example, reinforcer-elicited responses and the CRs that resemble them provide a ready measure of the acquisition process. Stimuli that elicit behavior, such as reflexes, are products of natural selection, and reproductive fitness clearly benefits when these responses are acquired in environments in which the reflexive behavior is relevant—as in the case of the Siamese fighting fish. Once the biological mechanisms of conditioning have been naturally selected, those same mechanisms are available to stimuli that do not elicit easily detectable responses. That is, once learning mechanisms have evolved, their behavioral expression is not necessary for them to be engaged by the environment. However, note that if the neural mechanisms that mediate conditioning were not *initially* correlated with overt behavior, those mechanisms could not have been naturally selected in the first place.

Most human behavior is reinforced by stimuli that do not evoke responses that are readily detectable at the behavioral level of analysis. The child whose letter writing becomes clearer following praise from the teacher does not have an easily detected response to praise—perhaps a subtle smile,

but not something as identifiable as a reflexively elicited response. The adult whose speaking is followed by attention from another person also does not have a readily identifiable response to the other's attention. And yet praise from a teacher and attention from another clearly function as reinforcers—letter writing improves and conversation continues. How can these stimuli that function as reinforcers be related to laboratory examples in which reinforcing stimuli elicit identifiable responses?

Both Pavlov and Skinner realized very early in their work that many stimuli that functioned as reinforcers outside the laboratory did not evoke responses that were readily identifiable at the behavioral level of observation. To investigate such reinforcers, they demonstrated that any of a wide range of stimuli could become reinforcers if they preceded a stimulus that was already a reinforcer. By being paired with a reinforcer, these formerly neutral stimuli became reinforcers themselves. Stimuli that acquire the ability to function as reinforcers are called **conditioned reinforcers,** because their reinforcing function is conditional upon experience. They also are called *secondary reinforcers,* as distinct from **unconditioned reinforcers,** or stimuli that evoke behavior because of natural selection, so-called *primary reinforcers.* Conditioned reinforcers are of critical importance for the acquisition of behavior in experienced learners outside of the laboratory. Even within the

▲ *For most people, handshakes, smiles, awards, and other forms of social approval serve as important forms of conditioned reinforcement.*

laboratory, conditioned reinforcers play an important role. For example, in Skinner's demonstrations of conditioning with food as a reinforcer (refer back to Figure 5.10), he first paired the presentation of food with the clicking sound of the mechanism that delivered the food. This established the click as a conditioned reinforcer. The click then sounded *immediately* after a lever press so that the delay between lever pressing and a reinforcer was minimized. If the immediate click had not been given, then other responses that intervened between lever pressing and eating the food might be strengthened more than lever pressing.

Neural Mechanisms of Unconditioned and Conditioned Reinforcement. Research conducted at the neural level of observation indicates that both unconditioned (primary) reinforcers, such as food, and conditioned (secondary) reinforcers, such as neutral stimuli paired with food, activate a common reinforcing system in the brain. Food stimulates taste and smell receptors whose axons eventually activate neurons located in nuclei in the ventral-tegmental area (VTA) of the midbrain. VTA neurons, in turn, send axons to widespread regions of the frontal lobes and other midbrain structures where they liberate the neuromodulator called **dopamine** (see Chapter 4). Dopamine is intimately involved in the cellular changes that alter the strengths of connections between neurons. Because of its widespread distribution, dopamine can change the strengths of connections between many neurons simultaneously (Donahoe & Palmer, 1994; Frey, 1997).

The effect of both unconditioned and conditioned reinforcers on dopaminergic (dopamine-releasing) neurons in the VTA has been shown in the laboratory. A light CS was presented to a monkey followed by the US of a squirt of orange juice into the monkey's mouth. During this training the experimenter monitored the activity of VTA neurons. The upper tracing of neural activity in **Figure 5•11** shows the increase in firing of a VTA neuron that occurred in response to the US alone at the beginning of conditioning. Shortly after the squirt of orange juice into the mouth, the firing of the VTA neuron increased. The firing of the VTA neuron to the CS after several CS–US pairings is shown in the lower tracing. Note that the VTA neuron now fired in response to the CS. CS-evoked firing indicates that the CS can function as a conditioned reinforcer, because the CS now stimulates the release of dopamine by the VTA neuron. Before the pairing of the CS with the US, the CS did not have this effect. If the CS were now to follow an operant response, such as lever pressing, the operant response would be reinforced by the CS. Note also in the lower tracing that the VTA neuron no longer fires when the US occurs. This is the neural basis of blocking: Once the CS activates VTA neurons, the US no longer activates them; similarly, any other stimulus that accompanied the light CS would not become a CS.

The neural pathways by which conditioned reinforcers activate VTA neurons are different from those of unconditioned reinforcers. The neural pathways mediating conditioned reinforcement arise from neurons in the frontal lobes that are activated by the CS. In human learners for whom many stimuli have acquired the ability to guide behavior, the opportunity for conditioned reinforcement via these pathways is enormous (Goldman-Rakic, 1996). As the environment changes with changes in a person's behavior, conditioned reinforcement via these pathways can be immediate and relatively continuous. Thus, behavior in the office at the beginning of the week is not, strictly speaking, reinforced by a paycheck at the end of the week, but by the immediate conditioned reinforcers that likely follow specific current responses. These immediate conditioned reinforcers include feedback from coworkers and that more subtle reinforcer of seeing a job well done.

Automatic Conditioned Reinforcement. The existence of conditioned reinforcement helps us understand the reinforcing effects of "seeing a job well done." Consider the acquisition of skills through trial and error. To begin with, if you wish to acquire a skill, you must be able to recognize the *target behavior*—the behavior that will ultimately be reinforced. Your first responses may produce stimuli that vaguely resemble those produced by the target behavior. These stimuli provide automatic (self-generated) conditioned reinforcers for approximations to the target behavior. Automatic conditioned reinforcement for approximations to the target behavior— automatic shaping—is not dependent on the intervention of another person. In nontechnical terms, you realize you are on the right path. When subsequent behavior even more closely approximates the target behavior, the stimuli that arise from these actions provide additional conditioned reinforcement. Skills such as the ability to draw a picture, catch a baseball, or make a bed all are behaviors that are aided by shaping with automatic

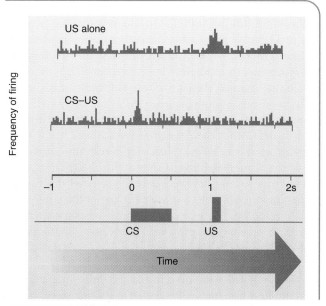

FIGURE 5•11 The frequency of firing of a single neuron in the ventral tegmental areas (VTA) of the midbrain. The upper tracing shows firing when the US was first presented. The lower tracing shows firing when a CS was presented after being paired with US.

reinforcement. This process is analogous to a lab experimenter's changing the criteria for reinforcers when training the behavior of an animal—except that no trainer is required, only the automatic feedback from stimuli produced when you make responses that ever more closely approximate the target behavior.

Automatic conditioned reinforcement plays a critical role in the acquisition of language. As an example, a child first learns to behave in response to the sound of a word—for example, to point to a dog in a picture book when a parent says, "Where's the dog?" Correct pointing behavior is reinforced by the parent. This sequence establishes the sound "dog" as a stimulus that guides behavior and, as such, also establishes hearing the word "dog" as a potential conditioned reinforcer. Later, as the child vocalizes, the closer its own speech sounds are to the sounds of adult speech, the greater the immediate and automatic reinforcement for the vocal responses that produced the sound.

Extinction

Thus far, we have considered the implications of basic reinforcement processes for the *acquisition* of behavior—for increases in the strength with which environmental stimuli guide behavior. But we know that experience can also weaken behavior. Learned behavior can also be lost, such as the French you learned in middle school or the calculus you learned only last week. There are many causes for losses in the ability of the environment to guide behavior. Here we will consider one important cause—extinction. In **extinction** a response that was previously reinforced is no longer reinforced, with the result that the behavior weakens.

To illustrate extinction, let's return to the well-controlled classical procedure I described earlier, in which a CS is presented to a rabbit followed by an aversive US applied in the region of the eye, thereby eliciting the UR of a nictitating-membrane response (Gibbs, Latham, & Gormezano, 1978). As shown in the left panel of **Figure 5•12**, when rabbits in three different groups were conditioned according to this procedure,

responding during the CS increased to a high level. This illustrates the effect of reinforcement on acquisition. The training procedure was then changed so that the percentages of CS presentations that were followed by the US were gradually decreased. One group of animals continued to receive the US after 100 percent of the CSs, but the second group was reduced to 50 percent and the third group to only 25 percent. As the middle panel of Figure 5.12 shows, slowly reducing the number of reinforcers had relatively little effect on the level of responding. This illustrates a general finding: Frequent reinforcers are required for rapid acquisition of behavior, but once established the behavior often may be maintained by less frequent reinforcers with relatively little loss in strength. (For other effects of decreases in reinforcement, however, see Nevin & Grace, 2005.)

The third panel of Figure 5.12 shows the effects of an extinction procedure. When the CS was no longer followed by any reinforcer at all, responding declined in strength until it reached low levels approximating those seen before conditioning. But look again at the extinction findings, and note that responding decreased in strength less rapidly if behavior had previously been maintained by *less* frequent reinforcement. This surprising finding is a general result: Responding that has been maintained by less frequent reinforcers is more resistant to the effects of extinction. Procedures in which not every instance of the behavior is followed by a reinforcer are known as **intermittent reinforcement** procedures, also known as *partial reinforcement* procedures. And research findings illustrate that intermittent reinforcement increases resistance to extinction. Many variables affect resistance to extinction. One is that training with intermittent reinforcement ensures that responses are reinforced under circumstances that more closely resemble those present during extinction, when reinforcers are absent altogether: Reinforcers are totally absent during extinction and are sometimes absent during intermittent reinforcement as well. The more similar the environment during learning is to the environment during extinction, the more persistent the behavior during extinction.

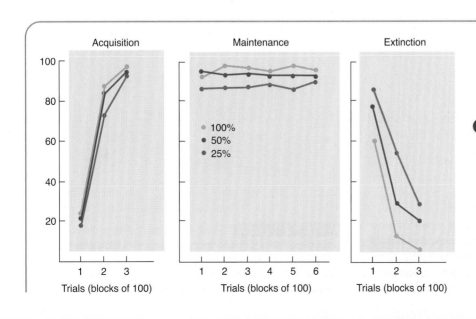

FIGURE 5•12 Conditioned responding during acquisition with CS–US pairings (left panel), during maintenance of conditioning with different percentages of CS–US pairings (middle panel), and during extinction when the US was not presented (right panel).

(Adapted from Gibbs, C. M., Latham, S. B., & Gormezano, I. (1978). Classical schedule and resistance to extinction. *Animal Learning and Behavior, 6,* 209–215.)

▲ *Highly skilled athletes make complicated behavior seem easy. Such skilled behavior is the result of thousands of hours of practice and comes with much effort and only intermittent reinforcement. Can the pattern of reinforcement make a difference between athletes who persevere and those who do not?*

It would be incorrect to conclude that extinction completely eliminates the effects of prior reinforcement. If reinforcement is reinstituted after the response has undergone extinction, the response rapidly recovers its former strength. Reacquisition after extinction is generally much more rapid than original acquisition. Also, if some time has elapsed between an extinction procedure and the test for retention, the learned response usually recovers some of its strength. The increase in responding on return to the training environment after an extinction procedure is called **spontaneous recovery**. Both rapid reacquisition and spontaneous recovery demonstrate that extinction does not completely remove the effects of prior learning.

As with resistance to extinction, rapid reacquisition and spontaneous recovery are affected by many variables (Donahoe & Palmer, 1994; Kehoe, 1988). One major variable is that all of the stimuli that acquired control of the response during acquisition may not be present during extinction. Both environmental and intraorganismic (internal) stimuli vary over time. If some of the stimuli that were present during acquisition were not present during extinction, then their control of behavior would not be eliminated: Responding would reemerge if these stimuli recurred. We saw an example of the recurrence of learned behavior with conditioned drug-withdrawal responses: These responses, which had been extinguished during drug rehabilitation, were again evoked by the environment when the addict returned to the settings in which the addiction had been acquired.

Stimulus Generalization

Until this point we have focused on behavioral changes that can be observed in the specific environment in which a behavior was reinforced. But the effects of experience must transcend the specifics of the environment during acquisition if the learning process is to be efficient. A child who learns to catch a green ball should also improve his or her skill to catch

a red ball. Experimental work has amply documented that the effects of reinforcement are not restricted to the specific environment in which learning takes place. The process by which learning in one environment affects behavior in similar environments is called **stimulus generalization**.

For a clear-cut example of stimulus generalization, let's return to the controlled environment of the animal laboratory. Experimenters used food as a reinforcer to train pigeons to peck a yellow-green disk (wavelength of 550 nanometers, or nm) located on the wall of a test chamber (Hanson, 1959). Training was conducted with intermittent reinforcement so that the operant response would be resistant to the effects of extinction. Once responding was stable, the color on the disk was occasionally varied during short periods in which reinforcers were not given. Evidence of stimulus generalization would be found if pecking occurred to test stimuli that differed from the yellow-green training stimulus. The results of the experiment are shown in **Figure 5•13**. Even though operant responding had been reinforced only during the yellow-green stimulus, responses occurred to other stimuli. Moreover, the degree to which responses occurred varied with the similarity of the test stimuli to the training stimulus. When the disk was green or yellow, it was pecked more often than when it was blue or orange.

Behavior that has been reinforced in one environment will occur in other environments if the other environments contain stimuli in common with those in which the behavior has previously been reinforced. Stimulus generalization has been demonstrated in the laboratory with a wide range of stimuli and learners, including humans (Thomas & Thomas, 1974). As experience accumulates, the mixture of environment–behavior relations that can occur in any given environment increases enormously. Stimulus generalization produces an increasingly rich mixture of behavior, whose constituents are available for strengthening and modification by other reinforcers— reinforcers that are increasingly conditioned reinforcers.

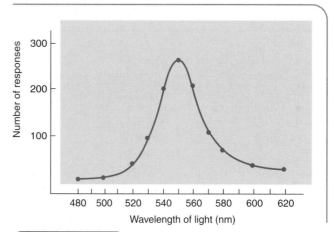

FIGURE 5•13 Generalized responding to various colors (wavelengths) after training to respond to a yellow-green color (550 nm).

(Adapted from Hanson, H. M. (1959). Effects of discrimination training on stimulus generalization. *Journal of Experimental Psychology, 38,* 1–16.)

Stimulus Discrimination Because similar behavior is often reinforced in similar environments, stimulus generalization benefits the learner. For example, the person who acquires good conversational skills with friends can use those same skills when meeting new people. However, similar behavior is not always reinforced in similar environments. Some people may not be interested in conversing, and even friends do not wish to converse in some situations. A friend may be in a bad mood or may be studying in the library. When experience causes behavior to change as the situation changes, a **stimulus discrimination** is said to be formed. Stimulus discrimination occurs when behavior has different consequences in different environments, even when the environments may be quite similar.

Again, the animal laboratory provides the clearest examples of the formation of stimulus discriminations. In the laboratory, we can better control prior experience with the various stimuli. As one example, pigeons whose pecking had been reinforced when the disk was yellow-green received additional training in which the yellow-green color (550 nm) on the disk alternated with a yellow color (555 nm). Unlike responding to the yellow-green color, responding during yellow was never followed by food (Hanson, 1959). That is, an extinction procedure was instituted during the yellow color. In contrast to the stimulus generalization shown in Figure 5.13, responding to the 555-nm yellow stimulus decreased during testing from about 200 responses to less than 25 responses, even though the test stimulus was very similar to the training stimulus. For more dissimilar stimuli—such as orange—responding fell to essentially zero. A procedure in which a response has different consequences in different environments is called a **differential conditioning procedure**. Differential conditioning produces stimulus discrimination. Stimuli that guide behavior after differential conditioning are called **discriminative stimuli**.

The differential conditioning procedure just described is an example of a *three-term contingency*. A simple classical procedure exemplifies a two-term stimulus–reinforcer contingency. A simple operant procedure exemplifies a two-term response–reinforcer contingency. The three terms in differential conditioning are stimulus–response–reinforcer. In the experiment with pigeons, differential conditioning was given in which responding was reinforced when the color was yellow-green, but not when it was yellow. We may ask what occurs when a differential conditioning procedure institutes still higher-order contingencies. As an example of a four-term contingency, suppose that during a green stimulus a response to a triangular form is reinforced, but not a response to a circular form. On other trials in which a red stimulus is present, the three-term contingency is reversed: A response to the circle is now reinforced, but not a response to the triangle (see **Figure 5.14**). In this procedure the consequences of responding depend on *both* color and shape, a four-term contingency—color–shape–response–reinforcer. As the color context changes, reinforcement for responding to the shapes changes as well. For this reason, procedures that implement four-term contingencies are also described as **contextual discriminations**.

Equivalence Classes Differential conditioning with the more complex procedures of contextual discriminations also has been studied in the laboratory. Four-term stimulus discriminations have been acquired by both animal and human learners. Of greatest interest, Sidman (1994) discovered that human learners who have acquired several four-term stimulus discriminations display emergent behavior that has not yet been found with nonhuman animals. Specifically, after a human learner has acquired multiple four-term discriminations—for example, an S1–S2–response–reinforcer contingency and an S2–S3–response–reinforcer contingency—the learner responds appropriately to new stimulus combinations such as S1–S1, S2–S1, or S3–S1 *without further training*. Consider the stimulus combination S3–S1. This notation signifies that in stimulus context S3 the learner responds to S1 when given a choice between responding to S1 and another stimulus. This occurs even though responding to S1 was never reinforced in the context of S3. Human learners with a history of multiple four-term stimulus discriminations respond to new combinations of stimuli as if they were equivalent to one another. Such emergent discriminations are taken as evidence that for humans the stimuli become members of an *equivalence class* that includes all of the sets of stimuli used in training. As mentioned earlier, despite substantial experimental work, these emergent contextual discriminations have not been unequivocally observed in nonhuman animals (Sidman et al., 1982). The origin of this difference is not known—whether it is due to prior experiences that are thus far unique to humans or to differences in brain structure (Donahoe & Palmer, 1994).

One application of research on equivalence classes has been a technique for teaching intellectually impaired children to read without explicit training in reading. In one case a mentally disabled boy could correctly respond with spoken words only to pictures of objects, not to the printed names of the objects. He was then trained to point to the correct printed word among several choices when he heard that word spoken by someone else. Note that the child had not been trained to respond to printed words with spoken words (that is, to read orally). Nevertheless, after acquiring these contextual discriminations, the child was able to speak the correct word when

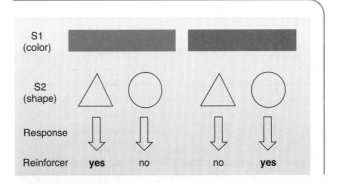

FIGURE 5·14 A contextual discrimination with which the shape (S2) to which responding is reinforced (either circle or triangle) depends on the color (S1) of the context (green or red).

FIGURE 5·15 After a child with mental disabilities had learned to speak the name of an object when seeing its picture (left panel) and to point to an object when seeing the printed word (middle panel), the child was able to speak the name of the object when seeing the printed word (right panel). That is, the child was capable of oral reading without explicit training.

Learned relation
picture = spoken word
S1 = S2

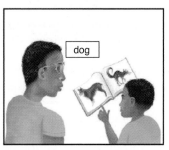

Learned relation
printed word = picture
S3 = S1

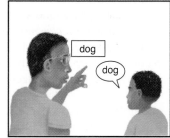

Emergent relation
printed word = spoken word
S3 = S2 (oral reading)

presented with the printed word. (See **Figure 5·15.**) That is, the child was capable of oral reading! Reading emerged without explicit training. Moreover, the child could then also pick out the correct picture when presented with the printed word (a measure of reading comprehension). This also occurred without additional training. Understandably, the study of stimulus discriminations with four-term contingencies is an active area of research because of both its theoretical and its practical implications (Hayes & Barnes-Holmes, 2001; Palmer, 2004).

Punishment

We have thus far considered only cases in which behavior is followed by a stimulus that strengthens the behavior. That is, the stimulus functions as a reinforcer. In the classical (Pavlov) procedure, when a tone is followed by food, salivation to the tone increases. In the operant (Thorndike) procedure, if a lever press is followed by food, lever pressing increases. In **punishment,** however, the presentation of an eliciting stimulus *weakens* the measured behavior. If an operant response is followed by an eliciting stimulus and the operant response decreases in strength, then the eliciting stimulus has functioned as a **punisher,** or punishing stimulus. Stimuli that function as punishers elicit **escape** or **withdrawal responses** as well as a variety of emotional responses mediated by the autonomic nervous system. In the animal laboratory, researchers can study punishment by occasionally following a food-reinforced response by a moderate electric shock. For example, a rat's lever pressing decreases from its food-reinforced level; shock has functioned as a punisher. In daily life a punishment procedure occurs when a child reaches for food cooking on a stove and the hot food burns the child's hand. Reaching for food on a stove decreases; the burn has functioned as a punisher.

How may we understand punishment in terms of the basic learning processes that we described earlier in the chapter? We can gain insight into punishment by recognizing that two sets of responses are acquired in an operant procedure—the

operant response that precedes the eliciting stimulus, and the elicited response that is evoked by the eliciting stimulus. Thus, when a lever press is followed by food, lever pressing increases in strength but so does salivation. When an eliciting stimulus functions as a reinforcer, these two responses—the operant and the CR—do not interfere with one another; a rat can press a lever and salivate at the same time. However, if food-reinforced lever pressing is followed by shock, a different situation arises. Now, the CRs conditioned to environmental stimuli include shock-elicited escape responses and an array of emotional responses mediated by the autonomic nervous system. The rat cannot simultaneously press the lever and escape from the region where the lever is located (that is, the region where the shock was administered). Because of interference between lever pressing and the various shock-elicited conditioned responses, lever pressing decreases in strength. Similarly with the child

▲ *Punishment occurs when an aversive stimulus immediately follows a response. Punishment need not involve a physically aversive event; social disapproval also can be punishing. Punishers elicit withdrawal, escape, and emotional behavior, so they must be used with caution.*

whose hand is burned while reaching for food on the stove. The child cannot simultaneously extend his hand (which would potentially be reinforced by attaining the food) and withdraw his hand (which is elicited by the hot food).

The interaction between operants and conditioned responses can be studied in the laboratory by the **conditioned-emotional response (CER)** procedure (Estes & Skinner, 1941), also known as the conditioned-suppression procedure. This procedure uses interference between operants and shock-elicited conditioned responses to provide an indirect measure of emotional responses. In the CER procedure, a stimulus (such as a tone) is paired with electric shock, and the tone is occasionally presented while an animal is engaged in reinforced operant behavior (such as food-reinforced lever pressing). After several tone–shock pairings, operant responding decreases during the tone even before the paired shock occurs. This decrease is taken as evidence that emotional responses are interfering with the operant. Scientists often use the CER procedure to evaluate drugs that are intended to reduce anxiety. If the drug is effective, responding during the tone does not decrease—presumably because the drug has suppressed the emotional responses that are conditioned to the tone.

An elicited response interferes with the operant response in the case of punishment. However, elicited responses can sometimes facilitate responding in an operant procedure. Consider the case in which pecking a lighted disk by a pigeon is followed by food. Here, the operant response is pecking, and the food-elicited unconditioned response is also pecking. Not surprisingly, acquisition of pecking is very rapid under these conditions. In fact, pigeons acquire a disk-pecking response even without an operant contingency. If the disk is illuminated just before food is presented (a classical contingency), the pigeon will come to peck the disk even though pecking the disk is not required to obtain the food. This phenomenon is called *autoshaping* (Brown & Jenkins, 1968). The contribution of reinforcer-elicited responses to autoshaping can be shown when different reinforcers are used. With food as the reinforcer, the pigeon opens its beak when it strikes the disk as if it were eating. With water as the reinforcer, the pigeon swallows when it strikes the disk as it were drinking. The relation between the operant response and responses elicited by the reinforcer must be considered outside the laboratory as well. As a particularly problematic example, spanking a child for crying attempts to punish crying by following it with a stimulus that evokes the very behavior that the parent is trying to decrease. In addition to its many other drawbacks, this is not an effective punishment procedure.

Punishment can be very effective, and the real-world environment provides many naturally occurring punishment contingencies. A child who touches hot food on a stove is unlikely to touch it again. The hand-withdrawal response elicited by the painful stimulus gains strength immediately and prevents the child from reaching for food on the stove in the future. Punishment contingencies also can be effective when implemented by the social environment—that is, by another person. When one person punishes the behavior of

▲ *Punishment takes many forms. The aversive consequences of a penalty reduce the likelihood of an infraction.*

another, it is often effective, at least temporarily. The offending behavior ceases, which immediately reinforces the behavior of the one administering the punishment. For example, a parent whose television viewing is interrupted by his child's talking can stop the talking by shouting, "Be quiet!" Remember, however, that the emotional responses elicited by shouting can become conditioned to the sight of the parent. The result is not only that the child stops the offending talking but also that the child is likely to avoid the parent in the future. The short-term consequences of punishers may be effective, but their longer-term effects are less so.

The example of the social punisher of shouting "Be quiet!" illustrates a second point. By being paired with unconditioned punishing stimuli, the loud voice of the parent and removal from the family room, a formerly neutral stimulus, such as the words, "Be quiet!," becomes a *conditioned punisher*. There are both conditioned punishers and unconditioned punishers, just as there are conditioned and unconditioned reinforcers. But conditioned punishers are not effective in the long run unless they are occasionally followed by an unconditioned punisher. Thus, "Be quiet!" becomes ineffective as a conditioned punisher if nothing is done when the behavior persists after the warning. The child will come to ignore the warning. Removal from the family room might reinstate "Be quiet" as an effective punisher, but it also would recondition withdrawal and emotional responses to the parent. To reduce the offending response of talking while the television is on, a parent is better advised to provide a young child with reinforcers for some behavior that competes with talking, such as the opportunity to play with a toy.

Figure 5•16 summarizes the possible procedural arrangements of appetitive and aversive stimuli with responses that produce or terminate them. The effects of these procedural

FIGURE 5•16 Possible arrangements between behavior with appetitive or aversive stimuli. Behavior may either produce or terminate the stimulus. The effects of the arrangements are shown by the arrows; an "up" arrow indicates that the behavior is strengthened, and a "down" arrow indicates that it is weakened.

	Appetitive Stimulus	Aversive Stimulus
Target response **produces** the stimulus	Positive reinforcement ⬆	Punishment (also positive punishment) ⬇
Target response **terminates** the stimulus	Negative punishment (also response cost) ⬇	Negative reinforcement ⬆

arrangements can be understood as combinations of the processes of reinforcement and punishment. In the figure, note that the term "reinforcement" is reserved for those arrangements that *increase* the strength of the target response, and "punishment" is reserved for those arrangements that *decrease* the target response. Consider negative reinforcement. **Negative reinforcement** occurs when a response that terminates an aversive stimulus produces an increase in the strength of that response. For example, suppose that in the laboratory a rat can terminate an electric shock by performing the target response of pressing a lever. All responses other than lever pressing are followed by shock. Under these conditions, lever pressing becomes stronger. As an illustration with human behavior, consider the case in which a parent is scolding a child for not doing his or her homework where doing homework is the target response. Doing homework terminates scolding and also allows the child—we hope—to receive the reinforcers that occur from seeing the homework completed. Scolding has negatively reinforced doing homework.

Negative punishment, in contrast, occurs when an appetitive stimulus is terminated by a target response with the result that the target response decreases in strength. For example, suppose that you are enjoying a pleasant conversation with an attractive person whom you have just met. You make a critical comment about someone else, not knowing that this person is a friend of your attractive new acquaintance. Your new acquaintance's smile suddenly disappears and is replaced by a frown. You quickly change the subject to a more pleasant

topic. In this case the target behavior (the critical comment) terminated an appetitive stimulus (your new acquaintance's smile) and the critical comments disappeared. Negative punishment procedures, also known as *response-cost* procedures, often are employed in applications outside the laboratory. For example, a child that is acting up in class is made to leave the classroom and go into a *time-out* room. Acting up, the target response, is punished by isolation in the time-out room—that is, by removal of the companionship and stimulation available in the regular classroom.

Evaluating Scientific Issues

What Is Insight?

Many problems that we solve in our daily lives require us to behave in ways that we have never done before. We may think about a problem, look at its elements, and try to imagine various solutions. We explore various options in our heads. Suddenly, we think of a new approach. We try it, and it works! In such cases we say that we solved the problem through insight.

But what is insight? Some people see it as almost a magical process: a sudden flash of inspiration, a bolt from the blue, an answer coming from nowhere. Most people regard insight as a particularly human ability—or, at least, as an ability that belongs to our species and perhaps to some other higher primates. But what if at least some instances of behavior that would be described as insightful are in fact the cumulative outcome of fundamental learning processes?

● **Insight in Other Primates**
During the early 1900s the German psychologist Wolfgang Köhler studied problem solving in chimpanzees. In one famous example (Köhler, 1927/1973), Köhler suspended some bananas from the ceiling of the cage housing Sultan, one of the chimps, just high enough to be out of reach. The cage also contained a large box. Sultan first tried to jump up to reach the bananas, then paced around the cage, stopped in front of the box, pushed it toward the bananas, climbed onto the box, and retrieved and ate the fruit. (See **Figure 5•17.**) Later, when the bananas were suspended even higher, he stacked up several boxes—and on one occasion when no boxes were present, he grabbed Köhler by the hand, led him over to the bananas, and climbed on top of him.

Köhler believed that Sultan had displayed insightful problem-solving behavior that could not be understood in

▲ *Our use of umbrellas when it is raining is a negatively reinforced behavior. Opening an umbrella blocks the rain that would otherwise fall on us.*

FIGURE 5•17 Insight in the chimpanzee. On observing the behavior of the chimpanzee Sultan, Köhler inferred the mental process he called "insight." Confronted with bananas suspended out of reach from the ceiling, Sultan moved a box under the bananas and climbed onto the box (or, in another instance, onto Köhler himself) to reach the bananas. (Photos © SuperStock)

terms of the basic learning processes studied by Thorndike. Thorndike's cats learned by trial and error, arriving at the solution by accident. Escape from the puzzle box and food served as reinforcing stimuli, and eventually the animals acquired the ability to operate the latch efficiently. The behavior of Sultan seemed very different. He would suddenly come up with a solution, often after simply looking over the situation and with little overt behavior. Köhler saw no evidence of accidental trial-and-error behavior. On the basis of his observations, Köhler proposed that a new mental process—insight—must be taking place.

● A Behavioral Interpretation of Insight

More recent work suggests that insight may be less mysterious than it appears, however. In fact, insight may actually be based on combinations of behaviors initially learned through trial and error. In one study with pigeons (Epstein, Kirshnit, Lanza, & Rubin, 1984), the researchers used operant procedures (with food as the reinforcer) to condition two behaviors: (1) pushing a box toward a green spot placed at various locations on the floor and (2) climbing onto a box and pecking at a miniature plastic banana that was suspended overhead. Flying up to peck the banana was never reinforced (an extinction procedure). Once the two target behaviors had been acquired, the researchers presented the pigeon with a new situation—the box was in one part of the chamber, without a spot on the floor, and the suspended banana was in a different part.

> At first, the bird appeared to be confused: It stretched toward the banana, turned back and forth from the banana to the box, and so on. Then, rather suddenly, it began to push the box toward the banana, sighting the banana and readjusting the path of the box as it pushed. Finally, it stopped pushing when the box was near the banana, climbed onto the box, and pecked the banana. (Epstein, 1985, p. 132)

The pigeon had acted in much the same way as Sultan. (See **Figure 5•18.**) If an observer had not known the learning history of the pigeon, the pigeon's behavior might also have been attributed to insight or some other mental process.

In a control experiment, other pigeons received food for standing on the box and pecking the plastic banana and for simply pushing the box around the chamber instead of pushing it toward particular locations marked by a spot on the floor. These birds usually did not "solve" the problem; they pushed the box aimlessly around the chamber, not to a location underneath the suspended banana. Thus, the learning history had to include a specific set of environment–behavior relations if the problem were to be solved. Epstein (1987) went on to reinforce even more complex responses in pigeons. A pigeon would receive food for (1) pecking a plastic banana, (2) climbing onto a box, (3) opening a door in the transparent chamber wall, and (4) pushing a box toward a spot on the floor. Then, the pigeon would be confronted with a banana hanging above its head, but the box would be behind the door. The pigeon now would combine all four behaviors: It would open the door, push the box into the chamber, move the box under the banana, climb onto the box, and peck the banana.

FIGURE 5•18   Insight in the pigeon. The pigeon was confronted with a small plastic banana suspended out of reach from the ceiling of the test chamber. During the pigeon's training, both pushing a box and pecking a reachable banana had been reinforced with food. (Flying to the banana had been extinguished.) After its training the pigeon pushed the box under the banana, climbed onto the box, and pecked the banana, even though the bird had never been trained to make this sequence of responses.

(Photos © Norman Baxley/Baxley Media Group.)

The demonstrations with pigeons indicate that so-called insightful behavior may emerge from combinations of previously discriminated environment–behavior relations. Only after the pigeons had acquired the individual responses were they able to solve the problems. Presumably, Sultan's prior experience had included moving objects around, climbing on objects, climbing on objects to reach other objects, and so on. Sultan had lived in the wild, and Köhler did not know Sultan's learning history. Therefore, we cannot interpret Sultan's behavior with the confidence that we can bring to the case of a lab pigeon whose history is known. However, other work with chimpanzees indicated that they solve problems such as Köhler's only if they have prior experience with the objects (Birch, 1945).

● **What Should We Conclude?**

In Chapter 2 you learned about the *nominal fallacy,* the mistaken belief that we can explain a phenomenon simply by naming it. So it is important to realize that simply labeling behavior as insightful does not help us to understand it. If we do not know the behavior that an animal has already acquired, a novel and complex sequence of responses may seem to come from nowhere. Our ignorance of the learner's history may lead us to attribute the complex behavior to something inside of the learner—to insight, rather than to the animal's history. To understand the conditions that are necessary for insight to occur, we need to know more than the current situation; we need to know the learner's conditioning history.

The scientist's challenge is to dissect even the most complex behavior to understand its true causes. Perhaps chimpanzees, like humans, can solve problems through some sort of mental imagery, testing possible solutions in their heads before trying them. But if such constructs as "mental imagery" and "testing solutions in their heads" are to be used, they too must be subjected to experimental analysis (Donahoe & Palmer, 1994). Whatever the case, neither humans nor chimpanzees can imagine or think about objects they have never seen or actions they have never taken.

Interim Summary

The Outcomes of Learning

The occurrence of an eliciting stimulus after a stimulus in the classical procedure or after a response in the operant procedure produces *acquisition* of responding. The eliciting stimulus has functioned as a reinforcer. With more complex behavior, acquisition often requires *shaping,* whereby the criteria for presenting the reinforcer gradually change to approximate the target behavior. Stimuli function as *unconditioned reinforcers* when they elicit behavior because of natural selection. Stimuli function as *conditioned reinforcers* when they evoke behavior because of prior learning, as occurs when a tone has been paired with food. Conditioned reinforcers play an increasingly important role in the acquisition of behavior as the learner gains experience. Conditioned reinforcers are available from both the environment and from stimuli produced by the learner's own behavior, as in the case of *automatic reinforcement*. Research at the neural level of investigation indicates that unconditioned and conditioned reinforcers exploit the same neural system of reinforcement—a widely projecting neuromodulatory system that changes the strengths of synaptic connections throughout large regions of the brain. The net effect of learning is to adapt the individual's behavior to the behavior required to obtain reinforcers in that environment.

After the environmental guidance of behavior has been changed by reinforcement, the strength of an acquired response decreases if reinforcers are no longer forthcoming for the behavior; that is, the response undergoes *extinction*. Extinction occurs less rapidly if intermittent reinforcement is used during acquisition. Extinction does not completely eliminate the effects of prior reinforcement on behavior, however. Responding can be rapidly reacquired if the response is again reinforced, and it also may recover some of its strength after the passage of time (*spontaneous recovery*). All of the various stimuli that are present when the response is reinforced must lose their ability to guide the response before the effect of prior reinforcement is undone.

Reinforcers do not simply change the strength of behavior; they change its strength in the environment in which the behavior was reinforced. To the extent that other environments contain stimuli that are shared with the environment in which behavior was reinforced, those other environments also guide behavior. This is called *stimulus generalization*. For behavior to be restricted to the environment in which it was reinforced, *stimulus discrimination* must occur. Stimulus discrimination occurs when behavior has different consequences in other environments. This is called *differential conditioning*. Differential conditioning occurs when behavior is followed by a reinforcer in one environment but is not followed by a reinforcer in similar environments; that is, when extinction occurs in similar environments. Differential conditioning restricts stimulus generalization of responding, and the acquired response now occurs in only those environments in which it was reinforced.

In a particularly interesting and potentially important instance of stimulus discrimination, human learners can acquire multiple *contextual discriminations*. In a contextual discrimination the response to a stimulus is reinforced only when it occurs in the presence of another stimulus (the context). After multiple contextual discriminations, appropriate responding occurs with new combinations of the stimuli that appeared during contextual-discrimination training. The emergence of these untrained discriminations has been interpreted to indicate that stimuli in the various contextual discriminations become members of an *equivalence class*. Evidence for the formation of equivalence classes is, as yet, largely restricted to humans.

Some eliciting stimuli that follow operant responses decrease rather than strengthen the operant. Such stimuli function as *punishers*. Punishers are aversive stimuli that elicit withdrawal and escape responses, which become conditioned to the stimuli accompanying the operant response; these withdrawal responses then interfere with the operant. Stimuli that have been paired with aversive stimuli can function as *conditioned punishers* for other behavior.

The basic conditioning processes involved in reinforcement and punishment can be implemented in several procedural arrangements. Behavior may be strengthened when it is followed by either presenting an appetitive stimulus or terminating an aversive stimulus—positive and negative reinforcement, respectively. Behavior may be weakened when it is followed by either presenting an aversive stimulus or terminating an appetitive stimulus—positive and negative punishment, respectively.

Finally, even complex behavior such as the solution of problems by novel sequences of responses—what Köhler called insight—may be understandable as the cumulative product of the fundamental learning processes.

QUESTIONS TO CONSIDER

1. Knowing what you do about the outcomes of learning, what are some things that you might do to increase the chances that, after rehabilitation in a drug treatment center, an addict does not relapse when returned to the community?

2. Comment on the following: Basic learning processes operate over only very short time intervals. Therefore, basic learning processes cannot explain why a person studies in college, because studying does not lead to a job until years later.

Cellular Mechanisms of Reinforcement

We have already encountered some of the neural systems that play a role in reinforcement. Reinforcers activate VTA neurons in the midbrain whose axons project widely throughout major portions of the brain. Both unconditioned reinforcers, such as food, and conditioned reinforcers, such as stimuli paired with food, have this effect, although conditioned and unconditioned reinforcers activate these midbrain neurons via different pathways. The axons of the midbrain neurons liberate the neuromodulator dopamine; and because of its widespread distribution, dopamine affects many synapses simultaneously. But how does dopamine affect transmission at the synapse?

A full account of the cellular mechanisms of reinforcement would be beyond the scope of this book, and research on these mechanisms is very much a work in progress in any case. Nevertheless, the general outlines of the answer are emerging, instigated in large part by the pioneering work of Eric Kandel (Pittenger & Kandel, 2003). Kandel began his work with a marine mollusk, *Aplysia*, whose nervous system was small and whose neurons could be individually identified. A simple nervous system offered the controlled conditions the researchers needed to isolate fundamental processes. Kandel's work on neural transmission during learning, which began back in the 1960s (Kandel & Spencer, 1968), was recognized with a Nobel Prize that he shared with two other scientists in 2000. With the development of new and more refined experimental techniques, much current work on the cellular mechanisms of reinforcement is focused on neurons in mammalian nervous systems and that is the work summarized here.

Long-Term Potentiation

Figure 5•19 depicts some of the cellular events that occur when a presynaptic neuron increases its ability to activate a postsynaptic neuron; that is, when synaptic efficacy increases. As you will recall from Chapter 4, neurons affect one another through the liberation of neurotransmitters, and the primary excitatory neurotransmitter in the brain is glutamate. An excitatory transmitter is a molecule that facilitates the production of an action potential in the postsynaptic neuron. Glutamate liberated by the presynaptic neuron acts on two main types of glutamate receptors in the cell membrane of a postsynaptic neuron. One glutamate receptor—the AMPA receptor—rapidly facilitates the initiation of a nerve impulse in the postsynaptic neuron. A second type of glutamate receptor—the NMDA receptor—plays a different role, but a role that is crucial if glutamate-induced firing is to produce long-lasting changes in synaptic efficacies. Normally, the channel in the NMDA receptor is blocked by a magnesium ion (Mg^{2+}). However, if the postsynaptic neuron is sufficiently stimulated through the action of AMPA receptors, the electrical potential across the membrane of the postsynaptic neuron changes, and the magnesium ion migrates out of the channel. The opening of the ion channel of the NMDA receptor permits calcium ions (Ca^{2+}) to enter the cell. When calcium enters the postsynaptic neuron, a sequence of intracellular events occurs—and one key event is the placement of a molecular "tag" on AMPA receptors that have just been acted upon by glutamate. This tag lasts for only several hours and marks those receptors as having been recently stimulated by glutamate (Bailey, Kandel, & Si, 2004; Frey & Morris, 1998).

If the neural pathways that have recently been activated are followed by behavior that produces a reinforcer, then dopaminergic neurons in midbrain nuclei are stimulated. The neuromodulator dopamine is liberated from *varicosities* (enlargements) distributed along the axons of these neurons. Dopamine diffuses into the extracellular space where it can act at the synapses of many neurons. When dopamine receptors are engaged at about the same time as AMPA and NMDA receptors, the concerted effect initiates a series of *second messengers* (intracellular events). The second messengers activate genes in the nucleus of the cell that lead to the synthesis of new proteins. These proteins migrate down the axon and, when they contact tagged receptors, produce long-lasting structural changes in these receptors. Following this sequence of intracellular events, when the presynaptic neuron subsequently liberates glutamate, there is a higher probability of initiating an action potential in the

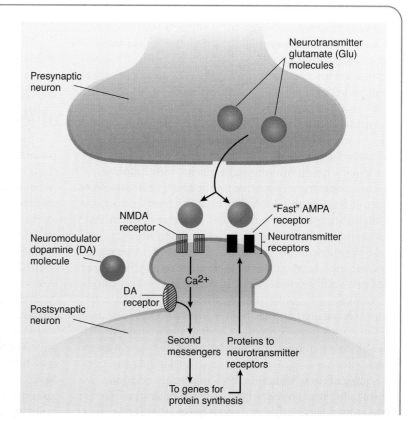

FIGURE 5•19 Some of the cellular events that take place during learning. As a result of the process diagrammed here, the presynaptic neuron becomes more able to activate the postsynaptic neuron. This process occurs during long-term potentiation.

postsynaptic neuron. Glutamate opens the ion channels in AMPA receptors for a longer time and/or more glutamate receptors are opened. The net result is that synaptic efficacies are increased along the pathways in which environmental stimuli have initiated neural activity that led to reinforced behavior. Note that the synaptic tags that mark recently active receptors allow the delayed synthesis of proteins to be distributed generally but to have effects that are specific to the AMPA receptors that were involved in the reinforced environment–behavior relation. Researchers can produce changes in synaptic efficacy in the laboratory by electrically stimulating presynaptic neurons to produce what is called **long-term potentiation** (Bliss & Lomø, 1973). As I noted earlier, the cellular mechanisms of reinforcement are more complex than described here, and they may involve changes in presynaptic as well as postsynaptic neurons (Frey, 1997). Nevertheless, a coherent picture of reinforcement is developing that extends from the intracellular to the neural to the behavioral level of observation.

Sensory Learning

Sensory learning is a process whereby an environment–environment relation is acquired by the learner. This chapter has focused on the acquisition of environment–behavior relations: In the presence of stimuli, some response occurs and is followed by a reinforcer. As a result, the response becomes stronger in the presence of these stimuli. However, organisms learn about the relations between environmental stimuli as well as between stimuli and responses. For example, if a rat is permitted to wander about a maze without receiving food for exploring, the rat nevertheless learns the maze faster if it is later given food for navigating the maze. This phenomenon is called **latent learning** (Tolman & Honzik, 1930). While exploring, the rat learned about the relation between stimuli in the maze, and this facilitated its learning to navigate the maze when running was reinforced. But the rat's learning about the relation between stimuli was not expressed in behavior until running was reinforced; that is, the learning was latent. How are stimulus–stimulus relations acquired?

As Chapter 8 will discuss, a brain structure called the hippocampus plays a very important role in memory. The hippocampus (shown in Figure 4.35) is a structure located within the temporal lobe of the brain that receives inputs from polysensory neurons of the sensory association cortex and sends multisynaptic outputs back to those same regions. Polysensory neurons are cells that can be activated by sensory inputs from more than one sensory channel—for example, from both visual and auditory neurons or from both color and location neurons within the visual system. It is thought that the coordinated stimulation of a polysensory neuron by its sensory inputs, when combined with the activity of inputs from the hippocampus, increases the likelihood that the polysensory neuron will fire. The joint firing of a polysensory neuron and its inputs causes synaptic efficacies to increase. In this way, polysensory neurons become cells that respond to the conjunction of stimuli. For example, a given group of polysensory neurons might fire on the conjunction of a light and a tone or on the conjunction of a

particular color at a particular location within the visual field. These polysensory neurons then become able to guide behavior when a response is reinforced after the co-occurrence of these stimuli. It is sometimes said that the process leads the animal to form *cognitive maps* of its environment.

Laboratory experimenters study the process whereby the co-occurrence of stimuli guide behavior by reinforcing a response when a tone and light are presented together, but not when either the tone or light is presented separately. This differential conditioning procedure is called a *stimulus patterning procedure*. Research indicates that the acquisition of stimulus patterning requires a properly functioning hippocampus (Rudy, 1991). Moreover, neuroanatomical research reveals that the dopamine-releasing neurons in the midbrain send projections to the hippocampus as well as to areas where they affect the synaptic efficacies of neurons that mediate environment–behavior relations (Swanson, 1982). In fact, the cells in the hippocampus that receive inputs from dopamine-releasing neurons are the very cells that have been most frequently studied in investigations of long-term potentiation. Although reinforcement may not be necessary for the development of polysensory cells in the cortex, it can facilitate changes in synaptic efficacies from sensory inputs to polysensory neurons (Donahoe, 1997). In this way, reinforcers coordinate the strengthening of environment–environment relations as well as environment–behavior relations.

Interim Summary

Cellular Mechanisms of Reinforcement

Instigated by the pioneering work of Eric Kandel, researchers are beginning to understand some of the important cellular processes that occur during learning. Much of this understanding comes from studying long-term potentiation, a laboratory phenomenon that is thought to involve the same cellular processes that occur during learning. The stimulation of receptors on a postsynaptic neuron by the neurotransmitter glutamate released from a presynaptic neuron can produce long-lasting changes in the structure of the glutamate receptor. The change in the glutamate receptor causes the postsynaptic neuron to become more responsive to stimulation by glutamate on future occasions. Long-lasting changes in the structure of the glutamate receptor occur when behavior produces reinforcers that cause liberation of the neuromodulator dopamine to accompany stimulation by glutamate. Over repeated occasions, these cellular processes change the synaptic efficacies along the neural pathways that mediate reinforced environment–behavior relations.

Behavior is often guided by complex combinations of environmental stimuli. Thus, behavioral change requires learning about relations between environmental stimuli as well as between the environment and behavior. Sensory learning occurs when neurons in sensory-association cortex become responsive to *combinations* of stimuli through the effects of inputs of neurons arising from the hippocampus. The hippocampus produces these changes most rapidly when reinforcers accompany the stimulation of sensory-association neurons, although some sensory learning takes place in the absence of reinforcers as in latent learning.

QUESTIONS TO CONSIDER

1. Substances that are commonly abused—such as cocaine, amphetamine, and alcohol—are all known to cause the release of dopamine. From what you know about the cellular mechanisms of learning, why might these substances promote drug-seeking behavior (addiction)?

2. From what you know about sensory learning, why might a passenger in a car not remember as much as the driver of the car about a new route that they have just traveled together?

Behavior in Experienced Learners

The science of behavior takes as its working hypothesis the premise that even the most complex human behavior is the cumulative product of fundamental evolutionary and learning processes. As experience accumulates, the learner acquires an ever richer repertoire of ways in which the environment can guide behavior and an ever larger number of environmental events that can function as reinforcers. As already noted, these reinforcers are increasingly conditioned as opposed to unconditioned reinforcers. In this final section of the chapter, we'll consider two products of an extensive history of reinforcement—instructional control and observational learning.

Instructional Control

In the complex behavior of humans, reinforcers do not generally await the random emission of "correct" responses. Instead, other persons provide stimuli, such as instructions, that make the to-be-reinforced response more likely—and hence the reinforcers more likely as well. **Instructional control** is the guidance of behavior by previously established discriminative stimuli, especially verbal stimuli such as rules. Skinner (1984) found it useful to distinguish between behavior that can best be understood as the result of its prior consequences, or contingency-governed behavior, and behavior that can best be understood as the result of its antecedents, or rule-governed behavior. The ability of discriminative stimuli such as instructions to guide behavior depends on a history of reinforcement for responding to instructions. Thus, rule-governed behavior is itself dependent on the fundamental learning processes that we have examined.

Researchers have studied the interaction between rules and reinforcers by giving false rules to study participants—that is, by inaccurately describing the behavior that is required for reinforcement. In such experiments people may behave in accordance with either the rule or the reinforcement contingency. In one study, for example, college students were told that they would receive a reinforcer if their responses occurred at least 15 seconds after the previous reinforcer (Buskist & Miller, 1986). In fact, at least 30 seconds had to elapse before the response became effective. Other students were told the truth about the procedure. At first the behavior of the misinformed students was guided by the instructions, with a response occurring about every 15 seconds. However, because "early" responses were extinguished, responding shifted to about once every 30 seconds. The students' behavior was no longer guided by the rule. Meanwhile, the students who received truthful instructions responded appropriately throughout.

Incorrect instructions or rules need not lose their ability to guide behavior, however. For another group of students, responding also could produce a reinforcer after 30 seconds had elapsed, but the instructions falsely stated that 60 seconds had to elapse. Guided by the false instructions, the students responded only after 60 seconds. Naturally, because 60 seconds was longer than the correct interval of 30 seconds, every response was reinforced. So more rapid responses never occurred and, as a result, could never be reinforced. Rules can guide human behavior not only when they describe correct reinforcement contingencies, but also when they prevent behavior from encountering the true contingencies. In general, the guidance of behavior by instructions depends—as does guidance by any other stimuli—on the specific contingencies of reinforcement with which the learner's behavior comes into contact (Catania, Mathews, & Shimoff, 1982). Behavior is shaped by realized contingencies, not potential contingencies.

Observational Learning

Human learners benefit from the experience of others not only through instructions but also through observation of the behavior of others. *Observational learning* occurs when changes in the observer's behavior take place after watching the behavior of others—including the stimuli present when the others' behavior occurred and the consequences of that behavior. A subset of observational learning is imitation. **Imitation** occurs when the behavior of an observer matches the behavior of the person or persons being observed.

Observational learning usually occurs without special training, but occasionally children who are severely disabled do not imitate the behavior of others. This unfortunate circumstance gives researchers an opportunity to investigate the conditions that foster imitation and, in so doing, to help the children as well. Three children who had never been seen to imitate and who did not imitate the actions of the experimenter when requested were exposed to an operant conditioning procedure in which the verbal stimulus "Do this" was followed by a reinforcer if the child emitted a response that was similar in form to the experimenter's (Baer, Peterson, & Sherman, 1967). The required responses were relatively simple actions such as hand-clapping or raising one arm. When the child failed to imitate, as was always the case at the beginning of the study, the experimenter shaped the response by guiding the movement and following it by reinforcers such as giving the child a bit of food and saying, "Good." Gradually, shaping was reduced until the child imitated the behavior without guidance. After more than 100 different responses had been reinforced in this manner, the children began to imitate new responses, such as pulling a window shade, when they heard "Do this." (See **Figure 5·20**.) In short, the cumulative effect of acquiring many different imitative responses led to *generalized imitation*.

How can we understand the acquisition of imitation and other observational learning by means of the basic learning processes described in this chapter? In order for any generalized

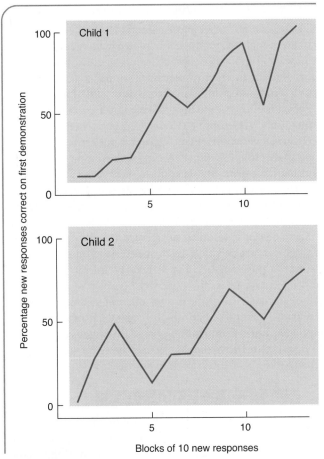

FIGURE 5·20 Training in imitation. Two children with severe disabilities, who did not imitate on their own, received explicit reinforcement for doing so. Gradually, after many different imitative responses were reinforced, the children began to imitate new actions on their first appearance.

(From Baer, D. M., Peterson, R. F., & Sherman, J. A. (1967). Development of imitation by reinforcing behavioral similarity to a model. *Journal of the Experimental Analysis of Behavior, 10*, 405–418.)

response to occur, that response must have been reinforced under similar conditions in the past. What are the similar conditions and reinforcers in this case? When we see another person behave, some of the stimuli produced by that behavior are similar to the stimuli that we see when we make the same response ourselves. A motion is in a given direction or directed toward a particular object, other people's limbs look similar to our own limbs, and so on. Consistent with this interpretation, electrical recordings of the activity of neurons in the motor association cortex of monkeys have revealed that some of the same neurons that are active when a monkey observes another monkey's movements are also active when the observer makes the movement itself. (See Brass & Heyes, 2005, for a review of such studies.) Furthermore, research with humans that uses less physiologically invasive procedures has shown that these areas of the brain are active only when the observed response is a response that humans make, such as biting but not barking. Finally, the activation of these brain areas is greater when the movements of others are viewed from the same angle as would be the case if the observer were viewing his or her own actions. Thus, the greater the similarity of the stimuli produced by others' movements to those produced by the observer's own movements, the more similar the motor activity initiated in the observer. The neural activity induced in the observer occurs at about the same time as the reinforcer for the responses of the other, which produces a conditioned reinforcer that strengthens the same neural activity in the observer that mediates that behavior in the observer. The neurons that are similarly activated by observed and executed behavior are called *mirror neurons*. Mirror neurons are so called because their activity in the observer's brain is the same as—that is, it "mirrors"—their activity when the observer actually makes the response. Although the interpretation of observational learning and other complex behavior remains incomplete, these forms of behavior do not appear to be beyond the reach of fundamental learning processes (Donahoe & Palmer, 1994).

Evaluating Scientific Issues

How Do Complex Outcomes Arise from Simple Processes?

Darwin introduced a new way of understanding complex phenomena: **selectionism**. Darwin proposed that rather than being the result of complex processes, complexity and order could result from the repeated action of simple processes acting over time. In the case of evolution, Darwin argued that from initial variation in inherited characteristics, those characteristics that benefited survival and reproduction would be selected and retained to contribute to the variation on which future selection would act. Over time, the cumulative effect of natural selection would adapt organisms to the demands of their environments. All of the diversity and complexity of nature is the result. Natural selection acts on a *population of different individuals* and on the genes that each individual carries. The process of evolution through natural selection does not ensure that any given individual survives to reproduce; only that—on average—an individual having certain characteristics is more likely to survive than others not having those characteristics. George Washington clearly had admirable qualities, but he left no children.

● Learning and Complex Behavior

Learning theory, beginning with Pavlov and Thorndike, and articulated most clearly by Skinner, makes a similar proposal. Instead of seeing complex behavior as the product of complex processes—intelligence, insight, memory, symbolic behavior, and the like—these investigators have proposed that the cumulative effect of reinforcement may yield complex behavior. From initial variation in a *population of environment–behavior relations in the same individual*, selection by reinforcement favors some relations and disfavors others. The favored variations are retained—through changes in synaptic efficacies, not gene frequencies—and contribute to the variation on which subsequent reinforcers may act. Again, there is no guarantee that the selection process will lead to effective behavior in every case. The behavior, or some approximation of it, must occur before it can be selected. Remember the vignette at the beginning of the chapter: Natalie's mother, who refused to scavenge the gowns of the dead because of her middle-class background, could not experience the warming effects of putting on a gown. Selection by reinforcement is sensitive not to possible cause–effect relations but to temporal coincidences. However, reliable coincidences often portend cause–effect relations; and for that reason, adaptation of individuals to the demands of their environments is often achieved. If this were not true—on average—natural selection would not have favored the biological mechanisms that underlie learning. Nevertheless, the limitations of selection processes must be kept in mind: Selection by reinforcement, like Darwinian natural selection, "prepares" us to live in the past—to live under the conditions that were present when selection took place. When the contingencies of the present are like those of the past, we behave adaptively. When the contingencies change, and particularly when they change quickly, species may go extinct; and, sometimes, good people such as Natalie's mother may die.

● What Should We Conclude?

Selection processes produce relative order out of relative chaos. Beginning with a varying population—whether of individuals, behaviors, or synapses—selection favors those members of the population that—on average—adapt the population to the demands of the environment. Natural selection by the ancestral environment among members of the population of individuals favors those members that display reproductive fitness. Selection by reinforcement by the individual environment among members of the population of environment–behavior relations favors those members that are followed by reinforcers. Selection at the cellular level among members of the population of synaptic efficacies favors those

members that are followed by neuromodulators. Thus, at whatever level, selection processes act upon the target population to produce adaptation to the contingencies of selection. When adaptation arises from selection processes, there is no guarantee that adaptation will be optimal, particularly for any individual member of the population. Natural selection can produce species that become extinct and selection by reinforcement can produce superstitions. Nevertheless, selection provides the most general account of how order and complexity may arise for the action of natural-science-based processes—processes that ultimately can all be traced to the environment (Donahoe, Burgos, & Palmer, 1993).

Interim Summary

Behavior in Experienced Learners

The behavior of experienced animals, most especially humans, is increasingly the product of reinforcement by conditioned reinforcers. With experience, behavior is guided by discriminative stimuli from prior learning, particularly verbal stimuli provided by other humans such as directions and instructions. Behavior of this origin is called rule-governed behavior to distinguish it from contingency-governed behavior that is the direct result of reinforcement. Of course, rule-governed behavior persists only if it is ultimately consistent with the contingencies of reinforcement. Another source of behavior in experienced learners is observational learning. Researched indicates that some of the same neurons are activated when we observe the behavior of others as when we execute the behavior ourselves. These neurons are called mirror neurons. When conditioned reinforcers are produced by the behavior of others, these reinforcers can strengthen the activity of mirror neurons and, thereby, strengthen the observed behavior in ourselves. Although much about the origins of complex human behavior remains unknown, basic biobehavioral processes appear to provide a firm foundation upon which understanding can be constructed. Even complex human behavior appears within reach of fundamental selection processes.

QUESTIONS TO CONSIDER

1. Others frequently offer advice about how we should live our lives. We tend to pay attention to some more than others. Using concepts from this section of the chapter, when are we most likely to follow that advice?

2. If behavior is a product of selection processes and selection processes can always be traced to the environment, does this mean that we have no control over our own destinies? Explain.

Suggestions for Further Reading

Donahoe, J. W., & Palmer, D. C. (2005). *Learning and complex behavior.* Richmond, MA.: Ledgetop Publishing. (Reprint of Donahoe, J. W., & Palmer, D. C. (1994). *Learning and complex behavior.* Boston: Allyn and Bacon. Supplementary additional material at http://www.LCB-online.org.)

This book describes basic biobehavioral processes and their implications for complex human behavior. The complex behavior includes stimulus classes ("concepts"), attending, perceiving, remembering, imagining, problem solving, and verbal behavior together with related findings from neuroscience and neuropsychology.

Skinner, B. F. (1953). *Science and human behavior.* New York: The Free Press.

Although originally published more than 50 years ago, this book is still a valuable interpretation of the behavior-analytic position. Skinner interestingly and clearly explains the basic principles of operant conditioning and their application to an understanding of a wide range of behaviors. *Science and Human Behavior* is an excellent choice if you wish to know more about Skinner's views.

Key Terms

acquisition (p. 135)

behavioral discrepancy (p. 131)

blocking design (p. 131)

classical procedure (p. 128)

conditioned emotional response (CER) (p. 143)

conditioned reinforcer (p. 137)

conditioned response (CR) (p. 129)

conditioned stimulus (CS) (p. 128)

conditioning (p. 129)

contextual discrimination (p. 141)

contingency (p. 136)

differential conditioning procedure (p. 141)

discriminative stimuli (p. 141)

dopamine (p. 138)

escape or **withdrawal response** (p. 142)

extinction (p. 139)

habituation (p. 135)

imitation (p. 150)

instructional control (p. 150)

intermittent reinforcement (p. 139)

latent learning (p. 149)

learning (p. 124)

long-term potentiation (p. 149)

negative punishment (p. 144)

negative reinforcement (p. 144)

operant chamber (p. 133)

operant procedure (p. 128)

orienting response (p. 135)

punisher (p. 142)

punishment (p. 142)

reinforcement (p. 135)

reinforcing stimulus (p. 130)

response chaining (p. 136)

selectionism (p. 151)

sensory learning (p. 149)

shaping (p. 136)

spontaneous recovery (p. 140)

stimulus discrimination (p. 141)

stimulus generalization (p. 140)

superstitious behavior (p. 133)

taste aversion (p. 136)

temporal contiguity (p. 128)

unconditioned reinforcer (p. 137)

unconditioned response (UR) (p. 129)

unconditioned stimulus (US) (p. 128)

6

SENSATION

Sensory Processing

Transduction • Sensory Coding • Psychophysics • *Evaluating Scientific Issues: Subliminal Self-Help*

The primary function of the sense organs is to provide information that can guide behavior. The translation of information about environmental events into neural activity is called transduction. In the nervous system sensory information must be translated into one of two types of neural code: anatomical or temporal. Psychophysics is the study of the relation between the physical characteristics of stimuli and the perceptions they produce. The term "subliminal perception" refers to the behavioral effects of a stimulus that cannot be consciously detected. There is no evidence that information presented subliminally can produce useful, practical learning.

Vision

Light • The Eye and Its Functions • Transduction of Light by Photoreceptors • Adaptation to Light and Dark • Eye Movements • Color Vision

Light is a form of electromagnetic radiation. Images of the visual scene are focused on the retina, the inner layer at the back of the eye. Photoreceptors, specialized neurons located in the retina, contain chemicals called photopigments that transduce light into neural activity. Chemical changes in the photopigments are responsible for our ability to see in dim or bright light. The eyes make small, involuntary movements that prevent the image from fading as well as three types of purposive movements. Light can vary in wavelength, intensity, and purity. Three types of cones in the retina, each most sensitive to a particular wavelength of light, detect colors. Most genetic defects affecting color vision result in the absence of one of the three photopigments found in cones.

Audition

Sound • The Ear and Its Functions • Detecting and Localizing Sounds in the Environment • Age-Related Losses in Hearing • *Biology and Culture: The Deaf Community*

Sound waves can vary in frequency, intensity, and complexity, giving rise to differences in perceptions of pitch, loudness, and timbre. The bones of the middle ear transmit sound vibrations from the eardrum to the cochlea, which contains the auditory receptors—the hair cells. The auditory system detects individual frequencies by means of place coding and rate coding. The ear locates a sound's source by detecting arrival time and differences in intensity. With age, people may lose the ability to hear sound against a noisy background and to hear certain frequencies. The Deaf community consists of deaf people who can comfortably and effectively communicate with one another through sign language.

Gustation

Receptors and the Sensory Pathway • The Five Qualities of Taste

Taste receptors on the tongue respond to bitterness, sourness, sweetness, saltiness, and *umami*. Together with the olfactory system, these receptors provide us with information about complex flavors.

Olfaction

Anatomy of the Olfactory System • The Dimensions of Odor

The olfactory system detects the presence of aromatic molecules. Recent discoveries suggest that several hundred different types of receptors may be involved in olfactory discrimination and thus that odor may have several hundred dimensions.

The Somatosenses

The Skin Senses • The Internal Senses • The Vestibular Senses

Sensory receptors in the skin provide information about touch, pressure, vibration, changes in temperature, and stimuli that cause tissue damage. Pain perception helps protect us from harmful stimuli. Sensory endings located in the internal organs, joints, and muscles convey information about our movements and about internal events in the body. The vestibular system helps us maintain our balance and helps prompt compensatory eye movements to help us maintain fixation when our heads move.

A lthough he didn't mention it at the time he told me this story, Ken Hill must have started his shift with a fear that the day would end in heartbreak. Ken is a social psychologist, but that day he was working in his other role: as a search-and-rescue manager for the Canadian province of Nova Scotia.

Ken's job is to prevent the tragedy that can occur in Canada's open spaces when someone loses her or his bearings in the wilderness and dies of exposure. There are many police and civilian agencies throughout Canada whose members assist in the search for lost persons. Shortly after moving to Nova Scotia, Ken had seen the tragedy that occurs when these efforts fail and a lost child is not found in time. Since then he had devoted his free time to learning search-and-rescue techniques and much of his professional time to the study of lost-person behavior. He had become one of the foremost experts in North America on search-and-rescue management.

But the search mission that day was not looking good. Ken's team was searching for a lost four-year-old boy who had been missing for three days after wandering away from his family. The weather had turned cold and rainy. Alone in such conditions, survival is problematic even for an adult. However, young children sometimes beat the odds by cuddling up in a warm place, whereas an older child might panic and wander far. That hope was keeping the searchers going.

Search-and-rescue doctrine emphasizes that, because a lost person may be hard to spot in heavy undergrowth, the searchers themselves should be as easy to detect as possible. Getting the lost person to spot you is as good as your spotting them. Searchers dress in bright clothing; use loud whistles; and, at night, wear bright headlights—all in an attempt to get a response from the person they are seeking. Also, searchers must be spaced far enough apart to cover ground quickly but not so far apart that they are out of earshot of each other.

For whatever reason, the searchers had failed to locate the lost boy over the last three days. But Ken's anxiety vanished with a single radio report. A truck bringing food to the searchers' camp found the boy when he stepped onto the road and flagged it down. "I want my mommy," the boy said. He was, all things considered, remarkably fit after his experience—even a little nonchalant about it.

Part of Ken's skill as a search manager arises from his attention to debriefing the lost person in order to learn what he or she did. Ken got a chance to talk to the four-year-old boy shortly after he was found. "What was it like being lost in the woods?" Ken asked.

"Oh, it was okay," the boy said. "Except at night. When the monsters came out."

"Monsters?" Ken asked. This was a wilderness risk new to him.

"Yes. They were tall and scary. I could see them at night moving around, because they had one big glowing eye on the tops of their heads. And what was worse was that they knew I was there. They kept calling out my name. Over and over again. I'm glad I found you first."

B ehavior does not exist in a vacuum, nor do our thoughts and emotions. Our actions are provoked, informed, and guided by events that occur in our environment, and we think about—and have feelings about—what is happening there. Our senses are the means by which we experience the world. Everything we learn is detected by sense organs and transmitted to our brains by sensory nerves. Without sensory input, a human brain would be utterly useless; it would learn nothing, think no thoughts, and have no experiences.

The sense organs and the sensory nerves have evolved to provide us with useful information about the external world. Using vision as their example, Milner and Goodale (1996) make this point succinctly: "Vision [evolved] to provide distal sensory control of the movements that the animal makes

▲ *Our senses are the means by which we experience the world.*

Sensory Processing

Traditionally, psychologists have distinguished between sensation and perception. Most define **sensation** as the detection of specific properties of stimuli, such as their intensity. For example, one star shines brighter in the night sky than others. Thunder grows louder as an electrical storm approaches. The soup can have too much salt or too little. The same can be said of perfume or cologne on a date. Too much exposure to the sun may produce a painful sunburn. In all these instances—visual, auditory, gustatory, olfactory, and somatosensory—sensory organs are reacting to the intensity of the stimuli and transmitting that information to the brain. **Perception** occurs when the sensory information is used by the brain to produce a response. It is one thing for the eye to react to red light reflected from an object (sensation). It is quite another for the brain to recognize the object as an apple or to recognize its color as red (perception) on the basis of the information provided by the eye. Similarly, the light from a moving object produces sensation when it enters our eyes, but recognizing that it is a soccer ball coming rapidly toward us (and that we need to move to the left in order to block it) is perception. As Ken Hill's story about the lost four-year-old demonstrates, detecting a sound is not the same as identifying its source as one-eyed monsters. Psychologists used to believe that sensation involved innate, "prewired" physiological mechanisms, whereas perception depended heavily on learning. However, neither physiological nor behavioral research has been able to establish this boundary clearly. Where sensation leaves off and perception begins is still a mystery.

in order to survive and reproduce in that world" (p. 11). That is, vision and other sensory systems make it possible for stimuli that exist outside the body to affect the body's movements. How they do this depends not only on the specific modality of the information, but also on the characteristics of the information and the state of the brain at the time the information arrives. Differences between sources of information in the environment have important consequences for the way sensory systems process that information.

For example, consider the difference between the world as we see it and as we hear it. The visual scene received by our eyes changes rapidly as we move our body, our head, and our eyes. Think of it as a visual picture frame, and consider how quickly it moves as we shift our eyes around a room. Yet we perceive our visual world as stable. The visual system must provide that stability in the face of rapid shifts in its input. Sound, on the other hand, is not so variable. While its intensity changes as we move toward or away from its origin, on the whole these changes are more gradual than those faced by the visual system. Furthermore, sounds can move around obstacles in ways that light cannot. Our auditory system, then, has more time to process signals. As we will see, the system uses this time to discriminate the complex waveforms that sounds contain.

Because they are attuned to different aspects of our world, the senses contribute to the richness of experience. Given the role that speech plays in human culture, audition is extremely important for social behavior. Together with vision, audition provides information about distant events—as does the sense of smell, which can tell us about sources of aromatic molecules far upwind. The other senses deal with events occurring much closer; for instance, the taste of our favorite foods or the touch of a loved one. The so-called body senses are closely tied to our own movements and to events at the body's surface and in its interior. When we touch an object while blindfolded, for example, the experience is active, not passive; we move our hands over the object to determine its shape, texture, and temperature. Information from specialized organs in the inner ear and from receptors in the muscles and joints actually arises from our movements. This information helps us maintain our balance while standing or on the move.

Chapter 7 will explore perception. Meanwhile, this chapter describes our sensory systems in detail: the visual, auditory, gustatory, olfactory, and somatosensory systems. By this traditional list, we have five senses; but in fact, we have several more. For example, the somatosensory system includes separate components that are able to detect touch, warmth, coolness, vibration, physical damage (pain), head tilt, head movement, limb movement, muscular contraction, and other events occurring within our bodies. But the question of whether to call each of these components a "sense" is a matter of whether to disturb the tradition.

Transduction

Your brain, floating in cerebrospinal fluid, swaddled in its protective sheath of meninges, and sheltered in a thick skull, is isolated from the world around you. The only sense receptors that the brain possesses detect local conditions such as the temperature and salt concentration of the brain's blood. These receptors cannot inform the brain about what is going on elsewhere. For that it is dependent on the information gathered by the sense organs that lie beyond it.

Sense organs detect stimuli such as light, sound, taste, odor, or touch. Information about these stimuli is transmitted to the brain through neural impulses—action potentials carried by the axons in sensory nerves. The task of the sense organs is to transmit signals to the brain that are coded in such a way as to represent certain features of events that have occurred in the environment. The task of the brain is to analyze this information and decide what has occurred.

Transduction (literally, "leading across") is the process by which the sense organs convert energy from environmental events into neural activity. Each sense organ responds to a particular form of energy given off by an environmental stimulus and translates that energy into neural firing to which the brain can respond. The means of transduction are as diverse as the kinds of stimuli we can transduce. In most senses, specialized sensory neurons called **receptor cells** release chemical transmitter substances that stimulate other neurons, thus altering the rate of firing of their axons. In the somatosenses ("body senses"), dendrites of neurons respond directly to physical stimuli without the intervention of specialized receptor cells. However, some of these neurons do have specialized endings that enable them to respond to particular kinds of sensory information. **Table 6•1** summarizes the types of transduction accomplished by our sense organs.

Sensory Coding

Sensory information must accurately represent the environment. But, as we saw in Chapter 4, nerves are bundles of axons, each of which can do no more than transmit action potentials. These action potentials are fixed in size and duration; they cannot be altered. Thus, different stimuli cannot be translated into different types of action potentials. Yet we can detect an enormous number of different stimuli with each of our sense organs. For example, we are capable of discriminating among approximately 7.5 million different colors. We can recognize up to 10,000 odors. We can also identify touches to different parts of the body; and we can further distinguish the degree of pressure involved and the sharpness or bluntness, softness or hardness, and temperature of the object touching us. But how, then, if action potentials cannot be

altered, do the sense organs tell the brain that, for instance, a red apple or a yellow lemon is present—or that the right hand is holding a small, cold object or a large, warm one? The information from the sense organs must somehow be coded in the activity of axons carrying information from the sense organs to the brain.

A *code* is a system of signals representing information. Spoken English, written Spanish, traffic lights, key presses on a cell phone, and the electrical zeros and ones in the memory of a computer are all examples of codes. As long as we know the rules of a code, we can convert a message from one medium to another without losing any information, as when we convert from the sound of spoken English to a meaningful message. Although we do not know the precise rules by which the sensory systems transmit information to the brain, we do know that the rules take two general forms: *anatomical coding* and *temporal coding*.

Anatomical Coding Since the early 1800s, when Johannes Müller formulated his doctrine of specific nerve energies (discussed in Chapter 1), we have known that the brain learns what is happening through the activity of specific sets of neurons. Sensory organs located in different places in the body send their information to the brain through different nerves. Because the brain has no direct information about the physical energy impinging on a given sense organ, it uses **anatomical coding** to interpret the location and type of sensory stimulus according to which incoming nerve fibers are active. For example, if you rub your eyes, you will mechanically stimulate the light-sensitive receptors they contain. This stimulation produces action potentials in the axons of the nerves that connect the eyes with the brain (the *optic nerves*). The visual system of the brain has no way of knowing that the light-sensitive receptors of the eyes have been activated by a nonvisual stimulus. As a result, the brain acts as if the neural activity in the optic nerves were produced by light—so you "see" stars and other flashes. Experiments performed during surgery have shown that artificial stimulation of the nerves that convey taste

TABLE 6•1 The Types of Transduction Accomplished by the Sense Organs		
Location of Sense Organ	**Environmental Stimuli**	**Energy Transduced**
Eye	Light	Radiant energy
Ear	Sound	Mechanical energy
Tongue	Taste	Recognition of molecular shape
Nose	Odor	Recognition of molecular shape
Skin	Touch	Mechanical energy
	Temperature	Thermal energy
	Vibration	Mechanical energy
	Pain	Chemical reaction
Internal organs; Muscle	Stretch	Mechanical energy
Vestibular system	Tilt and rotation of head	Mechanical energy

produces the perception of taste, electrical stimulation of the auditory nerve produces the perception of a buzzing noise, and so forth.

Through anatomical coding the brain distinguishes not only among the sensory modalities, but also among stimuli of the same sensory modality. Obviously, sensory coding for the body surface is anatomical: Different nerve fibers serve different parts of the skin. Thus, we can easily discriminate between a touch on the arm and a touch on the knee. As we saw in Chapter 4, the primary somatosensory cortex contains a neural "map" of the skin. Receptors in the skin in different parts of the body send information to different parts of the primary somatosensory cortex. Similarly, the primary visual cortex maintains a map of the visual field.

Temporal Coding **Temporal coding** is the coding of sensory information in terms of time. The simplest form of temporal code is *rate*. By firing at a faster or slower rate according to the intensity of a stimulus, an axon can communicate quantitative information to the brain. For example, a soft touch to the skin can be encoded by a low rate of firing and a more forceful touch by a high rate. Thus, signals produced by a particular set of neurons (an anatomical code) tell *where* the body is being touched; the rate at which these neurons fire (a temporal code) tells *how intense* that touch is. It is commonly assumed that all sensory systems use rate of firing to encode the intensity of stimulation.

Psychophysics

As you learned in Chapter 1, nineteenth-century Europe was the birthplace of **psychophysics,** the systematic study of the relation between the physical characteristics of stimuli and the psychological responses (or perceptions) they produce (thus the "physics of the mind"). To study perceptual phenomena, scientists had to find reliable ways to measure people's responses to stimuli. We will examine two of these methods—the just-noticeable difference and the procedures of signal detection.

The Principle of the Just-Noticeable Difference Ernst
Weber (1795–1878), a German anatomist and physiologist, investigated the ability of humans to discriminate between various stimuli. He measured the **just-noticeable difference (jnd)**—the smallest change in the magnitude of a stimulus that a person can detect. He discovered a principle that held true for many sensory systems: The jnd is directly related to the magnitude of the existing stimulus. For example, when he presented participants with two metal objects and asked them to say whether the objects differed in weight, the participants reported that the two weights felt the same unless they differed by a ratio of at least 1 in 40. That is, a person could just barely distinguish a 40-gram weight from a 41-gram weight, an 80-gram weight from an 82-gram weight, or a 400-gram weight from a 410-gram weight. Psychologically, the difference between a 40-gram weight and a 41-gram

weight is equivalent to the difference between an 80-gram weight and an 82-gram weight: one jnd. Different sensory systems had different ratios. For example, the ratio for detecting differences in the brightness of white light is approximately 1 in 60. These ratios are called **Weber fractions.**

Gustav Fechner (1801–1887), another German physiologist, used Weber's concept of the just-noticeable difference to measure people's perceptual experience. That is, he measured the absolute magnitude of perceptual experience in jnds.

For example, suppose we want to measure the strength of a person's experience of light of a particular intensity. We seat the participant in a darkened room facing two disks of frosted glass, each having a light bulb behind it; the brightness of the light bulbs is adjustable. One of the disks serves as the sample stimulus, the other as the comparison stimulus. We start with the sample and comparison stimuli turned off completely and increase the brightness of the comparison stimulus until our participant can just detect a difference. That level of brightness is one jnd. Then we set the sample stimulus to the same intensity (one jnd) and again increase the brightness of the comparison stimulus until our participant can just tell them apart. The new level of the comparison stimulus is two jnds. We continue making these measurements until the comparison stimulus is as bright as we can make it or until it becomes uncomfortably bright for the participant. Finally, we construct a graph indicating the perceived brightness (in jnds) in relation to the physical intensity of the stimulus. The graph, which relates the strength of a perceptual experience to physical intensity, might look something like **Figure 6•1**.

How should you interpret a graph such as Figure 6.1? First, note the two scales. The values along the X axis are measures of physical intensity—something measured with respect to the objective world. The values along the Y axis are very different. Each one is a jnd—a measure of the extent that

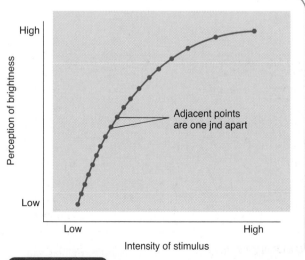

FIGURE 6•1 A hypothetical range of perceived brightness (in jnds) as a function of intensity.

the subjective experience is increasing. So, in other words, Figure 6.1 provides a mapping between the physical and the psychological worlds—it depicts a psychophysical function.

Second, notice that if you trace the distance between dots on the X axis, the distances become larger as you move to the right on the graph. This is a consequence of what Weber found; namely, that the amount of physical energy necessary to produce a jnd increases with the magnitude of the stimulus.

Finally, note the shape of the curve. It rises steeply at first, but then it begins to level off. This kind of curve is characteristic of the mathematical function known as a logarithm. Fechner's great contribution to psychology was to show how a logarithmic function could be derived from Weber's work. Norwich and Wong (1997) provide a technical overview of how these two perspectives—Weber's and Fechner's—relate to each other.

What would the function shown in Figure 6.1 look like if the situation were different? In some sensory systems (e.g., the pain from electric shock), it actually takes less energy to produce a jnd at higher intensities. The kind of function that describes this situation looks like the one in **Figure 6·2**. Notice that the levels of stimulus intensity that produce more intense perceptions are closer together at the higher levels. The shape of the curve is different as a result.

Is there a way to reconcile these two contrasting functions? Almost 100 years after Fechner's work, S. S. Stevens proposed another viewpoint, which has become very influential. Stevens (1975) suggested a power function rather than a logarithmic function to relate physical intensity to the magnitude of perception. In mathematical notation, if S is psychological magnitude and I is the intensity of the physical stimulus, then, according to Stevens's power function,

$$S = kI^b$$

The symbol k stands for a mathematical constant that adjusts for the way physical intensity is measured. The important change is that the intensity (I) is now raised to the power b.

The mathematical properties of a power function are such that when b is a number between zero and 1, the curve looks somewhat like Fechner's (see Figure 6.1). However, if the value of b is greater than 1, the curve looks like Figure 6.2. Stevens's power function, then, provides a single principle that can account for both types of results. The only substantive difference is the value of b.

An example comes from our sense of taste. The value of b for saccharin (a sugar substitute) is 0.8 (see Schiffman, 1996). What the power function implies, for this value, is that if we were to taste two solutions, one containing twice as high a concentration of saccharin as the other, the first solution would taste about 1.7 times as sweet as the second. In contrast, the value of b for salt is 1.3. A solution with twice the concentration of salt would therefore taste about 2.5 times as salty. The larger effect of doubling the concentration of salt compared to the effect of doubling the concentration of saccharin is reflected in the two exponents. The power law therefore provides a systematic way to compare different sensory systems and the perceptions they produce.

Signal Detection Theory Psychophysical methods rely heavily on the concept of a **threshold,** the thin line between not perceiving and perceiving. The just-noticeable difference can also be called a **difference threshold,** the minimum detectable difference between two stimuli. An **absolute threshold** is the minimum intensity of a stimulus that can be detected—that is, discriminated from no stimulus at all. Thus, the first comparison in the experiment described above—using two frosted disks and two lamps—measured an absolute threshold. The subsequent comparisons measured difference thresholds.

Even early psychophysicists realized that a threshold was not an absolutely fixed value. When a researcher flashes a very dim light, a participant may report seeing it on some trials but not on others. By convention, the absolute threshold is the point at which a participant detects the stimulus 50 percent of the time; the difference threshold, the point at which the difference is detected 50 percent of the time. This conventional definition is necessary because of the inherent variability of activity in the nervous system. Even when neurons are not being stimulated, they are never absolutely inactive; they continue to fire even when at rest. If a very weak stimulus occurs when neurons in the visual system happen to be less active, the brain is likely to detect it. But if the neurons are already quite active, the effects of the stimulus are likely to be lost in the "noise."

An alternative method of measuring a person's sensitivity to changes in physical stimuli takes account of random changes in the nervous system. According to **signal detection theory** (Green & Swets, 1974), every stimulus event requires discrimination between a *signal* (the stimulus) and *noise* (the

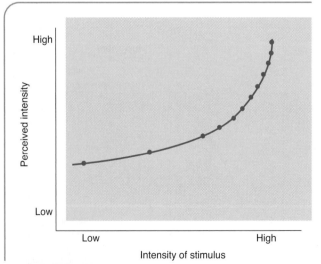

FIGURE 6·2 The relationship between stimulus and perception when less energy is required to produce a jnd at higher intensities.

▲ *According to signal detection theory, we must discriminate between the signal that conveys information and the noise contributed by background stimuli and random activity of our own nervous systems.*

combination of background stimuli and the random activity of the nervous system).

Signal detection theory takes into account our willingness to report detecting a signal. For example, suppose you are participating in an experiment. You are seated in a quiet room, facing a small warning light. The researcher tells you that when the light flashes, you *may* hear a faint tone one second later. Your task is to say yes or no after each flash of the warning light, according to whether you hear the tone. At first the task is easy: Some flashes are followed by an easily heard tone; others are followed by silence. You are confident about your yes and no decisions. But as the experiment progresses, the tone gets fainter and fainter, until it is so soft that you have doubts about how you should respond. The light flashes. What should you say? Did you really hear a tone, or were you only imagining it?

At this point your *response bias*—your tendency to say yes or no when you are not sure whether you detected the stimulus—can have an effect. According to the terminology of signal detection theory, *hits* are saying yes when the stimulus is presented; *misses* are saying no when it is presented; *correct negatives* are saying no when the stimulus is not presented; and *false alarms* are saying yes when the stimulus is not presented. Hits and correct negatives are correct responses; misses and false alarms are incorrect responses. (See **Figure 6•3**.) Suppose you want to be very sure that you are correct when you say yes, because you would feel foolish saying you have heard something that is not there. Your response bias will be to err in favor of avoiding false alarms, even at the risk of making misses. Someone else's response bias might be to err in favor of detecting all the stimuli, even at the risk of making false alarms.

A person's response bias can seriously affect the threshold of detection. A person with a response bias to avoid false alarms will appear to have a higher threshold than will some-

one who does not want to let a tone go by without saying yes. To avoid this problem, signal detection researchers have developed a method of assessing people's sensitivity, regardless of their initial response bias. They deliberately manipulate the response biases and observe the results of these manipulations on participants' judgments.

Suppose you were a participant and the researcher promised you a dollar every time you made a hit, with no penalty for false alarms. You would undoubtedly tend to say yes on every trial, even if you were not sure you had heard the tone; after all, you'd have nothing to lose and everything to gain. In contrast, suppose the researcher announced that she would fine you a dollar every time you made a false alarm and would give you nothing for making hits. You would undoubtedly say no every time, because you would have everything to lose and nothing to gain: You would be extremely conservative in your judgments.

Now consider your response bias under intermediate conditions. If you receive a dollar for every hit but also are fined 50 cents for every miss, you will say yes whenever you are reasonably sure you hear the tone. If you receive 50 cents for every hit but are fined a dollar for each false alarm, you will be more conservative. But if you are sure you heard the tone, you will say yes to earn 50 cents. (Note, however, that there are other, less expensive ways to change people's response biases, which is fortunate for researchers on limited budgets.) **Figure 6•4** graphs your performance over this range of payoff conditions.

The graph in Figure 6.4 is a **receiver operating characteristic curve (ROC curve),** named for its original use in research at the Bell Laboratories to measure the intelligibility of speech transmitted through a telephone system. The curve shows performance when the sound is difficult to detect. If the sound were louder, so that you rarely doubted you heard it, you would make almost every possible hit and very few false alarms. The few misses you made would be under the

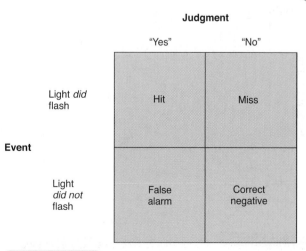

FIGURE 6•3 Four possibilities in judging the presence or absence of a stimulus.

FIGURE 6•4 A receiver operating characteristic curve (ROC curve): the percentage of hits and false alarms in judging the presence of a stimulus under several payoff conditions.

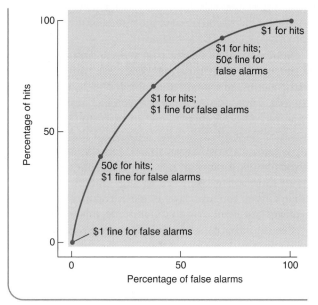

difference between the two curves demonstrates that the louder tone is easier to detect. Detectability is measured by the relative distances of the curves from a 45-degree line.

The signal detection method is the best way to determine a person's sensitivity to the occurrence of a particular stimulus. Note that the concept of threshold is not used. Instead, a stimulus is considered more or less detectable. The person *decides* whether a stimulus occurred, and the consequences of making hits or false alarms can bias this decision. Signal detection theory emphasizes that perceptual experience involves factors other than the activity of the sensory systems, factors such as motivation and prior experience.

low-payoff condition, when you wanted to be absolutely certain you heard the tone. The few false alarms would occur when guessing did not matter because the penalty for being wrong was low or nonexistent. In **Figure 6•5** the ROC curve (the magenta line) reflecting this new condition is shown together with the original curve (the blue line). The

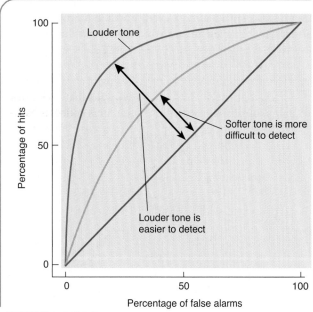

FIGURE 6•5 Two ROC curves, obtained by presenting a more discriminable stimulus (magenta curve) and a less discriminable stimulus (blue curve).

Evaluating Scientific Issues

Subliminal Self-Help

As you undoubtedly know, the market is full of self-help aids: Books, CDs, videotapes, DVDs, online courses, and professional seminars offer ways to increase your productivity, improve your self-image, enhance your memory, reduce stress, quit smoking, become fit, and lose weight. If you are afraid that achieving these goals might take some effort on your part, don't worry; no work is necessary. Or so say the makers of certain aids—subliminal self-help media (that is, audio or video materials that contain messages so faint that they cannot be consciously heard or seen).

The U.S. armed forces spend billions of dollars each year training their personnel, and they support research directed at developing more effective educational methods. In 1984 the Army Research Institute asked the National Academy of Sciences/National Research Council to investigate several methods purported to improve people's performance—including subliminal self-help procedures. These investigations provided an objective, scientific evaluation of these products (Druckman & Bjork, 1991).

● **Claims about Subliminal Self-Help Tapes**
According to the vendor of a subliminal self-help audiocassette, *Building Self-Confidence*, the message provided by the tape reaches

> the subconscious mind, which is the seat of all memories, knowledge, and emotions. The unconscious mind has a powerful influence on conscious actions, thoughts, feelings, habits, and behaviors, and actually controls and guides your life. If you want to make real, lasting changes and improvements in any area of your life, you must reach the subconscious mind where the changes begin. (Druckman & Bjork, 1991, p. 107)

The tape is rather pleasant to listen to; all the user hears is the sound of surf crashing on a beach, with the cries of seagulls in the distance. But according to the manufacturer, the tape also contains a voice making positive statements such as "I am a secure person. I believe in myself more and more every day, and my confidence naturally rises to the surface in every situation." The voice is inaudible, masked by the sound of the surf. To profit from these messages, says a notice on the cover, "Simply play the tapes while you work, play, drive, read, exercise, relax, watch TV, or even as you sleep. No concentration is required for the tapes to be effective" (Druckman & Bjork, 1991, pp. 107–108).

By the late 1980s there were at least 2,000 vendors of subliminal self-help tapes in North America, having sales of more than $50 million a year (Oldenburg, 1990). One catalogue of such tapes even promised to help restore hearing. Imagine, a deaf person restoring his or her hearing by listening to a subliminal message on an audiotape! What a remarkable claim—to say the least.

Several vendors offer subliminal videotapes and DVDs in which they present visual information so briefly that it cannot be consciously detected. One manufacturer even supplies an electronic device that plugs into a television set and superimposes subliminal messages on ordinary programs so that the viewer can effortlessly engage in self-improvement while watching reruns of, say, *Friends* or *Seinfeld*.

● **Evidence in Support of Subliminal Self-Help Media**

How would an experimenter determine whether subliminal self-help media work? Having read Chapter 2, you know that one possible method would be a double-blind study. For example, one group of participants would listen to a CD that contained a hidden message, and another group would listen to a CD that contained only the background. Neither the researchers nor the participants would know which CD contained the message. The researchers would make measurements of the personal characteristics relevant to the message before and after the course of treatment. For example, if the message was alleged to help people lose weight, participants could be weighed. If it was designed to lessen wrinkles or help people become better bowlers (this is a real claim!), their wrinkles could be counted or their bowling scores recorded.

What kind of evidence do the vendors provide? They provide *testimonials:* "I'm listening to my tape on pain reduction. It is marvelous. I had almost instant relief from pain on first using it a few days ago. It's much cheaper than a doctor and much better than medication. Phenomenal is what it has done for my spirits" (Druckman & Bjork, 1991, p. 113).

We need not doubt the sincerity of the satisfied customers; vendors do not usually need to write their own testimonials. But if a person is convinced that he or she received help from a subliminal tape, can we conclude that the system really works? Research—and simple logic—strongly suggest that the answer is no.

● **Why Do People Accept Subliminal Self-Help Claims?**

If subliminal self-help products don't work, why do their users endorse them? At least three phenomena can account for the fact that some customers will say they are satisfied. First, simply making a purchase indicates a commitment to self-improvement. (Interestingly, some people with emotional or behavioral problems show improvements in their feelings and behavior as soon as they make an appointment for psychotherapy—even before the therapy actually begins.) Second, social psychologists learned long ago that once people have expended effort toward reaching a goal, they tend to justify their effort by perceiving positive results. (We will encounter several examples of this phenomenon in Chapter 15.) Finally, if a person expects an effect to occur, he or she may be readily convinced that it really did.

The effect of expectation is demonstrated by a study that was carried out to follow up a famous hoax. In 1957 an advertising expert claimed that he had inserted subliminal visual messages in a showing of *Picnic,* a popular film. The messages, which said "Eat Popcorn" and "Drink Coke," supposedly caused people to rush to the refreshment stand and purchase these items. As you can imagine, this event received much attention and publicity. Several years later, the advertising expert revealed that he had invented the story in an attempt to get some favorable publicity for his firm (Weir, 1984).

In 1958, however, long before the advertising expert admitted his hoax, the Canadian Broadcasting Corporation commissioned a study to determine whether a subliminal message could really work (Pratkanis, Eskenazi, & Greenwald, 1990). At the beginning of a television show, an announcer described the "Popcorn" study and told the viewers that a test of subliminal persuasion would follow, with an unspecified message appearing on the screen. In fact, the message was "Phone now." According to the telephone company, no increase in the rate of phone calls occurred. But many viewers wrote to the network to say that they had felt compelled to *do something,* such as eat or drink. Obviously, the specific message "Phone now" did not get across to the viewers, but the expectation that they should feel some sort of compulsion made many of them report that they did.

In many ways, the claim that subliminal messages can affect consumer behavior is similar to claims that other media intentionally control behavior through secret coded messages. It has been asserted, for example, that rock music contains subversive instructions to listeners coded as backward speech. One rock group was even accused of encouraging suicide by supposedly including the command "Do it" recorded backward in the middle of one of their songs. Begg, Needham, and Bookbinder (1993) examined this possibility directly: They played messages backward or forward and tested whether people could recognize the message played backward and whether they agreed with the message played forward. The researchers found that indeed, hearing a message played backward helped a person recognize the same message when it was played backward again; its meaning, however, was not detected. As they put it:

Presumably, if participants heard music that included a backward version of "do it," they would find a backward version of "do it" more familiar than a backward version of an unheard phrase like "praise cows," but would be no more likely to commit suicide than to worship bovine images. (p. 9)

Is there any objective, scientific evidence that subliminal perception can occur? The answer is yes, there is. But the information transmitted by this means is very scanty. *Subliminal* literally means "below threshold," after the Latin *limen*, "threshold." The term **subliminal perception** refers to the behavioral effect of a stimulus that falls below the threshold of conscious detection; that is, below the absolute threshold. Although the person denies having detected a stimulus, the stimulus nevertheless has a measurable effect on his or her behavior. But the effects are subtle, and special procedures are required to demonstrate them.

For example, Cheesman and Merikle (1986) looked at the effect of presenting a word just before college students were asked to identify the color of a brief flash of light. When the word is a color name that is different from the color of the light, people usually take longer to identify the color—an effect called "incongruent priming." Cheesman and Merikle found that when the word was followed closely by a series of random letters before the light appeared, participants reported that they had a hard time identifying the word; they still, however, showed the incongruent priming effect. So, there is an effect of a stimulus—the word—even when it is presented in such a way that it is not consciously perceived.

Results such as these indicate that perception is a complex process—that when a stimulus is too weak to give rise to a conscious perception, it may still be strong enough to leave some traces in the brain that affect a person's perception of other stimuli. But this effect has a threshold of its own: If a word is presented too briefly, it has no effect at all on the perception of other stimuli. The phenomenon is real and involves the sensory receptors and normal physiological processes. (We'll look at the relation between consciousness, perception, and memories in more detail in Chapters 8 and 9.)

Psychologists have examined very few of the many thousands of different subliminal self-help materials that are available, but those they have examined seem to be ineffective. Some, according to Merikle (1988), contain stimuli that are simply too weak for the human ear to detect under any conditions. Others, when subjected to spectrographic analysis (which detects the presence of "voiceprints" in the sound track), were found to contain no message at all.

Perhaps this fact explains the results of the experiment by Pratkanis and colleagues (1990). The researchers recruited volunteers to listen to either a subliminal tape designed to improve memory or a tape designed to improve self-esteem. After the participants listened to the tapes for five weeks, the researchers asked them whether their memories or self-esteem had improved. About half of the participants in each group reported improvement—but none of the objective tests of memory or self-esteem administered by the researchers showed any effect. In addition, the researchers had switched tapes for half of the participants: Some of those who thought they had received a memory tape actually received a self-esteem tape and vice versa. The switch made no difference at all to the improvement ratings. Thus, a person's report of improvement is no indication that subliminal perception has really taken place.

● **What Should We Conclude?**

Only one conclusion seems reasonable: If you have been thinking about purchasing a subliminal self-help product, save your money—unless you think you will be content with a placebo effect caused by a personal commitment to change, a need to justify your efforts, or the expectation of good results.

Interim Summary

Sensory Processing

We experience the world through our senses. Our knowledge of the world stems from the accumulation of sensory experience and subsequent learning. All sensory experiences are the result of energy from events that is transduced into activity of receptor cells, which are specialized neurons. Transduction causes changes in the activity of axons of sensory nerves, and these changes in activity inform the sensory mechanisms of the brain about the environmental event. The information received from the receptor cells is transmitted to the brain by means of two coding schemes: anatomical coding and temporal coding.

To study the nature of subjective experience scientifically, we must be able to measure it. In nineteenth-century Germany Weber devised the concept of the just-noticeable difference, and Fechner used the jnd to measure perceived intensity of stimuli.

In the twentieth century Stevens modified this formulation and suggested a power function to describe the relation between the physical intensity of a stimulus and its perceived intensity. Signal detection theory gave rise to methods that enabled psychologists to assess people's sensitivity to stimuli despite individual differences in response bias. The methods of psychophysics apply to all sensory modalities, including sight, hearing, taste, smell, and touch.

The producers of subliminal self-help media suggest that material that is presented below the detection threshold can improve a variety of skills and attitudes. Evidence suggests, however, that the testimonials of satisfied customers are a result of people's commitment to change, their need to justify their efforts, and their expectation of good results. Subliminal perception does occur as long as the stimulus is not too weak, but the effects are subtle and are unlikely to produce useful changes in people's behavior.

1. Which sensory modalities would you least want to lose? Why?

2. If you could design a new sensory modality, what kind of information would it detect? What advantages would this new ability provide? Or do you think that our sense organs already detect all the useful information that is available? Why or why not?

Vision

The visual system performs a remarkable job. We take for granted the fact that in a quick glance we can recognize what there is to see: people, objects, and landscapes, in depth and in full color. Researchers who have tried to program computers to recognize visual scenes realize just how complex this task is. This section begins our tour of the visual system. We will consider the eye and its functions in this chapter, and we'll explore visual perception in Chapter 7. But first, let's start with the stimulus: light.

Light

The eye is sensitive to light. But what is light? Light consists of radiant energy similar to radio waves. Radiant energy oscillates as it is transmitted from its source. For example, the antenna that broadcasts the programs of your favorite FM station transmits radio waves that oscillate at 88.5 MHz (megahertz, or a million times per second). Because electromagnetic energy travels at 186,000 miles per second, the waves transmitted by the FM radio antenna are approximately 11 feet apart. (One 88.5 millionth of 186,000 miles equals 11.09 feet.) Thus, the **wavelength** of the signal from the station—the distance between the waves of radiant energy—is 11 feet.

The wavelength of visible light is much shorter, ranging from 380 through 760 nanometers (a nanometer, nm, is one

billionth of a meter). When viewed by the human eye, different wavelengths of visible light have different colors: for instance, 380-nm light looks violet and 760-nm light looks red.

All other radiant energy is invisible to our eyes. Ultraviolet radiation, X-rays, and gamma rays have shorter wavelengths than visible light has, whereas infrared radiation, radar, radio and television waves, and AC circuits have longer wavelengths. The entire range of wavelengths is known as the *electromagnetic spectrum*. The part our eyes can detect—the part we see as light—is referred to as the *visible spectrum*. (See **Figure 6•6**.)

The definition of the visible spectrum is based on the human visual system. Other species of animals would undoubtedly define the visible spectrum differently. For example, bees can see ultraviolet radiation that is invisible to us. Some plants have taken advantage of this fact and produce flowers that contain pigments that reflect ultraviolet radiation, presenting patterns that attract bees to them. Some snakes (notably, pit vipers such as the rattlesnake) have special organs that detect infrared radiation. This ability enables them to find their prey in the dark by detecting the heat emitted by small mammals in the form of infrared radiation.

The Eye and Its Functions

The eyes are important and delicate sense organs—and they are well protected. Each eye is housed in a bony socket and can be covered by the eyelid to keep out dust and dirt. The eyelids are edged by eyelashes, which help keep foreign matter from falling into the open eye. The eyebrows prevent sweat on the forehead from dripping into the eyes. Reflex mechanisms provide additional protection: The sudden approach of an object toward the face or a touch on the surface of the eye causes automatic eyelid closure and withdrawal of the head.

Figure 6•7 shows a cross-section of a human eye. The transparent **cornea** forms a bulge at the front of the eye and admits light. A tough white membrane called the **sclera** (from the Greek *skleros*, "hard") coats the rest of the eye. The **iris** consists of two bands of muscles that control the amount of light admitted into the eye. The brain controls these muscles and thus regulates the size of the pupil, which is the circular opening

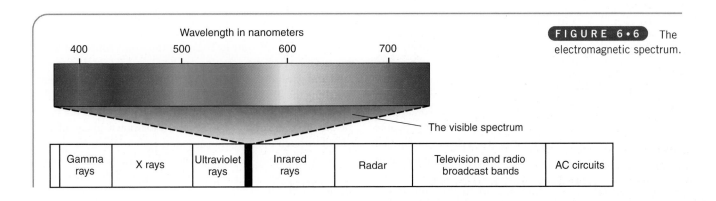

Wavelength in nanometers

400   500   600   700

The visible spectrum

| Gamma rays | X rays | Ultraviolet rays | Inrared rays | Radar | Television and radio broadcast bands | AC circuits |

FIGURE 6•6 The electromagnetic spectrum.

FIGURE 6•7 A cross-section of the human eye.

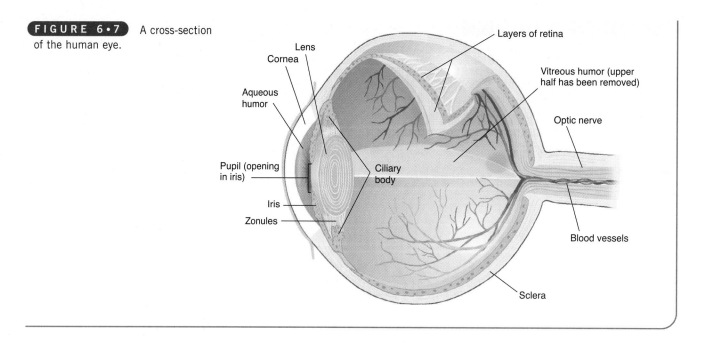

formed by the iris. The pupil constricts in bright light and dilates in dim light. The space immediately behind the cornea is filled with *aqueous humor,* which simply means "watery fluid." This fluid is constantly produced by tissue behind the cornea that filters the fluid from the blood. In place of blood vessels, the aqueous humor nourishes the cornea and other portions of the front of the eye; this fluid must circulate and be renewed. (If aqueous humor is produced too quickly or if the passage that returns it to the blood becomes blocked, the pressure within the eye can increase and cause damage to vision—a disorder known as *glaucoma.*) Because of its transparency, the cornea must be nourished in this unusual manner. Our vision would be less clear if the cornea had blood vessels within it.

The curvature of the cornea and of the **lens,** which lies immediately behind the iris, causes images to be focused on the inner surface of the back of the eye. Although this image is upside down and reversed from left to right, the brain compensates for this alteration and interprets the information appropriately. The lens has a special limitation: Because it must remain transparent, the lens contains no blood vessels and is therefore functionally dead tissue. The shape of the cornea is fixed, but the lens is flexible. A special set of muscles, the ciliary muscles, can alter its shape so that the eye can receive images of either nearby or distant objects. This change in the shape of the lens to adjust for distance is called **accommodation.**

Normally, the length of the eyeball from front to back matches the bending of light rays produced by the cornea and the lens so that the image of the visual scene is sharply focused on the **retina,** the interior surface of the eye. However, for some people these two factors are not matched, and the image on the retina is therefore out of focus. These people may need extra lenses (in the form of eyeglasses or contact lenses) to correct the discrepancy and bring the image into focus. Certain forms of eye surgery also can provide the needed correction. People whose eyes are too long are said to

be *nearsighted*; they need a concave lens to correct the focus. People whose eyes are too short are said to be *farsighted*; they need a convex lens. As people get older, the lenses of their eyes become less flexible, and it becomes difficult for them to focus on objects close to them. If older people already wear glasses, they may need to add reading glasses with convex lenses or to switch to bifocals. (See **Figure 6•8**.)

The retina performs the sensory functions of the eye. Embedded in the retina are more than 130 million **photoreceptors**—specialized neurons that transduce light into neural activity. The information from the photoreceptors is transmitted to neurons that send axons toward one point at the back of the eye—the **optic disk.** All axons leave the eye at this point and join the optic nerve, which connects to the brain. (See **Figure 6•9**, and refer again to Figure 6.7.) Because there are no photoreceptors directly in front of the optic disk, this portion of the retina is blind. If you have not discovered your own blind spots, you might want to try the demonstration shown in **Figure 6•10.**

Before the seventeenth century, scientists thought that the lens sensed the presence of light. Johannes Kepler (1571–1630), the astronomer who discovered the elliptical shape of the planets' orbits around the sun, is credited with suggesting that the retina, not the lens, contained the receptive tissue of the eye. It remained for Christoph Scheiner (another German astronomer) to demonstrate in 1625 that the lens is simply a focusing device. (Perhaps astronomers had a special interest in vision and gave some thought to it during the long nights spent watching the sky.) Scheiner obtained an ox's eye from a slaughterhouse. After carefully peeling the sclera away from the back of the eye, he was able to see an upside-down image of the world through the thin, translucent membrane that remained. As an astronomer, he was familiar with the fact that convex glass lenses could cast images, so he recognized the function of the lens of the eye.

FIGURE 6•8 Lenses used to correct nearsightedness and farsightedness.

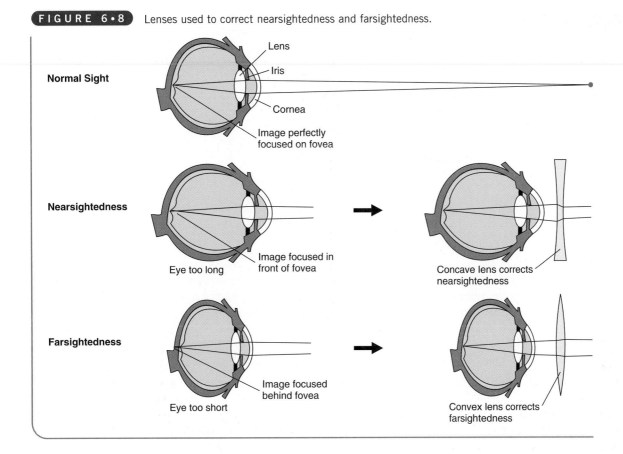

Normal Sight
- Lens
- Iris
- Cornea
- Image perfectly focused on fovea

Nearsightedness
- Eye too long
- Image focused in front of fovea
- Concave lens corrects nearsightedness

Farsightedness
- Eye too short
- Image focused behind fovea
- Convex lens corrects farsightedness

Figure 6•11 (on page 168) shows a schematic view of the retina. The retina has three principal layers. Light passes successively through the *ganglion cell layer* (front), the *bipolar cell layer* (middle), and the *photoreceptor layer* (back). Early anatomists were surprised to find the photoreceptors in the deepest layer of the retina. As you might expect, the cells that are located above the photoreceptors are transparent.

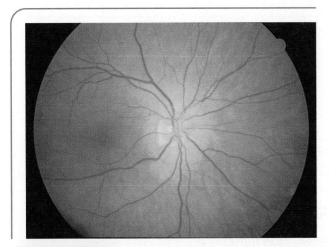

FIGURE 6•9 A view of the back of the eye. The photograph shows the retina, the optic disk, and blood vessels. (Courtesy of Douglas G. Mollerstuen.)

Photoreceptors respond to light and pass signals by means of a transmitter substance to the **bipolar cells,** the neurons with which they form synapses. Bipolar cells transmit this information to the **ganglion cells,** neurons whose axons travel across the retina to form the optic nerve. Thus, visual information passes through a three-cell chain to the brain: photoreceptor → bipolar cell → ganglion cell → brain.

A single photoreceptor responds only to light that reaches its immediate vicinity, but a ganglion cell can receive information from many different photoreceptors. The retina also contains other types of neurons that interconnect both adjacent photoreceptors and adjacent ganglion cells. (Refer to Figure 6.11.) The existence of this neural circuitry indicates that some kinds of information processing occur in the retina.

The human retina contains two general types of photoreceptors: approximately 125 million rods and 6 million cones, so called because of their shapes. **Rods** function mainly in dim light; they are very sensitive to light but are insensitive to differences between colors. **Cones** function when the level of illumination is bright enough to see things clearly. They also are responsible for color vision. The **fovea,** a small pit in the back of the retina approximately 1 millimeter in diameter, contains only cones. (Refer to Figure 6.8.) In most cases a cone sends signals to only one ganglion cell via the bipolar cell to which it is connected. As a consequence, the fovea is responsible for our finest, most detailed vision. When we focus on a specific point in our visual field, we move our eyes so

A test for the blind spot. With the left eye closed, look at the + with your right eye and move the page back and forth, toward and away from yourself. At about 8 inches the colored circle disappears from your vision because its image falls on your blind spot.

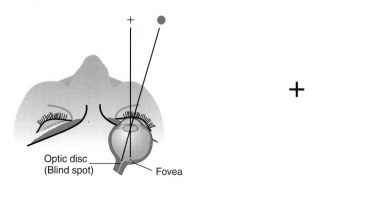

Optic disc
(Blind spot)   Fovea

that the image of that point falls directly on the cone-packed fovea.

Farther away from the fovea, the number of cones decreases and the number of rods increases. Up to 100 rods may send signals to a single ganglion cell. A ganglion cell that receives information from so many rods is sensitive to very low levels of light. Rods are therefore responsible for our sensitivity to very dim light, but the visual information they convey lacks the same sharpness produced by cones.

Transduction of Light by Photoreceptors

Although light-sensitive sense organs have evolved independently in a wide variety of animals—from insects to fish to mammals—the chemistry is essentially the same in all species: A molecule derived from vitamin A is the central ingredient in the transduction of the energy of light into neural activity. (Carrots are said to be good for vision because they contain a substance that the body easily converts to vitamin A.) In the absence of light, this molecule is attached to another molecule, a protein. The two molecules together form a **photopigment.** The photoreceptors of the human eye contain four kinds of photopigments (one for rods and three for cones), but their basic mechanism is the same. When a photon (a particle of light) strikes a photopigment, the photopigment splits apart into its two constituent molecules. This event starts the process of transduction. The splitting of the photopigment causes a series of chemical reactions that stimulate the photoreceptor and cause it to send a signal to the bipolar cell with which it forms a synapse. The bipolar cell sends a signal to the ganglion cell, which then sends a signal to the brain. (See **Figure 6•12**.)

An intact photopigment has a characteristic color. **Rhodopsin,** the photopigment of rods, is pink (*rhodon* means "rose" in Greek). However, once photopigments are split apart by the action of light, they lose their color—they become bleached. Franz Boll discovered this phenomenon in 1876 when he removed an eye from an animal and pointed it toward a window that opened onto a brightly lit scene. He then examined the retina under dim light and found that the image of the

scene was still there. The retina was pink where little light had fallen and pale where the image had been bright. Boll's discovery led others to suspect that a chemical reaction was responsible for the transduction of light into neural activity.

Photoreceptor Layer   Bipolar Cell Layer Ganglion Cell Layer

Photoreceptors

Cone

Rod

Back of Eye

Bipolar cell

Ganglion cell

Light

FIGURE 6•11   The cells of the retina.
(Redrawn by permission of the Royal Society and the authors from Dowling, J. E., & Boycott, B. B. (1966). *Proceedings of the Royal Society* (London), Series B, *166*, 80–111.)

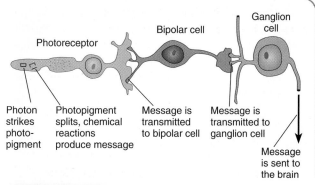

Photoreceptor

Bipolar cell

Ganglion cell

Photon strikes photopigment

Photopigment splits, chemical reactions produce message

Message is transmitted to bipolar cell

Message is transmitted to ganglion cell

Message is sent to the brain

FIGURE 6•12   Transduction of light into neural activity. A photon strikes a photoreceptor and causes the photopigment to split apart. This event initiates the transmission of information to the brain.

After light has caused a molecule of photopigment to split and become bleached, energy from the photoreceptor's metabolism causes the two molecules to recombine. The photopigment is then ready to be bleached by light again. Each photoreceptor contains many thousands of molecules of photopigment. The number of intact, unbleached molecules of photopigment in a given cell depends on the relative rates at which they are being split by light and being put back together by the cell's energy. The brighter the light, the more bleached photopigment there is and thus a decreased sensitivity to light.

Adaptation to Light and Dark

Think, for a moment, about how difficult it can be to find a seat in a darkened movie theater. If you have just come in from bright sunlight, your eyes do not respond well to the low level of illumination. However, after a few minutes you can see rather well—your eyes have adapted to the dark. This phenomenon is called **dark adaptation.**

As already stated, the detection of light requires that photons split molecules of rhodopsin or one of the other photopigments. When high levels of illumination strike the retina, the rate of regeneration of rhodopsin falls behind the rate of the bleaching process. With only a small percentage of the rhodopsin molecules intact, the rods are not very sensitive to light. If you enter a dark room after being in a brightly lit room or in sunlight, there are too few intact rhodopsin molecules for your eyes to respond immediately to dim light. The probability that a photon will strike an intact molecule of rhodopsin is very low. However, after a while the regeneration of rhodopsin overcomes the bleaching effects of the light energy. The rods become full of unbleached rhodopsin, and a photon passing through a rod is likely to find a target. The eye has become dark adapted.

Eye Movements

Our eyes are never completely at rest, even when our gaze is fixed on a particular location—the *fixation point.* Our eyes make fast, aimless, jittering movements, similar to the fine tremors our hands and fingers make when we try to keep them still. They also make occasional slow movements away from the target they are fixed on, which are terminated by quick movements that bring the image at the fixation point back to the fovea.

Although the small, jerky movements that the eyes make when at rest are random, they appear to serve a useful function. Riggs, Ratliff, Cornsweet, and Cornsweet (1953) devised a clever way to project *stabilized images* on the retina—images that remain in the same location on the retina. They mounted a small mirror on a contact lens worn by a research participant and projected a visual image onto the mirror. The image was reflected onto a white screen in front of the participant and from there to a series of mirrors mounted else-

where in the room and back into the participant's eye. The path of the reflections was arranged so that the image moved in perfect synchrony with the eye movements. If the eye moved, so did the image; thus, the image that the researchers projected always fell on precisely the same part of the retina despite the participant's eye movements. Under these conditions, the image began to disappear. At first, the image was clearly seen, but then a "fog" drifted over the participant's field of view, obscuring the image. After a while, the image could not be seen at all.

The disappearance of stabilized images suggests that certain elements of the visual system are not responsive to an unchanging stimulus. Retinal processes may cease to respond to a constant stimulus. The small, involuntary movements of our eyes keep the image moving and thus keep the visual system responsive to the details of the scene before us. Without these involuntary movements, our vision would become blurry soon after we fixed our gaze on a single point and our eyes became still.

The eyes also make three types of nonrandom movements: conjugate movements, saccadic movements, and pursuit movements. In **conjugate movements** both eyes remain fixed on the same target—or, more precisely, such movements keep the image of the target object focused on corresponding parts of the two retinas. If you hold up a finger in front of your face, look at it, and then bring your finger closer to your face, your eyes will make conjugate movements toward your nose. If you then look at an object on the other side of the room, your eyes will rotate outward, and you will see two separate blurry images of your finger. As you will learn in Chapter 7, conjugate eye movements assist the perception of distance.

When you scan the scene in front of you, your gaze travels from point to point as you examine important or interesting features. As you do so, your eyes make jerky **saccadic movements**—you shift your gaze abruptly from one point to another. (See **Figure 6•13.**) For example, when you read a line in this book, your eyes stop several times, moving very quickly between each stop. You cannot consciously control the speed of movement between stops; during each *saccade,* or jump, the eyes move as fast as they can. Scialfa and Joffe (1998) have found that these movements are important to the way we search for a visual object. Ross and Ma-Wyatt (2004) have suggested that saccadic movements help us remember the spatial relationships between objects in our visual field. These researchers found that saccadic movements enhance something called the McCollough effect—a phenomenon described later in the chapter.

Much of the time, the visual scene in front of us contains moving objects: other people, objects blown by the wind, automobiles, airplanes, animals. When we concentrate on one of these objects, we fix our gaze on it and track its movements with our eyes. These tracking movements, which follow the object and project its image onto the fovea, are called **pursuit movements.**

Color Vision

Among mammals, only primates have full color vision. A bull does not charge a red cape; he charges what he sees as an annoying gray object being waved at him. Many birds and fishes have excellent color vision; a brightly colored lure may really appeal to fish as much as to the angler who buys it.

Light (as we humans define it) consists of radiant energy having wavelengths between 380 and 760 nm. Light of different wavelengths gives rise to the perception of different colors. How are we able to tell the differences? Experiments have shown that there are three types of cones in the human eye, each containing a different type of photopigment. Each type of photopigment is most sensitive to light of a particular wavelength. That is, light of a particular wavelength most readily causes a particular photopigment to split. Thus, different types of cones are stimulated by different wavelengths of light. This is what enables us to perceive colors.

Wavelength is related to color, but the terms are not synonymous. For example, the *spectral colors* (the colors we see in a rainbow, which contains the entire spectrum of visible radiant energy) do not include all the colors that we can see, such as brown, pink, and the metallic colors silver and gold.

The fact that not all colors are found in the spectrum means that differences in wavelength alone do not account for the differences in the colors we can perceive.

The Dimensions of Color　Most colors can be described in terms of three physical dimensions: wavelength, intensity, and purity. Three perceptual dimensions corresponding to these physical dimensions—namely, hue, brightness, and saturation—describe what we see. The **hue** of most colors is determined by wavelength; for example, light having a wavelength of 540 nm is perceived as green. A color's **brightness** is determined by the intensity, or amount of energy, of the light that is present, all other factors being equal. A color of maximum brightness dazzles us; a color of minimum brightness is simply black. The third perceptual dimension of color, **saturation,** is roughly equivalent to purity. A fully saturated color consists of light of only one wavelength—for example, pure red or pure blue. Desaturated colors look pastel or washed out. (See **Table 6•2**.)

Saturation is probably the most difficult dimension of color to understand. White light consists of a mixture of all wavelengths of light, but we perceive it as colorless. White light is completely desaturated; no single wavelength is dominant. If we begin with light of a single wavelength (a pure, completely saturated color) and then mix it with a white light, we will have reduced the saturation of that color. For example, when white light is added to red light (700 nm), the result is pink light. The dominant wavelength of 700 nm gives the color a reddish hue, but the addition of white light to the mixture decreases the color's saturation. In other words, pink is a less saturated version of red. **Figure 6•14** illustrates how a color with a particular dominant wavelength (hue) can vary in brightness and saturation.

Color Mixing　Vision can be considered a *synthetic* sensory modality. That is, vision synthesizes (puts together) rather than analyzes (takes apart). When two wavelengths of light are present, we see an intermediate color rather than the two components. (In contrast, the auditory system can be considered *analytical*. If a high note and a low note are played together on a piano, we hear both notes instead of a single, intermediate tone.) The addition of two or more lights of dif-

TABLE 6•2	Physical and Perceptual Dimensions of Color	
Perceptual Dimension	**Physical Dimension**	**Physical Characteristics**
Hue	Wavelength	Length of oscillation of light radiation
Brightness	Intensity	Amount of energy of light radiation
Saturation	Purity	Intensity of dominant wavelength relative to total light energy

FIGURE 6•14 Hue, brightness, and saturation. The colors shown have the same dominant wavelength (hue) but different saturation and brightness.

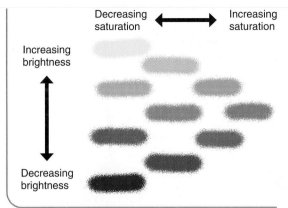

▲ *The spectral colors, contained in a rainbow, do not include all the colors we can see. Thus, differences in wavelength do not account for all the differences in the colors we can perceive.*

ferent wavelengths is called **color mixing.** If we pass a beam of white light through a prism, we break it into the spectrum of the different wavelengths it contains. If we recombine these colors by passing them through another prism (as Isaac Newton did), we obtain white light again. (See **Figure 6•15**.)

Do not confuse color mixing with pigment mixing—what we do when we mix paints. An object has a particular color because it contains pigments that absorb some wavelengths of light (converting them into heat) and reflect other wavelengths. For example, the chlorophyll found in the leaves of plants absorbs less green light than light of other wavelengths. When a leaf is illuminated by white light, it reflects a high proportion of green light and appears green to us.

When we mix paints, we are subtracting colors, not adding them. Mixing two paints yields a darker result (see **Figure 6•16**). For example, adding blue paint to yellow paint yields green paint, which certainly looks darker than yellow. But mixing two beams of light of different wavelengths always yields a lighter color. For example, when red and green light are shone together on a piece of white paper, we see yellow. In fact, we cannot tell a pure yellow light from a synthesized one made of the proper intensities of red and green light. To our eyes, both yellows appear identical.

To reconstitute white light, we do not even have to recombine all the wavelengths in the spectrum. If we shine a blue light, a green light, and a red light together on a sheet of white paper and properly adjust their intensities, the place where all three beams overlap will look perfectly white (refer to Figure 6.16). A color television or a computer screen uses this principle. When white appears on the screen, it actually consists of tiny dots of red, blue, and green light.

Color Coding in the Retina In 1802 Thomas Young (1773–1829), a British physicist and physician, noted that the human visual system can synthesize any color from almost any set of three colors of different wavelengths. Young proposed a **trichromatic theory** ("three-color" theory) of color vision. He hypothesized that the eye contains three types of color receptors, each sensitive to a different hue, and that the brain synthesizes colors by combining the information received from each type of receptor. He suggested that these receptors were sensitive to three of the colors that people perceive as "pure": blue, green, and red. (His theory ignored the fact that people also perceive yellow as a pure color; more about this fact later.) Young's suggestion was incorporated later into a more elaborate theory of color vision developed by Hermann von Helmholtz (1821–1894).

Experiments in recent years have shown that the cones in the human eye do contain three types of photopigments, each of which preferentially absorbs light of a particular wavelength: 420, 530, and 560 nm. Although these wavelengths actually correspond to blue-violet, green, and yellow-green,

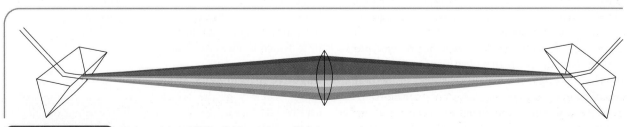

FIGURE 6•15 Color mixing. White light can be split into a spectrum of colors with a prism and recombined through another prism.

FIGURE 6•16 Additive color mixing and paint mixing. When red, blue, and green light of the proper intensity are all shone together, the result is white light. When red, blue, and yellow paints are mixed together, the result is a dark gray.

most investigators refer to these receptors as *blue, green,* and *red* cones. To simplify the discussion here, let's pretend that the three cones respond to these three pure hues. Red and green cones are present in about equal proportions. There are far fewer blue cones.

The eye uses the principle of the color television screen but in reverse: Instead of displaying colors, it senses them. If a spot of white light shines on the retina, it stimulates all three types of cones equally, and we perceive white light. If a spot of pure blue, green, or red light shines on the retina, it stimulates only one of the three classes of cones, and a pure color is perceived. If a spot of yellow light shines on the retina, it stimulates red and green cones equally well but has little effect on blue cones. (You can see in **Figure 6•17** on page 173 that yellow is located between red and green.) Stimulation of red and green cones, then, is the signal that yellow light has been received.

Other investigators after Young and Helmholtz devised theories that took into account the fact that people also perceive yellow as a pure hue. Late in the nineteenth century, Ewald Hering (1834–1918), a German physiologist, noted that the four primary hues appeared to belong to pairs of opposing colors: red/green and yellow/blue. We can imagine a bluish green or a yellowish green, or a bluish red or a yellowish red. However, it is more difficult to imagine a greenish red or a yellowish blue. Hering originally suggested that we cannot imagine these blends because there are two types of photoreceptors, one kind responding to green and red and the other kind responding to yellow and blue. (We'll look at the reasoning behind his statement shortly.)

Hering's hypothesis about the nature of photoreceptors was wrong, but he accurately described the characteristics of the information the retinal ganglion cells send to the brain. Two types of ganglion cells encode color vision: *red/green cells* and *yellow/blue cells.* Both types of ganglion cells fire at a steady rate when they are not stimulated. If a spot of red light shines on the retina, excitation of the red cones causes the red/green

ganglion cells to begin to fire at a high rate. Conversely, if a spot of green light shines on the retina, excitation of the green cones causes the red/green ganglion cells to begin to fire at a slow rate. Thus, the brain learns about the presence of red or green light by the increased or decreased rate of firing of axons attached to red/green ganglion cells. Similarly, yellow/blue ganglion cells are excited by yellow light and inhibited by blue light. Because red and green light, and yellow and blue light, have opposite effects on the rate of axon firing, this temporal coding scheme is called an **opponent process.**

Figure 6.17 provides a schematic account of the opponent-process coding that takes place in the retina. Stimulation of a red cone by red light excites the red/green ganglion cell, whereas stimulation of a green cone by green light inhibits the red/green ganglion cell. If the photoreceptors are stimulated by yellow light, both the red and green cones are stimulated equally. Because of the neural circuitry between the photoreceptors and the ganglion cells, the result is that the yellow/blue ganglion cell is excited, signaling yellow.

The retina contains red/green and yellow/blue ganglion cells because of the nature of the connections between the cones, bipolar cells, and ganglion cells. The brain detects various colors by comparing the rates of firing of the axons in the optic nerve that signal red or green and yellow or blue. Now you can see why we cannot perceive (and therefore would find it difficult to imagine) a reddish green or a bluish yellow: An axon that signals red or green (or yellow or blue) can either increase or decrease its rate of firing. It cannot do both at the same time. A reddish green would have to be signaled by a ganglion cell firing slowly and rapidly at the same time, which is obviously impossible.

Negative Afterimages **Figure 6•18** demonstrates an interesting property of the visual system: the formation of a **negative afterimage.** Stare at the cross in the center of the colorful but odd-looking image on the left for approximately 30 seconds. (Doing so will focus the image on the same retinal

FIGURE 6•17   Color coding in the retina. (a) Red light stimulating a "red" cone, which causes excitation of a red/green ganglion cell. (b) Green light stimulating a "green" cone, which causes inhibition of a red/green ganglion cell. (c) Yellow light stimulating "red" and "green" cones equally. The stimulation of "red" and "green" cones causes excitation of a yellow/blue ganglion cell. The arrows labeled E and I represent neural circuitry within the retina that translates excitation of a cone into excitation or inhibition of a ganglion cell. For clarity, only some of the circuits are shown.

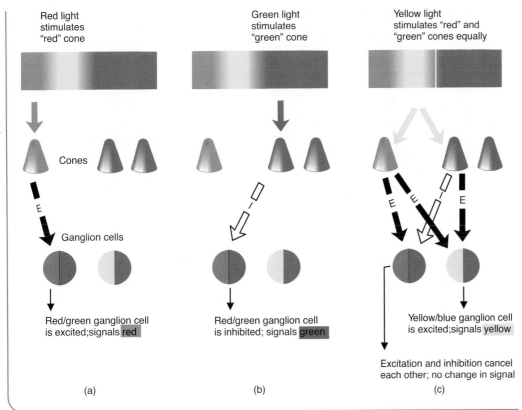

location in each eye.) Then quickly look at the cross in the center of the white rectangle on the right. You will have a fleeting experience of seeing the more familiar red and green colors of a radish—colors that are complementary, or opposite, to the ones on the left. Items that are complementary go together to make up a whole. In color vision, *complementary colors* are those that make white (or shades of gray) when added together.

The most important cause of negative afterimages is the adaptation in the rate of firing of retinal ganglion cells that occurs during prolonged exposure to the original stimulus. When ganglion cells are excited or inhibited for a prolonged period of time, they later show a *rebound effect,* firing faster or slower than normal. For example, the blue of the radish in Figure 6.18 inhibits some red/green ganglion cells. When this region of the retina is then stimulated by the neutral-colored

FIGURE 6•18   A negative afterimage. Stare for approximately 30 seconds at the cross in the center of the left figure; then quickly transfer your gaze to the cross in the center of the right figure. You will see colors that are complementary to the originals.

light reflected off the white rectangle, the red/green ganglion cells—no longer inhibited by the blue light—fire faster than normal. Thus, we see a red afterimage of the radish.

A related phenomenon is that of *contingent color aftereffects*. One type of contingent color aftereffect was discovered by Celeste McCollough in 1965. She asked people to look at two differently oriented and differently colored fields of lines. For example, a person was asked to look at a set of alternating black and red horizontal bars for three seconds and then asked to look at a set of alternating black and green vertical bars for another three seconds. After several minutes of this, the person was then asked to look at black bars that alternated with white ones. The usual result was that the white areas between the horizontal bars now seemed to be tinted with green, while the white areas between the vertical bars seemed pinkish. Known as the McCollough effect, this phenomenon is long lasting compared to the simple aftereffects of the radish; sometimes the McCollough effect persists for days. **Figure 6•19** shows the stimuli used in a related experiment by Ross and Ma-Wyatt (2004).

The explanation of contingent aftereffects is still debated. Dodwell and Humphrey (1990) suggested that the alternating colors of the lines act somewhat like the opponent processes of color. The visual system uses this information to adapt to the arbitrary correlation experienced between the bars and the color. Allan and colleagues (1997) have suggested that the different perceptions are associated in a way similar to classical conditioning. This account is interesting, because it suggests that perceptual experiences can serve as unconditioned stimuli (UCSs) in a classical conditioning paradigm (see Chapter 5). However, this account has been disputed by Humphrey, Herbert, Hazlewood, and Stewart (1998).

Defects in Color Vision

Approximately 1 in 20 males has some form of defective or anomalous color vision. These defects are sometimes called *color blindness,* but this term should probably be reserved for the very few people who cannot see any color at all. Males are affected more than females because many of the genes for producing photopigments are located on the X chromosome. Females have two X chromosomes, but males have only one; so in males a defective gene on that chromosome will always be expressed.

There are many different types of defective color vision. Two of the three we'll consider involve the red/green system. People with these defects confuse red and green. Their primary color sensations are yellow and blue; red and green both appear yellowish. **Figure 6•20** shows one of the figures from a commonly used test for defective color vision. A person who confuses red and green will not be able to see the number 5 in this image.

The most common defect in color vision, called **protanopia** (literally, "first-color defect"), appears to result from a lack of the photopigment for red cones. The fact that people with protanopia have relatively normal sharpness of vision suggests that they have red cones but that these cones are filled with green photopigment (Boynton, 1979). If red cones were missing, almost half of the cones would be gone from the retina, and vision would be less acute. To a protanope, red looks much darker than green. The second form of red/green defect, called **deuteranopia** ("second-color defect"), appears to result from the opposite kind of substitution: Green cones are filled with red photopigment.

As you can see, the nature of the problem for people with either protanopia or deuteranopia is that the red and green cones contain photopigments that respond similarly to light instead of responding differently. Normally, genetic coding on the X chromosome will produce a different photopigment for red cones than for green cones. Provided there is even a slight difference in the way each cone's photopigment absorbs light, the person will be able to distinguish red from green (Neitz, He, & Shevell, 1999); when the two are the same, however, red/green defects will result. Among mammals, only primates exhibit the genetic mechanisms by which red and green cones contain different photopigments (Mollon, 1989). The recent evolutionary development of this characteristic may be the reason that the two red/green color defects are more prevalent than the third form of color defect.

This third form of color defect, called **tritanopia** ("third-color defect"), involves the yellow/blue system and is much

Adapt   Test

FIGURE 6•19 A demonstration of the McCollough effect. Cover the red patch and gaze for a few seconds at the green patch. You should not fixate your gaze, as in the demonstration of negative afterimages; instead, move your eyes around the gray border now and then. Then cover the green patch and gaze at the red patch. Alternate gazing at these two patches. After a few minutes, look at the patch on the right. Does one half look a different color? How do the two sides differ in color? Some people report seeing this effect long after they have stopped looking at the colored patches on the left.

(Adapted from Ross, J., & Ma-Wyatt, A. (2004). Saccades actively maintain perceptual continuity. *Nature neuroscience, 7,* 65–69. Reprinted with permission.)

FIGURE 6·20 A figure commonly used to test for defective color vision. People with red/green color blindness will fail to see the number 5.
(Courtesy of American Optical Corporation.)

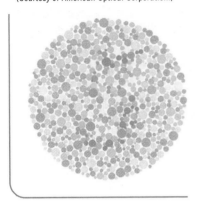

rarer: It affects fewer than 1 in 10,000 people. Tritanopes see the world in greens and reds; to them, a clear blue sky is a bright green, and yellow appears pink. The faulty gene that causes tritanopia is not carried on a sex chromosome; therefore, it is equally common in males and females. This defect appears to involve the loss of blue cones. There are far fewer of these than of red and green cones to begin with, and investigators have not yet determined whether tritanopes' blue cones are missing or are filled with one of the other photopigments.

Interim Summary

Vision

Imagine yourself watching a dance competition on television with a friend. The cornea and lens of each eye cast an image of the screen on your retinas, which contain photoreceptors: rods and cones. In bright illumination, only your cones gather visual information; your rods work only when the light is very dim. The energy from the light that reaches the cones in your retinas is transduced into neural activity when photons strike molecules of photopigment, splitting them into their two constituents. This event causes the cones to send information through the bipolar cells to the ganglion cells. The axons of the ganglion cells form the optic nerves and have synapses with neurons in the brain.

Vision requires the behavior of looking, which consists of moving your eyes and head. The eyes have a repertoire of movements that are important for visual perception. Experiments using stabilized images show that small, involuntary movements keep an image moving across the photoreceptors, thus preventing them from adapting to a constant stimulus. (As you will see later in this chapter, other sensory systems also respond better to changing stimuli than to constant ones.) As the TV images move, your eyes follow them with pursuit

movements. If you look at your friend, your eyes make rapid saccadic movements. These movements are conjugate, so that each eye is fixed on the same point. Your eyes also accommodate to changes in distance, adjusting the focus of their lenses.

When an image of the visual scene is cast on the retina, each part of the image has a different color, which can be specified in terms of its hue (corresponding to the dominant wavelength), brightness (intensity), and saturation (purity). Information about color is encoded trichromatically by your cones; the red, green, and blue cones respond in proportion to the amount of the appropriate wavelength contained in the light striking them. This information is transformed into an opponent-process coding, signaled by the firing rates of red/green and yellow/blue ganglion cells, and is transmitted to the brain. If you stare for a while at a colored image and then look at a blank wall, you will see a negative afterimage. If you are a male, the chances are about 1 in 20 that you will have some defect in red/green color vision. If this is the case, your red or green cones contain the wrong photopigment. Male or female, chances are very slim that you will have a blue/yellow defect caused by the absence of functioning blue cones.

QUESTION TO CONSIDER

Birds, certain species of fish, and some primate species have full, three-cone color vision. Why is color vision useful? What are its benefits for humans specifically?

Audition

Vision involves the perception of objects in three dimensions, at various distances, and with a multitude of colors and textures. These complex stimuli may occur at a single point in time or over an extended period. They also may involve either an unchanging or a rapidly changing scene. In contrast to vision, audition and the other senses analyze much simpler stimuli (such as an odor or a taste) or depend on time and stimulus change for the development of a complex perception. For example, to perceive a solid object in three dimensions by means of touch, we must manipulate it—turn it over in our hands or move our hands over its surface. The stimulus must change over time for a full-fledged perception of form to emerge. The same is true for audition: We hear nothing meaningful in an instant.

Sound

Sound consists of rhythmical pressure changes in air. As an object vibrates, it causes the air around it to move. The vibration creates waves of pressure, positive and negative, as molecules of air alternately undergo compression and rarefaction (thinning out). As a positive pressure wave arrives at your ear, it bends your eardrum in. The following wave of negative pressure causes your eardrum to bend out. (See **Figure 6·21**.)

FIGURE 6•21 Sound waves. Changes in air pressure from sound waves move the eardrum in and out. Air molecules are closer together in regions of higher pressure and farther apart in regions of lower pressure.

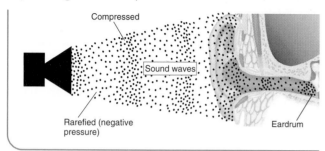

▲ *Sound consists of rhythmical pressure changes in air, which can convey an incredible diversity of auditory sensations.*

Sound waves are measured in frequency units of cycles per second or **hertz (Hz).** The human ear perceives vibrations between approximately 30 and 20,000 Hz. Sound waves can vary in intensity (amplitude) and frequency. These variations produce corresponding changes in our perception of a sound's loudness and of its pitch (highness or lowness). Consider a loudspeaker, a device that contains a paper cone moved back and forth by a coil of wire located in a magnetic field. Alternations in the electrical current transmitted from an amplifier to this coil cause the coil (and the paper cone) to move back and forth. If the vibrations become more intense (that is, if the cone moves in and out over a greater distance), the *loudness* of the sound increases. (See **Figure 6•22**.) If the cone begins vibrating more rapidly, the *pitch* of the sound rises. A third perceptual dimension, *timbre* (pronounced "TAM-ber"), corresponds to the complexity of the sound. We'll examine all three dimensions of sound waves in more detail later in the chapter.

The Ear and Its Functions

When people refer to the ear, they usually mean what anatomists call the *pinna*—the flesh-covered cartilage attached to the side of the head. (*Pinna* means "wing" in Latin.) But the pinna performs only a small role in audition. It helps funnel sound waves through the *ear canal* toward the middle and inner ear, where the business of hearing gets done. (See **Figure 6•23**.)

The *eardrum* (or, more properly, the *tympanic membrane*) is a thin, flexible membrane that vibrates back and forth in response to sound waves and passes these vibrations on to the receptor cells in the inner ear. The eardrum is attached to the first of a set of three middle ear bones called the **ossicles** (literally, "little bones"). The three ossicles are known informally as the *hammer*, the *anvil*, and the *stirrup*, because of their shapes. The technical terms are *malleus*, *incus*, and *stapes*, respectively. These bones act together, in lever fashion, to transmit the vibrations of the eardrum to the fluid-filled structure of the inner ear.

The bony structure that contains the auditory receptor cells is called the **cochlea** (pronounced "COKE-lee-uh"). *Kochlos* is a Greek word that means "snail," which accurately describes its shape; refer to Figure 6.23. The cochlea is filled with a liquid. A bony chamber (the *vestibule*) is attached to the cochlea and contains two openings, the oval window and the round window. The last of the three ossicles (the stirrup) presses against a membrane behind the **oval window,** thus transmitting sound waves into the liquid inside the cochlea. The cochlea is divided into three chambers by two membranes, one of which is the **basilar membrane**—a sheet of tissue that contains the auditory receptor cells. As the footplate of the stirrup presses back and forth against the membrane behind the oval window, pressure changes in the fluid above the basilar membrane cause the basilar membrane to vibrate. Because the basilar membrane varies in its width and flexibility, different frequencies of sound cause different

Physical Dimension	Perceptual Dimension				
Amplitude (intensity)	Loudness	∿∿∿	loud	∿	soft
Frequency	Pitch	∿	low	∿∿∿	high
Complexity	Timbre	∿∿	simple	∿	complex

FIGURE 6•22 The physical and perceptual dimensions of sound waves.

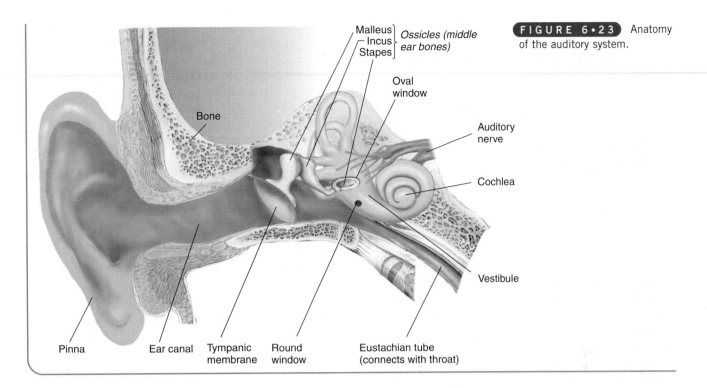

FIGURE 6·23 Anatomy of the auditory system.

parts of the basilar membrane to vibrate. High-frequency sounds cause the end near the oval window to vibrate, medium-frequency sounds cause the middle to vibrate, and low-frequency sounds cause the tip to vibrate. (See **Figure 6·24**.)

In order for the basilar membrane to vibrate freely, the fluid in the lower chamber of the cochlea must have somewhere to go—because unlike gases, liquids cannot be compressed. Free space is provided by the **round window.** When the basilar membrane moves down, the displacement of the fluid causes the membrane behind the round window to bulge out. In turn, when the basilar membrane moves up, the membrane behind the round window bulges in.

Some people suffer from a middle ear disease that causes bone to grow over the round window. Because their basilar membrane cannot easily move back and forth, these people have a severe hearing loss. However, their hearing can be restored by a surgical procedure called *fenestration* ("window making") in which the surgeon drills a tiny hole in the bone where the round window should be.

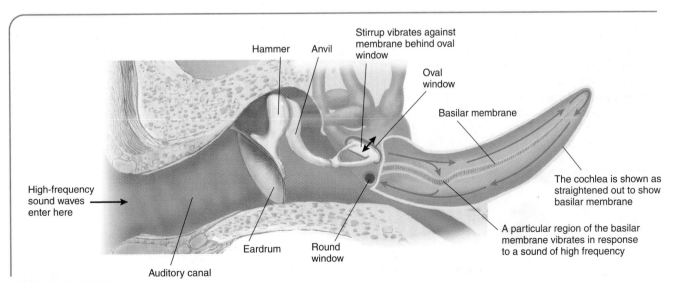

FIGURE 6·24 Responses to sound waves. When the stirrup pushes against the membrane behind the oval window, the membrane behind the round window bulges outward. Different high-frequency and medium-frequency sound vibrations cause flexing of different portions of the basilar membrane. In contrast, low-frequency sound vibrations cause the tip of the basilar membrane to flex in synchrony with the vibrations.

Sounds are detected by special neurons known as auditory hair cells, located on the basilar membrane. **Auditory hair cells** transduce mechanical energy caused by the movement of the basilar membrane into neural activity. These cells possess hairlike protrusions called **cilia** ("eyelashes"). The ends of the cilia are embedded in the **tectorial membrane**, a fairly rigid shelf that hangs over the basilar membrane like a balcony. When sound waves cause the basilar membrane to vibrate, the cilia are stretched.

This pull on the cilia of the auditory hair cells is translated into neural activity. (See **Figure 6•25.**) When a mechanical force is exerted on the cilia of a cell, the electrical charge across the cell's membrane is altered. What causes the change in potential is not fully known, although pressure on the cilia is known to increase calcium flow into the hair cell (Kennedy, Evans, Crawford, & Fettiplace, 2003). These calcium currents are very fast and may alter the temporal duration of the depolarization. The change in the electrical charge causes a transmitter substance to be released at a synapse between the auditory hair cell and the dendrite of a neuron, similar to the way that bipolar cells connect to a ganglion cell in the retina. However, one hair cell will be connected to many auditory neurons (Trussell, 2002); so, unlike the case with visual cells, one hair cell has a large effect on subsequent nerve activity. The auditory neurons project axons that form the auditory nerve.

Earlier we saw how stabilized visual stimuli can actually disappear; small movements of the eyes normally keep this from happening by changing the location of the stimuli on the retina. The auditory system does not have this capacity and must instead deal with sounds that persist for long intervals—intervals long enough to deplete the transmitter substance in a normal synapse. The synapses between the hair cells and neurons therefore differ in function from others in the central nervous system. They involve more synaptic vesicles and briefer effects. Also, the depolarization is stronger (Glowatzki & Fuchs, 2002). The result is a more reliable signal passed along the auditory nerve.

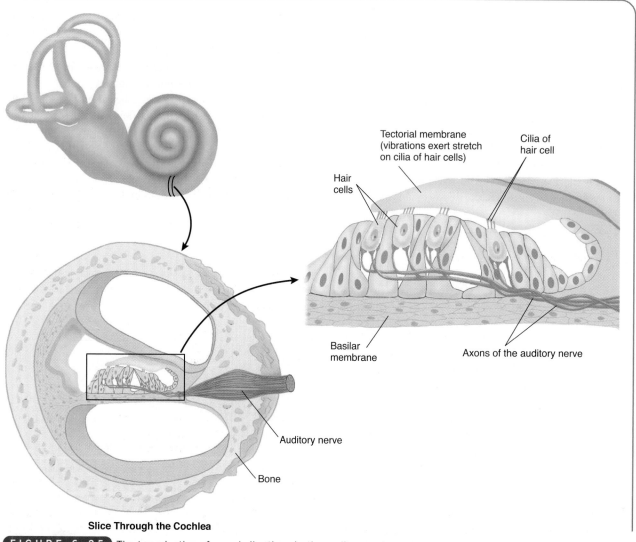

Slice Through the Cochlea

FIGURE 6•25 The transduction of sound vibrations in the auditory system.

Detecting and Localizing Sounds in the Environment

Sounds can differ in pitch, loudness, and timbre. They also come from particular locations in the auditory environment. How does the ear distinguish these characteristics? The ear's ability to distinguish sounds by their timbre depends on its ability to distinguish pitch and loudness. So let's examine these two characteristics first.

Pitch and Loudness Scientists originally thought that the sensory neurons of the auditory system represented pitch (frequency) by firing in synchrony with the vibrations of the basilar membrane. However, they subsequently learned that axons cannot fire rapidly enough to represent the high frequencies that we can hear. A good, young ear can hear frequencies of more than 20,000 Hz, but axons cannot fire more than 1000 times per second. Therefore, high-frequency sounds, at least, must be encoded in some other way.

High-frequency and medium-frequency sounds cause different parts of the basilar membrane to vibrate, as already noted. Thus, sounds of different frequencies stimulate different groups of auditory hair cells located along the basilar membrane. At least for high-frequency and medium-frequency sounds, therefore, the brain is informed of the pitch by the activity of different sets of axons in the auditory nerve that represent different groups of hair cells. When medium-frequency sound waves reach the ear, auditory hair cells located in the middle of the basilar membrane are activated. In contrast, high-frequency sounds activate auditory hair cells located at the base of the basilar membrane near the oval window. (Refer to Figure 6.24.)

Experiments have found that damage to specific sets of hair cells along the basilar membrane causes loss of the ability to perceive specific frequencies.

Although high-frequency and medium-frequency sounds are detected because they cause different sets of hair cells to respond, low-frequency sounds are detected by a different method. Kiang (1965) recorded the electrical activity of single axons in the auditory nerve and found many that responded to particular frequencies. Presumably, these axons originated in neurons stimulated by hair cells located on different regions of the basilar membrane. However, Kiang did not find any axons that responded uniquely to particular frequencies lower than 200 Hz—and yet tones lower than 200 Hz are easily perceived. How, then, are the lower frequencies encoded?

The answer is this: Frequencies lower than 200 Hz cause the tip of the basilar membrane to vibrate in synchrony with the sound waves. Neurons that are stimulated by hair cells located there are able to fire in synchrony with these vibrations, thus firing at the same frequency as the sound. The brain "counts" these vibrations (so to speak) and thus detects low-frequency sounds. This process is an example of temporal coding.

What about loudness (intensity, or amplitude)? The axons of the auditory nerve appear to inform the brain of the loudness of a stimulus by altering their rate of firing—another example of temporal coding. More intense vibrations stimulate the auditory hair cells more intensely. This stimulation causes them to release more transmitter substance, which results in a higher rate of firing by the axons in the auditory nerve.

This explanation works for the axons involved in anatomical coding of pitch; in this case, pitch is signaled by which neurons fire, and loudness is signaled by their rate of firing. However, the neurons that signal lower frequencies do so with their rate of firing alone. If they fire more frequently, they signal a higher pitch. Obviously, they cannot signal both loudness and pitch by the same means. Therefore, most investigators believe that the loudness of low-frequency sounds is signaled by the number of auditory hair cells that are active at a given time. A louder sound excites a larger number of hair cells.

Timbre You can easily distinguish between the sounds of a violin and a clarinet, even if they are playing tones of the same pitch and loudness. So, clearly, pitch and loudness are not the only characteristics of a sound. Sounds can vary greatly in complexity. They can start suddenly or gradually increase in loudness, be short or long, and seem thin and reedy or full and vibrant. The enormous variety of distinguishable sounds is in large part due to the important characteristic of sound called timbre.

The combining, or synthesizing, of two or more simple tones, each consisting of a single frequency, can produce a complex tone. For example, an electronic synthesizer produces simple tones of different frequencies, each of which can be varied in amplitude. Thus, it can synthesize the complex tones of a clarinet or violin or can assemble completely new sounds not produced by any other source. Conversely, complex tones that have a regular sequence of waves can be reduced by means of analysis into several simple tones. **Figure 6•26** (on page 180) shows a waveform produced by the sound of a clarinet (upper curve). The curves that appear beneath it depict the amplitude and frequency of the simple waveforms that, when combined, can be shown mathematically to produce the complex waveform of the sound made by a clarinet.

The kind of analysis shown in Figure 6.26 specifies the timbre of a sound. We can tell a clarinet from another instrument because each instrument produces sounds consisting of a unique set of simple tones called **harmonics** (also called *overtones*). Their frequencies are multiples of the **fundamental frequency,** or the basic pitch of the sound. **Timbre** is the distinctive combination of harmonics with the fundamental frequency. The fundamental frequency causes one part of the basilar membrane to vibrate, while each of the harmonics causes another portion to vibrate. Thus, a complex tone causes many different portions of the basilar membrane to vibrate simultaneously. The ear analyzes the tone as diagrammed in Figure 6.26. Information about the fundamental frequency and each of the harmonics is sent to the brain through the auditory nerve, and the person hears a complex

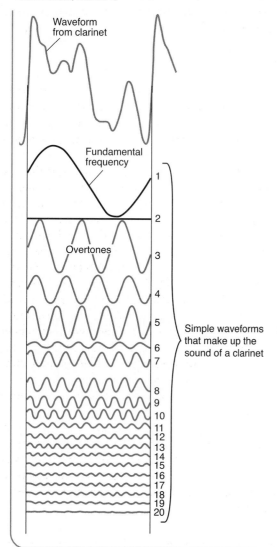

Waveform from clarinet

Fundamental frequency

1

2

Overtones

3

4

5

6
7

Simple waveforms that make up the sound of a clarinet

8
9
10
11
12
13
14
15
16
17
18
19
20

tone with a particular timbre. The process of listening to an orchestra and identifying several instruments playing simultaneously is analogous to the complex analysis performed by the auditory system.

There is a trade-off between time and complexity when the ear analyzes sound. Engineers speak of "filters" that can distinguish specific aspects of sound; a filter that is good at analyzing a brief sound may not be good at analyzing a longer one. Lewicki (2002) has examined the kinds of filters that can best discriminate among different kinds of sounds: environmental sounds such as twigs snapping, animal vocalizations such as hyena calls, and sounds in between such as human speech. He found that the human auditory system amounts to a theoretical combination of filters attuned to a mixture of sounds in which those of the environment predominate. Sig-

nificantly, this theoretical system performs quite well within the range of human speech sounds (100–2000 Hz).

Locating the Source of a Sound When we hear an unexpected sound, we usually turn our heads quickly to face its source. Even newborn infants can make this response with reasonably good accuracy. And once our faces are oriented toward the source of the sound, we can detect changes in its location by as little as 1 degree. To locate the source, we make use of two qualities of sound: relative loudness and difference in arrival time.

Relative loudness is the most effective means of perceiving the location of high-frequency sounds. Acoustic energy, in the form of vibrations, does not actually pass through solid objects. Low-frequency sounds can easily make a large solid object, such as a wall, vibrate, setting the air on the other side in motion and producing a *new* sound across the barrier. But large solid objects cannot vibrate rapidly, so they effectively damp out high-frequency sounds. They cast a "sound shadow," just as opaque objects cast a shadow in the sunlight. The human head is one such object, and it damps out high-frequency sounds so that they appear much louder to the ear nearer the source of the sound. Thus, if a source on your right produces a high-frequency sound, your right ear will receive more intense stimulation than your left ear will. The brain uses this difference to calculate the location of the source of the sound. (See **Figure 6•27**.)

The second method involves detecting differences in the arrival time of sound pressure waves at each eardrum. This method works best for frequencies below approximately 3000 Hz. A 1000-Hz tone produces pressure waves approximately 1 foot apart. Because the distance between a person's eardrums is somewhat less than half that, a source of 1000-Hz sound located to one side of the head will cause

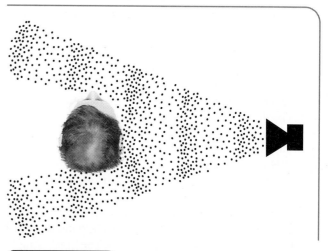

FIGURE 6•27 Localizing the source of high-frequency sounds. The head casts a "sound shadow" for high-frequency sound vibrations. The brain uses the difference in loudness to detect the location of the source of the sound.

one eardrum to be pushed in while the other eardrum is pulled out. In contrast, if the source of the sound is directly in front of the listener, both eardrums will move in synchrony. (See **Figure 6•28**.)

Researchers have found that when the source of a sound is located to the side of the head, as in Figure 6.28(a), axons in the right and left auditory nerves will fire at different times. The brain detects this disparity and so perceives the location of the sound at one side or the other. In fact, the brain can detect differences in firing times of a fraction of a millisecond. The easiest auditory stimuli to locate are those that produce brief clicks, which cause brief bursts of neural activity. Apparently, it is easiest for the brain to compare the arrival times of single bursts of sound.

Where does the brain compute this information? Initial processing occurs in the brain stem region known as the superior olive. Stimulation involving temporal disparity activates different areas of the superior olive; but, unlike the retina, these areas do not have a simple relationship to the locations of sounds in space (Oliver et al., 2003). Zatorre, Bouffard, Ahad, and Belin (2002) used a PET scan technique to examine cortical functioning as people listened to environmental sounds. When all sounds were the same but differed in location, no single part of the auditory cortex seemed to respond to differences in location. But when the sounds were different and came from different locations, the area at the top of the temporal cortex, close to the parietal lobe, showed a strong response. Recall from Chapter 4 that the parietal lobe is a region of the brain that helps us maintain a sense of spatial orientation.

Sound localization seems to show contingent aftereffects similar to those discussed earlier for color vision. Dong, Swindale, and Cynader (1999) asked people to listen to tones produced by a loudspeaker that moved back and forth in front of them. As the loudspeaker moved to the left, the frequency of the tone increased; as it moved to the right, the frequency decreased. After the participants underwent 10 minutes of adaptation, the researchers presented several test tones. Some of these tones were stationary in location but changed in pitch. Dong and colleagues found that participants judged stationary tones that increased in pitch as moving to the right. They judged stationary tones that decreased in frequency as moving to the left. That is, the apparent motion of the tone was, like a negative afterimage, opposite to the initial experience.

Age-Related Losses in Hearing

Earlier, I mentioned that visual acuity changes as the eye's lens becomes less flexible with age. The auditory system also changes with age, but the result is not merely a general loss of sensitivity. In absolute terms, significant hearing losses generally do not occur until the sixth or seventh decade of life (Cheesman, 1997). What is important, however, is the way these cumulative losses involve specific aspects of hearing.

Under laboratory conditions, if you are trying to hear a tone against background noise, your threshold is better if the noise goes to both ears rather than to one. The difference is called the masking-level difference (MLD), and it can be measured in various ways. Pichora-Fuller and Schneider (1998), among others, have found that older listeners (about 69 years of age) show smaller MLDs than younger listeners (about 23 years of age) over a wide range of noise levels. These results imply an age-related decline in the auditory system's ability to use loudness and arrival disparities to isolate a sound. The result is likely to be that the older listener will find it more difficult to follow a conversation in a noisy environment, or may confuse the sound of a telephone on television with a phone ringing in the kitchen.

Another age-related change is the loss of sensitivity to different bands of frequencies. Sensitivity to higher frequencies declines earlier and with more severity than sensitivity to lower frequencies. The result may be a loss in the ability to perceive the sounds that convey the information in speech (Schneider, 1997).

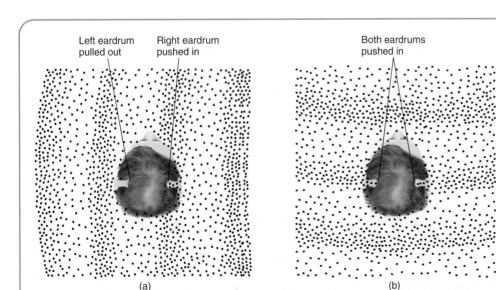

Left eardrum pulled out   Right eardrum pushed in

Both eardrums pushed in

(a)

(b)

FIGURE 6•28

Localizing the source of medium-frequency and high-frequency sounds through differences in arrival time. (a) Source of a 1000-Hz tone to the right. The pressure waves on each eardrum are out of phase; one eardrum is pushed in, while the other is pulled out. (b) Source of a sound directly in front. The vibrations of the eardrums are synchronized.

Biology and Culture

The Deaf Community

From 0.1 to 0.2 percent of children in the Western world are born deaf. By the time we're 80 years of age, half of us will have lost some or all of our hearing (Avraham, 1997). Deafness profoundly affects a person's ability to communicate with others; imagine trying to join a group of people whose voices you cannot hear. But now imagine that the other people are also deaf. It is only in the company of people who have normal hearing that deafness hinders a person's ability to communicate (Erting, Johnson, Smith, & Snider, 1989; Sachs, 1989; Schein, 1989).

Deaf people aren't just people who have a particular sensory loss. In fact, they share a common language. As we saw in Chapter 2, the term *culture* usually refers to a group of people who live close together in a common environment—who share customs, religious beliefs, and practices—and who often resemble each other genetically. Deaf people are extremely diverse. They live in different environments; they have different customs, religious beliefs, and practices; and they are genetically unrelated. Nevertheless, deaf people share a culture. What unites the Deaf community is the ability of its members to communicate with one another visually through sign language. In this way the Deaf community provides a remedy for what would seem the disadvantage of deafness: the inability to communicate readily with others.

Not all deaf people are members of the Deaf community. People who are *postlingually deaf*—people who become deaf later in life after they have learned oral and written language—are unlikely to learn sign language and join the Deaf community. (In this context, *lingual,* from the word for "tongue," refers to the acquisition of spoken language.) In addition, some *prelingually deaf* people—people who are born deaf or who become deaf during infancy—never learn sign language, primarily because they are "mainstreamed" in community schools or attend a school for the deaf that teaches oral communication.

What is a sign language? It is *not* English; nor is it French or Spanish or Chinese. The most common sign language in North America is American Sign Language (ASL). ASL is a full-fledged language, having signs for nouns, verbs, adjectives, adverbs, and all the other parts of speech contained in oral languages. People can converse rapidly and efficiently by means of sign language, can tell jokes, and can even make puns based on the similarity between signs. They can also use their language ability to think in words.

The grammar of ASL is based on its visual and spatial nature. For example, if a person makes the sign for *John* while holding her hands in one location in front of her and later makes the sign for *Mary* while holding her hands in another location, she can hold one hand in the *John* location and move it toward the *Mary* location while making the sign for *love.* In this way she is saying, "John loves Mary." Signers also can modify the meaning of signs through facial expressions or through the speed and vigor with which they make a sign. Many of the prepositions, adjectives, and adverbs found in spoken languages do not require specific words in ASL. The fact that sign languages are based on three-dimensional hand and arm movements accompanied by facial expressions means that their grammars are very different from those of spoken languages. Thus, a word-for-word translation from a spoken language to a sign language (or vice versa) is impossible.

There is no single, universal sign language. Deaf people from North America cannot communicate with deaf people from Great Britain. (They can write to each other, of course, but written English bears no relation to ASL or to the sign language used in Great Britain.) However, deaf people in France and North America can understand each other reasonably well, because ASL is partly based on the sign language that was used in France in the early nineteenth century.

Several attempts have been made (invariably by people who are *not* deaf) to "improve" sign languages. Deaf people resent such attempts, just as you might resent it if a foreigner tried to improve the English language by cleaning up its inconsistencies. Most people cherish their native languages, and deaf people are particularly proud of theirs.

The education of deaf persons poses special problems. Deafness follows the so-called 90 percent rule. That is, 90 percent of deaf children have parents who can hear, 90 percent of deaf people marry other deaf people, and 90 percent of deaf parents have children who can hear. Most parents of deaf children, not being themselves deaf, know nothing about the Deaf community. Thus, they are unable to transmit to their children the most important characteristic of this community: a sign language. The current practice of "mainstreaming" children who have disabilities—that is, placing them in neighborhood schools with the rest of the population—means that most deaf children's teachers have no experience educating deaf students. In fact, most of their teachers have never even met a deaf child before. Thus, deaf youngsters may not learn a sign language until late childhood or adolescence, when they finally meet other deaf people. Some never learn it.

Some schools for deaf students use the *oralist approach* to education. Children are taught to communicate orally with the rest of the population by reading lips and speaking. Both tasks are extremely difficult. Try watching a news broadcast with the sound turned off to see how much you can understand. Ask a friend to mouth, "bear, bar, pear," and see if you can detect the difference. Of course, you could get better with years of practice, but even a very skilled lip-reader must do a lot of guessing and anticipating. And you would be starting out knowing English as a native language, so you would know what words to look out for and anticipate. A congenitally deaf child taught with the oralist approach starts out with no knowledge of language at all, which makes the process doubly difficult. Also, learning to lip-read and to speak (without the opportunity to hear

▲ *Communication by means of American Sign Language is as rapid, efficient, and rich in nuance and detail as communication by means of any spoken language.*

yourself) takes so much time that not much of the school day is left for other academic subjects.

Most people in the Deaf community who communicate with one another by means of signing have negative reactions to oral communication. The difficult task of deciphering lip movements makes them feel tense. They also realize that their pronunciation is imperfect and that their voices sound strange to others. They feel at a disadvantage with respect to hearing people in a spoken conversation. In contrast, they feel relaxed and at ease when communicating with other deaf people by signing. A young man wrote about his experience when he entered Gallaudet University, an institution for deaf students that uses ASL:

> As I made my way through many educational and enjoyable semesters, learning a "new" way of communicating, I was enthralled. I was able to understand a person 100 percent of the time without having to lipread or depend on notes. It is a special feeling to relax and listen when in the past you have had to pay so much attention to the person you were speaking with that you could never really relax. (Mentkowski, 1983, p. 1)

Like other people who closely identify with their cultures, members of the Deaf community feel pride in their common heritage and become defensive when they perceive threats to it. Some deaf people say that if they were given the opportunity to hear, they would refuse it. Some deaf parents have expressed happiness when they learned that their children were born deaf: They no longer needed to fear that their children would not be included in their own Deaf culture.

A recent technological development, the cochlear implant, is perceived by most members of the Deaf community as a serious threat to their culture. A cochlear implant is an electronic device surgically implanted in the inner ear that can enable some deaf people to hear. It is most useful for two groups: people who became deaf in adulthood and very young children. Cochlear implants in postlingually deaf adults pose no threat to the Deaf community, because postlingually deaf persons never were members of Deaf

culture. Putting a cochlear implant in a young child, however, means that the child's early education will take the oralist approach. In addition, many deaf people resent the implication that deafness is something that needs to be repaired. They see themselves as different but never defective.

Interim Summary

Audition

The human auditory system is sophisticated enough to differentiate among a vast array of sounds. Audition translates the physical dimensions of sound—amplitude, frequency, and complexity—into the perceptual dimensions of loudness, pitch, and timbre for sounds ranging from 30 to 20,000 Hz. Sound pressure waves put the process in motion by setting up vibrations in the eardrum, which are passed on to the ossicles. Vibrations of the stirrup against the membrane behind the oval window create pressure changes in the fluid within the cochlea that cause the basilar membrane to vibrate. This causes the auditory hair cells on the basilar membrane to move relative to the tectorial membrane. The resulting pull on the cilia of the hair cells stimulates them to secrete a transmitter substance that excites auditory neurons and stimulates the auditory nerve, which, in turn, informs the brain of the presence of sound.

Two different methods of detection enable the brain to recognize the pitch of a sound. Different high-frequency and medium-frequency sounds are perceived when different parts of the basilar membrane vibrate in response to these frequencies. Low-frequency vibrations are detected when the tip of the basilar membrane vibrates in synchrony with the sound, which causes some axons in the auditory nerve to fire at that frequency.

Locating the source of a sound depends on two systems. The ear locates low-frequency sounds by differences in the arrival time of the sound waves in each ear. It locates high-frequency sounds by differences in intensity that result from the "sound shadow" cast by your head.

The auditory system analyzes sounds with complex timbre into their constituent frequencies, each of which causes a particular part of the basilar membrane to vibrate. All of these functions proceed automatically, so the brain can hear the sound of a clarinet or any other combination of fundamental frequency and harmonics. With age, people may lose some of their ability to hear sound against a noisy background and to hear certain frequencies.

The Deaf community consists of deaf people who communicate visually by means of a sign language. The social isolation that a deaf person may feel among oral communicators disappears in the company of other people who can sign. Communication by sign languages can be as accurate and efficient as spoken communication.

1. A naturalist once noted that when a male bird stakes out his territory, he sings with a very sharp, staccato song that says, in effect, "Here I am, and stay away!" In contrast, if a predator appears in the vicinity, many birds will emit alarm calls that consist of steady whistles that start and end slowly. Knowing what you do about the two means of localizing sounds, why do you think these two types of calls have different characteristics?

2. If you had a child who was born deaf, would you send him or her to a school that taught sign language or to a school that emphasized speaking and lip-reading? Why? Now imagine that you are deaf (or, if you are deaf, that you are hearing). Does your answer change? Why or why not?

Gustation

We have two senses specialized for detecting chemicals in our environment: taste and smell. Together, they are referred to as the **chemosenses**. Taste, or **gustation**, is the simplest of the sensory modalities. Taste is not the same as flavor; the flavor of a food includes its odor and texture as well as its taste. You have probably noticed that the flavors of foods are diminished when you have a head cold. This loss of flavor occurs not because your taste buds are inoperative but because mucus congestion makes it difficult for odor-laden air to reach your receptors for the sense of smell. Without their characteristic odors to serve as cues, onions taste much like apples (although apples do not make your eyes water).

Receptors and the Sensory Pathway

Taste reception begins with the tongue. The tongue has a corrugated appearance marked by creases and bumps. The bumps are called **papillae** (from the Latin, meaning "nipple"). Each papilla contains numerous taste buds (in some cases as many as 200). A **taste bud** is a small organ containing receptor cells shaped like the segments of an orange. The cells have hairlike projections called *microvilli* that protrude through the pore of the taste bud into the saliva that coats the tongue and fills the trenches of the papillae. (See **Figure 6•29**.) Molecules of chemicals dissolved in the saliva stimulate the receptor cells, probably by interacting with specialized receptors on the microvilli. The receptor cells form synapses with dendrites of neurons that send axons to the brain through three different cranial nerves.

The Five Qualities of Taste

The physical properties of the molecules that we taste determine the nature of the taste sensations (Lindemann, 2001). Traditionally, it has been thought that there were four taste qualities: sourness, sweetness, saltiness, and bitterness. Recently, however, investigators have found evidence for another taste: *umami* (a Japanese word that means "good taste"). Umami refers to the taste of monosodium glutamate; genes that code for its receptors have been identified (Chaudhari, Landin, & Roper, 2000). We experience these five taste qualities when different molecules stimulate different types of receptors. For example, all substances that taste salty ionize (break into charged particles) when they dissolve. The most important salty substance is, of course, table salt—sodium chloride (NaCl). Other chlorides, such as lithium or potassium chloride, and other salts, such as bromides or sulphates, also are salty; but none tastes quite as salty as sodium chloride. This finding suggests that the specific function of salt-tasting receptors is to identify sodium chloride. Most likely, salt-tasting receptors respond when sodium enters a taste cell through sodium channels in the membrane. The influx of sodium depolarizes the cell, causing it to release a transmitter substance. Sodium plays a unique role in the regulation of our body fluid. If the body's store of sodium falls too low, we cannot retain water, and our blood volume will decrease. One result can be heart failure. Loss of sodium stimulates a strong craving for the salty taste of sodium chloride.

Both bitter and sweet substances seem to consist of large, non-ionizing molecules. Scientists cannot predict merely on the basis of shape whether a molecule will taste bitter or sweet (or neither). Some molecules (such as saccharin, a sugar substitute) stimulate both sweet and bitter receptors. Most likely, the function of our sensitivity to bitterness is to avoid ingesting poisons. Many plants produce alkaloids that serve to protect them against being eaten by insects or browsing herbivores. Some of these alkaloids are poisonous to humans, and most of them taste bitter. In contrast, the sweetness receptor creates sensitivity to the sugar content of fruits and other nutritive plant foods. When sweet-loving animals gather and eat fruit, they tend to disperse the seeds and help propagate the plant; thus, the presence of sugar in the fruit is to the plant's advantage as well.

Most sour tastes are produced by acids—in particular, by the hydrogen ion (H+) contained in acid solutions. The sourness receptor probably serves as a warning device against substances that have undergone bacterial decomposition,

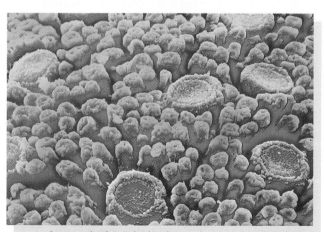

▲ *A photograph of taste buds taken with a scanning electron microscope.*

FIGURE 6•29 (a) Saliva makes contact with taste buds located in the papillae of the tongue. (b) Molecules of chemicals dissolved in saliva stimulate the receptor cells of taste buds.

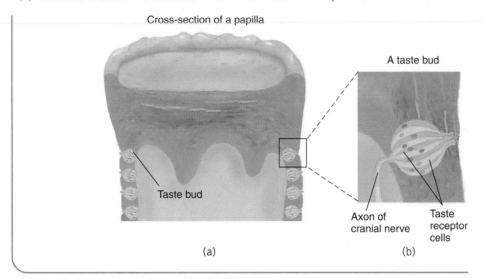

Cross-section of a papilla

A taste bud

Taste bud

Axon of cranial nerve

Taste receptor cells

(a)　　　(b)

most of which become acidic. In earlier times, most wholesome, natural foods were likely to taste sweet or salty, not bitter or sour. (Nowadays we can mix sweet-tasting and sour-tasting substances to make tasty beverages such as lemonade.)

You probably recognize monosodium glutamate—the chemical that stimulates the umami receptor—as a taste-enhancing agent used in many dishes, especially in Asian cuisines. Why would we have a gene for such a taste sensation? Glutamate is an abundant amino acid and is present in many proteins, which may explain why animals have evolved a taste for it (Lindemann, 2000). There also may be receptors for groups of amino acids (Nelson et al., 2002) to enhance our preference for fuel-rich meaty-tasting foods.

Olfaction

The sense of smell—**olfaction**—is one of the most puzzling sensory modalities and is unlike the other sensory modalities in two important ways. First, people have difficulty using words to describe odors. Second, odors have a powerful ability to evoke memories and feelings, even many years after an event (Chu & Downes, 2000). At some time in their lives, most people encounter an odor that they recognize as belonging to their childhood, even though they cannot identify it specifically. The phenomenon may occur because the olfactory system sends information to the limbic system, a part of the brain that plays a role in both emotions and memories.

The olfactory sense shows other interesting patterns as well. Women, for example, seem to have a more acute sense of smell than do men. And it is possible that we have not one but two olfactory systems. The second system would be the "accessory olfactory system" possessed by many mammals, which detects special chemicals called **pheromones** that regulate sexual and social behavior (Bartoshuk & Beauchamp, 1994). Humans possess the organ appropriate to an accessory olfactory system, and

there is evidence that women's menstrual cycles can be affected by chemical signals (Stern & McClintock, 1998). However, there is still uncertainty whether the anatomical components of a human accessory olfactory system are fully functional. For this reason we'll consider only the primary olfactory system here.

Olfaction, like audition, seems to be an analytical sensory modality. That is, when we sniff air that contains a mixture of familiar odors, we usually can identify the individual components. The molecules do not blend together and produce a single odor the way lights of different wavelengths produce a single color. For example, when visiting a carnival, we can distinguish the odors of popcorn, cotton candy, crushed grass, and diesel oil in a single sniff.

Although many other mammals, such as dogs, have more sensitive olfactory systems than humans do, we should not underrate our own. The olfactory system is second only to the visual system in the number of sensory receptor cells, with an estimated 10 million cells. We can smell some substances at lower concentrations than the most sensitive laboratory instruments can detect. One reason for the difference in sensitivity between our olfactory system and those of other mammals is that other mammals put their noses where odors are the strongest—just above the ground. For example, a dog following an odor trail sniffs along the ground, where the odors of a passing animal may have clung. Even a bloodhound's nose would not be very useful if it were located five or six feet above the ground, as ours is. That being said, though, it is true that dogs have vastly more olfactory receptors (Doty, 2001).

Anatomy of the Olfactory System

Figure 6•30 (on page 186) shows the anatomy of the olfactory system. The receptor cells lie in the **olfactory mucosa**, patches of mucous membrane on the roof of the nasal sinuses, just under the base of the brain. The receptor cells have cilia that are embedded in the olfactory mucosa. They also have axons that

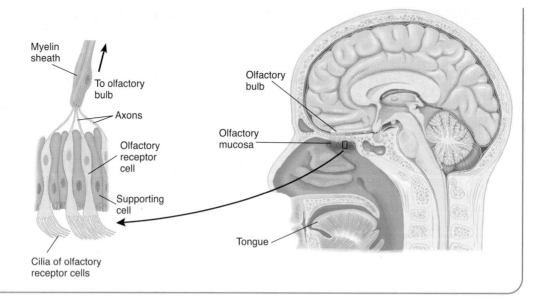

The olfactory system.

pass through small holes in the bone above the olfactory mucosa and form synapses with neurons in the olfactory bulbs. The **olfactory bulbs** are stalklike structures located at the base of the brain. They contain neural circuits that perform the first analysis of olfactory information.

The interaction between odor molecule and receptor cell appears to be similar to the interaction between transmitter substance and postsynaptic receptor on a neuron. That is, when a molecule of an odorous substance fits a receptor molecule located on the cilia of a receptor cell, the cell becomes excited. This excitation is passed on to the brain by the axon of the receptor cell. Thus, the mechanism for smell shares features with that for taste.

Unlike information from all other sensory modalities, olfactory information is not sent to the thalamus and then relayed to a specialized region of the cerebral cortex. Instead, olfactory information is sent directly to several regions of the limbic system—in particular, to the amygdala and to the limbic cortex of the frontal lobe. One intriguing clue about the way olfactory stimuli are processed is that olfaction shows *cross-modal* integration with taste stimuli. Dalton, Doolittle, Nagata, and Breslin (2000) tested people's sensitivity to benzaldehyde, an odor that smells like cherry and almonds. They found that the threshold for detecting the odor was lower when the participants in their study held a sweet solution of saccharin in their mouths. Dalton and colleagues suggested that the amygdala may be responsible for this increased sensitivity to an odor when it is paired with a particular flavor.

The Dimensions of Odor

We know that there are five qualities of taste and that a color can be specified in terms of hue, brightness, and saturation. Research in molecular biology suggests that the olfactory system uses up to 1000 different receptor molecules, located in the membrane of the receptor cells, to detect different categories of odors (Buck & Axel, 1991). Presumably, the presence of molecules of a substance with a particular odor produces a particular pattern of activity in the olfactory system. That is, the molecules will strongly stimulate some receptors but will stimulate others only moderately or not at all. This pattern of stimulation is transmitted to the brain, where it is recognized as a particular odor. Researchers do not yet know exactly which molecules stimulate which receptors; nor do they know how the information from individual olfactory receptor cells is put together. Araneda, Kini, and Firestein (2000) have found a receptor that responds to a large family of chemicals but rejects others. Sets of receptors may therefore serve a discriminative function similar to the three different kinds of cones in the visual system.

Interim Summary

Gustation and Olfaction

Both gustation and olfaction involve cells whose receptors respond selectively to various kinds of molecules. Taste buds have at least five kinds of receptors, which respond to molecules that we perceive as sweet, salty, sour, bitter, or umami. To most organisms sweet, umami, and moderately salty substances taste pleasant, whereas sour or bitter substances taste unpleasant. Sweet, umami, and salty receptors permit us to detect nutritious foods and sodium chloride. Sour and bitter receptors help us avoid substances that might be poisonous.

Olfaction is a remarkable sense modality. Olfactory information combines with information about taste to provide us with the flavor of a food present in our mouths. We can distinguish countless different odors and can recognize smells from childhood, even if we cannot remember when or where we first encountered them. Although we recognize similarities between different odors, most seem unique. Unlike visual stimuli such as colors, odors do not easily blend.

The detection of different odors appears to be accomplished by up to 1000 different receptor molecules located in the membrane of the olfactory receptor cells.

QUESTIONS TO CONSIDER

1. Bees and birds can taste sweet substances, but cats and alligators cannot. Obviously, the ability to taste particular substances is related to the range of foods a species eats. If, through the process of evolution, a species develops a greater range of foods, what do you think comes first, the food or the receptor? Would a species start eating something having a new taste (say, something sweet) and later develop new taste receptors by which to detect the taste, or would the taste receptors evolve first and then provide the animal with a new taste when it came across the food? Give reasons for your answer.

2. Odors have a peculiar ability to evoke memories—a phenomenon vividly described by Marcel Proust in his multivolume novel *Remembrance of Things Past*. Have you ever encountered an odor that you knew was somehow familiar, but you couldn't say exactly why? What explanations can you think of? Might this phenomenon have something to do with the fact that the sense of olfaction appeared very early during the evolutionary development of the human brain? Why or why not?

The Somatosenses

The body senses, or **somatosenses,** include our abilities to respond to touch, vibration, pain, warmth, coolness, limb position, muscle length and stretch, tilt of the head, and changes in the speed of head rotation. The precise number of sensory modalities in this list depends on definitions; but it does not really matter whether we say, for example, that we respond to warmth and coolness by means of one sensory modality or two. The important thing (in this example) is to understand how our bodies are able to detect changes in temperature.

Many experiences require simultaneous stimulation of several different sensory modalities. For example, taste and odor alone do not determine the flavor of spicy food; mild (or sometimes not-so-mild) stimulation of pain detectors in the mouth and throat gives hot food its special characteristic. Sensations such as tickle and itch are apparently mixtures of varying amounts of touch and pain. Similarly, our perception of the texture and three-dimensional shape of an object that we touch involves our senses of pressure, muscle and joint sensitivity, and motor control simultaneously (in order to manipulate the object). If we handle an object and find that it moves smoothly in our hand, we may conclude that it is slippery. If, after handling this object, our fingers subse-

quently slide across each other without much resistance, we perceive a feeling of oiliness. In contrast, if we perceive vibrations when we move our fingers over an object, we may consider it rough. And so on. If you close your eyes as you manipulate soft and hard, warm and cold, and smooth and rough objects, you can make yourself aware that the separate sensations interact and give rise to a complex perception.

The following discussion of the somatosenses groups them into three major categories: the skin senses, the internal senses, and the vestibular senses.

The Skin Senses

The entire surface of the human body is *innervated* (supplied with nerves) by the dendrites of neurons that transmit somatosensory information to the brain. Cranial nerves convey information from the face and the rest of the front portion of the head (including the teeth and the inside of the mouth and throat); spinal nerves convey information from the rest of the body's surface. All somatosensory information is detected by the dendrites of neurons; the system uses no separate receptor cells. However, some of these dendrites have specialized endings that modify the way they transduce energy into neural activity.

Figure 6·31 shows the sensory receptors found in hairy skin and in smooth, hairless skin (such as the skin on the palms of the hands or soles of the feet). The most common type of skin sensory receptor is the **free nerve ending,** which resembles the fine roots of a plant. Free nerve endings infiltrate the middle layers of both smooth and hairy skin and surround the hair follicles in hairy skin. If you bend a single hair on your forearm, you will see how sensitive the free nerve endings are.

The largest of the specialized skin receptors, called the **Pacinian corpuscle,** is actually visible to the naked eye. Pacinian corpuscles are very sensitive to touch. When they are moved, their axons fire a brief burst of impulses. Among the possible functions of Pacinian corpuscles is providing information about vibration.

Other specialized receptors detect different sensory qualities, including warmth, coolness, and pain.

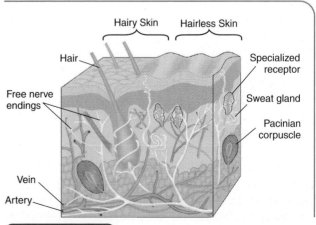

FIGURE 6·31 Sensory receptors in hairy skin (left) and in hairless skin (right).

Temperature There is general agreement that different sensory endings produce the perceptions of warmth and coolness. Detectors for coolness appear to be located closer to the surface of the skin. If you suddenly place your foot under a stream of rather hot water, you may feel a brief sensation of cold just before you perceive that the water is really hot. This sensation probably results from short-lived stimulation of the coolness detectors located in the upper layers of the skin.

The temperature detectors respond best to changes in temperature. Within reasonable limits, the temperature of the air around us—the ambient temperature—comes to feel "normal." Temporary changes in temperature are perceived as warmth or coolness. Thus, temperature detectors adapt to the temperature of the environment. This adaptation can be easily demonstrated. If you place one hand in a pail of hot water and the other in a pail of cold water, the intensity of the sensations of heat and cold will decrease after a few minutes. If you then plunge both hands into a pail of water that is at room temperature, it will feel hot to the cold-adapted hand and cold to the hot-adapted hand. It is the *change* in temperature that is the important information signaled to the brain. Of course, there are limits to the process of adaptation. Extreme heat or cold will continue to feel hot or cold no matter how long we experience it.

Pressure Sensory psychologists speak of touch and pressure as two separate senses. They define *touch* as the sensation of very light contact of an object with the skin and *pressure* as the sensation produced by more forceful contact. Sensations of pressure occur only when the skin is actually moving (being pushed in), which means that the pressure detectors respond only while they are being bent. Just how the motion stimulates the neurons is not known. If you rest your forearm on a table and place a small weight on your skin, you will feel the pressure at first, but eventually you will feel nothing at all, if you keep your arm still. You fail to feel the pressure not because your brain "ignores" incoming stimulation but because the sensory endings no longer send impulses to your brain. Studies that have measured very slow, very minute movements of a weight sinking down into the skin have shown that sensory transmission ceases when the movements stop. With the addition of another weight on top of the first one, movement and sensory transmission begin again (Nafe & Wagoner, 1941). A person will feel a very heavy weight indefinitely, but the sensation is probably pain rather than pressure.

Sensitivity to subtle differences in touch and pressure varies widely across the surface of the body. The most sensitive regions are the lips and the fingertips. The most common measure of tactile discrimination (the ability to tell touches apart) is the **two-point discrimination threshold.** To determine this measure, a researcher touches a person with one or both legs of a caliper and asks the person to say whether the sensation is coming from one or two points. (See **Figure 6•32.**) The farther apart the legs of the caliper must be before the person reports feeling two separate sensations, the lower the sensitivity of that region of skin.

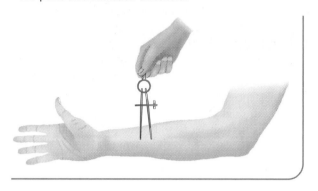

FIGURE 6•32 The method for determining the two-point discrimination threshold.

Pain Pain is a complex perception involving not only intense sensory stimulation but also emotion. That is, a given sensory input to the brain might be interpreted as pain in one situation and as pleasure in another. For example, when people are sexually aroused, they become less sensitive to many forms of pain and may even find such intense stimulation pleasurable.

Physiological evidence suggests that the sensory aspect of pain is quite different from the emotional reaction to pain. Opiates such as morphine diminish pain by stimulating opioid receptors on neurons in the brain; these neurons block the transmission of pain information to the brain. In contrast, some tranquilizers (e.g., Valium) depress neural systems that are responsible for the emotional reaction to pain but do not diminish the intensity of the pain. Thus, people who have received a drug such as Valium will report that they feel the pain but that it does not bother them much.

Evidence from surgical procedures also supports the distinction between the sensory and emotional factors in pain. Prefrontal lobotomy (a form of brain surgery), like the use of tranquilizers, blocks the emotional component of pain but does not affect the primary sensation. Therefore, operations similar to prefrontal lobotomy (but much less drastic) are sometimes performed to treat people who suffer from chronic pain that cannot be alleviated by other means.

Many noxious stimuli elicit two kinds of pain—an immediate sharp, or "bright," pain followed by a deep, dull, sometimes throbbing pain. Some stimuli elicit only one of these two kinds of pain. For example, a pinprick will produce only the superficial "bright" pain, whereas a hard blow from a blunt object to a large muscle will produce only the deep, dull pain. Different sets of axons transmit signals corresponding to these two types of pain.

Pain—or the fear of pain—is one of the most effective motivators of human behavior. It also serves us well in the normal course of living. As unpleasant as pain is, we would have difficulty surviving without it. For example, pain tells us if we have sprained an ankle or broken a bone or have an inflamed appendix.

A particularly interesting form of pain sensation occurs after a limb has been amputated: Up to 70 percent of amputees report that they feel as though their missing limbs still exist and that they often hurt. This phenomenon is referred to as the **phantom limb** (Melzack, 1992). People who have phantom limbs report that the limbs feel very real; that if they try to reach something with their missing limb, it feels as though the limb responded. Sometimes they perceive the limb as protruding, and they may feel compelled to avoid knocking the limb against a door frame or sleeping with the limb between them and the mattress. People have reported all sorts of sensations in phantom limbs, including pain, pressure, warmth, cold, wetness, itching, sweatiness, and prickliness.

Melzack suggests that the phantom limb perception is inherent in the organization of the parietal cortex. As we saw in Chapter 4, the parietal cortex is involved in our perception of our own bodies. Indeed, people who have sensory neglect, caused by lesions of the right parietal lobe, have been seen to push their own legs out of bed, believing that they actually belong to someone else. Melzack reports that some people who were born with missing limbs nevertheless experience the phantom limb. This suggests that our brains are genetically programmed to provide sensations from all four limbs—even if one or more limbs are absent.

The Internal Senses

Sensory receptors located in our internal organs, bones and joints, and muscles convey painful, neutral, and in some cases pleasurable sensory information. For example, the internal senses convey the pain of arthritis, the physical location of our limbs in three dimensions, the pangs of hunger, and the pleasure of a warm drink descending to our stomach.

Muscles contain special sensory receptors. One class of receptors, located at the junction between muscles and the tendons that connect them to the bones, provides information about the amount of force the muscle is exerting. These receptors protect the body by inhibiting muscular contractions when they become too forceful. During competition weight lifters may receive injections of a local anesthetic near the tendons of some muscles to eliminate this protective mechanism. This enables the athletes to lift even heavier weights. Unfortunately, tendons may snap or bones may break under the increased force.

Another stretch-detection system consists of spindle-shaped receptors distributed throughout the muscle. These receptors, appropriately called **muscle spindles,** inform the brain about changes in muscle length. Although we are not conscious of the specific information provided by the muscle spindles, the brain uses the information, together with information from joint receptors, to keep track of the location of parts of our body and to control muscular contractions.

The Vestibular Senses

What we call our "sense of balance" in fact involves several senses, not merely one. For example, if you stand on one foot and then close your eyes, you immediately realize how important vision is to balance. The **vestibular apparatus** of the inner ear provides additional sensory input that helps us remain upright.

▲ *Information from the internal senses, along with visual information, tells this skater about the location and movements of her body and helps her gauge the force she needs to exert to perform this intricate maneuver.*

The three liquid-filled **semicircular canals**—located in the inner ear and oriented at right angles to one another—detect changes in the rotation of the head. (See **Figure 6•33.**) Rotation of the head causes motion of the liquid, which stimulates the receptor cells located in the canals.

Another set of inner ear organs, the **vestibular sacs,** contain crystals of calcium carbonate that are embedded in a gelatin-like substance attached to receptive hair cells. In one sac the receptive tissue is on the wall; in the other, it is on the floor. When the head tilts, the weight of the calcium carbonate crystals shifts, producing different forces on the cilia of the hair cells. These forces change the activity of the hair cells, and the information is transmitted to the brain. However, it must also be coordinated with information from the semicircular canals. Taking a rapid step forward shifts the calcium carbonate crystals in the same way that tilting your head back does. Yet you probably don't feel as if you've accelerated forward when you only tilt your head back. Research evidence reviewed by Snyder (1999) suggests that the semicircular canals help to differentiate the information from the vestibular sacs.

The vestibular sacs help us maintain an upright head position. They also participate in a reflex that enables us to see clearly even when the head is moving. When we walk, our

FIGURE 6•33 The three semicircular canals and two vestibular sacs located in the inner ear.

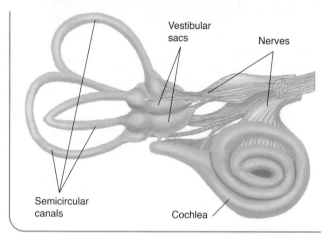

eyes are jostled back and forth. The movement of the head stimulates the vestibular sacs to cause reflex movements of the eyes that partially compensate for the head movement. You can see the effect of this reflex with the following demonstration. Hold this textbook steady and move your head from side to side. Notice that it is relatively easy to keep the text in the center of your vision. Now try keeping your head still and move the textbook from side to side. The relative motion is the same, but it is very difficult to keep the text in view. The reflexive eye movements are linked to the specific vestibular information from the head. People who lack this reflex because of localized brain damage must stop walking in order to see things clearly—for example, to read a street sign.

Interim Summary

The Somatosenses

The somatosenses gather several different kinds of information from different parts of the body. The skin senses of temperature, touch and pressure, vibration, and pain inform us about the nature of objects that come in contact with our skin. The sensitive Pacinian corpuscles in the skin detect vibration. The skin's temperature receptors convey the sense of warmth or coolness, responding chiefly to changes in temperature. Also in the skin, free nerve endings give rise to sensations of pain. The internal senses convey sensations such as hunger pangs or the pain of a kidney stone. Sensory receptors in our muscles and joints inform the brain of the movement and location of our arms and legs. The vestibular senses help us keep our balance.

QUESTION TO CONSIDER

Why does repetitive vestibular stimulation (like that provided by a boat ride on choppy water) sometimes cause nausea and vomiting? What useful functions might this response serve?

Suggestions for Further Reading

Beauchamp, G. K., & Bartoshuk, L. M. (Eds.). (1997). *Tasting and smelling (Handbook of perception and cognition)* (2nd ed.). San Diego, CA: Academic Press.

This chapter provides an authoritative review of research and theory related to these two often-overlooked sensory systems.

Bruce, V., Green, P. R., & Georgeson, M. A. (2003). *Visual perception: Physiology, psychology and ecology* (4th ed.). New York: Psychology Press.

While perhaps not as appealing as Gregory's book, Bruce et al. offer a comprehensive overview of the visual system.

Coren, S., Ward, L. M., & Enns, J. T. (2003). *Sensation and perception* (6th ed.). New York: Wiley.

After you have completed Chapter 6, this book will provide an excellent next step in enlarging your understanding of the sensory systems.

Gregory, R. L. (1997). *Eye and brain: The psychology of seeing* (5th ed.). Princeton, NJ: Princeton University Press.

This richly illustrated book offers a fascinating and highly readable introduction to the visual system and related psychological phenomena.

Gulick, W. L., Gescheider, G. A., & Frisina, R. D. (1989). *Hearing: Physiological acoustics, neural coding, and psychoacoustics.* New York: Oxford University Press.

This book builds on Stevens' and offers an updated technical view of the physiology and psychophysics of hearing.

Stevens, S. S. (1975). *Psychophysics: Introduction to its perceptual, neural, and social prospects.* New York: Wiley.

The world's first professor of psychophysics summarizes his research and theory at the conclusion of his brilliant career. Of particular interest is the material on the psychophysics of social judgment.

Yost, W. A. (2000). *Fundamentals of hearing: An introduction* (4th ed.). San Diego, CA: Academic Press.

If you are looking for a strong follow-up to the chapter's consideration of the auditory system, this book is highly recommended.

Key Terms

absolute threshold (p. 160)

accommodation (p. 166)

anatomical coding (p. 158)

auditory hair cell (p. 178)

basilar membrane (p. 176)

bipolar cell (p. 167)

brightness (p. 170)

chemosense (p. 184)

cilia (p. 178)

cochlea (p. 176)

color mixing (p. 171)

cone (p. 167)

conjugate movement (p. 169)

cornea (p. 165)

dark adaptation (p. 169)

deuteranopia (p. 174)

difference threshold (p. 160)

fovea (p. 167)

free nerve ending (p. 187)

fundamental frequency (p. 179)

ganglion cell (p. 167)

gustation (p. 184)

harmonic (p. 179)

hertz (Hz) (p. 176)

hue (p. 170)

iris (p. 165)

just-noticeable difference (jnd) (p. 159)

lens (p. 166)

muscle spindle (p. 189)

negative afterimage (p. 172)

olfaction (p. 185)

olfactory bulbs (p. 186)

olfactory mucosa (p. 185)

opponent process (p. 172)

optic disk (p. 166)

ossicles (p. 176)

oval window (p. 176)

Pacinian corpuscle (p. 187)

papilla (p. 184)

perception (p. 157)

phantom limb (p. 189)

pheromones (p. 185)

photopigment (p. 168)

photoreceptor (p. 166)

protanopia (p. 174)

psychophysics (p. 159)

pursuit movement (p. 169)

receiver operating characteristic curve (ROC curve) (p. 161)

receptor cell (p. 158)

retina (p. 166)

rhodopsin (p. 168)

rod (p. 167)

round window (p. 177)

saccadic movement (p. 169)

saturation (p. 170)

sclera (p. 165)

semicircular canal (p. 189)

sensation (p. 157)

signal detection theory (p. 160)

somatosenses (p. 187)

subliminal perception (p. 164)

taste bud (p. 184)

tectorial membrane (p. 178)

temporal coding (p. 159)

threshold (p. 160)

timbre (p. 179)

transduction (p. 158)

trichromatic theory (p. 171)

tritanopia (p. 174)

two-point discrimination threshold (p. 188)

vestibular apparatus (p. 189)

vestibular sac (p. 189)

wavelength (p. 165)

Weber fraction (p. 159)

7

PERCEPTION

Brain Mechanisms of Visual Perception

The Primary Visual Cortex • The Visual Association Cortex • Effects of Brain Damage on Visual Perception

The visual system of the brain is arranged hierarchically: Information is analyzed at each level, and the results are passed on to the next level for further analysis. The primary visual cortex contains a "map" of the retina and thus of the visual field. Visual images are broken down into small pieces, each analyzed by clusters of neurons that provide information about such features as lines, edges, and colors. Particular regions of the first level of the visual association cortex are responsible for the analysis of details of orientation, spatial frequency, movement, and color. The second level of the visual association cortex contains regions that recognize three-dimensional objects and the objects' location and direction of movement. Brain damage to a person's visual association cortex disrupts specific perceptual abilities, such as the perception of common objects, faces, colors, movements, and spatial locations.

Perception of Objects

Figure and Ground • Gestalt Laws of Perceptual Organization • Models of Pattern Perception • *Evaluating Scientific Issues: Does the Brain Work Like a Computer?* • Bottom-Up and Top-Down Processing: The Roles of Features and Context • Perceptual ("What") and Action ("Where") Systems: A Possible Synthesis

The Gestalt organizational laws of proximity, similarity, good continuation, closure, and common fate describe how the grouping of elements of the visual scene helps us distinguish between figure and ground—between objects and their backgrounds. Psychologists have proposed several models, including templates, prototypes, and distinctive features, to explain how we can recognize particular patterns of visual stimuli and thus identify particular objects. The fact that we can recognize complex objects such as faces as quickly as we can recognize simple geometric shapes suggests that the visual system performs many tasks at the same time. Cognitive research and research using computers provide evidence that the brain is a parallel processor. Neural networks have elements with properties similar to those of neurons. Bottom-up processing assembles a complex perception from simple elements provided by clusters of neurons in the primary visual cortex. Top-down processing refers to the powerful effect that context can have on the interpretation of the information about these simple elements. Top-down information may be provided by a system of object perception that is distinct from the system that guides controlled movement.

Perception of Space and Motion

Depth Perception • *Biology and Culture: Effects of Cultural Experience on Visual Perception* • Constancies of Visual Perception • Motion Perception

Although perceiving the shapes of objects is an important task, we also must perceive their locations in space and their movements in order for behavior to be effective. Depth perception relies on both binocular and monocular cues. Cultural factors may affect our visual perceptions, but probably not in a fundamental way. When there are changes in the brightness of the light that illuminates an object or when an object rotates or its distance from us changes, our perception of the object remains relatively constant. The perception of motion enables us to predict the future locations of objects. We can perceive shapes of objects even when we have only scanty information about the movements of their parts. We can also perceive nonexistent movement when two objects are alternately illuminated.

Dr. L., a young neuropsychologist, was presenting the case of Mrs. R. to a group of medical students doing a rotation in the neurology department at the medical center. The chief of the department had shown them Mrs. R.'s CT scans, and now Dr. L. was addressing the students. He told them that Mrs. R.'s stroke had not impaired her ability to talk or to move about, but it had affected her vision.

A nurse ushered Mrs. R. into the room and helped her find a seat at the end of the table.

"How are you, Mrs. R.?" asked Dr. L.

"I'm fine. I've been home for a month now, and I can do just about everything that I did before I had my stroke."

"Good. How is your vision?"

"Well, I'm afraid that's still a problem."

"What seems to give you the most trouble?"

"I just don't seem to be able to recognize things. When I'm working in my kitchen, I know what everything is as long as no one moves anything. A few times my husband tried to help me by putting things away, and I couldn't see them any more." She laughed. "Well, I could see them, but I just couldn't say what they were."

Dr. L. took some objects out of a paper bag and placed them on the table in front of Mrs. R.

"Can you tell me what these are?" he asked. "And," he added, "please don't touch them."

Mrs. R. stared intently at the objects. "No, I can't rightly say what they are."

Dr. L. pointed to one of them, a wristwatch. "Tell me what you see here," he said.

Mrs. R. looked thoughtful, turning her head one way and then the other. "Well, I see something round, and it has two things attached to it, one on the top and one on the bottom." She continued to stare at it. "There are some things inside the circle, I think, but I can't make out what they are."

"Pick it up."

She did so, made a wry face, and said, "Oh. It's a wristwatch." At Dr. L.'s request, she picked up the rest of the objects, one by one, and identified each of them correctly.

"Do you have trouble recognizing people, too?" asked Dr. L.

"Oh, yes!" she sighed. "While I was still in the hospital, my husband and my son both came in to see me, and I couldn't tell who was who until my husband said something—then I could tell which direction his voice was coming from. Now I've trained myself to recognize my husband. I can usually see his glasses and his bald head, but I have to work at it. And I've been fooled a few times." She laughed. "One of our neighbors is bald and wears glasses, too, and one day when he and his wife were visiting us, I thought he was my husband, so I called him 'honey.' It was a little embarrassing at first, but everyone understood."

"What does a face look like to you?" asked Dr. L.

"Well, I know that it's a face, because I can usually see the eyes, and it's on top of a body. I can see a body pretty well, by how it moves." She paused a moment. "Oh, yes, I forgot, sometimes I can recognize a person by how he moves. You know, you can often recognize friends by the way they walk, even when they're far away. I can still do that. That's funny, isn't it? I can't see people's faces very well, but I can recognize the way they walk."

Dr. L. made some movements with his hands. "Can you tell what I'm doing?" he asked.

"Yes, you're mixing something—like some cake batter."

He mimed the gestures of turning a key, writing, and dealing out playing cards, and Mrs. R. recognized them without any difficulty.

"Do you have any trouble reading?" he asked.

"Well, a little, but I don't do too badly."

Dr. L. handed her a magazine, and she began to read the article aloud—somewhat hesitantly, but accurately. "Why is it," she asked, "that I can see the words all right but have so much trouble with things and with people's faces?"

The primary function of the sense organs, as we saw in Chapter 6, is to provide information to guide behavior. But the sensory mechanisms cannot achieve this function by themselves. Consider vision, for example. The brain receives fragments of information from approximately 1 million axons in each of the optic nerves. It combines and organizes these fragments into the perception of a scene—objects having different forms, colors, and textures, residing at different locations in three-dimensional space. Even when our bodies or our eyes move, exposing the photoreceptors to entirely new patterns of visual information, our perception of the scene before us does not change. We see a world that is stable, not continually moving, because the brain keeps track of the body's movements and those of the eyes and compensates for the constantly changing patterns of neural firing that these movements cause. *Perception,* as explained in Chapter 6, is the process by which we recognize what is represented by the information that the sense organs provide. This process gives unity and coherence to sensory input.

Perception is a rapid, automatic, unconscious process; it is not a deliberate activity in which we puzzle out the meaning of what we see. We do not first see an object and then perceive it; we simply perceive the object. Although occasionally what we see is ambiguous, requiring us to reflect on what it might be or gather further evidence to determine what it is, this situation is more problem solving than perception. If we look at a scene carefully, we can describe the elements of the objects that are present, but we do not become aware of the elements before we perceive the objects and the background of which they are a part. Our awareness of the process of visual perception comes only after it is complete; we are presented with a finished product, not the details of the process.

The distinction between sensation and perception is not easy to make; in some respects the distinction is arbitrary. Probably because of the importance we give to vision and because of the richness of the information provided by our visual system, psychologists make a more explicit distinction between visual sensation and perception than they do for any other sensory system. Hence, this chapter on perception will focus primarily on the visual system, while recognizing that the other perceptual systems could be analyzed similarly. In fact, we will examine the most important task of auditory perception—recognizing spoken words—in Chapter 10.

Brain Mechanisms of Visual Perception

Although the eyes contain the photoreceptors that detect areas of different brightness and color in the visual field, perception takes place in the brain. As we saw in Chapter 6, the optic nerves send visual information to the thalamus, which relays the information to the primary visual cortex, located in the occipital lobe at the back of the brain. In turn, neurons in the primary visual cortex send visual information to two successive levels of the visual association cortex. The first level, located in the occipital lobe, surrounds the primary visual cortex. The second level is divided into two parts, one in the middle of the parietal lobe and one in the lower part of the temporal lobe. (See **Figure 7·1.**)

Visual perception by the brain is often described as a hierarchy of information processing. According to this scheme, circuits of neurons analyze particular aspects of visual information and send the results of their analysis to another circuit, which performs further analysis. At each step in the process, successively more complex features are analyzed. Eventually, the process leads to the perception of the scene and the objects in it. The higher levels of the perceptual process also interact with memories: The viewer recognizes familiar objects and learns to recognize new, unfamiliar ones.

The Primary Visual Cortex

Our knowledge about the characteristics of the earliest stages of visual analysis has come from investigations of the activity of individual neurons in the thalamus and the primary visual cortex. For example, Nobel Prize laureates David Hubel and Torsten Wiesel have inserted *microelectrodes*—extremely small wires with microscopically sharp points—into various regions of the visual systems of cats and monkeys to detect the action potentials produced by individual neurons (Hubel & Wiesel, 1977, 1979). The signals picked up by the microelectrodes are electronically amplified and sent to a recording device so that they can be studied later.

After positioning a microelectrode close to a neuron, Hubel and Wiesel presented various stimuli on a large screen in front of the open-eyed but anesthetized animal. The anesthesia

FIGURE 7•1 The visual system of the brain. Arrows represent the flow of visual information. Sensory information from the eye is transmitted through the optic nerve to the thalamus, and from there it is relayed to the primary visual cortex. The results of the analysis performed there are sent to the visual association cortex of the occipital lobe (first level) and then on to that of the temporal lobe and parietal lobe (second level). At each stage, additional analysis takes place.

From Carlson, N. R. (2004). *Physiology of Behavior,* 8/e. Published by Allyn and Bacon, Boston, MA. Copyright © 2004 by Pearson Education. Reprinted by permission of the publisher.

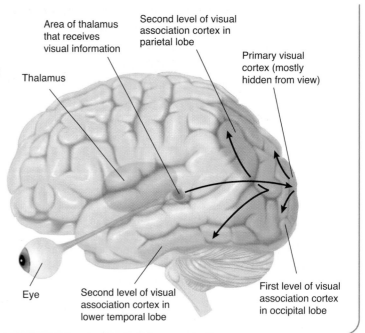

makes the animal unconscious but does not prevent neurons in the visual system from responding. The researchers moved a stimulus around on the screen until they located the point where it had the largest effect on the electrical activity of the neuron. Next, they presented stimuli of various shapes to learn which ones produced the greatest response from the neuron.

From their experiments, Hubel and Wiesel concluded that the geography of the visual field is retained in the primary visual cortex. That is, the surface of the retina is "mapped" on the surface of the primary visual cortex. However, this map on the brain is distorted, with the largest amount of area given to the center of the visual field. The map is actually like a mosaic—a picture made of individual tiles or pieces of glass. Each "tile" or, in neural terms, *module* consists of a block of tissue approximately 0.5 x 0.7 millimeters in size and containing approximately 150,000 neurons. All of the neurons within a module receive information from the same small region of the retina. The primary visual cortex contains approximately 2,500 of these modules.

Because each module in the primary visual cortex receives information from a small region of one retina, that means it receives information from a small region of the visual field—the scene that is currently projected onto the retina. If you closed one eye and looked at the scene in front of you through a drinking straw, this would be much like the amount of information received by an individual module. Hubel and Wiesel found that neural circuits within each module analyzed various characteristics of their own particular part of the visual field—that is, of their **receptive field**. Some circuits detected the presence of lines passing through the field and signaled the *orientation* of these lines (that is, the angle they made with respect to the horizon). Other circuits detected the

width or the *spatial frequency* of these lines. Others detected the movement of the lines and the direction of movement. Still others detected the lines' colors.

Figure 7•2 shows a recording of the responses of an orientation-sensitive neuron in the primary visual cortex. This neuron is located in a cluster of neurons that receive information from a small portion of the visual field. (That is, the neuron has a small receptive field.) The neuron responds maximally when a line oriented at 50 degrees to the vertical is placed in this location—especially when the line is moving through the receptive field. This response is highly specific to orientation; the neuron responds very little when a line having a 70-degree or 30-degree orientation is passed through the receptive field. Other neurons in this cluster share the same receptive field but respond to lines of different orientations. Thus, the orientation of lines that pass through this receptive field is signaled by an increased rate of firing of particular neurons in the cluster.

Because each module in the primary visual cortex receives information about only a restricted area of the visual field, the information must be combined somehow for perception to take place. This combination takes place in the visual association cortex.

The Visual Association Cortex

The first level of the visual association cortex, which surrounds the primary visual cortex (refer to Figure 7.1), contains several subdivisions, each of which contains a map of the visual scene and uses information received from both retinas. Each subdivision receives information from different types of neural circuits within the modules of the primary

FIGURE 7•2   Responses of a single cortical neuron to lines of particular orientations that are passed through its receptive field.

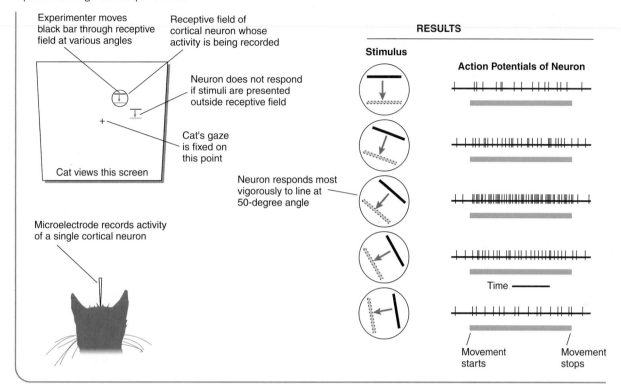

visual cortex. For instance, one subdivision receives information about the orientation and spatial frequency of lines and edges and is involved in the perception of shapes. Another subdivision receives information about movement and keeps track of the relative movements of objects; that is, their movements with respect to one another. This subdivision may help compensate for movements of our eyes as we scan the scene in front of us. Yet another subdivision receives information concerning color (Hadjikhani et al., 1998). (See **Figure 7•3**.)

The two regions of the second level of the visual association cortex put together the information gathered and processed by the various subdivisions of the first level. Information about shape, movement, and color are combined in

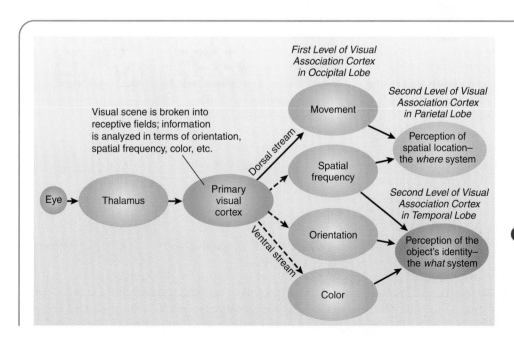

FIGURE 7•3   A schematic diagram of the types of analyses performed on visual information in the primary visual cortex and the various regions of the visual association cortex.

the visual association cortex in the lower part of the temporal lobe; this flow of information is the **ventral stream** shown in Figure 7.3. Three-dimensional perception of size, shape, orientation, and color takes place here. In essence, this is the "what" division of the brain's visual system. In contrast, the visual association cortex in the parietal lobe is responsible for perception of the *spatial location* of objects—their location in three dimensions. It integrates the flow of information from the first level of the visual association cortex—the **dorsal stream** that appears in Figure 7.1—with information from the motor system and the body senses about movements of the eyes, head, and body (Baizer, Ungerleider, & Desimone, 1991; Eskandar & Assad, 1999; Ungerleider & Mishkin, 1982). Thus, the dorsal stream could be considered the "where" division of the brain's visual system. It has been suggested that it is also part of the system that allows us to reach for and manipulate objects (Goodale & Humphrey, 1998). A later section of the chapter will discuss the "what" and "where" systems further.

Researchers have studied the anatomy and functions of the visual association cortex in laboratory animals. They have also used functional imaging (functional MRI and PET scans) to discover the locations of comparable subregions in the human brain. For example, when a person looks at a display containing irregular patches of different colors, one region of the visual association cortex becomes active. When a person looks at a display containing moving black-and-white squares, another region becomes active. Presumably, these regions are involved in the analysis of color and movement, respectively. (See **Figure 7•4**.)

Effects of Brain Damage on Visual Perception

The effects of damage to the primary visual cortex and to the visual association cortex support the general outline just described. When the primary visual cortex is damaged, a person becomes blind in some portion of the visual field. The exact location depends on where the brain damage is. However, even if the person loses a considerable amount of vision, he or she will be able to perceive objects and their backgrounds. This finding supports the conclusion that perception takes place in the visual association cortex and not in the primary visual cortex.

Try a simple demonstration that illustrates this principle. Close one eye, then take a drinking straw and look through it with the other eye as you would through a telescope. Move the straw around so that you scan the scene in front of you. Although you see only a part of the scene at any one time, you have no difficulty perceiving what is present. Your experience is like that of a person who has extensive damage to the primary visual cortex but whose visual association cortex has been spared: The result is a limited visual field but good perceptual ability.

In contrast, damage to the visual association cortex does not disrupt the person's ability to see fine details, but it does produce varying amounts of difficulty in perceiving shapes and objects or their particular visual characteristics. For example, damage to part of the visual association cortex can disrupt color vision—a condition known as **achromatopsia** (literally, "vision without color"). A person

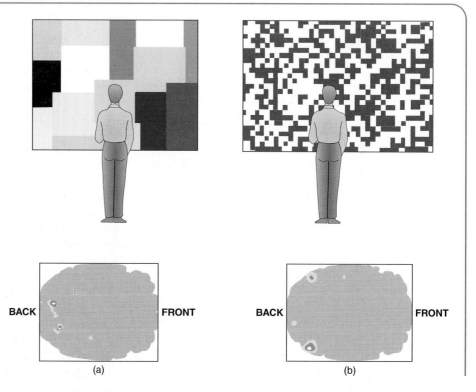

FIGURE 7•4 PET scans of a research participant's brain (seen from above) showing regions of increased metabolic activity (indicating increased neural activity) when the individual looked at multicolored patterns (a) and moving black-and-white rectangles (b).
(Adapted from Zeki, S. (1990). *La Recherche, 21,* 712–721. Adaped by permission of S. Zeki.)

BACK   FRONT   BACK   FRONT

(a)   (b)

who has achromatopsia can still see normally, but everything looks as if it had been filmed in black and white (Heywood & Cowey, 1998). Damage to only one side of the brain produces achromatopsia in the contralateral (opposite) visual field. Total achromatopsia occurs only after bilateral damage. (See **Figure 7•5**.) In addition, persons with achromatopsia are unable even to imagine colors or to remember the colors of objects they saw before the brain damage.

Damage to another subregion of the visual association cortex can make it difficult for a person to perceive movements and to keep track of moving objects. For example, Zihl, von Cramon, Mai, and Schmid (1991) studied a woman who had sustained bilateral damage to a region of the first level of the visual association cortex. The woman could see; she could recognize the shape, color, and location of objects in her environment. However, she had great difficulty perceiving movements. She was unable to cross a street when traffic was moving, because she could not judge the speed of the cars. When the investigators asked her to try to detect movements of a visual target in the laboratory, she said, "First the target is completely at rest. Then it suddenly jumps upwards and downwards" (p. 2244). She was able to see that the target was constantly changing its position, but she had no perception of its continuous motion.

If the visual association cortex in both posterior parietal lobes is damaged, a person will experience a disruption in the ability to keep track of the location of objects in the visual scene. This deficit is called **Balint's syndrome,** after its discoverer. People who have Balint's syndrome can recognize individual objects when they look directly at them but are unable to see where they are located. The scene in front of them is a jumble of individual objects, arranged in no particular order.

Damage to the visual association cortex of the temporal lobe can disrupt the ability to recognize objects without affecting the ability to see colors, movements, or fine details. This deficit, described in Chapter 4, is called *visual agnosia*. People who have visual agnosia may have normal visual acuity, but they cannot successfully recognize objects visually by their shape. Surprisingly, many people who have visual agnosia can read—just like Mrs. R., who was described in the opening vignette. (And, as we shall see in Chapter 10, many people who are unable to read because of brain damage have no difficulty recognizing objects by sight. These findings indicate that different brain mechanisms are involved in the recognition of words and objects.)

One form of visual agnosia makes it difficult or impossible for a person to recognize particular faces—a disorder called **prosopagnosia** (from the Greek *prosopon,* meaning "face"). For example, Mrs. R. was unable to recognize her husband by sight but could identify him by his voice as soon as he spoke. She could even recognize friends at a distance by observing the way they walked. Another patient reported that "I have trouble recognizing people from just faces alone. I look at their hair color, listen to their voices . . . I try to associate

FIGURE 7•5 A photograph illustrating the way the world would look to a person who had achromatopsia in the right visual field, caused by damage on the left side of the brain to the region of the visual association cortex shown in Figure 7.1.

(Photo courtesy of Neil Carlson.)

something with a person one way or another . . . what they wear, how their hair is worn" (Buxbaum, Glosser, & Coslett, 1999, p. 43). Most people who have prosopagnosia have difficulty recognizing other complex visual stimuli as well (Damasio, Tranel, & Damasio, 1990). They can easily recognize *categories* of objects (such as automobiles, animals, or houses) but have difficulty distinguishing between particular *individual* stimuli (their car, their dog, or their house). One woman with prosopagnosia could no longer distinguish between different makes of cars and so had to find her own in a parking lot by looking for the correct license plate. (Obviously, she could still distinguish numbers and letters.) Another person, a farmer, could no longer tell his cows apart.

Interim Summary

Brain Mechanisms of Visual Perception

Visual information proceeds from the retina to the thalamus, and then to the primary visual cortex. The primary visual cortex is organized into modules, each of which receives information from a small region of the retina. Neural circuits within each module analyze specific information from their part of the visual field, including the orientation and spatial frequency of lines, movements, and color.

The different types of information analyzed by the neural circuits in the modules of the primary visual cortex are sent to separate maps of the visual field in the first level of the visual association cortex. The information from these maps is combined in the second level of the visual association cortex:

perception of size and shape in the base of the temporal lobe and spatial perception in the parietal lobe.

Damage to specific regions of the primary visual cortex causes blindness in corresponding parts of the visual field. Damage to parts of the first level of the visual association cortex may cause achromatopsia (lack of color vision) or difficulty in perceiving movements. Damage to the visual association cortex of the parietal lobe causes Balint's syndrome, a deficit in the perception of spatial location. Damage to the visual association cortex of the temporal lobe can disrupt the perception of size and shape without affecting the ability to see, movements, colors, or fine details—a condition called visual agnosia.

QUESTIONS TO CONSIDER

1. Would you rather have your primary visual cortex or your visual association cortex partially (not totally) damaged? What would the symptoms be, and which symptoms would you find less disabling?

2. If you had one of the perceptual deficits described in this section, what coping strategies might you adopt? Suppose that you could not identify people by sight, or recognize your automobile. Or suppose that you could not recognize common objects but could read. How could you arrange things so that you would function at a high level of independence? Suppose that you had complete achromatopsia. What would you miss seeing? What difficulties would you face, and how would you cope with them?

Perception of Objects

When we look at the world, we do not see patches of colors, the frequency of lines, or shades of brightness. We see *things*—cars, streets, people, desks, books, trees, dogs, chairs, walls, flowers, clouds, televisions. We see where each object is located, how large it is, and whether it is moving. We recognize familiar objects; we also recognize when we see something we have never seen before. The visual system is able to perceive shapes and sizes, determine distances, and detect movements; it tells us what something is, where it is located, and what it is doing. This section considers the first task: perceiving an object's size and shape so that we know what it is.

Figure and Ground

We classify most of what we see as either object or background. *Objects* are things having particular shapes and particular locations in space. (In this context, people can be considered as objects.) *Backgrounds* are essentially formless and

serve mostly to help us judge the location of objects we see in front of them. Psychologists use the terms **figure** and **ground** to label an object and its background, respectively. The classification of an item as a figure or as a part of the background is not an intrinsic property of the item. Rather, it depends on the behavior of the observer. If you are watching some birds fly overhead, they are figures and the blue sky and clouds behind the birds are part of the background. If, instead, you are watching the clouds move, then the birds become background. If you are looking at a picture hanging on a wall, it is an object. If you are looking at a person standing between you and the wall, the picture is part of the background. Sometimes we receive ambiguous cues about what is object and what is background. For example, does the reversible figure in **Figure 7•6** illustrate two faces or a wine goblet?

What are the characteristics of the complex patterns of light—varying in brightness, saturation, and hue—that give rise to perceptions of figures, of *things*? One of the most important aspects of form perception is the existence of a *boundary*. If the visual field contains a sharp and distinct change in brightness, color, or texture, we perceive an edge. If this edge forms a continuous boundary, we probably will perceive the space enclosed by the boundary as figure rather than ground. (See **Figure 7•7**.)

Gestalt Laws of Perceptual Organization

Although most figures are defined by a boundary, the presence of a boundary is not necessary for the perception of an object. **Figure 7•8** demonstrates *illusory contours*—lines that do not

FIGURE 7•6 A drawing in which figure and ground can be reversed. You can see either two faces against a white background or a goblet against a dark background.

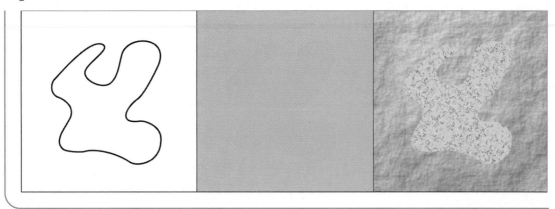

FIGURE 7·7 Object perception and boundaries. We immediately perceive even an unfamiliar figure when it is closed.

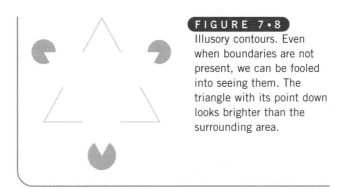

FIGURE 7·8
Illusory contours. Even when boundaries are not present, we can be fooled into seeing them. The triangle with its point down looks brighter than the surrounding area.

exist. In this figure, the orientation of the pie-shaped objects (resembling Pacman) and the three 45-degree segments produce the visual illusion of two triangles, one on top of the other. The illusory triangle that looks like it is superimposed on three green circles even appears to be brighter than the background.

Early in the twentieth century, a group of German psychologists developed a theory of perception based on our tendency to organize elements and empty spaces into cohesive forms. As Chapter 1 discussed, they called their movement *Gestalt psychology,* and they maintained that the task of perception was to recognize objects in the environment according to the organization of their elements. Gestaltists argued that in perception the whole is other than the sum of its parts. In other words, because of the characteristics of the visual system of the brain, visual perception does not consist simply of analyzing scenes into their elements. Instead, what we see depends on the *relationships* of these elements to one another.

The elements of a visual scene can be organized in various ways to produce different objects. Gestalt psychologists observed that several principles or laws can predict the organization of these elements. The fact that our visual system organizes visual elements is useful, because we can then perceive objects even if they appear fuzzy or incomplete. The real world presents us with objects partly obscured by other objects and with backgrounds that are the same color as

parts of the objects in front of them. Thus, the outlines of objects are very often indistinct. For example, suppose you look out the window of a classroom in summer and see a large bush against a background of trees. Countless shades of green may appear in the scene. It would be impossible to distinguish the bush from the trees behind it simply by differences in color. However, the outline of the bush is clear because of subtle differences in its texture (the leaves are smaller than those of the tree) and because the wind causes its branches to move in a pattern different from that of the tree branches. The laws of perceptual organization discovered by Gestalt psychologists describe this ability to distinguish a figure from its background.

Consider first the Gestalt **law of proximity,** which states that elements that are closest together will be perceived as belonging together. . . . What do you see when you look at the patterns shown in **Figure 7·9**? The number of dots in each pattern is the same, as is their arrangement in a 5 x 5 array. However, most people are inclined to see five vertical columns of dots when they first look at the pattern on the left but five horizontal rows when they look at the pattern on the right. We perceive the pattern on the left as columns because the dots are closer (more proximate) to their neighbors above and below them than to those located to the left and the right. On the other hand, the dots in the other pattern

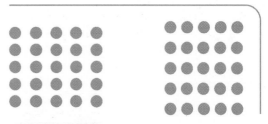

FIGURE 7·9 The Gestalt law of proximity. Different spacing of the dots produces five vertical or five horizontal lines.

are closer to their neighbors on the left and right than to those above and below.

The **law of similarity** states that elements that have a similar appearance will be perceived as part of the same object. We can easily see the diamond of circles inside the square of X's in **Figure 7•10**.

The **law of good continuation** refers to predictability or simplicity. Which of the two sets of gray dots best describes the continuation of the line of black dots in **Figure 7•11**? Most people choose the gray dots that continue the curve down and to the right. It is simpler to perceive the line as following a smooth course than as suddenly making a sharp bend.

Often, one object partially hides another, but we nevertheless perceive the incomplete image. The **law of closure** states that our visual system often supplies missing information and "closes" the outline of an incomplete figure. For example, **Figure 7•12** looks like it might be a triangle, but if you place a pencil on the page so that it covers both of the gaps, the figure is undeniably a triangle. (Try it.)

The final Gestalt law of organization relies on movement. The **law of common fate** states that elements that move in the same direction will be perceived as belonging together and forming a figure. In the forest, an animal is camouflaged if its surface is covered with the same elements found in the background—spots of brown, tan, and green—because its boundary is obscured. There is no basis for organizing the elements that belong to the animal alone. As long as the animal is stationary, it remains well hidden. However, once it moves, the elements on its surface will move together, and

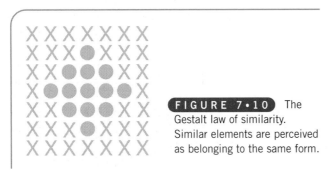

FIGURE 7•10 The Gestalt law of similarity. Similar elements are perceived as belonging to the same form.

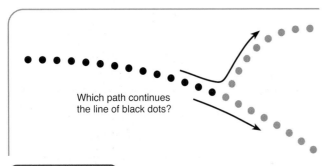

Which path continues the line of black dots?

FIGURE 7•11 The Gestalt law of good continuation. It is easier to perceive a smooth continuation than an abrupt shift.

FIGURE 7•12 The Gestalt law of closure. We tend to supply missing information in order to close a figure and separate it from its background. Lay a pencil across the two gaps and see how much stronger the perception of a complete triangle becomes.

the animal's size and shape will quickly be visible. A child's ability to distinguish figure from ground on the basis of motion seems to develop at a different rate from some of the other cues we have looked at, suggesting that motion-defined segregation may have different pathways in the human visual system (Giaschi & Regan, 1997). The evolutionary advantages and disadvantages posed by camouflage are obvious—for predators as well as their prey.

Alais, Blake, and Lee (1998) have found that the principle of common fate applies to changes other than movement. Visual objects stand out from their background to the extent that they exhibit contrasts in color or brightness. Alais and colleagues showed people several groups of lines and rapidly changed the contrast between the lines and their backgrounds. When this temporal variation in contrast was the same across different groups of lines, the participants perceived the different groups as belonging together. The researchers described this "common tempo" effect as a variation on the law of common fate.

In distinguishing the bush from the trees viewed from the classroom, the primary cues were differences in leaf size and in the movement induced by the wind—examples of the laws of similarity and common fate, respectively.

Models of Pattern Perception

Stimulus objects large and small can come together simultaneously or over time. As such, they can be said to form patterns. Most psychologists who study the perception of patterns call themselves cognitive psychologists. They are interested in the cognitive processes responsible for perception—the steps that take place between the time a person's eye is exposed to a stimulus and the time a perception of the pattern is formed, ready for the person to act on. They collect behavioral data and try to make inferences about the nature of these intervening processes. Let's look at some of the models cognitive psychologists have devised to explain pattern perception.

Templates and Prototypes   Our ability to recognize shapes of objects might be explained by special kinds of memories used by the visual system known as **templates**. A template is a type of pattern used to produce a series of similar objects. For example, a cookie cutter is a template used to cut out identical shapes from a flat piece of dough. According to the template model, the visual system reverses the process; when a particular pattern of visual stimulation is encountered, the visual system searches through its set of templates and compares each of them with the pattern. If it finds a match, the pattern is recognized as familiar. Connections between templates and memories in other parts of the brain could provide the name of the object and further information about it, such as its function, when it was seen before, and so forth.

The template model of pattern recognition has the virtue of simplicity. However, most cognitive psychologists do not believe that it could actually work—the visual system would have to store an enormously large number of templates. Consider a familiar object, such as a human hand. Hold your own hand in front of you and look at it. Turn it around, wiggle your fingers, clench your fist, and see how many different patterns you can project on your retinas. No matter what you do, you continue to recognize the patterns as your hand. How many different templates would your visual memory have to contain just to recognize one hand? And suppose that the hand was more or less hairy, darker or lighter, had longer or shorter fingers—you get the point.

A more flexible model of pattern perception suggests that the visual system compares patterns of stimuli with **prototypes** rather than templates. A prototype (Greek for "original model") is an idealized pattern; it resembles a template but is used in a much more flexible way. The visual system does not

▲ *We can recognize particular objects as well as general categories of objects.*

require an exact match between the pattern being perceived and a specific memory but accepts a degree of disparity. It accepts a variety of patterns produced when we look at a particular object—a hand, for example—from different viewpoints. All sufficiently resemble the hand prototype.

Most cognitive psychologists believe that visual pattern recognition involves prototypes, at least in some form. For example, you can probably identify maple trees, pine trees, and palm trees when you see them. In nature, any one tree looks different from all the others, but maples resemble other maples more than they resemble pines, and so on. A reasonable assumption is that the visual system has access to memories of the prototypical visual patterns that represent these objects. Recognizing particular types of trees, then, is a matter of finding the best fit between stimulus and prototype.

The visual system of the brain may indeed contain generic prototypes that help us recognize objects we have never seen before, be they coffee cups, maple trees, or human faces. But we do more than recognize categories of objects; we can recognize *particular* coffee cups, maple trees, or human faces. In fact, we can learn to recognize enormous numbers of objects. Think of how many different people you can recognize by sight, how many different buildings in your town or city you can identify, how many of the pieces of furniture in your house and in your friends' houses you are familiar with—the list will be very long indeed.

It is likely that many objects have to be represented by more than one prototype, such as side-profile and front views of a face. Perhaps there are even various levels of prototypes:

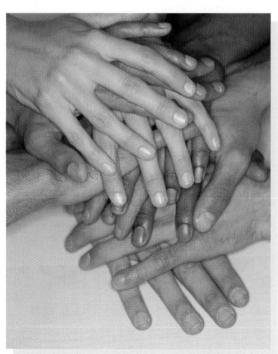

▲ *The template model for pattern recognition seems inadequate for explaining how we can recognize a human hand in its many sizes, colors, and positions.*

FIGURE 7•13 Distinctive features. We easily recognize all of these items as the letter *N*.

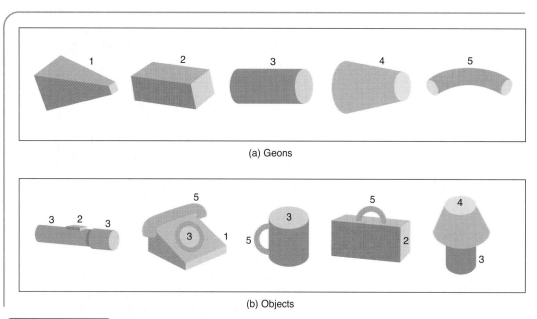

generic prototypes such as maples or human faces and more specific prototypes such as the tree in your backyard or the face of a friend. In fact, evidence from studies of nonhuman primates suggests that increased familiarity with categories of objects may lead to the development of specific types of prototypes (Humphrey, 2003).

Distinctive Features How complete does the information in a prototype have to be? Does a prototype have to contain a detailed representation of an image of the category of objects it represents, or can the representation exist in some shorthand way? Some cognitive psychologists suggest yet another way in which the visual system encodes images of familiar patterns; namely, in terms of **distinctive features**—collections of important physical features that specify particular objects. For example, **Figure 7•13** contains several examples of the capital letter *N*. Although the examples vary in size and style, you have no trouble recognizing them. How

do you do so? Perhaps your visual system contains a specification of the distinctive features that fit the criteria for an *N*: two parallel vertical lines connected by a diagonal line sloping downward from the top of the left one to the bottom of the right one. (Note, however, that one of the *N*s in the bottom row does not meet these criteria.)

An ambitious theory of feature-based object perception was proposed by Biederman (1995). Critical to the theory is a fixed set of "primitives," or feature detectors for specific three-dimensional geometrical shapes—called *geons*—that reside in the brain. A sample of geons appears in **Figure 7•14**, together with familiar objects that represent combinations of geons. The perception of an object occurs as the brain analyzes its visual image in terms of geons. In other words, specific relationships within the image are matched to (that is, mapped onto) a corresponding geon image. Because geons remain invariant in the face of shifts in perspective, Biederman argued, it is possible to decode all visual information, even the most complex—for example, a face—in terms of geons. The theory also specifies brain areas where geon detection may take place. Although the theory makes comprehensive claims, as you might expect, it is not without detractors (see Pinker, 1997).

A classic experiment by Neisser (1964) supports the hypothesis that perception involves analysis of distinctive features. **Figure 7•15** shows one of the tasks Neisser used. The figure shows two columns of letters. Scan through them until you find the letter *Z*, which occurs once in each column.

Chances are good that you found the *Z* much faster in the left column than in the right column, just as the participants

FIGURE 7•14 Geons for perception. (a) Several different geons. (b) The combination of two or three geons (indicated by the numbers) into common three-dimensional objects.

(Adapted from Biederman, I. In *An Invitation to Cognitive Science. Vol 2: Visual Cognition and Action*, edited by D. N. Osherson, S. M. Kosslyn, and J. Hollerbach. Copyright © 1990 by the Massachusetts Institute of Technology; published by MIT Press, Cambridge, Mass.)

in Neisser's study did. Perhaps you guessed why: The letters in the left column have few features in common with those found in the letter *Z*, so the *Z* stands out from the others. In contrast, the letters in the right column have many features in common with the target letter, and thus the *Z* is camouflaged, so to speak.

Some phenomena cannot easily be explained by the distinctive-features model. For example, the model of visual pattern recognition on the basis of distinctive features suggests that perception consists of analysis and synthesis: The visual system first identifies the component features of a pattern and then combines the features to determine what the pattern is. We might expect, then, that more complex patterns, having more distinctive features, would take longer to perceive. But in reality the addition of more features, in the form of contextual cues, often *speeds up* the process of perception. The tendency for certain stimuli to "pop out" during visual search of a larger display provides evidence that perception does not necessarily involve a strict search for features. Enns and Rensink (1991) found that the orientation of wire-frame objects like those in panel (a) in **Figure 7•16** was quickly detected in a search. If the vertices of the drawing were not connected, however, as in panel (b), orientation was much more difficult to detect. In another study Pilon and Friedman (1998) found that misaligned vertices, as at the bottom right of panel (c), were difficult to detect when wire-

FIGURE 7•16 Wire-frame figures similar to those used by Enns and Rensink (1991) and Pilon and Friedman (1998). Panel (a) depicts the wire-frame figures with connected vertices; panel (b) depicts figures with unconnected vertices. Pilon and Friedman used figures like those depicted in panel (c), in which the individual vertices in a figure were individually rotated and could be misaligned with the rest of the figure.

(Redrawn from Enns and Rensink (1991) and Pilon and Friedman (1998). Copyright 1998. Canadian Psychological Association. Reprinted with permission.)

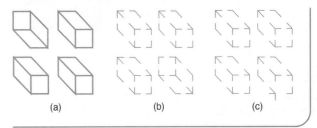

(a)   (b)   (c)

frame models were not connected. Presumably, only closing the figures with solid lines, and thus providing additional features, afforded sufficient detail to make orientation more immediately perceptible.

It also may be the case that prolonged exposure to particular features simplifies the perceptual task. For example, try to read the paragraph that appears in **Figure 7•17**. Most of the words in the paragraph have been scrambled—except for the first and last letters—yet you probably are able to make your way through the paragraph with only a slight slowing of your normal reading speed. Demonstrations such as this suggest that your ability to perceive the meaning of visual stimuli—in this case strings of letters—may eventually rely on

GDOROC	IVEMXW
COQUCD	XVIWME
DUCOQG	VEMIXW
GRUDQO	WEXMVI
OCDURQ	XIMVWE
DUCGRO	IVMWEX
ODUCQG	VWEMXI
CQOGRD	IMEWXV
DUZORQ	EXMZWI
UCGROD	IEMWVX
QCUDOG	EIVXWM
RQGUDO	WXEMIV
DRGOQC	MIWVXE
OQGDRU	IMEVXW
UGCODQ	IEMWVX
ODRUCQ	IMWVEX
UDQRGC	XWMVEI
ORGCUD	IWEVXM
QOGRUC	VMIWEX

FIGURE 7•15 A letter-search task. Look for the letter *Z* hidden in each column.

(Adapted from Neisser, U., *Scientific American*, 1964, *210*, 94–102. Copyright © 1964 by Scientific American. All rights reserved.)

> Aoccdrnig to rseerach at Cmabrigde Uinervtisy, it deosn't mttaer in waht oredr the ltteers in a wrod are, the olny iprmoatnt thing is taht the frist and lsat ltteer be at the rghit pclae. The rset can be a tatol mses and you can sitll raed it wouthit a porbelm. This is bcuseae the huamn mnid deos not raed ervey lteter by istlef, but the wrod as a wlohe. Amzanig huh?
>
> PS: Hwo'd you lkie to run tihs by yuor sepll ckehcer?

FIGURE 7•17 A paragraph in which the letters in each word have been scrambled except for the first and last letters.

("Are Reading and Writing Innate Skills?" http://www .brainconnection.com/content/198_1. Reprinted by permission of Scientific Learning Corporation.)

only some of the features that are present; for example, the "outer boundaries" of words. Dehaene (2003) has speculated that such ability derives from the innovative reuse of brain modules that originally served other functions, such as object recognition in the natural world. He used the term "neural recycling" to refer to this possibility.

Evaluating Scientific Issues

Does the Brain Work Like a Computer?

As we saw in Chapter 1, when we try to understand something extremely complicated (such as the functioning of the human brain), we tend to think in terms of things that are familiar to us. For example, René Descartes used the moving statues in the Royal Gardens at Saint-Germain-des-Prés as a basis for his hydraulic model of the nervous system. He saw an analogy between the nerves, muscles, and brain of the body and the pipes, cylinders, and valves of the statues, and he suggested that their principles of operation might be similar. Although cognitive psychology as a discipline dates back to the early twentieth century, most of its philosophy and methodology have developed since the mid-1960s. During this time the best known physical device that performs functions similar to those of the human brain has been the computer. The computer continues to provide much of the inspiration for the models of human brain function proposed by cognitive psychologists.

● **Using Computers to Model Cognitive Processes**
Computers can be programmed to store any kind of information that can be coded in numbers or words, can solve any logical problem that can be explicitly described, and can compute any mathematical equations that can be written. Therefore—in principle, at least—they can be programmed to do the things we do: perceive, remember, make logical deductions, solve problems. The power and flexibility of computers seem to make them an excellent source of models of mental processes. For example, psychologists, linguists, and computer scientists have constructed computer-inspired models of visual pattern perception, speech comprehension, reading, control of movement, and memory.

The creation of computer programs that simulate human cognitive functions belongs to a branch of cognitive science known as **artificial intelligence**. Research on artificial intelligence can help clarify the nature of cognitive functions. For instance, to construct a program that simulates the perception and classification of certain types of patterns, the investigator must begin with a model that specifies precisely what the task of pattern perception requires. If the program fails to recognize the patterns, then the investigator knows that something is wrong with the model or with the way it has been implemented in the program. The investigator revises the model, tries again, and keeps working until the program finally works (or until the researcher gives up the task as too ambitious). So far, no pattern-recognition program has been able to deal with more than a small fraction of the patterns a human can recognize.

Ideally, discovering the steps necessary for a computer program to simulate a particular human cognitive ability also would tell an investigator the kinds of processes the brain must perform. However, there is usually more than one way to simulate an ability, such as recognizing letters of the alphabet. Critics of artificial intelligence have pointed out that although it is entirely possible to write a program that performs a task that the human brain performs—and to show that the brain produces exactly the same results—the brain may perform the task in an entirely different way. In fact, given the way computers work and what we know about the structure of the human brain, some critics argue that the computer program is *guaranteed* to work differently (see, e.g., Dreyfus & Dreyfus, 2000).

● **How Does a Computer Work?**
Computers work one step at a time. In other words, they are *serial* processors. Each step takes time. A complicated program will contain more steps and will take more time to execute. But humans do some things extremely quickly that it takes computers a very long time to do. One of the best examples (appropriately enough, given the subject of this chapter) is visual perception. We can recognize a complex figure about as quickly as we can a simple one. For example, it takes about the same amount of time to recognize a friend's face as it does to identify a simple triangle. The same is not true at all for a computer program. It must operate serially, first analyzing the scene that is transmitted through an input device, such as a television camera. The program must convert information about the brightness of each point in the scene into a number and store the numbers in a memory location. Then it examines each memory location, one at a time, and does calculations that determine the locations of lines, edges, textures, and shapes. Finally, it tries to determine what these shapes represent. When a computer program follows these steps, one by one, recognizing a face takes *much* longer than recognizing a triangle.

● **An Alternative: The Parallel Processor**
If the brain were to operate in serial fashion like a computer, it could never keep up with a computer, because neurons cannot fire more than a thousand times per second (Rumelhart, McClelland, & the PDP Research Group, 1986). Obviously, when we perceive visual images, our brain is not processing information step-by-step.

Instead, the brain appears to be a **parallel processor,** in which many different modules (collections of circuits of neurons) work simultaneously at different tasks. In the brain a complex task is broken down into many smaller ones, and separate modules work on each of them. Because the brain consists of many billions of neurons, it can afford to devote different clusters of neurons to different tasks. With so many things happening at the same time, the task can be done in an instant.

● The Emerging Model: Neural Networks

It is one thing to say that the brain consists of many different modules, all working in parallel on separate pieces of a complicated task (such as recognizing someone's face), and another thing to explain how these modules work. In recent decades, psychologists have begun to devise models of mental functions that are based, more or less, on the way the brain seems to be constructed. These models are called **neural networks**. Donald Hebb (1949) developed the concept of a neural network long before the age of modern computers, but only more recently have cognitive psychologists begun to explore the implications of Hebb's ideas.

Investigators developing artificial neural networks construct a network of simple units that have properties like those of neurons. The units are connected to one another through junctions similar to synapses. Like synapses, these junctions can have either excitatory or inhibitory effects. When a unit is activated, it sends a message to the units with which it communicates, and so on. Some of the units of a network have input lines that can receive signals from the "outside," which could represent a sensory organ or the information received from another network. Other units have output lines, which could communicate with other networks or control muscles, producing behavior. Thus, particular patterns of input can represent particular stimuli, and particular patterns of output can represent responses. (See **Figure 7•18**.) The specific connections between units can be either strengthened or weakened by the extent to which the response matches the stimulus in some way. In this sense, neural networks not only mimic the structural connections between neurons in the brain but also simulate brain plasticity. Indeed, one of the hypotheses that Hebb developed for synaptic change (the so-called Hebbian rule of learning) is now recognized as a standard approach to constructing neural networks that can learn.

Cognitive psychologists do not construct physical networks. Instead, they write computer programs that simulate them. The programs track each unit and the state of each of its inputs and outputs and calculate what happens when a particular pattern of input is presented. Neural networks can be taught to "recognize" particular stimuli. A stimulus is presented, and the network's output is monitored. If the response is incorrect, the network receives a signal indicating the correct response. This signal causes the strength of some of the connections to be

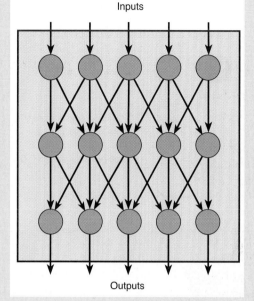

FIGURE 7•18 A simple neural network used as a model of brain function. The circles are units having properties similar to those of neurons. The connections (arrows) can be excitatory or inhibitory, depending on the particular network.

Inputs

Outputs

changed (a process known as "backward propagation"), just as learning is thought to alter the strength of synapses in the brain. After several repetitions, the network learns to make correct responses.

If the network uses a sufficiently large number of units, it can be trained to recognize several different patterns, producing the correct response each time one of the patterns appears. In addition, it will even recognize the patterns if they are altered slightly, or if only parts of the patterns are shown. Thus, neural networks can recognize not only particular patterns but also variations on that pattern. Some networks also appear to learn general rules about the occurrence of features within a pattern (Berkeley et al., 1995). Selectively disabling some of the network's connections can even produce errors similar to dyslexia, for example (Hinton & Shallice, 1991).

The simulation of visual perception using neural networks consists of a series of analyses, beginning with simple features and progressing to more complex ones. Each level of analysis involves a different neural network. Similarly, in the primary visual cortex the actual networks are small and local. Each one analyzes simple features—such as the orientation of lines and edges, color, and movement—within a restricted part of the visual field. In the subregions of the visual association cortex of the occipital lobes, larger networks process the information they receive from the primary visual cortex. For example, the

FIGURE 7•19 A neural network model of object perception. The stimulus in this sketch is an object like a bent paper clip. Successive layers in the network collect input from units in the previous layer. Some of these connections are added together to get the sum of excitatory and inhibitory influences (weighted sum), while others work on the principle that the strongest input determines the response (MAX).

(From Riesenhuber, M., & Poggio, T. (1999). *Nature Neuroscience, 2,* Figure 2.)

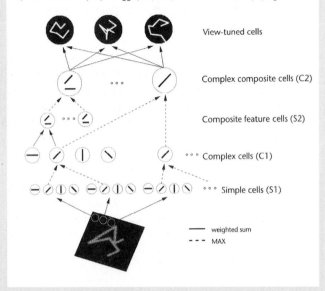

region that receives information about orientation of lines and edges recognizes shapes and patterns: squares, circles, ice cream cones, dogs, cats, faces. Other networks of neurons in the visual association cortex of the temporal lobes put all the information together and perceive the entire, three-dimensional scene, with objects having particular shapes, colors, and textures. Riesenhuber and Poggio (1999) have proposed a model along these lines, which is depicted in **Figure 7•19**. As you can see, the model is based on the general scheme of Figure 7.18. One modification, however, is that the connections between layers can either be *additive* (i.e., summing excitatory and inhibitory influences) or *maximum input (MAX),* wherein the strongest input determines the response.

● **What Should We Conclude?**

So what is the answer to the question posed at the beginning of this section? Does the brain work like a computer? The answer seems to be that it does, but not like the most familiar kind of computer—the serial processor—that cognitive psychologists first used as a basis for constructing models of brain function. The brain appears to be a parallel processor made up of collections of neural networks.

Bottom-Up and Top-Down Processing: The Roles of Features and Context

We often must perceive objects under conditions that are less than optimal; the object is in a shadow, camouflaged against a similar background, or obscured by fog. Nevertheless, we usually manage to recognize the item correctly. We are often helped in our endeavor by the context in which we see the object. For example, look at the four items in **Figure 7•20**. Can you tell what they represent? Now look at **Figure 7•21**, where with the aid of a context, the items are easily recognized.

Palmer (1975) showed that even more general forms of context can aid in the perception of objects. He first showed his participants familiar scenes, such as a kitchen. (See **Figure 7•22**.) Next, he used a device called a **tachistoscope** to show the participants drawings of individual items and asked them to identify the objects. (The word comes from Greek: *takhistos,* "most swift," and *skopein,* "to see.") A tachistoscope can present visual stimuli so briefly that they are very difficult to perceive. Sometimes the participants were shown an object that was appropriate to the scene, such as a loaf of bread. Other times, they were shown a similarly shaped but inappropriate object, such as a mailbox.

Palmer found that when the objects fit the context that had been set by the scene, the participants correctly identified about 84 percent of them. But when they did not, performance fell to about 50 percent. In the no-context control condition, under which participants did not first see a scene, performance was intermediate. Thus, compared with the no-context control condition, an appropriate context facilitated recognition and an inappropriate context interfered with it.

The context effects demonstrated by experiments such as Palmer's are not simply examples of guessing games. That is, people do not think to themselves, "Let's see, that shape could be either a mailbox or a loaf of bread. I just saw a picture of

FIGURE 7•20

Simple elements that are difficult to recognize without a context.

FIGURE 7•21

An example of top-down processing. The context facilitates our recognition of the items shown in Figure 7.20.

(Adapted from Palmer, S. E. in *Explorations in Cognition,* edited by Donald A. Norman and David E. Rumelhart. © 1975 by W. H. Freeman and Company. Used with permission.)

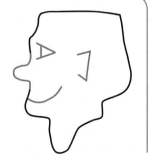

FIGURE 7·22 Stimuli from the experiment by Palmer (1975). After looking at the contextual scene, the participants were shown one of the stimuli below it very briefly by means of a tachistoscope.
(From Palmer, S. E. (1975). *Memory and cognition, 3,* 519–526. Reprinted by permission of the Psychonomic Society, Inc.)

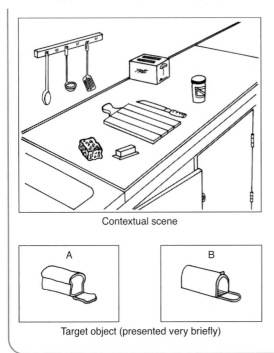

Contextual scene

A   B

Target object (presented very briefly)

coming up through the successive levels of the bottom-up system and finds the appropriate circuits already warmed up, so to speak, so that recognition occurs more readily.

Haenny, Maunsell, and Schiller (1988) obtained direct evidence that watching for a particular stimulus can, indeed, "warm up" neural circuits in the visual system. These researchers trained monkeys to look at a pattern of lines oriented at a particular angle, to remember that pattern, and then to pick it out from a series of different patterns presented immediately afterwards. A correct response was rewarded with a sip of fruit juice.

While the animals were performing the task, the researchers recorded the activity of individual neurons in the visual association cortex. They found that watching for a pattern of lines with a particular orientation affected the responsiveness of the neurons. For example, if the monkeys were watching for a pattern containing lines oriented at 45 degrees, neurons that detected lines of that orientation responded more vigorously than normal when that pattern was presented again. Haenny and colleagues found that this enhancement could even be produced if they let the monkeys feel the orientation of a pattern of grooves in a metal plate they could not see. When a subsequent visual pattern contained lines whose orientation matched that of the grooves, a larger neural response was recorded.

Perceptual ("What") and Action ("Where") Systems: A Possible Synthesis

Our examination of the perception of objects has brought us to a puzzle. It is clear that features play some role in our ability to identify objects, but it is less clear that theories of feature analysis can fully explain that ability. Top-down factors such as context exert powerful influences, but we still must ask how specific contextual states are activated.

In most cases perception would seem to consist of a combination of top-down and bottom-up processing. **Figure 7·23** shows several examples of objects that can be recognized only by a combination of both forms of processing. Our knowledge of the configurations of letters in words (top-down processing) provides us with the contexts that permit us to organize the flow of featural information from the bottom up. But concluding that the perception of objects requires the interaction of both types of processing still leaves unanswered the question of what that interaction is composed of. How do bottom-up and top-down processing come together to produce object recognition?

Perhaps this puzzle will remain unsolved for some time. But findings from cognitive neuroscience are providing some provocative hints about where to look. For example, Goodale and Milner (2004) have described a large number of observations of a woman named "Dee" with a condition that is the opposite of Balint's syndrome. Dee suffered an accident from carbon monoxide poisoning that left her unable

a kitchen, so I guess it's a loaf of bread." The process is rapid, unconscious, and automatic; thus, it belongs to the category of perception rather than of conscious problem solving, which is much slower and more deliberate. Somehow, seeing a kitchen scene sensitizes or primes the neural circuits responsible for the perception of loaves of bread and other items we have previously seen in that context.

Psychologists distinguish between two categories of information-processing models of pattern recognition: bottom-up processing and top-down processing. In **bottom-up processing,** also called *data-driven processing,* the perception is constructed out of the features—the bits and pieces—of the stimulus, beginning with the image that falls on the retina. The information is processed hierarchically by successive levels of the visual system until the highest levels (the "top" of the system) are reached, and the object is perceived. **Top-down processing,** also called *knowledge-driven* processing, involves the use of contextual information—the "big picture." For example, once the kitchen scene is perceived, information about kitchen-specific features is sent from the "top" of the system down through lower levels. This information excites neural circuits responsible for perceiving those objects normally found in kitchens and inhibits others. Then, when the participant sees a drawing of a loaf of bread, information starts

FIGURE 7·23 Examples of combined top-down/bottom-up processing. The effect of context enables us to perceive the letters despite the missing or ambiguous features. Note in the top example that a given letter may be perceived in more than one way, depending on the letters surrounding it.

(Adapted from McClelland, J. L., Rumelhart, D. E., & Hinton, G. E. in *Parallel Distributed Processing. Vol. I: Foundations,* edited by D. E. Rumelhart, J. L. McClelland, and the PDP Research Group. Copyright © 1986 by the Massachusetts Institute of Technology; published by the MIT Press Cambridge, Mass.)

to identify objects visually. Nonetheless, she is still able to reach for specific objects in a way that is behaviorally appropriate. For example, Dee would be unable to tell you whether the slot on a mailbox was oriented horizontally or vertically, but if you gave her an envelope and asked her to deposit it in the slot, her motor movements would be completely accurate. Chapter 9 will discuss the implications of similar findings; but for now, Goodale and Milner's work suggests a strong dissociation between what they describe as "vision for perception" (the "what" system) and "vision for action" (the "where" system)—the two streams that were introduced earlier in the chapter. One system, schematically represented in the lower part of Figure 7.3, provides us with information about objects and their meanings and involves pathways that lead to the temporal lobe—the ventral stream. The other, shown in the upper part of Figure 7.3, provides us with information necessary for acting on objects with guided movement and involves pathways leading through the parietal lobe—the dorsal stream.

Dee's brain damage apparently affected her perception of objects—her "what" system—but left intact her ability to respond to the location and orientation of objects—her

"where" system. The dorsal stream provides information necessary for guiding our actions toward objects but does not provide us with the ability to recognize or name them. Meaning is instead provided by the ventral stream. This differentiation produces some intricate differences between Dee's interaction with the world and yours. Suppose, for example, that you reach for either a screwdriver or a ruler on your workbench. Both are oblong and, as you reach for them, your wrist will orient your hand appropriately. Dee's wrist will do the same. But now suppose that the handle of the screwdriver faces away from you. Your object identification system knows that what you reach for is a screwdriver and that a screwdriver has a "handle part." As you reach for it, you will adjust your hand so that you grab the handle—even if it means an awkward backhand grasp. This is the ability that Dee has lost. Her object perception system is no longer fully functional. As a result, her reaching does not adjust to the position of the "handle part" of the screwdriver.

Goodale and Milner argue that our use of vision involves the interplay between these two systems. The dorsal stream shown in Figure 7.3 responds to the location and orientation of objects and coordinates the actions we take with respect to them. The ventral stream gives us visually derived information about what the objects are so that we know, for example, that the screwdriver we pick up will be heavier and will require more force to lift than the ruler. We have returned, then, to the theme with which Chapter 6 began—that our sensory systems function to provide us with the information necessary to control our behavior. To understand perception, we need to look at the kind of information that is necessary to move within our three-dimensional world of objects and to interact with it.

Interim Summary

Perception of Objects

Perception of objects requires, first, recognition of figure and ground. The Gestalt laws of proximity, similarity, good continuation, closure, and common fate describe some of the ways we distinguish figure from ground even when the outlines of the figures are not explicitly bounded by lines.

Psychologists have advanced hypotheses about the mechanism of pattern perception, or visual recognition of particular shapes. The first hypothesis suggests that our brain contains templates of all the shapes we can perceive. We compare a particular pattern of visual input with these templates until we find a fit. But can the brain hold infinitely many shapes? Another hypothesis suggests that our brain contains prototypes, which are more flexible than simple templates. According to a different hypothesis, prototypes are collections of distinctive features (such as the two parallel lines and the connecting diagonal of the letter *N*). One such view posits the brain's possession of a set of feature detectors known as geons. Further hypotheses are based on the neural network model and assert that the ability of neural networks to learn to recognize patterns of input is the best explanation of pattern perception.

Cognitive psychologists originally based their information-processing models of the human brain on the computer as a serial processor. However, the fact that a computer program can simulate a brain function does not mean that the brain and the computer perform the function in the same way. In fact, they do not. The brain consists of billions of interconnected neurons that operate comparatively slowly. However, by doing many things simultaneously, the brain can perform complex operations quickly. It acts as a parallel processor. Thus, more recent attempts to devise models of mental functions—especially pattern perception—have employed neural networks that operate in parallel fashion. This approach uses assemblies of units having properties similar to those of neurons.

Perception involves both bottom-up and top-down processing. Our perceptions are influenced not only by the details of the particular stimuli we see, but also by their relations to each other and by our expectations. Evidence from cognitive neuroscience suggests that our perceptions arise from a system that is specialized for object identification—the "what" system—that involves the ventral stream. A second system—the "where" system—involves the dorsal stream and may function independently to guide our actions in three-dimensional space.

QUESTIONS TO CONSIDER

1. Explore your visual environment to find examples of figure and ground. Can you change your focus of attention and make items previously seen as figures become part of the background and vice versa? Find some examples of when each of the Gestalt laws of perceptual organization helps you perceive particular objects.

2. How many unique objects do you think you can recognize? How many more do you think you will learn to recognize during the years ahead of you? What problem(s) does this potential of unlimited acquisition pose for a theory of object perception?

3. What do you do when you try to assemble the pieces of a complex picture puzzle? Relate this experience to the concepts of templates, prototypes, and distinctive features.

4. Suppose that Goodale and Milner are correct about a visual system that is specialized for movements such as reaching. Are you "aware" of orienting your hand when you reach for, say, a knife or a fork that is at an odd angle on a tabletop? What might this say about the role of consciousness?

Perception of Space and Motion

We not only are able to perceive the forms of objects in our environment (what) but also can judge quite accurately their relative location in space and their movements as well as our movements relative to them (where). Perceiving where things are and what they are doing are obviously important functions of the visual system.

Depth Perception

Depth perception requires that we perceive the distance between us and objects in the environment as well as their distance from one another. This is an impressive feat, given that the three-dimensional quality of depth perception must be derived from the two-dimensional images that fall on the retina in each eye. We accomplish this feat by means of two kinds of visual cues: binocular ("two-eye") and monocular ("one-eye"). *Binocular cues* arise from the fact that the visual fields of the two eyes overlap. Only animals that have eyes on the front of the head (such as primates, cats, and some birds) can obtain binocular cues. Animals that have eyes on the sides of their heads (such as rabbits and fish) can obtain only monocular cues.

Among the *monocular cues,* one involves movement and thus must be experienced in the natural environment or in a motion picture. The others can be represented in a drawing or a photograph. In fact, most of these cues were originally discovered by artists and only later studied by psychologists. Artists wanted to represent the world realistically, and they studied their visual environments to identify the features that indicated the distance of objects from the viewer. **Figure 7•24** on the next page provides a classification of the principal distance cues. Let's look more closely at each category.

Binocular Cues An important cue about distance is supplied by **convergence**. Recall from Chapter 6 that the eyes make conjugate movements so that both look at (*converge* on) the same point of the visual scene. If an object is very close to your face, your eyes are turned inward. If it is farther away, they turn straight ahead. Thus, the eyes can be used like range finders. The brain controls the extraocular muscles that move each eye, so it has information about the angle between them, which, in turn, is related to the distance between the object and the eyes. Convergence is most important for perceiving the distance of objects located close to us—especially those we can reach with our hands. (See **Figure 7•25**.)

Another important factor in the perception of distance is the information provided by **retinal disparity**. (*Disparity* means "unlikeness" or "dissimilarity.") Hold up a finger of one hand at arm's length and then hold up a finger of the other hand midway between your nose and the distant finger. If you look at one of the fingers, you will see a double

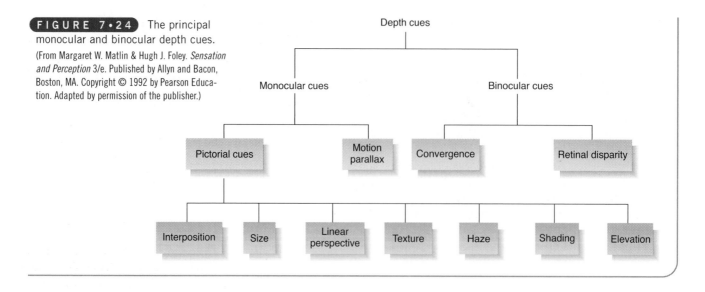

FIGURE 7·24 The principal monocular and binocular depth cues. (From Margaret W. Matlin & Hugh J. Foley. *Sensation and Perception* 3/e. Published by Allyn and Bacon, Boston, MA. Copyright © 1992 by Pearson Education. Adapted by permission of the publisher.)

image of the other one. (Try it.) Whenever your eyes are pointed toward a particular point, the images of objects at different distances will fall on different portions of the retina in each eye. The disparity between the images of an object on the two retinas provides an important clue about its distance from us.

Research on retinal disparity has sometimes utilized a *stereoscope,* a device that shows two slightly different pictures, one to each eye. The pictures are taken by a camera equipped with two lenses, located a few inches apart, just as our eyes are. When you look through a stereoscope, you see a three-dimensional image. In an ingenious experiment Julesz (1965) demonstrated that retinal disparity is what pro-

duces the effect of depth. Using a computer, he produced two displays of randomly positioned dots in which the location of some dots differed slightly. If some of the dots in one of the displays were displaced slightly to the right or the left, the two displays gave the impression of depth when viewed through a stereoscope.

Figure 7·26 shows a pair of these random-dot stereograms. If you look at them very carefully, you will see that some of the dots near the center have been moved slightly to the left. Some people can look at these figures without using a stereoscope and see depth. If you want to try this, hold the book at arm's length and look at the space between the figures. Now pretend you are looking "through" the

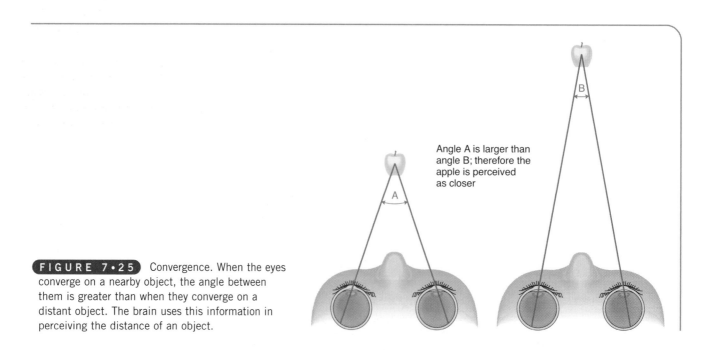

FIGURE 7·25 Convergence. When the eyes converge on a nearby object, the angle between them is greater than when they converge on a distant object. The brain uses this information in perceiving the distance of an object.

FIGURE 7•26 A pair of random-dot stereograms. (From Julesz, B. (1965). Texture and visual perception. *Scientific American, 12,* 38–48.)

book, into the distance. Each image will become double, because your eyes are no longer converged properly. If you keep looking, you may be able to make two of these images fuse into one, located right in the middle. Eventually, you may see a small square in the center of the image, raised above the background.

The necessary condition for this perception is that the two images are fused together so that the visual system can analyze the disparity. The single-image random-dot (SIRD) stereograms that were described in Chapter 2 induce a perception of depth by tricking the visual system into fusing different parts of the image together. If you have seen one of these stereograms, you have probably noticed how they show a kind of "wallpaper" structure, with repetitions of visual elements along the length of the image. The result is a little like staring at the tiles on your bathroom floor. Under the right conditions, the visual system may fuse an individual tile from one eye with the tile's neighboring image on the other eye. The SIRD stereogram is constructed to exploit this fusion by presenting additional disparity cues to provide the illusion of an object in depth (Schiffman, 1996).

Electrical recordings of the firing of individual neurons in the visual system of the brain have found a class of cells that receive information from both eyes and respond only when there is a slight disparity between the image of an object on both retinas. (This effect occurs if an object is slightly nearer or farther from you than the point at which you are gazing.) Thus, some neurons at this level apparently compare the activity of neurons with corresponding receptive fields for both eyes and respond when there is a disparity. These neurons participate in depth perception.

Monocular Cues One of the most important monocular sources of information about the relative distance of objects is **interposition** (*interposed* means "placed between"). If one object is placed between us and another object so that the closer object partially obscures our view of the more distant one, we can immediately perceive which object is closer to us.

Obviously, interposition works best when we are familiar with the objects and know what their shapes should look like. In **Figure 7•27** panel (a) can be seen either as two rectangles located one in front of the other—panel (b)—or as a rectangle nestled against an L-shaped object—panel (c). Because we tend to perceive an ambiguous drawing on the basis of shapes that are already familiar, we are more likely to perceive Figure 7.27(a) as two simple rectangles, one partly hiding the other.

Another important monocular distance cue is provided by our familiarity with the **sizes** of objects. For example, if an automobile casts a very small image on our retinas, we will perceive it as being far away. We already know how large cars are, so our visual system automatically computes the approximate distance based on the size of the retinal image.

Figure 7•28 shows two columns located at different distances. It demonstrates **linear perspective:** the tendency for parallel lines that recede from us to converge at a single point. Thus we perceive the columns as being the same size even though they produce retinal images of different sizes. We also perceive the segment of the wall between the columns as rectangular, even though the image it casts on the retina does not contain any right angles.

Texture provides another cue we use to perceive the distance of objects. A coarser texture looks closer, and a finer texture looks more distant (see **Figure 7•29**). The earth's atmosphere, which always contains a certain amount of **haze,** also can supply cues about the relative distance of objects or

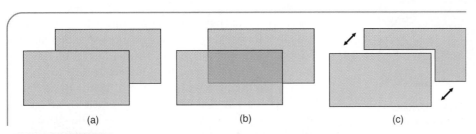

(a)   (b)   (c)

FIGURE 7•27 Interposition. The two objects shown in panel (a) could be two identical rectangles, one in front of the other, as shown in (b), or a rectangle and an L-shaped object, as shown in (c). The principle of good form states that we will see the ambiguous object in its simplest (best) form—in this case, a rectangle. As a result, the shape to the right is perceived as being partly hidden and thus farther away from us.

FIGURE 7•28 Linear perspective. The use of straight lines that converge to a single point gives the appearance of distance and makes the two inset columns look similar in size.

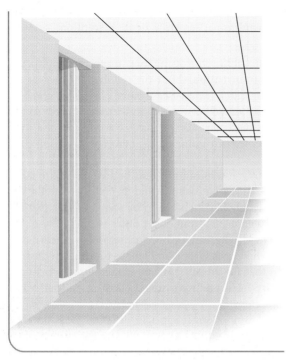

FIGURE 7•30 Cues from atmospheric haze. Variation in detail, owing to haze, produces the perception of distance.
(Photo © Mark Keller/SuperStock)

parts of the landscape. Parts of the landscape that are farther away become less distinct because of haze in the air (see **Figure 7•30**).

The patterns of light and shadow in a scene—its **shading**—can provide us with cues about distance. Although the cues that shading provides may not tell us much about the absolute distances of objects from us, they can tell us which *parts* of objects are closer and which are farther. **Figure 7•31** illustrates this phenomenon. Some of the circles look convex, as if they bulge out toward us (bumps); others look concave, as if they are hollowed out (dimples). You may notice a tendency to perceive this figure as a collection of dimples surrounded by bumps. Try turning the page upside down. The only difference is the direction of the shading, but your perception of the bumps and dimples changes. Our visual system appears to interpret such stimuli as if they were illuminated from above. Thus, the top of a convex object will be in light and the bottom will be in shadow. Actually, our visual system may be more specific than that. Using a "pop-out" image comparable to Figure 7.31, Sun and Perona (1998) found that dimples tended to pop out faster when the perceived direction of lighting was slightly from the top left. The next time you visit an art gallery, check the shadows on portraits and see if the artists have followed this convention.

When we are able to see the horizon, we perceive objects near it as being distant and those above or below it as

FIGURE 7•29 Textures. Variations in texture can produce the perception of distance. The stones diminish in size toward the top of the photo; we therefore perceive the top of the photo as being farther away from us.
(Photo © Bohdan Hrynewych/Stock Boston)

FIGURE 7·31 Depth cues supplied by shading. A viewer tends to interpret this configuration as a group of bumps surrounding a group of dimples.
(From Sun, J., & Perona, P. (1998). *Nature Neuroscience, 1*. Reprinted by permission from Macmillan Publishers, Ltd.)

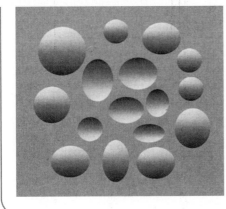

your eyes on an object close to you and move your head from side to side, your image of the scene moves back and forth behind the object. If you focus your eyes on the background while moving your head from side to side, the image of the object passes back and forth across the background. Head and body movements cause the images from the scene in front of us to change; the closer the object, the more it changes relative to the background.

Figure 7·33 illustrates the kinds of cues supplied when we move with respect to features in the environment. The top part of the figure shows three objects at different distances from the observer: a man, a house, and a tree. The lower part shows the views that the observer will see from five different locations (P_1–P_5). The changes in the relative locations of the objects provide cues concerning their distance from the observer. Note that the location of the man undergoes the largest change, followed by the house, and finally the tree. On this basis the man is perceived as closest and the tree farthest away.

being nearer to us. Thus, **elevation** provides an important monocular depth cue. For example, cloud B and triangle B in **Figure 7·32** appear farther away from us than cloud A and triangle A.

Another important source of distance information is **motion parallax** (*parallax* comes from a Greek word meaning "change"). Try the following demonstrations: If you focus

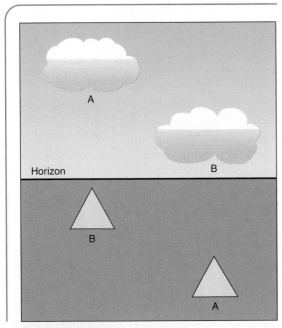

FIGURE 7·32 Depth cues supplied by elevation. The objects nearest the horizontal line appear farthest away from us.

(From Margaret W. Matlin & Hugh J. Foley. *Sensation and Perception* 3/e. Published by Allyn and Bacon, Boston MA. Copyright © 1992 by Pearson Education. Adapted by permission of the publisher.)

Biology and Culture

Effects of Cultural Experience on Visual Perception

As we saw in Chapter 4, the development of the nervous system is shaped by interplay between heredity and environment. In fact, normal development of the sensory systems of the brain *requires* experience. For example, if one of an animal's eyes is covered during the first few months after it is born, particular sets of neural connections fail to develop in the brain. As a result, the animal is unable to perceive normally with that eye after it is uncovered. If development of the brain can be so drastically affected by the temporary blocking of visual input, perhaps less drastic changes in sensory input can produce smaller but nevertheless real changes in perceptual ability.

The development of visual perception certainly involves learning. From birth onward, we explore our environment with our eyes. The patterns of light and dark, color, and movement produce changes in the visual system of the brain. Many psychologists and anthropologists have wondered what role cultural learning plays in the development of perceptual abilities. Chapter 2 explained that cultures differ with respect to two major classes of variables: biological and ecological. Biological variables—such as diet, genetics, and diseases common in a particular region—may affect perceptual development, but these variables have not received much attention from cross-cultural researchers. Ecological variables—particularly those associated with geography, cultural codes, and education—have received more attention.

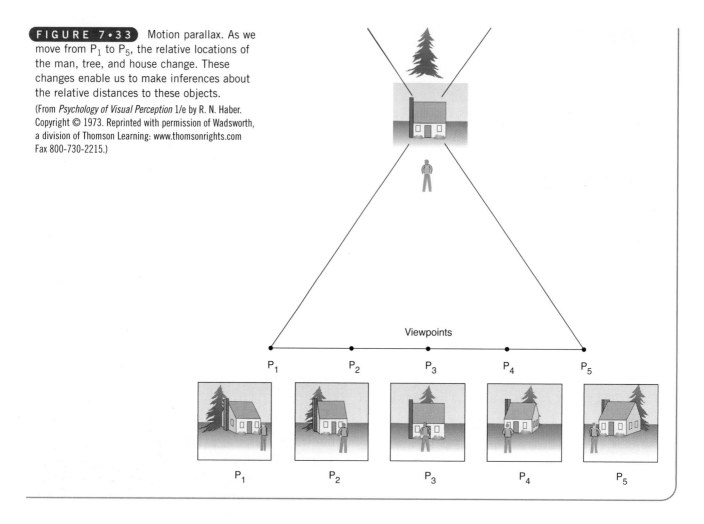

FIGURE 7•33 Motion parallax. As we move from P₁ to P₅, the relative locations of the man, tree, and house change. These changes enable us to make inferences about the relative distances to these objects.

(From *Psychology of Visual Perception* 1/e by R. N. Haber. Copyright © 1973. Reprinted with permission of Wadsworth, a division of Thomson Learning: www.thomsonrights.com Fax 800-730-2215.)

Viewpoints

P₁   P₂   P₃   P₄   P₅

P₁   P₂   P₃   P₄   P₅

Consider geographical variables. The visual stimulation we receive, particularly during infancy, affects the development of our visual system. If our environment lacks certain features—certain visual patterns—we may fail to recognize them if we encounter them later in life. For example, we might expect that people living in a treeless environment without pronounced vertical features would perceive the world differently from inhabitants of dense forests who are surrounded by vertical features but very seldom encounter vast, open fields.

The variance in cultural codes found in pictorial representations may also affect perceptual development. For example, as we saw earlier in this chapter, artists have learned to use the monocular depth cues (except motion parallax) in paintings. But not all these cues are represented in the traditional art of all cultures. For example, many cultures do not use linear perspective. Does the absence of particular monocular cues in the paintings of a particular culture mean that people from this culture will not recognize them when they see them in paintings from another culture?

The definitive answer to this question is not yet known. According to Berry, Poortinga, Segall, and Dasen (1992),

▲ *Perhaps people from cultures (such as that pictured here) whose art does not use linear perspective will not recognize this device when they see it in paintings from a culture where it is used.*

some reports suggest that Asians who are unfamiliar with art that incorporates linear perspective are more likely to misperceive the true shape of rectangles drawn in perspective. (Refer to Figure 7.28.) Much more cross-cultural research remains to be done.

A related question asks whether growing up in an environment having particular types of visual features affects the development of the visual system. So far, cross-cultural studies on this issue have revealed a few modest differences. For example, people who live in "carpentered worlds"—that is, worlds in which buildings are built from long, straight pieces of material that normally join each other at right angles—are more likely to be subject to the Müller-Lyer illusion, shown in **Figure 7.34**. Look at the two vertical lines and decide which is longer. (Actually, the lines are of equal length.)

Segall, Campbell, and Herskovits (1966) presented the Müller-Lyer illusion (and several others) to groups of participants from Western and non-Western cultures. Most investigators believe that the Müller-Lyer illusion is a result of our experience with the angles formed by the intersection of walls, ceilings, and floors. The angled lines can be seen as examples of linear perspective. (See **Figure 7.35**.) In fact, Segall and his colleagues *did* find that people from "carpentered" cultures were more susceptible to this illusion.

The effects on perception of another cultural code—language—have received close attention. In the mid-nineteenth century, the British statesman William Gladstone noted that the writings of the ancient Greeks did not contain words for brown or blue. Is it possible the ancient Greeks did not perceive these colors? At about the same time, Magnus (1880) investigated this hypothesis by gathering both linguistic and perceptual data. He sent questionnaires and color chips to colleagues living in the

FIGURE 7·35 The impact of culture on the Müller-Lyer illusion. People from "non-carpentered" cultures that lack rectangular corners are less likely to be susceptible to this illusion. Although the two vertical lines are actually the same height, the line on the right looks shorter.
(Photos courtesy of Neil Carlson)

Americas and asked them to test the abilities of the native people to distinguish among various colors. He assumed that the natives' language would reflect their perceptual ability. If a language did not contain words to distinguish between certain colors, then the people who belonged to that culture would not be able to distinguish these colors perceptually.

Magnus was surprised to discover very few cultural differences in people's ability to perceive the colors. Linguistic differences did not appear to reflect perceptual differences. The issue emerged again in the mid-twentieth century as the **linguistic relativity** hypothesis, sometimes called the *Whorfian hypothesis*. Briefly stated, this principle asserts that the language used by the members of a particular culture strongly influences the thoughts and perceptions that characterize the culture. The best-known proponent of this view, Benjamin Whorf, stated that "the background linguistic system . . . of each language is not merely a reproducing instrument for voicing ideas but rather is itself a shaper of ideas, the program and guide for the individual's mental activity, for his analysis of impressions, for his synthesis of his mental stock-of-trade" (Whorf, 1956, p. 212).

Supporters of linguistic relativity suggested that color names were cultural conventions—that members of a given

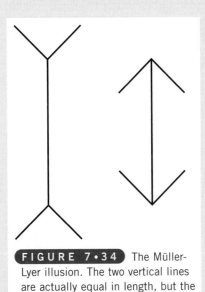

FIGURE 7·34 The Müller-Lyer illusion. The two vertical lines are actually equal in length, but the one on the left appears to be longer.

culture could divide the countless combinations of hue, saturation, and brightness that we call colors into any number of different categories. Each category was assigned a name, and when members of that culture looked out at the world they perceived each of the colors they saw as belonging to one of these categories.

Two anthropologists, Berlin and Kay, tested this hypothesis (Berlin & Kay, 1969; Kay, 1975). They studied a wide range of languages and found 11 primary color terms: black, white, red, yellow, green, blue, brown, purple, pink, orange, and gray. (Of course, the words for these terms are different in different languages. For example, Japanese speakers say *aka,* Navajos say *lichi,* Inuits say *aupaluktak,* and English speakers say *red.*) The authors referred to these as *focal colors.* Not all languages used all 11 terms (as English does). In fact, some languages used only two terms: black and white. If a language contained words for three primary colors, they were black, white, and red. If it contained words for six primary colors, they were black, white, red, yellow, green, and blue. The fact that all cultures had words for the focal colors suggests that the physiology of the visual system—and not arbitrary cultural conventions—is responsible for the selection of color names.

Other evidence supports this conclusion. Eleanor Heider (1971) reported that both children and adults found it easier to remember a color chip of a focal color (such as red or blue) than one of a nonfocal color (such as turquoise or peach). In her study of a specific culture—the Dani culture of New Guinea—Rosch (formerly Heider) found that the language of the Dani people has only two basic color terms: *mili* ("black") and *mola* ("white"). Rosch assembled two sets of color chips, one containing focal colors and the other containing nonfocal colors. She taught her participants arbitrary names that she made up for the colors. Even though the participants had no words in their language for any of the colors, the group learning names for focal colors learned the names faster and remembered them better (Heider, 1972; Rosch, 1973).

Rosch's experiments have been interpreted as evidence against linguistic relativity. Roberson, Davies, and Davidoff (2000) have found more supportive evidence, however. They compared British adults with adult speakers of Berinmo, a language spoken by a stone-age cultural group who live in Papua, New Guinea. Berinmo speakers have five basic color terms, including *nol,* which describes shades of green, blue, and purple, and *wor,* which covers yellow, orange, brown, and khaki. Unlike British adults, then, Berinmo speakers do not distinguish green and blue as colors with separate names, nor do they discriminate among the different colors denoted by the word *wor.*

Roberson and her colleagues showed participants from both linguistic groups three cards, each with a color on it, and asked them to pick the color that was different from the other two. For English speakers, when shown two

shades of green and a shade of blue, the choice was obvious: the shade of blue was different. For the Berinmo speakers, however, the distinction between two greens and a blue was arbitrary; all three were *nol* colors. They chose the blue only about half the time. However, when shown cards with a yellow, a khaki, and a green shade, the tables were turned. For the Berinmo speakers, the choice was between two *wor* cards and a *nol.* For the English speakers, the distinction looked arbitrary. Roberson and her colleagues found that each group of speakers could distinguish colors across its own linguistic category boundaries, but was only at a chance level when making decisions relevant in the other group's language.

Constancies of Visual Perception

An important characteristic of the visual environment is that it is almost always changing as we move, as objects move, and as lighting conditions change. However, despite the changing nature of the images the visual environment casts on our retinas, our perceptions remain remarkably constant. Here we consider the perceptual constancies of brightness, size, and shape.

Brightness Constancy Experiments have shown that people can judge the whiteness or grayness of an object very well, even if the level of illumination changes. If you look at a sheet of white paper either in bright sun-light or in shade, you will perceive it as white, although the intensity of its image on your retina will vary dramatically. A sheet of gray paper seen in sunlight may in fact reflect more light to your eye than a white paper in the shade, but you will still see the white paper as white and the gray paper as gray. This phenomenon is known as **brightness constancy.**

Katz (1935) provided an early demonstration of brightness constancy by constructing a vertical barrier and positioning a light source so that a shadow was cast to the right of the barrier. (See **Figure 7•36.**) In the shadow, he placed a gray square card on a white background. In the lighted area on the left of the barrier, he placed various shades of gray and asked participants to choose one that matched the gray square in the shadow. His participants matched the grays not in terms of the light the cards actually reflected but in terms of the light they *would have* reflected had both been viewed under the same level of illumination. In other words, they compensated fairly well for the dimness of the shadow. Compensations based on assumptions about the direction of lighting (refer to Figure 7.31) and color saturation also affect brightness constancies (Lotto & Purves, 1999).

FIGURE 7·36 Brightness constancy as demonstrated by the experiment by Katz (1935).

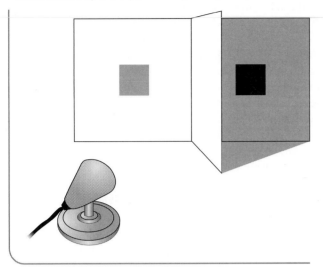

Motion Perception

Detection of movement is one of the most primitive perceptual abilities. It is exhibited even by animals whose visual systems do not obtain detailed images of the environment. In animals that must avoid obstacles and elude predators, accurate estimation of motion is essential. Pigeons are a good example, as they are prey to fast-moving predators able to catch them in flight. Sun and Frost (1998) found that the pigeon's visual system contains three distinct classes of neurons that separately carry information about looming objects. The information provided by these neurons provides a sort of "early warning" system of an impending collision, as well as an accurate estimate of the time to collision. Of course, the human visual system can detect more than the mere presence of movement. We can detect what is moving in our environment and the direction in which it is moving.

Adaptation to and Long-Term Modification of Motion Perception
One of the most important characteristics of all sensory systems is that they show adaptation and aftereffects. For example, when you stare at a spot of color, the adaptation of neurons in your visual system will produce a negative afterimage if you shift your gaze to a neutral background (recall the radish in Figure 6.18 in Chapter 6). Or if you put your hand in some hot water, warm water will feel cool to that hand immediately afterwards.

Motion, like other kinds of stimuli, can give rise to adaptation and illusory aftereffects. Perhaps you have stood on a foot bridge and stared at the water in the stream below you as it ran under the bridge. If you shifted your gaze and looked down at the bridge instead, it may have appeared to move in the direction opposite that of the water.

Size and Shape Constancies When we approach an object, or when it approaches us, we do not perceive it as getting larger. Even though the image of the object on the retina gets larger, we perceive this change as being due to a decrease in the distance between the object and ourselves. Our perception of the object's size remains relatively constant. This is known as **size constancy.**

Constancy also works for the rotation of an object. The drawing shown in panel (a) of **Figure 7·37** could either have the shape of a trapezoid or be a rectangle rotated away from us. However, the extra cues clearly identify the drawing in panel (b) of the figure as a window, and experience tells us that windows are rectangular rather than trapezoidal; thus, we perceive it as rectangular. This is an example of **shape constancy.**

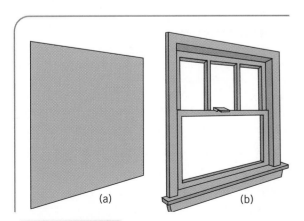

FIGURE 7·37 Shape constancy. (a) This figure can be perceived as a trapezoid. (b) Because we recognize this figure as a window, we perceive its shape as rectangular.

▲ *The combat soldier's survival depends on the ability to detect subtle movements in the environment.*

In 1834 a Mr. Adams reported what is now referred to as the *waterfall phenomenon* or *waterfall illusion* after watching the descent of a waterfall. When he shifted his gaze elsewhere, the objects in his view appeared to move upward at the same rate of speed as the falling water. Tootell, Reppas, Dale, and Look (1995) presented research participants with a display showing a series of concentric rings moving outward like the ripples in a pond. When the rings suddenly stopped moving, the participants had the impression of the opposite movement—that the rings were moving inward. During this time, the researchers scanned the participants' brains to measure the metabolic activity there. The scans showed increased activity in the motion-sensitive region of the visual association cortex, which lasted as long as the illusion of movement did. Thus, the neural circuits that give rise to this illusion appear to be located in the same region that responds to actual moving stimuli.

A study by Ball and Sekuler (1982) suggests that even the long-term characteristics of the system that detects movement can be modified by experience. The researchers first trained people to detect extremely small movements. Each person sat in front of a display screen. A series of dots appeared, scattered across the face of the screen, and either all moved a very small distance or all remained stationary. The dots always moved in the same direction, but the direction was different for each person. After several sessions, the researchers assessed sensitivity to movements of the dots in various directions. They found that each person was especially good at detecting movement *only in the direction in which he or she had been trained;* the training did not increase the participants' detection of movements in other directions. The effect was still present 10 weeks later.

Interpretation of a Moving Retinal Image As you read this book, your eyes are continuously moving. Naturally, the eye movements cause the image on your retina to move. You can also cause the retinal image to move by holding the book close to your face, looking straight ahead, and moving it back and forth. (Try it.) In the first case, when you were reading normally, you perceived the book as being still. In the second case, you perceived it as moving. Why does your brain interpret the movement differently in these two cases? Try another demonstration. Pick a letter on this page, stare at it, and then move the book around, following the letter with your eyes. This time you will perceive the book as moving even though the image on your retina remains stable. Thus, perception of movement requires coordination between movements of the image on the retina and those of the eyes.

Obviously, the visual system must know about eye movements in order to compensate for them in interpreting moving images on the retina. Another simple demonstration suggests the source of this information. Close your left eye and look slightly down and to the left. Gently press your finger against the outer corner of the upper eyelid of your right eye

and make your right eye move a bit. The scene before you appears to be moving, even though you know better. This sensation of movement occurs because your finger—not your eye muscles—moved your eye. When your eye moves normally, perceptual mechanisms in your brain compensate for this movement. Even though the image on the retina moves, you perceive the environment as being stationary. However, if the image moves because the object itself moves or because you push your eye with your finger, you perceive movement. (See **Figure 7•38**.)

We also perceive the movements of objects relative to one another, and sometimes we can be fooled. You may have sat in an automobile at a stoplight when the vehicle next to you appeared to start rolling backward. For a moment, you were uncertain whether you were moving forward or the other vehicle was moving backward. Only by looking at unmoving objects such as buildings or trees could you be sure.

If two objects of different size each move, the smaller object is perceived as moving and the larger as standing still. Normally, for example, we perceive people at a distance moving against a stable background and flies moving against an unmoving wall. Thus, when a researcher moves a frame that encloses a stationary dot, we tend to see the dot move, not the frame. This phenomenon is also encountered when we perceive the moon racing behind the clouds, even though we know that the clouds, not the moon, are moving.

Perception of relative movement can even help us perceive three-dimensional forms. Johansson (1973) demonstrated just how much information we can derive from movement. He dressed actors in black and attached small lights to several points on their bodies, such as their wrists, elbows, shoulders, hips, knees, and feet. He made movies of the actors in a darkened room while they were performing various behaviors, such as walking, running, jumping, limping, doing push-ups, and dancing with a partner who was also equipped with lights. Even though observers who

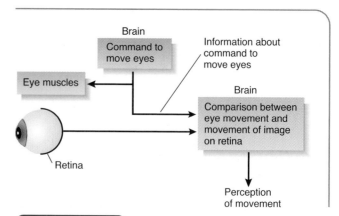

FIGURE 7•38 A schematic representation of the brain mechanisms responsible for the interpretation of a moving retinal image. This system must compensate for eye movements.

FIGURE 7·39 An impossible figure that seems plausible at first. Only after carefully studying the figure do we see that it cannot be a drawing of a real three-dimensional object.

watched the films could see only a pattern of moving lights against a dark background, they could readily perceive the pattern as belonging to a moving human and could identify the behavior the actor was performing. Subsequent studies (Kozlowski & Cutting, 1977; Barclay, Cutting, & Kozlowski, 1978) showed that people could even tell, with reasonable accuracy, the gender of the actor wearing the lights. The gender cues appeared to be supplied by the relative amounts of movement of the shoulders and hips as the person walked.

Earlier we saw that perception of the shapes of objects, their color, and their locations seems to involve different brain mechanisms. Bernstein and Robertson (1998) explored the way movement might be involved with these same mechanisms. They were testing a patient named R. M. who, as a result of a stroke, had the symptoms of Balint's syndrome. In fact, R. M. often exhibited "illusory conjunctions" of shapes with colors. For example, if he saw a red *X* and a green *S,* he might report seeing a green *X.* Bernstein and Robertson combined some of these displays involving shape and color with movement of the letters (e.g., the red *X* might move up and down and the green *S* move from side to side). R. M. would show illusory conjunctions of movement with the shape, as if the motion features of one letter could be detached and combined with a different letter. However, accurately reporting the shape and color of a letter did not mean an increase in accuracy of reporting its motion. The results suggest that these features are independently registered by the visual system and must be brought together to be integrated properly. The damage that R. M. had experienced as a result of his stroke apparently interfered with this integration. What is interesting about R. M.'s case is that this damage was to the second level of the visual system in the parietal lobe. Although the temporal areas may be important in associating shapes, colors, and movements, the parietal lobes may be instrumental in binding these features together into the perception of a single object.

As we saw in Chapter 6, when examining a scene, our eyes do not roam slowly around; rather, they make rapid, random movements called *saccades.* After each saccade, the eyes rest for a while, gathering information before moving again. These stops are called *fixations.* The visual system combines the information from each fixation and, in doing so, is able to perceive objects too large or too detailed to see in a single glance. Obviously, to do this, it must keep track of the location of each fixation.

To appreciate how saccades and fixations affect perception, consider the next two figures. **Figure 7·39** illustrates an *impossible figure* that appears plausible at first. That is, an artist can draw lines that, at first glance, we perceive as a three-dimensional object. However, on careful inspection we realize that the object cannot possibly exist. But the drawing in **Figure 7·40** creates a very different impression; it does not look at all like a unified three-dimensional object. The dif-

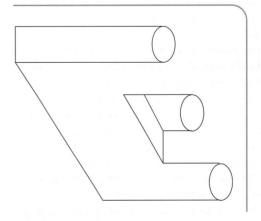

FIGURE 7·40 An unconvincing impossible figure. When the legs are short enough so that the entire figure can be perceived during a single fixation, the figure does not look paradoxical.

▲ *This lithograph,* Convex and Concave *by M. C. Escher, shows how contradictory depth clues can be combined to provide an "impossible" scene.*

ference in the two figures is that the details of the larger figure cannot be obtained in a single glance. Apparently, when we look from one end of the figure to the other, the information we gather from the first fixation is slightly modified to conform to the image of the second.

Combining Information from Vision and Audition

So far this chapter has concentrated on the visual perceptual system. Space and movement, however, often involve sound. You're probably familiar with the *Doppler effect,* in which an approaching sound, like that of the whistle of an oncoming train, increases in frequency, then decreases after it has passed by. Changes in both pitch and loudness are therefore good cues to whether a sound is coming toward you. And, as we saw in Chapter 6, our two ears receive slightly different versions of the same sound, allowing us to localize its source. So how does our *auditory* construction of space relate to our visual construction?

The fact that we have two auditory sense organs (that is, our two ears) seems to be recapitulated in our auditory perceptual system. Using the human ability to detect a temporal gap in an ongoing sound, Boehnke and Phillips (1999) found that we have two spatial channels for sound localization: one to each side, with about 30 degrees of overlap at the point directly in front of us. That means that we can tell more than whether sounds come from the left and right. Remember that we have only three kinds of color receptors and yet can distinguish a large number of hues. Similarly, on the basis of only two systems for sound localization, we can discriminate sounds coming from many directions around us (Recanzone, Makhamra, & Guard, 1998).

The **ventriloquism effect** demonstrates that the auditory system's ability to locate a sound interacts with our visual system. As stage performers have known for a long time, when

an auditory cue and a visual cue signal conflicting sources of a sound, the visual cue tends to dominate. That is, the source of the sound is judged to be closer to the apparent visual location (Vroomen, Bertelson, & de Gelder, 2001). Ventriloquists don't "throw" their voices as such; instead, they throw off our perception of their voices' source by the movements of the puppets (dummies) they hold.

This interaction occurs in other phenomena as well. Remember Mr. Adams's waterfall illusion? There is an auditory equivalent, in which rising or falling sounds are used to suggest movement. If that movement "stops," a person perceives the aftereffect as an opposing movement. This auditory waterfall illusion can be affected by visual cues: A visual cue for movement enhances the auditory aftereffect (Kitagawa & Ichihara, 2002).

Both of these observations suggest an important question: How do we connect visual with auditory sources? What leads us, for example, to think that the squeaky voice is coming from the ventriloquist's dummy rather than the human beside it? This issue is sometimes called the **binding problem,** because it is a puzzle to psychologists and neuroscientists at present. Clearly, when combining auditory and visual perceptions of space, the brain must connect these two sources of sensory input. How it accomplishes this connection is still a mystery, although the functional imaging techniques discussed in Chapter 4 are providing new insights. For example, Bushara and colleagues (2003) used fMRI procedures to look at one type of binding, depicted in **Figure 7·41.** In their experiment, people watched a screen. Two vertical lines moved from the edges toward the center. When the two lines reached the center, they then moved toward the edges at the same rate. Observers either perceived the lines as passing through each other or as colliding and bouncing back. The tendency to report a collision was greatly enhanced if a "crash" noise was sounded at the moment the two lines met. In other words, there was a binding of the noise with the visual image to produce a unique perception. Bushara and colleagues found, not surprisingly, that this binding was associated with activity in areas of the brain that respond to multimodal sensory input. However, binding was also associated with decreased activity in the auditory and visual cortical areas. The connection, then, between auditory and visual localities may be established early in spatial processing.

Perception of Movement When It Is Absent

If you sit in a darkened room and watch two small lights that are alternately turned on and off at a certain rate, your perception will be of a single light moving back and forth. You will not see the light turn off at one position and then turn on at the second position. If the distance and timing are just right, the light will appear to stay on at all times, quickly moving between the positions. This demonstration is known as the **phi phenomenon** and was originally studied by the Gestalt psychologists referred to earlier in the chapter. Theater mar-

FIGURE 7·41 A schematic of the procedure used in the study by Bushara and colleagues (2003). Study participants viewed a white rectangular window (a). At the beginning of a trial, two identical bars appeared at the left and right edges (b) and moved horizontally to the center. After coinciding at the center (c), the two bars continued moving away from each other (d) and disappeared at the opposite edges (e). Participants were asked to fixate their gaze at the center while attending to the bars' movement and to indicate whether the two bars bypassed each other or collided. A collision sound (the waveform indicated in the diagram) was synchronized with the point of overlap (c).

(From Bushara, K. O., Hanakawa, T., Immisch, I., Toma, K., Kansaku, K., & Hallett, M. (2003). Neural correlates of cross-modal binding. *Nature Neuroscience, 6,* 190–195.)

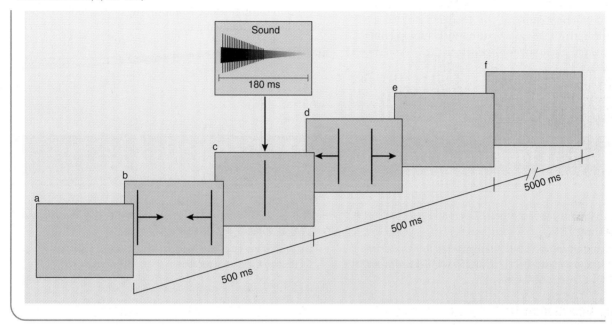

quees, "moving" neon signs, and computer animations make use of it.

This characteristic of the visual system accounts for the fact that we perceive the images in motion pictures and on television as continuous rather than discrete. The images actually jump from place to place, but we perceive smooth movement.

Interim Summary

Perception of Space and Motion

Our visual system accomplishes a remarkable feat: It manages to perceive objects accurately even in the face of movement and changes in levels of illumination. Because the size and shape of a retinal image—a two-dimensional image—vary with the location of an object relative to the eye, accurate form perception requires depth perception—perception of the locations of objects in three-dimensional space. Depth perception comes from binocular cues (from convergence and retinal disparity) and monocular cues (from interposition, size, linear perspective, texture, haze, shading, elevation, and head and body movements).

A person's culture may affect his or her perceptions, but probably not in a fundamental way. The linguistic relativity hypothesis, which suggested that language could strongly affect the way we perceive the world, has received limited empirical support. It is also possible that experience with some environmental features, such as particular geographical features or buildings composed of straight lines and right angles, may influence the way people perceive the world.

We perceive the brightness of an object relative to that of objects around it; thus, objects retain a constant brightness under a variety of conditions of illumination. In addition, our perception of the relative distance of objects helps us maintain both size and shape constancy.

Because our bodies may well be moving while we are visually following some activity in the outside world, the visual system has to make further compensations. It keeps track of the commands to the eye muscles and compensates for the direction in which the eyes are pointing. Movement is perceived when objects move relative to one another. In particular, a smaller object is likely to be perceived as moving across a larger one. Movement is also perceived when our eyes follow a moving object, even though its image remains on the same part of the retina.

Movement supplies important cues about an object's three-dimensional shape. In fact, we are much more sensitive to complex movements than we commonly realize, as illustrated by the research involving movies of actors wearing lights. Vision is not the only perceptual system that can locate objects; we also rely on sound. Usually, the two systems provide similar information—but when they conflict, as in the case of ventriloquism, the visual system usually dominates.

The phi phenomenon is our tendency to see a sequence of discrete images as a continuously moving object. Because of the phi phenomenon, we perceive television shows and movies as real motion, not as a series of disconnected images.

QUESTIONS TO CONSIDER

1. Why do you suppose that artists sometime hold their thumbs in front of them while looking at the scenes they are painting?
2. When we ride in an automobile and can see the sun or moon through a side window, why does it look as if these objects are following us?

Suggestions for Further Reading

Dowling, J. E. (2004). *The great brain debate: Nature or nurture?* Washington, DC: Joseph Henry Press.

A foremost expert on the visual system examines the development of visual perception in the context of the larger issue of gene-environment interaction.

Goodale, M., & Milner, D. (2004). *Sight unseen.* Oxford, UK: Oxford University Press.

Drawing from clinical observations of a patient with "blindsight," this provocative book introduces the concept of two visual systems: one for the perception of objects and the other for the control of movement.

Hoffman, D. D. (1998). *Visual intelligence: How we create what we see.* New York: Norton.

This is an authoritative work on visual perception as representation, that is, on how the visual system creates models of the visual world.

Hubel, D. H. (2004). *Brain and visual perception: The story of a 25-year collaboration.* New York: Oxford University Press.

One-half of the Nobel-prize winning team provides a marvelous summary of their work and its implications.

Pinker, S. (1997). *How the mind works.* New York: Norton.

If you only read one book about cognitive neuroscience, you'll do no better than this comprehensive, well-told introduction.

Sacks, O. (1998). *The island of the colorblind.* New York: Vintage.

The noted neurologist and superb storyteller weaves a fascinating tale of research findings in Micronesia and their larger, Darwinian implications. Part of the book is devoted to his observations of an isolated population of individuals with achromatopsia.

Key Terms

achromatopsia (p. 198)

artificial intelligence (p. 206)

Balint's syndrome (p. 199)

binding problem (p. 222)

bottom-up processing (p. 209)

brightness constancy (p. 218)

convergence (p. 211)

distinctive features (p. 204)

dorsal stream (p. 198)

elevation (p. 215)

figure (p. 200)

ground (p. 200)

haze (p. 213)

interposition (p. 213)

law of closure (p. 202)

law of common fate (p. 202)

law of good continuation (p. 202)

law of proximity (p. 201)

law of similarity (p. 202)

linear perspective (p. 213)

linguistic relativity (p. 217)

motion parallax (p. 215)

neural network (p. 207)

parallel processor (p. 206)

phi phenomenon (p. 222)

prosopagnosia (p. 199)

prototype (p. 203)

receptive field (p. 196)

retinal disparity (p. 211)

shading (p. 214)

shape constancy (p. 219)

size (p. 213)

size constancy (p. 219)

tachistoscope (p. 208)

template (p. 202)

texture (p. 213)

top-down processing (p. 209)

ventral stream (p. 198)

ventriloquism effect (p. 222)

8

MEMORY

Overview

Memory involves the cognitive processes of encoding, storage, and retrieval of information. Encoding involves putting stimulus information in a form that can be used by our memory system. Storage involves maintaining it in memory, and retrieval involves locating and using it. Memory has been described as taking at least three forms: sensory memory, short-term memory, and long-term memory.

Sensory Memory

Iconic Memory • Echoic Memory

Sensory memory stores newly perceived information for very brief periods. Although sensory memory appears to exist for all senses, visual (iconic) and auditory (echoic) memories have received the most empirical attention.

Short-Term or Working Memory

Encoding of Information: Interaction with Long-Term Memory • Primacy and Recency Effects • The Limits of Working Memory • Varieties of Working Memory • Loss of Information from Short-Term Memory

Information may enter short-term memory (also called working memory) from both sensory memory and long-term memory. Working memory works very well for items at the end of lists. Working memory holds about seven items and lasts for about 20 seconds, unless the information is rehearsed. Verbal and visual information in working memory appears to be represented phonologically (both acoustically and articulatorily) and is subject to manipulation by thought processes. An important cause of loss of information from working memory is displacement of older information to make room for newer information.

Learning and Encoding in Long-Term Memory

The Consolidation Hypothesis • The Levels-of-Processing Hypothesis • Improving Long-Term Memory through Mnemonics

Long-term memory likely involves permanent structural changes in the brain. Our ability to retrieve information from long-term memory is often determined by how that information is learned or encoded. Rehearsal helps us store information permanently, although some types of rehearsal seem to be more effective than others. Special techniques called mnemonics improve storage and retrieval of information in long-term memory.

The Organization of Long-Term Memory

Episodic and Semantic Memory • Explicit and Implicit Memory • The Biological Basis of Long-Term Memory

Research has distinguished among permanent memories for autobiographical information (episodic), conceptual information (semantic), information of which we are aware (explicit), and information of which we may be unaware (implicit). Studies involving amnesic people strongly suggest that the biological basis of long-term memory involves the hippocampus.

Remembering

Remembering and Recollecting • How Long Does Memory Last? • *Biology and Culture: Cultural Contexts for Remembering* • Reconstruction: Remembering as a Creative Process • Remembering and Interference • *Evaluating Scientific Issues: Hypnosis, Remembering, and Criminal Investigation*

In many instances remembering is automatic—we do not have to put forth much conscious effort to retrieve a memory. In other cases, though, we must actively search for and use cues that aid our retrieval of a memory. Forgetting of information is greatest during the first few years after the information is learned and decreases slowly afterwards. Remembering is influenced by aspects of culture, such as teaching practices and societal mores. The process of remembering complex information often is inaccurate, because it involves reconstruction of information from existing memories. Information contained in other memories may interfere with recall of a particular memory. Hypnosis may help people recall information, but it also may bias the accuracy of the information that is actually remembered.

accompanied my graduate student Fred to a hospital in a nearby town, where Fred had been studying several patients. We met Mr. P. in the lounge. Fred introduced us, and we walked to the room where he had set up his equipment. We sat down and chatted.

"How long have you been here?" Fred asked Mr. P.

"Oh, about a week."

"Uh-huh. What brought you here?"

"I'm having some work done on my teeth. I'll be going back home in a couple of days. I have to help my father on the farm."

I knew that Mr. P. had actually been in the hospital for 11 years.

He had been an alcoholic for a long time before that, and he was brought to the hospital in a severely malnourished condition. He was diagnosed with Korsakoff's syndrome, a state of physical and mental deterioration caused by excessive consumption of alcohol. Fred pointed to a slide projector and screen and asked Mr. P. whether he had seen them before.

He looked at them and said, "No, I don't think so."

Fred looked at me and said, "Say, have you met Dr. Carlson?"

Mr. P. turned around, stood up, and extended his hand. "No, I don't believe I have. How do you do, sir?" he said. We shook hands, and I greeted him in return.

"Mr. P., a few days ago you saw some pictures here," said Fred. Mr. P. looked doubtful but said politely, "Well, if you say so." Fred dimmed the lights and showed him the first slide.

Two pictures of two different automobiles were projected on the screen, side by side.

"Which one did you see before?" Fred asked.

"Neither of them."

"Well," Fred persisted, "point to the one you might have seen." Mr. P. looked nonplussed but pointed to the one on the right. Fred made a notation in his notebook and then showed the next slide, which showed views of two different trees.

"Which one?" he asked.

Silently, Mr. P. pointed to the one on the left. After showing 18 pairs of slides, Fred said, "That's it, Mr. P. Thanks for helping me. By the way, have you met Dr. Carlson?" Mr. P. looked at Fred and then followed his gaze, turned around, and saw me. He stood up, and we shook hands and introduced ourselves.

As we left the hospital, I asked Fred how Mr. P. had done. "He got 17 correct!" he exulted.

Overview

In this chapter we will attempt to understand the structure of **memory**—the cognitive processes of encoding, storing, and retrieving information. **Encoding** is the active process of putting stimulus information into a form that can be used by our memory system. **Storage** is the process of maintaining information in memory. **Retrieval** includes the active processes of locating and using information stored in memory.

When psychologists refer to the *structure* of memory, they are referring to two approaches to understanding memory—one approach literal and the other metaphorical (Howard, 1995). On the literal side, physiological psychologists and other neuroscientists are trying to discover the physiological changes that occur in the brain when an organism learns something. To them, the structure of memory has to do with these physiological changes. In contrast, cognitive psychologists study the structure of memory in a metaphorical sense. They have developed conceptual, information-processing models of memory. Most of the research described in this chapter involves these latter kinds of models. However, we will also examine research on the physiological nature of memory.

Recall from Chapter 5 that learning is the tendency for behavior to change as a result of experience; learning and performance reflect the brain's plasticity. Our ability to learn allows us to engage in an enormous variety of behaviors in response to an enormous variety of situations. But a lapse of time may occur between the act of learning and a change in behavior caused by that learning. For example, I may observe that a new restaurant has opened and then, some days later, visit that restaurant when I want to eat out. The usefulness of memory, then, manifests itself in behavior. Presumably, the sight of the restaurant has induced some changes in my brain, which we refer to as the encoding of the memory. These changes persist over time, showing that I have stored the memory. Later, when I think about what restaurant I would like to visit, I think about the new one (that is, I retrieve the memory) and I act. This chapter describes how we encode, store, and retrieve memories.

Back in the 1960s Richard Atkinson and Richard Shiffrin suggested a way of thinking about memory that psychologists have found useful. They proposed that memory takes at least three forms: sensory memory, short-term memory, and long-term memory (Atkinson & Shiffrin, 1968). **Sensory memory** is memory in which representations of the physical features of a stimulus are stored for a very brief time—perhaps for a second or less. This form of memory is difficult to distinguish from the act of perception. The information contained in sensory memory represents the original stimulus fairly accurately and contains all or most of the information that has just been perceived. For example, sensory memory contains a brief image of a sight we have just seen or a fleeting echo of a sound we have just heard. Normally, we are not aware of sensory memory; no analysis seems to be performed on the information while it remains in this form. The function of sensory memory appears to be to hold information long enough for it to become part of the next form of memory, short-term memory.

Short-term memory is an immediate memory for stimuli that have just been perceived. As we will soon see, its capacity is limited in terms of the number of items it can store and its duration. We can remember a new item of information, such as a telephone number, by rehearsing it. However, once we stop rehearsing the information, we may not be able to remember it later. Information soon leaves short-term memory, and unless it is stored in long-term memory it will be lost forever.

To demonstrate the fact that short-term memory can hold only a limited amount of information for a limited time, read the following numbers to yourself just once, and then close your eyes and recite them back.

1 4 9 2 3 0 7

You probably had no trouble remembering them. Now, try the following set of numbers, and go through them only once before you close your eyes.

7 2 5 2 3 9 1 6 5 8 4

Very few people can repeat 11 numbers; in fact, you may not have even bothered to try once you saw how many numbers there were. Even if you practice, you will probably not be able to recite more than seven to nine independent pieces of information that you have seen only once. Thus, short-term memory has definite limits. As we will see, of course, there are ways to organize new information so that you can remember more than seven to nine items; but in such cases the items can no longer be considered independent.

If you wanted to, you could recite the 11 numbers again and again until you had memorized them. You could rehearse the information in short-term memory until it was eventually part of **long-term memory**—memory in which information is represented on a permanent or near-permanent basis. Unlike short-term memory, long-term memory has no known limits; and, as its name suggests, it is relatively durable. For example, Standing (1973) showed people 10,000 color slides and found that they could recognize most of them weeks later, even though they had seen them just once. Presumably, long-term memory involves physical changes that take place in the brain. If we stop thinking about something we have just perceived (that is, something contained in short-term memory), we may not remember the information later. However, information in long-term memory need not be continuously rehearsed. We can stop thinking about it until we need the information at a future time.

I have been using the metaphorical conceptualization of memory to suggest that information flows from one type of memory to another. (See **Figure 8•1**.) This general conception of the memory system has been termed the "modal model" of memory. However, some cognitive psychologists argue that no real distinction exists between short-term and long-term memory; instead, they see them as different phases of a continuous process. So, although the next few sections will follow the general outline of Figure 8.1, you will see that psychologists have discovered memory is more complex than this model would have us believe (Healy & McNamara, 1996).

Sensory Memory

Under most circumstances we are not aware of sensory memory. Information we have just perceived remains in sensory memory just long enough to be transferred to short-term

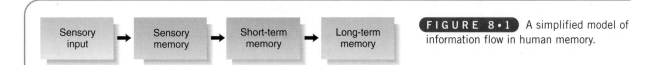

FIGURE 8•1 A simplified model of information flow in human memory.

▲ *Images to which we are briefly exposed, such as a bolt of lightning, linger momentarily in iconic memory.*

memory. We become aware of sensory memory only when information is presented so briefly that we can perceive its aftereffects. For example, a thunderstorm at night provides us with an opportunity to become aware of visual sensory memory. When a bright flash of lightning reveals a scene, we see things before we recognize them. That is, we see something first, then study the image it leaves behind. Although we probably have a sensory memory for each sense modality, research efforts so far have focused on the two most important forms: iconic (visual) and echoic (auditory) memory.

Iconic Memory

Visual sensory memory, called **iconic memory** (*icon* means "image"), is a form of sensory memory that briefly holds a visual representation of a scene that has just been perceived. Because the representation is so closely tied to the perception, this form of memory is sometimes called "visible persistence." To study this form of memory, Sperling (1960) presented visual stimuli to people by means of a tachistoscope. As you may recall from Chapter 7, a tachistoscope is an apparatus for presenting visual stimuli for extremely brief durations. Sperling flashed a set of letters (three rows of letters) on the screen for 50 milliseconds (see **Figure 8•2**). He then asked the participants to recall as many letters as they could,

a method known as the whole-report procedure. On average, participants could remember only four or five letters. They insisted that for a brief time they could see more; however, the image of the letters faded too fast for people to identify them all.

To determine whether the capacity of iconic memory accounted for this limitation, Sperling used a partial-report procedure. He sounded tones when presenting the stimuli, and he asked people to name the letters in only one of the three horizontal rows: Depending on whether a high, middle, or low tone was sounded, they were to report the letters in the top, middle, or bottom line. When the participants were warned beforehand to which line they should attend, they had no difficulty naming all three letters correctly. But then Sperling sounded the tone *after* he flashed the letters on the screen. The participants had to select the line from the mental image they still had: *They could use only information from memory.* With brief delays, they recalled the requested line of letters with high accuracy. For example, after seeing all nine letters flashed on the screen, they would hear the high tone, direct their attention to the top line of letters in their iconic memory, and "read them off" much as one might read the headlines in a newspaper. The participants' high level of performance indicated that there was little difference between having the letters physically present in front of them and having them present as a memory. However, Sperling also varied the delay between flashing the nine letters on the screen and sounding the high, medium, or low tone. If the delay was longer than one second, people could report only around 50 percent of the letters. This result indicated that the image of the visual stimulus fades quickly from iconic memory. It also explains why participants who were asked to report all nine letters failed to report more than four or five. They had to scan their iconic memory, identify each letter, and name it verbally. This process took time, and during this time the image of the letters was fading and the information becoming unreliable (Dixon, Gordon, Leung, & Di Lollo, 1997). Although their iconic memory originally contained all nine letters, participants had time to recognize and report only four or five before the mental image disappeared.

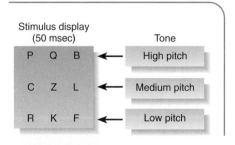

FIGURE 8•2 The critical features of Sperling's iconic memory study.

(Adapted from Sperling, G. (1960). The information available in brief visual presentations. *Psychological Monographs, 74,* 1–29.)

Echoic Memory

Auditory sensory memory, called **echoic memory,** is a form of sensory memory for sounds that have just been perceived. It is necessary for comprehending many sounds, particularly those that constitute speech. When we hear a word pronounced, we hear individual sounds, one at a time. We cannot identify the word until we have heard all the sounds, so acoustical information must be stored temporarily until all the sounds have been received. For example, if someone says "mallet," we may think of a kind of hammer; but if someone says "malice," we will think of something entirely different. The first syllable we hear—*mal*—has no meaning by itself in English, so we do not identify it as a word. However, once the last syllable is uttered, we can put the two syllables together and recognize the word. At this point, the word enters short-term memory. Echoic memory holds a representation of the initial sounds until the entire word has been heard. Although early use of partial-report procedures suggested that echoic memory lasts less than 4 seconds (Darwin, Turvey, & Crowder, 1972), more recent evidence employing repeated patterns of random, or "white," noise indicates that echoic memory can last up to 20 seconds (Kaernbach, 2004). Indeed, if you consider your ability to recognize a friend's voice over the telephone, there's a sense in which we retain sound patterns for much longer (Winkler & Cowan, 2005). This everyday phenomenon presents a problem for the simplified model that we've been discussing. To understand why, we need to consider the next stages in that model: short-term and long-term memory.

Interim Summary

Overview and Sensory Memory

Memory exists in three forms: sensory, short-term, and long-term. The characteristics of each form differ, which suggests that the three forms differ physiologically as well. Sensory memory is very limited—it provides temporary storage until newly perceived information can be stored in short-term memory. Short-term memory contains a representation of information that has just been perceived, such as an item's name. Although the capacity of short-term memory is limited, we can rehearse the information as long as we choose, thus increasing the likelihood that we will remember it indefinitely (that is, that it will enter long-term memory).

Information in iconic memory is considered to last for only a very short time. The partial-report procedure shows that when a visual stimulus is presented in a brief flash, all of the information is available for about a second. If the viewer is asked to recall one line of information after one second, the information is no longer present in iconic memory. Although echoic memory was originally considered as a similar type of memory for auditory stimulation, recent evidence suggests it can last longer.

QUESTIONS TO CONSIDER

1. It is easy to understand how we can rehearse verbal information in short-term memory—we simply say the information to ourselves again and again. But much of the information we learn is not verbal. Can we rehearse nonverbal information in short-term memory? How do we do so?

2. Suppose that your iconic memory malfunctioned—that instead of holding information only briefly, your iconic memory retained information for longer periods of time. What complications or problems might follow from such a malfunction? Would there be any advantages to this sort of malfunction?

Short-Term or Working Memory

Short-term memory has a limited capacity, and most of the information that enters it is subsequently forgotten. What, then, is its function? Before we try to answer this question, let us examine its nature a little more closely.

Encoding of Information: Interaction with Long-Term Memory

So far, the story I have been telling about memory has been simple: Information in sensory memory enters short-term memory, where it may be rehearsed for a while. The rehearsal process keeps the information in short-term memory long enough for it to be transferred into long-term memory. After that, a person can stop thinking about the information; it can be recalled later, when it is needed.

However, this simple story is incomplete. First of all, information does not simply "enter short-term memory." For example, read the letters below. Put them into your short-term memory, and keep them there for a few seconds while you look away from the book.

P X L M R

How did you keep the information in short-term memory? You would probably say that you repeated the letters to yourself. You may even have whispered or moved your lips. You are able to say the names of these letters because many years ago you learned them. But that knowledge is stored in long-term memory. Thus, when you see some letters, you retrieve information about their names from long-term memory, and then you hear yourself rehearse those names (out loud or silently, "within your head"). The five letters you looked at contain only visual information; their names came from your long-term memory, which means that the information put into short-term memory actually came from long-term memory.

To convince yourself that you used information stored in long-term memory to remember the five letters, study the symbols below, look away from the book, and try to keep them in short-term memory for a while.

$$\zeta \cap \partial \ni \wp$$

Could you do it? I certainly can't. I never learned the names of these symbols, so I have no way of rehearsing them in short-term memory. Perhaps, then, **Figure 8•3** more accurately represents the successive stages of the memory process than does the diagram you saw in Figure 8.1.

You can see now that short-term memory is more than a simple way station between perception and long-term memory. Information can enter short-term memory from two directions: from sensory memory or from long-term memory. In Figure 8.3 this feature is represented by arrows pointing to short-term memory from both iconic memory and long-term memory. Perhaps another example will clarify the process further. When we are asked to multiply 7 by 19, information about the request enters our short-term memory from our sensory memory. Actually performing the task, though, requires that we retrieve some information from long-term memory. What does *multiply* mean? What is *7*, and what is *19*? At the moment of the request, such information is not being furnished through our senses; it is available only from long-term memory. Note, however, that information is not recalled directly from long-term memory. It is first moved into short-term memory and then recalled.

The fact that short-term memory contains both new information and information retrieved from long-term memory, and also seems more than a passive recording of information, has led some psychologists, such as Alan Baddeley, to prefer the term **working memory** (Baddeley, 1993). Working memory does seem to work on what we have just perceived. In fact, working memory represents a sort of behavior that takes place within our heads. It represents our ability to remember what we have just perceived and to think about it in terms of what we already know (Haberlandt, 1994). We use this form of memory to remember what a person says at the beginning of a sentence until we finally hear the end. We use it to remember whether any cars are coming up the street after we look left and then right. We use it to think about what we already know and to come to conclusions on the basis of this knowledge. These behaviors are similar to what I have described as short-term memory, and from now on this chapter will use the terms *short-term memory* and *working memory* interchangeably. Some psychologists, however, prefer to distinguish the two forms of memory on the basis of the functions they serve (Kail & Hall, 2001).

Primacy and Recency Effects

Imagine yourself as a participant in a memory study. You are asked to listen to the researcher as she slowly reads words, one at a time, off a long list. As soon as she finishes reading the list, she asks you to write down each word that you can remember. (This task is called a *free-recall task*.) Which words in the list do you think you are most likely to remember? If you are like most people in free-recall tasks of this type, you will tend to remember the words at the beginning and the end of the list and forget the words in between. The tendency to remember the words at the beginning of the list is called the **primacy effect**; the tendency to remember words at the end of the list is called the **recency effect**.

What causes these effects? Research that has addressed this question points to two factors (Atkinson & Shiffrin, 1968). The primacy effect appears to be due to the fact that words earlier in a list have the opportunity to be rehearsed more than do words in the other parts of a list. This makes good sense—the first words are rehearsed more because, at the experiment's outset, these are the only words available to rehearse. The rehearsal permits them to be stored in long-term memory. As more and more words on the list are presented, short-term memory becomes more and more full, so words that come later have more competition for rehearsal time. Because the first words on the list are rehearsed the most, they are remembered better.

What about the recency effect? As Atkinson and Shiffrin (1968) point out, because the words at the end of the list were

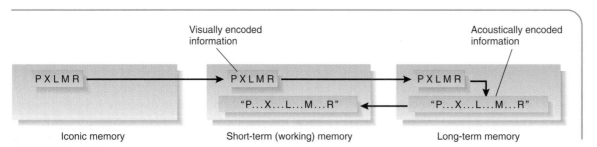

FIGURE 8•3 Relations between iconic memory, short-term memory, and long-term memory. Letters are read, transformed into their acoustic equivalents, and rehearsed as "sounds" in the head. Information can enter short-term memory from both iconic memory and long-term memory. Visual information enters short-term memory from iconic memory, but what is already known about that information (such as names of letters) is moved from long-term memory to short-term memory.

the last to be heard, they are still available in short-term memory. Thus, when you are asked to write the words on the list, the last several words are still available in short-term memory, even though they did not undergo as much rehearsal as words at the beginning of the list.

Earlier, I said that working memory is a sort of behavior—a type of behavior that takes place inside the head. The primacy and recency effects are important because they show the consequence of this behavior. Memory is not a random process that plucks information from the environment and stores it haphazardly in the brain. Instead, it follows predictable patterns and is dependent on the contributions of rehearsal and short-term memory. We cannot observe these behaviors directly, but we can observe their consequences.

The Limits of Working Memory

How long does information remain in working memory? The answer to this question was provided in a classic study conducted by Lloyd and Margaret Peterson (1959). The researchers presented people with a stimulus composed of three consonants, such as *JRG*. Not surprisingly, with rehearsal, people easily recalled the consonants 30 seconds later. The Petersons then made the task a bit more challenging: They prevented the participants in their study from rehearsing by assigning a distracter task: After they presented the participants with *JRG,* they asked them to count backward by 3s from a three-digit number they gave them immediately after they had presented the set of consonants. For example, they might present people with *JRG,* then say, "397." The participants would count out loud, "397 . . . 394 . . . 391 . . . 388 . . . 385," and so on until the researchers signaled them to recall the consonants. The accuracy of participants' recall was determined by the length of the interval between presentation of the consonants and the signal for recall (see **Figure 8•4**). When rehearsal was disrupted by backward counting—which prevented participants from rehearsing information in short-term memory—the consonants remained accessible in

▲ *Unless we actively rehearse the material we are studying, we are unlikely to remember it for very long: It is relegated to short-term memory, in which information is stored for relatively short periods of time.*

FIGURE 8•4 Limits of recall from working memory. Shown here is the percentage correct in the recall of the stimulus as a function of the duration of the distracter task used in the study by Peterson and Peterson.
(Adapted from Peterson, L. M., & Peterson, M. J. (1959). Short-term retention of individual verbal items. *Journal of Experimental Psychology, 58,* 193–198.)

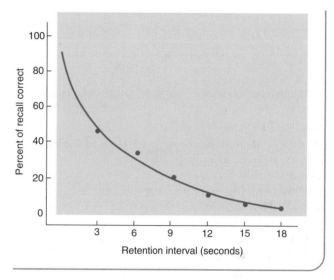

memory for only a few seconds. After a 15- to 18-second delay between the presentation of the consonants and the recall signal, recall dropped to near zero. So, for now at least, we can conclude that stimuli remain in working memory for less than 20 seconds *unless they are rehearsed.*

And what is the capacity of working memory? A while ago, I asked you to try to repeat 11 numbers, which you were almost certainly unable to do. In fact, Miller (1956), in a paper entitled "The Magical Number Seven, Plus or Minus Two," demonstrated that people could retain, on average, about seven pieces of information in their short-term memories: seven numbers, seven letters, seven words, or seven tones of a particular pitch. But if we can remember and think about only seven pieces of information at a time, how can we manage to write novels, design buildings, or even carry on simple conversations? The answer comes in a particular form of encoding of information that Miller called **chunking**. In chunking information is simplified by rules, which make the information easily remembered once the rules are learned.

A simple demonstration illustrates this phenomenon. Read the 10 numbers printed below and see whether you have any trouble remembering them.

1 3 5 7 9 2 4 6 8 0

These numbers are easy to retain in short-term memory because we can remember a rule instead of 10 independent numbers. In this case the rule concerns odd and even numbers. The actual limit of short-term memory is seven chunks, not necessarily seven individual items. Thus, the total amount of information we can store in short-term memory depends on the particular rules we use to organize it.

In life outside the laboratory (and away from the textbook), we are seldom required to remember a series of numbers. The rules that organize our short-term memories are much more complex than those that describe odd and even numbers. But the principles of chunking apply to more realistic learning situations. For example, say the group of words below, look away from the page, and try to recite the words from memory.

> along got the was door crept locked slowly he until passage the he to which

No doubt you found the task hopeless; there was just too much information to store in short-term memory. Now try the following group of words:

> He slowly crept along the passage until he got to the door, which was locked.

This time you were probably much more successful. Once the same 15 words are arranged in a sequence that makes sense, they are not difficult to store in short-term memory.

The capacity of short-term memory for verbal material is not measured in letters, syllables, or words. Instead, the limit depends on how much *meaning* the information has. The first set of words above merely contains 15 different words. Because few people can immediately recite back more than five to nine independent items, we are not surprised to find that we cannot store 15 jumbled words in short-term memory. However, when the items are related, we can store many more of them. We do not have to string 15 words together in a meaningless fashion. Instead, we can let the image of a man creeping down a passage toward a locked door organize the new information. Thus, we can read or hear a sentence, understand what it means, and remember that meaning.

This aspect of short-term memory suggests a way of making working memory more efficient in everyday use. If information can be organized into a more meaningful sequence, there is less to be remembered. McNamara and Scott (2001) taught people to chain unrelated words together as they listened to them. The chaining technique was simple: People were to imagine a story involving these words. This technique sharply improved short-term memory. Later in this chapter we will discuss similar strategies to improve long-term memory.

Varieties of Working Memory

So far, I have been referring to short-term or working memory in the singular. But evidence suggests that working memory can contain a variety of sensory information: visual, auditory, somatosensory, gustatory, and olfactory. It also can contain information about movements that we have just made (motor memories), and it may provide the means by which we rehearse movements that we are thinking about making. Is all this information contained in a single system, or do we have several independent working memories?

Baddeley (1993, 2000) has suggested that working memory consists of several components, all coordinated by a "central executive" function. One component maintains verbal information; another retains memories of visual stimuli. A third component might serve to store more general information, including memory for nonspeech sounds (such as the sound of your friend's voice over the telephone), touch, odors, or other types of information. Because we know most about memory for verbal and visual material, I will describe these two aspects of working memory and treat them as Baddeley does in his model.

Phonological Working Memory   Although we receive information from different senses, much of it can be encoded verbally. For example, we can see or smell a rose and think the word *rose*; we can feel the prick of a thorn and think the word *sharp*; and so on. Thus, seeing a rose, smelling a rose, and feeling a thorn can all result in words running through our working memory. How is verbal information stored in working memory? Evidence suggests that the short-term storage of words, whether originally presented visually or acoustically, occurs in **phonological short-term memory**—short-term or working memory for verbal information. The Greek word *phōnē* means both "sound" and "voice"; as the name implies, phonological coding could involve either the auditory system of the brain or the system that controls speech. As we shall see, it involves both.

In an experiment Conrad (1964) showed how quickly visually presented information becomes encoded acoustically. He briefly showed people lists of six letters and then asked them to write the letters. The errors these people made were almost always acoustical rather than visual. For instance, they sometimes wrote B when they had seen V (these letters sound similar), but they rarely wrote F when they had seen T (these letters look similar). Keep in mind that Conrad presented the letters visually. The results suggested that people read the letters, encoded them acoustically ("heard them in their minds"), and remembered them by rehearsing the letters as sounds. During this process, they might easily mistake a V for a B.

The fact that the errors seem to be acoustical may reflect a form of acoustical coding in working memory. That is, phonological memory may be produced by activity in the auditory system—say, circuits of neurons in the auditory association cortex. However, people often talk to themselves. Sometimes, they talk aloud; sometimes, they whisper or simply move their lips. At other times, no movements can be detected, but people still report that they are thinking about saying something. They are engaging in **subvocal articulation,** an unvoiced speech utterance. Even though no actual speech movement may occur, it is still possible that activity occurs in the neural circuits in the brain that normally control speech. When we close our eyes and imagine seeing something, the mental image is undoubtedly caused by the activity of neurons in the visual association cortex. Similarly, when we imagine saying something, the "voice in our head" is probably controlled by the activity of neurons in the motor association cortex.

In 1970 Conrad attempted to determine whether sub-vocal articulation played a role in phonological working memory by repeating his 1964 experiment—but this time with children who could not hear. The children had been deaf from birth and thus could not confuse the letters be-cause of their sounds. Nevertheless, some of the children made "acoustical" errors. The children who made these er-rors were those who were rated by their teachers as being the best speakers (Conrad, 1970). Therefore, the results sug-gested that the deaf children who could speak the best en-coded the letters in terms of the movements they would make to pronounce them.

This study provided clear evidence for an articulatory code in working memory. Of course, people who can both hear and speak may use both acoustic and articulatory codes: They may simultaneously hear a word and feel themselves saying it in their heads. Phonological codes stored in long-term memory also may help to strengthen the rehearsed in-formation (Roodenrys et al., 2002).

The best neurological evidence for the existence of phonological short-term memory comes from a disorder called **conduction aphasia,** which is usually caused by damage to a region of the left parietal lobe. Conduction aphasia ap-pears as a profound deficit in phonological working memory. People who have conduction aphasia can talk and can com-prehend what others are saying, but they are very poor at re-peating precisely what they hear. When they attempt to repeat words that other people say, they often get the meaning cor-rect but use different words. For example, if asked to repeat the sentence, "The cement truck ran over the bicycle," a per-son who has conduction aphasia may reply, "The concrete mixer got into an accident with a bike."

Most investigators believe that conduction aphasia is caused by brain damage that disrupts the connections be-tween two regions of the cerebral cortex that play important roles in people's language ability. These two regions are *Wern-icke's area,* which is concerned with the perception of speech, and *Broca's area,* which is concerned with the production of speech. (We'll look at these areas in more detail in Chapter 10.) As we've seen, phonological working memory appears to involve both articulatory and acoustical coding. Because the brain damage that produces conduction aphasia disconnects regions of the brain involved in speech perception and pro-duction, perhaps the damage disrupts acoustical short-term memory by making such subvocal verbal rehearsal difficult or impossible. (See **Figure 8•5.**)

Visual Working Memory Verbal information can be re-ceived by means of the auditory system or the visual system—that is, we can hear words or read them. As we saw in the pre-vious section, both forms of input produce acoustic and articulatory codes in phonological working memory. But much of the information we receive from the visual system is nonverbal. We recognize objects, perceive their locations, and find our way around the environment. We can look at objects, close our eyes, and then sketch or describe them. We can do

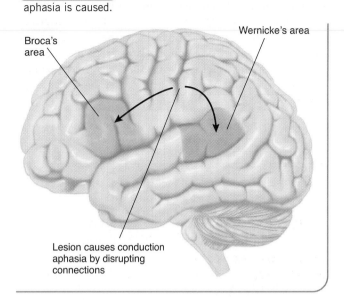

FIGURE 8•5 A diagram showing how conduction aphasia is caused.

Broca's area

Wernicke's area

Lesion causes conduction aphasia by disrupting connections

the same with things we saw in the past. Thus, we apparently possess a working memory that contains visual information, either obtained from the immediate environment by means of the sense organs or retrieved from long-term memory.

The chunking of information in working memory does not have to consist of words. Much of what we see is familiar; we have seen the particular items—or similar items—before. Thus, our visual working memory does not have to encode all the details, the way a photograph copies all the details in the scene gathered by the lens of a camera. For example, our short-term memory of the sight of a dog does not have to store every visual feature we saw, such as four legs, whiskers, ears, a tail. Instead, we already have mental images of dogs in our long-term memory. When we see a dog, we can select a prototype that fits the bill, filling in a few features to represent the particular dog we just saw.

DeGroot (1965) performed an experiment that pro-vides a nice example of the power of encoding visual infor-mation in working memory. He showed chessboards to ex-pert players and to novices. If the positions of the pieces represented an actual game in progress, the experts could glance at the board for a few seconds and then look away and report the position of each piece; the novices could not. However, if the same number of pieces had been placed haphazardly on the board, the experts recognized immedi-ately that their positions made no sense, and they could not remember their positions any better than a nonexpert could. Thus, the experts' short-term memories for the posi-tions of a large number of chess pieces depended on orga-nizational rules stored in long-term memory as a result of years of playing chess. Novices could not remember the lo-cation of the pieces in either situation, because they lacked long-term memories for patterns of chess pieces on a board and could not acquire the information as efficiently (Reingold, Charness, Pomplun, & Stampe, 2001).

Does this interplay between short-term and long-term memories apply just to the rarefied example of expert chess players? In a popular account of hockey star Wayne Gretzky's early years, author Peter Gzowski (1981) detected a similar process at work:

> What Gretzky perceives on a hockey rink is, in a curious way, more simple than what a less accomplished player perceives. He sees not so much a set of moving players as a number of situations—chunks. Moving in on the Montreal blueline, as he was able to recall while he watched a videotape of himself, he was aware of the position of all the other players on the ice. The pattern they formed was, to him, one fact, and he reacted to that fact. When he sends a pass to what to the rest of us appears an empty space on the ice, and when a teammate magically appears in that space to collect the puck, he has in reality simply summoned up from his bank account of knowledge the fact that in a particular situation, someone is likely to be in a particular spot, and if he is not there now he will be there presently.[1]

As this passage suggests, humans have a remarkable ability to manipulate visual information in working memory. Shepard and Metzler (1971) presented people with pairs of drawings that could be perceived as three-dimensional constructions made of cubes. The participants' task was to see whether the shape on the right was identical to the shape on the left; some were, and some were not. Even when the shapes were identical, the one on the right was sometimes drawn as if it had been rotated. For example, in **Figure 8•6** the shape on the right in panel (a) is identical but has been rotated clockwise 80 degrees, but in panel (b) the two shapes are different.

Shepard and Metzler found that people were very accurate in judging whether the pairs of shapes were the same or different. However, they took longer to decide when the right-hand shape was rotated. They reported that they formed an image of one of the drawings in their heads and rotated it until it was aligned the same way as the other one. (Mental manipulation of shapes is an important component of the ability to design and construct tools, buildings, bridges, and other useful objects.) If the participants' rotated images coincided with the other drawings, they recognized them as having the same shape. If they did not, they recognized them as being different (Shepard & Metzler, 1971).

Loss of Information from Short-Term Memory

The essence of short-term memory is its transience; hence, its name. Information enters from sensory memory and from long-term memory; is rehearsed, thought about, and modified; and then leaves. Some of the information controls ongoing

▲ *One advantage that experienced hockey players have over novice players is their superior long-term memory for different patterns of play on the ice. This information helps them both to anticipate the possible moves their opponent might make and to plan their responses.*

behavior and some of it causes changes in long-term memory, but ultimately it is lost from short-term memory. What causes it to leave?

As I mentioned earlier, psychologists have described working memory as a kind of behavior that we use to maintain information over the short term. This way of thinking about working memory provides a useful framework to explain how

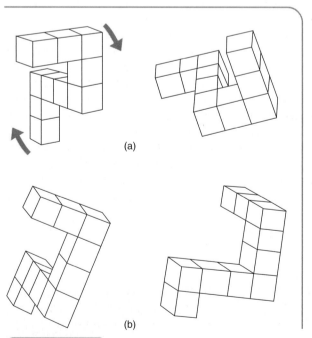

FIGURE 8•6 The mental rotation task. (a) The shape on the right is identical to the one on the left but rotated 80 degrees clockwise. (b) The two shapes are different.

(Adapted from Shepard, R. N., & Metzler, J. Mental rotation of three-dimensional objects. *Science*, 1971, *171*, 701–703. Reprinted with permission from AAAS. Copyright © 1971 by the AAAS.)

---

1. Excerpt from *The Game of Our Lives* (p. 188) by Peter Gzowski. Used by permission of McClelland & Stewart, Ltd.

▲ *Working memory has been compared to juggling. With greater skill or effort, more items can be juggled—unless a distraction occurs.*

we lose information, if we assume that information has a tendency to be degraded or to decay with time. Rehearsal activity of phonological short-term memory, such as subvocal articulation, prevents decay. Nairne (2002) has suggested a metaphor of how this might work. Working memory, Nairne says, is like a juggler trying to maintain several plates or balls in the air. As long as the juggler works actively at catching and throwing the plates, they don't fall and hit the ground (decay). With increased skill or more effort, the juggler can keep even more plates in the air. But any distraction or other competing behavior will reduce the number of plates that can be juggled.

If you accept this metaphor, then consider this: Anything that makes the plates easier to handle should decrease the risk that they will be dropped. With respect to words, shorter words are easier to articulate and therefore should be easier to rehearse. Psychologists have shown that shorter words are remembered better under conditions of short-term memory (e.g., Tehan, Hendry, & Kocinski, 2001)—a finding that supports the rehearsal-and-decay explanation.

However, as Nairne himself points out, "decay" is a nonspecific term and risks falling prey to the nominal fallacy discussed in Chapter 2. Why should information decay? Perhaps more active processes work to degrade the information or to make it more difficult to recall. Later in this chapter, after we have surveyed long-term memory, I will discuss one such possibility.

Interim Summary

Short-Term or Working Memory

Information in short-term memory is encoded according to previously learned rules. Information in long-term memory determines the nature of the encoding. Because short-term memory contains information retrieved from long-term mem-

ory as well as newly perceived information, many researchers conceive of it as working memory. Working memory is not simply a way station between sensory memory and long-term memory; it is where thinking occurs. When presented with a list of items, we tend to remember the items at the beginning of the list (the primacy effect) and at the end of the list (the recency effect) better than items in the middle of the list. The primacy effect presumably occurs because we have a greater opportunity to rehearse items early in the list and thus store them in long-term memory, and the recency effect because we can retrieve items at the end of the list that are still stored in short-term memory.

Working memory lasts for about 20 seconds and has a capacity of about seven items—give or take two. We often simplify large amounts of information by organizing it into "chunks" of information, which can then be more easily rehearsed and remembered.

Although each sensory system probably has a working memory associated with it, psychologists have devoted most of their attention to two kinds: phonological and visual working memory. The existence of acoustical errors (rather than visual ones) in the task of remembering visually presented letters suggests that information is represented phonologically in short-term memory. Because deaf people (but only those who can talk) also show this effect, the code appears to be articulatory. Phonological working memory is encoded acoustically as well. People who have conduction aphasia show a specific deficit in phonological short-term memory, apparently because their brain damage interrupts direct communication between Wernicke's area and Broca's area.

Visual working memory also is important and has been demonstrated in the laboratory by the ability of chess masters to remember a board and by research participants' ability to perform mental rotation of shapes.

The processes of working memory act to maintain information over time. Variables that affect rehearsal ability, such as the length of the items being remembered, affect short-term memory. This account, however, raises the question as to what might cause items to decay when they are not rehearsed.

QUESTIONS TO CONSIDER

1. Suppose that someone has sustained a brain injury that prohibits her from putting information into, and getting information out of, long-term memory. Would this injury affect only her long-term memory, or would her short-term memory be affected, too? Can you think of an experiment that you could perform that would answer this question?

2. Take a few moments to imagine the shortest route you can take to get from your home to your favorite restaurant. In terms of how your short-term memory operates, explain how you are able to accomplish this bit of mental imagery.

Learning and Encoding in Long-Term Memory

As we have seen, information that enters short-term memory may or may not be available later. It depends on the number of "chunks" of information and how much time has elapsed. But once information has successfully made its way into long-term memory, it remains relatively stable (Burt, Kemp, & Conway, 2001). Of course, we do forget things, but nevertheless, our brains have the remarkable ability to store vast amounts of information and numerous experiences from our past.

What kinds of information can be stored in long-term memory? To answer this question, let us consider the kinds of things we can learn. First, we can learn to recognize things: objects, sounds, odors, textures, and tastes. Thus, we can remember perceptions received by all of our sensory systems, which means that we have visual memories, auditory memories, olfactory memories, somatosensory memories, and gustatory memories. These memories can be combined and inter-connected; for example, a soft "meow" in the dark elicits an image of a cat. Perceptual memories also can contain information about the order in which events occurred, so we can remember the plot of a movie we saw or hear the melody of a song in our heads.

Second, we can learn from experience. We can learn to make new responses—as when we learn to operate a new machine, ride a bicycle, or say a new word—or we can learn to make old responses in new situations. Perceptual memories presumably involve alterations in circuits of neurons in the sensory association cortex of the brain—visual memories in the visual cortex, auditory memories in the auditory cortex, and so on. Memories that involve combinations of perceptual information presumably involve the establishment of connections between different regions of the association cortex. And motor memories (memories for particular behaviors) presumably involve alterations in circuits of neurons in the motor association cortex of the frontal lobes. Thus, learning to perform particular behaviors in particular situations likely involves the establishment of connections between the appropriate regions of the sensory and motor cortexes.

Memory involves both active and passive processes. Sometimes we use deliberate strategies to remember something (to encode the information into long-term memory), as when we rehearse the lines of a poem or memorize famous dates for a history course. At other times we simply observe and remember without any apparent effort, as when we tell a friend about an interesting experience we had. And memories can be formed even without our being aware of having learned something. What factors determine whether we can eventually remember information and experiences? Let's look at some hypotheses that have been proposed.

The Consolidation Hypothesis

The traditional view of memory is that it consists of a two-stage process (not counting sensory memory). Information enters short-term memory from the environment, where it is stored temporarily. Then, if the material is rehearsed long enough, it is transferred into long-term memory. Once the information is in long-term memory, we can safely stop thinking about it. The transfer of information from short-term memory into long-term memory has been called **consolidation** (Hebb, 1949). According to the consolidation hypothesis, short-term memory consists of the activity of neurons that encodes the information received from the sense organs. Once this activity subsides, the information will be forgotten. However, the neural activity can be sustained through rehearsal; and if enough time passes, the activity causes structural changes in the brain. These structural changes are more or less permanent and solid (hence, the term "consolidation"). They are responsible for long-term memory.

Some of the best evidence in favor of the consolidation hypothesis comes from events that disrupt brain functioning. From the earliest times people have observed that a blow to the head can affect memory. In such "closed-head injury" incidents, individuals forget what happened immediately before the injury. A blow to the head makes the brain bump against the inside of the skull, and this movement apparently disrupts its normal functioning. The blow disrupts short-term memory but not long-term memory. A lack of memory for events, particularly experiences that occurred just before an injury, is called **retrograde amnesia** (*retro-* means "backward": in this case, backward in time).

Head injury often disrupts people's memories for a period of time afterwards; if the injury is severe enough, retrograde amnesia can extend back for a period of days or even weeks. Obviously, the loss of memories in that case involves more than short-term memories. Why recent long-term memories are more vulnerable to injury than older long-term memories is a mystery.

The Levels-of-Processing Hypothesis

The consolidation hypothesis makes several assertions about the learning process. For one thing, it asserts that short-term memory and long-term memory are physiologically different. The evidence presented in the previous section supports this assertion, and few investigators doubt that information that has just been perceived is stored in the brain in a different way than information that was perceived some time ago. However, certain other features of the original consolidation hypothesis have been challenged. First, the hypothesis asserts that all information gets into long-term memory only after passing through short-term memory. Second, it asserts that the most important factor determining whether a particular piece of information reaches long-term memory is the amount of time it spends in short-term memory.

To refute these assertions, Craik and Lockhart (1972) developed a different model. They pointed out that the act of rehearsal may effectively keep information in short-term memory but does not necessarily result in the establishment of long-term memories. They suggested that people engage in two different types of rehearsal: maintenance rehearsal and elaborative rehearsal. **Maintenance rehearsal** is the rote repetition of verbal information—simply repeating an item over and over. This behavior serves to maintain the information in short-term memory but does not necessarily result in lasting changes. In contrast, when people engage in elaborative rehearsal, they think about the information and relate it to what they already know. **Elaborative rehearsal** involves more than new information. It involves deeper processing: forming associations, attending to the meaning of the information, thinking about that information, and so on. Thus, we *elaborate* on new information by recollecting related information already in long-term memory. Here's a practical example: You are more likely to remember information for a test by processing it deeply or meaningfully; simply rehearsing the material to be tested will not do.

The effectiveness of elaboration in remembering was nicely demonstrated in an experiment conducted by Craik and Tulving (1975). The investigators gave people a set of cards, each showing a printed sentence with a missing word, such as "The _____ is torn." After reading the sentence, the participants looked at a word flashed on a screen, then pressed a button as quickly as possible to signify whether the word fit the sentence. In this example, *dress* will fit, but *table* will not. The sentences varied in complexity. Some were very simple:

The _____ is torn.

She cooked the _____.

Others were more complex:

The great bird swooped down and carried off the
struggling _____.

The old man hobbled across the room and picked up
the valuable _____.

The sentences were written so that the same word could be used for either a simple or a complex sentence: "She cooked the chicken" or "The great bird swooped down and carried off the struggling chicken." All participants saw a particular word once, in either a simple or a complex sentence.

The researchers made no mention of a memory test, so there was no reason for the participants to try to remember the words. However, after responding to the sentences, they were presented with them again and were asked to recall the words they had used. The researchers found that the participants were twice as likely to remember a word if it had previously fit into a sentence of medium or high complexity than if it had fit into a simple sentence.

These results suggest that a memory is more effectively established if the item is presented in a rich context—a context that is likely to make us think about the item and imagine an action taking place. Consider the different images conjured up by these two sentences (Craik & Tulving, 1975):

He dropped the watch.

The old man hobbled across the room and picked up
the valuable watch.

The second sentence provides much more information. The word *watch* is remembered in the vivid context of a hobbling old man, and the word *valuable* suggests that the watch is interesting. Perhaps, because the man is old, the watch is too; it might be a large gold pocket watch attached to a gold chain. The image that is evoked by the more complex sentence provides the material for a more complex memory. This complexity makes the memory more distinctive and thus helps us pick it out from all the other memories we have. When the incomplete sentence is presented again, it easily evokes a memory of the image of the old man and of the watch.

In contrast with the traditional consolidation hypothesis, Craik and Lockhart (1972) proposed a levels-of-processing framework for understanding the way information enters long-term memory. They suggested that memory is a by-product of perceptual analysis. A central processor, analogous to the central processing unit of a computer, can analyze sensory information on several different levels. Craik and Lockhart conceived of the levels as being hierarchically arranged, from shallow (superficial) to deep (complex). A person can control the level of analysis by *paying attention* to different features of the stimulus. If a person focuses on the superficial sensory characteristics of a stimulus, then these features will be stored in memory. If the person focuses on the meaning of a stimulus and the ways in which it relates to other things the person already knows, then these features will be stored in memory. For example, consider the word written below.

tree

You can see that the word is written in black type, that the letters are lowercase, that the bottom of the stem of the letter *t* curves upward to the right, and so on. Craik and Lockhart referred to these characteristics as *surface features* and to the analysis of these features as **shallow processing**. Maintenance rehearsal is an example of shallow processing. In contrast, consider the meaning of the word *tree*. You can think about how trees differ from other plants, what varieties of trees you have seen, what kinds of foods and what kinds of wood they provide, and so on. These features refer to a word's meaning and are called *semantic features*. Their analysis is called **deep processing**. Elaborative rehearsal is an example of deep processing. According to Craik and Lockhart, deep processing generally leads to better retention than surface processing does.

Knowledge, Encoding, and Learning You might think that memory would be related to knowledge: As we gain more knowledge over time, our recall of that knowledge ought to improve. However, merely possessing knowledge

▲ *Taking notes while studying from a text (left) is a more active method of processing information than is merely highlighting important passages in the text (right). Note taking involves deep processing, and highlighting involves shallow processing.*

does not always facilitate recall; even the brightest people have problems with remembering things. What seems to be more important is what happens during the encoding of information. Remember, encoding involves getting material into memory. More than that, how we encode information is likely to affect our ability to remember it later. We have already seen that, to some degree, encoding information involves paying attention to it. We have also seen that if we can make material more meaningful during encoding, we may decrease the likelihood of forgetting that information later.

Automatic versus Effortful Processing. Psychologists and educators have long known that practicing or rehearsing information enhances retrieval. Practicing or rehearsing information, through either shallow or deep processing, is called **effortful processing**. As a student, you know that the more you concentrate on your studies, the more likely it becomes that you will do well on an exam. But your experience also tells you that you have stored information in memory that you never rehearsed in the first place. Somehow, without any effort, information is encoded into your memory. This formation of memories of events and experiences with little or no attention or effort is called **automatic processing**.

Information that is automatically processed includes frequency (How many times have you read the word *encode* today?), time (When did you first meet your best friend?), and place (Where in the textbook is the diagram of Sperling's study located?). Automatic processing helps us learn things with relative ease, which makes life a lot less taxing than it would be if we continually had to process information effortfully. Unfortunately, perhaps because of its complexity, most textbook learning is effortful, not automatic.

Encoding Specificity. When encoding is not automatic, it is effortful, and the most useful effort we can expend is to attempt to make the new material meaningful. We can think of making new or difficult material meaningful as elaborative encoding; you encountered this idea earlier as elaborative rehearsal. There are two conclusions that I'll offer concerning elaborative encoding. First, it seems clear that more rehearsal is better than less.

The second conclusion concerns **encoding specificity**, the principle that *how* we encode information determines our ability to retrieve it later. For example, suppose that someone reads you a list of words that you are to recall later. The list contains the word *beet* along with several terms related to music, such as *melody, tune,* and *jazz.* When asked if the list contained the names of any vegetables, you may report that it did not. Because of the musical context, you may have encoded *beet* as *beat* and never thought of the root vegetable while you were rehearsing the list (Flexser & Tulving, 1978).

Many experiments have made the point that meaningful elaboration during encoding is helpful and probably necessary for the formation of useful memories. Imagine, for example, trying to remember the following passage:

> With hocked gems financing him, our hero bravely defied all scornful laughter that tried to prevent his scheme. "Your eyes deceive," he had said. "An egg, not a table correctly typifies this unexplored planet." Now three sturdy sisters sought proof, forging along, sometimes through calm vastness, yet more often over turbulent peaks and valleys. Days became weeks as many doubters spread fearful rumors about the edge. At last, from nowhere welcome winged creatures appeared, signifying momentous success.

How do you think you would have done on this task? Could you have remembered this passage very well? Probably not, for it is phrased rather oddly. However, what if, *before* you read the paragraph, you were told that it had a title: "Columbus Discovers America"? Do you think you might have encoded the story differently and so improved your recall? (Read the passage again and you will see that *hocked gems* refers to the means by which Queen Isabella financed the expedition, *sturdy sisters* refers to the three ships, and *winged creatures* refers to the birds that signaled the proximity of land.) Dooling and Lachman (1971) found that people who were told the title of a story such as this remembered the information much better. But if they were given the title *after* they had read and processed the story, their recall was not improved (Bransford & Johnson, 1972). Apparently, the time to make information meaningful is during encoding.

Criticisms of the Levels-of-Processing Hypothesis

The concept of processing depth has been useful in guiding research efforts to understand how we learn and remember. However, many psychologists have noted that the distinction between shallow and deep processing has never been rigorously defined. The difference between looking at the shape of the letters of a word and thinking about its meaning is clear, but most instances of encoding cannot be so neatly categorized. The term *depth* seems to be metaphorical. It roughly describes the fact that information is more readily remembered when we think about it in relation to what we already know, but it is not exact and specific enough to satisfy most memory theorists.

Another problem with trying to understand exactly what is meant by a term such as *depth of processing* is that no matter what we may ask a person to do when we present a stimulus (for example, "Count the letters"), we have no way of knowing what else he or she may be doing that may aid recall of that item. In other words, researchers may not be able to control the depth to which a person processes information because they have no way of peering into his or her head and knowing exactly how the information is being manipulated. For each of us, our memory, its processes, and its contents are private. Memory, like all cognitive processes, is not an observable phenomenon.

Some psychologists have criticized the assertion that tasks that encourage people to focus on superficial features of stimuli inevitably lead to poorer memory than do tasks that encourage them to focus on deeper features. For example, after reading something new, people often can remember exactly where the information appeared on a page (Rothkopf, 1971). I have had students tell me, after failing to answer a question on a test, that they could picture the page on which the answer could be found, even though they could not remember what the words said. This example indicates good retention of information that had undergone shallow processing but poor retention of information that had undergone deep processing.

Improving Long-Term Memory through Mnemonics

When we can imagine information vividly and concretely, and when it fits into the context of what we already know, it is easy to remember later. Earlier, I described how chaining words together in a meaningful pattern can improve working memory. People have known for millennia that vividness and context can improve remembering and have devised mnemonic systems (from the Greek *mnemon,* meaning "mindful") that take advantage of this fact. **Mnemonic systems**—special techniques or strategies consciously used to improve memory—employ information already stored in long-term memory to make memorization an easier task.

Mnemonic systems do not simplify information; in fact, they make it more elaborate. More information is stored, not less. However, the additional information makes the material easier to recall. Furthermore, mnemonic systems organize new information into a cohesive whole so that retrieval of part of the information ensures retrieval of the rest of it. These facts suggest that the ease or difficulty with which we learn new information depends not on *how much* we must learn but on *how well it fits with what we already know*. The better it fits, the easier it is to retrieve.

Method of Loci

In Greece before the sixth century BCE, few people knew how to write, and those who did had to use cumbersome clay tablets. Consequently, oratory skills and memory for long epic poems (running for several hours) were highly prized, and some people earned their livings by cultivating these abilities. Because people could not carry around several hundred kilograms of clay tablets, they had to keep important information in their heads. To do so, the Greeks devised the **method of loci,** a mnemonic system in which items to be remembered are mentally associated with specific physical locations. (The word *locus* means "place"; the plural is *loci,* pronounced "low sigh.")

To use the method of loci, would-be memory artists first memorized the inside of a building. In Greece they would wander through public buildings, stopping to study and memorize various locations and arranging them in order, usually starting with the door of the building. After memorizing the locations they could make the tour mentally, just as you could make a mental tour of your house to count the rooms. To learn a list of words, they would then visualize each word in a particular location in the memorized building and picture the association as vividly as possible. For example, for the word *love,* they might imagine an embracing couple leaning against a particular column in a hall of the building. To recall the list, they would imagine each of the locations in sequence, "see" each word, and say it. To store a speech, they would group the words into concepts and place a "note" for each concept at a particular location in the sequence.

Suppose that you wish to remember a short shopping list without writing it down. Your list consists of five items: cheese, milk, eggs, taco sauce, and lettuce. To use the loci technique, you would first think of a familiar place, perhaps your house. Next, you would mentally walk through your house, visually placing different items from your list at locations—*loci*—in the house: a package of cheese hanging from a coat rack, milk dripping from the kitchen faucet, eggs lying in the hallway, a bottle of taco sauce on the kitchen chair, and a head of lettuce on the sofa (see **Figure 8•7**). Then, in the grocery store, you would mentally retrace your path through the house and note what you had stored at the different loci. Any familiar location will do the trick as long as you can visually and vividly imagine the items to be remembered in the various landmarks.

Peg-Word Method

A similar technique is the **peg-word method** (Miller, Galanter, & Pribram, 1960). As with the method of loci, the goal involves visually associating the new with the familiar. In the peg-word method, the familiar material is a set of "mental pegs" that you already have in memory. One way to create pegs is to take the numbers from 1 to 10 and rhyme each number with a peg word; for example, one is a bun, two is a shoe, three is a tree, four is a door, five is a hive, and so on. So for your grocery list you might imagine the package of cheese in a hamburger *bun,* a *shoe* full of milk, eggs dangling from a *tree,* taco sauce on a *door,* and the lettuce on top of a bee*hive* (see **Figure 8•8**). In the grocery store you would review each peg word in order and recall the item associated with it. At first this technique may seem silly, but there is ample research suggesting that it actually works (Marshark, Richman, Yuille, & Hunt, 1987).

Narrative Stories and Songs

Another useful aid to memory is to place information into a **narrative**—to link items to be remembered together by a story. Bower and Clark (1969) showed that even inexperienced people can use this method. The investigators asked people to try to learn 12 lists of 10 concrete nouns each. They gave some of the people the following advice:

> A good way to learn the list of items is to make up a story relating the items to one another. Specifically, start with the first item and put it in a setting which will allow other items to be added to it. Then, add the other items to the story in the same order as the items appear. Make each story meaningful to yourself. Then, when you are asked to recall the items, you can simply go through your story and pull out the proper items in their correct order. (Bower & Clark, 1969, p. 181)

Here is a typical narrative, described by one of the participants (list words are italicized): "A *lumberjack dart*ed out of the forest, *skate*d around a *hedge* past a *colony* of *ducks.* He tripped on some *furniture,* tearing his *stocking* while hastening to the *pillow* where his *mistress* lay."

People in the control group were merely asked to learn the lists and were given the same amount of time as the people in the "narrative" group to study them. Both groups could remember any given 10-word list equally well immediately afterwards. However, when all of the lists had been learned, recall of all 120 words was far superior in the group that had constructed narrative stories.

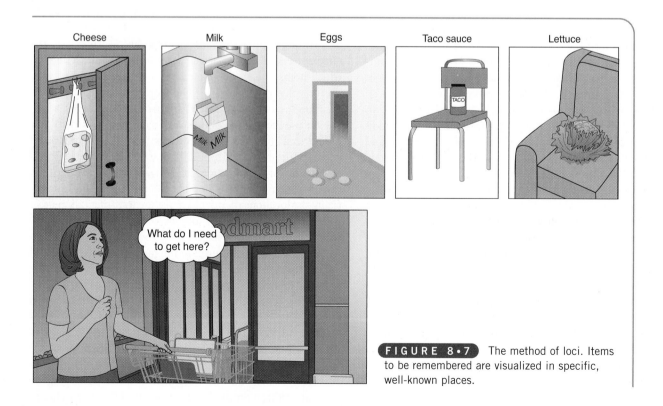

FIGURE 8•7 The method of loci. Items to be remembered are visualized in specific, well-known places.

FIGURE 8•8 The peg-word method. Items to be remembered are associated with nouns that rhyme with numbers.

When I started my description of aids to memory and referred to ancient singers of heroic poems, you may have thought of advertising jingles. Many advertisers use music with their messages, apparently believing that placing their slogan in a song will improve its memorability (Yalch, 1991). Music, like narrative, provides a structure for information. Songs that link melody to a sequence of words could serve the same role as the narrative elements of a story.

There is some evidence that supports this notion. Wallace (1994) asked people to learn the words to a ballad by listening to either a spoken or a sung version. She found that, provided people had a chance to learn the melody of the song, they learned the sung ballad more quickly than the spoken version. Changing the melody after each verse, in contrast, failed to improve learning.

Although hearing the melody of a song may improve your ability to learn its text, the effect may not be due to the structuring processes I noted when discussing the method of loci. A melody not only structures the text of a song but also alters the rate at which you hear the words. Using a sound editing program, Kilgour, Jakobson, and Cuddy (2000) found that, indeed, the rate of word presentation was important in determining the advantage that singing provides. When the words were spoken at the same rate that they were sung, study participants learned the text as fast as when they heard it sung. The basis of this mnemonic, then, is that it slows the rate at which you hear information, allowing you to encode the information better.

Obviously, mnemonic systems have their limitations. They are useful for memorizing information that can be reduced to a list of words, but not all information can easily be converted to such a form. For example, if you were preparing to take an examination on the information in this chapter, figuring out how to encode it into lists would probably take you more time than studying and learning it by the more traditional methods suggested in the study guide.

▲ *Long-term memory has no known limits. Shakespearean actors, like these actors performing a scene from* The Taming of the Shrew, *may remember their parts long after their performances are over.*

Interim Summary

Learning and Encoding in Long-Term Memory

Long-term memory appears to consist of physical changes in the brain—probably within the sensory and motor association cortexes. Consolidation of memories is likely caused by rehearsal of information, which sustains particular neural activities and leads to permanent structural changes in the brain. Data from head injuries provide evidence that long-term and short-term memory are affected differently by physical trauma: Short-term memories probably involve neural activity (which can be prolonged by rehearsal), whereas long-term memories probably involve permanent structural changes.

Craik and Lockhart's model of memory points out the importance of elaboration in learning. Maintenance rehearsal, or simple rote repetition, is usually less effective than elaborative rehearsal, which involves deeper, more meaningful processing. These theorists assert that long-term memory is a by-product of perceptual analysis. The level of processing can be shallow or deep and is controlled by changes in the amount of attention we pay to information. Having read a description of Craik and Tulving's experiment, you can probably remember the end of the sentence "The great bird swooped down and carried off the struggling _____."

Encoding of information to be stored in long-term memory may take place automatically or effortfully. Automatic processing of information is usually related to the frequency, timing, and place (location) of events. Textbook learning entails effortful processing, probably because of its complexity. The principle of encoding specificity—how we encode information into memory—determines the ease with which we can later retrieve that information. To produce the most durable and useful memories, information should be encoded in ways that are meaningful. However, critics of the levels-of-processing model point out that shallow processing sometimes produces very durable memories, and the distinction between shallow and deep has proved impossible to define explicitly.

Mnemonic systems are strategies used to enhance memory and usually employ information that is already contained in long-term memory as well as visual imagery. For example, to use the method of loci to remember a grocery list, you could visualize each item on the list at a specific location in your home. Other mnemonic systems include the peg-word method, which involves visually associating items to be remembered with a specific set of "mental pegs," and narrative stories, which involve weaving a story around the to-be-remembered items. Mnemonics are useful for remembering lists of items but are less useful for more complex material, such as textbook information.

QUESTION TO CONSIDER

Suppose that a friend comes to you for advice about studying for an upcoming English test. He explains to you that half of the test involves multiple-choice questions over key terms and the other half involves essay questions about the narrative of several short stories. Based on what you now know about encoding and memory, what suggestions might you offer him regarding how to prepare for the test? (Hints: Is there a difference between how rote information is best encoded and how more elaborate, complex information is best encoded? What role might the idea of levels of processing play in preparation for a test?)

The Organization of Long-Term Memory

As we just saw, memorization is not a simple, passive process. Many investigators believe that long-term memory consists of more than a simple pool of information. Instead, it is organized in terms of different systems: Different kinds of information are encoded differently and stored in different ways, possibly in response to evolutionary pressures (Sherry & Schacter, 1987).

Episodic and Semantic Memory

Long-term memory contains more than exact records of sensory experiences. It also contains information that has been transformed—organized in terms of meaning. A study by Sachs (1967) showed that as a memory of verbal material gets older, specific words become less important than their content or meaning. Sachs had participants listen to a passage of prose. At varying intervals after they had heard a particular sentence in the passage (the *test sentence*), she interrupted the participants, presented them with another sentence (the *comparison sentence*), and asked them whether it had appeared in the passage. The comparison sentence was sometimes the same as the test sentence and sometimes different. Differences might involve meaning or only word order. For example:

Test sentence: He sent a letter about it to Galileo, the great Italian scientist.

Comparison sentence, different meaning: Galileo, the great Italian scientist, sent him a letter about it.

Comparison sentence, same meaning but different word order: He sent Galileo, the great Italian scientist, a letter about it.

The results shown in **Figure 8•9** reveal that the participants accurately recognized changes when there was no delay between the test sentence and the comparison sentence. When

FIGURE 8•9 Memory for sensory information versus meaning. Graphed here is the percentage of correct judgments as a function of the delay between the test sentence and the comparison sentence. As memory for verbal material gets older, specific sensory information becomes less important than the underlying meaning.

(Based on data of Sachs, J. S. (1967). Recognition memory of syntactic and semantic aspects of connected discourse. *Perception and Psychophysics, 2,* 437–442.)

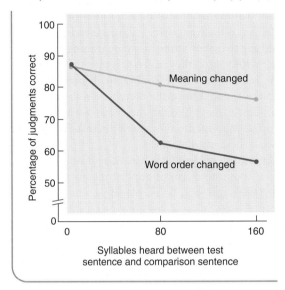

a delay was introduced, they had difficulty remembering the specific word order of the original sentence but made very few errors in meaning, even with a 160-syllable delay. Thus, as the sentence enters long-term memory, information about its *form* disappears faster than information about its *meaning*.

This distinction between information about specific sensory inputs (such as the sequence of words in their original order) and more general information about meaning has led to the suggestion that there are two kinds of long-term memory: episodic memory and semantic memory (Tulving, 1972). **Episodic memory** provides us with a record of our life experiences. Events stored there are autobiographical; episodic memory consists of memory about specific things we have done, seen, heard, felt, tasted, and so on. The memories are tied to particular contexts: this morning's breakfast, my fifteenth birthday party, the first time I went skiing, and so forth. **Semantic memory** consists of conceptual information; it is a long-term store of data, facts, and information, including vocabulary. Your knowledge of what psychology is, how human sensory systems operate, and how behavior is affected by its consequences is now part of your semantic memory. (If not, you need to review some of the material presented earlier in this book!) In other words, semantic memory contains information of the "academic" type. Semantic memories appear to interact with episodic ones. For example, when I come to work at the university, I park my car in the lot adjacent to the building. When I leave the building each evening, I have to remember where I parked my car that day. My semantic memory tells me that I always park in Lot 40. However, because I park in a different space each day, I must use information in episodic memory to find my car again. In particular, I must remember the most recent episode in which I parked the car.

The distinction between episodic and semantic memory reflects the fact that we make different uses of things we have learned: We describe things that happened to us or talk about facts we have learned. However, we cannot necessarily conclude that episodic memory and semantic memory are different memory systems. They may simply be different kinds of information stored in the same system. For example, I am a native English speaker, but I have also learned to speak French. Do I have an English memory system and a French memory system? Most likely not. Instead, my memory contains the information I need in order to recognize and speak

▲ Remembering the correct spelling of a word involves semantic memory—memory for academic-type information (a). Remembering important life events, such as an important social event, involves episodic memory—memory for specific events that occurred at a specific time (b).

both English and French words and to understand their meanings. The same system can handle both kinds of words. Nevertheless, many psychologists feel that episodic memory reflects a different system of the brain than that of semantic memory. They point to evidence like that supplied by K. C., a man now in his fifties who suffered a closed-head injury at age 30. As a result of the accident, K. C.'s ability to acquire new knowledge is severely impaired. His memory for things learned before the accident, however, shows a remarkable difference: general knowledge—the information of semantic memory—is relatively intact, whereas his knowledge about his life—the material that makes up episodic memory—has been completely obliterated. K. C. can recall knowledge about algebra and history that he learned at school, but cannot recall personal experiences such as the birthday parties he attended (Tulving, 2002).

Explicit and Implicit Memory

For many years, most cognitive psychologists studied memory as a conscious operation. Experimenters presented people with lists of words, facts, episodes, or other kinds of stimuli and asked them to recognize or recollect the items later. In many cases a verbal response was required. In recent decades, however, psychologists have come to appreciate the fact that an unconscious memory system, which is capable of controlling complex behaviors, also exists (Squire, 1992). Psychologists use the terms *explicit memory* and *implicit memory* when making this distinction. **Explicit memory** is memory of which we are aware; we know that we have learned something, and we can talk about what we have learned with others. (For this reason, some psychologists prefer to use the term *declarative memory*.) **Implicit memory** is unconscious; we cannot talk directly about its contents. However, the contents of implicit memory can affect our behavior—even our verbal behavior. (Some psychologists use the term *procedural memory*, because this system is responsible for remembering "how-to" skills such as bicycle riding; others use the term *nondeclarative memory*.) The distinction between implicit and explicit memory is important—because retrieval cues seem to influence implicit more than explicit memory, and the level of processing seems to influence explicit more than implicit memory (Blaxton, 1989; Roediger, 1990).

Implicit memory appears to operate automatically. It does not require deliberate attempts on the part of the learner to memorize something. It does not seem to contain facts; instead, it controls behaviors. If someone asks us a question about a fact or about something we have experienced, the question evokes images in the explicit memory system that we can then describe in words. For example, suppose that someone asks us which is larger, a boat or a bee. We have probably never answered that question before. But we can easily do so, perhaps by picturing both of these objects and comparing their size.

In contrast, implicit memory is not something about which we can answer questions. Suppose we learn to ride a bicycle. We do so quite consciously and develop episodic memories about our attempts: who helped us learn, where we rode, how we felt, how many times we fell, and so on. But we also learn to ride. We learn to make automatic adjustments with our hands and bodies that keep our center of gravity above the wheels. Most of us cannot describe the rules that govern our behavior. For example, what do you think you must do if you start falling to the right while riding a bicycle? Many cyclists would say that they compensate by leaning to the left. But they are wrong; what they really do is turn the handlebars to the right. Leaning to the left would actually make them fall faster, because it would force the bicycle even farther to the right. The point is that although they have learned to *make* the appropriate movements, they cannot necessarily describe in words what these movements are.

The acquisition of specific behaviors and skills is probably the most important form of implicit memory. Driving a car, turning the pages of a book, playing a musical instrument, dancing, throwing and catching a ball, sliding a chair backward as we get up from the dinner table—all of these skills involve coordination of movements with sensory information received from the environment and from our own moving body parts. We do not need to be able to describe these activities in order to perform them. We may not be aware of all the movements involved while we are performing them. Implicit memory may have evolved earlier than explicit memory. Our ancient ancestors were able to adapt their behavior to their environment long before they were able to talk.

The Biological Basis of Long-Term Memory

Psychologists agree that long-term memory involves more or less permanent changes in the structure of the brain (Fuster, 1995). Much of what we know about the biology of human memory has been derived from studies of people who suffer from memory loss—amnesia—or from studies of animals in which investigators surgically induce amnesia in order to learn more about the specific brain mechanisms involved in memory (Spear & Riccio, 1994).

Human Anterograde Amnesia   Damage to particular parts of the brain can permanently impair people's ability to form new long-term memories, a phenomenon known as **anterograde amnesia**. The brain damage can be caused by the effects of long-term alcoholism, severe malnutrition, stroke, head trauma, or surgery (Parkin, Blunden, Rees, & Hunkin, 1991). In general, people with anterograde amnesia can still remember events that occurred prior to the damage. They can talk about things that happened before the onset of their amnesia, but they cannot remember what has happened since. They never learn the names of people they subsequently meet, even if they see them daily for years. As we saw in the opening vignette, Mr. P. had been in the hospital for 11 years, but he thought he had actually been there for about a week. And 15 minutes after we were introduced, he could not remember meeting me.

One of the most famous cases of anterograde amnesia is that of patient H. M. (Corkin, Sullivan, Twitchell, & Grove, 1981; Milner, 1970; Scoville & Milner, 1957). H. M.'s case is interesting because his amnesia is both severe and relatively pure, being uncontaminated by other neuropsychological deficits. In 1953, when H. M. was 27, a neurosurgeon removed part of the temporal lobe on both sides of his brain. The surgery was performed to alleviate very severe epilepsy, which was not responding to drug treatment. The surgery cured the epilepsy, but it caused anterograde amnesia. (This type of operation is no longer performed.)

H. M. can carry on conversations and talk about general topics not related to recent events. He can also talk about his life prior to the surgery. However, he cannot talk about anything that has happened since 1953. He lives in an institution where he can be cared for and spends most of his time solving crossword puzzles and watching television. H. M. is aware that he has a memory problem. For example, here is his response to an investigator's question.

> Every day is alone in itself, whatever enjoyment I've had, and whatever sorrow I've had. . . . Right now, I'm wondering. Have I done or said anything amiss? You see, at this moment everything looks clear to me, but what happened just before? That's what worries me. It's like waking from a dream; I just don't remember. (Milner, 1970, p. 37)

Clearly, H. M.'s problem lies in his inability to store new information in long-term memory, not in his short-term memory. His verbal short-term memory is normal—he can repeat seven numbers forward and five numbers backward, which is about average for the general population.

Given that H. M. cannot remember much of his past, it is relevant to ask whether he retains a sense of self. Researcher Suzanne Corkin, who has known H. M. for many years, has an interesting discussion on this issue (Corkin, 2002). She feels that the answer is definitely yes. H. M. seems comfortable when he sees his image in a mirror (think of how *you* would feel if you saw yourself looking 50 years older than you remembered), and he exhibits strong moral and conscientious attitudes. Perhaps the most telling aspect is that he also has a sense of humor about his own condition. When once asked about how he remembers, he replied: "Well, that I don't know 'cause I don't remember (laugh) what I tried" (Corkin, 2002, p. 158).

At first investigators concluded that the problem was in memory consolidation and that the part of the brain that was destroyed during surgery was essential for carrying out this process. But subsequent evidence suggests that the brain damage disrupts *explicit* memory without seriously damaging *implicit* memory. Many studies performed with H. M. and with other people with anterograde amnesia have shown that implicit learning can still take place. For example, **Figure 8·10** shows sets of drawings. Almost no one can recognize these

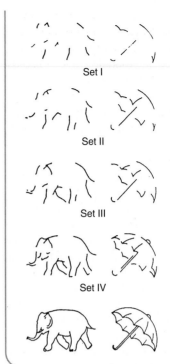

FIGURE 8·10
Broken drawings used to study implicit memory. Sets of the different versions of broken drawings presented to patient H. M.
(Reprinted with permission of author and publisher from Gollin, E. S. Developmental studies of visual recognition of incomplete objects. *Perceptual and Motor Skills*, 1960, *11*, 289–298. © Southern Universities Press 1960.)

Set I

Set II

Set III

Set IV

drawings when they see Set I or Set II. However, once they have seen the complete drawings, people can recognize the elephant and the umbrella if they later see only the incomplete versions. So can H. M.; seeing the complete versions leads to a long-term memory that aids his recognition (Milner, 1970).

Other investigators have found that people with anterograde amnesia can learn to solve puzzles, perform visual discriminations, and make skilled movements that require hand–eye coordination (Squire, 1987). Clearly, their brains are still capable of undergoing the kinds of changes that constitute long-term memory. But the people fail to remember having performed the tasks previously. For example, perhaps research participants learn a task on one occasion. The next day, the researcher brings them to the experimental apparatus and asks if they have ever seen it before. Like Mr. P. in the opening vignette, the participants say no, they have not. They have no explicit, episodic memory of having spent some time learning the task. But then they go on to perform the task well, clearly demonstrating the existence of implicit long-term memory.

Not all implicit memory abilities are spared in this way, however. Chun and Phelps (1999) asked people to find a T-like figure in a cluttered, multicolored display. Although the location of the target varied from trial to trial, its location could be predicted on some trials by the specific configuration of the distracting items. People without anterograde amnesia generally show two kinds of learning on this task: They get faster at finding and reporting the target on all trials, reflecting an improvement in procedural memory, and they also get faster on those trials where the location is predicted by the display. They are, however, unable to recognize explicitly the configurations that allow them to predict the location of the target, showing that this latter learning is an improvement in implicit memory. People with anterograde amnesia likewise show an improvement in procedural memory, but they do not learn the predictive relations of the task.

The evidence we've looked at so far, in sum, suggests that the brain damage causing anterograde amnesia disrupts the formation of all new explicit memories but spares the ability to form many, though not all, new implicit memories. The fact that amnesic patients can remember facts and describe experiences that occurred before the brain injury indicates that their ability to recall explicit memories acquired earlier is not severely disrupted. What parts of the brain are involved in the functions necessary for establishing new explicit memories? The most important part seems to be the hippocampus, one of the structures located deep within the temporal lobe that forms part of the limbic system. (Look back at **Figure 4•35.**)

The hippocampus receives information from all association areas of the brain and sends information back to them. In addition, the hippocampus has two-way connections with many regions in the interior of the cerebral hemispheres (Gluck & Myers, 1997). Thus, the hippocampal formation is in a position to know—and to influence—what is going on in the rest of the brain. Its role in memory may be to bind certain kinds of information together, especially when that information involves conscious awareness (Eichenbaum, 1999).

The hippocampus, like many structures of the brain, is not fully mature at birth. In fact, not until a child is two to three years old are most of these structures fully developed. As a result, many cognitive activities, such as the formation of semantic memories, are not well developed until this age. One reason that few people remember events that occurred during infancy may be the immaturity of the hippocampus.

The hippocampus also may be important for *maintaining* and *retrieving* explicit memories of episodic experiences. For example, Rosenbaum and colleagues (2000) tested the spatial memory of K. C., the man I discussed earlier who suffered a closed-head injury. This injury damaged the hippocampal area of K. C.'s brain. Consistent with his mostly intact semantic memory, K. C. can accurately draw a general map of his home neighborhood and can estimate distances between major landmarks. However, he has significant difficulty identifying landmarks of his neighborhood from photographs. He cannot recognize houses in his community that he would pass by every day, or even distinguish the general type of house found in his community from those of very different neighborhoods. For K. C., the hippocampal damage deprived him of the ability to use the incidental details of his home neighborhood that would normally provide a rich and individualized knowledge of his community.

Are there areas of the brain that, when damaged, produce impairments of implicit memory? Parkinson's disease is a degenerative disease that destroys the striatum, an area of the midbrain. Research by Doyon and colleagues (1998) has demonstrated that bilateral damage to the striatum in an individual with Parkinson's disease interferes with that person's ability to learn to perform a visual–motor task efficiently and automatically. Interestingly, people in the early stages of the disease, with unilateral damage, did manage to learn the task to an automatic level. But when these patients were tested on the task a year later, after the disease had damaged the striatum in both hemispheres, performance was poorer than among control participants. Explicit memory for the task (i.e., the ability to verbalize what the task required) was the same, however, for people both with and without Parkinson's disease. Similarly, people with damage to the cerebellum also had trouble learning and retrieving the implicit memory task but did not show a decline in explicit memory.

Explicit Memory in Animals Given that a key difference between implicit and explicit long-term memory seems to be whether we are able to talk about the memories, can we conclude that only humans have an explicit memory system? The answer seems to be no, although we need to consider how we would test for explicit memories in animals.

One summer, when I was between sixth and seventh grades, I spent two weeks at a summer camp on Orcas Island, north of Seattle, Washington. The beach at camp had a submerged rock in the deeper water. If you knew where it was, you could stand out of the water and fool newcomers into thinking the water was shallow. Knowing where the rock was involved lining up different landmarks on shore—definitely a form of explicit memory, as the water was too murky for you to see the rock itself.

Memory research has given rats an analogous opportunity to learn landmark information when locating a hidden platform. In some experiments, rats are placed in a large circular tank filled with water mixed with an opaque white powder. This apparatus is known as the "Morris water maze," after the investigator who developed it as a test of spatial learning (Morris, Garrud, Rawlins, & O'Keefe, 1982). In the Morris water maze, the rats could find a submerged platform if they could learn, as I did at summer camp, to line up a set of external landmarks. Normally, rats placed at random in the Morris water maze can do this, although it takes several trials before they can swim directly to the platform. But damage to the hippocampus seriously affects this learning (Duva et al., 1997; Eichenbaum, Stewart, & Morris, 1990).

If animals demonstrate explicit memory, do they also possess episodic (autobiographical) memory? Psychologists have thought of episodic memory as memory about actions of the self. Tulving (2002), for example, has called episodic memory a form of "time travel," because it enables us to relive episodes of our past. Some animals can perform similar feats of memory and remember places they have visited. For these animals, the hippocampus seems to be particularly important. Reviewing the literature on species of birds and rodents that store seeds in hidden caches for later retrieval, Sherry, Jacobs, and Gaulin (1992) reported that the hippocampal formation of these animals is larger than that of species who do not have this ability. Black-capped chickadees, for example, spend a lot of time in the fall hiding food in seemingly random places in their territories; later, through memory, they return to these sites to retrieve the food. Smulders, Sasson, and DeVoogd (1995) found that the size of the hippocampal formation in chickadees increased during the time of year when they are most active hiding food—a pattern that does not appear in birds that do not cache seeds (Lee et al., 2001).Whishaw and Wallace (2003) have pointed out that some forms of spatial behavior, involving a type of navigation called **dead reckoning,** may be based on similar types of memory. Dead reckoning is navigation by internal stimuli, such as vestibular cues of motion, that an organism uses to estimate the distance and direction of travel. When you walk through your room at night, turning to avoid unseen furniture, you are navigating by dead reckoning. Whishaw and Wallace suggest that, because dead reckoning requires memory of personal motion, it should be considered a form of episodic memory. This suggests a strong link between navigation ability and the role of the hippocampal formation. Remember the case of the London cab drivers discussed in Chapter 4? London taxi drivers train for years to acquire the expertise they need to find their way in the city's complex road network. Maguire and colleagues (2000) found the posterior hippocampus was larger in experienced taxi drivers than in control individuals. Moreover, the longer a taxi driver's experience, the greater was the volume of the posterior hippocampus.

The hippocampus, then, seems to be involved in memory for locations. Just as there are neurons in the visual centers of the brain that respond to very specific visual stimuli, so there are cells in the hippocampus that react to an animal's specific whereabouts. Using these cells, the hippocampus is capable of forming stable "maps"—even in the very disorienting environment of weightlessness aboard a spaceship. Knierim, McNaughton, and Poe (2000) recorded the activity of "place" neurons in the hippocampus of rats taken aboard a space shuttle mission. The rats' cages contained a special running track that the rats could crawl along in the microgravity environment of earth orbit. Normally, you can't return to a location after making only three 90-degree turns to the right. But, as you can see in the left half of **Figure 8•11,** it is possible when the running track is built in three dimensions. Despite this disorienting geometry, electrical recording of the brains of rat "astronauts" showed that there were hippocampal neurons that developed highly specific firing patterns. Like the neuron whose activity is depicted in the right half of Figure 8.11, these neurons would show high rates of activity whenever the rat was at a certain spot on the running track.

How does the hippocampus support such memories? Mice that, through genetic knockout techniques, have been bred without the NMDA receptors in hippocampal regions (discussed in Chapter 4) show strong deficits in spatial memory (Rampon et al., 2000)—a finding that suggests that these synapses play a central role. Other research evidence suggests

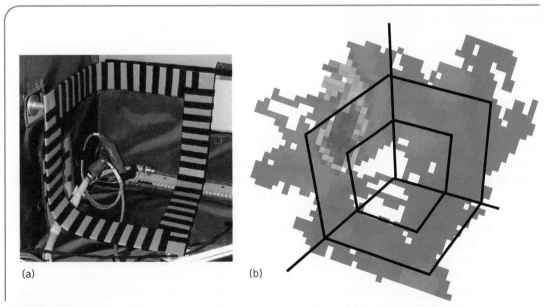

(a)   (b)

FIGURE 8•11   Runway track used to test the response of place cells in weightlessness. (a) Photograph of the staircase. Rats received brain stimulation reward for grasping the surface of the runway and crawling around its path. (b) Recordings from a cell in the hippocampus of one rat. Red indicates locations in three-dimensional space where the cell showed high activity, and blue indicates locations for which the cell never fired. Positions depicted outside the black outline were sampled when the rat's head moved away from the track.

(From Knierim, J. J., McNaughton, B. L., & Poe, G. R. (2000). Three-dimensional spatial selectivity of hippocampal neurons during space flight. *Nature Neuroscience, 3,* 211–212. Reprinted by permission from Macmillan Publishers, Ltd.)

that new cell growth also may play a role. The hippocampus is distinctive as a brain structure in that it produces new neurons during the adulthood of the individual. Gould and her colleagues (1999) looked at what happens to these new neurons in the weeks following their emergence. They gave rats either of two experiences. One involved the water maze as I described it, with landmarks needed to locate the hidden platform. For the other experience, the platform was clearly visible and needed no external landmarks to be located. Gould and her colleagues found that the survival rate of new hippocampal neurons was apparently higher in the former task—the experience requiring the learning of navigational landmarks.

The meaning of this latter finding is still unclear, but Greenough, Cohen, and Juraska (1999) have suggested an interpretation based on simulations using neural networks. As we saw in Chapter 7, these networks are capable of generalizing their information to new situations. However, this capacity is also a weakness, because the structural connections that allow neural networks to generalize also make them overly sensitive to new connections. It has been suggested that the hippocampus serves as a buffer that protects the older connections within association areas of the brain from being overwhelmed by new connections. Greenough, Cohen, and Juraska have proposed the interesting possibility that, to protect itself from being overwhelmed in turn, the hippocampus creates new neurons to represent new knowledge.

Interim Summary

The Organization of Long-Term Memory

Episodic and semantic memory involve different degrees of specificity in long-term memories: We can remember the time and place we learned an episodic memory but not a semantic memory. The study by Sachs (using the "Galileo" sentences) provided behavioral evidence in support of this distinction. Most psychologists believe that the distinction is important but do not necessarily believe that episodic and semantic memories are parts of different systems. Another distinction—between explicit and implicit memory—has received much attention. We use explicit memory when we remember facts and events that we can consciously describe. Implicit memory, in contrast, is unconscious; it is, for example, the memory system that we use when we acquire specific behaviors and skills.

Much of what we have learned about the biological basis of memory comes from studies involving humans with brain damage and from laboratory studies in which animals undergo surgical procedures that produce amnesia. Anterograde amnesia appears to reflect a deficit of explicit memory but not a major impairment of implicit memory. People with anterograde amnesia cannot talk about events that took place after their brain damage occurred, but they can learn to perform many tasks that do not require verbal rules, such as recognizing fragmentary pictures. The deficit in explicit memory appears to be strongly related to normal functioning of the hippocampus. The behavior of laboratory animals also demonstrates this distinction between episodic and other kinds of memories. If a rat's hippocampus has been destroyed, the animal has difficulty learning the location of important landmarks and the routes to them.

QUESTIONS TO CONSIDER

1. Does it make sense to you to suppose that there are different kinds of memory for different kinds of information and that different kinds of information require different kinds of encoding to be remembered? Can you propose alternative ways to think about how long-term memory might be organized (in contrast to the system we have described in this chapter)? Try it. (You may find it helpful to compose a list of all categories of information people can remember—people, places, things, words, events, and so on—and all ways that remembering can take place—fast, slow, with or without much effort, with or without awareness, using or not using retrieval cues, and so on.)

2. Suzanne Corkin says that the most frequent question she hears is "What does H. M. see when he looks in the mirror?" What would *your* reaction be if you looked in the mirror and saw yourself as 50 years older than you remembered yourself to be?

3. What would it be like to lack, as H. M. does, the ability to form new explicit memories? If, as has been suggested, implicit memory systems preceded explicit systems in our evolutionary history, do you think our ancestors were capable of conscious awareness independent of memory?

4. Since the mid-1980s, many researchers have investigated the question of whether nonhuman animals can think. We learned in this chapter that animals can remember and forget information. Does this mean that they can also think? Donald Hebb described both thinking and working memory in terms of the activity of cell assemblies. Would Hebb's model suggest that because animals possess memory, they also can think?

Remembering

So far, we have looked at research and theorizing on the act of learning and the nature of long-term memory. But what do we know about remembering—the process of retrieving information from long-term memory?

Remembering and Recollecting

Remembering is an automatic process. The word *automatic* means "acting by itself." But this definition implies that no special effort is involved. Thinking about examinations you may have taken—and the efforts you made to remember what you had studied—you may want to dispute that statement. Of course, you are right; sometimes we must work very hard to remember something. What is automatic is the retrieval of information from memory in response to the appropriate stimulus. What is sometimes effortful is the attempt to come up with the thoughts (the internal stimuli) that cause the information to be retrieved.

The retrieval of implicit memories is automatic: When the appropriate stimulus occurs, it automatically evokes the appropriate response. For example, when I open my car door, I do not have to think about how the latch works; my hand goes to the appropriate place, my fingers arrange themselves in the proper positions, and I make the necessary movements. But explicit memories, too, are retrieved automatically. Whisper your name to yourself. How did you manage to remember what your name is? How did you retrieve the information needed to move your lips in the proper sequence? Those questions simply cannot be answered by the method of introspection. The information simply pops out at us when the proper question is asked (or, more generally, when the appropriate stimulus is encountered).

Reading provides a particularly compelling example of the automatic nature of memory retrieval. When an experienced reader looks at a familiar word, the name of the word occurs immediately, and so does the meaning. In fact, it is difficult to look at a word and not think of its name. **Figure 8•12** contains a list of words that can be used to demonstrate a phenomenon known as the *Stroop effect* (MacLeod, 1991; Stroop, 1935). Look at the words and, as quickly as you can, say the *names of the colors in which the words are printed;* do not read the words themselves.

blue blue blue green
green yellow red
yellow yellow blue
red green yellow
yellow green yellow
yellow red yellow
green blue yellow
red blue green green
blue blue green red

FIGURE 8•12 The Stroop effect. Name the color in which each word is printed as quickly as you can; you will find it difficult to ignore what the words say.

Most people cannot completely ignore the words and simply name the colors; the tendency to think of the words and pronounce them is difficult to resist. The Stroop effect indicates that even when we try to suppress a well-practiced memory, it tends to be retrieved automatically when the appropriate stimulus occurs.

But what about the fact that some memories seem to be difficult to recall? For most people, remembering information is effortless and smooth. It is something we do unconsciously and automatically—most of the time. Occasionally, though, our memory of a name or a place or something else fails. The experience is often frustrating. We know that the information is "in there someplace," but we just cannot seem to get it out: "Oh, what is his name? I can see his face; he has a moustache, and he's skinny. It seems like his name starts with a *D:* Don? No. Dave? Nope. Dennis? No, that's not it either—what is his name?! Now I remember, his name is Doug. Doug Hoisington, a friend of mine in New York." This phenomenon is known as the **tip-of-the-tongue phenomenon** and has fascinated psychologists since the days of William James (1893). It was first studied carefully during the 1960s (Brown & McNeill, 1966), and since then we have learned a good deal about it (A. S. Brown, 1991). It is a common, if not universal, experience; it occurs about once a week and increases with age; it often involves proper names and knowing the first letter of the word; and it is solved during the experience about 50 percent of the time.

The active search for stimuli that will evoke the appropriate memory, as exemplified in the tip-of-the-tongue phenomenon, has been called *recollection* (Baddeley, 1982). Recollection may be aided by contextual variables, including physical objects, suggestions, or other verbal stimuli. These contextual variables are called **retrieval cues**. For example, as I was about to leave my house this morning, I remembered that I needed to stop by the grocery store on my way home from school later in the day to buy something, but I couldn't remember what it was that I was supposed to buy. So I went into the kitchen and began looking for clues (retrieval cues). Right away, I noticed the toaster and remembered that I was out of bread—that is what I needed to get at the store.

As you might guess, the usefulness of retrieval cues often depends on encoding specificity. Encoding specificity is quite general in its impact on retrieval. In one rather strange example, skilled scuba divers served as participants and learned lists of words either under water or on land (Godden & Baddeley, 1975). Their ability to recall the lists was later tested in either the same or a different environment. The variable of interest was *where* the participants learned the list: in or out of the water. When lists were learned under water, they were recalled much better under water than on land, and lists learned on land were recalled better on land than in the water. The context in which information is learned or processed influences our ability to recollect that information. The implication for studying is clear: To improve recall of material to be tested, the best study strategy is to review the material under conditions similar to those that will prevail during the test. If you are going to take all your psychology tests in a specific room, then you should study for those tests in that room.

Context and retrieval cues can be so powerful in recollection that they can even create *false memories*. Suppose that you were asked to learn this list of words: *bed, rest, awake, tired, dream, wake, night, blanket, doze, slumber, snore, pillow, peace, yawn, drowsy.* Now, without looking back, ask yourself: was *sleep* one of the words? You might find it hard to be sure it wasn't, because the context evoked by the entire set of words suggests the core idea of sleep. In a now-classic article, Roediger and McDermott (1995) found that people would spontaneously recall words after listening to a list of closely associated words. That is, they fall prey to an illusion, thinking that they remember something that did not happen.

Like genuine retrieval, false recall depends on encoding specificity. Goodwin, Meissner, and Ericsson (2001) asked people to learn lists that could suggest a core word. For example, a list of words like *hard, pillow, light,* and so on could suggest the word *soft.* And, indeed, people falsely recalled *soft* as a word that they had heard. However, if the associated words were paired with words that suggested an unrelated context, such as *hard hat, pillow case,* etc., then false recall was lower.

How Long Does Memory Last?

The question "How long does memory last?" has fascinated psychologists and other researchers for many years. In fact, Hermann Ebbinghaus reported the results of the first experiment to determine memory duration back in 1885. Using himself as a participant, Ebbinghaus memorized 13 nonsense syllables such as *dax, wuj, lep,* and *pib.* He then studied how long it took him to relearn the original list after intervals varying from a few minutes up to 31 days. **Figure 8•13** shows what he found. Much of what he learned was forgotten very quickly—usually within a day or two. But even after 31 days he could still recall some of the original information.

Ebbinghaus's research dealt with remembering nonsense syllables. What about remembering aspects of real life? For

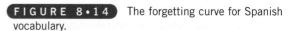

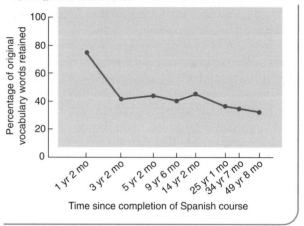

FIGURE 8•14   The forgetting curve for Spanish vocabulary.

(Adapted from Bahrick, H. P. (1984). Semantic memory content in permastore: Fifty years of memory for Spanish learned in school. *Journal of Experimental Psychology: General, 113,* 1–29.)

example, how long might you remember the important experiences of your youth? Bahrick addressed this issue by testing the memories of people of different ages, all of whom had accumulated similar information at different times in their past (Bahrick, 1983, 1984a, 1984b). For example, Bahrick was interested in his participants' ability to recall the names and faces of their high school classmates, the Spanish they had learned in high school or university, or significant aspects of the small town in which they all had been raised.

The recall tests were given to everyone in the study at about the same time. So, of course, the retention intervals for the older people were much longer than those for younger people. Bahrick found that his participants remembered considerable amounts of information without further use, elaboration, or rehearsal even almost 50 years after originally learning it. In fact, retention scores showed little decline for the period between 3 years and nearly 50 years after learning. (See **Figure 8•14.**) About the only factor that significantly

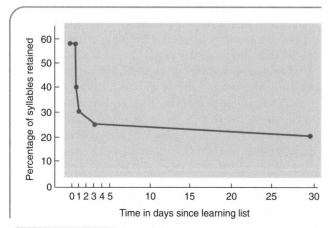

FIGURE 8•13   Ebbinghaus's (1885) forgetting curve.

(Adapted from Ebbinghaus, H. (1885/1913). *Memory: A contribution to experimental psychology.* (Translated by H. A. Ruger & C. E. Bussenius.) New York: Teacher's College, Columbia University.)

▲ *Researchers have found that there is little decline in recall of information such as names and faces, even after 50 years.*

affected people's ability to recall the information was the degree to which the original material was learned (which again shows us the importance of initial encoding). In general, the rate of forgetting of this kind of information, which also includes people's names, music, and special situations, is greatest in the first few years after it is learned and decreases slowly afterwards (Kausler, 1994).

Biology and Culture

Cultural Contexts for Remembering

Memory consists of a network of physical changes in our brains. As we have new experiences, biochemical changes occur in the brain that produce alterations in the neurons that constitute this network. Of course, different people have different experiences, so the physical changes in their brains are different, too. Although it is true that many people "know" the same things—the basic rules of arithmetic, the fact that the sun rises in the east, and so on—it is also true that the way we use our memory, the way we get information out of our memory, and the personal meaning of that information differ considerably from person to person. We should not be surprised to learn, then, that culture provides an important context for remembering.

In fact, some researchers, such as Mistry and Rogoff (1994), argue that "remembering is an activity that is defined . . . in terms of its function in the social and cultural system" (p. 141). According to this view, the act of remembering cannot be separated from its cultural context. In support of this position, let's consider two studies that compared the remembering abilities of Guatemalan Maya and American children.

In the first study (Rogoff & Waddell, 1982), the children were given a test of free recall of lists of material they had learned earlier. Not surprisingly, the American children performed better—after all, if there is one thing that American children learn in school, it is how to remember lists of information: names, dates, places, events, and so on. Maya children receive no such training. In their agriculturally based culture, this sort of information is of little practical value.

To compare how children from these two cultures would perform on a task that was not biased toward the experiences common to children in either culture, Rogoff and Waddell had the Maya and American children watch a local researcher place 20 small toy objects (cars, animals, and so on) in a model of a country village. After the children viewed the scene for a few minutes, the objects were removed and mixed in with 60 other objects from which the 20 items had been originally selected. After a short delay, each child was asked to reconstruct the scene the way the

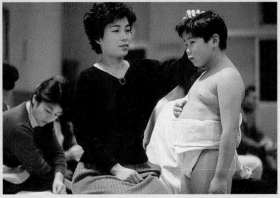

▲ *The culture in which we are raised plays an important role in providing us with learning experiences and memories of those experiences.*

researcher had constructed it. This time, the Maya children performed as well as the American children. (In fact, they did slightly better.) The cross-cultural differences were eliminated when the American children were not permitted to use well-practiced, culturally based mnemonic strategies. The Maya children did not have defective memories; their culture simply had not prepared them for learning long lists of unrelated items.

Cultural customs also seem to affect remembering. In a second study, Rogoff and Waddell asked American and Maya children to recall a story five minutes after hearing it told in their respective native languages by a local teenager. Although the story was taken from Maya oral history, neither the Maya nor the American children had heard the story before. Interestingly, though, the American children seemed to remember the story better than the Maya children did, as evidenced by their retelling of the story to an adult. For example, consider the responses of two children, one from each culture (as cited in Mistry & Rogoff, 1994).

As retold by the Maya child:

When the angel came, cha (so I have been told), from Heaven, well, when the angel came, he came to see the flood (The adult listener prompts: What else?) He ate the flesh of the people. . . . (and then?) He didn't return right away, cha. . . . (What else?) That's all. He threw up, cha, he threw up cha, the flesh. "I like the flesh," he said, cha. . . . (What else?) "Now you're going to become a buzzard," they told him, cha. . . . (With further prompts, the retelling continued similarly.) (p. 140)

Here is the same story as retold by an American child:

There once was a buzzard and he was an angel in heaven and God sent him down to . . . to take all the dead animals and um, and so the buzzard went down and he ate the animals and then he was so full he couldn't get back up to heaven and so he waited another day and then he flew back up to heaven and God said, "You're not an angel anymore," and he goes, "Why?" And . . . and he said that "you ate the raw meat and now you're a buzzard and you'll have and . . . and you'll have to eat the garbage," and . . . and he goes, "I didn't eat anything," and God said, "Open your mouth and let's see," and then he opened his mouth and there was all the raw meat and he goes, "It's true I did eat, I did eat the meat," and God goes, "That's . . . that's why you're the buzzard now," and the . . . and the . . . and . . . and so the buzzard flew down and he, um, then he ate all the trash and everything. (p. 139)

If you were asked to say which of these children retold the story better, clearly you would say the American child did. In fact, you would probably express some surprise at the Maya child's *inability to remember* the story any better than he did. What you might not know, though, is that in Maya culture children do not speak openly to adults. When they cannot avoid speaking to an adult, they must include the word *cha* (so I have been told) in their conversation to show to the adult that they are not behaving disrespectfully by having superior knowledge. Thus, the Maya child may have remembered the story, but the discomfort produced by having to retell it to an adult may have interfered with his ability to provide the adult with the story's details. In contrast, the American child, who undoubtedly was used to speaking freely to adults, *appeared* to have a better memory for the story.

Remembering or verbally expressing a memory is not an activity that occurs independently of cultural practices and rules. Culture influences remembering to the extent that it provides the context for what information is learned, the strategies for learning it, and social contingencies for expressing it.

Reconstruction: Remembering as a Creative Process

Much of what we recall from long-term memory is not an accurate representation of what actually happened. Many errors in memory, however, are not mere inaccuracies: They tend to show systematic patterns. Often, our recollection corresponds to what makes sense to us at the time we retrieve it. It becomes, in other words, a plausible account of what *might* have happened or even of what we think *should* have happened. Psychologists now recognize that the context of remembering is a very important determinant of memory.

The Role of Schemas   From my discussion about encoding specificity earlier in the chapter, you'll recall that when a retrieval cue is understood to have a different meaning at the time of remembering than it did at the time of encoding, it loses its effectiveness. Perhaps you remember from that discussion the passage about "three sturdy sisters" seeking proof. Knowing that the passage described Columbus's voyage helped you place the passage within a framework of knowledge involving people, places, and events. This type of framework is called a **schema**. Schemas help us encode information in more meaningful ways. But they also can induce systematic errors.

An early experiment by Bartlett (1932) called attention to this fact. The experimenter had people read a story or essay or look at a picture. Then he asked them on several later occasions to retell the prose passage or draw the picture. Each time, the participants "remembered" the original a little differently. If the original story had contained peculiar and unexpected sequences of events, people tended to retell it in a more coherent and sensible fashion, as if their memories had been revised to make the information accord more closely with their own schema for what the story was about. Bartlett concluded that people remember only a few striking details of an experience and that during recall they reconstruct the missing portions in accordance with their own interpretation of what was likely.

Eyewitness Testimony Elizabeth Loftus (1979) has investigated a different set of variables that affect the recall of details from episodic memory. Her research indicates that the kinds of questions used to elicit information can have a major effect on what people remember. In courts of law, lawyers are not permitted to ask witnesses leading questions—questions phrased so as to suggest what the answer should be. Loftus's research showed that even subtle changes in a question can affect people's recollections. For example, Loftus and Palmer (1974) showed people films of car accidents and asked them to estimate vehicles' speeds when they *contacted, hit, bumped, collided,* or *smashed* each other. As **Figure 8•15** shows, the people's estimates of the vehicles' speeds were directly related to the force of the impact suggested by the verb, such as *hit,* that appeared in the question.

In a similar experiment, when people were asked a week after viewing the film whether they saw any broken glass (there was none), people in the *smashed* group were most likely to say yes. Thus, a leading question that encouraged them to remember the vehicles going faster also encouraged them to remember that they saw nonexistent broken glass. The question appears to have modified the memory itself.

Another experiment indicates that how events are reviewed affects this suggestibility. Lane, Mather, Villa, and Morita (2001) showed people a videotape of a staged crime,

▲ *The questions asked during a pretrial investigation may affect an eyewitness's later testimony.*

then asked questions that were designed to suggest things that were not part of the video. For example, the witnesses might be asked, "At the beginning of the scene, a young man dressed in jeans, a T-shirt, and gloves entered the house. Did he enter through the door?" In the video, the thief did not wear gloves; the test was to see if witnesses would incorrectly include the gloves in their recall of the scene later on. Before recalling information about the scene, however, they were asked, as witnesses might reasonably be asked to do, to review the videotape mentally. Some were asked to review as much detail as possible; others were asked to review only the highlights. Instructions to focus on details led to an increased tendency to incorporate the suggested, and false, information, such as the presence of gloves. Apparently, after being asked to review details, eyewitnesses rehearse the suggestions and come to view these as true.

Experiments such as these have important implications for eyewitness testimony in courts of law. A judge can prevent a lawyer from asking leading questions during a trial, but he or she cannot undo the effects of leading questions put to the witness during pretrial investigations. Many experiments indicate that learning new information and recalling it later are active processes—we do not simply place an item of information in a mental filing cabinet and pick it up later. We organize and integrate information in terms of what we already know about life and have come to expect about particular experiences. Thus, when we recall the memory later, it may contain information that was not part of the original experience. Even more disturbing, our confidence in this new information may be quite high.

At first, this phenomenon may appear to be maladaptive because it means that we cannot always trust our own recollections, no matter how hard we try to be accurate. However, our tendency to reconstruct memories probably reflects the fact that information about an episode can be more efficiently stored by means of a few unique details. The portions of an episode that are common to other experiences, and hence resemble information already stored in long-term

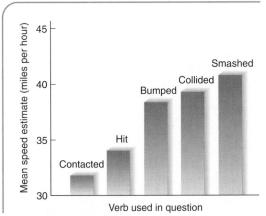

FIGURE 8•15 Leading questions and recall. Shown are the mean estimated speeds of vehicles as recalled by people in the study by Loftus and Palmer (1974).

(Based on data from Loftus, E. F., & Palmer, J. C. (1974). Reconstruction of automobile destruction: An example of the interaction between language and memory. *Journal of Verbal Learning and Verbal Behavior, 13,* 585–589.)

memory, need not be retained. If every detail of every experience had to be encoded uniquely in long-term memory, perhaps we would run out of storage space. Unfortunately, this process sometimes leads to instances of faulty remembering, both in the witness stand and in life in general.

Flashbulb Memories Are some memories immune to this reconstructive process? One possibility is that some episodic memories are acquired under such powerful personal experiences of emotion and surprise that they become especially vivid and long-lasting. Consider your personal memory of when you first heard about the attack on the World Trade Center on September 11, 2001. Can you recall where you were, what you were doing, and who gave you the news? Do you remember your personal feelings? The feelings of those around you? Can you recall what you did next?

Roger Brown and James Kulik provided a name for memories activated by events of extreme surprise and great person consequence: **flashbulb memories**. Using the assassination of President John F. Kennedy as an example, Brown and Kulik (1977) suggested that surprising events could result in the encoding of some (but not all) of the context surrounding the individual at the time. When they asked people in 1977 to recollect their personal situation at the time they heard of Kennedy's 1963 assassination, they discovered that most accounts included the information behind the six questions I asked you in the last paragraph. Brown and Kulik speculated that flashbulb memories were not only especially vivid but also, possibly, especially long-lasting or even permanent.

However, other evidence suggests that flashbulb memories are not immune to the effects of distortion and modification that I discussed in the previous section. Schmolck, Buffalo, and Squire (2000) looked at an event that, although it was less consequential than the Kennedy assassination or 9/11, nevertheless produced flashbulb memories in students at the University of California: the 1995 acquittal of O. J. Simpson in his trial for the murder of his wife, Nicole, and her friend Ron Goldman. The investigators asked the students to record their reactions to the event three days after it happened. Then, either 15 months or 32 months later, they asked them to recall the event again. In general, recollection after 15 months was accurate. After 32 months, however, more than 40 percent of the recollections were seriously distorted. Schmolck, Buffalo, and Squire found that of 50 individuals who could be described as having a flashbulb memory of the verdict, 38 percent could not remember it as they had originally described it three days after the event. A significant source of error in the years after the event was in people's recall of the source of the news, with many people misreporting that they had heard about the verdict from the media rather than from another person. Rather than saying they couldn't remember, these individuals apparently assumed that because they get much of their news from the media, they must have heard about the Simpson verdict the same way. This assumption was then incorporated into their memory of the event.

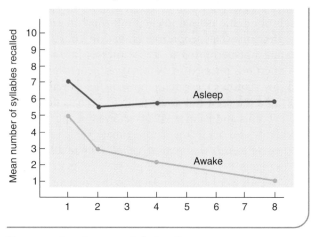

FIGURE 8•16   Interference in memory retrieval. The graph shows the mean number of nonsense syllables people recalled after sleeping or staying awake for varying intervals of time.

(Adapted from Jenkins, J. G., & Dallenbach, K. M. (1924). Oblivescence during sleep and waking. *American Journal of Psychology*, 1924, *35*, 605–612. Copyright 1924 by the Board of Trustees of the University of Illinois. Used with permission of the the the University of Illinois.)

Remembering and Interference

Although long-term memory appears to last for a long time, you have probably heard the notion that people often forget something they once knew because so much time has elapsed since the memory was last used that the memory has *decayed*. A similar term has been used to describe the loss of items from short-term memory when they are not rehearsed. But the notion that items are forgotten because they decay provides little explanation. Why does time have this effect? One popular alternative explanation for long-term memory failure is *interference*. (It has also been used to describe some aspects of short-term memory failure as well.)

The concept of interference is based on the well-established finding that some memories may interfere with the retrieval of others. An early study by Jenkins and Dallenbach (1924) showed that we are less likely to remember information after an interval of wakefulness than after an interval of sleep, presumably because of new memories that are formed when we are awake. (See **Figure 8•16**.)

Subsequent research soon showed that there are two types of interference in retrieval. Sometimes we experience **retroactive interference**—when we try to retrieve information, other information, which we have learned more recently, interferes. The top part of **Figure 8•17** charts how researchers test for the effects of retroactive interference. The experimental group first learns a list of words (we'll call the list "A"). Next, during the retention interval, the experimental group learns a second list of words, "B." Finally, the experimental group is asked to recall the first list of words ("A"). Meanwhile, the control group learns only the words in list "A"—the group is not asked to learn the words in list "B" during the retention interval. However, the control

Group	Initial learning	Retention interval	Retention test
Retroactive Interference			
Experimental	Learn A	Learn B	Recall A
Control	Learn A		Recall A

	Initial learning	Retention interval	Retention test
Proactive Interference			
Experimental	Learn A Learn B		Recall B
Control	Learn B		Recall B

FIGURE 8•17 Retroactive and proactive interference.

group is asked to recall the words in list "A" immediately following the retention interval. If the experimental group recalls fewer words during the test than does the control group, retroactive interference is said to have occurred in the people in that group.

To take a real-life example, you may have a hard time recalling the presents you received on your seventh birthday because you have had many birthdays since. If your seventh birthday had been just yesterday, you would likely show perfect recall. When memories that interfere with retrieval are formed *after* the learning that is being tested, we have retroactive interference.

At other times retrieval is impaired by **proactive interference,** in which our ability to recall new information is reduced because of information we learned previously. The bottom part of Figure 8.17 illustrates the experimental procedure used to test for proactive interference. In this procedure, before learning a list (we'll call it list "B" in this procedure) the experimental group learns the words in another list, "A." The control group learns only the words in list "B." Both groups then experience a retention interval before they are asked to recall the words in list "B." If the experimental group recalls fewer words in list "B" during the test than does the control group, proactive interference is said to have occurred.

For example, let us assume that you took French for several years in high school and that you are now taking a Spanish class in college. You find that some of the knowledge and study skills from high school are beneficial. But occasionally you discover that when you try to recall some Spanish, French pops up instead. Similarly, one reason that you may not be able to recall with certainty what birthday presents you received last year is that you have had so many birthdays before.

As reasonable and intuitive as the concept of interference may be, it has not gone unchallenged. Researchers agree that interference can affect retrieval, but some argue that the kinds of recall tasks people are asked to perform in the laboratory are exceptionally likely to be affected by interference. In real life, such effects may not be so powerful. For example, meaningful prose, such as the kind found in novels, is resistant to interference. Laboratory studies most often use lists of nonsense syllables and unrelated words.

Evaluating Scientific Issues

Hypnosis, Remembering, and Criminal Investigation

Daniel Schacter has suggested that memory can exhibit seven deficiencies or "sins." These sins of memory are transience, absent-mindedness, blocking, misattribution, suggestibility, bias, and persistence. The first three are deficiencies of omission: Transience is the weakening of memory over time; absent-mindedness is the failure to register information that needs to be memorized; and blocking is the failure to retrieve information we know we possess. The other four are deficiencies of commission and add wrong information to our memory: Misattribution confuses different sources of memory; suggestibility embellishes memory under the influence of misleading questions or statements from others; bias creates errors because of our own beliefs; and persistence brings to mind information that we would rather forget (Schacter, 2001; Schacter & Dodson, 2002).

Schacter's "seven sins" have particular relevance to the criminal justice system. In many criminal investigations—particularly those in which little or no physical evidence is available—the memory of witnesses becomes especially important. Their ability to remember events and faces can determine the success or failure of the investigation—and of the subsequent prosecution, should a suspect be brought to trial. But memories of eyewitnesses are transient, especially when the events in question are fast-paced, confusing, and frightening.

Hypnosis is a condition that induces special behaviors. It is a major topic of Chapter 9, which describes possible explanations for its special effects. However, one notable claim made by some people who use or study hypnotism is that it can produce enhanced recollection of events. It is not surprising that many criminal investigators have turned to hypnosis in an attempt to overcome Schacter's three sins of omission. As we will see, though, another issue is whether hypnosis also increases the likelihood of the other four.

Hypnotic Memory Enhancement

Some police departments employ officers trained in hypnosis or hire professionals as consultants. The idea is that if victims of crime or witnesses to crimes cannot supply the investigators with sufficient details to identify the criminal, hypnosis may help them recollect useful information. Several methods are used in this effort. The most common approach is to ask the witness to relax, imagine himself or herself at the scene of the crime, try to see things as they were, and describe all that happens. Almost always, the witness is told that hypnosis is a significant aid to memory and that he or she will become aware of information that was previously available only to the subconscious mind.

Sometimes the hypnotist uses a method called the *television technique*, so named because of its resemblance to the methods used in broadcasts of sporting or news events. Witnesses are told to "zoom in" on details they have forgotten (such as the criminal's face or the licence plates of the car involved in an accident) or to "freeze the frame" to examine fleeting details at their leisure (Reiser & Nielsen, 1980).

Police hypnotists have reported some successes with their techniques. One of the most famous was the capture and conviction of the kidnappers in a sensational case in California (Kroger & Doucé, 1979). In July 1976, three masked men kidnapped a busload of children in Chowchilla, California, and transferred them to a subterranean chamber they had prepared in an abandoned quarry. Eventually the bus driver and two of the older boys managed to dig their way out, and the other children were rescued. The driver had seen the licence plates on the two vans the criminals had used to transport him and the children, but the most he could remember during the subsequent investigation was three numbers (out of seven) from one of them.

Under hypnosis, the bus driver suddenly remembered the two licence plate numbers, which the police investigated. It turned out that one of the numbers was completely wrong, but the other one was correct except for one digit. The police found the kidnappers, who were then arrested, convicted, and sentenced to life imprisonment.

How Can Hypnosis Assist Memory?

Some advocates of hypnotic memory enhancement have made outrageous claims about its efficacy. But what can hypnosis actually do? First, let's be clear about what hypnosis cannot do: It cannot possibly help people remember events that they did not witness. It can only help people recollect information that they have already learned and are having trouble recalling. In other words, hypnosis helps only if the information has been perceived and has left a trace in the brain. It cannot enhance memories themselves; it can only enhance their recollection. The bus driver in the Chowchilla case was able to remember three more numbers from one of the licence plates only because he had actually seen the plates—and had, in fact, tried to memorize them at the time.

Hypnosis does provide a different protocol for interviewing eyewitnesses. Instead of standard police interrogations, where, for example, the interviewer might interrupt a witness, hypnosis may provide a more relaxed and "client-oriented" approach to memory reconstruction (Kebbell & Wagstaff, 1998). In other words, the style of interaction between interrogator and witness may be an important factor.

In fact, some investigators have developed methods for improving recall of memories that do not involve hypnosis but are based on the research findings of cognitive psychologists interested in memory. These methods appear to work just as well as hypnosis. The guided memory method of Malpass and Devine (1981) instructs witnesses to visualize the original environmental setting in which the events occurred and to try to imagine their mood, thoughts, and feelings at the time. Such a reconstruction often provides retrieval cues that help witnesses recall details they thought they had forgotten. The cognitive interview of Geiselman and colleagues (1984) also encourages a re-creation of the original environment and, in addition, has the witness try to describe the episode from different perspectives.

The Dangers of Hypnotic Memory Enhancement

Many people believe that even if hypnosis does not endow witnesses with special powers, it should perhaps be used routinely just in case it helps someone remember some unreported information. However, as Orne and colleagues point out, hypnosis does more than help people recollect memories. It can modify existing memories, increase people's confidence in their recollections, and even implant false memories. In one case, for example, a hypnotist interviewing a victim who had been raped by a masked man asked her to mentally "take off" his mask and report what his face looked like. She did, and the authorities even attempted to convict a man on the basis of her "eyewitness identification" (Orne, Whitehouse, Dinges, & Orne, 1988). Because the victim never saw the man's face, her hypnotic visualization of it was completely imaginary.

▲ *Eyewitnesses frequently provide valuable information. The issue is often how best to retrieve it.*

Most witnesses to a crime want very much to help the police in their investigation. The eagerness of the witness, who may even be the victim of the crime, along with a belief in the mythical powers of hypnosis and the expertise of the hypnotist, sometimes leads the witness to "see" details that were never present at the scene of the crime. In one case, after being hypnotized, a witness to a murder identified a person as the murderer. However, testimony later showed that the witness was 270 feet away. Under the lighting conditions present at the time, this witness could not possibly have seen the murderer's face beyond 25 feet (*People v. Kempinski*, 1980).

Laurence and Perry (1983) demonstrated that through suggestion hypnosis can induce false memories that people later sincerely come to believe. The researchers hypnotized people and asked them whether they had been awakened by some loud noises on a particular night. (They first ascertained that, in fact, the people had not been awakened then.) Most of the people reported that yes, they had heard some loud noises. When the people were interviewed by another researcher later, in a nonhypnotized condition, 48 percent said that they had heard some loud noises on the night in question. Even after the researcher told them that the hypnotist had *suggested* that the noises had occurred, almost half of them still insisted that the noises had occurred. One said, "I'm pretty certain I heard them. As a matter of fact, I'm pretty damned certain. I'm positive I heard these noises" (Laurence & Perry, 1983, p. 524).

The results of this and other studies (Scoboria, Mazzoni, Kirsch, & Milling, 2002) strongly suggest that the testimony of people who have been hypnotized by investigators to "help refresh their memories" is not always trustworthy. Fuzzy recollections become clear memories of events, and the witnesses become convinced that these events actually occurred. As we saw earlier, research on eyewitness testimony has shown that leading questions can affect the memories of people who are not hypnotized. Hypnosis adds to

this effect; under hypnosis people are especially suggestible, and subtle hints made by the examiner can inadvertently change the way witnesses recollect an event.

The eyewitness testimony of a person who appears to believe sincerely what he or she is saying is extremely compelling. Thus, it can have a strong effect on a jury. If, in addition, the person's testimony is full of precise details about the episode, the effects on a jury are even more powerful. Because an interview under hypnosis tends to fill in missing details, often with events that never really happened, and increases the witness's confidence in what he or she remembers, the potential dangers of permitting a previously hypnotized witness to testify before a jury should be obvious.

● **What Should We Conclude?**
The Council on Scientific Affairs (1985) of the American Medical Association concludes that although hypnosis may be useful in providing leads to guide further investigation, the dangers of contaminating the recollection of witnesses are very real. In fact, most courts in North America do not permit witnesses to testify once they have been hypnotized. Thus, if the police hypnotize a witness, they run the risk of rendering the person's testimony inadmissible. Even if the only goal of hypnosis is to provide clues, the police must be wary of the results of the interview. If they place too much credence in the statements of a hypnotized witness, they may end up following false leads and neglecting more productive avenues. They may even be deliberately misled by a witness who stands to gain by doing so. Contrary to popular belief, there is no way to be sure that a person is hypnotized and not merely pretending to be; and even genuinely hypnotized people can lie. Justice would probably best be served if, instead of interviewing people under hypnosis, the police pursued methods based on scientific research on the memory process. Indeed, some of this research is now being discussed as the basis for policy in police investigations (Yarmey, 2003).

Interim Summary

Remembering

Remembering is an automatic process, although we may sometimes work hard at generating thoughts that will help this process along. As Bahrick's research shows, the forgetting of information occurs primarily in the first few years after it is learned, and the rate of forgetting decreases slowly thereafter. Once we have learned something and retained it for a few years, chances are that we will remember it for a long time afterward. The process of remembering information is influenced by how cultures teach their members to learn about the world. In addition, a culture's customs governing social interaction may influence what people tell others about what they have learned.

Recalling a memory of a complex event entails a process of reconstruction that uses old information. And, as Loftus's research has established, our ability to recall information from episodic memory is influenced by retrieval cues, such as the questions lawyers ask people in courts of law to establish how an event occurred. Sometimes the reconstruction introduces new "facts" that we perceive as memories of what we previously perceived. Reconstructions also affect the recollection of flashbulb memories—especially vivid memories of surprising and consequential events. This reconstructive process undoubtedly makes more efficient use of the resources we have available for storage of long-term memories.

Sometimes retrieval of one memory is made more difficult by the information contained in another memory, a phenomenon known as interference. In retroactive interference, information that we have recently learned interferes with our recollection of information learned earlier. In proactive interference, information that we learned a while ago interferes with information we have learned more recently. Although interference has been demonstrated in the laboratory, interference may not operate so obviously in real life. Prose and other forms of everyday language appear to be more resistant to interference than the nonsense syllables often used in memory experiments.

Hypnosis has sometimes been used to improve the recall of persons who witness crimes. But, as research has shown, this can be a risky practice, if only because hypnotic suggestions given to the witness may bias his or her recall of the events. Hypnosis may modify a person's memory, increase a person's confidence in his or her recollections, and suggest false but believable memories. For these reasons, the testimony of witnesses who have been hypnotized to enhance their memories of a crime is not credible or admissible in court.

QUESTIONS TO CONSIDER

1. Given what you know about memory, was Ebbinghaus right to use nonsense syllables?
2. Recall a particularly important event in your life. Think about the activities that led up to this event and how the event has affected your life since. How much of the information you recall about this event is accurate? How many of the details surrounding this event have you reconstructed? How would you go about finding the answers to these questions?

Suggestions for Further Reading

Luria, A. R. (1968). *The mind of a mnemonist.* New York: Basic Books.

Given the importance of learning and forgetting in almost everyone's life, it is not surprising that many popular books have been written about human memory. This book is the great Russian neurologist's account of a man with an extraordinary memory.

Loftus, E. F., & Ketcham, K. (1994). *The myth of repressed memory: False memories and allegations of sexual abuse.* New York: St. Martin's.

Elizabeth Loftus is an internationally recognized authority on remembering. She has researched and written extensively on the errors people make in recalling events. This book deals with case studies of individuals who purportedly were able to recall significant events that had been "repressed" because of their traumatic nature. As Loftus and Ketcham note, such repressed memories likely never existed in the first place.

Haberlandt, K. (1997). *Cognitive psychology* (2nd ed.). Boston: Allyn and Bacon.

Schacter, D. L. (2001). *The seven sins of memory.* Boston: Houghton Mifflin.

The Haberlandt book is an upper-level undergraduate text that contains a well-written and thoughtful consideration of memory and its processes. The book's discussion of memory is placed in the larger context of cognitive psychology, along with coverage of other topics, especially language, decision making, reasoning, and problem solving. The Schacter book is an engaging overview of memory errors.

Key Terms

anterograde amnesia (p. 246)

automatic processing (p. 240)

chunking (p. 233)

conduction aphasia (p. 235)

consolidation (p. 238)

dead reckoning (p. 249)

deep processing (p. 239)

echoic memory (p. 231)

effortful processing (p. 240)

elaborative rehearsal (p. 239)

encoding (p. 228)

encoding specificity (p. 240)

episodic memory (p. 245)

explicit memory (p. 246)

flashbulb memories (p. 256)

iconic memory (p. 230)

implicit memory (p. 246)

long-term memory (p. 229)

maintenance rehearsal (p. 239)

memory (p. 228)

method of loci (p. 241)

mnemonic system (p. 241)

narrative (p. 242)

peg-word method (p. 242)

phonological short-term memory (p. 234)

primacy effect (p. 232)

proactive interference (p. 257)

recency effect (p. 232)

retrieval (p. 228)

retrieval cues (p. 251)

retroactive interference (p. 256)

retrograde amnesia (p. 238)

schema (p. 254)

semantic memory (p. 245)

sensory memory (p. 229)

shallow processing (p. 239)

short-term memory (p. 229)

storage (p. 228)

subvocal articulation (p. 234)

tip-of-the-tongue phenomenon (p. 251)

working memory (p. 232)

9

CONSCIOUSNESS

Consciousness as a Social Phenomenon

Can We Understand Consciousness? • The Adaptive Significance of Consciousness • Consciousness and the Ability to Communicate • *Evaluating Scientific Issues: Does Conscious Thought Control Behavior?* • Consciousness and Moral Reasoning

Although consciousness is a subjective phenomenon, it is a natural phenomenon that can be studied scientifically. Consciousness may be explained as a product of our ability to communicate symbolically with ourselves and with other people.

Selective Attention

Auditory Information • Visual Information • Brain Mechanisms of Selective Attention

Our ability to focus on particular categories of stimuli or stimuli in particular locations is called selective attention. The factors that control selective attention include novelty, verbal instructions, and significance. PET studies show that attention to a particular characteristic of a visual stimulus increases the activity of particular regions of the visual association cortex involved in the analysis of that characteristic.

Consciousness and the Brain

Isolation Aphasia: A Case of Global Unawareness • Visual Agnosia: Lack of Awareness of Visual Perceptions • The Split-Brain Syndrome

Studies of people with brain damage show that some mental processes can be lost from awareness. It is sometimes possible for people to lose the ability to understand words while retaining the ability to recognize and repeat them—or for people to perceive objects they are unaware of. People with split brains (those whose corpus callosum has been cut) cannot talk about perceptions or other mental processes that occur in their right hemispheres.

Hypnosis

Characteristics of Hypnosis • Theories of Hypnosis • *Biology and Culture: Control of Consciousness through Meditation, Attention, and Dishabituation*

Hypnotic phenomena include hallucinations and other changes in consciousness, posthypnotic suggestibility, and posthypnotic amnesia. The behavior of a hypnotized person depends both on the suggestions of the hypnotist and on the expectations of the individual. Hypnosis is related to people's ability to participate actively in a story that interests them and may be related to their ability to empathize with other people. It may also involve a special state in which awareness is dissociated from the mechanisms that control behavior. For many centuries, people of various cultures have discovered drugs and developed behavioral methods of increasing or decreasing their consciousness.

Sleep

The Stages of Sleep • Functions of Sleep • Dreaming • Brain Mechanisms of Sleep

Sleep consists of slow-wave sleep and REM sleep. One of the most important functions of slow-wave sleep may be to permit the cerebral cortex to rest. In adults, REM sleep may be involved in learning. Dreaming occurs during REM sleep. The brain contains two biological clocks that control circadian rhythms and rhythms of slow-wave sleep and REM sleep.

Laverne J. had brought her grandfather to see Dr. M., a neuropsychologist. Mr. J. had had a stroke that had left him almost completely blind; all he could see was a tiny spot in the middle of his visual field. Dr. M. had learned about the situation from Mr. J.'s neurologist and had asked Mr. J. to come to his laboratory so that he could do some tests for his research project.

Dr. M. helped Mr. J. find a chair and sit down. Mr. J., who walked with the aid of a cane, gave it to his granddaughter to hold for him. "May I borrow that?" asked Dr. M. Laverne nodded and handed it to him. "The phenomenon I'm studying is called blindsight," he said. "Let me see if I can show you what it is."

"Mr. J., please look straight ahead. Keep looking that way, and don't move your eyes or turn your head. I know that you can see a little bit straight ahead of you, and I don't want you to use that piece of vision for what I'm going to ask you to do. Fine. Now, I'd like you to reach out with your right hand and point to what I'm holding."

"But I don't see anything—I'm blind!" said Mr. J., obviously exasperated.

"I know, but please try, anyway."

Mr. J. shrugged his shoulders and pointed. He looked startled when his finger encountered the end of the cane, which Dr. M. was pointing toward him.

"Gramps, how did you do that?" asked Laverne, amazed. "I thought you were blind."

"I am!" he said, emphatically. "It was just luck."

"Let's try it just a couple more times, Mr. J.," said Dr. M. "Keep looking straight ahead. Fine." He reversed the cane, so that the handle was pointing toward Mr. J. "Now I'd like you to grab hold of the cane."

Mr. J. reached out with an open hand and grabbed hold of the cane.

"Good. Now put your hand down, please." He rotated the cane 90 degrees, so that the handle was oriented vertically. "Now reach for it again."

Mr. J. did so. As his arm came up, he turned his wrist so that his hand matched the orientation of the handle, which he grabbed hold of again.

"Good. Thank you, you can put your hand down." Dr. M. turned to Laverne. "I'd like to test your grandfather now, but I think it's safe to say that there's a lot more to your grandfather's vision than just luck."

What is consciousness, and why are we conscious? How do we direct our consciousness from one event to another, paying attention to some stimuli and ignoring others? What do we know about the brain functions responsible for consciousness? What is hypnosis—can another person really take control of our thoughts and behavior? Why do we regularly undergo the profound alternation in consciousness called sleep? We do not yet have all the answers to these questions, but we have made much progress. This chapter explores the nature of human consciousness: knowledge of our own perceptions, thoughts, and memories.

Consciousness as a Social Phenomenon

Why are we aware of ourselves—of our actions, our perceptions, our thoughts, our memories, and our feelings? Is some purpose served by our ability to realize that we exist, that events occur, that we are doing things, and that we have memories? Philosophers have puzzled over this question for centuries without finding a convincing answer. Early behaviorists approached the issue by denying that there was any-

▲ *When do we become aware of our own existence?*

Hebb, who stated that "consciousness, a variable state, is a present activity of thought processes in some form; and thought itself is an activity of the brain" (Hebb, 1980, p. 3). But Hebb rejected the notion that concepts like consciousness were "nothing but" neural impulses. For him, the psychological concepts were at a different level; understanding the neural level would enrich and enhance our understanding of the psychological.

The Adaptive Significance of Consciousness

To discover the functions of consciousness, we must not confuse consciousness with complex mental processes such as perceiving, thinking, or remembering. **Consciousness** is the *awareness* of these processes, not the processes themselves. Thus, consciousness is a characteristic that exists *in addition to* functions such as perception, thinking, memory, and planning.

It is difficult to see why a living organism having elaborate behavioral abilities plus consciousness would have any advantages over an organism that possessed the same abilities but lacked consciousness. If the behavior of these two types of organisms were identical in all situations, they should be equally successful. So let us put aside the search for useful functions of consciousness itself. A more fruitful approach might be to conceive of consciousness as a by-product of another characteristic of the human brain that does have useful functions. But what might this characteristic be?

Let us consider what we know about consciousness. First, although the word *consciousness* is a noun, it does not refer to a thing. The word *life* is a noun, too, but modern biologists know better than to look for "life." Instead, they study the characteristics of living organisms. Similarly, "consciousness" does not exist. What exists is a species with the ability to do something in particular: be conscious. So, then, what does it mean to be conscious? Consciousness is a private experience, which cannot be shared directly. We experience our own consciousness but not that of others. We conclude that other people are conscious because they are like us and because they can tell us that they, too, are conscious.

Another clue to the functions of consciousness is that we are not conscious of everything about ourselves, nor are we equally conscious of the same thing all the time. That is, *consciousness is not a general property of all parts of the brain.* The phenomenon discussed in the opening vignette, **blindsight,** is one example. Blindsight is the ability to reach for objects accurately while remaining unaware of seeing them. It is caused by damage to the visual cortex, or to some of the pathways leading into or from that area. Apparently, a part of the visual system can control our ability to react to the presence of objects, directing our eye movement, our limbs, and other behaviors, but without necessarily giving information needed for us to describe or to think about the objects. For other parts of our brain, awareness comes about with a special effort, as when we concentrate on or attend to certain experiences.

thing to explain. For them, the only subject matter for psychological investigation was behavior, they argued, and consciousness was not behavior. More recently investigators have begun to apply the methods of inquiry developed by psychology and neuroscience, and finally we seem to be making some progress.

Can We Understand Consciousness?

Historically, people have taken three philosophical positions about the nature of consciousness (Flanagan, 1992). The first, and earliest, position holds that consciousness is not a natural phenomenon. (Natural phenomena are those subject to the laws of nature that all scientists attempt to discover: laws involving matter and purely physical forces.) This position says that consciousness is something supernatural and miraculous, not to be understood by the human mind.

The second position maintains that consciousness is a natural phenomenon but also that, for various reasons, we cannot understand it. Consciousness exists because of the nature of the human brain, but just how this occurs is not known. Some people say that we can never understand consciousness, because our brains are simply not capable of doing so; it would take a more complex brain than ours to understand the biology of subjective awareness. Others say that we are probably capable of understanding consciousness but that at present we lack the means to study it scientifically. Still others say that, in principle, everything can be explained—including all aspects of the human brain—but that *consciousness* is a vague, poorly defined term. Before we can hope to study it with any success, we must define just what it is we want to study.

The third position is that people are indeed conscious, that this consciousness is produced by the activity of the human brain, and that there is every reason for us to be optimistic about our ability to understand this phenomenon. This was the position advocated for many years by Donald

With concentration, we can then describe these activities of the brain so as to convey them to other people.

In my opinion, it is no coincidence that the principal evidence we have of consciousness in other people comes through the use of language. I believe that the most likely explanation for consciousness lies in its relation to deliberate, symbolic communication. Our ability to communicate (through words, signs, or other symbolic means) provides us with self-awareness. Thus, consciousness—like communication—is, I believe, primarily a social phenomenon.

Consciousness and the Ability to Communicate

How does the ability to communicate symbolically give rise to consciousness? To answer this question, let us consider what can be accomplished through verbal communication. We can ask other people to help us get something we need. We can share our knowledge with others by describing our past experiences. We can make plans with other people to accomplish tasks that are beyond the abilities of a single person. We can warn other people of our intentions and in so doing avoid potential conflicts. In other words, we can express our needs, perceptions, thoughts, memories, intentions, and feelings to other people.

All of these accomplishments require two general capacities. First, we must be able to translate private events—our needs, thoughts, and other processes—into symbolic expressions. This means that the brain mechanisms we employ for communicating with others must receive input from the systems of the brain involved in perceiving, thinking, remembering, and so on. Second, our words (or other symbols) must have an effect on the person listening. Once the words are decoded in the listener's brain, they must affect the listener's own perceptions, thoughts, memories, and—ultimately—behavior. For example, if we describe an event that we witnessed, our listener will be able to imagine that event, too. The episode will become part of our listener's memory.

Of course, the world is not divided into talkers and listeners. We are all capable of expressing our thoughts symbolically and of decoding the symbols other people express. Having both of these capabilities enables us to communicate with ourselves, privately. We can make plans in words, think about the consequences of these plans in words, and use words to produce behaviors—all without actually *saying* the words. We *think* them.

As we saw in Chapter 8, thinking in words appears to involve subvocal articulation. Thus, the brain mechanisms that permit us to understand words and produce speech are the same ones we use to think in words. Similarly, investigators have noted that when deaf people are thinking to themselves, they often make small movements with their hands, just as those of us who can hear and speak sometimes talk to ourselves under our breath. Apparently, we exercise our expressive language mechanisms, whatever they may be, when we think.

So what does all this have to do with consciousness? My thesis is this: It is the ability to communicate with ourselves symbolically that gives rise to consciousness. We are conscious of those private events we can talk about, to ourselves or to other people: our needs, perceptions, thoughts, memories, intentions, and feelings.

For example, consider the experiment by Cheesman and Merikle (1986) that we encountered in Chapter 6. These researchers presented people with a word (the prime) that was either congruent or incongruent with the color of a subsequent stimulus (the target). People were asked to name the color of the target—a task that is more difficult when the prime is incongruent. Presented between the prime and the target on some trials, though, would be a random jumble of visual lines that would interfere with people's ability to report what the word was. (You'll recognize this as an example of the Stroop effect, described in Chapter 8.) Cheesman and Merikle found that incongruent primes produced a Stroop-like interference even when the jumble of lines had interfered with the ability to consciously identify the word.

Now, by itself, this may not be evidence of a role for consciousness. After all, the fact that the primes have an effect whether or not people are conscious of their meaning does not show that consciousness adds anything to our ability to process information. However, Cheesman and Merikle then presented the same experiment, but with many more congruent than incongruent primes. In other words, if the word "green" appeared, it was much more likely to be followed by a green patch than any other color. So, by using the prime, participants could predict what color was about to come. Now, when the prime was consciously perceivable, people used the predictive information of the prime. However, when it was not consciously perceivable, they failed to exploit this predictive arrangement. Conscious awareness, I suggest, has this property: We become able to describe, and thereby use, the psychological events that are private to ourselves.

Are humans the only living organisms having self-awareness? Probably not. The evolutionary process is incremental: New traits and abilities—including the ability of humans to communicate symbolically—build on attributes that already exist. Most forms of communication among animals other than humans—for example, mating displays and alarm calls—are automatic and probably do not involve consciousness. However, other forms of communication can be learned, just as we learn our own language. Certainly, your dog can learn to communicate with you. The fact that it can learn to tell you when it wants to eat, go for a walk, or play suggests that it, too, may be conscious. Obviously, humans' ability to communicate symbolically far surpasses that of any other species; thus, our consciousness is much more highly developed. But the underlying brain mechanisms, such as those of the explicit memory system we examined in Chapter 8, may be present in species closely related to ours (Moscovitch, 1995). And studies looking at the behavior of animals viewing mirror images suggest that some other primates may have a sense of self-awareness (see Boysen and Himes, 1999, for a review).

Could a computer ever be conscious? In principle, I do not see any reason to reject this possibility. I think most people would grant the possibility that alien species from another planetary system could be conscious. Their brains would be different from ours, so the design of our brain is not the only one capable of consciousness. Perhaps, then, the thought of a conscious computer is not far-fetched, either. The computer would have to possess devices that enabled it to perceive events in its environment, think about these events, remember them, and so on. The computer also would have to communicate symbolically with us (or with other computers), describing its perceptions, thoughts, and memories. Furthermore, when we described our own mental events, our words would have to evoke thoughts and perceptions in the computer, just as they do in the brain of a human. In an abstract sense, at least, many of the functions of computers can serve as metaphors for self-awareness. (Pinker, 1997, provides some good examples.)

Evaluating Scientific Issues

Does Conscious Thought Control Behavior?

In the past, psychologists have found fault with using consciousness to explain behavior. Many found it pointless to explain something that we could observe (behavior) in terms of something that we could not (consciousness). But this view has lately been reconsidered, largely because of the techniques of brain study described in earlier chapters. Today psychologists are more willing to address some of the deeper issues that figured in the discipline's early history.

Chapter 1 introduced René Descartes's view of human nature. Descartes believed that human actions were controlled by a nonmaterial mind. Although his dualism is not a productive way of explaining behavior, his idea that our conscious thoughts control our movements seems like common sense. But is it?

William James proposed a contrasting idea. As you will see in Chapter 13, James suggested that our emotional awareness comes after a physiological response. James wrote: "We feel sorry because we cry, angry because we strike, afraid because we tremble" (James, 1890, p. 449). James was speaking of emotion, but his theory provides an alternative way of thinking about consciousness.

● **Evidence for Distinguishing Action from Awareness**
Recent evidence from cognitive psychology and neuropsychology provides a way of thinking about the issue of conscious control of behavior. Some of this evidence uses the phenomenon of visual illusions that was discussed in Chapter 7. For example, consider the two crayons in **Figure 9•1**. Although they are both the same size, the horizontal crayon

FIGURE 9•1 The "top hat illusion" depicted with naturalistic objects. The two crayons are the same lengths; however, the vertically positioned crayon looks longer.

tends to look shorter—a visual illusion known as the "top hat illusion" because it is often demonstrated using judgments about the crown versus the brim of a top hat. Suppose, now, that I ask you to pick up each crayon by grasping the ends. Would you reach for the horizontal crayon with your fingers closer together?

Goodale and his colleagues have evidence that our actions are little affected by such visual illusions. In one experiment, Ganel and Goodale (2003) compared perceptual judgments of object shape with the ability to pick up the object. They simply showed people a wooden block on a table and asked them whether the block was wide or narrow. They then replaced the block with another and again asked for a judgment of width; this trial was repeated several times. It is easy to judge width under these conditions if the blocks all have the same length. But if the blocks vary in length, the task is more difficult. Shape, in other words, is holistic, in the sense meant by the Gestaltists discussed in Chapter 7. However, when Ganel and Goodale asked the participants of their study to grasp the blocks across the middle, their grasping action was not affected by variation in length. In other words, the distance between their fingers was the same for blocks perceived to be of varying widths. Our perceptual awareness of objects—their identity, their features, and so on—may be based on a different visual system than the one we use for actions.

● Does the Thought Cause the Action?

If our perceptual awareness differs from our actions, then what does this say about consciousness and behavior? When you reach for the coffee cup on your desk, is your action controlled by your conscious thoughts of picking it up? Certainly, the thought and the action go together. But remember the lesson from Chapter 2: Correlation does not necessarily imply causation. It could be that the conscious thought and the action are both caused by a third action of the brain (Wegner, 2003).

Some of the brain recording techniques discussed in Chapter 4 may provide insight into this possibility. In a set of experiments performed in 1983, Libet (2002) and his colleagues asked people to make a hand motion while watching a rapidly moving clock hand. They were to report where the clock hand was at the time they became aware of an intention to move. Their reports indicated that they experienced awareness of the intention about three-tenths of a second before the motion. However, Libet also measured the "readiness potential," the electrical brain activity of the motor cortex prior to the movement. This potential occurred about seven-tenths of a second before the motion—even earlier than the conscious intention. The brain seemed to be starting the movement before there was awareness of "willing" the motion.

There is considerable controversy over what these observations mean. Much of the debate concerns how to interpret the readiness potential. Recall that the readiness potential precedes a person's awareness of the intention to act. Does it reflect the brain's "decision" to initiate a movement? Haggard and Eimer (1999) reasoned that if the readiness potential was the cause of movement, then it should show covariation in time with awareness. They asked the participants in their study to move either their left hands or their right hands on a trial, and to report when they were aware of the intention to move. Haggard and Eimer looked at those occasions on which the report of awareness was "late" (that is, closer in time to the actual movement) to see if the readiness potential was also late. It was not. However, they also looked at another brain activity, the "lateralized readiness potential." Remember from Chapter 4 that motor control of the body is contralateral, with the left motor cortex controlling the right side of the body; the lateralized readiness potential measures activity specific to the side where the movement occurs. This potential did covary with the report of awareness. When awareness was late, the lateralized readiness potential also was late; when awareness was early, the potential occurred earlier.

So the lateralized readiness potential may reflect brain activity that leads to awareness about action. But it is specific to the side of the body that moves, which presumably means that it must follow a more general decision to make any movement. It may be only a part of a sequence of brain activity leading up to conscious awareness. To explore this sequence further, Haggard, Clark, and Kalogeras (2002) looked at awareness of both voluntary and involuntary movements. It is possible to induce muscle twitches by delivering magnetic impulses through the surface of the scalp. Haggard and his colleagues used this technique to produce involuntary movements of the hand and compared trials with stimulation to those in which a participant moved a hand voluntarily. As in the Libet experiment, each person watched a clock hand spinning around a dial and reported where the hand was when he or she felt either the intention to move or the involuntary movement produced by stimulation. On some trials, called "operant" trials, a tone came a quarter of a second after a movement and the person was asked to report the time of the tone.

An interesting pattern emerged. On the operant trials, reported times of voluntary movement were late, and reported times of the following tone were early. This was opposite to the involuntary trials, on which the reported time of the movement was early and the reported time of the tone was late. In other words, people's subjective experience of the sequence was that, on voluntary trials, the movement and the tone were close together. On involuntary trials, the perception was that they were farther apart. Our brain, therefore, must "bind together" the experience of voluntary movement with its external consequences. Perhaps this binding process helps us recognize those external events that are the consequences of our behaviors.

● What Can We Conclude?

Perhaps you've noticed that this discussion is somewhat different from others in the Evaluating Scientific Issues boxes. Consciousness is a difficult topic for scientific research, because the underlying behavior is not directly observable. Perhaps we will not be able to answer the question posed in the heading of this feature in any absolute way. But research employing the techniques of neuroscience has certainly advanced our understanding of the way in which brain activity is linked to our verbal reports (Rees, 2001). Such research may help us understand cases in which consciousness departs from our normal experiences—for example, in the case of hallucinations and mental disorders (Rees, Kreiman, & Koch, 2002).

Consciousness and Moral Reasoning

If one person callously and remorselessly killed another, would we be justified in saying that that person was "unconscious of right and wrong"? To answer this question in the framework I've described, we would examine the brain processes that communicate symbolic expressions of right and wrong.

At present, we do not have enough knowledge about the brain to understand how this occurs. But the imaging techniques described in Chapter 4 may help. For example, Anderson and colleagues (1999) studied the case of two individuals who, before they were two years of age, suffered damage to the prefrontal areas of the brain. In **Figure 9·2** you can see magnetic resonance image (MRI) of the brain of one of these individuals, taken when she was 20 years of age. Through a battery of neurological tests, both this woman and the other individual in this study, a male, showed normal intellectual functioning. But when asked to solve social and moral dilemmas or to describe standard norms of moral reasoning, both individuals showed poor factual recall of social and moral knowledge. What is significant about these two case studies is that both individuals had life histories showing poor social and moral adjustment. The woman whose brain is depicted in Figure 9.2, for example, could not retain a job, because she repeatedly violated the rules of her employers. Having engaged in risky sexual behavior as a teenager, she had become pregnant at age 18. She showed no evidence of maternal empathy toward her child and was dangerously insensitive to the infant's well-being. Yet she denied any problem with her own cognition or behavior, and blamed all her difficulties on others. The male member of this study frequently engaged in petty larceny, lied, and threatened and assaulted others. He too seemed completely unresponsive to the contingencies that regulate social conduct.

Note that these individuals do behave purposely—in a sense. They can feed themselves, answer the telephone, make short-term decisions, and so on. Their actions, however, seem not to relate to conventional norms for moral and ethical behavior. Does damage to the frontal lobes mean that symbolic information about right and wrong, and about the consequences of our actions to others, is not available to the parts of the brain that control actions? Perhaps. We just don't know yet (see Dolan, 1999). Later in this chapter we will consider studies of perception in which we can identify the role of consciousness more definitely. But regardless, thinking of consciousness as the result of the brain's activity will undoubtedly help us arrive at a better understanding of this elusive phenomenon.

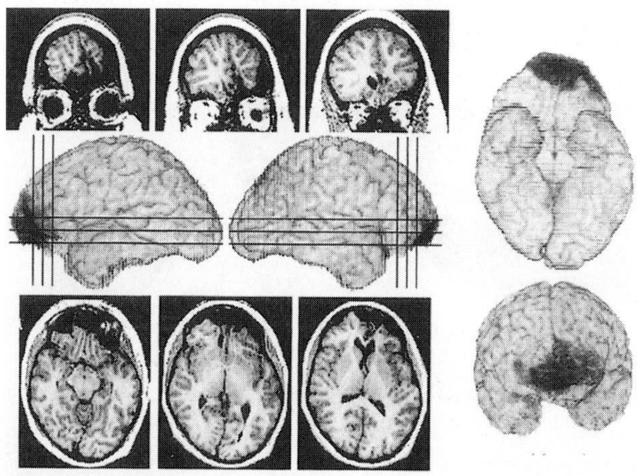

Interim Summary

Consciousness as a Social Phenomenon

Consciousness, as it is defined here, can be viewed as a by-product of our ability to communicate symbolically by using words or other signs. Its physiological basis is the activity of language mechanisms of the brain. The private use of language (thinking to oneself) is clearly conscious. Private nonverbal processes are conscious if we can describe them—that is, if their activities are available to the neural mechanisms of language. In the same way, we are conscious of *external* events only if we can think (and verbalize) about our perceptions of them. These perceptions may be different from the actions we take to interact with the external events. Even our awareness of "voluntary" movements may reflect a byproduct of other brain activities that initiate behavior.

This view of human self-awareness is only one of several, and it may finally be proved wrong. However, it does help present a unified picture of a variety of phenomena related to consciousness. Its primary value is that it relates a private and mysterious phenomenon to a set of behaviors that can be observed and studied.

QUESTIONS TO CONSIDER

1. What do you think about the possibility that members of other species may be conscious? What evidence would you look for to answer this question?
2. If my thesis is correct, babies acquire consciousness as they acquire language. Do you think this conclusion is somehow related to the fact that we cannot remember what happened to us when we were very young?
3. What would happen if a person were raised in isolation and never came in contact with (or communicated with) another person? That person would not be able to talk. What would that person's mental life be like? Would he or she be conscious?
4. We looked at consciousness in an ethical or moral context. Is being conscious of right and wrong different from being conscious of sensory experiences? Is it possible to have different types of consciousness?

FIGURE 9·2 Magnetic resonance images of the brain of a woman who suffered prefrontal damage as an infant. Note the bilateral damage in the frontal lobes.

(From Anderson, S. W. (1999). Impairment of social and moral behavior related to early damage in prefrontal cortex. *Nature Neuroscience, 2*(11), 1032–1037.)

Selective Attention

We do not become conscious of all the stimuli detected by our sensory organs. For example, if an angler is watching a large trout circling underneath an artificial fly she has gently cast on the water, she probably will not notice the chirping of birds in the woods behind her or the temperature of the water surrounding her legs or the floating twigs drifting by with the current. Her attention is completely devoted to the behavior of the fish, and she is poised to respond with the appropriate movements of her fly rod if the fish takes the bait. The process that controls our awareness of particular categories of events in the environment, to the exclusion of others, is called **selective attention.**

But now consider what happens if the fish takes the bait. The angler's task changes drastically to one of **divided attention:** She must monitor the tension on the line, control the rod, and watch her footsteps on the slippery rocks as she maneuvers into position to reel in her catch. Divided attention is the process by which we allocate our attention to two or more tasks in order to perform them simultaneously.

Attention, then, may be the means by which we become conscious of our experiences. Selective attention narrows our awareness to particular experiences, leaving us unaware of other experiences. Divided attention is basically a decision process of the brain that determines how our awareness will be apportioned to different experiences. Attention may be controlled automatically, as when an unexpectedly intense stimulus (such as a loud and novel sound) captures our attention. It may be controlled by instructions ("Pay attention to that one over there!"). Or it may be controlled by the demands of the particular task we are performing; for example, when we are driving a car, we pay special attention to other cars, pedestrians, road signs, and so on. Or we may try to divide our attention, as when we use a cell phone while driving—with possibly adverse consequences. Attention to visual events in particular tends to act like a spotlight, or perhaps a zoom lens, that highlights the events within some spatially contained area (McCormick, Klein, & Johnston, 1998). Our attentional mechanisms serve to enhance our responsiveness to certain stimuli and to tune out irrelevant information. And, as we saw in the case of blindsight, attention may be irrelevant to certain kinds of experiences or behaviors that can proceed without awareness.

Attention plays an important role in memory. By exerting control over the information that reaches short-term memory, it determines what information ultimately becomes stored in explicit long-term memory. But the storage of information in *implicit memory* does not require conscious attention. As a result, not all information is lost when we do not pay attention to it.

Why does attention exist? Why do we not simply process *all* of the information that is being gathered by our sensory receptors? After all, it sometimes happens that we miss something important because our attention is occupied else-where. The answer, according to Broadbent (1958), is that the brain mechanisms responsible for conscious processing of information have a limited capacity. There is only so much information that these mechanisms can handle at one particular moment. Thus, we need some system to serve as a gatekeeper, controlling the flow of information to this system. Broadbent suggested that the processes of attention solve this problem by *filtering* information—allowing information of one type (such as the visual information in my fishing example) to be processed while screening out anything else (such as the bird songs in that example). However, the nature of this gatekeeper—selective attention—is still the subject of ongoing research.

Auditory Information

The first experiments that investigated the nature of attention took advantage of the fact that we have two ears. Cherry (1953) devised a test of selective attention called **dichotic listening,** a task that requires a person to listen to one of two messages presented simultaneously, one to each ear. (*Dichotic* means "divided into two parts.") He placed headphones on his participants and presented recordings of different spoken messages to each ear. He asked the participants to **shadow** the message presented to one ear—to continuously repeat back what that voice was saying. Shadowing ensured that they would pay attention to only that message.

What happened to the information that entered the unattended ear? In general, it appeared to be lost. When questioned about what that ear had heard, participants responded that they had heard something, but they could not say what it was. Even if the voice presented to the unshadowed ear began to talk in a foreign language, they did not notice the change.

These results suggest that a channel of sensory input (in this case, one ear) can simply be turned off. Perhaps neurons in the auditory system that detect sound from the unattended ear are inhibited so that they cannot respond to sounds presented to that ear. (See **Figure 9•3(a).**)

▲ *This stock exchange broker must keep track of several different conversations and selectively attend to each of them, one after the other.*

FIGURE 9•3 Models of selective attention in the dichotic listening task. (a) Filtering of unattended sensory information immediately after it is received by the sensory receptors. This model cannot explain the fact that some information presented to the unattended ear enters consciousness. (b) Filtering of unattended sensory information after some preliminary analysis.

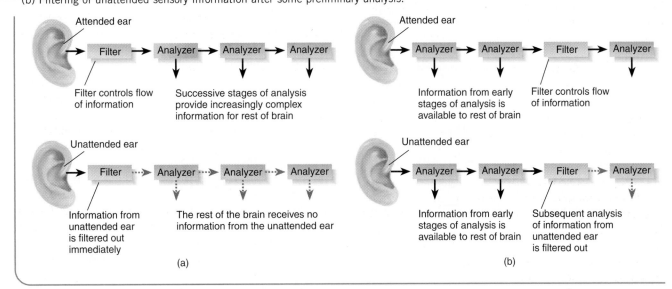

(a)   (b)

The story is not so simple, however. Other evidence shows that achieving selective attention is not simply a matter of closing a sensory channel. Some information, by its very nature, can break through into consciousness. For example, if a person's name is presented to the unattended ear, he or she will very likely hear it and remember it later (Moray, 1959). Or if the message presented to the unattended ear contains sexually explicit words, people tend to notice them immediately (Nielsen & Sarason, 1981). The fact that some kinds of information presented to the unattended ear can grab our attention indicates that even unattended information undergoes some verbal analysis. If the unattended information is "filtered out" at some level, this filtration must not occur until *after* the sounds are identified as words. (See **Figure 9•3(b)**.)

McKay (1973) showed that information presented to the unattended ear can influence verbal processing even when the listener is not conscious of this information. In the attended ear, participants heard sentences such as the following:

> They threw stones toward the bank yesterday.

While this sentence was being presented, the participants heard the word *river* or *money* in the unattended ear. Later, they were asked which of the following sentences they had heard:

> They threw stones toward the side of the river yesterday.

> They threw stones toward the savings and loan association yesterday.

Of course, the participants had heard neither of these sentences. But as Sachs (1967) showed (Chapter 8), people quickly forget the particular words a sentence contains, although they do remember the sentence's meaning for much longer. McKay found that the participants' choices were determined by whether the word *river* or *money* was presented to the unattended ear. They did not specifically recall hearing the words presented to the unattended ear, but obviously these words had affected their perception of the meaning of the word *bank*.

Besides being able to notice and remember some characteristics of information received by the unattended sensory channel, we are able to store information temporarily as it comes in. No doubt you have had the following sort of experience. You are intently reading or thinking about something, when you become aware that someone has asked you a question. You look up and say, "What?" but then answer the question before the other person has had a chance to repeat it. You first became aware that you had just been asked a question, but you did not know what had been asked. However, when you thought for a moment, you remembered what the question was—you heard it again in your mind's ear, so to speak. The information, held in temporary storage, was made accessible to your verbal system.

Treisman (1960) showed that people can follow a message that is being shadowed even if it switches from one ear to the other. Suppose a research participant is shadowing a message presented to the left ear, while the message to the right ear is unshadowed. (See **Figure 9•4**.) In the example given in Figure 9.4, the person will probably say "crept out of the swamp" and not "crept out of flowers." Apparently, the switch occurs when the message begins to make no sense. However, by the time the participant realizes that "crept out of flowers" makes no sense, the rest of the message, "the swamp," has already been presented to the right ear. Because the participant is able to continue the message without missing any words, he or she must be able to retrieve some words

FIGURE 9•4 Shadowing a message that switches ears. When the message switches, the person must retrieve from memory some words that were heard by the unattended ear.

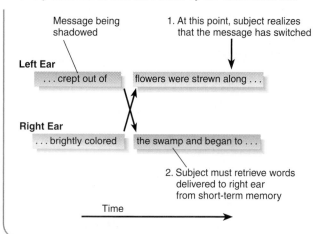

Message being shadowed

1. At this point, subject realizes that the message has switched

Left Ear

. . . crept out of   flowers were strewn along . . .

Right Ear

. . . brightly colored   the swamp and began to . . .

2. Subject must retrieve words delivered to right ear from short-term memory

Time

from memory. Thus, even though an unshadowed message cannot be remembered later, it produces some trace that can be retrieved if attention is directed to it soon after the words are presented. In other words, the "gatekeeping" role of selective attention is not that of an absolute filter; rather, nonattended sensory information is only reduced and can still be used under the right conditions.

Selective attention to auditory messages has practical significance outside the laboratory. For example, sometimes we have to sort out one message from several others without the benefit of such a distinct cue; we seldom hear one voice in one ear and another voice in the other. We may be trying to converse with one person while we are in a room with several other people who are carrying on their own conversations. Even in the situation shown in **Figure 9•5**, we can usually sort out one voice from another—an example of the **cocktail-party phenomenon**. In this case we are trying to listen to the person opposite us and to ignore the cross-conversation of the people

FIGURE 9•5 The cocktail-party phenomenon. We can follow a particular conversation even when other conversations are going on around us.
(Photo © Royalty-Free/CORBIS)

to our left and right. Our ears receive a jumble of sounds, but we are able to pick out the ones we want, stringing them together into a meaningful message and ignoring the rest. This task takes some effort, and following one person's conversation in such circumstances is even more difficult when what he or she is saying is not very interesting. If we overhear a few words of another conversation that seems more interesting, it is hard to strain out the cross-conversation.

Visual Information

Since the pioneering work on dichotic listening, experiments have studied the nature of visual attention. These experiments have shown that we can successfully attend either to the *location* of the information or to the *nature* of the information (revealed by its physical features, such as form or color).

Location Sperling's studies on sensory memory (see Chapter 8) were probably the first to demonstrate the role of attention in selectively transferring visual information into verbal short-term memory (or, for our purposes, into consciousness). Other psychologists have studied this phenomenon in more detail. For example, Posner, Snyder, and Davidson (1980) had people watch a computer-controlled video display screen. A small mark in the center of the screen served as a fixation point for the participants' gaze. The participants were shown a warning stimulus near the fixation point followed by a target stimulus—a letter displayed to the left or the right of the fixation point. The warning stimulus consisted of either an arrow pointing right or left or simply a plus sign. The arrows served as cues to the participants to expect the letter to occur either to the right or to the left. The plus sign served as a neutral stimulus, containing no spatial information. The participants' task was to press a button as soon as they detected the letter.

Eighty percent of the time, the arrow accurately pointed toward the location in which the letter would be presented. However, 20 percent of the time, the arrow pointed *away from* the location in which it would occur. The advance warning clearly had an effect on the participants' response times: When they were correctly informed of the location of the letter, they responded faster; and when they were incorrectly informed, they responded more slowly. (See **Figure 9•6**.)

This study shows that selective attention can affect the detection of visual stimuli: If a stimulus occurs where we expect it, we perceive it more quickly; if it occurs where we do *not* expect it, we perceive it more slowly. Thus, people can follow instructions to direct their attention to particular locations in the visual field. Because the participants' gaze remained fixed on the center of the screen in this study, this movement of attention was independent of eye movement. How does this focusing of attention work neurologically? The most likely explanation seems to be that neural circuits that detect a particular kind of stimulus are somehow sensitized so that they can more easily detect that stimulus. In this case the mechanism of selective attention sensitized the neural circuits that detect visual stimuli in a particular region.

FIGURE 9•6 Location as a cue for selective attention. Mean reaction time in response to a letter displayed on a screen after participants received a cue directing attention toward the location in which the letter appears was less than when no cue or an incorrect cue was received.

(Based on data from Posner, Snyder, and Davidson (1980).)

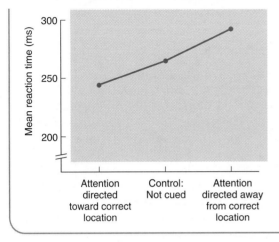

FIGURE 9•7 Schematic diagram of O'Donnell and Pratt's experiment. Each display was presented for the period of time noted on the right.

(Adapted from O'Donnell and Pratt (1996). From " Inhibition of return along the path of attention." *Canadian Journal of Experimental Psychology, 50,* 386–392. Copyright 1996. Canadian Psychological Association. Reprinted with permission.)

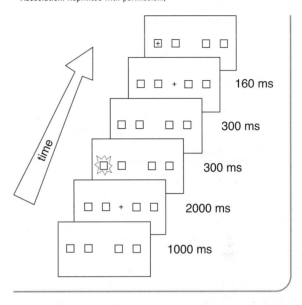

A possible clue to the way these attentional circuits work comes from an interesting extension of the task used by Posner and his colleagues. Suppose the arrow is completely nonpredictive (that is, it sometimes points to where the letter will be presented and sometimes does not). When the letter is presented right after the arrow, people are usually faster at identifying the letter when it appears where the arrow indicated. This seems similar to the attentional effect we've been discussing: Even though the arrow is sometimes correct and sometimes wrong, the attentional spotlight is directed by the arrow. However, if the interval between the presentation of the cue and the letter is a little longer (about 100 to 300 milliseconds), then recognition is slower when the letter appears at the location of the cue. Posner and his colleagues have called this phenomenon **inhibition of return**. Speaking loosely, the attentional spotlight sweeps momentarily over to the location of the cue, swings back, and is then inhibited from returning immediately to the same spot. It's as if, having shifted to the location of the cue, the attentional system is now slower to return to it.

"Sweep" is perhaps a good way to describe how attention is directed, based on the results of an experiment by O'Donnell and Pratt (1996). Their experiment, a variation on the inhibition-of-return procedure, is depicted in **Figure 9•7**. Individuals in this experiment sat in front of a video screen. Four gray boxes would appear on the screen and, 1000 milliseconds later, a small cross would appear in the center. The participants in this study were asked to fixate on this cross. Then, after 2000 milliseconds, the cross disappeared and one of the boxes changed to white for 300 milliseconds (the cue). After a brief delay of 300 milliseconds, the fixation cross then appeared in the center again and, 160

milliseconds later, it was turned on in one of the boxes. The target cross could be in any of the boxes, regardless of which one had been lit up as the cue. Participants were asked to press a key when they saw the cross appear in a box.

O'Donnell and Pratt found that when the cross appeared on the same side as the cue, recognition was slower than when the cross appeared on the other side. That is, the noninformative cue nevertheless caused an attentional process to be momentarily shifted to the side that the cue was on; this shift biased people against seeing the target on that side. A more detailed analysis, though, showed that inhibition of return occurred to the two inside boxes when the outside boxes were cues, but not the other way around. That is, when the outside boxes were cues, attention swept out, inhibiting return to any location along the path of the sweep. When the sweep was only to the inside box, the outside box was not along the path of the sweep and was not subsequently affected. Inhibition seemed to follow the spatial extent of the path.

The mechanisms that produce inhibition of return are still disputed. Although I have discussed it in terms of a general attentional process, it may be closely linked to motor circuits in the visual system. For example, although we can attend well to color features, color change alone does not seem to produce an effect like inhibition of return (Taylor & Klein, 1998).

Features The second dimension of visual attention is the nature of the object being attended to (Desimone & Duncan, 1995; Vecera & Farah, 1994). Sometimes, two events happen in close proximity, but we can watch one of them while ignoring the other. For example, Neisser and Becklen (1975) showed people a videotape that presented a situation similar to that confronted by a person trying to listen to the voice of one person at a cocktail party. The videotape contained two different actions presented one on top of the other: a basketball game and a hand game, in which people try to slap their opponents' hands, which are resting on top of theirs. The participants could easily follow one scene and remember what had happened in it; however, they could not attend simultaneously to both scenes. (See **Figure 9•8**.)

What happens to information that is not attended to? In the auditory system, information that is surprising, such as someone calling our name, can override attention to something else. Similarly, our name seems to jump out if it appears in print, even if it appears in text that we ignore (Neisser, 1969). Can surprising visual experiences likewise draw our attention?

Recent evidence suggests that the visual system is prone to surprising cases of **inattentional blindness,** a failure to perceive an event when attention is diverted elsewhere. We've probably all had the experience of going to something like, say, a basketball game, and being so engrossed in the action that we "looked right through" and failed to notice a good friend across the aisle. But suppose you were watching a basketball game and a woman in a gorilla suit walked right through the action, stopping in the middle to pound her chest? (See **Figure 9•9**.) You probably feel you would definitely notice that, right? Remarkably, half of the people who observed this action in a film sequence designed by Simons and Chabris (1999) failed to notice the gorilla. This was despite the fact that the unusual event was in the center of the action. Interestingly, the unusual nature of the event seemed to make it more likely to be missed: When a game was interrupted by a woman carrying an umbrella, more people noticed her.

Simons (2000) makes the general point that although our visual experience is rich with information, our ability to represent it in memory may be limited. We saw such limitations in the case of memory in Chapter 8. Perhaps when we focus our attention on a part of the external world, our consciousness relies on the stability of the rest of it. After all, people don't spontaneously change hair color or the clothes they're wearing just because we look away.

Would we notice it if they did? Surprisingly, the answer seems to be no under some circumstances. If visual displays are artificially changed during an eye movement or other disruption, **change blindness** often results: People often fail to notice significant changes in the picture (O'Regan, Rensink, & Clark, 1999). And in one very unusual study, people who were talking to a construction worker failed to notice when the person himself changed during a brief distraction (Simons & Levin, 1998).

Brain Mechanisms of Selective Attention

One possible explanation for selective attention is that some components of the brain's sensory system are temporarily

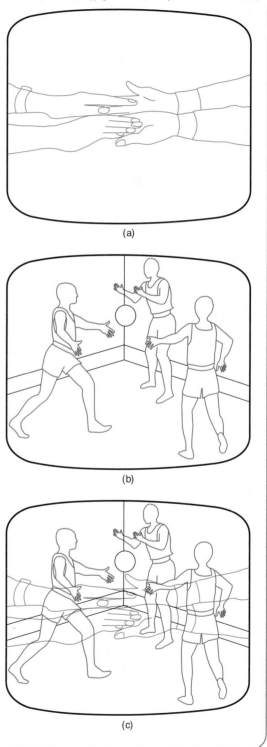

FIGURE 9•8 Drawings of the scenes from the videotapes in Neisser and Becklen's study. (a) The hand game. (b) The basketball game. (c) The two games superimposed.

(Reprinted from Neisser, U., & Becklen, R. (1975). *Cognitive Psychology, 1975, 7,* 480–494, copyright © 1975, with permission from Elsevier.)

(a)

(b)

(c)

FIGURE 9•9 A frame from the film constructed by Simons and Chabris for their study of inattentional blindness. Observers were asked to watch a basketball game being played by two teams and to count the passes between members of each team. As they watched, a woman wearing a gorilla suit walked in from the right, paused in the middle of the game facing the camera, and then walked out to the left. Half of the observers failed to notice this unusual event. To learn more about the "gorilla" study or to view the original video, go to www.viscog.net

(From Simons, Daniel. J., & Chabris, Christopher. F. (1999). Gorillas in our midst: Sustained inattentional blindness for dynamic events. *Perception, 28,* 1059–1074, Figure 3. Reprinted with permission from Pion Limited, London. Figure provided by Daniel Simons.)

sensitized, which enhances their ability to detect particular categories of stimuli. For example, if a person were watching for changes in shapes, colors, or movements (that is, if the person's attention were focused on one of these attributes), we might expect to see increased activity in the portions of the visual cortex devoted to the analysis of shapes, colors, or movements.

This result is exactly what Corbetta and colleagues (1991) found. These investigators had people look at a computerized display containing 30 colored rectangles, which could change in shape, color, or speed of movement. The participants were asked to say whether they detected a change. On some trials they were told to pay attention to only one attribute: shape, color, or speed of movement. The stimuli were counterbalanced so that the same set of displays was presented during each condition. Thus, the only difference between the conditions was the type of stimulus change the participants were watching for.

The investigators used a PET scanner to measure brain activity while these people were watching the display. They found that paying attention to shape, color, or speed of movement caused activation of different regions of the visual association cortex. The locations corresponded almost precisely to the regions other studies have shown to be activated by shapes, colors, or movements. Thus, selective attention toward different attributes of visual stimuli is accompanied by activation of the appropriate regions of the visual association cortex

Luck, Chelazzi, Hillyard, and Desimone (1993) obtained similar results in a study using monkeys. They recorded the activity of single neurons in the visual association cortex. When a cue indicated that the monkey should be watching for a stimulus to be presented in a particular location, neurons that received input from the appropriate part of the visual field began firing more rapidly, even before the stimulus was presented. These neurons seemed to be "primed" for detecting a stimulus in their part of the visual field.

Interim Summary

Selective Attention

As we saw in the first section of this chapter, consciousness can be analyzed as a social phenomenon derived through evolution of the brain mechanisms responsible for our ability to communicate with one another (and, in addition, with ourselves). However, because our verbal mechanisms can contain only a limited amount of information at one time, we cannot be conscious of all the events that take place in our environment. The process of selective attention determines which stimuli will be noticed and which will be ignored. The factors that control our attention include novelty, verbal instructions, and our own assessment of the significance of what we are perceiving. Dichotic listening experiments show that what is received by the unattended ear is lost within a few seconds unless something causes us to take heed of it; after those few seconds we cannot say what that ear heard. Studies using visually presented information indicate that attention can focus on location or on shape: We can pay attention to particular objects or to stimuli that occur in a particular place. Possibly because visual stimulation is so complex, distractions can produce inattentional blindness to certain kinds of visual experiences. A PET study found that when people pay attention to particular characteristics of visual stimuli, the activity of particular regions of the brain is enhanced.

QUESTIONS TO CONSIDER

1. Have you ever had an experience in which someone asked you a question that you weren't paying attention to, and then, before the question could be repeated, you realized what it was? How long do you think the unattended information lasts before it is eventually lost? Can you think of an experiment that would permit you to find out?

2. Let's reconsider the cocktail-party phenomenon. Suppose that someone is carrying on a conversation and then happens to overhear a word or two from another conversation that seems much more interesting. Wanting

to be polite, the person tries to ignore the other conversation but finds it difficult. Should we regard this example as a failure of the person's attentional mechanism? Or is it actually useful that we usually don't become so absorbed in one thing that we miss out on potentially interesting information?

3. Why do we feel that paying attention to something not very interesting takes some effort—that it requires work? And if we concentrate on something for a long time, we feel tired. Where does this tiredness take place? Do some circuits of neurons become "weary"? Why, then, do we not become tired when we are concentrating just as hard on something that interests us?

Consciousness and the Brain

As we have already seen, brain damage can alter human consciousness. For example, Chapter 8 described the phenomenon of anterograde amnesia, caused by brain damage—particularly to the hippocampus. Although people with this defect cannot form new verbal memories, they can learn some kinds of tasks. However, they remain unaware that they have learned something, even when their behavior indicates that they have. The brain damage does not prevent all kinds of learning, but it does prevent conscious awareness of what has been learned.

If human consciousness is related to speech, then it is probably related to the brain mechanisms that control comprehension and production of speech. This hypothesis suggests that for us to be aware of a piece of information, the information must be transmitted to neural circuits in the brain responsible for our communicative behavior. Several reports of cases of human brain damage support this suggestion. Let's consider some examples.

Isolation Aphasia: A Case of Global Unawareness

Geschwind, Quadfasel, and Segarra (1968) described the case of a woman who had suffered severe brain damage from inhaling carbon monoxide from a faulty water heater. The damage spared the primary auditory cortex, the speech areas of the brain, and the connections between these areas. However, the damage destroyed large parts of the visual association cortex and isolated the speech mechanisms from other parts of the brain. In fact, the syndrome that Geschwind and colleagues reported is referred to as *isolation aphasia,* a language disturbance in which a person is unable to comprehend speech or to produce meaningful speech but is able to repeat speech and to learn new sequences of words. Thus, al-

though the woman's speech mechanisms could receive auditory input and could control the muscles used for speech, they received no information from the other senses or from the neural circuits that contain memories concerning past experiences and the meanings of words.

The woman remained in the hospital for nine years, until she died. During this time she made few movements except with her eyes, which were able to follow moving objects. She gave no evidence of recognizing objects or people in her environment. She did not spontaneously say anything, answer questions, or give any signs that she understood what other people said to her. By all available criteria, she was not conscious of anything that was going on. However, the woman could *repeat* words that were spoken to her. And if someone started a poem she knew, she would finish it. For example, if someone said, "Roses are red, violets are blue," she would respond, "Sugar is sweet, and so are you." She even learned new poems and songs and would sing along with the radio. Her case suggests that consciousness is not simply activity of the brain's speech mechanisms; it is activity prompted by information received from other parts of the brain concerning memories or events currently occurring in the environment.

Visual Agnosia: Lack of Awareness of Visual Perceptions

The case I just described was of a woman who appeared to have completely lost her awareness of herself and her environment. In other instances people have become unaware of particular kinds of information. For example, some people with a particular kind of blindness caused by brain damage can point to objects they cannot see—or rather, that they are not aware of seeing. Two colleagues and I studied a young man with a different kind of disconnection between perception and awareness. His brain had been damaged by an inflammation of the blood vessels, and he consequently suffered from *visual agnosia* (Chapter 7)—the inability to recognize the identity of an object visually (Margolin, Friedrich, & Carlson, 1985). The man had great difficulty identifying common objects by sight. For example, he could not say what a hammer was by looking at it, but he quickly identified it when he was permitted to pick it up and feel it. He was not blind; he could walk around without bumping into things, and he had no trouble making visually guided movements to pick up an object that he wanted to identify. The simplest conclusion was that his disease had damaged the neural circuits responsible for visual perception.

However, the simplest was not the correct conclusion. Although the patient had great difficulty visually recognizing objects or pictures of objects, he often made hand movements that appeared to be related to the object he could not identify. For example, when we showed him a picture of a pistol, he stared at it with a puzzled look, then shook his head and said that he couldn't tell what it was. While continuing to study the picture, he clenched his right hand into a fist and began making movements with his index finger. When we asked him what he was doing, he looked at his hand, made a few tentative movements with his finger, then raised his hand in the air and moved it forward each time he moved his finger. He was unmistakably miming the way a person holds and fires a pistol. "Oh!" he said. "It's a gun. No, a pistol." Clearly, he was not aware of what the picture was until he paid attention to what his hand was doing. On another occasion he looked at a picture of a belt and said it was a pair of pants. We asked him to show us where the legs and other parts of the pants were. When he tried to do so, he became puzzled. His hands went to the place where his belt buckle would be (he was wearing hospital pajamas) and moved as if he were feeling one. "No," he said. "It's not a pair of pants—it's a belt!" The process might involve steps such as those shown in **Figure 9•10**.

The patient's visual system was not normal, yet it functioned better than we could infer from only his verbal behavior. That is, his perceptions were much more accurate than his words indicated. The fact that he could mime the use of a pistol or feel an imaginary belt buckle with his hands indicated that his visual system worked well enough to initiate appropriate nonverbal behaviors, though not the appropriate words. Once he felt what he was doing, he could name the object.

Although the patient had lost his ability to read, speech therapists were able to teach him to use finger spelling to read. He could not say what a particular letter was, but he could learn to make a particular hand movement when he saw it. After he had learned the finger-spelling alphabet used by deaf people, he could read slowly and laboriously by making hand movements for each letter and feeling the words that his hand was spelling out.

This case supports the conclusion that consciousness is synonymous with a person's ability to talk about his or her perceptions or memories. In this particular situation, disruption of the normal interchange between the visual perceptual system and the verbal system prevented the patient from being directly aware of his own visual perceptions. Instead, it was as if his hands talked to him, telling him what he had just seen.

The Split-Brain Syndrome

One surgical procedure demonstrates dramatically how various brain functions can be disconnected from one another and from verbal mechanisms. It is used for people who have severe epilepsy that cannot be controlled by drugs. In these people, violent storms of neural activity begin in one hemisphere and are transmitted to the other by the corpus callosum, the large bundle of axons that connects corresponding parts of the cortex on one side of the brain with those on the other. Both sides of the brain then engage in wild neural firing and stimulate each other, causing an epileptic seizure. These seizures can occur many times each day, preventing the patient from leading a normal life. Neurosurgeons discovered that the **split-brain operation**—cutting the corpus callosum to disconnect the two cerebral hemispheres—greatly reduces the frequency of the epileptic seizures.

Sperry (1966) and Gazzaniga and his associates (Gazzaniga, 1970; Gazzaniga & LeDoux, 1978) studied split-brain patients extensively. Normally, the cerebral cortexes of the left and right hemispheres exchange information through the corpus callosum. With one exception (described later), each hemisphere receives sensory information from the opposite side of the body and controls muscle movements on that side. The corpus callosum permits these activities to be coordinated, so that each hemisphere knows what is going on in the other hemisphere. After the two hemispheres are disconnected, they operate independently; their sensory mechanisms, memories, and motor systems can no longer exchange information. The effects of these disconnections are not obvious to a casual observer, for the simple reason that only one hemisphere—in most people, the left—controls speech. The right hemisphere of an epileptic person with a split brain can understand speech reasonably well, but it is poor at reading and spelling. And because Broca's speech area is located in the left hemisphere, the right hemisphere is totally incapable of producing speech.

Because only one side of the brain can talk about what it is experiencing, a casual observer will not detect the independent operations of the right side of a split brain. Even the patient's left brain has to learn about the independent existence of the right brain. One of the first things that these patients say they notice after the operation is that their left hand seems to have a mind of its own. For example, patients may find themselves putting down a book held in the left hand, even if they are reading it with great interest. At other times, they surprise themselves by making obscene gestures with the left hand. Because the right hemisphere controls the movements of the left hand, these unexpected movements puzzle the left hemisphere, the side of the brain that controls speech.

An exception to the crossed representation of sensory information noted earlier is the olfactory system. When a person sniffs a flower through the left nostril, only the left brain receives a sensation of the odor. Thus, if the right nostril of a patient with a split brain is closed and the left nostril is open, the patient will accurately identify odors verbally. Conversely, if the odor enters the right nostril, the patient will say that he or she smells nothing. But, in fact, the right brain has perceived the odor and can identify it. This ability is demonstrated by an experiment in which the patient is told to reach for some objects hidden from view by a partition. If asked to use the left hand, with the left nostril closed, he or she will select the object that corresponds to the odor— a plastic flower for a floral odor, a toy fish for a fishy odor, a model tree for the odor of pine, and so forth. But if the left nostril is closed, the right hand fails this test, because it is connected to the left hemisphere, which did not smell the odor. (See **Figure 9•11**.)

As we saw in Chapter 4, the left hemisphere, besides giving us the ability to read, write, and speak, is good at other tasks that require verbal abilities, such as mathematics and

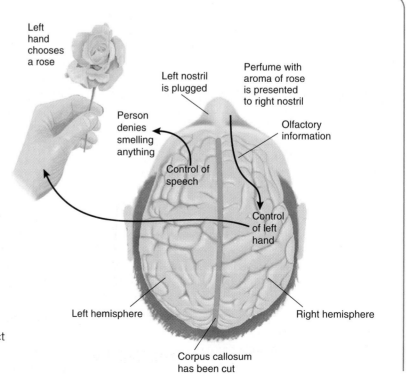

Left hand chooses a rose

Left nostril is plugged

Perfume with aroma of rose is presented to right nostril

Person denies smelling anything

Olfactory information

Control of speech

Control of left hand

Left hemisphere

Right hemisphere

Corpus callosum has been cut

FIGURE 9•11 Identification of an object by a person with a split brain in response to an olfactory stimulus.

logic. The right hemisphere excels at tasks of perception and has a much greater artistic ability. If a patient with a split brain tries to use his or her right hand to arrange blocks to duplicate a geometrical design provided by the researcher, the hand will hopelessly fumble around with the blocks. Often, the left hand (controlled by the right hemisphere) will brush the right hand aside and easily complete the task. It is as if the right hemisphere becomes impatient with the clumsy ineptitude of the hand controlled by the left hemisphere.

The effects of cutting the corpus callosum reinforce the conclusion that consciousness depends on the ability of speech mechanisms in the left hemisphere to receive information from other regions of the brain. If such communication is interrupted, then some kinds of information can never reach consciousness.

Interim Summary

Consciousness and the Brain

The suggestion that consciousness is a function of our ability to communicate with one another receives support from some cases of human brain damage. As we saw, people with certain kinds of damage can point to objects they say they cannot see; people with isolation aphasia can perceive speech and talk without apparent awareness; and a patient with a particular form of visual agnosia can make appropriate hand movements when looking at objects that cannot be consciously recognized. Thus, brain damage can disrupt a person's awareness of perceptual mechanisms without disrupting other functions performed by these mechanisms. And although a person whose corpus callosum has been severed can make perceptual judgments with the right hemisphere, he or she cannot talk about them and appears to be unaware of them.

QUESTIONS TO CONSIDER

1. Some people with split brains have reported that they can use only one hand to hold a book while reading. If they use the other hand, they find themselves putting the book down even though they want to continue reading. Which hand puts the book down? Why does it do so?
2. When a stimulus is presented to the right hemisphere of a person with a split brain, the person (speaking with his or her left hemisphere) claims to be unaware of it. Thus, the left hemisphere is unaware of stimuli perceived only by the right hemisphere. Because the right hemisphere cannot talk to us, should we conclude that it lacks conscious self-awareness? If you think it is conscious, has the surgery produced two independent consciousnesses where only one previously existed?

Hypnosis

Hypnosis is a specific and unusual form of verbal control that apparently enables one person to control some of another person's behavior, thoughts, and perceptions. Under hypnosis a person can be induced to bark like a dog, act like a baby, or tolerate being pierced with needles. Although these examples are interesting and amusing, hypnosis is important to psychology because it provides insights into the nature of consciousness; it also has applications in the fields of medicine and psychotherapy (Laurence & Perry, 1988).

Although hypnosis may have been used by religious cults in the times of classical Greece (Spanos & Chaves, 1991), the modern phenomenon of hypnosis, or *mesmerism,* was discovered by Franz Anton Mesmer (1734–1815), an Austrian physician. He found that when he passed magnets back and forth over people's bodies (in an attempt to restore their "magnetic fluxes" and cure them of disease), they often would have convulsions and would enter a trancelike state during which almost miraculous cures could be achieved. As Mesmer discovered later, the patients were not affected directly by the magnetism of the iron rods; they were responding to his undoubtedly persuasive and compelling personality. We now know that convulsions and trancelike states do not necessarily accompany hypnosis, and we also know that hypnosis does not cure physical illnesses. Mesmer's patients apparently had psychologically produced symptoms that were alleviated by suggestions made while they were hypnotized.

Characteristics of Hypnosis

A person undergoing hypnosis can be alert, relaxed, tense, lying quietly, or exercising vigorously. There is no need to move an object in front of someone's face or to say "You are getting sleepy"; an enormous variety of techniques can be used to induce hypnosis in a susceptible person. The only essential feature seems to be the participant's understanding that he or she is to be hypnotized.

Hypnotized people are very suggestible; their behavior will conform to what the hypnotist suggests, even to the extent that they may appear to misperceive reality. Generally, hypnotic suggestions are one of three types (Kirsch & Lynn, 1998):

- *Ideomotor* suggestions are those in which the hypnotist suggests that a particular action will occur without awareness of voluntary action, such as raising an arm.
- *Challenge* suggestions are suggestions that the hypnotized individual will be unable to perform a normally voluntary action.
- *Cognitive* suggestions are suggestions that the hypnotized person is undergoing distortions of sensory or cognitive experiences, such as not feeling pain or not being able to remember something.

FIGURE 9•12 The Ponzo illusion and hypnotic blindness. The short horizontal lines are actually the same length. Even when a hypnotic suggestion made the slanted lines disappear, the visual system still perceived the illusion.

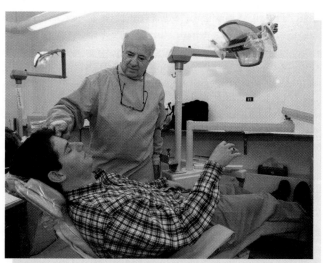

▲ *Is a hypnotized person really under the control of the hypnotist, or is the person simply acting out a social role?*

One of the most dramatic phenomena of hypnosis is **posthypnotic suggestibility,** in which a person is given instructions under hypnosis and follows those instructions after returning to a non-hypnotized state. For example, a hypnotist might tell a man that he will become unbearably thirsty when he sees the hypnotist look at her watch. She might also admonish him not to remember anything upon leaving the hypnotic state, so that **posthypnotic amnesia** is also achieved. After leaving the hypnotic state, the man acts normally and professes ignorance of what he perceived and did during hypnosis, perhaps even apologizing for not having succumbed to hypnosis. The hypnotist later looks at her watch, and the man suddenly leaves the room to get a drink of water.

Studies indicate that when changes in perception are induced through cognitive suggestions, the changes occur not in the people's actual perceptions but in their verbal reports about their perceptions. For example, Miller, Hennessy, and Leibowitz (1973) used the *Ponzo illusion* to test the effects of hypnotically induced blindness. Although the two parallel horizontal lines in the left portion of **Figure 9•12** are the same length, the top one looks longer than the bottom one. This effect is produced by the presence of the slanted lines to the left and right of the horizontal ones; if these lines are not present, the horizontal lines appear to be the same length. Through hypnotic suggestion, the researchers made the slanted lines "disappear." But even though the participants reported that they could not see the slanted lines, they still perceived the upper line as longer than the lower one. This result indicates that the visual system continues to process sensory information during hypnotically induced blindness; otherwise, the participants would have perceived the lines as equal in length. The reported blindness appears to occur not because of altered activity in the visual system but because of altered activity in the verbal system (and in consciousness).

Theories of Hypnosis

Hypnosis has been called a special case of learning, a transference of the superego, a goal-directed behavior shaped by the hypnotist, a role-playing situation, and a restructuring of perceptual–cognitive functioning. In other words, no one yet knows exactly what it is. Hypnosis has been described as a state of enhanced suggestibility, but that is simply a description, not an explanation. Several investigators have advanced theories of hypnosis. We will look at two general views.

The Sociocognitive Approach All of the behavioral and perceptual phenomena discussed so far in this book have obvious survival value for the organism; that is, functional analysis of any given behavioral phenomenon usually points to a plausible reason for the occurrence of the behavior. Therefore, if hypnotic phenomena occurred only when a person was hypnotized, it would be difficult to understand why the brain happened to evolve in such a way that it is susceptible to hypnosis. Does it seem plausible that this susceptibility first manifested itself in the eighteenth century when Mesmer discovered the phenomenon of hypnosis?

The answer is no, according to Spanos (1991) and others. The *sociocognitive view* of hypnosis developed by these theorists proposes that at least some aspects of hypnosis are related to events that can happen every day. Spanos argues that hypnosis should not be viewed as a special state of consciousness, in the way that sleep is a state of consciousness that differs from waking. Rather, "hypnotic behaviors" are social actions that reflect what the hypnotized individual believes to be characteristic of a hypnotized trance. The hypnotized person willingly adopts a role and enacts that role according to rules as he or she understands them. Some of the rules governing this role are supplied by the direct instructions of the hypnotist, others are indirectly implied by what the hypnotist says and does, and still others consist of expectations that the person already has about what hypnotized people do.

People's expectations about hypnosis do indeed play an important role in their behavior while under hypnosis. In lectures to two sections of an introductory psychology class,

Orne (1959) told one section (falsely) that one of the most prominent features of hypnosis was rigidity of the preferred (that is, dominant) hand. Later, he arranged a demonstration of hypnosis during a meeting of students from both sections. Several of the students who had heard that the dominant hand became rigid showed this phenomenon when hypnotized, but none of the students who had not heard this myth developed a rigid hand. Similarly, if people become willing to follow a hypnotist's suggestions, perhaps they do so because they believe that this suggested behavior is what is supposed to happen. Perhaps people willingly follow a hypnotist's suggestion to do something silly (such as bark like a dog) because they know that hypnotized people are not responsible for their behavior.

If hypnosis can be described as role playing, then why are so many people willing to play this role? Barber (1975) submits that the suspension of self-control that occurs during hypnosis is very similar to our "participation" in the story of a movie or a book. When we go to a movie or read a novel or even listen to a friend recounting an experience, we generally do so with the intent of being swept up in the story. We willingly let the filmmaker or storyteller lead us through a fantasy. When we hear a story or read a book, we even imagine the scenes and the events that occur in them. We feel happy when good things happen to characters that we identify with and like, and we feel sad when bad things happen to them. Certainly, we express a full range of emotions while watching a good movie or reading a good book. In fact, one of the criteria we use to judge a movie or book is whether it causes us to enter this fantasy world; if it does not, we regard the work as unsatisfactory. Perhaps these imagined events are similar to the hallucinations experienced during hypnosis.

The Dissociation Approach Other psychologists have adopted an approach to hypnosis based on the distinction between a psychological process and our *awareness* of that process. We have examined the distinction between explicit and implicit memory and have considered extraordinary cases, like visual agnosia, in which perception may occur without explicit awareness. *Dissociation theories* of hypnosis use this distinction. Basically, a hypnotized individual is assumed to be unaware of events and experiences that he or she would ordinarily be conscious of. Hypnotic induction is presumed to separate or isolate some psychological processes from conscious perception or control.

One version of this approach, developed by Hilgard (1991), places particular attention on the dissociation of sensory experiences from conscious awareness. Most of us have had episodes of "absent-mindedness"—moments when we suddenly catch ourselves with no clear awareness of events in the immediate past. Now consider how this kind of dissociation might relate to cognitive suggestions that distort perceptions, such as the perception of pain. (Psychologists can, under appropriate ethical guidelines, administer noninjurious pain, such as placing an arm in cold water, and then suggest to a hypnotized individual that the pain is not perceived.) Hilgard suggests that hypnosis is a particularly extreme example of "absent-minded" episodes, in which conscious awareness of ongoing stimulation—even pain—is suppressed by the suggestions of the hypnotist.

Other versions of this approach (Bowers & Davidson, 1991; Kihlstrom, 1998) have suggested that this dissociation may extend to conscious *control* of actions. I once received a call from my wife while I was at work; her first words to me were "What are *you* doing at Virginia's house?" She had consciously intended to dial her friend Virginia but, out of long habit, had dialed my university number instead. For this brief moment, her conscious intention was dissociated from her actions (see Koch and Crick, 2001, for some similar examples). Dissociated control theories of hypnosis interpret response to ideomotor and challenge suggestions in terms of similar states. The key assumption is that behavior may have a hierarchy of control centers; under hypnosis, higher levels of control become isolated from lower levels.

Psychologists who study hypnosis disagree as to whether the sociocognitive or the dissociative approach offers a better interpretation of hypnosis. Neither seems complete. The dissociative explanation, for example, does not provide a clear mechanism by which hypnotic induction can produce dissociation. It may be that, ultimately, some synthesis of the two approaches will provide a better account (Woody & Sadler, 1998). Regardless, some psychologists have adopted the position that, whatever its explanation, hypnosis can provide a tool for exploring issues related to brain functioning (Rainville et al., 1997). Conversely, advances in our knowledge of brain function may help us understand the specific neural pathways that produce some of the effects of hypnosis (Sandrini et al., 2000).

Biology and Culture

Control of Consciousness through Meditation, Attention, and Dishabituation

A craving for at least occasional changes in consciousness seems to be a widespread trait among members of our species. Every culture has its means for altering consciousness—even children enjoy spinning around to make themselves dizzy. Some means of altering consciousness have become commonplace, such as the ingestion of coffee, tea, alcohol, or tobacco. As we saw in Chapter 4, certain drugs, such as LSD and psilocybin, suppress the activity of serotonin-secreting neurons. Serotonin, in turn, inhibits the mechanisms of dreaming (a topic discussed later in this chapter). Because the inhibitory action of serotonin is reduced by these drugs, it is not surprising that the result can be visual hallucinations.

The expectations and customs of a society substantially influence the effects that drugs have on a person's consciousness. For example, when coffee drinking was associated with religious rituals long ago, it undoubtedly caused a much more striking change in consciousness than it does now when it is dispensed into a paper cup from the local

▲ *Different cultures have discovered different ways to alter their consciousness through meditation or repetitive movement. These Islamic Dervish monks, members of the Mevlevi sect, are participating in a dance in which spinning facilitates a trancelike state that connects them with Allah.*

vending machine. Similarly, when smoking tobacco was a part of the rites of indigenous American peoples, it almost certainly induced a greater change in consciousness than it does in the average cigarette smoker today.

Altering, expanding, or even escaping from consciousness does not require the use of drugs. Since the beginning of history, people have developed ways to change their consciousness by means of self-control. For example, the ancient Hebrews and early Christians often fasted for many days, undoubtedly because of the effects that their altered metabolism had on their consciousness. In earlier times there was also much more emphasis on ritualized chants and movements, such as those of the early Jewish Hasidim and Cabalists. In fact, the Christian Pentecostal and the Jewish Hasidic sects today practice dances and chanting that would not seem strange to thirteenth-century mystics, and these group rituals encourage the "taking over" of members' consciousness.

The one function that all methods of changing consciousness have in common is an alteration in attention. The various exercises can be divided into those that withdraw attention from the stimuli around us and those that increase attention to events that have become so commonplace that we no longer notice them—including behaviors of our own that have become automatic and relatively nonconscious. We refer to exercises in both categories as *meditation*. Forms of meditation have developed in almost every culture. Zen Buddhism, yoga, Sufism, and Taoism are best known and most influential in Eastern societies, where they first developed, but there is also a tradition of meditation and contemplation in the Western world, still carried on by Christian monasteries. Even the ritualized recitation of the rosary and the clicking of the beads serve to focus a person's attention on the prayer he or she is chanting.

● Techniques for Withdrawing Attention

The goal of most meditation exercises is to remove attention from all sensory stimuli—to think of absolutely nothing. The various techniques require that the meditator direct his or her attention to a single object (such as a specially prepared symbol), to a spoken or imagined word or phrase (such as a prayer or mantra), to a monotonous sound (such as the rushing of a waterfall), or to a repetitive movement (such as breathing or touching the tips of each of the four fingers with the thumb). A Tibetan monk might say, *"Om mani padme hum"*; a Christian monk might say, "Lord Jesus Christ, have mercy on me"; and a Sufi might say, *"La illa ill' Allahu."* Although the theologies are different, the basic effect of all the chants is the same.

By concentrating on an object, a sound, or a repetitive movement, we can learn to ignore other stimuli. We achieve this kind of focus to some degree when we read a book intently or attempt to solve a problem. The difference is that the book or problem supplies a changing form of stimulation. Thoughts, words, images, and ideas flow through our minds. In contrast, a person attempting to achieve a meditative trance selects an inherently static object of attention that leads to habituation. By concentrating on this unchanging source of information, continually bringing his or her attention back to it, the person achieves a state of utter concentration on *nothing*.

Withdrawal of attention appears to have two primary goals: to reduce verbal control over nonverbal functions of the brain and to produce afterward a "rebound phenomenon"—a heightening of awareness and an increase in attention. The second goal is identical to that of consciousness-increasing exercises.

● Techniques for Increasing and Dishabituating Consciousness

Habituation to most stimuli in our environment enables us to concentrate on those stimuli that are important to our survival. For instance, I can remember very little about showering, shaving, and dressing this morning or about driving back and forth between my home and office. When driving along a highway I do not concentrate on the position of my hands on the steering wheel, its texture under my fingers, or the road vibrations transmitted through my body. Neither do I notice the shape of the windshield, the color of the hood, the outline of the guardrails as I go past them, or any of the myriad other stimuli to which I could attend. Sometimes I drive over a very familiar route and suddenly arrive at my destination without being able to remember anything about the journey, or at least large parts of it. Obviously, I did all the right things, because I got there; but for all I can remember about the trip, I might as well have been unconscious. My attention is left free for noticing dangers that I must either respond to or be injured by. The relative infrequency of automobile accidents attests to the efficiency of our attentional mechanisms in monitoring the information that we must process in order to survive.

▲ *Doing something dangerous heightens self-awareness and awareness of one's surroundings.*

However, given our awareness that we all must grow older and eventually die, habituation to everything around us would prevent us from making the most of life. The beautiful things and special moments may not contain stimuli that are important to our survival, but they are certainly important to the enjoyment of life. Techniques for increasing awareness help reduce habituation.

The easiest way to reduce habituation and automatic functioning is to encounter novel stimuli. If we go to new places and have new experiences, we are more likely to be aware of what is going on around us. Moreover, there is a worthwhile side effect: When we return home, many of the old stimuli seem fresh and new again, at least for a while. We recover from some of our habituation.

Another way to notice things is to do them differently. Many ancient traditions suggest doing routine tasks in a different order or with the unaccustomed hand and making oneself concentrate on just what happens. By analyzing the details of the habituated stimuli, we force them into consciousness. For example, if this morning I had shaved before showering, had tried to hold my toothbrush in my left hand, and had put the left pant leg on before the right, I might have remembered more details of the start of my day.

Doing something dangerous, or at least something that places great demands on skill and coordination, also can heighten awareness by presenting unexpected stimuli to which we must react. Activities such as driving a car too fast, rock climbing, skiing, and hang gliding require us to be aware of what is going on around us and to remain vigilant at all times. Many people report that they never feel so "alive" as when they are in danger.

Finally, as I mentioned earlier, a very effective means of increasing our attention to the world around us is to remove ourselves from it temporarily. Almost all of the meditative traditions, new and old, stress that the world appears to be more real after a period of withdrawal of attention from it. This heightened awareness undoubtedly occurs because attentional mechanisms, which have been suppressed by concentration on an unchanging stimulus, now "rebound," and we notice much more than we previously did.

Interim Summary

Hypnosis

Hypnosis is a form of verbal control over a person's consciousness in which the hypnotist's suggestions affect some of the person's perceptions and behaviors. Although some people have viewed hypnosis as a mysterious, trancelike state, investigations have shown it to be similar to many phenomena of normal consciousness. There is no single way to induce hypnosis, and the responses depend very much on what the hypnotist says.

The sociocognitive approach to explaining hypnosis asserts that being hypnotized is similar to participating vicariously in a narrative, which is something we do whenever we become engrossed in a novel or a movie. When we are engrossed in this way, we experience genuine feelings of emotion, even though the situation is not "real." Dissociation theories of hypnosis, in contrast, consider hypnosis a specialized state in which awareness and conscious control centers of the brain become isolated from those controlling behavior.

Dissociative theories of hypnosis emphasize the extent to which the qualities of consciousness can be changed. Regardless of whether this is the best explanation of hypnosis, other phenomena point to ways of controlling consciousness. Techniques of meditation have been used since the beginning of history and include methods for increasing or decreasing attention to the external world. In meditative techniques a person pays strict attention to a simple stimulus such as a visual pattern, a word, or a monotonous, repetitive movement. As the response to the repeated stimulus habituates, the person is left with a relatively empty consciousness. The withdrawal of attention causes a rebound that leads the practitioner to look at his or her surroundings with revitalized awareness.

Some people prefer explanations that demystify puzzling phenomena such as hypnosis. Others resist such explanations; for them, an interesting phenomenon is spoiled by an explanation that places it in the realm of physics and biology. How do you feel about these two viewpoints?

Sleep

Sleep is not a state of unconsciousness. It is a state of *altered consciousness*. During sleep we have dreams that can be just as vivid as waking experiences, and yet we forget most of them as soon as they are over. Our amnesia leads us to think—incorrectly—that we were unconscious while we were asleep. In fact, there are two distinct kinds of sleep—and thus, two states of altered consciousness.

We spend approximately one-third of our lives sleeping—or trying to. You might therefore think that the reason we sleep would be clearly understood by scientists who study this phenomenon. And yet, despite the efforts of many talented researchers, we are still not completely sure why we sleep. Many people are preoccupied with sleep or with the lack of it (insomnia). Collectively, they consume large amounts of drugs each year in an attempt to get to sleep. Advertisements for nonprescription sleep medications imply that a night without a full eight hours of sleep is a physiological and psychological disaster. Is this worry justified? Does missing a few hours—or even a full night—of sleep actually harm us? As we will see, the answer seems to be a limited "no."

The Stages of Sleep

Sleep is not uniform. We can sleep lightly or deeply; we can be restless or still; we can have vivid dreams, or our consciousness can be relatively blank. Researchers who have studied sleep have found that its stages usually follow an orderly, predictable sequence.

Most sleep research takes place in sleep laboratories. Because a person's sleep is affected by his or her surroundings, a sleep laboratory contains one or more small bedrooms that are furnished and decorated to be as homelike and comfortable as possible. The most important apparatus of the sleep laboratory is the **polygraph,** a machine located in a separate room that records on paper the output of various devices that can be attached to the sleeper. You've undoubtedly seen depictions of one kind of polygraph, the instrument used to detect the physiological changes that often occur when a person tries to lie. (The word *polygraph* translates from its Greek roots as "much writing," and indeed, polygraph records can be extensive.) In sleep research the polygraph can record the electrical activity of the brain through small metal disks

pasted to the scalp, producing an *electroencephalogram (EEG)*. It can record electrical signals from muscles, producing an *electromyogram (EMG),* or from the heart, producing an *electrocardiogram (EKG)*. Or it can record eye movements through small metal disks attached to the skin around the eyes, producing an *electrooculogram (EOG)*. Other special transducers can detect respiration, sweating, skin or body temperature, and a variety of other physiological states.

Let us look at a typical night's sleep of a male college student on his third night in the laboratory. (Of course, we would obtain similar results from a female, with one exception, which I will note later.) The EEG electrodes are attached to his scalp, EMG electrodes to his chin, EKG electrodes to his chest, and EOG electrodes to the skin around his eyes. (See **Figure 9•13**.) Wires connected to these electrodes are plugged into the amplifiers of the polygraph. The output of each amplifier causes a pen on the polygraph to move up and down while a long, continuous sheet of paper moves by.

The EEG record distinguishes between alert and relaxed wakefulness. When a person is alert, the tracing looks rather irregular, and the pens do not move very far up or down. The EEG in this case shows high-frequency (15–30 Hz), low-amplitude electrical activity called **beta activity**. When a person is relaxed and perhaps somewhat drowsy, the record shows **alpha activity,** a medium-frequency (8–12 Hz), medium-amplitude rhythm. (See **Figure 9•14**.) Recall from Chapter 6 that the amplitude of a wave is the amount by which the electrical signal changes; the frequency of a wave activity is the number of waves in a second.

The technician leaves the room, the lights are turned off, and the student closes his eyes. As he relaxes and grows drowsy, his EEG changes from beta activity to alpha activity. The first stage of sleep (stage 1) is marked by the presence of some **theta activity,** EEG activity of 3.5 to 7.5 Hz. This stage is actually a transition between sleep and wakefulness; the EMG shows that the student's muscles are still active, and his EOG indicates slow, gentle, rolling eye movements. The eyes slowly

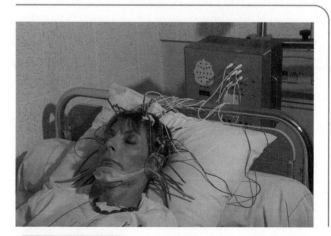

FIGURE 9•13 A participant prepared for a night's sleep in a sleep laboratory.

(Photo © Christian Voulgaropoulos/ISM/Photake, Inc.)

FIGURE 9•14 An EEG recording of the stages of sleep.

(Adapted from Horne, J. A. (1989). *Why We Sleep: The Functions of Sleep in Humans and Other Mammals.* Oxford, England: Oxford University Press, 1989. Copyright 1988 Oxford University Press. Reprinted by permission of Oxford University Press.)

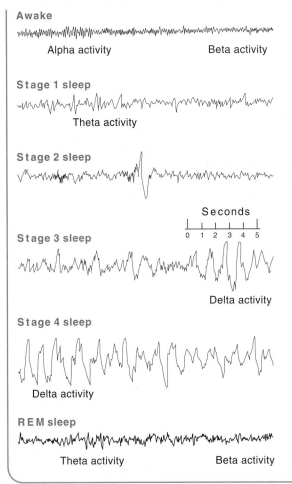

ronmental stimuli that caused him to stir during stage 1 produce little or no reaction during stage 4. The sleep of stages 3 and 4 is called **slow-wave sleep.**

Stage 4 sleep is reached in less than an hour and continues for as long as a half-hour. Then, suddenly, the EEG begins to indicate lighter levels of sleep, back through stages 3 and 2 to the activity characteristic of stage 1. The sleeper's heartbeat becomes irregular and his respiration alternates between shallow breaths and sudden gasps. The EOG shows that the participant's eyes dart rapidly back and forth, up and down. The EEG record looks like that of a person who is awake and active. Yet the sleeper is fast asleep, which is why, when this pattern of EOG and EEG was first discovered, the stage was called *paradoxical sleep.* Although his EMG is generally quiet, indicating muscular relaxation, the sleeper's hands and feet twitch occasionally.

At this point the sleeper is dreaming. He has entered another stage of sleep, called **rapid eye movement (REM) sleep.** It is such a significant part of the sleep cycle that often the other stages (stages 1–4) are simply labeled as **non-REM sleep.** The first episode of REM sleep lasts about 20 to 30 minutes and is followed by approximately one hour of slow-wave sleep. As the night goes on, the episodes of REM sleep get longer and the episodes of slow-wave sleep get shorter, but the total cycle remains at approximately 90 minutes. A typical night's sleep consists of four or five of these cycles. **Figure 9•15** shows a record of a person's stages of sleep; the dark blue shading indicates REM sleep.

As I noted, although a person in REM sleep exhibits rapid eye movements and brief twitches of the hands and feet, the EMG shows that the facial muscles are still. In fact, physiological studies have shown that, aside from occasional twitching, a person actually becomes paralyzed during REM sleep. Males are observed to have partial or full erections. In addition, women's vaginal secretions increase at this time.

open and close from time to time. Soon, the student is fully asleep. As sleep progresses, it gets deeper and deeper, moving through stages 2, 3, and 4. As shown in Figure 9.14, the EEG gets progressively lower in frequency and higher in amplitude. This pattern is interrupted between two and five times a minute by short bursts of waves of 12 to 14 Hz, known as *sleep spindles.* It has been suggested that sleep spindles represent the activity of a mechanism that is involved in keeping a person asleep (Nicolas, Petit, Rompre, & Montplaisir, 2001). Stage 2 sleep also is characterized by sudden and sharp waveforms known as *K complexes,* which occur about once a minute. The deepest stage of sleep, stage 4, consists mainly of **delta activity,** characterized by relatively high-amplitude waves occurring at less than 3.5 Hz. De Gennaro, Ferrara, and Bertini (2000) have suggested that the forerunner of delta activity may be the K complexes of stage 2. As our sleeper enters stage 4 sleep, he becomes less responsive to the environment, and it becomes more difficult to awaken him. Envi-

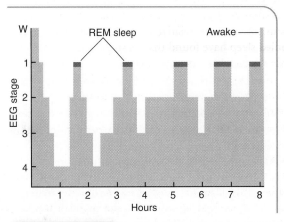

FIGURE 9•15 Typical progression of stages during a night's sleep. The dark blue shading indicates REM sleep.

(From Hartmann, E. (1967). *The Biology of Dreaming,* 1967. Courtesy of Charles C. Thomas, Publisher, Ltd., Springfield, Illinois.)

TABLE 9•1	Principal Characteristics of REM Sleep and Slow-Wave Sleep	
REM Sleep	**Slow-Wave Sleep**	
Rapid EEG waves	Slow EEG waves	
Muscular paralysis	Lack of muscular paralysis	
Rapid eye movements	Slow or absent eye movements	
Penile erection or vaginal secretion	Lack of genital activity	
Story and narrative dreams	Static, rarely narrative dreams; night terrors; sleepwalking	

These genital changes are usually not associated with sexual arousal or dreams of a sexual nature, however. **Table 9•1** lists the principal characteristics of REM sleep and the deeper stages of non-REM sleep, slow-wave sleep.

Functions of Sleep

Sleep is one of the few universal behaviors. All mammals, all birds, and some cold-blooded vertebrates spend part of each day sleeping. Sleep is seen even in species that would seem to be better off without sleep. For example, the Indus dolphin (*Platanista indi*) lives in the muddy waters of the Indus estuary in Pakistan (Pilleri, 1979). Over the ages it has become blind, presumably because vision is not useful in the animal's environment. (It has an excellent sonar system, which it uses to navigate and find prey.) The Indus dolphin never stops swimming; doing so would result in injury, because of the dangerous currents and the vast quantities of debris carried by the river during the monsoon season. However, despite the dangers caused by sleeping, sleep has not disappeared. Pilleri (1979) captured two Indus dolphins and studied their habits. He found that they slept a total of seven hours a day, in very brief naps of 4 to 60 seconds each. If sleep did not perform an important function, we might expect that it, like vision, would have been eliminated in this species through the process of natural selection.

The universal nature of sleep suggests that it performs some important functions. But just what are they? The simplest explanation for sleep is that it serves to *repair* the wear and tear on our bodies caused by moving and exercising. Perhaps our bodies just get worn out by performing waking activities for 16 hours or so.

One approach to discovering the functions of any activity is the deprivation study. Consider, for example, the function of eating. The effects of starvation are easy to detect: The person loses weight, becomes fatigued, and will eventually die if he or she does not eat again. By analogy, it should be easy to discover why we sleep by seeing what happens to a person who goes without sleep.

Unfortunately, sleep deprivation studies have not produced persuasive evidence that sleep is needed to keep the body functioning normally. Horne (1978) reviewed more than 50 experiments in which humans had been deprived of sleep. He reported that most of the results indicated that sleep deprivation did not interfere with people's ability to perform physical exercise. In addition, the studies found no evidence of a physiological stress response to sleep deprivation. If people encounter stressful situations that cause illness or damage to various organ systems, changes can be seen in such physiological measures as blood levels of cortisol and epinephrine. (The physiology of stress is described in more detail in Chapter 16.) Generally, these changes did not occur.

Although sleep deprivation does not seem to damage the body, and sleep does not seem to be necessary for athletic exercise, sleep may be required for normal brain functioning. Several studies suggest that sleep-deprived people are able to perform normally on most intellectual tasks, as long as the tasks are short. They perform more poorly on tasks that require a high level of cortical functioning after two days of sleep deprivation (Horne & Petit, 1985). In particular, they perform poorly on tasks that require them to be watchful, alert, and vigilant.

During stage 4 sleep the metabolic activity of the brain decreases to about 75 percent of the waking level (Sakai et al., 1979). Thus, stage 4 sleep appears to give the brain a chance to *rest*. In fact, people are unreactive to all but intense stimuli during slow-wave sleep and, if awakened, act groggy and confused—as if their cerebral cortex has been shut down and has not yet resumed its functioning. These observations suggest that during stage 4 sleep the brain is, indeed, resting.

Sleep deprivation studies of humans suggest that although the brain may need slow-wave sleep in order to recover from the day's activities, the rest of the body does not. Another way to determine whether sleep is needed for restoration of physiological functioning is to look at the effects of daytime activity on nighttime sleep. If the function of sleep is to repair the effects of activity during waking hours, then we should expect that sleep and exercise are related. That is, we should sleep more after a day of vigorous exercise than after a day spent quietly at an office desk.

In fact, evidence for a relation between sleep and exercise is not very compelling. For example, Ryback and Lewis (1971) found no changes in slow-wave or REM sleep of healthy participants who spent six weeks resting in bed. If sleep repairs wear and tear, we would expect these people to sleep less. Adey, Bors, and Porter (1968) studied the sleep of completely immobile quadriplegics and paraplegics and found only a small decrease in slow-wave sleep as compared to uninjured people.

Although bodily exercise has little effect on sleep, *mental* exercise seems to increase the demand for slow-wave sleep. In an ingenious study, Horne and Minard (1985) found a way to increase mental activity without affecting physical activity and without causing stress. The investigators told volunteers to show up for an experiment in which they were supposed to take some tests designed to assess reading skills. In fact, when the people turned up, they were told that the plans had been changed. They were invited for a day out, at the expense of the researchers. (Not surprisingly, they willingly accepted.) They spent the day visiting an art exhibition, a shopping center, a museum, an amusement park, a zoo, and an interesting mansion. After a scenic drive through the countryside, they watched a movie in a local theater. They were driven from place to place and certainly did not become overheated by exercise. After the movie they returned to the sleep laboratory. They said they were tired, and they readily fell asleep. Their sleep duration was normal, and they awoke feeling refreshed. However, their slow-wave sleep—particularly stage 4 sleep—was increased.

Dreaming

One of the most fascinating aspects of sleep is the fact that we enter a fantasy world several times each night during which we perceive imaginary events and perform imaginary behaviors. Why do we do so?

Consciousness during Sleep

A person who is awakened during REM sleep and asked whether anything was happening will almost always report a dream. The typical REM sleep dream resembles a play or movie—it has a narrative form. Conversely, reports of narrative, storylike dreams are rare among people awakened from slow-wave sleep. In general, mental activity during slow-wave sleep is more nearly static; it involves situations rather than stories, and generally the situations are unpleasant. For example, a person awakened from slow-wave sleep might report a sensation of being crushed or suffocated. It is during slow-wave sleep that some young children will experience *night terrors* (a vague but anguished emotion with no clear memory of its cause) and *sleepwalking*.

Unless a sleeper is heavily drugged, almost everyone has four or five bouts of REM sleep each night, with accompanying dreams. Yet if the dreamer does not happen to awaken while the dream is in progress, it is lost forever. Some people who claimed not to have had a dream for many years slept in a sleep laboratory and found that, in fact, they did dream. They were able to remember their dreams because the investigator awakened them during REM sleep.

The reports of people awakened from REM and slow-wave sleep clearly show that people are conscious during sleep, even though they may not remember any of their sleeping experiences. *Lack of memory of an event does not mean that it never happened; it only means that there is no permanent record accessible to conscious thought during wakefulness.* Thus, we can say that slow-wave sleep and REM sleep reflect two different states of consciousness.

Functions of Dreams

There are two major approaches to the study of dreaming: psychological analysis of the contents of dreams, and psychobiological research on the nature and functions of REM sleep. The psychological analysis is closely

▲ *Marc Chagall's painting depicts images and symbols that could occur in a dream. Freud's assertion that dreams provide an opportunity for unconscious desires to be expressed symbolically is challenged by many psychologists today.*

associated with Sigmund Freud's proposal that dreams symbolize desires of which we are not aware. The psychobiological approach considers dreams as the products of the brain's function as a information processor. Let us consider the psychological analysis first.

Dreaming as Wish Fulfillment. Since ancient times, people have regarded dreams as important, using them to prophesy the future, decide whether to go to war, or determine the guilt or innocence of a person accused of a crime. In the twentieth century Sigmund Freud proposed a very influential theory about dreaming. He said that dreams arise out of inner conflicts between unconscious desires (primarily sexual ones) and prohibitions against acting out these desires, which we learn from society. According to Freud, although all dreams represent unfulfilled wishes, their contents are disguised and expressed symbolically. The *latent content* of the dream (*latent* is from the Latin word for "hidden") is transformed into the *manifest content* (the actual storyline or plot). Taken at face value, the manifest content is innocuous, but a knowledgeable psychoanalyst can supposedly recognize unconscious desires disguised as symbols in the dream. For example, climbing a set of stairs or shooting a gun might represent sexual intercourse. The problem with Freud's theory is that it is not disprovable; even if it is wrong, a psychoanalyst can always provide a plausible interpretation of a dream that reveals hidden conflicts disguised in obscure symbols.

Dreaming as Pattern Construction. Hobson and Pace-Schott (2002) have developed a model of brain activity during sleep that explains dreaming without relying on unconscious conflicts or desires. As we will see later, research using laboratory animals has shown that REM sleep occurs when a circuit of acetylcholine-secreting neurons in the pons becomes active, stimulating rapid eye movements, activation of the cerebral cortex, and muscular paralysis. (Yes, other animals engage in REM sleep, and they appear to dream, too.) The activation of the visual system produces both eye movements and images. In fact, several experiments have found that the particular eye movements that a person makes during a dream correspond reasonably well with the content of a dream; that is, the eye movements are those that a person would be likely to make if the imaginary events were really occurring (Dement, 1974). The images evoked by the cortical activation often incorporate memories of episodes that have occurred recently or of things that a person has been thinking about lately. Presumably, the circuits responsible for these memories are more excitable because they have recently been active. Hobson and Pace-Schott (2002) suggest that both slow-wave sleep and REM sleep work together. Memories that are consolidated during slow-wave sleep are reactivated during REM sleep and consolidated with other memories. The activation of these brain mechanisms produces fragmentary images; our brains try to tie these images together and make sense of them by creating or synthesizing a more or less plausible story. This theory is known as the **activation–synthesis theory,** because it proposes that activation of the cortex by the pons causes the brain to create a subjective interpretation of what this activity means. When we communicate these interpretations to ourselves or to others, we call them dreams.

Dreaming as Learning.   As we saw, total sleep deprivation impairs people's ability to perform tasks that require alertness and vigilance. What happens when only REM sleep is disrupted? People who are sleeping in a laboratory can be selectively deprived of REM sleep. An investigator awakens them whenever their polygraph records indicate that they have entered REM sleep. The investigator must also awaken control participants just as often at random intervals to eliminate any effects produced by being awakened several times.

If someone is deprived of REM sleep for several nights and is then allowed to sleep without interruption, the onset of REM sleep becomes more frequent. It is as if a need for REM sleep builds up, forcing the person into this state more often. When the person is no longer awakened during REM sleep, a rebound phenomenon is seen: The person engages in many more bouts of REM sleep than normal during the next night or two, as if catching up on something important that was missed.

Several investigators have suggested that REM sleep may play a role in learning, a view consistent with the explanation for dreaming suggested by Hobson and Pace-Schott (2002). Smith and Lapp (1991) observed increased REM sleep in college students during examination periods, which would be a time of increased learning. In addition, many studies using laboratory animals have shown that deprivation of REM sleep does impair the ability to learn a complex task.

However, although animals deprived of REM sleep learn a complex task more slowly, they still manage to learn it. Thus, REM sleep is not necessary for learning. If REM sleep does play a role in learning, the effect appears to be subtle—at least in an adult. In fact, medical journals contain reports of several patients who showed little or no REM sleep after sustaining damage to the brain stem (Gironell, de la Calzada, Sagales, & Barraquer-Bordas, 1995; Lavie et al., 1984). The lack of REM sleep did not appear to cause serious side effects. One of the patients, after receiving his injury, completed high school, attended law school, and began practicing law.

Brain Mechanisms of Sleep

If sleep is a behavior, then some parts of the brain must be responsible for its occurrence. In fact, researchers have discovered several brain regions that have special roles in sleep stages and biological rhythms.

Let us first consider biological rhythms. All living organisms show rhythmic changes in their physiological processes and behavior. Some of these rhythms are simply responses to environmental changes. For example, the growth rate of plants is controlled by daily rhythms of light and darkness. In animals some rhythms are controlled by internal "clocks" located in the brain. Mammals have two biological clocks that play a role in sleep. One of these controls **circadian rhythms**—rhythms that oscillate once a day (*circa*, "about"; *dies*, "day").

▲ *Late-term fetuses and newborn infants spend much time in REM sleep, which has led some investigators to hypothesize that this activity plays a role in brain development.*

The second clock, which controls the cycles of slow-wave and REM sleep, oscillates several times a day.

The clock that controls circadian rhythms is located in a small pair of structures located at the bottom of the hypothalamus: the *suprachiasmatic nuclei (SCN)*. The activity of neurons in the SCN oscillates once each day; the neurons are active during the day and inactive at night. These changes in activity control daily cycles of sleep and wakefulness. If people are placed in a windowless room with constant lighting, they will continue to show circadian rhythms, controlled by the oscillations of their suprachiasmatic nuclei. However, because this biological clock is not very accurate, people's circadian rhythms will eventually get out of synchrony with the day/night cycles outside the building. But within a few days after leaving the building, their rhythms will be resynchronized with those of the sun. This resynchronization is accomplished by a direct connection between the eyes and the SCN. Each morning, when we see the light of the sun (or turn on the room lights), our biological clock resets and begins ticking off the next day.

The second biological clock in the mammalian brain runs considerably faster, and it runs continuously, unaffected by periods of light and darkness. In humans, this clock cycles with a 90-minute period. The first suggestion that a 90-minute cycle occurs throughout the day came from the observation that infants who are fed on demand show regular feeding patterns (Kleitman, 1961). Later studies found 90-minute cycles of rest and activity, including such activities as eating, drinking, smoking, heart rate, oxygen consumption, stomach motility, urine production, and performance on various tasks that make demands on a person's ability to pay attention. Kleitman termed this phenomenon the **basic rest–activity cycle (BRAC)**. (See Kleitman, 1982, for a review.) During the night, the clock responsible for the BRAC controls the alternating periods of REM sleep and slow-wave sleep.

Studies using laboratory animals have found that the clock responsible for the BRAC is located somewhere in the pons. The pons also contains neural circuits that are responsible for REM sleep. The neurons that begin a period of REM sleep release the neurotransmitter acetylcholine. The acetylcholine activates several other circuits of neurons. One of these circuits activates the cerebral cortex and causes dreaming. Another activates neurons in the midbrain and causes rapid eye movements. Yet another activates a set of inhibitory neurons that paralyze us and prevent us from acting out our dreams. The location of the two biological clocks is shown in **Figure 9•16**.

The first hint that REM sleep was turned on by acetylcholine-secreting neurons came from the observation that overdoses of insecticides that excite such neurons also cause visual hallucinations, like those of dreaming. Subsequent research using laboratory animals confirmed this suspicion. These acetylcholine-secreting neurons (referred to as *REM-ON* neurons) are normally inhibited by neurons that secrete another transmitter substance, serotonin. Thus, drugs that decrease the activity of serotonin-secreting neurons will per-

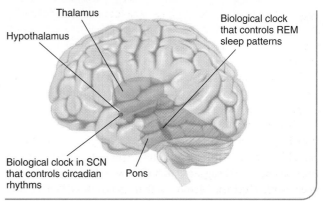

FIGURE 9•16 Two biological clocks in the human brain. The suprachiasmatic nucleus (SCN) of the hypothalamus is responsible for circadian rhythms. The clock in the pons is responsible for the basic rest–activity cycle (BRAC) and cycles of REM sleep and slow-wave sleep.

mit the REM-ON neurons to become active. LSD is one of these drugs, and this fact explains why people who take LSD experience visual hallucinations similar to those that occur during dreams. On the other hand, drugs that increase the activity of serotonin-secreting neurons will suppress REM sleep (see **Figure 9•17**). All antidepressant drugs have this effect, which suggests that excessive amounts of REM sleep may play a role in mood disorders. This hypothesis will be explored in more detail in Chapter 17.

What about the brain mechanisms responsible for slow-wave sleep? The brain region that regulates the slow-wave sleep stages seems to be the **preoptic area**, located just in front of the hypothalamus, at the base of the brain. (This region is named for the fact that it is located anterior to the point where some axons in the optic nerves cross to the other side of the brain.) If the preoptic area is destroyed, an animal will sleep much less (McGinty & Sterman, 1968; Szymusiak & McGinty,

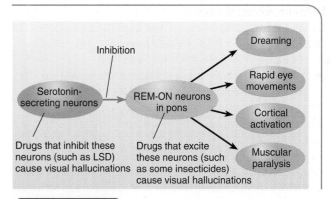

FIGURE 9•17 Control of REM sleep. REM sleep is produced by activation of the acetylcholine-secreting REM-ON neurons located in the pons. These neurons are normally inhibited by serotonin-secreting neurons.

1986). If it is electrically stimulated, an animal will become drowsy and fall asleep (Sterman & Clemente, 1962a, 1962b).

REM sleep during the night. A circuit of acetylcholine-secreting neurons in the pons, normally inhibited by serotonin-secreting neurons, turns on REM sleep. Slow-wave sleep is controlled by neurons in the preoptic area.

Interim Summary

Sleep

Sleep consists of several stages of slow-wave sleep, characterized by increasing amounts of delta activity in the EEG, and REM sleep. REM sleep is characterized by beta activity in the EEG, rapid eye movements, general paralysis (with twitching movements of the hands and feet), and dreaming. Sleep is a behavior, not simply an altered state of consciousness. Although evidence suggests that sleep is not necessary for repairing the wear and tear caused by physical exercise, sleep may play an important role in providing an opportunity for the brain to rest.

Although narrative dreams occur only during REM sleep, people often are conscious of static situations during slow-wave sleep. Freud suggested that dreams provide the opportunity for unconscious conflicts to express themselves through symbolism in dreams. An alternative suggestion is that dreams are the attempts of the brain to make sense of hallucinations produced by the activation of the cerebral cortex. The function of REM sleep in adults is uncertain, but it may be involved somehow in learning. The brain contains two biological clocks. One, located in the suprachiasmatic nucleus of the hypothalamus, controls circadian (daily) rhythms. This clock is reset when light strikes the retina in the morning. The second clock, located in the pons, controls the basic rest–activity cycle, which manifests itself in changes in activity levels during the day and in alternating periods of slow-wave sleep and

QUESTIONS TO CONSIDER

1. What does dreaming accomplish? Some researchers believe that the subject matter of a dream does not matter—it is the REM sleep itself that is important. Others believe that the subject matter does count. Some researchers believe that if we remember a dream, the dream failed to accomplish all of its functions; others say that remembering is useful, because it can give us some insights into our problems. What do you think of these controversies?

2. Some people report that they are "in control" of some of their dreams—that they feel as if they decide what comes next and are not simply swept along passively. Have you ever had this experience? And have you ever had a "lucid dream," in which you were aware of the fact that you were dreaming?

3. Until recently (that is, in terms of the evolution of our species), our ancestors tended to go to sleep when the sun set and to wake up when it rose. Once our ancestors learned how to control fire, they undoubtedly stayed up somewhat later, sitting in front of a fire. But it was only with the development of cheap, effective lighting that many members of our species adopted the habit of staying up late and waking several hours after sunrise. Considering that the neural mechanisms of sleep evolved long ago, do you think the changes in our daily rhythms affect any of our physical and intellectual abilities?

Suggestions for Further Reading

Damasio, A. (2000). *The feeling of what happens: Body and emotion in the making of consciousness.* New York: Harcourt Brace.

A leading neuroscientist looks at the topic of consciousness and offers an unconventional suggestion regarding its origins.

Dennett, D. C. (1992). *Consciousness explained.* Boston: Little, Brown.

This book provides a provocative look at consciousness from a philosophical, psychological, and computational viewpoint.

Jaynes, J. (2000). *The origin of consciousness in the breakdown of the bicameral mind.* Boston: Houghton Mifflin.

Jaynes's book presents the intriguing hypothesis that human consciousness is a recent phenomenon that emerged long after the evolution of the human brain as we know it now. You do not need to agree with Jaynes's thesis to enjoy reading this scholarly book.

Baker, R. A. (1990). *They call it hypnosis.* Buffalo, NY: Prometheus Books.

Laurence, J. R., & Perry, C. (1988). *Hypnosis, will, and memory: A psycholegal history.* New York: Guilford Press.

Sheehan, P. W., & McConkey, K. M. (1982). *Hypnosis and experience: The exploration of phenomena and process.* Hillsdale, NJ: Lawrence Erlbaum Associates.

If you would like to learn more about hypnosis, you will enjoy reading any of these books. The Sheehan and McConkey book provides a more advanced, scholarly approach.

Horne, J. (1988). *Why we sleep: The functions of sleep in humans and other mammals.* Oxford, UK: Oxford University Press.

Horne's book about sleep is excellent and interesting.

Key Terms

activation–synthesis theory (p. 288)

alpha activity (p. 284)

basic rest–activity cycle (BRAC) (p. 289)

beta activity (p. 284)

blindsight (p. 265)

change blindness (p. 274)

circadian rhythm (p. 288)

cocktail-party phenomenon (p. 272)

consciousness (p. 265)

delta activity (p. 285)

dichotic listening (p. 270)

divided attention (p. 270)

inattentional blindness (p. 274)

inhibition of return (p. 273)

non-REM sleep (p. 285)

posthypnotic amnesia (p. 280)

posthypnotic suggestibility (p. 280)

polygraph (p. 284)

preoptic area (p. 289)

rapid eye movement (REM) sleep (p. 285)

selective attention (p. 270)

shadowing (p. 270)

slow-wave sleep (p. 285)

split-brain operation (p. 277)

theta activity (p. 284)

10

LANGUAGE

Speech Comprehension and Production

Speech Recognition • Understanding the Meaning of Speech • Brain Mechanisms of Speech Production and Comprehension

Psycholinguists study verbal behavior and focus on cognitive mechanisms involved in language, including perception and memory. Words consist of smaller units of speech (phonemes and morphemes), are arranged into sentences that follow specific rules (syntax), and have meanings (semantics). Context plays an important role in the complex task of identifying individual words from continuous speech. Studies of patients with brain damage and PET studies of people engaging in verbal behavior suggest that some parts of the brain—especially Broca's area and Wernicke's area—play special roles in language-related behaviors.

Reading

Scanning of Text • Phonetic and Whole-Word Recognition: Evidence from Neuropsychology • Understanding the Meanings of Words and Sentences

Eye-tracking devices allow researchers to study people's eye movements during reading. Reading is accomplished by whole-word recognition and by phonetic decoding of the sounds represented by letters and groups of letters. Brain damage can produce acquired dyslexias, disrupting one or both of these processes. Developmental dyslexias may involve abnormal development of parts of the left hemisphere that play a special role in language abilities. The phenomenon of semantic priming has permitted researchers to investigate the interactions of neural circuits responsible for the recognition and understanding of spoken and written words.

Language Acquisition by Children

Evaluating Scientific Issues: Is There a Language Acquisition Device? • Recognition of Speech Sounds by Infants • The Prespeech Period and the First Words • The Two-Word Stage • How Adults Talk to Children • Acquisition of Adult Rules of Grammar • Acquisition of Meaning • *Biology and Culture: Communication with Other Primate Species*

Some psycholinguists believe that the human brain contains a language acquisition device that already contains universal rules of grammar, but the evidence for such a device is questionable. By the time babies are born, they have already learned something about language from what they have heard while in their mothers' uteruses. Language is very much a social behavior; babies learn to carry on "conversations" with caregivers even before they can utter real words, and they use movements, facial expressions, and sounds to communicate. During the two-word stage, children begin to combine words creatively, saying things they have never heard, including incorrect utterances. Infants learn how to communicate verbally from adults and older children, who use a special form of address known as child-directed speech. The question of whether language abilities are uniquely human is being addressed by researchers who have succeeded in teaching other primates some aspects of language.

O liver Sacks was feeling just a little bit scared. The celebrated neurologist from New York City had traveled the world, researching and writing about the normal and abnormal workings of the human brain. But at this moment, on a lonely highway in the interior of the Canadian province of British Columbia, he was most concerned about the moment-to-moment functioning of the brain belonging to the man in the driver's seat next to him, Carl Bennett.

Bennett lived and worked in British Columbia, and he had just taken Sacks to one of his favorite spots, a ranch in one of the spectacular mountain valleys of the interior ranges. Now they were driving back, and Bennett's behavior would have seemed bizarre, even shocking, to any observer who didn't know him. Jerking the wheel violently right and left, Bennett erratically steered the vehicle down the mountain road. He took his hands off the wheel for a few seconds at a time to tap the windshield frenetically. And his conversation was peppered with strange expressions like "hootey-hoot" and "hideous," repeated often and rhythmically. "Don't worry," he said to Sacks. "I've never had an accident driving." Oddly enough, Sacks found this comforting.

Bennett had been diagnosed with Tourette's syndrome—a psychological disorder marked by sudden nervous tics of behavior and language. The tapping, the readjustments of the steering wheel, and the spontaneous,

The noted neurologist and author, Oliver Sacks.

nonsensical words were manifestations of what Bennett himself described as "unpredictable dishabituations of motoric patterns." But all the more remarkable, and the source of Sacks's comfort on this otherwise terrifying journey, was that Bennett seemed quite capable of suppressing the erratic movements when absolutely necessary. Sacks knew. He had just seen Bennett wield a scalpel in a delicate operation at the hospital near Bennett's home. Bennett, you see, was a surgeon.

Bennett's language was a good example of the dissociations that he exhibited. He had discussed this with Sacks the day before, when he had invited the neurologist to his home to discuss the illness. His speech was normally peppered with bizarre expressions such as "Babaloo Mandel," and "Hideous." Bennett couldn't say what many of them meant or why they appeared. Take "hideous," for instance.

"It suddenly appeared one day two years ago. It'll disappear one day, and there will be another word instead. When I'm tired, it turns into 'Gideous.' One cannot always find sense in these words; often it is just the sound that attracts me. Any odd sound, any odd name, may start repeating itself, get me going. I get hung up with a word for two or three months. Then, one morning, it's gone, and there's another one in its place."

The random and sporadic appearance of these words was apparent when Sacks accompanied Bennett to the hospital. Conversations with nurses, colleagues, and patients had included these strange utterances, along with all the other verbal and motor tics that characterize a person with Tourette's. But they ceased the moment surgery started. Bennett's motions were smooth, decisive, controlled; his speech melded into the normal flow of operating room commands and observations. "It's like a miracle," one of his surgical assistants observed. "The way the Tourette's disappears."

True to his prediction, Bennett arrived back from the ranch without an accident. Still in the car, he looked over at a somewhat shaken Sacks. "I've got an idea. Your flight to New York leaves from Calgary International. To save you a long drive, I'll fly you to Calgary tomorrow in my private plane."

L anguage is the most complex ability humans possess. Steven Pinker has said that when we use language, "we can shape events in each other's brains with exquisite precision" (Pinker, 1994, p. 1). Yet, as Oliver Sacks's experience with Carl Bennett reminds us, our use of language is behavior.

Spoken words, by themselves, are highly organized patterns of motor activity. When randomly uttered under the influence of Tourette's syndrome, they mean no more than other random behaviors such as the shoulder twitches and finger tapping that Bennett engaged in. When organized as language, however,

▲ *People's earliest attempts at written communication took the form of stylized pictures, such as these petroglyphs located in the Great Gallery of Horseshoe Canyon in Utah.*

words can communicate the complex steps of a surgical procedure. Sacks's visit with Bennett (Sacks, 1995) nicely illustrates this distinction. Verbal tics, such as "hideous," are random utterances, without purpose. On the other hand, a surgeon's commands or a pilot's radio transmissions in flight require organization. Bennett's remarkable ability was his capacity to inhibit the random words whenever he needed to communicate clearly and precisely.

With the exception of sexual behavior (without which our genes would not survive), communication is probably the most important of all human social behaviors. Our use of language can be private—we can think to ourselves in words or write diaries that are meant to be seen by no one but ourselves—but language evolved through social contacts among early human ancestors. Speaking and writing are clearly social behaviors: We learn these skills from other people and use them in order to communicate with others. Language is a form of communication. The transmission and reception of signals provided by arbitrary sounds (spoken language) and marks (written language) can alter our own and others' behavior.

We also use language as a tool in remembering and thinking. As we saw in Chapter 8, we often encode information in memory verbally, that is, with words. In addition, we can extend our long-term memory for information by writing notes and consulting them later. Language also enables us to think about very complex and abstract issues by encoding them in words and then manipulating the words according to the rules of language.

Speaking, listening, writing, and reading are behaviors; so, as with other behaviors, we can study them directly. Linguists have studied the conventions or rules of language and have described precisely what we do when we speak or write. In contrast, researchers in **psycholinguistics,** a branch of psychology devoted to the study of verbal behavior, are more concerned with human cognition than with the particular rules that describe language. Psycholinguists also are interested in how children acquire language—how verbal behavior develops and how children learn to speak from their interactions with adults and other children. Additionally, psycholinguists study how adults use language and how verbal abilities interact with other cognitive abilities. These issues, rather than the concerns of linguists per se, are the focus of this chapter.

The chapter addresses three major topics. The first is speech—specifically, how the sounds of speech are recognized and produced and how recognition leads to meaning. Along the way the text introduces basic concepts from linguistics; the principal emphasis, however, is on the brain mechanisms associated with speech comprehension and production and on the clinical consequences when those mechanisms are impaired. The second topic is reading, with much the same interest in how the brain recognizes written text and produces meaning from it. We'll also consider clinical disorders of reading. The chapter's final topic is the acquisition of language and, specifically, the patterns that characterize the child's emergence as a fluent speaker of language within a brief span of years. Of particular interest is the possibility that the human brain possesses a language acquisition device. The chapter ends by exploring the question of whether other primate species can acquire language.

Speech Comprehension and Production

The ability to engage in verbal behavior confers decided advantages on our species. Through listening and reading, we can profit from the experiences of others, even from those of people who died long ago. Through talking and writing, we can share the results of our own experiences. We can request from other people specific behaviors and information that are helpful to us. We can give information to other people so that their behavior will change in a way that benefits them (or us).

Speech Recognition

When we speak to someone, we produce a series of sounds in a continuous stream, punctuated by pauses and modulated by stress and changes in pitch. We write sentences as sets of words, with spaces between them. But we say sentences as a string of sounds, emphasizing (stressing) some, quickly sliding over others, raising the pitch of our voice on some, lowering it on others. We maintain a regular rhythmic pattern of stress. We pause at appropriate times—for example, between phrases—but we do not pause after pronouncing each word. Thus, speech does not come to us as a series of individual words; we must extract the words from a stream of speech (Liberman, 1996; Miller & Eimas, 1995).

Recognition of Speech Sounds

The auditory system performs a formidably complex task in enabling us to recognize speech sounds. Human vocalizations are clearly distinguished from other sounds around us. They contain enough information that we can recognize individuals from the sounds of their speech. Furthermore, we can filter out the nonspeech sounds, such as coughs or chuckles, within an individual's vocalization. We do this despite the fact that the underlying sounds of speech vary according to the sounds that precede and follow them, the speaker's accent, and the stress placed on the syllables in which they occur. Like our ability to recognize faces visually, the auditory system recognizes the *patterns* underlying speech rather than just the sounds themselves (Sinha, 2002).

The functional imaging technologies described in Chapter 4 have provided new insight into how this happens. Using fMRI scans, Belin, Zatorre, and Ahad (2002) found that some regions of the brain responded more when people heard human vocalizations (both speech and nonspeech) than when they heard other sounds of the natural world. Regions in which there was a large difference were located in the temporal lobe, on the auditory cortex. (Refer to Figure 4.30). Interestingly, given what we saw in Chapter 9 regarding the results of the split-brain operation, both the left and right hemispheres showed this contrast between responses to vocalizations and responses to other sounds. However, when Belin, Zatorre, and Ahad studied the way the brain reacted to either natural speech or speech that had been scrambled in frequency, the auditory area on the left hemisphere showed a greater contrast in response. This suggests that when it comes to analyzing the detailed information of speech, the left hemisphere plays a larger role.

What is this detailed information? The analysis of speech usually begins with its elements, or phonemes. **Phonemes** are the basic elements of speech. For example, the word *pin* consists of three phonemes: /p/ + /i/ + /n/.

Many experiments have investigated how we discriminate among phonemes. Let us consider just one distinction that we can detect: **voice-onset time**, the delay between the initial sound of a consonant and the onset of vibration of the vocal cords. Voicing is the vibration of your vocal cords. The distinction between voiced and unvoiced consonants permits us to distinguish between /p/ and /b/, between /k/ and /g/, and between /t/ and /d/. Try to figure out the difference yourself by saying *pa* and *ba*. Pay attention to what the sounds are like, not to how you move your lips to make them.

The difference is very subtle. When you say *pa,* you first build up a little pressure in your mouth. When you open your lips, a puff of air comes out. The *ah* sound does not occur immediately, because the air pressure in your mouth and throat keeps air from leaving your lungs for a brief time. Your vocal cords do not vibrate until air from your lungs passes through them. When you say *ba,* you do not first build up pressure. Your vocal cords start vibrating as soon as your lips open. The delay in voicing that occurs when you say *pa* is very slight: only 0.06 second. Try saying *pa* and *ba* aloud a few more times and note the difference. Your vocal cords will start vibrating just a little later when you say *pa.*

Phonemic discriminations begin with auditory processing of the sensory differences, and this occurs in both hemispheres (Binder et al., 2004). However, regions of the left auditory cortex seem to specialize in recognizing the special aspects of speech. Scott, Blank, Rosen, and Wise (2000) identified some of these areas using PET scans. They played recordings of either natural speech, speech that was computer-distorted and unintelligible but contained the phonemic complexity of the sounds, or speech that was intelligible but lacked the normal frequencies of human speakers. Some brain areas responded to both natural and unintelligible speech; others responded only to speech that was intelligible—even if it was highly distorted. (See **Figure 10•1**.)

These latter regions of the auditory cortex must rely on information that transcends the distortions of individual phonemes. Perhaps this information is based on larger segments of speech, such as that provided by syllables. A behavioral experiment conducted by Ganong (1980) supports this suggestion. Ganong found that the perception of a phoneme

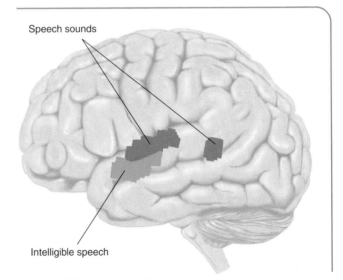

Speech sounds

Intelligible speech

FIGURE 10•1 Results of PET scans indicating regions of the superior temporal lobe that respond to speech sounds. Dark brown: Regions that responded to phonetic information (normal speech sounds or a computerized transformation of speech that preserved the complexity of the speech sounds but rendered it unintelligible). Light brown: Region that responded only to intelligible speech (normal speech sounds or a computerized transformation that removed most normal frequencies but preserved intelligibility).

(Adapted from Scott, S. K., Blank, E. C., Rosen, S., & Wise, R. J. S. (2000). *Brain, 123,* 2400–2406. By permission of Oxford University Press.)

is affected by the sounds that follow it. He used a computer to synthesize a novel sound that fell between those of the phonemes /g/ and /k/. When the sound was followed by *ift,* the participants heard the word *gift,* but when it was followed by *iss,* they heard *kiss.* These results suggest that we recognize speech sounds in pieces larger than individual phonemes. In addition, the results are analogous to the effects of context on visual stimuli (refer to Figure 7.22).

Recognition of Words in Continuous Speech: The Importance of Learning and Context

Phonemes combine to become **morphemes,** which are the smallest units of a language that convey meaning. *Pin* is a pair of morphemes—/p/ and /in/—containing the three phonemes. Adding another morpheme—/s/—changes the meaning to the plural of *pin.* Morphemes alone and in combination form the words of a language.

These larger units of speech are established by learning and experience. Sanders, Newport, and Neville (2002) examined brain wave activity when people listened to a continuous string of sounds. The sounds were composed of short two-letter syllables spliced together, such as the string

babupudutabatutibubabupubu

Sanders and her colleagues then took some of the sounds from the continuous stream (such as the sequence "dutaba") and designated them as "words." They asked their participants to study these nonsense words carefully. A special electrical signal, called the N100 wave, appears shortly after people hear the onset of a word. Sanders and her coworkers found that when people learned these nonsense sounds as words, they showed the N100 response—despite the fact that there were no additional auditory cues to segment the string of sounds.

In addition to learning the units of speech, words, we also learn its content. Even though speech is filled with hesitations, muffled sounds, and sloppy pronunciations, we are able to recognize the sounds because of the context. Context affects the perception of words through top-down processing. (Recall the discussion in Chapter 7.) Other contexts also affect word perception. For example, although we tend to think of a conversation as involving only sounds, we also use other types of cues present in the environment to help us understand what someone is saying. If we are standing at a snack shop at a beach, for example, and someone says, "I scream," we are likely to hear it as "ice cream" (Reynolds & Flagg, 1983).

Understanding the Meaning of Speech

The meaning of a sentence (or of a group of connected sentences that are telling a story) is conveyed by the words that are chosen, the order in which they are combined, the affixes (which are morphemes) attached to the beginnings or ends of the words, the pattern of rhythm and emphasis of the speaker, and knowledge about the world shared by the speaker and the listener. Let us examine some of these features.

Syntax   If we want a listener to understand our speech, we must follow the conventions or "rules" of language. We must use words with which the listener is familiar and combine them in specific ways. For example, if we say, "The two boys looked at the heavy box," we can expect to be understood; but if we say, "Boys the two looking heavy the box at," we will not be. Only the first sentence follows the rules of English grammar.

All languages have a *syntax,* or *grammar.* They all follow certain principles, which linguists call **syntactical rules,** for combining words to form phrases, clauses, or sentences. (*Syntax,* like *synthesis,* comes from the Greek *syntassein,* "to put together.") Syntax provides important information. Consider the following sentence: *A little girl picked the pretty flowers.* A linguist (or an English teacher) can analyze the sentence and identify the part of speech for each word. However, linguists and English teachers could *understand* sentences like this while they were still children—even before they learned such terms as *articles, noun phrases,* and so on. Our understanding of syntax is automatic. We are no more conscious of syntax when we listen to speech than a child is conscious of the laws of physics when he or she learns to ride a bicycle.

In Chapter 8 we saw that some memories (*implicit memories*) cannot be described verbally, whereas others (*explicit memories*) can. Apparently we learn the syntactical rules of our language implicitly. Later we can be taught to talk about these rules and to recognize their application (for example, in constructing diagrams of sentences), but we don't need to be able to explain the rules in order to speak or to understand the speech of others. In fact, Knowlton, Ramus, and Squire (1991) found that patients with anterograde amnesia were able to learn an artificial grammar even though they had lost the ability to form explicit memories. In contrast, as Gabrieli, Cohen, and Corkin (1988) observed, such patients are unable to learn the meanings of new words. Thus, learning syntax and learning word meaning appear to involve different types of memory—and, consequently, different brain mechanisms.

The syntactical rules of the English language are very complicated and by themselves do not tell us much about the psychology of verbal behavior. However, becoming acquainted with the types of cues we attend to in trying to understand things people say (or write) can be useful. Syntactical cues are *word order, word class, function words, content words, affixes, word meanings,* and *prosody.*

Word order is important in English. Thus, if we say, "The A X's the B," we are indicating that the agent is A, the object is B, and the thing being done is X. For example, in the sentences *The boy hit the ball* and *The ball hit the boy,* word order tells us who does what to whom. Word order does not play the same role in all languages, however.

Word class refers to the grammatical categories or parts of speech (such as noun, pronoun, verb, adjective) that we learn about in school. But a person need not learn to categorize words deliberately in order to recognize them and use them appropriately. For example, when we hear a sentence containing the word *beautiful,* we recognize that it describes a person or a thing; it could be categorized as an adjective. Consider these two sentences: *The beautiful girl picked the strawberries* and *The tablecloth was beautiful.* Although the word *beautiful* is used in two different word orders, at the beginning or end of the sentence, we have no trouble identifying what the word refers to.

Words can be classified as *function words* or *content words.* **Function words** include determiners, quantifiers, prepositions, and words in similar categories: *a, the, to, some, and, but, when,* and so on. **Content words** include nouns, verbs, and most adjectives and adverbs: *apple, rug, went, caught, heavy, mysterious, thoroughly, sadly.* Content words express meaning; function words express the relations between content words and thus are very important syntactical cues. As we shall see later, people with a particular type of brain damage lose the ability to comprehend syntax. Included with this deficit is the inability to understand function words or to use them correctly in speech.

Affixes are sounds that we add to the beginning (*prefixes*) or end (*suffixes*) of words to alter their grammatical function. For example, we add the prefix *un-* to the beginning of an adjective or verb to indicate an opposite meaning (*satisfied/unsatisfied; hinge/unhinge*). We add the suffix *-ed* to the end of a regular verb to indicate the past tense (*drop/ dropped*); we add *-ing* to a verb to indicate its use as a noun (*sing/singing*); and we add *-ly* to an adjective to indicate its use as an adverb (*bright/brightly*). We are very quick to recognize the syntactical function of words with affixes like these. For example, Epstein (1961) presented people with word strings such as the following:

> a vap koob desak the citar molent um glox nerf
>
> A vapy koob desaked the citar molently um glox nerfs.

People could more easily remember the second string than the first, even though letters had been added to some of the words. Apparently, the addition of the affixes *-y, -ed,* and *-ly* made the words seem more like a sentence, and they thus became easier to categorize and recall.

Word meanings, or **semantics,** also provide important cues to the syntax of a sentence. (*Semantics* comes from the Greek *sema,* "sign.") For example, consider the following set of words: *Frank discovered a louse combing his beard.* The *syntax* of this sentence is ambiguous. Is Frank combing Frank's beard? Is the louse combing Frank's beard? Is the louse combing the louse's beard? According to the rules of formal grammar, it's the louse doing the combing. But our knowledge of the world and of the usual meanings of words tells us that Frank was doing the combing, because people, not lice, have beards and combs.

Just as function words help us determine the syntax of a sentence, so content words help us determine its meaning. For example, even with its function words removed, the following set of words still makes pretty good sense: *man placed wooden ladder tree climbed picked apples.* You can probably fill in the function words yourself and get *The man placed the wooden ladder against the tree, climbed it, and picked some apples.* We can often guess at function words— which is fortunate, because they are normally spoken quickly and without emphasis and are therefore the most likely to be poorly pronounced.

The final syntactic cue is called **prosody**. It refers to the varying stresses, rhythms, and changes in pitch that accompany speech. Prosody can emphasize the syntax of a word or a group of words or even can serve as the primary source of syntactic information. Prosody is extremely important in language comprehension, because so much of our communication relies on spoken forms. Consider the following two sentences discussed by Steinhauer, Alter, and Friederici (1999):

> Since Jay always jogs five miles seems like a short distance to him.
>
> Since Jay always jogs five miles this seems like a short distance to him.

The first sentence probably seemed a bit harder to comprehend. That's because we lack the prosody cues conveyed by normal speech. A person speaking that sentence would normally slightly elongate the word *jogs,* lower the pitch of the voice at the end of the word, and pause briefly. These cues signal that the words *five miles* belong with *seems* rather than with *jogs.* Putting a comma between *jogs* and *miles* would accomplish in print what we would normally do in speech. Questions marks and periods have correspondence to speech; spoken questions generally end with a rising tone, whereas declarative sentences do not.

Although we don't normally notice these cues as we process spoken language, they are certainly part of our ability to segment speech and understand it. Using sentences in German (their study was conducted with German participants) that approximate the two English sentences above, Steinhauer and colleagues placed a verbal pause between *jogs* and *five* in the second sentence. In this case the syntactic cues to meaning conflicted with the prosody. People who heard this hybrid sentence were virtually unanimous in detecting the mismatch. Furthermore, electrical activity of the brain, recorded from exterior electrodes placed on the scalp, showed the kind of brain activity that accompanies unexpected experiences.

Relation between Semantics and Syntax There is more than one way to say something, and sometimes a particular sentence can mean more than one thing. In Chapter 8 we looked at an experiment by Sachs that showed that we soon forget the particular form a sentence takes but remember its meaning much longer. Noam Chomsky (1957, 1965), a noted linguist, suggested that newly formed sentences are represented in the brain in terms of their meaning, which he called their **deep structure.** The deep structure represents the kernel of what the person intended to say. In order to say the sentence, the brain must transform the deep structure into the appropriate **surface structure:** the particular form the sentence takes.

An example of a "slip of the tongue" recorded by Fromkin (1973) gives us some clues about the way a sentence's deep structure can be transformed into a particular surface structure.

Rosa always date shranks.

The speaker actually intended to say, "Rosa always dated shrinks" (meaning psychiatrists or clinical psychologists). We can speculate that the deep structure of the sentence's verb phrase was something like this: *date* [past tense] + *shrink* [plural]. The words in brackets represent the names of the syntactical rules that are to be used in forming the surface structure of the sentence. Obviously, the past tense of *date* is *dated,* and the plural of *shrink* is *shrinks.* However, something went wrong during the transformation of the deep structure (meaning) into the surface structure (words and syntax). Apparently, the past tense rule got applied to the word *shrink,* resulting in *shrank.* The plural rule also got applied, making the nonsense word *shranks.* (See **Figure 10•2.**)

Most psycholinguists agree that the distinction between surface structure and deep structure is important. As we saw in Chapter 8, people with a language disorder known as conduction aphasia have difficulty repeating words and phrases, but they can *understand* them. In other words, they can retain the deep structure, but not the surface structure, of other people's speech. Later in this chapter we will encounter more neuropsychological evidence in favor of the distinction. However, psycholinguists generally disagree with Chomsky about the particular nature of the cognitive mechanisms through which deep structure is transformed into surface structure and vice versa (Bohannon, 1993; Hulit & Howard, 1993; Tanenhaus, 1988).

Knowledge of the World   Comprehension of speech also involves knowledge about the world and about particular situations that we may encounter there (Carpenter, Miyake, & Just, 1995). Schank and Abelson (1977) suggested that this knowledge is organized into **scripts,** which specify various kinds of events and the event-related interactions that people have witnessed or have learned about from others. Once the speaker has established which script is being referred to, the listener can fill in the details. For example, consider the following sentences (Hunt, 1985): *I learned a lot about the bars in town yesterday. Do you have an aspirin?* To understand what the speaker means, you must be able to do more than simply understand the words and analyze the sentence structure. You must know something about a particular kind of bar; for example, that they serve alcoholic beverages and that "learning a lot about them" probably involved some drinking. You also must know that drinking these beverages can lead to a headache and that aspirin is a remedy for headaches.

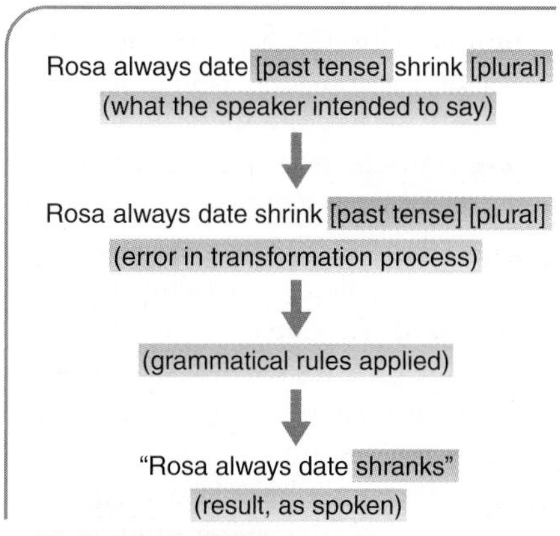

Brain Mechanisms of Speech Production and Comprehension

Studies of people with brain damage and PET studies of people engaged in verbal behavior suggest that mechanisms involved in producing and comprehending speech are located in different areas of the cerebral cortex. These studies have furthered our understanding of the processes of normal verbal behavior.

Speech Production and Comprehension: Evidence from Broca's Aphasia
Meaningful speech involves the expression of our perceptions, memories, and thoughts. The neural mechanisms that control speech production appear to be located in the frontal lobes. Damage to a region of the motor association cortex in the left frontal lobe (Broca's area) disrupts the ability to speak: It causes **Broca's aphasia,** a language disorder characterized by slow, laborious, nonfluent speech and named for Paul Broca (1824–1880), an influential nineteenth-century neurologist. (See **Figure 10•3** on the next page.) When trying to talk with patients who have Broca's aphasia, most people find it hard to resist supplying the words the patients are obviously groping for. But although these patients often mispronounce words, the words they do manage to come out with are meaningful. They have something to say, but the damage to the frontal lobe makes it difficult for them to express it.

Here is a sample of speech from a man with Broca's aphasia, who is telling the examiner why he has come to the hospital. As you will see, his words are meaningful, but what he says is certainly not grammatical. The dots indicate long pauses.

> Ah . . . Monday . . . ah Dad and Paul [patient's name] . . . and Dad . . . hospital. Two . . . ah doctors . . . and ah . . . thirty minutes . . . and yes . . . ah . . . hospital. And, er Wednesday . . . nine o'clock. And er Thursday, ten o'clock . . . doctors. Two doctors . . . and ah . . . teeth. Yeah, . . . fine. (Goodglass, 1976, p. 278)

Lesions that produce Broca's aphasia must be centered in the vicinity of Broca's area. However, damage restricted to the cortex of Broca's area does not appear to produce Broca's aphasia; the damage must extend to surrounding regions of

Rosa always date [past tense] shrink [plural]
(what the speaker intended to say)

Rosa always date shrink [past tense] [plural]
(error in transformation process)

(grammatical rules applied)

"Rosa always date shranks"
(result, as spoken)

FIGURE 10•2   Deep structure and surface structure. A possible explanation for the error in the sentence *Rosa always date shranks.*

FIGURE 10•3 The locations of Broca's area, Wernicke's area, and associated areas involved in language deficits.

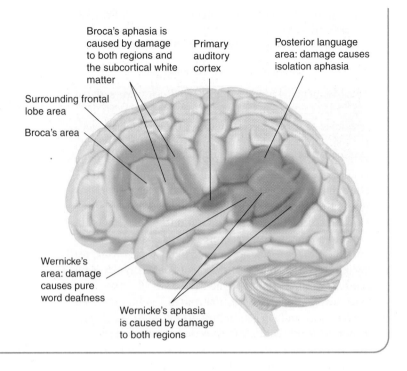

Broca's aphasia is caused by damage to both regions and the subcortical white matter

Surrounding frontal lobe area

Broca's area

Primary auditory cortex

Posterior language area: damage causes isolation aphasia

Wernicke's area: damage causes pure word deafness

Wernicke's aphasia is caused by damage to both regions

the frontal lobe and to the underlying subcortical white matter (Damasio, 1989; Naeser et al., 1989).

Karl Wernicke (1848–1905) suggested that Broca's area contains motor memories—in particular, memories of the sequences of muscle movements that are needed to articulate words. Talking involves rapid movements of the tongue, lips, and jaw, and these movements must be coordinated with one another and with those of the vocal cords; thus, talking requires some very sophisticated motor control mechanisms. Obviously, circuits of neurons somewhere in our brain will, when properly activated, cause these sequences of movements to be executed. The mechanisms that control these movements also adjust to somatosensory feedback (Tremblay, Shiller, & Ostry, 2003). Because damage to the lower left frontal lobe (including Broca's area) disrupts the ability to articulate words, this region is the most likely candidate for the location of these "programs." The fact that this region is located just in front of the part of the primary motor cortex that controls the muscles used for speech certainly supports this conclusion.

In addition to their role in the articulation of words, neural circuits located in the lower left frontal lobe appear to perform more complex functions. Damage to Broca's area often produces **agrammatism:** loss of the ability to produce or comprehend speech that employs complex syntactical rules. For example, people with Broca's aphasia rarely use function words. In addition, they rarely use grammatical markers such as *-ed* or auxiliaries such as *have* (as in *I have gone*). A study by Saffran, Schwartz, and Marin (1980) illustrates this difficulty. The following quotations are from agrammatic patients attempting to describe pictures:

Picture of a boy being hit in the head by a baseball

The boy is catch . . . the boy is hitch . . . the boy is hit the ball. (p. 229)

Picture of a girl giving flowers to her teacher

Girl . . . wants to . . . flowers . . . flowers and wants to . . . The woman . . . wants to . . . The girl wants to . . . the flowers and the woman. (p. 234)

So far, we have viewed Broca's aphasia as a disorder of speech production. In an ordinary conversation, Broca's aphasics seem to understand everything that is said to them. They appear to be irritated and annoyed by their inability to express their thoughts well, and they often make gestures to supplement their scanty speech. The striking disparity between their speech and their comprehension often leads people to assume that their comprehension is normal. But this is an error. To test individuals diagnosed with agrammatism for their speech comprehension, Schwartz, Saffran, and Marin (1980) showed them a pair of drawings, read a sentence aloud, and then asked the patients to point to the appropriate picture. The patients heard 48 sentences such as *The clown applauds the dancer* and *The robber is shot by the cop*. For the first sentence, one picture showed a clown applauding a dancer, and the other showed a dancer applauding a clown. On average, the brain-damaged individuals responded correctly to only 62 percent of the pictures (chance would be 50 percent). In contrast, the performance of normal people on such a simple task is close to 100 percent.

The correct pictures in the study by Schwartz and her colleagues were specified by a particular aspect of grammar: word order. The agrammatism that accompanies Broca's aphasia appears to disrupt patients' ability to use grammatical information, including word order, to comprehend the

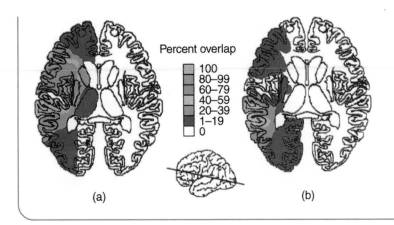

FIGURE 10•4 Evidence for involvement of the insular cortex in speech articulation. Percentage overlap in the lesions of 25 patients (a) with speech articulation difficulties and (b) without speech articulation difficulties. The only region common to all lesions that produced speech articulation difficulties was the precentral gyrus of the insular cortex.

(Reprinted with permission from Dronkers, N. F. (1996). *Nature, 384,* 159–161. Copyright 1996 Macmillan Magazines Limited.)

meaning of a sentence. Thus, these patients' deficit in comprehension parallels their deficit in production. If they hear a sentence such as *The mosquito was swatted by the man,* they can understand that it concerns a man and a mosquito and the action of swatting. And because of their knowledge of men and mosquitoes, they will have no trouble figuring out who is doing what to whom. But a sentence such as *The cow was kicked by the horse* does not provide any extra cues; if the grammar is not understood, neither is the meaning of the sentence (e.g., Zurif, 1990).

In sum, damage to Broca's area seems to affect a hierarchy of language functions. That is, on one level damage creates difficulty in sequencing the muscles of speech, producing articulation problems. At a higher level the problems involve appropriate grammatical sequences.

We might then expect brain areas critical to the articulation function to be located closer to the motor areas of the frontal cortex. Indeed, research evidence supports this possibility. Dronkers (1996) examined MRI and CT scans of 25 patients with severe speech articulation disorders. More than half of the cases involved the joint diagnosis of Broca's aphasia. Depicted in **Figure 10•4(a)** are the areas in which the brain damage overlapped across the different patients. You can see that all of the patients had damage in a region deep within the frontal cortex known as the insula. Compare this to Figure 4.30 on page 111 and you will see how close this region is to the motor areas of the lips and face. In contrast, Dronkers found no damage to this area among a group of individuals without speech articulation problems. (See **Figure 10•4(b)**.) Other studies have produced similar findings (Donnan, Darbey, & Saling, 1997).

The agrammatism that accompanies Broca's aphasia may be a consequence of damage to a different brain area. Caplan, Alpert, and Waters (1999) examined PET scans of individuals who were asked to decide whether various sentences made sense. Some of these sentences were syntactically more complex than others. Interpreting the syntactically more difficult sentences produced greater activity in a part of the frontal cortex just in front of the motor areas and coinciding with Broca's area.

This area may also be responsible for grammatical sequences that transcend speech, such as the sign language systems used by many people in the Deaf community, such as American Sign Language (see Chapter 6). Although they do not require verbal articulation, these languages depend on grammatical structure just as spoken languages do. In a remarkable comparison, Petitto and colleagues (2000) examined cerebral blood circulation (using PET scans) of both vocal and sign language users when they were asked to produce verbs in response to nouns. Both groups showed activation of the area identified by Caplan and colleagues (1999) as important to syntactical processing.

Speech Comprehension and Production: Evidence from Wernicke's Aphasia Comprehension of speech obviously begins in the auditory system, which is needed if the brain is to analyze sequences of sounds and to recognize them as words. Recognition is the first step in comprehension. Recognizing a spoken word is a complex perceptual task that relies on memories of sequences of sounds. This task appears to be accomplished by neural circuits in the upper part of the left temporal lobe—a region that has come to be known as **Wernicke's area.** (Refer to Figure 10.3.)

Brain damage in the left hemisphere that invades Wernicke's area as well as the surrounding region of the temporal and parietal lobes produces a disorder known as Wernicke's aphasia (Figure 10.3). The symptoms of **Wernicke's aphasia** are poor speech recognition and the production of meaningless speech. Unlike speech in Broca's aphasia, the speech associated with Wernicke's aphasia is fluent and unlabored; the person does not strain to articulate words and does not appear to be searching for them. The patient's voice rises and falls normally. When you listen to the speech of a person with Wernicke's aphasia, it appears to be grammatical. That is, the person uses function words such as *the* and *but* and employs complex verb tenses and subordinate clauses. However, these patients use few content words, and the words that they string together do not make sense. In extreme deficits speech deteriorates into a meaningless jumble sometimes referred to as "word salad," as in the following example:

Examiner: What kind of work did you do before you came into the hospital?

Patient: Never, now mista oyge I wanna tell you this happened when happened when he rent. His—his kell come down here and is—he got ren something. It happened. In thesse ropiers were with him for hi—is friend—like was. And it just happened so I don't know, he did not bring around anything. And he did not pay it. And he roden all o these arranjen from the pedis on from iss pescid. In these floors now and so. He hadn't had em round here. (Kertesz, 1981, p. 73)

Given the speech deficits of people with Wernicke's aphasia, assessment of their ability to comprehend speech must rely on their nonverbal behavior. That is, we cannot assume that they do not understand what other people say to them just because they do not give a lucid answer. In a commonly used test of comprehension, clinicians assess these patients' ability to understand questions by asking them to point to objects on a table in front of them. For example, they are asked to "point to the one with ink." If they point to an object other than the pen, they are assumed not to have understood the request. When tested this way, people with severe Wernicke's aphasia show poor comprehension of speech.

Because Wernicke's area is a region of the auditory association cortex, and because a comprehension deficit is so prominent in Wernicke's aphasia, this disorder has been characterized as a *receptive* aphasia. Wernicke suggested that the region that now bears his name is the location of memories of the sequences of sounds that constitute words. This hypothesis is reasonable; it suggests that the auditory association cortex of Wernicke's area makes it possible to recognize the sounds of words, just as the visual association cortex in the lower part of the temporal lobe makes possible the visual recognition of objects.

But why should damage to an area responsible for the ability to recognize spoken words disrupt people's ability to speak? Wernicke's aphasia, like Broca's aphasia, actually appears to consist of several deficits. The abilities that are disrupted include *recognition of spoken words, comprehension of the meaning of words,* and the *ability to convert thoughts into words.* Let us consider each of these abilities in turn.

Remember that *recognizing* a word is not the same as *comprehending* it. If you hear a foreign word several times, you will learn to recognize it; but unless someone tells you what it means, you may not comprehend it. Recognition is a perceptual task; comprehension involves retrieval of additional information from long-term memory. Damage to Wernicke's area produces a deficit in *recognition;* damage to the surrounding temporal and parietal cortex produces a deficit in the production of meaningful speech and comprehension of the speech of others.

Bilateral brain damage that is restricted to Wernicke's area and a comparable area in the right temporal lobe produces an interesting syndrome known as **pure word deafness**—a disorder of auditory word recognition that is uncontaminated by other

problems. Although people with pure word deafness are not deaf, they cannot understand speech. As one patient put it, "I can hear you talking, I just can't understand what you're saying." Another said, "It's as if there were a bypass somewhere, and my ears were not connected to my voice" (Saffran, Marin, & Yeni-Komshian, 1976, p. 211). These patients can recognize nonspeech sounds such as the barking of a dog, the sound of a doorbell, the chirping of a bird, and so on. Often they can recognize the emotion expressed by the intonation of speech, even though they cannot understand what is being said. More significantly, their own speech is excellent. They often can understand what other people are saying by reading their lips. They also can read and write, and sometimes they ask people to communicate with them in writing. Clearly, pure word deafness is not an inability to comprehend the meaning of words; if it were, people with this disorder would not be able to read people's lips or read written words.

What happens if the region around Wernicke's area is damaged, but Wernicke's area itself is spared? The person will exhibit all of the symptoms of Wernicke's aphasia *except* a deficit in auditory word recognition. (We encountered this disorder in Chapter 9.) Damage to the region surrounding Wernicke's area (henceforth identified as the *posterior language area*) produces a disorder known as **isolation aphasia,** in which a person cannot comprehend speech or produce

▲ *Recognition is not the same as comprehension. If you encounter a foreign word several times, you will learn to recognize it, but you will need additional information in order to comprehend it.*

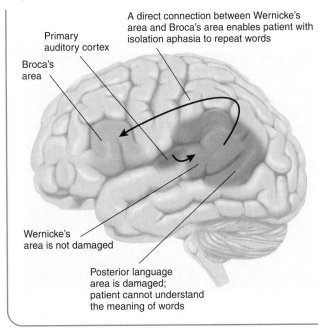

FIGURE 10•5 Connections among regions of the brain that play a special role in language. The arrows provide an explanation of the ability of people with isolation aphasia to repeat words without being able to understand them.

Primary auditory cortex

A direct connection between Wernicke's area and Broca's area enables patient with isolation aphasia to repeat words

Broca's area

Wernicke's area is not damaged

Posterior language area is damaged; patient cannot understand the meaning of words

meaningful speech but is able to repeat speech and learn new sequences of words. (Refer again to Figure 10.3.) The difference between isolation aphasia and Wernicke's aphasia is that patients with isolation aphasia can repeat what other people say to them; thus, they obviously can recognize words. However, *they cannot comprehend the meaning of what they hear and repeat; nor can they produce meaningful speech of their own.* Apparently, the sounds of words are recognized by neural circuits in Wernicke's area, and this information is transmitted to Broca's area so that the words can be repeated. In fact, a bundle of axons, the *arcuate fasciculus* ("curved bundle"), directly connects these two regions. But because the posterior language area is destroyed, the meaning of the words cannot be comprehended. (See **Figure 10•5**.)

Word Recognition and Production: PET and fMRI Studies

The results of studies using PET scans are generally consistent with the results of studies of language-impaired patients with

brain damage. First, several studies have found that patients with Broca's aphasia show abnormally low activity in the lower left frontal lobe; patients with Wernicke's aphasia show low activity in the temporal/parietal area of the brain (Karbe et al., 1989; Karbe, Szelies, Herholz, & Heiss, 1990; Metter, 1991; Metter et al., 1990). These results explain the fact that lesions in the depths of the frontal or temporal/parietal cortex can sometimes produce aphasia by disrupting normal activity there.

Other studies have used PET scanners to investigate the neural activity of people with no cerebral damage while they performed verbal tasks. **Figure 10•6** shows PET scans from a study by Petersen and colleagues (1988). Listening passively to a list of nouns activated the primary auditory cortex and Wernicke's area, while repeating the nouns activated the primary motor cortex and Broca's area. When people were asked to think of verbs that were appropriate to use with the nouns, even more intense activity was seen in Broca's area.

Brain imaging using fMRI scans has helped supplement this picture. Binder and colleagues (1997) produced comprehensive scans of individuals processing the semantic characteristics of spoken words. The scans showed activation of Wernicke's area, a result that supports the standard model we have been examining. But semantic decisions also activated large areas of the temporal and parietal areas outside Wernicke's area, as well as frontal lobe regions around Broca's area. Processing the meaning of words most likely involves other areas of the cortex as well.

Interim Summary

Speech Comprehension and Production

Language provides an orderly system of communication. The recognition of sounds in continuous speech is a complex process. Phonemes are recognized even though their pronunciation is affected by neighboring sounds, by accents and speech peculiarities, and by stress. Studies have shown that we distinguish between voiced and unvoiced consonant phonemes by means of voice-onset time. Research has also shown that the primary unit of analysis is not individual phonemes but combinations of phonemes. Learning and contextual information are additional factors in recognizing what we hear.

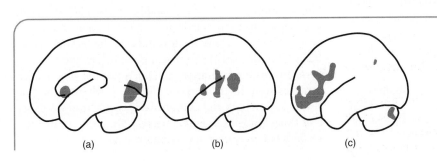

(a) (b) (c)

FIGURE 10•6 PET scans of participants in a study by Petersen and colleagues (1988). (a) Listening passively to a list of nouns. (b) Silently reading a list of nouns. (c) Thinking of verbs related to a list of nouns.

Morphemes are the smallest units of meaning. Meaning is a joint function of syntax and semantics. All users of a particular language observe syntactical rules that establish the relations of the words in a sentence to one another. These rules are not learned explicitly. In fact, research indicates that people can learn to apply rules of an artificial grammar without being able to state the rules. The most important features that we use to understand syntax are word order, word class, function words, content words, affixes, word meanings (semantics), and prosody. Content words refer to objects, actions, and the characteristics of objects and actions and thus can express meaning even in sentences with ambiguous syntax.

Chomsky has suggested that speech production entails the transformation of deep structure into surface structure. Most psycholinguists disagree with the details of Chomsky's explanation but consider the distinction between deep and surface structure to be important.

Speech comprehension requires more than an understanding of syntax and semantics; it also requires knowledge of the world. When we are listeners, we must share knowledge about the world with the speaker if we are to understand what she or he is referring to.

The effects of brain damage suggest that memories of the sounds of words are located in Wernicke's area and that memories of the muscular movements needed to produce them are located near Broca's area. Thus, Wernicke's area is necessary for speech comprehension, and Broca's area is necessary for speech production. Function words and other syntactical features of speech related to motor operations involve mechanisms in the frontal lobes. Broca's aphasia (caused by damage that extends beyond the boundaries of Broca's area) is characterized by nonfluent but meaningful speech that is scarce in function words but rich in content words.

Wernicke's aphasia (caused by damage that extends beyond the boundaries of Wernicke's area) is characterized by fluent but meaningless speech that is scarce in content words but rich in function words. Agrammatism is a disorder marked by the inability to produce and comprehend speech that involves complex syntax. Damage restricted to Wernicke's area does not produce aphasia; instead, it produces pure word deafness, a deficit in speech comprehension unaccompanied by other language deficits. Damage to the temporal/parietal region surrounding Wernicke's area produces isolation aphasia—loss of the ability to produce meaningful speech or to comprehend the speech of others but retention of the ability to repeat others' speech. The results of studies of patients with brain damage have been supported by PET and fMRI studies.

QUESTIONS TO CONSIDER

1. Suppose that you were asked to assess the abilities and deficits of people with aphasia. What tasks would you include in your assessment to test for the presence of particular deficits?

2. What would the thoughts of a person with severe Wernicke's aphasia be like? These people produce speech that has very little meaning. In what ways could you test these people to see if their thoughts were any more coherent than their words?

Reading

Although the comprehension and production of spoken language have a long history in the human past, the comprehension and production of written language are much more recent. Initially written language was pictorial. Arbitrary symbols gradually made their appearance as cues to pronunciation when a pictorial symbol was ambiguous. With the notable exception of Chinese (and other Asian writing systems based on Chinese), most modern languages use alphabetic writing systems in which a small number of symbols represent the sounds used to pronounce words. For example, most European languages are represented by the Roman alphabet, originally developed to represent the sounds of Latin and subsequently adopted by peoples ruled or otherwise influenced by the Roman Empire. The Roman alphabet was adapted from the Greek alphabet, which in turn was adapted from the Phoenician alphabet, which was the first alphabet. For example, the letter *D* has its origin in the Phoenician symbol *daleth,* which meant "door." At first the symbol literally indicated a door, but it later came to represent the phoneme /d/. The Greeks adopted the symbol and its pronunciation but changed its name to *delta.* Finally, the Romans altered its shape into the one that is found in English today.

Scanning of Text

As we saw in Chapter 6, our eyes make rapid jumps, called *saccades,* as we scan a scene. These same rapid movements occur when we read. In fact, a French ophthalmologist discovered saccadic eye movements while watching people read (Javal, 1879).

We do not receive information from the visual environment while the eyes are actually moving but only during the brief **fixations** that occur between saccades. The average fixation lasts about 250 milliseconds (ms, 1/1000 of a second), but duration can vary considerably. **Figure 10•7** shows the patterns of fixations made by a good reader and a poor reader. The ovals above the text indicate the locations of the fixations in the line of text that appears below, and the numbers indicate their duration (in ms). All of the good reader's saccades were in the forward direction, whereas the poor reader looked back and examined previously read words several times (indicated by the arrows). In addition, the good reader's fixations were, on average, considerably shorter.

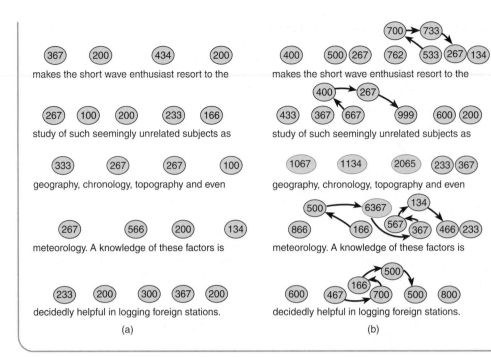

FIGURE 10•7 The pattern of fixations made by two readers. Ovals indicate the locations of fixations in the line of text below them; the numbers within the ovals indicate durations of the fixations (in milliseconds). Arrows indicate backtracking to text already examined. (a) A good reader. (b) A poor reader. (After Buswell (1937). From M. A. Just and P. A. Carpenter, *The Psychology of Reading and Language Comprehension.* Published by Allyn and Bacon, Boston, MA. Copyright © 1987 by Pearson Education. Reprinted by permission of the publisher.)

What do we look at when we read? Research with eye-tracking cameras has shown that college students typically fixate on most of the words in a text when they are asked to read it carefully enough to understand its meaning. They fixate on 80 percent of the content words but on only 40 percent of the function words (Reichle, Pollatsek, Fisher, & Rayner, 1998). Of course, function words are generally shorter than content words, but the difference is not simply a matter of word size. Readers are more likely to skip over short function words such as *and* or *the* than over short content words such as *ant* or *run* (Carpenter & Just, 1983).

Eye movements provide an excellent window into the dynamics of the reading process. Apparently, as we read a sentence, we analyze it word by word (Rayner & Pollatsek, 1989). Of course, some words contribute more to our understanding than others do. And sometimes we must wait to see how a sentence turns out in order to understand its beginning. The less frequently a word occurs in normal usage, the greater the fixation time (e.g., Rayner, Sereno, & Raney, 1996); presumably, we take longer to recognize and understand unusual words. For example, the word *sable* has a longer fixation than the word *table*. The word that follows an unusual word does not receive a longer-than-usual fixation, which indicates that the reader finishes processing the word before initiating the next saccade (Thibadeau, Just, & Carpenter, 1982). Fixation time also is influenced by the predictability of the words in a text, as measured by readers' ability to guess a missing word. Gaze time is longer for unpredictable than for predictable words, even when comparison words in experiments are matched for word length and frequency of usage (Reichle et al., 1998).

Besides spending a longer time fixating on unusual words, readers spend more time fixating on *longer* words. In fact, if word familiarity is held constant, the amount of time a word receives is proportional to its length (Carpenter & Just, 1983). In addition, Just, Carpenter, and Wu (1983) found that the amount of time that Chinese readers spent

▲ *When people read Chinese, the amount of time they fixate on each character is proportional to its complexity — the number of brushstrokes used to make it.*

fixating on a character in the traditional Chinese writing system was proportional to the number of brushstrokes used to make it. Because Chinese characters are of approximately the same size, the increased fixation time appears to reflect the visual complexity of a character rather than the amount of space it occupies.

Phonetic and Whole-Word Recognition: Evidence from Neuropsychology

Most psychologists who study the reading process believe that readers have two basic ways to recognize words: phonetic and whole-word recognition. **Phonetic reading** involves the decoding of the sounds that letters or groups of letters make. For example, most readers of English would probably pronounce *praglet* in approximately the same way. Our ability to pronounce this nonsense word depends on our knowledge of the relation between letters and sounds in the English language. We use such knowledge to "sound the word out." But do we have to "sound out" familiar, reasonably short words such as *table* or *grass*? It appears that we do not; we recognize each of these words as a whole. In other words, we also engage in **whole-word reading**

If a reader is relatively inexperienced, he or she will have to sound out most words and, consequently, will read rather slowly. Experienced readers will have had so much practice

▲ *Most school systems teach children phonetic reading skills so that they can sound out words they do not recognize.*

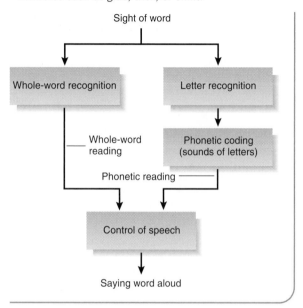

FIGURE 10•8 A simplified model of the reading process, showing whole-word and phonetic reading. The model considers only reading a single word aloud. Whole-word reading is used for most familiar words; phonetic reading is used for unfamiliar words and for nonwords such as *glab*, *trisk*, or *chint*.

looking at words that they will quickly recognize most of them as whole units. During reading, phonetic and whole-word reading may alternate. If the word is familiar, the whole-word method will suffice. If the word is unfamiliar, the whole-word method will fail, and the reader will turn to the phonetic method long enough to read the word. **Figure 10•8** illustrates elements of the reading process, although in admittedly oversimplified fashion.

Whole-word recognition not only is faster than phonetic decoding but also is absolutely necessary in a language (such as English) in which spelling is not completely phonetic. Consider the following pairs of words: *cow/blow, bone/one, post/cost, limb/climb.* Obviously, no single set of rules can account for the pronunciation of both members of each pair. In this case the rules are phonological (*phonology*—loosely translated as "laws of sound"—refers to the relation between letters and the sounds they represent in a particular language). But all of these words are familiar and easy to read. If we did not have the ability to recognize words as wholes, we would not be able to read irregularly spelled words, which are rather common in English. Some languages, such as Italian, have far fewer irregularities. Speakers of these languages apparently process speech in different brain areas than speakers of phonetically irregular languages like English (Paulesu et al., 2000).

The best evidence demonstrating that people can read words without sounding them out comes from studies of patients with acquired dyslexias. *Dyslexia* means "faulty reading." *Acquired* dyslexias are those caused by damage to the

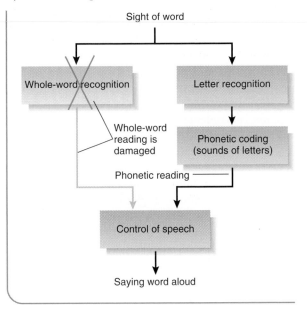

FIGURE 10·9 A model of surface dyslexia. Only phonetic reading remains.

brains of people who already know how to read. In contrast, *developmental* dyslexias are reading difficulties that become apparent when children are learning to read. Developmental dyslexias may involve anomalies in brain circuitry and will be discussed later in the chapter.

Investigators have reported several types of acquired dyslexias. We will look at three of them here. All are caused by damage to the left parietal lobe or left temporal lobe, but the precise anatomy of dyslexias is not well understood. **Surface dyslexia** is a deficit in whole-word reading (Marshall & Newcombe, 1973; McCarthy & Warrington, 1990). The term "surface" reflects the fact that people with this disorder make errors related to the visual appearance of the words and to phonological rules, not to the meaning of the words, which could be considered "deeper" than their appearance. Because patients with surface dyslexia have difficulty recognizing words as wholes, they are obliged to sound them out. Thus, they can easily read words with regular spelling, such as *hand, tablet,* or *chin.* However, they have difficulty reading words with irregular spelling, such as *sew, pint,* or *yacht.* In fact, they may read these words as *sue, pinnt,* and *yatchet.* They have no difficulty reading pronounceable nonwords, such as *glab, trisk,* and *chint.* (See **Figure 10·9**.)

Patients with **phonological dyslexia** have the opposite problem; they can read by the whole-word method but cannot sound out words. Thus, they can read words that they are already familiar with, but they have great difficulty figuring out how to read unfamiliar words or pronounceable nonwords (Beauvois & Dérouesné, 1979; Dérouesné & Beauvois, 1979). People with phonological dyslexia may be excellent readers if they have already acquired a good reading vocabulary before their brain damage occurs. (See **Figure 10·10**.)

Phonological dyslexia provides evidence that whole-word reading and phonetic reading involve different brain mechanisms. Phonetic reading, which is the only way we can read nonwords or words we have not yet learned, entails letter-to-sound decoding. It also requires more than decoding of the sounds produced by single letters; for example, some sounds are transcribed as two-letter sequences (such as *th* or *sh*), and the addition of the letter *e* to the end of a word lengthens an internal vowel (*can* becomes *cane*). Further, there is some evidence from PET scans that phonetic reading activates the left frontal lobe in the area associated with Broca's aphasia (see Fiez, Balota, Raichle, & Petersen, 1999).

We know that recognizing a spoken word is different from understanding it. For example, patients with *transcortical sensory aphasia* can repeat what is said to them even though they show no signs of understanding what they hear or say. **Direct dyslexia** resembles isolation aphasia, except that the words in question are written, not spoken (Lytton & Brust, 1989; Schwartz, Marin, & Saffran, 1979). People with this disorder can read words aloud *even though they cannot understand the words they are saying.* After sustaining a stroke that damaged his left frontal and temporal lobes, Lytton and Brust's (1989) patient lost the ability to communicate verbally; his speech was meaningless and he was unable to comprehend what other people said to him. However, he could read words with which he was already familiar. He could *not* read pronounceable nonwords; thus, he had lost the ability to read phonetically. His comprehension deficit seemed complete; when the investigators presented him with a word and several pictures, one of which corresponded to the word, he correctly read the word aloud but had no idea which picture went with it.

The symptoms of developmental dyslexias resemble those of acquired dyslexias. They first manifest themselves in

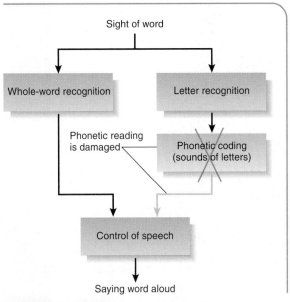

FIGURE 10·10 A model of phonological dyslexia. Only whole-word reading remains.

childhood and tend to occur in families, which suggests the presence of a genetic (and hence biological) component. Several studies have found evidence that brain abnormalities in a portion of Wernicke's area may be responsible for developmental dyslexias (Galaburda, 1993; Galaburda & Kemper, 1979; Galaburda et al., 1985). In addition, Galaburda, Menard, and Rosen (1994) found evidence that structural differences in the auditory system of the brain may play a role in this disorder. Brain imaging data indicate that people with developmental dyslexias can use both Broca's area and Wernicke's area for language processing. However, these individuals lack the degree of synchrony of neural activity in the two areas shown by people without dyslexia (Paulesu et al., 1996). Dyslexic patients may not be able to combine information from the two areas.

As I mentioned earlier, PET studies have shown that the auditory association cortex is activated by the sound of words but not by other sounds. Petersen, Fox, Snyder, and Raichle (1990) obtained similar results using visual stimuli. These investigators presented people with four types of visual stimuli: unfamiliar letterlike forms, strings of consonants, pronounceable nonwords, and real words. They found that although all visual stimuli activated the primary visual cortex, one region of the visual association cortex was activated only by pronounceable nonwords or by real words; that is, by familiar combinations of letters. Presumably, damage to this region, or faulty development of the neural circuits located there, is responsible for some forms of dyslexia. (See **Figure 10•11**.)

Understanding the Meanings of Words and Sentences

Recognizing a word is a matter of perception. The primary task is visual. But, as described in the previous section, when we encounter an unfamiliar word we use phonological codes to "sound it out." Either way though, once we recognize a word, the next step in the reading process is understanding its meaning.

We learn the meanings of words through experience. The meanings of content words involve memories of objects, actions, and their characteristics—visual, auditory, somatosensory, olfactory, and gustatory. These memories of the meanings of words are distributed throughout the brain. For example, our understanding of the meaning of the word *apple* involves memories of the sight of an apple; the way it feels in our hands; the crunching sound we hear when we bite into it; and the texture, taste, and odor we experience when we chew it. Our understanding of the meanings of adjectives, such as the word *heavy*, involves memories of objects that are difficult or impossible to lift. The image evoked by the phrase *heavy package* undoubtedly involves memories of our own experience with heavy packages, whereas the image evoked by the phrase *heavy rocket* (with which we have had no personal experience) is understood in terms of visual size and bulk.

What about the understanding of abstract content words, such as the nouns *honesty* and *justice*? These words are probably first understood as adjectives: An *honest student* is someone who does not cheat on exams or plagiarize when writing

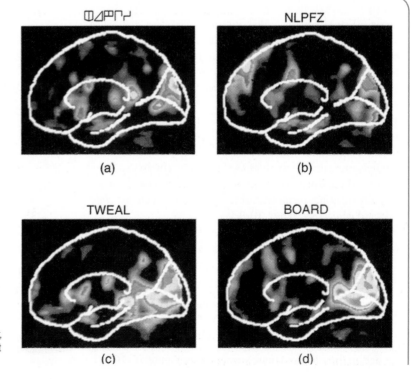

FIGURE 10•11 PET scans of the medial surface of the brains of people who read (a) letterlike forms, (b) strings of consonants, (c) pronounceable nonwords, and (d) real words.
(Reprinted with permission from Petersen, S. E., Fox, P. T., Snyder, A. Z., & Raichle, M. E. *Science*, 1990, *249*, 1041–1044. Copyright © 1990 AAAS.)

papers, an *honest bank clerk* does not steal money, and so on. Our understanding of these words depends on our direct experience with such people or on our vicarious experience with them through stories we read or hear about. By itself, the word *honesty* is abstract; it does not refer to anything concrete.

The understanding of most function words is also abstract. For example, the word *and* serves to link two or more things being discussed; the word *or* indicates a choice; the word *but* indicates that a contradiction will be expressed in the next phrase. The meanings of such words are difficult to imagine or verbalize, rather like the rules of grammar. The meanings of prepositions, such as *in, under,* or *through,* are more concrete and are probably represented by images of objects in relation to each other.

As we read (or hear) a sentence, the words and phrases we encounter activate memories that permit us to understand their meanings. Unless we have to pause to figure out an obscure allusion (which should not happen very often in the case of good writing and speaking), memory activation is an automatic, unconscious process. When we read the sentence *She opened her mouth to let the dentist examine her aching tooth,* we very quickly picture a specific scene. Our understanding depends not only on comprehension of the specific words but also on our knowledge of dental chairs, dentists, toothaches and their treatment, and so on.

A phenomenon known as **semantic priming** gives us some hints about the nature of activation of memories triggered by the perception of words and phrases. Semantic priming is a facilitating effect: The presentation of a word facilitates the recognition of words having related meanings (Tulving & Schacter, 1990). The process involves similarities in the *meanings* of words. For example, if a person sees the word *bread,* he or she will be more likely to successfully recognize a fuzzy image of the word *butter* or an image that is presented very briefly by means of a tachistoscope (Johnston & Dark, 1986). Presumably, the brain contains circuits of neurons that serve as "word detectors" involved in visual recognition of particular words (McClelland & Rumelhart, 1981; Morton, 1979). Reading the word *bread* activates word detectors and other neural circuits involved in memories of the word's meaning. Apparently the activation spreads to circuits denoting related concepts, such as *butter.* Thus, our memories must be linked according to our experience regarding the relations between specific concepts.

Figure 10•12 suggests how neural representations of concepts may be linked together in a network. The concept "piano" has many different features, including the sounds a piano makes, its size, the shapes it can have, its parts, people who play it or tune it or move it, and so on. Depending on the context in which it is perceived, the word *piano* can activate various subsets of these features. For example, the sentences *The piano was tuned* and *The piano was lifted* presumably activate neural representations of different features.

Context effects, an example of top-down processing, have been demonstrated through semantic priming. For example, Zola (1984) asked people to read either of two sentences such as the following while he recorded their eye movements with an eye-tracking camera.

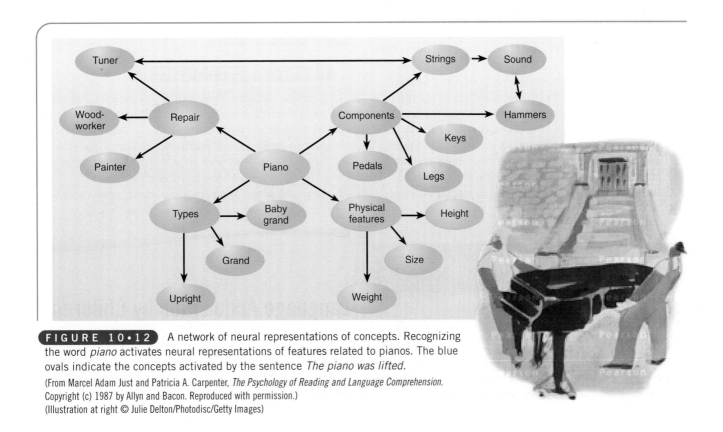

FIGURE 10•12 A network of neural representations of concepts. Recognizing the word *piano* activates neural representations of features related to pianos. The blue ovals indicate the concepts activated by the sentence *The piano was lifted.*

(From Marcel Adam Just and Patricia A. Carpenter, *The Psychology of Reading and Language Comprehension.* Copyright (c) 1987 by Allyn and Bacon. Reproduced with permission.)

(Illustration at right © Julie Delton/Photodisc/Getty Images)

1. Movie theaters must have adequate popcorn to serve their patrons.

2. Movie theaters must have buttered popcorn to serve their patrons.

Zola found that people made a significantly shorter fixation on the word *popcorn* in sentence 2. Let us consider why they did so. The word *adequate* is not normally associated with the word *popcorn*, so the people who read sentence 1 were unprepared for this word when they got to it. However, *buttered* certainly goes with *popcorn*, especially in the context of a movie theater. Thus, the context of the sentence must have provided some activation of the word detector for *popcorn*, making it easier for people to recognize the word.

Semantic priming studies have also shed some light on another aspect of the reading process—the development of a *mental model*. Many investigators believe that as a person reads some text, he or she generates a mental model of what the text is describing (see Johnson-Laird, 1985, for a discussion of mental models). For example, if the text contains a narrative, the reader will imagine the scenes, the people, and the actions that are being recounted. Glenberg, Meyer, and Lindem (1987) asked participants to read the following sentences. Some saw the words *put on*; others saw *took off*:

> John was preparing for a marathon in August. After doing a few warm-up exercises, he *put on/took off* his sweatshirt and went jogging. He jogged halfway around the lake without too much difficulty.

After the participants had read the last sentence, the researchers flashed the word *sweatshirt* on a screen and measured the participants' reaction times. Those participants who had read *put on* recognized the word faster than did those who had read *took off*. Presumably, the mental model of the first group of participants contained a man wearing a sweatshirt; thus, the word detector for *sweatshirt* was primed.

Reading may therefore involve two types of memory. As we scan text, we use memory for the words in the sentences to discern the meanings of other words, as in the *buttered popcorn* example. But we also retain a memory for the mental model we construct from the narrative. Singer and Ritchot (1996) suggest that these are two different abilities, and that they make independent contributions to reading efficiency.

Once a word has been perceived, recognition of its pronunciation and meaning takes place. Long or unfamiliar words are sounded out—that is, they are read phonetically. In contrast, short, familiar words are recognized as wholes. In fact, only whole-word reading will enable us to know how to pronounce words such as *cow* and *blow*, or *bone* and *one*, which have irregular spellings. Experienced readers use both whole-word and phonetic reading. If a word is recognized as a whole, readers move on; if not, they continue to decode phonetically. The distinction between these two forms of recognition is supported by behavioral data and by studies of people with acquired dyslexias. People with surface dyslexia have difficulty with whole-word reading, whereas people with phonological dyslexia have difficulty sounding out unfamiliar words or pronounceable nonwords. In addition, people with direct dyslexia can read words but cannot understand their meaning. Developmental dyslexias appear to be caused by abnormal development of parts of the left hemisphere and may reflect an inability to combine information from Broca's area and Wernicke's area.

The meanings of words are learned through experience. Concrete content words are represented by memories of objects, actions, and their characteristics. Abstract content words are probably first understood as adjectives that refer to properties of concrete concepts. Function words are understood by their grammatical roles or by the relations they represent. The phenomenon of semantic priming suggests that some neural circuits recognize the visual form of words, whereas other circuits encode various aspects of the meanings of words. Connections between these circuits are responsible for our ability to recognize meaningful associations. Semantic priming has been used to study the processes of word recognition and comprehension of meaning.

QUESTIONS TO CONSIDER

1. Suppose someone close to you received a head injury that caused phonological dyslexia. What would you do to try to help her read better? (Hint: It would probably be best to build on her remaining abilities.) Suppose she needed to learn to read some words she had never seen before. How would you help her do so?

2. Young children (and even some adults) often move their lips while they read. Why do you think they do so?

Interim Summary

Reading

Recognition of written words is a complex perceptual task. The eye-tracking camera allows researchers to study people's eye movements and fixations and to learn about the reading process. For example, we analyze a sentence word by word as we read it, pausing longer on long or unusual words.

Language Acquisition by Children

How do children learn to communicate verbally with other people? How do they master the many rules needed to transform a thought into a coherent sentence? How do they learn the meanings of thousands of words? And *why* do they do all

▲ *A young child's direct interaction with adult speakers is a critical feature of language acquisition.*

of these things? Do other people shape children's babble into words by appropriately reinforcing their behavior, or do innate mechanisms ensure children's acquisition of language without reinforcement? This section addresses these and other questions related to children's verbal development.

Evaluating Scientific Issues

Is There a Language Acquisition Device?

The linguistic accomplishments of young children are remarkable. Even a child who may do poorly after entering school has previously learned the rules of grammar and the meanings of thousands of words. Some children fail to work hard at school, but no typical child fails to talk fluently or to understand others' talk. And this happens despite the fact that much of everyday language is ungrammatical, hesitating, and full of unfinished sentences. What shapes this learning process, and what motivates it?

Many linguists have concluded that the ability to learn language is innate. A child must only live in the company of speakers of a language to acquire that language. To explain how this happens, linguists have proposed that a child's brain contains a "language acquisition device" that embodies rules of "universal grammar"; because each language expresses these rules in slightly different ways, the child must learn the details, but the basics are already there in the brain (Chomsky, 1965; Lennenberg, 1967; McNeill, 1970; Miller, 1987).

● Do We Have Special Cognitive Structures for Language?

The assertion that an innate language acquisition device guides children's acquisition of a language is part of a general theory about the cognitive structures responsible for

language and its acquisitions (Pinker, 1990, 1994). The most important components are as follows:

1. Children who are learning a language make hypotheses about the grammatical rules they need to follow. These hypotheses are confirmed or disconfirmed by the speech they hear.

2. An innate language acquisition device (a part of the brain) guides children's hypothesis formation. Because they have this device, there are certain types of hypothetical rules they will never entertain and certain types of sentences they will never utter.

3. The language acquisition device makes reinforcement unnecessary; the device provides the motivation for the child to learn a language.

4. There is a critical period for learning a language. The language acquisition device works best during childhood; after childhood, languages are difficult to learn and almost impossible to master.

● Evidence Concerning the Language Acquisition Device Hypothesis

At present we have no way to evaluate the first assertion—that children make and test hypotheses about grammatical rules. No serious investigator believes that these hypotheses are conscious and deliberate; thus, we cannot simply ask children why they say what they do. We should probably view this concept of hypothesis testing as a working assumption based on the fact that children's speech sometimes follows one rule or another. During one stage of language acquisition, for example, children often apply the regular past-tense rule even to irregular verbs, saying "I catched it" or "She hitted me." Some researchers would say that the children are testing the hypothesis that all events in the past are expressed by adding *-ed* to the word that denotes the action.

A more important—and testable—assertion is that the child's hypothesis testing is guided by the language acquisition device. The most important piece of evidence in favor of this assertion is the discovery of **language universals:** characteristics that can be found in all languages that linguists have studied. Some of the more important language universals include the existence of noun phrases (*The quick brown fox . . .*); verb phrases (*. . . ate the chicken*); grammatical categories of words such as nouns and adjectives; and syntactical rules that permit the expression of subject–verb–object relations (*John hit Andy*), plurality (*two birds*), and possession (*Rachel's pen*).

But the fact that all languages share certain characteristics does not mean that they are the products of innate brain mechanisms. For example, Hebb, Lambert, and Tucker (1973) observed that language universals may simply reflect realities of the world. Objects come in slightly different shapes, sizes, and colors, so we can expect languages to develop ways (such as adjectives) to distinguish among them.

Similarly, when people deal with one another and with nature, their interactions often take the form of an agent's acting on an object. Thus, the fact that all languages have ways of expressing these interactions is not surprising. It is not unreasonable to suppose that the same kinds of linguistic devices have been independently invented at different times and in different places by different cultures. After all, archaeologists tell us that similar tools have been invented by different cultures all around the world. People need to cut, hammer, chisel, scrape, and wedge things apart, and different cultures have invented similar devices to perform these tasks. We need not conclude that these inventions are products of a "tool-making device" located in the brain.

But even if *some* language universals are dictated by reality, others could indeed be the result of a language acquisition device. For example, consider the following sentences (Pinker, 1990):

A1. *Irv drove the car* into the garage.

A2. Irv drove the car.

B1. Irv *put the car* into the garage.

B2. Irv put the car.

Someone (such as a child learning a language) who heard sentences A1 and A2 could reasonably infer that sentence B1 could be transformed into sentence B2. But the inference obviously is false; sentence B2 is ungrammatical. The linguistic rules that say that sentence A2 is acceptable but that sentence B2 is not are very complex; and their complexity is taken as evidence that they must be innate, not learned. As Pinker (1990) concludes, "The solution to the problem [as to why children do not utter sentence B2] must be that children's learning mechanisms ultimately do not allow them to make the generalization" (p. 206).

This conclusion rests on the assumption that children use rules similar to the ones that linguists use. How, the reasoning goes, could a child master such complicated rules at such an early stage of cognitive development unless the rules were already wired into the brain? But perhaps the children are not following such complex rules. Perhaps they learn that when you say *put* (*something*), you must always go on to say *where* you put something. Linguists do not like rules that deal with particular words, such as *put* (*something*) (*somewhere*); they prefer abstract and general rules that deal with *categories:* clauses, prepositions, noun phrases, and the like. But children learn particular words and their meanings—why should they not also learn that certain words must be followed (or must never be followed) by certain others? Doing so is certainly simpler than learning the complex and subtle rules that linguists have devised. It would seem that both complex and simple rules (or innate or learned ones) could explain the fact that children do not utter sentence B2.

The third assertion is that language acquisition occurs without the need of reinforcement—or even of correction. Brown and Hanlon (1970) recorded dialogue between children and parents and found that adults generally did not show disapproval when the children's utterances were ungrammatical or approval when they were grammatical. Instead, approval appeared to be contingent on the truth or accuracy of the children's statements. But if there is no differential reinforcement, how can we explain the fact that children eventually learn to speak grammatically?

It is undoubtedly true that adults seldom say, "Good, you said that right" or "No, you said that wrong." However, adults do distinguish between grammatical and ungrammatical speech of children. A study by Bohannon and Stanowicz (1988) found that adults are likely to repeat children's grammatically correct sentences verbatim but to correct ungrammatical sentences. For example, if a child says, "That be monkey," an adult would say, "Yes, that is a monkey." Adults were also more likely to ask for clarifications of ungrammatical sentences. Thus, adults *do* provide the information children need to correct faulty speech.

It is also the case that adults talk differently to children than they do to other adults; specifically, they speak in ways that would seem to be optimal for promoting learning. According to Newport, Gleitman, and Gleitman (1977), almost all speech that a young child hears (at least, in industrialized English-speaking societies) is grammatically correct. If that is so, why should we hypothesize that a language acquisition device exists? Because, say some researchers, not all children are exposed to child-directed speech. "In some societies people tacitly assume that children aren't worth speaking to and don't have anything to say that is worth listening to. Such children learn to speak by overhearing streams of adult-to-adult speech" (Pinker, 1990, p. 218).

Pinker's statement is very strong; it says that children in some cultures have no speech directed toward them until they have mastered the language. It implies that the children's mothers do not talk with them and ignores the fact that older children may not be quite so choosy about their conversational partners. To conclude that such an extreme statement is true would require extensive observation and documentation of child-rearing practices in other cultures. One of the strongest biological tendencies of our species is for a mother to cherish, play with, and communicate with her offspring. If there really is a culture in which mothers do *not* do so, we need better documentation of it.

In fact, children do *not* learn a language that they simply overhear. Bonvillian, Nelson, and Charrow (1976) studied children of deaf parents whose only exposure to spoken language was through television or radio. This exposure was not enough; although the children could hear and did watch television and listen to the radio, they did not learn to speak English. It takes more than "overhearing streams of adult-to-adult speech" to learn a language. The way that parents talk to their children is closely related to the children's language acquisition (Furrow & Nelson, 1986; Furrow, Nelson, & Benedict, 1979). Thus, the question is, Just how much instruction (in the form of child-directed speech) do children need?

The final assertion—that the language acquisition device works best during childhood—has received the most experimental support. For example, Newport and Supalla (cited in Johnson & Newport, 1989) studied the ability of people who were deaf from birth to use sign language. They found that the earlier the training began, the better the person was able to communicate. Also, Johnson and Newport (1989) found that native Korean and Chinese speakers who moved to North America learned English grammar better if they arrived during childhood. The advantage did not appear to be a result of differences in motivation to learn a second language. Such results are consistent with the hypothesis that something happens to the brain after childhood that makes it more difficult to learn a language.

As you learned in Chapter 2, observational studies such as these do not prove that a cause-and-effect relation exists between the variables in question. Johnson and Newport suggest that people's age (in particular, the age of their brain) affects their language learning ability. But other variables also are correlated with age. For example, the Korean and Chinese speakers who moved to North America as children spent several years in school; perhaps the school environment is a particularly good place to learn a second language. In addition, adults are generally more willing to correct the grammatical errors made by children than those made by adolescents or other adults; thus, children may get more tutoring. It is certainly possible that the investigators are correct, but their results cannot be taken as *proof* that the brain contains an innate language acquisition device.

● **What Should We Conclude?**

In one sense, a language acquisition device does exist. The human brain *is* a language acquisition device; without it, languages are not acquired. The real controversy is over the characteristics of this language acquisition device. Is it specialized for universal rules of grammar, and does it provide innate motivation that makes reinforcement unnecessary?

The answer to the first question may be emerging in the increased resolution of the techniques of functional brain imaging. An fMRI study by Musso and colleagues (2003) shows what is now possible. Musso and colleagues examined the brain activity of native German speakers as they learned one of two types of language: a real but unfamiliar language (such as Italian or Japanese) or an artificial language that used Italian or Japanese words but violated grammatical principles common to both languages. Of course, German and, say, Italian differ in several ways. For example, in the sentence "I eat a pizza," the *I* is explicitly stated in German ("*Ich esse ein Pizza*") but not in Italian ("*Mangio una pizza*"). However, the variation is within the range of universal rules of grammar that recognize the deeper structure of the meaning. In contrast, Musso and colleagues constructed their artificial languages to contain arbitrary and bizarre grammatical conventions based solely on linear word order. For example, to construct a question, the word order of a sentence simply would be reversed. To ask whether Paolo is eating the pizza, the artificial language would read *Pizza la mangia Paolo?* Or to construct a negative statement, the word *no* would be added after the third word of a sentence, as in *Paolo mangia la no pizza* ("Paolo eats the no pizza").

As you might imagine, it can be difficult for an adult to learn any language, let alone one that violates what we might regard as conventional grammatical rules. But which areas of the brain control this learning? Musso and colleagues found that only the real languages triggered activity in a definite region—Broca's area. Learning the artificial grammar produced only nonspecific activity across large areas of the brain. Apparently, when we learn the hierarchical rules of grammar we rely specifically on the regions of the brain around Broca's area.

What about the rules of reinforcement? Certainly, we need not deliberately teach our children to speak or place them in a formal setting such as that of the experiment I just described. Does this make verbal behavior different from all other kinds of behavior? That issue will not be resolved until we know much more about the role of reinforcement in other types of behaviors that are learned through observation and imitation.

After all, reinforcement need not be consciously and intentionally delivered; it can be provided by attention and other social stimuli, and it may even be provided by the efficiency a child gains in talking the way others do.

Perhaps the best position on the issue of the language acquisition device is to keep an open mind. The ease with which young children learn a language must be explained. It may be that our evolutionary history shaped some regions of our brain so that they were well equipped to handle the special characteristics of linguistic behaviors (see Dunbar, 2004, for a short commentary). But the precise nature of both the brain mechanisms and the environmental contributions remains for us to discover.

Recognition of Speech Sounds by Infants

Language development starts even before birth. Although the sounds that reach a fetus are somewhat muffled, speech sounds can still be heard. The voice that a fetus hears best and most often is obviously that of its mother. DeCasper and Spence (1986) found that newborn infants preferred hearing their mothers reading a passage they had read aloud several times before the babies were born to hearing them read a passage they had never read before. Presumably, the infants had learned something about the rhythm and intonation of the passage they had heard *in utero*. There is also some evidence that newborns can learn to discriminate speech sounds while they sleep (Cheour et al., 2002).

Developmental psychologists have devised a clever technique to determine what sounds a very young infant can

TABLE 10•1	Examples of Responses Infants Make to Various Speech Sounds
First Age of Occurrence	**Response**
Newborn	Is startled by a loud noise
	Turns head to look in the direction of sound
	Is calmed by the sound of a voice
	Prefers mother's voice to a stranger's
	Discriminates among many speech sounds
1–2 months	Smiles when spoken to
3–7 months	Responds differently to different intonations (e.g., friendly, angry)
8–12 months	Responds to name
	Responds to "no"
	Recognizes phrases from games (e.g., "Peekaboo," "How big is baby?")
	Recognizes words from social routines (e.g., waves in response to "bye-bye")
	Recognizes some words

Source: Berko Gleason, J. (1993). *The development of language.* New York: Macmillan Publishing Company. Used by permission.

perceive. A special pacifier nipple is placed in the baby's mouth. The nipple is connected by a plastic tube to a pressure-sensitive switch that converts the infant's sucking movements into electrical signals. These signals can be used to turn on auditory stimuli. Each time the baby sucks, a particular sound is presented. If the auditory stimulus is novel, the baby usually begins to suck at a high rate. If the stimulus remains the same, its novelty wears off (habituation occurs), and the rate of sucking decreases. With another new stimulus, the rate of sucking may again suddenly increase, unless the baby cannot tell the difference. If the two stimuli sound the same to the infant, the rate of sucking remains low after the change.

Using this technique, Eimas, Siqueland, Jusczyk, and Vigorito (1971) found that one-month-old infants could tell the difference between the sounds of the consonants *b* and *p*. They presented the sounds *ba* and *pa*, synthesized by a computer. The infants discriminated between speech sounds having voice-onset times that differed by only 20 ms. Even very early during postnatal development, the human auditory system is able to make very fine discriminations.

Table 10•1 lists some of the responses infants make to various speech sounds.

The Prespeech Period and the First Words

Kaplan and Kaplan (1970) have outlined the progression of early vocalizations in infants. The first sound that a baby makes is crying. As we will see in Chapter 12, this aversive stimulus serves an important function: It produces useful reactions from the baby's caregivers. At about one month of age, infants start making other sounds, including *cooing* (so called because of the prevalence of the *oo* sound). Often during this period, infants also make a series of sounds that resemble a half-hearted attempt to mimic the sound of crying.

At around six months, an infant's sounds begin to resemble those that occur in speech. Even though their *babbling* does not contain words—and does not appear to involve attempts to communicate verbally—the sounds infants make, and the rhythm in which the sounds are articulated, reflect the adult speech that infants hear. At this age they also show evidence of long-term memory for the sound patterns of words read to them (Jusczyk & Hohne, 1997).

A study by Kuhl and colleagues (1992) provides further evidence of the effect of children's verbal environment on their language development. Native speakers learn not to distinguish between slight variations of sounds present in their language. In fact, they do not even *hear* the differences. For example, Japanese contains a sound that comes midway between /l/ and /r/. Different native speakers pronounce the sound differently, but all pronunciations are recognized as examples of the same phoneme. When native speakers of Japanese learn English, they have great difficulty distinguishing the sounds /l/ and /r/; for example, *right* and *light* sound to them like the same word. Presumably, the speech sounds a child hears alter the brain mechanisms responsible for recognizing them so that minor variations are not even perceived.

The question is, When does this alteration occur? Most researchers suppose that it happens after children begin to learn the meanings of words at around 10 to 12 months of age. Kuhl and her colleagues found, however, that the alteration takes place much earlier. These researchers studied six-month-old infants in the United States and Sweden. The infants were seated in their mothers' laps, where they watched a researcher sitting nearby, playing with a silent toy. Every two seconds a loudspeaker located to the infant's left presented the sound of a vowel. From time to time the sound was altered. If the infant noticed the change and looked at the loudspeaker, the researcher reinforced the response by activating a toy figure that pounded on a miniature drum. Thus, the procedure provided a test of infants' ability to distinguish slight differences in vowel sounds. (See **Figure 10•13**.)

The researchers presented two different vowel sounds, one found in English but not in Swedish and the other found in Swedish but not in English. From time to time, they varied the sound slightly. The reactions of the Swedish infants and the American infants were strikingly different. Swedish infants noticed when the English vowel changed but not when the Swedish vowel changed; American infants did the opposite. In other words, by the age of six months, the infants had learned not to pay attention to slight differences in speech sounds of their own language but were still able to distinguish slight differences in speech sounds they had never heard. Even though they were too young to understand the *meaning* of what they heard, the speech of people around them had affected the development of their auditory perception.

FIGURE 10·13 A child being tested in the experiment by Kuhl and her colleagues (1992).

(Photo © James Wilson/Woodfin Camp & Associates)

The experiment by Kuhl and her colleagues used synthetic sounds to produce changes from either the English or the Swedish vowel. Does this effect generalize to actual vowels that differ in sound? Using a similar procedure with infants raised in English-speaking households, Polka and Werker (1994) examined the ability of infants to distinguish between two English vowels or between two German vowels. They found that the ability to distinguish vowels in both languages was present in four-month-old infants. By six months of age, however, the infants had become more language-specific, showing little ability to distinguish between the German vowels. Thus, language acquisition seems to be a matter of becoming *less* discriminating of speech sounds when they do not form part of the child's native language. Furthermore, this *tuning* seems to occur very early in life.

Brain activity shows the effects of tuning. Cheour and colleagues (1998) examined how infants' brains respond to changes in vowels that are either part of their native language or not. Using Finnish and Estonian vowels with one-year-old babies from both linguistic groups, Cheour and colleagues found that the brain showed a specific change in electrical activity when a native vowel was changed to another native vowel. The same change was not elicited when a native vowel was followed by a non–native vowel sound.

These results are, in a sense, puzzling. Very young infants seem highly sensitive to sound differences in speech. But as infants begin to learn words from sound patterns and to associate those words with objects, they become less discriminating. Perhaps acute sensitivity to sound differences is necessary in the early stages of language acquisition in order to provide the brain with the means of organizing speech experiences. As the infant begins to represent speech in new ways, this sensitivity either is no longer necessary or perhaps even becomes detrimental (Stager & Werker, 1997).

Infants babble before they talk. They often engage in "serious conversations" with their caregivers, taking turns "talking" with them. Infants alter the stream of sounds they make, almost as if they are using a secret language (Menn & Stoel-Gammon, 1993). They are also able to discriminate and categorize sounds with respect to rhythm and tempo (Trehub & Thorpe, 1989).

At about one year of age, a child begins to produce words. The first sounds children use to produce words appear to be similar across all languages and cultures: The first vowel is usually the soft *a* sound of *father,* and the first consonant is a *stop consonant* produced with the lips—*p* or *b.* Thus, the first word is often *papa* or *baba.* The next feature to be added is *nasality,* which converts the consonants *p* or *b* into *m.* Thus, the next word is often *mama.* Naturally, mothers and fathers all over the world recognize these sounds as their children's attempts to address them.

The first sounds used in words contain the same phonemes that are found in the babbling sounds the child is already making; thus, speech emerges from prespeech sounds. Yet although young children learn words from their caregivers and from older children, they often invent their own **protowords,** unique strings of phonemes that serve wordlike functions. Children use these protowords consistently in particular situations (Menn & Stoel-Gammon, 1993). For example, Halliday (1975) reported that when his son Nigel wanted something, he would reach for it with an intent facial expression and say "Na! Na!" until he was given the desired object.

The development of speech sounds continues for many years. Some sequences are added quite late. For example, the *str* of *string* and the *bl* of *blink* are difficult for young children to produce; they usually say *tring* and *link,* omitting the first consonant. Most children recognize sounds in adult speech before they can produce them. Consider this conversation (Dale, 1976):

> *Adult:* Johnny, I'm going to say a word two times and you tell me which time I say it right and which time I say it wrong: *rabbit, wabbit.*
>
> *Child: Wabbit* is *wight* and *wabbit* is *wong.*

Although the child could not pronounce the r sound, he clearly could recognize it.

Early language acquisition, then, takes place within a context of changing perceptual, motor, and cognitive abilities. Werker and Tees (1999) have suggested that humans are born with a perceptual system that is especially attuned to the requirements of speech but that also interacts with the infant's linguistic environment and other developmental changes. Speech perception, word comprehension, and babbling work in concert to establish the foundation for more sophisticated speech.

The Two-Word Stage

At around 18 to 20 months of age, children start putting two words together, and their linguistic development takes a leap forward. It is at this stage that linguistic creativity become more apparent; children begin to say things they have never heard. Consider the creativity in *allgone outside,* said by a child when the door was closed.

Like first sounds, children's two-word utterances are remarkably consistent across all cultures that have been observed. Children use words in the same way, no matter what language their parents speak. Even deaf children who learn sign language from their parents put two words together in the same way as children who can hear (Bellugi & Klima, 1972). And deaf children whose parents do not know sign language invent their own signs and use them in orderly, "rule-governed" ways (Goldin-Meadow & Feldman, 1977). Thus, the grammar of children's language at the two-word stage appears to be universal (Owens, 1992).

For many years developmental psycholinguists described the speech of young children in terms of adult grammar, but researchers now recognize that children's speech simply follows different rules. Young children are incapable of forming complex sentences—partly because their vocabulary is small, partly because their short-term "working" memory is limited (they cannot yet encode a long string of words), and partly because their cognitive development has not yet reached a stage at which they can learn complex rules of syntax (Locke, 1993). As a result, their utterances in the two-word stage are dominated by content words. The absence of function words gives their language an abbreviated but nevertheless efficient form, much like that found in telegrams. For that reason, it is sometimes referred to as *telegraphic speech*.

How Adults Talk to Children

Parents do not talk to children the way they talk to adults; they use only short, simple, well-formed, repetitive sentences and phrases (Brown & Bellugi, 1964). In fact, such speech deserves its own label: **child-directed speech,** also known as *motherese* (Snow, 1986). In a comprehensive review of the literature, deVilliers and deVilliers (1978) found that adults' speech to children is characterized by clear pronunciation, exaggerated intonations, careful distinctions between similar-sounding phonemes, relatively few abstract words and function words, and a tendency to isolate constituents that undoubtedly enables young children to recognize them as units of speech.

Another important characteristic of child-directed speech is that it tends to refer to tangible objects the child can see, to what the child is doing, and to what is happening around the child (Snow et al., 1976). Words are paired with objects the child is familiar with, which is the easiest way to learn them. For example, caregivers make statements and ask questions about what objects are called, what noises they make, what color they are, what actions they are engaging in, whom they belong to, and where they are located. Their speech contains more content words and fewer function words (Newport, 1975; Snow, 1977).

Adults often expand children's speech by imitating it while putting it into more complex forms. This undoubtedly helps the child learn about syntactical structure (Brown, 1973; Brown & Bellugi, 1964). Consider the following exchange:

Child: Baby highchair.

Adult: Baby is in the highchair.

Child: Eve lunch.

Adult: Eve is having lunch.

Child: Throw daddy.

Adult: Throw it to daddy.

The most important influence on adults' speech to children is the child's attentiveness. Both adults and children are very sensitive to whether another person is paying attention to them. As Snow (1986) notes, although people may talk *at* children, they generally talk *with* them. When a child looks interested, we continue what we are saying. When we notice signs of inattention, we advance or simplify our level of speech until we regain the child's attention. Stine and Bohannon (1983) found that when children give signs that they do not understand what an adult is saying, the adult adjusts his or her speech, making it simpler.

Infants also exert control over what their caregivers talk about. The topic of conversation usually involves what the infant is playing with or is guided by what the infant is gazing at (Bohannon, 1993). This practice means that infants hear speech that refers to what they are already attending to, which undoubtedly facilitates language acquisition. In fact, Tomasello and Farrar (1986) found that infants of mothers who talked mostly about the objects of their infants' gazes uttered their first words earlier than other infants and also developed larger vocabularies early in life. Werker, Pegg, and McLeod (1994) found that when infants were shown a video of a Cantonese speaker talking to either an infant or to an adult, babies from both Cantonese- and English-speaking homes preferred to look at the infant-directed communication.

Acquisition of Adult Rules of Grammar

The first words children use tend to be content words, probably because these words are emphasized in adult speech and because they refer to objects and actions that children can directly observe (Brown & Fraser, 1964). As children develop past the two-word stage, they begin to learn and use more and more of the grammatical rules that adults use. The first form of sentence lengthening appears to be the expansion of object nouns into noun phrases (Bloom, 1970). For example, *That ball* becomes *That a big ball*. Next, verbs get used more often, articles are added, prepositional phrases are mastered, and sentences become more complex. These changes involve the use of inflections and function words. Function words, you recall, are the little words (*the, to, and,* and so on) that help shape the syntax of a sentence. **Inflections** are special suffixes we add to words to change their syntactical or semantic function. For example, the inflection *-ed* changes most verbs into the past tense (*change* becomes *changed*), *-ing* can turn a verb into a noun (*make* becomes *making*), and *-'s* indicates possession (*Paul's truck*).

The rules that govern the use of inflections or function words are rarely made explicit. That is, a parent seldom says,

"When you want to use the past tense, add *-ed* to the verb"— nor would a young child understand such a pronouncement. Instead, children must listen to speech and figure out how to express such concepts as the past tense.

Studies of children's speech have told us something about this process. Interestingly, the most frequently used verbs in most languages are *irregular*. Forming the past tense of such verbs in English does *not* involve adding *-ed*. (Examples are *go/went, throw/threw, buy/bought, see/saw,* and *can/could*.) The past tenses of such verbs must be learned individually. Because irregular verbs get more use than regular ones do, children learn them first, producing the past tense easily in sentences such as *I came, I fell down,* and *She hit me*. Soon afterward, they discover the regular past tense inflection and expand their vocabulary, producing sentences such as *He dropped the ball*. But they also begin to say *I comed, I falled down,* and *She hitted me*—all examples of *overgeneralization errors*. Having learned a rule, they apply it to all verbs, including the irregular ones that they were previously using correctly. In fact, it takes children several years to learn to use the irregular past tense correctly again (Pinker, 1999).

English-speaking children as young as three years of age know how to combine nouns to describe relationships between objects. Nicoladis (2003) showed children pictures that could be described by compound nouns. (See **Figure 10•14**.) She asked: "What is this?" Three- and four-year-old children generally gave three types of responses: Compound nouns such as *fish shoes* were the most frequent, followed by prepositional phrases (e.g., *fish on shoes*) or single words (e.g., *shoes*). Three-year-olds were just as likely as four-year-olds to create compound words—although, somewhat surprisingly, they were less likely to comprehend compound words or to choose them from a set of alternatives.

Acquisition of Meaning

How do children learn to use and understand words? The simplest explanation is that they hear a word spoken at the same time that they see (or hear, or touch) the object to which the word refers. After several such pairings, they add a word to their vocabulary. In fact, children first learn the names of things with which they interact, or things that change (and thus attract their attention). For example, they are quick to learn words like *cookie* or *blanket* but are slow to learn words like *wall* or *window* (Pease, Gleason, & Pan, 1993; Ross, Nelson, Wetstone, & Tanouye, 1986).

Suppose that we give a boy a small red plastic ball and say "ball." After a while, the child says "ball" when he sees it. Yet we cannot conclude from this behavior that the child knows the meaning of *ball*. So far, he has encountered only one referent for the word: a small ball made of red plastic. If he says "ball" when he sees an apple or an orange, or even the moon, we must conclude that he does not know the meaning of *ball*. This type of error is called **overextension**—the use of a word to denote a larger class of items than is appropriate. If the boy uses the word to refer only to the small red

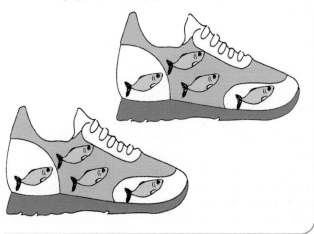

FIGURE 10•14   An object that could be described by a compound noun.

(Reprinted from Nicoladis, E., What compound nouns mean to preschoool children, *Brain and Language, 84*, 38–49, copyright © 2003 with permission from Elsevier.)

plastic ball, his error is called an **underextension**—the use of a word to denote a smaller class of items than is appropriate.

Both overextensions and underextensions are normal; a single pairing of a word with the object does not provide enough information for accurate generalization. Suppose that someone is teaching you a foreign language. She points to a penny and says "*pengar*." Does the word mean "penny," "money," "coin," or "round"? You cannot decide from this one example. Without further information, you may overextend or underextend the meaning of the word if you try to use it. If your teacher then points to a dollar bill and again says "*pengar*," you will deduce (correctly) that the word means "money."

Caregivers often correct children's overextensions. The most effective type of instruction occurs when an adult provides the correct label and points out the features that distinguish the object from the one with which the child has confused it (Chapman, Leonard, & Mervis, 1986). For example, if a child calls a yo-yo a "ball," the caregiver might say, "That's a yo-yo. See? It goes up and down" (Pease, Gleason, & Pan, 1993, p. 130).

Graham, Baker, and Poulin-Dubois (1998) looked at how children 16 to 19 months of age interpret these adult utterances. They provided artificial names for objects, then observed whether children would gaze at another object that matched a given item categorically or thematically. For example, a child would be shown a baby stroller while the researcher said, "This is a wug." Then a picture of another stroller would appear on one side of the child and a picture of a baby would appear on the other. At the same time, the researcher would say, "Find the wug." Looking at the picture of the second stroller was more prolonged when the artificial label was used than when no label was used. In contrast, the amount of time spent looking at the baby was not affected by the use of a label. Graham and her colleagues interpreted these results as indicative of children's tendency to assign the language labels spoken by adults to basic categories. Their sensitivity to categorical references and their ability to use them seem to underlie children's rapid acquisition of vocabulary between the ages of two and six years (Poulin-Dubois, Graham, & Sippola, 1995).

Biology and Culture

Communication with Other Primate Species

The members of most species can communicate with one another. Even insects communicate: A female moth that is ready to mate can release a chemical that will bring male moths from miles away. A dog can tell its owner that it wants to go for a walk by bringing its leash in its mouth and whining at the door. And many of the higher primates, such as gorillas, use gestures to communicate (Pika, Liebal, & Tomasello, 2003). But until recent decades humans were the only species that used languages to communicate.

In the 1960s Beatrice and Roger Gardner, of the University of Nevada, began Project Washoe (Gardner & Gardner, 1969, 1978), a remarkably successful attempt to teach sign language to a female chimpanzee named Washoe. Previous attempts to teach chimps to learn and use human language had focused on speech (Hayes, 1952). These attempts had failed, because chimps lack the control of tongue, lips, palate, and vocal cords that humans have and thus cannot produce the variety of complex sounds that characterize human speech.

Gardner and Gardner realized this limitation and decided to attempt to teach Washoe a *manual language*—a language that makes use of hand movements. Chimps' hand and finger dexterity is excellent, so the only limitations on Washoe's ability would be cognitive factors. The manual language the Gardners chose was based on American Sign Language, one of the sign languages used by deaf people. ASL is a true language: It contains function words and content words and has regular grammatical rules.

Washoe was one year old when she began to learn sign language; by the time she was four, she had a vocabulary of more than 130 signs. Like children, she used single signs at first; then she began to produce two-word sentences such as *Washoe sorry, gimme flower, more fruit,* and *Roger tickle.* Sometimes she strung three or more words together, using the concept of agent and object: *You tickle me.* She asked and answered questions, apologized, made assertions—in short, did the kinds of things that children would do while learning to talk. She showed overextensions and underextensions, just as human children do. Occasionally Washoe even made correct generalizations by herself. After learning the sign for the verb *open* (as in *open box, open cupboard*), she used it to say *open faucet* when requesting a drink. She made signs to herself when she was alone and used them to "talk" to cats and dogs, just as children will do. Nevertheless, although it is difficult to compare her progress with that of human children (the fairest comparison would be with that of deaf children learning to sign), humans clearly learn language much more readily than Washoe did.

Inspired by Project Washoe's success, several other investigators have taught individuals from other Great Ape species to use sign language. For example, Patterson began to teach a gorilla (Patterson & Linden, 1981), and Miles (1983) began to teach an orangutan. Washoe's training started relatively late in her life, and her trainers were not, at the beginning of the project, fluent in sign language. Other chimpanzees, raised from birth by humans who are native speakers of ASL, have begun to use signs when they are three months old (Gardner & Gardner, 1975).

Many psychologists and linguists have questioned whether the behavior of these animals can really be classified as verbal behavior. For example, Terrace, Petitto, Sanders, and Bever (1979) argue that the apes simply learned to imitate the gestures made by their trainers and that sequences of signs such as *please milk please me like drink apple bottle* (produced by a young gorilla) are nothing like the sequences that human children produce. Others have challenged these criticisms (Fouts, 1983; Miles, 1983; Stokoe, 1983), blaming much of the controversy on the method Terrace and his colleagues used to train their chimpanzee.

Certainly, the verbal behavior of apes cannot be the same as that of humans. If apes could learn to communicate verbally as well as children can, then humans would not have been the only species to have developed language. The usefulness of these ape studies rests in what they can teach us about our own language and cognitive abilities. Through such research we may discover what abilities animals need to communicate as we do. Ape studies also may help us understand the evolution of these capacities.

The work has already provided useful information. For example, Premack (1976) taught chimpanzees to "read" and "write" by arranging plastic tokens into "sentences." Each token represents an object, action, or attribute such as color or shape, much the way words do. His first trainee, Sarah, whom he acquired when she was one year old, learned to understand complex sentences such as *Sarah insert banana in pail, apple in dish.* When she saw the disks arranged in this order, she obeyed the instructions.

Chimpanzees apparently can use symbols to represent real objects and can manipulate these symbols logically. These abilities are two of the most powerful features of language. For Premack's chimpanzees, a blue plastic triangle means "apple." If the chimpanzees are given a blue plastic triangle and asked to choose the appropriate symbols denoting its color and shape, they choose the ones that signify "red" and "round," not "blue" and "triangular." Thus, the blue triangle is not simply a token the animals can use to obtain apples; it *represents* an apple for them, just as the word *apple* represents it for us.

Even though humans are the only primates that can pronounce words, other species can *recognize* them. Sue Savage-Rumbaugh (1990) taught Kanzi, a bonobo or pygmy chimpanzee, to communicate with humans by pressing buttons that contained symbols for words. Kanzi's human companions talked with him, and he learned to understand them. Although the structure of his vocal apparatus prevented him from responding vocally, *he often tried to do so.* During a three-month period, Savage-Rumbaugh and her colleagues tested Kanzi with 310 spoken sentences, 302 of which the chimpanzee had never heard before. Only situations in which Kanzi could not have been guided by nonverbal cues from the human companions were counted; often, Kanzi's back was to the speaker. He responded correctly 298 times. **Table 10·2** presents specific examples of these sentences and the actions that Kanzi took.

Savage-Rumbaugh and her colleagues took an interesting further step by comparing Kanzi's language performance with that of a two-year-old human girl (Savage-Rumbaugh et al., 1993). The test was a stringent one. Both Kanzi and the child (over a period of time) were given more than 600 commands in oral English. All of the commands were novel. Care was taken to avoid methodological flaws. For example, Kanzi could not see the person who

▲ *Researcher Sue Savage-Rumbaugh taught her chimp, Kanzi, to communicate using a special keyboard.*

gave him his commands, removing the possibility that he would merely read subtle behavioral cues rather than understand the spoken commands. Likewise, to avoid observer bias, the person who scored reactions to the commands could not hear the commands. Kanzi and the child performed equally well, although with time the girl progressed beyond Kanzi's

TABLE 10·2 Semantic Relations Comprehended by Kanzi, a Pygmy Chimpanzee

Semantic Relations	N*	Examples (Spoken)
Action–object	107	*"Would you please carry the straw?"* Kanzi looks over a number of objects on the table, selects the straw, and takes it to the next room.
Object–action	13	*"Would you like to ball chase?"* Kanzi looks around for a ball, finds one in his swimming pool, takes it out, comes over to the keyboard, and answers "Chase."
Object–location	8	*"Would you put the grapes in the swimming pool?"* Kanzi selects some grapes from among several foods and tosses them into the swimming pool.
Action–location	23	*"Let's chase to the A-frame."* Kanzi is climbing in trees and has been ignoring things that are said to him. When he hears this he comes down rapidly and runs to the A-frame.
Action–object–location	36	*"I hid the surprise by my foot."* Kanzi has been told that a surprise is around somewhere, and he is looking for it. When he is given this clue, he immediately approaches the speaker and lifts up her foot.
Object–action	9	*"Kanzi, the pine cone goes in your shirt."* Kanzi picks up a pine cone and puts it in his shirt.
Action–location–object	8	*"Go the refrigerator and get out a tomato."* Kanzi is playing in the water in the sink. When he hears this he stops, goes to the refrigerator, and gets a tomato.
Agent–action–object	7	*"Jeannine hid the pine needles in her shirt."* Kanzi is busy making a nest of blankets, branches, and pine needles. When he hears this, he immediately walks over to Jeannine, lifts up her shirt, takes out the pine needles, and puts them in his nest.
Action–object–recipient	19	*"Kanzi, please carry the cooler to Penny."* Kanzi grabs the cooler and carries it over to Penny.
Other: object–action–recipient, action–recipient–location, etc.	68	

*N = number of sentences to which Kanzi responded correctly.

Source: From Savage-Rumbaugh, E. S. (1990). *Developmental Psychobiology, 23,* 599–620. Copyright © 1990. Reprinted with permission of John Wiley & Sons, Inc.

abilities. Nevertheless, Kanzi made a good showing in comparison to the child—an impressive feat for a nonhuman, and an achievement that quelled some critics' concerns about the credibility of Kanzi's language performance.

One conclusion that has emerged from the studies of primates is that true verbal ability is a social behavior. It builds on attempts at nonverbal communication in social situations. The most successful attempts at teaching a language to other primates are those in which the animal and the trainer have established a close relationship and can successfully communicate nonverbally by means of facial expressions, movements, and gestures. Chimpanzees, gorillas, orangutans, and bonobos clearly perceive people as other beings who can be loved, trusted, or feared. Their interactions with humans naturally lead to attempts at communication; signs (or spoken words) will be learned most readily if they serve to make communication easier and more effective.

One of the most interesting questions asked of researchers in this area is whether animals who learn to communicate by means of signs will teach those signs to their offspring. The answer appears to be yes. Fouts, Hirsch, and Fouts (1983) obtained a 10-month-old infant chimpanzee, Loulis, whom they gave to Washoe to "adopt." Within eight days the infant began to imitate Washoe's signs. To be certain that Loulis was learning the signs from Washoe and not from humans, the investigators used only the signs for *who, what, want, which, where, sign,* and *name* in his presence. As Fouts (1983) reported:

> [A] sign, *food* [which he now uses], was . . . actively taught by Washoe. On this occasion Washoe was observed to sign *food* repeatedly in an excited fashion when a human was getting her some food. Loulis was sitting next to her watching. Washoe stopped signing and took Loulis' hand in hers, molded it into the *food* sign configuration, and touched it to his mouth several times. (pp. 71–72)

Interim Summary

Language Acquisition by Children

Some researchers believe that a child learns language by means of a brain mechanism called a language acquisition device, which contains universal grammatical rules and motivates language acquisition. Although children's verbal performance can be described by complex rules, it is possible that simpler rules—which children could reasonably be expected to learn—can also be devised. Everyone agrees that deliberate reinforcement is not necessary for language learning, but a controversy exists about just how important child-directed behavior is. A critical period for language learning may exist, but the evidence is not yet conclusive.

Studies using the habituation of a baby's sucking response have shown that the human auditory system is capable of discriminating among speech sounds soon after birth. Human vocalization begins with crying, then develops into cooing and babbling, and finally results in patterned speech. During the two-word stage, children begin to combine words creatively.

Child-directed speech is very different from that directed toward adults; it is simpler and clearer, and it generally refers to items and events in the present environment. As young children gain more experience with the world and with the speech of adults and older children, their vocabulary grows and they learn to use adult rules of grammar. Although the first verbs they learn tend to have irregular past tenses, once they learn the regular past tense rule (add *-ed*), they apply this rule even to irregular verbs they previously used correctly.

Studies of the ability of other primates to learn language enable us to analyze some of the types of experiences necessary for the acquisition of the skills involved in producing and understanding speech. To the extent that apes can be taught at least some of the rudiments of language, their behaviors provide some hints about the ways humans acquire these skills.

QUESTIONS TO CONSIDER

1. Think of examples of child-directed speech that you may have overheard (or engaged in yourself when talking with a young child). How would you feel if you were talking with a baby who suddenly lost interest in you? Would you be motivated to do something to regain the baby's attention? What would you do?

2. Do you think it is easier for a young child to learn a language than it is for an adult? How could we make a fair comparison of the interactions that young children and adults have with the people they talk to? Could a modified form of child-directed language be developed as an effective way of tutoring adults who attempt to learn a second language? Would this be effective? Why or why not?

3. Would you like to talk with a chimpanzee? If so, what would you like to talk about? What would it take to convince you that the animal was using something like a simplified human language, as opposed to simply repeating words and phrases learned by rote? Some people seem to be uncomfortable with the idea that the difference in the ability of humans and other primates to communicate may be a matter of degree and not an all-or-nothing matter. How do you feel about this issue? Finally, does teaching a chimpanzee a human language confer special responsibilities on the investigator? If so, what are they?

Suggestions for Further Reading

Berko Gleason, J. (2004). *The development of language.* Boston: Allyn and Bacon.

A noted developmental psycholinguist offers an excellent overview of language acquisition during infancy and childhood.

Calvin, W. H. (2004). *A brief history of the mind: From apes to intellect and beyond.* New York: Oxford University Press.

If you are intrigued by the evolutionary origins of cognition and language, this book provides a stimulating introduction.

Carter, R. (1998). *Mapping the mind.* London: Weidenfeld & Nicolson.

This book provides a beautifully illustrated introduction to brain areas and their correlated psychological functions, including language.

Just, M. A., & Carpenter, P. A. (1987). *The psychology of reading and language comprehension.* Boston: Allyn and Bacon.

Experts in eye-movement research focus on the psychology of written language, including reading disorders.

Miller, G. A. (1987). *Spontaneous apprentices: Children and language.* New York: Seabury Press.

This brief memoir by a highly regarded founder of cognitive science offers poignant reflections on his serious search for an elusive target: how children acquire a first language.

Pinker, S. (1994). *The language instinct: How the mind creates language.* New York: William Morrow.

A highly readable introduction to linguistics and psycholinguistics.

Rayner, K., & Pollatsek, A. (1994). *The psychology of reading.* Mahwah, N.J.: Lawrence Erlbaum and Associates.

A companion piece to Just and Carpenter, this book provides a richly referenced summary of research and theory on the acquisition of reading and the liabilities that accompany it.

Savage-Rumbaugh, E. S., Shanker, S., & Taylor, T. J. (1998). *Apes, language, and the human mind.* New York: Oxford University Press.

Savage-Rumbaugh is a central figure in the ape language controversy, which is the focus of this wide-ranging summary of research and theory.

Key Terms

affix (p. 298)

agrammatism (p. 300)

Broca's aphasia (p. 299)

child-directed speech (p. 316)

content word (p. 298)

deep structure (p. 298)

direct dyslexia (p. 307)

fixation (p. 304)

function word (p. 298)

inflection (p. 316)

isolation aphasia (p. 302)

language universal (p. 311)

morpheme (p. 297)

overextension (p. 317)

phoneme (p. 296)

phonetic reading (p. 306)

phonological dyslexia (p. 307)

prosody (p. 298)

protoword (p. 315)

psycholinguistics (p. 295)

pure word deafness (p. 302)

script (p. 299)

semantic priming (p. 309)

semantics (p. 298)

surface dyslexia (p. 307)

surface structure (p. 298)

syntactical rule (p. 297)

underextension (p. 317)

voice-onset time (p. 296)

Wernicke's aphasia (p. 301)

Wernicke's area (p. 301)

whole-word reading (p. 306)

INTELLIGENCE AND THINKING

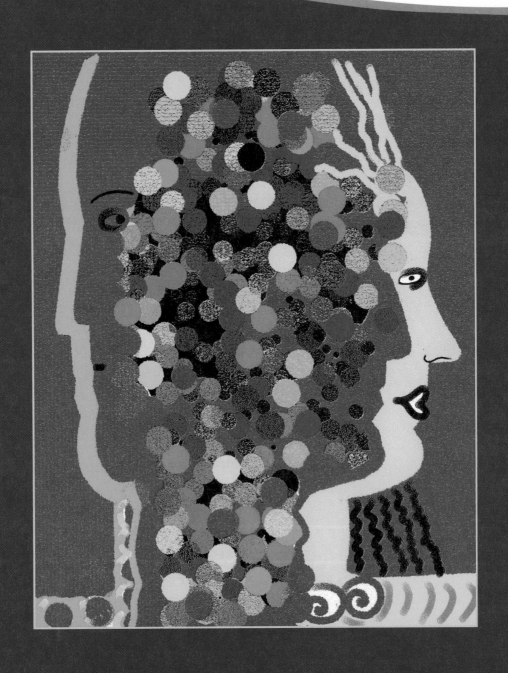

Intelligence: Global or Componential?

Spearman's *g* Theory • Evidence from Factor Analysis • Sternberg's Triarchic Theory of Intelligence • Gardner's Theory of Multiple Intelligences • *Biology and Culture: Definitions of Intelligence*

Spearman's theory proposes that intelligence consists of a global general factor (*g*) and specific task-related factors. Factor analysis suggests that one or two general factors of intelligence may exist. Sternberg's triarchic theory of intelligence applies the information-processing approach and emphasizes adaptability to the demands of natural and social environments. Gardner's theory emphasizes the categories of aptitudes and skills (physical as well as cognitive) that permit people to thrive in their cultures. Researchers are coming to recognize that different environments require different types of skills; thus, different cultures have different definitions of intelligence.

Intelligence Testing

From Mandarins to Galton • Intelligence Tests • Reliability and Validity of Intelligence Tests • The Use and Abuse of Intelligence Tests

Binet's attempts to identify schoolchildren who needed special attention led him to develop a series of tests that eventually became the Stanford-Binet Scale. Binet and his colleague Simon developed the concept of norms with which to compare a particular individual and formulated the concept of mental age. Wechsler developed an intelligence test that could be applied to adults (the WAIS) and another for children (the WISC). The reliability of modern intelligence tests is excellent. Their validity is difficult to assess, however, because we have no single criterion of intelligence. One way intelligence tests may be used is to identify gifted students and students with special needs so that they may be enrolled in appropriate educational programs. Intelligence tests may be abused if teachers and administrators expect little from students labeled as "unintelligent" and so fail to encourage such students to achieve highly.

The Roles of Heredity and Environment

The Meaning of Heritability • Sources of Environmental and Genetic Effects during Development • Results of Heritability Studies • *Evaluating Scientific Issues: The Issue of Race and Intelligence*

Variability in people's intellectual abilities is produced by three sources: environmental variability, genetic variability, and the interaction between the two. Environmental variability has its origins even before birth; it includes factors that affect prenatal development and physical development during childhood as well as sources of formal education and intellectual stimulation. Genetic variability affects the structure and development of the brain and also affects people's resistance to diseases and other environmental events that can affect the development and functioning of the brain. Studies of genetic relatedness between individuals have been useful in estimating the heritability of intelligence; that is, the proportion of variation in test scores that is attributable to genetic variation among test takers. The topic of race and intelligence has been the subject of considerable passion and debate, much of which has been illogical and misinformed. Environmental factors appear to play a larger role than hereditary ones in racial differences in performance on intelligence tests.

Thinking and Problem Solving

Categorization and Generalization • Formal and Natural Concepts • Deductive Reasoning • Inductive Reasoning • Problem Solving

Psychologists interested in the process of thinking have studied the formation and recognition of concepts, deductive reasoning, inductive reasoning, and problem solving. Formal as well as natural concepts exist at the basic, subordinate, and superordinate levels, but we mostly think about basic-level concepts. Concepts are more than simple collections of essential features; they can involve complex relationships. Deductive reasoning consists of applying general principles to specific instances and requires the ability to construct and manipulate mental models that represent a problem. Inductive reasoning consists of inferring general principles from particular facts; people use various forms of hypothesis testing to infer general principles. Problem solving requires a person to form a concept of a goal and to evaluate whether particular behaviors will promote attainment of that goal and any subgoals that may emerge.

Mr. V., a 72-year-old man, has suffered a massive stroke in his right hemisphere that has paralyzed the left side of his body. At his doctor's office, Mr. V. is seated in a wheelchair equipped with a large tray on which his right arm rests; his left arm is immobilized in a sling, to keep it out of the way. He greets his doctor politely, almost formally, articulating his words carefully with a slight European accent.

Mr. V. seems intelligent, and this impression has been confirmed for his doctor by the results of some of the subtests of the Wechsler Adult Intelligence Scale (WAIS-III) that were administered by a psychologist. The subtests showed that Mr. V. could define rather obscure words, provide the meanings of proverbs, supply critical information, and do mental arithmetic. In fact, his verbal intelligence appears to be in the upper 5 percent of the population. The fact that English is not his first language makes his performance even more remarkable. However, he did poorly on simple tasks that required him to deal with shapes and geometry. He could not solve even the sample problem for the block design subtest, in which colored blocks must be put together to duplicate a pattern shown in a drawing.

An interesting aspect of Mr. V.'s behavior is his lack of reaction to his symptoms. When his doctor asks him some simple questions about himself and his lifestyle—for example, about his favorite pastime, Mr. V. answers, "I like to walk. I walk at least two hours each day around the city, but mostly I like to walk in the woods. I have maps of most of the nearby parks on the walls of my study, and I mark all the trails I've taken. I figure that in about six months I will have walked all of the trails that are short enough to do in a day. I'm too old to camp out in the woods."

"You're going to finish up those trails in the next six months?" asks his doctor.

"Yes, and then I'll start over again!" Mr. V. replies.

"Mr. V., are you having any trouble?" asks the doctor.

"Trouble? What do you mean?"

"I mean physical, medical, difficulties."

"No." Mr. V. gives him a slightly puzzled look.

"Well, what are you sitting in?"

Mr. V. gives his doctor a look that indicates he thinks the question is rather stupid—or perhaps insulting. "A wheelchair, of course," he answers.

"Why are you in a wheelchair?"

Now Mr. V. looks exasperated; he obviously does not like to answer foolish questions. "Because my left leg is paralyzed!" he snaps.

Mr. V. talks about continuing his walking schedule when he obviously knows that he can't walk. Does he think that he will recover soon?

"No, that's not it," says Mr. V.'s doctor. "He knows what his problem is, but he doesn't really understand it. The people at the rehabilitation hospital are finding it difficult because he keeps trying to go outside for a walk.

"The problem Mr. V. experiences stems from the fact that intelligence is made up of a variety of skills that must be coordinated, and the results of their use must be synthesized. The right hemisphere is specialized in seeing many things at once: in seeing the parts of a geometric shape and grasping its overall form or in recognizing the elements of a situation and understanding what it means. That is what's wrong. He can tell you about his paralyzed leg, about the fact that he is in a wheelchair, and so on, but he does not put these facts together and realize that his days of walking are over. Mr. V. is very intelligent, but his judgment can be lacking because of the stroke damage."

What is intelligence? We can easily tell that some people are more intelligent than others, but just what do we mean by that? In general, if people do well academically or succeed at intellectual tasks, we consider them to be intelligent. Thus, a critic who writes a witty, articulate review of an artist's exhibition of paintings is said to demonstrate intelligence, whereas the painter is said to show talent. Psychologists often define **intelligence** as a person's ability to learn and remember information, to recognize concepts and their relations, and to apply the information and recognition by behaving in an adaptive way. Recently, psychologists have pointed out that any definition of intelligence depends on cultural judgments of adaptiveness (e.g., Berry, 2001; Sternberg & Grigorenko, 2001). Analyses of the types of skills that enable people to survive and flourish in different cultures suggest that we may need to broaden the generally accepted definition to include a wider range of abilities.

Intelligence: Global or Componential?

People vary in many ways, such as in their abilities to learn and use words, to solve arithmetic problems, and to perceive and remember spatial information. Psychologists have assumed that we can best investigate the nature of intelligence by studying the ways in which people differ on tests of such intellectual abilities. But is intelligence a single, overarching—that is, *global*—trait that affects all types of intellectual performance? Or is it a composite of separate, independent abilities?

Psychologists have devised intelligence tests that yield a single number, usually called an intelligence quotient or IQ score. But the fact that the tests provide a single score does not itself mean that intelligence is a global characteristic. For example, suppose that we wanted to devise a test of athletic ability. We could have people run, jump, throw and catch a ball, lift weights, balance on a narrow beam, and perform other athletic feats. We could measure their performance on each task and add these numbers up, yielding a total score that we would call the *AQ*, or *athleticism quotient*. But would this single measure be useful in predicting who would be the best skier, or baseball player, or swimmer, or gymnast? Because athletic ability consists of a variety of skills, and different sports require different combinations of skills, the AQ could turn out to be a useful predictor for some sports but useless for others. Similarly, the controversy among psychologists is whether intelligence should be considered a global trait, singular and indivisible, or whether it should be considered the composite of several abilities that may or may not be independent of one another. Even those who believe that intelligence is a global trait may acknowledge that people also have specific intellectual abilities and that these abilities are at least somewhat independent. For example, a person can be excellent at spatial reasoning but poor at solving verbal analogies (such as telling how a cat is like a brick). Do these

▲ *Different cultures have different definitions of intelligence. Members of the Aitutaki tribe from the Cook Islands have particular respect for a person's ability to obtain food from the sea.*

abilities have something in common, or are they distinct? We will examine three theories of intelligence: a general factor theory, an information-processing theory, and a neuropsychological theory.

Spearman's *g* Theory

The British psychologist Charles Spearman (1863–1945) proposed that a person's performance on a test of intellectual ability is determined by two factors: the **g factor,** which is a general factor, and the **s factor,** which is a factor specific to a particular test (Spearman, 1927). We consider only the *g* factor here. Spearman did not call the *g* factor "intelligence"; he considered the term too vague. Instead, he defined the *g* factor in terms of three "qualitative principles of cognition": apprehension of experience, eduction of relations, and eduction of correlates. (*Eduction,* not "edu*cation,*" is the process of drawing or bringing out—that is, of figuring out from given facts.) A common task on tests of intellectual abilities—solving analogies—requires all three principles (Sternberg, 1988a, 1997). For example, consider the following analogy:

LAWYER : CLIENT :: DOCTOR : _____

This analogy problem is read as "LAWYER is to CLIENT as DOCTOR is to _____." Spearman's term *apprehension of experience* refers to people's ability to perceive and understand what they experience; thus, reading and understanding each of the words in the analogy requires apprehension of experience. In this example, *eduction of relations* refers to the ability to perceive the relation between LAWYER and CLIENT; namely, that the lawyer works for the client. *Eduction of correlates* refers to the ability to apply a rule inferred from one case to a similar case. Thus, the person whom a doctor works for is obviously a PATIENT. Because analogy problems require all three of Spearman's principles of cognition, he advocated their use in intelligence testing.

Empirical evidence for Spearman's two-factor theory comes from correlations among various tests of particular intellectual abilities. The logic is as follows: Suppose that we administer 10 different tests of intellectual abilities to a group of people. If each test measures a separate, independent ability, the scores these people make on any one test will be unrelated to their scores on any other; the correlations between different pairs of tests should be approximately zero. However, if the tests measure abilities that are simply different manifestations of a single trait, the scores should be perfectly related; the correlations will be close to 1.0. In fact, the correlations from a group of tests of intellectual abilities are neither zero nor 1.0. Instead, most of these tests are at least moderately correlated, that is, they are in the range from 0.3 to 0.7. This means that a person who scores well on a vocabulary test also tends to score better than average on other tests, such as arithmetic or spatial reasoning. In fact, the correlations among various tests of intellectual ability usually fall in the moderate range. On the basis of this finding, Spearman concluded that a general factor (*g*) accounted for the correlations between different tests of ability.

Recent work by Gottfredson (2004) has extended Spearman's claim for the centrality of *g* in intellectual performance. Gottfredson contends that *g* predicts performance well beyond the domain of IQ testing and influences personal success in virtually all important areas of life. She identifies four areas in particular—work, daily self-maintenance, chronic illness, and accidents—in which the ability to deal with complexity provides individuals with higher levels of *g* an advantage. In addition, she argues that *g* is a robust predictor: that information about an individual's more specific mental abilities or socioeconomic status, for example, adds little to what *g* predicts alone.

Evidence from Factor Analysis

Together with Karl Pearson (1852–1936), an illustrious statistician, Spearman developed a statistical procedure known as **factor analysis**. This procedure permits researchers to identify underlying intellectual factors that contribute to performance on intelligence tests. Suppose that a group of people take several different tests of intellectual ability. If each person's scores on several of these tests correlate with one another, we can conclude, as previously stated, that the tests are measuring a single factor. Factor analysis determines which tests can be grouped together. For example, Birren and Morrison (1961) administered the Wechsler Adult Intelligence Scale (WAIS, described in the next section) to 933 people. This test at that

time consisted of 11 different subtests. The researchers calculated the correlations each subtest had with every other subtest and then applied factor analysis to the correlations.

Table 11•1 lists the results of the 1961 factor analysis. It revealed three factors, labeled A, B, and C. The numbers in the three columns in the table are called *factor loadings;* they express the degree to which a particular test is related to a particular factor. On factor A, the largest factor loading is for vocabulary, followed by information, comprehension, and similarities. (For detailed descriptions of the subtests, see Table 11.5 on p. 335) The intermediate loadings are for picture completion, arithmetic, picture arrangement, and digit symbol. Digit span, object assembly, and block design have the lowest loadings. Because verbal subtests have the heaviest loading on factor A, that factor might be labeled *verbal ability*. But because all tests have at least a moderate loading, it may be reasonable to call A *general intelligence*. Digit span has a heavy loading on factor B (.84), and arithmetic and digit symbol have moderate loadings. Perhaps factor B contributes to *maintaining information in short-term memory* and *manipulating numbers*. Factor C appears to apply mainly to block design, object assembly, picture completion, and picture arrangement. A good name for this factor might be *spatial ability*.

Although factor analysis generates clues about the nature of intelligence, by itself it is not a theory of intelligence, as it can never be more meaningful than the individual tests from which it derives. To identify the relevant factors in human intelligence, it is obviously necessary to include an extensive variety of tests in the factor analysis. And although many are available (Daniel, 1997) factor analysis can never reveal other important abilities that are *not* measured by the tests it is used

TABLE 11•1	Three Factors Derived by Factor Analysis of Scores on WAIS Subtests		
	Factors		
Subtest	**A**	**B**	**C**
Information	.70	.18	.25
Digit span	.16	.84	.13
Vocabulary	.84	.16	.18
Arithmetic	.38	.35	.28
Comprehension	.63	.12	.24
Similarities	.57	.12	.27
Picture completion	.41	.15	.53
Picture arrangement	.35	.18	.41
Block design	.20	.14	.73
Object assembly	.16	.06	.59
Digit symbol	.24	.22	.29

Source: Adapted from *Multivariate Statistical Methods,* 4th edition by D. F. Morrison. © 2005. Reprinted with permission from Brooks/Cole, a division of Thomson Learning. www.thomsonrights.com. Fax 800-730-2215.

to investigate. For example, the WAIS does not contain a test of musical ability. If it did, factor analysis might reveal an additional factor related to that ability.

The results of factor analyses over the history of intelligence testing have revealed a range of specific factors. For example, Louis Thurstone (1938) administered a battery of 56 tests to 218 college students. In a factor analysis he extracted seven factors, which he labeled *verbal comprehension, verbal fluency, number, spatial visualization, memory, reasoning,* and *perceptual speed.* At first Thurstone thought that his results contradicted Spearman's hypothesized *g* factor. However, Hans Eysenck (1939) suggested that a second factor analysis could be performed on Thurstone's factors. If the analysis found one common factor among the factors, then Spearman's *g* factor would receive support. In other words, if Thurstone's seven factors themselves had a second-order factor in common, this factor might be conceived of as general intelligence.

Raymond Cattell (1963) performed just such a second-order factor analysis and found not one but two major factors. He called these factors *fluid intelligence* (g_f) and *crystallized intelligence* (g_c). **Fluid intelligence** largely has to do with detecting relationships in limited informational contexts, such as classifying figures or seeing patterns in a repeating series of items. **Crystallized intelligence** involves drawing on previously acquired information and skills, such as vocabulary, arithmetic, and general information—the kind of thing learned in schools. Cattell regarded fluid intelligence as closely related to a person's native capacity for intellectual performance; in other words, to the individual's potential ability to learn and solve problems. In contrast, crystallized intelligence is what a person has already developed through the use of his or her fluid intelligence—what he or she has learned. Horn's (1994) interpretation differs. He cites evidence suggesting that both factors are learned but that g_f refers to informal learning while g_c refers to culture-specific, school-centered learning.

According to both Cattell and Horn, if two people share similar experiences, the person with the greater fluid intelligence will develop the greater crystallized intelligence. However, a person with a high fluid intelligence exposed to an intellectually impoverished environment will develop a poor crystallized intelligence. **Table 11•2** presents a summary of tests that load on g_f and g_c.

Sternberg's Triarchic Theory of Intelligence

Robert Sternberg (1996, 1997, 2003a, 2003b) has devised a *triarchic* ("ruled by three") theory of intelligence that derives from the information-processing approach used by many cognitive psychologists. Consequently, the theory focuses on the ways in which people perceive, analyze, store, and apply information in their daily interactions with the environment. According to Sternberg, the degree of success that people achieve in life is strongly affected by the extent to which they

effectively analyze and manage their unique combinations of strengths and weaknesses. The theory identifies three major aspects of intelligence: analytic intelligence, creative intelligence, and practical intelligence. As you will see, these three components go beyond the abilities measured by most tests of intelligence. Taken together, they contribute to what Sternberg (1996, 1999, 2002) calls **successful intelligence,** which is a person's ability to (a) analyze his or her strengths and weaknesses, (b) use the strengths to greatest advantage, and (c) minimize the impact of weaknesses by overcoming or compensating for them.

Analytic intelligence consists of the mental mechanisms people use to plan and execute tasks. Verbal ability and deductive reasoning, as revealed by factor analysis, are facets of

TABLE 11•2 Summary of Tests with Large Factor Loadings on g_f or g_c		
Test	g_f	g_c
Figural relations: Deduction of a relation when this is shown among common figures	.57	.01
Memory span: Reproduction of several numbers or letters presented briefly	.50	.00
Induction: Deduction of a correlate from relations shown in a series of letters, numbers, or figures, as in a letter series test	.41	.06
General reasoning: Solving problems of area, rate, finance, and the like, as in an arithmetic reasoning test	.31	.34
Semantic relations: Deduction of a relation when this is shown among words, as in an analogies test	.37	.43
Formal reasoning: Arriving at a conclusion in accordance with a formal reasoning process, as in a syllogistic reasoning test	.31	.41
Number facility: Quick and accurate use of arithmetical operations such as addition, subtraction, and multiplication	.21	.29
Experiential evaluation: Solving problems involving protocol and requiring diplomacy, as in a social relations test	.08	.43
Verbal comprehension: Advanced understanding of language, as measured in a vocabulary reading test	.08	.68

Source: Adapted from Horn, J. L. (1968). Organization of abilities and the development of intelligence. *Psychological Review, 75,* 242–259. Copyright 1968 by the American Psychological Association.

analytic intelligence. Sternberg suggests that the components of analytic intelligence serve three functions. *Metacomponents* (higher-level components) are the processes by which people decide what an intellectual problem is about, select a strategy for solving it, and allocate their resources to that solution. For example, good readers vary the amount of time they spend on a passage according to how much information they need to extract from it; this is the metacomponent (Wagner & Sternberg, 1983). *Performance components* are the processes actually used to perform the task—for example, word recognition or rehearsal in working memory. *Knowledge acquisition components* are the processes that the person uses to gain new knowledge, including sifting through information, extracting what is relevant, and integrating it with what he or she already knows.

The second part of Sternberg's theory deals with **creative intelligence** (Sternberg, 2003b). This is the ability to deal effectively with novel situations or to solve familiar problems automatically. According to Sternberg's theory, people with high creative intelligence are able to deal more effectively with novel situations than individuals with low creative intelligence can. They can better analyze a situation and bring cognitive resources to bear on the problem, even if encountering it for the first time. After solving a particular type of problem several times, the person with good creative intelligence is also able to "automate" the procedure so that similar problems can be solved without much thought, freeing cognitive resources for more demanding work. Sternberg suggests that the distinction between initially working out a solution and automating it is closely related to the distinction between fluid and crystallized intelligence (Carroll, 1993; Horn, 1994; Horn & Cattell, 1966). According to Sternberg, tasks that require fluid intelligence demand novel approaches, whereas tasks drawing on crystallized intelligence demand cognitive processes that have become automatic. Another interesting dimension of

creative intelligence is that people high in such intelligence are willing to tolerate criticism and the initial rejection of their new ideas (Sternberg & Lubart, 1996). Because new ideas often threaten those who have the power to implement them, creative people must learn when the time is right to press their ideas.

The third part of Sternberg's theory deals with **practical intelligence**—intelligence reflecting the behaviors that were subject to natural selection in human evolutionary history. Practical intelligence takes three forms: adaptation, selection, and shaping. The first, *adaptation,* consists of initially fitting into a given environment by developing useful skills and behaviors. In different cultural contexts, adaptation will take different forms. For example, knowing how to distinguish between poisonous, edible, and medicinal plants is an important skill for members of the Malaysian Sarawak hunter–gatherer tribe. For many people in the United States, knowing how to find grocery bargains and have prescriptions filled with low-priced generic drugs are important skills. Sternberg argues forcefully that sociocultural and physical contexts have a strong impact on the development and manifestation of practical intelligence (e.g., Sternberg & Grigorenko, 2001). Other writers go so far as to say that context underpins intelligence—"smart contexts" make "smart people" (Barab & Plucker, 2002).

The second form of practical intelligence, *selection,* involves a person's ability to find his or her own niche in the environment. Most of us have known students who, although seemingly brilliant, never found agreeable interests in life and fell far short of what they seemed capable of achieving. They seem like brilliant but tragic dreamers. Sternberg's theory stresses the importance of actively finding a good match between self and environment. For example, Feldman (1982) studied some of the child prodigies who appeared on radio and television shows called *Quiz Kids* during the 1940s and 1950s. The youngsters were selected originally for their ability to answer factual-knowledge questions quickly, and they had very high IQ scores. Feldman's follow-up study indicated that the former prodigies who went on to have the most distinguished careers were those who had found something that uniquely interested them and held their attention for extended periods of life. Those who failed to do so accomplished very little, despite their high IQs. According to Sternberg, the difference was a reflection of differences in the selective aspect of practical intelligence.

Sternberg's is an optimistic approach, in that it states that when the environment is not a good match (adaptation does not work) or people cannot find a good alternative environment (selection does not work), they often can change their environment to better suit their abilities. This third form of practical intelligence is *shaping*. For example, a person whose talents are not appreciated by his or her employer may decide to start his or her own business.

Observations of people with damage to their frontal lobes support Sternberg's emphasis on practical intelligence.

▲ *Knowing how to distinguish between poisonous plants, edible plants, and plants with medicinal properties is an important skill. This woman, a member of the Sarawak tribe, is collecting medicinal herbs in a Malaysian rain forest.*

TABLE 11·3	An Outline of Sternberg's Triarchic Theory of Intelligence

Analytic Intelligence

Metacomponents (e.g., planning)

Performance components (e.g., word recognition)

Knowledge acquisition components (e.g., adding new words to vocabulary)

Creative Intelligence

Novel tasks

Automated tasks

Practical Intelligence

Adaptation (fitting in to a given environment)

Selection (finding a niche in the environment)

Shaping (changing the environment)

Even after sustaining massive damage to the frontal lobes (for example, after a car or snowmobile accident), people often continue to score well on standard intelligence tests. Thus, we may be tempted to conclude that their intelligence is unimpaired. But such people lose the ability to plan their lives or even their daily activities. For example, consider the case of a formerly successful physician who had received a head injury that severely damaged his frontal lobes. Even though he still had a high IQ as measured by intelligence tests, he could no longer perform his job as a physician. He became a delivery truck driver for his brother, who owned a business. He was able to carry out this job only because his brother did all the planning for him, carefully laying out his route and instructing him to call if he encountered any trouble. The man's behavior lost its previous flexibility and insightfulness. If he found the front door locked at a store where he had gone to deliver an order, it would not occur to him to go around to the back; his brother had to suggest that by telephone. Clearly, the man's behavior lacked a crucial component of practical intelligence. The fact that practical intelligence is not a part of most intelligence tests may indicate that these tests are neglecting something of considerable importance (Sternberg, 1996; Sternberg & Kaufman, 1998). **Table 11·3** provides a summary of the key concepts of Sternberg's triarchic theory.

Gardner's Theory of Multiple Intelligences

Howard Gardner (1983, 1993, 1999) has formulated a theory of multiple intelligences, which rejects the idea of a single or even a few primary types of intelligence. From Gardner's perspective intelligences are situated within cultures; that is, intelligences are potentials that may or may not be activated in the individual, depending on the extent to which the individual's culture values the expression of those potentials. Gardner believes that each of the intelligences he identifies is the result of evolution and has separate, unique neuropsychological underpinnings. One of the criteria for identifying an intelligence is distinctive evidence of a neurological substrate. Gardner argues that there are cases in which brain damage impairs one type of intelligence but leaves others intact and vice versa. We have seen in previous discussions that localized brain damage can indeed impair specific types of abilities. For example, damage to various regions of the left hemisphere can impair verbal abilities, and damage to various regions of the right hemisphere can impair spatial orientation. Another example of ability-specific isolation is that people with damage to the frontal or temporal lobes—especially of the right hemisphere—may have difficulty evaluating the significance of social situations but are still able to function quite well in other situations.

Findings such as this led Gardner (1999) to identify eight separate intelligences that meet his criteria. (See **Table 11·4**.) Three of Gardner's intelligences—*logical–mathematical intelligence, verbal–linguistic intelligence, and visual–spatial intelligence*—are not unusual, having been identified previously by others and often included to a greater or lesser extent in intelligence tests that were developed independently of Gardner's work (e.g., see Table 11.5 on p. 335). You may also notice an overlap with Sternberg's notion of *practical intelligence*. For example, Gardner's *naturalist intelligence* fits well with Sternberg's notion of adaptation as a part of practical intelligence when applied to the specific example of being able to distinguish edible and poisonous plants. The difference is that Sternberg's adaptation is a quality broadly associated with practical abilities, whereas Gardner assigns naturalist intelligence independent status among the other intelligences.

Psychologists generally have not recognized the remainder of Gardner's intelligences as distinct potentials. For example, they have tended not to consider skill in moving the body as a measure of intelligence, although this talent was undoubtedly selected during the evolution of the species. Individuals who could more skillfully prepare tools, hunt animals, climb trees, descend cliffs, and perform other tasks requiring physical skills were more likely to survive and reproduce. Psychologists have developed mechanical aptitude tests, primarily to help employers choose prospective employees, but such skills have generally been regarded as representing something other than intelligence per se. Yet Gardner's theory has the advantage of recognizing the cultural situatedness of intelligence, especially in non-Western cultures. For example, the ability of a member of the Puluwat culture of the Caroline Islands to navigate across the sea by the stars serves as an example of naturalistic intelligence (Gladwin, 1970).

Although Gardner himself prefers not to be involved personally in the development of formal measures that reflect elements of his intelligences (Gardner, 1999), that has not deterred others. The Bar-On Emotional Intelligence Inventory (Bar-On, 1997), for example, draws on elements of Gardner's interpersonal and intrapersonal intelligences and

TABLE 11•4 An Outline of Gardner's Theory of Multiple Intelligences

Type of Intelligence	Description	Relevant Activities and Professions
Logical–mathematical intelligence	Ability to reason logically and to process mathematical equations	Conduct systematic investigations; scientists, mathematicians, logicians
Verbal–linguistic intelligence	Ability to use language, sensitivity to meanings and sounds of words	Learn new languages easily, write and speak clearly; writers, teachers, lawyers
Visual–spatial intelligence	Ability to understand patterns in closed or open spaces	Organize objects and activities in three-dimensional space; sculptors, architects, pilots
Naturalist intelligence	Ability to understand patterns in nature	Identify and categorize plants and animals, notice regularities of weather conditions; taxonomists, farmers, hunters, herbal medicine practitioners, meteorologists
Bodily–kinesthetic intelligence	Ability to control the body precisely	Use of the body to solve problems and create; athletes, dancers, actors, mechanics, surgeons
Musical intelligence	Ability to understand and create musical patterns	Composition and performance of music; composers, lyricists, musicians
Intrapersonal intelligence	Ability to understand the self, including awareness of skills, emotions, thoughts, and intentions	Personal integrity, strength of character; can be manifested in many different life contexts, but may not be obvious to outsiders
Interpersonal intelligence	Ability to recognize differences among people and to understand others' emotions, intentions, and motivations	Leadership and interpersonal problem solving; politicians, clergy, mediators, psychologists

on complementary work by Salovey and Mayer (e.g., Salovey & Mayer, 1989–1990; Mayer & Salovey, 1993). Dawda and Hart (2000) reported research suggesting that the scale may indeed be useful for measuring differences among people on the interpersonal and intrapersonal dimensions.

Biology and Culture

Definitions of Intelligence

What intelligence consists of is determined by culture. Most Western societies include academic skills such as verbal ability and formal reasoning in their definitions of intelligence and regard nonacademic abilities as something else, such as talents. But this Western view may not be applicable in some cultures.

For example, the **syllogism,** a tool for measuring deductive logic (that is, reasoning from already established

premises), is often found in tests of intelligence. A syllogism is a logical construction that consists of a major premise (e.g., *All birds have feathers*), a minor premise (e.g., *A goose is a bird*), and a conclusion (e.g., *A goose has feathers*). The major and minor premises are assumed to be true. The problem is to decide whether the conclusion is true or false. Several studies suggested that unschooled people in remote villages in various parts of the world were unable to solve syllogistic problems. Scribner (1977) visited two tribes of people in Liberia, West Africa, the Kpelle and the Vai. She found that indeed, the tribespeople gave what Westerners would consider wrong answers.

This is not to say, however, that the people could not reason logically. They simply approached problems differently. For example, Scribner presented the following problem to a Kpelle farmer. At first glance, this appears to be a reasonable problem even for a person without formal schooling, because it refers to the farmer's own tribe and to an occupation he is familiar with.

All Kpelle men are rice farmers. Mr. Smith is not a rice farmer. Is he a Kpelle man?

The man replied:

Subject: I don't know the man in person. I have not laid eyes on the man himself.

Experimenter: Just think about the statement.

Subject: If I know him in person, I can answer that question, but since I do not know him in person, I cannot answer that question.

Experimenter: Try and answer from your Kpelle sense.

Subject: If you know a person, if a question comes up about him you are able to answer. But if you do not know the person, if a question comes up about him it's hard for you to answer. (Scribner, 1977, p. 490)

The farmer's response did not show that he was unable to solve a problem in deductive logic. Instead, it indicated that as far as he was concerned, the question was unreasonable. In fact, his response contained an example of logical reasoning: "If you know a person . . . you are able to answer." Luria (1977) received a similar answer from an unschooled Uzbekistanian woman, who was asked the following:

In the far north all bears are white.

Novaya Zemlya is in the far north.

What color are the bears there?

The woman replied, "You should ask the people who have been there and seen them. We always speak of only what we see; we don't talk about what we haven't seen."

Scribner found that sometimes people without formal schooling would reject the premises of her syllogism, replace them with what they knew to be true, and then solve the new problem *as they had defined it.* For example, she presented the following problem to a Vai tribesperson:

All women who live in Monrovia are married.

Kemu is not married.

Does she live in Monrovia?

The answer was yes. The respondent said, "Monrovia is not for any one kind of people, so Kemu came to live there." The suggestion that only married women live in Monrovia was absurd, because the tribesperson knew otherwise. Thus, if Kemu wanted to live there, she could—and did.

Clearly, it may be a serious error to measure the intellectual ability of people in other cultures against our own cultural standards. Among traditional tribal peoples, problems may be solved by the application of logical reasoning to facts gained through direct experience. The deductive-reasoning ability of such peoples is not necessarily inferior to ours; it is simply different (see Diamond, 1997, for a remarkable extension of this basic idea).

Interim Summary

Intelligence: Global or Componential?

Although intelligence often is represented by a single score, the IQ, modern investigators do not deny the existence of specific intellectual abilities. What is controversial is whether a general factor also exists. Spearman thought so; he named the factor *g* and demonstrated that people's scores on various specific tests of ability were correlated. Thurstone performed a factor analysis on 56 individual tests that revealed the existence of seven factors, not a single *g* factor. Eysenck reasoned that because these factors were themselves correlated, a factor analysis on them was justified. Cattell performed such an analysis and obtained two factors, and he confirmed this result with factor analyses of tests of his own construction. The nature of the tests that loaded heavily on these two factors suggested the factors he named fluid intelligence (g_f) and crystallized intelligence (g_c), with the former representing a person's native ability and the latter representing what a person learns.

Sternberg's triarchic theory of intelligence relies on information-processing mechanisms as they are applied in natural and cultural environments. According to Sternberg, we use analytic intelligence to plan and execute tasks. We use creative intelligence to apply past strategies to new problems. Finally, we use practical intelligence to adapt to, select, or shape our environment. Gardner's theory of multiple intelligences begins with neuropsychology and is based primarily on the types of skills that can be selectively lost due to brain damage. His definition of intelligence includes many abilities that are commonly regarded as "skills" or "talents." Like Sternberg's theory, Gardner's theory emphasizes the significance of the cultural contexts in which behavior occurs.

People in preliterate societies are less likely than Westerners to approach a logical problem abstractly. Instead, they tend to base their conclusions on what they have experienced and not on hypothetical or abstract situations.

QUESTIONS TO CONSIDER

1. How do you define intelligence in your everyday life? Would your definition work as well for someone from a preliterate society as for someone from the culture in which you live? Why or why not?
2. How would you define the deficits exhibited by Mr. V. in the opening vignette in terms of one or more of the theories of intelligence discussed in this section?
3. Gardner has considered the possibility of a "spiritual" intelligence. What do you think about the possibility that such a thing exists? What criteria could Gardner use to decide whether to add spiritual intelligence to his list?

Intelligence Testing

Intelligence testing is a controversial topic because of its importance in modern society. Many employers use specialized aptitude tests, which are modifications of intelligence tests, to help them select employees. Because the scores achieved on these tests have major implications for the quality of people's adult lives, testing has become one of the most important areas of applied psychology (e.g., Hough & Oswald, 2000). Today there are hundreds of tests of specific abilities, such as manual dexterity, spatial reasoning, vocabulary, mathematical aptitude, musical ability, creativity, and memory. There are also general tests of scholastic aptitude, some of which you have probably taken yourself. All these tests vary widely in reliability, validity, and ease of administration, as will be evident in what follows.

From Mandarins to Galton

Undoubtedly, humans have been aware of individual differences in abilities since the species first evolved.

Some people were more efficient hunters, others more efficiently gathered, some were more skillful at constructing tools and weapons, and some were more daring and clever in battle. As early as 2200 BCE, Chinese emperors tested civil servants (mandarins) periodically to be sure that their abilities still qualified them for their jobs. But in Western cultures differences in social class were far more important than individual differences in ability—until the Renaissance, when the modern concept of individualism arose.

Sir Francis Galton (1822–1911), a man of extraordinarily wide-ranging interests, was the most important early investigator of individual differences in ability. He was strongly influenced by his cousin, Charles Darwin, who stressed the importance of inherited differences in physical and behavioral traits related to a species' survival. Galton observed that there were family differences in ability within Great Britain and concluded that intellectual abilities were heritable. Having noted that people with low ability were poor at making perceptual discriminations, he was confident that tests involving such discriminations would provide valid measures of intelligence.

In 1884 Galton established the Anthropometric ("human-measuring") Laboratory at the International Health Exhibition in London. His exhibit was so popular that his laboratory later became part of the South Kensington Museum. It was the first laboratory devoted to **psychometrics,** the measurement of individual differences in psychological characteristics. Galton tested more than 9000 people on 17 variables, including height and weight, muscular strength, and the ability to perform perceptual discriminations. One task involved detecting small differences in the weights of objects of the same size and shape.

The use of simple tests of discrimination fell into disfavor among subsequent researchers in the field of intelligence,

and Galton's program was not continued after his death. Nevertheless, Galton made very important contributions to science and mathematics. His systematic evaluation of large numbers of people inspired the development of statistical tests now used in all branches of science. His observation that the distribution of most human traits closely resembles the normal curve (which was developed by the Belgian statistician Lambert Quételet, 1796–1874, and was discussed in Chapter 2) is the foundation for inferential tests of statistical significance. (See **Figure 11•1**.)

Galton also outlined the logic of a measure he called *correlation:* the degree to which variability in one measure is related to variability in another. From this analysis Karl Pearson (who also collaborated with Spearman, as noted earlier) derived the correlation coefficient (symbolized as *r*) that is widely used to assess the degree of statistical relation between

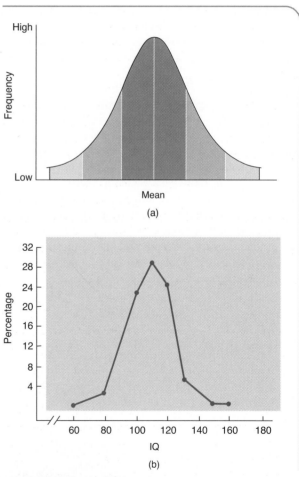

FIGURE 11•1   The normal curve and data from intelligence testing. (a) A mathematically derived normal curve. (b) A curve showing the distribution of IQ scores of 850 children 2.5 years of age.

a pair of variables. In addition, Galton developed the logic of *twin studies* and *adoption studies* to assess the heritability of a human trait. We will discuss these methods later in the chapter. (You also read about them in Chapter 3.)

Intelligence Tests

Modern intelligence tests began in France, with the work of the psychologist Alfred Binet (1857–1911). Binet's test, later adapted by American psychologists, is still used today. Another psychologist, David Wechsler, devised two new intelligence tests, one for adults (the WAIS) and another for children (the Wechsler Intelligence Scale for Children or WISC), both of which we'll look at in more detail later in the chapter.

The Binet-Simon Scale

Alfred Binet disagreed with Galton's conception of human intelligence. He suggested (see Binet & Henri, 1896) that a group of simple perceptual tests could not adequately determine a person's intelligence. Binet recommended measuring a variety of psychological abilities (such as imagery, attention, comprehension, imagination, judgments of visual space, and memory for various stimuli) that appeared to be more representative of the traits that distinguished people of high and low intelligence.

The French government asked Binet to look into problems associated with teaching children who had learning difficulties. To identify children who were unable to profit from typical classroom instruction and who therefore needed special attention and programs, Binet and a colleague, Théodore Simon, assembled a collection of tests, many of which had been developed by other psychologists and educators, and published the **Binet-Simon Scale** in 1905. The word *scale* refers to the fact that the purpose of testing is measurement. The tests were arranged in order of difficulty, and the researchers obtained norms for each test. **Norms** are data obtained from large numbers of individuals. They permit the score of any one individual to be assessed relative to his or her peers. In this case the norms consisted of distributions of scores obtained from children of various ages. Binet and Simon also provided a detailed description of the testing procedure, which was essential for obtaining reliable scores. Without a standardized procedure for administering a test, different test givers may obtain different scores from the same child.

Binet revised the 1905 test in order to assess the intellectual abilities of both typical children and those with learning problems. The revised versions provided a procedure for estimating a child's **mental age**—the average level of intellectual development for a child of a particular age. For example, if a child of 8 scores as well as average 10-year-old children, his or her mental age is 10 years. Binet did not develop the concept of IQ, which relies on the notion of mental ages as well as the child's chronological age. Nor did he believe that the mental age derived from the test scores expressed a simple trait called "intelligence." Instead, he conceived of the overall score as the average of several different abilities.

The Stanford-Binet Scale

In the United States, Lewis Terman of Stanford University translated and revised the Binet-Simon Scale. The revised group of tests, published in 1916, became known as the **Stanford-Binet Scale**. Revisions by Terman and Maud Merrill were published in 1937 and 1960. In 1996, an entirely new version was published. The Stanford-Binet Scale, which is widely used in North America, consists of various tasks grouped according to mental age. Simple tests include identifying parts of the body and remembering which of three small cardboard boxes contains a marble. Intermediate tests include tracing a simple maze with a pencil and repeating five digits orally. Advanced tests include explaining the difference between two abstract words that are close in meaning (such as *fame* and *notoriety*) and completing complex sentences.

The 1916 Stanford-Binet Scale contained a formula for computing IQ, a measure devised by Stern (1914). The **intelligence quotient (IQ)** is based on the idea that if test scores indicate that a child's mental age is equal to his or her chronological age (that is, calendar age), the child's intelligence is average; if the child's mental age is above or below his or her chronological age, the child is more or less intelligent than average. This relation is expressed as the quotient of mental age (MA) and chronological age (CA). The result, when multiplied by 100, is called the **ratio IQ:**

$$IQ = MA \div CA \times 100$$

Multiplication by 100 is a convenience for eliminating fractions. For example, if a child's mental age is 10 and the child's chronological age is 8, then his or her ratio IQ is $(10 \div 8) \times 100 = 125$.

The 1960 version of the Stanford-Binet Scale replaced the ratio IQ with the **deviation IQ**. The aim was to avoid various problems that had become apparent with the ratio IQ, such as the fact that mental age tends not to increase in adulthood even though chronological ages does. Instead of using the ratio of mental age to chronological age, the deviation IQ compares a test taker's score with those received by other people of the same chronological age. (The deviation IQ was created by David Wechsler, whose work is described in the next section.) For example, suppose that a child's score is one standard deviation above the mean for his or her age. The standard deviation of the ratio IQ scores is 16 points, and the score assigned to the average IQ is 100 points. (See Chapter 2 for a description of the standard deviation, a measure of variability.) If a child's score is one standard deviation above the mean for his or her age, the child's deviation IQ score is 100 + 16 (the standard deviation) = 116. A child who scores one standard deviation below the mean has a deviation IQ of 84 (100–16). (See **Figure 11•2**.)

Wechsler's Tests

While chief psychologist at New York City's Bellevue Psychiatric Hospital, David Wechsler (1896–1981) developed several widely used tests of intelligence. His goals were to devise tests of intelligence that were not limited to a single performance index, that were not limited to verbal

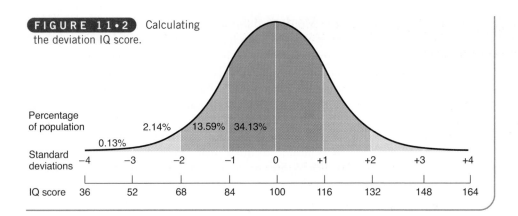

FIGURE 11•2 Calculating the deviation IQ score.

content, and that avoided cultural and linguistic biases. The Wechsler-Bellevue Scale, published in 1939, was revised in 1942 for use in the armed forces and was superseded in 1955 by the **Wechsler Adult Intelligence Scale (WAIS)**. This test was revised in 1981 (the WAIS-R) and again in 1997 (the WAIS-III). The **Wechsler Intelligence Scale for Children (WISC)**, first published in 1949 and revised most recently in 2003 (the WISC-IV), closely resembles the WAIS. Wechsler also devised an intelligence test for preschool children, a memory scale, and other measures of ability.

The WAIS-III consists of several subtests, divided into two categories: verbal and performance. **Table 11•5** lists the subtests and a typical question or problem for each. The norms obtained for the WAIS-III permit the test giver to calculate a deviation IQ score.

The WAIS has become the most popular individually administered adult intelligence test. An important advantage is that it tests verbal and performance abilities separately. Neuropsychologists often use it, because people with brain damage tend to score very differently on the performance and verbal tests; thus, comparisons of performance and verbal test scores may suggest the presence of undiagnosed brain damage. Conversely, because people who have had few educational and cultural opportunities often do worse on the verbal tests than on the performance tests, the WAIS helps indicate what these individuals' scores might have been had they been raised in more favorable environments.

Reliability and Validity of Intelligence Tests

As you will recall from Chapter 2, the adequacy of a measure is defined by its reliability and validity. In the case of intelligence testing, researchers assess reliability in terms of the correlation between the scores people receive on the same test on two different occasions; perfect reliability is 1.0. High reliability is achieved by means of standardized test administration and objective scoring: All test takers are exposed to the same conditions during testing, and all test givers score responses in the same way. The acceptable reliability of a modern test of intellectual ability should be at least .85.

The validity of an intelligence test is assessed by the strength of the correlation between test scores and the **criterion**—an independent measure of the variable that is

being assessed, such as grades in school. The importance of criterion validity can be illustrated by the research literature on self-reported intelligence. What is the validity of people's self-reports of their own intelligence? The typical research approach to this question is to obtain self-ratings of intelligence as well as scores for the same people from established IQ tests. The IQ test scores provide the *criterion* against which the self-report measures of intelligence are assessed. Paulhus, Lysy, and Yik (1998), for example, asked college students to estimate their own intelligence, but did not find correlations greater than .30 between the self-report scores and the criterion IQ scores. Their conclusion: At least for college students, self-reports of intelligence cannot stand in as valid "proxies" for formal IQ test results.

There is no single criterion measure with which to assess validity, not least because there is no single definition of intelligence. We can, however, look at Binet's original goal of intelligence testing—the prediction of scholastic aptitude; that is, the prediction of success in school subjects. The evidence is reasonably clear. School performance, as measured by grades, has a correlation of about .50 with IQ scores (Neisser et al., 1996). Keep in mind, though, that this correlation does not mean that IQ *determines* school performance. A correlation of that size means that about 75 percent of the variability among students in their school performance is due to factors other than IQ. The proportion of the variance explained by IQ scores equals the square of the correlation coefficient: $(.50)^2 = .25$ or 25 percent. This leaves 75 percent of the variance unexplained. The list of potential influences other than IQ on scholastic success is lengthy—but probably includes quality of instruction, family emphasis on education, personal interest and motivation, effort and persistence, and peer group attitudes toward school. Many of us know students who obtained stellar IQ scores but who performed wretchedly in school because they were uninterested or lacked motivation. Likewise, we know people who never posted more than average aptitude scores but who, through hard work and perseverance, have achieved remarkable success in school. The same pattern of variability occurs for other potential criterion measures. For example, IQ scores account for less than half of the variability on income and job performance measures (Neisser et al., 1996). Once again, motivation and social variables will account for at least as much as IQ by itself.

TABLE 11·5   WAIS-III Subtests and Typical Questions or Problems

Subtest	Typical Question or Problem
Verbal	
Information	"What is the capital of France?"
Digit span	"Repeat these numbers back to me: 46239."
Vocabulary	"What does the word *conventional* mean?"
Arithmetic	"Suppose you bought six postcards for thirteen cents each and gave the clerk a dollar. How much change would you receive?" (Paper and pencil cannot be used.)
Comprehension	"Why are we tried by a jury of our peers?"
Similarities	"How are goldfish and canaries similar to each other?"
Letter/number search	The test giver reads a list of out-of-sequence letters and numbers and instructs the person to repeat the items back in sequence.
Performance	
Picture completion	The test giver shows the person a picture with a missing part (such as a mouse without its whiskers) and says, "Tell me what's missing."
Picture arrangement	The test giver shows a series of cartoon pictures (without words) and instructs the person to arrange them in the proper sequence.
Block design	The test giver shows a picture and four or nine blocks divided diagonally into red and white sections, then instructs the person to arrange the blocks so that they match the design in the picture.
Object assembly	The test giver gives the person pieces of cardboard cut like a jigsaw puzzle and instructs him or her to assemble them. (When properly assembled, the pieces form the shape of a common object.)
Digit symbol	The test giver presents a set of 10 symbols paired with the 10 digits and instructs the person to write the corresponding symbols beneath each of a long series of numerals.
Symbol search	The test giver presents a string of symbols, then instructs the person to say whether either of two symbols shown separately also appears in the string of symbols.
Matrix reasoning	The test giver shows the person a matrix containing designs in three of the quadrants and instructs him or her to select the correct missing design from five options.

Differential patterns of brain activity may offer new criteria for the validation of IQ tests. In one experiment Haier and colleagues (Haier, White, & Alkire, 2003) recorded the brain activity of participants who were watching videos. Certain brain regions were more active for participants who performed well on the nonverbal Raven's Advanced Progressive Matrices test than for participants who performed poorly. In related work using fMRI scans, Haier, Jung, Yeo, Head, and Alkire (2004) found that individuals with higher IQ scores had proportionately higher volumes of gray matter in certain regions of the brain than individuals with lower scores.

The Use and Abuse of Intelligence Tests

Schools that group students according to ability usually do so on the basis of scores on intelligence tests. Schools also administer tests to students who appear to have learning disabilities in order to assess needs that may require special programs. At selective academic institutions, aptitude test scores usually serve as an important criterion for admission. Similarly, many corporations use tests to screen job candidates. Because test scores have such important consequences for people's opportunities, we must know whether intelligence tests are valid and whether they are being used appropriately. You have seen that much of the variability on grades and job performance is due to factors other than IQ. The best and fairest practice is to consider IQ as one of several predictors relevant to such decisions—and to recognize both the problems and the utility of IQ testing. Let's look more closely at some problems as well as some valid uses of tests.

The Problem of Cultural Bias   Critics of intelligence testing have argued that the results of some tests are strongly affected by what people have learned (e.g., Miller-Jones, 1989), not just by the test takers' inherent abilities. Consider the effects of a person's family background and culture on his or her ability to answer questions such as "Who wrote *Romeo and Juliet*?" "What is a hieroglyph?" and "What is the meaning of *catacomb*?" (Vernon, 1979, p. 22). Obviously, a child from a family with a strong educational background is much more likely to be able to answer these questions than is an equally intelligent child from a less educated family. The worst form of this bias occurs when entire groups of people are disadvantaged because the content of the test material is foreign to their own cultural contexts.

Test makers have responded to the criticism of cultural bias, and tests are now less likely to contain questions that are obviously biased (see Helms, 1997). But this is not to say that problems of cultural bias have disappeared. It is hard to make bias-free tests, because test makers (like the rest of us) are strongly socialized in their cultures to assume that what they themselves know is common knowledge. For example, the 2002–2003 Miller Analogies Test sample set includes the following analogy:

_____ : SHADE :: INOCULATION : PARASOL

Knowing the meaning of "parasol" likely varies with cultural background. (The keyed answer to this problem is "immunity." A parasol produces shade, and an inoculation produces immunity.) And cultural bias in intelligence testing is not limited to issues of surface vocabulary. Darou (1992) tells a story of presenting a standard analogy question to a tribal councilor in a remote Arctic village: "Saw is to whine, as snake is to . . ." (p. 97), for which the scored correct answer would be "hiss." The person questioned could not generate the correct answer. The reason? Most saws that people in that particular region had experience with were handsaws and chain saws, neither of which whine like a power saw. Clinching the cultural inappropriateness of the question was the fact that there were no snakes in the area.

Even when questions having obvious cultural bias are excluded from tests, different experiences can lead to different test-taking strategies in subtler ways (e.g., Helms, 1992). For example, as we saw earlier, Kpelle tribespeople approach hypothetical logical problems very differently from people in literate societies. Their "failure" to solve such problems indicates cultural differences, not necessarily intellectual differences.

The Problem of Self-Fulfilling Prophecies

There are ways in which intelligence testing can be potentially harmful even if the tests are free of cultural bias. There is good reason to believe that knowledge about children's intelligence scores can set in motion the *self-fulfilling prophecy* phenomenon. A self-fulfilling prophecy occurs when people's expectations about what will happen lead them to act in ways that make the expectations come true, even if the expectations were unfounded in the first place (Merton, 1948). In short, if teachers learn that a child has a low intelligence test score, they may see encouragement of and special attention to the child as a waste of time—time perhaps better spent with students who have greater ability. Likewise, parents who learn that their child has scored low on an intelligence test may try to persuade the child away from academic pursuits. The reactions of both teachers and parents would be ill advised, because we know that intelligence scores are just part of the overall picture of a child's intellectual aptitude. Failure to provide the child with special attention and encouragement

could in fact seal the child's fate, and, ironically, produce the poor academic performance that was expected on the basis of the intelligence test scores. The prophecy (i.e., the expectation) of academic failure would be fulfilled, even though the child might well have been able to do well academically, given proper support. Although ethical considerations prevent direct testing of this possibility, related research strongly suggests that these concerns are well placed (e.g., Madon et al., 2001; Rosenthal, 1985).

Children, too, can fulfill their own prophecies. You can imagine the discouraging effects when a child learns that the result of an intelligence test was a low score. Expecting not to perform well academically could produce actual performance that was far short of the child's actual capacity. (See Chapter 15 for further discussion of self-fulfilling prophecy.)

Identifying Specific Learning Needs

Intelligence testing can bring important benefits when it is used for Binet's original purpose: to identify students who require special instruction. Children with severe learning problems may develop a sense of inferiority if they are placed in mainstream classes without appropriate specialized teaching support. These tests can also identify exceptionally bright students who are performing poorly because they are bored with the pace of instruction or who have been labeled as troublemakers by their teachers.

Many otherwise bright children have learning disabilities. Some have trouble learning to read or write; some perform poorly at math or motor skills. For example, some children have developmental dyslexias that make learning to read difficult for them. They often are frustrated by the contrast between their inability to read and their competence in other realms. They may express this frustration through disruptive behavior at school and at home, or they may simply stop trying to excel at anything. As a result, they are sometimes labeled as mentally retarded and are placed in inappropriate educational programs. By identifying a specific learning disability in an otherwise bright child, testing helps ensure remedial intervention and prevents mislabeling.

Identifying Degrees of Mental Retardation

In keeping with Binet's original purpose—to identify children who needed special educational opportunities—intelligence tests remain an accepted means of evaluating the extent of mental disabilities and thus, of indicating the most appropriate remedial program for a child.

The term **mental retardation** ("mental delay") was originally applied to children with severe learning problems because such children appeared to achieve intellectual skills and competencies at a significantly later age than children typically do. People with mental retardation were formerly relegated to a bleak and hopeless existence in institutions. Fortunately, there are many more options today for people with intellectual deficiencies.

People with mental retardation face a double problem. Because they have a demonstrable degree of intellectual dis-

▲ *With appropriate education, most people with mild mental retardation can lead independent lives and perform well at jobs.*

ability, they may have difficulty—in some cases, extreme difficulty—with the usual tasks of living. They also must deal with prejudice and discrimination. Being intelligent is a highly valued quality in Western societies, and people with intellectual deficits often are the target of derision. Unfortunately, being different often translates into being "bad." Many people also believe that if a person has an intellectual disability, he or she lacks normal emotions, desires, and needs. These beliefs are, of course, false. Nevertheless, the term *mental retardation* is still the professionally accepted label and is used here for the purpose of describing the degrees of this disability. In other contexts, *cognitive disability* or *intellectual disability* is often a better term.

According to the American Psychological Association, degrees of mental retardation are defined jointly by IQ scores and adaptive limitations in everyday living (Jacobson & Mulick, 1996). The most severe classification, *profound mental retardation*, is applied when a person has an IQ score below the range of 20. This is a very rare level of disability that involves problems in all domains of life and also is associated with motor difficulties. The person shows little cognitive development during his or her early years. People with this degree of disability require permanent supervision and care. The next category is *severe mental retardation*, which is used when a person's IQ score is between 20 and 34. This degree of disability includes difficulty with speech development during the early years. People with severe mental retardation can profit from special education programs and can contribute to their own care, although they almost always need close supervision. People with *moderate mental retardation* have IQ scores between 35 and 54, are able to learn most basic life skills, are able to hold well-supervised jobs, and can live semi-independently with some supervision and assistance. The vast majority of people with mental retardation (about 90 percent) are classified as having *mild mental retardation*. IQ scores for this level fall between 55 and 70. Although people with mild mental retardation may need assistance and sup-

port from time to time, they generally are able to live independently and to learn the skills and responsibilities needed to maintain employment. It is important to recall again that IQ by itself does not determine a person's achievement and satisfaction with life. Families, neighbors, schools, communities, and special programs are all significant contributors to the well-being of people with intellectual disabilities.

Interim Summary

Intelligence Testing

Although the earliest known use of ability testing was by the ancient Chinese, modern intelligence testing dates from the efforts of Francis Galton to measure individual differences in psychological characteristics—an area of study known as psychometrics. Galton made an important contribution to the field of measurement, but his tests of simple perceptual abilities were abandoned in favor of tests that attempt to assess more complex abilities, such as memory, logical reasoning, and vocabulary.

Alfred Binet developed a test that was designed to assess students' intellectual abilities in order to identify children with special educational needs. Although the test that later superseded his, the Stanford-Binet Scale, provided for calculation of IQ, Binet believed that "intelligence" was actually a composite of several specific abilities. For him the concept of mental age was a convenience, not a biological reality. Wechsler's two intelligence tests, the WAIS-III for adults and the WISC-IV for children, are widely used today. The information provided by the verbal and performance scores helps neuropsychologists diagnose brain damage and can provide at least a rough estimate of the innate ability of poorly educated people.

The reliability of modern intelligence tests is excellent, but assessing their validity is still difficult. Because no single criterion measure of intelligence exists, analysts often validate intelligence tests by comparing test takers' scores with other measures of achievement, such as scholastic success.

Intelligence tests can have both good and bad effects on the people who take them. The principal benefit is identifying children with special needs (or special talents) who will profit from special programs. The principal danger is that stigmatizing those who score poorly can deprive them of the opportunity for good jobs or further education. Tests are also used for the classification of individuals whose very low scores indicate disabilities ranging from mild to profound mental retardation.

QUESTIONS TO CONSIDER

1. Would you like to know your own IQ score? Why? What difference(s) would knowing your IQ score make in your life? How would you feel if your IQ score were "average"?

2. Suppose you wanted to devise an intelligence test of your own. What kinds of tasks would you include? What abilities would these tasks measure?

The Roles of Heredity and Environment

Abilities of various kinds—intellectual, athletic, musical, and artistic—appear to run in families. Why? Are the similarities due to heredity, or are they the result of a common environment, including similar educational opportunities and exposure to people with similar kinds of interests? We considered this problem briefly in Chapter 3; now we will examine it in more detail. As you will see, both hereditary and environmental factors play a substantial role.

The Meaning of Heritability

When we ask how much influence heredity has on a given trait, we are usually asking about the heritability of the trait. As we saw in Chapter 3, **heritability** is a statistical measure that applies to a population. It is the proportion of the observed variability in a trait within that population that is directly produced by the genetic variability in the population. The value of this measure can vary from 0 to 1.0. The heritability of many physical traits in most cultures is very high; for example, eye color is affected almost entirely by hereditary factors and little, if at all, by the environment. Thus, the heritability of eye color is close to 1.0.

Heritability is a concept that many people misunderstand. It does not describe the extent to which one's genes are responsible for producing a particular trait. It measures the relative contributions of differences in genes and differences in environmental factors to the overall observed *variability* of the trait in a particular population. An example may make this distinction clear. Consider the heritability of hair color among Inuit. Assume that all young Inuit have black hair. Because all members of the population possess the same versions of the genes that determine hair color, there is no genetic variability in the population. Therefore, the heritability of hair color among Inuit is zero. This may sound odd to you, because you know that hair color is genetically determined. How can a trait be genetically determined, indeed inherited, but have zero heritability? The key point is that genetic determination and heritability are not the same thing. The word *heritability* refers only to the genetic influence on the distribution of differences in a trait—the variability—within a population. If there are no genetic differences among individuals in the population, then a trait has a heritability of zero.

We measure the heritability of intelligence through observation of the trait within a population. By measuring the correlation between IQ scores and various genetic and environmental factors, it is possible to estimate the heritability of IQ. Clearly, even if hereditary factors do influence intelligence, the heritability of this trait will be considerably less than 1.0, because so many environmental factors (including the mother's prenatal health and nutrition, the child's nutrition, the educational level of the child's parents, and the quality of the child's school) can influence it.

A person does not inherit a certain IQ score. Rather than IQ, you inherit genes that influence the development of intelligence. The life you experience early in the womb, your home, your schools, and your neighborhood all influence your IQ in conjunction with your genes. Most important, remember that heritability estimates do not apply to individuals (see Sternberg & Grigorenko, 1999, for an interesting discussion of this point). The estimates apply only to populations. Also keep in mind that knowing the heritability of a trait is .50 does not mean that 50 percent of the trait is inherited by an individual. Rather, we would say that half of the variability in the trait, as measured in the population, can be accounted for by the genetic variability that exists there. Again, heritability refers to populations, not to individuals.

When we consider studies that attempt to measure the heritability of intellectual abilities, we should remember the following considerations:

1. The heritability of a trait depends on the amount of variability of genetic factors in a given population. If there is little genetic variability, genetic factors will appear to be unimportant. Because the ancestors of people living in developed Western nations came from all over the earth, genetic variability is likely to be much higher in those nations than in an isolated community of people in a remote part of the world. Therefore, if a person's IQ score is affected by genetic factors, the measured heritability of IQ will be higher in, say, North America than in an isolated community.

2. The relative importance of environmental factors in intelligence depends on the amount of environmental variability that occurs in the population. If environmental variability is low, then environmental factors will appear to be unimportant. In a hypothetical society with low variability in the environmental factors relevant to intellectual development—a society in which, à la Lake Wobegon, all children are raised in the same way by equally skilled and conscientious caregivers, all schools are equally good, all teachers have equally effective personalities and teaching skills, and no one is discriminated against—the effects of environmental variability will be small and those of genetic variability will be large. In contrast, in a society in which only a few privileged people receive a good education, environmental factors will be responsible for much of the variability in intelligence: The effects of environmental variability would be large relative to those of genetic variability.

3. Heritability is affected by the degree to which genetic inheritance and environment interact. Genetic factors and environmental factors often affect each other. For example, suppose that because of genetic differences some children are mellow and others are excitable. Suppose that the excitable children will profit most from a classroom in which distractions are kept to a minimum and teachers are themselves mellow and soothing. Further suppose that the mellow students will profit most from an exciting classroom that motivates them to work their hardest. In this situation, the actual performance of the students will be based on an interaction between heredity and environment. If all students are taught in a mellow classroom, the excitable children will learn more and obtain better IQ scores. If all students are taught in an exciting classroom, the mellow children will do better and obtain the higher scores. In an ideal world, of course, a child's learning environment would be optimal for his or her hereditary predispositions.

Sources of Environmental and Genetic Effects during Development

Donald Hebb (1949, 1966) set the stage for our current understanding of how genetics and environment contribute to intelligence. In his neuropsychological theory of behavior, Hebb explained that both biological and environmental factors occurring before and after birth can affect intellectual abilities. His view was that the term "intelligence," as used by psychologists, reflects two components. The first component (*Intelligence A*) is the hereditary, biological potential for intellectual development. The second component (*Intelligence B*) reveals the effect of biological development coupled with environmental influences on intellectual functioning. Intelligence B, then, is what we measure with IQ tests. From this perspective, newborn infants cannot be said to possess any substantial intellectual abilities; rather, they are more or less capable of developing these abilities as they grow older. Therefore, prenatal influences affect a child's potential intelligence by affecting the development of the brain. Factors that impair brain development will necessarily also impair the child's potential intelligence.

The factors that control the development of a human organism are incredibly complex. For example, the most complicated organ—the brain—consists of billions of interconnected neurons, all of which are connected to other neurons. In addition, many of these neurons are connected to sensory receptors, muscles, or glands. During development, neurons must establish the proper connections so that the eyes send their information to the visual cortex, the ears send theirs to the auditory cortex, and the nerve cells controlling movement connect with the appropriate muscles.

As the axons of developing neurons grow, they thread their way through a tangle of other growing cells, responding to physical and chemical signals along the way, much as a salmon swims upriver to the tributary in which it was spawned. During this stage of prenatal development, differentiating cells can be misguided by false signals. For example, if a woman contracts rubella during early pregnancy, toxic chemicals produced by the disease virus may adversely affect the development of the fetus. Sometimes these chemicals misdirect the interconnections of brain cells and produce mental retardation. Thus, although development of a human organism is programmed genetically, environmental factors can affect development even before a person is born.

Harmful prenatal environmental factors include physical trauma (for instance, injury to the mother in an automobile accident) and toxins. A developing fetus can be exposed to toxins from diseases contracted by the mother during pregnancy (such as rubella) or from other sources. A pregnant woman's intake of drugs can have disastrous effects on fetal development. For example, alcohol, opiates, cocaine, and the chemicals present in cigarettes can harm fetuses. There is some evidence that even a single alcoholic binge during a critical stage of pregnancy can cause permanent damage to the fetus. One of the most common drug-induced abnormalities is **fetal alcohol syndrome,** which afflicts the offspring of women who are chronic alcoholics. Children with fetal alcohol syndrome are much smaller than average, have characteristic facial abnormalities, and, more significantly, have cognitive disabilities.

Genetic abnormalities can also impair development. The best-known example is Down syndrome, which was described in Chapter 3. Although it is a genetic disorder, it is not hereditary; it results from imperfect division of the 21st pair of chromosomes during the development of an ovum or (more rarely) a sperm. Chapter 3 also described phenylketonuria (PKU), an inherited metabolic disorder that disrupts brain development. If left untreated, PKU can result in severe mental retardation. However, although PKU is a genetic disease, a person born with PKU can eliminate its effects by

▲ *Children born with fetal alcohol syndrome are at much higher risk for several health-impairing conditions as well as mental retardation.*

limiting dietary intake of phenylalanine, underscoring the point that environmental interventions (in this case, eliminating phenylalanine from food) may completely overcome otherwise ill effects.

A child's brain continues to develop from birth onward. Environmental factors can either promote or impede that development. Postnatal factors such as birth trauma, diseases, or toxic chemicals can prevent optimum development and thereby affect the child's intelligence. For example, encephalitis (inflammation of the brain), when contracted during childhood, can result in mental retardation. So can the ingestion of poisons such as mercury or lead, as well as malnutrition.

Educational influences in the environment, including home life and schooling (to mention only two), can nurture a child's intelligence. By contrast, a less-than-optimum environment prevents the fullest possible realization of intellectual potential. Research with people who have mental retardation demonstrates this point. Known causes account for only about 25 percent of cases of mental retardation. Moreover, people with mental retardation that has no obvious physical cause are likely to have close relatives who also have mental retardation. These findings strongly suggest that some of the remaining 75 percent of cases have hereditary origins. However, shared environmental conditions (such as poor nutrition or the presence of environmental toxins) can produce brain damage in members of the same family; thus, not all cases of mental retardation within families are necessarily hereditary.

In sum, the interactive effects of environmental and genetic factors are complex. The effects of hereditary factors on adult intellectual ability are necessarily indirect, and many environmental factors exert their effects throughout the journey to adulthood. Because an adult's intellectual abilities are the product of a long chain of events, we cannot isolate the effects of the earliest factors. The types of genetic and environmental factors that influence potential intelligence at each stage of development are summarized below.

Conception. A basic genetic endowment sets in place the potential for the later development of intellectual abilities.

Prenatal development. Good nutrition and a normal pregnancy result in optimal fetal brain development and optimal intellectual potential. Drugs, maternal disease, toxic substances, poor nutrition, and physical accidents can impair fetal brain development, thus lowering that potential. Genetic disorders such as Down syndrome and phenylketonuria also can impair brain development.

Birth. Anoxia (lack of oxygen) or head trauma can cause brain damage.

Infancy. The brain continues to develop and grow. Good nutrition continues to be important. Sensory stimulation and interaction with responsive physical and social environments are important for cognitive development. An infant's environment and brain jointly determine his or her intelligence.

Childhood and later life. A person's intelligence continues to be jointly determined by environmental factors and brain structure and chemistry. Rich environmental stimulation continues to be vital to intellectual abilities into old age. Advancing years bring an increased risk of senile dementia—a class of diseases characterized by the progressive loss of cortical tissue and a corresponding loss of cognitive functions. (*Senile* means "old"; *dementia* literally means "an undoing of the mind.") The most common causes of *dementia* are *Alzheimer's disease* (discussed in Chapter 12) and *multiple infarcts*—the occurrence of many small strokes, each of which damages a small amount of brain tissue. In addition, as we will see in Chapter 12, cognitive deterioration can also be produced by depression, a psychological disorder. Unlike Alzheimer's disease or multiple infarcts, depression can be treated with drugs and with psychotherapy.

Results of Heritability Studies

Estimates of the degree to which heredity influences a person's intellectual ability come from several sources. As we saw in Chapter 3, the two most powerful methods are comparisons between identical and fraternal twins and comparisons between adoptive and biological relatives. As you read the evidence about heritability, remember what heritability *does* and *does not* mean. If we find that the heritability of a trait is .50, it does not mean that 50 percent of the trait was inherited. It means that 50 percent of the variance for that trait in a population is determined by the genetic variance. A very high heritability estimate does not mean that environmental influences are unimportant. Rather, it means that, under environmental conditions favorable to the expression of the trait, a great deal of variability in the population will be attributable to genes. But environments are variable, and in the real world some environments will promote the genetic expression of the trait and some will inhibit that expression.

General Intelligence Table 11•6 presents correlations for IQ scores between people with varying degrees of kinship. The data in the table were obtained from a summary of several studies by Henderson (1982). As you can see, the correlation between two people is indeed related to their genetic similarity. For example, the correlation between identical twins is larger than that between fraternal twins. The correlation between a biological parent and a child is approximately the same regardless of whether or not the child is raised by the parent (.35 versus .31). The correlation, in turn, is higher than that between an adopted child and the parent who raises him or her (.16).

Genetics clearly make a difference, but how much?

Neisser and colleagues (1996) summarized the evidence on the heritability of IQ and estimated it to be at about .45 in childhood and about .75 in late adolescence. In other

TABLE 11·6 Correlations between IQ Scores for Members of Various Kinship Pairs

Relationship	Rearing	Percentage of Genetic Similarity	Correlation
Same individual	—	100	.87[a]
Identical twins	Together	100	.86
Fraternal twins	Together	50	.62
Siblings	Together	50	.41
Siblings	Apart	50	.24
Parent–child	Together	50	.35
Parent–child	Apart	50	.31
Adoptive parent–child	Together	?	.16

[a] The correlation is not 1.0 because a person's score may vary from one test to another on account of tiredness, distraction, etc. Nevertheless, such a high correlation shows the high reliability of IQ tests.

Source: Adapted from Henderson, N. D. *Human behavior genetics,* pp. 403–440. Reprinted, with permission, from the *Annual Review of Psychology,* Volume 33. © 1982 by Annual Reviews,www.annualreviews.org.

words, it appears that heritability of IQ increases with age. Studies of people in their eighth and ninth decades likewise show higher IQ heritability estimates than typically seen for children (McClearn et al., 1997). How could this be? The answer suggested by Neisser and colleagues and other researchers (e.g., Sternberg & Grigorenko, 1999) is that until early adulthood a person is subject to the authority and decisions of many other people and institutions. The environment therefore stands to play a relatively important role in the de-

velopment of the individual's intellectual abilities. When people become independent, however, they can begin to choose their own environments. To the extent that those choices reflect the heritable component of intelligence, the influence of the chosen environments becomes less distinct from genetic influence.

Specific Abilities So far, we have looked at the effects of genetic factors on tests of intelligence. Scarr and Weinberg (1978) compared specific intellectual abilities of parents and their adopted and biological children and of children and their adopted and biological siblings. To do so, they administered four of the subtests of the Wechsler Adult Intelligence Scale: arithmetic, vocabulary, block design, and picture arrangement. (Table 11.5 described these subtests.) **Table 11·7** shows the results. As you can see, the correlations between biological relatives were considerably higher than those between adoptive relatives, indicating that genetic factors played a more significant role than shared environmental factors. In fact, with the exception of vocabulary, adopted children showed little resemblance to other members of their adoptive family.

These results suggest that a person's vocabulary is more sensitive to his or her home environment than are other specific intellectual abilities. Presumably, such factors as the availability of books, parental interest in reading, and the complexity of vocabulary used by the parents have a significant effect on the verbal skills of all members of the household, whether or not they are biologically related.

▲ *Although heredity plays some role in the development of intelligence, children's home environments can also influence the extent to which they achieve their full intellectual potential.*

TABLE 11·7 Correlations between IQ Scores in Adoptive and Biological Families

WAIS Subscale	Relationship		
	Father–Offspring	Mother–Offspring	Sibling
Adoptive family correlations			
Arithmetic	.07	−.03	−.03
Vocabulary	.24	.23	.11
Block design	.02	.13	.09
Picture arrangement	−.04	−.01	.04
Biological family correlations			
Arithmetic	.30	.24	.24
Vocabulary	.39	.33	.22
Block design	.32	.29	.25
Picture arrangement	.06	.19	.16

Source: Adapted from Scarr, S., & Weinberg, R. A. (1978). *American Sociological Review, 43,* 674–692.

Evaluating Scientific Issues

The Issue of Race and Intelligence

The fact that heredity plays an important role in people's intellectual capacities raises the question of whether people of some racial or ethnic groups are generally more intelligent than those of others. The harmful effects that racism has had on the lives of countless people make this far from an academic question. A word in advance: As I'll discuss shortly, it is actually inaccurate to refer to a "race" of people. But because discussion on this subject generally employs the word *race* rather than another term, I will use that word here.

● Are There Racial Differences in Intelligence?

Many studies have established that there are racial differences in scores on various tests of intellectual abilities. For example, people in the United States who are identified as "black" generally score an average of 85 on IQ tests, whereas people who are identified as "white" score an average of 100 (Jensen, 1985; Lynn, 1978). Remember from Chapter 2, however, that averages, or means, do not tell us about the variability of scores. This is an especially important point in the socially significant context of differences between races. What the means fail to tell us is that the variation of scores *within* each race is far greater than the variation *between* the two races. In other words, IQ scores of the two races overlap much more than they differ. Some whites score higher than blacks, and some blacks score higher than whites. But there is a seemingly reliable difference on average.

The issue is not the difference in average scores themselves but what those differences *mean*. The simplest explanation, and the one most widely accepted, has been that the historical and continued disadvantaged status of some black people in the United States suppresses the intellectual development of a large enough proportion that a mean difference in test scores is predictable and understandable.

A more provocative stance is the thesis that the racial differences in scores on intelligence tests reflect heritable factors. *The Bell Curve*, a book written by American social scientists Richard Herrnstein and Charles Murray (1994), provoked a furor among psychologists and in the news media. The book asserted that psychologists agree that a single general factor corresponding to intelligence exists, that IQ is for all intents and purposes genetically determined, that racial differences in IQ are the result of heredity, and that IQ is almost impossible to modify through education and special programs. However, many influential psychologists (e.g., Horn, 2002; Sternberg, 1995) vehemently disagree with these conclusions.

● What Is the Evidence for Racial Differences in Intelligence?

Sternberg (1995) examined *The Bell Curve*'s claims and claimed to find scientific evidence against all of them. As we have already seen in this chapter, most psychologists believe that intelligence cannot be accounted for by a single factor. And if you ask people what they mean by the word *intelligence*, three factors rather than one will emerge in their responses: verbal ability, practical problem-solving ability, and social competence (Sternberg, Conway, Ketron, & Bernstein, 1981). Different cultures emphasize these factors differently; some think that social competence is more important, whereas others value competence on cognitive tasks (Berry, 1984, 2001; Okagaki & Sternberg, 1993; Ruzgis & Grigorenko, 1994).

What about the assertions that IQ is almost impossible to modify? In fact, special programs *have* been successful in raising children's IQ scores—on the order of 8 to 20 points (see Ramey, 1994; Wahlsten, 1997b). Herrnstein and Murray (1994) went farther by claiming that there are diminishing returns on the advanced education of black people, but there are data to show otherwise (Myerson, Rank, Raines, & Schnitzler, 1998). The gain in general cognitive ability from college education is actually greater for blacks than for whites.

And what about genes? There are many reasons why we *cannot* conclude that the observed racial differences in average test scores are the result of heredity. We will examine the two most important considerations here: the definition of race and the role of the environment.

First, let's examine the concept of *race*. Biologists use the term to identify a population of plants or animals that has some degree of reproductive isolation from other members of the species. For example, collies, cocker spaniels, and beagles constitute different races of dogs (although we usually refer to them as breeds). In this case the reproductive isolation has been imposed by humans.

Any isolated group of organisms will, as a result of chance alterations in genes and differences in local environment, become genetically differentiated over time. Groups of humans whose ancestors mated only with other people who lived in a restricted geographical region tend to differ from other groups on a variety of hereditary traits, including stature, hair color, skin pigmentation, and blood type. However, subsequent migrations and invasions caused mating between many different groups of people. As a result, human racial groups have become much more similar than they are different.

Many researchers have used the trait of skin pigmentation to classify people by race. Two chemicals, melanin (a pigment) and keratin (a fibrous protein), cause skin to be black and yellow, respectively; a combination produces brown skin, and lighter-colored skin contains little of either substance. Evidence suggests that the selective value of greater skin pigmentation is related to its ability to protect against the effects of sunlight (Loomis, 1967). Such protection was important near the equator, where the sun is intense all year, but was less important in temperate zones. Because vitamin D is synthesized primarily through the action of sunlight on deep layers of the skin, lack of pigmentation was advantageous to residents of northern latitudes—except to those living in Arctic regions, where vitamin D was readily available from fish and seal meat. The selective advantage of differences in skin pigmentation is obvious. But there is no necessary reason to expect these differences to be correlated with intellectual ability.

The second reason why we cannot conclude definitively that racial differences in test scores are caused by heredity is the existence of cultural differences. Most of the data used in the studies cited in *The Bell Curve* come from the United States; extensive data from other countries and cultures are not included in those studies.

A study by Scarr and Weinberg (1976) provided evidence that environmental factors can substantially increase the measured IQ of an American black child. Scarr and Weinberg studied 97 black children who were adopted while they were young into white families of higher-than-average educational and socioeconomic status. The expected average IQ of black children in the same area (Minnesota) who were raised in black families was approximately 90. The average IQ of the adopted group was 105. A decade later, Weinberg, Scarr, and Waldman (1992) studied many of the same children and concluded that the IQ differences they had observed earlier had disappeared. The average IQ of the adopted black children was 89.

● **What Should We Conclude?**

Some authors have flatly stated that there are no racial differences in biologically determined intellectual potential. But this claim, like the assertion that blacks are inherently less intelligent than whites, has received mixed support at best. Although we know that American blacks and whites can experience different environments and that a black child raised in an environment similar to that of a white child may receive a higher IQ score, the question of whether any hereditary differences exist has not been answered. However, given that there is at least as much variability in intelligence between two people selected at random as there is between the average black person and the average white person, knowing a person's race tells us little if anything about how intelligent he or she may be.

Still, Murray (2005), after careful consideration of the major interventions designed to reduce the black–white IQ difference in the United States, points to the persistence of that difference and argues that additional research must be pursued to help us understand the difference and its implications for the larger culture.

More interesting and more valid questions concerning race may be those addressed by social psychologists and anthropologists—questions concerning issues such as the prevalence of prejudice, ethnic identification and cohesiveness, fear of strangers, and the tendency to judge something (or someone) that is different. Chapter 15 discusses the topic of prejudice.

Interim Summary

The Roles of Heredity and Environment

Variability in all physical traits is co-determined by genetic variability, environmental variability, and an interaction between genetic and environmental factors. A measure of the degree to which genetic variability is responsible for the observed variability of a particular trait in a particular population is called heritability. Heritability is not an indication of the degree to which the trait is determined by genetic factors.

Intellectual development is affected by many factors both prenatally and postnatally. A person's heredity, because of its effect on brain development, affects his or her intellectual potential. This potential can be permanently reduced during prenatal or postnatal development by injury, toxic chemicals, poor nutrition, or disease. In order for a person to achieve his or her intellectual potential, it is necessary for the person to interact with an environment that will foster the learning needed to function successfully in society.

Twin studies and studies comparing biological and adoptive relatives indicate that both genetic and environmental factors affect intellectual ability. Correlations in IQ scores of pairs of individuals vary with their biological relatedness.

Some people have suggested that racial differences in intellectual ability are the result of differences in heredity. However, the available data do not support this suggestion unequivocally. First, race is almost always defined culturally, not genetically. Second, we cannot rule out the effects of environmental differences. Because performance on IQ tests can be influenced by what people have learned, it reflects environmental factors as well as genetic ones. Members of some racial groups have fewer opportunities for environmental interactions that promote intellectual growth. For that reason, it is difficult to draw conclusions about whether the racial differences in IQ are hereditary. The little evidence we do have suggests that when educational opportunities are equalized, the difference in test scores narrows.

QUESTIONS TO CONSIDER

1. What types of early human environments may have favored natural selection of particular kinds of abilities—for example, mathematical ability, spatial ability, perceptual ability, or ability to memorize stories?
2. Among continuing contested issues in education is the system of "tracking"—assigning students with different levels of intellectual ability to different classes. Take the point of view of students who have (a) high or (b) low levels of ability, and state arguments for and against this practice.

Thinking and Problem Solving

One of the most important components of intelligence is thinking, which includes categorizing, reasoning, and solving problems. Thinking is an activity that takes place where no one can see it—inside our heads. Because thinking is private, we know what we ourselves think but can only infer what others think from their behavior. When we think, we classify, manipulate, and combine information. As a result, after thinking we may know something we did not know before (although this new knowledge could be incorrect).

The purpose of thinking is, in general, to solve problems. The problems may involve simple classifications (*What is that, a bird or a bat?*). They may involve decisions about courses of action (*Should I buy a new car or pay to fix the old one?*). Or they may require the construction, testing, and evaluation of complex plans of action (*How am I going to manage to earn money to support my family, help raise our children, and continue my education so that I can get out of this dead-end job—and still be able to enjoy life?*). Much, but not all, of our thinking involves language. We certainly think with words, but we also think with shapes and images. Thus, it's important to consider verbal as well as nonverbal processes in thinking (Holyoak & Spellman, 1993; Reber, 1992).

In this section we consider the important elements and goals of thinking: classification and concept formation, logical reasoning, and problem solving.

Categorization and Generalization

When we categorize, we classify things according to their characteristics. When we attempt to solve a problem involving a particular object or event, we often use information that we have already learned about similar objects or events. To take a very simple example, when we enter someone's house for the first time, we recognize chairs, lamps, tables, and other pieces of furniture even though we may have never seen these particular versions of those objects before. Because we can classify them, we know where to sit, how to increase the level of illumination, where to place our coffee mug, and so on.

A **concept** is a category of objects, actions, events, or states of being that share certain attributes. Each of the following is a concept: cat, comet, team, destroying, playing, forgetting, happiness, truth, justice. Most thinking deals with the relations and interactions among concepts. For example, *The hawk caught the sparrow* describes an interaction between two birds; *Studying for the examination was fun* describes an attribute of a particular action related to an event; and *Youth is a carefree time of life* describes an attribute of a state of being.

Concepts exist because they have consequences for us. For example, *mean dogs* may hurt us, whereas *friendly dogs* may give us pleasure. *Mean dogs* tend to growl, bare their teeth, and bite, whereas *friendly dogs* tend to prance around, wag their tails, and invite our attention. Thus, when we see a dog that growls and bares its teeth, we avoid it because it might bite us; but if we see one prancing around and wagging its tail, we may try to pet it. We have learned to avoid or approach dogs that display different sorts of behavior directly (through personal experience with dogs) or indirectly (through what other people tell us or by watching other people interact with dogs). The point is, once we have learned the concepts of mean and friendly dogs, we can then respond appropriately to other dogs throughout life. Our experiences with particular dogs *generalize* to others.

Formal and Natural Concepts

A **formal concept** is a category defined by a list of essential characteristics, as in a dictionary definition. For example, dogs have four legs, tails, fur, and wet noses; are carnivores; can bark, growl, whine, and howl; pant when they are hot; bear live young; and so on. Thus, a formal concept is a category that has rules of membership and exclusion.

Psychologists have studied the nature of formally defined concepts, such as species of animals. Collins and Quillian (1969) suggested that such concepts are organized hierarchically in semantic memory (see Chapter 8 for a discussion of this category of memory). Each concept in a hierarchy is defined by a set of characteristics. Consider the hierarchy of concepts related to animals shown in **Figure 11•3**. At the top is the general concept *animal*. It is associated with the characteristics common to all animals, such as *has skin, can move around, eats, breathes,* and so on. Linked to the concept animal and subordinate to it are specific groups of animals, such as *birds, fish,* and *mammals,* along with their characteristics. Nested lower in the hierarchy are still more specific concepts, such as types of birds and types of fish.

Collins and Quillian assumed that the characteristics common to all concepts at a particular level of the hierarchy would be remembered not at that level but at the next higher level. Such an arrangement would produce an efficient and economical organization of memory. For example, all birds have wings. Thus, we need not remember that a canary, a blue jay, a robin, and an ostrich all have wings; we need only remember that each of these concepts belongs to the category of *bird* and that birds have wings.

Collins and Quillian tested the validity of their model by presenting questions about the characteristics of various concepts, such as the concept *canary*. They asked their study participants to respond "true" or "false" to statements such as *A canary eats*. When the question dealt with characteristics that were specific to canaries (such as *can sing* or *is yellow*), the participants responded quickly. If the question dealt with a characteristic that was associated with the more general concept *animal* (such as *has skin* or *breathes*), the participants took a longer time in answering. The researchers inferred that, when asked a question about a characteristic that ap-

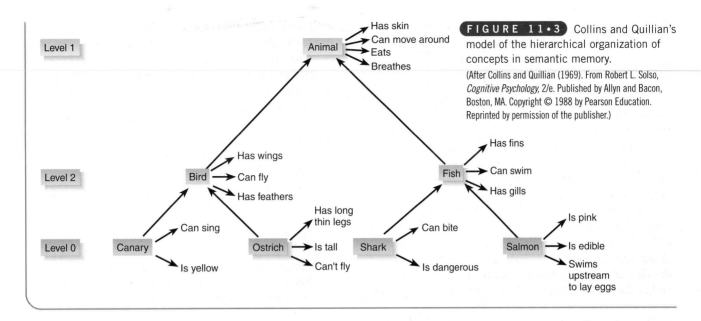

FIGURE 11·3 Collins and Quillian's model of the hierarchical organization of concepts in semantic memory.

(After Collins and Quillian (1969). From Robert L. Solso, *Cognitive Psychology*, 2/e. Published by Allyn and Bacon, Boston, MA. Copyright © 1988 by Pearson Education. Reprinted by permission of the publisher.)

plied to all birds or to all animals, the participants had to "travel up the tree of concepts" from the entry for *canary* until they found the level that provided the answer. The farther they had to go, the longer the process took.

This model of hierarchical structure has an appealing simplicity to it, but further research suggests that human brains do not follow such tidy, logical schemes in classifying concepts and their characteristics. For example, although people may indeed conceive of objects in terms of a hierarchy, a particular person's hierarchy of animals need not resemble that compiled by a zoologist. For example, Rips, Shoben, and Smith (1973) found that people said yes to *A collie is an animal* faster than they did to *A collie is a mammal*. According to Collins and Quillian's model, *animal* comes above *mammal* in the hierarchy, so the results should have been the opposite.

Thus, although categories and subcategories must somehow be linked in memory, the structure appears not to be straightforwardly logical and systematic. For example, Roth and Mervis (1983) found that people judged *Chablis* to be a better example of *wine* than of *drink*, but they judged *champagne* to be a better example of *drink* than of *wine*. This inconsistency clearly reflects people's experience with the concepts. Chablis is obviously a wine: It is sold in bottles that resemble those used for other wines, it looks and tastes similar to other white wines, the word *wine* is found on the label, and so on. Given these characteristics, champagne appears not to belong, even though a wine expert would categorize champagne as a particular type of wine. The average person may not be well acquainted with the fact that champagne is made from fermented grape juice and may encounter champagne only as something to drink on a special occasion, something to christen ships with, and so on. Thus, to most people, champagne's characteristics are rather different from those of Chablis.

Eleanor Rosch (1975, 1999, 2002; Mervis & Rosch, 1981), whose work was discussed in Chapter 7, suggested that people do not look up the meanings of concepts in their heads the way they do in dictionaries. In addition, the concepts we use in everyday life are *natural concepts,* not the formal categories known to experts who have examined characteristics most of us are not aware of. **Natural concepts** are categories based on personal perceptions and interactions with the real world. For example, some things in the world have wings, beaks, and feathers, and they fly, build nests, lay eggs, and make high-pitched noises. Other things are furry, have four legs and tails, and run around on the ground. Formal concepts consist of carefully defined sets of rules governing membership in a particular category; natural concepts are collections of memories of particular examples with shared similarities that may not be especially well defined. Formal concepts are used primarily by experts (and by people studying to become experts), whereas natural concepts are used by ordinary people in their daily lives.

Rosch further suggests that people's natural concepts consist of collections of memories of *particular examples,* called **exemplars,** that share similarities. The boundaries between formal concepts are precise, whereas those between natural concepts are fuzzy—the distinction between a member and a nonmember is not always clear. For this reason, to nonexperts, not all members of a concept are equally good examples of that concept. A robin is a good example of *bird;* a penguin or an ostrich seems a poor one. Although we may ultimately acknowledge that a penguin is a bird because we have been taught that it is, we often qualify that acknowledgment by making statements such as "*Strictly speaking,* a penguin is a bird." Exemplars represent the important characteristics of a concept—characteristics that we can readily perceive when we encounter a member of the category.

According to Rosch, natural concepts vary in their level of precision and detail. Somewhat as in the structure proposed by Collins and Quillian, they are arranged in a hierarchy that ranges from very detailed to very general. When we think and talk about concepts, we usually deal with **basic-level concepts.** For example, *chair* and *apple* are basic-level concepts. They belong to more general concepts, such as *furniture* and *fruit,* which are called **superordinate concepts.** Concepts that refer to types of items within a basic-level category, such as *lawn chair* and *Granny Smith apple,* are called **subordinate concepts.** (See **Figure 11•4**.)

The basic-level concept tends to be what people spontaneously name when they see a member of the category. That is, all types of chairs tend to be called "chair," unless there is a special reason to use a more precise label (for example, if you wanted to buy a particular kind of chair). People tend to use basic-level concepts for a very good reason: *cognitive economy.* The use of subordinate concepts wastes time and effort on meaningless distinctions, and the use of superordinate concepts lacks essential information. In one study Rosch and colleagues (1976) presented participants with various concepts from all three levels and gave them 90 seconds to list as many attributes as they could for each concept. The participants supplied few attributes for superordinate concepts but were able to think of many for basic-level concepts. Subordinate concepts evoked no more responses than basic-level concepts did. Thus, basic-level concepts, because they are associated with a collection of subordinate concepts and their characteristics, provide us with the most information in the most efficient manner. When people think in terms of basic-level concepts, they do not have to travel up or down a tree, as they would in the structure proposed by Collins and Quillian, to find the attributes that belong to the concept. The attributes are directly attached to the exemplars that constitute each concept.

It is important to recognize that concepts can represent something more complex than simple exemplars or collections of attributes. Goldstone, Medink, and Gentner (1991) showed

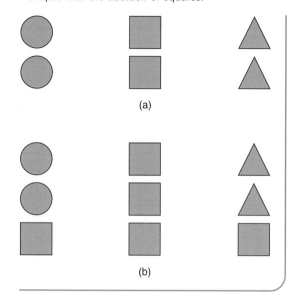

FIGURE 11•5 Concept formation. Participants were asked which of the groups of shapes (shown in the columns) were most similar. (a) Three pairs of geometrical shapes. (b) The same shapes with the addition of squares.

research participants groups of figures and asked them to indicate which were most similar to each other. When they showed the participants pairs of triangles, squares, and circles, the participants said that the squares and triangles were most similar, presumably because both contained straight lines and angles. However, when they added a square to each of the pairs, the participants said that the two most similar groups were the triangles plus square and the circles plus square. (See **Figure 11•5**.) The concept this time was "two things and a square." If the participants had been simply counting attributes, then the addition of a square to the pairs should not have changed their decision. As this study shows very clearly, concepts can include relations among elements that cannot be described by the mere enumeration of shared attributes.

Deductive Reasoning

Concepts are the raw material of thinking; they are what we think in terms of. *Reasoning* involves the manipulation and combination of concepts. Among its most common forms are deductive reasoning and inductive reasoning.

Deductive reasoning produces specific conclusions from general principles or rules. Series problems and syllogisms are often used to study deductive reasoning. Consider the following series problem:

John is taller than Phil.

Sue is shorter than Phil.

Therefore, John is taller than Sue.

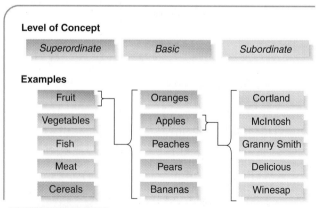

FIGURE 11•4 Examples of basic-level, subordinate, and superordinate concepts.

Application of simple logical principles will have led you to recognize that the conclusion to this series problem is correct as stated.

Let's try a syllogism. As you remember, a syllogism consists of two premises from which a conclusion can be drawn. Is the conclusion in the following syllogism correct?

All mammals have fur.

A bat is a mammal.

Therefore, a bat has fur.

Most people understand that the conclusion is indeed justified by the premises. But now look at these two:

All Xs are Y.

Z is an X.

Therefore, all Xs are Z.

and

All nemots have some hair.

A zilgid has some hair.

Therefore, all zilgids are nemots.

Although the conclusions are not warranted on logical grounds for the latter two syllogisms, many people endorse them as true. For the first of these, try replacing X with "planet," Y with "round," and Z with "Jupiter." The last syllogism is just as difficult, but here is the solution: The first premise says only that all nemots have hair—it leaves open the possibility that no nemot is a zilgid. Still not clear? Try substituting "cat" for *nemot* and "dog" for *zilgid*. How is it possible that we make such mistakes when the answers become so obvious after we make the concrete substitutions? A possible answer lies in the concept of mental models.

Mental Models Psychologists used to believe that people solved deductive reasoning problems by applying formal rules of logic. If people did so, however, it should not matter whether they dealt with letters of the alphabet, planets, cats and dogs, or numbers; they would identify the underlying structure of the problem and solve it forthwith. However, Philip Johnson-Laird and his colleagues (Johnson-Laird, 1995, 1999, 2001; Johnson-Laird, Byrne, & Schaeken, 1992) suggest that in reality people approach problems involving logical deduction by creating **mental models.**

You can think of a mental model of a situation as the representation of a *possibility* (Johnson-Laird, 1999); that is, of what might be true given certain premises. A mental model includes semantic information, because most problems involve meaningful content, specify relations among elements of the problem, and rely more or less on knowledge about the world. Spatial arrangements also play a central role in the theory of mental models. Johnson-Laird (1985) maintains that syllogistic reasoning is much more highly correlated with spatial ability than with verbal ability. Spatial ability includes the ability to visualize shapes and

to manipulate them mentally. For example, read the following problem and answer it. *A is less than C. B is greater than C. Is B greater than A?* In order to compare A with B, you must remember the order of the three elements. One kind of mental model is an imaginary line going from small to large on which you mentally place each item as you encounter it. Then, with all three elements in a row, the possibilities are mentally arrayed before you, and you can answer the question. (See **Figure 11·6**.) Let's attach more meaningful content to another problem. *The pie is sweeter than the cake. The custard is not as sweet as the cake. Is the custard sweeter than the pie?* You may have found it easier to produce a mental model in which the pastries were arrayed in a line and consequently found it easier to answer the question. Having concrete objects to array on your mental line should have made this example easier for you. You can now see the problem with the nemods and zilgids in the earlier syllogism. Since they were unfamiliar words, it became very difficult to construct a mental model with which to solve the syllogism.

An interesting feature of mental models that involve the comparison of a series of items is that we may attend more to the model than to the facts it is supposed to represent. For example, read the following passage:

Although the four craftsmen were brothers, they varied enormously in height. The electrician was the

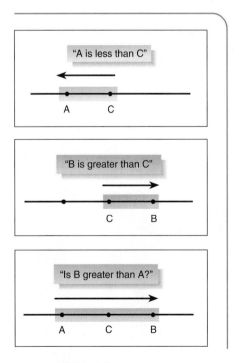

FIGURE 11·6 A mental model. People often solve logical problems by imagining a spatial representation of the facts.

very tallest, and the plumber was shorter than him. The plumber was taller than the carpenter, who, in turn, was taller than the painter. (Just & Carpenter, 1987, p. 202)

After reading this passage, people answer questions about differences in heights that can only be inferred more easily than they answer questions about differences that were directly stated. For example, they are faster to answer the question "Who is taller, the electrician or the painter?" than the question "Who is taller, the plumber or the carpenter?" The passage explicitly states that the plumber is taller than the carpenter. Answering this question requires only accessing memory for that specific bit of information. Answering the question about the electrician and painter, however, *requires an inference* and therefore should take more time than merely repeating what you were told. Yet Just and Carpenter's study shows that the result of an inference can be more readily available than information explicitly given. How can this be? The most plausible explanation is that when people read the passage, they construct a mental model that represents the four brothers arranged in order of height. The painter is clearly the shortest and the electrician is clearly the tallest. Thus, a comparison involving extremes can be made very quickly. (See **Figure 11•7**.)

Here is a different type of problem to illustrate the point: *What do you call your mother's sister's son?* Most people report that they answer this question by constructing a mental family tree, with their mother above them, their mother's sister to the side, and her son below her. Then, comparing that location with their own, they can easily see that the answer is "cousin." (See **Figure 11•8**.) Consistent with the idea that spa-

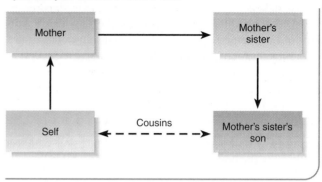

FIGURE 11•8 A spatial model of reasoning: "What do you call your mother's sister's son?"

tial representation is a significant feature of mental models, Luria (1973) found that people with damage to the parietal lobes had difficulty answering such questions. As you learned in Chapter 4, the parietal lobes are involved with somatosensory and spatial abilities.

Finally, consider another complex problem, adapted from an experiment by Wason and Johnson-Laird (1972), that is known as a *selection task*. The instructions accompany a set of four cards and read as follows:

> Your job is to determine which of the cards you need to turn over in order to test the following rule decisively:
>
> If there is a vowel on one side of a card, there is an even number on the other side.
>
> You have only one opportunity to make this decision. You are not permitted to inspect the cards one at a time. You must name the card or cards that you absolutely must see in order to test the rule.

The participants were shown four cards like those illustrated in **Figure 11•9**. Read the problem again, look at the cards, and decide which card or cards you would have to see.

Most people in the experiment said that they would need to see card (a) (the letter A), and they were correct: If there is *not* an even number on the back of card (a), then the rule is not correct. However, many participants failed to realize that card (a) is not enough. Card (d) (the number 7) also must be inspected. True, there is no even number on this card, but what if there is a vowel on the other side? If there is, then the

FIGURE 11•7 A mental model of the craftsmen experiment. Although the passage describing the craftsmen explicitly compared the heights of the plumber and the carpenter, people had to infer that the electrician was taller than the painter. Nevertheless, participants could judge the relative heights of the electrician and the painter faster than those of the plumber and the carpenter.

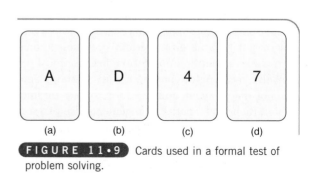

FIGURE 11•9 Cards used in a formal test of problem solving.

rule is again proved wrong. Many participants also wanted to see card (c) (the number 4), but there is no need to do so. The hypothesis says nothing about whether an even number can be on one side of the card without there being a vowel on the other side.

The card task is very abstract, and we have already seen that concreteness can increase the ease with which people reach "logical" conclusions, even if they do not do so using formal logic. Would relating the card–vowel problem to familiar, concrete content make it easier? The answer comes from research such as a study conducted by Griggs and Cox (1982). These experimenters asked people to decide which cards should be turned over to test the following rule: "If a person is drinking beer, she or he must be over age 21." As shown in **Figure 11•10**, the cards represented people who were drinking; their age was on one side and their beverage (beer or Coke) on the other. Which card(s) would you turn over?

Most participants correctly chose cards (a) and (d). They knew that if someone were drinking beer (a), they had to check that she or he was over the age of 21 in order for the rule to be true. Similarly, if someone was 16 years old (d), they knew that they needed to check the card to see that she or he was not drinking beer in order for the rule to be true. The participants readily recognized the fact that they did not need to know the age of someone drinking Coke, and that someone 22 years old can drink whatever beverage she or he prefers.

One explanation for the greater ease of this more concrete problem comes from the mental models. It would seem to be much easier to construct and manipulate cognitive representations of Coke, beer, and teenagers than to think about vowels and numbers. There are, however, other explanations. Cheng and Holyoak (1985), for example, proposed that people have sets of helpful mental rules ("pragmatic reasoning schemas") that center on issues of causality, permission, and obligation. According to Cheng and Holyoak, these schemas are more likely to be evoked with the meaningful beer–age task, which requires consideration of whether an action (drinking) is permitted or not, than in the more abstract vowel–number task. But the jury is still out on a generally accepted explanation of the selection task, which, as Johnson-Laird (1999) commented, "has launched a thousand studies." For example, Cosmides (1989), an evolutionary psychologist, has suggested that people solve the beer–age problem more easily not simply because it is more concrete than the vowel–number problem but because it allows them to apply a detection rule. Specifically, the rule applies to social situations involving costs and benefits. A person who obtains a benefit without meeting the necessary requirement may be considered a cheater. Thus, an under-age beer drinker is a cheater. According to Cosmides, natural selection has provided humans with the ability to detect cheaters. It is this ability that allows us to solve the beer–age problem more easily.

Many creative scientists and engineers report that they use mental models to reason logically and to solve practical and theoretical problems (Krueger, 1976). For example, physicist and Nobel laureate Richard Feynman said that he favored bizarre mental models when keeping track of the characteristics of complex mathematical theorems. Such models allowed him to see whether the theorems were logical and consistent. Among his many highly quotable statements was this: "What I cannot create, I cannot understand." Here is how Feynman described his reasoning:

> When I'm trying to understand . . . I keep making up examples. For instance, the mathematicians would come in with a . . . theorem. As they're telling me the conditions of the theorem, I construct something that fits all the conditions. You know, you have a set (one ball)—disjoint (two balls). Then the balls turn colors, grow hairs, or whatever, in my head as they [the mathematicians] put more conditions on. Finally, they state the theorem, which is some . . . thing about the ball which isn't true for my hairy green ball thing, so I say "False!" (Feynman, 1985, p. 70)

▲ *The noted physicist Richard Feynman was a member of the expert panel that investigated the* Challenger *disaster.*

FIGURE 11•10 Cards used in a socially situated version of the problem-solving test.

Beer (a)   Coke (b)   22 (c)   16 (d)

Such use of mental models by a gifted theorist strengthens the conclusion that being able to convert abstract problems into tangible mental models is an important aspect of intelligent thinking. It was Feynman, after all, who first brought to light the cause of the tragic deaths of the *Challenger* astronauts (Feynman, 2001).

Inductive Reasoning

Deductive reasoning involves applying the rules of logic to produce conclusions from general principles or rules. This type of reasoning works well when general principles or rules have already been worked out. But how do we accumulate new knowledge and formulate new general principles or rules? Having read Chapter 2 of this book, you already know the answer—by following the scientific method. But few people know the rules of the scientific method, and even those who do may seldom follow them in their daily lives.

Inductive reasoning is, in some ways, the opposite of deductive reasoning; it consists of inferring general principles or rules from specific facts. A well-known laboratory example of inductive reasoning works like a guessing game (see Bruner, Goodnow, & Austin, 1956). The participants are shown cards that contain figures differing in several characteristics, such as shape, number, and color. On each trial the participants are given two cards and asked to choose the one that represents a particular concept. After they choose a card, the researcher says "right" or "wrong." (See **Figure 11•11**.)

One trial is not enough to recognize the concept. For example, if the first trial reveals that card (a) is correct, then the concept could be *red,* or *four,* or *triangle,* or some combination of these, such as *red triangle, four red shapes,* or even *four red triangles.* Information gained from the second trial permits the participant to rule out some of these hypotheses—for example, if on the second trial four red squares is a correct card choice, it appears that shape does not matter, but color and number do. The participant uses steps to solve the problem much the way a scientist does: Form a hypothesis on the basis of the available evidence and test that hypothesis on subsequent trials. If it is proved false, abandon it, try to think of a hypothesis consistent with what went before, and test the new hypothesis.

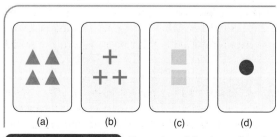

FIGURE 11•11 Examples of the type of cards used in a test of inductive reasoning.

Logical Errors in Inductive Reasoning Obviously, people can be trained to follow the rules of the scientific method. However, without special training, they follow commonsense rules, some of which work and some of which do not. Psychologists interested in human inductive reasoning have identified several tendencies that lead us astray. It is precisely because of such tendencies that we need to learn specific rules (such as those of the scientific method) so that we can have confidence in our conclusions.

Two of the tendencies that interfere with our ability to reason inductively are the failure to seek information that would be provided by a comparison group and the disinclination to seek evidence that would indicate whether a hypothesis is false. (In Chapter 15 we'll investigate two others: the representativeness and availability heuristics.)

Failure to Consider a Comparison Group. A tendency that interferes with people's efforts to reason inductively is their failure to consider a comparison group. Suppose that you learn that 79 percent of the people with a particular disease get well within a month after taking a new experimental drug (Stich, 1990). What will you conclude? Is the drug effective? The correct answer to this question is, "We cannot conclude anything—we need more information." What we need to know is what happens to people with the disease if they do not take the drug. If we find that only 22 percent of these people recover within a month, we can conclude that the drug is effective; 79 percent is much greater than 22 percent. On the other hand, if we find that 98 percent recover without taking the drug, we must conclude that the drug is worse than useless—it actually interferes with recovery. In other words, we need a control group. But most people are perfectly willing to conclude that, because 79 percent seems like a high figure, the drug must work. Seeing the necessity for a control group does not come naturally; unless people are explicitly taught about control groups, they will not recognize the need for them.

Failure to seek or use information that would be provided by a control group has been called *ignoring the base rate;* the term *base rate* refers to the rate of occurrence of a phenomenon in the absence of a particular intervention. In the drug example, the rate of recovery in a control group would provide a base rate. As several researchers have suggested, the problem here may be that we engage in two types of reasoning (Kahneman, 2003; Reber, 1992). One is deliberate and conscious and involves the explicit memory of rules that we can describe verbally. The other type of reasoning is unconscious and uses information we have learned implicitly. (The distinction between explicit and implicit memories and their relation to consciousness was discussed in Chapters 8 and 9.) Because the explicit and implicit reasoning systems may involve different brain mechanisms, information from one system cannot easily interact with information from the other system. In fact, even if people observe actual occurrences of the events in question (that is, if they directly acquire information about the base rate of occurrence), they do not include the base rate in their decisions (Holyoak & Spellman, 1993).

Confirmation Bias. Another tendency that interferes with inductive reasoning is a disinclination to seek evidence that would indicate whether a hypothesis is false. Instead, people tend to seek evidence that might confirm their hypothesis; that is, they exhibit the **confirmation bias.** For example, Wason (1968) presented study participants with the series of numbers "two, four, six" and asked them to try to figure out the rule to which the numbers conformed. The participant was to test his or her hypothesis by making up series of numbers and reciting them to the researcher, who would respond with "yes" or "no." Then, whenever the person decided that enough information had been gathered, he or she could state what the hypothesis was. If the answer was correct, the problem was solved. If it was not, the person was to think of a new hypothesis and test it in turn.

Several rules could explain the series "two, four, six." The rule could be "even numbers," or "each number is two more than the preceding one," or "the middle number is the mean of the first and third number." When people tested their hypotheses, they almost always did so by presenting several sets of numbers, *all of which were consistent with their hypotheses*. For example, if they thought that each number was two more than the preceding one, they might say, "ten, twelve, fourteen" or "sixty-one, sixty-three, sixty-five." *Very few* participants tried to test their hypotheses by choosing a set of numbers that did *not* conform to the hypothesized rule, such as "twelve, fifteen, twenty-two." In fact, the series "twelve, fifteen, twenty-two" does conform to the actual rule. The rule was so simple that few people figured it out: Each number must be larger than the number preceding it.

The confirmation bias is very strong. Unless people are taught to do so, they tend not to think of or to test possible counterexamples that might disprove their hypotheses—as scientists would. The point is that evidence that disconfirms a hypothesis is conclusive, whereas evidence that merely confirms it is not. Suppose that you thought the answer to the problem just described was "even numbers." You could give ascending lists of three even numbers hundreds of times, and each list would be correct. But, of course, your rule would still be wrong. If you gave just one counterexample—say, "five, six, seven"—the researcher would say "yes" and you would immediately know that the rule was not "even numbers."

The confirmation bias in inductive reasoning has a counterpart in deductive reasoning. For example, consider the following sentences (Johnson-Laird, 1985):

> All the pilots are artists.
>
> All the skiers are artists.
>
> True or false: All the pilots are skiers.

Many people say "true." They test the truth of the conclusion by imagining a person who is a pilot and an artist and a skier—and that person complies with the rules. Therefore, they decide that the conclusion is true. But if they would try to disconfirm the conclusion—to look for an example that would fit the first two sentences but not the conclusion—they would easily find one. Could a person be a pilot but not a skier? Of course; the first two sentences say nothing to rule out that possibility. There are artist–pilots and there are artist–skiers, but nothing says that there must be artist–pilot–skiers.

Problem Solving

The ultimate function of thinking is to solve problems. We are faced with an enormous variety of problems in our daily lives. The ability to solve problems is related to academic success, vocational success, and overall success in life—so trying to understand how to do so is an important undertaking.

The Spatial Metaphor According to Holyoak (1990), a problem exists when we have a goal but do not have a clear understanding of how to attain it. Recall Johnson-Laird's contention that mental models are often spatial. Indeed, when we talk about problems, we often use spatial metaphors to describe them (Lakoff & Turner, 1989). For example, we may think of the solving of a problem as *finding a path to the solution*. We may have to *get around roadblocks* that we encounter or *backtrack* when we *hit a dead end*. If we *get lost*, we may try to *approach the problem from a different angle*. If we have experience with particular types of problems, we may know some *shortcuts to the solution*.

Newell and Simon (1972) used spatial metaphors to characterize the problem-solving process. At the beginning of a person's attempt to solve a problem, the *initial state* is different from the *goal state*—if it were not, there would be no problem. The person solving the problem has a number of *operators* available. Operators are actions that can be taken to change the current state of the problem; metaphorically, operators move the current state from one position to another. Knowledge of the operators that are available depends on education and experience. In addition, there may be various costs associated with different operators; some may be more difficult, expensive, or time consuming than others. The *problem space* consists of all possible states that can be achieved if all possible operators are applied. A *solution* is a sequence of operators (a "path") that moves from the initial state to the goal state.

Figure 11•12 illustrates this process schematically. The circles represent the current or possible states of affairs while the problem is being solved. The arrows represent the operators—the actions that can be taken. Some actions are reversible (double arrows); others are not. A solution follows a path from the initial state to the goal state.

FIGURE 11·12   Newell and Simon's spatial conceptualization of the problem-solving process.

(Adapted from Holyoak, K. J. in *An Invitation to Cognitive Science: Volume 3: Thinking*, edited by D. N. Osherson and E. E. Smith. Cambridge, MA: MIT Press, 1990. Copyright © 1990.)

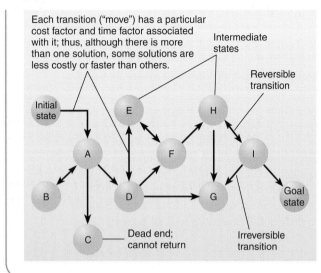

Algorithms and Heuristics

Some kinds of problems can be solved by following a sequence of operators known as an algorithm. **Algorithms** are procedures that consist of series of steps that, if followed in the correct sequence, will provide a solution. For example, you are undoubtedly familiar with an algorithm known as "long division." If you properly apply the steps of this algorithm (which involves the operators of division and subtraction) to divide one number by another, you will obtain the correct answer. But many problems are not as tidy or as easy to solve as those in long division. When there is no algorithm to follow, we must follow a *heuristic* to guide our search for a path to the solution. **Heuristics** (pronounced "hyoo-ris-tiks," derived from the Greek *heuriskein*, "to discover") are general rules, or "rules of thumb," that are useful in guiding our search for a path to the solution of a problem. Heuristics tell us what to pay attention to, what to ignore, and what strategy to take. As such, they may be considered shortcuts.

Heuristical methods can be very specific, or they can be quite general, applying to large categories of problems. For example, business management courses try to teach students problem-solving methods they can use in a wide variety of contexts. Newell and Simon (1972) suggest a general heuristic that can be used to solve *any* problem: **means–ends analysis**. The principle behind means–ends analysis is that a person should look for differences between the current state and the goal state and seek ways to reduce these differences. The steps of this method are as follows (Holyoak, 1990, p. 121):

1. Compare the current state to the goal state and identify differences between the two. If there are none, the problem is solved; otherwise, proceed.

2. Identify possible operators and select one that would reduce one of the differences.

3. If the operator can be applied, do so; if not, set a new subgoal of reaching a state at which the operator could be applied. Then apply means–ends analysis to this new subgoal until the operator can be applied or the attempt to use it is abandoned.

4. Return to step 1.

Suppose that the problem is to clear two feet of snow off your driveway. Rejecting several possible operators because they are too time consuming or too costly (*dig the snow off with my hands* or *melt the snow with a propane torch*), you may decide to apply the operator *start the snowblower and run it up and down the driveway.* Unfortunately, you find that the snowblower will not start, which means that the operator you have chosen cannot be applied. Thus, you set up a subgoal: *Fix the snowblower.*

One possible operator that will get you toward that subgoal is *put the snowblower in the car and take it to a mechanic,* but the snow on the driveway precludes that option. Therefore, you decide to fix the snowblower yourself. In order to fix it, you have to know what its problem is. You consider some possible actions, including *take the engine apart to see whether something inside is broken,* but you decide to try some simpler steps, such as *see whether the wire is attached to the spark plug* or *see whether there is gasoline in the tank.* You find the wire attached but the gas tank empty. The only operator that will get you to your subgoal is *fill the tank with gasoline.* But you have no gasoline. Therefore, you construct another subgoal: *Get some gasoline.*

What are the possible sources of gasoline? A gas station? No, you can't move the car. A neighbor? The snow is so deep that you do not want to fight your way through the drifts. The tank of your car? That's it. New subgoal: *Remove some gasoline from the car's fuel tank.* How do you get it out? New subgoal: *Find rubber hose to siphon the gasoline into the tank of the snowblower.* You do so, you start the engine, and you clear the snow off the driveway. Voilà! The problem is solved. And at that point you may be ready to establish a new goal—*take a nap.*

As in the example, in means–ends analysis the individual's activity is oriented at all times toward reducing the distance between the current state and the goal state. If problems are encountered along the way (that is, if specific operators cannot be applied), then subgoals are created and means–ends analysis is applied to solving that newly emerged problem—and so on, until the goal is reached.

Successful problem solving involves more than applying various operators to see whether they bring us closer to the goal, however. It also involves *planning.* When we plan, we may act vicariously, "trying out" various actions in our heads before acting on one of them or not. Obviously, planning requires that we know something about the consequences of the actions we are considering. For that reason experts are usually better at planning than novices are. If we do *not* know the con-

▲ *Problem solving takes many forms. When a snow-blower's gas tank is empty, starting it can be a problem. The heuristic method of means–ends analysis may well provide a solution.*

collections of memories of particular examples, called exemplars. Natural concepts exist at the basic, subordinate, and superordinate level. Most of our thinking occurs at the level of basic concepts.

Deductive reasoning consists of reaching conclusions on the basis of general principles. That is, we take information that is already known and determine whether particular occurrences are consistent with that information. One of the most important skills in deductive reasoning is the ability to construct mental models to represent the problems we are attempting to solve.

Inductive reasoning attempts to infer general principles from particular information. This form of thinking involves generating and testing hypotheses. Without special training (such as learning the rules of the scientific method), people often ignore the necessity of determining base rates or show a confirmation bias—the tendency to look only for evidence that confirms a given hypothesis. Problem solving is often best pursued spatially: We follow a path in the problem space from the initial state to the goal state, using operators to get to each intermediate state. Sometimes a problem fits a particular mold and can be solved with an algorithm—an already formulated set of steps to follow. In most cases, however, we must attack a problem by following a heuristic—a general rule that helps guide our search for a path to the solution of a problem. A useful heuristic is means–ends analysis, which involves taking steps that reduce the distance from the current state to the goal. If obstacles are encountered, subgoals are created and attempts are made to reach them.

sequences of particular actions, we will be obliged to try each action (apply each operator) and see what happens. Planning is especially important when many possible operators are present, when they are costly or time consuming, or when they are irreversible. If we take an irreversible action that brings us to a dead end, we have failed to solve the problem.

Interim Summary

Thinking and Problem Solving

Thinking often is directed at problem solving. To think requires the use of concepts. Formal concepts are concepts defined explicitly by the essential characteristics of objects and events. In everyday life we use natural concepts instead—

QUESTIONS TO CONSIDER

1. Think of a new concept you have learned recently. Describe its characteristics. Then think of an exemplar. Which was easier to do? Why?

2. Chapter 2 described the scientific method. Some of the rules and procedures you learned in that chapter were designed to prevent the errors in logical thinking that were described in this chapter. Relate the scientific method to these errors.

3. Over the next few days, try to catch yourself making one of the errors of reasoning described in this section. Describe your experience, then indicate how you will attempt to prevent the same error in the future.

Suggestions for Further Reading

Aiken, L. (2006). *Psychological testing and assessment* (12th ed.). Boston: Allyn and Bacon.

This authoritative guide to the construction and use of psychological tests is a next step if you have a serious technical interest in psychometrics.

Diamond, J. (1997). *Guns, germs, and steel: The fates of human societies.* New York: W. W. Norton.

This best-selling essay attempts to answer the question of how certain civilizations came to dominate others without there being large differences in intelligence between them. It does so in scholarly, provocative fashion.

Gardner, H. (1999). *Intelligence reframed: Multiple intelligences for the 21st century.* New York: Basic Books.

This is the founding work for what has become a major alternative to psychometric theories of intelligence; highly readable and humane.

Kaplan, R. M., & Saccuzzo, D. P. (2005). *Psychological testing: Principles, application, and issues* (6th ed.). Pacific Grove, CA: Brooks/Cole.

Like Aiken's book, this book offers a comprehensive overview of the types of psychological tests, their construction, their interpretation, and attendant controversies.

Polya, G. (2004). *How to solve it: A new aspect of mathematical method.* Princeton, NJ: Princeton University Press.

This book is a classic, a still timely introduction to practical problem solving in mathematics; a trove of insights and clever, heuristical applications. You will sense a master teacher at work.

Sternberg, R. J. (2003). *Wisdom, intelligence, and creativity synthesized.* New York: Cambridge University Press.

An influential, information processing–based theory of intelligence and its measurement unfolds in the pages of this book.

Key Terms

algorithm (p. 352)

analytic intelligence (p. 327)

basic-level concept (p. 346)

Binet-Simon Scale (p. 333)

concept (p. 344)

confirmation bias (p. 351)

creative intelligence (p. 328)

criterion (p. 334)

crystallized intelligence (p. 327)

deductive reasoning (p. 346)

deviation IQ (p. 333)

exemplar (p. 345)

factor analysis (p. 326)

fetal alcohol syndrome (p. 339)

fluid intelligence (p. 327)

formal concept (p. 344)

g factor (p. 325)

heritability (p. 338)

heuristic (p. 352)

inductive reasoning (p. 350)

intelligence (p. 325)

intelligence quotient (IQ) (p. 333)

means–ends analysis (p. 352)

mental age (p. 333)

mental model (p. 347)

mental retardation (p. 336)

natural concept (p. 345)

norms (p. 333)

practical intelligence (p. 328)

psychometrics (p. 332)

ratio IQ (p. 333)

s factor (p. 325)

Stanford-Binet Scale (p. 333)

subordinate concept (p. 346)

successful intelligence (p. 327)

superordinate concept (p. 346)

syllogism (p. 330)

Wechsler Adult Intelligence Scale (WAIS) (p. 334)

Wechsler Intelligence Scale for Children (WISC) (p. 334)

12

LIFE-SPAN DEVELOPMENT

Prenatal Development

Stages of Prenatal Development • Threats to Normal Prenatal Development

During the prenatal period the fertilized ovum develops into a fetus, a human in miniature. Crucial factors in the fetus's development are the mother's diet and chemicals in her blood; the presence of toxins in the prenatal environment can cause the fetus to be born with physical and cognitive defects.

Physical and Perceptual Development in Infancy and Childhood

Motor Development • Perceptual Development

Timing and experience are two key elements in normal motor and perceptual development. For normal development to occur, a child must encounter stimulation from the environment during a specific time interval. If stimulation does not occur during this period, normal development is impeded, perhaps permanently.

Cognitive Development in Infancy and Childhood

The Importance of a Responsive Environment • The Work of Jean Piaget • Vygotsky's Sociocultural Theory of Cognitive Development • Applying Information-Processing Models to Cognitive Development • *Evaluating Scientific Issues: The Effects of Television Viewing on Children's Cognitive Development*

In Piaget's view, a child passes through four distinct intellectual stages, which coincide with changes in a child's nervous system and with a child's experience, on his or her way to becoming an adult. According to Vygotsky, a child's cognitive development is strongly influenced by sociocultural variables, especially language. Information-processing models of cognitive development center on how brain maturation influences the development of cognitive processes and on the development of knowledge in specific domains.

Social Development in Infancy and Childhood

Behaviors of the Infant That Foster Attachment • The Nature and Quality of Attachment • Interactions with Peers • Approaches to Child Rearing

Attachment is the social and emotional bond that develops between infant and caregiver during infancy. The quality of attachment depends largely on the nature of infants' relationships with their caregivers. Social development during childhood is influenced by both the child's interactions with peers and the parent's style of child rearing.

Development of Gender Roles

The Nature of Gender Differences • *Biology and Culture: The Causes of Gender Role Differences*

Evolution appears to have shaped differences in brain development for males and females: Males tend to have stronger spatial abilities, and females tend to have stronger communication skills. Socialization processes such as parenting are involved in shaping gender-specific behavior. However, most gender differences in behavior are small.

Moral Development

Piaget's Theory of Moral Development • Kohlberg's Theory of Moral Development • Evaluation of Piaget's and Kohlberg's Theories of Moral Development

Piaget concluded that people pass through two stages of moral development: The first is marked by egocentrism and adherence to rules, and the second is marked by empathy. Kohlberg argued that a person moves through three levels of moral development, initially defining morality externally, then considering how the social system relates to morality, and finally understanding the principles on which moral rules are based. Although neither theory is universally accepted, the description of moral development as a progression is considered useful.

Adolescence

Physical Development • Social Development • Cognitive Development

Adolescence begins with sexual maturation, which brings with it marked changes in social behavior. Females tend to build relationships based on trust, whereas males tend to seek social support in becoming more independent. A key aspect of adolescent social development involves the formation of an identity. Cognitive development in adolescence may reflect development of two reasoning systems and the ability to choose when to use each of them.

Adulthood and Old Age

Physical Development • Cognitive Development • Social Development

Our physical abilities peak in early adulthood and decline gradually thereafter, although maintaining a healthy lifestyle can delay loss of these abilities. Compared to young adults, older adults perform worse on tests of abstract reasoning but better on tests related to general knowledge and abilities related to experience. Success in love, family, and work is the yardstick by which most people measure their satisfaction in life.

A visual cliff. The child does not cross the glass bridge.

One day a colleague of mine, Dr. D., approached me in the hall and asked me about my young daughter. When I told him she was an energetic crawler, he asked whether my wife and I would mind if he used her for a demonstration in his child development class. I said it would be fine with me, and I was sure my wife would agree also.

The next week my wife brought our daughter to the psychology building at the appointed time. Dr. D. ushered them into a small room that contained a large, square table. Part of the surface of the table was a strip of plywood about a foot wide, which ran along one edge. It was painted in a bright red-and-black checkerboard pattern. The rest of the tabletop consisted of an enormous piece of glass. The floor under the glass, about three feet below, was painted in the same checkerboard pattern.

Dr. D. asked my wife to place our daughter at one corner of the table, on the end of the plywood platform. After my wife had done so, and after she had reassured our daughter that everything was all right, Dr. D. asked my wife to go to the opposite corner of the table and stand there. He glanced up at the one-way glass that separated the room from the adjoining classroom, which contained a small group of students who were watching the procedure.

"Now ask her to come to you," he said.

"Come here, Kerstin," said my wife in a cheerful tone.

Kerstin grinned, made a happy noise, and scampered across the glass, making slapping sounds with her hands as she crawled. She seemed heedless of the three-foot drop beneath the glass.

My wife picked her up, smiled at Dr. D., and realized from the expression on his face that something had gone wrong. He glanced at the one-way glass, cleared his throat, and said, "Let's try it again."

The second trial was like the first. In fact, this time Kerstin did not even wait for my wife to get to her corner before she started across the glass. Clearly, she knew how the game was played.

"Kerstin hasn't done this before, has she?" asked Dr. D.

"No, she hasn't," my wife replied. "But I think I know why she wasn't afraid of crawling onto the glass. That was what you expected, wasn't it?"

"Yes," he said.

"We have a glass-topped coffee table in the living room at home, and Kerstin likes to play there. She used to like to lie on the floor under it and look up through the glass, and the past couple of months we've put her on top of it and let her crawl around."

Dr. D. looked relieved. "That explains it," he said. "She has learned to trust her sense of touch, even though she undoubtedly could perceive that the floor under the glass was far away." He paused a few seconds. "Actually," he said, "this provides a nice demonstration of the interaction between experience and development. Although children change in predictable ways as they mature, their development is shaped by their encounters with their environment."

He thanked my wife and turned toward the classroom. He was obviously thinking about how he would take advantage of this unexpected happening in the rest of his lecture.

Growing older is a matter not only of aging, but also of changing—physically, intellectually, and socially. We can see different aspect of change by looking at our grandparents, our parents, our friends, our brothers and sisters, and our children. (See **Table 12•1**.) Developmental psychologists study both the similarities and the differences among people as they develop and change. In this chapter we will examine when and how these similarities and differences occur.

The work of developmental psychologists reflects two complementary perspectives on the understanding of behavior. One approach seeks to describe and explain the changes that are of interest to different areas of psychology, providing a developmental perspective on the psychology of perception, or of memory, or of social behavior. The other approach focuses on the individual, describing the processes and patterns of change that occur over the individual's life. This latter approach is sometimes called *life-span developmental psychology,* and I will use it as a means of organizing the material of this chapter. We will examine each of the major developmental periods of a person's life—prenatal development, infancy and childhood, adolescence, adulthood, and old age—and will look at the psychological processes that change over these periods.

Because they study change, developmental psychologists employ special strategies of research. In a **cross-sectional study,** individuals of different ages are simultaneously compared

TABLE 12•1	Phases of the Life Span	
Phase	**Approximate Age**	**Highlights**
1. Prenatal period	Conception through birth	Rapid physical development of both nervous system and body
2. Infancy	Birth to 2 years	Motor development; attachment to primary caregiver
3. Childhood	2 years to 12 years	Increasing ability to think logically and reason abstractly; refinement of motor skills; peer influences
4. Adolescence	13 years to about 20 years	Thinking and reasoning becomes more adultlike; identity search; continued peer influences
5. Adulthood	20 years to 65 years	Love, committed relationship; career; stability and then decrease in physical abilities
6. Old age	65 years and older to death	Reflection on life's work and accomplishments; physical health deteriorates; preparation for death; death

with respect to some test or observation. For example, a developmental psychologist might present mathematical problems to groups of five-, seven-, and nine-year-olds to measure the children's grasp of the concept of negative numbers. The children of one group are different from those of the other groups, but each group is tested under conditions that are as identical as possible. Differences between the groups imply age-related changes in the understanding of the concept. In contrast, a **longitudinal study** compares observations on the same individuals at different times of their lives. A longitudinal study of children's grasp of negative numbers might test a group of children when they were five years of age, and then repeat the test on the same children at seven and then at nine.

Cross-sectional studies are usually more convenient to carry out, and they avoid the problems associated with repeatedly testing or observing the same individuals. However, they contain a subtle problem in interpretation. I will discuss this problem in connection with a concrete issue later in this chapter. Meanwhile, let's begin our consideration of life-span development by exploring the prenatal period.

Prenatal Development

The **prenatal period** extends over the approximately nine months between conception and birth. The length of a normal pregnancy is 266 days, or 38 weeks. The prenatal period involves three developmental stages: The fertilized egg becomes a zygote, then an embryo, and finally a fetus. Normal development at each stage requires a healthy uterine environment.

Stages of Prenatal Development

The union of the ovum (egg) and sperm, or conception, is the starting point for prenatal development. During the **zygotic stage,** which lasts about two weeks, the *zygote,* or the single new cell that is formed at conception, divides many times, and the internal organs begin to form. By the end of the first week, the zygote consists of about a hundred cells. Many of the cells are arranged in two layers: one layer for the skin, hair, nervous system, and sensory organs and the other for the digestive and respiratory systems and glands. Near the end of this stage, a third layer of cells appears that will eventually develop into muscles and the circulatory and excretory systems.

The **embryonic stage** of prenatal development, the second stage, begins at about two weeks and ends about eight weeks after conception. During this stage the zygote is transformed into an embryo, and development occurs at an incredibly rapid pace. By a month after conception, a heart has begun to beat, a brain and spinal cord have started to function, and most of the major body structures are beginning to form. By the end of this stage, the major features that define the human body—arms, hands, fingers, legs, toes, shoulders, head, and eyes—are discernible. Behaviorally, the embryo can react

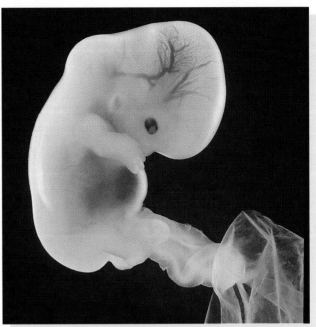

▲ *As this photograph of a six-week-old fetus illustrates, most of the major features that define the human body are present near the end of the embryonic stage of development (which starts at about two weeks and ends about eight weeks after conception).*

reflexively to stimulation. For example, if the mouth is stimulated, the embryo moves its upper body and neck. This stage also is noteworthy because it is now that the embryo is most susceptible to chemicals that can cause birth defects, including alcohol and other drugs, or toxins produced by diseases such as rubella (German measles). These substances are **teratogens** (from the Greek *teras,* meaning "monster"). The term *teratogens* refers to any substance, agent, or event that can cause mental or physical birth defects.

The beginning of sexual development occurs during the embryonic stage. Recall from Chapter 3 that the 23rd chromosome pair determines the sex of the embryo. The female partner always contributes an X chromosome to this pair at conception, whereas the male partner contributes either an X or a Y chromosome. If the male partner contributes a Y chromosome, the embryo will become a male (XY); if it is an X, the embryo will become a female (XX). Early in prenatal development the embryo develops a pair of gonads that will become either ovaries or testes. (The word *gonad* comes from the Greek *gonos,* "procreation.") If a Y chromosome is present, a gene located on it causes the production of a chemical signal that makes the gonads develop into testes. Otherwise, the gonads become ovaries.

The presence or absence of testes determines the development of the other sex organs. If testes are present, they begin to secrete a class of sex hormones known as **androgens** (*andros* means "man"; *gennan* means "to produce"). The most important androgen is *testosterone.* Androgens bring about the development of the male internal sex organs, the

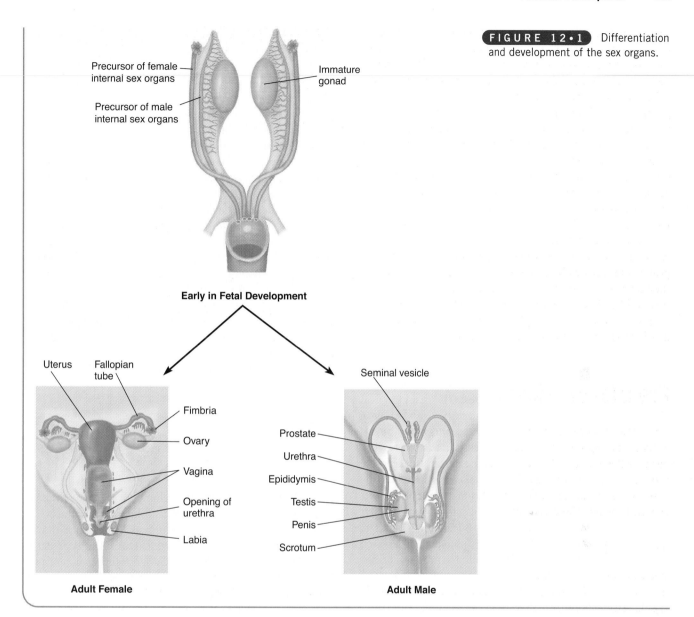

FIGURE 12•1   Differentiation and development of the sex organs.

penis, and the scrotum. These hormones are therefore absolutely necessary for the development of a male. The development of female sex organs (uterus, vagina, and labia) occurs on its own; it does not need to be stimulated by a hormone. (See **Figure 12•1.**)

The **fetal stage** is the final period of prenatal development and lasts about seven months. It officially begins with the appearance of bone cells and ends with birth. At the end of the second month of pregnancy, the fetus is about one and a half inches long and weighs about one ounce. By the end of the third month, the development of major organs is completed and the bones and muscles are beginning to develop. The fetus is now three inches long and weighs about three ounces. The fetus may show some movement, especially kicking.

By the end of the fourth month, the fetus is about six inches long and weighs about six ounces. It is also now sleep-ing and waking regularly. Fetal movements also become strong enough to be felt by the mother, and the heartbeat is loud enough to be heard through a stethoscope. Sound and light sensitivity will emerge within a few weeks. During the sixth month, the fetus grows to more than a foot long and weighs about one and a half pounds. The seventh month is a critical month: If the fetus is born prematurely at this point, it has a fair chance of surviving. A newborn at this age would almost certainly require help breathing. However, fetuses mature at different rates; some seven-month-old fetuses may be mature enough to survive premature birth, whereas others may not.

During the last two months of prenatal development, the fetus gains weight at the rate of about half a pound per week. On average the fetus is about 20 inches long and weighs about seven pounds at the end of this period. The fetus is ready to be born.

Threats to Normal Prenatal Development

The prenatal environment normally provides the correct supply of nutrients to the fetus. Probably the single most important factor in the fetus's development is the mother's diet: The food she eats and the vitamins and minerals she ingests are the fetus's only source of nutrition. If the mother is extremely malnourished, the fetus's nervous system develops abnormally, and intellectual deficits may result.

Not only malnutrition but teratogens, as mentioned earlier, can cause birth defects. Psychologists who study birth defects are very interested in how drugs affect the fetus, because drug taking is a behavior that is directly under the control of the mother. Certain antibiotics, especially when taken in large quantities over long periods, can produce fetal defects. For example, tetracycline, a common antibiotic, can cause irregularities that develop later in the bones and in the coloration of the teeth. Certain tranquilizers may produce a cleft palate.

A pregnant woman's cigarette smoking is another behavior that can affect the fetus. The carbon monoxide contained in cigarette smoke reduces the supply of oxygen to the fetus. Reduced oxygen levels are particularly harmful to the fetus during the last half of pregnancy, when the fetus is developing most rapidly and its need for oxygen is greatest. The main physical effects of mothers' smoking are increased rates of miscarriages, low-birth-weight babies, premature births, and births by cesarean section (Floyd et al., 1993; Kirchengast & Hartmann, 2003). Research suggests that prenatal exposure to cigarette smoking may produce lowered arousal levels in newborns (Franco et al., 2000), and there are indications of relatively uncommon but statistically related birth defects, such as cleft palate (e.g., Chung, Kowalski, Kim, & Buchman, 2000). The possible psychological effects of mothers' smoking are less well known. Nevertheless, prenatal exposure to the products of cigarette smoking may be related to behavior problems in adolescence, even when other correlated risk factors are considered (e.g., Weissman, Warner, Wickramaratne, & Kandel, 1999).

Cocaine use by mothers during pregnancy produces dramatic effects. If a pregnant woman uses cocaine, there is an increased risk of premature birth, low birth weight, and a smaller-than-normal head circumference. One study showed that growth deficits attributable to prenatal cocaine exposure were still remarkable in children at age seven (Covington et al., 2002). Research evidence also suggests that prenatal exposure to cocaine interferes with neural development, and that there may be long-term consequences in the areas of arousal and attention (Bard, Coles, Plaatzman, & Lynch, 2000; Mayes, Cicchetti, Acharyya, & Zhang, 2003; Potter, Zelazo, Stack, & Papageorgiou, 2000; Singer et al., 2002). Further, some babies are born addicted and show withdrawal symptoms such as hyperactivity, irritability, tremors, and vomiting (Zuckerman & Brown, 1993). The symptoms make the baby harder to care for, which, in turn, makes attachment between mother and baby difficult.

Although a woman's regular use of any psychoactive drug during her pregnancy is likely to harm the fetus, the damaging effects of alcohol use during pregnancy have been most widely studied (Janzen, Nanson, & Block, 1995; Kelly,

Day, & Streissguth, 2000; Nanson & Hiscock, 1990; Steinhausen & Spohr, 1998; Streissguth, 2001). These effects can include both pre- and postnatal growth deficits, deformations of the eyes and mouth, low brain mass, other brain and central nervous system abnormalities, and heart deformation—the problems collectively known as *fetal alcohol syndrome (FAS)*. Even if children with FAS are reared in healthy environments with regular, nutritious meals, their physical and intellectual development still falls short of that of normal children. Research with laboratory animals shows widespread neural damage as a result of prenatal alcohol exposure (Ikonomidou, 2000; Olney et al., 2002).

There is disappointing evidence that many women drink during pregnancy—and that the proportion who do drink has been stable or slightly increasing since the early 1990s, despite relatively good publicity about the link between alcohol and FAS (Centers for Disease Control, 1995, 1997, 2002; Habbick et al., 1996). Drinking as little as two ounces of alcohol a day early in pregnancy can produce some symptoms of FAS (Astley et al., 1992). That's just a bit more than an airline-type miniature bottle contains. The best advice should be clear: Don't drink during pregnancy.

Interim Summary

Prenatal Development

The three stages of prenatal development span the time between conception and birth. In just nine months, the zygote grows from a single cell, void of human resemblance, into an embryo and then a fully developed fetus. Gender is determined by the sex chromosomes. Male sex organs are produced by the action of a gene on the Y chromosome that causes the gonads to develop into testes. The testes secrete androgens, which stimulate the development of male sex organs. If testes are not present, the fetus develops as a female. The most important factor in normal fetal development is the mother's nutrition. Normal fetal development can be disrupted by the presence of teratogens, which can cause intellectual deficits and physical deformities. One well-studied teratogen is alcohol, which, when consumed by a pregnant woman, may lead to fetal alcohol syndrome.

QUESTIONS TO CONSIDER

1. Each of us experiences similar prenatal developmental stages and processes, so why do differences among people start to emerge from this very early period?
2. Suppose that you are a psychologist working in a pediatric clinic. A woman, pregnant with her first child, asks you for advice on what she can do to care for her unborn child. Based on what you now know about prenatal development, what advice would you give her?

Physical and Perceptual Development in Infancy and Childhood

The term "infant" applies to babies up to the age of two years. A newborn human infant is helpless and absolutely dependent on adult care. Recent research has shown, however, that newborns do not passively await the ministrations of their caregivers. They quickly develop skills that shape the behavior of the adults with whom they interact. This section will look at motor development and perceptual development in infancy and early childhood; in the next section we'll examine some influential theories of cognitive development.

Motor Development

At birth, the infant's most important movements are *reflexes*—automatic movements in response to specific stimuli. The most important reflexes are the rooting, sucking, and swallowing responses. If a baby's cheek is lightly touched, the baby will turn its head toward the direction of the touch (the *rooting* response). If the object makes contact with the baby's lips, the baby will open its mouth and begin *sucking*. When milk or any other liquid enters the mouth, the baby will automatically make *swallowing* movements. Obviously, these reflexes are important for the

baby's survival. As we will see later in this chapter, these behaviors are important for an infant's social development as well.

Normal motor development follows a distinct pattern, which appears to be dictated by maturation of the muscles and the nervous system. The term **maturation** refers to any relatively stable change in thought, behavior, or physical growth that is due to the aging process and not to experience. Although individual children progress at different rates, their development follows the same basic maturational pattern (see **Figure 12•2**). Development of motor skills requires two ingredients: maturation of the child's nervous system and practice. Development of the nervous system is not complete at birth; considerable growth occurs during the first several months (Dekaban, 1970). In fact, important changes in brain structure occur throughout the life span as a result of experience (Kolb, Gibb, & Robinson, 2003; Kolb & Whishaw, 1998).

Particular kinds of movements must await the development of the necessary neuromuscular systems. But motor development is not merely a matter of using these systems once they develop. Instead, physical development of the nervous system depends to a large extent on the ways the baby moves while interacting with the environment. In turn, more complex movements depend on further development of the nervous system, creating an interplay between motor and neural development. Thus, different steps in motor development are both an effect of previous development and a cause of further development (Thelen & Corbetta, 2002).

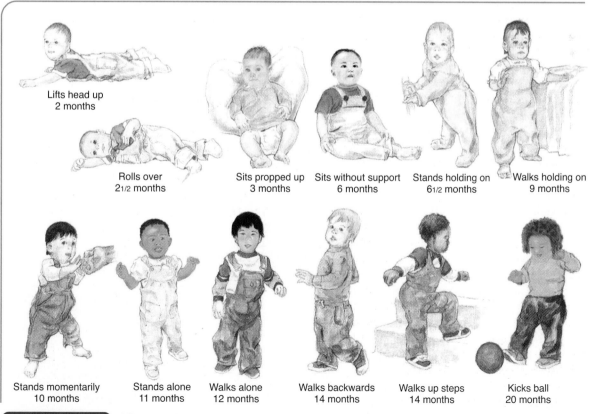

Lifts head up
2 months

Rolls over
2½ months

Sits propped up
3 months

Sits without support
6 months

Stands holding on
6½ months

Walks holding on
9 months

Stands momentarily
10 months

Stands alone
11 months

Walks alone
12 months

Walks backwards
14 months

Walks up steps
14 months

Kicks ball
20 months

FIGURE 12•2   Milestones in a child's motor development.

(Adapted from Shirley, M. M. (1933). *The first two years: Vol. 2. Intellectual development.* Minneapolis: University of Minnesota Press.)

Perceptual Development

We have known for a long time that fetal experience with sensory stimuli can prepare the way for the newborn's experience (e.g., Kisilevsky et al., 2003) and that a newborn's senses are already functioning at least to a certain extent (e.g., Maurer & Maurer, 1988). We know that the newborn's auditory system can detect sounds, because the baby will show a startle reaction when presented with a sudden loud noise. Similarly, a bright light will elicit eye closing and squinting. A cold object or a pinch will produce crying, so the sense of touch must be present. If held firmly and tilted backwards, a baby will stiffen and flail his or her arms and legs, indicating that babies have a sense of balance.

We also know that newborn infants have a sense of taste, because they indicate their taste preferences by facial expression and by choosing to swallow or not to swallow different liquids. When an infant is given a sweet liquid, its face relaxes in an expression rather like a smile; but when an infant is given a sour or bitter liquid, the face indicates displeasure.

Infants also have an early-developing ability to distinguish odors, an ability that can be seen as an element of mother–infant bonding. For example, infants show a preference for the odor of their mother's breast shortly after birth (Porter & Winberg, 1999), at two weeks can distinguish their own mother from other lactating women by breast odor (Porter, Makin, Davis, & Christensen, 1992), prefer their mother's breast over that of other lactating women, but prefer the smell of any lactating woman over that of any nonlactating woman (e.g., Porter & Winberg, 1999). This facility with odors extends to the learning of preferences very soon after birth. For instance, Sullivan and colleagues (1991) presented one-day-old infants with a citrus odor and then gently stroked them. The next day, these infants (but not control infants) turned toward a cotton swab containing the odor that had been paired with the stroking.

We also know that infants very early on can recognize and prefer their mother's voice (e.g., DeCasper & Fifer, 1980). Research shows that preference and discrimination likely develop before birth as a result of the fetus's in utero exposure to the mother's voice (Kisilevsky et al., 2003).

Observations such as these establish the sensory abilities of infants. But when do infants develop the capacity to interpret sensory signals? Is perception present at birth? Developmental psychologists have looked at many perceptual systems to answer this question. I'll consider two systems: the perception of forms and the perception of distance.

Form Perception Researchers study the visual perceptual abilities of infants by observing their eye movements with an eye-tracking device while showing them visual stimuli. A harmless spot of infrared light, invisible to humans, is directed onto the baby's eyes. A special television camera, sensitive to infrared light, records the spot and superimposes it on an image of the display that the baby is looking at. The technique is precise enough to enable experimenters to tell which parts of a stimulus the baby is scanning. For example, Salapatek (1975) reported that a one-month-old infant tends not to look at the inside of a figure. Instead, the baby's gaze seems to be "trapped" by the edges. By the age of two months, the baby scans across the border to investigate the interior of a figure. **Figure 12•3** shows a reconstruction of the paths followed by the eye scans of infants of these ages. (The babies were looking at real faces, not the drawings shown in the figure.)

The work by Salapatek and his colleagues suggests that at the age of one or two months, babies are probably not perceiving complete shapes; their scanning strategy is limited to fixations on a few parts of the object at which they are looking. By three months, however, babies show clear signs of pattern recognition. For example, by this age they prefer to look at stimuli that resemble the human face (Rosser, 1994), and by four or

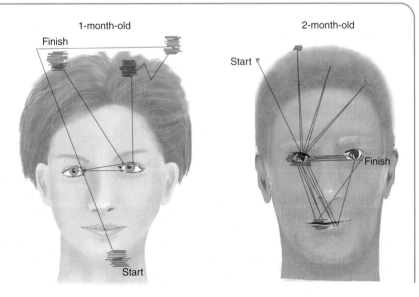

FIGURE 12•3 The scanning sequence used by infants viewing faces.

(From Salapatek, P. (1975). Pattern perception in early infancy. In *Infant Perception: From Sensation to Cognition, Vol 1: Basic Visual Processes*, edited by L. B. Cohen and P. Salapatek. New York: Academic Press. Copyright © 1975. Reprinted with permission from Elsevier.)

five months they can discriminate between even very similar faces (Bornstein & Arterberry, 2003; Fagan & Singer, 1979).

Distance Perception The ability to perceive three-dimensional space comes at an early age. Gibson and Walk (1960) placed six-month-old babies on what they called a *visual cliff*—the table that I described in the opening vignette. On one side is a platform containing a checkerboard pattern. The platform adjoins a glass shelf mounted three or four feet over a floor that also is covered by the checkerboard pattern. Most babies who could crawl would not venture out onto the glass shelf. The infants acted as if they were afraid of falling; that is, they could perceive the distance between themselves and the floor.

Remember from Chapter 7 that several different types of cues in the environment contribute to depth perception. One cue arises from *retinal disparity.* As explained in Chapter 7, under normal circumstances points on objects that are different distances from the viewer fall on slightly different points of the two retinas—the phenomenon known as retinal disparity. The perception of depth occurs when the two images are fused through visual processing (Poggio & Poggio, 1984). This form of depth perception, *stereopsis* ("solid vision"), is the kind obtained from a stereoscope or a three-dimensional movie. The brain mechanisms necessary for stereopsis will not develop unless animals have experience viewing objects with both eyes during a period early in life.

The dependence of stereopsis on retinal disparity has important implications for the development of normal vision. If an infant's eyes are crossed, causing the same points on the two retinas to receive the same information (i.e., producing no disparity), the infant will not experience depth perception via stereopsis. This appears to be true even if the eyes are later positioned normally through surgery. Banks, Aslin, and Letson (1975) studied infants whose eye deficits were later corrected surgically. Their results show that the crucial developmental period ends sometime between one and three years of age. If surgery occurs before this time, stereoscopic vision will develop. If the surgery occurs later, it will not.

Critical and Sensitive Periods in Perceptual Development Psychologists use the term **critical period** to denote a specific time during which certain experiences must occur if an individual is to develop normally. Stereopsis exhibits a critical period because, as we have seen, retinal disparity must occur between one and three years of age to ensure normal development of this ability. Many other perceptual, behavioral, and cognitive abilities are subject to critical periods. For example, as we shall see later in this chapter, if infants are not exposed to a stimulating environment and do not have the opportunity to interact with caregivers during the first two years of their lives, their cognitive development will be impaired.

Other abilities may show a weaker dependence on experience: The ability in question may develop in response to experience that occurs any time within a broad range, but the effect may be stronger during some periods than during others. This weaker form of dependency is often referred to as a **sensitive period.** Acquisition of a second language seems to be

such a case. A person can learn a second language throughout life; but, as we saw in Chapter 10, a second language is learned more easily in childhood than later.

Critical periods and sensitive periods demonstrate that human development is more than an unfolding of a genetically determined program. *It consists of a continuous interaction between physical maturation and environmental stimulation.*

Interim Summary

Physical and Perceptual Development in Infancy and Childhood

A newborn infant's first movements are actually reflexes that are crucial to its survival. For example, the rooting, sucking, and swallowing reflexes are important in finding and consuming food. More sophisticated motor skills develop and are refined through natural maturation and practice.

A newborn's senses appear to be at least partially functional at birth. However, normal development of perceptual abilities, like that of motor abilities, depends on experience. Genetically, an infant has the potential to develop motor and sensory abilities that coincide with the maturation of its nervous system. But in order for this potential to be realized, the infant's environment must give the infant opportunities to test and practice these skills. If an infant is deprived of the opportunity to practice them during a critical or sensitive period, these skills may fail to develop fully, which will affect his or her performance as an adult.

QUESTION TO CONSIDER

Suppose you are expecting your first child. How might you design your child's room (or nursery) to facilitate motor and perceptual development? What kinds of toys would you include in the room? What sorts of experiences might you wish to have with your child to promote normal motor and sensory development?

Cognitive Development in Infancy and Childhood

As children grow, their nervous systems mature and they undergo new experiences. Perceptual and motor skills develop in complexity and competency. Children learn to recognize people and their voices, begin to talk and respond to the speech of others, and learn how to solve problems. Infants as young as 12 months are even able to form memories of specific events (see Bauer, 2002). In short, their cognitive capacities develop.

This section will begin by highlighting the importance of a responsive environment to cognitive development; then we will turn to Piaget's theory, Vygotsky's theory, the information-processing model, and the controversial question of television's impact on cognitive development.

The Importance of a Responsive Environment

Cognitive development is the process by which infants get to know things about themselves and their world. Although cognitive development appears to involve both evolutionary and environmental variables (Geary, 1995), I will focus mainly on environmental factors in this section. I will discuss evolutionary contributions to development later in the chapter.

One of the first steps in a baby's cognitive development is for the baby to learn that events in the environment can be dependent on its own behavior. It appears, in fact, that the type of setting that is most effective in promoting cognitive development is an environment in which the infant's behavior has tangible effects. In an experimental test of this hypothesis, Watson and Ramey (1972) presented three groups of infants with a mobile 10 minutes per day for 14 days. A pillow containing a pressure-sensitive switch was placed under each baby's head, and the mobile was suspended above the baby's face. For one group, the mobile automatically rotated whenever the infant moved its head and activated the switch. For another group, the mobile remained stationary. For a third group, the mobile intermittently moved on its own (but not in response to infant head movements). So the first group of infants had experience controlling the mobile's movements, whereas the other two groups experienced no association between their own actions and the mobile's movement.

The babies were tested again. This time, the mobile was connected to the pillow switch for infants in all three of the experimental groups. Infants who had learned the contin-

gency between head turning and mobile movement again turned their heads when they saw the mobile. They seemed to have learned that they could control its movements. In contrast, when the babies in the second and third groups were given the opportunity to make the mobile move by turning their heads, they did *not* learn to do so. It was as if they had learned from their prior experience that they could not affect whether the mobile would move.

Research using similar methods found that infants were visibly pleased when they controlled the onset of a *Sesame Street* music video (Lewis, Alessandri, & Sullivan, 1990). Losing this type of contingent control, on the other hand, produces facial expressions of anger (Lewis et al., 1990; Sullivan & Lewis, 2003).

Findings from research on infant control of stimuli in their environments are consistent with a great deal of other evidence about adults (as you will see in later chapters). For each of us, the abilities to extend ourself and to affect objects and other people are important aspects of personal and social functioning. There are implications here for infant-rearing practices as well. In some tragic cases, babies have been raised in unresponsive, unstimulating settings. Several decades ago, infants in an institution in Beirut, Lebanon, were cared for physically but were raised in cribs that visually isolated them from one another. The infants had very limited opportunities to learn that they could affect others. Although their physical needs were fulfilled, they received no individual attention from their caregivers (Dennis, 1973). The children raised under these conditions were extremely impaired in cognitive, language, and motor development. Dennis (1973) found that when children were adopted from the nursery and reared in a normal home environment, they showed significant gains in physical and intellectual development. However, there was evidence for a critical period. Infants adopted before two years of age eventually achieved a normal level of development, whereas children who were adopted after the age of two years remained behind normally reared children.

The Work of Jean Piaget

The most influential student of child development has been Jean Piaget (1896–1980), a Swiss researcher, who viewed cognitive development as a maturational process. Piaget formulated the most complete and detailed description of the process of cognitive development that we now have. His conclusions were based on his observations of the behavior of children—first of his own children at home, and later of other children at his Center of Genetic Epistemology in Geneva. Piaget noticed that children of similar ages tend to engage in similar behaviors and to make the same kinds of mistakes in problem solving. He concluded that these similarities are the result of a sequence of development that all normal children follow. Completion of each period, with its corresponding abilities, is the prerequisite for entering the next period.

Piaget considered himself a philosopher concerned with the development of knowledge rather than a developmental

▲ *Watson and Ramey's experiment using mobiles demonstrated the importance of a responsive environment in promoting cognitive development.*

psychologist. He was also strongly influenced by James Mark Baldwin's attempt to describe the mind in biological and evolutionary contexts. As a result, Piaget's theories of cognitive development use terms that overlap, but do not always coincide with, the meanings psychologists give to those same terms. For example, Piaget often spoke of mental structures, as Wundt and the other structuralists did; however, in Piaget's use the term carried strong connotations about the actions and purposes of these constructs, much as the functionalists emphasized (Moessinger, 2000). Nevertheless, as you will see, Piaget's contributions continue to exert an enormous impact on the study of early development.

Piaget proposed that as children develop, they acquire mental representations or frameworks that are used for understanding and dealing with the world and for thinking about and solving problems. As Chapter 8 explained, a mental framework that organizes and synthesizes information about a person, place, or thing is known as a *schema*. Piaget proposed that schemas are first defined in terms of objects and actions but that later they become the basis of the concrete and abstract concepts that constitute adult knowledge. For example, a baby girl is said to have a "grasping schema" when she is able to grasp a rattle in her hand. Once she has learned how to grasp a rattle, she can then apply the same schema to other objects. Later, she can incorporate the "grasping schema" with others to accomplish the behavior of picking an object up. At this point she will possess a "picking up schema."

I will discuss how the acquisition and enlargement of schemas occur after I introduce another important component of Piaget's theory, the notion of an **operation.** In the field of both logic and mathematics, an operation is a transformation of an object or thing. For example, multiplication by 2 transforms 6 into 12. Similarly, saying "Rhonda is my sister" transforms your conception of "Rhonda" into another conception, that of "my sister." For Piaget an important logical characteristic of an operation is that it is *invertible;* that is, it can be reversed. By inverting the operation of multiplication into division, I can transform 12 back to 6. According to Piaget, an important aspect of cognitive development is whether a child possesses the ability to use operations of different types.

Let's consider schemas. Infants acquire schemas by interacting with their environment. According to Piaget, two processes help a child adapt to his or her environment: assimilation and accommodation. **Assimilation** is the process by which new information is incorporated into existing schemas. For example, suppose that a young boy has schemas for what adults are like and for what children are like. Adults are tall and drive cars. Children are short and ride bikes. When this child meets new children and adults, they will usually fit, or be assimilated, into his existing schemas and will be properly categorized. But our child will be challenged when he meets his mother's older sister Marge, who is no taller than the average 12-year-old and rides a bike. The child will need to account for the fact that Aunt Marge is nevertheless identifiably an

▲ *According to Piaget, children develop schemas, such as schemas for grasping objects or putting them into their mouths, that become the basis for understanding current and future experiences.*

adult. The process by which existing schemas are changed by new experiences is called **accommodation**. Our child's schemas for children and adults will have to change to include the possibility that some short people are adults rather than children. As you continue in this chapter, keep in mind that assimilation and accommodation apply not just to categorization of people and objects, but to methods of doing things and even to abstract concepts as well.

Piaget's Four Periods of Cognitive Development

Although development is a continuous process, Piaget argued that at three key points in an individual's life (at 2 years, 7 years, and 11 years of age), the two processes of assimilation and accommodation fail to adjust adequately to the child's knowledge of the world. At these points, by a process that Piaget labeled *equilibration,* the individual's schemas are radically reorganized.

Thus, Piaget divided cognitive development into four periods: sensorimotor, preoperational, concrete operational, and formal operational. (See **Table 12•2.**) What a child learns in one period enables him or her to progress to the next period. Crucially, it matters whether the schemas of an earlier period can be reorganized in a way that will permit operations to occur in the next. The periods in Piaget's theory are more than just intervals of time; they are necessary *stages* in a progression from primitive sensory knowledge to abstract reasoning.

The Sensorimotor Period. The **sensorimotor period,** which lasts for approximately the first two years of life, is the first stage in Piaget's theory of cognitive development. It is marked by an orderly progression of increasingly complex cognitive development ranging from reflexes to symbolic

TABLE 12•2	The Four Periods of Piaget's Theory of Cognitive Development	
Period	**Approximate Age**	**Major Features**
Sensorimeter	Birth to 2 years	Grasp of object permanence; deferred imitation; rudimentary symbolic thinking
Preoperational	2 to 6 or 7 years	Increased ability to think symbolically and logically; egocentrism; cannot yet master conservation problems
Concrete operational	6 or 7 years to 11 years	Mastery of conservation problems; understanding of categorization; cannot think abstractly
Formal operational	11 years upward	Ability to think abstractly and hypothetically

thinking. During this period, cognition is closely tied to external stimulation, including that produced by physical objects and people (see Muller & Carpendale, 2000). An important development in the sensorimotor period is the child's grasp of **object permanence:** the realization that objects do not cease to exist when they are out of sight. Until about six months of age, children appear to lose all interest in an object that disappears from sight—the saying "out of sight, out of mind" seems particularly appropriate. In addition, cognition is inseparable from action or behavior: Thinking is doing.

At first infants do not appear to have a concept for the permanence of objects. They can look at visual stimuli and will turn their heads and eyes toward the source of a sound, but hiding an object elicits no particular response. At around three months, infants become able to follow moving objects with their eyes. If an infant's doll disappears behind a barrier, the infant will continue to stare at the place where the doll has disappeared but will not search for it.

At around five months, infants can grasp and hold objects and gain experience with manipulating and observing them. They also can anticipate the future position of a moving object. If a doll is made to pass behind a screen, infants will turn their eyes toward the far side of the screen, seeming to anticipate the doll's reappearance on the other side.

During the last half of the first year, infants develop much more complex concepts concerning the nature of physical objects. They grasp objects, turn them over, and investigate their properties. By looking at an object from various angles, they learn that the object can change its visual shape and still be the same object. In addition, if an object is hidden, infants will actively search for it; their object concept now contains the rule of object permanence. For infants at this stage of development, a hidden object still exists. Out of sight is no longer out of mind. In the game of peekaboo, babies laugh because they know that after momentarily disappearing, you will suddenly reappear and say, "Peekaboo!"

By early in the second year, awareness of object permanence is well enough developed that infants will search for an object in the last place they saw it hidden. However, at this stage infants can keep track of changes only in a hiding place they can see. For example, if an adult picks up an object, puts it under a cloth, drops the object while his or her hand is hidden, closes the hand again, and removes the hand from the

cloth, infants will look for the object in the adult's hand. When they do not find the object there, they look puzzled or upset and do not search for the object under the cloth. (See **Figure 12•4.**)

Two other interesting developments take place near the end of the sensorimotor period. First, toddlers develop the ability to imitate actions that they have seen others perform, a behavior that Piaget called **deferred imitation.** This ability is due to children's increasing ability to form mental representations of actions that they have observed. Children may then recall these representations at a later time to direct particular imitative actions and symbolic play, such as pretending to feed a doll or taking a stuffed animal for a walk. Second, as is clear from the fact that a two-year-old has an imagination, children at this stage begin to think symbolically. They can use words to represent objects such as balls and animals. This is a critical developmental step, because symbolic thinking is crucial to language development.

The Preoperational Period. Piaget's second period of cognitive development, the **preoperational period,** lasts from approximately age two to age seven and involves the ability to think logically as well as symbolically. This period is characterized by rapid development of language ability and of the ability to represent things symbolically. The child arranges toys in new ways to represent other objects (for example, a row of blocks can represent a train), begins to classify and categorize objects, and starts learning to count and to manipulate numbers.

According to Piaget the development of symbolism actually begins during the sensorimotor period, when a child starts imitating events in his or her environment. For example, a child might represent a bird by extending her arms in a flapping motion or imitate her mother driving by making circling movements with her hands. Symbolic representations like these are called *signifiers:* The motor act represents (signifies) the concept, because it resembles either the movements the object makes or the movements the child makes when interacting with the object. However, symbolic thinking is not fully developed until it loses this intrinsic connection with the actions and behaviors of the sensorimotor period. During the preoperational period schemas are reorganized around a different kind of referent: words.

FIGURE 12•4   Object permanence. An infant will not realize that the object has been left under the cloth.

(Adapted from Bower, T. G. R. (1972). *Development in infancy* (2nd ed.). © 1982 by W. H. Freeman and Company. Used with permission.)

Object is in researcher's hand.

Researcher closes hand...

...puts hand under cloth...

...removes hand, leaving object under the cloth.

Infant looks in researcher's hand.

Obviously upset, infant quits.

Words are symbols that have no physical resemblance to the concept they represent; Piaget referred to such abstract symbols as *signs*. Signifiers are personal, derived from the child's own interactions with objects. Therefore, only the child and perhaps members of his or her immediate family will understand a child's signifiers. In contrast, signs are social conventions. They are understood by all members of a culture. A child who is able to use words to think about reality has made an important step in cognitive development.

Egocentrism, a child's belief that others see the world in precisely the way he or she does, is another important characteristic of the preoperational period. A preoperational child sees the world only from his or her own point of view. For example, a preoperational child playing hide-and-seek may run to a corner, turn his back to you, and "hide" by covering his eyes. Although in plain sight of you, he believes that because he cannot see you, you must not be able to see him.

A third important characteristic of the preoperational period—and the reason for its name—is that the child's schemas do not permit invertible operations. For example, if I take a stack of pennies on a table and spread them out all over the tabletop, I have transformed them into a different array. A child in the preoperational period cannot conceptualize that this operation can be reversed. Instead, he or she believes that I have radically changed something about the pennies.

Piaget's work demonstrated this belief quite clearly and, in doing so, showed that a child's representation of the world is strikingly different from that of an adult. For example, most adults realize that the volume of water remains constant when the water is poured from a short, wide container into a taller, narrower container, even though its level is now higher. However, early in the preoperational period, children will fail to recognize this fact; they will say that the taller container contains more water. (See **Figure 12•5**.) The ability to realize that an object retains volume, mass, length, or number when it undergoes various transformations is referred to as a grasp of **conservation;** the transformed object *conserves* its original properties. **Figure 12•6** depicts three additional tests of children's understanding of conservation.

Piaget concluded that the abilities to perceive the conservation of volume, mass, length, and number are manifestations of operational thinking. His studies showed that understanding of number conservation generally develops by age 6, whereas most children do not grasp conservation of volume until age 11. Presumably, the reason that conservation of number comes first is that children can verify the stability of number once they learn to count.

The Period of Concrete Operations.   Piaget's third stage of cognitive development, the **period of concrete operations,** spans approximately ages 7 to 11 and involves children's developing

FIGURE 12•5 Conservation. In the preoperational period, a child does not grasp the fact that the volume of a liquid remains the same even if the liquid is poured into a different-shaped container.

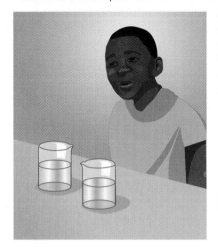
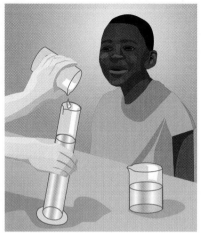

understanding of the conservation principle and other concepts, such as categorization. The end of this period marks the transition from childhood to adolescence. The period of concrete operations is characterized by the emergence of the ability to perform logical analysis, by an increased ability to empathize with the feelings and attitudes of others, and by an understanding of more complex cause-and-effect relations.

The child becomes much more skilled at the use of symbolic thought. For example, even before the period of concrete operations, children can arrange a series of objects in order of size and can compare any two objects and say which is larger. However, if they are shown that stick A is larger than stick B and that stick B is larger than stick C, they cannot infer that stick A is larger than stick C. Children become capable of making such inferences during the early part of this period. At this stage, however, although they can reason with

respect to concrete objects, such as sticks that they have seen, they cannot do so with hypothetical objects. For example, they cannot solve the following problem: "Judy is taller than Frank, and Frank is taller than Carl. Who is taller, Judy or Carl?" The ability to solve such problems awaits the next period of cognitive development.

The Period of Formal Operations. During the **period of formal operations**, which begins at about age 11, children first become capable of abstract reasoning. They can now think and reason about hypothetical objects and events. They also begin to understand that under different conditions their behavior can have different consequences. Formal operational thinking is not "culture free"; that is, it is influenced by cultural variables, especially formal schooling (Piaget, 1972; Rogoff & Chavajay, 1995). Without exposure to the principles of

Conservation of Mass	The researcher presents two balls of clay.	The researcher rolls one ball into a "sausage" and asks the child whether they still contain the same amount of clay.
Conservation of Length	The researcher presents two dowels.	The researcher moves one dowel to the right and asks the child whether they are still the same length.
Conservation of Number	The researcher presents two rows of poker chips.	The researcher moves one row of chips apart and asks the child whether each row still contains the same number.

FIGURE 12•6
Various tests of conservation.
(Adapted from *Of Children: An Introduction to Child Development,* 4th ed., by Guy R. Lefrancois, Belmont, CA: Wadsworth Publishing Company.)

▲ *Formal operational thinking is influenced by cultural variables, especially formal schooling.*

scientific thinking, such as those taught in middle school and high school science classes, people do not develop formal operational thinking.

As evidence that children think differently as they progress through the different periods of cognitive development, consider the answers that three of my children gave to the question "If you were to go to the moon today, what would it be like?"

> *Caden* (age 7, but still preoperational because he cannot solve the water conservation problem): "I don't know, what do you think?"
>
> *Colin* (age 9, concrete operational because he easily solves the water conservation problem): "I don't know because I've never been to the moon."
>
> *Tara* (age 11, early formal operational): "It would be cold, dark, scary, and lonely if I were there by myself."

The differences between Colin's and Tara's answers are significant. Colin doesn't know the answer to the question because he's never been to the moon, a clear indication of concrete operational thinking. But Tara can *imagine* what it's like, partly because she has learned something about the moon in school (it's cold and dark) and partly because she can hypothetically place herself on the moon and imagine that it's also a lonely and scary place. At age 11 Tara is at the beginning of the formal operations period.

Not all people pass through all four of Piaget's stages and reach the formal operational period, even as physically mature adults. In some cases, adults show formal operational thought only in their areas of expertise. Thus, a mechanic may be able to think abstractly while repairing an engine but not while solving math or physics problems. A physicist may be able to reason abstractly when solving physics problems but not while reading poetry. However, once an individual does reach the formal operational level of thinking, he or she will always (except in the case of damage to the brain from injury or disease) perform intellectually at that level.

Evaluation of Piaget's Contribution Piaget's theory has had an enormously positive impact, stimulating interest and research in developmental psychology and educational psychology (e.g., Brainerd, 2003; Voyat, 1998). Not all of Piaget's conclusions have been universally accepted, however. One criticism leveled at Piaget is that he did not always define his terms operationally. Consequently, it is difficult for others to interpret the significance of his generalizations. Many of his studies lack the proper controls discussed in Chapter 2. Thus, much of his work was not experimental, which means that cause-and-effect relations among variables cannot be identified with certainty.

As well, research evidence suggests that a child's ability to understand conservation of various physical attributes occurs earlier than Piaget supposed. For example, Gelman (1972) found that when the appropriate task is used, even three-year-old children are able to demonstrate a grasp of conservation of number. As in other areas of psychology, testing methods make a difference.

Piaget also appears to have underestimated the ability of young children to understand another person's point of view. In other words, children are less egocentric at early ages than Piaget thought (Flavell, 1992). For example, Flavell, Everett, Croft, and Flavell (1981) found that even a three-year-old child realizes that a person looking at the opposite side of a card the child is examining will not see the same thing the child sees. Clearly, the child recognizes the other person's point of view. Other research shows that children as young as two years old make inferences about other people's knowledge that require understanding what the others could or could not have seen happen (O'Neill, 1996).

Despite the fact that Piaget's method of observation led him to underestimate some important abilities, his meticulous observations of child behavior have been extremely important in the field of child development and have had a great influence on educational practice.

Vygotsky's Sociocultural Theory of Cognitive Development

Another important contributor to our understanding of cognitive development was the Russian psychologist Lev Vygotsky (1896–1934). Vygotsky agreed with Piaget that experience with the physical world is an important factor. But he disagreed that this is the whole story. He argued that the culture in which a child lives also plays a significant role in the child's cognitive development (Vygotsky, 1934/1987). Although Vygotsky's work was conducted during the 1920s and early 1930s, his writings continue to influence present-day conceptualizations of cognitive development during childhood (Kozulin & Falik, 1995). In this section we will briefly examine some of Vygotsky's ideas.

Vygotsky argued that children do not learn to think about the physical world in a vacuum. The cultural context—what they hear others say about the world and how they see others interact with physical aspects of the world—matters (Behrend, Rosengren, & Perlmutter, 1992; Thomas, 1996). Thus parents, teachers, friends, and many others help children acquire ideas about how the world works. We would expect, then, that the development of children raised in non-stimulating environments devoid of interesting interactions with other people, with books, and, yes, with television would lag behind that of children raised in more stimulating environments. And this is exactly what has been found (Rymer, 1992).

Vygotsky further believed that children's use of speech also influences their cognitive development. Children up to about age seven often talk to themselves. When drawing in a coloring book, a child may say, "I'll color her arms and face green and her pants black." Piaget would focus on such talk as reflecting egocentrism. Vygotsky's focus would be different. He would say that the child's talk reflects a cognitive developmental process—the child is developing a mental plan that will serve as a guide to subsequent behavior. According to Vygotsky, language is the basis for cognitive development, including the abilities to remember, to solve problems, to make decisions, and to formulate plans.

After about age seven, children stop vocalizing their thoughts and instead carry on what Vygotsky labelled *inner speech*. Inner speech represents the internalization of words and the mental manipulation of them as symbols for objects in the environment. As children interact with their parents, teachers, and peers, they learn new words to represent new objects. Given Vygotsky's linking of language with thought, this increased facility with language would imply better cognitive skill as well.

These two themes of Vygotsky's theory—the interconnection between thought and language, and the importance of society and culture—led him to propose a developmental distinction important to educational psychologists. The skills and problem-solving abilities that a child can show on his or her own indicate the level of development that the child has mastered. Vygotsky called this the **actual developmental level**. For Piaget, this level would represent the limit of the child's cognitive skill. However, Vygotsky argued that a patient parent or a skilled mentor could assist a child to achieve a potentially higher level. Perhaps you've had the experience of studying for the Scholastic Aptitude Test and being stumped by a particular kind of problem. That would, loosely, define your actual developmental level. But now suppose a teacher shows you a method for solving the problem that not only makes perfect sense to you but also helps you to solve similar problems. That increased capacity for problem solving resulting from guided help Vygotsky called the **zone of proximal development**. And indeed, as the "expertise" of the people they interact with increases, so do the children's cognitive skills. For example, Rogoff and her colleagues (e.g., Rogoff, 1990) have shown that children become better problem solvers if they practice solving problems with their parents or with more experienced children than if they practice the problems alone or with children of similar cognitive ability.

Thus, whereas Piaget argued for a primarily maturational view of children's cognitive development, Vygotsky stressed the importance of sociocultural influences, such as language and interactions with other people, on cognitive development. As we have seen, research partially supports both theorists' ideas. Piaget's descriptions of the milestones involved in cognitive development have proved to be fairly accurate. However, Vygotsky's work has gone beyond Piaget's theory in explaining how cultural variables, especially language, influence cognitive development.

Applying Information-Processing Models to Cognitive Development

Vygotsky argued that proficiency with language accompanied greater cognitive ability. This may have struck you as a familiar assertion. Earlier, in Chapter 8, I described how chunking could increase our ability to remember objects in working memory. You also saw how important meaning and depth of processing were to human memory. As our knowledge about human memory has expanded since the time of Piaget and Vygotsky, developmental psychologists have examined how an information-processing perspective on human sensation, perception, and memory might fit within an account of human development. One approach is to consider how processes of memory might change during development, and what effects these changes might have. Another approach has looked not at the processes of cognition per se, but rather at the knowledge base that children have at different ages. Presumably, if we knew how a child understood the world, we would be able to know how he or she would encode, store, and retrieve the semantic information required to adjust to it.

Changes in Cognitive Processes Can infants remember? Piaget's observations on the concept of object permanence seemed to indicate that infants younger than six months do not encode objects; therefore, they cannot remember them. Rovee-Collier and her colleagues, however, have challenged this conclusion using a variation of the mobile task I described at the start of this section (e.g., Rovee-Collier, 1999). Infants from two to six months of age were shown a mobile that they could move by means of a ribbon attached to one of their legs. After varying amounts of time they would be shown the mobile again, but with the ribbon disconnected. If the infant kicked at a rate higher than normal, Rovee-Collier would conclude that that infant recognized the mobile on the second presentation. Infants 6 to 18 months of age were tested in a similar way using a mechanical switch to operate a toy train.

Rovee-Collier proved not only that memory is present in infants, but also that the retention span increases systematically

FIGURE 12·7 Retention of memory of the sight of an infant mobile or a toy train by infants 2 to 18 months of age. Blue circles depict data from infants tested with a mobile that they could move by leg motions. Orange circles depict data from infants trained with the toy train. Six-month-old infants were tested with both the mobile and the train.

(From Rovee-Collier, C. (1999). The development of infant memory. *Current Directions in Psychological Science, 8,* 80–85. © 1978 American Psychological Society.)

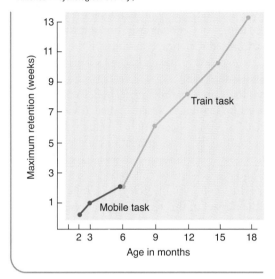

over the 2- to 18-month period of life (Rovee-Collier, 1999). **Figure 12·7** shows data from both the mobile and train test situations; the maximum delay over which the infants show retention is plotted against their age. Using a similar procedure, Rovee-Collier and her colleagues have shown that retrieval cues increase retrieval in infants—and that infants apparently demonstrate an implicit/explicit differentiation similar to that discussed in Chapter 8.

Case (1992, 1998) claims that cognitive development is a matter of a child's becoming more efficient in using memory and other cognitive processes. The heart of Case's model is a hypothetical information-processing construct similar to short-term or working memory, whose chief function is the processing of information from the external world. According to Case, as the brain matures, so does its capacity to process greater amounts of information using memory. First, maturation of the brain, specifically the increasing number of networks of neural connections and increasing myelinization of neurons, also enhances more efficient processing of information. Second, as children become more practiced at using schemas, less demand is placed on cognitive resources, which can now be devoted to other, more complex cognitive tasks. For example, when children first learn to ride a bicycle, they must focus entirely on keeping their balance and steering the bike in a straight line. But after they have acquired these skills, they no longer have to devote so much attention to

steering the bike and not falling off. Now they can look around, talk to other bike riders, and so on. Third, schemas for different objects and events become integrated, so children now think in novel ways about these objects and events. The net result of such integration is the acquisition of central conceptual structures—networks of schemas that allow children to understand the relationships among the objects and events represented by the schemas. As increasingly complex central conceptual structures are formed, children advance to higher levels of cognitive development, as represented in Piaget's stages.

Changes in Cognitive Content The increased complexity of children's knowledge as they develop has figured prominently in development theories. Contemporary research based on information-processing models of memory has clarified the importance of the specific knowledge an individual can use to encode information, store it, or retrieve it. We have seen, for example, that elaborative rehearsal is more effective in maintaining information than simple repetition. As Case suggests, increased cognitive ability is facilitated by a richer knowledge of the world surrounding the child. This simple proposition has encouraged many developmental psychologists to examine the content of infants' and children's knowledge in certain areas or *domains.*

One important domain is the world of physics and mechanical action. In Chapter 8 you discovered how hard it was to remember a disconnected set of words as compared to a set of words linked to a physical train of action. Think how hard it might be to remember an experience if the individual events of that experience could occur in any order. Our knowledge of what is physically or logically connected helps us to structure experiences and thereby to organize them in ways that improve memory.

Infants show knowledge of at least some of the laws of physics at an early age. One very simple law is an optical one: When one object passes behind another, it gets occluded, or blocked from view. But where there is a gap in the occluding object, the object should be visible. Luo and Baillargeon (2005) found that infants develop this knowledge piece by piece. They discovered this using the fact that even young infants will react to unexpected events by prolonged looking. By comparing the amount of time infants spend looking at one scene as opposed to another, it's possible to infer what infants consider to be "normal" and what is "unexpected."

To understand Luo and Baillargeon's experiment, think of an old-fashioned theater stage with a main curtain across the front and side curtains on the left and right. If I were to wave at you, walk behind the left side curtain, and later emerge at the edge of the right side curtain, you would find nothing unusual about that sequence. But if the central curtain were raised and you saw me enter one side and exit the other without seeing me cross the open stage, you'd be pretty surprised, right? It would appear that I had teleported from behind the left curtain to the right curtain. Piaget's early work on object permanence notwithstanding, two-and-a-half-month-old infants apparently know that such unseen teleportation is impossible. When Luo and Baillargeon (2005) used a bit of stage magic to accomplish what I just described, infants of this age spent a lot of time looking at the scene.

But this knowledge about occlusion is only partially present in infants. Luo and Baillargeon performed another test, similar to what the stage would be like if the central curtain were only half raised. Now, you would expect to see my legs as I walked across the stage. Infants two and a half months of age, however, are not surprised if they don't see this partial occlusion (although infants of three months are). Rather, the younger infants are surprised if they *do* see the partial occlusion. They seem to treat a partial gap as if it were no gap at all. Apparently, knowledge about optical occlusion develops incrementally, as infants acquire an understanding about the solidity and continuity of occluding objects.

Another important domain, especially as the infant or child encounters social settings, is knowledge about others' beliefs or state of mind. For example, when I lecture, I keep a whiteboard marker in a drawer of the classroom podium. If you came to the classroom early and saw the professor before me pick up my marker and leave with it, you would still expect me to look for the marker in the drawer. You have developed expectations about how my experiences relate to my beliefs, something that developmental psychologists describe as **theory of mind**.

Four-year-olds seem capable of correctly inferring how events can shape the state of mind or beliefs of another. But three-year-olds do not: They use their own beliefs to predict the beliefs and actions of others. Developmental psychologists have observed this difference in a procedure sometimes called the "Sally-Anne" test (e.g., Baron-Cohen, Leslie, & Frith, 1985). A child is shown two dolls—Sally and Anne. The Sally doll is shown placing a marble in a basket within a doll house and then shown leaving the house. While she is away, the Anne doll takes the marble and places it in a box. The Sally doll returns to the house, and the child is asked: "Where will Sally look for her marble?" A three-year-old girl watching this little drama would think that, since *she* knows where the marble is, another, such as Sally, would know that too. She has, in other words, not differentiated her own beliefs from another's. By the following year, however, she will have developed a type of "naive psychology" by which she will recognize that other people's behaviors follow patterns based on their own beliefs (Kail, 2001; Slaughter & Repacholi, 2003).

The term "naive psychology" is not meant to imply anything negative. When a child develops a theory of mind, he or she acquires a sophisticated tool for predicting the actions of others. Think of your own ability to understand a friend's nuanced reaction to a forgotten birthday greeting and you'll recognize the significance of this developmental change. Indeed, it's been suggested that the lack of a theory of mind may underlie some severe developmental disorders (Baron-Cohen, Leslie, & Cohen, 1985).

Evaluating Scientific Issues

The Effects of Television Viewing on Children's Cognitive Development

Cognitive development is influenced by many factors, including a child's parents' education and occupational status, the number of siblings in the family, social class of playmates, the nature of the neighborhood, the availability of educational resources such as books in the home, opportunities for travel, and the quality of schooling the child receives. These factors vary enormously, but almost all children in industrialized societies, even those in the poorest households, are exposed for several hours a day to a near-universal factor—television.

Although there are certainly other modern media that resemble television's visual experience, such as video games and web broadcasts, it has been argued that television is especially important to the development of children because it is present in almost every home, occupies a large part of a child's time, and is accessible to children across a wide span of their lives (Huston & Wright, 1998). It is important to understand the impact of this technological presence on a child's cognitive development.

● **What Are the Effects of Television Viewing on Children?** There are two issues that concern us here—the *content* of television programs and the general effects of the *medium* itself. Let us consider content first. There is no question that television does not do the good it could, and there is a strong probability that it does some harm. One of the best examples of the good it can do is demonstrated by *Sesame Street*, a program that was devised to teach school-readiness skills such as counting, letter recognition, and vocabulary. Research indicates that the program has succeeded in its goals; children who watch *Sesame Street* have better vocabularies, have better attitudes toward school, adapt better to the classroom, and have more positive attitudes toward children of other races (Fisch & Truglio, 2001). (*Sesame Street* emphasizes multiculturalism in its choice of characters and in the activities and interests they display.) Rice, Huston, Truglio, and Wright (1990) studied a large sample of three- to five-year-old children from a wide range of socioeconomic backgrounds and found that children of all backgrounds profited from watching *Sesame Street*—the advantages were not restricted to middle-class children.

On the other hand, many television programs are full of violence, and watching them may well promote aggressiveness and impatience with nonviolent resolution of disagreements in the children who watch such shows (Huesmann, Moise-Titus, Podolski, & Eron, 2003). (We will examine more research on this issue in Chapter 13.) In addition, commercial television affects consumer behavior. Sponsors target many of their commercial messages at children (McNeal, 1990). Furthermore, sponsors produce commer-

▲ *Does television viewing promote or retard cognitive development in children?*

cials that encourage children to demand that their parents purchase particular snack foods, toys, and other items (Taras et al., 1989). Interestingly, commercials related to the purchase and consumption of alcoholic beverages and those containing antidrinking messages do not appear to influence children's attitudes about the positive or negative effects of alcohol (Lipsitz, Brake, Vincent, & Winters, 1993)—perhaps because these ads are not specifically targeted at very young audiences. Nonetheless, we can ask ourselves whether sponsors are likely to find it in their interests to educate children to be informed consumers.

● **Criticisms That Claim That Television Impairs Cognitive Development**

The second issue that people have raised about children and television regards the nature of the medium itself, and it is this issue that we will examine in the rest of this feature.

Many people who have written about the potential effects of television as a medium on children's cognitive development have concluded that the medium is generally harmful. Anderson and Collins (1988) summarize some of the criticisms these people have made:

- Television has a mesmerizing power over children's attention; this power is exerted by the movement, color, and visual variety typical of television.

- Children do not think about television programs; that is, they do not engage in inferential and reflective thought while viewing television.

- Children get overstimulated by television; by some accounts this leads to hyperactivity, and by other accounts this leads to passivity.

- Television viewing displaces valuable cognitive activities, especially reading and homework.

- Attention span is shortened, probably because of the rapid pace at which visual images are presented.

- Creativity and imagination are reduced, perhaps because reading and viewing television are incompatible.

- Reading achievement is reduced, perhaps because reading and viewing television are incompatible.

● **Does the Evidence Support These Criticisms of Television as a Medium?**

In a review of their own research and of that of others, Anderson and Collins (1988) conclude that there is little evidence to support these criticisms. In fact, the evidence directly contradicts some of them. Let us examine four of the most important criticisms: that television mesmerizes children, that it overstimulates them, that it displaces valuable cognitive activities, and that it reduces children's reading achievement.

Before we look at the evidence concerning these issues, we should ask just how much of a child's time is dominated by the medium. Estimates vary according to the method used. Studies of two-year-olds have shown that on average they view up to two hours of television per day (Hollenbeck, 1978), and studies of older children have shown that they may watch a little more than three hours of television per day (Nielsen, 1990). Boys tend to view more television than do girls; and, across all ages, children with low IQs from low-income families watch more television than do other children (Huston, Watkins, & Kunkel, 1989; Huston et al., 1990).

The most objective measures of the amount of time children spend watching television are those that researchers have obtained by placing a time-lapse video camera and VCR in people's homes next to their television sets so that the viewers can be recorded. Back in the mid-1980s, Anderson and colleagues (1985) used this method to measure television viewing by members of 99 families in a New England city. They found that on average the children in the study watched television about 16 hours per week.

According to Anderson and Collins (1988), while watching television, children often are engaged in other activities: They eat, play with toys, draw or color pictures, read, play games, sleep, talk with others, or do their homework. They often enter and leave the room while the television is on. Thus, although the children do watch television a substantial amount of the time, it is probably inaccurate to say that the average North American child spends more time watching television than attending school.

Mesmerization. Winn (2002) metaphorically described television and related computer technologies as the "plug-in drug." Some critics go further and argue that television is "addictive" and "mesmerizing," that children who watch it have "glazed eyes" and are "spaced out" (Moody, 1980). In fact, studies that actually observe children who are watching television find no such effects. Children are rarely "glued" to the television set. They look away from it between 100 and 200 times each hour (Anderson & Field, 1983). They rarely look at the screen for much more than one minute at a stretch. Their viewing behavior is related to program content: They tend to pay attention when they hear other children's voices, interesting sound effects, or peculiar voices, and when they see movement on the screen. They tend not to pay attention when they hear men's voices or see no signs of activity on the screen (Anderson & Lorch, 1983).

The selectivity shown by young viewers is certainly not consistent with the behavior of children who have been "mesmerized." The fact that the sound track of a television program has so much effect on children's looking behavior suggests that children have learned to use auditory cues to help them decide whether to watch, especially when they are time sharing—alternating their attention between the television and another activity. If they hear certain kinds of sounds, they turn their attention away from the alternative activity and look at the screen to see whether something interesting is happening. The child is an active viewer, using the sights and sounds of the program to choose when to pay attention (Bickham, Wright, & Huston, 2001).

Overstimulation. Moody (1980) states that "television is an intense kaleidoscope of moving light and sound. It can create extreme excitement in the brain and, after prolonged viewing, it can produce a 'drugged state'" (p. 18). Anderson and Collins (1988) found no evidence to support such claims. And the fact that children look away from television so often suggests that if they found television too stimulating they would have an easy means for reducing potential overarousal—simply looking away from the screen. Certainly, an exciting program can excite the viewer, but no evidence suggests that "kaleidoscopic images" act like drugs on the brains of young children.

Displacement of Activities That Stimulate Cognitive Development. Perhaps television takes up time that would otherwise be spent on activities that would stimulate children's cognitive development (Singer, 1993; Singer & Singer, 1990). Some evidence with respect to this possibility comes from research in Canada, in which investigators made observations before and after television was available in remote regions of the country (Williams & Boyes, 1986). Television viewing primarily displaced social and recreational activities. It had little effect, however, on time spent reading. As most parents undoubtedly know, many children do their homework in front of the television set, switching their attention back and forth between the screen and their studies. In general, children are more likely to use television as a backdrop for their math homework than for reading (Patton, Stinard, & Routh, 1983). Surprisingly, there is no evidence that the quality of the homework suffers.

Reduction in Children's Reading Achievement. The fact that children are less likely to watch television while doing homework that involves reading suggests that reading and viewing are at least somewhat incompatible. Indeed, one criticism of television—that it retards children's reading achievement—has received some support. Measurements of children's reading skills before and after television became available suggested that television viewing decreased the reading skills of young children (Corteen & Williams, 1986).

However, the effects were slight and were not seen in older children. Perhaps, then, television viewing does interfere with reading achievement in young children. And, as our parents told us when we were young, trying to read with the television on in the background is not conducive to comprehension and learning (Armstrong & Chung, 2000).

● **What Should We Conclude?**

Although children spend a considerable amount of time watching television, the negative effects of their viewing appear to be negligible. Children do not appear to become mesmerized or overstimulated by television. Nor does television viewing appear to detract significantly from other activities that would stimulate children's cognitive development or substantially reduce their reading achievement.

However, the possibility exists that television programs could do more to stimulate children's cognitive development. We have focused on the potential *harm* that may be done by watching television, not on the potential *good* that could be achieved through this medium. Educational programs and other shows that take into account children's developmental needs would seem to be especially conducive to the stimulation of children's imagination, creativity, language skills, and prosocial behavior. This, of course, is a hypothesis, and like the hypothesis of negative effects, would need to be empirically tested.

Interim Summary

Cognitive Development in Infancy and Childhood

The first step in a child's cognitive development is learning that many events are contingent on his or her own behavior. This understanding occurs gradually and is controlled by the development of the nervous system and by increasingly complex interactions with the environment.

Piaget hypothesized that a child's cognitive development is divided into four periods. The periods are determined by the joint influences of the child's experiences with the physical and social environment and the maturation of the child's nervous system. An infant's earliest cognitive abilities are closely tied to the external stimuli in the immediate environment; objects exist for the infant only when they are present. Gradually, infants learn that objects exist even when hidden. The development of a grasp of object permanence leads to the ability to represent things symbolically, which is a prerequisite for the use of language. Next to develop is the ability to perform logical transformations on concepts. A key aspect of these transformations is that that they are reversible. Piaget designated these transformations as concrete operations and felt that their appearance was accompanied by the recognition that some properties were preserved across physical transformations. Around the age of 11, a child develops more adultlike cognitive abilities—abilities that may allow the child to solve difficult problems by means of abstract reasoning, or formal operations.

Critics point out that in some cases Piaget's tests of cognitive development underestimated children's abilities. For example, if tested appropriately, it is evident that children understand the conservation of various properties earlier than Piaget thought, and that their egocentrism is less pronounced than his tests indicated. Nevertheless, his conclusions continue to have a profound impact on the field of child development.

Vygotsky's writings and the research they have stimulated have showed that the sociocultural context in which children grow up has a significant impact on their cognitive development. In particular, language appears to influence how children learn to think, solve problems, formulate plans, make decisions, and contemplate ideas.

Information-processing accounts of cognitive development have been developed more recently. These accounts describe how cognitive development proceeds according to the brain's information-processing capacity. Capacity expands because of three factors: brain maturation, practice using schemas, and the integration of schemas for different objects and events. Such models essentially reinterpret Piaget's theory in the language of information processing.

Along with increased capacity to process information, children also acquire notions about physical and psychological causes. Even young infants demonstrate some knowledge about physical laws, and by the time they are four years old, children can reason about the mental beliefs of others. Luo and Baillargeon have suggested that knowledge of the physical domain develops incrementally.

A survey of the scientific literature by Anderson and Collins made the medium of television look like less of a threat to children's cognitive development than many people believe. Studies that actually examined the viewing behavior of children rather than speculating about television's harmful effects showed that children are not passive recipients of whatever the medium offers them. They watch what interests them and look away at other times, and they engage in a variety of other behaviors while sitting in front of the set. Fortunately, children are more discerning in their watching than many people have believed.

QUESTIONS TO CONSIDER

1. In a Question to Consider earlier in this chapter, I asked you to design a home environment that would facilitate your child's motor and perceptual development. How might you also construct that environment to facilitate your child's cognitive development? What types of toys would you give your child, and what kinds of personal interactions would you want to have with him or her?

2. Suppose that you want to develop a test for determining which of Piaget's periods of cognitive development a child

is in. What kinds of activities would you include in such a test, and how would the child's behavior with respect to those activities indicate the child's stage of development?

Social Development in Infancy and Childhood

The first adults with whom infants interact are usually their parents. In most families one parent serves as the primary caregiver. As many studies have shown, a close relationship called *attachment* is extremely important for infants' social development. **Attachment** is a social and emotional bond between infant and caregiver. It involves both the warm feelings that the parent and child have for each other and the comfort and support they provide for each other, which become especially important during times of fear or stress. This interaction must work both ways, with each participant fulfilling certain needs of the other. Formation of a strong and durable bond depends on the behavior of both people in the relationship. According to theorist John Bowlby (1907–1990), the innate capacity for the development of attachment is a part of the native endowment of many organisms (Bowlby, 1969, 1988). Bowlby and Mary Ainsworth have developed an approach that has succeeded in identifying many of the variables that influence attachment in humans (Ainsworth & Bowlby, 1991). We are going to look at what Bowlby, Ainsworth, and other researchers have learned about human attachment.

Be mindful that cultural variables strongly influence the development of attachment. Interactions between infant and

▲ *Attachment is the cornerstone of an infant's social development, and it has important implications for the parent's social behavior as well.*

parent produce different sorts of attachment behaviors that vary from culture to culture. For example, in an extensive comparison of cross-cultural attachment patterns, Harwood (Harwood, Miller, & Irizarry, 1995; Miller & Harwood, 2002) found that white American mothers want their children to be self-sustaining individuals and so emphasize independence, self-reliance, and self-confidence in their interactions with their children. In contrast, Puerto Rican mothers want their children to be polite and law-abiding and thus stress the importance of respect, courtesy, interdependence, and tact in interacting with their children.

Behaviors of the Infant That Foster Attachment

Newborn infants rely completely on their parents (or other caregivers) to supply them with nourishment, keep them warm and clean, and protect them from harm. And nearly all parents anticipate the birth of a child with the expectation that they will love and cherish their baby; when a child is born, most parents do exactly that. As time goes on, and as parent and child interact, they become strongly attached to each other. What factors cause this attachment to occur? Evidence suggests that human infants are innately able to produce special behaviors that shape and even control the behavior of their caregivers. As Bowlby (1969) noted, the most important of these behaviors are sucking, cuddling, looking, smiling, and crying.

Sucking

A baby must be able to suck in order to obtain milk. But not all sucking is related to nourishment. Piaget (1952) noted that infants often suck on objects even when they are not hungry. Nonnutritive sucking appears to be an innate behavioral tendency in infants that serves to inhibit a baby's distress. In modern societies most mothers cover their breasts between feedings or feed with a bottle, so a baby's nonnutritive sucking must involve inanimate objects or the baby's own thumb.

Cuddling

Infants of all species of primates have special reflexes that encourage front-to-front contact with their mothers. For example, a baby monkey clings to its mother shortly after birth. This clinging leaves the mother free to use her hands and feet. Human infants are carried by their parents and do not hold on by themselves. However, infants do adjust their posture to mold themselves to the contours of the parent's body. This cuddling response plays an important role in reinforcing the behavior of the caregiver.

Psychologist Harry Harlow (1905–1981) conducted a series of experiments on infant monkeys and showed that clinging to a soft, cuddly form appears to be an innate response (Harlow, 1974). Harlow and his colleagues isolated baby monkeys from their mothers immediately after birth and raised them alone in cages containing two mechanical surrogate mothers. One surrogate mother was made of bare

wire mesh but contained a bottle that provided milk. The other surrogate was padded and covered with terry cloth but provided no nourishment.

The babies preferred to cling to the cuddly surrogate and went to the wire model only to eat. If they were frightened, they would rush to the cloth-covered model for comfort. These results suggest that close physical contact with a cuddly object is a biological need for a baby monkey, just as food and drink are. A baby monkey clings to and cuddles with its mother because the contact is innately reinforcing, not simply because she provides food.

Looking

In human infants, looking serves as a signal to parents: Even very young infants seek eye-to-eye contact with their parents. If a parent does not respond when eye contact is made, the baby usually shows signs of distress. Tronick and colleagues (1978) observed face-to-face interactions between mothers and their infants. When the mothers approached their babies, they typically smiled and began talking in a gentle, high-pitched voice. In return, infants smiled and stretched their arms and legs. The mothers poked and gently jiggled their babies, making faces at them. The babies responded with facial expressions, wiggles, and noises of their own.

To determine whether the interaction was really two-sided, the researchers had each mother approach her baby while keeping her face expressionless or masklike. At first, the infant made the usual greetings, but when the mother did not respond, the infant turned away. (See **Figure 12•8**.) From time to time the infant would look at her again, giving a brief smile, but again would turn away when the mother continued to stare without changing her expression. These interactions were recorded on videotape and were scored by raters who did not know the purpose of the experiment, so the results were not biased by the researchers' expectations.

Every mother found it difficult to resist her baby's invitation to interact. In fact, some of the mothers broke down and smiled back. Most of the mothers who managed to hold out (for three minutes) later apologized to their babies, saying something like, "I am real again. It's all right. You can trust me again. Come back to me" (Tronick et al., 1978, p. 10). This study clearly showed that the looking behavior of an infant is an invitation for the mother to respond.

Smiling

By the time an infant is five weeks old, visual stimuli begin to dominate as elicitors for smiling. A face (especially a moving one) is a more reliable elicitor of a baby's smile than a voice is; even a moving mask will cause an infant to smile. At approximately three months of age, specific faces—those of people to whom the infant has become attached—will elicit smiles. The significance of these observations should be obvious. An infant's smile is very rewarding. Almost every parent reports that parenting becomes a real joy when the baby starts to smile as the parent approaches—the infant is now a "person."

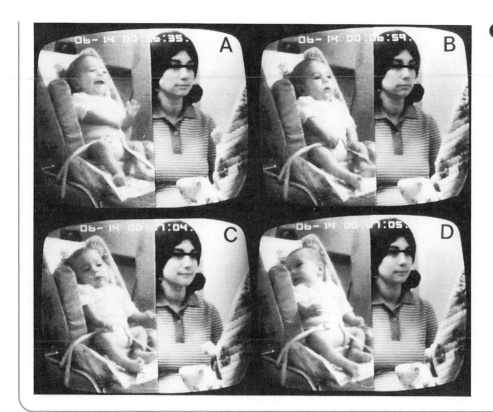

FIGURE 12·8 Reaction of an infant to its mother's expressionless face. Although each panel shows mother and infant side by side, they actually faced each other. The infant greets the mother with a smile and, getting no response, eventually turns away from her.

(From Tronick, E., Als, H., Adamson, L., Wise, S., & Brazelton, T. B. The infant's response to entrapment between contradictory messages in face-to-face interaction. *Journal of the American Academy of Child Psychiatry*, 1978, *17*, 1–13. © 1978 American Academy of Child Psychiatry.)

Crying For almost any adult, the sound of an infant's crying is intensely distressing or irritating. For a baby the event that most effectively terminates crying is being picked up and cuddled, although unless the baby is fed and made more comfortable, he or she will soon begin crying again. Because picking up the baby stops the crying, the parent learns through negative reinforcement (see Chapter 5) to pick up the infant when he or she cries. Thus, crying serves as a useful means for a cold, hungry, colicky, or wet child to obtain assistance.

The nature of the *onset* of crying seems to provide North American caregivers with important information. If a baby suddenly begins crying intensely, caregivers are more likely to assume that the baby is afraid or in pain. If the cry begins more gradually, caregivers suspect hunger, sleepiness, or the need for a diaper change. Individual differences in how caregivers perceive distress in an infant's crying is another important quality that determines adult reactions and is influenced by context and expectations. Wood and Gustafson (2001), for example, found that adults responded more quickly to infant cries that they personally interpreted as communicating distress; they somewhat inhibited their response to the same cries if they believed the infant needed sleep.

Although an infant's behavioral repertoire is limited, it is apparent that a complex process is at work. At a very early age, perhaps through innate mechanisms, infants perform behaviors that their adult caregivers find reinforcing. The baby, in other words, is partially teaching the parent. From the baby's perspective, what is the object of this? Evolutionary psychologists would respond that the baby is teaching the parent to behave in ways that enhance the baby's chances to survive and eventually reproduce.

The Nature and Quality of Attachment

For an infant the world can be a frightening place. The presence of a primary caregiver provides a baby with considerable reassurance when he or she first becomes able to explore the environment. Although the unfamiliar environment produces fear, the caregiver provides a secure base that the infant can leave from time to time to see what the world is like. Let's look at two categories of behavior that develop as infants explore their world: first, stranger anxiety and separation anxiety; and second, reactions to strange situations.

Stranger Anxiety and Separation Anxiety Babies are born prepared to become attached to their primary caregivers, which in most cases are their mothers. Attachment appears to be a behavior pattern that is necessary for normal development (Ainsworth, 1973; Bowlby, 1973). However, although attachment appears to be an inherited disposition, infants do not have a natural inclination to become attached to any one specific adult. Rather, the person to whom the baby becomes attached is determined through learning; the individual who serves as the infant's primary caregiver is usually the object of the attachment.

Attachment partially reveals itself in two specific forms of infant behavior: stranger anxiety and separation anxiety.

Stranger anxiety, which usually appears in infants between the ages of 6 and 12 months, consists of wariness and sometimes fearful responses, such as crying and clinging to their caregivers, that infants exhibit in the presence of strangers. **Separation anxiety** is a set of fearful responses, such as crying, arousal, and clinging to the caregiver, that an infant exhibits when the caregiver attempts to leave the infant. Separation anxiety first appears in infants when they are about 6 months old and generally peaks at about 15 months—a finding consistent across many cultures (Kagan, Kearsley, & Zelazo, 1978). Like stranger anxiety, separation anxiety can occur under different conditions with different degrees of intensity. For example, if an infant is used to being left in a certain environment, say a day-care center, he or she may show little or no separation anxiety (Maccoby, 1980). The same holds true for situations in which the infant is left with a sibling or other familiar person (Bowlby, 1969). However, if the same infant is left in an unfamiliar setting with unfamiliar people, he or she is likely to show separation anxiety (Bowlby, 1982). Familiarity, then, at least for infants, breeds attachment.

Ainsworth's Strange Situation
Ainsworth and her colleagues (Ainsworth, Blehar, Waters, & Wall, 1978) developed a test of attachment based on unfamiliar situations called the **Strange Situation**. The Strange Situation is a standardized test that consists of a series of eight episodes, during which a baby is exposed to various events that might cause some distress related to attachment and security. In different episodes the researcher introduces the infant and its parent to an unfamiliar playroom and then leaves, the parent leaves and later is reunited with the infant, or a stranger enters the playroom with or without the parent present. The Strange Situation is based on the idea that if the attachment process has been successful, an infant should use his or her mother as a secure base from which to explore an unfamiliar environment. The episodes permit the observation of separation anxiety, stranger anxiety, and the baby's reactions to comforting by both the parent and the stranger. The use of the Strange Situation led Ainsworth and her colleagues to identify three patterns of attachment; a fourth was identified later by Main and Solomon (1990). **Secure attachment** is the ideal pattern: The infants show a distinct preference for their caregiver over the stranger. Infants may cry when their caregiver leaves, but they stop crying and seek contact when she returns. The majority of babies form a secure attachment. Babies may also form three types of insecure attachments. Babies with **resistant attachment** show tension in their relations with their caregiver. Infants stay close to their caregiver before the caregiver leaves but show both approach and avoidance behaviors when the caregiver returns. Infants continue to cry for a while after their caregiver returns and may even push them away. Infants with **avoidant attachment** generally do not cry when they are left alone, and they tend to react to strangers much as they react to their caregiver. When their caregiver returns, these infants are likely to avoid or ignore her. They tend not to cling and cuddle when they are picked up. Babies with

disoriented attachment are the least attached and appear to be the most troubled. They react to their caregiver in confused and contradictory ways. They may stop crying when held, but they may show no emotion on their faces, turn their heads away from their caregiver, or become rigid. A common way of describing the emotional tone of such infants is that they appear dazed.

Although infants' personalities certainly affect the nature of their interactions with their caregivers and hence the nature of their attachment, mothers' behavior appears to be the most important factor in establishing a secure or insecure attachment (Ainsworth, Blehar, Waters, & Wall, 1978; Pederson, Gleason, Moran, & Bento, 1998; Pederson & Moran, 1996). Mothers of *securely* attached infants tend to be those who respond promptly to their crying and who are adept at handling them and responding to their needs. The babies apparently learn that their mothers can be trusted to react sensitively and appropriately. Mothers who do not modulate their responses according to their infants' own behavior— who appear insensitive to their infants' changing needs—are most likely to foster *avoidant* attachment. Mothers who are impatient with their infants and who seem more interested in their own activities than in interacting with their offspring tend to foster *resistant* attachment. There is some evidence that mothers who interfere with their infants' behaviors, but without sensitivity to their infants' needs, are likely to foster disoriended attachment (Carlson, 1998).

There is good evidence that the type of attachment formed during infancy has implications for later life (Belsky & Cassidy, 1994; Belsky & Fearon, 2002). For example, the nature of attachment during infancy seems to produce an enduring trace in how people form relationships with others, at least through early adulthood (e.g., Waters et al., 2000). Adults who were securely attached as infants remember their childhood in more positive terms and value attachment relationships more than those who were insecurely attached.

Of course, mothers are not the only people who can form close attachments with infants; so do fathers (see Parke, 2000) and other adults who interact with them. Parke and Tinsley (1981), for example, observed that fathers are just as likely as mothers to touch, talk to, and kiss their babies. However, when the mother serves as the primary caregiver, fathers tend to play somewhat different roles. In general, they tend to engage in more physical games, lifting, tossing, and bouncing their babies. This difference may account for the fact that babies tend to seek out their mothers when they are distressed but look for their fathers when they want to play (Clarke-Stewart, 1978).

In our culture secure attachment would seem to be more adaptive in terms of getting along with both peers and adults than would insecure attachment. It has become clear that attachment plays an influential role in social relationships, including those that we form in adolescence and adulthood, such as romantic love (Feeney & Noller, 1991). Among women, insecure attachment in infancy seems to be correlated with clinical depression and difficulties in coping with stress in adult life (Barnas, Pollina, & Cummings, 1991).

Effects of Child Day Care   This recognition of the importance of attachment inevitably leads to the question of whether child day care has deleterious effects on a child's development. In recent decades many families have entrusted their infants to day care because both parents work. In 2004, for example, 53 percent of mothers of children younger than one year were employed outside the home (United States Department of Labor, 2005). Thus, because so many infants spend many of their waking hours away from their families, the question of the effects of day care is not simply academic.

Without question, the quality of care provided in a day-care setting is critical (Zaslow, 1991). High-quality day care either produces no impairment of attachment or actually benefits social development (Broberg, Wessels, Lamb, & Hwang, 1997; Field, 1994; National Institute of Child Health and Human Development, 1997), although it is difficult to generalize this conclusion across the full range of day care programs available, because this latter issue is measured by correlational methods (NICHD Early Child Care Research Network, 2003). Nevertheless, high-quality day care is expensive, and there are not enough subsidized spaces available for all of the families that need them. Worldwide, the day care available to low-income families is generally of lower quality than that available to middle- or upper-income families. Regrettably, the infants who receive the poorest day care tend to be members of unstable households, often headed by single mothers. Thus, they are at risk of receiving a double dose of less-than-optimal care.

Interactions with Peers

Although the attachment between an infant and his or her primary caregiver is the most important social interaction in early life, a child's social development also involves other people. A normal infant develops attachments with other adults, and with older siblings if there are any. But interaction with peers—children of a similar age—is especially important to social development.

Harlow and his colleagues (e. g., Harlow, 1974) showed that social contact with peers is essential to an infant monkey's social development. An infant monkey that is raised with only a cuddly surrogate mother can still develop into a reasonably normal adult if it has peers to play with. However, an isolated monkey that does not interact with other juveniles before puberty shows severe deficits. When a previously isolated adolescent monkey is introduced to a colony of normally reared age mates, it will retreat with terror and huddle in a corner in a desperate attempt to hide.

Approaches to Child Rearing

When I discussed the cognitive development theory of Vygotsky, I mentioned his concept of the *zone of proximal development*—the idea that a child's cognitive functioning can be increased by effective mentoring. Of course, it is usually the case that a child's closest mentor is one or both parents. Our

▲ *Notwithstanding the importance of attachment, high quality day care can benefit social development.*

consideration of social development has emphasized the way the child and the parents affect each other. A family, in other words, is a type of *system* in which the members have interacting roles. The parents provide the support for the child's attachment. However, the child also controls much of the parent's behavior through reactions that are intrinsically reinforcing. It is a developmental partnership.

As Vygotsky recognized, the child–parent partnership works best when the parent provides **scaffolding** for the child's development. Scaffolding is the matching of the mentor's efforts to the child's developmental level. For example, a mother practicing scaffolding provides guidance when the child requires it, but also allows the child to innovate and apply new skills to new situations. When well practiced, scaffolding is generally the most effective form of parent–child instruction or mentoring (Meadows, 1996).

Social adjustment is a type of skill, and it is interesting to consider what type of child-rearing practices best support its development. The notion of scaffolding would imply that there must be certain approaches to parenting that will work best in the child–parent partnership. What might those approaches be?

Parents seem to adopt one of four approaches when raising their children: authoritarian, permissive, authoritative, or indifferent (Baumrind, 1983, 1991). *Authoritarian parents* establish firm rules and expect them to be obeyed without question. Disobedience is met with punishment. *Permissive parents* adopt the opposite strategy: They impose few rules and do little to influence their children's behavior. *Authoritative parents* also establish rules and enforce them, but not merely through punishment. Instead, they seek to explain the relationship between the rules and punishment. Authoritative parents also allow for exceptions to the rules. They set rules not as absolute or inflexible laws, but rather as general behavioral guidelines. *Indifferent parents* exhibit a lack of interest in their children's behavior, to the point of possible neglect.

Suppose that a 10-year-old boy has just broken a neighbor's window by accidentally hitting it with a ball. How would the four kinds of parents react to the child? Perhaps it would go something like this:

Authoritarian parents: "You know better than that! Don't you ever play with a ball in the yard again. Now go to your bedroom and don't come out until I tell you to. And I'm withholding your allowance until the window is paid for."

Permissive parents: "Well, don't worry about it. These things happen; it was an accident. I'll talk to our neighbor."

Authoritative parents: "You know better than that—you agreed not to play with the ball in the yard. Now you know why we made that rule. Go get the broom and the dustpan and offer to clean up this mess. When you finish, go to your bedroom and wait for me. I want to talk to you some more about how we're going to pay for the window."

Indifferent parents: "Now you're in trouble. I don't care what you do about it, but just don't come crying to me about it!"

Not surprisingly, authoritarian parents tend to have children who are more unhappy and distrustful than are children of permissive or authoritative parents. You might imagine that children of permissive parents would be the most likely to be self-reliant and curious. Not so. In fact, they appear to be the least so, probably because they never received parental encouragement and guidance for developing these sorts of behaviors. Rather, they are left on their own without the benefit of learning directly from an adult's experience and without the guidance needed to learn self-control. Authoritative parents bring up their children in an environment in which individuality and personal responsibility are encouraged, and so they tend to rear children who are self-controlled, independent, and socially competent. Psychologically, then, one important element in raising happy and independent children is an open line of communication between parent and child. As you might expect, children of indifferent parents tend to be the least competent (Baumrind, 1991).

Interim Summary

Social Development in Infancy and Childhood

Because babies are totally dependent on their parents, the development of attachment between parent and infant is crucial to the infant's survival. A baby has the innate ability to shape and reinforce the behavior of the parent. To a large extent, the baby is the parent's teacher. In turn, parents reinforce the baby's behavior, which facilitates the development of a durable attachment between them.

Some of the behaviors that babies possess innately are sucking, cuddling, looking, smiling, and crying. These behaviors promote parental responses and are instrumental in satisfying physiological needs.

Normally, infants show both stranger anxiety and separation anxiety. They also tend to be afraid of novel stimuli, but the presence of their caregiver provides a secure base from which

they can explore new environments. Ainsworth's Strange Situation allows a researcher to determine the nature of the attachment between infant and caregiver. By using this test, several investigators have identified some of the variables—some involving infants and some involving mothers—that influence secure or insecure attachment. Fathers, as well as mothers, can form close attachments with infants. Excellent child care by outsiders will not harm a child's social development, but less-than-excellent child care, especially if it begins in the child's first year of life, can adversely affect attachment.

Development also involves the acquisition of social skills. Interaction with peers is probably the most important factor in social development among children and adolescents. However, a caregiver's style of parenting also can have strong effects on the social development of children and adolescents, especially when the caregiver engages in scaffolding. Authoritative parents, compared to authoritarian, permissive, and indifferent parents, tend to rear more competent, self-reliant, and independent children.

QUESTION TO CONSIDER

We know that attachment occurs in humans and other primates. Do you think it occurs in other species, especially other mammalian species, as well? What kind of evidence would you need to collect to say that it does? Could you develop a test like Harlow's for researching attachment in other species? Develop your answer with a specific species in mind; for example, cats or dogs.

Development of Gender Roles

Physical development as a male or a female is only one aspect of sexual development. The social side of sexual development also is important. **Gender identity** is a person's private sense of being male or female and consists primarily of the person's acceptance of membership in a particular group of people: males or females. Acceptance of this membership does not necessarily indicate acceptance of the gender roles or gender stereotypes that may accompany it. For example, a dedicated feminist may fight to change the rights and responsibilities of women in her society but still clearly identify herself as a woman. **Gender roles** are cultural expectations about the ways in which men and women should think and behave. Closely related to them are **gender stereotypes**—beliefs about differences between the behaviors, abilities, and personality traits of males and females. Society's gender stereotypes have an important influence on the behavior of its members. In fact, many people unconsciously develop their gender identity and gender roles based on gender stereotypes they learned as children. This section considers the part gender stereotypes play in influencing the nature and development of gender roles.

▲ *Many people acquire their gender identities and gender roles as a result of the gender stereotypes they learn as children.*

Berk (2002) notes that by age three many children perceive themselves as being a boy or a girl. At that same age, boys and girls (though girls more than boys) have a fairly good grasp of gender roles and stereotypes (e.g., O'Brien et al., 2000). In the process of learning what it means to be boys or girls, children associate, in a stereotypical manner, certain toys, games, attitudes, and behaviors, such as being aggressive or compliant, with one gender or the other (Huston, 1983; Jacklin & Maccoby, 1983; Picariello, Greenberg, & Pillemer, 1990). For example, consider an experiment conducted by Montemayor (1974), who invited children between the ages of six and eight to play a game that involved tossing marbles into a clown's body. Some of the children were told that they were playing a "girls' game," some were told it was a "boys' game," and others were told nothing. Boys and girls both said that the game was more fun when it had been described as appropriate to their gender, and they even attained better scores when it was.

Where do children learn gender stereotypes? Although a child's peer group and teachers are important, parents play an especially important role in the development of gender stereotypes (Deaux, 1999). For example, parents tend to encourage and reward their sons for playing with "masculine" toys such as cars and trucks and objects such as baseballs and footballs (Fagot & Hagan, 1991). And parents tend to encourage and reward their daughters for engaging in "feminine" activities that promote dependency, warmth, and sensitivity, such as playing house or hosting a make-believe tea party (Dunn, Bretherton, & Munn, 1987; Lytton & Romney, 1991). Parents who do not actively promote these kinds of stereotypical activities tend to have children whose attitudes and behavior reflect fewer gender stereotypes (Weisner & Wilson-Mitchell, 1990).

The Nature of Gender Differences

The origin and nature of gender differences has long been and is likely to continue to be a controversial topic in psychology (Eagly & Wood, 1999; Shibley Hyde & Plant, 1995; Wood & Eagly, 2005). Part of the controversy stems from the way differences between males and females are measured and the apparent magnitude of those differences, and part of it stems from the sociopolitical implications of the differences (for example, sexism). In this section we will consider only those differences that have strong empirical support at present.

Berk (2005) reviewed the research on gender differences and concludes that the most reliable differences are the following: On average, girls show earlier verbal development, more effective expression and interpretation of emotional cues, and a higher tendency to comply with adults and peers. Boys show stronger spatial abilities, more aggression, and greater tendency toward risk taking. Boys also are more likely to show developmental problems such as language disorders, behavior problems, or physical impairments.

These differences are unlikely to be wholly biologically determined. In fact, socialization undoubtedly has a strong influence. Gender differences for many psychological characteristics are small. For example, after reviewing scores obtained from the Wechsler Intelligence Scales and the California Achievement Tests between 1949 and 1985, Feingold (1993) concluded that cognitive gender differences were small or nonexistent in preadolescent children and small in adolescents. Deaux (1985) reported that on average only 5 percent of the variability in individual differences among children can be attributed to gender; the other 95 percent is due to individual genetic and environmental factors. Therefore, gender, by itself, is not a very good predictor of a person's talents, personality, or behavior.

Biology and Culture

The Causes of Gender Role Differences

As the text points out, children readily learn gender stereotypes and adopt the roles that society deems appropriate for their gender. Two causes—biology and culture—may be responsible.

● Biological Causes

One possible explanation for children's ready acceptance of gender roles focuses on biological differences. Perhaps some of the observed differences between males and females can be attributed to chromosomal differences or to the effects of sex hormones. After all, these factors produce differences in the bodies of males and females, so perhaps they could affect their behavior, too.

A likely site of biologically determined gender differences is the brain. Studies using laboratory animals have shown that the exposure of a developing brain to male sex hormones has long-term effects. The hormones alter the development of the brain and produce changes in the animals' behavior, even in adulthood (Carlson, 1995). In addition, the human brain shows some structural gender differences. These too are probably caused by exposure to different patterns of hormones during development (Kolb & Stewart, 1995), although the precise effects of these differences on the behavior of males and females are not well understood at present. As well, investigations using fMRI techniques show neural activation differences between men and women during navigation in a virtual maze; men show greater activation of the left hippocampus, and women show greater involvement of right hemispheric structures (Grön et al., 2000).

Gender differences in two types of cognitive ability—verbal ability and spatial ability—may be at least partly caused by differences in the brain. Girls tend to learn to speak and to read sooner than boys, and boys tend to be better at tasks requiring spatial perception. Kimura (1999) suggests possible reasons for these sex differences. When the human brain was evolving into its present form, our ancestors were hunter–gatherers, and men and women probably had different roles. Women, because of restrictions on their movements imposed by childbearing, were more likely to work near the home, performing fine manual skills with small objects. Men were more likely to range farther from home, engaging in activities that involved coordination of body movements with respect to distant objects, such as throwing rocks or spears or launching darts toward animals. In addition, men had to be able to keep track of where they were so they could return home after following animals for long distances.

These specializations may have favored the evolution of gender differences. In particular, we might expect women's movements to be better integrated with nearby objects, whereas men's movements might be better integrated with

objects located at a distance. And indeed, as I've mentioned, fMRI scans do suggest gender differences in neural activation during a maze task. If Kimura's (1999) reasoning is correct, it is easy to see why, on average, men's spatial abilities would be better than those of women. But why would females learn to speak and read sooner than males? Many researchers believe that our ancestors used hand gestures long before verbal communication developed. Kimura suggests that fine motor control and speech production are closely related—that the neural circuits that control the muscles we use for speech may be closely related to those we use to move our hands. Presumably, then, women would be better at both.

Buss (1995) argues that other differences in the adaptive challenges that men and women have faced in the course of evolution also have led to gender differences. As you learned in Chapter 3, chief among these adaptive challenges are issues tied to reproduction. For women, such challenges include identifying and attracting a mate who is willing to invest his resources (time, energy, property, food, and so on) in her and her children. For men, they include identifying and attracting a fertile mate who is willing to copulate with him. Buss argues that over the course of evolution, men and women have come to differ because the challenges posed by reproduction and child rearing require different strategies for their successful resolution.

Kimura's and Buss's accounts are based on evolutionary arguments that can only be tested indirectly. However, they provide a good example of the biological approach—in particular, the functional, evolutionary approach—to an understanding of human behavior.

● Cultural Causes

Although evolutionary forces may have laid the groundwork for gender differences in brain mechanisms associated with verbal ability and spatial ability, practice at and training in tasks involving these abilities can improve people's performance at them (Hoyenga & Hoyenga, 1993). In fact, most psychologists believe that socialization plays the most significant role in the establishment of gender role differences. First adults and then peers teach, by direct instruction and by example, what is expected of boys and girls. These expectations are deeply ingrained in our culture and unconsciously affect our perceptions and our behavior. When someone announces the birth of a baby, most of us immediately ask, "Is it a boy or a girl?" Parents often dress their infants in clothing that makes it easy for strangers to recognize the infant's gender. And once we find out a baby's sex, we interact with the child in subtly (and not so subtly) different ways.

For example, Condry and Condry (1976) showed college students video of a baby crying. The participants tended to see the crying as "angry" if they believed that the baby was a boy and "fearful" if they thought the baby was a girl. Obviously, these judgments were the results of their gender stereotypes and not of their perceptions.

The effect of gender on an adult's *perception* of infants is clear and has been confirmed in many studies. What about differences in the *behaviors* adults direct toward boys and girls? The strongest difference in the way parents socialize their sons and daughters appears to lie in their encouragement of gender-typed play and their choice of "gender-appropriate" toys. As I've mentioned, many parents encourage their boys to play with trucks, blocks, and other toys that can be manipulated; they encourage their girls to play with dolls. However, a cross-cultural review of 172 studies conducted in North America, Australia, and Western Europe concluded that parents do not consistently treat their sons and daughters differently in any other important ways (Lytton & Romney, 1991).

Although parents do encourage "gender-appropriate" play, there is evidence that biological factors may play an initial role in children's preferences. Although fathers are less likely to give dolls to one-year-old boys than to one-year-old girls, the boys who do receive the dolls are less likely to play with them (Snow, Jacklin, & Maccoby, 1983). Perhaps, as Lytton and Romney (1991) suggest, adults' expectations and encouragement build on children's innate tendencies, producing an amplifying effect. Then, because boys' toys provide more opportunity for developing motor skills, spatial skills, and inventiveness, and girls' toys provide more opportunity for nurturance and social exchange, some important differences in gender roles may become established.

Once children begin to play with other children outside the home, peers have a significant influence on the development of their gender roles. In fact, Stern and Karraker (1989) found that the behavior of two- to six-year-old children toward a baby was influenced by the children's knowledge of the baby's gender even more than was the behavior of adults. By the time children are three years old, they reinforce gender-typed play by praising, imitating, or joining in the behavior. In contrast, they criticize gender-inappropriate behavior (Langlois & Downs, 1980). Parents indirectly encourage gender-stereotyped play by seeking out children of the same gender as playmates for their children (Lewis, Young, Brooks, & Michalson, 1975).

Of course, all of the research I have cited in this section describes *tendencies* of parents and children to act in a particular way. Some parents make a conscious attempt to encourage their children's interest in both "masculine" and "feminine" activities, with the hope that doing so will help keep all opportunities for achievement and self-expression open to them, regardless of their gender.

Almost everywhere men and women are treated unequally. In most industrialized countries, laws prohibit overt sexual discrimination. But despite these laws women have more difficulty obtaining prestigious jobs, and the higher levels of government and industry tend to be dominated by men. Society may indeed be moving toward a time in which gender neither hinders nor favors a person's aspirations, but clearly this time has not yet arrived.

Interim Summary

Development of Gender Roles

Children's gender roles tend to conform to their society's gender stereotypes. Very few real differences exist between the sexes, and those that do are relatively small. Females tend to show earlier verbal development, are better at expressing emotion and interpreting emotional cues, and show more compliance with adults and peers. Males tend to have better spatial abilities, are more aggressive, and tend to take more risks.

Some of these differences may have biological roots. Kimura suggests that the different tasks performed by our ancestors shaped brain development and favored men with better spatial skills and women with better fine motor skills. Buss argues that challenges related to reproduction and child rearing have caused gender differences in how these challenges are solved. Socialization undoubtedly plays a significant part in gender role differences.

Research has shown that both parents and peers tend to encourage children to behave in "gender-appropriate" ways—especially with regard to play activities and toys. However, scientific studies have revealed few other reliable differences in the ways parents treat young boys and girls.

QUESTIONS TO CONSIDER

1. Can you imagine an alternative course of human evolution in which gender roles would have developed along different lines? What events in the course of human evolution could have happened (but did not, of course) that would have changed the nature of gender roles as we know them today?
2. Imagine that you were born the opposite gender—that instead of being a male, you are a female, or vice versa. In what significant ways would your life be different? For example, in what important ways would your social, emotional, and intellectual experiences be different? (Be careful not to base your answer on stereotypes you have of the other gender.)

Moral Development

The word *morality* comes from a Latin word that means "custom." Moral behavior is behavior that conforms to a generally acknowledged set of rules. With very few exceptions, by the time a person reaches adulthood, the person has accepted his or her culture's rules about personal and social behavior. These rules vary in different cultures and may take the form of codified laws or of informally accepted taboos (Chasdi, 1994). Let us begin our look at moral development by considering the way a child acquires a concept of morality. The pioneer in this field, as in cognitive development, was Jean Piaget.

Piaget's Theory of Moral Development

According to Piaget, the first stage of moral development (ages 5 to 10 years) is **moral realism,** which is characterized by egocentrism, or self-centeredness and blind adherence to rules. Egocentric children can evaluate events only in terms of their personal consequences. The behavior of children at this stage is not guided by the effects it might have on someone else, because young children are not capable of imagining themselves in the other person's place. Thus, in Piaget's view young children do not consider whether an act is right or wrong but only whether it is likely to have good or bad consequences for them personally. Punishment is a bad consequence, and the fear of punishment is the only real moral force at this age. A young child also believes that rules come from parents (or other authority figures, such as older children or God) and that rules cannot be changed.

As children mature, however, two changes occur. First, older children judge an act by the intentions of the actor as well as by the consequences of the act—unlike young children, who consider only an act's objective outcomes, not the subjective intent that lay behind the act. For example, Piaget told children two stories, one about John, who accidentally broke 15 cups, and another about Henry, who broke one cup while trying to do something that was forbidden to him. When young children were asked which of the two boys was the naughtiest, they said that John was, because he broke 15 cups. They did not take into account the fact that the act was entirely accidental, as more mature individuals would.

Second, as children mature cognitively, they become less egocentric. Their lack of egocentrism makes them more capable of empathy. Children who are no longer egocentric (older than age 7) can imagine how another person feels. This shift away from egocentrism means that children's behavior may be guided not merely by the effects their actions have on the children themselves but also by the effects they have on others. At around 10 years of age, children enter Piaget's second stage of moral development, **morality of cooperation.** During this stage rules become more flexible; the child is more empathic but also understands that many rules (such as those that govern games) are social conventions that may be altered by mutual consent.

Kohlberg's Theory of Moral Development

Piaget's description of moral development was considerably elaborated on by the psychologist Lawrence Kohlberg (1927–1987). Kohlberg studied boys between 10 and 17 years of age, and he studied the same boys over the course of several years. He presented the children with stories involving moral dilemmas. For example, one story described a man named Heinz whose wife was dying of a cancer that could be treated only by a medication discovered by a druggist living in the same town. The man could not afford the price demanded by the druggist, so the distraught man broke into the druggist's store and stole enough of the drug to save his wife's life. The boys were asked what Heinz should have done and why he should have done it. On the basis of his research, Kohlberg decided that moral development progressed through three levels, which he divided into seven stages. (See **Table 12•3**.)

Kohlberg's first two stages belong to the **preconventional level,** during which morality is externally defined. During stage 1, *morality of punishment and obedience,* children blindly obey authority and avoid punishment. When asked to decide what Heinz should do, children at this stage base their decisions on fears about Heinz's being punished for letting his wife die or for committing a crime. During stage 2, *morality of naive instrumental hedonism,* children make moral choices egocentrically, guided by the pleasantness or unpleasantness of the consequences of a behavior. Heinz's dilemma is reduced to a weighing of the probable risks and benefits of stealing the drug.

The next two stages belong to the **conventional level,** which includes an understanding that the social system has an interest in people's behavior. During stage 3, *morality of maintaining good relations,* children want to be regarded by people who know them as good, well-behaved children.

TABLE 12•3	Levels and Stages of Kohlberg's Theory of Moral Development	
Level and Stage	**Highlights**
Preconventional Level	
Stage 1: Morality of punishment and obedience	Avoidance of punishment
Stage 2: Morality of naive instrumental hedonism	Egocentric perspective; weighing of potential risks and benefits
Conventional Level	
Stage 3: Morality of maintaining good relations	Morality based on approval from others
Stage 4: Morality of maintaining social order	Morality defined by rules and laws
Postconventional Level	
Stage 5: Morality of social contracts	Recognition that societal rules are for the common good, although individual rights sometimes outweigh laws
Stage 6: Morality of universal ethical principles	Perception of societal laws and rules as based on ethical values
Stage 7: Morality of cosmic orientation	Adoption of values that transcend societal norms

Moral decisions are based on perceived social pressure; so either Heinz should steal the drug because people would otherwise regard him as heartless, or he should not steal it because they would regard him as a criminal. During stage 4, *morality of maintaining social order,* laws and moral rules are perceived as instruments for maintaining social order and, as such, must be obeyed. Thus, both protecting a life and respecting people's property are seen as rules that help maintain social order.

Kohlberg also described a final level of moral development—the **postconventional level,** during which people realize that moral rules reflect important underlying principles that apply to all situations and societies. During stage 5, *morality of social contracts,* people recognize that rules are social contracts, that not all authority figures are infallible, and that individual rights can sometimes take precedence over laws. During stage 6, *morality of universal ethical principles,* people perceive rules and laws as being justified by abstract ethical values, such as the value of human life and the value of dignity. In stage 7, the *morality of cosmic orientation,* people adopt values that transcend societal norms. This stage represents the zenith of moral development. As Kohlberg noted, only a very few people ever reach stage 7. In fact, Kohlberg believed that not all people reach the postconventional level of moral development.

Evaluation of Piaget's and Kohlberg's Theories of Moral Development

Piaget's and Kohlberg's theories have greatly influenced research on moral development, but they also have come under some criticism. For example, Piaget's research indicated that children in the first stage (moral realism) respond to the magnitude of a transgression rather than to the intent behind it. But even adults respond to the magnitude of a transgression, and rightly so. The theft of a few postage stamps by an office worker is not treated in the same way as the embezzlement of hundreds of thousands of dollars.

Kohlberg's conclusions also have been challenged. For example, Sobesky (1983) found that changes in the wording of Heinz's dilemma would drastically change people's responses. If a researcher underscored the possibility of imprisonment, study participants tended to make more responses belonging to the preconventional level. Similarly, Carpendale (2000) points out that it is not uncommon for people to perform at less than their highest level of achieved moral reasoning, although Kohlberg believed that people would use lower levels only if extreme conditions undermined their higher moral sense. Many researchers agree with Rest (1979), who concluded that Kohlberg's "stages" are not coherent entities but do describe a progression in the ability of children to engage in more and more complex moral reasoning.

A different type of criticism was leveled by Carol Gilligan (1982), who suggested that Kohlberg's theory is gender biased. According to her, Kohlberg's studies indicated that men (in general) adhered to universal ethical principles, whereas women (in general) preferred to base their moral judgments on the effects these judgments would have on the people involved. Men's judgments were based more on abstract ideas of *justice,* whereas women's judgments were based more on concrete considerations of *caring and concern for relationships.*

However, most researchers have *not* found that men's and women's moral judgments tend to be based on different types of values (see Walker, de Vries, & Trevethan, 1994). For example, Donenberg and Hoffman (1988) found that boys and girls were equally likely to base their moral judgments on justice or caring and that the gender of the main character in the moral dilemma had no effect on their judgments. Walker (1989) tested 233 participants ranging in ages from 5 to 63 years and found no reliable gender differences. Thus, the available evidence does not appear to support Gilligan's conclusion that moral values are related to a person's gender.

Interim Summary

Moral Development

Piaget suggested that moral development consists of two principal stages: moral realism, characterized by egocentrism and blind adherence to rules, and morality of cooperation, characterized by empathy and a realization that behavior is judged by the effects it has on others. Kohlberg suggested that moral development consists of three levels, each further divided into stages. During the preconventional level, morality is based on the personal consequences of an act. During the conventional level, morality is based on the need to be well regarded and on sharing a common interest in social order. During the postconventional level, which is achieved by only a few people, morality becomes an abstract, philosophical virtue.

Critics of Piaget and Kohlberg point out that the stages of moral development are, to a certain degree, products of the measuring instruments. Subtle changes in the way that moral dilemmas are posed can produce very different responses from research participants. One criticism—that the theories attribute a different basis of moral judgments to men and women—has not been supported.

QUESTION TO CONSIDER

Laticia's parents are going away for the weekend and ask her to go with them. Laticia, who is 15 years old, says that she can't go because she has a special soccer practice on Saturday. Disappointed, her parents accept her answer; they agree to let her stay home, because they know how important soccer is to her. Later, after they return, they learn that Laticia lied to them about the practice. When they confront her, she tells them that she knows that she lied to them but that she did it so as not to hurt their feelings—she really did not want to go away with them for the weekend. Laticia's parents say that they understand her dilemma but that they feel they must punish her anyway for breaking an important family rule. How do you suppose that Piaget and Kohlberg would explain Laticia's level of morality? How would they explain her parents' level of morality?

Adolescence

After childhood comes adolescence, the threshold to adulthood. (In Latin, *adolescere* means "to grow up.") The transition between childhood and adulthood is as much social as it is biological. In some societies people are considered to be adults as soon as they are sexually mature, at which time they may assume adult rights and responsibilities, including marriage. In most industrialized societies, in which formal education often continues into the late teens and early twenties, adulthood officially comes several years later. The end of adolescence is difficult to judge, because the line between adolescence and young adulthood is fuzzy: There are no distinct physical changes that mark this transition. In this section we'll explore the physical, social, and cognitive changes that mark the adolescent years.

Physical Development

Puberty (from the Latin *puber*, meaning "adult"), the period during which people's reproductive systems mature, marks the beginning of the transition from childhood to adulthood. Many physical changes occur during this stage: People reach their ultimate height, develop increased muscle size and body hair, and become capable of reproduction.

Sexual Maturation The internal sex organs and genitalia do not change much for several years after birth, but they begin to develop again at puberty. When boys and girls reach about 11 to 14 years of age, their testes or ovaries secrete hormones that begin the process of sexual maturation. This activity of the gonads is initiated by the hypothalamus, the part of the brain to which the pituitary gland is attached. The hypothalamus instructs the pituitary gland to secrete hormones, which in turn stimulate the gonads to secrete sex hormones. These sex hormones act on various organs of the body and initiate the changes that accompany sexual maturation.

The sex hormones secreted by the gonads cause growth and maturation of the external genitalia and of the gonads themselves. In addition, these hormones cause the maturation of ova and the production of sperm. All of these structures are considered *primary sex characteristics*, because they are essential to the ability to reproduce. The sex hormones also stimulate the development of *secondary sex characteristics*, the physical changes that distinguish males from females. Before puberty, boys and girls look much the same—except, perhaps, for their

hairstyles and clothing. At puberty, adolescent males' testes begin to secrete testosterone; this hormone causes their muscles to develop, their facial hair to grow, and their voices to deepen. Females' ovaries secrete estradiol, the most important estrogen, or female sex hormone. Estradiol causes women's breasts to grow and their pelvises to widen, and it produces changes in the layer of fat beneath the skin and in the texture of the skin itself.

Development of the adult secondary sex characteristics takes several years, and not all characteristics develop at the same time. The process begins in girls at around age 11. The first visible change is the accumulation of fatty tissue around the nipples, followed shortly by the growth of pubic hair. The spurt of growth in height commences, and the uterus and vagina begin to enlarge. The first menstrual period, menarche, begins at around age 12 on average—at about the time a girl's rate of growth in height begins to decline. In boys sexual maturation begins slightly later. The first visible event is the growth of the testes and scrotum, followed by the appearance of pubic hair. A few months later the penis begins to grow, and the spurt of growth in height starts. The larynx grows larger, which causes the voice to become lower. Sexual maturity in males occurs at around age 15. The growth of facial hair usually occurs later; often a full beard does not grow until the late teens or early twenties.

In industrialized societies the average age at the onset of puberty has been declining. For example, girls' average age at the onset of menstruation was between 14 and 15 years in 1900 but is between 11 and 13 years today. The most important reason for this decline is better childhood nutrition. It appears that this decline is leveling off in industrialized societies, but in many developing countries the age of the onset of puberty is beginning to fall as these countries enjoy increasing prosperity.

Behavioral Effects of Puberty The changes that accompany sexual maturation have a profound effect on young people's behavior and self-concept. They become more sensitive about their appearance. Many girls worry about their weight

▲ *The transition between childhood and adulthood is as much social as it is biological.*

TABLE 12•4	Erikson's Eight Stages of Psychosocial Development		
Period	**Stage**	**Outcome**	
		Positive Resolution	**Negative Resolution**
Childhood	1. Crisis of trust vs. mistrust 2. Crisis of autonomy vs. self-doubt 3. Crisis of initiative vs. guilt 4. Crisis of competence vs. inferiority	Trust, security, confidence, independence, curiosity, competence, industry	Insecurity, doubt, guilt, low self-esteem, sense of failure
Adolescence	5. Crisis of identity vs. role confusion	Strong sense of self-identity	Weak sense of self
Adulthood	6. Crisis of intimacy vs. isolation 7. Crisis of generativity vs. stagnation 8. Crisis of integrity vs. despair	Capacity to develop deep and meaningful relationships and care for others; consideration for future generations; personal sense of worth and satisfaction	Isolation, unhappiness, selfishness, stagnancy, sense of failure and regret

and the size of their breasts and hips. Many boys worry about their height, the size of their genitals, their muscular development, and the growth of their beards. In addition, most adolescents display a particular form of egocentrism that develops early in the transition into the stage of formal operations: *self-consciousness*. Some developmental psychologists believe that self-consciousness results from teenagers' difficulty in distinguishing their own self-perceptions from the views other people have of them.

Because the onset of puberty occurs at different times in different individuals, young adolescents can find themselves more or less mature than some of their friends, and this difference can have important social consequences. An early study by Jones and Bayley (1950) found that early-maturing boys tended also to become more socially mature and were most likely to be perceived as leaders by their peers. Late-maturing boys tended to become hostile and withdrawn and often engaged in negative attention-getting behavior. Later studies have generally confirmed these findings (Brooks-Gunn, 1988; Peterson, 1985). The effect of age of maturity in girls is less clear. Some studies indicate that early-maturing girls may benefit from higher status and prestige; but they also are more likely to engage in norm-breaking behaviors such as stealing, cheating on exams, staying out late, and using alcohol (Brooks-Gunn, 1989). Brooks-Gunn suggests that the primary cause of the norm-breaking behaviors is the fact that early-maturing girls are more likely to become friends with older girls.

Social Development

During adolescence a person's behavior and social roles change dramatically. As a child, a person is dependent on parents, teachers, and other adults. As an adolescent, he or she is expected to assume more responsibility. Relations with peers also suddenly change; members of a teenager's own sex become potential rivals for the attention of members of the other sex. Adolescence is not simply a continuation of childhood, then; it marks a real transition from the dependency of childhood to

the relative independence of adulthood. Adolescence is also a period during which many young people seek out new experiences and engage in reckless behavior—behavior that involves psychological, physical, and legal risks for them as well as for others, such as driving too fast, having sexual relations, or using illegal drugs (Arnett, 1995). These behaviors often reflect the great challenges teenagers face as they search for an identity, focus on self-perceptions, cope with their emerging sexuality, and adjust to new relationships with peers and parents.

Forming an Identity You have probably heard the term "identity crisis," as in "She's having an identity crisis." The phrase was coined by Erik Erikson, a psychoanalyst who studied with Anna Freud, Sigmund Freud's daughter. Based on his observations of patients in his psychoanalytical practice and on his research with children, Erikson developed a theory of psychosocial development that divides human development into eight stages. Erikson proposed that people encounter a series of crises or conflicts in their social relations with other people and that the way these conflicts are resolved determines the nature of development. In fact, according to Erikson, the resolution of these conflicts *is* development. If a given conflict is resolved positively, the outcome is happy; if it is not resolved or is resolved negatively, the outcome is unhealthy and impairs development. Because the nature of people's social relations changes throughout life, their psychosocial development does not end when they become adults. **Table 12•4** lists Erikson's eight stages of development, the nature of the crisis that defines each stage, and the possible consequences.

Erikson argued that the primary crisis faced by adolescents is identity versus role confusion. If young people are able to develop plans for accomplishing career and personal goals and to decide which social groups they belong to, they have formed a personal identity. Failure to form an identity leaves a teenager confused about his or her role in life.

Erikson's concept of the identity crisis has been researched extensively by Marcia (1980, 1994; Bradley & Marcia, 1998), who has asserted that developing an identity consists of two components, crisis and commitment. A *crisis* is a period during which an adolescent struggles intellectually to resolve issues related to personal values and goals. For example, a teenager who questions his or her parents' religious and moral values is experiencing a crisis. *Commitment* is a decision based on consideration of alternative values and goals that leads to a specific course of action. For instance, a teenager who decides to go to a different religious institution than his or her parents is said to make a commitment. In this case, the teenager also is said to identify with the beliefs of that institution.

Marcia hypothesized that adolescents experience different degrees and combinations of crisis and commitment. Some teenagers never experience crises, and others do but may never resolve them. Marcia developed four main possibilities, which he called *identity statuses* (see **Figure 12•9**). As shown in the figure, in Marcia's model adolescents who experience a crisis, consider alternative solutions to it, and are committed to a course of action based on personal values are said to be *identity achievers*. Identity achievers are self-confident and have a high level of moral development (Dellas & Jernigan, 1990). Adolescents who experience a crisis but do not resolve it and therefore cannot become committed are said to be in *moratorium*. Teenagers who are in moratorium will express doubts about an identity but are still seeking information regarding it. Adolescents who have not experienced a crisis but who are nonetheless committed to a course of action are said to be in *foreclosure*. Teenagers in foreclosure are typically adolescents who identify strongly with people such as their parents and never consider alternatives to those identities. They can be dogmatic in their views and may feel threatened by others who challenge their identities (Frank, Pirsch, & Wright, 1990). Adolescents who do not experience a crisis and who do not become committed are said to experience *identity diffusion*. Teenagers who are identity diffused, especially over a long period, tend to be immature and impulsive and to have a sense of hopelessness about the future (Archer & Waterman, 1990). Erikson would probably have considered these people identity confused.

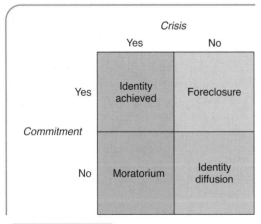

FIGURE 12•9 Marcia's four identity statuses. Different combinations of crises and commitment yield four different identity statuses.

Marcia's research has shown that adolescents move in and out of the different statuses as they experience new situations and crises. A teenager does not necessarily move progressively from one status to another. For example, after thinking about whether to major in business or engineering, a college student may decide on engineering because she thinks that she will like the work and earn good money. In terms of this decision, she is an identity achiever. However, after taking several engineering courses, she may decide that she really doesn't like engineering after all. Now she must decide whether to keep her major or to change it. She is now no longer committed; she is in moratorium.

Marcia's research is interesting for two reasons. First, it shows that most adolescents do indeed experience crises in their search for an identity—although "crisis" may be too strong a word for it, as many teens resolve its challenges without stress. Second, it shows that a teenager's psychological reaction to a crisis depends on the time at which he or she is dealing with it. That there are four possible avenues that can be involved in achieving an identity testifies to the complexity of "finding oneself."

Marcia's work, then, buttresses Erikson's view of adolescence. However, Erikson's theory would have us believe that teenagers are searching for an identity on their own, independent of parents and others. As Gilligan (1982) contends, this is more likely to be true for boys than for girls. Her point is that girls are more likely than boys to seek and develop close relationships with others. In her view a girl's search for identity is strongly influenced by the desire to be involved in close relationships with others. Gilligan's hypothesis reinforces many researchers' belief in the social nature of identity development: The search for an identity is enmeshed in a social context that may strongly influence how a teenager responds to a crisis.

Identity and Self-Perception The search for a personal identity brings with it changes in self-concept and self-esteem (Berk, 2005). During childhood children tend to perceive themselves in terms of both physical traits, such as "I am a boy and have brown hair and blue eyes," and individual personality characteristics, such as "I am honest" or "I am smart" (Damon & Hart, 1992). During adolescence teenagers become more focused on their social relationships and tend to perceive themselves more in terms of their interactions with others. They may use phrases such as "I am outgoing" or "I am trustworthy" to describe themselves. In late adolescence teenagers begin to perceive themselves more in terms of the values that they hold. They may now describe themselves in terms of their political, social, or philosophical views, as in "I am a conservative" or "I am an environmentalist."

As a teenager strives to develop an identity, earlier self-perceptions, including those held during childhood, are incorporated into his or her emerging self-concept. Newer self-perceptions do not merely replace older ones. Instead, the newer ones augment the older ones; for example, a teenage girl may perceive herself to be a blond-haired young woman who is shy, trustworthy, and moderate in her political views.

An adolescent's identity, then, seems inextricably bound to his or her perceptions of self.

Sexuality Sexuality has become a very evident component of modern culture in most industrialized societies. Displays of sexual attractiveness play an important role in advertisements in magazines and on television; sexual activities are portrayed in books and films; personal sexual practices are discussed in print and during talk shows on radio and television. Sexuality was always a part of life (after all, our species has managed to propagate during all periods of history), but since the latter part of the twentieth century, it has become much more open and evident than it was previously—and this is notably the case among adolescents. With so many examples of adult sexual behaviors given them, it is not surprising that adolescents adopt sexuality as part of their identity. According to the Center for Disease Control and Prevention, 30 percent of female teens between the ages of 15 and 17 have had sexual intercourse; 31 percent of male teens of this age also reported having experienced sex (Abma, Martinez, Mosher, & Dawson, 2004).

A timely but complex issue concerns the sex of the partner involved. Chapter 13 discusses possible explanations of the development of heterosexual or homosexual orientations in more detail, but one possible source of sexual orientation may be reflected in the way an individual reacts to sexuality. Sexual orientation appears to be largely determined by the time an individual reaches adolescence and seems to be correlated with childhood affiliation with "masculine" or "feminine" peers and behaviors. Bem (1996) has suggested that boys and girls who affiliate primarily with boys during childhood come to view girls as exotically different. As they mature sexually, their perception of girls as exotic is channeled into a perception that girls are also sexually attractive. (Bem calls this explanation the "exotic becomes erotic" theory.) A similar description would describe girls and boys who affiliate with girls during childhood: They would regard boys as exotic and, later, as sexually attractive. Therefore, although sexual orientation would be manifest in adolescence and early adulthood, Bem would identify its origins in the socialization and gender identity processes of childhood.

Friendships and Relations with Parents The nature of friendship changes during adolescence, and it changes in different ways for boys and girls. For girls the most important function of childhood friendships is having someone with whom to do things—someone with whom to share activities and common interests. At around the age of 14 years, girls begin to seek companions who can provide social and emotional support. As girls become aware of their growing sexuality and the changes in their relationships with boys, close friends serve as confidants—as sounding boards who help define their behavior and social roles. Adolescent boys' friendships are likely to be less intense than those of girls. Boys are more concerned with establishing and asserting their independence and defining their relation to authority; thus, groups of friends serve as allies—as mutual-aid societies, so to speak.

As adolescents begin to define their new roles and to assert them, they almost inevitably come into conflict with their parents. Some writers have claimed that changes in modern society have given rise to a "youth culture" that is apart from the rest of society and that a "generation gap" separates young people from their elders. However, research indicates that most of the differences between people of different generations are in style rather than in substance. Adolescents and their parents tend to have similar values and attitudes toward important issues (Youniss & Smollar, 1985). Unless serious problems occur, family conflicts tend to be provoked by relatively minor issues, such as messy rooms, loud music, clothes, curfews, and household chores. These problems tend to begin around the time of puberty; if puberty occurs particularly early or late, so does the conflict (Paikoff & Brooks-Gunn, 1991).

Cognitive Development

I discussed physical and social development in adolescence to make a point that will surely be familiar to you: Adolescence is a period of remarkable change. We've seen this with respect to physical change, sexual maturation, and identity formation. The adolescent's cognitive abilities likewise demonstrate a pronounced shift.

Early in adolescence, an individual's brain begins a period of growth of structures in the frontal lobe (Sowell et al., 1999). As we saw in Chapter 4, the frontal lobe is associated with regions related to control and planning. These are also the areas that most distinguish *homo sapiens* from the other primates. So, in a way, the changes in the brain during adolescence are the changes that especially define us as human (Keating, 2004). What are these changes?

As Piaget saw it, adolescents' cognitive changes were based on the logical power of abstract reasoning. In late childhood, said Piaget, a child entered the stage of formal operations. Adolescence, then, should be characterized as a sort of Sherlock Holmesian phase in which adolescents apply deductive skills to problems. There is certainly evidence that this period of development is marked by increased facility with the tools of formal reasoning. As one example, consider the difference between the things you know from experience and the things you know from logic. If I were to say, "I have blue eyes and brown hair," you would know that you would need to obtain empirical evidence (e.g., to meet me or see my picture) to prove the statement true or false. On the other hand, if I said, "I have blue eyes or have nonblue eyes," you would know from logic that this had to be true. Young children don't make this distinction, tending to think of propositions like this as matters of evidence. Children on the threshold of adolescence (i.e., 11- and 12-year-olds) do distinguish these statements and recognize when statements can be decided logically (Morris & Sloutsky, 2002).

However, as we saw in Chapter 11, formal logic does not necessarily dominate adult thinking, let alone that of adolescents. We use heuristics, biases, and mental models in place of, or as supplements to, formal logic. The prevalence of these strategies for reasoning has led some investigators (e.g., Klaczynski, 2004) to suggest that there are two reasoning systems: an **analytic processing system** and an **experiential processing system**. The analytic processing system is the basis of deliberate, abstract, and higher-order reasoning. It provides the capacity to remove a problem from its context and to apply logical rules to solve it. The experiential processing system, on the other hand, is rapid, mostly unconscious, and heuristic. It provides the memories for particular solutions to problems and forms the basis for the biases and stereotypes that we may apply to problems.

Adolescence may be the time at which we not only develop our analytic abilities but also become good at knowing when they must be used. The two systems give us a large number of reasoning tools, which work in some cases but not in all. Thus, cognitive development during adolescence is marked by choice: The individual shows increased capacity to select consciously the mode of reasoning appropriate to the context (Keating, 2004).

Interim Summary

Adolescence

Adolescence is the transitional stage between childhood and adulthood. Puberty is initiated by the hypothalamus, which causes the pituitary gland to secrete hormones that stimulate maturation of the reproductive system as well as secondary sex characteristics.

Puberty marks a significant transition, both physically and socially. Early maturity appears to be socially beneficial to boys, because early maturers are more likely to be perceived as leaders. The effects of early maturity in girls are mixed; although their advanced physical development may help them acquire some prestige, early-maturing girls are more likely to engage in norm-breaking behavior.

A focal point in adolescent development is the formation of an identity. Both Erikson and Marcia argue that adolescents face an identity crisis, the outcome of which determines the nature and level of identity that teenagers will form. Marcia argues that forming an identity has two primary components—the crisis itself and the commitment or decision that a young person takes regarding a course of action after considering possible alternatives. The extent to which a teenager experiences a crisis and the way in which he or she resolves it lead to identity achievement, moratorium, foreclosure, or identity diffusion. An adolescent's identity also may be influenced by gender-related factors, such as females' greater tendency to desire to form close relationships with others. An adolescent's identity is bound to his or her perceptions of self which, during this time of life, will often be based on social relationships.

Sexuality becomes important in adolescence, and many people engage in sexual intercourse in their teens. The nature of friendship changes. Girls seek out confidants rather than playmates, and boys join groups that provide mutual support in their quests to assert their independence.

Although adolescence brings conflicts between parents and children, these conflicts tend to be centered on relatively minor issues. Most adolescents hold the same values and attitudes concerning important issues as their parents do.

Conflict of a different sort may underlie cognitive development. Just before adolescence, children develop the tools of logical reasoning. However, adult reasoning uses a variety of reasoning strategies, of which logic is just one. Adolescence may be a period of growth in our capacity to choose among these strategies.

QUESTIONS TO CONSIDER

1. What important behavioral effects did you experience as a result of your own sexual maturation? In what ways did your social and emotional lives change? How does your experience compare to those of your friends who underwent puberty before or after you did?

2. It is often said (by adults) that adolescents act as if they are incapable of properly judging risk. Do you think this is true? Could it be, instead, that adolescents are using different modes of reasoning, such as the strategies discussed in Chapter 11?

Adulthood and Old Age

It is much easier to outline child or adolescent development than adult development; children and adolescents change faster, and the changes are closely related to age. Adult development is much more variable. Physical changes in adults are more gradual. Mental and emotional changes during adulthood are more closely related to individual experience than to age. In the social realm, some people achieve success and satisfaction with their careers; others hate their jobs. Some marry and have happy family lives; others never adjust to the roles of spouse and parent. No single description of adult development will fit everyone.

Physical Development

As we grow older, there is one set of changes that we can count on—physical alterations. Our physical abilities peak at around age 30 and decline gradually thereafter. By maintaining a well-balanced diet, exercising regularly, and not smoking, drinking, or using drugs, we can, in large measure, help our bodies maintain some of their physical vigor even into old age. This is not to say that good diet and exercise habits

▲ *Loss of physical ability during adulthood can be minimized by following a program of regular exercise.*

can make a 70-year-old look and feel like a 25-year-old. But if we don't eat well and exercise regularly, we will have less physical energy and poorer muscle tone than if we do. And apparently, staying in shape as a younger adult pays off in later life. Older people who were physically fit as younger adults are generally in better health and feel better about themselves than those who weren't (Perlmutter & Hall, 1995).

Unfortunately, though, even prudent diets and exercising cannot reverse the physical changes that accompany aging. People in their later 40s, 50s, and 60s often experience decreases in visual acuity and in depth perception, hearing, sensitivity to odors and flavors, reaction time, agility, physical mobility, and physical strength.

Muscular strength peaks during the late 20s or early 30s and then declines slowly thereafter as muscle tissue gradually deteriorates. By age 70 strength has declined by approximately 30 percent in both men and women (Young, Stokes, & Crowe, 1984). However, age has much less effect on *endurance* than on strength. Both laboratory tests and athletic records reveal that older people who remain physically fit show remarkably little decline in the ability to exercise for extended periods of time (Spirduso & MacRae, 1990).

Although it is easy to measure a decline in the sensory systems (such as vision or hearing), older people often show very little *functional* change in these systems. Most people learn to make adjustments for their sensory losses, using additional cues to help them decode sensory information. For example, people with hearing loss can learn to attend more carefully to other people's gestures and lip movements; they also can profitably use their experience to infer what is said.

Functional changes with age are also minimal in highly developed skills. For example, Salthouse (1984, 1988) found that experienced older typists continued to perform as well as younger ones, despite the fact that they performed less well on standard laboratory tests of sensory and motor skills, including the types of skills that might be expected to be important in typing. The continuous practice these typists re-

ceived enabled them to develop strategies to compensate for their physical decline. For example, they tended to read farther ahead in the text they were typing, which enabled them to plan in advance the patterns of finger movements they would have to make.

With regular exercise and a flexible attitude, individuals can accommodate their interests and activities to the inevitable changes in physical abilities brought by aging. There is no reason why a reasonably healthy person of *any* age should stop enjoying life because of physical limitations.

Cognitive Development

Psychologists have studied the effects of education and experience on intellectual abilities and have questioned whether intelligence inevitably declines with age. Most of us can conceive of a future when we can no longer run as fast as we do now or perform well in a strenuous sport, but we do not like to think of being outperformed intellectually by younger people. And, in fact, research indicates that people can get old without losing their intellectual skills.

Cognitive Development and Brain Disease

Before we consider the normal effects of aging in a healthy individual, we should look at some changes that can be caused by disease. As people get older, they have a greater risk of developing *dementia* (literally "an undoing of the mind")—a class of diseases characterized by the progressive loss of cortical tissue and a corresponding loss of mental functions. The most prevalent form of dementia is **Alzheimer's disease**. About 3 percent of the population in their late sixties or early seventies show diagnostic evidence of Alzheimer's disease (Evans et al., 1989), but that prevalence rate doubles with every five years of additional age (e.g., Wilson et al., 2002). There appear to be three relatively distinct subgroups of Alzheimer's patients (Fisher, Rourke, & Bieliauskas, 1999). The disease may manifest itself through (1) global deficits, or it may be most evident in functions identified with (2) the left hemisphere or (3) the right hemisphere. In general, though, Alzheimer's disease is characterized by progressive loss of memory and other mental functions (Ashford, Schmitt, & Kumar, 1996). At first the person may have difficulty remembering appointments and may sometimes fail to come up with words or people's names. As time passes, the individual shows increasing confusion and increasing difficulty with tasks such as balancing a checkbook. In the early stages of the disease, memory deficit involves recent events; but as the disease progresses, even old memories are affected. If the person ventures outside alone during the advanced stages of the disease, he or she is likely to get lost. Eventually the person becomes bedridden, becomes completely helpless, and finally dies (Khachaturian & Blass, 1992; Terry & Davies, 1980).

Geneticists have discovered an association between defects on chromosomes 14, 19, and 21 and at least one kind of Alzheimer's disease, which seems to involve reduced levels

FIGURE 12•10 Alzheimer's disease. A computer-enhanced photograph of a slice through the brain of a person who died of Alzheimer's disease (left) and a normal brain (right). Note that the grooves (sulci and fissures) are especially wide in the Alzheimer's brain, indicating degeneration of the brain.

(Photo © Alfred Pasieka/Photo Researchers, Inc.)

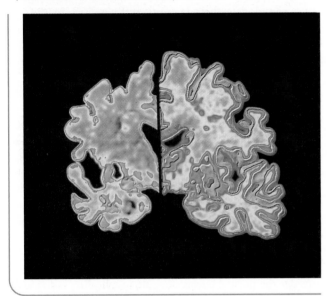

of the neurotransmitter acetylcholine (Cruts & Van Broeck-hoven, 1996; Gottfries, 1985; Poduslo & Yin, 2001; Selkoe, 1989; Shellenberg, 1997). Alzheimer's disease produces severe degeneration of the hippocampus and cerebral cortex, especially the association cortex of the frontal and temporal lobes. **Figure 12•10** shows a computer-enhanced photograph of a slice through a normal brain (right) and the brain of a patient who died of Alzheimer's disease (left). You can see that much of the tissue of the Alzheimer's brain has been lost; the grooves in the brain (sulci and fissures) are much wider.

An even more common cause of mental deterioration in old age is depression, a psychological disorder. Some people find old age an extremely unpleasant condition: They are declining physically; they lose their mobility; they no longer have jobs or family-related activities that confirm their usefulness to other people; and many old friends have died, are infirm, or have moved away. With this sense of loss or deprivation, some older people become depressed; they lose their appetite for food and for living in general, have trouble concentrating, and suffer losses in memory. Too often these symptoms of depression are diagnosed as dementia. Yet unlike dementia, depression is treatable with psychotherapy and drugs, as we will see in Chapters 17 and 18.

Cognitive Development and Normal Aging Aging affects different intellectual abilities to different degrees. Schaie (1990), describing the results of the Seattle Longitudinal Study of Aging, reports that on average, people's scores on five tests of intellectual abilities showed an increase until their late 30s or early 40s, then a period of stability until their mid-50s or early 60s, followed by a gradual decline. **Figure 12•11** shows the participants who maintained stable levels of performance on each of the tests over a seven-year period. As you can see, the performance of most of the participants—even the oldest—remained stable, although there were some reductions. Subsequent results from the Seattle Longitudinal Study of Aging (Schaie, 1996) suggest that these declines are due to the way different intellectual abilities change with age. Some abilities, such as the ability to perform rapid numerical or perceptual tasks, decline markedly as age increases. Verbal ability, as measured by vocabulary, shows little change. Other abilities, such as verbal memory, show a moderate decline at advanced age.

Related research by Kirasic (1991) has shown that, at least for performance on spatial tasks, deficits in short-term

FIGURE 12•11 Results from the Seattle Longitudinal Study of Aging. Percentage of participants of various age groups who maintained stable levels of performance on each of five tests of intellectual ability over a seven-year period.

(From Schaie, K. W. In *Handbook of the Psychology of Aging*, 3rd ed., edited by J. E. Birren and K. W. Schaie. San Diego: Academic Press, 1990. Reprinted with permission from Elsevier.)

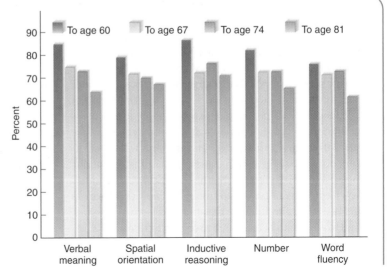

memory may coincide with aging. For example, Kirasic and Bernicki (1990) showed young and older adults 66 slides of a walk through a real neighborhood. Sometimes the slides were in the correct order; at other times they were mixed up. All participants were then asked to make distance estimates between some of the scenes shown in the slides. Both younger and older participants performed equally well in estimating distances for the slides presented in logical order. But older participants performed less well than younger participants when the slides were scrambled.

Kirasic and Bernicki concluded that information from the slides presented in normal order was encoded into short-term memory similarly for both sets of participants. However, the scrambled presentation of slides taxed available resources in the older participants' short-term memory, resulting in performance decline.

If memory shows wear with age, one might reasonably suspect that intelligence, too, would show a similar decline. This was once thought to be true, based on results from cross-sectional studies (studies that compare different age groups on the same task). However, we now know that intelligence does not decline until late adulthood, largely thanks to the work of Schaie and Strother (1968), who compared results from a cross-sectional approach with results from a longitudinal approach (a study in which researchers follow a group of participants over time in order to identify developmental changes that occur). For example, look at **Figure 12·12**, which shows performance on a verbal abilities subsection of an intelligence test plotted as a function of age. (Here, *verbal abilities* means the ability to understand ideas represented by words.) The cross-sectional data indicate that intelligence scores decrease—and rather precipitously so—after age 50. But the longitudinal data paint a different picture: Scores increase until about age 55, then decline gradually.

Why would different methods produce these different patterns of results? Cross-sectional studies do not take into account possible *cohort effects*—the fact that the people being tested were reared in different time periods. Thus, one explanation for these disparate results is that the older people tested had not had the same educational and career opportunities as their younger counterparts might have had. The longitudinal method takes this possibility into consideration by testing the same people at regular intervals spanning many years. In doing so, it gives a more accurate picture of the relationship between age and intelligence.

Many investigators believe that intelligence can be divided into two broad categories. In general, older people in good health do well on tests of *crystallized intelligence*—of the mental abilities that depend on knowledge and experience. Vocabulary, the ability to see similarities between objects and situations, and general information all are aspects of crystallized intelligence. On the other hand, *fluid intelligence*—the capacity for abstract reasoning—appears to decline with age (Baltes & Schaie, 1974; Horn, 1982). The abilities to solve puzzles, to memorize a series of arbitrary items such as unrelated words or letters, to classify

▲ *Studies of aging must take into account the possbility that people of different ages were reared in different time periods and may have had different educational experiences.*

figures into categories, and to change problem-solving strategies easily and flexibly are aspects of fluid intelligence.

The facts that older people excel in crystallized intelligence and that younger people excel in fluid intelligence are reflected in the kinds of intellectual endeavors for which the two age groups seem to be best suited. For example, great mathematicians usually make their most important contributions during their 20s or early 30s; apparently the ability to break out of the traditional ways of thinking and to conceive

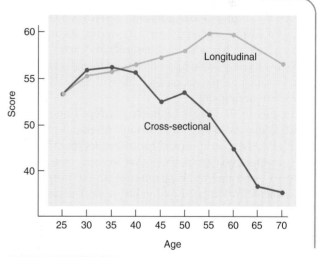

FIGURE 12·12 A comparison of cross-sectional and longitudinal data concerning changes in verbal ability with age. In contrast to the cross-sectional data, the longitudinal data show that verbal ability increased gradually to about age 55 and then decreased gradually.

(Based on Schaie, K. W., & Strother, C. R. (1968). A cross-sequential study of age changes in cognitive behavior. *Psychological Bulletin, 70,* 675. Reprinted with permission from K. Warner Schaie.)

new strategies is crucial in such achievements. In contrast, great contributions to literature and philosophy, in which success depends heavily on knowledge and experience, tend to be made by older people.

Another aspect of intellectual ability is speed. Older people have difficulty responding and performing quickly. When time pressures prevail, their performance is worse than that of younger people. When time requirements are relaxed, however, the performance of older people improves much more than does that of younger people (Arenberg, 1973; Botwinick & Storandt, 1974).

Part of the age-related decline in speed can be attributed to deterioration in sensory functions and to difficulty in changing strategies to meet new demands. But another important reason for decreased speed is caution; older people appear to be less willing to make mistakes. In some endeavors, this caution is valuable. In fact, many societies reserve important decision-making functions for older people, because they are less likely to act hastily. A study by Leech and Witte (1971) illustrates the effect of caution on performance. The investigators found that older people who were paid for each response they made—correct or incorrect—learned lists of pairs of words faster than did older people who were paid only for correct responses. The payment for incorrect responses increased their willingness to make a mistake, and this relaxation of their normal caution paid off in an increased speed of learning.

Social Development

Recall from Table 12.4 that Erikson believed that the adult years consist of three psychosocial stages during which the conflicts are intimacy versus isolation, in which people succeed or fail in loving others; generativity versus stagnation, in which people either withdraw inwardly and focus on their problems or reach out to help others; and integrity versus despair, in which people review their life with either a sense of satisfaction or despair.

In the 1970s Daniel Levinson developed another approach to understanding stages of adult development (Levinson et al., 1978). Levinson and his colleagues interviewed 40 men—business executives, blue-collar workers, novelists, and biologists—and analyzed biographies of famous men and stories of men's lives as portrayed in literature. The researchers claimed to have discovered a pattern common to most men's lives. Instead of proceeding smoothly, men's lives were characterized by several years of stability punctuated by crises. The crises were periods during which the men began to question their *life structures:* their occupations, their relations with their families, their religious beliefs and practices, their ethnic identities, and the ways they spent their leisure time. During these times of transition—which caused considerable anxiety and turmoil—the men reevaluated the choices they had made and eventually settled on new patterns that guided them through another period of stability. Periods of transition

lasted around four or five years, whereas the intervening periods of stability lasted six or seven years.

Levinson claimed that the most important crises occur early in adulthood, when men must make choices about career and marriage, and at midlife (during the early to mid-40s), when men must finally face realities about their life structure. Although Levinson did not invent the notion of the midlife crisis, he certainly helped bring it to the attention of the general public and helped make the term a part of everyone's vocabulary. Levinson concluded that the midlife crisis happens to all men. Men whose life structures do not yet meet their prior goals and expectations realize that the future probably will not bring the success that up until then has eluded them. Men who *have* succeeded begin to question whether the goals they first set for themselves were meaningful and worthwhile. All men, successful or not, also begin to confront the fact that they are getting older. They are starting to detect some signs of physical decline, and deaths are occurring among their older family members and acquaintances.

Several researchers have defined objective criteria for the presence of a midlife crisis and have looked for its presence in representative samples of participants. For example, Costa and McCrae (1980) administered a Midlife Crisis Scale to a total of 548 men aged 35 to 79 years. The scale contained items asking whether the participants were experiencing any of the symptoms of a midlife crisis, such as dissatisfaction with job and family, a sense of meaninglessness, or a feeling of turmoil. The investigators found no evidence for a midlife crisis. Some people did report some of the symptoms, but they were no more likely to occur during the early to mid-40s than at any other age. A study of 60 women (Reinke, Holmes, & Harris, 1985) also found no evidence of a midlife crisis. This finding does not mean that middle-aged people do not periodically contemplate or question the important issues in their lives; of course they do. But there appears to be no crisis—in the dramatic sense—to these reflective periods.

Adult development occurs against the backdrop of what many developmental psychologists consider to be the two most important aspects of life: love and work. For most of us, falling in love is more than just a compelling feeling of wanting to be with someone. It often brings with it major responsibilities, such as marriage and children. Work, too, is more than just a way to pass time. It involves setting and achieving goals related to income, status among peers, and accomplishments outside the family. For most adults, overall satisfaction with life reflects the degree to which they have been successful in marriage, raising a family, and achieving goals. With this in mind, let's look briefly at how love and work ebb and flow over the course of adult development.

Marriage and Family Most young people envision themselves falling in love and getting married. And, despite recent increases in numbers of never-married adults and in the prevalence of cohabiting, the vast majority of people do get married. Although divorce rates in North America have risen sharply over the last generation, they do not indicate the end of marriage; the majority of divorced people remarry.

Newlyweds are generally happy with their marriages and seem to become happier when children enter the picture (Rollins & Feldman, 1970). However, as children begin to demand more of their parents' time and emotional resources, couples report increasing unhappiness in marriage. Generally speaking, mothers assume more responsibilities than fathers for the day-to-day care of children (Biernat & Wortman, 1991). As a result, they spend more time doing housework and less time talking to their husbands (Peskin, 1982), which can place strain on their marital happiness. However, if husband and wife can find time together in the evenings, and if the husband is able to share in the parenting and household chores, the stress of adapting to family life is lessened considerably (Daniels & Weingarten, 1982).

As children grow older and become more self-sufficient, the day-to-day burdens of raising a family taper off and husbands and wives are able to spend more time with each other. However, adolescents pose new problems for their parents: Teenage offspring may question parental authority, and their burgeoning social agendas may put a wrinkle in their parents' personal and social calendars. For many parents, rearing adolescents, particularly during the years just before young people leave home, represents the low point of marital happiness (Cavanaugh, 1990).

Generally speaking, once a family's youngest child has left home, marital happiness increases—and it continues to do so through the remainder of the couple's life together. It once was thought that the "empty nest" posed problems for the middle-aged couple, particularly for the mother, who in earlier generations was thought to define her role mainly around her children. Although parents may miss daily contact with their children, however, they also feel happy (not to mention relieved) that a major responsibility of life—raising self-reliant children who become responsible members of

▲ *For most adults, satisfaction with life reflects the degree to which they have been successful in marriage, raising a family, and achieving goals.*

society—has been completed successfully. Just as important, the parents now have time for each other and freedom to pursue their own interests. Empty-nest couples report an increase in marital happiness. And, if they maintain frequent contact with their children, they also report increased satisfaction with life (White & Edwards, 1990).

Work The task of raising a family must be balanced against the demands of work outside the home. In fact, events that occur in the workplace often affect the quality of home life. A promotion and a raise can mean that the family can now do things that they could not before—they can now pursue a new hobby or travel together. Working long hours to get that raise can decrease the amount of time that a couple can spend together with their children.

With the dramatic increase in the number of women who work outside the home since the early 1970s, many psychologists have focused their research efforts on understanding *dual-earner marriages*—those in which both parents work full- or part-time. Compared to single-earner marriages, dual-earner families generally have a better standard of living in terms of material possessions and are better able to save money for their children's college education and for retirement.

Death Death is the final event of life. It is both a biological and a social event—family and friends are affected in many ways by the death of a loved one. Although a death may claim a life at any time, most people die when they are old. One question that developmental psychologists have asked about death and dying among the elderly is, How do old people view the inevitability of their own deaths?

At one time or another, most of us contemplate our own deaths. Some of us may contemplate death more than others, but the thought of death crosses everyone's mind at least occasionally. As you might expect, elderly people contemplate their deaths more often than do younger people. For the most part, they fear death less than their younger counterparts do (Kalish, 1976). Why? No one knows for sure, but a tentative explanation may be that older people have had more time to review the past and to plan for the future in the knowledge that death is close at hand. Thus, they are able to prepare themselves psychologically (and financially) for death.

Contemplating and preparing for death, though, is not like knowing that you are actually dying. The changes in attitudes that terminally ill people experience have been studied by Elisabeth Kübler-Ross (1969, 1981). After interviewing hundreds of dying people, Kübler-Ross concluded that people undergo five distinct phases in psychologically coping with death. The first stage is *denial*. When terminally ill people learn of their condition, they generally try to deny it. *Anger* comes next—people go through a period of resenting the certainty of death. In the third stage, *bargaining*, people attempt to negotiate their fate with God or others, pleading that their lives be spared. But even while bargaining, they actually realize that they are, in fact, going to die. This leads to *depression*, the fourth stage, which is characterized by a sense of hopelessness and loss. The fifth and final stage, *acceptance*, is marked by a more peaceful resignation to reality.

Kübler-Ross's work points up the psychological factors involved in dying and has provided an interesting model of how the dying come to grips with their fate. Her conclusions, though, have not escaped criticism. Her research was not scientific—her method for interviewing people was not systematic, and her results are largely anecdotal. Moreover, of the five stages, only denial appears to be universal. Apparently, not all terminally ill people have the same psychological responses to the fact that they are dying.

Despite its flaws, however, Kübler-Ross's work is important because it has enhanced awareness, both scientific and public, of the experiences undergone by people who are terminally ill. The scientific response, as you might guess, has been to do medical research in the hope of prolonging the lives of people with cancer and other terminal illnesses. The public response has emphasized attempts to provide support for dying individuals and their families, often through *hospice services* (Aiken, 2001). In past centuries hospices were places where strangers and pilgrims could find rest and shelter. Today, hospice programs provide invaluable medical and psychological support for dying persons and their families.

Interim Summary

Adulthood and Old Age

Up to the time of young adulthood, human development can reasonably be described as a series of stages: a regular sequence of changes that occur in most members of our species. However, development in adulthood is much more variable, and few generalizations apply. Aging brings with it a gradual deterioration in people's sensory capacities as well as changes in physical appearance that many people regard as unattractive. The effects of these changes can be minimized by vigorous participation in life's activities.

Although older people are more likely than young people to develop dementia because of illnesses such as Alzheimer's disease, severe intellectual deterioration is often caused by depression, which usually can be treated successfully. Rather than undergoing sudden intellectual deterioration, older people are more likely to exhibit gradual changes, especially in abilities that require flexibility and the learning of new behaviors. Intellectual abilities that depend heavily on crystallized intelligence—an accumulated body of knowledge—are much less likely to decline than are those based on fluid intelligence—the capacity for abstract reasoning.

Erikson and Levinson both have proposed that people encounter a series of crises that serve as turning points in development. Erikson's stages span the entire life cycle, from infancy to old age, whereas Levinson's stages concentrate on midlife development. There appears to be no evidence that supports the idea that people usually experience a midlife crisis. Adult social development occurs within the context of love, marriage, family, and work. Marriages seem to be happiest just after the birth of children and after the children have left home. They appear to be unhappiest just before the children leave home—possibly due to the emotional and time demands that adolescents place on their parents. Many families have parents who both work, which helps ease the financial burdens of raising a family and meeting long-term financial obligations.

Older people have less fear of death than younger people, perhaps because they have had more time to contemplate and prepare for it. In interviews with terminally ill people, Kübler-Ross found that many people seem to go through a five-stage process in facing the reality that they are going to die. Although her research has been found to have some methodological flaws, it has drawn both scientific and public attention to the plight of terminally ill individuals and the necessity of properly caring for them.

QUESTION TO CONSIDER

Imagine that you are the director of a new community mental health program for adults. The focus of this program is on prevention—on minimizing the negative effects of the aging process on adults who participate in the program. Your first task is to design a comprehensive plan to maximize adults' physical, social, emotional, and intellectual capacities. What activities would you include in such a plan? Why?

Suggestions for Further Reading

Berk, L. E. (2005). *Infants, children, and adolescents* (5th ed.). Boston: Allyn and Bacon.

This text presents an excellent overview of research and theory in the fields of infant, childhood, and adolescent development.

Lemme, B. H. (2006). *Development in adulthood* (4th ed.). Boston: Allyn and Bacon.

A well-written and thorough introduction to the major issues involved in the study of adult development.

Hoyenga, K. B., & Hoyenga, K. T. (1993). *Gender-related differences: Origins and outcomes*. Boston: Allyn and Bacon.

This book examines gender differences from evolutionary, physiological, and cultural perspectives.

Harwood, R. L., Miller, J. G., & Irizarry, N. L. (1997). *Culture and attachment: Perceptions of the child in context*. New York: Guilford Press.

As its title implies, this book considers cultural variables that influence the development of attachment between infants and their caregivers, including socioeconomic status, perceptions of different attachment behaviors, and perceptions of children themselves.

Key Terms

accommodation (p. 367)

actual developmental level (p. 372)

Alzheimer's disease (p. 393)

analytic processing system (p. 392)

androgens (p. 360)

assimilation (p. 367)

attachment (p. 377)

avoidant attachment (p. 380)

conservation (p. 369)

conventional level (p. 386)

critical period (p. 365)

cross-sectional study (p. 359)

deferred imitation (p. 368)

disoriented attachment (p. 380)

egocentrism (p. 369)

embryonic stage (p. 360)

experiential processing system (p. 392)

fetal stage (p. 361)

gender identity (p. 382)

gender role (p. 382)

gender stereotypes (p. 382)

longitudinal study (p. 360)

maturation (p. 363)

moral realism (p. 386)

morality of cooperation (p. 386)

object permanence (p. 368)

operation (p. 367)

period of concrete operations (p. 369)

period of formal operations (p. 370)

postconventional level (p. 387)

preconventional level (p. 386)

prenatal period (p. 360)

preoperational period (p. 368)

puberty (p. 388)

resistant attachment (p. 380)

scaffolding (p. 381)

secure attachment (p. 380)

sensitive period (p. 365)

sensorimotor period (p. 367)

separation anxiety (p. 380)

Strange Situation (p. 380)

stranger anxiety (p. 380)

teratogens (p. 360)

theory of mind (p. 374)

zone of proximal development (p. 372)

zygotic stage (p. 360)

13

MOTIVATION AND EMOTION

What Is Motivation?

Motivation involves a group of phenomena that affect the nature, strength, and persistence of an individual's behavior.

Motivation and Reinforcement

What Initiates Behavior? • What Determines the Strength of Behavior? • What Determines the Persistence of Behavior?

Motivation is importantly affected by the processes of reinforcement and punishment. Environments initiate behavior when behavior has previously been reinforced in their presence. The strength and persistence of behavior in an environment depends on the particular conditions that obtained when the behavior produced its consequences, how deprived the learner is of those consequences, and the availability of reinforcers for other behavior.

Aggressive Behavior

Ethological Studies of Aggression • Hormones and Aggression • Environmental Variables That Affect Human Aggression

Ethological studies show that aggression serves useful purposes in most species of animals. In males of most species, male sex hormones have both organizational and activational effects on aggressive behavior. Field studies suggest that violence in the mass media may promote aggression.

Sexual Behavior

Effects of the Brain's Reinforcement System on Sexual Behavior • *Evaluating Scientific Issues: What Is the Role of Chance in Scientific Breakthroughs?* • Effects of Sex Hormones on Sexual Behavior • Sexual Orientation

Both brain neurotransmitters and sex hormones play an important role in motivating sexual behavior. Important findings about the role of the brain's reinforcement system in sexual behavior resulted from an accidental discovery. Sex hormones have organizational effects on prenatal development and activational effects in adulthood. Although testosterone is the most important male sex hormone, it stimulates sexual desire in both men and women. The development of sexual orientation appears to have biological roots, both hormonal and genetic.

Emotion

Emotions as Response Patterns • Social Judgments: Role of the Orbitofrontal Cortex • Measuring Emotional Responses: Lie Detection in Criminal Investigation

An emotion is a particular pattern of behaviors, physiological responses, and feelings evoked by a situation that has motivational relevance. Emotional response patterns have three components: behavioral, autonomic, and hormonal. Fearful response patterns are particularly dependent on a brain structure called the amygdale; social response patterns are particularly dependent on the orbitofrontal cortex. Polygraphic lie detection attempts to identify emotional reactions associated with deception, but studies show that the technique gives unreliable results.

Expression and Recognition of Emotions

The Social Nature of Emotional Expression in Humans • Situations That Produce Emotions: The Role of Cognition • *Biology and Culture: Are Emotional Expressions Innate?*

Expressions of emotion are largely innate social responses that communicate important information between individuals. Although emotional reactions are automatic responses that are seen in many species, cognition plays an important role in people's recognition of emotion-inducing situations. Cross-cultural studies show that people in all cultures display similar facial expressions, although cultural rules determine under what circumstances people should let their feelings show.

Feelings of Emotion

Theories of Emotion • The James-Lange Theory • Effects of Spinal Cord and Autonomic-System Damage • *Evaluating Scientific Issues: Is Cognition Essential for Emotion?*

According to the James-Lange theory, feelings of emotion are caused by feedback from the body when a situation causes an emotional reaction. This feedback comes from behavior and from responses controlled by the autonomic nervous system. Research findings on the effects of spinal cord injury on feelings of emotion tend to support the James-Lange theory.

Eating

Regulatory Control Systems • What Starts a Meal? • What Stops a Meal? • Obesity • Anorexia Nervosa and Bulimia Nervosa

The motivation to eat involves both social and physiological factors. The most important physiological factor is the detection of a fall in the level of nutrients available in the blood. Short-term control of eating involves detectors in the stomach that monitor the level of nutrients received during a meal. Long-term control appears to involve a hormone released by overnourished fat cells. Both genetic and environmental factors are responsible for obesity. Anorexia nervosa is a serious, often life-threatening disorder whose causes are not well understood.

Some deceptive psychologists (you will see why I call them deceptive in a minute) asked a psychiatrist to comment on the motivation of a woman on a ward in a mental hospital. The psychiatrist noticed that wherever she went on the ward, the woman carried a broom; however, she was never seen to sweep the floor. After observing the woman for some time, the psychiatrist "explained" the behavior as follows:

> "Her constant and compulsive pacing, holding a broom in the manner she does, could be seen as a ritualistic procedure, a magical action. . . . Her broom would be then: (1) a child that gives her love and she gives him in return her devotion, (2) a phallic symbol, (3) a scepter of an omnipotent queen. . . . This is a magical procedure in which the patient carries out her wishes, expressed in a way that is far beyond our solid, rational and conventional way of thinking. . . ." (cited in Allyon, Haughton, & Hughes, 1965, p. 3)

What, in fact, was the woman's motivation? Unknown to the psychiatrist, the psychologists had previously occasionally given the woman a cigarette if she happened to be carrying the broom at that moment. (The woman was addicted to the nicotine in cigarettes.) In technical terms, broom-carrying behavior had been intermittently reinforced with a cigarette. But what was the psychologists' motivation in deceiving the psychiatrist?

Perhaps another example will help answer this last question: I asked students in an advanced psychology course to view the behavior of two pigeons and to comment on each. I brought the first pigeon in from the hallway and placed it in an operant chamber that had several clear plastic walls so that we could observe the bird's behavior. As soon as the pigeon was placed in the chamber, it began to rapidly peck a disk located on the one metal wall. Occasionally, a peck would be followed by the delivery of a small amount of grain into a food cup located under the disk. After several minutes I removed the pigeon from the chamber and took it outside the classroom. The students variously described the pigeon as "extremely hungry," "highly motivated," "well trained," and "very eager." I then went back into the hallway, brought in a second bird, and placed it in the same chamber. Unlike the first bird, this bird did not peck the disk rapidly. Instead, it spent most of its time wandering about the chamber with only a very occasional peck at the disk. These pecks were followed by food about the same number of times as for the first bird. After the second pigeon had been returned to its cage in the hallway, the students described it as "not as highly motivated as the first bird," "not as hungry," "lazy," and so on.

What, in fact, was responsible for the difference in the behavior of the "two" birds? To begin with, there was only one bird. After the bird had first performed, I simply went into the hallway and returned with the same bird. (One pigeon looks pretty much like another unless you are a pigeon.) What differed between the two tests was the color of a light behind the disk—a color that the birds could see but that the students could not. During prior training, when the disk was green, pecking occasionally produced food if *less than 2 seconds* had elapsed since the previous peck. When the disk was red, pecking occasionally produced food if *more than 10 seconds* had elapsed since the prior peck. In summary, the pigeon had learned to peck rapidly when the disk was green and slowly when it was red.

These examples teach several lessons (in addition to the fact that sometimes psychologists are not to be trusted). First, attempting to infer motivation—whether of humans or nonhumans—is a risky business in the absence of knowledge of their histories of reinforcement. Because we are usually ignorant of those histories, we should treat our inferences about motivation with considerable skepticism. Second, because we are often unaware of the histories of others, we tend to attribute their behavior—which we can see—to internal causes—which we cannot. The psychiatrist thought the woman on the hospital ward carried the broom because she was engaged in "magical" thinking; the students thought the bird responded rapidly at some times and slowly at others because of differences in "hunger." In fact, both behaved as they did because of the behavior that had been reinforced in their past—a past that was unknown to the observer.

We are all capable of a wide range of behavior, a range whose breadth is ever increasing as we gain experience. However, our full behavioral repertoire is not expressed at every moment. At one moment, we behave in one way and at another moment in a different way—even when the environment is constant. In everyday language, we say that we were *motivated* to act differently at different times.

What Is Motivation?

Motivation is a term we all use informally, but I restrict it here to refer to the major factors that affect whether and how we behave at a given time. **Motivation** has to do with the instigation, strength, and persistence of behavior and is derived from a Latin word meaning "to move." A person eats or not depending on how long it has been since the last meal or whether he

or she is dieting. People talk to others depending on whether they are friends or strangers. Because *motivation* is a term from the everyday vocabulary, not the laboratory, and because the factors that affect the likelihood of a given behavior are numerous, the topic includes a diverse set of phenomena.

As we'll see in this chapter, some motivational phenomena are primarily dependent on the individual environment (selection by reinforcement), and others are primarily dependent on the ancestral environment (natural selection). Of course, all behavior is affected by both reinforcement and natural selection. Because so many factors influence which behavior occurs out of the many of which we are capable, some motivational phenomena are treated in later chapters—such as dissonance reduction in social behavior (Chapter 15). Among the aspects of motivation considered in the present chapter are reinforcement, aggression, and sexual behavior. We shall also consider emotion, a frequent accompaniment of motivation that includes feelings, expressive behavior, and related physiological changes. Finally, we shall discuss eating and its complex motivational and emotional aspects.

Motivation and Reinforcement

There are many reasons for differences in behavior even when the environment is constant. Let's look at how reinforcement affects the initiation of behavior and its strength and persistence.

What Initiates Behavior?

Motivation cannot be separated from reinforcement and punishment. As explained in Chapter 5, we are motivated to perform operant behavior that has been followed by attaining a reinforcer or escaping a punisher. However, the initiation of behavior is determined by the environment that was present when we experienced these consequences. In short, the initiation of learned behavior depends on the presence of discriminative stimuli for the behavior. When the present environment contains these stimuli, the behavior occurs. When it does not, the behavior does not occur. Because people vary in their histories of differential conditioning (see Chapter 5), they often respond differently in the same environment. An observer, not knowing their different histories, attributes different motivations to the two individuals.

Consider two boys presented with the same homework assignment. One boy does the homework and the other does not. We are tempted to describe the first child as "hard-working" and the second as "lazy." However, these children may have very different reinforcement histories. The first boy may have acquired all the skills necessary to do the homework because of praise from teachers and family for doing prior assignments. As he works on his homework, his behavior produces results that have been reinforced in the past, and the stimuli arising from these results serve as conditioned reinforcers to maintain the behavior until he finishes the assignment. By contrast, the second boy may not have such a history. His prior schooling and his family may not have provided experiences that led to the acquisition of the requisite skills, with the result that he does not complete the assignment. Instead of attributing the boys' differences in behavior to different levels of inner motivation—industry or laziness—we should understand the differences as differences in reinforcement history.

Children whose schooling has provided very different histories of reinforcement are not treated "fairly" when, at some later date, they are exposed to the same contingencies of reinforcement. Unless their entering histories are comparable, their behavior will not bring them reinforcers in the same way. An example from the animal learning laboratory may illustrate the point. Suppose that two pigeons are placed in individual operant chambers and that each pigeon receives food after it has pecked a disk 100 times. One pigeon has had a history in which, at first, a single peck is required for food, then 5 pecks, then 10 pecks, and so on. That is, an increasing number of pecking responses has been shaped. It is likely that this pigeon will eventually receive the food even though 100 pecks are required. The second pigeon, however, has had a history in which only a single peck was required for food. It is likely that responding by the second pigeon will extinguish before the 100th peck has occurred. Thus, the first pigeon appears motivated and the second unmotivated, even though the opportunity for reinforcement is seemingly the same for both birds.

Untoward Effects of Reinforcement   Can would-be reinforcers ever have an undesired effect on motivation? Usually, people apply reinforcement contingencies when they are necessary to maintain behavior that would not otherwise occur or persist. I know that reinforcement is important with a new puppy, for example, to strengthen the likelihood that she will go to the back door and yip when she needs to use the outdoor facilities. I must be attentive to her yipping and must reinforce it by praising her, patting her head, and, most importantly, opening the door. A similar idea often applies to people. Children might never keep their rooms tidy if they did not receive encouragement for this behavior. *Extrinsic* reinforcers (stimuli produced by natural environmental contingencies or by others) may initially be needed to encourage and maintain behavior if *intrinsic* reinforcers (stimuli produced by the person's own behavior) are lacking.

Some psychologists have hypothesized, however, that providing extrinsic rewards for behavior that is already maintained by intrinsic rewards may actually weaken the target behavior (e.g., Deci & Ryan, 1987; Lepper, Greene, & Nisbett, 1973; Ryan & Deci, 2002; Vallerand & Ratelle, 2002). This is called the **overjustification effect**. The general idea behind the concept of overjustification is that the superfluous application of extrinsic rewards for behavior that is intrinsically motivated creates a shift to extrinsic rewards, the net result being a loss of intrinsic motivation. As long as the extrinsic rewards are available, an observer may not notice a difference: The behavior may continue as it did before the extrinsic rewards became available. But what happens when extrinsic rewards are no longer provided? The overjustification theory predicts that after a shift occurs from intrinsic to extrinsic motivation and extrinsic rewards disappear, the person will lose interest in the activity. That is, if the behavior has become maintained by the extrinsic rewards, the behavior will weaken when these rewards are no longer available.

A study by Lepper, Greene, and Nisbett (1973) was among the first of many to demonstrate the overjustification effect. The investigators first carefully documented the free-play activities preferred by a large number of children in a day-care setting. Among the favorite activities was drawing with large felt markers on sheets of newsprint. Drawing, therefore, showed behavioral evidence of intrinsic motivation. The children did not need to play with the art materials, but they did so without any extrinsic consequences. Two weeks after this preliminary assessment, the researchers returned and for one day randomly assigned the children to one of three conditions. In one condition each child was asked to produce a drawing to win a prize. Thus, the prize was contingent on the children's performing the requested behavior. Moreover, the children expected to receive prizes for drawing. Children in a second condition also were asked to make a drawing but were not offered the extrinsic reward. However, they unexpectedly received the same prize as children in the first condition when they had completed drawing. In a third condition the children were neither offered nor given the prize.

After a delay of one or two weeks, the researchers returned and unobtrusively observed children during their normal free playtime. Remember that during free-play periods, no one was present who might offer or give extrinsic rewards to the children—they were on their own. The results of these observations revealed a strong overjustification effect. Children who had previously received an expected prize played with the drawing materials less than did children in the other two groups. In terms of overjustification, they showed less intrinsic motivation during their free-play period. The children who received an unexpected prize in the prior session showed no evidence that their intrinsic motivation had been undermined. They spent about the same amount of time drawing as before. When the prize was unexpected, no shift from intrinsic to extrinsic motivation occurred. This finding has been replicated with children and adults across a variety of activities, and in laboratory and field settings (see Ryan & Deci, 2000).

Other research with both adults and children shows an important qualification of the overjustification effect. Extrinsic rewards that depend on the quality of performance and are not offered coercively may increase intrinsic motivation (e.g., Enzle & Ross, 1978; Karniol & Ross, 1977; Vallerand & Reid, 1984). Indeed, direct verbal praise can enhance intrinsic motivation, provided that it is sincere, that it conveys competence, and that it does not coerce the learner into engaging in the behavior (Henderlong & Lepper, 2002).

What can we conclude? Extrinsic rewards are obviously essential, but judiciousness is required as learners gain experience. Parents, educators, and employers should be careful not to use rewards in ways that shift attention from intrinsic to extrinsic reinforcers. Rewards can help instigate and maintain behavior that would otherwise not occur. Related phenomena may be found in earlier findings from the animal learning laboratory. For example, if a rat's lever pressing is originally acquired and maintained with a small amount of food as a reinforcer and then lever pressing is followed by a larger reinforcer, a return to the small reinforcer causes lever pressing to fall below its original level (Flaherty, 1982). Also, stimuli are known to be effective as reinforcers only when they are unexpected (Rescorla & Wagner, 1972). Of course, interpretations of human behavior in terms of findings from the animal laboratory are always complicated by the extensive and incompletely known histories of humans.

Learned Helplessness Organisms with a history in which their behavior has been ineffective in determining its conse-

quences become less sensitive to the consequences of their behavior. That is, they lose motivation, because they have learned that they are powerless to affect their own destinies. Maier and Seligman (1976) reported a series of animal experiments that demonstrated this effect, which is called **learned helplessness**. Learned helplessness involves learning that the consequences of behavior are independent of one's behavior—that an aversive outcome cannot be avoided or escaped or that an appetitive outcome cannot be achieved.

The basic experiment in this area was conducted by Overmeier and Seligman (1967). These researchers placed dogs in an apparatus in which unavoidable shocks were given. Next, they placed each dog in another apparatus in which the animal underwent a series of trials that provided a warning stimulus before an electrical shock. In this second situation, the animals could avoid the shocks by stepping over a small barrier to the other side of the apparatus. Dogs in a control group quickly learned to step over the barrier and avoid the shock. However, dogs that had previously received inescapable shocks in the other apparatus failed to learn. They just squatted in the corner and took the shock as if they had learned that it made no difference what they did. They had learned to be helpless. A related effect was found with appetitive stimuli: Acquisition of a learned response is impaired if animals receive food regardless of their behavior before experimenters make food contingent on the response (Engberg, Hansen, Welker, & Thomas, 1972).

Some psychologists believe that learned helplessness has important implications for human motivation (Seligman, 1975; Seligman & Nolen-Hoeksema, 1987). When people have experiences in which they are powerless to control the events that happen to them, they may become depressed, and their motivational level may decrease. The change in motivation occurs because the helplessness training reduces their expectation that performing a task will bring success. Learned helplessness has also been likened to a personality trait; that is, people who have had major experiences with unsolvable dilemmas may not try to succeed in other types of tasks, including problems they could solve (Overmeier, 1998). Findings from the animal laboratory may again be relevant, such as the finding that expected stimuli have diminished reinforcing effects. Finally, variables that are specific to the species used in the original demonstrations of learned helplessness may have affected the result. For example, dogs that receive aversive stimuli in the presence of other dogs later show a canine submissive response to those dogs, cowering and remaining immobile. If canine submissive behavior was conditioned to stimuli in these experiments when the shock was inescapable, it may have impeded the later acquisition of avoidance behavior.

What Determines the Strength of Behavior?

We often make assumptions about people's level of motivation from the rate at which responding occurs. If we see others responding without interruption or at a high rate, we take this as evidence that they are "highly motivated." If they respond only occasionally or at a low rate, we describe them as "unmotivated" or even "lazy." As an example, when you look around the library, you may see some students hunched over their books, intently reading, making notes, and so on; others may be staring off into space or idly looking about. You may be tempted to conclude that the first group is motivated and the second is not. But recall the behavior of the pigeon in the green-light–red-light demonstration. The same pigeon responded rapidly when placed in the test chamber the first time, but slowly the second time. You now know that different rates of pecking had different histories of reinforcement during the two colors—food followed rapid responses in one case and slow responses in the other. That is, the specific circumstances under which pecking was reinforced changed as the color changed.

Schedules of Intermittent Reinforcement

In technical terms, what changed in the piegon's green–red training was the schedule of reinforcement. A **schedule of reinforcement** specifies the conditions that must occur before a response produces a reinforcer. It turns out that many behavioral characteristics that are conventionally ascribed to differences in motivation are actually products of the schedules of reinforcement under which a response was acquired. When we do not know the schedule of reinforcement under which the response was acquired, we often attribute the strength of responding to the level of motivation. Let's look at some of the common schedules of reinforcement that have been studied in the laboratory and the patterns of responding they produce.

If every instance of a response is followed by a reinforcer, the schedule is a *continuous (consistent) reinforcement schedule.* For example, if every peck of a pigeon produces food, or if every time a child correctly reads a word the teacher says, "Good," the behavior is being reinforced on a schedule of continuous reinforcement. Our concern here, however, is primarily with the effects of schedules of *intermittent* reinforcement—schedules in which only *some* responses are followed by a reinforcer. The study of intermittent schedules is of general importance because the reinforcement contingencies that behavior encounters in the natural environment are usually intermittent, not continuous. Sometimes passing the butter at dinner is followed by a "Thank you," but often it is not. Sometimes casting a fishing line catches a fish; very often it does not.

The classic schedules of intermittent reinforcement were devised by B. F. Skinner (Ferster & Skinner 1957). These schedules manipulate two major variables—the number of *responses* and the amount of *time* required before a response produces a reinforcer. Schedules that manipulate response requirements are called **ratio schedules**. An everyday example of a ratio-type schedule is sawing a board. A piece of wood of the proper size (the reinforcer) is produced only after a number of saw-strokes has been executed. Ratio schedules are so named because they specify a particular *ratio* between responding and reinforcers. If it takes 10 saw-strokes to produce a piece of wood of the proper size, then the ratio is 10 to 1. Schedules that manipulate

temporal variables are called **interval schedules**. They vary the amount of time that elapses before a response produces a reinforcer. As an example of an interval schedule, picture yourself glancing to see if the bus has arrived to take you to school. A glance produces seeing the bus (the reinforcer) only after a set amount of time has elapsed. Unlike sawing, increasing the number of glances will not produce the reinforcing stimulus more quickly.

Schedules of reinforcement—whether ratio or interval—are often somewhat variable. The number of saw-strokes to cut a board varies with the hardness of the wood; the time before the bus arrives varies with the amount of traffic. For that reason, laboratory studies of schedules of reinforcement have investigated the patterns of responding produced by both fixed and variable schedules. In fixed schedules, the response produces a reinforcer after a constant number of responses (*fixed-ratio schedules*) or the passage of a constant amount of time (*fixed-interval schedules*). In variable schedules, the response produces a reinforcer after a varying number of responses (*variable-ratio schedules*) or a varying amount of time since the prior reinforcer (*variable-interval schedule*).

Illustrative examples of the patterns of behavior produced by these four combinations of ratio and interval, and fixed and variable schedules of reinforcement are shown in Figure 13.1.

Figure 13•1 plots responding on a different type of graph than we have seen previously. This graph is a **cumulative record** of responses. In a cumulative record, every response moves the curve upward as time passes. Cumulative records allow us to readily detect patterns in responding over time. Inspection of these cumulative records reveals two major trends. First, ratio schedules generally produce higher rates of responding than interval schedules. This may be one reason that many union contracts outlaw so-called piece-work agreements in which pay is dependent on the number of goods produced. Such agreements produce more work for less pay. Management also has concerns about ratio (piece-work) schedules of pay because high rates of production can lower the quality of work unless there is considerable oversight. Second, variable schedules produce more uniform rates of responding than do fixed schedules. In fixed schedules, the learner comes to discriminate that responses are not reinforced after a response has been recently reinforced. Research has shown that the failure to respond at the beginning of a fixed-interval or fixed-ratio schedule becomes more pronounced as the response or time requirement grows larger. Once responding has begun, however, it continues at a substantial rate, particularly with fixed-ratio schedules. (See Figure 13.1.) Something similar occurs when we have a large project to complete. Beginning the project is the most difficult part. We find every excuse not to begin—the room is too warm, the neighbors are too noisy, and so on. However, once we begin, we often consistently work for prolonged periods of time.

Research with schedules of reinforcement has shown that the conditions that immediately precede the reinforced response acquire the greatest control of the response. These

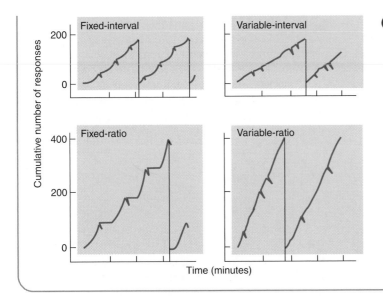

FIGURE 13·1 Cumulative records of the effect of different reinforcement schedules on operant responding. Interval schedules are shown in the top row, ratio schedules in the bottom row. Fixed schedules are shown in the left column, variables schedules in the right column. When a curve reached its maximum, it returned to the baseline level and then increased again as responding continued.

(From Donahoe, J. W., and Palmer, D. C. (1994). *Learning and Complex Behavior.* Boston, MA: Allyn and Bacon. Reprinted with permission from J. W. Donahoe.)

conditions include not only the environmental events at the moment of reinforcement but any persisting effects of prior environmental and behavioral events. For example, because the times of emission of responses are always somewhat variable, the response that satisfies a ratio requirement is more likely to be part of a "burst" of responses than to be a single discrete response. Accordingly, responding in bursts (rapid responding) is more apt to be followed by a reinforcer than is a single response (Williams, 1968). Thus, high rates of responding are differentially produced by ratio schedules.

Modern work on schedules of reinforcement does not often use the original procedures of Ferster and Skinner. These procedures were limited by the sorts of equipment available at the time. Through the introduction of computers, research on schedules began to better control the precise conditions present when a response was reinforced (Blough, 1966; Platt, 1973). A major conclusion from the work on schedules of reinforcement is that many of the differences in the strength of responding that were formerly attributed to differences in the level of motivation are due to differences in the schedule under which the behavior was acquired. Consider a child at the grocery store who repeatedly asks a parent to buy candy, even after the parent has said no many times. We might be tempted to attribute the child's persistence to a high motivation to obtain candy. It is more likely that repeated requests have, in the past, eventually led to the parent's buying the candy. Thus, the parent has unintentionally reinforced pleading for candy on a variable-ratio schedule, and the behavior now occurs at high rate and for long periods of time without reinforcement.

Deprivation of Reinforcers Our level of motivation, as reflected by our rate of responding, is affected by factors other than the schedule of reinforcement. Another major factor is **deprivation** of a reinforcer—how long it has been since we contacted a particular reinforcer. The opportunity to eat a

piece of cake may be an effective reinforcer, but it will be less so if you have just eaten a piece of the cake. The chance to play a video game may be an effective reinforcer, but it will be less so if you already have been playing for several hours. Absence does, in fact, make the heart grow fonder.

Ethical considerations usually preclude the study of deprivation with humans, but the effect of deprivation of reinforcers on levels of motivation can be studied quite precisely under the controlled conditions of the animal laboratory. For example, the lever-pressing behavior of rats was studied with different levels of food deprivation (Clark, 1958). Lever pressing produced food on a one-minute variable-interval schedule. Because an interval schedule of reinforcement was used, changes in the rate of responding had no effect on the rate at which food occurred—lever pressing could not produce food until an average of one minute had passed. Thus the rate of lever pressing shows the effect of deprivation of the reinforcer unaffected by other variables. **Figure 13·2** depicts the results of the experiment. Clearly, as the level of deprivation increased, the rate of responding increased, even though the increase did not produce more reinforcers. Deprivation of a reinforcer, whether of food or a loved one, increases the level of motivation.

Availability of Reinforcers for Other Behavior The level of motivation for a response is affected not only by the scheduling and deprivation of reinforcers but also by the availability of competing reinforcers for other responses. A piece of vanilla cake may be an effective reinforcer, but less so if chocolate cake is also available. Playing Pac-Man may be reinforcing, but less so if Quake or The Sims is also available (to say nothing of Grand Theft Auto). Again, animal experiments most clearly reveal the effect of this variable. Pigeons were placed in a test chamber in which either of two disks could be pecked. Pecking either disk was reinforced with food, but according to different schedules of reinforcement for each disk.

FIGURE 13•2 Effect of hours of food deprivation on the rate of responding on a variable-interval schedule of reinforcement. The rate of responding could not affect the rate of reinforcement.

(Clark, F. C. (1958). The effect of deprivation and frequency of reinforcement on variable interval responding. *Journal of the Experimental Analysis of Behavior, 1,* 221–228. Copyright © 1958 by the Society for the Experimental Analysis of Behavior, Inc. Reprinted by permission.)

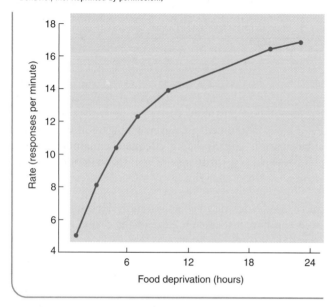

FIGURE 13•3 Effect of the relative rate of reinforcement on the relative rate of responding under concurrent reinforcement schedules. Two alternative operant responses were available, each with its own schedule of reinforcement. The proportion of responses for an alternative matched the proportion of reinforcers received for responding to that alternative.

(Herrnstein, R. J. (1970). On the law of effect. *Journal of the Experimental Analysis of Behavior, 13,* 7, 243–266. Copyright © 1970 by the Society for the Experimental Analysis of Behavior, Inc. Reprinted by permission.)

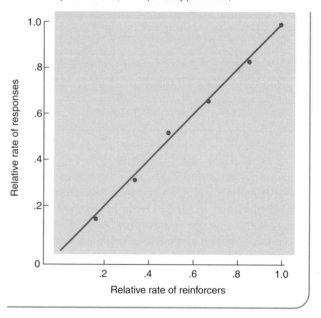

Schedules of reinforcement in which more than one operant is measured are called **concurrent schedules**. The world outside the laboratory typically confronts us with complex concurrent schedules in which several alternative responses are available, each with its associated schedule of reinforcement, and we must choose between the alternatives.

In the pigeon experiment, responding was reinforced on each disk according to different variable-interval reinforcement schedules. Once again, the use of variable-interval schedules ensured that the pigeons' rate of responding had little effect on the rate at which reinforcers occurred, thus revealing the effect of the alternative source of reinforcement while controlling other variables. **Figure 13•3** shows changes in the relative rate of responding to an alternative as a function of the relative rate of reinforcers for that response (Herrnstein, 1961, 1970). The choice of an alternative clearly depended on how the reinforcers for that response compared with the reinforcers for the other response. Choice matched the relative reinforcers for the alternative. This result, known as the **matching relation,** has been found in a wide range of studies, including studies with humans (Baum, 1974). In laboratory trials the reinforcement of individual responses can produce matching as its cumulative effect (Shimp, 1969; Staddon & Hinson, 1983). For example, suppose that during an hour 10 reinforcers are available for responding to the first of two alternatives but only 5 reinforcers (half as many) for the second alternative. Under these conditions 40 minutes will be spent on the first alternative and only 20 minutes (half

as long) on the second. However, if the second alternative provides 50 reinforcers to the first alternative's 10, the time spent on the first alternative will be reduced to only 10 minutes. In summary, the motivation to engage in an activity depends on the reinforcers for other concurrently available activities.

What Determines the Persistence of Behavior?

Another common measure of motivation is the persistence of behavior when responding is challenged in various ways—by the withholding of reinforcers, by reinforcement of competing behavior, and so on (Nevin & Grace, 2000). In Chapter 5 we saw that behavior acquired with intermittent reinforcement was more resistant to extinction than behavior acquired with continuous reinforcement. What happens during intermittent reinforcement that makes behavior more persistent?

Among the important factors is the particular *sequence* of reinforced and unreinforced responses during training (Capaldi, Haas, Miller, & Martins, 2005). Studies have shown that if intermittent training ensures that a reinforced response occurs only after a series of unreinforced responses, resistance to extinction is greatly enhanced. Training that

▲ *One meaning of motivation is persistence—working steadily on projects that take much time and effort to complete.*

consists of the same number of unreinforced responses, but in which the reinforcers do not occur after long series of unreinforced responses, does not produce behavior that is nearly as resistant to extinction. In other words, succeeding after several failures causes the learner to resist the effects of subsequent failure. As applied to human behavior outside the laboratory, these findings suggest that experiencing failure in our past facilitates persistence of later performance, but only if failure was eventually followed by success. The "school of hard-knocks" does not by itself teach us to endure in the face of adversity. On the contrary, experiencing tough times can lead us to give up unless success sometimes occurs.

In studies of extinction, psychologists discovered another motivational effect: Environmental stimuli that are present during extinction become aversive. The aversive properties of these stimuli are evident in several ways. First, it has long been known that laboratory animals acquire responses if they allow them to escape environments in which extinction is scheduled. The motivational effects of extinction are called **frustration** (Amsel, 1962). Second, if another animal is present when the learner's responses undergo extinction, the other animal may be attacked—a finding that has been confirmed in humans (Kelly & Hake, 1970). In fact, under such circumstances the learner will acquire a new response if, by so doing, the learner will gain an opportunity for aggression (Azrin, Hutchison, & Hake, 1966). This phenomenon is called **extinction-induced aggression**. Extinction causes other members of the species to become eliciting stimuli for aggressive behavior and thereby establishes the opportunity to aggress as a reinforcing stimulus. For obvious reasons, most studies on frustration and extinction-induced aggression have been conducted with nonhumans; however, their findings' applicability to human behavior seems clear. The husband who berates his partner on returning home from a day at work where "nothing went right" is probably displaying extinction-induced aggression. A similar phenomenon also may occur when groups within society who are not prospering blame other groups for their misfortune, as in scapegoating.

Interim Summary

Motivation and Reinforcement

Motivation is a general term for a group of phenomena affecting the *nature, strength,* and *persistence* of behavior. It includes a tendency to perform responses that bring an individual into contact with an appetitive stimulus or that move it away from an aversive one. Very often we infer an organism's level of motivation from differences in the rate or vigor of responding, but these may simply reflect differences in the schedule of reinforcement under which the behavior was acquired. Behavior is initiated when the environment contains stimuli that were present when the behavior was reinforced. However, giving reinforcers when a behavior is already being adequately maintained may actually lower performance when those reinforcers are withdrawn. Extrinsic reinforcers sometimes undermine the effect of intrinsic reinforcers, a phenomenon known as overjustification. Also, a history in which behavior does not affect the occurrence of important events may foster learned helplessness.

The strength of behavior, as reflected in the rate and timing of its occurrence, is often the result of the schedule of reinforcement under which the behavior was acquired and not the level of motivation. Common schedules of intermittent reinforcement vary the response requirements (ratio schedules) or time requirements (interval schedules) before a response produces a reinforcer.

Deprivation of contact with reinforcers—whether they be food or friends—increases the reinforcing value of those stimuli. The presence of competing reinforcers for other responses, in contrast, weakens the effectiveness of a reinforcer.

The persistence of responding when reinforcers are infrequent or absent is enhanced if the behavior was acquired with an intermittent schedule of reinforcement. The increase in persistence is greatest when the reinforcer occurs after a series of unreinforced responses.

QUESTIONS TO CONSIDER

1. What are some of the ways that you might seek to explain the following behavior, given what you know about schedules of reinforcement? A child keeps asking his parents to take him out to play even after the parents say that they are busy and will go out to play later. Again, making use of what you know about schedules of reinforcement, what could the parents do to make this behavior less likely in the future?

2. Evaluate the following statement: When people have tough times as they are growing up, they can better withstand life's later difficulties. When might this be true, and when might it not?

Aggressive Behavior

Aggression is a serious problem in human society. Every day, we hear of incidents involving violence and cruelty. If we are to live in a safer world, we must learn about the causes of aggressive behavior. Many factors influence a person's tendency to commit acts of aggression, including frustration when our behavior is no longer reinforced, childhood experiences, exposure to violence in the media, and physiological factors. Various aspects of aggressive behavior have been studied by biological, behavioral, and social scientists. We will examine some of the key variables that affect human aggression; but first, let's look at research on nonhuman animals in their natural environments.

Ethological Studies of Aggression

Violence and aggression are seen in many species other than our own. If aggression were harmful to survival of a population, we would not expect it to be so prevalent in nature. Ethologists—zoologists who study the behavior of animals in their natural environments—have analyzed the causes of aggression and have shown that in many cases aggressive behavior does, in fact, have value for the survival of species.

The Social Relevance of Intraspecific Aggression

Intraspecific aggression is aggression by one animal against another member of its own species. Ethologists have shown that intraspecific aggression has several biological advantages. First, it tends to disperse a population of animals, forcing some into new territories. The adaptations required by these new environments increase the flexibility of the species. Second, rivalry among males for mating opportunities perpetuates the genes of the healthier, more vigorous animals. The human situation, of course, is somewhat different from that of other species because of culture. Culture, through learning, provides a means whereby the selecting effects of previous environments may be transmitted to the next generation by other than genetic means. Perhaps intraspecific aggression has outlived whatever usefulness it may have had for humans.

Threat and Appeasement Ethologists studying aggression have discovered a related set of behaviors in many species: ritualized threat gestures and appeasement gestures. **Threat gestures** communicate an animal's aggressive intent to other members of the species before actual violence begins. For example, if one dog intrudes on another's territory, the defender growls and bares its teeth, raises the fur on its back (presumably making it look larger to its opponent), and stares at the intruder. Almost always, the dog defending its territory drives the intruder away. Threat gestures are particularly important in species whose members are able to kill one another (Eibl-Eiesfeldt, 1980; Lorenz, 1966). For example, wolves often threaten each other with growls and bared teeth but rarely bite each other. Because an all-out battle between two wolves would probably end in the death of one and serious injury to the other, the tendency to perform ritualized displays has an obvious advantage to the survival of the species.

To forestall an impending attack, one of the animals must behave in such a way as to show that it will not fight—that it will accept defeat. The submissive animal makes an **appeasement gesture**. For example, if two wolves get into a fight, one animal usually submits to the other by lying down and exposing its throat. The sight of a helpless and vulnerable opponent terminates the victor's hostility, and the fight ceases. The aggression of the dominant animal is appeased.

Hormones and Aggression

In birds and most mammals, male sex hormones (androgens, such as testosterone) exert a strong effect on aggressiveness. In nonhuman species testosterone exerts an **organizational effect** on the brain during development and an **activational effect** on some forms of aggressive behavior during adulthood. (We'll look more closely at these effects later in the chapter.) As shown in **Figure 13•4,** for example, a normal adult male mouse will fiercely attack other male mice that intrude into its territory; but if a male mouse is castrated early in life, before its brain has matured, it will not attack another male later, even if given injections of

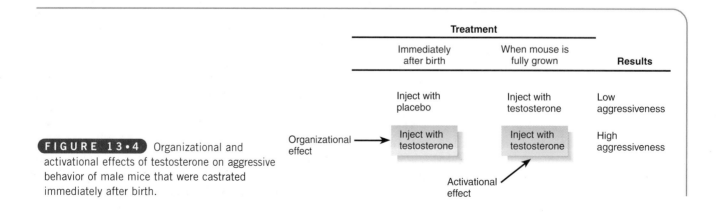

FIGURE 13•4 Organizational and activational effects of testosterone on aggressive behavior of male mice that were castrated immediately after birth.

testosterone (Conner & Levine, 1969). As always, natural selection and learning interact to determine behavior. As an illustration, pigeons establish literal pecking orders that determine the ranks of birds in the colony. In one study low-ranking male pigeons increased their rank after they had been injected with testosterone *and* their aggressive behavior (pecking another pigeon) had been reinforced with food in another situation. However, neither testosterone alone nor reinforcing aggressive behavior alone had such an effect (Lumia, 1972).

Do hormones also influence aggressive behavior in humans? On average, men are more physically aggressive than women (see Eagly & Steffen, 1986), and persons of either sex with higher testosterone levels appear to be more aggressive (Starzyk & Quinsey, 2001). Some male perpetrators of sexual assault have been treated with drugs that block androgen receptors and thus prevent androgens from exerting their normal effects. The rationale is based on animal research that indicates that androgens promote both sexual behavior and aggression in males. The efficacy of such treatment of humans with antiandrogens has yet to be established (Bain, 1987).

One way to determine whether androgens affect aggressiveness in humans is to examine the testosterone levels of people who exhibit varying levels of aggressive behavior. What is the evidence? Dabbs and colleagues (Dabbs, Carr, Frady, & Riad, 1995; Dabbs, Frady, Carr, & Besch, 1987) measured the testosterone levels of male prison inmates and found a significant correlation with several measures of violence, including the nature of the crimes for which inmates were convicted, the frequency or severity of inmates' infractions of prison rules, and ratings of inmates' "toughness" by their peers. These relations are also seen in female prison inmates. Women prisoners who had histories of unprovoked violence and had several prior convictions also showed higher levels of testosterone (Dabbs & Hargrove, 1997; Dabbs, Ruback, Frady, & Hopper, 1988). Women and men both can produce androgens from the adrenal glands.

We must remember that correlation does not necessarily indicate causation. A person's environment can affect his or her testosterone level. For example, one very thorough study found that the blood testosterone levels of a group of five men confined on a boat for 14 days changed as the men established a dominance–aggression ranking among themselves: The higher the rank, the higher the testosterone level (Jeffcoate, Lincoln, Selby, & Herbert, 1986). Yet in a correlational study such as this, we cannot be sure that high testosterone levels cause people to become dominant or violent; perhaps their success in establishing a position of dominance increases their testosterone levels relative to those of the people they dominate.

Some athletes have taken anabolic steroids in order to increase their muscle mass and strength and, supposedly, their competitiveness. Anabolic steroids include natural androgens and synthetic hormones that have androgenic ef-

fects. This would lead us to expect increases in aggressiveness among these athletes. And indeed, several studies have found exactly that effect. For example, male weight lifters who were taking anabolic steroids were more aggressive and hostile than those who were not (Yates, Perry, & Murray, 1992). Again, bear in mind that we cannot be certain that the steroid was responsible for the increased aggressiveness: Perhaps it was the men who were already more competitive and aggressive who chose to take the steroids. Taken together, however, the research findings strongly suggest (although they do not prove) that androgens stimulate aggression in humans as in other animals.

Environmental Variables That Affect Human Aggression

Environmental variables, including the behavior of family members and peers as well as the impact of the media, can play a part in human aggression.

Imitation of Aggression

Consider the following conversation:

> *Parent:* I don't know what to do with Johnny. His teacher says he is simply impossible. He just can't keep from hitting and kicking other children.
>
> *Friend:* Perhaps he needs more discipline.
>
> *Parent:* But I spank him all the time!

Why does Johnny persist in being aggressive even though this behavior is regularly punished? Some psychologists suggest that, instead of suppressing his violent behavior, frequent spankings *teach* Johnny to be aggressive. When his parents become upset with his behavior, they resort to physical violence. Johnny then learns by observation and imitation (see Chapter 5).

A large percentage of nonviolent people may have been spanked when they were children with no obvious harm. However, when parents habitually resort to aggression, their children may learn to do the same. To take an extreme example, many (though by no means all) parents who beat their children have themselves been victims of child abuse. It is important to note, however, that most adults who were physically abused as children manage to avoid repeating the pattern with their own children.

Most parents do not beat their children or even spank them frequently. But there is another opportunity for imitation in our society: violent behavior on television and in movies, comic books, and video games. The heroes in these media often disdain peaceful solutions to their problems and instead seek to resolve them through fighting. On average, North American children witness between 100,000 and 200,000 violent acts on television by the age of 18, with half that number viewed before the age of 12 (Plagens, Miller, Foote, & Yoffe, 1991; Sleek, 1994). Most people agree that it would be unfortunate if real people were as violent as the characters we see portrayed on television and in films. Does the continued observation of violence in the mass media lead children to choose aggressive means to solve their problems? Or are the television networks and movie studios correct when they argue that children have no trouble separating fact from fantasy and that the mass media only give us what we want anyway?

Psychologists and sociologists have shown keen interest in this question. Numerous researchers have studied the possible effects of media violence using correlational methods in both real-life environments and the laboratory. What can be concluded from the hundreds of investigations? Generally, there is a positive correlation between the amount of violent media programming that children watch and subsequent aggressive behavior (see Bushman & Huesmann, 2001). The relationship holds even when people are tracked from childhood to adulthood (Huesmann, Moise-Titus, Podolski, & Eron, 2003; Johnson et al., 2002). The obvious conclusion would seem to be that violent media programming causes increased violence among those who watch it. Yet as suggestive as such studies are, we must be careful to observe the fundamental problem with correlational studies (see Chapter 2). Again, correlation does not prove causation. Any effort at reducing violence in society requires that we make the right decisions about where to put our resources and attention. If media violence is a major culprit, then that is where a great deal of our attention and efforts should go. However, another possibility is that causation flows in the opposite direction. We must ask whether the results of the media violence studies might simply show that the degree to which people are predisposed to violence causally affects the amount of violent programming they choose to watch (e.g., Freedman, 2002). For example, it would not be surprising if aggressive boys chose to watch more aggressive programming than nonaggressive boys did. People watch programs that interest them. Thus, the alternative hypothesis about causal directionality is plausible. It may be that violent programming does substantially increase violence and aggression in our society, but the research carried out to date has not established this beyond a doubt.

Interim Summary

Aggressive Behavior

In many species aggression serves useful purposes within limits. Ethological studies of other species reveal the presence of mechanisms to limit violence: Threat gestures warn of an impending attack, and appeasement gestures propitiate the potential aggressor. In males of most species of animals,

androgens clearly have effects on aggressive behavior. The same is probably true of humans.

Parental and media violence may affect aggression in society through the process of imitation. In the case of media, correlational data cannot establish whether watching violent programming produces aggression against others or innate aggressiveness produces watching violent programming.

QUESTION TO CONSIDER

From the point of view of evolution, aggressive behavior and a tendency to establish dominance have useful functions. In particular, they increase the likelihood that only the healthiest and vigorous animals will reproduce. Can you think of examples of good and bad effects of these tendencies among members of our own species?

Sexual Behavior

The motivation to engage in sexual behavior can be very strong. (Most people agree with this statement, because those who disagree have left few offspring.) However, sexual behavior is not motivated by a biological need in the way that eating is, for example. Eating is necessary for the survival of the individual to the age of mating. Sexual behavior is necessary for the survival of the species and, in a sense, is the ultimate purpose of eating. Because reproduction requires both behavior and a nervous system that supports that behavior, natural selection has favored the selection of both.

Effects of the Brain's Reinforcement System on Sexual Behavior

Research has shown that the brain regions that are important for reinforcement are also important for sexual behavior. In fact, these same brain regions are involved in the effects of all reinforcers—naturally occurring reinforcers (such as food, water, and sexual contact), man-made reinforcers (such as heroin, alcohol, and cocaine), and the innumerable conditioned reinforcers that arise from experience. The normal function of the neural reinforcing system is to strengthen connections between neurons that detect discriminative stimuli (such as the sight of a lever) and those that mediate operant behavior (such as lever pressing). Experimenters have found that the reinforcing system can be stimulated not only by environmental stimuli but also by internal stimuli from electrodes implanted in the brain. In fact, the first evidence that activity in these brain regions was involved in reinforcement came from studies using electrical stimulation (see **Figure 13·5** and the Evaluating Scientific Issues feature describing this discovery).

FIGURE 13·5 Overview of the brain's reinforcement system. Electrical brain stimulation activates the system.

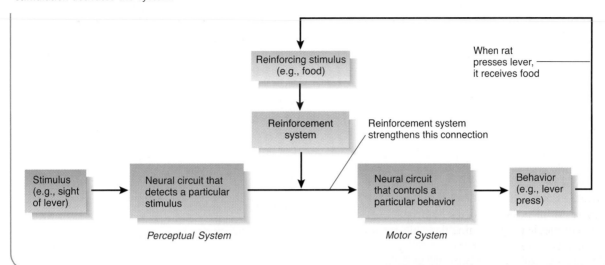

As described in Chapter 5, researchers discovered that an essential component of the reinforcement system consists of neurons that release the neuromodulator dopamine. All reinforcing stimuli appear to trigger the release of dopamine in the brain, including sexual stimulation. **Figure 13·6** illustrates the effects of sexually related stimuli and sexual activity on the release of dopamine from neurons in a part of the brain known to be involved in reinforcement. As shown in the figure, the dopamine levels in a male rat's brain increased when stimuli from the test chamber indicated that sexual stimulation was forthcoming and increased still further when the rat experienced additional stimuli.

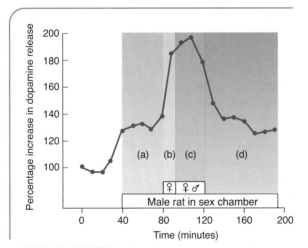

FIGURE 13·6 Release of dopamine produced by reinforcing stimuli. The graph indicates levels of dopamine in a region of a male rat's forebrain. (a) Rat is placed in apparatus in which it has mated before. (b) Receptive female is placed behind a wire-mesh partition. (c) Partition is removed; the animals copulate. (d) The female is removed.

Evaluating Scientific Issues

What Is the Role of Chance in Scientific Breakthroughs?

James Olds, then a young assistant professor of McGill University, designed an experiment in 1954 to determine if the reticular formation of the brain (a region in the brain stem) played a role in learning. Olds implanted an electrode in the brains of rats to stimulate the reticular formation with electricity. He thought that this stimulation might boost the rats' ability to learn a maze, because activity in the reticular formation was thought to enhance attention. If the stimulated animals learned the task faster than control animals that were not stimulated, the attention hypothesis would be supported.

Olds enlisted the aid of Peter Milner, a graduate student who was acquainted with the new surgical procedure needed to implant electrodes in the brain. But because the procedure had only recently been developed and was not very accurate, one electrode wound up in the wrong place—near the opposite end of a rat's brain, in fact. This turned out to be a lucky accident, because through it Olds and Milner discovered a phenomenon that they would not have encountered if the electrode had been placed where they intended.

● A Lucky Mistake

Olds and Milner had previously heard a talk by another psychologist, Neal Miller, who had discovered that electrical stimulation of some parts of the brain was aversive. That is, animals worked to avoid stimulating these parts of the brain. The investigators tested their rats to ensure that their stimulation did not have an aversive effect, because such an effect would interfere with performance in the maze. The behavior of most animals was unremarkable, but the one rat with a misplaced electrode produced a surprise. To test for possible aversive effects, experimenters gave the animal electrical stimulation when it entered one corner of the test area. Instead of avoiding that corner, however, the rat returned to the corner time and time again.

Realizing that they had seen something very important, Olds followed up the initial observations with, in his words, "the help of Hess's technique for probing the brain and Skinner's for measuring motivation":

> The first animal in the Skinner box ended all doubts in our minds that electric stimulation applied to some parts of the brain could indeed provide a reward for behavior. The test displayed the phenomenon in bold relief where anyone who wanted to look could see it. Left to itself in the apparatus, the animal (after about two to five minutes of learning) stimulated its own brain regularly about once every five seconds, taking a stimulus of a second or so every time. After thirty minutes the experimenter turned off the current, so that the animal's pressing of the lever no longer stimulated the brain. Under these conditions the animal pressed it about seven times and went to sleep. We found that the test was repeatable as often as we cared to apply it. When the current was turned on and the animal was given one shock as an hors d'oeuvre it would begin stimulating its brain again. When the electricity was turned off, it would try a few times and then go to sleep. (Olds, 1956, pp. 107–108)

Olds and Milner put electrodes in the same region of the brain in other rats and allowed them to press a lever that caused the region to be stimulated. The rats quickly learned to press the lever at a rate of more than 700 times per hour. The reinforcing effect of the electrical brain stimulation was extremely potent. When given a choice between pressing the lever for stimulation and eating, drinking, or copulating, the animals chose the lever!

● **What Should We Conclude?**

Olds and Milner's (1954) discovery had a greater impact on behavioral science than any other experiment in physiological psychology. James Olds fully appreciated the impact of the finding, dropped his work on attention, and embarked on an extremely productive career pursuing the neural mechanisms of reinforcement. As with Pavlov before him, Olds had stumbled on an observation that he had the good sense to appreciate and that caused him to drop his prior line of research to pursue new goals. In the words of Neal Miller, "His initial and greatest discovery resulted from having the wit to notice and exploit a totally unexpected outcome—an important aspect of science and inadequately understood by the general public or by those legislators who believe that it is efficient to concentrate most research on specific planned programs to attack targeted practical problems" (Miller, 1977). Unfortunately, James Olds died in 1976, at the age of 54, in a sailing accident off the coast of California. If he had lived, it is quite likely that his work would have been recognized with a Nobel Prize. Chance brought him a great discovery, but it also robbed him of the full benefits of that discovery.

Effects of Sex Hormones on Sexual Behavior

The motivation to perform sexual behavior is affected not only by the brain's reinforcement system but also by the sex hormones. Sex hormones, which are primarily secreted by the testes and ovaries, have effects on cells throughout the body. In general, these effects are related to reproduction. For example, they cause the production of sperm, build up the lining of the uterus, trigger ovulation, and stimulate the production of milk. Sex hormones also affect nerve cells in the brain, however, thereby affecting sexual behavior.

Sex hormones do not by themselves *cause* sexual behavior. Behavior consists of responses to particular situations and is affected by experience. What sex hormones affect is the *motivation* to perform particular classes of reproductive behaviors.

Effects of Androgens

As we saw in Chapter 12, androgens such as testosterone are necessary for male sexual development. During prenatal development the testes of male fetuses secrete testosterone, which causes the male sex organs to develop. This hormone also affects the development of the brain. The prenatal effects of sex hormones, as mentioned earlier, are called organizational effects, because they alter the organization of the sex organs and the brain. Studies using laboratory animals have shown that if the organizational effects of androgens on brain development are prevented, the animal later fails to exhibit male sexual behavior. Androgens enable the development of certain brain and other structures (*masculinization*) and disable the development of others (*defeminization*). In addition, in adulthood androgens have activational effects whereby the hormones activate sex organs and brain circuits that have already been developed. Males cannot have erections and engage in sexual intercourse unless testosterone is present in adulthood (see **Figure 13•7**).

To study the activational effects of testosterone on sexual behavior, Davidson, Camargo, and Smith (1979) performed a carefully controlled double-blind study on men whose testes were not then secreting normal amounts of androgens. The men were given monthly injections of a placebo or one of two different dosages of a long-lasting form of testosterone.

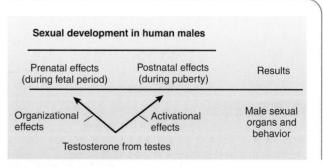

FIGURE 13•7 Organizational and activational effects of testosterone on male sexual development and behavior in humans.

(A placebo has no true treatment effect but provides a control for events that accompany the treatment, such as the injection in this case.) When the men receiving testosterone were compared with the men in the control group, testosterone had large effects on total number of erections and attempts at intercourse during the month following the injection. Larger doses produced more of an effect than did smaller doses. Thus, we may conclude that testosterone definitely affects male sexual performance. Although testosterone affects sexual motivation, it does not determine the *object* of sexual desire. A homosexual man who receives injections of testosterone does not suddenly become interested in women. If testosterone has any effect, it increases his interest in sexual contact with other men. We'll consider the effects of testosterone on sexual orientation shortly.

Androgens appear to affect sexual motivation in women as well as in men, although the evidence is mixed. Salmon and Geist (1943) reported that testosterone had a stimulating effect on sexual desire and on the sensitivity of the clitoris to touch. Persky and colleagues (1978) studied the sexual activity of 11 married couples ranging in age from 21 to 31. The participants kept daily records of their sexual feelings and behavior, and the researchers measured their blood levels of testosterone twice a week. Couples were more likely to engage in intercourse when the woman's testosterone level was at a peak. In addition, the women reported finding intercourse more gratifying during these times. Androgens appear to affect female sexual behavior through amplifying the effects of the female sex hormone, estradiol (Shifren et al., 2000).

Effects of Progesterone and Estrogen
Unlike the organization of the male brain, the organization of the female brain is not dependent on the presence of sex hormones from either the mother or the fetus. However, in most species of mammals, the activation of female sexual behavior is affected by female sex hormones. The levels of estradiol and progesterone fluctuate during the menstrual cycle of primates and the **estrous cycle** (ovulatory cycle) of other female mammals. The difference between these two types of cycles is primarily that the lining of the primate uterus—but not that of other mammals—builds up during the first part of the cycle and sloughs off at the end. A female mammal of a nonprimate species—for example, a laboratory rat—receives the advances of a male only when the levels of estradiol and progesterone are high. This condition occurs around the time of ovulation, when copulation is most likely to result in pregnancy. During this time the female stands still when the male approaches; if he attempts to mount her, she arches her back and moves her tail to the side. This provides access to the genitalia.

A female rat whose ovaries are removed is normally nonreceptive—even hostile—to the advances of a male. However, if she is given injections of estradiol and progesterone to duplicate the hormonal condition of the receptive part of her estrous cycle, she receives the male or even pursues him. Thus, the presence of hormones during development was not necessary for the formation of the neural circuits that mediate female sexual behavior.

Women and other female primates display a distinctive pattern of sexual behavior. They may engage in sexual behavior at any time during the reproductive cycle. In higher primates (including our own species), the ability to mate is not strictly controlled by estradiol and progesterone. Most studies report that changes in the level of estradiol and progesterone have less pronounced effects on sexual behavior in female primates than in other female mammals. However, sexual activity does tend to peak around the time of ovulation, when estradiol levels are highest (Van Goozen et al., 1997; see also Kelley & Byrne, 1992, and Meyers et al., 1990). Some investigators believe that this difference in the pattern of sexual receptivity in primates was favored by evolution because of the longer dependency of primate infants on parental care. That is, because of the continued sexual receptivity of the female, the male is more likely to remain with the female and less likely to search out other partners.

Sexual Orientation

When children reach puberty, the effects of sex hormones on the maturing body and brain increase the likelihood of sexual interest. As sexual interest increases, most people develop a heterosexual orientation. Why does attraction to the other sex occur? And why does same-sex attraction sometimes occur? Research is only beginning to answer these questions.

Homosexual behavior (engaging in sexual activity with members of the same sex; from the Greek *homos*, "same") is seen in male and female animals of many species. Humans, however, are apparently the only species in which some members regularly exhibit homosexual behavior exclusively. Other animals, if they are not exclusively heterosexual, are likely to be bisexual, engaging in sexual activity with members of both sexes. In contrast, the number of men and women who describe themselves as exclusively homosexual exceeds the number who describe themselves as bisexual.

Traditional theories of sexual orientation have stressed the importance of the early environment. During much of the twentieth century, mental health professionals often saw homosexuality as a disorder caused by a faulty home environment—for example, as the result of being raised by an overprotective mother and an indifferent father. Research has refuted these theories, however.

First, there is no evidence that homosexuality is a disorder. The adjustment problems of some homosexuals occur because the larger society to which they belong treats them differently. Therefore, even if more behavioral disorders were found in homosexuals than in heterosexuals, we could not conclude that their difficulties were directly related to their sexual orientation. In a society that was indifferent to a person's sexual orientation, homosexuals might be as well adjusted as heterosexuals.

In fact, a large number of homosexuals are well adjusted and happy (Bell & Weinberg, 1978). An ambitious project reported by Bell, Weinberg, and Hammersmith (1981) studied a large number of male and female homosexuals. The participants were asked about their relationships with their parents, siblings, and peers and about their feelings, gender identification, and sexual activity. The results provided little or no support for traditional theories of homosexuality. The major conclusions of the study:

1. Sexual orientation was determined before adolescence and before any homosexual or heterosexual activity. The most important single predictor of adult homosexuality was a self-report of homosexual feelings, which usually occurred three years before a person's first genital homosexual activity.

2. There is a strong relation between gender nonconformity in childhood and the development of homosexuality. Gender nonconformity is characterized by an aversion in boys to "masculine" behaviors and in girls to "feminine" behaviors.

The results of the study are consistent with the hypothesis that homosexuality is at least partly determined by biological factors. That is, biological variables predispose a child to behavior that is more typical of the other sex and eventually to sexual arousal by members of his or her own sex.

Is there evidence of what these biological causes of homosexuality may be? We can immediately eliminate the possibility that male homosexuals have insufficient levels of testosterone; well-adjusted male homosexuals have normal levels of testosterone. There do not appear to be any meaningful differences in hormone levels between heterosexuals and homosexuals (Garnets & Kimmel, 1991).

One of the likely causes of male homosexuality is the pattern of exposure of the developing brain to androgens. Some experiments show that if a female rat is subjected to stress during pregnancy, the secretion of androgens by male fetuses is decreased and their sexual development is affected. As a result these offspring are more likely to show female patterns of behavior as adults (Anderson, Fleming, Rhees, & Kinghorn, 1986; Ward, 1972). Additional evidence comes from postmortem studies of the brains of deceased homosexual men. Compared to the brains of heterosexual males, these brains show differences in the size of two subregions of the hypothalamus and of a bundle of axons that connects the right and left temporal lobes (Allen & Gorski, 1992; LeVay, 1991; Swaab & Hofman, 1990). These findings do not necessarily implicate these brain areas in sexual orientation. However, they do suggest that the brains of homosexuals were exposed to lower levels of androgens before birth or that their brains were relatively insensitive to these hormones (e.g., Berenbaum & Snyder, 1995).

Although less research has been done on the origins of female homosexuality, prenatal exposure to higher levels of androgens from either the mother or fetus is associated with an increased incidence of homosexuality in females (e.g., Meyer-Bahlburg et al., 1995; Money, Schwartz, & Lewis, 1984). These higher androgen levels can come from excessive production of these hormones by the adrenal glands. Thus, sexual orientation in females may also be affected by biological factors.

Genetics also may play a role in sexual orientation. Bailey and Pillard (1991) studied pairs of male twins in which at least one twin identified himself as homosexual. As discussed in Chapter 3, if both twins share a trait, they are said to be *concordant* for this trait. If only one has the trait, the twins are said to be *discordant*. Thus, if homosexuality has a genetic basis, the percentage of identical twins concordant for homosexuality should be higher than the percentage of fraternal twins. And this is exactly what Bailey and Pillard found. The concordance rate for male homosexuality was 52 percent for identical twins and 22 percent for fraternal twins. In a subsequent study Bailey, Pillard, Neale, and Agyei (1993) found evidence that heredity plays a role in female homosexuality too. The concordance rates for female identical and fraternal twins were 48 percent and 16 percent, respectively.

The evidence on human sexual orientation implicates two biological factors—prenatal hormonal exposure and heredity. These findings contradict the view that a person's sexual orientation is a matter of choice and hence a moral issue. Homosexuals appear to be no more responsible for their sexual orientation than heterosexuals.

Interim Summary

Sexual Behavior

The reinforcing effects of engaging in sexual behavior involve many of the same neural circuits in the brain as other reinforcing activities. James Olds's initially chance discovery of the reinforcement system of the brain has important implications for a wide range of behavior.

Testosterone has two major effects on male sexual motivation and behavior: organizational and activational. In the fetus testosterone organizes the development of male sex organs and of some neural circuits in the brain; in the adult testosterone activates these structures and permits erection and ejaculation to occur. The sexual behavior of most female mammals with estrous cycles depends on estradiol and progesterone. These hormones do not exert organizational effects on the brain or elsewhere. Female sex hormones have some activational effects on sexual behavior, although women's sexual motivation is affected by androgens as well.

The development of sexual orientation appears to have biological roots. A large-scale study of homosexuals failed to find evidence that child-rearing practices fostered homosexuality. Studies have identified regions of the brain that differ in size between homosexual and heterosexual males. These results suggest that the brains of these two groups may have experienced different androgen levels or reacted differently to androgens prenatally. Twin studies indicate that both male and female homosexuality have a genetic component as well.

QUESTIONS TO CONSIDER

1. Whatever the relative roles of biological and environmental factors in sexual orientation, most investigators believe that sexual orientation is not a matter of choice. Why do you think so many people consider sexual orientation a moral issue?

2. Given the rapid pace of scientific and technical advances in genetics and allied fields, consider the possibility that one day parents might be able to control the sex and sexual orientation of their offspring through treatments in utero. Do you think that such control should be exercised? In answering this question, consider the benefits and dangers of exercising such control.

Emotion

Until this point we have focused on forms of behavior that are most intimately related to motivation—the operant behavior instigated by reinforcement, the aggressive behavior instigated by aversive stimuli, and the reproductive behavior instigated by sexual stimuli. However, these same stimuli also produce a constellation of other important effects. These effects fall under the heading of emotion. The word **emotion** refers to the expressive behavior (for example, facial expressions), physiological reactions, and subjective feelings that accompany motivated behavior. When we are motivated, we display a wide range of emotional reactions—happiness, sadness, fear, and so forth. Different emotions are evoked by specific kinds of situations and provide distinctive stimuli that affect the subsequent behavior of the person experiencing the emotion and the behavior of others who detect the emotion. We are aware of whether we are smiling or frowning, but so are others. Most psychologists who study emotion have focused on the following questions: What kinds of situations produce emotions? What kinds of feelings do people experience during emotions? What kinds of behavior are prompted by emotions? What physiological changes occur during emotions?

Psychologists generally use the word *emotion* to denote experiences and behavior that are evoked when important events happen to people. *Emotion,* like *motivation,* is not a term that arises from scientific work. Nevertheless, the word serves to refer to an important set of phenomena that any complete account of human behavior must address. Emotions are often relatively brief and occur in response to events that have motivational relevance. Emotions may be evoked by current actions or by events that remind us of past actions. Emotions are the consequences of events that motivate us. When we encounter reinforcing or punishing stimuli that motivate us to act, we express and experience positive or negative emotions.

We will consider three aspects of emotions in this section: the response patterns elicited by emotional stimuli, the role of the orbitofrontal cortex in emotional appropriateness, and the measurement of emotional responses. The next section will examine the expression and recognition of emotions—the ways in which emotional behavior communicates emotional states to others. Finally, a third section on emotion will explore subjective feelings of emotion.

Emotions as Response Patterns

If asked to define the word *emotion,* you would probably talk about the feelings that accompany motivated behavior. But feelings and the other accompaniments of motivated behavior are produced by natural selection to provide patterns of behavior appropriate to particular situations. These patterns of emotional reactions contribute to the survival of the individual.

Emotional reactions have three components—behavioral, autonomic, and hormonal. The *behavioral* component consists of muscular movements appropriate to the situation that elicits them. For example, a parent seeing his or her child bullied on a playground would intervene to protect the child. The *autonomic* component consists of changes in the activity of the autonomic nervous system, changes that facilitate the behavioral component through mobilizing energy for vigorous movement. As a consequence, the parent's heart rate increases, the arteries that supply blood to the muscles increase in diameter, and the arteries that supply blood to the digestive organs constrict. In addition, autonomic activity causes secretion of *hormones* from the adrenal glands that further increase heart rate and blood flow to the muscles and causes increases in glucose levels in the blood, which facilitates muscle activity.

Conditioned Emotional Responses Like other behavior, emotional responses can be modified by experience. For example, once we have learned that a particular situation is dangerous, we become frightened when we next encounter that situation. This type of response, acquired through a classical procedure, is called a conditioned emotional response.

A **conditioned emotional response** is produced when a neutral stimulus is paired with an emotion-producing stimulus. For example, suppose you are helping a friend prepare a meal. You put your hand on the base of the food processor to begin mixing cake batter. Before you can turn the unit on, it makes a sputtering noise and then gives you a painful electrical shock. Your first response will be a defensive reflex: You let go of the unit, which ends the shock. This response is *specific;* it is aimed at terminating the painful stimulus. The painful stimulus also elicits *nonspecific* responses controlled by your autonomic nervous system: Your eyes dilate, your heart rate increases, your blood pressure increases, your breathing becomes faster, and so on. The painful stimulus also triggers the secretion of stress-related hormones, another nonspecific response.

Now suppose that when you next visit your friend, you are again asked to make a cake. Your friend assures you that the food processor is now perfectly safe—it has been fixed. Just seeing the food processor and thinking of touching it makes you a little nervous, but you accept your friend's assurance and put your hand on it. Just then, it makes the same sputtering noise it did when it shocked you. What will your response be? Almost certainly, you will let go of the unit again, even if it does not give you a shock. Moreover, your pupils will dilate, your heart rate and blood pressure will increase, and your endocrine glands will secrete stress-related hormones. In other words, the sputtering sound will trigger a conditioned emotional response. Moreover, the movement to let go of the unit occurs in less time than is required to instigate the cortical activity underlying a conscious decision.

Research by physiological psychologists indicates that a particular brain region plays an important role in the expression of conditioned emotional responses. This region is the *amygdala*, which is located in the temporal lobe, just in front of the hippocampus (refer to Figure 4.35). The amygdala is a region of convergence between sensory systems and systems responsible for behavioral, autonomic, and hormonal components of conditioned emotional responses (Kapp, Gallagher, Applegate, & Frysinger, 1982; LeDoux, 1995).

Studies with animals have found that damage to the amygdala disrupts components of conditioned emotional responses. If this region is destroyed, animals no longer show signs of fear when confronted with stimuli that have been paired with aversive events. In addition, they act tame when handled by humans, their blood levels of stress hormones are lower, and they are less likely to develop stress-induced illnesses (Coover, Murison, & Jellestad, 1992; Davis, 1992; LeDoux, 1992). These effects have been confirmed in humans that have suffered damage to the amygdala through stroke or otherwise (Bechara et al., 1995). Conversely, when the amygdala is stimulated by means of electrodes or by the injection of an excitatory drug, animals show physiological and behavioral signs of fear and agitation (Davis, 1992) and humans report feelings of fear. Such findings indicate that the autonomic and hormonal components of emotional responses are affected by the amygdala and may contribute to the harmful effects of long-term stress. (We will examine the topic of stress in Chapter 16.)

Social Judgments: Role of the Orbitofrontal Cortex

Conditioned emotional responses can be elicited by simple stimuli, but our emotions are often reactions to very complex situations. Situations involving other people are especially complex. Perceiving the meaning of social situations—and thus experiencing appropriate emotional responses—is obviously more complex than seeing a light or hearing a tone. Perceiving social situations involves experiences and memories, inferences and judgments. These skills are not localized in any one part of the cerebral cortex, although research suggests that the right hemisphere is more important than the left. However, one region of the brain, the orbitofrontal cortex, plays a special role.

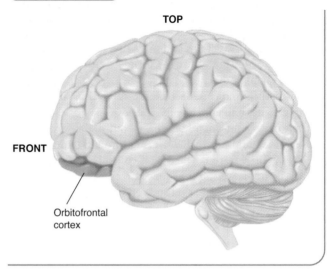

FIGURE 13•8   The orbitofrontal cortex.

TOP

FRONT

Orbitofrontal cortex

The **orbitofrontal cortex** is located at the base of the frontal lobes. It covers the part of the brain just above the *orbits*—the bones that form the eye sockets. (See **Figure 13•8**.) The orbitofrontal cortex receives information from sensory systems and from the regions of the frontal lobes that control behavior. Thus, neurons in the orbitofrontal cortex can integrate activity between the environment and behavior, including plans to respond to environmental events. This cortical region also communicates extensively with the limbic system, which plays an important role in emotions. In particular, connections to the amygdala can affect the activity of the amygdala, which, as we've seen, plays a critical role in emotional responses.

The important role of the orbitofrontal cortex in emotional behavior is shown when damage occurs to this region. The first and most famous clinical case occurred in the mid-nineteenth century. Phineas Gage, a Vermont quarry worker, was using a steel rod to ram a charge of dynamite into a hole drilled in solid rock. The charge accidentally exploded and drove the rod into his cheek, through his brain, and out the top of his head. (See **Figure 13•9**.) The accident largely destroyed Gage's orbitofrontal cortex. Gage survived, but he was a different man. Before his injury he was serious, industrious, and energetic. Afterward, he became childish, irresponsible, and thoughtless of others. He was unable to make or carry out plans, and his actions appeared to be capricious and whimsical.

In the decades that followed, physicians reported several cases similar to that of Phineas Gage. In general, damage to the orbitofrontal cortex reduces inhibitions and self-concern. People with damage to the orbitofrontal cortex become indifferent to the consequences of their actions. In addition, although they remain aware of noxious stimuli, they no longer produce an emotional reaction.

The application of scientific knowledge to societal and individual problems must be done with great care, however. In 1935 a report of a related experiment on a chimpanzee triggered a series of very unfortunate events. Jacobsen, Wolf, and Jackson (1935) tested chimpanzees on a task that required the animals to remain quiet and remember the location of food that had been placed behind a screen. One animal, Becky, displayed a violent emotional reaction whenever she made an error while performing this task. "[When] the experimenter lowered . . . the opaque door to exclude the animal's view of the cups, she immediately flew into a temper tantrum. . . . After a few such reactions during the training period, the animal would make no further responses. . . ." The experimenters removed the chimpanzee's frontal lobes (including the orbitofrontal cortex) to see if this diminished her emotional reactions. The investigators then found that the chimp became a model of good comportment. "If the animal made a mistake, it showed no evidence of emotional disturbance but quietly awaited the loading of the cups for the next trial" (Jacobsen, Wolf, & Jackson, 1935, pp. 9–10).

These findings were reported at a scientific meeting in 1935, which was attended by Egas Moniz, a Portuguese neuropsychiatrist. Another report presented at the same meeting indicated that radical removal of the frontal lobes in a human patient (frontal lobotomy, performed because of a tumor) did not appear to produce intellectual impairment (Brickner, 1936). Taken together, these two reports suggested to Moniz that frontal lobotomy reduced pathological emotional reactions without serious consequences for the patient's intellect. One of Jacobsen's colleagues reported that "Dr. Moniz . . . asked if frontal-lobe removal . . . eliminates frustrational behavior,

why would it not be feasible to relieve anxiety states in man by surgical means?" (Fulton, 1949, pp. 63–64). In fact, Moniz did persuade a neurosurgeon to perform such surgery, and about a hundred operations were eventually carried out under his supervision. Rather than the complete removal of frontal lobes, a refinement was developed in which connections were severed between the bases of the frontal lobes and the remainder of the brain (refer to Figure 4.30). This form of psychosurgery is called prefrontal lobotomy, and Moniz received the Nobel Prize in 1949 for his role in developing the procedure.

Only after many years did careful studies reveal the disastrous side effects of the procedure. They showed that although standard tests of intellectual ability did not reveal a loss, serious changes in personality occurred. The patients became irresponsible and childish, unable to carry out plans and unemployable. In short, they became like Phineas Gage. For obvious reasons, prefrontal lobotomy was abandoned (Jasper, 1995; Pressman, 1998; Valenstein, 1986).

The key point for our understanding of emotional responses is that a person whose orbitofrontal cortex has been damaged by disease or accident can accurately assess the significance of particular situations, but cannot respond appropriately to the situation. For example, Eslinger and Damasio (1985) found that a patient with bilateral damage to the orbitofrontal cortex displayed, in the abstract, excellent social judgment. For example, when these researchers described hypothetical situations that required decisions about what should be done—situations involving moral and ethical dilemmas—the patient gave reasonable answers and justified them appropriately. His own life, on the other hand, was a disaster. He frittered away his life savings on investments that his family and friends pointed out were bound to fail. He lost one job after another because of his irresponsibility. He became unable to distinguish between trivial decisions and important ones, spending hours trying to decide where to have dinner but failing to use good judgment in situations that concerned his occupation and family life. As Eslinger and Damasio (1985) noted, "He had learned and used normal patterns of social behavior before his brain lesion, and although he could recall such patterns when he was questioned about their applicability, *real-life situations failed to evoke them*" (p. 1737). Thus, it appears that the orbitofrontal cortex is not directly involved in our making judgments and conclusions about events (these involve additional areas in the brain) but that it *translates our judgments into appropriate feelings and behavior*.

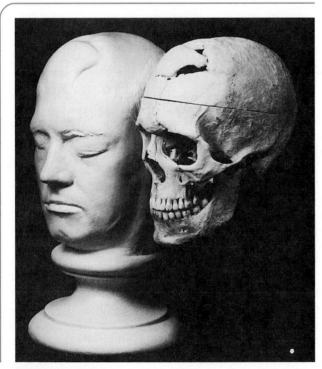

FIGURE 13•9 A bust and the skull of Phineas Gage. The steel rod entered his left cheek and exited through his left forehead.

(Photo © Warren Anatomical Museum, Countway Library of Medicine, Harvard Medical School. Reprinted by permission.)

Measuring Emotional Responses: Lie Detection in Criminal Investigation

In criminal investigations, authorities often interrogate witnesses and suspects to determine who is telling the truth. If we had a procedure that could reveal emotional responses connected with lying, we could be sure that the guilty would be convicted and the innocent would go free. Professional

▲ *Research indicates that the accuracy of lie detector tests is not very high.*

polygraphers (people who operate "lie detector" machines) say that we *do* have a method to detect emotions that indicate deception. A polygraph records many physiological reactions associated with people's emotional responses: heart rate, blood pressure, breathing, and skin conductance (a measure of sweating). The polygrapher asks suspects questions about a crime and measures these physiological reactions during their answers. But can lying be accurately detected by such a procedure?

In 1986, the CBS television network hired four different polygraphers to find out which of four employees of a photography magazine (which the network owned) had stolen an expensive camera (Lykken, 1988). Each of the polygraphers was told that one of the four employees was suspected but that definite proof was lacking. Sure enough, each polygrapher identified a targeted suspect—but a different person in each case! Because no camera had in fact been stolen, the test could not be definitive. However, the outcome of the test did raise serious questions about the validity of the procedure.

Lykken (1988, 1998) reviewed the scientific literature on the validity of polygraph tests and found that although most cases of lying were correctly identified, the incidence of *false positives*—of incorrect indications that people were lying—was almost 50 percent. Moreover, the tests were carefully performed by well-trained examiners. You can see why most countries do not accept polygraph tests as evidence in criminal trials. The tests can identify most of the guilty parties who falsely claim innocence, but half the time they also mark innocent people as guilty. The reason: Questions about crimes evoke emotional reactions from innocent as well as guilty persons.

Interim Summary

Emotion

The word *emotion* refers to behavior, physiological reactions, and feelings evoked by motivating stimuli. Emotional re-

sponse patterns consist of responses to particular situations and physiological reactions (both autonomic and hormonal) that support those responses. The amygdala organizes behavioral, autonomic, and hormonal responses to a variety of situations, including those that produce fear or anger. Stimulation of the amygdala leads to emotional responses, and its destruction disrupts them.

The orbitofrontal cortex plays an important role in social judgments and emotional reactions. People with damage to this region can explain the implications of complex social situations but are unable to respond appropriately to these situations. Thus, this region appears to be necessary for translating judgments about the significance of events into appropriate actions and emotional responses.

The cases of prefrontal lobotomy and lie detection by means of the polygraph sound cautionary notes about the uses of scientific findings. Laboratory research showed that destruction of the orbitofrontal cortex reduced fearful emotions but failed at first to reveal the procedure's adverse effects on patients' ability to manage their lives. Laboratory research demonstrated that emotional reactions can be detected by polygraphs but did not reveal at first that questioning can induce emotional reactions in both the innocent and the guilty.

QUESTIONS TO CONSIDER

1. Phobias are dramatic examples of conditioned emotional responses. We can acquire these responses without direct experience with an aversive stimulus. For example, a child who sees a parent show signs of fright in the presence of a dog may also develop a fear reaction to dogs. Do you think that some prejudices might be learned in this way, too?

2. If you were falsely accused of a crime, would you want to submit to a lie detector test to try to prove your innocence? Why or why not?

Expression and Recognition of Emotions

Thus far I have described emotions as organized response patterns (behavioral, autonomic, and hormonal) that are produced by environmental stimuli that are motivating. For example, being confronted with a threat not only motivates escape behavior but also evokes various emotional responses. At the same time, emotions exist, in part, because expressions of emotion communicate important information to other members of the species. Members of many species (including humans) convey their emotions to others by means of postural changes and facial expressions. Such responses tell other individuals how we feel and—more to the point—what we are likely to do. For example, they warn when we are angry and should be left alone or when we are sad and would welcome comfort. This section reviews research on the expression and recognition of emotions.

The Social Nature of Emotional Expression in Humans

The expression of emotions is inherently social. For example, Kraut and Johnston (1979) showed that people are more likely to express signs of happiness in the presence of other people than when they are alone. The investigators unobtrusively observed whether people smiled in three situations: while bowling and making a strike or missing one, while watching a hockey game and seeing the home team score or be scored against, and while walking down a street on a beautiful day or on a hot and humid day. They found that the happy situations (making a strike, seeing the home team score, or experiencing a beautiful day) produced only small signs of happiness when people were alone. However, when the people were interacting socially with others, they were much more likely to smile. Bowlers who made a strike usually did not smile when the ball hit the pins but did smile when they turned around to face their companions. When we express emotions, they tend to be displayed toward other people.

Situations That Produce Emotions: The Role of Cognition

Emotions rarely occur spontaneously; they are provoked by particular stimuli, as we saw with conditioned emotional responses. For humans the emotions evoked by eliciting stimuli can recur in later situations if they engage cognitive processes such as memory. For example, we reexperience emotions by remembering things that happened to us or by imagining events that might occur. Emotions are the products of cognitive processes as well. For example, suppose that someone appears to pay you a compliment. You will have a pleasurable emotional reaction at the time. But suppose you later think about the remark and realize it was actually a disguised insult. This realization—a product of your cognitive processes—will cause you to become angry.

Many investigators believe that humans share many of their emotional expressions with other mammals, especially other social mammals. If you have ever had a dog, you know that it expresses fear, anger, happiness, sadness, surprise, shame, and other emotions in ways that we recognize as somewhat similar to our own. However, we differ substantially from other mammals in the *types of stimuli* that evoke these emotions. For example, an animal may become frightened by the presence of a large group of strangers, but only humans can become frightened by having to perform in front of a television camera. Only humans realize that they are confronting an unseen audience.

Humans often experience emotions on the basis of their judgments about the significance of particular situations. For example, a pianist who is satisfied with her performance may perceive applause as praise for outstanding artistry, judging the applause to be a positive evaluation of her own worth. She will feel pride and gratification. In this case her emotional state is produced by social reinforcement—the expression of approval and admiration by other people. However, if the pianist believes that she has performed poorly, she may judge the applause as the mindless enthusiasm of people who have no taste and for whom she feels only contempt. Furthermore, the page-turner is also present on the stage and thus also perceives the applause. However, because he does not evaluate the applause as praise for anything he did, the page-turner does not experience the emotions the pianist feels. The applause may even make him feel jealous. Clearly, a given set of stimuli does not always elicit the same emotion. Judgments about the significance of the stimuli determine the emotion the person feels.

Biology and Culture

Are Emotional Expressions Innate?

Charles Darwin (1872/1965) suggested that expressions of emotion have evolved similarly across mammalian species owing to common ancestors. He said that emotional expressions are largely innate, unlearned responses consisting of a complex set of movements, principally of the facial muscles. From this perspective, a human's sneer and a wolf's snarl are both biologically organized response patterns that are controlled by innate brain mechanisms, as are coughing and sneezing. (Of course, humans sneer and wolves snarl for quite different reasons.) Some expressive behavior closely resembles the elicited and operant responses themselves, and may have evolved from them. For example, a snarl shows an animal's teeth and can be seen as an anticipation of biting. Less obviously, a yawn when an animal is anxious also bares the teeth and warns the observer to tread with caution.

● **Cross-Cultural Expression and Recognition of Emotions**

Darwin performed what was probably the first cross-cultural study of behavior. He observed his own children and corresponded with people living in various isolated cultures around the world. He reasoned that if people all over the world show the same facial expressions of emotion, the expressions must be inherited instead of learned. The argument goes like this: When groups of people are isolated for many years, they develop different languages. Thus, we can say that the words that people use are arbitrary; there is no biological basis for particular words' representing particular concepts. However, if facial expressions are inherited, they should take approximately the same form in people from all cultures. And indeed, Darwin did find that people in different cultures used the same patterns of movements of facial muscles to express particular emotional states.

▲ *Darwin suggested that a person's sneer and a wolf's snarl are both biologically determined response patterns.*

In 1967 and 1968, Paul Ekman and Wallace Friesen carried out cross-cultural observations that validated Darwin's work (Ekman, 1980). They visited an isolated tribe in a remote area of Papua New Guinea—the South Fore tribe. This group of 319 adults and children had never been exposed to Western culture. They had never seen a movie, lived in a Western country, or worked with someone from another culture. If they were able to identify accurately the emotional expressions of Westerners as well as they could identify those of members of their own tribe, and if their own facial expressions were the same as those of Westerners, then the researchers could conclude that these expressions were not culturally determined.

Because translations of single words from one language to another are not always accurate, Ekman and Friesen told the tribespeople brief stories to describe emotions. They would tell a story to a participant, present three photographs of Westerners depicting three different emotions, and asked the participant to choose the appropriate image. Read the captions of **Figure 13•10** and match them to the photographs shown there.

I am sure you had little trouble—and neither did the members of the South Fore tribe. In a second study, Ekman and Friesen asked South Fore people to imagine how they would feel in certain situations, and videotaped their facial expressions. They showed photographs of the videotapes to American college students, who also had no trouble identifying the emotions. (See **Figure 13•11**.)

Other researchers have compared the facial expressions of blind and normally sighted children. They reasoned that if the facial expressions of both groups were similar, the expressions would be natural for our species and would not require learning by imitation. (Studies of blind adults could not be conclusive, because adults would have heard enough descriptions of facial expressions to pose them.) The facial

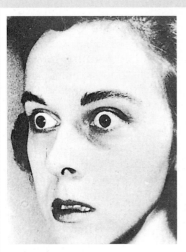

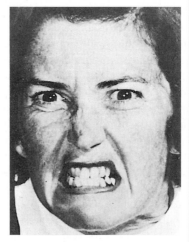

FIGURE 13•10 Recognizing emotional expressions. Ekman and Friesen asked members of the South Fore tribe of Papua New Guinea to match the following stories with the appropriate photographs. Fear: She is sitting in her house all alone and there is no one else in the village; and there is no knife, axe, or bow and arrow in the house. A wild pig is standing in the door of the house and . . . she is afraid the pig will bite her. Happiness: Her friends have come and she is happy. Anger: She is angry and is about to fight.

(From Ekman, 1980, *The face of man: Expressions of universal emotions in a New Guinea village.* New York: Garland STPM Press. Photos reprinted with permission of the estate of Silvan Tomkins. Photos by Ed Gallob.)

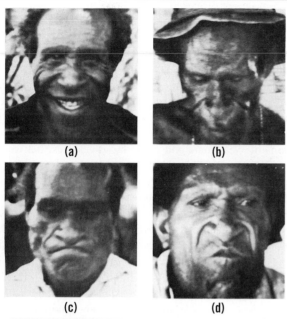

(a)   **(b)**

(c)   **(d)**

FIGURE 13·11 Portraying emotions. Ekman and Friesen asked South Fore tribesmen to make faces (shown in the photographs) when they were told stories. (a) "Your friend has come and you are happy." (b) "Your child has died." (c) "You are angry and about to fight." (d) "You see a dead pig that has been lying there a long time."

(From Ekman, 1980, *The face of man: Expressions of universal emotions in a New Guinea village.* New York: Garland STPM Press. Photos © Paul Ekman 1972–2004. Reprinted with permission.)

expressions of young blind and sighted children are very similar. As blind children grow older, however, their facial gestures tend to become somewhat less expressive (Izard, 1971; Woodworth & Schlosberg, 1954). This finding suggests that social reinforcement is important in the maintenance of expressive behavior. However, the evidence also clearly shows that we do not have to learn to smile, frown, or show other feelings.

The adaptiveness of correctly identifying expressive behavior such as facial displays of emotion is clear. It is important to know whether the people in our lives are happy or sad, amazed or angry. In an interesting elaboration of this reasoning, Hansen and Hansen (1988) proposed that people should be especially adept at noticing threatening (angry) facial displays. Knowing whether someone is likely to harm us is more important than knowing that someone might wish us a nice day. Hansen and Hansen showed study participants photographs in which an angry face was unique in a crowd of happy faces and photographs in which a happy face was embedded in a crowd of angry ones. Participants were simply asked to find the face that differed from the others. As Hansen and Hansen had predicted, participants more quickly noticed the discrepant angry face in the crowd than the discrepant happy face (also see Fox et al., 2000).

● Cultural Control of Emotional Expression: Display Rules

Because other people are able to recognize our expressions of emotions, we sometimes try to hide our true feelings. Suppose that a poker player has four aces; it is clearly not in his interest to let opponents know this by grinning broadly. Under such conditions the player may try to appear impassive or even to display an emotion different from what he feels. As with other behavior, expressive behavior is instigated by motivation-provoking stimuli but is also affected by its own consequences. The consequences of grinning because of a good poker hand are that the opponents drop from the hand and the player receives a smaller payoff. Under other circumstances, in contrast, we may exaggerate expressive behavior to make certain that others see how we feel. For example, if a friend tells us about a devastating experience, we make sure that our facial expression conveys sadness and sympathy.

Attempting to hide expressive behavior is called **masking**. Exaggerating or minimizing the expression of an emotion is called **modulation**. An attempt to express an emotion that we do not actually feel is called **simulation**. According to Ekman and Friesen (1975), these variations in the expression of emotions often follow culturally determined **display rules**. Display rules prescribe the situations when we should or should not display signs of particular emotions. Although the patterns of muscular movements that accompany particular feelings are biologically determined, these movements can, to a certain extent, be controlled by the situation—the environmental context and the consequences of the expressive behavior.

Each culture has its own set of display rules. For example, in Western society, it is impolite for a winner to show too much pleasure or for a loser to show too much disappointment. (These display rules are not absolute, however; witness the antics of some athletes after scoring a touchdown or dunking over an opponent.) Also, in many societies, gender matters: In many cultures it is considered unmanly to cry or to show fear and unfeminine to show anger.

Ekman and his colleagues (Ekman, Friesen, & Ellsworth, 1972; Friesen, 1972) studied culturally determined display rules. They showed a distressing film to Japanese and American university students when they were alone or when they were in the presence of a stranger. The researchers recorded the facial expressions of the students with hidden cameras while they viewed the film, which depicted a gruesome and bloody coming-of-age rite in a preliterate tribe.

Because Japanese culture discourages public displays of emotion, the researchers expected that the Japanese students would show fewer facial expressions of emotion when with another person than when alone. The results were as predicted. When alone, American and Japanese participants showed the same facial expressions. When they were with another person, the Japanese students were less likely than the Americans to express negative emotions and were more likely to mask these expressions with polite smiles. Thus, people from the two societies used the same facial expressions of emotion, but they were subject to different display rules.

When people try to mask the expression of a strongly felt emotion, they usually are unable to do so completely. That is, there is some **leakage,** or subtle sign of the emotion (Ekman & Friesen, 1969). Ekman and Friesen (1974) showed an unpleasant film of burns and amputations to female nursing students. After watching the film, the students were interviewed by a researcher who asked them about the film. Some had been instructed to pretend to the interviewer that they had seen a pleasant film. The researchers videotaped the students during the interviews and showed these tapes to a separate group of raters; they asked the raters to determine whether the students were being honest or deceptive. The raters saw either videos of only the faces of the participants or videos of only their bodies with the faces obscured. Surprisingly, the raters detected deception better when they saw only the students' bodies than when they saw only their faces. Apparently, people are able to mask signs of emotion shown in their facial expressions better than signs shown by muscles in other parts of their bodies. Presumably, people recognize the attention paid to the face and acquire some control over their facial expressions.

Research shows that in trying to detect deceit purely from facial expressions, most people perform little better than they would do by chance (e.g., DePaulo, 1994). Surprisingly, many people whom we would expect to be experts at detecting deception from facial expressions, such as police officers and customs agents, fare no better than the rest of us in controlled tests of accuracy (e.g., Ekman & O'Sullivan, 1991). There are interesting exceptions, however. Members of some professional groups that have a special interest in deception (e.g., clinical psychologists and judges) do detect lying from facial expressions at better than chance levels (Ekman, O'Sullivan, & Frank, 1999). Exactly why this is so is unclear. Perhaps people who are especially good at detecting deception gravitate to positions where that skill can be successfully used—or perhaps certain professional contexts provide excellent on-the-job training for the detection of deception.

Interim Summary

Expression and Recognition of Emotions

Expressive behavior communicates important information about emotions to other people. An observational study of humans indicated that smiles appear to occur most often when someone is there to see the smile. This finding supports the social nature of emotional expression.

Emotions are provoked by particular motivational stimuli, and in humans these stimuli include those from cognitive processes as well as observable behavior. For example, emotions can be produced by memories of previous emotion-arousing situations.

Darwin believed that the expression of emotion by facial gestures was innate and that these muscle movements were inherited behavioral patterns. Ekman and his colleagues showed that members of the South Fore tribe recognized facial expressions of Westerners and made facial gestures that were clear to Westerners. These findings, together with observations of blind children, indicate that emotional expressions do involve innate behavior patterns.

Expressions of emotion are not always valid indications of a person's emotional state. Expressive behavior can be masked, modulated, or simulated according to culturally determined display rules. Cultural differences exist, as the study comparing Japanese and American students demonstrated. Even when a person attempts to mask emotional expression, some leakage occurs, particularly in movements of the body. Presumably, we learn to control facial expressions because of the attention other people pay to these expressions. Indeed people have a great deal of trouble detecting lying from facial expressions alone.

QUESTION TO CONSIDER

We can move our facial muscles to simulate expressions of emotions, but these expressions are usually less convincing than spontaneous ones. Have you ever tried to suppress a smile when you wanted to seem serious or to look happy when you were really feeling sad? If you wanted to be an actor, how might you try to develop realistic expressions of emotions?

Feelings of Emotion

We have discussed two aspects of emotions—the patterns of behavioral, autonomic, and hormonal responses that are produced by a motivating situation and the communication of emotional states to others. The final aspect of emotion we will consider is the subjective component—*feelings* of emotion.

Emotions are accompanied by physiological reactions, and these reactions can evoke feelings of emotion. We can easily understand why. Strong emotions increase the heart rate and can produce irregular breathing, queasy feelings in the internal organs, trembling, sweating, reddening of the face, or even fainting. We may ask whether these physiological reactions *constitute* the emotion or are merely symptoms of some other underlying process. That is, do we feel frightened because we tremble, or do we tremble because we feel frightened? This section will explore some theories and research findings that address these questions.

Theories of Emotion

Two somewhat different approaches to feelings of emotion are the theory developed by the physiologists Walter Cannon and Phillip Bard and the earlier theory proposed by the psychologist William James and the physiologist Carl Lange. The **James-Lange theory** proposed that the physiological and behavioral responses to emotion-arousing stimuli produced feelings of emotion (James, 1884; Lange, 1887). The **Cannon-Bard theory** contended that feelings of emotion were relatively independent of the physiological and behavioral responses to emotion-arousing stimuli (Cannon, 1927).

Cannon and Bard, based on the evidence available at the time, incorrectly believed that autonomic and behavioral responses to emotion-arousing stimuli were too slow and too indistinct to affect the rapidly occurring and often subtle differences in feelings of emotion. As an illustration of the difference between the theories, Cannon and Bard took the position that the sight of an approaching bear evokes both physiological/behavioral responses and, largely independently, feelings of fear.

In contrast, James and Lange believed that the sight of the bear evokes physiological/behavioral responses and that stimuli produced by these responses, in turn, evoke feelings of fear. That is, the sight of the bear first evokes running and increases in heart rate and then, after these changes are sensed, feelings of fear. Let's look more closely at this theory.

The James-Lange Theory

In essence, the James-Lange theory states that emotion-producing situations elicit an appropriate set of physiological responses, such as trembling, sweating, and increased heart rate. The situations also elicit behaviors, such as clenching of fists or fighting. The brain receives sensory feedback from the muscles and from the organs that produce these responses, and it is this feedback that constitutes our subjective feelings of emotion. As James put it:

> The bodily changes follow directly the perception of the exciting fact, and . . . our feelings of the same changes as they occur is the emotion. Common sense says we lose our fortune, are sorry, and weep; we meet a bear, are frightened, and run. . . . The hypothesis here to be defended says that this order of sequence is incorrect. . . . The more rational statement is that we feel sorry because we cry, angry because we strike, afraid because we tremble, and not that we cry, strike, or tremble because we are sorry, angry or fearful, as the case may be. (James, 1890, p. 449)

James's approach is closely related to a process called *attribution,* which we will encounter in Chapter 15. Attribu-

tion theory in social psychology is concerned with how we draw conclusions about the causes of other people's behavior. The James-Lange theory says that we go through much the same process when we draw conclusions about our own behavior. We observe our own physiological and behavior responses and, based on that information, attribute feelings to ourselves. Our emotional feelings are based on what we find ourselves doing and on the sensory feedback we receive from the activity of our muscles and internal organs. Where feelings of emotions are concerned, we are self-observers. Thus, patterns of emotional responses and expressions of emotions give rise to feelings of emotion. By this reasoning, emotional feelings are the products of emotional responses. (See **Figure 13•12**.)

James's description of the process by which emotional feelings are produced may seem odd. We usually believe that we directly experience feelings without physiological or behavioral intermediaries. We tend to see the outward manifestations of emotions as secondary events. But have you ever found yourself in an unpleasant confrontation with someone and discovered that you were trembling, even though you did not think that you were so upset by the encounter? Or were you ever surprised to find yourself blushing in response to some remark? Or did tears ever come to your eyes while watching a film that you did not think was affecting you? What might you conclude about the causes of your emotional feelings in situations like these? Would you ignore the evidence of your own physiological and behavioral reactions?

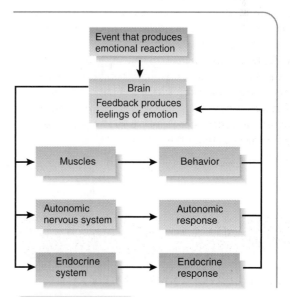

FIGURE 13•12 A diagrammatic representation of the James-Lange theory of emotion. An event in the environment triggers behavioral, autonomic, and endocrine responses. Feedback from these responses produces feelings of emotions.

Effects of Spinal Cord and Autonomic-System Damage

The way to evaluate the James-Lange theory of feelings of emotion is to assess the feelings of individuals with diminished sensory feedback from physiological and behavioral responses. Hohman (1966) collected data about the intensity of emotional feelings of people who had suffered damage to their spinal cords. If feedback from the body was important, Hohman reasoned, then emotional feelings would be less intense if the injury were high up in the spinal cord, thereby eliminating most bodily sensations, than if it were low in the cord, thereby permitting some bodily sensations. This result is precisely what the data showed: The higher the injury, the less intense the feelings. (See **Figure 13•13**.)

The comments of patients with high spinal cord injuries suggested that the severely diminished feedback did change their feelings, although not necessarily their behavior.

> I was at home alone in bed one day and dropped a cigarette where I couldn't reach it. I finally managed to . . . put it out. I could have burned up right there, but the funny thing is, I didn't get all shook up about it. I just didn't feel afraid at all. . . .
>
> Sometimes I act angry when I see some injustice. I yell and cuss and raise hell, because if you don't . . . I've learned people will take advantage of you, but it doesn't have the heat to it that it used to. It's a mental kind of anger. (Hohman, 1966, pp. 150–151)

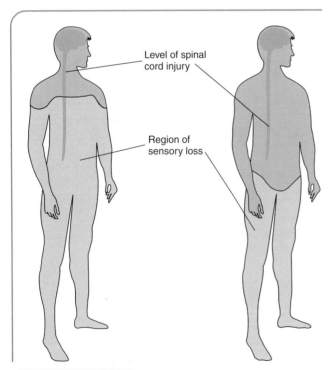

FIGURE 13•13 Hohman's investigation of emotion in people with spinal cord damage. The higher the spinal cord damage, the less intense was the person's feeling.

Anecdotal evidence also supports a contribution of bodily sensations to emotional feelings. As part of the treatment of a cardiovascular disorder, the sympathetic nerves (a part of the autonomic nervous system) of a music lover were severed on one side of his spinal cord (Sweet, 1966). The man reported that the shivering feeling of pleasure that he had previously experienced when hearing a thrilling piece of music was now felt only on the side of his body where the nerves were intact. He still enjoyed listening to music, but the feelings of emotion were diminished. This and other accounts suggest that people do not engage in emotional behavior because of their feelings but have feelings because they sense their emotional behavior and physiological reactions. Even when the feelings are diminished or absent, the behavior is still evoked by motivational stimuli.

Evaluating Scientific Issues

Is Cognition Essential for Emotion?

A controversy among psychologists interested in feelings of emotion is the relative importance of automatic processes (such as those produced by classical conditioning procedures) versus that of more complex processes such as those involved in cognition (especially conscious thought). Some psychologists believe that emotions are produced only by cognitive processes—by mental activities such as anticipating, experiencing, or imagining the outcomes of important interactions with the environment. Other psychologists hold that cognitive appraisal is not necessary and that emotions are automatic, species-typical responses that are heavily influenced by basic conditioning processes.

● **Conditioning or Cognition?**
In reality, both automatic processes and conscious deliberation can play a role in the behavioral expressions and feelings of emotion. Some examples of emotions clearly involve cognitive processes. For instance, as mentioned earlier in this chapter, a person can become angry after realizing that someone's "kind words" were actually a subtle insult. This anger is a result of cognition. However, emotional reactions and their associated feelings sometimes occur automatically: We may act and feel hostile and angry but without realizing why. The person who comes home after a frustrating day at work may argue with his partner because of extinction-produced aggression but may not be aware of the true causes and may blame his partner's behavior. In this instance, even if cognitive processes were involved in the person's anger, they were by no means conscious or deliberate.

What is the evidence regarding the role of cognition in feelings of emotion? The person most responsible for directing attention to the interaction between cognitive and physiological reactions in feelings of emotions is Stanley Schachter. Schachter (1964) took the sensible position that feelings of emotions are determined *jointly* by perception of physiological responses and by cognitive assessment of the situation. Thus, for Schachter, emotion is cognition plus perception of physiological arousal.

Schachter and Singer (1962) tested this view by inducing physiological reactions in groups of participants and then placing them in different situations. All participants were told that they would be taking part in an investigation of the effects of a vitamin called "suproxin" on visual perception. (No such vitamin exists.) The investigators gave some participants injections of adrenaline, a hormone that stimulates a variety of autonomic reactions associated with arousal, such as increased heart rate and blood pressure, irregular breathing, warming of the face, and mild trembling. Other participants received a control injection of a salt solution that had no physiological effects.

Next, the researchers placed some participants in an anger-provoking situation in which they were treated rudely and subjected to obnoxious test questions such as: "How many men, besides your father, has your mother slept with? *(a)* one, *(b)* two, *(c)* three, *(d)* four or more." Other participants were treated politely in the presence of another "participant" (a confederate of the researchers) who acted silly and euphoric. The researchers hoped that these two situations, together with the physiological reactions produced by the injections of adrenaline, would produce different feelings of emotion. In addition, some of the participants were correctly informed that the injections produce side effects such as trembling and a pounding heart, whereas others were told to expect unrelated side effects or none at all.

Schachter and Singer predicted that the participants who knew what side effects to expect would correctly attribute their physiological reactions to the drug and would not experience a change in emotional feelings. On the other hand, those who were misinformed would detect their physiological reactions and interpret them as feelings of anger or happiness depending on the situation. At the end of the session, all participants reported their emotional feelings in a questionnaire.

The results were complex. The adrenaline did not simply increase the intensity of the participants' emotional feelings. Instead, people who expected to experience physiological reactions as a result of the injection reported much less change in their feelings than those who did not expect it. Participants' expectations of physiological reactions had this effect *whether they had received the adrenaline or the placebo.* In other words, the participants who expected side effects felt less angry or happy after having been exposed to one of the emotional situations no matter what their actual physiological reaction. These results suggest that we *interpret* the significance of our physiological reactions rather than simply experiencing them as emotions.

Nisbett and Schachter (1966) demonstrated that we can be fooled into attributing naturally occurring physiological reactions to a drug and thus into feeling less "emotional." First, these researchers gave all study participants a placebo pill. They told half of the participants that the pill would make their hearts pound, their breathing increase, and their hands tremble; they told the other half (the control participants) nothing about possible side effects. Then the researchers gave all the participants electrical shocks through electrodes attached to the surface of their skin. Thus, all participants experienced feelings of pain and fear as well as physiological reactions such as increase in heart rate and breathing, trembling, and so on. They found that participants who perceived their reactions as drug induced tolerated stronger shocks than control participants. They also reported less pain and fear. Thus, once again, cognition can affect emotional feelings, even sensations of pain.

The precise nature of the interaction between cognition and physiological reactions has not been determined. For example, in the Nisbett and Schachter experiment, verbal instructions about effects of the placebo did affect the reactions to pain, but they did not appear to do so through a cognitive process. Nisbett and Wilson (1977) later reported that participants did not consciously attribute their increased tolerance of pain to the effects of the pill. When participants were asked whether they had thought about the pill while receiving the shocks or whether it had occurred to them that the pill was causing some physical effects, they typically gave answers such as "No, I was too worried about the shock." Even after the researchers explained the experiment and its rationale in detail, participants typically reported "that the hypothesis was very interesting and that many people probably would go through the process that the experimenter described, but so far as they could tell, they themselves had not" (Nisbett & Wilson, 1977, p. 237).

● What Should We Conclude?

Schachter's major contribution to the study of emotion was to encourage other psychologists to consider the interactions between basic conditioning processes and cognitive processes. These interactions are responsible for the ways in which we experience and perceive emotional feelings.

Too often, scientists—like most people—incorrectly see complex phenomena in terms of simple dichotomies. For example, there is a tendency to see behavior as the result of nature *or* of nurture, not both. Similarly, if we find that emotions are affected by cognitive factors, we need not conclude that emotions are not also affected by basic conditioning processes. Nor should we conclude that cognitive processes are irrelevant just because we find that some emotions are the result of conditioning processes. Perhaps the best way to understand emotions is to remember that they are responses to events that are important to us. Different events are important for different reasons. The emotional reactions to some of these events involve complex cognitive processes. Other events have a simple, direct relation to our well-being. In these cases, basic conditioning processes are sufficient to produce emotional reactions.

Interim Summary

Feelings of Emotion

Emotions are accompanied by feelings that come from inside the body. James and Lange suggested that the physiological and behavioral reactions to emotion-producing situations were perceived as feelings. Thus, feelings of emotion were not the causes but the results of these reactions. Hohman's study of people with spinal cord damage was consistent with the James-Lange theory. People who could no longer feel reactions from most of the body reported that they no longer experienced intense emotional feelings. However, the loss of feelings did not necessarily affect their behavior. Thus, emotional feelings and behavior are somewhat independent.

Although emotional feelings may be produced by basic conditioning processes, the perception of our own feelings is not determined solely by feedback from physiological and behavioral reactions. Feelings are also determined by cognitive assessment of the situations in which we find ourselves. Schachter and his colleagues demonstrated that information about the expected physiological effects of drugs (or placebos) influenced people's reports about their emotional state. In one study, people expecting side effects even tolerated more intense electrical shocks, apparently discounting their fear because of their expectations. These results do not support any single comprehensive theory of emotion, but they do underscore the importance of cognitive factors in emotional feelings. Emotions undoubtedly involve cognitive processes as well as basic conditioning processes.

QUESTIONS TO CONSIDER

1. As you know, we tend to become accustomed to our present circumstances. If we finally achieve a goal we have been striving for—a car, a well-paying job, a romantic attachment with a wonderful person—we find that the happiness it brings us is not permanent. But if we then lose what we have gained, we are even less happy than we were in the first place. Is it ever possible for a person to be happy all the time?
2. We can control the display of our emotions, but can we control our feelings? Can you think of any ways to make yourself feel happy or stop feeling angry?

Eating

We come to the last major topic of the chapter on motivation and emotion—the topic of eating. Freud chose to emphasize the importance of sexual motivation in human behavior, because he thought that sexual behavior was expressed in more different ways than any other motivation. But in this section we shall see that the regulation and expression of eating is at least as complex as any other motivation. In addition, I have saved eating for last because all other motivations are dependent on it. If life were not sustained by eating, other motivations would be irrelevant.

Regulatory Control Systems

It is probably no accident that dopamine, the same neuromodulator that plays such an important role in learning and in all motivated behavior, is intimately involved in the regulation of contractions of the smooth muscles of the stomach and intestines. The dopamine-mediated learning of behavior related to eating has been critical throughout evolutionary history.

It is helpful to consider eating as the result of a regulatory system whose components are analogous to those found in control systems in engineering. A regulatory system has four essential features: the **system variable** (the characteristic to be regulated), a **set point** (the optimum value of the system variable), a **detector** that monitors the value of the system variable, and a **correctional mechanism** that restores the system variable to the set point. A simple example of such a regulatory system is a thermostat that controls the temperature of a room by monitoring departures from the temperature at which it is set. When the room temperature falls below the desired temperature, the heat is turned on; when the temperature rises above the desired temperature, the heat is turned off. The temperature information that causes the turnoff is known as **negative feedback**. The system variable is the temperature of the room, and the detector is the thermostat. (See **Figure 13•14**.) Although the control of eating is much more complex than the control of heating by a thermostat, the basic elements are similar. There are several system variables to be controlled—body weight, caloric intake, energy output, body temperature; several detectors—receptors in the gastrointestinal tract, liver, and brain; and several correctional mechanisms—behavioral and social as well as physiological.

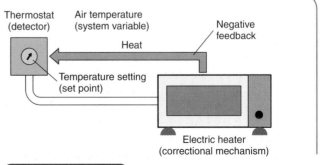

FIGURE 13•14 An example of a regulatory system.

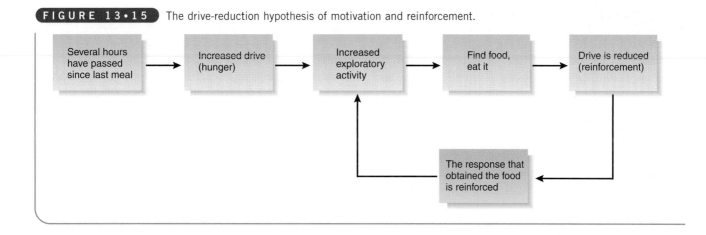

FIGURE 13•15 The drive-reduction hypothesis of motivation and reinforcement.

The earliest systematic attempt to explain eating and other motivational systems was **drive-reduction theory** (Hull, 1943). This theory stated that deprivation of a biological need creates a **drive** and that reduction of drives motivates behavior. That is, behavior is learned when it reduces a drive. For example, food deprivation creates a need for food, this need induces a drive called hunger, and behavior that produces food is reinforced because it reduces hunger. According to this view, all behavior is directed toward the reduction of drives (see **Figure 13•15**). Although drive-reduction theory enjoyed a brief vogue, it quickly became apparent that not all learned behavior is the result of drive reduction. For example, behavior reinforced by sexual stimulation is an obvious exception. One experiment revealed that male rats learned a response that allowed them to mount a female even though the male was removed from the female before ejaculation could occur (Sheffield, Wolff & Backer, 1951). The sight of a receptive female is an eliciting stimulus, however, so the finding presents no problem for current accounts of reinforcement.

Faced with such findings, some psychologists proposed that it was not the reduction of a drive that was critical but the maintenance of the drive at some optimal level. However, **optimal-level theory** (Berlyne, 1966; Hebb, 1955) fared no better, for a reason it shared with drive-reduction theory: Neither drive-reduction theory nor optimal-level theory provided a means to assess the level of drive independently of the behavior that the theory sought to explain. If behavior was acquired, the drive was assumed to have been reduced or to have returned toward its optimal level. However, the change in drive level could not be independently measured, so the theories were essentially untestable. The theories fell victim to circular reasoning: The behavior was said to be acquired if an appropriate change in drive level occurred, but the only way to assess the change in drive level was if the behavior was acquired.

In general, eating and other motivated behavior cannot be ascribed to any one theoretical variable. Each motivated behav-

ior requires us to ferret out the particular antecedents of the behavior, the particular consequences that maintain the behavior, and the particular physiological mechanisms that interrelate the antecedents, the behavior, and their consequences.

What Starts a Meal?

Hunger and satiety (the state of being fed to capacity) might appear to be two sides of the same coin, but investigations have shown that the factors that cause a meal to begin are not the same as the factors that end it. Therefore, this discussion will consider separately the factors that begin and end a meal.

Physiological Factors The reasons for beginning a meal must somehow be related to the fact that the body needs nourishment: Physiological factors clearly are involved in eating. But how do physiological factors help determine *when* to eat?

Cannon and Washburn (1912) proposed that eating begins when we have an empty stomach. They suggested that the walls of an empty stomach rub against each other to produce what are commonly called "hunger pangs." Some skeptics called Cannon's explanation of hunger "the rumble theory." But observations of surgical patients indicated that there was more to the onset of eating than hunger pangs. Removal of the stomach did not abolish hunger pangs, and these patients reported the same feelings of hunger and satiety that they had experienced before surgery (Inglefinger, 1944). (The patients had their stomachs removed because of cancer or large ulcers, and their esophagi had been attached directly to their small intestines.) Although the patients ate small, frequent meals because they had no stomachs to hold food, their reports of feelings of hunger and their total food intake were essentially normal.

Depletion of the body's store of nutrients is a more likely cause of hunger. The primary fuels for the cells of our body are glucose (a simple sugar) and fatty acids (compounds produced by the breakdown of fats). If the digestive system contains food, these nutrients are absorbed into the blood and nourish our cells. But the digestive tract is sometimes empty; in fact, it is empty when we wake up every morning. There must be a reservoir that stores nutrients to keep the cells of the body nourished when the gut is empty. Indeed, there are two reservoirs—a short-term reservoir and a longer-term reservoir. The short-term reservoir stores carbohydrates, and the long-term reservoir stores fats.

The short-term reservoir is located in the cells of the muscles and the liver, and it is filled with a carbohydrate—a form of animal starch called **glycogen**. When glucose is present in the bloodstream after the digestion of a meal, some glucose is used for fuel, but some is converted into glycogen and stored in the liver. The longer-term reservoir is the adipose tissue (fat tissue) found beneath the skin and in various locations in the abdomen. Adipose tissue consists of cells capable of absorbing nutrients from the blood, converting them to triglycerides (fats), and storing them. Fat cells can expand enormously in size to store triglycerides. In fact, the

primary difference between obese and normal-weight persons is the *size* of their fat cells, not their number.

The long-term reservoir keeps us alive during prolonged fasting. Once the level of glycogen in our short-term reservoir of carbohydrates is depleted, fat cells release fatty acids and a carbohydrate called *glycerol*. Brain cells metabolize glucose exclusively, whereas the other cells of the body can metabolize fatty acids. Because glycerol converts into glucose, the brain is nourished even after the short-term reservoir has been depleted. (See **Figure 13•16**.)

Because of the importance of glucose as a fuel, Mayer (1955) proposed the glucostatic hypothesis of hunger. According to the **glucostatic hypothesis,** hunger occurs when the level of glucose in the blood falls below a set point, which occurs when the glycogen in the short-term reservoir has been depleted. Mayer proposed that the decrease in blood sugar was detected by receptors on glucose-sensitive neurons in the brain called *glucostats.* (The term *glucostat* is analogous to *thermostat* but refers to the detec-

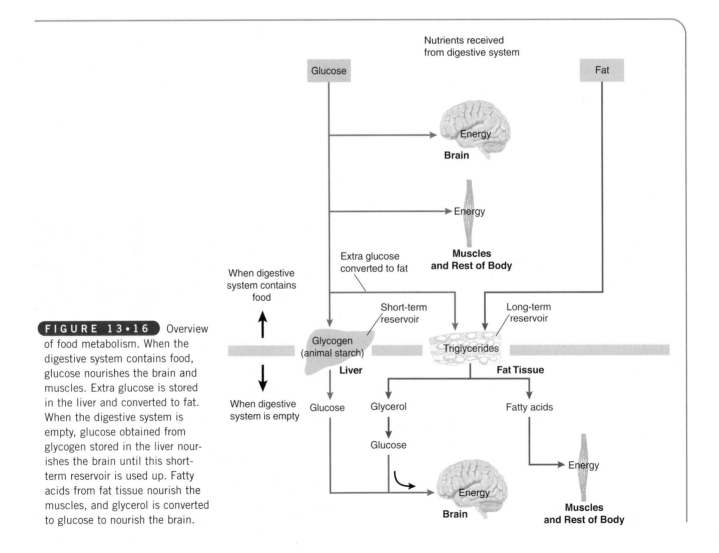

FIGURE 13•16 Overview of food metabolism. When the digestive system contains food, glucose nourishes the brain and muscles. Extra glucose is stored in the liver and converted to fat. When the digestive system is empty, glucose obtained from glycogen stored in the liver nourishes the brain until this short-term reservoir is used up. Fatty acids from fat tissue nourish the muscles, and glycerol is converted to glucose to nourish the brain.

tion of glucose rather than of temperature.) Mayer suggested that these detectors activate neural circuits that make a person hungry and stimulate the correctional mechanism of eating.

Subsequent research with both rats and humans demonstrated that the glucostatic hypothesis was too simple. Eating can be instigated in a number of different ways. An empty stomach causes a hormone, ghrelin, to be secreted. This hormone is a potent simulator of eating (Ariyasu et al., 2001; Kojima et al., 1999). Also, the liver contains two different types of nutrient receptors, one that detects the level of glucose and the other that detects the level of fatty acids (see Langhans, 1996). Both sets of receptors activate pathways that project to the brain; these pathways, in turn, activate neural circuits that initiate eating. For example, if a drug that blocks glucose receptors is injected into the vein that brings blood from the intestines to the liver, eating occurs immediately (Novin, VanderWeele, & Rezek, 1973). Moreover, if the nerves (vagus nerves) that carry information from these receptors to the brain are cut, eating fails to occur. Finally, the brain itself contains receptors that detect the level of glucose, and blocking these receptors also induces eating (Ritter, Dinh, & Zhang, 2000). Because the control of eating is so important to survival, natural selection has produced multiple interrelated mechanisms whereby eating is initiated.

Cultural and Social Factors Most people in Western society eat three times a day. As the time approaches for a meal, we become hungry and eat. This regular pattern of eating is not determined solely by biological need; it is at least partially determined by habit. For many of us, eating is initiated not by deprivation of nutrients but by environmental stimuli, such as the time shown by the clock on the wall.

If you have ever had to miss a meal, you may have noticed that your hunger did not continue to grow indefinitely. Instead, it subsided some time after the meal would normally have been eaten, only to grow again just before the scheduled time of the next one. Hunger, then, can wax and wane according to a learned schedule controlled by environmental stimuli.

Besides learning *when* to eat, we learn *what* to eat. What we accept as food depends on our culture and location. Our tastes also are shaped by habits acquired early in life. A child whose family exclusively eats a meat-and-potatoes diet will probably not become a venturesome gastronome.

Our social environment also affects our eating. We are more likely to feel hungry and to consume more food in the presence of companions who are doing the same. Even a chicken that has finished its meal will start eating again if it is placed among other chickens that are busily eating. Similarly, you may sometimes join friends at their table just after you have eaten. You say, no, you don't want to eat . . . well, perhaps just a bite to keep them company—and you eat almost as much as they do.

▲ *What we eat and how we eat are determined by cultural factors.*

What Stops a Meal?

We have seen that several factors—both behavioral and physiological—can initiate a meal, but what *ends* it? What brings a meal to a conclusion? Consider what happens when you eat. Your stomach fills with food, and the digestive process begins. However, about an hour passes before significant amounts of nutrients are absorbed into the bloodstream from the intestines. Therefore, the body's supply of fuel is not replenished until a considerable time after the meal begins. If you were to continue to eat until the nutrients actually entered the bloodstream, your stomach would burst. Other factors must be responsible for stopping the meal.

The physiological factors that stop a meal are divided into two groups—those that arise from the immediate effects of eating a meal and those that are produced by the longer-term consequences. The primary immediate cause of satiety is the stimulation of receptors by a distended stomach. In experiments with rats, eating does not occur if food is directly introduced into the stomach, even though the food was neither tasted nor smelled. Also, if procedures are used to remove food from the stomach after it has been eaten, eating continues unabated (Deutsch & Gonzales, 1980). The stomach rather precisely measures the volume of its contents. Food-deprived rats were allowed to eat their fill, then some of the contents of the stomach were removed via a tube. When the rats were again allowed to eat, they ate almost exactly as much as had been taken out (Davis & Campbell, 1973).

The stomach appears to contain receptors that inform the brain about the chemical nature as well as the quantity of its contents. The ability to detect the nutritional value of food is important; eating should stop relatively soon if the food is nutritious but should continue for a longer time if it is not. In one experiment researchers injected either milk or a dilute salt solution into the stomachs of food-deprived rats and 30 minutes later allowed them to eat (Deutsch, Young, & Kalogeris, 1978). The animals that had received milk ate less than those that had received the salt solution. Because the animals could not taste what had been put in their stomachs, the nutritional value had to be detected by receptors in the stomach. You can try an experiment of your own: Drink two glasses of water when you are hungry, and see what effect that has on your appetite.

The intestines also contain receptors that detect the presence of nutrients. The duodenum, the portion of the intestines into which the stomach empties, secretes a hormone called CCK that suppresses eating (Smith & Gibbs, 1992). And, further along the sequence of events that occur after a meal, the liver also has receptors that detect nutrients. After nutrients have been absorbed from the stomach and intestines, they enter the bloodstream and stimulate the receptors in the liver. If investigators stimulate these receptors by directly injecting nutrients into the veins supplying the liver of a rat, the rat's eating is reduced even though its stomach is empty (Langhans, Grossmann, & Geary, 2001; Tordoff & Friedman, 1988).

Even longer-term signals for satiety are produced by the adipose tissue that stores fat. The discovery of this signal came after studies with a strain of genetically obese mice. The *ob mouse* (as the strain is called) has a low metabolism, overeats, and becomes extremely fat. As these mice age, they develop diabetes, as do many obese humans both young and old. Researchers in several laboratories have discovered a genetic basis for the obesity of these animals (Campfield et al., 1995; Halaas, Gajiwala, Maffei, & Cohen, 1995; Pelleymounter et al., 1997). These animals have a mutation in a gene, called OB, that normally produces a protein known as *leptin* (from the Greek word *leptos*, meaning "thin"). Leptin is secreted by fat cells that have absorbed a large amount of triglyceride and acts on receptors in the hypothalamus to inhibit hunger. But because of their mutant OB gene, ob mice are unable to synthesize leptin.

Leptin has profound effects on metabolism and eating, acting as an antiobesity hormone. If ob mice are given daily injections of leptin, their metabolic rates increase, their body temperatures rise, they become more active, and they eat less. As a result, their weight returns to normal. The treatment works even when the leptin is injected directly into the brain,

FIGURE 13•17 The effects of leptin on obesity in mice of the ob (obese) strain. The ob mouse on the left is untreated; the one on the right received daily injections of leptin.

(Photo courtesy of Dr. J. Sholtis, The Rockefeller University. Copyright © 1995 Amgen, Inc.)

indicating that the chemical acts directly on the neural circuits that control eating and metabolism (see Woods, Seeley, Porte, & Schwartz, 1998). **Figure 13•17** shows an untreated ob mouse and an ob mouse that has received injections of leptin.

Maffei and colleagues (1995) found that leptin is secreted in humans and that the level of leptin in the blood is correlated with obesity. But if leptin is produced by human fat cells, why do some people nevertheless overeat and become obese? Much ongoing research continues to be devoted to the puzzle of obesity, to which we now turn.

Obesity

The physiological mechanisms that control eating are generally effective. Nevertheless, eating is not well regulated in many people, who become either too fat or too thin. Does what we have learned about the normal regulation of food intake help us understand these problems?

Studies in the United States indicate that the percentage of the population judged as obese by the body mass index (BMI) was 30 percent in 2000 (Ogden, Carroll, & Flegal, 2003), a percentage that had doubled in only 20 years. The BMI varies with the person's age, height, and weight. Obesity is a significant factor in coronary artery disease, hypertension, stroke, diabetes, several cancers, and many other conditions. The human costs of obesity are sobering: illness, suffering, dependency, and early death.

Obesity is extremely difficult to treat. The extraordinary financial success of diet books, spas devoted to weight loss, and commercial weight-reduction programs attests to the trouble people have losing weight. Kramer, Jeffery, Forster, and Snell (1989) reported that four to five years after adults participated in a 15-week behavioral weight-loss program, fewer than 3 percent continued to follow the program and maintain their weight loss. To make matters worse, studies with humans and nonhuman animals suggest that repeated bouts of weight loss and gain make subsequent weight loss more difficult (e.g., Brownell, Greenwood, Stellar, & Shrager, 1986; Steen, Oppliger, & Brownell, 1988).

Many psychological variables have been suggested as causes of obesity, including relatively low impulse control, inability to delay gratification, and maladaptive eating styles (primarily eating too fast). However, in a review of the literature, Rodin, Schank, and Striegel-Moore (1989) found that none of these suggestions has received empirical support. Unhappiness and depression seem to be *effects* of obesity, not its causes, and dieting may make these problems worse.

As with the factors that stop eating, there is no single explanation for obesity, but there are many partial ones. Habit plays an important role in the control of food intake. Early in life, when we are most active, we form our ideas about how much food constitutes a meal. Later in life, we become less active, but we do not always reduce our food intake accordingly. We fill our plates according to what we think is a proper-sized meal (or perhaps the plate is filled for us), and we eat everything, ignoring the satiety signals that might tell us to stop before the plate is empty. These behavioral factors may also help explain why people have so much difficulty losing weight.

Metabolic factors also play an important role in obesity. (The word *metabolism* refers to the physiological processes that produce energy from nutrients.) Just as cars differ in their fuel efficiency, so do people. Rose and Williams (1961) studied pairs of individuals who were matched for weight, height, age, and activity. One member of a pair might consume twice as many calories per day as their partner but nevertheless maintain the same weight. People with an efficient metabolism deposit excess calories in the long-term nutrient reservoir, fat cells. Over time the reservoir grows, and the individuals become obese. In contrast, people with an inefficient metabolism can eat large meals without getting fat. All of their calories are spent to maintain muscles and heat production. Whereas a fuel-efficient automobile is desirable, a fuel-efficient body runs the risk of becoming obese in many modern-day environments in which calories are plentiful.

We saw earlier that large fat cells secrete a protein, leptin, that lowers weight by increasing metabolic rate (that is, by making the metabolism less efficient) and decreasing food intake. Why, then, do some people become fat? Are they like ob mice, with defective OB genes? In most cases the answer is no (Maffei et al., 1995). The fat cells of most obese people do secrete leptin; the receptors in the brain that normally detect leptin, however, may be deficient. For leptin to reduce weight, the brain must contain functioning leptin receptors. But it is too soon to know if the discovery of leptin and leptin receptors will aid in the treatment of obesity.

There may well be an evolutionary basis for high metabolic efficiency—whatever the factors that produce it. Food was only intermittently available during human prehistory.

The ability to store up extra nutrients in the form of fat when food was available would therefore have been a highly adaptive trait (e.g., Assanand, Pinel, & Lehman, 1998). In addition, the known variability in metabolism among people today may reflect the specific environments in which their ancestors lived (e.g., James & Trahurn, 1981). A relative scarcity of food would promote the evolution of efficient metabolisms that would allow people to function on a relatively small number of calories per day. In an example from the late twentieth century, researchers found that in Gambia physically active (even lactating) women were able to maintain their weight on only 1500 calories per day (Whitehead et al., 1978). This level of intake would be considered a low-calorie diet and would cause weight loss in physically active adults in Western countries.

Another evolutionary consideration in the origins of obesity has been developed by Pinel, Assanand, and Lehman (2000). They observe that the evolutionary response to intermittently available food was fat storage during periods of high food availability and fat use during periods of food scarcity. Today, therefore, high rates of obesity are occurring in many countries because we regularly store energy in the form of fat but do not suffer the scarcities that would cause us to draw on those stores. In other words, our biological heritage promotes overeating and excess storage of fat because the environments of the present differ from the environments of the past in which natural selection took place.

Anorexia Nervosa and Bulimia Nervosa

Overeating is the most common eating problem in Western societies today. However, some people have the opposite problem: They suffer from **anorexia nervosa,** a disorder characterized by a severe decrease in eating (Uyeda, Tyler, Pinzon, & Birmingham, 2002). Both males and females can be afflicted with anorexia nervosa, but the disorder is at least 10 times more common in women. The literal meaning of the word *anorexia* is a loss of appetite, but people with this disorder generally do *not* lose their appetites. They limit their intake of food despite intense preoccupation with food and its preparation. They may enjoy thinking about food and preparing meals for others to consume; they may even hoard food that they do not eat. However, they have an intense fear of becoming obese, and this fear continues even if they become dangerously thin. Many reduce weight by cycling, running, or almost constant walking and pacing.

The fact that anorexia nervosa is seen primarily in young women has prompted both biological and social explanations. The disorder sometimes runs in families, and current studies estimate that more than 50 percent of the variation in the occurrence of anorexia nervosa is affected by genetic factors (Klein & Walsh, 2004). Many psychologists believe that the emphasis Western cultures place on slimness—especially in women—is largely responsible for this disorder (see Pinhas et al., 1999). One account states that if a young person responds to this pressure with excessive dieting and exercise,a

▲ *Anorexia nervosa: Mary-Kate Olsen, the actress, required treatment for the disorder during her freshman year in college, according to news reports.*

complex biological and behavioral pattern emerges that produces self-starvation (Epling & Pierce, 1991; Pierce & Epling, 1997). People with anorexia often suffer from osteoporosis and resulting bone fractures. When the weight loss becomes severe, menstruation stops. Anorexia nervosa is difficult to treat; as many as 6 percent of people with anorexia nervosa die from causes related to the disorder (Neumarker, 1997).

Another eating disorder, **bulimia nervosa,** is characterized by a loss of control of food intake and is again more common in women. (The term *bulimia* comes from the Greek words *bous,* meaning "ox," and *limos,* meaning "hunger.") People with bulimia nervosa periodically gorge themselves with food, especially desserts and snack foods, especially in the afternoons or evenings. These binges are usually followed by self-induced vomiting or the use of laxatives accompanied by feelings of depression and guilt (Halmi, 1996; Mawson, 1974; Steiger, Lehoux, & Gauvin, 1999). With this combination of bingeing and purging, the net nutrient intake of bulimics varies considerably. Weltzin, Hsu, Pollice, and Kaye (1991) report that 19 percent of bulimics undereat, 37 percent eat a normal amount, and 44 percent overeat. Episodes of bulimia are sometimes seen in patients with anorexia nervosa. Bulimia nervosa is seldom fatal, but it can result in poor health outcomes. Its causes are as uncertain as those of anorexia nervosa.

Interim Summary

Eating

Hunger is the emotional feeling that motivates and accompanies eating. Eating is a complex regulatory system with many variables to be controlled and many controlling factors. Eating occurs for both physiological and cultural-social reasons. Physiologically, the most important event appears to be the detection of a lowered supply of nutrients available in the blood. Detectors in the liver measure glucose and fatty acid levels, and detectors elsewhere in the body measure the level of fatty acids. Both sets of detectors inform the brain of the need for food and arouse hunger. Social factors and habit are perhaps the most important day-to-day instigators of hunger and eating in a society in which food is plentiful. We stop eating for different reasons. Detectors responsible for satiety, located in the walls of the stomach and in receptors in the liver and brain, monitor both the quality and the quantity of the food that has been eaten. Long-term control of eating appears to be regulated by a hormone known as leptin, which is released by fat cells and detected by cells in the brain. The effects of this hormone decrease meal size and increase metabolic rate, thus helping the body metabolize its supply of triglycerides.

Sometimes normal control mechanisms fail, and people gain too much weight. For any individual, genetic and environmental factors interact to cause the person's weight to deviate from the norm. People differ in the efficiency of their metabolisms, and this efficiency can lead to obesity. Experiences such as repeated bouts of weight loss and gain may promote obesity.

Anorexia nervosa is a serious, sometimes life-threatening disorder. Most anorexic patients are young women. Although they avoid eating, they remain preoccupied with food. Psychologists believe that a social emphasis on thinness may be an underlying factor that contributes to the development of the disorder. However, physiological and genetic factors are also implicated. Bulimia nervosa is another disorder, and is characterized by bingeing followed by self-induced purging. It, too, can result in poor health outcomes.

QUESTIONS TO CONSIDER

1. One of the last prejudices that people admit to publicly is a dislike of fat people. Is this fair, given that genetic differences in metabolism are an important cause of obesity?
2. Do you think that the fact that most people with anorexia nervosa are female is caused entirely by social factors (such as the emphasis on thinness in our society)? Do you think that biological factors (such as hormonal differences) also play a role? Can you think of any ways to answer these questions experimentally?

Suggestions for Further Reading

Carlson, N. R. (2006). *Physiology of Behavior* (9th ed.). Boston: Allyn and Bacon.

This is a good intermediate-level text that describes in detail the physiological bases of motivation and emotion.

Ekman, P. (2003). *Emotions revealed: Recognizing faces and feelings to improve communication and emotional life.* New York: Times Books/Henry Holt and Co.

Ekman offers a very readable account of his work on facial expressions of emotion.

Franken, R. E. (2002). *Human motivation* (5th ed.). Pacific Grove, CA: Brooks/Cole Publishing.

Examines the general principles of motivation as well as specific types of motivated behavior.

Logue, A. W. (2005). *The psychology of eating and drinking* (3rd ed.). New York: W. H. Freeman.

This book covers alcohol abuse as well as eating and eating disorders.

LeVay, S. (1993). *The sexual brain.* Cambridge, MA: MIT Press.

A well-written book on sexual behavior and the social and biological variables that affect it.

Jenkins, J. M., Catley, K., & Stein, N. L. (Eds.). (1998). *Human emotions: A reader.* Malden, MA: Blackwell Publishers.

This book contains chapters by many experts in the field of emotion.

Lykken, D. T. (1998). *A tremor in the blood: Uses and abuses of the lie detector.* New York: Plenum Press.

Lykken uses an informal style and provides a wealth of interesting details and vivid examples.

Key Terms

activational effect (p. 410)

anorexia nervosa (p. 433)

appeasement gesture (p. 410)

bulimia nervosa (p. 434)

Cannon-Bard theory (p. 425)

concurrent schedule (p. 408)

conditioned emotional response (p. 417)

correctional mechanism (p. 428)

cumulative record (p. 406)

deprivation (p. 407)

detector (p. 428)

display rule (p. 423)

drive (p. 429)

drive-reduction theory (p. 429)

emotion (p. 417)

estrous cycle (p. 415)

extinction-induced aggression (p. 409)

frustration (p. 409)

glucostatic hypothesis (p. 430)

glycogen (p. 430)

interval schedules (p. 406)

intraspecific aggression (p. 410)

James-Lange theory (p. 425)

leakage (p. 424)

learned helplessness (p. 405)

masking (p. 423)

matching relation (p. 408)

modulation (p. 423)

motivation (p. 403)

negative feedback (p. 428)

optimal-level theory (p. 429)

orbitofrontal cortex (p. 418)

organizational effect (p. 410)

overjustification effect (p. 404)

ratio schedules (p. 406)

schedule of reinforcement (p. 406)

set point (p. 428)

simulation (p. 423)

system variable (p. 428)

threat gesture (p. 410)

14

PERSONALITY

Trait Theories of Personality

Personality Types and Traits • Identification of Personality Traits

Trait theories of personality stress that personality consists of enduring characteristics evident in behavior in many situations. Several researchers have identified traits that appear to form the core of personality, including extroversion, neuroticism, psychoticism, openness, agreeableness, and conscientiousness.

Psychobiological Approaches

Heritability of Personality Traits • Brain Mechanisms in Personality

Psychobiological approaches to the study of personality focus on the role of inherited factors and brain mechanisms in personality development. Although most of the variability in personality traits is due to heredity, some is also due to the interaction of heredity and environment. Genetic factors may also underlie the individual patterns of behavior seen during infancy. The neural systems responsible for reinforcement, punishment, and arousal appear to underlie the personality traits of extroversion, neuroticism, and psychoticism. Other research shows that shyness may have its roots in a neural mechanism that includes the amygdala.

Social Cognitive Approaches

Expectancies and Observational Learning • Reciprocal Determinism and Self-Efficacy • Person Variables • Locus of Control • *Evaluating Scientific Issues: Traits versus Situations as Predictors of Behavior*

The social cognitive approach to the study of personality represents a mixture of behavioral and cognitive concepts. Bandura asserts that personality development involves both the imitation of others' behavior and expectations about potential reinforcing and punishing contingencies. Bandura also argues that the interaction of behavioral, environmental, and cognitive variables ultimately determines personality. Prominent among these variables is self-efficacy, or a person's expectations of success in a given situation. Mischel extended Bandura's emphasis on cognitive variables to include five other factors: competencies, encoding strategies and personal constructs, expectancies, subjective values, and self-regulatory systems and plans. Rotter's work has shown that locus of control, or the extent to which people perceive that the outcomes they experience are controlled by internal variables or external variables, also plays an important role in personality. Current thinking in psychology stresses that behavior results from the interaction of dispositional and situational variables.

The Psychodynamic Approach

The Development of Freud's Theory • Structures of the Mind: Id, Ego, and Superego • Defense Mechanisms • Freud's Psychosexual Theory of Personality Development • Further Development of Freud's Theory: The Neo-Freudians • Some Observations on Psychodynamic Theory and Research

The psychodynamic approach to the study of personality began with the work of Freud, who proposed that personality development is based on psychosexual tensions that are present from birth. Freud theorized that personality develops as psychosexual tensions express themselves during different stages of development. Defense mechanisms reduce the anxiety produced by conflicts among the id, ego, and superego. The neo-Freudians accepted some parts of Freud's theory but rejected others. Although Freud's theory influenced many Western conceptions of human nature, it has not been subjected to extensive scientific examination, largely because the theory itself is difficult to test.

The Humanistic Approach

Maslow and Self-Actualization • Rogers and Conditions of Worth • Some Observations on the Humanistic Approach

Humanistic psychologists are interested in personal growth, satisfaction with life, and positive human values. Maslow argued that self-actualization (reaching our fullest potential) first requires satisfaction of basic needs, such as food, safety, love, and esteem. Rogers maintained that self-actualization is best realized in circumstances characterized by unconditional positive regard. The humanistic approach remains empirically untested.

Assessment of Personality

Objective Tests of Personality • Projective Tests of Personality • Evaluation of Projective Tests • *Biology and Culture: Gender Differences in Personality*

Two types of tests have been developed with which to assess personality. Objective tests, such as the MMPI and the NEO-PI, contain multiple-choice and true/false questions that are aimed at revealing the extent to which the test taker possesses specific traits. Projective tests, such as the Rorschach Inkblot Test and the Thematic Apperception Test, present the test taker with ambiguous stimuli; it is assumed that test takers will "project" aspects of their personalities into their responses to these stimuli. Although projective tests are widely used, they have relatively low reliability and validity.

The reunion of this pair of twins, the Jims, prompted Dr. Thomas Bouchard to initiate the Minnesota Study of Twins Reared Apart.

The identical twin boys were separated at the age of 37 days and were adopted by two different working-class families. Coincidentally, both were named Jim by their adoptive families. They did not meet each other again until they were 39 years old. Both Jims liked math in school, but neither liked spelling. At 10 years of age, they both developed sinus headaches; a few years later they both developed migraine headaches. They both used the same words to describe their head pain. The twins had identical pulse rates and blood pressures, and both put on 10 pounds of weight at the same time in their lives. Both Jims were clerical workers who enjoyed woodworking, served as volunteers for police agencies, enjoyed spending their vacations in the tropics, had married and divorced women named Linda, chewed their nails, owned dogs named Toy, and drove Chevrolets.

Bridget and Dorothy, also identical twins, were 39 years old when they were reunited. Each came to their meeting wearing seven rings on her fingers, two bracelets on one wrist, and a watch and a bracelet on the other. Although the two women were raised by families of widely different socioeconomic levels, their personalities were very similar. The most striking difference between them was that the twin raised by the family of modest means had problems with her teeth.

Oskar and Jack were born in Trinidad. Their mother, a German, took Oskar back to Germany, where he was raised as a Catholic. He became a member of a Nazi youth group. Jack was raised by his father in the Caribbean as a Jew. He spent part of his adolescence on a kibbutz in Israel. At the time of their reunion, Oskar lived in Germany and Jack in southern California. When the twins met at the airport, both were wearing wire-rimmed glasses and two-pocket shirts with epaulets. Both had moustaches. They both liked spicy foods and sweet liqueurs, tended to fall asleep while watching television, kept rubber bands on their wrists, thought it funny to sneeze in a crowd of people, flushed the toilet before using it, and read magazines from back to front. Although their backgrounds were very different, their scores on a widely used personality test were similar.

These striking cases of identical twins reunited in adulthood suggest that heredity plays an important role in shaping personality. However, like all pieces of anecdotal evidence, such case histories must be regarded as clues, subject to confirmation by careful scientific evaluation. The Minnesota Study of Twins Reared Apart is one of several research projects designed to determine the roles of heredity and environment in the development of personality.

Each semester, I ask students in my introductory psychology class to respond, anonymously and in writing, to different psychological questions. One question I recently asked was "Are you a happy person, and why or why not?" Consider two answers that I received:

> I have always been a happy person. I don't really remember ever not being happy. Even as a kid I had lots of friends; nobody ever seemed to get mad at me. I like other people a lot. It seems the more I like people, the more I try to help them, the more they like me, and the happier I am.

> I wouldn't say that I am not happy. It's just that what makes me happy doesn't usually seem to be the same kinds of things that make my parents or even some of my friends happy. I would rather stay at home and read a novel or watch a movie by myself than go to a party . . . I like people but I don't necessarily find my happiness in them.

How would you respond to this question? Would your own response be the same as one of the answers given above? Probably not. After all, people differ so much. People have different styles of thinking, of relating to others, and of working, all of which reflect differences in personality—differences crucial to defining us as individuals. Common experience tells us that there is no one else just like us. There may even be significant differences in the personal characteristics of identical twins.

Everyday observations like these provide a starting point for psychology's study of personality. But psychology's approach to studying personality is considerably more calculated than these informal observations. For example, to many people personality is nothing more than "what makes people different from one another." But to psychologists the concept generally has a much more specific definition: **Personality** is a particular pattern of behavior and thinking that prevails across time and situations and differentiates one person from another.

Psychologists do not draw inferences about personality from casual observations of people's behavior. Rather, their assessment of personality is derived from results of special tests designed to identify particular personality characteristics. The goal of psychologists who study personality is to discover the causes of individual differences in behavior.

In this chapter we will explore what is currently known about personality. First I will present an overview of the major theories of personality. Next I will describe the methods used by psychologists to study individual differences in personality.

What types of research efforts are necessary to study personality? Some psychologists devote their efforts to the development of tests that can reliably measure differences in personality. Others try to identify the events—biological and environmental—that cause people to behave as they do. Thus, research on human personality requires two kinds of effort: identifying personality characteristics and determining the variables that produce and control them (Buss, 1995). Keep in mind that in the study of personality, we must be careful to avoid the nominal fallacy. As you'll recall from Chapter 2, the nominal fallacy is the false belief that the causes of an event are explained by simply naming and identifying them. Merely *identifying* and *describing* a personality characteristic is not the same as *explaining* it.

Trait Theories of Personality

Trait theories of personality are not, nor do they claim to be, all-encompassing explanations of behavior. But in all science categorization must come before explanation; we must know what we are dealing with before we can go about providing explanations.

The word *personality* means different things to different people. Trait theorists use the term much in the way we often think of personality in everyday life—to denote a set of personal characteristics that determine the different ways we act and react in a variety of situations (Sneed, McCrae, & Funder, 1998). However, as you will see, trait theorists do not all agree on exactly which characteristics are included in the set. Let's begin by differentiating personality *types* from personality *traits*.

Personality Types and Traits

The humoral theory of personality types, proposed by the Greek physician Hippocrates in the fourth century BC and refined by his successor Galen in the second century AD, is the earliest known explanation for individual differences in personality. The theory was based on then-common medical beliefs that originated with the ancient Greeks. The body was thought to contain four humors, or fluids: yellow bile, black bile, phlegm, and blood. People were classified according to the disposition supposedly produced by the predominance of one of these humors in their systems. Choleric people, who had an excess of yellow bile, were bad-tempered and irritable. Melancholic people, who had an excess of black bile, had gloomy and pessimistic temperaments. Phlegmatic people, whose bodies contained an excessive amount of phlegm, were sluggish, calm, and unexcitable. Sanguine people had a preponderance of blood (*sanguis*), which made them cheerful and passionate. (See **Figure 14•1**.)

Later biological investigations, of course, discredited the humoral theory. However, the notion that people could be divided into different **personality types**—different categories into which personality characteristics can be assigned based on factors such as developmental experiences—persisted long afterward. For example, Freud's theory, which maintains that people go through several stages of psychosexual development, predicts the existence of different types of people, each type having problems associated with one of these stages.

Personality types are useful in formulating hypotheses, because when a theorist is thinking about personality variables, extreme cases are easily brought to mind. But after identifying and defining personality types, theorists must determine whether these types actually exist and whether knowing an individual's personality type can lead to valid predictions about his or her behavior in different situations.

And in fact, most investigators today reject the idea that people can be assigned to discrete categories. Instead, they generally conceive of individual differences in personality as being differences in degree, not kind. Tooby and Cosmides (1990) also argue that the nature of human reproduction makes the evolution of specific personality types unlikely—sex produces a reshuffling of the genes in each generation, making it highly unlikely that a single, unified set of genes related to personality type would be passed from one generation to the next. In addition, nearly all behavioral scientists agree that many personality differences must be traced to the impact of environmental factors (Ehrlich & Feldman, 2003). (As in so much of psychology, in trait research, nature/nurture is the subject of intensive investigation. A later section, "Psychobiological Approaches," will explore work on biological versus environmental influences.)

Rather than focusing on types, many current investigators prefer to measure the degree to which an individual expresses a particular personality trait. A **personality trait** is an enduring personal characteristic that reveals itself in a particular pattern of behavior in different situations. A simple example illustrates the difference between types and traits. We could classify people into two different *types*: tall people and short people. Note that this is an either/or categorization. And indeed, we do use these categorical terms in everyday language. But we all recognize that height is best conceived of as a *trait*—a dimension on which people differ along a wide range of values. If we measure the height of a large sample of people, we will find instances all along the distribution, from very short to very tall, with most people falling in between the extremes. (See **Figure 14•2**.) It is not that people are only either tall or short (analogous to personality types) but that people vary in the extent to which they show tallness or shortness (analogous to personality traits).

We've all had experiences with people who behave in different characteristic ways: Some are friendly, some are mean, some are lazy, some are timid, and some are reckless. Trait theories of personality fit this commonsense view. However, personality traits are not the same as patterns of behavior: They are factors that underlie these patterns and are responsible for them; they produce physical or material states that are the causes of our behaviors. This does not mean that the

FIGURE 14•1 Characteristics of the four humors, according to a medieval artist: (a) choleric—violent and aggressive temperament; (b) melancholic—gloomy and pessimistic temperament; (c) phlegmatic—sluggish, relaxed, and dull temperament; and (d) sanguine—outgoing, passionate, and fun-loving temperament.
Illustrations © Bettman/CORBIS.

FIGURE 14•2 The distribution of height. We can measure people's heights, a trait, on a continuous scale. We can also look at the extremes and divide people into the categories of short and tall types.

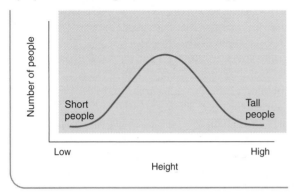

acquisition of personality traits is strictly biological and that learning is not involved. However, if our personality traits are changed through learning, those changes must have a neurological basis in the brain. In other words, we carry our personality traits around with us in our heads—or, more exactly, in our brains.

Identification of Personality Traits

Trait theorists are still in the process of discovering, describing, and naming the regular behavior patterns that people exhibit. In this section I'll introduce several influential trait categorization models: the theories of Gordon Allport, Raymond Cattell, and Hans Eysenck as well as the five-factor model proposed by other trait psychologists.

Allport's Search for Traits Gordon Allport (1897–1967) was one of the first psychologists to search systematically for a basic core of personality traits. He began his work by identifying all words in an unabridged dictionary of the English language that described aspects of personality (Allport & Odbert, 1936); he found approximately 18,000 such entries. Allport then conducted analyses that identified those words that described only stable personality characteristics. He eliminated words that represented temporary states, such as *flustered*, or evaluations, such as *admirable*.

Why did Allport undertake this exercise? He believed that the considerable extent to which trait labels appear in human languages attests to the importance of traits in how people think about themselves and others. Indirectly, then, the wealth of trait terms in English helped confirm his belief that a well-developed trait theory would have value in understanding human functioning. In fact, Allport believed that traits are neuropsychological properties that lead to behavioral consistency over time and contexts by producing functional similarity in the way each of us interprets and experiences events. That is, people with a particular trait react similarly across situations, because they experience a unique

sense of similarity across those situations that guides their feelings, thoughts, and behavior. There is evidence that some traits persist over time. In a 44-year longitudinal study, researchers found that creativity and some aspects of personality remained consistent over time (Feist & Barron, 2003).

According to Allport, some traits have greater influence on their possessors than others. The most powerful of all are those he termed *cardinal traits*. Cardinal traits exercise a strong unifying influence on a person's behavior. Allport believed that these traits are rare but that people characterized by them clearly stand out from the crowd. Examples include Adolf Hitler and his relentless exercise of oppressive power, Nelson Mandela's commitment to justice, and Mother Teresa's selfless devotion. In contrast, *central traits* are less singular in their influence than cardinal traits but capture important characteristics of an individual. When we say that someone is honest and warm in order to distinguish that person from others, we capture Allport's meaning of central traits. Finally, Allport's category of *secondary traits* includes characteristics that have only a minor influence on the consistency of individual behavior. An example would be a person's tendency to frequently change jobs.

Allport's research stimulated other psychologists to think about personality in terms of traits or dispositions. In fact, most modern trait theories can be traced to Allport's earlier theoretical work. Like Allport, modern trait theorists maintain that only when we know how to describe an individual's personality will we be able to explain it.

Cattell: Sixteen Personality Factors Raymond Cattell (1905–1998) used Allport's list of 18,000 trait words as a starting point for his own theory of traits. Cattell winnowed this large word set down to 171 adjectives that he believed made up a relatively complete set of distinct *surface traits* (those that are apparent in observable behaviors). He then used the process of factor analysis (see Chapter 11) to identify clusters of these traits that he believed in turn represented

▲ *Surface traits, such as friendliness, are those traits that are obvious to others.*

FIGURE 14●3 A hypothetical personality profile using Cattell's 16 personality factors.

(Adapted from the 16PF® Practitioner Report. Copyright © 2005 by the Institute for Personality and Ability Testing, Inc., Champaign, Illinois, USA. Reproduced with permission. All rights reserved.)

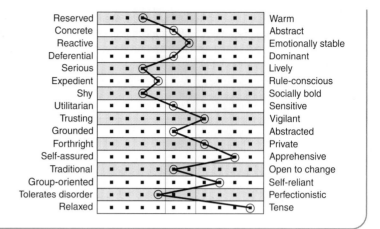

underlying traits. Cattell analyzed questionnaire responses from thousands of people in this manner; eventually he identified the 16 key personality factors shown in **Figure 14●3**. He referred to these 16 traits as *source traits*, because in his view they were the cornerstones on which personality is built. Figure 14.3 illustrates a personality profile of a hypothetical individual rated on Cattell's 16 factors. Think of someone you know well. Do you think you would be able to predict how they would score on these factors? Do you think these factors would help you predict the behavior of someone you did not know?

Eysenck: Three Factors

Hans Eysenck (1916–1997) also used factor analysis to devise a theory of personality (Eysenck, 1970; Eysenck & Eysenck, 1985). His research identified three important factors: extroversion, neuroticism, and psychoticism. These factors are bipolar dimensions. That is, extroversion is the opposite of introversion, neuroticism is the opposite of emotional stability, and psychoticism is the opposite of self-control. Individuals are rated on a continuum between the poles of these factors. People high in **extroversion** have an outgoing nature and a high level of activity. In general, extroverts like people and socializing, are spontaneous, and take risks. **Introversion** is at the opposite end of the scale: Introverts are shy, reserved, and careful. People at the high end of **neuroticism** are fraught with worry and guilt and are moody and unstable. Those who score low on neuroticism are eventempered and are characterized by **emotional stability. Psychoticism** involves an aggressive, egocentric, and antisocial nature; in contrast, a person with **self-control** has a kind and considerate nature and is obedient of rules and laws. Note that Eysenck's use of the term "psychoticism" is different from its use by most clinical psychologists; his term refers to antisocial tendencies, not to a mental illness. A person at the extreme end of the distribution of psychoticism in Eysenck's model would receive the diagnosis of antisocial personality disorder. (We'll look at this disorder in more detail in Chapter 17.)

Table 14●1 lists some questions that have high correlations or factor *loadings* (see Chapter 11 for a description of factor loadings) on Eysenck's three dimensions. The best way

to understand the meaning of these traits is to read the questions and to imagine the kinds of people who would answer yes or no to each group. If a factor loading is preceded by a minus sign, it means that people who say no receive high scores on the trait; otherwise, high scores are obtained by those who answer yes.

Eysenck argued that the most important aspects of a person's personality are determined by the combination of that person's positions on the three dimensions of extroversion, neuroticism, and psychoticism—just as colors are produced by the combinations of the three dimensions of hue, saturation, and brightness. **Figure 14●4** illustrates the effects of various

TABLE 14●1 Some Items from Eysenck's Tests of Extroversion, Neuroticism, and Psychoticism	
Factor	**Loading**
Extroversion	
Do you like mixing with people?	.70
Do you like plenty of bustle and excitement around you?	.65
Are you rather lively?	.63
Neuroticism	
Do you often feel "fed up"?	.67
Do you often feel lonely?	.60
Does your mood often go up and down?	.59
Psychoticism	
Do good manners and cleanliness matter much to you?	−.55
Does it worry you if you know there are mistakes in your work?	−.53
Do you like taking risks for fun?	.51

Source: Adapted from Eysenck, H. J., & Eysenck, M. W. (1985). *Personality and individual differences: A natural science approach.* New York: Plenum Press. Reprinted with kind permission from Springer Science and Business Media and from the H. J. Eysenck Memorial Fund.

FIGURE 14•4 Eysenck's theory illustrated for two factors. According to Eysenck, the two dimensions of neuroticism (labeled here as stable versus unstable) and introversion–extroversion combine to form a variety of personality characteristics. The four personality types based on the Greek theory of humors are shown in the center.

(From Eysenck, H. J. (1973). *The inequality of man*. London: Temple Smith. Reprinted with permission from the H. J. Eysenck Memorial Fund.)

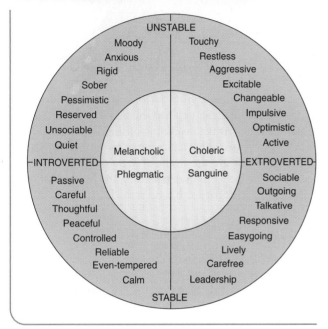

The Five-Factor Model

Recall that Allport attempted to discover personality traits through an analysis of the words we use in everyday language to talk about personality. Languages reflect the observations of members of a culture; that is, people invent words to describe distinctions they notice. An analysis of such distinctions by Tupes and Christal (1961), replicated by Norman (1963), has led to the five-factor model (Costa & McCrae, 1998a; McCrae & Costa, 1997, 1999, 2004). The **five-factor model** proposes that personality is composed of five primary dimensions: neuroticism, extroversion, openness, agreeableness, and conscientiousness. These factors are measured by the **Neuroticism, Extroversion, and Openness Personality Inventory** or (**NEO-PI-R**). (The name was chosen before the factors of agreeableness and conscientiousness were added, and the "R" stands for "revised." If you want a more useful mnemonic to remember the dimensions, think of the acronym OCEAN for openness, conscientiousness, extroversion, agreeableness, and neuroticism.)

The NEO-PI-R consists of 240 items that can potentially be used to describe the person being evaluated. The test items can be answered by the participant or by someone he or she knows well (Costa & McCrae, 1998b). (Studies have shown that self-ratings agree closely with ratings by spouses and other people who know a person well.) The test items are brief sentences, such as "I really like most people I meet" or (for ratings by someone else) "She has a very active imagination." The person completing the test rates the accuracy of each item on a scale of 1 to 5, from strong disagreement to strong agreement. The sums of the answers to different sets of items represent scores on each of the five factors.

McCrae, Costa, and Busch (1986) attempted to validate the five-factor model by performing a factor analysis on a list of adjectives contained in a test called the California Q-Set. This test consists of 100 brief descriptions (such as "irritable," "cheerful," "arouses liking," and "productive"). The items were provided by many psychologists and psychiatrists who found the words useful in describing people's personality characteristics. Thus, the words are not restricted to a particular theoretical orientation. Factor analysis yielded the same five core factors as the analysis based on everyday language: neuroticism, extroversion, openness, agreeableness, and conscientiousness. Indeed, the five-factor model is regarded by many personality psychologists as a robust model of personality (Paunonen, 2003; Wiggins & Pincus, 2002; Wiggins & Trapnell, 1997) that has considerable cross-cultural applicability (e.g., Allik & McCrae, 2002, 2004; McCrae et al., 1998).

Is there a biological basis for these five factors? A rapidly accumulating body of evidence points to a very strong degree of heritability (Jang, Livesley, & Vernon, 1996; Livesley, Jang, & Vernon, 2003; Loehlin, McCrae, Costa, & John, 1998; McCrae et al., 2000). To date, this research suggests that environmental factors pale beside genetic influences as far as the five personality factors are concerned.

Do the five factors predict anything of importance? DeNeve and Cooper (1998) showed that the five factors can be used to predict subjective well-being, and Vollrath (2000)

combinations of the first two of these dimensions—extroversion and neuroticism—and relates them to the four dispositions described by Hippocrates and Galen.

More than most other trait theorists, Eysenck emphasized the biological nature of personality (Eysenck, 1998). Eysenck believed that the functioning of a neural system located in the brain stem produces different levels of arousal of the cerebral cortex. Consider the introversion–extroversion dimension, which, according to Eysenck, is based on an optimum arousal level of the brain. Introverts have relatively high levels of cortical excitation, while extroverts have relatively low levels. Thus, in order to maintain the optimum arousal level, the extrovert requires more external stimulation than does the introvert. The extrovert seeks stimulation from external sources by interacting with others or by pursuing novel and highly stimulating experiences. The introvert avoids external stimulation in order to maintain his or her arousal level at an optimum state. In other words, Eysenck's theory hypothesizes that different states of arousal lead to different values of the extroversion trait for different people.

Eysenck's theory has received considerable support, especially from his own laboratory, which was highly productive. Most trait theorists accept the existence of his three factors, because they have emerged in factor analyses performed by many different researchers.

found moderate predictability for responses to "daily hassles" experienced by college students. Barrick, Mount, and Judge (2001) reported a meta-analysis of studies measuring job performance relative to the five personality dimensions. Generally speaking, extroversion seems to predict success in jobs that require leadership (managerial positions) or in jobs demanding the ability to improvise in order to reach goals (sales positions). Not surprisingly, conscientiousness predicts success across job classifications.

Finally, five is not necessarily the final number of fundamental personality dimensions. Jackson (Jackson & Tremblay, 2002) argues that a six-factor model may be more appropriate. According to Jackson, the conscientiousness factor in the traditional five-factor model actually represents two distinct dimensions (e.g., Jackson, Ashton, & Tomes, 1996; Jackson, Paunonen, Fraboni, & Goffin, 1996). One of these component dimensions, *methodicalness,* reflects planfulness and a need for orderliness. The other, *industriousness,* is characterized by perseverance and achievement orientation.

Interim Summary

Trait Theories of Personality

We can conceive of personality characteristics as types or traits. The earliest theory of personality classified people into types according to their predominant humor, or body fluid. Today most psychologists conceive of personality differences as being matters of degree, not of kind.

Personality traits are the factors that underlie patterns of behavior. Presumably these factors are biological in nature, although learning as well as heredity may enter in. The search for core personality traits began with Allport, who studied how everyday words are used to describe personality characteristics. Although Allport never isolated a core set of traits, his work inspired others to continue the search for such traits. Several researchers developed their trait theories through factor analysis. Cattell's analyses indicated the existence of 16 personality factors. Eysenck's research suggested that personality is determined by three dimensions: extroversion (versus introversion), neuroticism (versus emotional stability), and psychoticism (versus self-control). McCrae and Costa's five-factor model, based on an analysis of words used to describe people's behavioral traits, includes extroversion, neuroticism, agreeableness, openness, and conscientiousness. Ongoing research may identify additional fundamental personality dimensions.

QUESTIONS TO CONSIDER

1. Think of one personality trait that you are sure you possess. How did you come to possess this trait? To what extent does possessing this trait explain the kind of person you are?

2. Make a list of all of the personality traits that you feel describe you. Which approach to personality—Cattell's, Eysenck's, or the five-factor model—do you feel best represents the personality traits you possess? What are the reasons for your answer?

Psychobiological Approaches

The statistical evidence from factor analysis provides a description of consistent patterns of behaviors that we can identify as traits. At the beginning of the chapter, I said that we carry our personality traits around in our brains. That is, personality traits are the result of actions of the brain. Although we are far from understanding the psychobiology of personality, some progress has been made.

Heritability of Personality Traits

Cattell and Eysenck, among other trait theorists, have asserted that a person's genetic history has a strong influence on his or her personality. Many studies have shown that some personality traits are strongly heritable (e.g., Bouchard & Hur, 1998; Krueger, Markon, & Bouchard, 2003).

Psychologists assess the heritability of a trait by comparing identical and fraternal twins, comparing twins raised together and twins raised apart, and comparing twins raised by biological and adoptive relatives (see Chapter 3). Many studies have found that identical twins are more similar to each other on a variety of personality measures than are fraternal twins, which indicates that these characteristics are heritable (e.g., Jang et al., 2002; Livesley, Jang, & Vernon, 2003; McCrae et al., 2000). **Figure 14•5** shows correlations for "big five" personality traits between members of identical and fraternal twin pairs. Identical

▲ *Research into the genetic basis of personality suggests that traits such as extroversion may be inherited.*

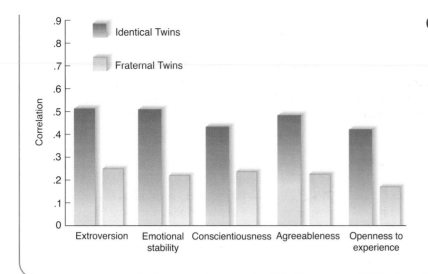

FIGURE 14·5 Correspondence between personality traits of identical and fraternal twins. These data show the degree to which the scores of identical and fraternal twins are correlated on each of the "big five" personality traits. The correlations for identical twins are more than double those of fraternal twins on each trait. This indicates that genes we receive from our parents do influence personality structure.

(Adapted from Bouchard, T. J. Jr. (1997). *The genetics of personality.* In K. Blum & E. P. Noble (Eds.), *The handbook of psychiatric genetics* (pp. 273–296). Boca Raton, FL: CRC Press Inc. Reproduced by permission of the Routledge/Taylor & Francis Group, LLC, and T. J. Bouchard.)

twins' personality traits correlate much more than those of fraternal twins. In fact, Bouchard (1997) found that identical twins' personality traits generally correlated nearly twice as much as those of fraternal twins. The similarities shown by the three pairs of identical twins described at the beginning of this chapter—Jim and Jim, Bridget and Dorothy, and Oskar and Jack, all of whom were separated early in life and united many years later—attest to the strength of genetic factors in influencing personality. Although each member of each pair of twins was reared in a separate and indeed very different environment, his or her personality was found to be amazingly similar to that of his or her identical twin.

Zuckerman (1991) compiled the results of 11 studies using various tests of Eysenck's personality factors of extroversion, neuroticism, and psychoticism. Every study found that identical twins were more similar than fraternal twins on every measure. According to Zuckerman's calculations, the best estimates of the heritability of these three traits are, for extroversion, 70 percent; for psychoticism, 59 percent; and for neuroticism, 48 percent. The results of these studies suggest that heredity is responsible for 50 to 70 percent of the variability in these three personality traits. Thus, it might appear that the remaining 30 to 50 percent of the variability would be caused by differences in environment. In other words, some family environments should tend to produce extroverts, others should tend to produce introverts, and so on.

But research indicates that the matter is not so simple. If family environment has a significant effect on personality characteristics, then identical twins raised together should be more similar than those raised apart. But in the studies reviewed by Zuckerman (1991), they were not. Several of those studies measured the correlation in personality traits of pairs of identical twins raised together and apart. Taken as a group, these studies found no differences—indicating that differences in family environment seem to account for none of the variability of personality traits in the twins who were tested. Researchers are now developing more sensitive measures of family environment

variables (e.g., Vernon, Jang, Harris, & McCarthy, 1997). As these techniques evolve, we should be better able to examine the relative contributions of genetics and experience to personality.

As we saw in Chapter 3, heredity and environment do interact. In fact, the major source of the interaction seems to be the effect that people's heredity has on their family environments (Plomin & Asbury, 2001; Plomin & Bergeman, 1991). That is, a person's genetic endowment plays an important role in determining how family members interact with him or her. **Figure 14·6** shows correlations between the ratings of various

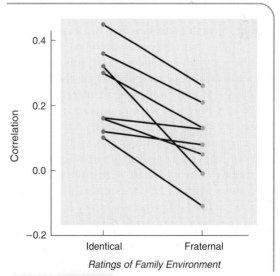

FIGURE 14·6 Correlations between members of pairs of twins on ratings of characteristics of their family environments. Individual pairs of data points represent ratings of cohesion, expressiveness, conflict, achievement, culture, activity, organization, and control.

(Based on data from Plomin, R., & Bergeman, C. S. (1991). The nature of nurture: Genetic influence on environmental measures. *Behavioral and Brain Sciences, 14,* 373–427.)

characteristics of the family environment made by pairs of identical and fraternal twins. The family characteristics that they rated included cohesion, expressiveness, conflict, achievement, culture, activity, organization, and control. The identical twins agreed on their ratings much more than the fraternal twins did; that is, identical twins were much more likely to report having experienced similar family environments.

There are two possible explanations for these results: The family environments could have been more similar for identical twins than for fraternal twins, or the family environments could have really been the same in all cases but simply have been *perceived* as different by the fraternal twins. Evidence suggests that the first possibility is correct. That is, the family environments really were more similar for identical twins (Loehlin, 1992).

How can this be? One might think that each family has a certain environment and that everyone in the household would come equally under its influence. But even within a family, each member experiences different social interactions. Although there are aspects of a family that are shared by the entire household, the factors that play the largest role in shaping personality development appear to come from unique social interactions between an individual and other family members. Because of hereditary differences, one child may be more sociable; this child will be the recipient of more social interactions. Another child may be abrasive and disagreeable; this child will be treated more coldly. In the case of identical twins, who have no hereditary differences, the amount and style of social interaction with each twin is likely to be similar.

Even physical attributes (which are largely hereditary) will affect a child's environment. A physically attractive child will receive more favorable attention than will an unattractive child. In fact, studies that examined videotaped interactions between mothers and their children have confirmed that heredity does have an important influence on the nature of these interactions (Plomin & Bergeman, 1991). Thus, although a child's environment plays an important part in his or her personality development, hereditary factors play a large role in determining the nature of this environment.

One caution about this interpretation is in order. Although the studies I have cited have been replicated in several cultures, none of them has investigated the effects of the full range of cultural differences in family lives. That is, when comparisons have been made between twins raised together and those raised apart, almost all have involved family environments *within* the same culture. It is possible that cultural differences in family environments could be even more important than the differences produced by a person's heredity; only cross-cultural studies will be able to test this possibility.

Should we assume that all personality traits are a product, direct or indirect, of a person's heredity? The answer is no. Some attributes and attitudes show a strong effect of shared environment but almost no effect of genetics. For example, twin studies have found a strong influence of family environment, but not of heredity, involvement in religion, masculinity/femininity, attitudes toward racial integration, and intellectual interests (Loehlin & Nichols, 1976; Rose, 1995). Thus, people tend to *learn* from their family environments some important social attitudes that contribute to their personalities.

Another way of examining the question of heredity is to look at personality early in life, in infancy. The NEO-PI-R was not designed to be administered to infants, but there is a related concept that psychologists use to describe the behaviors of infants—**temperament**, or each infant's individual pattern of behaviors and emotional reactions. Parents often will characterize their infant children in terms of temperament (as when your mother recalls you as a "fussy" or "quiet" baby), and there exist several scales for measuring temperaments in infants and preschool children. For example, in one assessment questionnaire, caregivers are asked a variety of questions, such as "When your child was being approached by an unfamiliar adult while shopping or out walking, how often did your child show distress or cry?" Unlike the case with personality, there is as yet no commonly agreed-on description of temperament; however, one measure, the Toddler Behavior Assessment Questionnaire, proposes that temperament can be measured with respect to five dimensions: activity level, pleasure, social fearfulness, anger proneness, and interest/persistence.

Using this questionnaire, Goldsmith, Buss, and Lemery (1997) examined the temperaments of infants and toddlers who were twins. For most of the dimensions, the correlation of scores between members of monozygotic (identical) twin pairs was higher than between dizygotic (fraternal) twin pairs. For example, the correlation between monozygotic twins for Activity Level scores was .74; the same correlation for dizygotic twins was .40. The higher monozygotic correlation indicates that variability in activity level is largely genetic in origin. Similar differences occurred for social fearfulness, anger proneness, and interest. However, there was little difference between monozygotic and dizygotic twins for pleasure, suggesting that twins who were similar in their expression of happiness were alike because of shared environmental influences.

Brain Mechanisms in Personality

We know that brain damage can produce permanent changes in personality; also, drugs that affect particular neurotransmitters can alter people's moods and anxiety levels. Thus, brain mechanisms are clearly implicated in personality traits. But what particular brain mechanisms are involved, and what personality traits do they affect? Several psychologists have attempted to relate the personality dimensions of extroversion, neuroticism, and psychoticism to underlying physiological mechanisms (Eysenck & Eysenck, 1985; Gray, 1991; Zuckerman, 1991).

Zuckerman (1991) suggests that extroversion, neuroticism, and psychoticism are determined by the neural systems responsible for reinforcement, punishment, and arousal. People who score high on extroversion are particularly sensitive to reinforcement—perhaps their neural reinforcement systems are especially active. Infants who later become extroverts show higher activity levels, whereas adult extroverts show more reinforcement-seeking behavior. Adult extroverts participate in more social activities and tend to shift from one type of activity to another. They are optimistic; they expect that their pursuits will result in reinforcing outcomes. However, unlike people who score high on psychoticism, they are sensitive to the effects of punishment and can learn to act prudently.

People who score high on neuroticism are anxious and fearful. If they also score high on psychoticism, they are hostile as well. These people are particularly sensitive to the punishing effects of aversive stimuli. Zuckerman therefore suggests that the personality dimension of neuroticism is controlled by the sensitivity of the neural system responsible for punishment, which appears to involve the amygdala. As we saw in Chapter 13, an important function of the amygdala is to organize the behavioral, autonomic, and hormonal components of conditioned emotional responses. If this system were oversensitive, a person would be expected to be especially fearful of situations in which he or she might encounter aversive stimuli. The amygdala is also involved in aggression. Thus, neurotics who also score high on psychoticism will tend to express their fear in the form of aggression.

People who score high on psychoticism have difficulty learning when not to do something. As Zuckerman suggests, they have a low sensitivity to punishment. They also have a high tolerance for arousal and excitation; in other words, we could say that their optimum level of arousal is abnormally high. As we saw in Chapter 13, some theorists hypothesize that people seek situations that provide an optimum level of arousal: Too much or too little arousal is aversive. Therefore, a person with a high optimum level of arousal (a high tolerance for excitement) seeks out exciting situations and performs well in them. (A neurotic would find these situations aversive, and his or her behavior would become disorganized and inefficient.) A person with a high tolerance for excitement makes a good warrior but does not fit in well in civilized society. **Table 14•2** summarizes Zuckerman's hypothetical explanations for the three major personality dimensions.

Few studies have directly tested the hypothesis that personality differences can be accounted for by biological differences. However, research using laboratory animals has provided support for Zuckerman's suggestions concerning neuroticism. A neurotic person avoids unfamiliar situations because he or she fears encountering aversive stimuli, whereas an emotionally stable person is likely to investigate unfamiliar situations to see whether anything interesting will happen. The same is true for other species. For example, about 15 percent of kittens avoid novel objects, and this tendency persists

when they become adults; some adult cats are timid, whereas others are bold. When a timid cat encounters a novel stimulus (such as a rat), the neural circuits in its amygdala responsible for defensive responses become more active (Adamec & Stark-Adamec, 1986). (Yes, some cats are afraid of rats.)

Kagan, Reznick, and Snidman (1988) investigated the possibility that timidity in social situations (shyness) has a biological basis in humans. They noted that about 10 to 15 percent of normal children between the ages of two and three become quiet, watchful, and subdued when they encounter an unfamiliar situation. In other words, like the kittens, they are shy and cautious in approaching novel stimuli. Childhood shyness seems to be related to two personality dimensions: a low level of extroversion and a high level of neuroticism (Briggs, 1988).

Kagan and his colleagues (1988) selected two groups of 21-month-old and 31-month-old children according to their reactions to unfamiliar people and situations. The shy group consisted of children who showed signs of inhibition, such as clinging to their mothers or remaining close to them, remaining silent, and failing to approach strangers or other novel stimuli. The children in the non-shy group showed no such inhibition; these children approached the strangers and explored the novel environment. The children were similarly tested for shyness several more times, up to the age of 7.5 years.

The investigators found shyness to be an enduring trait: Children who were shy at the ages of 21 or 31 months continued to be shy at the age of 7.5 years. In addition, the two groups of children showed differences in their physiological reactions to the test situation. Shy children were more likely to show increases in heart rate, their pupils tended to be more dilated, their urine contained more norepinephrine, and their saliva contained more cortisol. (Norepinephrine and cortisol are two hormones secreted during times of stress. Furthermore, their secretion in fear-provoking situations is controlled by the amygdala.) Obviously, the shy children found the situation stressful, whereas the non-shy children did not.

This study suggests that the biological basis of an important personality characteristic during childhood—shyness—may be the excitability of neural circuits that control

TABLE 14•2	Zuckerman's (1991) Hypothetical Biological Characteristics That Correspond to Personality Dimensions
Personality Trait	**Biological Characteristics**
Extroversion	High sensitivity to reinforcement
Neuroticism	High sensitivity to punishment
Psychoticism	Low sensitivity to punishment; high optimum level of arousal

avoidance behaviors. Of course, the researchers did not actually observe the children's brains, so we cannot be sure about the nature of the brain differences between the two groups of children. Studies of prenatal influences also reveal something about the biological bases of differences among people on dimensions such as shyness. Gortmaker, Kagan, Caspi, and Silva (1997), for example, examined the effects of maternal exposure to daylight on thousands of New Zealand children between the ages of one and seven years. They found that the children of mothers who experienced short day lengths during their pregnancies were especially prone to act shy. These researchers speculate that this effect may be due to neurotransmitters that are sensitive to day length.

Interim Summary

Psychobiological Approaches

Studies of twins indicate that personality factors, especially extroversion, neuroticism, and psychoticism, are affected strongly by genetic factors. However, there is little evidence for an effect of common family environment, largely because each individual's family environment is strongly affected by hereditary factors, such as personality and physical attributes. Family environment does have an influence on social attitudes. Study of infants' temperaments suggests that activity level, social fearfulness, anger proneness, and interest have a genetic component; genetic similarity, however, was less predictive of similarity in expressing happiness.

Important personality traits are likely to be the products of neural systems responsible for reinforcement, punishment, and arousal. Zuckerman believes that extroversion by a sensitive reinforcement system, neuroticism by a sensitive punishment system (which includes the amygdala), and psychoticism by the combination of a deficient punishment system and an abnormally high optimum level of arousal.

Research on shyness indicates that childhood shyness is a relatively stable trait that can be seen in the way children react to strangers and strange situations. The differences between shy and non-shy children manifest themselves in physiological responses controlled by the amygdala that indicate the presence of stress.

QUESTIONS TO CONSIDER

1. I have identical twin boys. One is much more outgoing than the other. If personality traits are heritable, how would you explain this difference—how can my twins share 100 percent of their genes yet have different "personalities"?
2. Are you a thrill seeker? To what extent do you seek out situations that might be considered risky or at least

mildly exciting? Depending on your answers to these questions, what might Zuckerman say about your personality (in terms of psychoticism)?

Social Cognitive Approaches

Trait psychologists such as Cattell and Eysenck are primarily interested in how people differ from one another. Factor analysis provides a statistical answer to this question. Trait psychologists chose the five factors of neuroticism, extroversion, openness, agreeableness, and conscientiousness, for example, because they measure how one person's responses on a personality questionnaire differ from someone else's. Trait theorists' general objective is to find a small set of measurements that will describe most people's responses—and that also will be distinctive with respect to any given individual. Furthermore, these trait measurements should describe the parts of an individual that don't change as the person grows older, acquires new friends, changes homes, and so on.

Other psychologists view personality differently, seeing it as the result of a behavioral learning process in which environmental variables act on the individual to produce behaviors. We might interpret certain behaviors in terms of traits like "extroversion," but the key question is why "extrovert behaviors" are frequently emitted by a particular person, and why that person might emit them in one situation but not in another.

Models that interpret personality as behavior stem partially from B. F. Skinner's experimental analysis of behavior (see Chapter 5). Although Skinner's work has influenced contemporary personality theory, he should not be mistaken for a personality theorist. Personality was definitely not Skinner's focus. But his ideas have relevance when we consider personality as a description for a certain set of behaviors.

Skinner believed that behavior is explained *entirely* in terms of its consequences. Environmental variables, therefore, are those that define the contingencies between stimuli, behaviors, and outcomes. Behavior is consistent from one situation to the next if it is maintained by similar kinds of consequences across those situations. Behavior changes only when the consequences change.

Behaviorists influenced by Skinner's approach have attempted to apply the experimental analysis of behavior to social contingencies and social behaviors. However, many choose to apply a behavioral approach by blending it with cognitive theory. The result is **social cognitive theory,** which embodies the idea that both the consequences of behavior and an individual's beliefs about those consequences determine personality. One such researcher is Albert Bandura (b. 1925) who combined elements of learning theory with cognitive concepts to explain social behavior.

▲ *At the heart of the social learning theory account of personality is the idea that personality develops as we observe and imitate the actions of others. Our observation of a model performing a behavior leads to an expectancy that our performance of the same behavior will produce a favorable result.*

Expectancies and Observational Learning

Bandura's theory is based on **observational learning,** which is learning through observation of the consequences that others (usually called *models*) experience as a result of their behaviors. Observational learning was described in Chapter 5 and is undoubtedly important in animal species whose young must learn a behavior before they are physically able to perform it. Mother cats, for example, teach their kittens which prey to hunt through observational learning. The kittens observe the mother modeling the behavior and imitate it—first in play and then later in actual predation. Your own experience is no doubt filled with examples of observational learning—it is partly through observation that we learn to dance, to make a paper airplane, to write in cursive, and to engage in many other activities. The more complex the behavior, *the more times we must observe it being executed, and practice what we have observed,* before we can learn it well. Learning to tie a shoelace requires more attention to details than learning to roll a ball across the floor.

Observational learning is more than just imitation. It also depends on reinforcement, as in other forms of learning. The nature of the reinforcement differs, however, in that it is the model who is reinforced. In other words, reinforcement is *vicarious,* and not directly experienced by the observer. The vicarious nature of some learning experiences is obvious in children as they imitate the actions of others. A three-year-old who applies deodorant to herself does so not because this behavior has been reinforced in the past, but rather because after watching her mother do it, she expects it would be "fun" for her to do so, too.

Vicarious reinforcement is made possible, in Bandura's theory, through cognition (Bandura, 1986, 1995, 2002; Bandura

& Locke, 2003). In particular, individuals can form an expectancy based on their behaviors. An **expectancy** is an individual's belief that a specific consequence will follow a specific action. To put it another way, expectancy has to do with how someone perceives the contingencies of reinforcement for his or her own behavior. If a person does something, it may be because he or she expects to be rewarded or punished. In different situations, expectancies may vary. For example, a young boy may learn that he can get what he wants from his younger sister by hitting her. However, on one occasion his parents may catch him hitting his sister and punish him. His expectancy may now change: He may still get what he wants by behaving aggressively, but if he is caught, he'll be punished. This new expectancy may influence how he behaves toward his sister in the future, especially when his parents are present.

Reciprocal Determinism and Self-Efficacy

Bandura, unlike many other theorists, does not believe that either personal characteristics (traits) or the environment alone determines personality (Bandura, 1978). Rather, he argues for **reciprocal determinism**—the idea that behavior, environmental variables, and cognitive variables interact to determine personality. (See **Figure 14•7.**) We know that our actions can affect the environment. We also know that the environment can affect our behavior. Likewise, our perceptions may affect the ways in which we behave to change the environment, and in turn those changes can influence our perceptions. For example, when our acts of kindness are met with kindness in return, we perceive the environment as friendly and are apt to show kindness under other, similar circumstances. Likewise, when we are treated rudely, we perceive the environment as unfriendly (perhaps hostile) and will likely attempt to avoid or change similar environments in the future.

The term **self-efficacy** refers to a person's beliefs about his or her ability to act as required in a particular situation

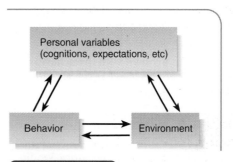

FIGURE 14•7 Patterns of interaction in reciprocal determinism. According to Bandura, behavior, environment, and cognitive variables, such as expectations and perceptions, interact to determine personality.

in order to experience satisfying outcomes (Bandura, 1982, 1997). According to Bandura, our degree of self-efficacy is an important determinant of whether we will attempt to make changes in our environment. Each day we make many decisions based on our perceptions of the extent to which our actions will produce reinforcement. Our actions are based on our evaluation of our competency. Moreover, self-efficacy not only determines whether we will engage in a particular behavior; it also determines the extent to which we will maintain that behavior in the face of adversity. For example, if you believe that you are underqualified for a job as ski instructor at a fancy Vail resort, even though you really want the job, you are not apt to apply for an interview—nothing good could come of the effort. However, if you are confident of your qualifications, you will surely attempt to get an interview. And even if you are turned down for that job, you may interview for a position at another resort, because you are sure of your abilities. Eventually your abilities will produce the outcome you want. Low self-efficacy can hamper both the frequency and the quality of behavior-environment interactions, whereas high self-efficacy can facilitate both.

Related to self-efficacy is the extent to which an individual feels optimistic or pessimistic about his or her life's circumstances. Seligman and Schulman (1986) studied life insurance salespeople and found that people who can see something positive in less-than-desirable circumstances are generally more successful than are people who view those circumstances negatively. It seems that otherwise cheerless circumstances stimulate optimists to seek creative means of "putting the circumstances right." Pessimists are more likely to throw up their hands in despair and give up. Thus, if there is a solution to be found for a problem, the optimist has the better chance of finding it.

Person Variables

Earlier I said that trait theorists seek to explain two aspects of personality: the distinctiveness of any one individual, and the aspects of personality that stay the same within that individual. But is this second objective reasonable? Is there stability to personality? Can the introverted high school student become a social star in college?

One extreme position, consistent with the behavior approach, is to assume that the behaviors that make up our personality are specific to a given situation and are not the result of any persevering traits. This position is known as **situationism**. In Chapter 5 we examined how discriminative stimuli control behaviors; perhaps personality is likewise dependent on the stimuli that control behaviors. Would a person high in conscientiousness stop at a red light at 3:00 in the morning with no one around and no chance of being caught? If you think the answer is "no," then you probably see the point.

This question is amenable to empirical test and has been the subject of much research (see the Evaluating Scientific Issues feature later in this section). In response to this research, some personality psychologists have argued for theories that represent the situation as part of the rules that govern behavior. Stability in personality, in this view, is a consequence of stability in the underlying rules. Variation results from the way the situation activates those rules.

One possible scheme along these lines is the model proposed by Walter Mischel (b. 1930). Mischel, like Bandura, believes that much of personality is learned through interaction with the environment. Also like Bandura, Mischel emphasizes the role of cognition in determining how people learn the relationship between their behavior and its consequences. In addition, though, Mischel argues that individual differences in cognition, or **person variables** as he calls them, account for differences in personality. Five person variables figure prominently in this version of social cognitive theory (Mischel, 1990, 2003; Mischel, Cantor, & Feldman, 1996):

- *Competencies.* We each have different skills, abilities, and capacities. What we know and the kinds of behaviors that have been reinforced in the past influence the kinds of actions in which we will likely engage in the future.

- *Encoding strategies and personal constructs.* We also differ in our ability to process information. The way we process information determines how we perceive different situations. One person may perceive going on a date as fun, and so may look forward to it; another person may perceive going on a date as potentially boring, and so may dread it.

- *Expectancies.* On the basis of our past behavior and our knowledge of current situations, we form expectancies about the effects of our behavior on the environment. Expecting our behavior to affect the environment positively leads to one action; expecting our behavior to affect it negatively leads to another.

- *Subjective values.* The degree to which we value certain reinforcers over others influences our behavior. We seek those outcomes that we value most.

- *Self-regulatory systems and plans.* We monitor our progress toward achieving goals and subject ourselves to either self-punishment or self-reinforcement, depending on our progress. We also modify and formulate plans regarding how we feel a goal can best be achieved.

Mischel's is a dynamic view; it envisions people's thoughts and behaviors undergoing constant change as they interact with the environment. New plans are made and old ones are reformulated; people adjust their actions in accordance with their competencies, subjective values, and expectancies of behavior–environment interactions. Between these periods of change, however, person variables provide stable rules for behavior akin to those described by trait theories.

Locus of Control

Social cognitive theorist Julian Rotter (1966, 1990) has focused on the extent to which people perceive themselves to be in control of the consequences of their behavior. Theories of **locus of control** (plural: loci of control) focus on whether people believe that the consequences of their actions are controlled by internal person variables or by external environmental variables. A person who expects to control his or her own fate—or, more technically, who perceives that rewards are dependent on his or her own behavior—has an *internal locus of control*. A person who sees his or her life as being controlled by external forces unaffected by his or her own behavior has an *external locus of control*. (See **Figure 14·8.**)

Rotter developed the *I-E Scale,* which assesses the degree to which people perceive the consequences of their behavior to be under the control of internal or external variables. The I-E Scale contains 29 pairs of statements to which a person indicates his or her degree of agreement. A typical item on the scale might look something like this:

> The grades that I get depend on my abilities and how hard I work to get them.

> The grades that I get depend mostly on my teacher and his or her tests.

Researchers score the scale by counting the number of choices consistent with either the internal or the external locus of control orientation. Scores may range from 0 to 23, with lower scores indicative of greater internal locus of control. The highest possible score is 23, because six of the choice pairs are nonscored "filler" items. Of all the populations Rot-

▲ *People having internal orientations are more likely to engage in good health practices.*

ter has assessed with the I-E Scale, a group of U.S. Peace Corps volunteers showed the highest level of internal locus of control (Rotter, 1966).

When Rotter published his work on the I-E Scale in 1966, the concept captured the imaginations of researchers; it seemed to be an antidote to what was perceived in the 1960s as an overemphasis on drive and motivational concepts (Lefcourt, 1992). The attraction has been long-lived, and the scale has been used in hundreds if not thousands of studies of social behavior in a wide variety of situations. Consider some of

Internal Locus of Control		**External Locus of Control**	
Poor performance on test	Good performance on test	Poor performance on test	Good performance on test
It's my own fault. I should have spent more time studying.	Great! I knew all that studying would pay off.	These tests are just too hard. The questions are impossible.	Did I get lucky or what? The teacher must really have gone easy on the grading.

FIGURE 14·8   Internal and external loci of control. People having internal loci of control perceive themselves as able to determine the outcomes of the events in their lives. People having external loci of control perceive the events in their lives as determined by environmental variables.

the findings obtained from research using the I-E Scale (Lefcourt, 1966, 1992):

- People with an internal locus of control orientation believe that achievement of their goals depends on their personal efforts toward accomplishing those goals.

- People having an internal locus of control orientation will work harder to obtain a goal if they believe that they can control the outcome in a specific situation. Even when people with external orientations are told that a goal can be obtained with their own skill and effort, they tend not to try as hard as those having internal orientations.

- People having internal orientations also are more likely to be aware of and to engage in good health practices. They are more apt to take preventive medicines, to exercise regularly, to diet when appropriate, and to quit smoking than are people having external orientations.

- People having high internal locus of control tend to have strong academic achievement goals and to do well in school. They are, however, also likely to blame themselves when they fail, even when failure is not their fault. People with an external locus of control tend to blame others for their failures.

Evaluating Scientific Issues

Traits versus Situations as Predictors of Behavior

Social cognitive theorists stress the importance of the environment as an influence on behavior and tend to place less emphasis on the role of enduring personal traits. They argue that the situation often plays a strong role in determining behavior. In contrast, trait theorists argue that personality traits are stable characteristics of individuals and that knowing something about these traits permits us to predict an individual's behavior in a variety of situations.

● The Case for Situationism

Mischel (1968, 1976) has suggested that stable personality traits do not exist—or that if they do, they are of little importance. Situations, not traits, best predict behavior, Mischel argues. He asks us to consider two situations: (1) a party to celebrate someone's winning a large sum of money in a lottery and (2) a funeral. People will be much more talkative, cheerful, and outgoing at the party than at the funeral. How much will knowing a person's score on a test of introversion–extroversion enable you to predict whether that person will be talkative and outgoing? In this case, knowing the situation has much more predictive value than knowing the test score.

Mischel can cite a wealth of empirical research evidence for his position. One of the first of these studies was performed back in the 1920s. Hartshorne and May (1928) designed a set of behavioral tests to measure the traits of honesty and self-control and administered them to more than 10,000 students in elementary and high schools. The tests gave the children the opportunity to be dishonest—for example, to cheat on a test, lie about the amount of homework they had done, or keep money with which they had been entrusted. In all cases the researchers had access to what the children actually did. They found that a child who acted honestly (or dishonestly) in one situation did not necessarily act the same way in a different situation.

Mischel (1968) reviewed evidence from research performed after the Hartshorne and May study and found that most personal characteristics showed the same low cross-situational consistency—.30 or lower. He concluded that the concept of personality trait was not very useful.

● The Case for Personality Traits

Other psychologists disagree with Mischel. For example, Epstein (1979, 1986) claimed that personality traits are more stable than some of the studies had suggested. He noted that assessments of cross-situational consistency usually test a group of people on two occasions and correlate their behavior in one situation with their behavior in the other. Epstein showed that repeated measurements across several days yielded much higher correlations. In a study of his own, a group of 28 undergraduates kept daily records of their most pleasant and most unpleasant experiences for a month. For each experience they recorded the emotions they felt, their impulses to action, and their actual behavior. The correlation between a given participant's emotions, impulses, or behavior on any two days was rather low—on the order of .30. However, when Epstein grouped measurements (that is, correlated the ratings obtained on odd-numbered days with those obtained on even-numbered days), the correlation rose dramatically—to around .80. That is, the correlation became much higher when the records of a group of days were compared to those of a different group of days than when a single day was compared to another single day.

Despite his skepticism about the value of the concept of personality traits, Mischel has acknowledged that some personality traits may be important predictors of behavior (Mischel, 1977, 1979). He has also pointed out that some situations by their very nature severely constrain a person's behavior, whereas others permit a wide variety of responses. For example, red lights cause almost all motorists to stop their cars. In this case, knowing the particular situation (the color of the traffic light) predicts behavior better than knowing something about the personality characteristics of the drivers. Conversely, some situations have less control over people's behavior. As Zuckerman (1991) points out, a yellow light is such a situation; when drivers see a yellow light, some will stop if they possibly can, and others will accelerate and rush through the intersection. The difference between the two behaviors is likely determined by individual personality traits.

● A Reconciliation?

Mischel and Shoda (1998) characterized the debate between supporters of the trait approach and social cognitive approaches in the following way:

The uneasy, often even antagonistic relationship between these two approaches over many decades in part reflects that their advocates tend to be committed passionately to different goals that seem to be in intrinsic conflict and even mutually preemptive. Consequently, the field has long been divided into two subdisciplines, pursuing two distinct sets of goals—either personality processes or personality dispositions—with different agendas and strategies that often seem in conflict. . . . (p. 231)

Mischel and Shoda (1995, 1998) propose a move toward reconciliation of the approaches in the form of what they call the cognitive–affective processing system approach (CAPS). Still being developed, the CAPS approach would have to recognize the multiple influences of biology, affect, cognition, and learning. Mischel and Shoda appear to extend the olive branch. Ongoing theory development and research in personality could constitute a very interesting chapter in the history of psychology.

● What Should We Conclude?

Most psychologists now acknowledge the stability of personality across many situations as well as the interaction between personality and situations, and most agree that the original question, "Which is more important in determining a person's behavior, the situation or personality traits?" has proved too simplistic. Some types of personality traits will prevail in most situations; some situations will dictate the behavior of most people. But some interactions between situation and personality require the analysis of both variables. An integration of the two approaches seems likely to shed more light on the causes of behavior than either approach alone.

include competencies, encoding strategies and personal constructs, expectancies, subjective values, and self-regulatory systems and plans. Rotter's research has shown that locus of control—the extent to which people believe that their behavior is controlled by person variables or by environmental variables—is also an important determinant of personality.

In the past, psychologists disagreed about the relative importance of situations and personality traits in determining a person's behavior. It now appears that personality traits are correlated with behavior, especially when multiple observations of particular behaviors are made. In addition, some situations (such as a funeral or a stoplight) are more powerful than others, exerting more control on people's behavior. Traits and situations interact: Some people may be affected more than others by a particular situation, and people tend to choose the types of situations in which they find themselves.

QUESTIONS TO CONSIDER

1. Think of a situation in which you modeled your behavior after someone else's. What factors led you to imitate this behavior? To what extent did you form an expectancy that imitating this behavior would lead to a particular consequence?
2. Provide a personal example of reciprocal determinism. Explain the interaction of behavior, environmental variables, and cognitive variables in this example.
3. Do you feel that you have an internal or an external locus of control? Give an example of a recent decision that you made or a social interaction that you had. How would your life be different if you adopted the opposite of locus of control orientation?

Interim Summary

Social Cognitive Approaches

Social cognitive theory blends Skinner's notion of reinforcement or other approaches to learning with cognitive concepts such as expectancy to explain social interaction and personality. According to Bandura, people learn the relation between their behavior and its consequences by observing how others' behavior is rewarded and punished. Bandura also believes that personality is the result of reciprocal determinism—the interaction of behavior, environment, and cognitive variables. The extent to which a person is likely to attempt to change his or her environment is related to self-efficacy, the expectation that the individual will be successful in producing the change. People with low self-efficacy tend not to try to alter their environments; just the opposite is true for people with high self-efficacy.

Mischel has argued that personality differences are due largely to individual differences in cognition. These variables

The Psychodynamic Approach

For many people, the name Sigmund Freud is synonymous with psychology. Indeed, his work has had profound and lasting effects on Western culture. Terms such as *ego, libido, repression, rationalization,* and *fixation* are as familiar to many laypeople as to clinicians. Before Freud formulated his theory, people believed that most behavior was determined by rational, conscious processes. Freud was the first to claim that what we do is often irrational and that the reasons for our behavior are seldom conscious. The mind, to Freud, was a battleground for the warring factions of instinct, reason, and conscience; the term **psychodynamic** refers to this struggle. As you will soon see, although Freud's work began with the clinical treatment of patients with psychological problems, it later provided a framework for explaining how psychodynamic factors determine personality.

The Development of Freud's Theory

Sigmund Freud (1856–1939) was a Viennese physician who acquired his early training in neurology in the laboratory of Ernst Wilhelm von Brücke, an eminent physiologist and neuroanatomist. Freud's work in the laboratory consisted mostly of careful anatomical observation rather than experimentation. Careful observation also characterized his later work with human behavior; he made detailed observations of individual patients and drew inferences about the structure of the human psyche from these cases. (As Chapter 1 mentioned, *psyche*, from the Greek word for "breath" or "soul," refers to the mind.)

Freud left Vienna briefly and studied in Paris with Jean Martin Charcot, who was investigating the usefulness of hypnosis as a treatment for hysteria. Patients with hysteria often experience paralysis of some part of the body or loss of one of the senses, and no physiological cause can be detected. The fact that hypnosis could be used either to produce or to alleviate hysterical symptoms suggested that these symptoms were of psychological origin. Charcot proposed that hysteria was caused by some kind of psychological trauma. Freud was greatly impressed by Charcot's work and became even more interested in problems of the mind.

He then returned home to Vienna, opened his medical practice, and began an association with the prominent physician Josef Breuer. They published a seminal book called *Studies on Hysteria*, and one of the cases cited in it, that of Anna O., provided the evidence that led to some of the most important tenets of Freud's theory. Breuer had treated Anna O. 12 years before he and Freud published their book. She suffered from a staggering number of symptoms, including loss of speech, disturbances in vision, headaches, and paralysis and loss of feeling in her right arm. Under hypnosis Anna was asked to think about the time when her symptoms had started. Each of her symptoms appeared to have begun just when she was unable to express a strongly felt emotion. While under hypnosis she experienced these emotions again, and the experience gave her relief from her symptoms. It was as if the emotions had been bottled up, and reliving the original experiences uncorked them. This release of energy (which Breuer and Freud called *catharsis*) presumably eliminated her symptoms.

The story of Anna O. is one of the most frequently and thoroughly discussed cases in the annals of psychotherapy. Interestingly, Breuer's original description appears to be inaccurate in some of its most important respects (Ellenberger, 1972). Apparently, the woman was not cured. Ellenberger discovered hospital records indicating that Anna O. continued to take morphine for the distress caused by the disorders Breuer had supposedly cured. Freud appears to have eventually learned the truth, but this fact did not become generally known until recently. Breuer's failure to help Anna O. with her problems does not really undermine Freud's approach, however. The Freudian theory of personality must stand or fall on its own merits, despite the fact that one of its prime teaching examples appears to be largely fiction.

Freud concluded from his observations of patients that all human behavior is motivated by instinctual drives, which, when activated, supply "psychic energy." This energy is aversive, because the nervous system seeks a state of quiet equilibrium. According to Freud, if something prevents the psychic energy caused by activation of a drive from being discharged, psychological disturbances will result.

Freud believed that instinctual drives are triggered by events in a person's life. Many of these events, and the reactions they cause, will be mundane and part of the normal fabric of life. Traumatic events, however, may seriously threaten the desired state of psychic energy equilibrium. During a traumatic event, a person may try to deny or hide a strong emotional reaction rather than express it. Indeed, sometimes we must hide and not act on strong emotions, according to Freud. Strong anger, for example, could lead to violence or even murder. But there is a cost to hiding emotional reactions and suppressing the psychic energy that fuels them: The emotion may be expressed neurotically—that is, with excessive anxiety. The individual will not be able to recall the extreme emotional reactions, because they will be embedded in the **unconscious,** the inaccessible part of the mind. Unconscious emotions, however, still exert control over conscious thoughts and actions. As we will see later, according to Freud the ways in which those emotions eventually find a degree of release will help define our unique personalities.

Freud also believed that the mind actively prevents unconscious memories of traumatic events from reaching conscious awareness. That is, the mind *represses* the memories of anxiety-provoking traumatic events from being consciously discovered. Freud used the metaphor of an iceberg to describe the mind. Only the tip of an iceberg is visible above water; the much larger and more important part is submerged. Likewise, the conscious mind hides a larger and more important part of the mind—the unconscious. To understand someone's personality, we must tap into that individual's unconscious.

Freud, then, argued that our personalities are determined by both conscious and unconscious powers, with the unconscious exerting considerable influence on the conscious. To understand how the unconscious exerts its control over conscious thought and action, we need to explore Freud's view of the structure of personality.

Structures of the Mind: Id, Ego, and Superego

Freud was struck by the fact that psychological disturbances could stem from events that a person apparently could no longer consciously recall, although the events could be revealed during hypnosis. This phenomenon led him to conclude that the mind consists of unconscious, preconscious, and conscious elements. The *unconscious* includes mental events of which we are not aware, the *conscious* entails mental events of which we are aware, and the *preconscious* involves mental events that may become conscious through effort.

FIGURE 14•9 Freud's conception of the structure of the mind. Freud compared the conscious portion of the mind to the tip of an iceberg and the unconscious portion to the larger part of the iceberg below the water's surface. The id is completely unconscious, but both the ego and the superego may be partially conscious and partially unconscious. In addition, Freud argued that part of the mind is preconscious (not shown in this figure), containing information that may be brought into consciousness through effort.

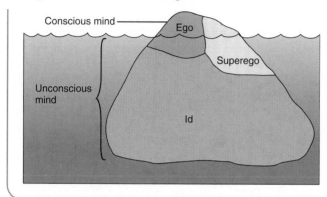

Conscious mind

Ego

Superego

Unconscious mind

Id

Freud divided the mind into three structures: the id, the ego, and the superego (see **Figure 14•9**). The operations of the **id** are completely unconscious. The id contains the **libido,** which is the primary source of instinctual motivation for all psychic forces; this force is insistent and is unresponsive to the demands of reality. The id obeys only one rule—to obtain immediate gratification in whatever form it may take—called the **pleasure principle.** If you are hungry, the id compels you to eat; if you are angry, the id prompts you to strike out or to seek revenge or to destroy something; if you are sexually aroused, the id presses for immediate sexual gratification. It is important to understand that for Freud the id was a source of unrestrained, uncivilized, and ultimately harmful behavior. Freud (1933) conceived of the id as

> ... the dark, inaccessible part of our personality.... We approach the id with analogies: we call it a chaos, a cauldron full of seething excitations.... It is filled with energy reaching it from the instincts, but it has no organization, produces no collective will, but only a striving to bring about the satisfaction of the instinctual needs subject to the observance of the pleasure principle. (p. 65)

The **ego** is the thinking, planning, and protective self; it controls and integrates behavior. It acts as a mediator, negotiating a compromise among the pressures of the id, the counterpressures of the superego (described next), and the demands of reality. The ego's functions of perception, cognition, and memory perform this mediation. The ego is driven by the **reality principle**—the tendency to satisfy the id's demands realistically, which almost always involves compromising the demands of the id and the superego. Adherence to

the reality principle involves delaying gratification of a drive until an appropriate goal is located. To ward off the demands of the id when these demands cannot be gratified, the ego uses defense mechanisms (described later). Some of the functions of the ego are unconscious.

The **superego** is subdivided into the conscience and the ego-ideal. The **conscience** is the internalization of the rules and restrictions of society. It determines which behaviors are permissible and punishes wrongdoing with feelings of guilt. The **ego-ideal** is the internalization of what society values and what the person will strive to achieve.

Freud believed the mind to be full of conflicts. A conflict may begin when one of the two primary drives, the sexual instinctual drive or the aggressive instinctual drive, is aroused. The id demands gratification of these drives but often is held in check by the superego's internalized prohibitions against the behaviors the drives tend to produce. *Internalized prohibitions* are rules of behavior learned in childhood that protect the person from the guilt he or she would feel if the instinctual drives were allowed to express themselves.

The result of the conflict is *compromise formation,* in which a compromise is reached between the demands of the id and the suppressive effects of the superego. According to Freud, phenomena such as dreams, artistic creations, and slips of the tongue (we now call them Freudian slips) are examples of compromise formation. Consider the following slip committed by a student in one of my introductory psychology classes: At the end of the term, after nearly failing the course, the student approached me, extended his hand, and clearly said, "Great course, professor—I'd like to break your hand." According to Freud, the student was working hard to suppress his aggressive impulses toward me and trying to behave magnanimously, but his underlying feelings nevertheless emerged.

In what many consider to be his greatest work, *The Interpretation of Dreams,* Freud wrote, "The interpretation of dreams is the royal road to a knowledge of the unconscious activities of the mind" (Freud, 1900, p. 647). To Freud, dreams were motivated by repressed wishes and urges. Through the analysis of dreams, Freud thought, repressed wishes and memories could be rediscovered. For example, Freud believed that the **manifest content** of a dream—its actual story line—is only a disguised version of its **latent content**—its hidden message, which is produced by the unconscious. The latent content usually will be related to unexpressed wishes generated by instinctual drives.

For example, a person may want to hurt or injure another person, perhaps a competitor for a job promotion. However, acting out this scenario in a dream would lead to guilt and anxiety. Therefore, the aggressive wishes of the unconscious are transformed into a more palatable form—the manifest content of the dream might be that the coworker accepts a different job offer, removing any competition for the promotion. The manifest content of this dream manages to express, at least partly, the latent content supplied by the unconscious.

In addition to analyzing his patients' dreams, Freud also developed the technique of free association to probe the unconscious mind for clues of intrapsychic conflict. **Free association** is a method of analysis in which patients are asked to relax, clear their minds of what they are currently thinking, and then report all thoughts, images, perceptions, and feelings that come to mind. During free association Freud looked for particular patterns in patients' reports that might reveal wishes, fears, and worries that the patients' minds might be keeping hidden. For example, someone's free association might reveal, among other things, the thought of beating someone up, an image of a knife, and perhaps a feeling of relief. Recognizing a pattern in his patient's report, Freud might then develop hypotheses about the client's hidden desire to harm someone and about the reasons motivating both that desire and the relief experienced once the aggressive urge was satisfied. These hypotheses would then guide the therapy.

Defense Mechanisms

According to Freud, the ego contains **defense mechanisms**— mental systems that become active whenever the id's unconscious instinctual drives come into conflict with the superego's internalized prohibitions. The signal for the ego to use one of its defenses is the state of anxiety produced by an intrapsychic conflict, which motivates the ego to apply a defense mechanism and thus reduce the anxiety. **Table 14•3** presents six important defense mechanisms; let's look at each of them in turn.

As mentioned previously, **repression** is responsible for keeping threatening or anxiety-provoking memories from our conscious awareness. For example, repression of memories of a childhood sexual assault might provide the child with periods of freedom from the otherwise paralyzing fear of future assaults. Freud believed that repression was perhaps the most powerful of the defense mechanisms.

Reaction formation involves replacing an anxiety-provoking idea with its opposite. An often-cited example of a reaction formation is that of a person who is aroused and fascinated by pornographic material but whose superego will not permit this enjoyment; he or she therefore becomes a militant crusader against pornography. Reaction formation can be a very useful defense mechanism in this situation, permitting acceptable interaction with the forbidden sexual material. The crusader against pornography often studies the salacious material to see just how vile it is so that he or she can better educate others about its harmful nature. Thus, enjoyment becomes possible without feelings of guilt.

Projection involves denying our own unacceptable id-based desires and finding evidence of these desires in others' behavior. For example, a woman who is experiencing a great deal of repressed hostility may perceive the world as being full of people who are hostile to her. In this way she can blame someone else for her own aggression when she verbally lashes out at somebody. That is, it would be unacceptable to the superego for her to initiate aggression, but perfectly acceptable for her to take preemptive action in self-defense.

Sublimation is the diversion of psychic energy from an unacceptable drive to an acceptable substitute. For example, a person may feel strong sexual desire but find its outlet unacceptable because of internalized prohibitions. Despite the barring of the originally desired outlet for the drive, the psychic energy remains and finds another outlet, such as artistic or other creative activity. Freud considered sublimation an important factor in artistic and intellectual creativity. He believed that people have a fixed amount of drive available for motivating all activities; therefore, surplus sexual instinctual drive that is not expended in its most direct fashion can be used to increase a person's potential for creative achievement.

Rationalization is the process of inventing an acceptable reason for a behavior that is really being performed for an-

TABLE 14•3	Freudian Defense Mechanisms	
Defense Mechanism	**Description**	**Example**
Repression	Unconsciously barring memories of traumatic experiences from reaching conscious awareness.	Being unable to remember traumatic childhood sexual abuse or other traumatic events that occurred earlier in life.
Reaction Formation	Replacing an anxiety-provoking idea with its opposite.	Having intense feelings of dislike for a person but acting friendly and kind toward him or her.
Projection	Denying your unacceptable feelings and desires and finding them in others.	Denying your hostility toward a person but believing that that person is hostile toward you.
Sublimation	Channelling psychic energy from an unacceptable drive into a more acceptable one.	Diverting energy from the sex drive to produce a work of art.
Rationalization	Creating an acceptable reason for a behavior that is actually performed for a less acceptable reason.	Asserting that you enjoy a wrestling match as an athletic contest when in fact you enjoy the vicarious violence.
Denial	Negating or dismissing the reality of an unpleasant truth.	Asserting that a loved one is not dead but is missing in action and unable to communicate.

This table shows several of the most frequently used defense mechanisms.

▲ *Freud argued that creativity was often the result of sublimation—the redirection of psychic energy from unacceptable actions, such as unrestrained sexual behavior, to acceptable actions, such as the jointly sensual and creative work shown here.*

other, less acceptable reason. For example, a woman who goes to a wrestling match after a frustrating day at the office might say, "I really go because I admire the athleticism of the wrestlers."

In **denial** we refuse to acknowledge a fact in order to preserve the ego from unpleasant truths. In wartime, when families receive the tragic news of a death of a loved one, it is not uncommon for a family member to deny the possibility that death has occurred. Such a person may invent elaborate scenarios to explain why a son or daughter is "missing" rather than dead.

Interestingly, researchers have found that the use of defense mechanisms predicts personality changes in later adulthood (Cramer, 2003). The investigators measured participants' personality traits over a 24-year period using the five-factor model. Although most personality traits remained reasonably stable, the use of defense mechanisms such as denial and projection correlated with an increased neuroticism, decreased extroversion, and decreased agreeableness among some study participants in later adulthood. The use of these defense mechanisms was not found to be negative in all cases, though. Among participants who used defense mechanisms, low scores on IQ tests were found to correlate with positive personality traits.

Freud's Psychosexual Theory of Personality Development

Freud believed that personality development involves passing through several *psychosexual stages* of development—stages in which the individual seeks pleasure from specific parts of the body called *erogenous zones*. As we will see, each stage of personality development involves deriving physical pleasure from a different erogenous zone. (Freud used the term "sexual" to refer to physical pleasures and to the many ways an individual might seek to gratify an urge for such pleasure. When referring to children, he did not use the term to refer to adult sexual feelings or orgasmic pleasure.)

Freud's theory of personality development has been extremely influential because of its ability to explain personality disorders in terms of whole or partial **fixation**—arrested development due to a person's failure to pass completely through a given stage of development. Freud believed that a person becomes fixated at a particular stage of development when he or she becomes strongly attached to the erogenous zone involved in that stage. Although ideal personality development involves passing successfully through all of the psychosexual stages, Freud maintained that most people develop some degree of fixation during their early development. Let's take a closer look at Freud's psychosexual stages and the kinds of fixation that may develop in them.

Because newborn babies can do little more than suck and swallow, their sexual instinctual drive finds an outlet in these activities. Even as babies become able to engage in more complex behaviors, they continue to receive most of their sexual gratification orally. (Remember that by "sexual" in this context, Freud meant the physical pleasure derived from reducing the hunger drive.) We can think of infants at this stage as being dominated by the id. Over- or undergratification of the hunger drive during this **oral stage** can result in fixation. Undergratification might result from early weaning and overgratification from too zealous attempts by parents to feed the infant. According to Freud, too little gratification during the oral stage will set in motion the development of personality traits related to dependency—what we commonly refer to as "clinging vine" characteristics. Too much gratification, or overstimulation, will lay the groundwork for the development of aggressive personality characteristics. Other oral stage fixation activities include habits such as smoking, hoarding, and excessive eating.

The **anal stage** of personality development begins during the second year of life. According to Freud, sensual pleasure derives from emptying the bowels. But around this time most parents place demands on their toddlers to control their bowels, to delay their gratification, through toilet training. The stage is set for the early development of ego functions—the deliberate management of id impulses (in this case, the desire to vacate the bowels as soon as the urge arises). The way that parents toilet train their infants will again have a stage-setting effect on later personality development. Harsh toilet training characterized by punishment when a child fails to reach the toilet may lead to fixation at this stage. The personality characteristics that start to develop will center on orderliness and a need for control. In their adult form we would refer to these characteristics as compulsiveness and, at an extreme, megalomania (a single-minded need for power and control). Mild toilet training, the preferred method, involves encouraging

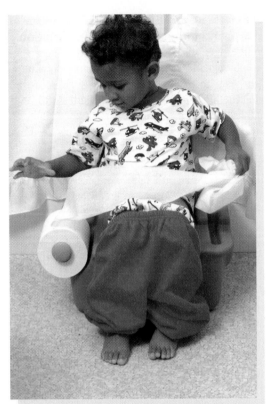

▲ *Does toilet training affect personality development? Freud thought so: He asserted that improper toilet training caused personality development to become fixated during the anal stage of psychosexual development.*

and praising the infant for successfully producing the bowel movement at the right place and time. The stage is set for pride in the expression of id needs coupled with appropriate ego control. Personality characteristics that should evolve include creativity and emotional expressiveness.

At around age three a child discovers that it is pleasurable to play with his penis or her clitoris (again, an immature sexuality), and enters the **phallic stage**. (*Phallus* means "penis," but Freud used the term "phallic stage" for children of both genders.) Children during this stage form strong immature sexual attachments to the parent of the opposite sex. This occurs, according to Freud, because mothers predominantly nurture male children and fathers predominantly nurture female children. In other words, opposite-sex parents become the focus of sensual pleasure for children during this stage. These attachments become the focus of psychological and interpersonal conflicts that Freud called *complexes*. According to Freud, children experience jealousy of their same-sex parent's close relationship with the opposite-sex parent—the parent that children want exclusively for themselves.

The process diverges for boys and girls beyond this point. A boy's love of his mother is mixed with hostility toward and, importantly, fear of his rival father. Freud believed that boys unconsciously fear being punished by their fathers for their desire for their mother, including the ultimate punishment—castration. These elements constitute the *Oedipus complex* (after the king of Greek mythology who unknowingly married his mother after killing his father). This rich mix of emotions demands resolution.

A girl's love of her father and envy of her mother, Freud said, is complicated by her discovery that she does not have a penis. This discovery, Freud theorized, leads to *penis envy* and girls' magical belief that they can acquire a penis through their attachment to their father. The underlying reasoning for Freud's notion of penis envy is that girls at this age typically are not knowledgeable enough to realize that children of both sexes have genitals but that they differ in appearance. Rather, girls simply conclude that boys have something and that they have nothing. Imagine the impact of this incorrect conclusion. What, a little girl might wonder, is wrong with her (and with her mother)? According to Freud, girls register this difference between themselves and males (inaccurately) as personal deficiency and weakness. They then gravitate even more strongly toward their fathers, who have the organ they do not, in order to associate with power and compensate for their self-perceived weakness. These powerful emotions are what Freud called the *Electra complex*. (In Greek mythology, Electra, aided by her brother, killed her mother and her mother's lover to avenge her father's death.) Again, there must be some resolution.

The conflict for both girls and boys is resolved through a process called *identification*. According to Freud, children of both sexes turn their attention to their same-sex parent—the father for boys and the mother for girls. They begin to imitate their same-sex parent in many ways and in a sense to idolize them. The effect of this imitation is to build a strong bond between the flattered and approving parent and the attentive, hero-worshipping son or heroine-worshipping daughter. Fear and envy are resolved. Gender roles are learned, and anxiety over the genitals is resolved. This process of identification is also the initial source of *superego* development. Through their admiration and imitation of their same-sex parent, children learn society's fundamental principles of right and wrong (as interpreted by the parents, of course).

After the phallic stage comes a **latency period** of several years, during which the child's sexual instinctual drive is mostly submerged. Following this period is the onset of puberty. The child, now an adolescent, begins to form adult sexual attachments to young people of the other sex. Because the sexual instinctual drive now finds its outlet in heterosexual genital contact, this stage is known as the **genital stage**.

According to Freud, the results of psychosexual development amount to the building blocks of personality and general psychological functioning. Children develop basic ego and superego functions and gender role identities. Their own special mixes of fixations will follow them through life and manifest themselves as distinctive personality traits.

Further Development of Freud's Theory: The Neo-Freudians

As you might imagine, Freud's theory created quite a controversy in the Victorian era when it was unveiled. Its emphasis on childhood sexuality and on seething internal conflicts seemed preposterous and offensive to many. Yet the theory's proposal that adults' thoughts and behavior stem from unconscious forces as well as from early childhood experiences was revolutionary and was recognized by many scholars as a genuinely original idea. Freud attracted many followers who studied his work closely but did not accept it completely. Each of these people agreed with Freud's view on the dynamic forces operating within the psyche. Each of them disagreed with Freud, though, on how much importance to place on the role of unconscious sexual and aggressive instincts in shaping personality. Five psychodynamic theorists—Carl Jung, Alfred Adler, Karen Horney, Erik Erikson, and Melanie Klein—have been particularly influential in elaborating psychodynamic theory.

Carl Jung

Many scholars and physicians of the early twentieth century were influenced by Freud's psychodynamic theory and studied with him. One of these people was Carl Jung (1875–1961). Freud called Jung "his adopted eldest son, his crown prince and successor" (Hall & Nordby, 1973, p. 23). However, Jung developed his own version of psychodynamic theory, in which he deemphasized the importance of sexuality. He also disagreed with his mentor on the structure of the unconscious. Freud had little tolerance, and often much sarcasm, for those who disagreed with him. After 1913 he and Jung never saw each other again. Jung continued to develop his theory after the split, drawing ideas from mythology, anthropology, history, and religion, as well as from an active clinical practice in which he saw people with psychological disorders.

In Jung's view the libido is a positive creative force that propels people toward personal growth. He also believed that forces other than the id, ego, and superego, including what he called the *collective unconscious,* form the core of personality. Jung believed that the ego is totally conscious and contains the ideas, perceptions, emotions, thoughts, and memories of which we are aware. One of Jung's more important contributions to psychodynamic theory, however, was his idea of the **collective unconscious,** which contains shared ("collective") memories and ideas inherited from our ancestors. Stored in the collective unconscious are **archetypes,** inherited and universal thought forms and patterns that allow us to notice particular aspects of our world. From the dawn of our species, all humans have had roughly similar experiences with things such as mothers, evil, masculinity, and femininity. Each one of these is represented by an archetype. For example, the *shadow* is the archetype containing basic instincts that allow us to recognize aspects of the world such as evil, sin, and carnality. Archetypes are not stored images or ideas—we are not born with a picture of evil stored somewhere in our brains—but inherited dispositions to behave, perceive, and think in certain ways.

Alfred Adler

Alfred Adler (1870–1937), like Jung, studied with Freud. Also like Jung, Adler felt that Freud had overemphasized sexuality. Adler argued that feelings of inferiority play the key role in personality development. At birth we are dependent on others for survival. Early in our development we encounter mostly older, more experienced people who are more capable than we are in almost every aspect of life. The inferiority we feel may be social, intellectual, physical, or athletic. These feelings create tension that motivates us to compensate for the deficiency. Emerging from this need to compensate is a **striving for superiority,** which Adler believed to be the major motivational force in life. In Adler's theory superiority connotes a "personal best" approach rather than defining achievement merely in terms of outperforming others. Our unique experiences with inferiority, and our consequent strivings for superiority, become organizing principles in our lives and therefore define our personalities.

According to Adler (1939), an individual's striving for superiority is affected by another force, *social interest,* which is an innate desire to contribute to society. Social interest is not wholly instinctual, because it can be influenced by experience. Nevertheless, although individuals have a need to seek personal superiority, they have a greater desire to sacrifice for causes that benefit the society as a whole. Thus, whereas Freud believed that people act in their own self-interests, motivated by the id, Adler believed that people desire to help others, directed by social interest. In asserting that positive rather than negative motives direct personality, Adler's ideas represented a sea change in psychodynamic theory.

Karen Horney

Karen Horney (1885–1952), like other Freudian dissenters, did not believe that sex and aggression are the primary determinants of personality. She did agree with Freud, though, that anxiety is a basic problem that people must address and overcome.

According to Horney, individuals suffer from basic anxiety caused by insecurities in relationships. People often feel alone, helpless, or uncomfortable in their interactions with others. For example, a person who begins a new job is often unsure of how to perform his or her duties, whom to ask for help, and how to approach his or her new coworkers. Horney theorized that to deal with basic anxiety, the individual has three options (Horney, 1950):

- *Moving toward others.* Accept the situation and become dependent on others. This strategy may entail an exaggerated desire for approval or affection.

- *Moving against others.* Resist the situation and become aggressive. This strategy may involve an exaggerated need for power, exploitation of others, recognition, or achievement.

- *Moving away from others.* Withdraw from others and become isolated. This strategy may involve an exaggerated need for self-sufficiency, privacy, or independence.

Horney believed that these three strategies corresponded to three basic orientations with which people approach their lives. These **basic orientations** reflect different personality characteristics. The *self-effacing solution* corresponds to the moving-toward-others strategy and involves the desire to be loved. The *self-expansive solution* corresponds to the moving-against-others strategy and involves the desire to master oneself. The *resignation solution* corresponds to the moving-away-from-others strategy and involves striving to be independent of others. For Horney, personality is a mixture of these three strategies and basic orientations. As the source of anxiety varies from one situation to the next, so may the strategy and basic orientation used to cope with it. In Horney's view, to understand personality, it is necessary to consider not only psychodynamic forces within the mind, but also the environmental conditions to which those forces are reacting.

Erik Erikson

Erik Erikson (1902–1994) studied with Anna Freud, Sigmund Freud's daughter. Erikson emphasized social aspects of personality development rather than biological factors. He also differed with Freud about the timing of personality development. For Freud the most important development occurs during early childhood. Erikson emphasized the ongoing process of development throughout the lifespan. As we saw in Chapter 12, Erikson proposed that people's personality traits develop as a result of a series of crises they encounter in their social relations with other people. Because these crises continue throughout life, psychosocial development does not end when people become adults. Erikson's theory of lifelong development has been very influential, and his term "identity crisis" has become a familiar, although possibly overextended household word (see Table 12.4 in Chapter 12).

Melanie Klein and Object-Relations Theory

Yet another dissenter from Freud's ideas was Melanie Klein (1882-1960), although she preferred to think of herself as extending Freud's theory. Klein felt that the psychodynamic battleground that Freud proposed occurs very early in life, during infancy. Furthermore, its origins are different from the basis Freud proposed. An infant begins life utterly dependent upon another. That other person, of course, is the infant's mother. The interactions between infant and mother are so deep and intense that they form the focus of the infant's structure of drives. Some of these interactions provoke anger and frustration (as when the mother withdraws the feeding infant from her breast); others provoke strong emotions of dependence as the child begins to recognize that the mother is more than a breast to feed from. These reactions threaten to overwhelm the individuality of the infant. The way in which the infant resolves the conflict, Klein believed, is reflected in the adult's personality (Gomez, 1997).

Klein's theories put her in sharp disagreement with classical Freudian conceptions of personality development, because she emphasized a much earlier progression through psychosexual stages and because she stressed that Freudian drives coalesce around specific objects of the drives (Greenberg & Mitchell, 1983). Klein's work stimulated a contrasting school of psychodynamic theory called **object-relations theory**. According to object-relations theory, adult personality reflects the relationships that the individual establishes with others when the individual is an infant. The term "object" is not confined to inanimate things; rather, it includes the people, especially the mother, that the infant must relate to. For object-relations theorists, relationships are the key to personality development. An individual forms a mental representation of his or her self, of others, and of the relationships that tie them together. For many object-relations theorists, the need that drives the development of personality is not sexual gratification, as Freud believed, but rather the need for other human beings (Westen, 1998).

Some Observations on Psychodynamic Theory and Research

Sigmund Freud's theory has profoundly affected psychological theory, psychotherapy, and literature. His writing, although sexist and outmoded in some respects, is lively and stimulating in others. His ideas have provided many people with food for thought. However, his theory has received little empirical support, mainly because he used concepts that are difficult to operationalize. How can anyone study the ego, the superego, or the id? How can a researcher prove (or disprove) through experimentation that an artist's creativity is the result of a displaced aggressive or sexual instinctual drive? Although the theories of Jung, Adler, Horney, Erikson, and Klein have their followers, they have not led to much in the way of scientific research. On the other hand, some of Freud's fundamental concepts are alive and well today. In later chapters you will read about evidence for unconscious processing of social information and about the impact on well-being of discussing traumatic events.

Interim Summary

The Psychodynamic Approach

Freud proposed that the mind is full of conflicts between the primitive urges of the id, the practical concerns of the ego, and the internalized prohibitions of the superego. According to Freud these conflicts tend to be resolved through compromise formation and through ego defenses such as repression, sublimation, and rationalization. Freud's theory of psychosexual development, a progression through the oral, anal, phallic, and genital stages, provided the basis for a theory of personality and personality disorders.

Freud's followers—most notably Jung, Adler, Horney, Erikson, and Klein—embraced different aspects of Freud's theory, disagreed with other aspects of it, and embellished still other aspects. Jung disagreed with Freud about the structure of the unconscious and the role of sexuality in personality development, and he saw libido as a positive life force. Adler also disagreed with Freud on the importance of sexuality; instead, he emphasized our need to compensate for our inferiority and our innate desire to help others as the major forces in personality development. Horney argued that personality is the result of the strategies and behaviors people use to cope with anxiety, which she believed is the fundamental problem that all people must overcome in the course of normal personality development. Erikson maintained that personality development is more a matter of psychosocial processes than of psychosexual processes. He viewed personality development as involving eight stages, each of which requires resolution of a major conflict or crisis. Resolving the conflict allows the person to pass to the next stage; failing to resolve it inhibits normal personality development. Klein suggested that psychodynamic conflict occurs early in infancy and centers on the relation between the infant and the mother. Her work formed the basis for object-relations theory, which posits that relationships with others constitute the fundamental basis of personality.

QUESTIONS TO CONSIDER

1. Have you ever found yourself using any of the Freudian defense mechanisms discussed in this chapter? If so, under what circumstances do you tend to use them, and what unconscious conflict do you suppose you might be protecting yourself from?

2. Do you possess any behaviors that might represent fixations? If so, what are they, and what fixations do they represent?

3. Which neo-Freudian view on personality development makes the most sense to you? Why do you feel this way—what is your rationale for concluding that one view is more sensible than the others? Which of the theories best explains your own personality development? Provide an example.

The Humanistic Approach

The **humanistic approach** to the study of personality emphasizes the positive, fulfilling elements of life. Humanistic psychologists are interested in nurturing personal growth, life satisfaction, and positive human values. These theorists believe that people are innately good and that each of us has an internal drive for **self-actualization**—the realization of our true intellectual and emotional potential. The two most influential humanistic theorists have been Abraham Maslow and Carl Rogers.

Maslow and Self-Actualization

For both Freud and Abraham Maslow (1908–1970), motivation is one of the central aspects of personality. However, where Freud saw strong instinctual urges generating tensions that cannot be completely resolved, Maslow saw positive impulses that can easily be overwhelmed by negative forces within a person's culture. According to Maslow (1970), human motivation is based on a hierarchy of needs. Our motivation for different activities passes through several levels, with entrance to subsequent levels dependent on our first satisfying needs in previous levels. (See **Figure 14•10.**) If an individual's needs are not met, he or she cannot scale the hierarchy and so will fail to attain his or her true potential.

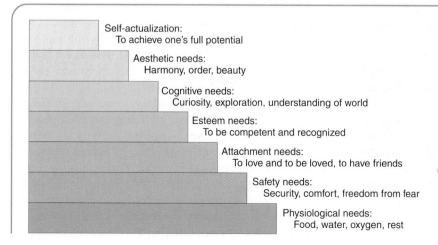

Self-actualization:
  To achieve one's full potential

Aesthetic needs:
  Harmony, order, beauty

Cognitive needs:
  Curiosity, exploration, understanding of world

Esteem needs:
  To be competent and recognized

Attachment needs:
  To love and to be loved, to have friends

Safety needs:
  Security, comfort, freedom from fear

Physiological needs:
  Food, water, oxygen, rest

FIGURE 14•10 Maslow's hierarchy of needs. According to Maslow, every person's goal is to become self-actualized. In order to achieve this goal, individuals must first satisfy several basic needs.

In Maslow's view, understanding personality requires understanding this hierarchy. Our most basic needs are *physiological needs,* including needs for food, water, oxygen, rest, and so on. Until these needs are met, we cannot be motivated by needs found in the next level (or any other level). If our physiological needs are met, we find ourselves motivated by *safety needs,* including needs for security and comfort as well as for peace and freedom from fear. Once the basic survival and safety needs are met, we can become motivated by *attachment needs,* the need to love and to be loved, to have friends and to be a friend. Next, we seek to satisfy *esteem needs*—to be competent and recognized as such. You are probably beginning to get the picture: We are motivated to achieve needs higher in the hierarchy only after first satisfying lower needs. If we are able to lead a life in which we possess food, shelter, love, esteem, intellectual stimulation, and beauty, then we are free to pursue self-actualization.

Maslow based his theory partially on his own assumptions about human potential and partially on his case studies of historical figures whom he believed to be self-actualized, including Albert Einstein, Eleanor Roosevelt, and Frederick Douglass. Maslow examined the lives of each of these people in order to assess the common qualities that led each to become self-actualized. In general, he found that these individuals were very accepting of themselves and of their life circumstances; were focused on finding solutions to pressing cultural problems rather than to personal problems; were open to others' opinions and ideas; were spontaneous in their

▲ *Abraham Maslow considered Albert Einstein to possess qualities representative of self-actualization, including self-acceptance, a focus on finding solutions to cultural problems, open-mindedness, and spontaneity.*

emotional reactions to events in their lives; had strong senses of privacy, autonomy, human values, and appreciation of life; and had a few very close, intimate friendships rather than many superficial ones.

Maslow (1964) believed that the innate drive for self-actualization is not specific to any particular culture. He viewed it as a fundamental part of human nature. In his words, "Man has a higher and transcendent nature, and this is part of his essence . . . his biological nature of a species which has evolved" (p. xvi).

Rogers and Conditions of Worth

Carl Rogers (1902–1987) also believed that people are motivated to grow psychologically, aspiring to higher levels of fulfillment as they progress toward self-actualization (Rogers, 1961). Like Maslow, Rogers believed that people are inherently good and have an innate desire to become better. Rogers, though, did not view personality development in terms of satisfying a hierarchy of needs. Instead, he believed that personality development centers on our *self-concept,* or our opinion of ourself, and on the way we are treated by others.

Rogers argued that all people have a need for *positive regard,* or approval, warmth, love, respect, and affection flowing from others. Young children, in particular, show this need when they seek approval for their actions from parents and siblings. The key to developing a psychologically healthy personality is for us to develop a positive self-concept or image of ourself. How do we do this? Rogers's answer is that we are happy if we feel that others are happy with us. Likewise, we also are unhappy with ourselves when others are disappointed in or unsatisfied with us. Thus, our feelings toward ourselves depend to a large extent on what others think of us. And as children, we learn that there exist certain conditions or criteria that must be met before others give us positive regard. Rogers called these criteria **conditions of worth**.

Positive regard is often conditional. For example, parents may act approvingly toward their young son when he helps in the kitchen or in the yard but not when he pinches his younger sister or tells a fib about how many cookies he has taken from the cookie jar. The boy learns that what others think of him depends on his actions. Soon, too, he may come to view himself as others view him and his behavior: "People like me when I do something good and they don't like me when I do something bad."

Although conditions of worth are a necessary part of the socialization process, they can have negative effects on personality development if satisfying them becomes the individual's major ambition. In Rogers's view, children often want others to like them to the extent that gaining positive regard is a major focus of their lives. So long as any individual focuses chiefly on seeking positive regard from others, he or she may ignore other aspects of life, especially those that lead to positive personality growth. In Rogers's view, then, conditions of worth may stand in the way of self-actualization. Individuals may devote their lives to satisfying the expectations and demands of others in lieu of working toward realizing their potential. In this sense, the need for positive regard may smother a person's progress toward self-actualization.

According to Rogers, the solution to this problem is **unconditional positive regard,** or love and acceptance that has no strings attached. In a family setting, this means that parents may establish rules and expect their children to obey them, but not through methods that compromise the children's feelings of worth and self-respect. For example, if a child misbehaves, the parents should focus on the child's behavior and not on the child. The parent is free to stop destructive behavior but should not implicitly undermine the child's self-concept through negative labeling ("What a stupid thing to do," "You're such a bad girl," "You must want to hurt Mommy").

Parents have an enormous responsibility. By distinguishing between the behavior and the child, parents can help children learn that their behavior is unacceptable but that their parents still love them. Implementing unconditional regard in this way permits children to explore life within reasonable bounds and thereby to realize their inherent potential. Rogers would say that parents need to understand and believe that their children are intrinsically good. Bad behavior, in his view, results only when the child's positive potential is being undermined or constrained by the social environment.

In developing his theory, Rogers used unstructured interviews in which the client, not the therapist, directed the course of the conversation. Rogers believed that if the therapist provides an atmosphere of unconditional positive regard, clients will eventually reveal their *true selves,* the kind of people they now are, as well as their *ideal selves,* the kind of people they would like to become. Rogers also gave the *Q sort test* to many of his clients. This test consists of a variety of cards, each of which contains a statement such as "I am generally an optimistic person" or "I am generally an intolerant person." The client's task is to sort the cards into several piles that vary in degree from "least like me" to "most like me." The client sorts the cards twice, first on the basis of his or her real self and next in terms of his or her ideal self. The difference between the arrangements of the cards in the piles is taken as an index of how close a client is to reaching his or her ideal self. Rogers's goal as a therapist was to facilitate clients' becoming their ideal selves. We will examine Rogers's approach to therapy in more detail in Chapter 18.

Some Observations on the Humanistic Approach

The humanistic approach is impressive because of its emphasis on individuals' quest for a healthy and positive life for themselves and others. Indeed, the approach has wide appeal to those who seek an alternative to the more mechanistic biologically or environmentally determined views of human nature. However, critics point out two closely related problems with the humanists' approach.

First, many of the concepts used by humanistic psychologists are defined subjectively and so are difficult to test empirically. For example, how might we empirically examine the nature of self-actualization? Few published studies have even attempted to answer this question. By now you know the hallmark of a good scientific theory—the amount of research it generates. On this count the humanistic approach comes up short by scientific standards. Keep in mind, though, that humanistic theorists are aware that the structure of their theories hinders the use of scientific research methods. Maslow, for instance, simply did not care—in fact, he believed that the scientific method was a hindrance to the development of psychology.

A second criticism of the humanistic approach is that it cannot account for the origins of personality. It is subject to the nominal fallacy; it describes personality, but it does not explain it. Humanistic psychologists believe that the impulse toward self-actualization is an innate tendency, but there is no research that shows this to be so. Conditions of worth are said to hamper a child's quest for self-actualization and thus to alter the course of personality development away from positive psychological growth. However, the humanistic approach provides no objective explanation of this process.

▲ *According to Rogers, all people have a basic need for approval, warmth, and love from others. This need is best met through unconditional positive regard: love and acceptance with no strings attached.*

TABLE 14•4   **A Summary of the Major Personality Theories**

Theory	Primary Figures	Primary Emphases	Primary Strengths	Primary Limitations
Trait	Allport, Cattell, Eysenck, McCrae, Costa	An individual's traits determine personality.	Focuses on stability of behavior over long periods; attempts to measure traits objectively.	Largely descriptive; ignores situational variables that may affect behavior.
Psychobiological	Zuckerman, Plomin, Kagan	Genetics and the brain and nervous system play important roles in personality development.	Emphasizes the interaction of biology and environment in determining personality; uses rigorous empirical approach.	Relies on correlational methods in determining the role of genetics in personality.
Social Learning	Bandura, Mischel, Rotter	Personality is determined by both the consequences of behavior and our perception of those consequences.	Focuses on direct study of behavior and stresses rigorous experimentation.	Ignores biological influences on personality development; often more descriptive than explanatory.
Psychodynamic	Freud, Jung, Adler, Horney, Erikson, Klein	Personality is shaped by unconscious psychic conflicts and the repression of anxiety-provoking ideas and desires.	Argues that behavior may be influenced by forces outside conscious awareness.	Built on basic concepts that are not empirically testable.
Humanistic	Maslow, Rogers	Positive aspects of human nature and the quest to become a better person are central to personality.	Proves useful in therapeutic settings.	Contains untestable concepts; primarily descriptive.

Before moving on to the next section, take a few moments to examine **Table 14•4,** which reviews each of the major theories of personality I have discussed.

Interim Summary

The Humanistic Approach

The humanistic approach attempts to understand personality and its development by focusing on the positive side of human nature and on self-actualization, or people's attempts to reach their full potential.

Maslow argued that self-actualization is achieved only after the satisfaction of several other important but lower-level needs; for example, physiological, safety, and attachment needs. Maslow's case study analyses of people whom he believed to be self-actualized revealed several common personality characteristics, including self-acceptance, a focus on addressing cultural rather than personal problems, spontaneity, preservation of privacy, an appreciation for life, and possession of a few intimate friendships.

According to Rogers, the key to becoming self-actualized is developing a healthy self-concept. The primary roadblocks in this quest are conditions of worth—criteria that we must meet to win the positive regard of others. Rogers maintained that too often people value themselves only to the extent that they believe other people do. As a result, they spend their lives seeking the acceptance of others instead of striving to become self-actualized. Rogers proposed that only by treating others with unconditional positive regard can we help people to realize their true potentials.

Although the humanistic approach emphasizes the positive dimensions of human experience and the potential that each of us has for personal growth, it has been faulted for being unscientific. Critics argue that its concepts are vague and untestable and that it is more descriptive than explanatory.

QUESTIONS TO CONSIDER

1. Are you a self-actualized person? If not, what obstacles might be standing in the way of your reaching your true potential?
2. Describe some of the conditions of worth that others have imposed on you as you have developed into an adult. Explain how your experience confirms or disconfirms Rogers's idea that conditions of worth are impediments to personal growth and to the development of a healthy self-concept.

Assessment of Personality

Think for a moment about your best friend. What is he or she like? Outgoing? Impulsive? Thoughtful? Moody? You can easily respond yes or no to these alternatives, because you have spent enough time with your friend to know him or her quite well. After all, one of the best ways to get to know people—what they are like and how they react in certain situations—is to spend time with them. Obviously, psychologists do not have the luxury of spending large amounts of time with people in order to learn about their personalities. Generally, in fact, they have only a short period to accomplish this goal. From this necessity personality tests were first developed. The underlying assumption of any personality test is that personality characteristics can be measured. This final section of the chapter describes the two primary types of personality tests—objective tests and projective tests—and discusses the three tests most frequently used by clinical psychologists (Watkins, Campbell, Nieberding, & Hallmark, 1995).

Objective Tests of Personality

Objective personality tests are similar in structure to classroom tests. Most contain multiple-choice and true/false items, although some allow test takers to indicate the extent to which they agree or disagree with an item. The responses that participants can make on objective tests are constrained by the test design. The questions asked are unambiguous, and explicit rules for scoring the participants' responses can be specified in advance.

One of the oldest and most widely used objective tests of personality is the **Minnesota Multiphasic Personality Inventory (MMPI)**, originally devised in 1939. The purpose for developing the test was to produce an objective, reliable method for identifying various personality traits that were related to mental health. The developers believed that this test would be valuable in assessing people for a variety of purposes. For instance, it would provide a specific means of determining how effective psychotherapy was. Improvement in people's scores over the course of treatment would indicate that the treatment was successful.

The test was developed by administering several hundred true/false items to several groups of people in mental institutions in Minnesota who had been diagnosed as having certain psychological disorders. Clinicians had arrived at these diagnoses through psychiatric interviews with the patients. Such interviews are expensive, so a simple paper-and-pencil test that accomplished the same result would be valuable. The control group consisted of relatives and friends of the patients, who were tested when they came to visit them. (Whether these people constituted the best possible group of normal participants is questionable.) The responses were analyzed empirically, and the questions that correlated with various diagnostic labels were included in various scales. For example, if people who had been diagnosed as paranoid tended to answer "true" to "I

believe I am being plotted against," this statement would become part of the paranoia scale.

The current, revised version of this test, the MMPI-2, has norms based on a sample of people that is much more representative ethnically and geographically than the original sample was (Butcher et al., 2000; Graham, 1990). It includes 567 questions, grouped into 10 *clinical scales* and several *validity scales*. A particular item can be used on more than one scale. For example, both people who are depressed and people who are hypochondriacal tend to agree that they have gastrointestinal problems. The clinical scales include terms traditionally used to label psychiatric patients, such as hypochondriasis, depression, and paranoia.

Four validity scales were devised to provide the tester with some assurance that participants are answering questions reliably and accurately and that they can read the questions and pay attention to them. The ? scale ("cannot say") is simply the number of questions not answered. A high score on this scale indicates either that the person finds some questions irrelevant or that the person is evading issues he or she finds painful.

The L scale ("lie") contains items such as "I do not read every editorial in the newspaper every day" and "My table manners are not quite as good at home as when I am out in company." A person who disagrees with questions like these is almost certainly not telling the truth. A high score on the L scale suggests the need for caution in interpreting other scales and also reveals something about the participant's personality.

The F scale ("frequency") consists of items that are answered one way by at least 90 percent of the normal population. The usual responses are "false" to items such as "I can easily make other people afraid of me, and sometimes do it for the fun of it" and "true" to items such as "I am liked by most people who know me." A high score on this scale indicates carelessness, poor reading ability, or very unusual personality traits.

The K scale ("defensiveness") was devised to identify people who are trying to hide their feelings to guard against internal conflicts that might cause them emotional distress. A person receives a high value on the K scale by answering "false" to statements such as "Criticism or scolding hurts me terribly" and "At times, my mind seems to work more slowly than usual."

As well as being used in clinical assessment, the MMPI has been employed extensively in personality research, and several other tests, including the California Psychological Inventory and the Taylor Manifest Anxiety Scale, are based on it. However, the MMPI has its critics. As we saw earlier, the five-factor model of personality has received considerable support. Some advocates of the five-factor model have noted that the MMPI misses some of the dimensions measured by the NEO-PI-R, which includes tests of neuroticism, extroversion, openness, agreeableness, and conscientiousness (Johnson, Butcher, Null, & Johnson, 1984). Thus, these dimensions will be missed by a clinician or researcher who relies only on the MMPI.

Projective Tests of Personality

Projective tests of personality are different in form from objective ones and are derived from psychodynamic theories of personality. Psychoanalytically oriented psychologists believe that behavior is determined more by unconscious processes than by conscious thoughts or feelings. Thus, they believe that a test that asks straightforward questions is unlikely to tap the real roots of an individual's personality characteristics. **Projective tests** are designed to be ambiguous; the hope is that test takers' answers will be more revealing than simple agreement or disagreement with statements provided by objective tests. The assumption of projective tests is that individuals will "project" their personalities into the ambiguous situations and thus will make responses that give clues to their personalities. In addition, the ambiguity of the tests makes it unlikely that participants will have preconceived notions about which answers are socially desirable. Thus, it will be difficult for participants to give biased answers in an attempt to look better (or worse) than they actually are.

The Rorschach Inkblot Test One of the oldest projective tests of personality is the Rorschach Inkblot Test, published in 1921 by Hermann Rorschach, a Swiss psychiatrist. The **Rorschach Inkblot Test** consists of 10 pictures of inkblots. Rorschach published these pictures from images made by spilling ink on a piece of paper and then folding the paper in half, producing blots that were symmetrical in relation to the line of the fold. Five of the inkblots in the test are black and white, and five are colored. (See **Figure 14•11**.) The participant is shown each card and asked to describe what it looks like. Then the cards are shown again, and the participant is asked to point out the features he or she used to determine what was seen. The responses and the nature of the features the participant uses to make them are scored on several dimensions.

In the following example described by Pervin (1975), a person's response to a particular inkblot (not the example shown in Figure 14.11) might be "Two bears with their paws touching one another playing pattycake or could be they are fighting and the red is the blood from the fighting." The classification of this response, also described by Pervin, would be: Large detail of the blot was used, good form was used, movement was noted, color was used in the response about blood, an animal was seen, and a popular response (two bears) was made. A possible interpretation of the response might be:

> Subject starts off with popular response and animals expressing playful, "childish" behavior. Response is then given in terms of hostile act with accompanying inquiry. Pure color response and blood content suggest he may have difficulty controlling his response to the environment. Is a playful, childlike exterior used by him to disguise hostile, destructive feelings that threaten to break out in his dealings with the environment? (Pervin, 1975, p. 37)

Although the interpretation of people's responses to the Rorschach Inkblot Test was originally based on psychoanalytical theory, many investigators have used it in an empirical fashion. That is, a variety of different scoring methods have been devised, and the scores obtained by these methods have been correlated with clinical diagnoses, just as investigators have done with people's scores on the MMPI. When this test is used empirically, the style and content of the responses are not interpreted in terms of a theory (as Rorschach interpreted them) but are simply correlated with other measures of personality.

The Thematic Apperception Test Another popular projective test, the **Thematic Apperception Test (TAT),** was developed in 1938 by psychologists Henry Murray and C. D. Morgan to measure various psychological needs. People are shown a picture of a very ambiguous situation and are asked to tell a story about what is happening in the picture—to explain the situation, what led up to it, what the characters are thinking and saying, and what the final outcome will be. The idea is

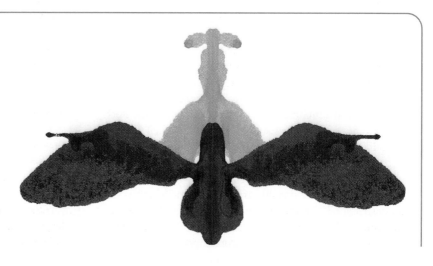

FIGURE 14•11 An inkblot similar to one of the blots that appear in the Rorschach Inkblot Test.

that test takers will "project" themselves into the scene and that their stories will therefore reflect their own needs.

As you might imagine, scoring is difficult and requires a great deal of practice and skill. The tester attempts to infer the psychological needs expressed in the stories. Consider the responses of one woman to several TAT cards, along with a clinician's interpretation of these responses (Phares, 1979). The questions asked by the examiner are in parentheses.

> Card 3BM. Looks like a little boy crying for something he can't have. (Why is he crying?) Probably because he can't go somewhere. (How will it turn out?) Probably sit there and sob hisself to sleep. Card 3GF. Looks like her boyfriend might have let her down. She hurt his feelings. He's closed the door on her. (What did he say?) I don't know. Card 10. Looks like there's sorrow here. Grieving about something. (About what?) Looks like maybe one of the children's passed away.

> Interpretation: The TAT produced responses that were uniformly indicative of unhappiness, threat, misfortune, a lack of control over environmental forces. None of the test responses were indicative of satisfaction, happy endings, etc. . . . In summary, the test results point to an individual who is anxious and, at the same time, depressed. (Phares, 1979, p. 273)

The pattern of responses in this case is quite consistent; few people would disagree with the conclusion that the woman is sad and depressed. However, not all people provide such clear-cut responses, and interpreting differences in the stories of people who are relatively well adjusted is much more difficult. As a result, distinguishing among people with different but normal personality traits is hard.

Evaluation of Projective Tests

Most empirical studies have found that projective tests such as the Rorschach Inkblot Test and the TAT have poor reliability and little validity. For example, Eron (1950) found no differences between the scores of people in mental hospitals and the scores of college students. (No, I'm not going to make a joke about that.) Entwisle (1972) reported that "recent studies . . . yield few positive relationships between need achievement [measured by the TAT] and other variables" (p. 179). Lundy (1988) suggests that in many of the situations used to validate the TAT, test takers are likely to realize that they are talking about themselves when they tell a story about the cards and may be careful about what they say.

Even if people taking the TAT are not on their guard, their scores are especially sensitive to their moods (Masling, 1960, 1998). Therefore, the scores they receive on one day are often very different from those they receive on another day. But a test of personality is supposed to measure enduring traits that persist over time and in a variety of situations. The TAT also has been criticized for potential gender bias, mostly because of male-dominated themes, such as power, ambition, and status, used to score the test (Worchel, Aaron, & Yates, 1990).

The reliability and validity of the Rorschach Inkblot Test also are rather low. One study that used the most reliable scoring method found little or no correlation between participants' scores on the Rorschach and their scores on six objective tests of personality (Greenwald, 1990, 1999).

If projective tests such as the Rorschach and the TAT have been found to be of low reliability and validity, why do many clinical psychologists and psychiatrists continue to use them? The primary reason seems to be tradition. The use of these tests has a long history, and the rationale for the tests is consistent with psychodynamic explanations of personality. Many psychodynamic and clinical psychologists still argue that the tests provide them with valuable tools for discovering and evaluating inner determinants of personality (Watkins, 2000).

Biology and Culture

Gender Differences in Personality

From a very early age, people in all cultures learn that boys and girls and men and women are different in at least two ways—physically and psychologically. The psychological differences often are more difficult to detect than the physical differences, but nonetheless, males and females tend not only to perceive aspects of their environments differently, but also to behave differently under some circumstances.

● **What Gender Differences in Personality Actually Exist?**
People in all cultures hold certain beliefs, called *stereotypes*, about differences between males and females (see Chapter 12). A stereotype is a belief that people possess certain qualities because of their membership in a particular group—in this case, a gender. (We will look more closely at stereotypes and their origins in Chapter 15.) In general, stereotypes about men are more flattering than those about women: Men are stereotyped as being more competent, independent, decisive, and logical. Women are stereotyped as being less competent, competitive, ambitious, independent, and active (Broverman et al., 1994).

Thousands of psychological studies of gender differences do not confirm most of these stereotypes. In terms of personality, males and females are actually more alike than different. For instance, there seem to be few significant differences between the genders in terms of the personality variables, such as introversion and extroversion, associated with intelligence (Snow & Weinstock, 1990), friendships (Jones, 1991), or perceived career success (Poole, Langan-Fox, & Omodei, 1991).

Numerous studies have revealed gender differences in personality characteristics related to social behavior, however. One social behavior that shows large gender differences is aggression. During play young boys react to provocation with greater anger than do young girls (Fabes, Eisenberg,

▲ *A higher level of aggressive behavior in males is one of the few important psychological differences between males and females.*

Smith, & Murphy, 1996). In a longitudinal study of elementary and high school students, males were shown to be more aggressive than females, and patterns of aggression were found to be less stable for males than for females (Woodall & Matthews, 1993).

Even so, gender differences in aggression may vary in different cultures. In one study of preschoolers, for example, American and Israeli girls were shown to start fewer fights than did their respective male counterparts, but Israeli girls started more fights than did American boys (Lauer, cited in Bower, 1991). The higher levels of aggression among Israeli children may be due in part to their country's constant preparation for and frequent participation in military conflicts. In addition, in some cultures and subcultures, girls may join gangs that are involved in aggressive activities. For example, in Chihuahua, Mexico, a girl being initiated into a gang must fist-fight a gang member (Bower, 1991). Girl gangs often join their "brother" gangs in defending their turf against other male gangs. Girl gangs also fight other girl gangs, and such fights may involve knife fighting and rock throwing as well as fist fighting.

Several other gender differences related to personality and social behavior have been documented. Males tend to emerge as leaders when the groups to which they belong need to accomplish a specific task. Females tend to emerge as leaders when the groups to which they belong stress interpersonal relationships (Eagly & Karau, 1991). Males

tend to report higher thresholds for pain than females, and females on average report a greater willingness to report pain than the typical male (Wise et al., 2002). Females tend to be more empathetic and tend to offer assistance to others when the situation demands comforting others. Men are more likely to offer assistance when the situation demands physical aid (Eisenberg et al., 1991). Likewise, males tend to be less intimate, while females tend to be more empathetic and expressive in their relationships (Buss, 1995).

● Biological Origins of Personality Differences

As I noted earlier in this chapter, personality traits appear to have a strong heritable component. For example, in a review of behavior genetic research related to personality, Rose (1995) concluded that heredity accounts for a large segment of the variability in personality traits among individuals and may also explain continuity and changes in personality over the life span.

Unfortunately, however, not much is known about how genes influence gender differences in personality and behavior. The only thing we can say with any certainty is that personality differences between the sexes seem likely to have evolved as a direct result of the biological differences between males and females with respect to the division of labor required by sexual reproduction, as described in Chapter 3 (Loehlin, 1992; Tooby & Cosmides, 1990). For example, because of their greater physical and biological investment in reproduction, females may have developed tendencies to become more empathetic and interpersonally skilled. Possession of these traits may have helped females solicit support from the father and others during pregnancy and child rearing (Buss, 1995). And because of their larger size and greater strength, males may have evolved tendencies toward hunting, fighting, and protecting their families and social units. In modern times, these behaviors may translate into aggression and leadership tendencies. Females still have strong tendencies to be empathetic and skilled interpersonal communicators, most likely because cultural evolution has favored these behaviors.

● Cultural Origins of Personality Differences

Whereas the genetic and evolutionary contributions to gender differences in personality remain matters of speculation, the cultural origins of such differences seem clearer and would appear to center on the histories, environmental conditions, economic structures, and survival needs of different cultures (Wade & Tavris, 1994). That is, the behavioral tendencies and personality traits of males and females vary from culture to culture, depending on the specific conditions under which members of each culture live.

For example, consider how males and females in three different Papua New Guinea tribes are expected to act (Harris, 1991). Among the Arapesh, both men and women are expected to be cooperative and sympathetic, much as Western cultures expect the ideal "mom" to be. Among the Mundugumor, both men and women are expected to be

▲ *To a large extent, the specific culture in which people live influences the gender-linked behavioral tendencies and personality traits of males and females.*

fierce and aggressive, similar to what we might expect of the men in our culture whom we call "macho." Finally, among the Tchambuli, women shave their heads, are boisterous, and provide food; the men tend to focus on art, their hairstyles, and gossiping about women.

As living conditions change, so does a culture's conception of the behaviors and personality traits appropriate to gender. For instance, as Wade and Tavris (1994) point out, the twentieth century witnessed two unprecedented advances in technology, both of which have important implications for what most Western cultures consider gender-appropriate traits. First, because of advances in contraceptive technology, women may choose to limit the number of children they bear and make plans for when they bear them. Second, in today's job market, less emphasis is placed on physical skills and more on intellectual skills.

Combined, these two factors allow women to compete head-to-head with men not only for employment but also for leadership positions in today's global economy. And, as a result, we are finding that the stereotypes we once held of both men and women are breaking down. Many women have personality characteristics that were once thought to be exclusively male traits, such as extroversion, assertiveness, competitiveness, and ambitiousness. In fact, in the not-too-distant future, personality psychologists may

discover that gender differences in aggression, empathy, and other personality characteristics related to social behavior will no longer exist.

Interim Summary

Assessment of Personality

Objective tests contain items that can be answered and scored objectively, such as true/false or multiple-choice questions. One of the most important objective personality tests is the Minnesota Multiphasic Personality Inventory, which was devised in 1939 to discriminate empirically among people who had been assigned various psychiatric diagnoses. The MMPI has been used widely in research on personality. More recently, researchers interested in personality have turned to tests not based on people with mental disorders, such as the NEO-PI-R.

Projective tests, such as the Rorschach Inkblot Test and the Thematic Apperception Test, contain ambiguous items that elicit answers that supposedly reveal aspects of personality. Because answers on these tests can vary widely, test administrators must receive special training to interpret them. Unfortunately, evidence suggests that the reliability and validity of projective tests are not particularly high.

What few gender differences exist in personality seem to be related to social interaction. Although personality traits have been shown to have high heritability, cultural variables—living conditions related to a specific culture's traditions, economy, environmental conditions, and survival needs—also play a powerful role in shaping gender-related personality and behavior. As these conditions change, so do the types of personality traits and behaviors necessary for males' and females' survival during cultural change. Thus, we should not be surprised when both males and females behave in ways that are contrary to the common stereotypes we hold regarding gender-specific personality characteristics.

QUESTIONS TO CONSIDER

1. Which kind of personality inventory—objective tests or projective tests—do you suppose would be more effective in revealing important aspects of your personality? Why?
2. If your results on a personality inventory revealed that you possess a personality trait that you didn't think you had (especially if it is a negative trait), how would you react? Would you tend to disparage the test, or would you admit that in fact this trait is part of your personality?
3. What kinds of personality differences between males and females have you noticed? Are these differences genuine, or do your observations reflect the stereotypes you hold of the sexes? How do you know?

Suggestions for Further Reading

Buss, A. H. (1995). *Personality: Temperament, social behavior, and the self.* Boston: Allyn and Bacon.

Carver, C. S., & Scheier, M. F. (2003). *Perspectives on personality* (5th ed.). Boston: Allyn and Bacon.

Wiggins, J. S. (Ed.). (1996). *The five-factor model of personality: Theoretical perspectives.* New York: Guilford Press.

Theories of personality, personality testing, and research on the determinants of personality receive thorough coverage in these three texts.

Bandura, A. (1986). *Social foundations of thought and action: A social cognitive theory.* Englewood Cliffs, NJ: Prentice-Hall.

In this book, Bandura presents his account of social cognition and social behavior, which is derived from the behaviorist tradition and cognitive psychology.

Freud, S. (1957). *General introduction to psychoanalysis* (J. Riviere, Trans.). New York: Permabooks.

Jones, E. (1953). *The life and work of Sigmund Freud.* New York: Basic Books.

The best resource on Freud's theories of personality is Freud himself. Jones provides an interesting discussion of Freud's life as well as of his writings.

Key Terms

anal stage (p. 457)

archetypes (p. 459)

basic orientations (p. 460)

collective unconscious (p. 459)

conditions of worth (p. 462)

conscience (p. 455)

defense mechanisms (p. 456)

denial (p. 457)

ego (p. 455)

ego-ideal (p. 455)

emotional stability (p. 442)

expectancy (p. 449)

extroversion (p. 442)

five-factor model (p. 443)

fixation (p. 457)

free association (p. 456)

genital stage (p. 458)

humanistic approach (p. 461)

id (p. 455)

introversion (p. 442)

latency period (p. 458)

latent content (p. 455)

libido (p. 455)

locus of control (p. 451)

manifest content (p. 455)

Minnesota Multiphasic Personality Inventory (MMPI) (p. 465)

neuroticism (p. 442)

Neuroticism, Extroversion, and Openness Personality Inventory (NEO-PI-R) (p. 443)

object-relations theory (p. 460)

objective personality tests (p. 465)

observational learning (p. 449)

oral stage (p. 457)

person variables (p. 450)

personality (p. 439)

personality trait (p. 440)

personality types (p. 440)

phallic stage (p. 458)

pleasure principle (p. 455)

projection (p. 456)

projective tests (p. 466)

psychodynamic (p. 453)

psychoticism (p. 442)

rationalization (p. 456)

reaction formation (p. 456)

reality principle (p. 455)

reciprocal determinism (p. 449)

repression (p. 456)

Rorschach Inkblot Test (p. 466)

self-actualization (p. 461)

self-control (p. 442)

self-efficacy (p. 449)

situationism (p. 450)

social cognitive theory (p. 448)

striving for superiority (p. 459)

sublimation (p. 456)

superego (p. 455)

temperament (p. 446)

Thematic Apperception Test (TAT) (p. 466)

unconditional positive regard (p. 463)

unconscious (p. 454)

15

SOCIAL
PSYCHOLOGY

Social Cognition

Impression Formation • The Self • Attribution • Attributional Biases • Attribution, Heuristics, and Social Cognition

Our perceptions, feelings, thoughts, and beliefs about the world are organized as schemas that help us form impressions about our social world. Our self-concept is based on the schemas that frame the personal knowledge and feelings we have about ourselves. In making attributions about the causes of our own or another person's behavior, we consider the relative contributions of dispositional and situational factors. However, we tend to overestimate the role of dispositional factors and underestimate the role of situational factors in attributing the causes of others' actions—a phenomenon called the fundamental attribution error. We also often misapply heuristics when making attributions.

Attitudes: Their Formation and Change

Formation of Attitudes • Attitude Change and Persuasion • Cognitive Dissonance • Self-Perception

Attitudes have affective, behavioral, and cognitive components; attitudes may be learned through mere exposure to objects and through classical conditioning. To understand any explicit attempt to change a person's attitude, we must consider both the source of the message and the message itself. A message tends to be persuasive if its source is credible or attractive and if it correctly addresses its intended audience. How critically we consider persuasive arguments determines their impact in changing our attitudes. Cognitive dissonance is an aversive state that occurs when our attitudes and behavior are inconsistent. A change of attitude may reduce dissonance. Self-perception theory also accounts for attitude change by suggesting that people perceive the causes of their own actions in much the same way they perceive the causes of others' actions: Where situational cues are weak, attributions tend to be dispositional.

Stereotypes and Prejudice

The Origins of Prejudice • Self-Fulfilling Prophecies • Hope for Change

A prejudice is an attitude toward a particular group based on characteristics of that group. Stereotypes are schemas in which certain characteristics of other people are overgeneralized and therefore erroneous. Discrimination often results from prejudice. Prejudice is related to competition, self-esteem, and social cognition and may have evolutionary roots as well. A self-fulfilling prophecy occurs when a person acts in ways congruent with a stereotype that he or she holds; members of the stereotyped group then seem to confirm the stereotype. Teaching people to think about members of other groups as individuals and to consider them in terms of their personal situations and characteristics can reduce prejudice.

Social Influences and Group Behavior

Conformity • Social Facilitation • Social Loafing • Commitment and Compliance • Obedience to Authority • Group Decision Making • Resisting Social Influences

The phenomena of conformity and bystander intervention reflect our tendency to be directly influenced by the action or inaction of others. The presence of others also can enhance the performance of a well-learned behavior but may interfere with the performance of complex or only partially learned behavior. When a group of people must collectively perform a task, any one individual often puts in less effort than we would have expected had the individual attempted the task alone, a behavior known as social loafing. We tend to honor commitments we make to others, respond positively to requests made of us by attractive people and authority figures, and identify with group values and goals. Unscrupulous persons often exploit these tendencies for their own gain. Effective group decision making can be hampered by elements of the discussion preceding the decision, which may result in group polarization or groupthink. A recognition of how people may try to exploit the rules of social influence is helpful in reducing the effectiveness of such exploitation.

Interpersonal Attraction and Loving

Interpersonal Attraction • *Evaluating Scientific Issues: Arousal and Interpersonal Attraction* • Loving • *Biology and Culture: Evolution and the Likelihood of Love*

We are attracted to others who think positively of us; who live, work, or play near us; who are similar to us; and who are physically attractive. Attraction is also related to arousal. Sternberg's theory of love describes how the elements of intimacy, passion, and commitment are involved in the different kinds of love. From an evolutionary perspective, gender-specific mate preferences play an important role in reproduction and child rearing.

T his vignette is from the anonymous annals of new-car buyers who also happen to be psychologists.

A few years ago it was time for me to buy a new car. I had done my background research and had a good idea of what the dealer cost was for the model I wanted and what would be a decent commission for a salesperson. I went to a dealer near my home, took a test drive, and settled down with my salesman, Greg, to negotiate the deal.

Greg quoted an unbelievably low price. I had to ask him to repeat himself. Even with factory-to-dealer discounts and incentives, I couldn't imagine how they were going to make any money. "Deal!" I said. We completed the formal offer; I gave Greg a check for several thousand dollars to seal the agreement; and then from Greg came the dreaded salesperson phrase, "I'll have to go get the manager to approve this."

I knew then that I was in the middle of a process called "lowballing," a technique whereby a salesperson quotes a very low price, only to find a reason (for example, a mistake reading the invoice) to raise the price later. The down payment check is meant to commit the buyer to the deal (more about this later in the chapter). I was supposed to sit in the salesperson's office, happily daydreaming about my new car, psychologically developing a sense of ownership. Being a psychologist, though, I knew better. I sat there getting more and more irritable while Greg had a cup of coffee or whatever he did other than talking to the manager.

Sure enough, Greg returned and said, "Geez, I really messed this up. I usually work in used cars. I'm not up on these prices. My manager really blew a gasket. Your car is $8000 more than I told you. You're going to have to come close to that. I can knock off maybe $500."

"No," I said, "I'm only willing to pay what we agreed on."

Greg countered with, "No, the car is worth way more than that. You have to up your offer."

"No," I said again, "you need to stand behind your first offer to me, or I'm going home. I teach about lowballing in my class at the university. I know what you're doing, and you can stop it now."

To my surprise, Greg immediately caved in, and I got the car for the price he originally quoted. While I was signing the final papers, two other salespeople teased Greg in front of me about blowing the deal and needing to spend more time on the used car lot.

M ost human activities are social: We spend many of our waking hours interacting with other people. Our behavior affects the way others act, and their behavior in turn affects our actions. The subdiscipline within psychology that studies these effects, as you may recall from Chapter 1, is called **social psychology.** Social psychology is, in the words of Gordon Allport (1968), the examination of "how the thoughts, feelings, and behavior of individuals are influenced by the actual, imagined, or implied presence of others" (p. 3).

This chapter's discussions reflect two principal concerns of social psychology. The first is social cognition and evaluation—how we think about others, how we account for what others do, and how we evaluate or form attitudes about others. The second concern focuses on how others' actions affect our own—on our relationships with people in groups both large and small, including the dyad (two people) in love. These concerns revolve around social interactions and their effects. Interactions with other people affect all aspects of human behavior from infancy through old age. The important people in our lives shape our perceptions, emotions, thoughts, and personalities. Social psychologists have found that even the most personal and seemingly subjective aspects of our lives, such as interpersonal attraction, can be studied with an impressive degree of scientific rigor.

Social Cognition

Understanding a person's social behavior requires considerable attention to that person's environment, both physical and social. The ability of a person to size up a social situation depends on many of the cognitive processes you have already studied. Among these are memory for people, places, and events (see Chapter 8); concept formation skills (Chapter 11); and, more fundamentally, the sensory and perceptual abilities you learned about in Chapters 5, 6, and 7 (also see Bodenhausen, Macrae, & Hugenberg, 2003; Fiske & Taylor, 1991; Kunda, 1999). Social psychologists apply knowledge of these basic psychological processes to research on **social cognition**— to understanding how people perceive, think about, and respond to the social world. Important areas of study in social cognition are impression formation, self-concepts, and attribution processes.

Impression Formation

All of us form impressions of others: friends, neighbors, colleagues, and even strangers—virtually everyone we meet or learn about through the reports of others. In doing so we assign characteristics to people. We may, for example, think of someone as friendly or hostile, helpful or selfish. A major task of social psychology is to understand how we form these impressions. In Solomon Asch's (1952) words, "How do the

▲ *Forming impressions of others involves sensory and perceptual processes as well as memory and concept formation skills, including schemas.*

perceptions, thoughts, and motives of one person become known to other persons?" (p. 143). To answer this question, psychologists study **impression formation,** the way in which we integrate information about another person's characteristics into a coherent sense of who the person is. As noted by Asch more than half a century ago, we form our impressions of others on the basis of rules that are more complex than mere sums of the characteristics we observe.

Schemas   As you saw in Chapter 12, a central concept in the study of cognitive development is that of the *schema,* a set of rules or representations by which we organize and synthesize information about a person, place, or thing (Markus, 1977; Olson, Roese, & Zanna, 1996; Wyer & Srull, 1994). We use schemas to interpret the world. The first time you visited a professor in his or her office, for example, there were probably few surprises. Your "professor" schema successfully guided your interactions with the individual you encountered. However, you probably would have been surprised had your professor's office been filled with soccer trophies, autographed photos of rock stars, or paintings of Elvis on black velvet—furnishings inconsistent with your schema.

To appreciate how schemas guide our interpretations, try to understand what the following passage is describing:

> The procedure is actually quite simple. First you arrange things into different groups. Of course, one pile may be sufficient depending on how much there is to do. . . . It is important not to overdo things. That is, it is better to do too few things at once than too many. In the short run this may not seem important, but complications can easily arise. A mistake can be expensive as well. At first the whole procedure will seem complicated. Soon, however, it will become just another facet of life. (Bransford & Johnson, 1972, p. 722)

Did this passage make sense to you? What if you learn that the title of the passage is "Washing Clothes"? The sentences make perfect sense within the context of your schema for washing clothes.

Central Traits   In the same way that your schema for washing clothes clarified an otherwise obscure description, your social schemas aid you in making sense of other people and their actions. Information about specific traits affects your overall sense of what a person is like. If a person is described as "witty, smart, and warm," your general impression of the person probably will be quite positive. But what would your reaction be if the person were described instead as "witty, smart, and cold"? What would account for the difference? Asch (1946) proposed that certain traits, called **central traits,** organize and influence our impressions of a person to a greater extent than do other traits. Note the similarity between Asch's concept of central traits and that of Gordon Allport as defined in Chapter 14. Asch (1946) tested the concept using the warm–cold trait dimension. In one study, for example, he provided all participants with the same basic list of adjectives describing a hypothetical person: Participants heard that the person was intelligent, skillful, industrious, determined, practical, and cautious. Some participants were told that the person was also "warm," whereas others were told that the person was also "cold." Overall, those who heard the list that included "warm" formed more positive impressions of the imaginary person than did those who heard "cold." Participants in the "warm" condition also were more likely to speculate that the person was also generous, happy, and altruistic. When the words "polite" and "blunt" were substituted for "warm" and "cold" in the list, no differences were observed in the participants' impressions. Traits such as "politeness" and "bluntness" thus are known as *peripheral traits* (or, in Allport's terminology, as *secondary traits*).

Results parallel to Asch's findings for the warm–cold variable were found in a natural setting in which a researcher privately described a real person to some people as "warm" and to others as "cold," although the person's actions and demeanor were identical in both cases (Kelley, 1950). More recent work suggests that the negative influence of the "cold" trait is stronger than the positive influence of the "warm" trait (Singh, Onglatco, Sriram, & Tay, 1997; Singh & Teoh, 2000). This imbalance may occur because people tend to have a general bias toward positivity in forming impressions of others (e.g., Heyman & Giles, 2004; Sears, 1983). Thus, negative information, such as that conveyed by a negative central trait, may be more salient in the context of a generally positive impression than another piece of positive information about the person would be (Skowronski & Carlston, 1989).

The Primacy Effect Getting to know someone takes time, because it requires multiple interactions. Suppose that the first time you see a young man is at a party, where he is loud and boisterous and having a good time with his friends. But later you learn that he is a math major with excellent grades who is actually quite reserved. What is your impression of this person: Loud and boisterous, or bright and shy? Seeking to determine whether first impressions might overpower later impressions, Asch (1946) presented one of the following lists of words to each of two groups of people:

> Intelligent, industrious, impulsive,
> critical, stubborn, envious

> Envious, stubborn, critical,
> impulsive, industrious, intelligent

Notice that these lists describe the same traits but in reverse order. After the participants heard the list, Asch asked them to describe the personality of a person having these characteristics. People who heard the first list thought of the person as someone who was able and productive but who possessed some shortcomings. The person

described by the second list, however, was seen as someone who had serious problems. The tendency to form an impression of a person based on the initial information we learn about him or her is called the **primacy effect** (not to be confused with the primacy effect discussed in Chapter 8, which had to do with remembering lists of words). The primacy effect reflects the greater attention we give to information about traits that is presented early as opposed to later (Belmore, 1987; Park, 1986). Consistent with this attentional interpretation, Webster, Richter, and Kruglanski (1996) found that the primacy effect was more pronounced for participants who were mentally fatigued than for those who were relatively alert.

We seldom receive lists of traits in the way Asch and others provided them to research participants. How do we develop impressions in the absence of lists? The most intuitive answer may be that as we observe what a person does and says, we think about what our observations reveal about the person's qualities (e.g., Carlston & Skowronski, 1994). Alternatively, Brown and Bassili (2002) suggest that people generate trait labels from their observations and that the labels become associated with other stimuli that happened to occur at the same time that the person's behavior was observed. Most often, observed behavior will be closely associated with the person who performs it, so memories will link the person and the trait labels. When the observer later thinks about the person, the trait information will be recalled. This linking by association is quite different from a spontaneous but purposeful attempt to decipher what a person is like. In a study of their associationistic interpretation, Brown and Bassili (2002) showed that trait labels from behavioral descriptions may become associated with almost any stimulus, including inanimate ones. For example, they found that people associated personality traits with bananas that were part of the situation when personal impressions were formed. This interpretation calls into question the intuitive view that we form impressions of others solely by observing them and what they do.

The Self

If you are asked who you are, how do you respond? You might state your name, say that you are a student, and perhaps add that you are from a certain place or have a certain interest. Alternatively, you could say something about your family, nationality, ethnicity, or religion. There are many ways you could potentially describe yourself, all of which would reflect your **self-concept**—your knowledge, feelings, and beliefs about yourself. The **self** per se is a person's distinct individuality. Your self-concept, then, is your "self-identity"—your perception of your distinct individuality in the context of events that are relevant to defining who you are. The self-concept is represented by the **self-schema**—a cognitive structure that organizes the knowledge, feelings, and beliefs you have about your self (Markus, 1977).

The self-concept is dynamic; it changes with experience. Some researchers, such as Markus and Nurius (1986), argue that the self-concept is a work in progress; it changes as we have new experiences or receive new feedback from others. That is, each of us has many potential selves that we may become depending on experience. Can you imagine the different twists and turns your life might take and how your self-concept could be affected as a result? Can you imagine the circumstances that might lead you to change your major, drop out of school, or get married or divorced—and how your self-concept would be affected in turn? In one study researchers asked people who had experienced a traumatic life event (for example, the death of a family member or friend) to describe their current and possible future selves (Markus & Nurius, 1986; Ruvolo & Markus, 1992). All of the participants reported that they were worried, upset, and depressed and lacked control over their lives. That is, everyone described similar *current* selves. Nonetheless, different participants described different sorts of possible *future* selves. Those who had not yet recovered from the traumatic event predicted that they would be unhappy and lonely. Those who had recovered predicted just the opposite: They saw themselves as happy, self-confident, and having many friends. Thus, thinking of ourselves only in terms of who we are at present often does not accurately reflect how we will think of ourselves in the future or the kind of person we might become. More recently, Wilson and Gilbert (2003) have summarized evidence showing that people typically make inaccurate predictions as to how readily they will recover from negative events—something the authors refer to as *affective forecasting*.

Identifying the complex interchange between biological, familial, social, and cultural influences on the self is a daunting challenge, but social psychologists have taken up the task with particular enthusiasm (e.g., see Berry, 2003;

▲ *People in many Eastern cultures are more likely than people in Western cultures to construe their self-concepts in terms of the social interactions they have with others.*

Lehman, Chiu, & Schaller, 2004; Matsumoto, 2003). Among the issues researchers have addressed are the formation of the self-concept, the perceptions people form of others, and the extent to which others may influence the development of a person's self-concept (Heine, 2001; Markus & Kitayama, 2003). For example, in North America parents sometimes encourage their children to eat all of their dinner by admonishing them to "think about all the starving children in the world and how lucky you are not to have to go hungry," whereas in Japan parents often urge reluctant eaters to "think of the farmer who worked so hard to produce this rice for you; if you don't eat it, he will feel bad, for his efforts will have been in vain" (Markus & Kitayama, 1991). As this example shows, Western cultures often emphasize our uniqueness as individuals and the ways in which we are different from others. In contrast, Japanese and other Eastern cultures often emphasize paying attention to others and to our relatedness to them.

Markus and Kitayama (1991) have conceptualized categories of self-concepts that reflect such cultural differences. What they call *independent construal* emphasizes the uniqueness of each person's self, the self's autonomy from others, and self-reliance. Thus, although other people have an influence on a person's behavior, a person's self-concept is largely defined independently of others. By contrast, *interdependent construal* emphasizes the interconnectedness of people and the roles that others play in developing a person's self-concept. In the interdependent construal, what others think of the individual or do to the individual matters.

In related research, Markus and Kitayama (1991) found that students from India judge themselves as more similar to others, whereas American students judge themselves as more dissimilar. Campbell and colleagues (1996) suggested that Eastern and Western cultures also may differ in terms of the *clarity* of self-concepts—that is, in terms of how confident people are that they possess particular attributes, how sharply defined they believe those attributes are, and how internally and temporally consistent they think the attributes are. The researchers proposed that high clarity more closely matches an independent construal of self than an interdependent construal. In fact, they found that college students in Canada expressed greater self-concept clarity than did students in Japan, for example.

Another study considered the implications of the two types of construals for the common experiences of temporary successes and failures in life. Heine and colleagues (2001) reasoned that people with an independent construal of self would view their traits and abilities as relatively stable. People with an interdependent construal, on the other hand, should view their traits and abilities as relatively unstable and likely to shift. And indeed, the researchers found that Canadian students of European descent were more likely to persist on a task after a successful experience than after failure, whereas Japanese students from Kyoto University were more likely to persist following a failure than a success. If people believe that their abilities are likely to persist, then success will likely breed further efforts to succeed. If, on the other hand, people believe that abilities can change, then endeavoring to change in the wake of failure may lead to success.

If you are from a Western culture, you may have interpreted the theory and research I've been describing to mean, "People from Western cultures have better self-concepts and approaches to life than do people from Eastern cultures." Such a conclusion would follow from the way your culture values and encourages independence and stability of the self. A reader from an Eastern culture, however, could well read these same paragraphs and conclude: "People from Eastern cultures have better self-concepts and approaches to life than do people from Western cultures." Eastern cultures tend to value and emphasize the changing nature and demands of interpersonal relations. Indeed, well-being and satisfaction among Eastern students have been found to be strongly correlated with interpersonal behaviors and socially focused emotions such as friendliness (Kitayama, Markus, & Kurakawa, 2000; Markus & Kitayama, 1991). In contrast, well-being and satisfaction among Western students are more strongly correlated with individual achievement and self-reflective emotions such as pride (see also Wilson, 2003).

Attribution

We are all, in some ways at least, implicit social psychologists (Jones, 1990). Each of us constructs *folk theories* (informal theories) about the nature and causes of other people's behavior. On any given day we are confronted by thousands of individual acts performed by other people. Some acts are important to us, because they provide clues about others' personality characteristics and about how others are likely to perceive us and interact with us. But if we had to pay close attention to each of these acts, then classify them, think about their significance, and compare them to previous observations, we would quickly come to a halt. Instead, we use social schemas to reach conclusions and thus save much time and effort. This process by which we infer the causes of other people's behavior is called **attribution**.

Disposition versus Situation
According to attribution theorists, the primary distinction that we make concerning the causes of a person's behavior is between *situational* (or external) and *dispositional* (or internal) *factors* (Heider, 1958). **Situational factors** include stimuli found in the physical and social environments, such as living conditions, other people, societal norms, and laws. **Dispositional factors** include a person's traits, needs, and intentions. As we grow up, one of our tasks during the process of socialization is to learn the behaviors that are normally expected in various kinds of situations. Once we learn that in certain situations most people act in a specific way, we develop schemas for how to act in those situations and how to expect others to act. For example, in

American culture, when two people are introduced, they are expected to look at each other, smile, say something like "How do you do?" or "It's nice to meet you," and perhaps offer to shake the other person's hand. If people act in conventional ways in given situations, we are not surprised. Their behavior appears to conform to social custom according to the characteristics of the situation.

As we get to know other people, we learn to characterize them as friendly, generous, suspicious, pessimistic, or greedy by observing their behavior across a variety of situations. We also can make inferences from a single observation (Krull & Erickson, 1995). For example, if someone's behavior is very different from the way most people would act in a particular situation, we may attribute his or her behavior to dispositional (internal) factors. That is, if we see someone refuse to hold a door open for someone in a wheelchair, we're likely to attribute negative personal characteristics to that individual.

Kelley's Theory of Attribution
Kelley (1967) suggested that we attribute the behavior of other people to situational or dispositional causes on the basis of three types of information: consensus, distinctiveness, and consistency.

Consensus is the extent to which we have observed a behavior to be common to other people in a given situation. When consensus exists, we usually attribute behavior to situational causes. For example, if you hear Bill praise a new off-campus club and you also have heard other people say the same things (high consensus), you will likely attribute Bill's praise to the qualities of the club (a situational attribution). What if everyone else disagrees with Bill's evaluation (low consensus)? Now you will be likely to view Bill's opinion of the club as reflecting something personal about him (a dispositional attribution). Maybe he has bad taste in clubs, or maybe something unique about this club appealed to him alone.

We also base our attributions on **distinctiveness**—the extent to which a person performs a particular behavior only during a particular type of event or toward a particular person or thing. If you have never heard Bill praise anything as highly as he praises the new club, his behavior has high distinctiveness, and you will probably see Bill's praise for the new club as reflecting the quality of the club itself (a situational attribution). But if Bill praises every place he's ever visited as highly as he praises this club, you will attribute his evaluation to something dispositional in Bill. Perhaps he is quick to praise or very easily entertained.

Finally, we base our attributions on **consistency**—on whether a person's behavior occurs reliably over time. Suppose that Bill's behavior is characterized by high distinctiveness and high consensus. Both signs point to an attribution to the situational entity—the club. Bill likes this new club more than he likes any others, and most other people rave about the new club. If Bill likes the club every time he goes (high consistency), then your conclusion is clear: It's a great

TABLE 15•1	Kelley's Theory of Attribution	
	Dispositional Attribution	**Situational Attribution**
Consensus	Low. Jose is smiling broadly while talking with Maria; most people do not smile while talking with her.	High. Jose is smiling broadly while talking with Maria; most other people do as well.
Distinctiveness	Low. Jose smiles like this while talking with most people.	High. Jose does not smile like this when talking with most other people.
Consistency	High. Jose always smiles like this when he talks with Maria.	High. Jose always smiles like this when he talks with Maria.
Conclusion (Attribution)	Jose is smiling at Maria because he is a happy person who enjoys talking with people.	Jose is smiling at Maria because there is something about her that makes him happy.

club (situational attribution). But consider what happens if low consistency combines with high distinctiveness and high consensus. Suppose that the next time Bill goes to the club, he tells you he hates it—but then he goes again and tells you it's the best place he's ever been. Now your attribution may well be dispositional—something peculiar to Bill is affecting his experience at the club. On the other hand, you may have reason to think that circumstances at the club tend to shift, making Bill's alternately liking and hating it understandable. In this case your attribution will be situational. **Table 15•1** summarizes Kelley's ideas about attributions using another example.

When people are presented with examples of social behavior that include information about consensus, distinctiveness, and consistency, they answer questions about dispositional and situational factors in the way Kelley's theory predicts (e.g., Hazelwood & Olson, 1986; McArthur, 1972). But such results do not mean that we always engage in this type of attribution (e.g., Brown & Bassili, 2002). Overall, the evidence suggests that people are more likely to engage in inferential decisions like those described by Kelley when they are asked questions directly about why someone behaved as he or she did (e.g., Enzle & Schopflocher, 1978), when the events they are exposed to are unexpected or abnormal (Hilton & Slugoski, 1986), or when they believe it is important for the advancement of their personal interests to understand the cause of others' behaviors (e.g., Burger & Hemans, 1988; Kunda, 1990).

Attributional Biases

It is important to realize that when we make attributions, we do not function as impartial, dispassionate observers. There are biases in the attribution process that affect our conclusions about the persons whose behavior we observe. Two kinds of bias are those associated with the fundamental attribution error and false consensus.

The Fundamental Attribution Error   When attributing a person's behavior to possible causes, we tend to *overestimate*

the significance of dispositional factors and *underestimate* the significance of situational factors. This bias is called the **fundamental attribution error** (Ross, 1977).

This bias toward dispositional attribution is a potent factor in our thinking about people. Even when evidence indicates otherwise, we seem to prefer dispositional to situational attributions. For example, consider a study by Jones and Harris (1967). College students read essays that had supposedly been written by other students. The topic of the essay was Fidel Castro's rule of Cuba. Half of the students read an essay that was very positive toward Castro (the "pro" version), and the other half read a very negative account of Castro's leadership (the "con" version). The key manipulation in the experiment was information about the circumstances under which the writer supposedly composed the essay. Half of the students who read either the pro or the con version of the essay were told that the writer had been *assigned* a position (i.e., pro or con) to take when writing the essay. The remaining students were told that the writer *chose* the orientation. After reading the essay, all participants were asked to estimate the essay writer's *true* attitudes toward Castro. Amazingly, the participants reported that the essay writer's attitudes matched the pro or con stance of the essay regardless of whether the stance in the essay had been assigned to or chosen by the writer. For example, if the writer's statements about Castro were positive, participants attributed those statements to the writer's beliefs, even though the writer had been assigned to produce those statements. Participants did not take into account the situational demands on the writer who was assigned a position. Subsequent research has replicated this finding with many different methods and across cultures (e.g., Krull et al., 1999; Miyamoto & Kitayama, 2002). In fact, it is extremely difficult to eliminate the fundamental attribution error.

Victim-blaming is a common form of the fundamental attribution error, particularly when the victim is not actually responsible for his or her misfortune. According to Lerner (1980), victim-blaming occurs because, whether we're aware of it or not, most of us have a **belief in a just world**. That is, we erroneously assume that the world is a fair place in which people get what they deserve. One result of this error is that we tend to blame victims when misfortune or tragedy strikes. Why? An innocent victim would threaten the stability of our belief system (see Hafer, 2000a). Blaming the victim establishes a just outcome (bad things happen to bad people) and therefore protects the belief that the world, and life, are fair (and safe).

Belief in the world as a just place also may help motivate people to persist in the pursuit of their goals. According to Hafer (2000b, 2002), just-world beliefs assure people that their efforts toward reaching long-term goals will ultimately be rewarded. Hafer's (2000b) research supports this view by showing that focusing college students on the relationship between their present efforts and the successful achievement of their long-term (postgraduation) goals increased the extent to which they blamed innocent victims for their trials and tribulations. In other words, participants who were sensitized to long-term fairness concerns sought to maintain their belief in justice by insisting that an innocent victim was not innocent but deserved to be harmed.

Attorneys and mental health practitioners are all too familiar with victim-blaming. Innocent victims of crime often are blamed for their misfortunes. People who are raped, for example, often must cope with being blamed for their own assault (Bell, Kuriloff, & Lottes, 1994; Wakelin & Long, 2003). Complex social problems such as poverty (e.g., Guimond & Dube, 1989) seem prone to the same blaming phenomenon. By blaming poor people for their own predicament, others can maintain their sense that the world is just and can avoid having to deal with the difficult underlying causes of poverty. Interestingly, in a study of people from 12 different countries, Furnham (1992) discovered that the tendency to blame victims was positively correlated with status and wealth.

In contrast, when trying to explain our own rather than others' behavior, we are much more likely to attribute it to characteristics of the situation than to our own personal characteristics. We tend to see our own behavior as relatively variable and strongly influenced by the situation, whereas we see the behavior of others as more stable and due to dispositional factors. In other words, when we try to explain our own behavior, we are not likely to make the fundamental attribution error (Sande, Goethals, & Radloff, 1988). This phenomenon is called the **actor–observer effect**.

A study of college-age male–female couples demonstrated the actor–observer effect (Orvis, Kelley, & Butler, 1976). Each person was asked separately to describe disagreements in the relationship, such as arguments and criticism. Each was also asked to explain his or her attribution of the underlying causes of the disagreements. When describing their own behavior, the participants tended to refer to environmental factors, such as financial problems or not getting enough sleep. When describing their partners' behavior, however, the participants often referred to specific negative personal characteristics, such as selfishness or low commitment to the relationship.

Why do we tend to commit the fundamental attribution error when we observe the behavior of others but not when we explain the causes of our own behavior? Jones and Nisbett (1971) suggested two possible reasons. First, we have a different focus of attention when we view ourselves. We tend to see the world around us more clearly than we observe our own behavior. However, when we observe someone else doing something, we focus our attention on what is most salient and relevant: that person's behavior, not the situation in which he or she is placed.

A second possible reason is that different types of information are available to us about our own behavior and that of other people. We have more information about our own behavior and are thus more likely to realize that it is often inconsistent. After all, it is typically easy to access our own thoughts and feelings. We also have a better notion of which stimuli we are attending to in a given situation. This difference in information may lead us to conclude that the behavior of other people is typically consistent and thus a product of their personalities, whereas our behavior, given the inconsistency, is a product of the situation in which we find ourselves.

There is an important exception to our strong preference for situational self-attributions: When we attempt to attribute our behavior, we tend to attribute our accomplishments and successes to dispositional factors and our failures and mistakes to situational factors, a phenomenon called the **self-serving bias** (Miller & Ross, 1975). Suppose that you receive an outstanding test score. If you are like most people, you will consider the score well deserved. After all, you are a smart individual who studied hard. Your attributions reflect dispositional factors. Now suppose that you receive a failing score on the test—what sorts of attributions do you tend to make? Again, if you are like most people, you may blame your low score on the fact that it was a difficult, even "unfair" test, or on the teacher for being so picky about the answers he or she considered wrong. Your attributions in this case point

▲ *Victims who testify in court may elicit victim-blaming by members of a jury who believe in a just world.*

▲ *Attributing your own and others' performances on an exam is likely to involve the fundamental attribution error, the actor–observer effect, and self-serving bias.*

to situational factors. A possible explanation for the self-serving bias is that people are motivated to protect and enhance their self-esteem (Brown & Rogers, 1991; Robins & Beer, 2001). Simply put, we protect our self-esteem when we blame failures on the situation, and we enhance it when we give ourselves credit for our successes. Moreover, self-enhancement has the short-term effect of promoting positive mood (Robins & Beer, 2001).

False Consensus

Another attributional bias is our frequent tendency to perceive our own responses to things as representative of the general consensus—an error called **false consensus** (Gilovich, 1990). For example, McFarland and Miller (1990) asked psychology students to choose one of two unpleasant experiments in which to participate. Regardless of their choice, participants believed that the majority of other students would select the same experiment they had. They overestimated the similarity of others' preferences.

One proposed explanation for false consensus points to self-esteem. Presumably, people do not like to think of themselves as being too different from other people and thus think that most will act the way they do. Another explanation derives from the fact that people tend to place themselves in the company of others who are similar to themselves (Ross, 1977). For this reason they are apt to think that others share their tastes and views.

Attribution, Heuristics, and Social Cognition

As you learned in Chapter 11, we tend to follow general rules of thumb, or *heuristics*, when making decisions. This is especially evident when we make judgments about other people and our interactions with them. Most of the time, social heuristics serve us well. However, they sometimes lead us astray. When they do, we refer to them as biases or fallacies.

The Representativeness Heuristic As noted earlier in the chapter, when we meet someone for the first time, we observe the person's clothes, hairstyle, posture, manner of speaking, hand and facial gestures, and other characteristics. Based on our previous experience, we use this information to make tentative judgments about characteristics that we cannot immediately discern. In doing so, we attempt to match the characteristics we can observe to schemas for different types of people. If the person seems to fit a particular schema, then we may come to a conclusion as to what he or she is likely to be or to do (Lupfer, Clark, & Hutcherson, 1990). In reaching this conclusion, we use the **representativeness heuristic**—we classify the person using the category that she or he appears to fit best.

Sometimes the representativeness heuristic can mislead us, however. Consider the following example: A professor swims laps in the pool during every lunch hour. He also likes to play tennis; if he can find a willing opponent, he will play in the dead of winter if the court can be swept clear of snow. Which of the following is his academic field: sports medicine or psychology?

If you said "psychology," you were more likely to be right, because there are many more professors of psychology than of sports medicine. Simply in view of the actual frequency of professors in these two fields, there is a strong likelihood that your guess is correct. Yet you might have said sports medicine, or at least seriously considered it. The *image* of an athletic person is such a distinctive cue that it is difficult not to conclude that the professor specializes in sports medicine. The image of the swimmer and tennis player suggests involvement in sports more than in psychology. Here, paying too much attention to the more representative image is an example of the **base-rate fallacy**—the error we commit when we fail to consider the actual likelihoods involved.

The Availability Heuristic When people attempt to assess the importance or the frequency of an event, they tend to be guided by the ease with which examples of that event can be recalled—by how available these examples are to memory. This shortcut is called the **availability heuristic**. In general, the things we are able to think of most easily are more important and occur more frequently than things that are difficult to remember. Thus, the availability heuristic works well—most of the time. But it can lead to mistakes as well.

Amos Tversky and Daniel Kahneman (1982) demonstrated how the availability heuristic can cause errors by asking people to estimate whether English words starting with *k* were more or less common than words with *k* in the third position (for example, *kiss* versus *lake*). Most people said that there were more words starting with *k*. In fact, there are more than twice as many words having *k* in the third position as those having *k* in the first. But because thinking of words that start with a particular letter is easier

TABLE 15•2 **The Availability Heuristic in Operation**

Does this list contain more men's or women's names? The answer may surprise you: There are fifteen male names and only fourteen female names. Because of the *availability heuristic*, however, most people tend to guess that female names are more numerous. The women listed are more famous than the men, so it is easier to bring their names to mind; this leads to overestimates of their frequency in the list.

Louisa May Alcott	Henry Vaughan
Allan Nevins	John Dickson Carr
Kate Millet	Jane Austen
Emily Dickinson	Eudora Welty
Henry Crabb Robinson	Thomas Hughes
Richard Watson Gilder	Joseph Lincoln
Laura Ingalls Wilder	Harriet Beecher Stowe
Emily Brontë	Jack Lindsay
Pearl Buck	Arthur Hutchinson
Edward George Lytton	Amy Lowell
James Hunt	Margaret Mitchell
Robert Lovett	Erica Jong
Michael Drayton	Edna St. Vincent Millay
Brian Hooker	Edith Wharton
George Jean Nathan	

Source: From Robert A. Baron, *Psychology*, 5/e. Published by Allyn and Bacon, Boston, MA. Copyright © 2001 by Pearson Education. Reprinted with permission of the publisher.

than thinking of words that contain the letter in another position, people are misled. **Table 15•2** shows another example, based on a study by Tversky and Kahneman (1974), of how the availability heuristic works.

The availability heuristic also explains why encounters with other people tend to have an especially strong effect on our decision making. For example, suppose that you have decided to transfer to another university for your last two undergraduate years. You have narrowed your choices down to two schools. You read *U.S. News & World Report*'s latest annual rankings, which clearly favor one of the two universities. You decide to apply to that school and mention the fact to an acquaintance later that day. She says, "Oh, no! Don't go there! I went there for two terms. The profs are distant. Badly prepared TAs do all the lectures. The grading system is unfair and way too competitive. The general atmosphere is appalling. I couldn't wait to leave." Will her report affect your decision about where to transfer?

It would not be unusual to take this personal information very seriously. Even though it consists of the experiences of only one person, whereas the *U.S. News & World Report* rankings are based on large numbers of interviews and summaries of data, a vivid personal encounter is much more available and memorable than a large array of statistics and tends to have a disproportionate effect on people's behavior (Borgida & Nisbett, 1977).

Interim Summary

Social Cognition

Social cognition involves our perception and interpretation of information about our social environment and our behavior in response to that environment. Our experiences give rise to schemas, rules, or representations by which we organize and synthesize information about our interactions with others. Characterizing people in terms of central traits helps us to form impressions of them. The initial information we learn about someone plays an important part in forming our impressions—a tendency called the primacy effect.

A person's self-concept represents his or her knowledge, feelings, and beliefs about himself or herself. At the center of the self-concept is the self-schema by which we process and interpret information about the self. Our self-concepts change with our personal experiences and are influenced by the culture in which we live. In fact, different cultures often have different ways of conceptualizing the self. Western cultures emphasize the self's uniqueness, while Eastern cultures emphasize the interdependence of the self and others.

We attribute particular instances of behavior to two types of factors: dispositional and situational. A behavior that is high in consensus (many other people act the same way), high in distinctiveness (occurs only in the particular situation), and consistent over time is usually attributed to the situation. Behavior low in consensus, low in distinctiveness, and consistent over time is usually attributed to disposition.

The fundamental attribution error occurs because we tend to overemphasize dispositional factors and underemphasize situational factors in judging the causes of others' behavior. We are most likely to make the fundamental attribution error about others than about ourselves because we are less aware of the situational factors that affect others' behavior. One example of the fundamental attribution error is the belief that people get what they deserve in life; that is, the belief in a just world. Our tendency to see our own behavior as influenced more by situational than by dispositional factors and others' behavior as due more to dispositional than to situational factors is called the actor–observer effect. However, when it comes to our successes and failures, we display the self-serving bias: We tend to attribute our successes to dispositional factors and our failures to situational factors. The error known as false consensus is our tendency to believe that others act and believe much as we do, even when they do not.

The representativeness heuristic is a mental shortcut in which we seize on a few especially salient characteristics in order to categorize a person or situation. Thus, we sometimes ignore other evidence and may commit the base-rate error. When we rely on the availability heuristic, we judge the importance or the frequency of events by the ease with which examples are recalled. Personal testimony about a topic often has high availability and thus may outweigh less vivid—but more representative—evidence.

1. What factors have been most influential in the development of your self-concept? What sorts of experiences do you think will influence the continued development of your self-concept during your college years? How will they do this?

2. How much of your social behavior do you engage in unconsciously—that is, without self-awareness? In answering this question, consider the phenomena of attribution (such as the fundamental attribution error) and heuristics (such as representativeness). What effect do you suppose being more conscious of social cognition in your social interactions would have? Why?

3. Imagine you are the first person to arrive at the scene of an auto accident in which several people have been badly injured. What factors—situational or dispositional or some combination of the two—would influence your response?

Attitudes: Their Formation and Change

The study of **attitudes**—evaluations of persons, places, and things—and of how our attitudes form and change constitutes an important part of social psychology (Petty, Wegener, & Fabrigar, 1997; Wood, 2000).

Formation of Attitudes

Attitudes are generally considered to have three components: affect, behavior, and cognition (Eagly & Chaiken, 1998; Zanna & Rempel, 1988). The affective (emotional) component consists of the kinds of feelings that a particular stimulus arouses. The behavioral component consists of a tendency to act in a particular way toward a particular stimulus. The cognitive component consists of a set of beliefs about the stimulus. (See **Figure 15•1**.) Social psychologists have studied all three aspects of attitudes, and we will examine their findings in this section, particularly with respect to ethnicity and social issues.

Affective Components of Attitudes The affective components of attitudes can be strong and pervasive. The bigot feels unease in the presence of people from a certain religious, racial, or ethnic group; the nature lover feels exhilaration from a pleasant walk through the woods. Like other emotional reactions, these feelings are strongly influenced by direct or vicarious classical conditioning (see Chapter 5) (Rajecki, 1990).

Direct classical conditioning of attitudes is straightforward. Suppose that you meet someone who seems to take delight in embarrassing you. She makes clever, sarcastic remarks that disparage your intelligence, looks, and personality. Unfortunately, her remarks are so clever that your attempts to defend yourself make you appear even more foolish. After a few encounters with this person, the sight of her or the sound of her voice is likely to elicit feelings of dislike and fear. Your attitude toward her will be negative.

In contrast, vicarious classical conditioning undoubtedly plays a major role in transmitting parents' attitudes to their children. People are skilled at detecting even subtle signs of fear, hatred, and other negative emotional states in other people, especially when they know them well. Thus, children often perceive their parents' prejudices and fears even if these feelings are unspoken. Children who sense their parents' distaste at the sight of members of some ethnic group are likely to learn to react in the same way.

Even without conditioning, simply being exposed repeatedly to an otherwise neutral object or issue over time may cause us to develop a positive attitude toward it. This preference

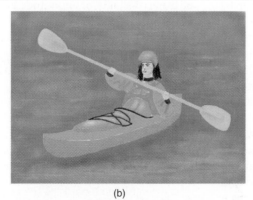
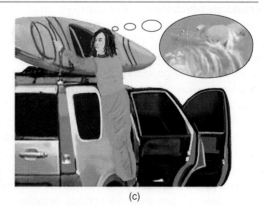

(a)   (b)   (c)

FIGURE 15•1 The three components of attitude: affect, behavior, and cognition. (a) Affective component (feelings): Enjoys kayaking. (b) Behavioral component (actions): Pursues kayaking as a hobby. (c) Cognitive component (beliefs): Believes that kayaking has an element of risk but is fun.

for the familiar is what Robert Zajonc (pronounced "zi-onze"; 1968) called the **mere exposure effect.** One of the first studies to demonstrate this effect used several neutral stimuli—toward which there were initially no positive or negative feelings—such as nonsense words, photographs of the faces of unknown people, and Chinese characters (Zajonc, 1968). The more the participants saw the stimuli, the more they liked them. Research also shows that the mere exposure effect is stronger when stimuli are presented below participants' threshold of awareness (Murphy, Monahan, & Zajonc, 1995) and that the positive affect produced in this way generalizes to similar stimuli (Monahan, Murphy, & Zajonc, 2000).

Note that the effect of mere exposure is limited to initially neutral stimuli. The effect of mere exposure does not apply to stimuli that are initially disliked. Repeated exposure to things or people we do not like seems only to confirm that we do not like them (Perlman & Oskamp, 1971).

Behavioral Components of Attitudes

People do not always behave as their expressed attitudes and beliefs would lead us to expect. In a classic example, LaPiere (1934) drove through the United States with a Chinese couple. They stopped at more than 250 restaurants and lodging places and were refused service only once. Several months after their trip, LaPiere wrote to the owners of the places they had visited and asked whether they would serve Chinese people. The response was overwhelmingly negative; 92 percent of those who responded said that they would not. Clearly, their behavior gave less evidence of ethnic bias than their expressed attitudes did. This study has been cited as proof that attitudes do not always influence behavior. However, more recent research indicates that there is a definite relation between attitudes and behavior, but that the relation is influenced by several factors: the specificity, motivational relevance, and accessibility of the attitudes as well as possible constraints on the related behavior.

Degree of Specificity. Measuring a person's general attitude toward a stimulus may not enable you to predict his or her behavior (e.g., Haddock, Zanna, & Esses, 1994). Behaviors, unlike attitudes, are specific events. As the attitude being measured becomes more specific, the person's behavior becomes more predictable. For example, Weigel, Vernon, and Tognacci (1974) measured people's attitudes toward a series of topics that increased in specificity from "a pure environment" (that is, a clean or unpolluted environment) to "the Sierra Club" (a pro-environment organization). They used the participants' attitudes to predict whether they would volunteer for various activities to benefit the Sierra Club. A person's attitude toward environmentalism was a poor predictor of whether he or she would volunteer; the person's attitude toward the Sierra Club itself was a much better predictor. (See **Table 15•3.**) For example, a person might favor the preservation of wilderness but might also dislike organized clubs or have little time to spare for meetings. This person would express a positive attitude toward wilderness but would not join the Sierra Club or volunteer for activities that support it.

▲ *A protest is one example of a situation in which a person's attitude on an issue corresponds to his or her behavior—in this case, demonstrating against abortion and for abortion rights.*

Motivational Relevance. Expressing a particular attitude takes less effort than does acting on that attitude. In other words, "Talk is cheap." Sivacek and Crano (1982) demonstrated the importance of motivational relevance by asking students to volunteer their time to help campaign against a pending law that would raise the drinking age from 18 to 20. Although almost all of the students were opposed to the new drinking law, younger students, who would be affected by its passage, were much more likely to volunteer their time and effort. Thus, attitudes are more likely to motivate behaviors if the effects of the behaviors are relevant to the individual.

Accessibility. Another variable that affects the relation between attitude and behavior is an attitude's accessibility, which refers to the readiness with which an attitude is expressed. Suppose you have a negative attitude toward forest clear-cutting but have never expressed that attitude before. If you are asked for the first time to support a forest-preservation group, it is unlikely that you will act (make a donation to the group, for instance) in a way that is consistent with your attitude (e.g., Fazio & Roskos-Ewoldsen, 1994). An important aspect of the accessibility of an attitude is how quickly it comes to

TABLE 15•3	Correlation between Willingness to Join or Work for the Sierra Club and Various Measures of Related Attitudes
Attitude Scale	**Correlation**
Importance of a pure environment	.06
Concern about pollution	.32
Support for conservation	.24
Positive attitude toward the Sierra Club	.68

Source: Based on Weigel, R. H., Vernon, D. T. A., & Tognacci, L. N. (1974). Specificity of the attitude as a determinant of attitude–behavior congruence. *Journal of Personality and Social Psychology, 30,* 724–728.

mind. Some theorists consider the period of time between the stimulus relevant to the attitude and a person's statement of his or her attitude to be a good predictor of attitude–behavior consistency. For example, Bassili (1993, 1995) found that each one-second delay in an interviewee's response to questions about whom he or she favored in an upcoming election translated into a nearly 10 percent mismatch with the candidate the interviewee actually voted for in the elections. The longer the latency, the greater the inconsistency between attitudes and behavior.

Constraints on Behavior. Other, more obvious factors, such as existing circumstances, also produce discrepancies between attitudes and behaviors. For example, a young man may have a very positive attitude toward a certain young woman. If he is asked specifically, he may express a very positive attitude toward kissing her. However, he never kisses her, because she has plainly shown that she is not interested in him. No matter how carefully we measure the young man's attitudes, we cannot predict his behavior without considering additional information that is available (in this case, information about the young woman's receptiveness).

Cognitive Components of Attitudes

The cognitive components of attitudes are conscious beliefs. We acquire most beliefs about a particular stimulus quite directly: We hear or read a fact or opinion, or other people reinforce statements in which we ourselves express a particular attitude. A group of racially prejudiced people will probably ostracize a person who makes positive statements about the group or groups against which they are prejudiced. Conversely, conscientious parents may applaud their child's positive statements about other ethnic groups or about social issues such as environmental conservation.

Attitude Change and Persuasion

Once attitudes are formed, people often attempt to persuade us to change them. Two aspects of persuasive messages have received special attention from social psychologists: the sources of the messages and the messages themselves.

A message tends to be more persuasive if its source is credible. Source credibility is high when the source is perceived as knowledgeable and is trusted to communicate this knowledge accurately. For example, in a classic study, people developed a more favorable attitude toward different types of medicine when information about the medicines appeared in the prestigious *New England Journal of Medicine* than when the same information appeared in a mass-circulation tabloid (Hovland & Weiss, 1951).

Messages also seem to have more impact when their sources are attractive. For example, physically attractive people are more likely than physically unattractive people to persuade others to sign a petition (Chaiken, 1979). Individuals who are asked to endorse products for advertisers are almost always physically attractive or appealing in other ways. Addi-

tionally, the likability of the communicator, independent of physical attractiveness, has a similar effect on persuasion (Roskos-Ewoldsen & Fazio, 1992).

Aspects of the message itself also are important in determining its persuasive appeal. For example, is an argument that provides only one side of an issue more effective than an argument that presents both sides? The answer depends on the audience. If the audience either knows very little about the issue or already holds a strong position with respect to it, one-sided arguments tend to be more effective. If the audience is well informed about the issue, however, a two-sided argument tends to be more persuasive (McAlister et al., 1980).

How effective is the use of scare tactics in persuasive messages? This question was addressed when a program called Scared Straight was implemented in New Jersey in an effort to persuade youthful offenders to abandon their delinquent lifestyles. The program entailed an afternoon visit to Rahway State Prison and a distressing, intimidating encounter with selected prison inmates. Although the program initially appeared successful, the majority of the offenders exposed to the program eventually returned to delinquent activities (Hagan, 1982). Other research has shown that scare tactics may be effective in bringing about change, but only when combined with instructive information about how to change behavior (Gleicher & Petty, 1992). Also, messages are most effective in changing attitudes when they contain both affective and cognitive components.

The **elaboration likelihood model** offers an explanation of how attitudes may be changed through persuasion (Cacioppo, Petty, & Crites, 1993; Petty & Wegener, 1999; Petty, Wheeler, & Tormala, 2003). (See **Figure 15·2**.) According to this model, persuasion can take either a *central* or a *peripheral* route. The central route requires a person to think critically

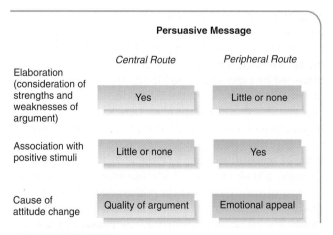

FIGURE 15·2 The elaboration likelihood model of attitude change. Persuasive messages may center either on a substantive argument that requires an individual to think critically about its strengths and weaknesses (the central route) or on a superficial association with positive stimuli (the peripheral route).

about the argument or arguments being presented, to weigh their relative strengths and weaknesses, and to elaborate on the relevant themes. At issue is the actual substance of the argument, not its emotional appeal. The peripheral route, on the other hand, involves attempts at persuasion in which the desired attitudinal change is specifically associated with positive stimuli—a professional athlete, a billionaire, an attractive model—that actually may have nothing to do with the substance of the argument. Sales pitches that associate products with attractive people or imply that buying the product will result in emotional, social, or financial benefits are examples of the use of peripheral techniques to change attitudes.

Cognitive Dissonance

Although we usually assume that our attitudes cause our behavior, behavior also affects attitudes. Two major theories attempt to explain the effects of behavior on attitude formation and attitude change. The earlier theory is **cognitive dissonance theory**, developed by Leon Festinger (1957). According to this theory, when we experience a discrepancy between an attitude and a behavior, between a behavior and our self-image, or between two attitudes, an aversive state of tension called *dissonance* results. For example, a person may believe that he has overcome his racial prejudices only to find himself disapproving of a racially mixed couple he sees in a shop. According to cognitive dissonance theory, the person should experience tension between his belief in his own lack of prejudice and the simultaneous evidence of prejudice from his reaction to the couple. McGregor, Newby-Clark, and Zanna (1999) argue that this simultaneity maximizes the degree of dissonance we feel. To some extent, we must be focused on the discrepancy for the aversiveness of dissonance to be experienced.

In Festinger's view, *dissonance reduction* can be a powerful motive. A person can achieve dissonance reduction by *(a)* reducing the importance of one of the dissonant elements, *(b)* adding consonant elements, or *(c)* changing one of the dissonant elements.

Suppose that a student believes he is very intelligent, but he receives a failing grade in an important course. Because the obvious expectation is that an intelligent person will get good grades, the discrepancy causes the student to experience dissonance. To reduce this dissonance, he may decide that grades are not important or that intelligence is not very closely related to grades. He is using strategy *a,* reducing the importance of one of the dissonant elements. Or he can dwell on the belief that his professor was unfair or that his job left him little time to study for the exam. In this case, he is using strategy *b,* reducing dissonance by adding consonant elements—factors that can account for his poor performance and hence explain the discrepancy between his perceived intelligence and grades. Finally, he can use strategy *c* to change one of the dissonant elements: He can either start getting good grades in the course or revise his opinion of his own intelligence.

Justification Cognitive dissonance theoretically occurs when a person's behavior is inconsistent with his or her attitudes. But the degree of dissonance a person experiences will depend on whether other factors can justify one of the dissonant elements. Being paid handsomely for doing something you dislike can justify your behavior and, on balance, reduce the dissonance between doing one thing and believing another. Being paid a very small amount, on the other hand, may not justify your behavior and can leave you with considerable cognitive dissonance. For example, an executive of a commercial television network may know that the programs she produces are sleazy, mindless drivel, but she is so well paid that she experiences little or no dissonance. Her high salary justifies her job and the programs she creates, making the inconsistency between her evaluation of the programs and her continued creation of them tolerable. But consider a poorly paid vacuum cleaner salesperson who constantly tells prospective customers that the merchandise he knows to be shoddy is actually marvelous. The absence of a strong financial incentive leaves room for a great deal of dissonance produced by the inconsistency between the salesperson's verbal behavior (saying the merchandise is great) and his attitude (that the merchandise is crummy). One way for the salesperson to reduce the dissonance is to change his attitude: to believe that the merchandise really is as good as he says. The other option is to quit his job and thus end the lying.

In a classic experiment, Festinger and Carlsmith (1959) tested the effects of justification on the strength of cognitive dissonance and resultant attitude change. These researchers had college students perform very boring tasks, such as putting spools on a tray, dumping them out, putting them on the tray again, dumping them out again, and so on. After the students had spent an hour in this type of activity, the researchers asked each student in two experimental conditions whether he or she would help out by trying to convince the next participant, who was waiting outside the room, that the boring tasks actually were enjoyable. Some students were offered the paltry sum of $1 for lying to the next participant (a very low justification for saying the tasks were enjoyable); others were offered $20 for doing so (a very high justification, in 1959 dollars, for lying). The next "participant" was actually a paid confederate of the researchers who listened attentively to the real participants' claims about how interesting the tasks were. Following this phase of the experiment, the researcher paid the participants the agreed-on amount. No mention of deceiving another participant or of payment was made to the participants in a third, control condition.

At the end of the experiment, all participants were asked to rate how much they, in truth, had enjoyed the activity they had engaged in. Festinger and Carlsmith predicted that those who were paid only $1 would consider the activity relatively interesting. Because they had been induced to praise the activity to another person without a sufficient justification, they should have experienced strong cognitive dissonance: Their original attitude about the activity and their oral behavior were inconsistent. Because the participants could not take back their oral behavior, the only thing left to change was their attitude toward the activity. The well-paid participants, on the other hand, had a perfect justification for their oral behavior and should not have experienced much cognitive dissonance.

As predicted, the poorly paid participants did in fact rate the activity as more enjoyable than did those who were well paid. You can see in **Figure 15•3.** that being paid a lot left people with about the same attitude toward the boring activity as existed among participants in the control condition—who experienced no dissonance because they never told anyone the tasks were enjoyable.

Arousal and Attitude Change Festinger hypothesized that dissonance reduction is motivated by an aversive drive; that is, by a strong inclination to remove the unpleasant tension. A study by Croyle and Cooper (1983) produced physiological evidence to support this hypothesis. These researchers studied college students who *disagreed* with the assertion that alcohol should be banned at campus clubs and eating establishments. Each student was induced to write an essay containing strong arguments either in favor of the assertion or in opposition to it. While the participants were writing the essay, the researchers measured the electrical conductance of their skin, which, as noted in Chapter 13, is a good indicator of the physiological arousal that accompanies stress. Some participants were instructed to write the essay in a way that led them to believe that they had no choice but to do so. Other participants were told that their participation was completely voluntary and that they were free to leave at any time; they even signed a form emphasizing the voluntary nature of the task. Those in the first group should have perceived sufficient justification for the content of their essays, because they were following the researcher's imperative. They would thus be expected to experience less dissonance than those who believed that they had exercised a free choice in deciding to participate.

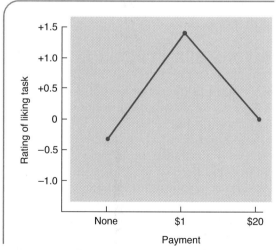

FIGURE 15•3 Effects of induced compliance on justification. People who received $1 to lie about a boring task later indicated that they liked the task more than did people who received $20 or people in the control group.

(Based on data from Festinger, L., & Carlsmith, J. M. (1959). Cognitive consequences of forced compliance. *Journal of Abnormal and Social Psychology, 58,* 203–210.)

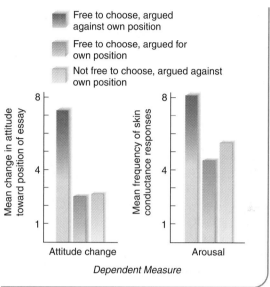

FIGURE 15•4 Physiological evidence for cognitive dissonance. Graphed here are mean changes in attitude toward the position advocated by the essay and mean frequency of skin conductance responses (a physiological index of arousal) in people who argued for or against their own positions.

(Based on data from Croyle, R. T., & Cooper, J. (1983). Dissonance arousal: Physical evidence. *Journal of Personality and Social Psychology, 45,* 782–791.)

Students in the "voluntary" group who wrote essays contradicting their original opinions showed both a change in attitude and evidence of physiological arousal. In contrast, those who were told to write the essay or who wrote arguments that they had originally agreed with showed little sign of either arousal or attitude change. (See **Figure 15•4.**)

Attitudes and Expenditures Festinger's theory of cognitive dissonance accounts for another relation between behavior and attitudes; namely, our tendency to value something more if it costs us time, effort, or other resources such as money. For example, some people buy extremely expensive brands of cosmetics even though the same ingredients are used in much cheaper brands. Presumably, they believe that if an item costs more, it must be better. Following the same rationale, animal shelters often sell their stray animals to prospective pet owners, not only because the money helps defray their operating costs, but also because they believe that a purchased pet will be valued more and treated better than a free pet.

Self-Perception

A second major theory concerning the relationship between behavior and attitudes is *self-perception theory*. Daryl Bem (1972) defined **self-perception theory** in the following way:

Individuals come to "know" their own attitudes, emotions, and other internal states partially by inferring them from observations of their own overt behavior and/or the circumstances in which this behavior occurs. Thus, to the extent that internal cues are weak, ambiguous, or uninterpretable, the individual is functionally in the same position as an outside observer, an observer who must necessarily rely on those same external cues to infer the individual's inner states. (Bem, 1972, p. 2)

In other words, an observer who attempts to make judgments about someone's attitudes, emotions, or other internal states necessarily must examine the person's behavior for clues. For example, if you cannot ask someone why he or she is doing something, you must analyze the situation in which the behavior occurs to try to determine the motivation. Bem suggested that people analyze their own internal states in a similar way, making attributions about the causes of their own behavior.

Think about how Bem would explain Festinger and Carlsmith's results in which students who were paid only $1 later rated a boring activity as more interesting than did those who were paid $20. Suppose that an observer watches a person who has been paid $1 to deliver a convincing speech about how interesting a dull activity was. Because being paid such a small sum is not an acceptable reason for calling a dull activity interesting, the observer will probably conclude that the speaker actually enjoyed it. Lacking good evidence for situational attributions, the observer will attribute the behavior to a dispositional factor—genuine interest in the activity. Bem argued that in this instance the speaker would make the same inference about himself or herself: "I wasn't paid enough to justify lying, so I must have enjoyed the activity." The principal advantage of self-perception theory is that it makes fewer assumptions than does dissonance theory. It does not postulate a motivating aversive-drive state. Perhaps self-perception and cognitive dissonance occur under different situations, producing attitude changes for different reasons. Further evidence will be needed to determine whether the two theories are competing or complementary (see also Wegner, 2002, on this issue).

Interim Summary

Attitudes: Their Formation and Change

Attitudes have affective components; behavioral components, which are affected by specificity, motivational relevance, accessibility, and constraints and are primarily formed through direct or vicarious classical conditioning; and cognitive components.

Explicit attempts to change our attitudes often involve persuasion. We tend to be persuaded by arguments that have a credible source, such as an expert on a particular topic, or an attractive source, such as a celebrity. Aspects of the message being delivered in a persuasive appeal also are important. If we know little about an issue or hold a strong opinion about it, then we are likely to be persuaded by a one-sided argument. However, if we are already well informed about the issue, then we are likely to find a two-sided argument more persuasive. Scare tactics appear to work best when they include information that is instructive (that is, that explains how to change behavior) as well as emotional. According to the elaboration likelihood model, persuasive messages follow a central route, a peripheral route, or both.

Festinger's theory of cognitive dissonance suggests reasons for interactions between attitudes and behavior. It proposes that discrepancies between attitudes and behavior, or between one attitude and another, lead to the unpleasant state of cognitive dissonance. We can reduce dissonance by reducing the importance of dissonant elements, adding consonant elements, or changing one of the dissonant elements.

Bem's alternative to cognitive dissonance—self-perception theory—suggests that many of our attitudes are based on self-observation. When our attitudes are ambiguous, we look to the situation for motivational clues.

QUESTIONS TO CONSIDER

1. Attitudes have sometimes been described as "predispositions to act." What does this phrase mean? Does the phrase accurately describe attitudes? Why or why not?

2. What kinds of arguments would be effective in persuading you to change your attitude toward a prominent political figure? Would they follow a central route, a peripheral route, or both? How would they do so?

3. Have you ever experienced cognitive dissonance? If so, what factors made you feel this way, and how did you eventually reduce the dissonance?

Stereotypes and Prejudice

A **prejudice** is a particular form of attitude. The dictionary defines prejudice as a preconceived opinion, a bias, or a partiality toward a person or group, which may be favorable or unfavorable. However, people usually use the term to refer to an unfavorable bias, and that's the sort of prejudice we're concerned with in this section: a negative evaluation of a group of people who are defined by their racial, ethnic, or religious heritage or by their gender, language, occupation, sexual orientation, level of education, or place of residence. A prejudice (literally, a "prejudgment") is essentially a heuristic by which we may focus on a few salient features of a person (such as skin color, accent, family name, or manner of dressing) and assume that the person also possesses other, mainly negative, characteristics. In this way a prejudice is an insidious example of the representativeness heuristic.

Stereotypes contribute to prejudice. In fact, the meanings of the two terms overlap. But strictly speaking, a prejudice is a negative evaluation of a particular group, whereas a **stereotype** is essentially an overgeneralized, and therefore potentially false, schema for the characteristics of the group. (Although some stereotypes are positive, we usually think of them as negative.) Many of the regional cultural differences in the United States, for example, are subject to stereotyping. Although a given stereotype may be true in a specific instance, stereotyping generalizes characteristics to entire groups of people and thus overgeneralizes. The error of thinking in terms of stereotypes lies in the failure to consider individual differences. The same is true of prejudices.

Sometimes people use stereotypes to exert control over others and to justify maintaining them in their present social condition (Fiske, 1993). For example, a male employer who holds a stereotype of women as "followers" rather than "leaders" effectively ensures that the women in his employ will not be promoted to management positions.

Prejudice often leads to discrimination. In other contexts, *to discriminate* can mean simply "to distinguish." In the present social context, however, the word **discrimination** refers to behaviors, not to attitudes; it means treating people differently because of their membership in a particular group (Dion, 2003). Thus, we can discriminate favorably or unfavorably according to our attitudes. Prejudice occurs any time members in one group, referred to as the *in-group*, exhibit negative attitudes toward members of another group, called the *out-group*. Discrimination occurs any time members of the in-group display behavior intended to prevent members of the out-group from getting something, such as a vote, a job, an education, or a home in a particular neighborhood.

At the level of nations, prejudice, stereotypes, and discrimination give rise to **ethnocentrism**—the notion that our own cultural, national, racial, or religious group is superior to or more deserving than others. Ethnocentric attitudes and behaviors often cause conflict in the form of war, terrorism, or other forms of violent confrontation.

The Origins of Prejudice

Unfortunately, prejudice seems to be an enduring characteristic of the human species. It exists in every realm, from education, business, and athletics to politics and religion. History has shown that even groups of people who have been oppressed, if they manage to overthrow their oppressors, go on to commit their own version of ethnocentric exploitation. Why is prejudice such a widespread trait?

The Role of Competition in Prejudice Affiliation and prejudice are two sides of the same coin. That is, along with the tendency to identify with and feel close to members of our own group or clan, there is the tendency to be suspicious of others. A classic experiment by Muzafer Sherif and colleagues (1961) demonstrated just how easily intergroup mistrust and conflict can arise. The study took place at a remote summer camp. The participants, 11-year-old boys, were arbitrarily as-

signed to one of two cabins. The two groups were initially isolated from each other. During the first week the boys in each cabin spent their time together as a group, fishing, hiking, swimming, and otherwise enjoying themselves. The boys formed two cohesive groups and named themselves the Rattlers and the Eagles. They became attached to their groups and strongly identified with them.

Next, the researchers sowed the seeds of dissension. They set up a series of competitive events between the two groups. The best team would win a trophy and individual prizes for its members. As the competition progressed, the teams began taunting and insulting each other. Then the Eagles burned the Rattlers' flag, and in retaliation the Rattlers broke into the Eagles' cabin and scattered or stole their belongings. Although further physical conflict was prevented by the researchers, the two groups continued to abuse each other verbally and seemed to have developed a genuine mutual hatred.

Finally, the researchers arranged for the boys to work together. The researchers sabotaged the water supply for the camp and had the boys fix it. They also arranged for the boys to repair a truck that had broken down, and they induced them to pool their money in order to rent a movie. The boys' joint efforts on cooperative rather than competitive ventures brought a reduction in intergroup conflicts.

The Role of Self-Esteem in Prejudice Most social psychologists believe that competition is an important factor in the development of prejudice. The competition need not be for tangible goods; it can be motivated by a desire for social superiority. People's tendency to perceive their own group (the in-group) as superior and that of others (the out-group) as inferior may be based on their need to enhance their self-esteem. Thus, people who belong to groups that preach racial hatred tend to be those whose own social status is rather low.

▲ *Members of in-groups often demonstrate similarities that distinguish them from members of out-groups.*

An experiment performed with members of ethnic groups supports this conclusion. Meindl and Lerner (1985) exposed English-speaking participants to a situation designed to threaten their self-esteem. The participants were asked to walk across a room to get a chair. For those in the experimental group, the chair was rigged so that a pile of old-style computer data cards would be knocked over and scattered on the floor. In a situation like this, most people feel clumsy and foolish—and a bit guilty about making trouble for the person who has to put the cards back in order. After this experience, the participants were asked about their attitudes toward the French-speaking individuals. Participants in the experimental group, who had toppled the cards, rated the "others" more negatively than did those in a control group, who had not toppled the cards in retrieving the chair. The researchers reasoned that by viewing the the French-speakers as members of a group inferior to their own, the participants partially compensated for their temporary loss of self-esteem. Of course, levels of self-esteem have been shown to vary from culture to culture (e.g., Feather & McKee, 1993). Thus, the effects found by Meindl and Lerner (1985) might not generalize to more interdependent or collectivist societies, for example.

The Role of Social Cognition in Prejudice   Research on social cognition has provided further information about the origins of prejudice. As noted earlier, when we use heuristics, we sometimes make errors of judgment. We've also seen that stereotypes are overgeneralized, usually negative schemas for the characteristics of an out-group. Stereotypes are convenient, because they provide a way for us to classify others quickly. Doing so is seductive: Making a general point about a group is often easier to state and cognitively easier, than dealing with the actual complexities of a problem we are trying to explain (Macrae, Milne, & Bodenhausen, 1994). For example, attributing slow traffic movement to older drivers as a group is easier than analyzing the truly complex effects of roadway engineering, traffic flow patterns, and differences among all people in driving skills. The problem is that stereotypes are usually false in their application to all members of the out-group.

In many cases people first learn stereotypes through communications with family members, friends, and acquaintances. Research also has shown that stereotypical information becomes more and more stereotypical as it passes from one person to another (Ruscher, 1998). The mass media are a prominent source of stereotypes. Thompson, Judd, and Park (2000) found that stereotypes tend to be more extreme when acquired through such sources than through direct contact with the out-group. Also, when members of ethnic or regional groups are portrayed in movies or television shows as having criminal tendencies, as having low-status jobs, as being prone to substance abuse, or as being rather comic and stupid, people may acquire stereotypes without being aware of it. Stereotyped beliefs are unlikely to be examined closely and changed to reflect reality. Even when faced with contradictory evidence, people seem to resist changing their stereo-

types. For example, Kunda and Oleson (1997) gave participants information that challenged their stereotypes and found that they maintained the original stereotypes by creating special subcategories for the "exceptions that proved the rule." Other work suggests that people use stereotypes selectively to support and maintain desired impressions of others (Kunda & Sinclair, 1999).

The availability heuristic, as we saw earlier, involves the use of distinctive, easily recalled material in decision making. This phenomenon probably explains why Americans typically overestimate both the rate of violent crime and the relative numbers of violent crimes committed by members of minority groups. Violent acts certainly are distinctive events, and minority group members often are conspicuously depicted in the media. Both the crimes and the minorities stand out; as a result, they may be perceived as causally related. This perception is an example of an **illusory correlation**—an apparent relation between two distinctive elements that does not actually exist (see Spears & Haslam, 1997).

Another fallacy that promotes the formation and maintenance of stereotypes is the **illusion of out-group homogeneity:** People tend to assume that members of out-groups are more similar than are members of their in-group (Ostrom & Sedikides, 1992). For example, men tend to perceive women as being more alike than men are, and women do the opposite (Park & Rothbart, 1982). The same is true for young people and old people (Linville, Fischer, & Salovey, 1989). Most of us resist being stereotyped but nevertheless engage stereotypes when thinking about members of other groups.

The Role of Evolution in Prejudice   Finally, a very different explanation of in-group biases toward out-groups (including prejudice, stereotypes, and discrimination) has been devised by Krebs and Denton (1997). These authors propose that cognitive structures that are biased in favor of the in-group, and against out-groups, were selected in the course of early human evolution because those structures had adaptive value.

The basic argument will be familiar to you by now. Early humans are usually characterized as living in small cooperative groups that were in competition with one another for scarce resources. An ability to make rough-and-ready characterizations of others as belonging to someone's own group or to another group presumably would facilitate both in-group cooperation and competitive effectiveness against out-groups. A positive bias toward members of the in-group would contribute to cohesiveness. A negative bias against other groups would motivate in-group members to keep out-groups under close scrutiny in order to detect dangers to themselves.

Krebs and Denton (1997) point out that in modern life these once-adaptive biases can produce difficulties by perpetuating conflict even though cooperative solutions are now possible. Moreover, our contemporary sense of humanity and justice is offended when people engage in undeserved negative evaluation and treatment of others simply because they belong to other groups.

Research using the Implicit Association Test (Greenwald, McGhee, & Schwartz, 1998) has revealed the existence of ethnic biases of which individuals are otherwise unaware (see Greenwald, Nosek, & Banaji, 2003). Though study participants profess to be free of such prejudices, the test results indicate otherwise. Such findings may be seen to support the existence of the deeply ingrained biases suggested by evolutionary psychologists. Moreover, they suggest the possibility that these biases may be difficult to eliminate entirely (but see Dasgupta & Greenwald, 2001, for a more hopeful appraisal

Self-Fulfilling Prophecies

We encountered self-fulfilling prophecies in the discussion of intelligence testing in Chapter 11. In the context of stereotyping and prejudice, a **self-fulfilling prophecy** begins when a person holds stereotypes of what other people are like. The person then acts in a manner consistent with the stereotypes. The behavior of the individuals whom the stereotypes describe then tends to confirm them.

A memorable example of the self-fulfilling prophecy was demonstrated in an experiment by Snyder, Tanke, and Berscheid (1977). The researchers asked male participants to engage in telephone conversations with female participants. Just before each conversation took place, each male participant was shown a photograph of the young woman to whom he would talk. In fact, the photographs were not those of participants but rather were images of other women, some attractive and some unattractive, that the researchers had selected. The conversations that took place were recorded, and the voices of the female participants were played to independent observers, who rated their impressions of the young women.

Based on the vocal characteristics of the female participants and what they said, the independent observers rated the women whose male conversation partners believed them to be attractive as being more friendly, likable, and sociable than those whose partners believed them to be unattractive. Obviously, the male participants talked differently to women they thought were attractive or unattractive. Their words had either a positive or negative effect on the women, a difference that could be detected by the independent observers.

Hope for Change

Prejudices are maintained because they can justify exploitation of the out-group by the in-group. If the out-group can be portrayed as "stupid," "dependent," or "irresponsible," the in-group can justify the exploitation of the out-group as being in the out-group's own best interest—or at least can conclude that its treatment of the out-group is the best that the out-group can reasonably expect. When exploitative practices lead to material advantages in the form of cheap labor or unequal access to resources, the prejudices will tend to persist.

Change in this pattern may be possible, however. Many instances of personal prejudice may be inadvertent; as noted earlier, people may be unaware of their stereotypes and prejudices. But if people can be made aware of their prejudices, they may be persuaded (though with difficulty) that their attitudes are unjustified. It may be possible to teach people to become more reflective, to take time to analyze their biases. For example, Langer, Bashner, and Chanowitz (1985) gave a group of sixth-grade children specific training in thinking about the problems of people with disabilities. The children were asked to think about the way in which a person with disabilities might drive a car or about the reasons a blind person might make a good newscaster. After this training, the children were more willing to go on a picnic with a person with disabilities than were children who did not receive the training. They were also more likely to perceive the specific consequences of particular disabilities than to view people with disabilities as uniformly "less fit." Thus, at the individual level, it may be possible for people to learn to recognize their prejudices and to take steps to overcome them.

Interim Summary

Stereotypes and Prejudice

A prejudice is a negative evaluation of a group of people defined by such characteristics as race, ethnicity, religion, gender, socioeconomic status, or sexual orientation. An important component of prejudice is the existence of stereotypes that include false beliefs about the characteristics possessed by members of a particular group. Prejudices often lead to discrimination—actual behaviors injurious to the members of the group. Intergroup conflicts often have at their core the belief that individuals' own group (the in-group) is superior to or more deserving than another group (the out-group).

One of the primary causes of prejudice appears to be competition between groups for limited resources and the increased self-esteem that results from affiliating with a group perceived to be better than other groups. The study at the boys' camp by Sherif and his colleagues indicates just how easily prejudices can form, even when the groups consist of similar individuals.

Heuristics guide our social encounters. One reason we tend to view out-group members negatively is our use of the availability heuristic: Negative behaviors often are more vivid than positive behaviors, and out-group members are especially noticeable. Thus, when out-group members commit a deviant act, we are more likely to notice it and to remember it. We then incorrectly conclude that such behavior is a characteristic of the out-group as a whole. Such a conclusion is referred to as an illusory correlation.

People also are susceptible to the illusion of out-group homogeneity. Although they realize that their in-group contains members who are very different from one another, they tend to view members of out-groups as similar to one another.

Some social psychologists suggest an evolutionary explanation of in-group and out-group biases. They propose that earlier in human evolution competitive needs favored the development of cognitive structures that quickly (and unconsciously) categorized in-group and out-group members. Research with the Implicit Association Test has confirmed the existence of prejudices of which individuals are unaware.

Prejudices have many harmful effects, such as the self-fulfilling prophecy, in which being perceived and treated as inferior leads the victim of prejudice to act that way. Although many instances of prejudice may be inadvertent, when people are taught to think about members of out-groups as individuals having specific characteristics, they can learn to avoid injurious conduct toward an out-group.

QUESTIONS TO CONSIDER

1. Think about a prejudice that you have. (It could be toward a place or a thing; it doesn't have to be directed toward a particular group of people.) What factors have caused this prejudice? To what extent are stereotypes involved in it?
2. How different are the members of your family compared to those of another family that you know? Describe how the illusion of out-group homogeneity may or may not apply in this instance.

Social Influences and Group Behavior

A **group** is a collection of individuals who generally have common interests and goals. For example, the members of the American Association of Retired Persons (AARP) have a different set of interests and goals than do members of the American Cancer Society, although some of their interests and goals may overlap. The behaviors, emotions, and cognitions that define each of us as an individual are strongly influenced, often without our awareness, by those with whom we interact. Frequently this influence is unintentional: Other people may be equally unaware of how they are influencing us. At other times this influence is intentional and is designed to manipulate us in some way (Santos, Leve, & Pratkanis, 1994). In this section we'll examine various means by which we influence, and are influenced by, others.

Conformity

The most powerful social influence on our attitudes and behavior may well be the behavior of other people. If we see people act in a particular way, we may imitate them. Sometimes we observe that people are not performing a particular behavior, and so we refrain from performing it. In other words, we *conform* to what others are doing. Changing our attitudes or behavior to be similar to those of a social group is called **conformity**. Let's consider why conformity occurs and look at the dangers posed by this very human tendency.

Social Norms   Although most of us cherish our independence and like to think that we do what we do because we want to do it, none of us is immune to social influences. Moreover, most instances of conformity benefit us all. In fact, many of the rules that govern our social behavior are formally codified as laws that we are legally obligated to follow. Many other conventions that influence our behavior, however, are not formal laws but are instead unwritten. These informal rules that define the expected and appropriate behavior in specific situations are called **social norms,** or, when applied to members of a particular group, *group norms.* How we look at strangers, the way we talk to our friends or to our supervisors at work, and the kinds of food that we eat all are influenced by the norms of the society in which we live. Despite the fact that they are not spelled out in formal or legal documents, norms are very powerful sources of social influence.

▲ *Our manner of dress and grooming often reflects the prevailing norms of the group or groups with which we most strongly identify ourselves.*

A study by Sherif (1936) demonstrated the power of social influence in establishing group norms. Sherif's study was based on a perceptual illusion, originally discovered by astronomers, called the *autokinetic effect:* A small stationary light, when projected on a screen in an otherwise completely darkened room, appears to move. The illusion is so strong that even if someone is aware of the effect, the apparent movement often still persists.

Sherif first placed people in the room individually and asked each of them how far the light was moving at different times. The answers were quite variable; one person might see the light move three inches on average, while another might see it move a couple of feet. Next, Sherif asked groups of three participants to observe the light together and make joint decisions about the extent of the movement. Finally, all of the participants again observed the light individually. The most interesting result of the study was that after participants had taken part in the group decision, their individual judgments tended to resemble those that the group had made. That is, the groups of three had established what Sherif called a *collective frame of reference.* Even when tested by themselves on a different day, the group members still conformed to the frame of reference each group had previously established.

Sherif's findings are not all that surprising if we consider that the participants found themselves in an uncertain situation. When you are not sure what is going on, it makes sense to use others' opinions or judgments as a guide. But just how strongly do group norms influence our individual behavior when the situation is unambiguous—when we are certain that we perceive things as they really are? An answer to this question was provided in a series of elegant studies conducted by Asch (1951, 1952, 1955).

Several groups of seven to nine college students were asked to estimate the lengths of vertical lines presented on a poster. A sample line was shown at the left, and the students were to choose which of the three lines to the right matched it. (See **Figure 15•5**.) The participants gave their answers orally.

In fact, there was only one real student in each group; all other participants were confederates of the researcher. The

seating was arranged so that the real student answered last. Under some conditions, the confederates made incorrect responses. When they made incorrect responses on at least 6 of the 12 trials in an experiment, 76 percent of the students went along with the group on at least one trial. Under control conditions, when the confederates responded accurately, only 5 percent of the participants made an error.

Group pressure did not affect the students' perceptions; it affected their behavior. That is, they went along with the group decision even though the choice still looked wrong to them—and even though the other people were complete strangers. When the students were questioned later, they said that they had started doubting their own eyesight or had thought that perhaps they had misunderstood the instructions. The students who did not conform felt uncomfortable about disagreeing with the other members of the group. Asch's results show how strong the tendency to conform can be.

Two of the most important reasons why people conform so readily to social norms are the desire to be liked and the desire to be right (Baron, Vandello, & Brunsman, 1996; Cialdini & Goldstein, 2004). As we will see later, people tend to like other people who are similar to themselves, especially those who act like them and share their attitudes and beliefs. Because most of us prefer to be liked, we tend to conform to the norms or expectations of others. In addition, most of us prefer to be right rather than wrong.

Bystander Intervention Conformity can sometimes have disastrous consequences. In New York City in 1964, a woman named Kitty Genovese was robbed and repeatedly stabbed by an assailant, who took 35 minutes to finally kill her. The woman's screams went unheeded by 38 eyewitnesses, who watched from behind their apartment windows. No one tried to stop the attacker; no one even made an anonymous telephone call to the police until after the attacker had left. When the eyewitnesses were questioned later, they could not explain their inaction.

As you can imagine, people were appalled and shocked by the eyewitnesses' response to the Genovese murder. Media commentators concluded from the apparent indifference of the eyewitnesses that society, especially in urban areas, had become cold and apathetic. But interviews with the eyewitnesses suggested otherwise. They were not uncaring. They were distressed and confused by what happened and by their failure to intervene.

Experiments performed by social psychologists suggest that the apathy explanation is wrong—people in cities are not generally indifferent to the needs of other people. The fact that Kitty Genovese's attack went unreported is not remarkable because 38 eyewitnesses were present; instead, it is precisely *because* so many eyewitnesses were present that it went unreported.

John Darley and Bibb Latané ("lat-an-AY") studied the phenomenon of **bystander intervention**—the actions (or inaction) of people who witness a situation in which someone appears to require assistance. Their experiments showed

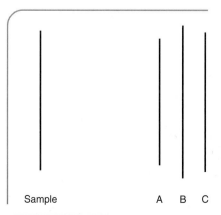

FIGURE 15•5 An example of the stimuli used by Asch (1951).

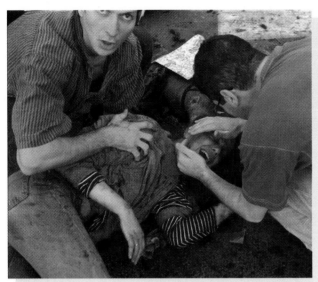

▲ *Not all bystanders are indifferent to the plight of people in danger. Two men administer aid to the victim of a terrorist attack.*

that in such situations, the presence of people who are doing nothing inhibits others from giving aid. For example, Darley and Latané (1968) staged an "emergency" during a psychology experiment with college students. Each participant took part in a discussion about personal problems associated with university life. The discussions included one, two, or five other people, who talked by means of an intercom. The researcher explained that the participants would sit in individual rooms so that they would be anonymous and hence more likely to speak frankly. The researcher would not listen in but would learn the participants' reactions to the conversation later in a questionnaire. Actually, only one real student was present; the other voices were tape recordings. During the discussion one "participant" who had previously mentioned that he sometimes had seizures apparently did experience a seizure. His speech became incoherent, and he stammered out a request for help.

Almost all participants left the room to help the victim when they were the only witness to the seizure. When the group was larger, however, the true participants were much less likely to help. In addition, those who did try to help reacted more slowly if they believed that other people were present. (See **Figure 15•6**.) This finding has been replicated in dozens of experiments. When people are alone and an emergency occurs, they are very responsible, not apathetic.

Darley and Latané reported that the students who did not respond were not indifferent to the plight of their fellow student. Indeed, when the researcher entered the room, they usually appeared nervous and emotionally aroused, and they asked whether someone was helping the victim. The researchers concluded that the students were still in conflict, trying to decide whether they should do something.

Thus, it seems that whether bystanders will intervene in an emergency depends, at least in part, on how they perceive the situation and on whether they witness the event alone or in the presence of others. Latané and Darley (1970) proposed a model describing a sequence of steps bystanders face when confronted with a potential emergency:

They must notice and correctly interpret the event.

They must assume responsibility for helping the victim.

They must consider the possible courses of action and conclude that the costs of intervening are not prohibitively high.

Finally, they must actually implement the chosen course of action.

Of course, this sequence takes place rapidly and without much awareness on the bystander's part, much like other situations to which we respond each day.

Unfortunately, at least from the perspective of the victim, obstacles may arise at any stage in this decision-making process that make it unlikely that a bystander will intervene. In many cases a bystander who is aware that others are available to help may not feel sufficient personal responsibility to do so. This phenomenon, called **diffusion of responsibility,** is considered to be responsible for the finding that people are less likely to offer help when there are several bystanders present. In addition, a bystander may not feel competent to intervene or may be fearful of doing so; consequently, the person may take no action in the belief that he or she will worsen the situation or that someone else is more competent

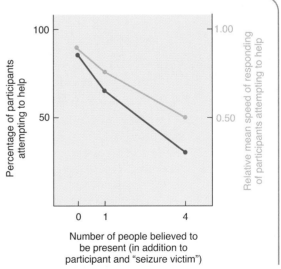

FIGURE 15•6 Bystander intervention and diffusion of responsibility. The percentage of participants attempting to help is a function of the number of other people the participant believes to be present.

(Based on data from Darley, J. M., & Latané, B. (1968). Bystander intervention in emergencies: Diffusion of responsibility. *Journal of Personality and Social Psychology, 8,* 377–383.)

to act. For example, Shotland and Heinold (1985) staged an accident in which a person seemed to be bleeding. Bystanders who had received formal training in first aid were much more likely to come to the victim's aid, and they did so whether or not other bystanders were present. Because they knew how to recognize an emergency and knew what to do, they were less likely to fear doing the wrong thing and did not need to rely on others.

Social Facilitation

Even the mere presence of other people can affect a person's behavior. Triplett (1898) published the first experimental study of **social facilitation**—the enhancement of a person's performance by the presence of other people. Triplett asked people to perform simple tasks, such as turning the crank of a fishing reel. He found that his participants turned the crank faster and for a longer time if other people were present. Although many other studies found the same effect, some investigators reported just the opposite phenomenon: If the task was difficult and complex, the presence of an audience impaired participants' performance.

Zajonc (1965) has offered an explanation of these different effects of social facilitation. In his view, the presence of people who are watching a performer (or of people whom the performer perceives as watching) raises the performer's arousal level. Presumably, the increase in arousal has the effect of increasing the probability that the individual will perform dominant responses—the responses that are most likely to occur in a particular situation. When the task is simple, the dominant response is generally the correct response, so an audience improves performance. When the task is complex, however, a person can perform many different responses and must decide which behavior is appropriate. The presence of the audience makes the selection of the appropriate behavior more difficult, because the increased arousal tends to cause the person to perform the dominant response, which may not be correct under the circumstances.

Subsequent experiments have supported Zajonc's explanation. For example, Martens (1969) tested the prediction that the presence of a group increases a person's level of arousal. While participants performed a complex motor task either alone or in the presence of 10 people, the researcher determined physiological arousal by measuring the amount of sweat present on the participants' palms. The result: Those who performed in front of other people had sweatier palms.

Such arousal may contribute to costly mistakes. For example, in a study of residential burglars, Cromwell, Marks, Olson, and Avery (1991) found that burglars who worked in groups were five times more likely to get caught than burglars who worked alone. The researchers argued that burglary is a complex task that cannot be "well learned," because each burglary is different. The complexity of the burglary, combined with high levels of arousal produced by the group's presence, may have contributed to errors in planning and execution of the crimes.

Social Loafing

In still another form of social influence, the presence of a group sometimes results in diminished effort, or **social loafing**. In an early study, Ringelmann (cited by Dashiell, 1935) measured the effort that people made when pulling a rope in a mock tug-of-war contest against a device that measured the exerted force. Presumably, the force exerted by eight people pulling together would be at least the sum of their individual efforts when each was tested alone—or even somewhat greater than that sum, because of social facilitation. However, Ringelmann found that the total force exerted by eight people was only about half of what would have been predicted by the simple combination of individual efforts. His participants exerted less force when they worked in a group.

More recent studies have confirmed these results and have extended them to other behaviors. This research indicates that several variables determine whether the presence of a group will produce social facilitation or social loafing.

One of the most important variables is *individual identifiability*. Williams, Harkins, and Latané (1981) asked people to shout as loud as they could individually or in groups. (Participants in the "group" condition could not see or hear the others.) People shouted less loudly in groups than they did individually when they believed that the recording equipment could measure only the total group effort. But when they were informed that the equipment would measure individual effort, people in groups shouted just as loudly as they did when alone. These results suggest that a person's efforts in a group activity are affected by whether his or her individual efforts can be observed by others. If they can, social facilitation is likely to occur; if they cannot, then social loafing is more likely.

Two additional variables that affect social loafing are *group cohesiveness* and *individual responsibility*. For example, Karau and Hart (1998) showed that groups that share a common position on an issue (and therefore are cohesive) do not exhibit social loafing. Noncohesive groups do show it, however. To examine social responsibility, Harkins and Petty (1982) tested the hypothesis that if a person's efforts are duplicated by those of another person (and if his or her individual efforts are not identifiable), the first person is likely to exert a less-than-maximum effort. The researchers asked people to work in groups of four on a task that required them to report whenever a dot appeared in a particular quadrant of a video screen. In one condition each person watched an individual quadrant and was solely responsible for detecting dots that appeared there. In the other condition all four participants watched the same quadrant; thus, the responsibility for detecting dots was shared. People did not loaf when they were solely responsible for their own quadrants.

Karau and Williams (1995) found that *gender and culture* also appear to moderate people's tendency to become social loafers. Although all people are susceptible to social loafing, the effect is smaller in women than in men and smaller in people living in Eastern cultures than in those living in Western cultures. According to Karau and Williams (1995), across cultures women tend to be more group oriented than men. Also, people of both genders living in Eastern cultures tend to be more group oriented in their attitudes and behavior than people of both genders living in Western cultures. So it seems that people living in Eastern cultures, and women in general, tend to place greater importance on participating in group activities, which partially buffers them from social loafing effects.

Commitment and Compliance

Another form of social influence is the impact of commitment on compliance. Once people commit themselves by making a decision and acting on it, they usually are reluctant to renounce their commitment. For example, have you ever joined one side of an argument on an issue that you do not really care about, only to find yourself vehemently defending a position that until then meant almost nothing to you? This phenomenon was demonstrated in a clever study by Knox and Inkster (1968). The researchers asked people at the betting windows of a racetrack how confident they were that their horses would win. They questioned half the people just before they had made their bets, the other half just afterwards. The people who had already made their bets were more confident than were those who had not yet paid. In other words, their commitment had increased the perceived likelihood of a specific outcome.

Compliance is engaging in a behavior at another person's request. And an experiment by Freedman and Fraser (1966) showed that commitment has a long-lasting effect on people's tendency to comply with requests. For example, suppose you answer a knock on your door to find a person who explains that he is a volunteer for Mothers Against Drunk Driving (MADD). He asks you to place a small sign in your front window to encourage responsible driving, and you agree to his request. Then, two weeks later, the same person returns and asks if you would allow volunteers from MADD to install a billboard on your front lawn. He shows you a photograph of an attractive house that is almost completely hidden by a huge, ugly, poorly lettered sign that says "DRIVE CAREFULLY." Do you think you would agree to this second request? Freedman and Fraser (1966) reported the powerful effects of just this type of approach. Three-fourths of their participants agreed to the second request! In contrast, in a control condition in which no initial small request was made, only 17 percent of participants agreed to have the billboard installed. Freedman and Fraser referred to the sequence of a small request followed by a large request as the *foot-in-the-door technique.*

Commitment increases people's compliance even when the reason for the original commitment is removed. For example, recall this chapter's opening vignette, in which I described my experience when negotiating the price of a new car. I made a commitment—I signed a formal offer to purchase the car at the proposed price and handed the salesperson a check to show my good-faith intention. However, when the salesperson returned, supposedly from talking with his manager, he said that he had made a mistake on the price and then quoted a new price many thousands of dollars higher. All too often, the customer is taken in by this ruse and agrees to the higher price. This technique is called *lowballing.*

Another tactic for using commitment to gain compliance is referred to as the *door-in-the-face technique* (Cialdini, 2000). In this case, instead of making a small initial request followed by a larger request (as in the billboard example), the would-be influencer deliberately starts with a large initial request. Now, most often it will be rejected. Once rejection occurs, it is followed by a smaller request, which is agreed to. For example, a teenager may initially ask a parent for $100 to take several friends out for pizza. Following the parent's stout refusal, the teenager follows up with "Well, how about ten dollars then?" In these circumstances the parent is much more likely to provide the money than if the teenager had asked for $10 at the outset.

Obedience to Authority

People tend to comply with the requests of people in authority and to be persuaded by their arguments. Society generally approves of obedience to authority when the authority figures are respected and trustworthy. And it is usually the case that authority figures are well intentioned. We are aware of exceptions to this generality, however, including the genocidal regimes of tyrants ancient and modern, perhaps most darkly illustrated by those who were "just following orders" during the Nazi regime in Germany.

A disturbing example of commonplace obedience to the illegitimate demands of an authority comes from a famous series of experiments performed by Stanley Milgram (1963). Milgram had recruited participants by advertising in local newspapers—a research strategy designed to obtain as representative a sample as possible. The participants served as "teachers" in what they were told was a memory experiment. A confederate (a middle-aged professional actor) serving as the "learner" was strapped into a chair "to prevent excessive movements when he was shocked," and electrodes were attached to his arm. The participants were told that "although the shocks can be extremely painful, they cause no permanent tissue damage."

After viewing the learner, a participant was shown to a separate room housing an apparatus with dials, a lighted display of the learner's responses, and a series of switches that supposedly delivered shocks ranging from 15 to 450 volts. The participant was instructed to use this apparatus to deliver shocks, in increments of 15 volts for each "mistake," to the learner in the other room. Beneath the switches were descriptive labels ranging from "Slight Shock" to "Danger: Severe Shock" to the ominous "XXX."

The learner gave answers to a series of questions by pressing the appropriate lever on the table in front of him. Each time he made an incorrect response, the researcher told the participant to throw another switch and give a larger shock.

 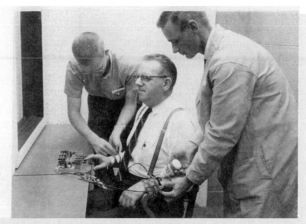

▲ Left: *The teacher's console in Milgram's experiments. The box on top of the console displayed the learner's answers to the questions.* Right: *A view of the teacher and researcher readying the learner for the experiment.*

At the 300-volt level, the learner pounded on the wall and then stopped responding to questions. The researcher told the participant to consider "no answer" as an incorrect answer. At the 315-volt level, the learner pounded on the wall again. If the participant hesitated in delivering a shock, the researcher said, "Please go on." If this admonition was not enough, the researcher said, "The experiment requires that you continue"; then, "It is absolutely essential that you continue"; and finally, "You have no other choice; you must go on." The question of interest was how long people would continue to administer shocks to the hapless victim. A majority of participants gave the learner what they believed to be the 450-volt shock, despite the fact that he pounded on the wall twice and then stopped responding altogether. (See **Figure 15·7**.)

In a later experiment, when the confederate was placed in the same room and the participant could witness his struggling and apparent pain, 37.5 percent of the participants still obeyed the order to administer further shocks (Milgram, 1974). Thirty percent were even willing to hold the learner's hand against a metal plate to force him to receive the shock.

Milgram's experiments indicate that a significant percentage of people will follow the orders of authority figures, no matter what the effects are on other people. Milgram had originally designed his experimental procedure to understand why ordinary people in Germany had participated in the murders of millions of innocent people during the Second World War. He had planned to perfect the technique in the United States and then travel to Germany to continue his studies. The results he obtained made it clear that he did not have to leave home.

Most people find the results of Milgram's studies surprising. They can't believe that for such a large proportion of people the social pressure to conform to the researcher's orders is stronger than the participant's own desire not to

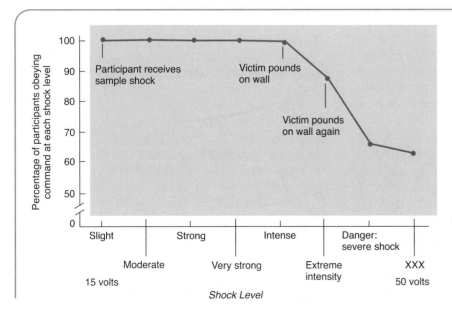

FIGURE 15·7 Data from one of Milgram's studies of obedience.

(After Milgram, 1963. From Baron, R. A. & Byrne, D. *Social Psychology*, 8/e. Published by Allyn and Bacon, Boston, MA. Copyright © 1997 by Pearson Education. Reprinted by permission of the publisher.)

hurt someone else. As Ross (1977) points out, this misperception is an example of the fundamental attribution error. People tend to *underestimate* the effectiveness of situational factors and to *overestimate* the effectiveness of dispositional ones. Clearly, the tendency to obey an authority figure is amazingly strong.

A great deal of attention has been paid to the ethical questions raised by Milgram's research (e.g., Elms, 1995). Psychologists and nonpsychologists alike have questioned whether Milgram should have conducted his experiments. For example, some critics point out that Milgram's results gave participants extremely negative information about themselves (specifically, about their capacity for harmful obedience)—information that they might never have learned had it not been for their participation in the research. In Milgram's defense, it must be stressed that he exercised a high degree of care with his participants—a practice followed by social psychologists today. At the end of each experimental session, he conducted an extensive debriefing in which the actual purpose of the experiment was explained to the participants. He made sure that participants understood that they were not deviant and that the situation had been very powerful. In addition, participants were later sent a detailed written report of the experimental procedure and a follow-up questionnaire asking them about their feelings regarding their participation. Interestingly, at least some people considered the enhanced insight into their own behavior to be a positive aspect of their participation. Eighty-four percent said that they were glad to have taken part in the experiment, and only 1.3 percent indicated that they wished they had not been involved.

Group Decision Making

We have seen how groups affect conformity, social facilitation, and social loafing. Let's consider certain phenomena associated with decision making in groups.

The process by which members of a group reach a decision is different from the process involved in individual decision making, if only because decisions in groups are usually preceded by discussion. However, discussion of issues relevant to a decision does not always guarantee that the best decision will be made. Two problems associated with group decision making are group polarization and groupthink.

Group Polarization In some group decision-making situations, discussion of alternative choices leads to decisions that are either riskier or more conservative than the group's initial position on the issue at hand. In general, if the initial inclination of group members is to make a risky decision, group discussion will lead to an even riskier decision. Conversely, if the initial inclination is to make a conservative decision, group discussion will usually lead to an even more conservative decision. This tendency for the initial position of a group to become exaggerated over the course of the discussion preceding a decision is called **group polarization**. For example, Myers and

Bishop (1970) found that initial levels of racial prejudice voiced by groups were altered through group discussion. Discussion caused a group with an initially low level of prejudice to become even less prejudiced, whereas discussion caused a group with an initially high level of prejudice to become even more prejudiced.

What causes discussion to produce polarization? Although several explanations have been offered, three seem particularly plausible: informational influence, repeated exposure, and normative influence (Isenberg, 1986). *Informational influence* is the impact of new information pertinent to the decision to be made. The new information may favor a particular decision, increasing the likelihood that more members of the group will become convinced that it is the best decision. In addition, the fact that the information is new to them may make it all the more persuasive, moving them to a more extreme position than they would have taken in the absence of the new information (Stasser, 1991).

Mere *repeated exposure* to information may play a role. When group members discuss issues, they tend to repeat the points that have been identified as relevant to the decision. Brauer, Judd, and Gliner (1995) showed that the repeated expression of attitudes during group discussion was positively related to the extremity of group polarization—a finding that is consistent with the claim discussed earlier in the chapter that mere exposure can increase the strength of attitudes.

Normative influence occurs when we compare our individual views with the group norm. People in groups receive social reinforcement for agreeing with the views of others. The more that group members wish to achieve group cohesion in decision making, the greater the tendency for individual group members to embrace the majority decision—no matter how extreme that decision might be.

Groupthink Irving Janis has studied a related phenomenon that sometimes occurs in group decision making—**groupthink**, the tendency to avoid dissent so as to achieve group consensus (Janis, 1972, 1982). Janis developed the theory of groupthink after analyzing the ineffective decision making that led U.S. President John F. Kennedy to order an ill-fated attempt to overthrow Fidel Castro's regime in Cuba in 1961. The decision to embark on the Bay of Pigs invasion was made by Kennedy and a small group of advisers. Janis studied the conditions that led to this decision as well as other important group decisions that altered the course of twentieth-century history.

Janis's theory specifies the conditions necessary for groupthink as well as its symptoms and consequences. As shown in **Figure 15•8**, the conditions that foster groupthink include a stressful situation in which the stakes are very high, a group of people who already tend to think alike and who are isolated from others who could offer criticism of the decision, and a strong group leader who makes his or her position well known to the group. In the Bay of Pigs example, the overthrow of a dictator seen as an archenemy of the United

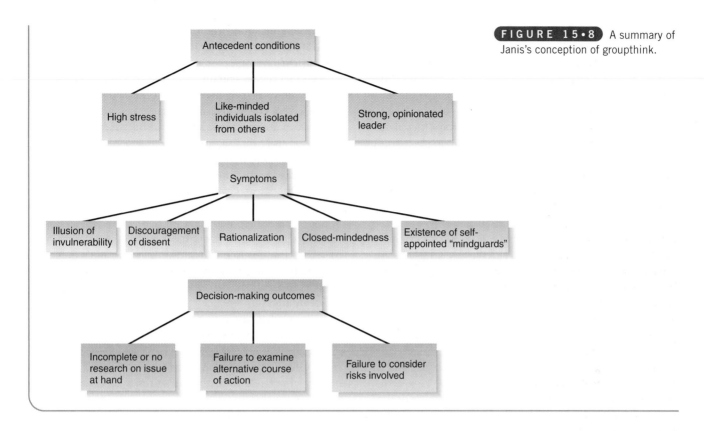

FIGURE 15•8 A summary of Janis's conception of groupthink.

States was at stake, Kennedy's advisers were like-minded regarding the invasion and met in secret, and Kennedy was a forceful and charismatic leader who made his intentions to invade Cuba known to them.

Janis also notes five symptoms of groupthink, all of which were present during the decision to invade Cuba. First, group members share the illusion that their decision is sound, moral, and right—in a word, invulnerable. Second, dissent from the leader's views is discouraged, further supporting the illusion that the group's decision is right. Third, instead of assessing the strengths and weaknesses of the decision, group members rationalize their decision, looking only for reasons that support it. Fourth, group members are closed-minded—they are not willing to listen to alternative suggestions and ideas. And fifth, self-appointed "mindguards" exist within the group and actively discourage dissent from the group norm.

Combined, these symptoms lead to flawed decision making. People caught up in groupthink tend to conduct only incomplete or no research on the issue at hand; often fail to examine alternative courses of action specified by the decision; and, finally, often fail to consider potential risks inherent in the decision.

Janis argues that groups can avoid groupthink by taking several precautions. First, group leaders should encourage criticism by group members. Second, the group should seek relevant input from appropriate people who are not members. Third, the group should break into smaller subgroups in which different ideas and opinions can be generated and developed. And fourth, the group leader should avoid overstating his or her position on the matter and should be on guard for rationalization, closed-mindedness, and illusions of invulnerability.

Resisting Social Influences

At first glance, social influence may appear to be negative; perhaps we would be better off if our behavior were always under rational, conscious control. But as Robert Cialdini (1993) points out, this conclusion is not warranted. Most of the time, humans profit from our tendency to be fair in our interactions with others, to take our cues for acting from one another, to honor our commitments, to obey authority figures, and to cooperate in group interactions. If we had to expend time and effort in consciously deciding what to do in every situation, we would be exhausted before the end of the day. For most normal people in most situations, the automatic, unconscious reaction is the best and most efficient response. We should save our cognitive efforts for the times when they count the most.

However, no general rule works all of the time; exceptions can occur that have bad effects. For example, an authority figure can order us to do things that hurt ourselves or others, and advertisers and sales representatives who know the rules of social influence can induce us to make unnecessary and costly expenditures.

Cialdini suggests that the best way to defend ourselves from the unscrupulous use of social influence is to be sensitive to ourselves and to the situation. Whenever we are spending money or committing ourselves to do something that will cost us time and effort, we should ask ourselves whether we feel any discomfort. Do we feel pressured? Do we feel tense? Do we wish we were somewhere else? If so, someone is probably trying to manipulate us. We should try to relax and step back from the situation. Does the other person stand to profit from what he or she is trying to get us to do? If we could go back to the time just before we got into this situation, would we put ourselves where we are now, or would we avoid this situation? If we would avoid it, then now is the time to leave. The feeling that we have to keep going, that we have to live up to our commitment, is exactly what the other person is counting on.

We must realize that when someone is trying to manipulate us, the rules that govern normal social interchanges are off. Of course, we should be polite and honest—just as we want other people to be with us—but we are not obliged to return "favors" from someone who is trying to sell us something. If someone tricks us into making a commitment, we should feel no compunction about breaking it. If someone tries to abuse our natural tendencies to be fair in our interactions with others, we should fight back. Otherwise, we run the risk of becoming cynical in our dealings with other people who are not trying to take advantage of us. Forewarned is forearmed.

Interim Summary

Social Influences and Group Behavior

The experiments of social psychologists have shown us just how potent social influences can be. We tend to do what others do, conforming to social norms and preferring not to disagree with attitudes and judgments expressed by others. This tendency undoubtedly serves us well most of the time, but the fact that people are less likely to assist someone if other bystanders are present shows that others' influence can also have unfortunate effects.

When people are part of a group or are observed by others, they act differently than when they are alone. In general, the presence of observers increases arousal, which increases the likelihood that a performer will make the dominant response called for by the task; depending on the complexity of the task, this effect can either facilitate or inhibit successful performance. When performing as part of a group, a person will often make less vigorous efforts if individual contribution cannot be identified—a phenomenon known as social loafing. Three important interpersonal variables that reduce social loafing are individual identifiability, group cohesiveness, and individual responsibility.

When we commit ourselves to a course of action, we tend to persist in the commitment. Research has revealed sev-

eral techniques for promoting compliance by exploiting commitment, including the foot-in-the-door, lowballing, and door-in-the-face approaches. Milgram's famous research showed that people will obey outlandish, even inhumane, requests from those perceived as authority figures.

Effective group decision making may be hampered by both group polarization and groupthink. In group polarization, the initial inclination of the group becomes exaggerated to one extreme or the other. Informational influence, repeated exposure, and normative influence tend to promote polarization. Groupthink develops in highly stressful situations in which the group making a decision includes an opinionated leader and like-minded individuals who are isolated from others. Groupthink is characterized by feelings that the group's decision is invulnerable, by lack of dissent, by rationalization, by closed-mindedness, and by "mindguards" who actively discourage differences of opinion. Although our tendency to be influenced socially is generally in our best interest, sometimes unscrupulous persons take advantage of this tendency in attempts to exploit us. The best way to protect ourselves from such persons is to become more reflective about the situations in which such exploitation is likely to occur and to resist others' manipulativeness directly.

QUESTIONS TO CONSIDER

1. How would social life be different if people tended not to conform to social norms? Think of an instance in which your behavior conformed to a social norm. How might the outcome of this social interaction have been different had you not conformed?

2. In life-saving and cardiopulmonary resuscitation (CPR) classes, students are taught to take control in emergency situations. For example, in a situation in which a person appears to be drowning, they learn to assign onlookers specific responsibilities, such as calling 911, fetching rescue equipment, and so on. To what extent does taking control in this manner enhance bystander intervention? What effect might it have on the onlookers' tendency toward diffusion of responsibility?

3. Suppose that you have been asked by your psychology professor to organize a small group of class members to prepare a presentation. As the leader of the group, what steps might you take to prevent the individual members of your group from becoming social loafers?

Interpersonal Attraction and Loving

When an individual conforms to a group norm, it is the individual, not the group, who is being influenced. When you comply with the request of a car salesperson or obey the dictates of

▲ *Several factors may contribute to the interpersonal attraction reflected in informal neighborhood gatherings.*

an authority figure, the influence flows in one direction; it is your behavior that is being influenced. However, many kinds of social influence are reciprocal. As we shall see in this section, the behavior of two individuals may produce a mutual, although not necessarily equal, influence.

Interpersonal Attraction

Many factors determine **interpersonal attraction,** or people's tendency to approach each other and evaluate each other positively. Although the factors that influence interpersonal attraction are complex and not yet fully understood, they appear to involve social reinforcement. People learn to act in ways that reinforce friends and lovers in order to maintain and strengthen their ties with them. So some factors in attraction are characteristics of the individuals themselves; others are determined by the socially reinforcing aspects of the environment. We'll consider the factors of positive evaluation, familiarity, similarity, and physical appearance.

Positive Evaluation Humans like to be evaluated positively—to be held in high regard by other people. This tendency is expressed in interpersonal attraction. There is no surprise in the fact that we like those who treat us well and dislike those who punish us.

Familiarity In order for an attraction to form between people, they must meet each other. Festinger, Schachter, and Back (1959) found that the likelihood of friendships between people who lived in an apartment house was related to the closeness between the apartments in which they lived—their *proximity*. The closer the apartments, the more likely the friendship was. People also were unlikely to have

friends who lived on a different floor unless their apartments were next to a stairway, where they would meet people going up or down the stairs.

Repetition generally increases our preference for a stimulus (the mere exposure effect). This phenomenon applies to the attraction between people as well. Even in the brief time it takes to participate in an experiment, familiarity affects interpersonal attraction. Saegert, Swap, and Zajonc (1973) asked college women to participate in an experiment that supposedly involved the sense of taste. Pairs of female students entered booths, where they tasted and rated various liquids. The movements of the students from booth to booth were arranged so that pairs of women were together from 0 to 10 times. Afterwards, the participants rated how likable each of the other students in the experiment was. Likability was directly related to the number of interactions any two participants had had—the more interactions a student had had with a fellow participant, the more likable she found her. (See **Figure 15•9**.)

Similarity Another factor that influences interpersonal attraction is similarity—in looks, interests, and attitudes (e.g., Byrne, 1997). There is a tendency for people in close relationships to be similar in physical attractiveness. Research indicates that couples who are mismatched in this respect are the most likely to break up (White, 1980). Although it might seen reasonable for people to seek the most attractive partners they could find, the fear of rejection and ridicule often prevents this from occurring. Men tend to be afraid of approaching attractive women (Bernstein, Stephenson, Snyder, & Wicklund, 1983).

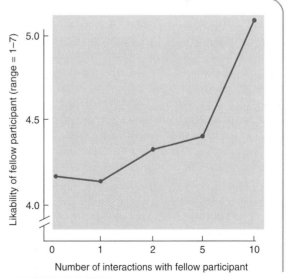

FIGURE 15•9 Familiarity, exposure, and attraction. The rated likability of a fellow participant as a function of the number of interactions.

(Based on data from Saegert, S. C., Swap, W., & Zajonc, R. B. (1973). Exposure, context, and interpersonal attraction. *Journal of Personality and Social Psychology, 25,* 234–242.)

Couples also tend to be similar in personality, attitudes, and intelligence (Brehm, 1992)—and the greater the similarity between the partners, the more enduring their relationship (Hatfield & Rapson, 1993). Presumably, a person who shares our attitudes is likely to approve of us when we express them. Also, having friends who have similar attitudes guarantees that our opinions are likely to find a positive reception; we tend to avoid the unpleasant experience of saying things that bring disapproval from others.

Other kinds of similarities are also important, such as age, occupational status, and ethnic background. Friends tend to have similar backgrounds as well as similar attitudes.

Physical Appearance People commonly judge one another to some extent on the basis of a characteristic that is supposed to be only skin deep—attractive physical appearance. In general, we are attracted more to good-looking people than to those who are not (Albright, Kenny, & Malloy, 1988). In fact, the beautiful-person stereotype has a strong influence (see, e.g., Dion, 1986; Dion, Berscheid, & Walster, 1972), especially in the United States and Canada, where beautiful people are seen as happier, more intelligent, and more socially skilled than those who are less physically attractive (e.g., Eagly, Ashmore, Makhijani, & Longo, 1991).

This bias extends to at least one Eastern culture, although there are interesting differences. Wheeler and Kim (1997) found that college students in Korea shared most of the biases shown by North Americans, but also saw beautiful people as more trustworthy and concerned for others, differences not found in North America. And Korean students did not share the North American bias toward perceiving beautiful people as more self-assertive and dominant than plainer people. Recall the earlier assertion that in collectivist cultures (such as Korea) great value is placed on the interconnectedness of people, whereas in individualist cultures independence and personal achievement are more valued.

Walster, Aronson, Abrahams, and Rottman (1966) studied the behavioral effects of physical appearance at a college dance where couples were randomly paired by a computer. Midway through the evening, the researchers asked each member of a couple to rate the attraction she or he felt toward the other member and to say whether she or he would like to see the other member in the future. For both genders, the only characteristic that correlated with felt attraction was physical appearance. Intelligence, grades, and personality variables had no significant effect.

When people publicly discuss the factors that are important in dating partners, they usually do not dwell on physical attractiveness. Why? One possibility is that they are perfectly aware that physical appearance strongly affects their choices and desires, but social norms and common wisdom (e.g., "beauty is only skin deep") inhibit them from dwelling on its prime importance. They do not want to appear superficial. Another possibility is that although people are aware of the stereotype of beauty, they do not believe that it affects their personal decisions and behavior—it's something that influences other people. Hadjistavropoulos and Genest (1994) examined these possibilities by using a special measurement system that encourages honest answering. Participants who responded under this system indicated a stronger influence of physical appearance on their attraction to others than did control participants who responded to conventional questioning.

Physically attractive people seem to benefit in many ways from this stereotype. Being good-looking can open many doors. But would it surprise you to know that most elements of the stereotype are wrong? Being beautiful guarantees none of the correspondingly beautiful qualities (Feingold, 1992).

Evaluating Scientific Issues

Arousal and Interpersonal Attraction

People may become attracted to one another under almost any circumstances. Hollywood often idealizes romantic relationships by showing us how they unfold under the most dire situations. Against a backdrop of war, earthquake, shipwreck, alien invasion, or jealous rivals, the spark of love ignites between the hero and heroine, who then brave all manner of difficulties to keep their love alive. Melodramatic, perhaps . . . and yet, as Walster and Berscheid (1971) put it, "Passion sometimes develops in conditions that would seem more likely to provoke aggression and hatred" (p. 47). How is it that love can spring forth from a less-than-optimal beginning?

● **Extraneous Sources of Arousal and Interpersonal Attraction**

Consider a well-known study conducted by Dutton and Aron (1974), who arranged for an attractive young woman to briefly interview male college students as they walked across a narrow suspension bridge. The bridge was about 5 feet wide, 400 feet long, and 200 feet above a gorge. It swayed and wobbled erratically when someone walked across it. The same woman also interviewed control participants on a more conventional, sturdier bridge that spanned a 10-foot drop. The interviewer gave her telephone number to all participants with the suggestion that they call her if they wanted to discuss the experiment further.

The men who were interviewed on the suspension bridge apparently found the woman more attractive than did those who were interviewed on the ordinary bridge—they were much more likely to telephone her later. These results suggest that the anxiety produced by walking across the suspension bridge increased the men's attraction toward the woman. Dutton and Aron explained their findings in terms of attribution theory: A man experiences increased arousal in the presence of a woman; he attributes the arousal to the most obvious stimulus—the woman—and concludes that he is attracted to her. Later, he acts on this conclusion by telephoning her. Arousal—pleasant or aversive—tends to increase interpersonal attraction between men and women. This is not a new idea. An ancient Roman expert advised men to take their women to the Coliseum to see the gladiators fight because the experience would increase their romantic inclinations.

● What Can We Conclude?

Interpersonal attraction is very complex. It develops under many different conditions—not always under ideal conditions, and not merely when one person helps reduce the other's fear or anxiety. There is much to learn about how interpersonal attraction is transformed into love.

Loving

The relationships we have with others generally are marked by two different kinds of emotion: **liking,** a feeling of personal regard, intimacy, and esteem toward another person, and **loving,** a combination of liking and a deep sense of attachment to another person. Loving someone does not necessarily entail romance. You may have several close friends whom you love dearly yet have no desire to be involved with romantically.

Romantic love, also called **passionate love,** is an emotionally intense desire for sexual union with another person (Hatfield, 1988). Feeling romantic love generally involves experiencing five closely intertwined elements: desiring intimacy with another person, feeling passion for that person, being preoccupied with thoughts of that person, depending emotionally on that person, and feeling wonderful if that person feels romantic love toward you or dejected if not.

"Falling in love" and "being in love" are common expressions that people use to describe their passionate desires for each other. Passionate love may occur at almost any time during life, although people involved in long-term cohabitation or marriages seem to experience a qualitatively different kind of love. The partners may still make passionate love to one another, but passion is no longer the defining characteristic of the relationship. This kind of love is called **companionate love** and is characterized by a deep, enduring affection and caring for another. Companionate love is also marked by a mutual sense of commitment, that is, a strong desire to maintain the relationship. How passionate love develops into companionate love is presently an unanswered question, although odds are that the sort of intimacy that punctuates romantic love is still a major

▲ *Growing older need not be a barrier to interpersonal attraction.*

force in the companionate relationship. An important feature of intimacy is *self-disclosure,* or the ability to share deeply private feelings and thoughts with another. Indeed, part of loving another is feeling comfortable sharing deeply personal aspects of yourself with that person.

Robert Sternberg has developed a "triangular" theory of how intimacy, passion, and commitment may combine to produce liking and several different forms of love (Barnes & Sternberg, 1997; Sternberg, 1988b). According to this theory, as shown in **Table 15•4.** liking involves only intimacy, infatuation involves only passion, and empty love involves only commitment. Combining any two of these elements produces still other kinds of love. Romantic love entails both intimacy and passion but no commitment. Companionate love

TABLE 15•4	Sternberg's Theory of Love		

According to Robert Sternberg, love is based on different combinations of intimacy, passion, and commitment. These elements may combine to form eight different kinds of relationships.

	Intimacy	Passion	Commitment
Nonlove			
Liking	*****		
Infatuated love		*****	
Empty love			*****
Romantic love	*****	*****	
Companionate love	*****		*****
Fatuous love		*****	*****
Consummate love	*****	*****	*****

***** indicates that the element is present in the relationship; a blank space indicates that the element is not present or is present only at a low level in the relationship.

Source: After Sternberg, R. J. (1986). A triangular theory of love. *Psychological Bulletin, 93,* 119–135.

entails both intimacy and commitment but no passion. Fatuous love (a kind of love marked by complacency in the relationship) entails both passion and commitment but no intimacy. The highest form of love, consummate love, contains all three elements.

Sternberg's theory is descriptive. It characterizes different kinds of love, but it does not explain their origins. What function has love served in human evolution? The answer can be summed up succinctly: procreation and child rearing. Although love of any kind for another person is not a necessary requirement for sexual intercourse, a man and a woman who passionately love each other are more likely to have sex than are a man and a woman who do not. And if their union produces a child, then love serves another function—it increases the likelihood that both parents will share in the responsibilities of child rearing. Our capacity for loving, then, contributes in very practical ways to the continued existence of our genes.

Biology and Culture

Evolution and the Likelihood of Love

Are you married? If not, are you interested in becoming married? You may not be married now, and you may not be interested in getting married, at least right away. But chances are that one day the "right" person will come along and that you will fall in love with that person, perhaps get married, and perhaps have children. What will that person be like—what will make that person right for you?

An answer to this question may be found in evolutionary psychological research, which, as you may recall from Chapter 3, is the study of the biological basis of social behavior. Evolutionary psychological theory predicts that gender makes a difference in what people find attractive in their potential mates. Gender matters because males and females differ in their biological and psychological "investments" in reproduction and child rearing.

As Chapter 3 pointed out, the costs of sexual behavior and reproduction are enormously greater for females than for males (Kenrick, Groth, Trost, & Sadalla, 1993). Evolutionary psychologists argue that because of this difference, natural selection has favored different mating strategies for each gender. Because male reproductive success rests on mating with fertile females, men seek potential mates who are capable of reproduction (Buss, 1992). But there is a problem here—how can males tell if a female is fertile? As Buss (1989) and Symons (1979) have argued, males should prefer younger females to older ones because age is highly correlated with female fertility. And a clue to a woman's age is her physical appearance: smooth skin, absence of gray hair, girlish figure, white teeth, and high energy level (Buss, 1992). Thus, in their quest to find a mate, males place a premium on these features (e.g., Li, Bailey, Kenrick, & Linsenmeier, 2002).

In contrast, because the female's reproductive success is dependent on her investment of biological resources, women seek potential mates who can provide other types of resources, such as food, shelter, protection, and, in general, social and economic resources. And how can a female tell if a potential mate has and is willing to provide these resources? Evolutionary psychologists assert that her best clues will be primarily the male's socioeconomic status and, to a lesser extent, his ability to work hard, his intelligence, and his kindness (Buss, 1992; Kenrick, Neuberg, Zierk, & Krones, 1994).

Research has shown that in evaluating potential mates males do place a greater emphasis on physical appearance than do females and that females stress social status more than do males. For example, in a cross-cultural study Buss (1990) asked people from 37 different cultures to assess which characteristics they found most desirable in a mate. Males from all cultures ranked physical attractiveness higher than females did, and females in 36 of the 37 cultures placed a greater emphasis on socioeconomic status than males did. These results confirm earlier findings showing that the physical attractiveness of a woman is a better predictor of the socioeconomic status of her husband than is her intelligence, education, or wealth (Elder, 1969). Buss's cross-cultural data also support the prediction that males will prefer younger females: The mean age difference between males and females on their wedding days was 2.99 years—with the bride being younger.

Buss also has shown that these tendencies translate into actual differences in the tactics men and women choose to attract potential mates (Buss & Schmitt, 1993; Schmitt & Buss, 1996). In the context of short-term relationships, males use tactics involving displays of their resources—flashing money, taking their dates to fancy restaurants for dinner, and driving expensive cars. In contrast, females use tactics that enhance their physical attractiveness—dieting, wearing makeup, and wearing flattering clothing. When the issue is long-term loving relationships, females offer sexual fidelity and males offer the resources necessary for secure living.

These differences in the importance men and women assign to physical attractiveness and socioeconomic status in mate selection also turn out to have an important effect on how people evaluate their partners in existing relationships. In a study conducted by Kenrick, Neuberg, Zierk, and Krones (1994), nearly 400 male and female college students involved in heterosexual dating relationships viewed photographs and read accompanying descriptions of people of the opposite gender. The students were told that they were helping the researchers improve the format for a university-sponsored dating service. In actuality, the researchers wished to learn how viewing the photographs and reading the descriptions would influence the participants' perceptions of their current dating partners.

The people depicted in the photographs were either highly attractive professional models or rather average-looking students. The descriptions accompanying the

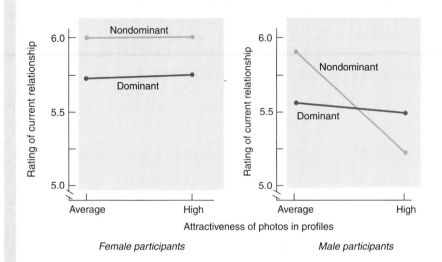

FIGURE 15•10 Results of Kenrick and colleagues' study of the effects of gender, dominance, and physical attractiveness on college students' evaluations of their current dating relationships. Males shown photographs of physically attractive, nondominant females rated their commitments to their current dating relationships lower than when shown photographs in the other three categories. Females who viewed photographs of dominant males, regardless of the males' physical attractiveness, rated their commitments to their current dating relationships lower.

(From Kenrick, D. T., Neuberg, S. L., Zierk, K. L., & Krones, J. M. (1994). Evolution and social cognition: Contrast effects as a function of sex, dominance, and physical attractiveness. *Personality and Social Psychology Bulletin, 20,* 210–217. Copyright 1994. Reprinted by permission of Sage Publications, Inc.)

photographs varied only according to a score on a personality test of dominance that the researchers defined as representing the person's natural leadership abilities. Participants were told that a high dominance score meant that the person in the photograph was "authoritative and masterful" and that a low score meant that the person was "obedient and submissive." The photographs and descriptions were arranged to produce four combinations: physically attractive and high in dominance; physically attractive and low in dominance; average-looking and high in dominance; and average-looking and low in dominance.

Kenrick and his colleagues found clear gender differences in their participants' evaluations of their current dating relationships following exposure to the photographs. (See **Figure 15•10.**) Compared to men who saw the photographs of average-looking women, men shown the photographs of physically attractive women rated their current dating relationships less favorably when the women were described as low in dominance. (Dominant physically attractive women had no effect on the men's evaluations of their current dating relationships.) In contrast, women who viewed photographs of dominant men—be they average-looking or handsome—tended to rate their current dating relationships as less satisfactory than did women who viewed photographs of the men described as being low in dominance.

In sum, it can be argued that evolution has shaped gender-specific social cognition—that is, gender-specific ways of attending to, perceiving, interpreting, and responding to information in our social environment (Kenrick, Li, & Butner, 2003). The reason is that each gender makes different contributions to courtship and child rearing. Our attraction to members of the opposite sex and our choice of a mate do not occur by chance. Although chance and circumstance may determine where we live and what people we meet, our evolutionary history has provided the social and cognitive mechanisms through which we become attracted to and fall in love with the "right" person.

Interim Summary

Interpersonal Attraction and Loving

Interpersonal attraction involves social reinforcement. It is increased by positive evaluation by the other person, familiarity, proximity, similarity, shared attitudes, and physical good looks.

Loving someone entails a combination of liking and strong feelings of attachment. Sternberg's theory of love describes how different combinations of intimacy, passion, and commitment give rise to liking and to different kinds of love. For example, romantic love involves both intimacy and passion, but infatuation involves only passion. The combination of all three elements is referred to as consummate love.

From an evolutionary standpoint, love serves both procreative and child-rearing functions. Evolutionary psychologists have observed that men and women differ with respect to the social-cognitive cues they use when selecting potential mates. Men prefer potential mates to be young and physically attractive, because attractive young women tend to be fertile. Women prefer potential mates who control socioeconomic resources because these resources are important in the support of offspring.

QUESTIONS TO CONSIDER

1. To what kinds of people are you most attracted? What factors, internal or external, appear to be most important in your relationships?

2. Is Sternberg's theory of love an accurate account of your own experience with different kinds of love? If so, provide an example. Are there kinds of love that you have experienced that are not included in his theory? If so, what are they?

Suggestions for Further Reading

Baron, R. A., Byrne, D., & Branscombe, H. R. (2005). *Social psychology* (11th ed.). Boston: Allyn and Bacon.

This textbook offers a solid, comprehensive introduction to social psychology and enlarges on the topics in this chapter.

Buss, D. M. (2003). *The evolution of desire: Strategies of human mating*. New York: Basic Books.

A leading evolutionary psychologist summarizes his large-scale (37 cultures) survey of human mating preferences and argues that the results confirm the natural selection of gender-specific preferences.

Cialdini, R. B. (2000). *Influence: Science and practice* (4th ed.). Boston: Allyn and Bacon.

In this best seller, a leading social psychologist serves up an entertaining recital of forms of social influence and illustrates each with numerous and often humorous anecdotes.

Milgram, S. (1974). *Obedience to authority*. New York: Harper & Row.

The author of perhaps the best known social psychology experiment recounts his rationale for the research, its design, and its results, while also providing a theoretical account of his findings and discussing their moral implications.

Nisbett, R. (2003). *The geography of thought: How Asians and Westerners think differently . . . and why*. New York: Free Press.

The author's early work on social inference led to a major study of the cognitive differences, particularly in perceptual search and memory, that exist between East Asians and Westerners. He discusses the implications in terms of cultural histories and practices.

Smith, P. B. (2006). *Understanding social psychology across cultures: Living and working in a changing world*. Thousand Oaks, CA: Sage Publications.

This textbook provides a wide-ranging intercultural perspective on several of the topics found in this chapter.

Wilson, T. D. (2002). *Strangers to ourselves: Discovering the adaptive unconscious*. Cambridge, MA: Harvard University Press.

A fascinating, very readable essay introduces the theory of the adaptive unconscious (the aspect of the person that controls what she or he does but remains unreportable) and adduces support for the theory from several areas of social psychological research.

Key Terms

actor–observer effect (p. 480)

attitude (p. 483)

attribution (p. 478)

availability heuristic (p. 481)

base-rate fallacy (p. 481)

belief in a just world (p. 479)

bystander intervention (p. 493)

central traits (p. 475)

cognitive dissonance theory (p. 486)

companionate love (p. 503)

compliance (p. 496)

conformity (p. 492)

consensus (p. 478)

consistency (p. 478)

diffusion of responsibility (p. 494)

discrimination (p. 489)

dispositional factors (p. 478)

distinctiveness (p. 478)

elaboration likelihood model (p. 485)

ethnocentrism (p. 489)

false consensus (p. 481)

fundamental attribution error (p. 479)

group (p. 492)

group polarization (p. 498)

groupthink (p. 498)

illusion of out-group homogeneity (p. 490)

illusory correlation (p. 490)

impression formation (p. 475)

interpersonal attraction (p. 501)

liking (p. 503)

loving (p. 503)

mere exposure effect (p. 484)

passionate love (p. 503)

prejudice (p. 488)

primacy effect (p. 476)

representativeness heuristic (p. 481)

self (p. 476)

self-concept (p. 476)

self-fulfilling prophecy (p. 491)

self-perception theory (p. 487)

self-schema (p. 476)

self-serving bias (p. 480)

situational factors (p. 478)

social cognition (p. 475)

social facilitation (p. 495)

social loafing (p. 495)

social norms (p. 492)

social psychology (p. 474)

stereotype (p. 489)

16

LIFESTYLE, STRESS, AND HEALTH

Cultural Evolution: Lifestyle Choices and Consequences

The behavior of an individual, in aggregate, defines that person's lifestyle. Our lifestyles have been shaped by environmental changes influenced by both cultural evolution and our biology. Although lifestyles significantly affect individual survival, many of their consequences occur after an individual's reproductive years, at an age where natural selection pressures are less significant. Hence, reinforcement, which operates in the short term, may be a more important factor.

Healthy and Unhealthy Lifestyles

Nutrition • Physical Fitness • Cigarette Smoking • Drinking Alcoholic Beverages • Sexually Transmitted Diseases and AIDS • *Biology and Culture: Cultural Reactions to Contagious Diseases*

In the long run, healthy behaviors enhance longevity and quality of life. Unhealthy behaviors, such as eating poorly, not exercising properly, smoking, excessive use of alcohol, and practicing unsafe sex, tend to affect our lives negatively in the long run but can affect them "positively" in the short run. Unhealthy behaviors are acquired and maintained because of their immediately reinforcing effects. Cultural reactions to persons with life-threatening contagious diseases are the result of powerful societal and psychological variables.

Preventing Unhealthy Lifestyles through Self-Control

We are often faced with a choice between an immediate, small reward and a delayed, but larger reward. Prior commitment to a course of action that allows us to obtain the delayed but larger reward constitutes self-control.

Stress and Health

The Biological Basis of Stress • Cognitive Appraisal and Stress • Stressful Lifestyles and Impaired Health • *Evaluating Scientific Issues: Is There a Cancer-Prone Personality?*

Our responses to stressful stimuli are governed by the autonomic nervous system, which produces changes in the activity of many organs, and by our perception of the extent to which a stimulus poses a threat to our physical or psychological well-being. Prolonged stress can lead to chronic heart disease; weakening of the immune system, which increases our susceptibility to infectious diseases; and, in some cases, an anxiety disorder called post-traumatic stress disorder. Personality variables, especially those involved in coping with stress, appear to be related to the development, if not the initial formation, of cancers.

Coping with Everyday Stress

Sources of Stress • Coping Styles and Strategies • Stress Inoculation Training

Stress can be caused by a wide variety of sources—positive experiences as well as negative ones. The levels of stress that we experience can be controlled by the use of specific coping strategies. Stress inoculation training is a form of stress management that teaches people how to develop and implement effective coping strategies for handling stressful situations before they occur.

My future wife (let's call her "FW") lived in an up-down duplex when I met her. During one of my first visits to her place, she introduced me to the upstairs tenant, Leif. Leif was about 30, looked at times like he was 18, and much of the time acted like he was 15. But he could be totally engaging. He bounced around on the balls of his feet, and anytime he came downstairs to visit, a party threatened to break out.

Leif was a freelance interior designer who, through dumpster diving and much talent, had transformed his flat into a place of magic and fantasy. I have vivid images of billowing fabric, mosaic surfaces, golden highlights, and stars on the ceiling. He asked my opinion about a few of the projects he was working on for clients. By and large, I thought his ideas were wonderful.

Leif had problems, though. That first time I met him, he was sporting a nasty abrasion on his forehead. He had tripped, he said. He might have, but I soon became familiar with a pattern of injuries. Leif would go to the bar and get drunk, and eventually someone would feel obliged to beat him up. His eyes were blackened several times during the few months I knew him. Leif drank too much. He drank all the time.

Leif lost most of his contract jobs because of his drinking. He drank late, slept late, and was late at best with his work. Although his clients liked his ideas, they had to cut him loose in order to meet their own deadlines.

Slowly but surely, Leif's circle of friends narrowed. In the long run, his positive qualities could not fully compensate for his alcohol-induced irresponsibility, unpredictability, and neediness.

When all of this jelled for FW and me, we decided to do an "intervention." We chose a time when Leif was sober and engaged him in straight talk. We told him how much we liked him and cared for him and how talented and valuable he was. We told him that he suffered from alcoholism and that there were choices to be made that only he could make. He could continue on the path he was on and be doomed to a lifetime of unhappiness, ill health, trouble, and disappointment. FW was even more specific—she told him that his very life was in danger. We discussed with him the common underpinnings of alcoholism, the resources available to him in our city, the first steps he needed to take, and how we would support him in that direction. We assured him that he could succeed. He passed on our advice and declined our help. We tried again later, with the same result.

After FW moved to my house, new tenants moved into her flat, and we lost track of Leif for a period of time. We stopped by FW's old place one day, though, to visit neighbors. We learned that Leif had recently endangered the lives of everyone in the house by turning on his gas oven without lighting it—an apparent suicide attempt. He had then disappeared into the night. Several months later we learned that he had been found dead on the side of a road, hundreds of miles from friends and family, of a drug and alcohol overdose.

Throughout this book we have seen that human behavior and thought are the result of the interaction of biological and environmental variables. Psychology encompasses both the study of this interaction and the application of the resulting knowledge to improving our lives. In this chapter I wish to emphasize these points again with issues that may be closer to home for you—personal behaviors that have serious implications for your long-term physical health and your psychological well-being. The central theme of this chapter is that the particular behaviors that make up an individual's lifestyle have important consequences for that person's quality of life. As illustrated in the opening vignette, these consequences go beyond the individual; they also affect the lives of many others.

We will look first at how cultural evolution shapes our lives, especially in terms of the sorts of lifestyle choices we make. Next, we will study these choices as they relate to our personal health and safety and will consider strategies for making choices that benefit us in the long term. We will also examine stress, including its biological and psychological effects, and we'll explore ways to cope with it.

Cultural Evolution: Lifestyle Choices and Consequences

Cultural evolution, as explained in Chapter 3, is a culture's adaptive change to recurrent environmental pressures. Unlike biological evolution, which is driven by biological forces, cultural evolution is driven mainly by psychological forces. Cultural evolution is a product of human intellect and physical capacity, both of which have strong genetic components. As you may recall from Chapter 3, cultural evolution has been the guiding force behind social, cultural, and technical innovation in such areas as law, the arts, science, medicine, and engineering. As a culture faces new problems, solutions are proposed and tested. Solutions that work are passed from generation to generation through imitation, books, oral histories, and, most recently, in electronic forms—as bits of information stored on computer chips. Some solutions are modified by future generations so that they work more effectively. Those that don't work are abandoned.

Cultural evolution has been the primary agent involved in shaping **lifestyle,** the aggregate behavior of a person, or the way a person leads his or her life. The ways in which we interact with others, the kinds of work we pursue, the hobbies and personal interests we enjoy, the habits we develop, and the decision to marry and raise a family or to remain single are characteristics of our lifestyles.

For our prehistoric ancestors lifestyle was pretty much the same for everyone. When earlier humans were hungry, they hunted and gathered food; they walked or ran to get from one place to another; they worked hard to stay alive. Different options for accomplishing these tasks arose only as the pace of cultural evolution increased. That is, our ancestors learned more about creating more effective means of transportation, growing and storing food, and building homes from durable materials. Today, there is no predominant lifestyle; cultural evolution has afforded us the luxury of choosing among many alternatives. We can hunt or gather food if we want, but we can also buy it in grocery stores or go to restaurants. When we want to go somewhere, we can walk or run, but more often we ride on planes, trains, and automobiles. Most of us in Western cultures no longer worry only about how to stay alive; we now worry about how to spend our spare time, or about how to have more of it. Grocery stores, transportation, medicine, and leisure time are innovations spawned through cultural evolution.

Cultural evolution has given many societies a much higher standard of living than that of our prehistoric or even our relatively modern ancestors. However, cultural evolution has also produced threats to our health and safety. People can be hit and killed by cars and trucks. The manufacture of many goods contributes to pollution, which may cause disease. Many of the chemical agents we use for lubrication and cleaning are poisonous. It falls as a personal responsibility to each of us to avoid these threats. Failure to do so carries the risk of injury or death.

Cultural evolution has therefore added many threats to survival that our ancestors did not face, making our choice of lifestyle all the more important. Some choices can result in an unhealthy lifestyle, as when we eat fast foods to save the time of preparing a meal or consume alcohol because it provides a quick diversion from stress. In contrast, other choices can produce a healthier lifestyle, in which our nutritional needs, fitness requirements, psychological desires, and sexual relationships promote a longer and more satisfying life.

Why do some of us maintain unhealthy lifestyles, if doing so diminishes our physical and psychological well-being? How do we acquire those unhealthy behaviors in the first place? After all, they appear to work against the process of natural selection. The answer to this question is complicated, so I will offer only a general response here. Although the consequences of unhealthy lifestyle behaviors have obvious negative *biological* implications, the behaviors themselves can be acquired and maintained by both *biological* and *psychological* factors.

It is easy to misinterpret biological evolutionary theory and argue that genes that give rise to unhealthy lifestyles should eventually become extinct. But remember that natural selection operates on traits that affect the ability to reproduce. Most adaptations resulting from biological evolution concern only those behaviors that are relevant to surviving to sexual maturity, reproducing, and rearing offspring until they become self-sufficient. Many, if not most, of the consequences of unhealthy lifestyles—heart disease, cancer, and the other negative effects of poor nutrition, inactivity, alcoholism, and smoking—do not appear until people are well beyond reproductive age. Thus, it may be that genes that promote many unhealthy lifestyles are functionally overlooked by biological evolution—they are simply not relevant to reproduction.

Reinforcement (see Chapter 5) undoubtedly plays a powerful role in cultural evolution, too; indeed, its impact appears to be analogous to the role of natural selection in biological evolution. Behaviors that produce favorable consequences tend to be repeated and behaviors that produce unfavorable consequences tend not to be repeated. Cultural practices and customs that result in reinforcement tend to be maintained, if not elaborated. Exercising, eating nutritious foods, getting sufficient rest, and other healthy behaviors are acquired and maintained because of the reinforcing consequences enjoyed by the people who practice them. But how do the principles of reinforcement apply if unhealthy lifestyles have negative consequences?

Unfortunately, many unhealthy behaviors have *reinforcing consequences in the short run* and *damaging consequences in the long run.* Many unhealthy behaviors are maintained because

▲ *Cultural evolution affords us many choices in matters related to our survival. Although most of us prefer to buy our food at the supermarket, some people prefer to pick their food fresh from the field.*

they tend to be available on a version of revolving credit—instead of "buy now, pay later," it's "enjoy now, suffer later." For example, teens who smoke cigarettes receive immediate rewards—physiological and psychological pleasure and perhaps a sense of acceptance from their peers. It is only many years later, when they are in their 40s or 50s, that the negative effects of smoking may appear. In the meantime, they have become physiologically addicted to the nicotine contained in the cigarette smoke. Reinforcement partially accounts for why those who adopt unhealthy lifestyles are not weeded out through cultural evolution. As we've seen, reinforcement can actually work against us sometimes.

Interim Summary

Cultural Evolution: Lifestyle Choices and Consequences

Our lifestyles—the ways in which we interact with others; the kinds of work, hobbies, habits, and personal interests we pursue; and our decisions to marry or remain single—are the results of the cumulative effects of cultural evolution on our society. Cultural evolution includes advances in technology and medicine and changes in social and cultural customs that are passed from one generation to the next. Although cultural evolution has improved the standard of living of many of us relative to that of our ancestors, it has also produced threats to our health and safety. These threats manifest themselves in particular lifestyle choices we make regarding our diet; physical activity; use of tobacco, alcohol, and other drugs; sexual behavior; and personal safety.

Biological evolution cannot weed out individuals who adopt unhealthy lifestyles, because the consequences are not usually experienced until after people have passed their childbearing years. Many of the consequences of unhealthy behaviors are reinforcing in the short run but life-threatening in the long run. Thus, unhealthy behaviors are acquired and maintained because of their immediately reinforcing effects. It is usually only after many years that the cumulative negative effects of these lifestyles threaten a person's health.

QUESTIONS TO CONSIDER

1. What kinds of lifestyle choices have you made? Have they been generally healthy or unhealthy? What personal, social, and cultural factors influenced you to make the decisions you have?
2. How has the law of effect operated in lifestyle decisions you have made? Can you explain some of your habits—good, bad, or otherwise—in terms of their immediately reinforcing effects? If you have an unhealthy habit, and you know it is unhealthy, why do you continue to engage in it? What steps might you take to break this habit?

Healthy and Unhealthy Lifestyles

A healthy lifestyle, you will recall, is a pattern of living that enhances an individual's well-being, both physical and psychological; an unhealthy lifestyle is a pattern that diminishes physical and psychological well-being. The top five causes of deaths in 2002 among persons in the United States were heart disease, cancer, stroke, lower respiratory disease, and accidental injury (National Center for Health Statistics, 2004). The first three of these were similarly ranked 25 years ago. Yet there is increasing evidence from the health sciences that most, if not all, of these five causes can be linked in some way to unhealthy lifestyles.

To make this connection, we need to consider specific components of a lifestyle: the behaviors that diminish well-being. We all know that on occasion a child develops brain cancer or a physically fit athlete dies of a heart attack, but these are the exceptions: Generally speaking, over the long term, our lifestyle choices do affect our physical and psychological well-being. Our focus here will be on choices related to nutrition, physical fitness, tobacco use, alcohol abuse, and sexual practices.

Nutrition

Until very recently our species consumed a low-fat, high-fiber diet. Our ancestors lived mainly on fruits, vegetables, nuts, and lean meats. In the last 150 years or so, though, our diets have changed; they are now considerably higher in fats and lower in fiber, largely because of the consumption of processed foods, fried foods, and sweets. Although we eat foods like bananas, broccoli, and lean beef, we also consume foods like hot fudge sundaes, doughnuts, and fried chicken. Diets too high in saturated fats (fats found in animal products and in a few vegetable oils) and too low in fiber have been linked with specific health disorders, such

▲ *Due to changes in our diets over the years, we now consume foods that are higher in fat and lower in fiber.*

as **coronary heart disease (CHD),** the narrowing of blood vessels that supply nutrients to the heart, and **cancer,** in which malignant growths destroy body organs and tissue. Heart disease and stroke are the leading causes of death in developed countries (World Health Organization, 2003). Recent estimates indicate that approximately 20 percent of annual deaths in the United States are attributable to CHD, and 23 percent are attributable to cancer (National Heart, Lung, and Blood Institute, 2004).

The chief culprit in CHD is **serum cholesterol,** a fatlike compound that occurs naturally in the bloodstream, where it serves as a detoxifier. Cholesterol is also present in the lipid membranes of cells and in steroid hormones. Thus, it is a vital substance. Blood cholesterol has two major forms: *HDL* (high-density lipoprotein) and *LDL* (low-density lipoprotein). HDL is sometimes called "good" cholesterol, because high levels are inversely associated with CHD; it seems to play a protective role. LDL is often called "bad" cholesterol, because high levels are associated with the formation of atherosclerotic plaques, which clog arteries. It has been estimated that lowering serum cholesterol to acceptable levels by reducing fat in-

take could extend the lives of about 2 percent of Americans who die in a given year and could be supported by a modest public health program (Browner, Westernhouse, & Tice, 1991; Tosteson et al., 1997).

Around the world, the cultures with the highest death rates due to breast cancer are those whose citizens consume relatively large amounts of fats (Cohen, 1987). **Figure 16•1** shows the correlation between death due to breast cancer and daily fat consumption for 40 countries. As you can see, people in the United States have both a relatively high fat intake and relatively high death rates due to breast cancer. In contrast, people in countries such as Japan and Thailand have both relatively low fat intake and relatively low death rates due to breast cancer. Remember, these data are correlational. We know there is a relationship between high fat intake and breast cancer, but these data do not prove that high fat intake is the cause of the cancer.

Nutrition plays an important role in good health and is pivotal to a healthy lifestyle. Based on Cohen's work, we would seem likely to decrease our risk for both CHD and cancer by choosing to eat foods that are not only low in fat but also high

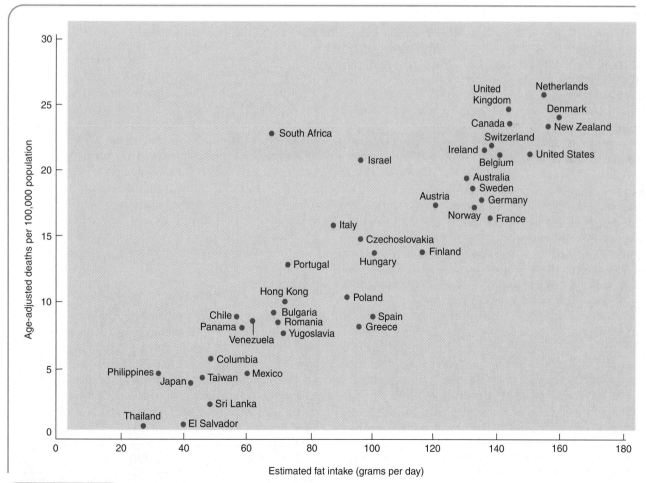

FIGURE 16•1 The correlation between diet and breast cancer. Nations whose citizens consume diets rich in fats generally show higher rates of death due to breast cancer.

(Adapted from Cohen, L. A. (1987). Diet and cancer. *Scientific American, 102,* 42–48. Reprinted with permission from Slim Films, New York City.)

FIGURE 16•2 The revised USDA food pyramid. In April 2005, the Center for Nutrition Policy and Promotion of the U.S. Department of Agriculture released a comprehensive set of recommendations regarding nutrition and lifestyles, symbolized by this new "food pyramid." The diagram depicts the variety of foods that should be consumed each day. The widths represent the relative proportions of each group that are needed daily for good health. The wider base signifies that inactive people should eat more foods that do not contain solid fats or added sugars; however, a more active person can "ascend" the pyramid and eat foods with more solid fats and added sugars. The website address printed below the graphic provides a link that will customize recommendations for your age, sex, and activity level.

Anatomy of MyPyramid

One size doesn't fit all
USDA's new MyPyramid symbolizes a personal approach to healthy eating and physical activity. The symbol has been designed to be simple. It has been developed to remind consumers to make healthy food choices and to be active every day. The different parts of the symbol are described below.

Activity
Activity is represented by the steps and the person climbing them, as a reminder of the importance of daily physical activity.

Moderation
Moderation is represented by the narrowing of each food group from bottom to top. The wider base stands for foods with little or no solid fats or added sugars. These should be selected more often. The narrower top area stands for foods containing more added sugars and solid fats. The more active you are, the more of these foods can fit into your diet.

Personalization
Personalization is shown by the person on the steps, the slogan, and the URL. Find the kinds and amounts of food to eat each day at MyPyramid.gov.

Proportionality
Proportionality is shown by the different widths of the food group bands. The widths suggest how much food a person should choose from each group. The widths are just a general guide, not exact proportions. Check the Web site for how much is right for you.

Variety
Variety is symbolized by the 6 color bands representing the 5 food groups of the Pyramid and oils. This illustrates that foods from all groups are needed each day for good health.

Gradual improvement
Gradual improvement is encouraged by the slogan. It suggests that individuals can benefit from taking small steps to improve their diet and lifestyle each day.

MyPyramid.gov
Steps to a healthier you

U.S. Department of Agriculture
Center for Nutrition Policy
and Promotion
April 2005   CNPP-16

| Grains | Vegetables | Fruits | Oils | Milk | Meat and beans |

---

in fiber. Fiber is an important dietary component that may help reduce LDL cholesterol levels. How should we balance our diets between foods that contain fat or fiber? **Figure 16•2** depicts the food pyramid derived by the U.S. Department of Agriculture to assist individuals with this decision.

Unfortunately, many of our favorite foods are high in fat and low in fiber. For example, to many people, the appeal of a candy bar or a few doughnuts is far greater than that of a tofu burger and an apple. In the long run, however, a diet centered on sweet and fatty foods is unhealthy. The immediate effect of eating these foods is to delight the palate, but over the years more serious consequences may occur: poor health, obesity, and possibly even early death. Why might our evolutionary past explain our innate preference for high-fat foods and sweets? In the past, our ancestors who faced starvation would be best served by eating fat, which provides high caloric value. In addition, sweet tastes usually indicate that food is safe, not poisonous. Thus, preferences for high-fat foods and for sweets were adaptive for early humans. These preferences have been passed

genetically along to us, but because our living conditions differ from those of our ancestors, they are not always adaptive now.

Physical Fitness

Our ancestors were probably in better physical shape than most people in developed nations today. Hunting, gathering, and a nomadic existence ensured plenty of exercise. Most people in Western societies today lead more sedentary lives. They may get little exercise other than walking to and from their cars. Like high-fat, low-fiber diets, lack of exercise is correlated with increased risk of CHD (Peters et al., 1983; Powell, Thompson, Caspersen, & Kendrick, 1987). People who exercise regularly appear to accumulate less body fat and to be less vulnerable to the negative effects of stress (Brown, 1991; Hoffman, 1997).

Kaplan (2000) has summarized the extensive research literature as showing that physical fitness decreases the risk of early death due to a wide variety of causes, including diabetes mellitus, CHD, and cystic fibrosis. According to a long-term longitudinal study of the lifestyles of 17,000 Harvard University alumni, people who exercise regularly are likely to live longer (Paffenbarger, Hyde, Wing, & Hsieh, 1986). Paffenbarger and his colleagues periodically questioned the study participants about their exercise patterns (type of exercise, frequency, and so on) and physical health. Here is a sample of their results:

1. During the first 16 years of surveillance, 1413 of the original 17,000 participants died, 45 percent from CHD and 32 percent from cancer. Significantly more of these deaths occurred in participants who had led sedentary lives.

2. Alumni who reported that they exercised the equivalent of 30 to 35 miles of running or walking per week faced *half* as much risk of dying prematurely as that faced by those who reported exercising the equivalent of 5 or fewer miles per week.

3. On average, those who exercised moderately (an equivalent of 20 miles' running or walking per week) lived about two years longer than those who exercised less than the equivalent of 5 miles.

Of course, these results do not mean that everyone who exercises regularly will live an extra two years. However, because regular exercise reduces blood pressure, increases lung capacity, and decreases the ratio of bad (LDL) to good (HDL) cholesterol, Paffenbarger's results suggest that regular exercise engenders good health. In addition, more recent research indicates that prolonged exercise activates dopamine (Hoffman, 1997), an endorphin that helps reduce negative emotions and promote positive feelings (DePue et al., 1994).

Research also shows that aerobic exercises such as running, walking, bicycling, and swimming are superior to other forms of exercise for improving cardiovascular health (Cooper, 1968, 1985). **Aerobic exercise** is activity that expends considerable energy, increases blood flow and respiration, and thereby stimulates and strengthens the heart and lungs and increases the body's efficiency in using oxygen. According to Cooper (1985), running at least three miles in less than 20 minutes four times a week (or any equivalent aerobic exercise) significantly increases cardiovascular health. One study showed that aerobic exercise had an additional benefit: reduced heart response to mental stress (Kubitz & Landers, 1993). Two groups of students who had not exercised for at least three months before the study were divided into two groups. One group rode an exercycle three times a week for 40 minutes for eight weeks; the other group did not perform any aerobic exercise. At the end of the eight-week period, both groups were given timed color perception and math tests in order to provoke moderate stress reactions. Students who had participated in the aerobic exercise program showed lower absolute heart rates in response to the tests than did the students who had not exercised. Bray and Born (2004) provided further evidence that exercise is beneficial for students. These researchers found that students who reported lower levels of

physical activity also reported higher levels of fatigue and tension. Unfortunately, although nearly two-thirds of high school students report adequate levels of exercise, this figure drops to less than half during the first eight weeks of college. Does this ring a bell with you?

Although exercise levels tend to decline for students in their first year of college, aerobic exercise has become a common activity for millions of people throughout the world. Countless people walk, jog, cycle, and take part in other aerobic forms of exercise thanks to research demonstrated the many health benefits of aerobic activity. The fact that work like Cooper's could have such a profound effect on the everyday activities of people testifies to the power of scientific research in producing positive changes in lifestyle. In the next section, we will see similar results: In many countries research on the hazards of cigarette smoking has helped reduce the number of people who smoke.

Cigarette Smoking

Although tobacco products have been used in one form or another for many centuries, we have only in the last few decades discovered just how harmful they can be. It is estimated that in the United States approximately 438,000 people die prematurely each year from diseases related to smoking (Centers for Disease Control and Prevention, 2005). In addition to the risk of lung cancer and heart disease, people who use tobacco also show increased rates of bronchitis, emphysema, and strokes. We know that the severity of these risks is directly related to the amount of carbon monoxide and tars contained in cigarette smoke.

Nonsmokers share the health risks created by cigarette smoking. Everyone is familiar with the problem of *passive smoking,* the inhalation of smoke from others' cigarettes. Hirayama (1981) showed that nonsmoking wives of husbands who smoked cigarettes were more at risk of developing lung cancer than were nonsmoking wives of nonsmoking husbands. Scores of studies have replicated this finding (e.g., Brennan et al., 2004; Hackshaw, Law, & Wald, 1997; Zhong, Goldberg, Parent, & Hanley, 2000) and have documented many other health risks attributable to breathing others' smoke (Steenland, 1999). We know, for example, that passive smoking is related to coronary heart disease (He et al., 1999; Steenland, Thun, Lally, & Heath, 1997), to an increased risk of brain hemorrhage (Anderson et al., 2004), and to nasal and sinus cancer (Benninger, 1999). Children are particularly susceptible to the effects of secondhand smoke. In addition to risking cancer and heart disease, children who live in homes where adults smoke are more likely to develop middle-ear disease (Adair-Bischoff & Sauve, 1998), lower respiratory tract infections (Li, Peat, Xuan, & Berry, 1999), and allergies (Kramer et al., 2004). And let's not forget Fido and Fluffy. Pets are at risk from passive smoking, too (Bertone, Snyder, & Moore, 2003; Rief, Bruns, & Lower, 1998).

Given the health risks of smoking and the fact that people in Western societies are knowledgeable about these risks, it is surprising that smoking is still as popular as it is. **Table 16•1** shows the prevalence of cigarette smoking by age and sex in the United States for 2002. Despite some encouraging declines in the rate of smoking over the last half century, the death toll from tobacco use continues to overshadow that caused by automobile accidents and other causes of premature death.

Why do people—especially adolescents—begin smoking? We know that peer pressure strongly contributes to the acquisition of the smoking habit during adolescence (Barber, Bolitho, & Bertrand, 1999; Biglan & Severson, 2003). As well, adolescents who have favorable impressions of a smoker are likely to imitate that person's actions, including smoking. A best friend who smokes can be a strong source of influence (e.g., Aloise-Young, Graham, & Hansen, 1994; Hirschman, Leventhal, & Glynn, 1984). There also is good evidence of intergenerational transmission of a tendency to smoke, particularly of a positive relationship between the smoking patterns of mothers and their children (Chassin, Presson, Rose, & Sherman, 1998; Nichols, Graber, Brooks-Gunn, & Botvin, 2004).

Cigarette manufacturers in the United States capitalize on young people's propensity to imitate respected others: They portray smoking as a glamorous, mature, independent, and sometimes even rebellious behavior. Billboard and magazine advertisements generally portray cigarette smokers as young, healthy, attractive, and exciting people. It is difficult to assess the impact of such advertising on smoking uptake. Perhaps the best indicator available comes from work by Pierce and his colleagues. These researchers have found a strong positive relationship between amount of exposure to cigarette advertising and smoking among adolescents in the United States (Pierce et al., 1998). Pierce also has found another interesting relationship between advertising and smoking in the United States: Smoking uptake among male youths increases after major cigarette marketing campaigns directed toward males, and uptake among female youths increases after campaigns directed toward females (Pierce & Gilpin, 1995). Not surprising, perhaps, but such findings seem to invalidate the tobacco industry's claim that advertising affects brand choice but not smoking uptake. If smoking among adolescents were merely experimentation, little harm would

be done. But adolescents who try smoking are twice as likely to smoke when they become adults, and 7 of 10 adolescents who smoke regularly maintain the habit into adulthood (Chassin, Presson, Sherman, & Edwards, 1990).

Cigarette smoking, like other forms of drug use, is addictive. To say that a person is addicted to a drug means two things. First, it means that the person's nervous system may have developed a tolerance to the drug (for some drugs, such as cocaine, sensitization, not tolerance, occurs). The term *tolerance* simply means that the neurons in the central nervous system (CNS) respond progressively less and less to the presence of the drug; larger doses of the drug therefore are required to produce the same CNS effects that smaller doses produced earlier. Second, an addicted person has become physically dependent on the drug. *Physical dependence* means that CNS neurons now require the presence of the drug to function normally. Without the drug in the CNS, the individual will experience *withdrawal symptoms*, or uncomfortable physical conditions such as sweating, tremors, and anxiety.

In addition to tolerance and physical dependence, many drugs, including the nicotine in cigarette smoke, produce *psychological dependence,* a craving to use the drug for its pleasurable effects. In other words, obtaining and using the drug become focal points of an individual's life. You may have been around people who "needed" a cigarette but were unable to get one at that moment. You likely noticed how getting a cigarette or thoughts of smoking preoccupied their attention. Another, perhaps more objective, way of describing psychological dependence is to say that it involves behavior that is acquired and maintained through positive reinforcement. Positive reinforcement—a pleasant sensation—provided by a drug strengthens or maintains the behavior that constitutes seeking, acquiring, and using the drug.

Nicotine from cigarette smoke exerts powerful effects on the CNS and heart by stimulating postsynaptic receptors sensitive to acetylcholine, a neurotransmitter. This stimulation produces temporary increases in heart rate and blood pressure, decreases in body temperature, changes in hormones released by the pituitary gland, and the release of adrenaline from the adrenal glands. And, in common with all reinforcers, natural and artificial, nicotine also causes dopamine to be secreted in the brain. As we saw in Chapters 5 and 13, the release of dopamine in the brain is reinforcing, so this effect contributes to the maintenance of cigarette smoking. Cigarette smoking also may be maintained by *negative reinforcement*. People who try to quit smoking usually suffer from withdrawal symptoms, including headaches, insomnia, anxiety, and irritability. These symptoms are relieved by smoking another cigarette. Such negative reinforcement appears to be extremely powerful. More than 60 percent of all smokers have tried to quit smoking at least once but have lit up again to escape the unpleasant withdrawal symptoms.

Nicotine alone cannot be blamed for the health risks posed by cigarette smoking. These risks are caused by the combination of nicotine and other toxic substances, such as the carbon monoxide and tars found in cigarette smoke. For

TABLE 16•1	Percentages of Persons in the United States Who Smoke, Grouped by Age and by Sex	
Age Range (years)	Males (%)	Females (%)
18–24	32	25
25–34	28	22
35–44	30	24
45–64	25	21
65 years and older	10	9

Source: National Center for Health Statistics (2004). *Health, United States, 2004, with chartbook on trends in the health of Americans.* Hyattsville, MD: Author.

example, while nicotine causes an increase in heart rate, the carbon monoxide in smoke deprives the heart muscle of the oxygen it needs to perform its work properly. The smoker's heart undergoes stress, because it is working harder with fewer nutrients than normal. Over a period of years, this continued stress weakens the heart, making it more susceptible to disease than is the heart of a nonsmoker.

Many smokers believe that they can diminish the health risks posed by their habit by switching to low-nicotine cigarettes. Unfortunately, this strategy is undermined by the fact that smokers develop a tolerance to nicotine; so they typically smoke more low-nicotine cigarettes and inhale more deeply to make up for the decreased nicotine content of their new brand. The only worthwhile approach is to cease smoking.

Most people who endeavor to quit smoking try to do so on their own (Schachter, 1982). A survey of more than 4000 adults who smoked (Zhu et al., 2000) revealed that only about one-fifth of those trying to quit were using any form of assistance (e.g., counseling, nicotine replacement therapy, etc.). One year later the researchers found that people who had used assistance were more than twice as likely to have abstained from smoking as those who had not used any form of assistance. Although underused, there are many programs available to help people stop smoking. A popular medical approach to smoking cessation is the *transdermal nicotine patch*, a bandage-like patch that allows nicotine to be absorbed through the skin. Over several months the nicotine levels of the patches are reduced, and finally the individual is weaned from nicotine altogether. This treatment is sometimes combined with the drug bupropion hydrochloride (marketed as Zyban), which reduces the desire for cigarettes in some people. Success rates are reasonably high, with 20 to 30 percent of those who quit still not smoking after six months. You may think this rate low, but consider that the long-run success rate of other treatment approaches is only about 12 percent (Pomerleau, 1992).

Quitting smoking has both immediate and long-term positive effects, even if the individual has been smoking for a long time. **Table 16·2** shows the time frame of the body's recovery from cigarette smoking. As little as 20 minutes after a person smokes a cigarette, the body begins to show recovery, including a return to normal blood pressure, pulse rate, and body temperature in the extremities. After 72 hours breathing becomes easier, partially because of increased lung capacity. After five years the risk of death by lung cancer is reduced by almost 50 percent.

Although smoking cessation is a positive change in lifestyle, it is better never to have started in the first place. Psychologists and other health researchers are therefore interested not only in designing programs to help people quit smoking, but also in developing prevention programs to help people, especially adolescents, resist the temptation to start smoking. Prevention programs are generally aimed at mitigating social influences such as imitation, peer pressure, and advertisements that can initially induce people to light up. Such programs involve educating adolescents about the disadvantages of cigarette smoking and teaching them how to

TABLE 16·2	**The Body's Response to Stopping Cigarette Smoking**
Within 20 minutes of last puff	
Blood pressure and pulse decrease to normal levels. Body temperature of extremities increases to normal levels.	
Within 1 day	
Risk of heart attacks decreases.	
Within 2 days	
Nerve endings begin regenerating. Taste and smell acuity increases.	
Within 3 days	
Breathing becomes easier because of relaxing of bronchial tubes. Lung capacity increases.	
From 2 weeks to 3 months	
Blood circulation improves. Walking and other exercises begin to seem easier. Lung efficiency increases as much as 30 percent.	
After 5 years	
Risk of death due to lung cancer decreases by 47 percent.	

Source: It's never too late to quit. (1989). *Living Well, IX*(4). Kalamazoo, MI: Bob Hope International Heart Research Institute.

respond negatively to people who encourage them to smoke. On a positive note, there is evidence that these programs may be having an impact. Chassin, Presson, Sherman, and Kim (2003) compared samples of grade 7 and grade 11 students in 1980 and 2001. The researchers found that smoking among adolescents had decreased and that beliefs about smoking had generally become more negative. In comparison to the 1980 sample, adolescents in 2001 not only viewed smoking more negatively, but also saw it as more addictive and as having more negative social consequences.

One antismoking program, the Waterloo Smoking Prevention Project (Flay et al., 1985), originally appeared especially effective in reducing the number of adolescents who experimented with smoking. Flay and colleagues first asked sixth grade students in southwestern Ontario, Canada, to seek out information about smoking and to think about their beliefs regarding smoking. Next, they taught the students about the social pressures involved in smoking and gave them explicit training in how to resist those pressures, including the role-playing of resistance strategies. The researchers also asked each student to make a commitment regarding whether he or she would start smoking. They then monitored the students five times over the next two years to see how many of them had experimented with smoking. By the end of the two-year period, fewer than 8 percent of the students who had been involved in the prevention program had experimented with smoking. In contrast, almost 19 percent of the students who had not gone through the program had experimented with smoking. The program obviously had a very positive initial impact.

What happened in the longer run? Flay and colleagues obtained information about smoking behavior at grades 11 and 12 for more than 80 percent of the original participants. Unfortunately, the initial gains had been lost (Flay et al., 1989). This is not a rare outcome. Wiehe, Garrison, Christakis, Ebel, and Rivara (2005) reviewed eight school-based programs that included long-term follow-up of participants and found that only one of these showed significant lasting effects. One promising suggestion (Murray, Pirie, Luepker, & Pallonen, 1989) is that occasional "booster" sessions may be necessary to maintain the effects of initial prevention exercises. This makes sense. After a prevention program for adolescents ends, peer pressure and smoking by family members can continue to be important sources of temptation to smoke, whereas resistance strategies may be forgotten over time or may become inappropriate to contemporary circumstances as the adolescent ages. Booster sessions could be helpful in upgrading and strengthening the original resistance strategies.

Drinking Alcoholic Beverages

The psychological effects of alcohol (and other drugs) have been known to humanity longer than have those of nicotine. Alcohol has been used for thousands of years for its euphoria-inducing properties.

Alcohol is widely abused today. To abuse a substance means to use it in a way that poses a threat to the safety and well-being of the user, society, or both. Most people who use alcohol do not abuse it, and not all people who abuse alcohol are alcoholics. For example, people who drive under the influence of alcohol pose a serious threat to both themselves and others, but they may not be alcoholics.

Alcoholism is an addiction to ethanol, the psychoactive agent in alcoholic beverages. A psychoactive substance is any substance that affects brain and CNS functioning. Alcoholism can be a serious problem for many. About half of Americans over the age of 11 report having an alcoholic drink within the past 30 days of being asked, and almost 7 percent report having consumed at least five drinks on the same occasion on at least 5 days during a 30-day period (Substance Abuse and Mental Health Services Administration, 2005).

Table 16•3 describes some of the very real and serious physical, psychological, and social consequences of alcohol abuse. For example, in regard to cultural consequences, alcohol often plays a role in relationship conflicts (MacDonald, Zanna, & Holmes, 2000). When asked to think about a past conflict in a romantic relationship, people who had been intoxicated at the time felt more negatively about the incident and believed that their partners were more upset.

Because consumption of moderate to heavy amounts of alcohol suppresses neuronal activity of the brain and reduces inhibitory controls on behavior, individuals who are drinking

TABLE 16•3 Potential Physical, Psychological, and Social Consequences of Alcohol Abuse
Physical
Cirrhosis, which results in death
Poor nutrition
Impaired sexual functioning
Psychological
Gradual deterioration of cognitive functioning
Increased feelings of anxiety and irritability
Aggressive behavior
Social
Impaired social skills and interpersonal functioning
Divorce
Employee absenteeism and decreased productivity
Death in alcohol-related traffic accidents

become more relaxed and more outgoing, show impaired motor coordination, and have difficulty thinking clearly. As they consume more alcohol, neuronal activity in the brain is depressed further, producing distortions in perception, slurred speech, memory loss, impaired judgment, and poor control of movement. Ingesting large amounts of alcohol over a relatively short period of time can even result in unconsciousness and death.

Alcohol is rapidly absorbed from the stomach and intestinal tract. Because alcohol is a small fat- and water-soluble molecule, it is quickly and evenly distributed throughout the body via the circulatory system. Blood alcohol levels are affected by body mass and muscularity. Generally speaking, a large person will have to consume more alcohol than a smaller person to attain the same level of intoxication; but at a given weight, a muscular person will have to consume more than a person with a higher proportion of body fat. In addition, regardless of body characteristics, blood levels of alcohol increase more slowly in people who drink on a full stomach than in those having little or no food in their stomachs. Food in the stomach impairs absorption of substances through the gastrointestinal tract.

A person's degree of inebriation is related to the manner in which alcohol is metabolized by the body. Unlike most other drugs, alcohol is metabolized by the liver at a constant rate, regardless of how much alcohol has been consumed. For example, in one hour, the body will metabolize the alcohol in about 12 ounces of beer or 1 ounce of 80 to 100 proof liquor. Hence, if a person consumes more than 12 ounces of beer or 1 ounce of liquor in an hour, his or her blood alcohol level rises beyond the level caused by the first drink, and he or she may begin to become intoxicated. When blood alcohol levels reach 0.3 to 0.4 percent (roughly the effect of 10 drinks consumed over a short period), people lose consciousness. At 0.5

percent, neurons in the brain that control the respiratory and circulatory systems stop functioning, causing death. Tests for driving under the influence of alcohol measure blood alcohol concentration (BAC); in the United States it is illegal to drive with a BAC greater than 0.08 percent. Research has shown that even at "safe" legal levels, alcohol consumption may increase drivers' risk-taking behaviors and increase the likelihood of an accident (Burian, Liguori, & Robinson, 2002). Consuming alcohol can also make people more tolerant in their attitudes toward drinking and driving (MacDonald, Zanna, & Fong, 1995), a truly lethal combination. In the United States, thirty percent of traffic crash fatalities in 2002 were alcohol-related (Yi, Williams, & Smothers, 2004).

Although you have probably heard the oft-quoted phrase that "drinking and driving don't mix," you may or may not have heard that "drinking and using other drugs don't mix." Drinking and using other drugs can be deadly. **Table 16•4** describes some of the dangerous consequences of mixing alcohol with other drugs, including over-the-counter medications.

Heavy drinkers who attempt to quit drinking sometimes suffer *delirium tremens*—the DTs—a pattern of withdrawal symptoms that includes trembling, irritability, hallucinations, sleeplessness, and confusion. In many cases alcoholics become so physically dependent on the drug that abrupt cessation of drinking produces convulsions and sometimes death.

As you learned in Chapter 3, an individual's tendency to develop alcoholism may have a genetic basis (McKim, 1991; Vaillant, 2002). Vaillant and Milofsky (1982), in a long-term study of adopted boys, found that biological sons of chronic alcoholics had a greater tendency to become alcoholics themselves, despite the fact that their adoptive parents were nonalcoholics. Cloninger (1987) found that biological children of alcoholic parents adopted at birth into nonalcoholic homes were about four times more likely to abuse alcohol than were other adopted children whose biological parents were nonalcoholics. However, although we know that genes are involved

in alcoholism, we are far from understanding their precise role (Parsian & Cloninger, 1995).

As pointed out in Chapter 12, women who drink moderate to heavy quantities of alcohol during pregnancy risk giving birth to children who suffer from *fetal alcohol syndrome*. Alcohol crosses the placental barrier and enters the fetal blood supply, where it retards the development of the fetus's nervous system. Fetal alcohol syndrome is characterized by decreased birth weight and physical malformations. It is the third leading cause of birth defects involving mental retardation, and it is completely preventable. Simply put, a woman will not give birth to a child with fetal alcohol syndrome if she does not drink during her pregnancy.

Alcohol use and cigarette smoking are prompted by many of the same factors: chiefly imitation and peer pressure. Many young people view drinking as the thing to do, both because it seemingly represents maturity, independence, and rebelliousness and because it is associated with having fun. For example, beer advertisements portray people drinking together at the end of a hard day's work, at festive parties, and to celebrate special occasions. To their credit, some brewers are now using their advertisements also to inform consumers of the potential dangers of alcohol abuse.

Treatment programs for drug abuse, including treatment for smoking and drinking, take several forms. Some programs involve aversion therapy (see Chapter 18); others consist of less intrusive forms of therapy and include extensive counseling. In the latter type of treatment, the psychologist's or counselor's general aim is to teach the individual to

1. identify environmental cues or circumstances that may cause the addictive behavior to occur or recur;

2. learn to behave in ways that are incompatible with the undesired behavior;

3. have confidence that he or she can overcome the addiction; and

TABLE 16•4   The Effects of Mixing Alcohol with Other Drugs

Drug	Example	Possible Consequences of Using Simultaneously with Alcohol
Narcotics	Codeine or Percodan	Increased suppression of CNS functions and possible death due to respiratory failure
Minor pain relievers	Aspirin or Tylenol	Stomach irritation and bleeding; increased likelihood of liver damage from acetaminophen
Antihistamines	Actifed	Increased drowsiness, making operation of motor vehicles and power equipment more dangerous
CNS stimulants	Caffeine, Dexedrine	Reversal of some of the depressive effects of alcohol, but without increasing sobriety
Antipsychotics	Largactil	Impaired control of motor movements and possible death due to respiratory failure
Antianxiety drugs	Valium, Librium	Decreased arousal; impaired judgment, which can lead to accidents in the home or on the road

Source: Based on Palfai, T., & Jankiewicz, H. (1991). *Drugs and human behavior.* Dubuque, IA: Wm. C. Brown. Also on data from the National Institute for Alcohol Abuse and Alcoholism Clearinghouse for Alcohol Information (1982).

4. view setbacks in overcoming the addiction as temporary and as learning experiences in which new coping skills can be acquired.

Treatment programs for people with addictive behaviors are only moderately successful. For example, many alcohol management programs have about a 30 to 50 percent success rate. Recall that smoking cessation programs (not including those that use the nicotine patch) fare even worse: They have about a 12 percent success rate (Pomerleau, 1992). As you might guess, an important goal for psychologists in the twenty-first century is to develop more effective programs for treating addictive behaviors.

Sexually Transmitted Diseases and AIDS

Human infectious diseases are products of evolution. They exist because viruses and bacteria exploit our physiology to reproduce. Behavioral patterns can be exploited too; a germ that can spread as a result of a behavior may benefit if that behavior is frequent or common. Sexual behavior is clearly crucial to our survival. It's not surprising, then, that it also is the route by which many diseases spread from one individual to another. **Table 16•5** lists the causes, symptomatology, and treatment of four such diseases, collectively known as *sexually transmitted diseases,* or STDs.

The most life-threatening STD is acquired immune deficiency syndrome (AIDS), which can be spread not only through sex but also through tainted blood transfusions and the sharing of hypodermic needles among intravenous drug users. AIDS is the last stage of the illness triggered by the human immunodeficiency virus (HIV). That is, AIDS is the disease; HIV is the cause. HIV attacks the human immune system, which is the body's basic defense against infection. (We'll examine the immune system later in this chapter.) By itself, AIDS does not kill. Rather, HIV compromises the human immune system to such an extent that other diseases, such as cancer and pneumonia, can more readily infect and kill the person who has it.

Once prevalent mainly among homosexual men in the western hemisphere, AIDS has spread among heterosexuals as well. The World Health Organization (2003) estimated that 40 million people were infected with HIV at the beginning of 2003. In that year there were nearly 5 million new cases of HIV infection, and approximately 3 million people died from AIDS. According to estimates from the Centers for Disease Control and Prevention (2004), 46 percent of AIDS cases in the United States diagnosed in 2003 were the result of male-to-male homosexual contact, 22 percent were the result of the sharing of contaminated needles among injection drug users (not including the cases also involving sexual contact), and 31 percent were the result of heterosexual contact.

Behavioral changes known as *safe sex practices* can reduce a person's risk of contracting an STD, including HIV and consequent AIDS. These practices include limiting the number of sexual partners, finding out the sexual history of partners before engaging in sexual relations, and using a condom during sex; of course, abstaining from sex altogether will provide complete safety. In the case of AIDS, the necessary lifestyle changes involve not only safe sex practices but also behaviors

TABLE 16•5 **Four STDs: Their Causes, Symptomatology, and Treatment**

STD	Cause	Symptoms	Treatment
Gonorrhea	Gonococcus bacterium	Appear 3 to 5 days after sexual contact with afflicted person. In both sexes, discharges of pus. Urination accompanied by a burning sensation. In female, pelvic inflammatory disease. If untreated, fevers, headaches, backaches, and abdominal pain develop.	Penicillin and other antibiotics can cure this disease.
Genital herpes	Herpes simplex types I and II virus	Small blisters appear around point of sexual contact. Blisters burst, causing pain. Symptoms recur every 1 to 2 weeks.	Acyclovir and similar drugs can suppress but do not cure this condition.
Syphilis	Treponema pallidum bacterium	Chancre or lesion develops where bacteria first entered body. If untreated, the bacteria penetrate body tissue, including the brain. May result in insanity and death.	Penicillin and other antibiotics can cure this disease.
AIDS	Human immunodeficiency virus (HIV)	Virus destroys body's immune system, allowing diseases like cancer and pneumonia to infect the body.	A combination of protease-inhibiting drugs can suppress the HIV load and improve immunologic functioning, lessen symptoms, and reduce the risk of transmission to newborns. There is no cure for the syndrome, however.

▲ *Behavioral changes—safe sex practices—can reduce a person's risk of contracting an STD. The key question is how to bring about these changes.*

that will prevent nonsexual transmission of the AIDS virus, such as refusing to share hypodermic needles.

If everyone engaged in safe sex practices, and if injection drug users refused to share hypodermic needles, the AIDS threat would be reduced significantly. The problem, of course, is that it is one thing to talk about safe sex and clean needles but another thing actually to act. Why is this so? For the intravenous drug user, the answer is clear: The most important thing in life is getting high. Nothing else really matters. For the couple about to engage in casual sex, the issue is less clear. Although each individual's behavior is motivated by a wish for sexual gratification, the social awkwardness involved in discussing each other's sexual history may lead to a failure to engage in safe sex behaviors.

One way to reduce this problem may be to establish prevention programs in which people role-play safe sex practices so as to overcome the feelings of uneasiness involved in asking a prospective partner about his or her sexual history (Bosarge, 1989). Most importantly, prevention programs must accomplish four main goals (e.g., Fisher & Fisher, 1992, 2000):

1. Teach people the relationship between their behavior and their risk of contracting STDs, including AIDS.

2. Familiarize people with safe sex behaviors, such as the proper way to use a condom.

3. Break down barriers to the use of safe sex practices, such as people's refusal to inquire about partners' sexual history, their assumption that they are invulnerable to STD or HIV infection, and/or their belief in myths about using condoms (such as that only wimps use them).

4. Provide encouragement and support in order to motivate behaviors that reduce STD and AIDS risks.

Although prevention programs have had some success in reducing high-risk sexual behaviors, such programs are least successful in situations in which people's personal or cultural values prevent them from engaging in safe sex practices (Herdt, 2001; Herdt & Lindenbaum, 1992). These values generally involve misperceptions of what practicing safe sex means. Some males refuse to wear condoms because they feel that doing so would detract from their conception of what it means to be a man. These individuals perceive that practicing safe sex robs them of their masculinity. Also, many people, especially young people, have the mistaken belief that they are invulnerable to any type of misfortune, including contracting an STD. They believe, in essence, that "things happen to other people, not me." The illusion of control seems to play a role as well. Some people falsely believe that they can tell by looking at another person whether he or she is infected, and therefore whether safe sex practices are necessary (e.g., Thompson, Kent, Thomas, & Vrungos, 1999). Other research shows that familiarity breeds a false sense of safety. Misovich, Fisher, and Fisher (1996) found that college students believed that simply knowing a partner well reduced the need to use condoms. The situation worsens with alcohol consumption. Alcohol consumption can create what Steele and Josephs (1990) call *alcohol myopia*. In the context of sex, alcohol myopia means that the salient attractions of sexual activity remain clear to the drinker, but the more distant risks of fatal infection recede to the blurry horizon (MacDonald, Zanna, & Fong, 1998; MacDonald, MacDonald, Zanna, & Fong, 2000). One result is that people fail to use condoms, thus increasing their risk of HIV and other STD infection. The challenge for psychologists and counselors is to help people reorient these types of thinking and understand the connection between their sexual behavior and its possible negative consequences.

Biology and Culture

Cultural Reactions to Contagious Diseases

Because we live in a closely connected world, contagious diseases can potentially spread rapidly and virulently. The risk of pandemics such as avian flu and severe acute respiratory syndrome (SARS) has been the topic of much public discussion. Beyond the issues of detection and control, however, are the social and cultural implications of how we would respond to the prospect of large segments of our society becoming potential carriers of deadly diseases. Our recent history of coping with the spread of HIV and AIDS provides some clues as to how we might react to another global epidemic.

Imagine that you are at a shopping mall and that you are so perceptive that you can identify the illness of everyone in the mall who is sick. You have been shopping for a while and wish to rest for a few minutes. You approach an area that has two benches, each of which is just wide enough for two people. Each bench is already occupied by a middle-aged woman. You can tell that the woman sitting on one bench has coronary heart disease, and that the woman on the other bench has AIDS. On which bench will you choose to sit?

Although knowledge of the routes of possible infection of HIV and AIDS is improving, there still are people who would not sit next to someone if they know that the person has AIDS (Bishop, 1994; Rushing, 1995). But why? Perhaps you know that AIDS is a contagious disease and that heart disease is not. If you know that, perhaps you also know that there is absolutely no evidence that AIDS can be transmitted through casual contact, such as by sitting next to an HIV-infected woman on a bench at the mall. Yet many people would not feel comfortable sitting next to the woman with AIDS for fear that somehow they could catch the disease. Even health care professionals may be prone to this feeling: A survey of persons with HIV infections during the mid-1990s found that 26 percent of those responding reported experiencing some discrimination against them by health care practitioners (Schuster et al., 2005).

Unfortunately, segments of our culture translated some of these feelings into political actions, calling for quarantines (for example, refusing to let children with AIDS attend school), ostracizing people with AIDS, or trying to get laws enacted that would force them to be registered by name as carriers of the disease. Despite widespread media coverage of the AIDS epidemic throughout the world and instructional programs designed to educate the public about AIDS, it remains the most feared, stigmatized, and publicly misunderstood contagious disease of our time (Rushing, 1995). Being identified as a member of a "AIDS carrier" group can lead to rejection by the dominant society, self-doubt, and lessened self-esteem (Santana & Dancy, 2000) and the threat of being stigmatized may lessen the likelihood that an individual will voluntarily seek testing for HIV infection (Herek, Capitanio, & Widaman, 2003).

When negative behavior of this sort occurs, especially on a collective, widespread social basis, it is referred to as *fear of contagion*. Historical analyses of previous epidemics, such as the Black Death (bubonic plague), that struck Europe during the fourteenth century, have shown that fear of contagion is likely to occur only when four conditions are met: The disease must be deadly, it must appear suddenly, it must have no apparent explanation, and people must believe that many people are at risk of contracting it (Rushing, 1995).

The AIDS epidemic meets these four conditions. First, it is deadly. Second, it appeared suddenly: The first cases of AIDS in the United States were reported in 1981. Through the year 2003 the Centers for Disease Control and Prevention estimate that there were about 930,000 cases of AIDS and over 500,000 deaths from the disease in the United States. Third, AIDS still is not completely understood. We know that a virus causes it, but we don't know how to completely eradicate it—for this disease there is no equivalent of the polio vaccine. And finally, as AIDS makes strong inroads into heterosexual populations, more and more people now see themselves and others like them as being at risk of contracting the disease. As a result, fear of contagion tends to foster the false belief that AIDS can be transmitted through casual contact (Bishop, 1991a, 1991b; Boone et al., 2003).

Interim Summary

Healthy and Unhealthy Lifestyles

The kinds of food we eat, how much exercise we get, the extent to which we use tobacco and alcohol, and our sexual practices have profound implications for our health and longevity. Eating right, exercising regularly, not smoking, consuming alcohol moderately, and practicing safe sex do not guarantee a long and healthy life, but they do improve our chances.

People who eat high-fat, low-fiber diets tend to be more susceptible to CHD and cancer than are people who eat low-fat, high-fiber diets. But many of the foods we like the most are high in fat and low in fiber. In the short run, eating these foods may delight our palate, but over the long run, eating these foods may lead to weight gain and increased LDL cholesterol levels, both risk factors for CHD and cancer. A well-balanced diet in combination with regular exercise reduces the risk of CHD and cancer. Aerobic exercise is particularly helpful to health. Research indicates that running at least three miles in less than 20 minutes four times a week significantly increases cardiovascular health.

Poor eating habits and sedentary living are not the only lifestyle aspects that put people at risk for developing CHD and cancer. Cigarette smoking and alcohol abuse have similar effects. Why do people start and continue to do these things? In everyday language, these behaviors can make people feel good. In addition to being reinforcing, these behaviors are addictive—the body may become dependent on the chemicals contained in cigarette smoke and alcohol for normal, day-to-day functioning.

Another threat to health and longevity is sexually transmitted disease. People have been advised to take precautionary measures against contracting any STD by practicing safe sex. In the case of AIDS, people who inject themselves with drugs also are advised not to share hypodermic needles. Programs aimed at preventing the spread of AIDS and other STDs focus on teaching people the relationship between their behavior and the likelihood of contracting one or more of these diseases, and on instruction in safe sex strategies.

Fear of contagion is influenced by four factors: The disease must be deadly, it must appear suddenly, it must have no apparent explanation, and people must believe that many are at risk of contracting it. Despite education efforts to inform the public about AIDS, fear of contagion with respect to AIDS remains a serious problem.

QUESTIONS TO CONSIDER

1. What kinds of unhealthy behaviors are part of your lifestyle? What psychological processes influenced how these behaviors developed? Why do you keep engaging in these behaviors?
2. Would a global pandemic based on a disease like avian flu trigger fear of contagion? Would cultural differences play a role in how different countries might respond to such a threat?

Preventing Unhealthy Lifestyles through Self-Control

As we've seen, our lifestyles are not always wholly adaptive; some aspects of our lifestyles are detrimental to both our longevity and our quality of life. We have seen that unhealthy aspects of our lifestyles include poor nutrition, physical inactivity, cigarette smoking, alcohol abuse, and failure to use safe sex practices. Behaviors that make up our lifestyles are partly a consequence of the environmental conditions created by cultural evolution and partly a result of our genetic and physiological constitution.

We can avoid unhealthy lifestyles. The problem, of course, is motivating ourselves to substitute healthy behaviors for unhealthy ones and to make positive lifestyle changes. Cultural evolution, or, more specifically, technological progress, offers choices to people in developed societies: to use a condom or not, to eat foods rich in vitamins and minerals or to follow a poor diet, to smoke or not, and so forth.

How do we decide whether we should eat fattening and unhealthy foods now or follow a prudent diet and lose weight and become healthier over the long run? The essence of each of these choices is whether to opt for the *small, short-term reward* produced by one action or the *larger, longer-term reward* produced by another, necessarily incompatible action. You can have unprotected sex now with a partner you do not know very well and run the risk of getting an STD or AIDS, or you can practice safe sex and enhance the likelihood that you will remain healthy. What really is at issue here is **self-control,** behavior that produces a larger, long-term reward when we are faced with the choice between it and behavior producing a small, short-term reward.

▲ *Jared Fogle has learned the benefits of self-control—in this case, choosing the long-term benefits of weight loss over the short-term rewards of overeating. Jared became known as "The Subway Guy" by sticking to a diet of sandwiches from Subway.*

Rachlin (1970) and Ainslie (1975) proposed a clear and conceptually useful model of self-control. This model, based on laboratory research using animals, captures well the essence of most self-control decisions that we face. Look at **Figure 16·3**. In each panel the vertical axis represents the value of a reward to us; the horizontal axis represents the passage of time. In panel (a) the curve represents a large, long-term reward—for example, acquiring and maintaining good physical health. Let us assume either that you are not in very good physical health (you have a high level of blood cholesterol because you eat a lot of high-fat, low-fiber foods, you smoke and drink more than you would like, and you don't get much exercise) or that you are in good condition and wish to remain that way. That is, the curve in Figure 16.3(a) represents a goal you wish to achieve or a condition you wish to maintain *in the long run.* Now look at panel (b). This curve represents a smaller, short-term reward; for example, the pleasure derived from eating a hot fudge sundae or fried chicken, smoking a cigarette, drinking a beer, or watching

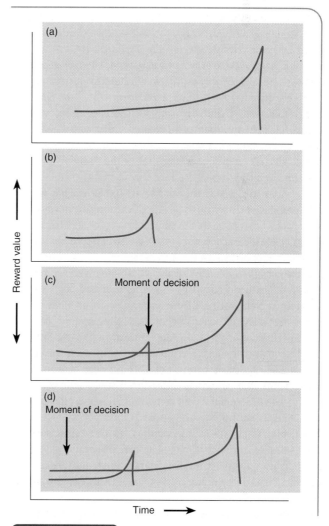

FIGURE 16·3 The relationship between commitment and self-control. (a) Value of the long-term, delayed reward. (b) Value of short-term, immediate reward. (c) No commitment, no self-control. (d) Self-control and commitment.

TV for three hours. The curve representing the value of the short-term reward in (b) looks smaller than the curve representing the long-term reward in (a), and it is—some of the time.

But now look at what happens when the two curves are placed in the same graph in panel (c): There comes a point in time at which the value of the small, short-term reward seems greater than that of the larger, long-term reward. How can that be?

Suppose that you are dieting. Further suppose that your roommate or spouse is baking your favorite kind of cookies. You are drawn to the kitchen, where a dozen freshly baked cookies, giving off a tantalizing aroma, are sitting on the counter. Your roommate (or spouse) says, "Have one." Now you are faced with a choice: Do you eat a cookie or two—or perhaps more—and consume more calories than your diet calls for? Or do you say, "No, thanks"? The temptation you face here is captured in Figure 16.3(c). At this moment the value of the small, short-term reward (the cookies) temporarily rises above that of the larger, long-term reward (maintaining or losing weight). But you cannot regularly consume more calories than your diet calls for *and* maintain or lose weight.

Many psychologists argue that if you wait until you are faced with the choice between the small, short-term reward and the larger, long-term reward (the *moment of decision*), you will most likely opt for the small, short-term reward. The most effective way to exercise self-control is to somehow avoid having to make that choice in the first place. Self-control is a *prior commitment to a course of action that precludes making this decision.* According to this model, the best way to exercise self-control is to move the moment of decision to some time *before* you are confronted with the choice between the two rewards. (See Figure 16.3(d).) That way, at the moment of decision, the value of the long-term reward is higher than the value of the short-term reward. Setting your alarm clock the night before you have to get up early (as opposed to making the decision to get up in the morning when you are groggy) and enrolling in a payroll savings plan (as opposed to getting your paycheck and deciding then to put some of it in savings) are forms of prior commitment. If you haven't set the alarm clock or enrolled in the savings plan, future events (the larger, long-term reward) may have little influence on your behavior at the moment of decision. In the case of dieting, prior commitment might lead you to avoid being home at times when your roommate or spouse is baking cookies or to enter a contract with that person stating that he or she will not offer you goodies. Other possible self-control strategies also exist for coping with situations like this. For example, you might imagine yourself saying no over and over again to such a temptation and feeling happy about your answer, then follow this model when actually faced with the temptation.

As you have learned, many treatment programs are unsuccessful at getting people to make lasting commitments to changes in their lifestyles. What is sorely needed is the development of effective commitment strategies that encourage people to make choices that benefit their health. Developing these strategies is a preeminent goal of **health psychology,** the branch of psychology concerned with the promotion and maintenance of sound health practices such as eating well, exercising regularly, not smoking or drinking, and engaging in safe sex practices. Once people begin viewing life as consisting of a series of choices between small, short-term rewards and larger, long-term rewards, they can begin to see clearly how the choices they make now influence the consequences they will face later.

Interim Summary

Preventing Unhealthy Lifestyles through Self-Control

We can avoid the negative consequences of unhealthy behaviors by exercising self-control—by opting to engage in behavior that produces the larger, but often delayed, reward when we are confronted with the choice between it and the smaller, more immediate reward. According to the model of self-control developed by Rachlin and Ainslie, self-control is most likely when we make a prior commitment to a course of action that leads only to the larger, long-term reward.

QUESTIONS TO CONSIDER

1. Think of an aspect of your life in which you would like to exercise more self-control. Explain how you might implement the model of self-control described in this section to help you with this aspect of your life. What barriers might prevent you from implementing this model in your life?
2. Many people believe that exercising self-control is a matter of "willpower." What is willpower, and how does it differ from the model of self-control you have just read about? From your point of view, is self-control due to willpower? Why or why not?

Stress and Health

At some point, we've all experienced stress, whether it was taking a difficult exam or coping with the loss of a friend. **Stress** is a pattern of physiological, behavioral, emotional, and cognitive responses to real or imagined stimuli that are perceived as blocking a goal or endangering or otherwise threatening our well-being. These stimuli are generally aversive and are called **stressors**. Stress is a product of natural selection. It is a behavioral adaptation that helped our ancestors fight or flee from wild animals and enemies. Likewise, stress often helps us confront or escape threatening situations (Linsky, Bachman,

▲ *Stressors, such as the flooding of the homes and businesses of New Orleans residents in the aftermath of Hurricane Katrina in 2005, threaten our normal life routine and well-being.*

& Straus, 1995). Although stress is not a direct product of cultural evolution, the changes in the environment wrought by cultural evolution have helped make stress commonplace.

Stressors come in many forms. They may be catastrophic in nature (see Meichenbaum, 1995), or they may belong to the class of trivial everyday irritations. Stressors are not always bad. Some stressors, such as athletic competition and class exams, can affect behavior in positive ways. When stress is extended over long periods, however, it can have negative effects on both psychological and physical health (Selye, 1991).

The Biological Basis of Stress

Our physiological response to stressors is governed by the autonomic nervous system, which is controlled by the hypothalamus. When an individual senses a stressor, the hypothalamus sends signals to the autonomic nervous system and to the pituitary gland, both of which respond by stimulating body organs to change their normal activities:

1. Heart rate increases, blood pressure rises, blood vessels constrict, blood sugar levels rise, and blood flow is directed away from extremities and toward major organs.

2. Breathing becomes deeper and faster and air passages dilate, allowing more air to enter the lungs.

3. Digestion stops and perspiration increases.

4. The adrenal glands secrete adrenaline (epinephrine), which stimulates the heart and other organs.

Accompanying these physiological changes can be a pattern of behaviors, emotions, or cognitive responses. The physiological changes prepare us for some action. We may also feel the stress response as an emotion, although the emotion may depend upon the nature of the stressor; stress may make us feel frightened in some situations or exhilarated in others. Finally, our cognitive state may be altered, as when we respond to fright with anticipation of danger.

Collectively, these physiological responses produce a heightened psychological and physical state of alertness and readiness for action. Regardless of the nature of the stressor, and whether we confront the stressor or run from it, the biological response is the same. Whether you find yourself in a dark alley confronted by a man with a knife or facing your next psychology exam, the autonomic nervous system and the pituitary gland stimulate the body to respond.

There are two cases in which such responses can be maladaptive. First, stress can produce anxiety, which may impair your ability to perform a task. As you may have experienced yourself, anxiety can make it more difficult to perform on an exam, deliver a public speech, compete during an athletic event, or remember lines in a play.

The second case, as I've mentioned, involves the effects of prolonged and severe stress. Many people's lifestyles place them in situations in which they are confronted with stressors daily. As we will see shortly, such lifestyles place these people at increased risk of illness.

Selye's General Adaptation Syndrome   Much of what we know about the effects of dealing with prolonged and severe stressors on the body stems from the work of endocrinologist Hans Selye. Through his work with laboratory animals, Selye found that chronic exposure to severe stressors produces a sequence of three physiological stages: *alarm, resistance,* and *exhaustion.* (See **Figure 16•4.**) Selye (1956/1976, 1993) referred to these stages collectively as the **general adaptation syndrome.**

The responses in the *alarm stage* involve arousal of the autonomic nervous system and occur when an organism is first confronted with a stressor. During this stage the organism's resistance to the stressor temporarily drops below normal, and the organism may experience shock—impairment of normal physiological functioning. With continued exposure to the stressor, the organism enters the *stage of resistance,* during which its autonomic nervous system returns to normal functioning. Resistance to the stressor increases and eventually plateaus at above-normal levels. The stage of

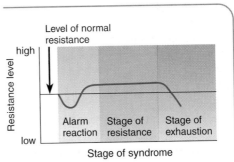

FIGURE 16•4   The general adaptation syndrome as proposed by Hans Selye.

(Figure 3, the three phases of the general adaptation syndrome, from *Stress without Distress* by Hans Selye, M.D. Copyright © 1974 by Hans Selye, M.D. Reprinted by permission of HarperCollins Publishers.)

resistance, then, reflects the organism's adaptation to environmental stressors. However, with continued exposure to the stressor, the organism enters the *stage of exhaustion*. During this stage the organism loses its ability to adapt, and resistance plummets to below-normal levels, leaving the organism susceptible to illness and even death.

Biologically speaking, we are able to adapt to the presence of environmental stressors for only so long before we become susceptible to exhaustion and illness. The extent to which people can adapt varies across individuals and depends on how the stressor is perceived.

Chapter 13 pointed out that emotional responses evolved because they are useful and adaptive. Why, then, can they harm our health? The answer appears to be that our emotional responses are designed primarily to cope with short-term events. The physiological responses that accompany negative emotions prepare us to threaten or fight rivals or to run away from dangerous situations. Harvard physiologist Walter Cannon (1953) popularized the phrase **fight-or-flight response,** which refers to the physiological reactions that prepare us for the strenuous efforts required by fighting or running away. Normally, once we have bluffed or fought with an adversary or run away from a dangerous situation, the threat is over and our physiological condition can return to normal. As long as the responses are brief, the physiological responses do not have adverse long-term effects. But when the threatening situations are continuous rather than episodic, they produce a more or less continuous stress response. This continued state of arousal can lead to CHD and other physical problems.

Several studies have demonstrated the deleterious effects of stress on health. For example, survivors of concentration camps, who were obviously subjected to long-term stress, have generally poorer health later in life than do other people of the same age (Cohen et al., 1953). Holocaust survivors who were children during the Second World War are more likely to display psychosocial problems and post-traumatic symptoms today (Cohen, Brom, & Dasberg, 2001). Air traffic controllers who work at busy airports with relatively high danger of collisions show a greater incidence of hypertension, which gets worse as they grow older (Cobb & Rose, 1973). (See **Figure 16•5.**)

Physiological Mechanisms Involved in Stress

Why does prolonged stress affect physical health? Let's look more closely at the physiological mechanisms involved in the stress response. As Chapter 13 discussed, emotions consist of behavioral, autonomic, and hormonal responses. The latter two components—autonomic and hormonal—are the responses that can have adverse effects on health. (Of course, the behavioral components can, too, if a person rashly gets into a fight with someone much bigger and stronger.) Because threatening situations generally call for vigorous activity, the autonomic and hormonal responses help make the body's energy resources available. The sympathetic branch of the autonomic nervous system is activated, and the adrenal glands secrete epinephrine, norepinephrine, and steroid stress hor-

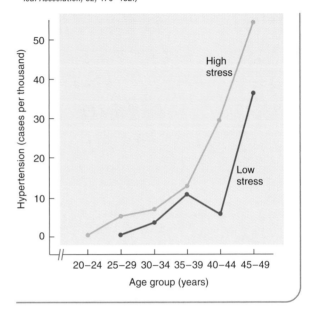

FIGURE 16•5 Stress and hypertension in air traffic controllers. Graphed are rates of hypertension in air traffic controllers in various age groups at high-stress and low-stress airports.

(Based on data from Cobb, S., & Rose, R. M. (1973). Hypertension, peptic ulcer, and diabetes in air traffic controllers. *Journal of the American Medical Association, 82,* 476–482.)

mones. Because the effects of sympathetic activity are similar to those of the adrenal hormones, I will limit my discussion to the hormonal responses.

Epinephrine releases the stored form of glucose that is present in the muscles, thus providing energy for strenuous exercise. Along with norepinephrine, epinephrine also increases blood flow to the muscles by increasing the output of the heart, which also increases blood pressure. In the short term, these changes are beneficial, because they prepare the body for fight-or-flight responses. Over the long term, however, these changes contribute to CHD. The other stress-related hormone is cortisol, a steroid secreted by the cortex of the adrenal gland. Cortisol is called a **glucocorticoid,** one of a group of steroids that have profound effects on glucose metabolism, effects similar to those of epinephrine. In addition, glucocorticoids help break down protein and convert it to glucose, help make fats available for energy, increase blood flow, and stimulate behavioral responsiveness, presumably by affecting the brain. They have other physiological effects, too, some of which are only poorly understood. Almost every cell in the body contains glucocorticoid receptors, which means that few parts of the body are unaffected by these hormones. (See **Figure 16•6.**)

Glucocorticoids do more than help an animal react to a stressful situation—they help it survive. When a rat's adrenal glands are removed, it becomes much more susceptible to the negative effects of stress. A stressful situation that a normal rat would take in its stride may kill an animal whose adrenal glands have been removed. Physicians know they must provide addi-

FIGURE 16·6 Control and effects of the secretion of epinephrine, norepinephrine, and cortisol by the adrenal glands.

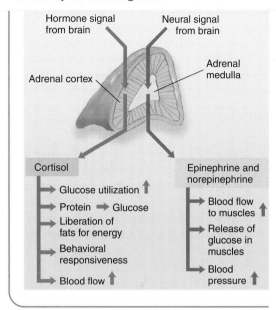

tional amounts of glucocorticoid, when treating people whose adrenal glands have been damaged or removed, if these individuals are subjected to stress (Tyrell & Baxter, 1981).

The most harmful effects of stress are caused by the prolonged secretion of glucocorticoids (Selye, 1956/1976). Although the short-term effects of glucocorticoids are essential, the long-term effects are damaging. These effects include elevated blood pressure, damage to muscle tissue, one form of diabetes, infertility, stunted growth, inhibition of the inflammatory responses, and suppression of the immune system. High blood pressure can lead to heart attacks and stroke. Children subjected to prolonged stress may not attain their full height. Inhibition of the inflammatory response makes it more difficult for the body to heal itself after an injury, and suppression of the immune system makes an individual vulnerable to disease.

Extreme stress has even been shown to cause brain damage in young primates (Uno et al., 1989). The investigators studied a colony of vervet monkeys housed in a primate center in Kenya. They found that some monkeys died, apparently as a result of stress. Vervet monkeys have a hierarchical society, and monkeys near the bottom of the hierarchy are picked on by the others; thus, they are almost continuously subjected to stress. (Ours is not the only species with social structures that cause stress in some of its members.) The deceased monkeys had enlarged adrenal glands, a sign of chronic stress. In addition, neurons in a particular region of their hippocampal formations were completely destroyed. Stress-induced damage of this nature is especially worrying, because the hippocampus plays a vital role in learning and memory (Sapolsky, 1996). Severe stress appears to cause brain damage in humans as well. Jensen, Genefke, and Hyldebrandt (1982)

found evidence of brain degeneration in CT scans of people who had been tortured. Victims of mass violence show similar results (Weinstein, Fucetola, & Mollica, 2001).

Cognitive Appraisal and Stress

We have seen that many of the harmful effects of long-term stress are caused by our own reactions—primarily the secretion of stress hormones. Some events that cause stress, such as prolonged exertion or extreme cold, cause damage directly. These stressors will affect everyone; their severity will depend on each person's physical capacity. Selye's model has been useful for understanding the biological components involved in stress, but it does not explain the role of psychological components in stress. The effects of other stressors, such as situations that cause fear or anxiety, depend on people's perceptions and emotional reactivity. That is, because of individual differences in temperament or experience with a particular situation, some people may find a situation stressful and others may not. In these cases, it is the *perception* that counts.

Richard Lazarus argues that our *perception* of the stressor determines, to a large extent, the stress we experience (Lazarus, 2000; Lazarus & Folkman, 1984). According to Lazarus, an individual's stress levels are affected by his or her **cognitive appraisal,** or perception, of the stressful situation. According to this model, cognitive appraisal is a two-stage process. In the first stage, **primary appraisal,** we evaluate the threat: We attempt to judge the seriousness of the perceived threat posed by the stressor. If we decide that the threat is real, we pass to the second stage, **secondary appraisal,** during which we assess whether we have the resources necessary to cope adequately with the threat. The extent to which we believe both that the stressor is serious and that we do *not* have the resources necessary to deal with it determines the level of stress we will experience. The belief that we cannot deal effectively with a stressor perceived as extremely dangerous leads to the highest levels of stress. Because different people may evaluate differently both the stressor and their ability to cope with it, they are likely to show different levels of stress when faced with the same stressor. We know from common experience that this is true. For example, people vary tremendously in their reactions to snakes: A harmless garter snake will arouse intense fear in some people and none in others.

Selye's findings, then, do not apply to all people; there are individual differences in how people react to prolonged exposure to stress. Some people, in fact, show little, if any, risk of becoming ill during or after chronic stress. Kobasa and her colleagues (Kobasa, 1979; Kobasa, Maddi, Puccetti, & Zola, 1994) refer to these people as *hardy* individuals. In a study of how business executives coped with long-term stress, Kobasa found that some became ill and some did not. She wanted to determine what caused this difference. Through detailed analyses of her participants' responses to different psychological inventories, she found that the hardy executives viewed the stressors in their lives as challenges and that they met these challenges head-on—they did not avoid them or become anxious about them. They also felt that they had control over the challenges (stressors) rather than that the challenges had control over them.

In other words, Kobasa's findings support Lazarus's idea of the importance of cognitive appraisal in dealing with stress: How we initially size up the stressor, how we tackle it, and the extent to which we believe that we can control the stressor seem to influence whether we become at risk for illnesses related to being chronically stressed.

Interestingly, Kobasa and Maddi (Maddi, 2002; Maddi & Kobasa, 1991) argue that the nature of early family home life is the cornerstone of hardiness. The development of a hardy personality is correlated with the combination of parental warmth, a stimulating home environment, and family support.

Stressful Lifestyles and Impaired Health

Selye's research showed that animals exposed to chronic and intense stressors became seriously ill during the stage of exhaustion. Can prolonged exposure to severe stressors produce similar effects in humans? Many studies investigating the relationship of lifestyle to health have shown that the answer to this question is yes. This section will look at the connections between stressful lifestyles or life experiences and increased risk of CHD, post-traumatic stress disorder, impaired immune system functioning, infectious diseases, and cancer.

These connections have important implications given the model of lifestyle choice we considered earlier. The long-term consequences of exposure to stressors can seriously compromise our health. But, as we have seen, choices that produce rewards in the long term often are overshadowed by more immediate short-term rewards. Similarly, we often make choices that reduce an immediate stressor but fail to reduce or avoid a larger, more chronic future threat. For example, we may fall into the habit of relying on all-night cramming sessions to manage a series of exams rather than developing more strategic studying behaviors that would give us better mastery at the time of the final. As we examine the links between stress-filled lifestyles and health, consider how the self-control mechanisms presented earlier could apply.

Stress Reactions and CHD One of the leading causes of death in Western societies is CHD—diseases of the heart and blood vessels. CHD can cause heart attacks and strokes. Heart attacks occur when the blood vessels that serve the heart become blocked, while strokes involve the blood vessels in the brain. The two most important risk factors in CHD, as you know, are high blood pressure and a high level of cholesterol in the blood.

The likelihood that a person will suffer from CHD may depend partly on how he or she reacts to stress. For example, Wood, Sheps, Elveback, and Schirder (1984) examined the blood pressure of people who had been subjected to a cold pressor test when they were children. The cold pressor test reveals how people's blood pressure reacts to the stress caused when their hand is placed in a container of ice water for one minute. Wood and his colleagues found that 70 percent of

their study participants who hyperreacted to the stress when they were children had high blood pressure as adults, compared with 19 percent of those who showed little reaction to the stress as children.

Research on primates also demonstrated individual differences in emotional reactivity as a risk factor for CHD. Manuck and colleagues (Manuck, Kaplan, & Clarkson, 1983; Manuck, Kaplan, & Matthews, 1986) fed a high-cholesterol diet to a group of monkeys, to increase the likelihood of their developing coronary artery disease, a component of CHD. The researchers measured the monkeys' emotional reactivity by threatening to capture them. (Monkeys avoid contact with humans, and they perceive being captured as a stressful situation.) The animals that showed the strongest negative reactions eventually developed the highest rates of CHD. Presumably, these monkeys reacted more strongly to all types of stress, and their reactions had detrimental effects on their health.

Given that certain physiological reactions to stress are associated with CHD, then other behavioral, emotional, or cognitive stress responses may be as well. In the mid-twentieth century, while trying to find the reason why some patients developed CHD and others did not, Friedman and Rosenman (1959, 1974) identified a behavior pattern that appeared to differentiate the two groups. They characterized the relatively CHD-prone individuals with the **type A behavior pattern** as persons with excessive competitive drive, an intense disposition, impatience, hostility, fast movements, and rapid speech. People with the **type B behavior pattern** were less competitive; less hostile; and more patient, easygoing, and tolerant; they moved and talked more slowly, and they also were less likely to suffer from CHD. Friedman and Rosenman developed a questionnaire that distinguished between these two types of people. The test is rather interesting, because the person who administers it is not a passive participant. The interviewer asks questions in an abrupt, impatient manner, interrupting the test taker if he or she takes too much time to answer a question. The point of such tactics is to try to elicit type A behavior.

The possibility of a relation between type A personality and CHD has generated a great deal of research. For example, the Western Collaborative Group Study (Rosenman et al., 1975, 1994) examined 3154 healthy men for 8.5 years. Among many other results, the Group found that the type A behavior pattern was associated with twice the rate of CHD of non–type A behavior patterns. Back in the early 1980s, findings such as these led an independent review panel to classify the type A behavior pattern as a risk factor for CHD (Review Panel, 1981). However, contradictory results have sometimes been obtained since then, and it is important to disentangle them.

An emerging understanding of these inconsistent results focuses on how the type A personality is measured. Researchers tend to find positive links between the type A pattern and CHD when they identify type A individuals through observation and evaluation of their behaviors during interviews, but not when they rely on self-report questionnaires (e.g., Pitts & Phillips, 1998). There are many plausible explanations for the conflicting evidence, then. For example, direct observation of type A–related behaviors simply may be a better measure of type A style than the self-descriptive method of classification. Or perhaps the two measurement methods identify only partially overlapping components of type A style, and only the behavioral component is related strongly to CHD risk.

Although the relation between CHD and the type A behavior pattern remains unresolved, several studies have found relationships between personality variables and particular risk factors, as distinct from a direct connection between type A personality and CHD. For example, Howard, Cunningham, and Rechnitzer (1976) found that people who exhibited extreme type A behavior were more likely to smoke and to have high blood pressure and high blood levels of cholesterol. Weidner and colleagues (1987) confirmed high blood cholesterol in a sample of men and women with the type A behavior pattern, and Irvine, Garner, Craig, and Logan (1991) confirmed the association between type A behavior and high blood pressure. Lombardo and Carreno (1987) found that type A smokers held the smoke in their lungs longer, leading to a high level of carbon monoxide in their blood.

How can we understand these research findings? The generally agreed-upon conclusion is that personality variables are involved in susceptibility to heart attack but that we need a better definition of just what these variables are. In addition, it is possible that different personality variables are associated with different risk factors, which makes it difficult to tease out the relevant variables. Personality factors certainly play an important role in CHD, but the precise nature of this role is still emerging through ongoing research.

Post-Traumatic Stress Disorder The aftermath of traumatic events, such as those that occur in wars or natural disasters, often includes psychological symptoms that persist long after the stressful events are over. **Post-traumatic stress disorder (PTSD)** is an anxiety disorder in which the individual has feelings of social withdrawal accompanied by atypically low levels of emotion; it is caused by prolonged exposure to a stressor such as a catastrophe. The symptoms produced by such exposure include recurrent dreams or recollections of the event, feelings that the traumatic event is recurring ("flashback" episodes), and intense psychological distress. These dreams, recollections, or flashback episodes lead the person to avoid thinking about the traumatic event, which often results in diminished interest in social activities, feelings of detachment from others, suppressed emotional feelings, and a sense that the future is bleak and empty. Psychological symptoms of PTSD include outbursts of anger, heightened reactions to sudden noises, sleep problems, and general difficulty concentrating.

Although PTSD is commonly associated with war, the disorder can be caused by many events. For example, many victims of rape, torture, natural disasters, and motor accidents suffer from PTSD (e.g., Korol, Kramer, Grace, & Green, 2002; Pulcino et al., 2003; Rheingold, Acierno, & Resnick, 2004). The severity of PTSD depends on factors such as the gender of the sufferer, the severity of the event, past psychiatric illness, and the person's level of educational achievement (Ba-

▲ *Peacekeepers, whose military mission does not include a combat role, nevertheless face most of the same stressors as those who engage in conflict, and are just as susceptible to post-traumatic stress disorder (Lamerson & Kelloway, 1996).*

soglu, Salclogle, & Livanou, 2002). Post-traumatic stress disorder can strike people at any age. Children may show symptoms not usually seen in adulthood, including loss of recently acquired language skills or toilet training and/or somatic complaints such as stomachaches and headaches. Usually the symptoms begin immediately after the traumatic event, but sometimes they are delayed for months or years (Pelcovitz & Kaplan, 1996). Whatever the context, the greater the severity of the trauma, the higher the risk that a person will develop PTSD (Berwin, Andrews, & Valentine, 2000).

The social support that people receive (or do not receive) after being exposed to an unusually stressful situation also can affect the likelihood of their developing post-traumatic stress disorder (Berwin, Andrews, & Valentine, 2000). As a result, mental health professionals try to seek out victims of natural disasters and of crimes such as rapes or shooting sprees to provide them with treatment in hopes of preventing future psychological disorders (e.g., Flannery, 1999; Mitchell, 1999).

Research has shown that excessive use of alcohol tends to co-occur with PTSD (e.g., Stewart, Mitchell, Wright, & Loba, 2004). One possibility for this association is that people with PTSD try to treat their own disorder with alcohol. People may use alcohol in an effort to manage negative moods and to block terrifying memories of the traumatic event(s). The problem, of course, is that such tactics will not work well in the long run, and excessive alcohol use itself will generate additional mental and physical health problems. The far better alternative is professional assistance.

Psychoneuroimmunology As we have seen, long-term stress can be harmful to a person's health and can even result in brain damage. The most important causes are elevated levels of glucocorticoids, epinephrine, and norepinephrine. But in addition, stress can impair the functions of the immune system—the system that protects us from illnesses caused by viruses, microbes, fungi, and other types of invaders. The branch of science that studies the interactions between the immune system and behavior (mediated by the nervous system, of course) is called **psychoneuroimmunology.**

The Immune System. The **immune system,** a network of organs and cells that protects the body from invading bacteria, viruses, and other foreign substances, is one of the most complex systems of the body. Its function is to protect us from infection. Because infectious organisms have developed devious tricks through the process of evolution, our immune system has evolved devious tricks of its own. The description I'll provide here is abbreviated and simplified, but it presents some of the important elements of the system.

The immune system depends on special white blood cells, called lymphocytes, that develop in the bone marrow and in the thymus gland. Some of the cells, produced in bone marrow and called **B lymphocytes,** roam through the blood or lymph glands and sinuses; others, produced in the thymus and called **T lymphocytes,** reside permanently in one place. If we think of the immune system as if it were the police department of the body, then B lymphocytes serve the function of mobile patrols, whereas T lymphocytes are like a stakeout team that stays in one place. The immune reaction occurs when the body is invaded by a foreign organism. There are two types of specific immune reactions: chemically mediated and cell mediated. Chemically mediated immune reactions involve antibodies. All bacteria have unique proteins on their surfaces called **antigens.** These proteins serve as the invaders' calling cards, identifying them to the immune system. Through exposure to the bacteria, the immune system learns to recognize these proteins. The result of this learning is the development of special lines of cells that produce specific **antibodies**— proteins that recognize antigens and help kill the invading microorganism. One type of antibody is released into the circulation by B lymphocytes, which receive their name from the fact that they develop in bone marrow. These antibodies, called **immunoglobulins,** are chains of protein. Each of five dif-

▲ *A T lymphocyte at work destroying tumor cells.*

ferent types of immunoglobulin is identical except for one end, which contains a unique receptor. A particular receptor binds with a particular antigen, just as a molecule of a hormone or a transmitter substance binds with its receptor. When the appropriate line of B lymphocytes detects the presence of an invading bacterium, the cells release their antibodies, which bind with the bacterial antigens. The antibodies either kill the invaders directly or attract other white blood cells, which then destroy the invaders. (See **Figure 16•7(a).**) This type of defense is described as chemically mediated because it is accomplished by the immunoglobulins.

The other type of defenses mounted by the immune system, cell-mediated immune reactions, are produced by T lymphocytes. These cells also produce antibodies, but the antibodies remain attached to the outside of their membranes. When antigens bind with their surface antibodies, the cells either directly kill the invaders or signal other white blood cells to come and kill them. (See **Figure 16•7(b).**) T lymphocytes primarily defend the body against fungi, viruses, and multicellular parasites.

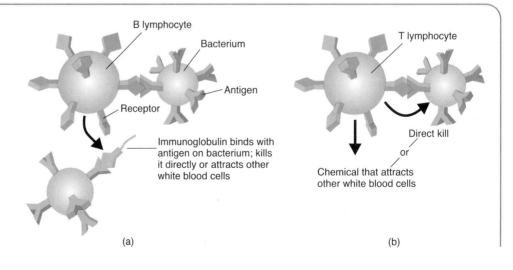

FIGURE 16•7

Immune reactions.
(a) Chemically mediated reaction. The B lymphocyte detects an antigen on a bacterium and releases a specific immunoglobulin.
(b) Cell-mediated reaction. The T lymphocyte detects an antigen on a bacterium and kills it, either directly or by attracting other white blood cells.

B lymphocyte

Bacterium

Antigen

Receptor

Immunoglobulin binds with antigen on bacterium; kills it directly or attracts other white blood cells

T lymphocyte

Direct kill

or

Chemical that attracts other white blood cells

(a)

(b)

In addition to the immune reactions produced by lymphocytes, *natural killer cells* continuously prowl through tissue. When they encounter a cell that has been infected by a virus or that has become transformed into a cancer cell, they engulf and destroy it. Thus, natural killer cells constitute an important defense against viral infections and the development of malignant tumors.

Our immune system normally protects us; however, there are times when it can cause us harm. Allergies provide a good example. Allergic reactions occur when an antigen from some substance causes cells of the immune system to overreact, releasing a particular immunoglobulin that produces a localized inflammatory response. The chemicals released during this reaction can enter general circulation and cause life-threatening complications. Allergic responses are harmful, and why they occur is unknown.

The immune system can do something else that harms the body—it can attack the body's own cells. **Autoimmune diseases** occur when the immune system becomes sensitized to a protein present in the body and attacks the tissue that contains this protein. Exactly what causes the protein to be so targeted is not known. What is known is that autoimmune diseases often follow viral or bacterial infections. Presumably, in learning to recognize antigens that belong to the infectious agent, the immune system develops a line of cells that treat one of the body's own proteins as foreign. Some common autoimmune diseases include rheumatoid arthritis, diabetes, lupus, and multiple sclerosis.

Neural Control of the Immune System. Stress can suppress the immune system, resulting in greater vulnerability to infectious diseases, and it can also aggravate autoimmune diseases. It may even affect the growth of cancers. What is the physiological explanation for these effects? One answer, and probably the most important one, points to neural control—and indeed to the brain.

Stress increases the secretion of glucocorticoids, and these hormones directly suppress the activity of the immune system. Because the secretion of glucocorticoids is controlled by the brain, the brain is obviously responsible for the effect of these hormones on the immune system. All types of white blood cells have glucocorticoid receptors, and suppression of the immune system is presumably mediated at least in part by these receptors (Solomon, 1987). For example, in a study of rats, Keller and colleagues (1983) found that the stress of inescapable shock decreased the number of lymphocytes in the animals' blood. But this effect was abolished by removal of the adrenal gland. Thus, the decrease in lymphocytes appears to have been caused by the release of glucocorticoids triggered by the stress. (See **Figure 16·8(a)**.)

However, the same authors found that removal of the adrenal glands did not abolish the effects of stress on another type of immune response: stimulation of lymphocytes by an antigen. (See **Figure 16·8(b)**.) Thus, not all effects of stress on the immune system are mediated by glucocorticoids; there must be additional mechanisms. These other mechanisms may involve direct neural control. The bone marrow, the thymus gland, and the lymph nodes all receive neural input. Although researchers have not yet obtained direct proof that this input modulates immune function, it would be surprising if it did not.

The immune system also appears to be sensitive to chemical compounds produced by the nervous system. The best

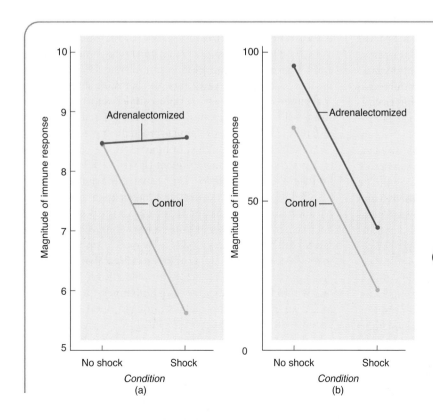

FIGURE 16·8 Effects of the removal of rats' adrenal glands on immune-system suppression produced by stress (inescapable shocks). (a) Number of white blood cells (lymphocytes) found in the blood. (b) Stimulation of lymphocyte production after exposure to an antigen.

(Based on data from Keller, S. E., Weiss, J. M., Schleifer, S. J., Miller, N. E., & Stein, M. (1983). Stress-induced suppression of immunity in adrenalectomized rats. *Science, 221,* 1301–1304.)

evidence comes from studies of the opioids produced by the brain. In research with rats, Shavit and colleagues (1984) found that inescapable intermittent shock produced both analgesia (decreased sensitivity to pain) and suppression of the production of natural killer cells. These effects both seem to have been mediated by brain opioids, because both effects were abolished when the researchers administered a drug that blocks opiate receptors. Shavit and colleagues (1986) found that they could suppress natural killer cell activity by injecting morphine directly into an animal's brain; thus, the effect of the opiates appears to take place in the brain. We do not yet understand the mechanism by which the brain affects the natural killer cells. As you can see, the links between stress and the immune system are complex and involve multiple mechanisms (Moynihan, 2003; Schleifer, Keller, & Stein, 1985).

Infectious Diseases You may have noticed that when a married person dies, his or her spouse often dies soon afterward. The cause frequently is an infection. In fact, a wide variety of stress-producing events can increase people's susceptibility to infectious diseases. For example, Glaser and colleagues (1987) found that medical students were more likely to contract acute infections—and to show evidence of suppression of the immune system—during final examinations. In addition, autoimmune diseases often get worse when a person is subjected to stress, as Feigenbaum, Masi, and Kaplan (1979) found for rheumatoid arthritis. In a laboratory study, Rogers and colleagues (1980) found that when they stressed rats by handling them or exposing them to a cat, the rats developed more severe cases of an artificially induced autoimmune disease than did control rats who were not exposed to the same stressors.

Stone, Reed, and Neale (1987) attempted to see whether stressful events in people's daily lives might predispose them to upper respiratory infection—that is, to catching colds. If a person is exposed to a microorganism that can cause a cold, the symptoms do not occur for several days; that is, there is an incubation period between exposure and signs of the actual illness. The researchers therefore reasoned that if stressful events suppressed the immune system, there should be a higher likelihood of respiratory infections several days after such stress.

To test their hypothesis, Stone and colleagues had volunteers keep daily records of desirable and undesirable events in their lives for 12 weeks. The volunteers also kept a daily record of any discomfort and illness symptoms. And indeed, Stone and colleagues (1987) found that the people who showed symptoms of an upper respiratory infection had experienced an increased number of undesirable events and a decreased number of desirable events three to five days before. (See **Figure 16•9**.) The researchers suggested that this effect was caused by decreased production of a particular immunoglobulin that is present in the secretions of mucous membranes, including those in the nose, mouth, throat, and lungs. This immunoglobulin serves as the first defense against infectious microorganisms that enter the nose or mouth. Stone and colleagues ˙nd that this immunoglobulin, known as IgA, is associated ˙ood. When people are unhappy or depressed, their IgA

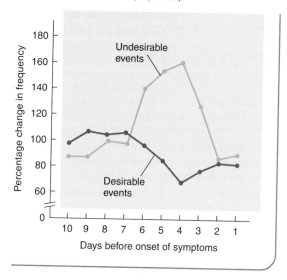

FIGURE 16•9 Mean percentage change in frequency of undesirable and desirable events during the 10-day period preceding the onset of symptoms of upper respiratory infections.
(Based on data from Stone, A. A., Reed, B. R., & Neale, J. M. (1987). Changes in daily event frequency precede episodes of physical symptoms. *Journal of Human Stress, 13,* 70–74.)

levels are lower than normal. In a parallel fashion, desirable events appear to increase levels of IgA (Stone et al., 1996). These results suggest that by suppressing the production of IgA, relatively chronic stress caused by undesirable life events may lead to a rise in the likelihood of upper respiratory infections (e.g., Cohen & Hamrick, 2003). Other work also shows that preexisting stress also exacerbates the severity of symptoms once a viral infection (influenza A) is already contracted (Cohen, Doyle, & Skoner, 1999).

Wu and colleagues (1999) demonstrated a direct association between stress and the immune system. These investigators found that caregivers of family members with Alzheimer's disease—who certainly underwent considerable stress—showed weaker immune systems, based on several different laboratory tests. Similar research shows that the effect of chronic stress on the immune system can last years after the stressor is no longer present (Esterling, Kiecolt-Glaser, Bodnar, & Glaser, 1994; Vitaliano, Zhang, & Scanlan, 2003).

People who are widowed have higher-than-average rates of cancer and other illnesses. To investigate the possibility that bereavement suppresses the immune system, Schleifer and several other researchers (1983) drew blood samples from 15 men whose wives were dying of breast cancer. Two blood samples were drawn, the first before the wife's death and the second within two months afterward. Both times, the researchers mixed an agent that normally stimulates blood lymphocyte activity with the lymphocytes and measured the resultant level of activity. On average, the activity level of blood lymphocytes after the wife's death was less than before her death, which meant that the bereaved husbands were more susceptible to

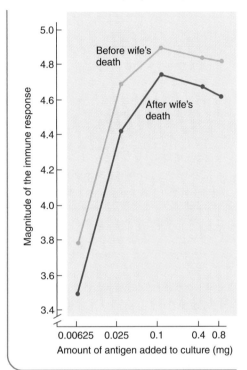

FIGURE 16·10 Stimulation of white blood cell (lymphocyte) production by an antigen in the blood of husbands before and after their wives' deaths.

(Adapted from Schleifer, S. J., Keller, S. E., Camerino, M., Thornton, J. C., & Stein, M. (1983). Suppression of lymphocyte stimulation following bereavement. *Journal of the American Medical Association, 250*, 374–377.)

illness. (See **Figure 16·10**.) Taken together, the results of these studies (and many other similar studies) suggest a strong link between stress and weakening of the immune system.

Evaluating Scientific Issues

Is There a Cancer-Prone Personality?

I have mentioned the connection between certain lifestyle choices and the incidence of cancer, as well as the connection between stress and cancer. Many people, both professionals and laypeople, believe that psychological factors play a role in determining whether people develop cancer—or, if they do develop cancer, in determining whether they can "beat" the disease. Some professionals have even suggested that there is such a thing as a "cancer-prone personality." Is there any truth to this assertion?

● **Do Personality Characteristics Increase Susceptibility to Cancer?**

The idea that personality is related to the development of cancer is not new. During the second century AD, Galen, the Greek anatomist and physician, concluded that "melancholic" women were more likely than optimistic women to develop cancer (Bastiaans, 1985). Physicians in more recent times have reported similar relations between cancer proneness and personality, but it was not until the 1950s that investigators attempted to do systematic studies (Gil, 1989). Several studies (e.g., Kissen, 1963; LeShan & Worthington, 1956) suggested that cancer-prone people had difficulty expressing emotions (especially anger and hostility) and had low self-esteem.

The concept of the **type C personality,** or cancer-prone personality, was introduced in the 1980s (Morris, 1980) to explain apparent differences among cancer survivors in the patterns of responses they showed to the diagnosis. According to Temoshok and colleagues (1985), the type C pattern is shown by a person "who is cooperative, unassertive, patient, who suppresses negative emotions (particularly anger), and who accepts/complies with external authorities" (p. 141). Temoshok and her colleagues conceive of the type C personality as the polar opposite of the type A pattern.

Proponents of the cancer-prone personality concept assert that there is a direct physiological connection between personality characteristics and cancer. That is, they believe that the coping styles characterizing the type C personality may be maladaptive in that they seem to cause physiological events that favor the development of cancer. For example, Temoshok (1987) suggests that the chronically blocked expressions of emotions in people with the type C personality cause the release of certain chemicals in the brain (neuropeptides) that disrupt the body's homeostatic mechanisms and impair the body's ability to defend itself against the growth of cancer cells. Eysenck (1988, 1994) suggested that negative emotions cause the release of glucocorticoids—which, as you know, suppress the immune system and interfere with its ability to destroy cancer cells.

● **What Is the Evidence for the Cancer-Prone Personality?**

Several studies have found a relation between personality variables and the presence or severity of cancer. For example, Temoshok and colleagues (1985) measured type C personality characteristics in a group of patients who had been referred to a hospital for assessment and treatment of malignant melanoma—a form of skin cancer that tends to metastasize (spread to other parts of the body). They found that the nonverbal type C personality cluster was related to the thickness of the tumor. People who scored high on nonverbal type C tended to be slow, lethargic, passive, and sad. Presumably, the existence of these personality variables favored the growth of the melanoma.

Most of the studies investigating the role of personality variables in cancer proneness have examined people who have already been identified as cancer patients. Some studies, such as the research done by Temoshok and colleagues, have related the personality characteristics to severity of the disease; others have compared the personality variables of cancer patients with those of people without cancer. As I'll discuss shortly, however, all such studies share some methodological problems. A more clear-cut approach is to administer personality tests to a large group of people and then follow them for several years, seeing who develops cancer and who does not. Grossarth-Maticek, Bastiaans, and Kanazir (1985) carried out a large-scale study of this type on 1353 residents of a small town in the former Yugoslavia. They administered psychological tests and questionnaires about current health status and habits such as smoking and drinking in 1966 and then followed the participants for 10 years. Their results showed that people with type C personality characteristics were most likely to develop cancer—especially lung cancer.

Grossarth-Maticek and his colleagues began an even more ambitious longitudinal study in 1974, when they administered personality tests to 19,000 residents of Heidelberg, Germany. The study was designed to examine many different issues, cancer being only one of them (Grossarth-Maticek & Eysenck, 1995). However, results indicate that a personality test can identify people who are likely to develop cancer (Grossarth-Maticek & Eysenck, 1990). Examples of the questions that tend to be answered "yes" by people who later develop cancer include "I prefer to agree with others rather than assert my own views," "I am unable to express my feelings and needs openly to other people," and "I often feel inhibited when it comes to openly showing negative feelings such as hatred, aggression, or anger."

● Evaluating Evidence for the Cancer-Prone Personality
Let's consider a methodological limitation of many of the studies that have reported an association between personality variables and cancer. Simply put, evidence from studies that test people who already have cancer cannot prove that personality variables affect the onset or progression of the disease. Physicians have known for a long time that malignancies can have physiological effects that alter people's emotions and personality, and these changes can occur even before the cancer is detected (Borysenko, 1982; Shakin & Holland, 1988). Thus, what may look like a cause of the disease may actually be an effect.

However, because Grossarth-Maticek and his colleagues administered personality tests to healthy people and looked for the subsequent development of cancer, their studies are not subject to this criticism. Indeed, this approach is the very best way to see whether a cause-and-effect link exists between personality and cancer. Yet even if the link exists, we cannot be sure that cancer proneness is a direct result of people's emotional reactions—that it is produced by suppression of the immune system, for instance. Instead, the effect could be caused by differences in people's behavior. For example, people who were passive might not take responsibility for their own health. Believing that someone else was responsible for their health, they might not bother to try to maintain a healthy lifestyle. They might not be alert for warning signs of cancer or might even disregard them until became so blatant that they could not be ignored. They

might be less likely to comply with the treatments recommended by their physicians; after all, it would be the doctor's responsibility to take care of them, not their own.

In any event, most investigators believe that if the immune system plays a role in the possible link between personality variables and cancer, it affects the *growth* of tumors, not their *formation*. Most of the studies using laboratory animals that have shown that stress can promote the growth of cancer have investigated tumors induced by viruses—and viruses do not appear to play a significant role in the formation of tumors in humans (Justice, 1985). Thus, this research may not be directly relevant to cancer in humans. The most important defense against the formation of tumors in humans appears to be carried out by mechanisms that help repair damaged DNA, and no one has yet shown a connection between stress and these mechanisms.

● What Should We Conclude?
The weight of the evidence suggests that personality variables, particularly those relevant to people's coping styles in the face of unpleasant and stressful situations, can affect the development of cancer. What we do not know is whether these variables do so *directly,* by altering the activity of the immune system, or *indirectly,* by affecting people's health-related behavior.

If personality traits play a role in the development of cancer, perhaps it may be possible to develop a form of psychotherapy that would alter these traits and help prevent or combat cancer. In fact, one careful study did find that psychotherapy can increase the survival rate of cancer patients. Spiegel, Bloom, and Yalom (1981) designed an experiment to see whether psychotherapy could help people cope with the anxiety, fear, and pain produced by their disease. (They did not intend the therapy to help the patients survive their disease.) The investigators randomly selected two groups of women with advanced breast cancer; one group received psychotherapy and the other did not. All 86 patients received standard medical treatment, including surgery, radiation, and chemotherapy. The psychotherapy did indeed help the women in the experimental group cope with their cancer—they became less anxious and depressed and learned to reduce their pain. Thirteen years later, Spiegel and his colleagues decided to examine the medical records of the 86 patients to see whether the psychotherapy had affected the course of their disease (Spiegel, Bloom, Kraemer, & Gottheil, 1989). They expected to find that it had not. But it had; those who received a year of therapy lived an average of 37 months, compared with 19 months for the patients who did not receive psychotherapy. Three of the women were still alive, and all of them had received the psychotherapy.

According to Spiegel, we cannot necessarily conclude that the psychotherapy prolonged the patients' survival time solely because it reduced stress. The psychotherapy could also have encouraged them to comply better with their physicians' orders concerning medication and diet, and the reduction in pain might have made it possible for them to exercise more and maintain their general health. Clearly, these findings are important. Identifying the factors that helped retard the course of the illness could lead to the development of even more effective therapies.

Although Spiegel's report is encouraging, advocating and publicizing the belief that thinking negatively causes illnesses and thinking positively cures them can have harmful side effects. Some people may be tempted to forgo medical treatment, hoping that they can make their tumors wither away by thinking positively. Variables such as heredity and exposure to carcinogens are by far the most important risk factors in tumor formation, and standard medical treatments provide by far the most effective forms of therapy. Because early medical treatment is important, any delays in beginning treatment may reduce the likelihood of a cure. In addition, a belief in the power of positive thinking can too easily turn into a game of "blame the victim." If someone tries to beat his or her cancer and fails to do so, the implication is that the person simply did not try hard enough or had the wrong attitude. People dying of cancer should certainly not be led to believe that they are responsible for being unable to cure themselves.

Interim Summary

Stress and Health

Stress consists of our physiological, behavioral, emotional, and cognitive responses to stressors—stimuli that either prevent us from obtaining a goal or endanger our well-being. Selye's well-known model describes how prolonged exposure to stress can lead to illness and sometimes death. The stress response, which Cannon called the fight-or-flight response, is useful as a short-term response to threatening stimuli but is harmful in the long term. This response includes increased activity of the sympathetic branch of the autonomic nervous system and increased secretion of epinephrine, norepinephrine, and glucocorticoids by the adrenal glands.

Although increased levels of epinephrine and norepinephrine can raise blood pressure, most of the harm to health comes from glucocorticoids. Prolonged exposure to high levels of these hormones can increase blood pressure, damage muscle tissue, lead to infertility, inhibit growth, inhibit the inflammatory response, and suppress the immune system. It can also damage the hippocampus. Because the harm caused by most stressors comes from our own response to them, individual differences in psychological variables can alter the effects of stressful situations. An individual's perception of stress is especially important. Hardy individuals, who cope well with stress, view stressors as challenges over which they have control.

Research on the type A behavior pattern suggests that some personality variables can predict the likelihood of CHD. However, the research findings are mixed, and some studies suggest that health-related behaviors may be more important than patterns of emotional reactions.

Post-traumatic stress disorder is a serious reaction to unusually intense stress that sometimes does not occur until several months after the stressful event. Research has demonstrated the beneficial effects of social support after the stressful event.

Psychoneuroimmunology is a field of study that investigates interactions between the immune system, as mediated by the nervous system, and behavior. The immune system includes several types of white blood cells that produce chemically mediated and cell-mediated responses. The immune system can cause harm when it triggers an allergic reaction or when, in autoimmune diseases, it attacks the body's own tissues.

Increased blood levels of glucocorticoids are the most important mechanism by which stress impairs immune functioning. Neural input to the bone marrow, lymph nodes, and thymus gland also may play a role; and naturally occurring opioids appear to suppress the activity of internal killer cells.

A wide variety of stressful situations have been shown to increase people's susceptibility to infectious diseases. For example, the stress associated with the loss of a spouse appears to contribute to increased infections.

Several investigators have suggested that a type C (cancer-prone) personality exists. Although the evidence is mixed, some careful, long-term studies suggest that cancerous tumors may develop faster in passive people who suppress the expression of negative emotions. A study on the effects of psychotherapy suggests that learning to cope with the pain and stress of cancer can increase survival rates. We do not know whether personality variables affect the growth of cancer directly, through internal physiological processes, or whether they affect people's health-related behavior, such as exercise, avoidance of smoking, and compliance with medical treatment.

QUESTIONS TO CONSIDER

1. What kinds of stressors do you face in your life? When confronted with a stressor, what kinds of physiological, emotional, cognitive, and behavioral reactions do you experience? What makes some stressors more aversive to you than others?

2. Has the stress response outlived its usefulness to our species? It seems as though this response was more useful to our prehistoric ancestors in avoiding predators and finding food than it is to us in our work and play. In your opinion, would our lives be better off without this response? Explain.

Coping with Everyday Stress

Regardless of our lifestyle, stress is a fact of everyday life. As we've seen, how much stress we experience and the degree to which stress impairs our health depends to a large extent on our perception of the threat posed by the stressor. In this section we will look at two general categories of everyday stress, major stressors and ordinary day-to-day hassles; then we'll consider various coping strategies, including the method known as stress inoculation training.

Sources of Stress

Depending on the individual, almost any aspect of the environment can be perceived as a stressor. But there is a difference between a major stressor such as a house fire and an everyday nuisance such as traffic.

Major Life Stressors Life changes that threaten or otherwise complicate life constitute a major source of stress. The death of a loved one, being fired from a job, getting married, having a child, and sustaining a personal injury or illness are examples of significant life changes that cause stress and disrupt everyday life (Miller & Rahe, 1997). Some evidence has accumulated that suggests that if some individuals experience enough of these major changes in lifestyle over a short time period, they are likely to develop physical illnesses within the next two years (Rahe & Arthur, 1978). But not every person who encounters a series of significant stressors over a short period is at risk for illness (DePue & Monroe, 1986; Santed et al., 2003). Why? Once again, the answer is the way in which people perceive stressors. Recall Lazarus's idea of cognitive appraisal: The amount of stress induced by a stimulus perceived to be a stressor is determined by how significant we *believe* its threat to be and whether we feel able to cope with it.

Ordinary Life Stressors Stressors do not have to be catastrophic or cause significant changes in lifestyle to induce stress. Research has even shown that mothers of grade school children may be at risk of health problems because of the daily hassles associated with raising children in this age group (Stuart & Garrison, 2002). Often the everyday hassles we experience are enough to leave us feeling stressed out. Locking our keys in the car, being late for an appointment, or having a disagreement with a friend are examples of stressful everyday events.

A common source of daily stress comes simply from making routine choices about what to do, how to do it, or when to do it. Consider, for example, a choice between studying for tomorrow's test and going to a party with friends. You want to do both, but you can do only one; you are back in the classic self-control situation again—the choice between a small, short-~~m~~ reward and a larger, long-term reward. Psychologists refer ~~...~~ situation as an *approach–approach conflict,* because the ~~...~~lves two desirable outcomes. Other choices involve ~~..~~*idance conflicts*—one outcome is desirable and the

other is not. For example, perhaps you want to visit England but you are afraid of flying. Still other choices involve *avoidance–avoidance conflicts* in which both outcomes are undesirable. For instance, choosing between having a root canal and having a tooth extracted creates stress: You do not want either procedure, yet you must submit to one or the other in order to maintain your health. People appear to have their own favored methods of dealing with such conflicts. Some people tend to deal with stressful conflicts through strategies that either provide more information about the outcome or substitute a distracting activity to blunt its impact (e.g., Rutherford & Endler, 1999).

Holmes and Rahe (1967) developed one of the first measures of life stressors, the Social Readjustment Rating Scale (SRRS). The SRRS was constructed on the assumption that any *change* in a person's life—for better or worse—is a stressor. The test asks people to rate the amount of change or adjustment caused by recent events in their lives, such as getting married or divorced, getting a new job or being fired, moving to a new location, or losing a loved one. Responses are given in terms of life-change units (LCUs)—how much change or adjustment is caused by specific events. Once a person completes the SRRS, the LCUs are summed, resulting in a single score. High scores indicate high levels of stress, and low scores represent low levels of stress. People who score high on the SRRS have been shown to have more health-related illnesses and adjustment problems than those who score low (Holmes & Rahe, 1967; Monroe & Hadjiyannakis, 2002).

The Daily Hassles and Uplifts Scale (DeLongis, Folkman, & Lazarus, 1988), another commonly used scale, measures daily events that are either troublesome (hassles) or pleasant (uplifts). This scale has people rate, at each day's end, the extent to which an event—such as the weather, deadlines, family, or physical appearance—served as a hassle or an uplift for them on that day. By filling this scale out daily over extended periods, people provide a picture of how the routine events of everyday life create stress. And it turns out that daily hassles yield a more accurate prediction of physical illness and adjustment problems than do either daily uplifts (DeLongis, Folkman, & Lazarus, 1988; Stuart & Garrison, 2002) or major life events (Garrett, Brantley, Jones, & McKnight, 1991).

Coping Styles and Strategies

So far, we have focused on the bad news about stress—its damaging effects on the body and mind. Let's now consider some good news: Each of us can learn to control stress or to change our perception of it. We may not always be able to predict when and where we will encounter stressors or to control their intensity, but we can mitigate their damaging effects by adopting coping strategies that are consistent with our lifestyles. A **coping strategy** is simply a plan of action that we follow, either in anticipation of encountering a stressor or as a direct response to stress as it occurs, and which is effective in reducing the level of stress we experience.

According to Lazarus and Folkman (1984; Folkman & Lazarus, 1991), there are two types of coping responses: problem-focused and emotion-focused. **Problem-focused coping** is directed toward the source of the stress. For example, if the stress is job-related, a person might try to change conditions at work or might take courses to acquire skills that will enable him or her to obtain a different job. **Emotion-focused coping** is directed toward our own personal reaction to the stressor. For example, a person might try to relax and forget about the problem or find solace in the company of friends. Obviously, if a stress-producing problem has a potential solution, problem-focused coping is the best strategy. If it does not, then emotion-focused coping is the only option.

Health psychologists have shown that several common emotion-focused coping techniques are effective in controlling stress; namely, aerobic exercise, cognitive reappraisal, progressive relaxation training, and social support.

Aerobic Exercise

As discussed earlier, aerobic exercise has many benefits. People who engage regularly in aerobic exercise are likely to live longer than people who do not exercise regularly (Paffenbarger, Hyde, Wing, & Hsieh, 1986). Those who consistently make time for aerobic exercise also tend to report reduced stress. Consider the results of an experiment involving mildly depressed female university students (McCann & Holmes, 1984). The students were assigned to one of three groups: a control group that received no treatment for depression, a group that received relaxation training, and a group that engaged in aerobic exercise (jogging and dancing). The students rated their depression levels at the beginning of the experiment and then again 10 weeks later. As expected, self-reported levels of depression in the control condition showed no change. Students given relaxation training showed a slight decrease in depression. Those who participated in aerobic exercise showed a large decrease in depression.

Although we know that aerobic exercise is effective in reducing stress, we do not yet know exactly how it reduces stress. One possibility is that increased heart and lung efficiency coupled with the lower blood pressure that results from aerobic exercise simply makes people feel better. Another possibility is that people who can adjust their schedules to make room for regular workouts have a greater sense of control than do those who cannot find the time for exercise. People who make exercise a priority in their schedules have to control other aspects of their lives to ensure that they do indeed exercise. As Chapter 14 described, people who have an internal locus of control ("internals") take responsibility for the course of their lives. One possibility, then, is that internals, more than externals, will attend to threats to their health and initiate steps to prevent illness (Avison & Cairney, 2003; Lefcourt & Davidson-Katz, 1991). A special locus of control scale developed by Wallston, Wallston, and DeVellis (1978) focuses on health behaviors. People with strong internal locus of health control have been found to engage in more health-promoting behaviors, including exercise, than do those with external orientations (e.g., Norman, Bennett, Smith, & Murphy, 1998).

▲ *Aerobic exercise, such as jogging, not only has positive effects on physical health but also reduces stress and promotes feelings of well-being.*

Cognitive Reappraisal

Aerobic exercise is not the coping strategy of choice for everyone. Some people find that simply altering their perceptions of the threat posed by stressors reduces stress. This coping strategy is called **cognitive reappraisal** (or *cognitive restructuring*) and is an extension of Lazarus and Folkman's (1984) idea of cognitive appraisal. The rationale underlying this strategy is easy to grasp: If our cognitive appraisal of a stressor is a determining factor in stress, then *reappraising* that stressor as less threatening should reduce stress. Sometimes simply learning to substitute an incompatible response, such as replacing a negative statement with a positive comment, is sufficient to reduce stress (Lazarus, 1971; Meichenbaum, 1977). For example, students who suffer from test anxiety perceive tests as extremely threatening. They may say to themselves "I am going to flunk the test tomorrow" or "That test is going to be so hard." To reappraise the stressor in this case would involve replacing these statements with remarks such as "I'm going to pass that test tomorrow" or "Sure, that test will be hard, but I'm ready for it."

Cognitive reappraisal is an effective coping strategy because it is often a more realistic approach to interpreting the threat posed by stressors than is the original appraisal. We have good reason to appraise a charging bear as a real threat, but not a psychology exam. After all, we may not be able to deal well with the bear, but we can always learn how to take tests and improve our study habits. An additional benefit of cognitive reappraisal is that it teaches the individual that he or she can take control of stressful situations.

Relaxation Training

A third coping strategy is simply learning to relax when confronted with a stressor. Relaxing is based on the same principle as cognitive reappraisal: Substitute an incompatible response for the stress reaction. Consider the following example. You are anxious to get home, but you are caught in rush hour traffic. Your blood pressure rises, you begin to perspire, and you feel a knot forming in your stomach. What would happen if you were to relax? First, the chain of responses started by the hypothalamus would gradually recede; second, you would feel less stress.

One procedure for producing relaxation is the **progressive relaxation technique**. It involves three steps: (1) recognizing your body's signals informing you that you are experiencing stress; (2) using those signals as a cue to begin relaxing; and (3) relaxing by focusing your attention on different groups of muscles, beginning with those in the head and neck and proceeding to those in the arms and legs. Here is an example of how relaxation may be used to reduce feelings of stress. Suppose that when confronted by a stressor—for example, a test—you respond by tensing certain muscles: those in your hand and fingers that you use to hold your pen or pencil and those around your mouth that you use to clench your teeth. Once you become aware of these responses, you can use them as cues to relax the muscle groups involved.

Social Support Although all of us experience stress, the experience is a subjective and private matter. Nobody else can truly know what we feel inside. However, being confronted by a stressor and coping with stress are often social matters. We learn as children to seek others—parents, siblings, and friends—when we need help. This is a pattern of coping that continues over the life span.

Social support, the help that we receive from others in times of stress, is an important coping strategy for many people for two reasons. First, we can benefit from the experience of others in dealing with the same or similar stressors. We may learn how to reappraise the situation if others show us

▲ *Seeking help from family members in times of stress is one type of coping strategy.*

how to cope. Second, other people can provide encouragement and incentives to overcome the stressor when we might otherwise fail to cope with the stressful situation.

Stress Inoculation Training

According to psychologist Donald Meichenbaum, the best way to cope with stress is to take the offensive—to have a plan in mind for dealing with stressors before you are actually confronted by them. In other words, people should not wait until they are faced with a stressor to cope with it. Instead, they should anticipate the kinds of stressors most likely to affect them and develop the most effective possible coping plan for dealing with specific stressors. Meichenbaum (1985, 1993), in fact, has devised a problem-focused coping method called **stress inoculation training,** which focuses on helping people develop coping skills that will decrease their susceptibility to the negative effects of stress. Stress inoculation training has been found to be effective in reducing stress levels among people working in a variety of settings, including nurses, teachers, police trainees (Bishop, 1994), military personnel (Armfield, 1994), bankers (Cambronne, Shih, & Harri, 1999), social workers (Keyes, 1995), and athletes (Newcomer & Perna, 2003).

In Meichenbaum's words, stress inoculation training

> is analogous to the concept of medical inoculation against biological diseases. . . . Analogous to medical inoculation, [stress inoculation training] is designed to build "psychological antibodies," or coping skills, and to enhance resistance through exposure to stimuli that are strong enough to arouse defenses without being so powerful as to overcome them. (1985, p. 21)

Stress inoculation training usually occurs in a clinical setting involving a therapist and a client. As shown in **Table 16•6,** the process takes place over three phases and aims at achieving seven goals.

Suppose that like many people, you are uncomfortable in new social situations. You feel comfortable around friends and people you know well, but you become anxious or nervous when you meet people for the first time. In fact, you become so nervous that it interferes with your ability to function socially—you may even avoid social situations in which you are likely to meet new people. How might you use Meichenbaum's system to deal with this stressor?

The first phase of the system is called the *conceptualization phase* and involves two basic goals. Goal 1 involves learning about the *transactional* nature of stress and coping. Stress and coping are strongly influenced by the interaction of cognitive and environmental variables. A person experiences stress to the extent that he or she appraises the stressor—an environmental variable—as taxing or overwhelming his or her ability to cope with it—a cognitive variable. In Meichenbaum's view, coping is any behavioral–cognitive attempt to overcome, eliminate, or otherwise control the negative effects caused by the stressor (see also Lazarus & Folkman, 1984).

TABLE 16·6	Summary of the Phases and Goals of Meichenbaum's Stress Inoculation Training Program

Conceptualization Phase

Goal 1: Learning the transactional nature of stress and coping.

Goal 2: Learning to become better at realistically appraising stressful situations by cultivating self-monitoring skills with respect to negative or maladaptive thoughts, emotions, and behaviors.

Skills Acquisition and Rehearsal Phase

Goal 3: Learning problem-solving skills specific to the stressor.

Goal 4: Learning and rehearsing emotion-regulation and self-control skills.

Goal 5: Learning how to use maladaptive responses as cues to implement the new coping strategy.

Application and Follow-Through Phase

Goal 6: Learning to practice imagery rehearsal, using progressively more difficult or stressful situations.

Goal 7: Learning to apply new coping skills to other, perhaps unexpected, stressors.

Source: Adapted from Meichenbaum, D. (1985). *Stress inoculation training.* New York: Pergamon Press, pp. 21–26.

If, as in our example, you are uncomfortable in new social situations, you will therefore begin by understanding the transactional nature of stress. In this case, you perceive meeting new people as stressful. You may avoid going to parties and other social functions, which makes you feel better because the anxiety goes away. Although you really want to become more outgoing, you become anxious in such social situations: Your stomach tenses, your palms sweat, and you worry about what to say and how to act. In other words, specific environmental variables—social functions, meeting new people, and so on—cause cognitive and emotional discomfort, such as anxiety and nervousness. You feel inadequate in coping with these types of social situations.

Goal 2 involves becoming better at realistically appraising stressful situations by taking stock of, or self-monitoring, patterns in maladaptive thinking, feeling, and behaving. A person may keep a diary, or a "stress log," to record stressful events, the conditions under which these events occur, and his or her reactions to these events. In our example, you would approach this goal by asking yourself several questions: Which social situations make you feel the most nervous? Do you feel more anxious meeting same-sex or opposite-sex people? Are there instances when meeting new people is not anxiety provoking? Do you feel less anxious when you are forced to meet people on your own or when a friend introduces you to others? By answering questions such as these, you learn more about the specific elements of the social situation that are stressful.

The second phase outlined in Table 16.6 is called the *skills acquisition and rehearsal phase* and includes Goals 3 through 5. Goal 3 involves learning specific problem-solving skills aimed at reducing stress. For example, a person may learn to identify and define a specific stressor and outline a plan for dealing with it in behavioral terms. This planning process should include developing alternative ideas for dealing with the stressor and considering the possible consequences of each alternative. At this point, a person may find relaxation training and self-instructional training, in which he or she learns to make positive self-statements when confronted by a stressor, helpful. With respect to our social anxiety example, you might identify meeting a person of the opposite sex as a specific social stressor. You might think about attending a party a friend of yours is having next Friday night. You could resolve to introduce yourself to the first person of the opposite sex that you meet there. Your specific fear might be that after introducing yourself, you'll have nothing further to say. The skill you must learn is to consider what you might say and what topics might be mutually interesting.

Goal 4 involves learning and rehearsing emotion-regulation and self-control skills. These skills help people remain calm and rational when confronted with a stressor. For example, when meeting new people, try to focus on what you must do to meet people rather than on your own anxiety. Goal 5 involves learning how to use maladaptive responses as a cue to invoke the new coping strategy. For example, when faced with a social stressor, you may feel yourself getting tense. This feeling of tension is your cue to implement specific aspects of your inoculation training, which should help reduce your level of stress.

The *application and follow-through phase* is the third and final phase of Meichenbaum's program and includes Goals 6 and 7. Goal 6 involves *imagery rehearsal*, in which a person practices coping with the stressor by imagining being confronted by that stressor in progressively more difficult situations. The purpose of rehearsing the coping skills is to build confidence in your

▲ *The first step in applying a stress inoculation program to social shyness is to understand the transactional nature of social stressors and coping behaviors.*

ability to use the new coping strategy. In our social example, you would picture yourself meeting someone who you have seen before but do not know, and you would imagine how you would respond if the person asked you a particular question.

Goal 7 involves learning to apply new coping abilities to both expected and unexpected stressors. To accomplish this you might imagine additional social situations in which you would feel anxious; imagine implementing the coping strategy in response to the anxiety; and, finally, imagine feeling relieved as a result of coping with the stressor. After such imagery rehearsal, going to a real party and meeting new people should be less stressful. You may not become the life of the party, but you should be more comfortable mingling with your fellow partygoers.

Stress is an inevitable consequence of environmental change. Both large changes, such as a natural disaster or a new job, and small changes, such as remembering that we have a quiz tomorrow, contribute to the overall level of stress that we experience at any one time. Whether stress impairs our health depends on three variables: the extent to which we appraise the stressor as threatening, the extent to which we engage in good health practices, and the extent to which we use coping strategies effectively.

Interim Summary

Coping with Everyday Stress

Stress may stem from a wide variety of sources. Even positive events such as getting married can produce stress. Stress may lead to physical illness when a person undergoes several stressful events over a short period of time. However, the extent to which people become ill appears to depend on the extent to which they perceive a stressor as a threat to their well-being and the extent to which they believe they can cope with that threat.

Lazarus and Folkman have identified two types of coping. Problem-focused coping involves trying to reduce stress by attempting to change the event or situation producing the stress. Emotion-focused coping centers on changing our personal reaction to the stressful event or situation. Emotion-focused coping may involve activities such as aerobic exercise, cognitive reappraisal, and relaxation training. Seeking social support also can help reduce stress.

Meichenbaum's stress inoculation training program is a problem-focused coping strategy that prepares people to cope with anticipated stressors. The program involves three phases and seven goals. In the first phase people learn how to conceptualize the transactional nature of stress. In the second phase they build coping skills specific to the stressors in their lives and practice or rehearse these skills in hypothetical situations. In the third phase people prepare to implement these coping skills in real-life situations. The seven goals of stress inoculation training focus on specific kinds of knowledge, cognition, behavior, and coping strategies designed to help people anticipate, confront, and reduce the threat posed by stressful situations.

QUESTIONS TO CONSIDER

1. Which general approach do you take to coping with the stress in your life, a problem-focused or an emotion-focused strategy? What led you to develop this style of coping? How effective are you at coping with stress?

2. What stressors do you seem to be able to handle better than your friends? What stressors are some of your friends better at handling than you? To what extent do differences in perception of the threat posed by these stressors account for these differences in coping success?

3. Think of a stressor that is especially difficult for you to deal with. Develop an outline for coping with it based on Meichenbaum's stress inoculation training program. Explain why your program may or may not be effective.

Suggestions for Further Reading

Meichenbaum, D. (1985). *Stress inoculation training.* New York: Pergamon Press.

This brief book outlines Meichenbaum's program for managing stress. Although intended for practitioners, it is written plainly enough for everyone to understand.

Monat, A., & Lazarus, R. S. (Eds.). (1991). *Stress and coping: An anthology.* New York: Columbia University Press.

A collection of highly readable articles by the foremost experts on stress and coping, this anthology focuses on both biological and psychological components of stress and methods of coping.

Rushing, W. A. (1995). *The AIDS epidemic: Social dimensions of an infectious disease.* Boulder, CO: Westview Press.

Rushing provides an overview of the impact of AIDS on social behavior. The book explores both the social causes of the disease and cultural reactions to it.

Key Terms

aerobic exercise (p. 515)

alcoholism (p. 518)

antibodies (p. 530)

antigens (p. 530)

autoimmune diseases (p. 531)

B lymphocytes (p. 530)

cancer (p. 513)

cognitive appraisal (p. 527)

cognitive reappraisal (p. 537)

coping strategy (p. 536)

coronary heart disease (CHD) (p. 513)

emotion-focused coping (p. 537)

fight-or-flight response (p. 526)

general adaptation syndrome (p. 525)

glucocorticoid (p. 526)

health psychology (p. 524)

immune system (p. 530)

immunoglobulins (p. 530)

lifestyle (p. 511)

post-traumatic stress disorder (PTSD) (p. 529)

primary appraisal (p. 527)

problem-focused coping (p. 537)

progressive relaxation technique (p. 538)

psychoneuroimmunology (p. 530)

secondary appraisal (p. 527)

self-control (p. 523)

serum cholesterol (p. 513)

stress (p. 524)

stress inoculation training (p. 538)

stressors (p. 524)

T lymphocytes (p. 530)

type A behavior pattern (p. 528)

type B behavior pattern (p. 528)

type C personality (p. 533)

17

THE NATURE AND CAUSES OF MENTAL DISORDERS

Classification and Diagnosis of Mental Disorders

What Is "Abnormal"? • Perspectives on the Causes of Mental Disorders • The DSM-IV-TR Classification Scheme • Some Problems with DSM-IV-TR Classification • The Need for Classification • *Evaluating Scientific Issues: Clinical versus Actuarial Diagnosis*

Abnormal behavior is any behavior that departs from the norm, which is culture-specific. Psychologists who study mental disorders work with individuals whose abnormality is often extreme. Several perspectives on the causes of mental disorders exist. The DSM-IV-TR is a classification system that describes psychological conditions on the basis of criteria that must be met before any given individual should be diagnosed as having a mental disorder. Because the DSM-IV-TR is based on the medical model of abnormal behavior, it may overlook environmental and cognitive causes of abnormal behavior. However, clinicians need to employ some form of classification of abnormal behavior in their efforts to diagnose and treat mental disorders. Although researchers have developed statistical methods for diagnosing mental disorders, many clinical psychologists still prefer to rely on their clinical experiences to make such diagnoses.

Anxiety, Somatoform, and Dissociative Disorders

Anxiety Disorders • Somatoform Disorders • Dissociative Disorders • *Biology and Culture: Culture-Bound Syndromes*

Several mental disorders involve unrealistic and excessive anxiety, fear, or guilt. These disorders may involve generalized anxiety, intense fear of specific objects, intrusive thoughts, compelling urges to engage in ritual-like behavior, physical problems with no biological basis, and sudden disruptions in consciousness that affect a person's sense of identity. Culture-bound syndromes are mental disorders that are present in only one or a few cultures.

Personality Disorders

Antisocial Personality Disorder

People with personality disorders exhibit traits that impair normal functioning. The most serious personality disorder is the antisocial personality disorder. Persons with this disorder are dishonest and irresponsible, are incapable of feeling empathy or sympathy for others, and feel no remorse for their misdeeds.

Substance-Related Disorders

Description • Possible Causes

Substance-related disorders include both abuse of and addiction to drugs and alcohol. Both heredity and brain chemistry play prominent roles in these disorders.

Schizophrenia

Description • Types of Schizophrenia • Early Signs of Schizophrenia • Possible Causes

Schizophrenic symptoms include disorganized thought, delusions, hallucinations, and disturbances of motor activity. Each of the five types of schizophrenia is diagnosed according to specific criteria based on these symptoms. Signs or characteristics of schizophrenia may appear during childhood. Researchers have found that heredity, environmental stressors, brain damage, and biochemical factors play crucial roles in the different types of schizophrenia.

Mood Disorders

Description • Possible Causes

Mood disorders involve extreme depression or swings between depression and mania. Mood disorders appear to involve one or more of the following: faulty cognition, heredity, brain biochemistry, and sleep/wake cycles.

A son describes his experience with his schizophrenic father:

"It happened when I was about seven years old. It was a Sunday afternoon and I was watching television. I heard a lot of yelling and screaming in the kitchen. I ran to see what was the matter. They were in the midst of a fight. When they saw me, I turned and ran into the bedroom.

"That was the last time I really remember seeing my father until I was about 21. I'm told that my sister and I visited him after the divorce, but it's all pretty fuzzy to me. I know that shortly after my parents' big fight, my dad was institutionalized for the first time. His diagnosis: paranoid schizophrenia. My father has been in and out of mental institutions over the past 30 years. He is currently treated on an outpatient basis with chlorpromazine, a drug that reduces the symptoms of his disorder. He manages pretty well as long as he takes his medication.

"I didn't go looking to reestablish a relationship with my father; it was all his doing. I was going to college out west at the time. Somehow, he got my address and wrote to me. He told me very little about the past 14 years. He simply wanted to start with me anew. When I returned home for the Christmas holidays, I went to see him. He was in the intensive care unit of the local hospital. He had attempted suicide. His first words to me, after not seeing me for nearly a decade and a half, were, 'I can't do anything right—not even kill myself.'

"Despite the situation, we managed to get reacquainted. He wanted to take the relationship a little faster than I did, which brings me to the point I wish to make. About a year after I saw him at the hospital, I received a phone call from him (I was then back at school, 3000 miles away). He said he had saved some money and wanted to come to visit me. I was stunned: I thought to myself, 'What would my friends think of me having a crazy father? I can't let him come out here.' So I told him that this was a really bad time for me, that I was overloaded with schoolwork, and that I had several exams coming up—all lies. I was simply embarrassed about having a father with a mental disorder. Disappointed, he said he understood about my heavy workload at school and that he would make other plans.

"About two weeks later, I received another call from him. He told me that he had just returned home from visiting the city in which I was living, where he had spent the previous week. He said that he knew how busy I was, but that he just wanted to learn a little more about me and my life. He told me that after spending time in the town where I lived—walking the same streets that I walked and seeing the same mountains I saw every day—he felt closer to me and could identify with me much more. And I had told him not to come. I now look back at the situation with a deep sense of humiliation and regret.

"My sharing of such a personal experience with you might have made you feel at least a bit uncomfortable. That was part of my intention. If I had told you about my father's experience with surgery for, say, a back problem, would you have felt uncomfortable? Probably not. Yet, when I tell you about my father's mental disorder you do. Why? That's a question I will leave for you to answer."

Life is complex, and things do not always go smoothly. We are all beset by major and minor difficulties at one time or another, and our responses are not always perfect. Sometimes we find ourselves behaving irrationally, having trouble concentrating on a single topic, or experiencing feelings that do not seem appropriate for the circumstances. Occasionally we may brood about imaginary disasters or harbor hurtful thoughts about people we love. For most of us, however, these problems remain occasional, and we usually manage to cope with them.

But the lives of some people, like that of the father described in the opening vignette, are dominated for long years by disordered thoughts, disturbed feelings, or inappropriate behaviors. The problems become so severe that these individuals cannot cope with life. They may withdraw from life; they may seek the help of others; or they may be judged unfit by society and be placed in institutions.

What causes such problems? Some mental disorders—especially the less severe ones—appear to be caused largely by environmental factors, such as stressors or unhealthy family interactions, or by a person's perception of these factors. For example, a child who is constantly criticized by an overbearing, demanding parent may learn to be passive and nonresponding. This strategy may be adaptive in interactions with the parent but will be maladaptive in other social situations. In contrast, many of the more severe mental disorders appear to be caused largely by hereditary and other biological factors that disrupt normal thought processes or produce inappropriate emotional reactions.

This chapter begins with a section on the classification and diagnosis of mental disorders; it then describes the nature of some of the more important disorders and discusses research on their causes. (Chapter 18 will discuss the treatment of mental disorders and the efforts of psychiatrists, clinical psychologists, and other mental health professionals to help people with problems of daily living.) The essential features of the more important mental disorders are simplified here for the sake of clarity. In addition, many of the cases that clinicians encounter are less clear-cut than the conditions described here and are thus not so easily classified (Carson, Butcher, & Mineka, 2000). Moreover, social factors—such as problems of marriage and family life, social inequities, war, and personal adjustment—may cause high levels of stress and personal disruption without leading to a diagnosis of a specific mental disorder. It is important to realize that, as more and more people now understand, the line dividing normal and abnormal behavior is not sharp. And a person need not be "sick" to benefit from professional advice concerning his or her feelings and behavior.

Classification and Diagnosis of Mental Disorders

To understand, diagnose, and treat psychological disorders, clinicians need some sort of classification system. The need for a comprehensive classification system of psychological disorders was first recognized by Emil Kraepelin (pronounced "kray-puh-leen"; 1856–1926), who provided his version in a textbook of psychiatry published in 1883. The Association of Medical Superintendents of American Institutions for the Insane, a forerunner of the American Psychiatric Association, later incorporated Kraepelin's ideas into a classification system of its own. Several of Kraepelin's original categories are retained in the DSM-IV-TR, the classification system most widely used today.

Before examining the DSM-IV-TR, let's consider different perspectives on what constitutes "abnormality" and on the underlying causes of mental disorders.

What Is "Abnormal"?

Mental disorders are characterized by abnormal behavior, thoughts, and feelings. The term *abnormal* literally refers to any departure from the norm. Thus, a short or tall person is "abnormal," and so is someone who is especially intelligent

▲ *The dividing line between normal and abnormal behavior is not always clear.*

or talented. By this definition, Albert Einstein was "abnormal," and so were composer Beethoven and baseball player Babe Ruth. But, as you know, the term *abnormal* has taken on a pejorative connotation: We use it to refer to characteristics we dislike or fear.

Perhaps you have friends who insist that their pets understand them or who have to check several times to be sure everything is turned off before they leave their homes. Are these behaviors abnormal? If so, are they abnormal enough to be considered signs of mental disorders? The distinction between normal and abnormal behavior can be highly subjective. Clinical psychologists remind us that the most important feature of a mental disorder is not whether a person's behaviors, thoughts, and feelings are "abnormal"—different from those of most other people—but whether they are *maladaptive*. Maladaptive behaviors, thoughts, and feelings cause distress or discomfort and interfere with people's ability to lead satisfying, productive lives. They often make it impossible for people to hold jobs, raise families, or relate to others socially. In this way, persons with mental disorders are at odds with the basic expectations of the majority of other people about how to conduct themselves acceptably with others. You might rightly point out that a person who holds an unpopular religious or political belief that violates a social norm may be ostracized by the community and may find it impossible to get a job or to make friends. Clearly, the person's behavior is maladaptive. But does this mean that the person has a mental disorder? Not by itself. Depending on our point of view, we may be tempted to label the behavior as courageous and wise or as misguided and foolish. Simply disagreeing with the government, with established religious practices, or with popular beliefs, while potentially maladaptive, is not sufficient evidence for a diagnosis of mental illness.

Although such a diagnosis should be as objective as possible, it may never be completely free from social and political judgments. For example, in many societies today experiences such as receiving direct messages from God and being transported on mystical voyages to the afterlife would probably be labeled as hallucinatory or delusional, whereas in other times and places such experiences might be taken as signs of holiness and devotion. If historical records are accurate, the behavior of many people who are now venerated as prophets or saints would be regarded quite differently if they were alive today. Understanding cultural differences in beliefs is important, especially in a multicultural society such as ours. Still, the fact that diagnoses are affected by social or cultural contexts does not mean that they are invalid (Arrindell, 2003; Lopez & Guarnaccia, 2000; Widiger & Sankis, 2000). People have mental disorders: They have delusions and hallucinations, they have thought disorders, they experience wildly inappropriate emotions. And this has been going on for a very long time (Jaynes, 1976).

As I have mentioned before (and will emphasize again later), the disorders that will be considered in this chapter are typically complex. And the descriptions in a text such as this may draw distinctions that are not necessarily easy to make in real life. Drawing such distinctions may require that the dividing line between normalcy and mental disorder be sharpened. At the extremes, it is not hard to tell a person with a phobic disorder, schizophrenia, or a mood disorder from a person without those disorders. But most people do not fall at the extremes. All of us should recognize aspects of our own behavior in this chapter's descriptions of people with mental disorders.

Perspectives on the Causes of Mental Disorders

There is no single cause of mental disorders. In general, they are caused by the interaction of biological, cognitive, and environmental factors, where biological factors include genetic factors and physiological factors such as the nervous system. In some cases the genetic component is strong, and a given individual is likely to develop a mental disorder even in a very benign environment. In other cases the cognitive and environmental components are highly influential. Once genetic factors have been identified, for example, the researcher faces the task of determining the physiological effects of the relevant genes and the consequences of these effects on a person's susceptibility to a mental disorder. Understanding the cognitive factors involved in mental disorders requires identification of the origins of distorted perceptions and maladaptive thought patterns. Environmental factors range from a person's family history and present social interactions to diet, exposure to drugs or alcohol, and childhood diseases, as we will see later in this chapter.

Psychologists and other mental health professionals approach the study of mental disorders from different perspectives, each of which places more or less emphasis on each of these three sets of factors. The perspectives differ primarily in their explanation of the *etiology,* or origin, of mental disorders. Several of these perspectives were previously discussed in Chapters 1 and 14 and will receive only brief mention here as they pertain to mental disorders.

The Medical Perspective   The origins of the medical perspective lie in the work of the ancient Greek physician Hippocrates. Recall from Chapter 14 that Hippocrates formulated the idea that excesses of the four humors (black bile, yellow bile, blood, and phlegm) led to emotional problems. Other physicians, Greek and Roman alike, extended Hippocrates' ideas and developed the concept of mental illness—illnesses of the mind. Eventually, specialized institutions or asylums were established where persons with mental disorders were confined. Most early asylums were poorly run, and the patients' problems were poorly understood and often mistreated. The conditions of asylums were so poor they may have further contributed to patients' disorders, rather than treating them. During the eighteenth and nineteenth centuries, massive reforms in the institutional care of people with mental disorders took place in several countries, including the United States. The quality of the facilities and compassionate attention to patients improved, and physicians, including neurosurgeons and psychiatrists who were specifically trained in the medical treatment of mental disorders, were hired to care for these patients.

The medical perspective continues to be highly influential in the treatment of mental disorders today. As we will see in Chapter 18, however, most individuals with severe mental disorders are no longer confined to mental institutions. Instead, they are treated on an outpatient basis with drugs that help decrease, and in some cases eliminate, the presenting symptoms of mental disorders. Usually, only people with severe and intractable mental problems—that is, problems that do not respond to treatment—are institutionalized for long periods of time.

The medical model is based on the idea that mental disorders are caused by specific abnormalities of the brain and nervous system; may or may not involve other bodily systems; and, in principle, should be treated in the same way as physical illnesses are. As we shall see, biological factors are known to contribute to the development of mental disorders, including schizophrenia and the bipolar disorders, and drugs are usually used for treatment. We shall also see that genes play a pivotal role in the development of some of these disorders.

However, not all mental disorders can be traced so directly to physical causes. For that reason, other perspectives, which focus on the cognitive and environmental factors involved in mental disorders, have emerged.

The Psychodynamic Perspective   According to the psychodynamic perspective, which is based on Freud's early work, mental disorders originate in intrapsychic conflict produced by the three components of the mind—the id, ego, and superego (see Chapter 14). These conflicts may center on attempts to control potentially harmful expressions of sexual or aggressive impulses; they also may arise from attempts to cope with external dangers and traumatic experiences. For some people the conflict becomes so severe that the ego's defense mechanisms cannot produce a resolution that is adequate for mental health. The result is that the defense mechanisms themselves distort reality. Or the individual begins to function in some areas of life in a manner characteristic of an earlier stage of development. The mental disorders that result may involve extreme anxiety, obsessive thoughts and compulsive behavior, depression, distorted perceptions and patterns of thinking, or paralysis or blindness for which there is no physical cause. As Chapter 18 will describe, psychodynamic therapists attempt to make their clients aware of their intrapsychic conflicts and defense mechanisms as part of the process of regaining mental health.

The Cognitive–Behavioral Perspective The cognitive–behavioral perspective holds that mental disorders are *learned* maladaptive behavior patterns that we can best understand by focusing on environmental factors and a person's perception of those factors. In this view a mental disorder is not something that arises spontaneously within a person. Instead, it is caused by the person's interaction with his or her environment. For example, a person's excessive use of alcohol or other drugs may be reinforced by the relief from tension or anxiety that often accompanies intoxication.

Recall from Chapter 1 that the behaviorist and cognitive approaches have different historical roots. Consequently, behaviorists and cognitive psychologists have different, often opposing, views on the causes of behavior. Interestingly, these approaches have become intertwined in the treatment of mental disorders. According to the cognitive–behavioral perspective, it is not merely the environment that matters. What also counts is a person's ongoing subjective interpretation of the events taking place in his or her environment. Therapists operating from the cognitive–behavioral perspective therefore encourage their clients to replace maladaptive outlooks with more adaptive thoughts and behaviors.

The Humanistic Perspective As Chapter 14 discussed, proponents of the humanistic perspective argue that successful personality development occurs when people experience unconditional positive regard. Conversely, according to this view, mental disorders arise when people perceive that they must earn the positive regard of others. Thus, they become overly sensitive to the demands and criticisms of others and come to define their personal value primarily in terms of others' reactions to them. They lack confidence in their abilities and feel as though they have no demonstrable value as persons. They may come to feel that they have no control over the outcomes of the important (and even not-so-important) events in their lives. Such feelings often accompany depression. The goal of humanistic therapy, as we will see in Chapter 18, is to persuade people that they do have intrinsic value and to help them achieve their own unique, positive potential as human beings.

▲ *Cultural norms dictate what is appropriate in any given culture. For example, in the Sudan the scars on this girl's forehead are considered normal. In North America, however, such markings are apt to draw stares.*

The Sociocultural Perspective Psychologists and others in the field of mental health are finding that the cultures in which people live play a significant role in the development of mental disorders (e.g., Lopez & Guarnaccia, 2000; Manson & Kleinman, 1998; Rosenfarb et al., 2004). As you have seen throughout this book, psychologists today are paying more attention to the role of sociocultural factors in their attempts to understand how people think and behave. The study of mental disorders is no exception. Also, proper treatment may require an understanding of cultural variables that influence the extent to which people interpret their own behaviors as normal or abnormal (Dana, 2000). What is considered normal in one culture may be considered abnormal in another. Moreover, certain mental disorders appear to occur only in certain cultures—a phenomenon called *culture-bound syndromes*. We will examine this topic in depth at a later point.

The Diathesis–Stress Model of Mental Disorders How should we make sense of these different perspectives on the causes of mental disorders? Are disorders caused by conflict within the individual? Are they caused by genetic factors or by abnormalities of the brain and nervous system, or both? Are they caused by learning, by faulty subjective interpretations of

▲ *According to the diathesis–stress model, stress that exceeds an individual's coping abilities may trigger the development of a mental disorder, and particularly so in people who are predisposed toward that disorder by genes and early learning experiences.*

environmental events, or by the way our particular culture says we should think and behave?

No single perspective is completely adequate in accounting for the origins of mental disorders. This is not to say that any perspective is unimportant, however. Different approaches can be combined to form larger, more comprehensive, perspectives. For example, the widely cited **diathesis–stress model** sees the combination of a person's genes and early learning experiences as producing a predisposition (a *diathesis*) for a particular mental disorder. However, the disorder will emerge only if that person is confronted with stressors that exceed his or her coping abilities. In other words, a person may be predisposed toward a mental disorder yet not develop it, either because he or she has not encountered sufficient stressors to trigger its development or because he or she possesses cognitive-behavioral coping skills adequate to counter the stressors that are present.

The DSM-IV-TR Classification Scheme

The classification of mental disorders can be difficult, as it is possible to classify these conditions in many ways. The system most commonly used is found in the American Psychiatric Association's *Diagnostic and Statistical Manual of Mental Disorders, Fourth Edition, Text Revision* (DSM-IV-TR, 2000). *Psychiatry* is a medical specialty devoted to the treatment of mental disorders. The corresponding specialty within psychology is called *clinical psychology*. **Table 17•1** lists the DSM-IV-TR classifications; several subclassifications were omitted for the sake of simplicity.

The DSM-IV-TR is the latest version of a classification scheme that aims to provide a reliable and comprehensive set of diagnostic categories with criteria that are specified as explicitly as possible. The DSM-IV-TR gives descriptions of

psychological conditions using five different sets of criteria, called *axes*. Individuals undergoing psychiatric or psychological evaluation are assessed on each of the axes. Axis I contains information specific to major psychological disorders that require clinical attention, including disorders that may develop during childhood. Personality disorders and mental retardation are found on Axis II. Diagnoses can include both Axis I and Axis II disorders; they also can include more than one disorder on either axis. For example, major depressive disorder and alcohol dependence are both Axis I disorders, and both may characterize an individual at a specific point in time. It is also possible for the same person to suffer different disorders at different points in time.

Axes III through V address other aspects of the condition and life circumstances of the individual. Axis III is used to pinpoint any physical disorders, such as skin rashes or heightened blood pressure, that accompany the psychological disorder. Axis IV identifies the severity of stress that the person has experienced (usually within the last year). This axis details the source of stress (for example, family or work) and indicates its severity and approximate duration. Axis V assesses the person's overall level of psychological, social, or occupational functioning. The purpose of Axis V is to estimate the extent to which a person's quality of life has been diminished by the disorder. Ratings are made on a 100-point "Global Assessment of Functioning" (GAF) scale on which 100 represents the absence or near absence of impaired functioning, 50 represents serious problems in functioning, and 10 represents impairment that may result in severe injury to the individual or to others.

The DSM-IV-TR offers clinicians a systematic means of compiling and evaluating a variety of personal and psychological information about any one specific individual. Let's consider an example to demonstrate the interrelationship among the five axes. Alcohol dependence (Axis I) often leads to marital problems, which may also be partly associated with an antisocial personality disorder (Axis II). Marital problems may lead to divorce, and these problems and the divorce are themselves stressors (Axis IV) that subsequently may contribute to an episode of major depression (Axis I). Alcohol dependence may eventually lead to physical problems, such as cirrhosis (Axis III). These problems, now acting in concert, are likely to lead to an increased impairment of overall life functioning (Axis V); eventually the individual may have only a few friends, none of them close, and may be unable to keep a job. The evaluation of this person might be summarized as follows:

Axis I: Alcohol Dependence
              Major Depressive Disorder

Axis II: Antisocial Personality Disorder

Axis III: Alcoholic cirrhosis

Axis IV: Severe stress—divorce, loss of job

Axis V: GAF evaluation = 30, which represents a
              very serious impairment of functioning

TABLE 17·1 Summary of the DSM-IV-TR Classification Scheme for Axes I and II

Axis I—Major Clinical Syndromes

- *Disorders usually first diagnosed in infancy, childhood, or adolescence.* Any deviation from normal development, including autism, attention-deficit disorder with hyperactivity (ADHD), excessive fears, speech problems, and highly aggressive behavior.

- *Delirium, dementia, and amnestic, and other cognitive disorders.* Disorders due to deterioration of the brain because of aging, disease (such as Alzheimer's disease, which was discussed in Chapter 12), or ingestion or exposure to drugs or toxic substances (such as lead).

- *Substance-related disorders.* Psychological, social, or physical problems related to abuse of alcohol or other drugs, not including symptomless recreational use. (Psychoactive substance use and abuse was discussed in Chapters 1, 3, 4, and 16 and is also discussed in this chapter.)

- *Schizophrenia and other psychotic disorders.* A group of disorders marked by loss of contact with reality, illogical thought, inappropriate displays of emotion, bizarre perceptions, and usually some form of hallucinations or delusions.

- *Mood disorders.* Disorders involving extreme deviations from normal mood including severe depression (major depression), excessive elation (mania), or alternation between severe depression and excessive elation (bipolar disorder).

- *Anxiety disorders.* Excessive fear of specific objects (phobia); repetitive, persistent thoughts accompanied by ritualistic behavior that reduces anxiety (obsessive-compulsive disorder); panic attacks; generalized and intense feelings of anxiety; and feelings of dread caused by experiencing traumatic events such as natural disasters or combat (post-traumatic stress disorder, discussed in Chapter 16).

- *Somatoform disorders.* Disorders involving pain, paralysis, or blindness for which no physical cause can be found; also excessive concern about health issues, as in persons with hypochondriasis.

- *Factitious disorders.* False reports of physical symptoms, as with Munchausen's syndrome, in which the individual is frequently hospitalized because of his or her claims of illness.

- *Dissociative disorders.* Loss of personal identity and changes in normal consciousness, including amnesia and dissociative identity disorder, in which two or more independently functioning personality systems exist.

- *Sexual and gender identity disorders.* Disorders involving fetishes, sexual dysfunction (such as erectile or orgasmic dysfunctions), and problems of sexual identity (such as transsexualism).

- *Eating disorders.* Disorders related to excessive concern about body weight, such as anorexia nervosa (self-starvation) and bulimia (alternating periods of eating large amounts of food and vomiting). (Eating disorders were discussed in Chapter 13.)

- *Sleep disorders.* Disorders including severe insomnia, chronic sleepiness, sleepwalking, narcolepsy (suddenly falling asleep), and sleep apnea.

- *Impulse control disorders.* Disorders involving compulsive behaviors such as stealing, fire setting, or gambling.

- *Adjustment disorders.* Disorders stemming from difficulties adjusting to significant life stressors, such as death of a loved one, loss of a job or financial difficulties, or family problems, including divorce. (Some adjustment disorders, as they pertain to difficulty in coping with life stressors, were discussed in Chapter 16.)

Axis II—Personality Disorders

- *Personality disorders.* Long-term, maladaptive, and rigid personality traits that impair normal functioning and involve psychological stress. Two examples are antisocial personality disorder (lack of empathy or care for others; lack of guilt for misdeeds; antisocial behavior; and persistent lying, cheating, and stealing) and narcissistic personality disorder (inflated sense of self-worth and importance and persistent seeking of attention).

- *Mental retardation* (which was discussed in Chapter 11).

Some Problems with DSM-IV-TR Classification

Although the DSM-IV-TR is the most widely used classification system for mental disorders, it is not flawless. Reflecting the fact that the development of the DSM-IV-TR has been strongly influenced by psychiatrists, the manual tends to be consistent more with the medical perspective on mental disorders than with other perspectives. This means that diagnosis and treatment based on the DSM-IV-TR emphasize biological factors; as a result, potential cognitive and environmental determinants may be overlooked.

Another potential problem with the DSM-IV-TR (and perhaps with any classification scheme) is its reliability. *Reliability* in this context means, as it did in the context of intelligence testing (see Chapter 11), consistency across applications. If the DSM-IV-TR were perfectly reliable, users would be able to diagnose each case in the same way. But evaluating psychological disorders is not so easy. Using the

DSM-IV-TR is not like using a recipe; it is more like navigating your way through an unfamiliar city with a map that includes only partial details. Using this map, you may or may not reach your ultimate destination. Mental disorders do not have distinct borders that allow a mental health professional to diagnose each disorder in a person with 100 percent accuracy. For example, the diagnosis of post-traumatic stress disorder requires the persistence of symptoms for more than 30 days. If symptoms similar to those found in post-traumatic stress disorder end before the 30-day cutoff, the diagnosis will be acute stress disorder instead. The necessity of having two separate classifications for the same symptoms has been questioned by some psychiatrists (see, e.g., Marshall, Spitzwer, & Liebowitz, 1999).

There will probably always be a downside to the classification of mental disorders. No classification scheme is likely to be perfect, and no two people with the same diagnosis will behave in exactly the same way. Moreover, once people are labeled, they are likely to be perceived as having all the characteristics assumed to accompany that label; their behavior will probably be perceived selectively and interpreted in terms of the diagnosis (Rosenhan, 1973). Obviously, much that is regrettable can occur in this process. An experiment by Langer and Abelson (1974) illustrated how labeling someone can affect clinical judgments. A group of psychoanalysts were shown videotape of a young man who was being interviewed. Half of the psychoanalysts were told that the man was a job applicant, while the other half were told that he was a patient. Although both groups of clinicians watched the same man exhibiting the same behavior, those who were told that he was a patient rated him as more disturbed—that is, less well adjusted.

As you may have recognized, there are potential problems inherent in any system that labels human beings. It is easy to lapse into the mistaken belief that labeling mental disorders explains why people are the way they are. But diagnosing the disorder only describes the presenting symptoms of the disorder; it does not explain the underlying causes and the psychological processes that may be at work. To say, for example, that Joe speaks incoherently "because he's schizophrenic" does not explain his behavior at all. Rather, the way Joe speaks is one of the symptoms of the disorder known as schizophrenia. Consequently, we need to be on guard against labeling people with the *names* of disorders rather than with their *symptoms*. Thus, it is more appropriate to talk about Joe as "having a schizophrenic disorder" than to call him "a schizophrenic." Labeling Joe "a schizophrenic" ignores the other aspects of Joe. If Joe were suffering from a physical problem such as a broken bone, would it make sense to label him only by his injury? "Joe's a broken bone" makes no sense.

The Need for Classification

Because labeling can have negative effects, some psychiatrists have suggested that we should abandon all attempts to classify and diagnose mental disorders. In fact, Thomas Szasz (1960, 2002) has argued that the concept of mental illness has done more harm than good because of the negative effects it has on those people who are said to be mentally ill. For example, Szasz (pronounced "sazz") notes that labeling people as having a mental illness places the responsibility for their care with the medical establishment, thereby relieving such people of responsibility for their condition—for their "problems of living," as Szasz puts it—and for taking personal steps toward improvement.

However, proper classification has advantages for a patient. One advantage is that, with few exceptions, the recognition of a specific diagnostic category precedes the development of successful treatments for that disorder. Treatments for physical diseases such as diabetes, syphilis, tetanus, and malaria were found only *after* the disorders could be reliably diagnosed. A patient may have a multitude of symptoms, but before the cause of the disease can be discovered, the primary symptoms must be identified. For example, persons with Graves' disease may show irritability, restlessness, confused and rapid thought processes, and occasionally delusions and hallucinations. Little was known about the endocrine system during the nineteenth century, when Robert Graves identified the disease; we now know, however, that this syndrome results from oversecretion of thyroxine, a hormone produced by the thyroid gland. Treatment involves prescription of antithyroid drugs or surgical removal of the thyroid gland, followed by administration of appropriate replacement doses of thyroxine. Graves devised his classification scheme for the symptoms many years before anyone understood the physiological basis of the disease. But once enough was known about the effects of thyroxine, physicians were able to treat Graves' disease and strike it from the roll of mental disorders.

Evaluating Scientific Issues

Clinical versus Actuarial Diagnosis

Clinical psychologists and other mental health professionals are often asked to make diagnoses and to predict people's future behavior. These decisions are important; for example, they can determine whether someone receives a treatment that may have significant side effects, whether someone receives parole, whether someone stands trial for a crime, or whether someone is placed in a psychiatric hospital. Two activities contribute to diagnoses and predictions: collection of data and interpretation of data. Accuracy is essential in both activities; unreliable or irrelevant data make interpretation questionable, and even good data can be misinterpreted.

Mental health professionals have many ways to collect data. They can observe people and note the presence or absence of particular behaviors. They can request medical tests such as EEG, CT, or MRI scans. They can interview

▲ *Most psychotherapists still prefer the clinical method for diagnosing mental disorders even though the actuarial method has been shown to be more accurate.*

people and take note of their facial expressions and their responses to questions. They can administer objective and projective personality tests (see Chapter 14). They can examine documents that already exist, such as medical records, criminal records, or reports of behavior from mental or penal institutions.

Once data are gathered, clinicians can interpret them in two ways: using the *clinical method* or using the *actuarial method*. Although a considerable amount of scientific research indicates that the actuarial method is superior, many mental health professionals still prefer to use the clinical method. Let's look at the difference between these two methods, survey the research that compares them, and consider why the use of the actuarial method is not more widespread.

● How Do These Methods Differ?

Clinical judgments are diagnoses based on an expert's experience. The information that is collected may come from many sources, but it is not the *source* of information that distinguishes the clinical method from the actuarial method—it is the *processing* of that information. Clinical judgments are based on experts' own memories of similar cases and, of course, on their knowledge of the symptoms that predict particular types of outcomes.

Actuarial judgments utilize statistical rules that relate particular indications (symptoms, test scores, or personal characteristics such as age, sex, and medical history) to particular outcomes. The actuarial method was first devised for setting the rates for life insurance policies. For example, an insurer can estimate a person's longevity by knowing his or her age, height, weight, sex, and health-related habits such as smoking. Although the estimate may be wrong about a particular person (for example, a person may be killed in a traffic accident or may stop smoking), actuarial judgments work very well when applied to large groups of people and to the prediction of average outcomes.

● Comparing the Clinical and Actuarial Methods

Mental health professionals are asked to make predictions about *individuals*, not groups of people. Does the actuarial method work well in such cases? According to research on the subject, the answer is yes (Dawes, Faust, & Meehl, 2002).

For a fair comparison of clinical and actuarial judgments, both methods must be applied to the same data. In addition, the eventual outcomes must be known—there must be a way to determine which judgments were right and which were wrong (Meehl, 1954). Goldberg (1968) performed one of the first studies to make such a comparison using data from clinical psychology. He analyzed the relation between patients' scores on the MMPI and the diagnoses they finally received when they were discharged from mental institutions. (You will recall from Chapter 14 that the MMPI, or Minnesota Multiphasic Personality Inventory, is extensively used in the diagnosis of mental disorders.) Goldberg found that a single actuarial rule effectively distinguished people who were diagnosed psychotic from those who were diagnosed neurotic. This was the rule: Add the scores from three of the scales of the MMPI (Lie, Paranoia, and Schizophrenia) and subtract the scores from two others (Hysteria and Psychasthenia). If the score exceeds 45 points, the person is diagnosed as psychotic, otherwise as neurotic. (Note that the DSM-IV-TR has discontinued the use of neurosis as a category of mental disorders; thus the distinction between psychotic and neurotic does not appear there.)

Goldberg obtained the MMPI scores of 861 patients and sent them to 239 clinicians (experts and novices) who made diagnoses based on the scores. On average, the clinicians' judgments were correct for 62 percent of the patients. The best judge was correct for about 67 percent of the cases. Goldberg's actuarial rule was superior, however. It was correct 70 percent of the time, which was better than the best of the expert clinical judges.

Leli and Filskov (1984) compared clinical and actuarial judgments on an important diagnosis—the presence of a progressive brain dysfunction such as Alzheimer's disease. As you can imagine, telling a family that one of its members does or does not have such a disorder has important consequences. The investigators used statistical methods to predict the presence of the disorder from scores on tests of intellectual abilities and were able to correctly identify 83 percent of the cases. Experienced clinicians who used the same information to make clinical judgments were correct only 58 percent of the time.

According to Dawes, Faust, and Meehl (2002), the hundreds of studies comparing actuarial and clinical judgments—not just in mental health but in the social sciences more generally—overwhelmingly show actuarial judgments to be superior. The criterion measures predicted in these studies included college grade point average, parole violation, response to particular forms of therapy, length of psychiatric hospitalization, and violent behavior. As Meehl (1986) noted earlier, "There is no controversy in social science that shows such a large body of qualitatively diverse studies coming out so uniformly . . . as this one" (p. 373).

● **Why Is the Actuarial Method More Accurate?**
There are several reasons why actuarial judgments tend to be more accurate than clinical judgments. First, their reliability is always higher. Because a decision is based on a precise rule, the actuarial method always produces the same judgment for a particular set of data. On the other hand, an expert making a clinical judgment may make different decisions about the same set of data on different occasions, or may allow personal bias to influence his or her analysis of the data (Rohling, Langhinrichsen-Rohling, & Miller, 2003). Experts may become tired; their judgment may be influenced by recent cases in which they were involved; or the order in which the information is presented to them may affect which factors they consider in making their decisions.

Another reason for inaccuracy in clinical judgment is the difficulty of sifting through a mass of data and retaining useful information while discarding useless or unreliable information. Clinicians rarely receive feedback about the accuracy of their judgments; if they do receive it, the feedback usually comes after a long delay. This makes it difficult for them to update their decision rules with any regularity.

In Chapter 11 we saw that when people make decisions, they usually follow heuristical rules. And as we saw in Chapter 15, these rules can lead people astray. For example, we tend to pay too much attention to particularly striking incidents and to ignore or underuse valuable information about base rates. Also, we have a common tendency to pay too much attention to information that is consistent with our own hypotheses and to ignore or minimize contradictory information (Greenwald, Pratkanis, Leippe, & Baumgardner, 1986). These same tendencies likely contribute to the inaccuracy of experts' judgments.

● **Why Do Practitioners Still Prefer the Clinical Method?**
More and more mental health professionals are using the actuarial method for diagnosis. For example, consulting firms have developed actuarial methods for scoring clinical tests such as the MMPI or the Rorschach. Clinicians can send the raw scores to these firms and receive a report, or they can purchase software for their own use that will analyze the data on the spot.

Even though the research consistently touts the actuarial method as superior, most mental health professionals still use clinical more than actuarial methods of prediction. Indeed some clinicians *avoid* the actuarial method (Guilmette, Faust, Hart, & Arkes, 1990). Why? According to Dawes, Faust, and Meehl (2002), some clinicians may be unaware of the research showing the inferiority of the clinical method. Others find the actuarial method dehumanizing; they believe that the method ignores the fact that each person is unique. And perhaps experts prefer to use their own judgment for a perfectly understandable reason: They find it difficult to accept that their diagnostic skills, developed over a long period of training and practice, can be bested by a rule embodied in a computer program.

● **What Should We Conclude?**
Scientific studies have shown that clinical judgments are consistently inferior to actuarial judgments. What do these results say about the role clinicians should play in trying to diagnose symptoms and make predictions? It is clear that clinicians play an essential role in collecting data and in identifying new variables that may be important predictors. After all, the actuarial approach must have useful data if it is to work. And humans are unexcelled in their ability to recognize complex visual patterns such as facial expressions; subtle indications of emotion in tones of voice and choice of words; and alterations in posture, gestures, or style of walking, which may provide useful information for diagnostic purposes.

But perhaps experts should concentrate their efforts on what they do best and what a data-derived rule cannot do: observing people's behavior, developing new and useful measurement instruments, and providing therapy. After all, helping people is the clinician's most important role. Perhaps routine diagnosis—a time-consuming activity—should be left to the actuarial method in the types of cases for which it has been shown to be superior.

Interim Summary

Classification and Diagnosis of Mental Disorders

The definition of abnormality is both context- and culture-specific. The causes of mental disorders involve biological, cognitive, and environmental factors. Mental health professionals view the causes of mental disorders from several different perspectives. The medical perspective asserts that mental disorders have an organic basis, just as physical illnesses do. The psychodynamic perspective holds that mental disorders arise from intrapsychic conflict that overwhelms the ego's defense mechanisms. The cognitive–behavioral perspective maintains that mental disorders are learned patterns of maladaptive thinking and behaving. The humanistic perspective suggests that mental disorders arise from the demands of others; specifically, from a need to meet others' demands in order to obtain their positive regard. The sociocultural perspective focuses on how cultural variables influence the development of mental disorders and people's subjective reactions to them. Many elements of these perspectives are integrated into the diathesis–stress model of mental disorders. This model suggests that people's genes and early learning experiences predispose them to develop mental disorders.

However, these disorders are only expressed if an individual encounters stressors that overwhelm her or his capacities to cope with them. Thus, even though some people may be predisposed toward a disorder, the coping skills they have acquired through experience may be sufficient to prevent the development of the disorder.

The principal classification scheme for mental disorders is the DSM-IV-TR, which provides explicit criteria along five dimensions called axes. Axis I includes the major psychological disorders of clinical significance and Axis II the personality disorders and mental retardation. The three remaining axes provide information about the individual, such as the presence of physical disorders, the level of stress, and the overall level of functioning.

Although clinical diagnosis is influenced by social norms, we should not abandon the practice. The value of classification and diagnosis lies in the potential identification of disorders with common causes. Once disorders are classified, research can be carried out with the goal of finding useful therapies. Clinical diagnosis and prediction of a person's behavior require the collection and interpretation of information. The interpretation can involve clinical or actuarial judgments. Clinical judgments are diagnoses based on experts' own experience and knowledge. Actuarial judgments are based on statistical analysis of the relation between available data and known clinical outcomes. Although research has consistently found the actuarial method of diagnosis superior, most clinicians do not use it. Some psychologists believe that clinicians should concentrate on developing new measurement instruments and making observations of behavior that only humans can make, then employ actuarial methods to produce the diagnosis.

QUESTION TO CONSIDER

The Evaluating Scientific Issues section discussed the diagnosis of mental disorders and the pros and cons of basing diagnoses on clinical versus actuarial judgments. This discussion was written from the perspective of the clinical psychologist. Let us turn the tables and consider the matter from the client's perspective. Suppose that you were the client whose mental health was in question. Which method would you prefer your therapist to use in reaching a judgment about you? Why?

Anxiety, Somatoform, and Dissociative Disorders

Once referred to as *neuroses* (particularly from the psychoanalytic perspective), anxiety, somatoform, and dissociative mental disorders constitute three of the categories on Axis I

of the DSM-IV-TR. All three of these clusters of disorders can be considered personal strategies of perception and behavior that have gotten out of hand. They are characterized by maladaptive increases in anxiety. From the psychoanalytic perspective, anxiety disorders may result from an inadequate number of defense mechanisms, from immature defenses that cannot cope with the anxiety, or from defense mechanisms applied so rigidly that they have become maladaptive. People with these disorders experience anxiety, fear, and depression, and generally are unhappy. However, unlike people who have *psychotic disorders,* such individuals do not suffer from delusions or severely disordered thought processes. Furthermore, they almost always realize that they have a problem. They may not know that the source of their difficulty is psychological, but they know that they are unhappy and that their strategies for coping with the world are not working very well. Typically, they tend to avoid problems rather than confront them. To avoid dealing with potential stressors, people with these disorders often turn unconsciously to strategies such as imagined illnesses, oversleeping, forgetfulness, and so forth.

Anxiety Disorders

Several important types of mental disorders are classified as anxiety disorders, which have fear and anxiety as their most prominent symptoms. **Anxiety** is a sense of apprehension or doom that is accompanied by certain physiological reactions, such as accelerated heart rate, sweaty palms, and tightness in the stomach. Anxiety is a normal reaction to many stresses of life, and none of us is completely free from it. In fact, anxiety is undoubtedly useful in causing us to be more alert and to take important things seriously. The anxiety we all feel from time to time, though, is significantly different

▲ *For most of us, anxiety is a typical reaction to circumstances that we perceive to be dangerous—for example, walking along a narrow ledge hundreds of feet above the ground—and is not considered abnormal. However, when anxiety interferes with our carrying out day-to-day activities, it may be considered a type of mental disorder.*

from the intense extremes experienced by a person with an anxiety disorder. Let's look at the nature and causes of three general types of anxiety disorders: panic disorder, phobic disorder, and obsessive-compulsive disorder.

Panic Disorder: Description

Panic is a feeling of extreme fear mixed with hopelessness or helplessness. We sometimes feel this way when we are trapped suddenly in an elevator or are in a car accident. Many people feel a tinge of panic when in a jet flying through turbulent air space. For most people, panic can be linked to these types of events.

People with **panic disorder** suffer from episodic attacks of acute anxiety—periods of acute and unremitting terror that grip them for lengths of time lasting from a few seconds to a few hours. According to the DSM-IV-TR, the *lifetime prevalence rate* for panic disorder is estimated to be between 1 and 2 percent. This means that 1 to 2 percent of individuals have reported the symptoms of panic disorder at least once in their lives. Women are approximately twice as likely as men to suffer from panic disorder. The disorder usually has its onset between the late teen years and the mid-20s; it rarely begins after a person reaches his or her 40s.

Shortness of breath, clammy sweat, irregularities in heartbeat, dizziness, faintness, and feelings of unreality are often symptoms of panic attacks. The victim of a panic attack often feels that he or she is going to die. The symptoms are sometimes mistaken for a heart attack rather than psychological distress. Leon (1977) described a 38-year-old man who suffered from frequent panic attacks:

> During the times when he was experiencing intense anxiety, it often seemed as if he were having a heart seizure. He experienced chest pains and heart palpitations, numbness, shortness of breath, and he felt a strong need to breathe. He reported that in the midst of the anxiety attack, he developed a feeling of tightness over his eyes and he could only see objects directly in front of him (tunnel vision). He further stated that he feared that he would not be able to swallow.
>
> . . . The intensity of the anxiety symptoms was very frightening to him and on two occasions his wife had rushed him to a local hospital because he was in a state of panic, sure that his heart was going to stop beating and he would die. His symptoms were relieved after he was given an injection of tranquilizer medication. . . . He began to note the location of doctors' offices and hospitals in whatever vicinity he happened to be . . . and he became extremely anxious if medical help was not close by. (Leon, 1977, pp. 112, 117)

Between panic attacks, people with panic disorder tend to suffer from **anticipatory anxiety**—a fear of having a panic attack. Because attacks can occur without apparent cause, these people worry about when the next one might strike them. Sometimes a panic attack that occurs in a particular situation can cause the person to fear that situation; that is, a panic attack can cause a phobic response, presumably through classical conditioning.

Panic Disorder: Possible Causes

Panic disorder is difficult to explain, as it is obviously maladaptive. Researchers attribute the disorder to biological or cognitive factors or to interactions between the two.

Genetic and Physiological Causes. Because the physical symptoms of panic attacks are so overwhelming, many patients reject the suggestion that they have a mental disorder, insisting that their problem is medical. They may be correct: A considerable amount of evidence implicates biological influences in the development of panic disorder. The disorder appears to have a substantial hereditary component; there is a higher concordance rate for the disorder between identical twins than between fraternal twins (Knowles, Kaufmann, & Rieder, 1999; Torgerson, 1983), and a significant number of the first-degree relatives of a person with panic disorder also have panic disorder (Hettema, Neale, & Kendler, 2001). (*First-degree relatives* are a person's parents, children, and siblings.) According to Crowe, Noyes, Pauls, and Slymen (1983), a pattern of panic disorder within a family tree suggests that the disorder may be caused by a single dominant gene.

People with panic disorder show distinctive physiological characteristics as well. They periodically breathe irregularly both when awake (e.g., Ley, 2003) and when asleep (e.g., Stein, Millar, Larsen, & Kryger, 1995). An Internet survey found that 95 percent of respondents reported breathing changes during a panic attack; and nearly 70 percent suffered from dyspnea, a disorder with symptoms including breathing discomfort or significant breathlessness (Anderson & Ley, 2001). Although irregular breathing itself does not appear to cause panic attacks, its presence is consistent with underlying biological processes. Researchers also have found that they can trigger panic attacks in people with histories of panic disorder by giving them injections of lactic acid (a by-product of muscular activity) or by having them breathe air containing an elevated amount of carbon dioxide (Biber & Alkin, 1999; Nardi, Lopes, & Valenca, 2004; Nardi et al., 2002). People with family histories of panic attacks are more likely to react to lactic acid, even if they have never had a panic attack previously (Cowley, Dager, & Dunner, 1995; Peskind et al., 1998). Some researchers believe that what is inherited is a tendency to react with alarm to bodily sensations from sources that would not disturb most other people.

As usual, it is important to note that biological factors alone are unlikely to provide a full account of this disorder. There is considerable room left for environmental influence after we take into account the likely heritable component of the disorder. Thus, the amounts of stress people experience and the ways in which people have learned to cope with stress probably influence the expression of biological factors.

Cognitive Causes. The cognitive approach to panic disorder focuses on *expectancies*. People who suffer from panic attacks appear to be extremely sensitive to any element of risk or danger in their environments: They expect to be threatened by environmental stressors and downplay or underestimate their abilities to cope with them (Mogg & Bradley, 2003; Mogg, Bradley, Williams, & Matthews, 1993). The expectation of having to face stressors that they fear may overwhelm their coping abilities leads these people to develop a sense of dread. Soon a full-blown panic attack results. Thus, merely anticipating that something bad is about to happen can precipitate a panic attack.

Phobic Disorder: Description *Phobias*—named after the Greek god Phobos, who frightened people's enemies—are persistent, irrational fears of specific objects or situations. Because phobias can be so specific, clinicians have coined a variety of inventive names for them, as shown in **Table 17•2.**

At one time or another almost all of us have had one or more irrational fears of specific objects or situations. It is not a simple matter to draw a line between these fears and phobic disorders. If someone is afraid of spiders but manages to lead a normal life by avoiding them, it seems inappropriate to say that the person has a mental disorder. Similarly, many otherwise normal people are afraid of speaking in public. The term **phobic disorder** should be reserved for people whose fear makes their lives difficult.

The DSM-IV-TR recognizes three types of phobic disorder: agoraphobia, social phobia, and specific phobia. Agoraphobia (*agora* means "open space") is the most serious of these disorders. Most cases of agoraphobia are associated with panic attacks. It can be classified with them (Panic Disorder with Agoraphobia) or separate from them (Agoraphobia without History of Panic Disorder). The DSM-IV-TR defines the essential feature of **agoraphobia** as "anxiety about, or avoidance of, places or situations from which escape might be difficult (or embarrassing) or in which help may not be available in the event of having a panic attack or panic-like symptom" (p. 429). Agoraphobia can be severely disabling. Merely thinking about leaving home can produce profound fear, dread, and physical symptoms such as nausea and profuse sweating. Imagine yourself unable to go to the store, let alone to school or work, without battling what feels like a case of food poisoning combined with the most extreme fear you have ever felt. Some people with this disorder have stayed inside their houses or apartments for years, afraid to venture outside (Arieti, 1979).

Social phobia is an exaggerated "fear of one or more situations . . . in which the person is exposed to possible scrutiny by others and fears that he or she may do something or act in a way that will be humiliating or embarrassing." Most people with social phobia are only mildly impaired. Thinking about social encounters and engaging in them still produce significant anxiety, but most people with the disorder might simply appear to the outsider to be reclusive or shy. There appears to be a self-perpetuating aspect to this disorder. Even after successful, positive interactions with others, people with social phobia feel less positive and more negative affect than people without the phobia (Wallace & Alden, 1997). People with a social phobia also tend to focus on threats in social situations (Mogg, Philippot, & Bradley, 2004). Social phobia can be general, causing fear of most social encounters; or it can be specific to certain situations, such as public speaking.

Males and females are equally likely to exhibit social phobias, but females are more likely to develop agoraphobia. Phobias that begin to develop in childhood or in early adolescence (primarily specific phobias) are likely to disappear, whereas those that begin to develop after adolescence are likely to endure. Social phobia tends to begin during the teen years, whereas agoraphobia tends to begin during a person's middle or late 20s. These disorders rarely make their first appearance after age 30.

Specific phobia is an umbrella term for all other phobias, such as fear of snakes, darkness, or heights. These phobias often are caused by a specific traumatic experience. The lifetime prevalence rate for specific phobia is estimated to be about 15 percent for women and about 7 percent for men (Magee et al., 1996), but approximately a third of the general population *sometimes* exhibits phobic symptoms (Goodwin & Guze, 1996). Let's try to understand what a specific phobia is really like from both an insider's and an outsider's point of view. Suppose that a colleague of yours is a woman with acrophobia (fear of heights). After you both attend a meeting in a new city, you invite her to take an aerial tram ride to a lookout point above the city. She hems and haws and says that she would rather not—that she wants to buy some souvenirs in a nearby shop instead. Subsequent invitations to ride the tram at other times finally make her quite upset. She reveals that the thought of taking the *tram* makes her ill with apprehension. It turns

TABLE 17•2	Names and Descriptions of Some Common Phobias
Name	**Object or Situation Feared**
Acrophobia	Heights
Agoraphobia	Open spaces
Algophobia	Pain
Astraphobia	Storms, thunder, lightning
Claustrophobia	Enclosed spaces
Hematophobia	Blood
Monophobia	Being alone
Mysophobia	Dirt or germs
Nyctophobia	Darkness
Ochlophobia	Crowds
Pathophobia	Disease
Pyrophobia	Fire
Taphophobia	Being buried alive
Triskaidekaphobia	The number thirteen
Zoophobia	Animals, or a specific animal

out that her fear is specific to circumstances in which she has a view of the ground dropping away from her feet. She is fine while in the aisle seats of airplanes and in most elevators—but she would not ever ride a tram. Like many people with phobias, she has become proficient at avoiding the experiences that frighten her.

Phobic Disorder: Possible Causes

What are the causes of phobic disorders? According to psychoanalytic theory, phobias arise from distress caused by intolerable unconscious impulses or from *displacement*—the redirection of objective fears toward symbolic objects (e.g., the displacement of fear of an abusive parent onto some object in the physical environment). According to the cognitive–behavioral perspective, people learn phobias by means of either direct or vicarious classical conditioning (see Chapter 5). *Direct classical conditioning* occurs when someone is exposed directly to an especially unpleasant situation. *Vicarious classical conditioning* occurs when a person observes another person (especially a parent or someone else to whom the person is closely attached) show fright in a particular situation.

Environmental Causes—Learning.

To say that phobias are learned through classical conditioning does not explain phobic disorder completely (Mineka & Zinbara, 2006). Many people have traumatic, frightening experiences, but not all of them develop phobic disorder; thus, it appears that not all people are likely to develop phobias. Also, many people with phobias do not remember having had specific early life experiences with the objects they fear (e.g., Kheriaty, Kleinknecht, & Hyman, 1999). (Of course, they may simply have forgotten the experiences.)

In addition, some objects are more likely to be feared than are others. People tend to fear animals (especially snakes, spiders, dogs, or rodents), blood, heights, and closed spaces. They are less likely to fear automobiles or electrical outlets, which are potentially more dangerous than some of the common objects of phobias, such as snakes and spiders. For this reason, evolutionary psychologists assert that phobias are more likely to involve objects and situations that affected survival in ancestral environments; see Genetic Causes, below.

The same classes of drugs useful in treating panic attacks also reduce the symptoms of agoraphobia, as Chapter 18 will discuss. However, the results that last longest are obtained from behavior therapy.

Genetic Causes.

Some investigators suggest that a tendency to develop a fear of certain kinds of stimuli may have a biological basis that reflects the evolution of the human species (Seligman, 1971). The general idea is that because of our ancestors' history in relatively hostile natural environments, a capacity evolved for especially efficient fear conditioning to certain classes of dangerous stimuli (e.g., snakes). Öhman and his colleagues have reported a well-integrated series of experiments that support this analysis. Participants

▲ *In obsessive-compulsive disorder, compulsive behaviors, such as ritualized hand-washing that occurs many times per day, may relieve obsession-induced anxiety while detracting from the quality of life overall.*

in these experiments were typically assigned either to a condition in which they were shown pictures of fear-irrelevant stimuli (e.g., plants) or to a condition in which they saw pictures of fear-relevant stimuli (e.g., snakes). The dependent variable was skin conductance, an index of emotional reactivity. A central finding was that pairing the pictures with a mild electric shock resulted in conditioned emotional responses to the fear-relevant but not to the fear-irrelevant stimuli, even though the pictures had been presented in such a way that participants could not consciously identify the content (Öhman & Soares, 1998; Soares & Öhman, 1993). Importantly, conditioning to the fear-relevant stimuli appeared more resistant to extinction than did conditioning to the fear-irrelevant stimuli. Thus, participants showed not only a special proclivity for conditioned fear to fear-relevant stimuli, but they did so without awareness. Another study in the series showed that participants who were already afraid of snakes and spiders reacted with higher skin conductance to pictures of these fear-relevant animals, again even when they had no conscious awareness of having seen the images, than did nonfearful participants (Öhman & Soares, 1994).

Obsessive-Compulsive Disorder: Description

People with an **obsessive-compulsive disorder** (OCD) suffer from **obsessions**—thoughts that will not leave them—and **compulsions**—behaviors that they cannot keep from performing. Major classes of obsessions and compulsions include impaired control of mental activities, incessant checking, urges involving loss of motor control, and feeling contaminated, according to a study of a large sample of American college students (Sternberger & Burns, 1990). The DSM-IV-TR estimates a lifetime prevalence rate of 2.5 percent among adults.

Unlike people with panic disorder, people with obsessive-compulsive disorder have a defense against anxiety—their compulsive behavior. Unfortunately, the need to perform this behavior often demands more and more of their time, to the point that it interferes with their daily lives, social relationships, and careers. Obsessions are seen in many mental disorders, including schizophrenia. However, unlike persons with schizophrenia, people with obsessive-compulsive disorder generally recognize that their thoughts and behaviors have become excessive and are unreasonable.

Consider the case of Beth, a young woman who had become obsessed with cleanliness.

> Beth's concern for cleanliness gradually evolved into a thorough cleansing ritual, which was usually set off by her touching her genital or anal area. In this ritual, Beth would first remove all of her clothing in a pre-established sequence. She would lay out each article of clothing at specific spots on her bed and examine each for any evidence of "contamination." She would thoroughly scrub her body, starting at her feet and working meticulously up to the top of her head, using certain washcloths for certain areas of her body. Any articles of clothing that appeared to have been "contaminated" were thrown into the laundry. Clean clothing then was put on the bed locations that were vacant. She would then dress herself in the opposite order from which she took the clothes off. If there were any deviations from this order, or if Beth began to wonder if she might have missed some contamination, she would go through the entire sequence again. It was not rare for her to do this four or five times in a row on some evenings. (Meyer & Osborne, 1982, p. 158)

Females are slightly more likely than males to have this diagnosis. Like panic disorder, obsessive-compulsive disorder most commonly begins in young adulthood (Sturgis, 1993). People with this disorder are unlikely to marry, perhaps because of the common obsessional fear of dirt and contamination—or perhaps because the shame associated with the rituals they are compelled to perform causes people with OCD to avoid social contact (Turner, Beidel, Stanley, & Heiser, 2001).

There are two principal kinds of obsessions: obsessive *doubt* or *uncertainty,* and obsessive *fear of doing something prohibited.* We all experience doubts about future activities (such as whether to look for a new job, whether to eat at one restaurant or another, or whether to wear a raincoat or take an umbrella) and about past activities (such as whether we have turned off a burner on the kitchen range or whether we remembered to lock the door on leaving home). But these uncertainties, both trivial and important, preoccupy some people with obsessive-compulsive disorder almost completely. Others are plagued with the fear that they will do something terrible—swear aloud in church, urinate in someone's living room, kill themselves or a loved one, or jump off a bridge—although they seldom actually do anything antisocial. And even though they are often obsessed with thoughts of killing themselves, few actually attempt suicide.

Most compulsions fall into one of four categories: *counting, checking, cleaning,* or *avoidance.* For example, some people feel they must count every step between their car and any building they plan to enter. Others may repeatedly check burners on the range to see that they are off or doors to be sure they are locked. Some people wash their hands hundreds of times a day, even when they become covered with painful sores. Some become afraid to leave home and refuse to touch other members of their families for fear of contamination. If they do accidentally become "contaminated," they usually perform lengthy purification rituals, as in the case of Beth.

Obsessive-Compulsive Disorder: Possible Causes Several possible causes have been suggested for obsessive-compulsive disorder. Unlike simple anxiety states, this disorder can be understood in terms of the defense mechanisms identified by psychoanalytic theory. From another perspective, some cognitive theorists have suggested that obsessions serve as devices to occupy the mind and displace painful thoughts. This strategy can be seen in normal behavior: A person who "psychs himself up" before a competitive event by telling himself about his skill and stamina is also keeping out self-defeating doubts and fears. Like Scarlett O'Hara in *Gone with the Wind,* who repeatedly told herself, "I'll think about it tomorrow," we all say, at one time or another, "Oh, I'll think about something else" when our thoughts become painful.

Cognitive–Behavioral Causes. Cognitive researchers also point out that persons with obsessive-compulsive disorder often believe that they should be competent at all times, avoid any kind of criticism at all costs, and worry about being punished for behavior that is less than perfect (Sarason & Sarason, 1999).

Thus, one reason people who have obsessive-compulsive disorder may engage in checking behavior is to reduce the anxiety caused by fear of being perceived by others as incompetent or to avoid others' criticism that they have done something less than perfectly. And if painful, anxiety-producing thoughts become frequent, but turning to alternative patterns of thought reduces anxiety, then the principle of reinforcement predicts that the person will turn to these patterns more frequently. Just as an animal learns to jump a hurdle to escape a painful foot shock, a person can learn to think about a "safe topic" in order to avoid painful thoughts. If the habit becomes firmly established, the obsessive thoughts may persist even after the original reason for turning to them—the situation that produced the anxiety-arousing thoughts—no longer exists. A habit can thus outlast its original causes.

Genetic Causes. Evidence is beginning to accumulate suggesting that obsessive-compulsive disorder may have a genetic origin (Pato, Pato, & Pauls, 2002; Pauls & Alsobrook, 1999). Whatever the degree of heritability may turn out to be, the disorder has a strong tendency to be transmitted within families. Nestadt and colleagues (2000) report that obsessive-compulsive disorder is found almost five times more frequently among first-degree relatives of those with the disorder than among first-degree relatives of people who do not have the disorder. Family studies also have found that this disorder is associated symptomatically with a neurological disorder called **Tourette's syndrome,** which appears during childhood (Leckman et al., 2003; Pauls & Leckman, 1986; Alsobrook & Pauls, 1997; Cath et al., 2000). Tourette's syndrome is characterized by muscular and vocal tics such as making facial grimaces, squatting, pacing, twirling, barking, sniffing, coughing, grunting, or repeating specific words (especially vulgarities). Pauls and his colleagues believe that the two disorders are produced by the same single, dominant gene. However, it is not clear why some people with the gene would develop Tourette's syndrome in childhood and others would develop obsessive-compulsive disorder later in life. There also is evidence that elevated glucose metabolic rates in certain areas of the brain occur in people suffering from obsessive-compulsive disorder (Saxena & Rauch, 2000). As well, disorders that involve basal ganglia dysfunction, such as Tourette's, often are associated with obsessive-compulsive disorder symptoms. This pattern supports the idea that the disorder may have a biological basis (Swedo, Rapaport, & Cheslow, 1989).

Not all cases of obsessive-compulsive disorder have a genetic origin. The disorder sometimes occurs after brain damage caused by birth trauma, encephalitis, or head trauma (Hollander et al., 1990). Obsessive-compulsive disorder has been treated by psychosurgery, drugs, and behavior therapy (see Chapter 18). These treatments are sometimes effective, but the disorder often persists despite therapeutic efforts. One of the problems in treating obsessive-compulsive disorder is that people are hesitant to seek treatment (Mayerovitch et al., 2003).

Somatoform Disorders

The primary symptoms of a **somatoform disorder** are bodily or physical problems (*soma* means "body") for which there is no physiological basis. We'll look at three types of somatoform disorders: somatization disorder, hypochondriasis, and conversion disorder.

Somatization Disorder: Description **Somatization disorder** involves complaints of wide-ranging physical ailments for which there is no apparent biological basis. Regier and colleagues (1988) found that the incidence of somatization disorder was extremely rare. In a sample of more than 18,000 people, it occurred in less than 1 percent of women and was essentially nonexistent in men. However, somatization disorder is usually chronic and may last for decades.

The disorder is characterized by persistent complaints of serious symptoms for which no physiological cause can be found. Obviously, a proper diagnosis can be made only after medical examination and laboratory tests indicate the lack of disease. The DSM-IV-TR requires that the person have a history of complaining about the physical symptoms for several years. The complaints must include at least 13 symptoms from a list of 35, which fall into the following categories: gastrointestinal symptoms, pain symptoms, cardiopulmonary symptoms, pseudoneurological symptoms, and sexual symptoms. These symptoms must also have led the woman to take medication, see a physician, or substantially alter her life. Almost every woman who receives the diagnosis of somatization disorder reports that she does not experience pleasure from sexual intercourse. Although all of us have physical symptoms from time to time that cannot be explained by a medical examination, few people chronically experience 13 or more unexplained symptoms. A woman with somatization disorder may consult many physicians and will do so frequently, often for the remainder of her life, following the onset of the disorder. Although women with somatization disorder often make suicide attempts, they rarely actually kill themselves.

Somatization Disorder: Possible Causes Somatization disorder tends to run in families. Coryell (1980) found that approximately 20 percent of first-degree female relatives of women with somatization disorder also had the disorder. In addition, many studies have shown that somatization disorder is closely associated with antisocial personality disorder (which I will describe later in this chapter). First-degree male relatives of women with somatization disorder have an increased incidence of alcoholism or antisocial behavior, and first-degree female relatives of convicted male criminals have an increased incidence of somatization disorder (Guze, Wolfgram, McKinney, & Cantwell, 1967; Woerner & Guze, 1968). These findings suggest that a particular environmental or genetic history leads to different pathological manifestations in men and women.

Hypochondriasis: Description Somatization disorder resembles another somatoform disorder called **hypochondriasis.** People who suffer from hypochondriasis, more frequently women than men, interpret minor physical sensations as signs that they have a serious underlying disease. For example, a person who experiences very minor stomach discomfort may interpret the sensations as a definite sign of a malignant tumor. Normal fatigue on another occasion then seems to be consistent with the self-diagnosis: The person decides that the fatigue is the result of a cancerous growth. The person worries a great deal about the presumed illness and often believes that he or she is facing death. This is more than the typical anxiety that most people have when they experience a symptom of illness and consult their doctors. With hypochondriasis, reassurances by physicians will have only short-term ameliorative effects on the person's anxiety.

One important distinction between somatization disorder and hypochondriasis is that in somatization disorder a person complains of many symptoms of many possible underlying disorders, whereas in hypochondriasis the person worries about a small number of symptoms. In addition, the anxiety accompanying somatization disorder tends to focus on the symptoms themselves (e.g., "I'm nauseous almost every day and want it to stop"), whereas with hypochondriasis the person usually focuses on the dangerous disease that the overinterpreted symptoms seem to implicate (e.g., "I'm going to die of stomach cancer"). Like the person with somatization disorder, the person with hypochondriasis will seek medical attention frequently.

Conversion Disorder: Description

In **conversion disorder** a person experiences physical problems that resemble neurological disorders but have no underlying physiological basis—problems such as blindness, deafness, loss of feeling, or paralysis. According to the DSM-IV-TR, a diagnosis of conversion disorder requires that there be an apparent psychological reason for the symptoms: The symptoms must occur in response to an environmental stimulus that produces a psychological conflict, or they must permit the person to avoid an unpleasant activity or to receive support and sympathy. The term *conversion*, when applied to a mental disorder, derives from psychoanalytic theory, which states that the energy of an unresolved intrapsychic conflict can be converted into a physical symptom. The symptoms themselves often are related to individuals' personal and work lives. For example, a telephone operator may become unable to speak, a surgeon may find her hands paralyzed, or a person with a history of doing volunteer work for music festivals may find that he cannot hear. Hofling (1963) described one such case:

> The patient had taken the day off from work to be at home with his wife and [newborn] baby. During the afternoon, he had felt somewhat nervous and tense, but had passed off these feelings as normal for a new father. . . .
>
> . . . The baby awoke and cried. Mrs. L. said that she would nurse him. . . . As she put the baby to her breast, the patient became aware of a smarting sensation in his eyes. He had been smoking heavily and attributed the irritation to the room's being filled with smoke. He got up and opened a window. When the smarting sensation became worse he went to the washstand and applied a cold cloth to his eyes. On removing the cloth, he found that he was completely blind.
>
> . . . Psychotherapy was instituted. . . . The visual symptoms disappeared rather promptly, with only very mild and fleeting exacerbations during the next several months. . . .
>
> . . . He had been jealous of the baby—this was a difficult admission to make—and jealous on two distinct counts. One feeling was, in essence, a sexual jealousy, accentuated by his own sexual deprivation during the last weeks of the pregnancy. The other was . . . a jealousy of the maternal solicitude shown the infant by its mother. (Hofling, 1963, pp. 315–316)

Although the sensory deficits or paralyses of people with conversion disorder are not caused by damage to the nervous system, these people are not faking their illnesses. People who

deliberately pretend they are sick in order to gain some advantage (such as avoiding work) are instead said to be *malingering*. Malingering is not defined as a mental disorder by the DSM-IV-TR. Although it is not always easy to distinguish malingering from conversion disorder, two criteria are useful. First, people with conversion disorder are usually delighted to talk about their symptoms in great detail, whereas malingerers are reluctant to do so for fear of having their deception discovered. Second, people with conversion disorder usually describe the symptoms with great drama and flair but do not appear to be upset about them.

Somatization disorder consists of complaints of medical problems, but the examining physician is unable to detect any symptoms that would indicate physical illness. In contrast, a patient with conversion disorder gives the appearance of specifically having a neurological disorder such as blindness or paralysis.

The particular physical symptoms of people with conversion disorder change with the times. For example, around the turn of the nineteenth century, patients commonly developed "glove" or "stocking" anesthesias, in which the skin over their hands or feet would become perfectly numb. It is physiologically impossible for these anesthesias to occur as a result of nerve damage; the patterns of anesthesia produced by such damage would be very different. Today people seldom suffer these specific symptoms.

Conversion Disorder: Possible Causes

As noted earlier, psychoanalytic theory suggests that conversion disorder occurs when the psychic energy of unresolved conflicts (especially those involving sexual desires the patient is unwilling or unable to admit to having) becomes displaced into physical symptoms. In other words, psychoanalysts regard conversion disorder as primarily sexual in origin.

Behavior analysts, on the other hand, have suggested that conversion disorder can be acquired for many reasons—and acquired through learning. This assertion gains support from the finding that people with this disorder usually suffer from physical symptoms of diseases with which they are already familiar (Ullman & Krasner, 1969). A patient often mimics the symptoms of a friend, for example. Furthermore, the patient must receive some kind of reinforcer for having the disability; that is, he or she must derive some benefit from it.

Ullman and Krasner (1969) cited a case that was originally reported by Brady and Lind (1961). A soldier developed an eye problem that led to his being discharged with a small disability pension. He worked at a series of menial jobs, returning periodically to the hospital for treatment of his eye condition. He applied for a larger disability pension several times but was turned down because his vision had not become worse. After 12 years the man, who was being forced by his wife and mother-in-law to spend his spare evenings and weekends doing chores around the house, suddenly became "blind." Because of his total disability, he was given special training for the blind and received a larger pension. He also received a family allowance from the community and no longer had to work around the house. In this case, both of the criteria described by Ullman and Krasner were met: The patient was familiar with the disorder (indeed, he had a real eye disorder), and his symptoms were reinforced.

Dissociative Disorders

In somatoform disorders people avoid anxiety by experiencing the symptoms of physical disorders. In **dissociative disorders**, people reduce anxiety by undergoing a sudden disruption of consciousness, which in turn may produce changes in their memory or even in their personal identity.

Description A relatively simple form of dissociative disorder is called **dissociative amnesia.** Amnesia (loss of memory) can, of course, be produced by physical causes such as brain damage, epilepsy, or intoxication. But dissociative amnesia is related instead to traumatic life events. For example, shortly before onset of the disorder, a person may be the victim of violence, suffer a non-neurologic injury, commit an act that he or she finds repulsive, or experience a significant personal loss. The amnesia is typically confined to the traumatic event. The person will not be able to remember, for example, being attacked and disfigured or even who the attacker was. If people's own actions are the source of guilt or other stress, they may be unable to remember committing the act, where they were at the time, or who was with them.

A more extreme form of dissociative amnesia is called **dissociative fugue** (pronounced "fyoog"). This disorder produces considerable confusion, consternation, and worry for family, friends, and coworkers of the afflicted person. The conditions of onset are the same as for dissociative amnesia, but the symptoms are much more extensive. Following the stressful incident, the person cannot identify himself or herself, and cannot remember his or her past; the person may relocate to a new area, adopt a new identity, and establish a new family and career. Imagine your reaction if a friend who lived in your community, an apparently stable and well-functioning person, simply disappeared one night. Your thoughts would turn to the possibilities of accidents or death or perhaps kidnapping. And then imagine your reaction if you learned through coincidence that your friend had a new career and family thousands of miles away. When the fugue state ends, as often happens, the person resumes his or her normal personality and memory, except that he or she has no memory for events during the fugue (Coons, 2000). At that point the person may be just as confused and worried about what happened as family and friends were.

Dissociative identity disorder (previously known as *multiple personality disorder*) is a very rare but very striking dissociative disorder in which the patient displays two or more separate personalities, either of which may be dominant at any given time. An intriguing instance of dissociative identity disorder is the case of Billy Milligan, as told in the book *The Minds of Billy Milligan* (Keyes, 1981). Milligan was accused of rape and kidnapping but was deemed not guilty by reason of insanity. His psychiatric examination showed him to have 24 different personalities. Two were women and one was a young girl. Of these, one was British, another Australian, and the third Yugoslavian. One woman, a lesbian, was a poet. The Yugoslav was an expert on weapons and munitions, and the British and Australian personalities were minor criminals.

Dissociative identity disorder has received much attention; people find it fascinating to contemplate the phenomenon of several different personalities, most of whom are unaware of one another, existing within the same individual. Bliss (1986) suggests that dissociative identity disorder is a form of self-hypnosis, established early in life, that permits escape from painful experiences. Indeed, Ross, Miller, Bjornson, and Reagor (1991) reported that of 102 people diagnosed with dissociative identity disorder in the United States and Canada, 95 percent reported childhood sexual or physical abuse, or both. Note that such data do not mean that childhood abuse *causes* dissociative identity disorder. Rather, they identify a strong commonality among those who report symptoms of the disorder. Because the disorder is very rare, the rate of childhood abuse is many times higher than the incidence of dissociative identity disorder; most people who are abused as children do not develop multiple personalities. It is useful to consider this point for a moment, because statistical reports of this kind are fairly common. To say that 95 percent of those with a particular disorder share a specific childhood experience is *not at all* to say that any other person who has the same experience has a 95 percent chance of developing the disorder. Investigation of the link between childhood trauma and dissociative identity disorder remains an active and important theoretical and empirical concern (Ross, 1997).

As we saw in Chapter 9, some psychologists believe that hypnosis is not a state but a form of social role-playing. In a similar vein, Nicholas Spanos (1996) advanced the theory that North Americans have learned the concept of dissociative identity disorder and that cultural knowledge of the disorder provides a conceptual framework in which people can organize a variety of problems. Spanos argued that in attempts to understand their emotions and behaviors, people sometimes create multiple identities if doing so will help them explain themselves in a congruent fashion to others. Thus, a person confused by his or her own emotional and behavioral instability may be especially prone to develop and enact the role of someone with dissociative identity disorder. In this way the person's confusing actions and emotions become understandable both to himself or herself and to others.

But do people have the knowledge to enact the symptoms of dissociative identity disorder? In one study Spanos and his colleagues asked people to do just that. They found that when given appropriate instructions, participants could effectively simulate two different personalities (Spanos, Weekes, & Bertrand, 1985). Participants adopted a new name for the new personality, and they gave different patterns of answers on a personality test when the second personality was "in control." Although observers are often impressed by the remarkable differences among the various personalities of someone with dissociative identity disorder, it is within the ability of most people to put on a convincing act. That is not to say that everyone with dissociative identity disorder is faking. Research suggests that clinicians should be open-minded when they encounter patients who appear to have multiple personalities (Lindsay, 1999).

Possible Causes Dissociative disorders are usually explained as responses to severe trauma. Partly because they are rare, dissociative disorders are among the least understood of the mental disorders. In general, the dissociation is advantageous to the person; preserving it may be reinforced. Amnesia enables the person to forget about a painful or unpleasant life. A person with fugue not only forgets what has occurred but may also relocate to start a new life, quite unaware of doing so. However, multiple personalities may allow a person to do things that he or she really feels a need to do but cannot because of the strong guilt feelings that would ensue. The alternative personality can be that of a person with a weak conscience, unmoved by guilt.

▲ *This Inuit man and his son show no signs of* nangiarpok, *a culture-bound syndrome that is today observed only rarely.*

Biology and Culture

Culture-Bound Syndromes

People in all societies have specific rules for categorizing behavior, and these rules can differ, often considerably, from culture to culture (Simons, 1996; Simons & Hughes, 1993). How behavior is categorized and whether an instance of behavior is considered "abnormal" are strongly influenced by social norms and values that exist in a given setting at any moment in time (Bohannan, 1995). Many kinds of aberrant behavior—behavior that deviates from cultural norms— are not included in official diagnostic manuals, such as the DSM-IV-TR, yet are considered pathological within a given culture. That is, there seem to exist highly idiosyncratic mental disorders called **culture-bound syndromes,** which are found only within one or a few cultures. They do not exist across cultures, as schizophrenia and several other mental disorders appear to (Al-Issa, 1995). For example, consider the following two individual cases:

> I. A. is a young Nigerian man. He recently met a stranger, whom he greeted with a handshake. He now claims that his genitals have fallen off. After a medical examination, the physician tells I. A. that his genitals are, in fact, still where they are supposed to be. But I. A. is unconvinced. He reports that his genitals are not the same since shaking hands with the stranger.
>
> I. L. was an Inuit hunter living in western Greenland. He hunted in the open sea from his kayak. He

stopped because of *nangiarpok* ("nahn-jee-are-poke"), or an intense fear; in this case, a fear of capsizing and drowning in a kayak. He withdrew socially from his people and eventually committed suicide. Although once common among western Greenlanders, *nangiarpok* is now rare because of changes in Greenlandic culture, especially with respect to hunting and fishing, introduced through exposure to Western culture.

Many other such culture-bound syndromes appear to exist. Some Polynesian Islanders suffer from *cafard* ("ka-fawr"), a sudden display of homicidal behavior followed by exhaustion; some male Southeast Asians develop *koro*, an intense fear that the penis will retract into the body, resulting in death (they will often hold their penises firmly to prevent this from happening); some Japanese develop an intense fear that their appearance, body odors, or behaviors are offensive to others, a condition called *taijin kyofusho* ("ta-ee-jeen ki-yo-foo-sho") (Suzuki et al., 2004).

What causes culture-bound syndromes? This is a very difficult question to answer for several reasons. First, a worldwide classification scheme of mental disorders does not exist, which means that an exhaustive taxonomy of mental disorders also does not yet exist. Second, many culture-bound syndromes have only recently been discovered, and only a few have received empirical scrutiny. Third, we do not yet have a complete explanation for major mental disorders that affect millions of people, such as schizophrenia and depression, so it is not unreasonable to expect that the study of mental disorders that afflict fewer people, as culture-bound syndromes do by definition, will be neglected. And fourth, and perhaps most important, many culture-bound syndromes are often described—and treated— using "alternative" (non-Western traditional) medical treatments. For example, in Japan, *taijin kyofusho* is treated in a ritual that involves, among other things, massage and sweating. Because practices based on folk medicine are widely accepted by members of the culture, other explanations or therapies for culture-bound syndromes, based on Western scientific methods, are neither sought nor readily accepted when offered.

Nonetheless, we may speculate about the origins of culture-bound syndromes. Those described here are specific to certain environmental events or situations and appear similar in nature to phobias. Thus, it appears unlikely that these problems have either a strong hereditary or a physiological basis. Syndromes such as *nangiarpok, koro,* and *taijin kyofusho* seem similar to what is described by the DSM-IV-TR as a specific phobia, suggesting that they are learned responses to fear-eliciting stimuli.

Certainly culture-bound syndromes are phenomena worthy of investigation. Understanding their development in the cultures in which they occur may help us learn more about how cultures influence individuals' mental states, whether normal or abnormal (Kleinknecht et al., 1997).

Interim Summary

Anxiety, Somatoform, and Dissociative Disorders

People with anxiety, somatoform, and dissociative mental disorders can be thought of as having adopted strategies that offer some immediate payoff but are maladaptive in the long run. We can understand most of these problems as exaggerations of our own. Although fears and doubts may be unrealistic, they can become outrageously extreme.

Anxiety disorders include panic disorder, phobias, and obsessive-compulsive disorder. All anxiety disorders (except specific phobia and social phobia) appear to have a genetic component. Panic disorder is the least adaptive of all these disorders; the person has no defense against his or her discomfort. In contrast, obsessive-compulsive disorder involves thoughts and behaviors that prevent the person from thinking about painful subjects or that ward off anxiety.

Simple phobias can probably be explained by classical conditioning: An experience (usually early in life) causes a particular object or situation to become a conditioned aversive stimulus. The fear associated with this stimulus leads to escape behaviors, which are reinforced because they reduce the person's fear. Agoraphobia is a much more serious disorder and is apparently not caused by a specific traumatic experience. Social phobia is a fear of being observed or judged by others; in its mildest form it involves a fear of speaking in public. Specific phobia is narrowly defined in terms of a particular fear-inducing stimulus, such as a spider or snake.

Somatoform disorders include somatization disorder and conversion disorder. Somatization disorder involves persistent complaints of symptoms of a large variety of illnesses without underlying physiological causes. It afflicts women almost exclusively. In hypochondriasis the person worries about a small set of symptoms and the serious disease they seem to implicate. Conversion disorder involves specific neurological symptoms, such as paralysis or sensory disturbance, that are not produced by a physiological disorder. In most cases the patient derives some gain from his or her disability.

Dissociative disorders are rare. Dissociative amnesia (with or without fugue) appears to be a withdrawal from a painful situation or from intolerable guilt. Because amnesia is a common symptom of brain injury or neurological disease, clinicians must rule out physical factors before accepting a diagnosis of dissociative amnesia. The multiple personalities found in dissociative identity disorder are even rarer and may occur because they permit a person to engage in behaviors contrary to his or her customary code of conduct.

Culture-bound syndromes are mental disorders that appear to be idiosyncratic to only one or a few cultures. These disorders frequently involve fear of specific objects or situations. The precise origins of culture-bound syndromes are unknown, but it seems likely that they involve learned responses that reduce or eliminate anxiety or stress.

QUESTIONS TO CONSIDER

1. When was the last time you felt especially anxious about something? Did the anxiety disrupt your behavior, even momentarily? In what ways was your anxiety similar to and different from that that might be experienced by a person with an anxiety disorder, such as panic disorder or phobic disorder?

2. Do you have a specific fear—heights, dark places, insects, snakes, or other things or situations? If you do, is it severe enough to be considered a phobia? How do you know?

3. Reflect for a minute on Beth, the woman who had an obsessive-compulsive cleaning ritual. How would you explain her behavior, given what you now know about the causes of obsessive-compulsive behavior?

Personality Disorders

As shown in Table 17.1, Axis II of the DSM-IV-TR also classifies *personality disorders*—abnormalities that impair social or occupational functioning. (Axis II also includes mental retardation, which we considered in Chapter 11.) Although there are several types of personality disorders, I will address one in detail here. It has the most impact on society: *antisocial personality disorder.* **Table 17•3** provides a brief description of several other personality disorders.

TABLE 17•3	Brief Descriptions of Personality Disorders
Personality Disorder	**Description**
Paranoid	Suspiciousness and extreme mistrust of others; enhanced perception of being under attack by others.
Schizoid	Difficulty in social functioning—social withdrawal and lack of caring for others.
Schizotypal	Unusual thought patterns and perceptions; poor communication and social skills.
Borderline	Lack of impulse control; drastic mood swings; inappropriate anger; tendency to become bored easily and for prolonged periods; suicidal tendencies.
Histrionic	Attention-seeking; preoccupation with personal attractiveness; proneness to anger when attempts at attracting attention fail.
Narcissistic	Self-promotion; lack of empathy for others; attention-seeking; grandiosity.
Avoidant	Oversensitivity to rejection; little confidence in initiating or maintaining social relationships.
Dependent	Discomfort with being alone or in terminating relationships; pattern of placing others' needs above own in order to preserve the relationship; indecisiveness.
Obsessive-compulsive	Preoccupation with rules and order; tendency toward perfectionism; difficulty relaxing or enjoying life.

Source: Adapted from Carson, R. C., Butcher, J. N., & Mineka, S. *Abnormal psychology and modern life* (11th ed.). Published by Allyn and Bacon, Boston, MA. Copyright © 2000 by Pearson Education. Reprinted by permission of the publisher.

Antisocial Personality Disorder

There have been many different labels for what we now call **antisocial personality disorder.** It is characterized by failure to conform to common standards of decency, repeated lying and stealing, failure to sustain long-lasting and loving relationships, low tolerance of boredom, and a complete lack of guilt (Cleckley, 1976; Hare, 1998; Harpur, Hart, & Hare, 2002). Prichard (1835) used the term "moral insanity" to describe people whose intellect was normal but in whom the "moral and active principles of the mind are strongly perverted and depraved . . . and the individual is found to be incapable . . . of conducting himself with decency and propriety." Koch (1889) introduced the term "psychopathic inferiority," which soon became simply "psychopathy"; a person who displayed the disorder was called a "psychopath." The first version of the DSM (the DSM-I) used the term "sociopathic personality disturbance," which was subsequently replaced by the present term, "antisocial personality disorder." Most clinicians still refer to such people as *psychopaths* or *sociopaths.*

Description Antisocial personality disorder contributes to a considerable amount of social distress. Many criminals can be diagnosed as psychopaths, and most psychopaths have a record of criminal behavior. The diagnostic criteria of the DSM-IV-TR call for evidence of at least three types of antisocial behavior before age 15 and at least four types after age 18. The adult forms of antisocial behavior include inability to sustain consistent work behavior; lack of ability to function as a responsible parent; repeated criminal activity, such as theft, pimping, or prostitution; inability to maintain enduring attachment to a sexual partner; volatility and violence, including fights or assault; failure to honor financial obligations; impulsiveness and failure to plan ahead; habitual lying or use of aliases; and consistently reckless or drunken driving. In addition to meeting at least four of these criteria, the person must have displayed a "pattern of continuous antisocial behavior in which the rights of others are violated, with no intervening period of at least five years without antisocial behavior." Clearly, individuals with antisocial personality disorder are people most of us do not want to be around.

▲ *Paul Bernardo, convicted of the brutal rapes and murders of two teenage girls, is considered by many psychologists to be a classic example of the antisocial personality disorder.*

TABLE 17•4 **Diagnostic Criteria for 301.7 Antisocial Personality Disorder**

A. There is a pervasive pattern of disregard for and violation of the rights of others occurring since age 15 years, as indicated by three (or more) of the following:

   (1) failure to conform to social norms with respect to lawful behaviors as indicated by repeatedly performing acts that are grounds for arrest

   (2) deceitfulness, as indicated by repeated lying, use of aliases, or conning others for personal profit or pleasure

   (3) impulsivity or failure to plan ahead

   (4) irritability and aggressiveness, as indicated by repeated physical fights or assaults

   (5) reckless disregard for safety of self or others

   (6) consistent irresponsibility, as indicated by repeated failure to sustain consistent work behavior or honor financial obligations

   (7) lack of remorse, as indicated by being indifferent to or rationalizing having hurt, mistreated, or stolen from another

B. The individual is at least age 18 years.

C. There is evidence of Conduct Disorder . . . with onset before age 15 years.

D. The occurrence of antisocial behavior is not exclusively during the course of Schizophrenia or a Manic Episode.

(Reprinted with permission from *The Diagnostic and Statistical Manual of Mental Disorders,* Fourth Edition, Text Revision (Copyright 2000). American Psychiatric Association.)

The lifetime prevalence rate for antisocial personality disorder is estimated to be about 5 percent for men and 1 percent for women (Golomb, Fava, Abraham, & Rosenbaum, 1995). However, we cannot be sure of the accuracy of such estimates, because psychopaths do not voluntarily visit mental health professionals for help. Indeed, most of them feel no need to change their ways.

Cleckley (1976), a prominent expert on psychopathy, has listed 16 characteristics of antisocial personality disorder. As shown in **Table 17•4**, the list of features provides a picture of what most psychopaths are like. They habitually tell lies, even when there is no apparent reason for doing so and even when the lie is likely to be discovered. They steal things they do not need or even appear to want. When confronted with evidence of having lied or cheated, psychopaths do not act ashamed or embarrassed and usually shrug the incident off as a joke, or simply deny it, however obvious their guilt may be. They are unconcerned for other people's feelings and suffer no remorse or guilt if their actions hurt others. Although they may be superficially charming, they do not form real friendships; thus, they often become swindlers or confidence artists.

Psychopaths do not easily learn desirable behavior from experience; they tend to continue getting into trouble throughout their lives (Hare, 1999), although there is something of a

decline in criminal activities around age 40 (Hare, McPherson, & Forth, 1988). People with this disorder also do not appear to be *driven* to perform their antisocial behaviors; instead, they often give the impression that they are acting on whims. When someone commits a heinous crime such as a brutal murder, normal people expect that the criminal had a compelling motive, however repellent it might be, for doing so. Criminal psychopaths, though, are typically unable to supply a reason more urgent than "He had money and I needed money," "He disrespected me," or "I just felt like it." They do not show much excitement or enthusiasm about what they are doing and do not appear to derive much pleasure from life.

Possible Causes Cleckley (1976) suggested that the psychopath's defect "consists of an unawareness and a persistent lack of ability to become aware of what the most important experiences of life mean to others. . . . The major emotional accompaniments are absent or so attenuated as to count for little" (p. 371). Some investigators have hypothesized that this lack of involvement is caused by an unresponsive autonomic nervous system. If a person feels no anticipatory fear of punishment, he or she is perhaps more likely to commit acts that normal people would be afraid to commit. Similarly, if a person feels little or no emotional response to other people and to their joys and sorrows, he or she is unlikely to establish close relationships with them.

Physiological Causes and Learning. Many experiments have found that psychopaths do show less reactivity in emotional situations. For example, psychopaths were found to be relatively unresponsive, behaviorally and physiologically, to emotional words (Williamson, Harpur, & Hare, 1991). Psychopaths' speech also tends to be less emotional than that of other people. Psychopaths generally speak more quietly and do not change their vocal emphasis between neutral and emotional words (Louth et al., 1998). In other work, Hare (1965) demonstrated that psychopaths show fewer signs of anticipatory fear. All participants in Hare's study watched the numerals 1 through 12 appear in sequential order in the window of a device used to present visual stimuli. They were told that they would receive a very painful shock when the numeral 8 appeared. Psychopathic participants showed much less anticipatory responsiveness than did normal controls or nonpsychopathic criminals.

An important early study by Schmauk (1970) showed that although psychopaths are poor at learning to avoid aversive stimuli, they readily learn to avoid a loss of an appetitive stimulus. Schmauk trained people on an avoidance task, using three types of aversive stimuli: a physical stimulus (a painful electrical shock), a social stimulus (the researcher's saying, "Wrong"), and loss of money (the researcher taking a quarter from a pile of quarters that he had given to the participant). Control participants, who were neither psychopaths nor criminals, readily learned the task in response to all three types of aversive stimuli. Nonpsychopathic criminals also learned the task well, except in their responses to the aversive social stimulus; apparently they were not disturbed when the researcher said, "Wrong." But psychopathic criminals learned the task only if the correct response allowed them to avoid the loss of money; they did not learn to avoid a painful electrical shock and were not affected by the researcher's saying, "Wrong." Thus, we can conclude that psychopaths are perfectly capable of learning an avoidance task but that social stimuli or the fear of physical pain are largely ineffective.

Genetic Causes. We do not yet know what causes the deficits in emotion and empathy displayed by psychopaths, but genes may be involved. These people often (but not always) come from grossly disturbed families that contain alcoholics and other psychopaths. Mednick, Gabrielli, and Hutchings (1983) examined the criminal records of men who had been adopted early in life and found that the likelihood of their being convicted of a crime was directly related to the number of convictions of their biological fathers. (See **Figure 17•1**.)

Environmental Causes—Parenting. Parenting and childhood experiences also appear to play a role in antisocial personality disorder. The quality of parenting, especially as it relates to supervision of children, is strongly related to the development of antisocial personality disorder. In particular, children whose parents ignore them or leave them unsu-

pervised for prolonged periods often develop patterns of misconduct and delinquency. When the parents do pay attention to their children, the attention tends to consist of harsh punishment or verbal abuse in response to their misdeeds. Thus, the children of these parents live in an environment that ranges from no attention to attention in the form of physical punishment and tongue-lashings. In response, the children develop a pattern of behavior that is characterized by increased aggression, distrust of others, concern only for themselves, and virtually no sense of right and wrong (MacMillan et al., 2001).

Cognitive–Behavioral Causes. Children with conduct problems tend to have a different view of their environments from that of well-adjusted children. They perceive the world as hostile and interpret others' actions, even the actions of other children, as aggressive and threatening. They may strike out at someone else (whoever may be the object of their misperception) to avoid being attacked first. Their attack then leads to retaliation, either in the form of punishment by a parent or a teacher or in the form of a counterattack by their peer. These children soon develop reputations for being aggressive and unlikable, which further strengthens their antisocial attitudes and behaviors.

Thus, a child may be biologically predisposed to behave aggressively and to have conduct problems. The key people in the child's environment may attempt to punish these actions with a commensurate level of physical or verbal punishment. The child, in turn, perceives his or her environment as hostile and reacts even more aggressively, perhaps due to a maladaptive perception of what is necessary for his or her personal survival. Eventually, a cycle may be established that is marked by behaviors and thoughts characteristic of antisocial personality disorder.

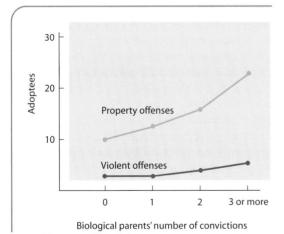

FIGURE 17•1 An adoption study of convicted criminals. Graphed here is the percentage of male adoptees convicted of violent crimes or crimes against property as a function of the number of convictions of their biological fathers.

(From Mednick, S. A., Gabrielli, W. F., & Hutchings, B. (1983). Genetic influences in criminal behavior: Some evidence from an adoptive cohort. In K. T. Van Dusen and S. A. Mednick (Eds.), *Prospective studies of crime and delinquency*. Hingham, MA: Martinus Nijhoff. With kind permission of Springer Science and Business Media.)

Interim Summary

Personality Disorders

Antisocial personality disorder is one of numerous personality disorders described in the DSM-IV-TR. Also called psychopathy or sociopathy, antisocial personality disorder is a serious problem for society. Many criminals are psychopaths, and many psychopaths become criminals. Psychopaths exhibit an apparent indifference to the effects of their behavior on other people, impulsiveness, failure to learn from experience, and habitual lying. Some psychopaths are superficially charming, and many make a living cheating others out of their money.

Psychopathy tends to run in families, and it seems likely that both heredity and a poor home environment may contribute to its development. The disorder is difficult to treat because psychopaths do not see any reason for changing.

QUESTION TO CONSIDER

Suppose that you have been hired as a screenwriter for a movie about a psychopath. Before you start work in earnest, the head of the film company wants to see a sample of what you have in mind for this character and asks you to write a few paragraphs describing the opening scene of the movie. What would you write? What would your character be doing in this scene?

Substance-Related Disorders

Substance-related disorders are closely related to personality disorders. In fact, many people who abuse alcohol and other drugs also have personality disorders. According to the Axis I of DSM-IV-TR, **substance-related disorders** include *substance use disorders*, or what is usually called "addiction," and *substance-induced disorders*, which are less severe but which still cause social, occupational, or medical problems.

Description

The lifetime prevalence rates for substance-related disorders vary by substance but overall are estimated to average about 27 percent (Kessler et al., 1994). The DSM-IV-TR estimates the lifetime prevalence rate for alcoholism to be about 15 percent. And although their alcohol use may not be severe enough to warrant a diagnosis of substance use disorder, as many as 25 percent of adults in North America experience problems due to alcohol consumption (Cunningham, Wild, Bondy, & Lin, 2001).

Substance-related disorders have grave social consequences. Consider some of the disastrous effects caused by the abuse of humankind's oldest drug, alcohol: automobile accidents, fetal alcohol syndrome, cirrhosis, increased rate of heart disease, and increased rate of cerebral hemorrhage. Smoking (nicotine addiction) greatly increases smokers' chances of dying of lung cancer, heart attack, and stroke; and women who smoke give birth to smaller, less healthy babies. Cocaine addiction often causes psychosis, brain damage, and death from overdose; it produces babies born with brain damage and consequent psychological problems. Competition for lucrative drug markets terrorizes neighborhoods, subverts political and judicial systems, and causes many deaths. People who take drugs intravenously run a serious risk of contracting AIDS. Why do people use these substances and subject themselves to these dangers?

Possible Causes

People abuse certain drugs because the drugs activate the reinforcement system of the brain, which is normally activated only by natural reinforcers such as food, warmth, and sexual contact. Dopamine-secreting neurons are an important component of this system. Some drugs, such as crack cocaine, activate the reinforcement system rapidly and intensely, providing immediate and potent reinforcement. For many people the immediate effects of drug use outweigh the prospect of dangers that lie in the future. As we saw in Chapter 4, although withdrawal symptoms make it more difficult for an addict to break his or her habit, these unpleasant symptoms are not responsible for the development of the addiction itself.

Genetic and Physiological Causes Not everyone is equally likely to become addicted to a drug (Bickel & Voinovich, 2000). Many people manage to drink alcohol moderately, and even many users of potent drugs such as cocaine and heroin use them "recreationally" without becoming dependent on them. There are only two possible sources of individual differences in any characteristic: heredity and environment. Obviously, environmental effects are important. People raised in a squalid environment without any real hope for a better life are more likely than other people to turn to drugs to escape from the unpleasant world that surrounds them. But even in a given environment, whether poor or privileged, some people become addicts and some do not. Some of these behavioral differences are a result of genetic differences.

Most of the research on the effects of heredity on addiction has been devoted to alcoholism. As we learned in Chapters 3 and 16, most people drink alcohol sometime in their lives and thus receive firsthand experience of its reinforcing effects. The same is not true for cocaine, heroin, or other drugs that have even more potent effects. In most countries alcohol is freely and legally available, whereas cocaine and heroin must be purchased illegally. From what we now know about the effects of addictive drugs on the nervous system, it seems likely that the results of studies on the genetics of alcoholism will apply to other types of drug addiction as well.

As Chapter 3 discussed, both twin studies and adoption studies have shown that susceptibility to alcoholism is heritable (e.g., Kendler, Prescott, Neale, & Pedersen, 1997; Prescott & Kendler, 1999; Rhee et al., 2003). In a review of the literature, Cloninger (1987) notes that there appear to be two principal types of alcoholics: those who have antisocial and pleasure-seeking tendencies—people who cannot abstain but drink consistently—and those who are anxiety-ridden—people who are able to go without drinking for long periods of time but are unable to control themselves once they start. (For convenience, these two groups are referred to as *steady drinkers* and *bingers*.) Binge drinking is also associated with emotional dependence, behavioral rigidity, perfectionism, introversion, and guilt feelings about the drinking behavior. Steady drinkers usually begin their alcohol consumption early in life, whereas binge drinkers begin much later. (See **Table 17•5**.) More generally, the age at which a person has his or her first drink correlates strongly

TABLE 17·5	Characteristic Features of Two Types of Alcoholism	

| | Types of Alcoholism | |
Feature	Steady	Binge
Usual age of onset (years)	Before 25	After 25
Spontaneous alcohol seeking (inability to abstain)	Frequent	Infrequent
Fighting and arrests when drinking	Frequent	Infrequent
Psychological dependence (loss of control)	Infrequent	Frequent
Guilt and fear about alcohol dependence	Infrequent	Frequent
Novelty seeking	High	Low
Harm avoidance	Low	High
Reward dependence	Low	High

Source: Reprinted with permission from Cloninger, C. R. (1987). Neurogenetic adaptive mechanisms in alcoholism. *Science, 236*, 410–416. Copyright 1987 by the American Association for the Advancement of Science.

with future alcohol abuse. Researchers found a quick progression to alcohol-related harm among those who reported having had their first drink between the ages of 11 and 14 (DeWit, Adlaf, Offord, & Ogborne, 2000). Among adults who had consumed alcohol at the age of 11 or 12, the study found that 13.5 percent met the criteria for alcohol abuse in adulthood, and nearly 16 percent were diagnosed as alcohol dependent.

An adoption study carried out in Sweden (Cloninger, Bohman, Sigvardsson, & von Knorring, 1985) found that men with biological fathers who were steady drinkers were almost seven times more likely to become steady drinkers themselves than were men whose biological fathers did not abuse alcohol. Family environment had no measurable effect; the boys began drinking whether or not the members of their adoptive families drank heavily. A related adoption study (Bohman, Cloninger, von Knorring, & Sigvardsson, 1984) found that women tended not to become steady drinkers. Instead, the daughters of steady-drinking fathers tended to develop somatization disorder (see also Kriechman, 1987). Thus, genes that may predispose a man to become a steady-drinking alcoholic (antisocial type) may predispose a woman to develop somatization disorder. The reason for this interaction with gender is not known.

Unlike steady drinking, binge drinking is influenced more readily by environment. The Swedish adoption study found that having a biological parent who was a binge drinker had little effect on the development of binge drinking unless the child was exposed to a family environment in which there was heavy drinking. This effect was seen in both males and females.

When we find an effect of heredity on behavior, we have good reason to suspect a biological marker of some kind.

That is, genes affect behavior only by affecting the body. A susceptibility to alcoholism could conceivably be caused by differences in the ability to digest or metabolize alcohol or by differences in the structure or biochemistry of the brain.

Most investigators believe that differences in brain physiology are most likely to play a role. Cloninger (1987) notes that many studies show that people with antisocial tendencies, including steady drinkers, show a strong tendency to seek novelty and excitement. These people are disorderly and distractible (many have a history of hyperactivity as children) and lack restraint in their behavior. They don't fear dangerous situations or social disapproval and are easily bored. On the other hand, binge drinkers tend to be anxious, emotionally dependent, sentimental, sensitive to social cues, cautious and apprehensive, fearful of novelty or change, rigid, and attentive to details. Their EEGs show little slow alpha activity (see Chapter 9), which suggests that they are aroused and anxious (Propping, Kruger, & Mark, 1981). When they take alcohol, they report a pleasant relief of tension (Propping, Kruger, & Janah, 1980).

The brains of steady drinkers may be unresponsive to danger and to social disapproval, due to an undersensitive punishment mechanism. They also may have an undersensitive reinforcement system; this may lead them to seek more intense thrills (including those provided by alcohol) in order to experience pleasurable sensations. Thus, they seek the euphoric effects of alcohol. On the other hand, binge drinkers may have an oversensitive punishment system. Normally, they avoid drinking because of the guilt they experience afterwards; but once they start, and once the sedative effect begins, the alcohol-induced suppression of the punishment system makes it impossible for them to stop.

Animal models have proved useful in the study of the physiology of addiction. Through selective breeding, researchers have developed two different strains of rats that differ in their response to alcohol. Alcohol-preferring rats do just what their name implies: If given a drinking tube containing a solution of alcohol along with their water and food, they become heavy drinkers. The alcohol-nonpreferring rats abstain. Fadda, Mosca, Colombo, and Gessa (1990) found that alcohol appeared to produce a larger release of dopamine in the brains of alcohol-preferring rats than in the brains of alcohol-nonpreferring rats. This result suggests that the reinforcing effect of alcohol is stronger in alcohol-preferring rats.

Cognitive Causes Cooper, Russell, and George (1988) have argued that people develop patterns of heavy drug use because of what they believe about the *positive* benefits of using drugs. For example, people who believe that alcohol will help them cope with negative emotions and who also expect that alcohol will make them more likable, sociable, or attractive may use alcohol to obtain these perceived positive effects. In fact, people may abuse alcohol in order to moderate both positive and negative emotions (Cooper, Frone, Russell, & Mudar, 1995). In this view, drug abuse or dependence is a way of avoiding perceived *negative* effects such as having negative emotions, not being outgoing enough, feeling uncomfortable around others, and so on. The influence of alcohol or other drugs provides an escape from such feelings. The relief negatively reinforces the use of drugs. But the effect is temporary. The negative feelings return with sobriety, leading to further drug use. Soon, the person may be intoxicated or high most or all of the time.

Interim Summary

Substance-Related Disorders

Drug addiction is one of the most serious problems society faces today. Apparently, all substances that produce addiction do so by activating the reinforcement system of the brain, which involves the release of dopamine. Most people who are exposed to addictive drugs—even those with high abuse potentials—do not become addicts. Evidence suggests that the likelihood of addiction, especially to alcohol, is strongly affected by heredity. There may be two types of alcoholism: one related to an antisocial, pleasure-seeking personality (steady drinking) and another related to a repressed, anxiety-ridden personality (binge drinking). A fuller understanding of the physiological basis of reinforcement and punishment may help us understand the effects of heredity on susceptibility to addiction. Some researchers also point to a role for cognition—beliefs about the benefits of drug use—in the development of addiction.

QUESTION TO CONSIDER

Steady and binge drinkers appear to have different kinds of personality characteristics. Do you think the presence of these characteristics might predict which kind of alcoholic a nonalcoholic person could become if he or she developed a tendency to drink? Why or why not?

Schizophrenia

Schizophrenia, the most common of the psychotic disorders, described in Axis I of the DSM-IV-TR, includes several subtypes, each having a distinctive set of symptoms. For many years controversy has existed over whether schizophrenia is one disorder with various subtypes or whether each subtype constitutes a distinct disorder. Because the prognosis differs for the various subtypes of schizophrenia, they appear to differ at least in severity. However, a particular individual may, at different times, meet the criteria for different subtypes. Some

experts have referred to schizophrenia as the "quintessential" psychological disorder. By this they refer not only to its universal incidence but also to the characteristic tragic ways in which it transforms the lives of schizophrenic individuals and their families.

Description

Schizophrenia involves distortions of thought, perception, and emotion; bizarre behavior; and social withdrawal. It is a disorder with no borders (see Murphy, 1976). According to the DSM-IV-TR, schizophrenia has a prevalence of 0.5 to 1.5 percent worldwide. It typically makes its appearance in the period from the late teens to the early 30s. Earlier onset, especially in children, is rare.

Descriptions of symptoms in historical writings indicate that this disorder may have existed as early as medieval times (Heinrichs, 2003). However, the word *schizophrenia* is widely misused. The word literally means "split mind," but it does *not* imply a split or multiple personality. People often say that they "feel schizophrenic" about an issue when they really mean that they have mixed or divided feelings about it. A person who sometimes wants to build a cabin in the woods and live off the land and at other times wants to take over the family restaurant may be undecided, but he or she is not schizophrenic. The psychiatrist who invented the term, Eugen Bleuler (pronounced "oi-gun bloi-lur"), intended to refer to a split with reality caused by extreme mental disorganization—a condition in which thoughts and feelings no longer worked together normally.

Schizophrenia is characterized by two categories of symptoms, positive and negative. The distinction is important. A **positive symptom** of schizophrenia emerges and makes itself known by its *presence*. Positive symptoms include thought disorders, delusions, and hallucinations. A **thought disorder**—a pattern of disorganized, irrational thinking—is probably the most definitive symptom of schizophrenia. People with schizophrenia have great difficulty arranging their thoughts logically and sorting out plausible conclusions from absurd ones. In conversation they may jump from one topic to another spontaneously. Sometimes they utter meaningless words or apparently choose words for their rhyme rather than for their meaning.

A *delusion* is a belief that is contrary to fact. Although there are debates about the exact nature of delusions (e.g., Leeser & O'Donohue, 1999; Mullen, 2003), these false beliefs are readily identifiable in the context of mental illness and tend to appear in three forms. *Delusions of persecution* are false beliefs that others are plotting and conspiring against the individual. *Delusions of grandeur* are a person's false beliefs in his or her own power and importance, such as a conviction that the person has godlike powers or has special knowledge that no one else possesses. *Delusions of control* are related to delusions of persecution; a person may believe, for example, that he or she is being controlled by others through such means as radar or tiny radio receivers implanted in the brain.

Hallucinations—the perception of stimuli that are not actually present—constitute the third positive symptom of schizophrenia. When filmmakers depict hallucinations, they typically use a device to let viewers know that the sound or sight is not real. For example, they may show visual hallucinations as ghostlike and give imaginary sounds an eerie quality. For the person with schizophrenia, cues like these would likely be a relief. Unfortunately, to someone with this disorder the hallucinated perceptions and sensations seem perfectly real, as real and as substantial as this textbook (Nasar, 1998).

Hallucinations can involve any of the senses. The common feature of hallucinations is that they are negative experiences. Visual hallucinations are usually threatening, frightening, or at least confusing. Gustatory (taste) and olfactory (smell) hallucinations usually are disgusting (e.g., of feces). The most common hallucinations in schizophrenia are auditory. The typical schizophrenic hallucination consists of voices talking to the person. Sometimes the voices order the person to do something; sometimes they criticize and humiliate the person for being unworthy, unclean, or immoral; sometimes they just utter meaningless phrases. People with schizophrenia may hear a voice that keeps a running commentary on their behavior.

In contrast to these positive symptoms, the **negative symptoms** of schizophrenia consist of the absence of normal behaviors: flattened emotional response, poverty of speech, lack of initiative and persistence, inability to feel pleasure, and social withdrawal. Negative symptoms are not specific to schizophrenia; they are seen in many neurological disorders that involve brain damage, especially to the frontal lobes.

As we will see later in this chapter, evidence suggests that positive and negative symptoms result from different physiological disorders. Positive symptoms appear to involve excessive activity in some neural circuits that include dopamine as a neurotransmitter. Negative symptoms appear to be caused by brain damage. Many researchers suspect that these two sets of symptoms involve a common set of underlying causes, but these causes have yet to be identified with certainty.

Types of Schizophrenia

According to the DSM-IV-TR, there are five types of schizophrenia: paranoid, disorganized, catatonic, undifferentiated, and residual.

The pre-eminent symptoms of **paranoid schizophrenia** are delusions of persecution, grandeur, or control. The word *paranoid* is so widely used in ordinary language that it has come to mean "suspicious." However, not all paranoid schizophrenics believe that they are being persecuted. Some believe that they hold special powers that can save the world—that they are Superman, Napoleon, or Joan of Arc. And some hold complementary delusions of grandeur and persecution.

People with paranoid schizophrenia are among the most intelligent of those who have psychotic disorders; so, not surprisingly, they often build up delusional structures incorporating a wealth of detail. They tend to interpret even the most trivial event in terms of a grand scheme, whether of persecution or grandeur or both intertwined. The way a person walks, a facial expression or movement, even the shapes of clouds can acquire special significance.

Disorganized schizophrenia is a serious progressive and irreversible disorder characterized primarily by disturbances of thought. People with disorganized schizophrenia often display signs of emotion, especially silly laughter, that are inappropriate to the circumstances. Also, their speech tends to be a jumble of words: "I came to the hospital to play, gay, way, lay, day, bray, donkey, monkey" (Snyder, 1974, p. 132). This sort of speech is often referred to as a *word salad*. Hallucinations and delusions are common.

Catatonic schizophrenia (from the Greek *katateinein*, meaning "to stretch or draw tight") is characterized by various motor disturbances, including both extreme excitement and stupor. People with this form of schizophrenia will display *catatonic postures*—bizarre stationary poses that may be maintained for many hours—and *waxy flexibility*, in which the person's limbs can be molded into new positions, which are then maintained for long periods.

Many patients are diagnosed as having **undifferentiated schizophrenia;** that is, they have delusions, hallucinations, and disorganized behavior but do not meet the criteria for paranoid, disorganized, or catatonic schizophrenia. In addition, some patients' symptoms change after an initial diagnosis, and their classification changes accordingly.

Residual schizophrenia is the diagnosis when at least one episode of one of the four other types of schizophrenia has occurred but no single, prominent positive symptom is currently observable. However, negative symptoms are observable, as are muted forms of positive symptoms. Residual schizophrenia may mark a transition from a full-blown schizophrenic episode to remission (the absence of any symptoms). But it also may continue to linger year after year.

Early Signs of Schizophrenia

Bleuler (1950), a pioneer in the diagnosis and study of schizophrenia, divided the disorder into *reactive* and *process* forms. Bleuler designated patients with a general history of good mental health as having **reactive schizophrenia,** on the assumption that their disorder was a reaction to stressful life situations. Typically, these patients soon recovered, and few experienced another episode. Patients with indications of mental illness early in life, however, were designated as having **process schizophrenia,** which was considered a chronic disorder.

If process schizophrenia has its roots in early life, an important task is to determine what the early predictors or risk factors are. In theory the ability to identify people with a high risk of schizophrenia while they are still young will allow clinicians to implement some form of therapy before the disorder becomes advanced. The early signs also may indicate whether the causes of schizophrenia are biological, environmental, or both.

In fact, many studies of people who develop schizophrenia in adulthood have found that they were different from others even in childhood. However, these studies do not tell us whether these differences resulted from physiological disorders or from the behavior of other family members when those who were later diagnosed with schizophrenia were in infancy and childhood. One remarkable study obtained home movies of people with adult-onset schizophrenia when they were children (Walker & Lewine, 1990). Although schizophrenia did not manifest itself until adulthood, viewers of the films (six graduate students and one professional clinical psychologist) did an excellent job of identifying the children who would later develop it. The viewers commented on the children's poor eye contact, relative lack of responsiveness and positive affect, and generally poor motor coordination. Clearly, something was different about these patients' behavior even early in life.

Possible Causes

For more than a century, research into the causes of all kinds and forms of schizophrenia has reflected the challenge that psychologists face in attempting to understand how psychological and biological factors interact to influence behavior. The diathesis–stress model of mental disorders, discussed earlier in the chapter, is a widely referenced account: Schizophrenia appears to result from one or more inherited biological predispositions that are activated by environmental stressors.

Genetic Causes Advances in genetics and research involving twin and adoption studies have established the heritability of schizophrenia—or, more precisely, the high heritability of a *tendency* toward schizophrenia (Gottesman & Reilly, 2003). Identical twins are much more likely to be concordant for schizophrenia than are fraternal twins, and the children of parents with schizophrenia are more likely themselves to become schizophrenic, even if they were adopted and raised by nonschizophrenic parents (Gottesman & Moldin, 1998). Twin studies of schizophrenia compare the concordance rates of monozygotic (MZ) or identical twins with the concordance rates of siblings of different genetic relatedness who were reared either together or apart. (Recall from Chapter 3 that twins are concordant for a trait if neither or both express it and discordant if only one expresses it.) According to Gottesman and Shields (1982) and Gottesman (1991), schizophrenia concordance rates for MZ twins are about 50 percent, but they are less than about 20 percent for dizygotic (DZ) or fraternal twins (see **Table 17•6**).

If a person has been diagnosed with schizophrenia, there exists the possibility that other family members have the disorder too. It is important to note that although the

TABLE 17•6 Summary of Major European Studies of the Genetics of Schizophrenia in Families and Twins	
Relation to Person Identified as Schizophrenic	**Percentage with Schizophrenia**
Spouse	1.0
Grandchild	2.8
Niece/nephew	2.6
Child	9.3
Sibling	7.3
Fraternal twin	12.1
Identical twin	44.3

Source: Davison, G. C., & Neale, J. M. (1990). *Abnormal psychology.* New York: John Wiley & Sons.

likelihood of developing schizophrenia increases if a person has relatives with schizophrenia, this disorder is not a simple trait, like eye color, that is inherited. In fact, 63 percent of people suffering from schizophrenia do not have a first- or second-degree relative who also has the disorder (Gottesman & Erlenmeyer-Kimling, 2001). Even if both parents have schizophrenia, the probability that their child will develop it is 30 percent or less.

Most investigators believe that a person inherits a *predisposition* to develop schizophrenia. In their view, most environments will foster normal development, whereas certain environments will trigger various disorders, including schizophrenia. If the diathesis–stress model is valid as it applies to schizophrenia, we would expect that some people carry a "schizophrenia gene" but do not express it. Their environments do not trigger schizophrenia, or they have acquired the coping skills to deal successfully with environmental stressors. Such a person might be the nonschizophrenic member of a pair of MZ twins discordant for schizophrenia.

The logical way to test this model is to examine the children of both members of discordant pairs of MZ twins. Gottesman and Bertelsen (1989) found that the percentage of schizophrenic children was nearly identical for both members of such pairs (16.8 percent for the schizophrenic parents; 17.4 percent for the nonschizophrenic parents). In contrast, for parents who were fraternal (DZ) twins and discordant for schizophrenia, the percentages were dissimilar— 17.4 when the parent was schizophrenic and 2.1 when the parent was nonschizophrenic. These results provide strong evidence that schizophrenia is heritable but also support the conclusion that carrying a "schizophrenia gene" does not mean that a person will necessarily develop schizophrenia. (See **Figure 17•2**.) As suggested by the diathesis–stress model, environmental factors are also likely to be involved.

Physiological Causes—The Dopamine Hypothesis

Cocaine and amphetamines can produce the symptoms of

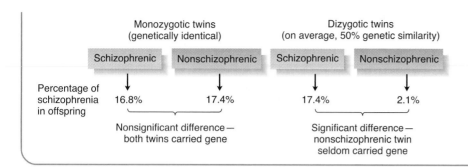

FIGURE 17·2 Heritability of schizophrenia. As shown in this diagram, people can have an unexpressed "schizophrenia gene."

schizophrenia, both in people who have schizophrenia and in people who do not. Antipsychotic medications reduce those symptoms in people who have schizophrenia. Because cocaine and amphetamine can affect the neural pathways that contain dopamine, researchers have formulated the **dopamine hypothesis:** the proposal that abnormal activity of dopamine-containing neurons is a causal factor in schizophrenia. That is, the positive symptoms of schizophrenia are produced by the overactivity of dopamine-transmitting synapses. Amphetamines, cocaine, and the antipsychotic drugs act on synapses—the junctions between nerve cells—in the brain. As you may recall from Chapter 4, one neuron passes on excitatory or inhibitory messages to another by releasing a small amount of neurotransmitter from its terminal button into the synaptic cleft. The chemical activates receptors on the surface of the receiving neuron, and the activated receptors either excite or inhibit the receiving neuron. Drugs such as amphetamine and cocaine *stimulate* receptors for dopamine. In contrast, antipsychotic drugs *block* dopamine receptors and prevent them from becoming stimulated.

Physiological Causes—Neurological Disorders

Although the dopamine hypothesis has long been the dominant biological explanation for schizophrenia, other evidence suggests that it offers only a partial explanation. Antipsychotic drugs alleviate positive, but not negative, symptoms of schizophrenia (Angrist, Rotrosen, & Gershon, 1980). Perhaps those patients who do not improve with medication have primarily negative symptoms.

Once researchers began paying more attention to negative symptoms, they discovered evidence for brain damage in patients exhibiting these symptoms. In several studies the CT or MRI scans of patients revealed larger than normal cerebral ventricles among schizophrenic patients (Sullivan et al., 1998; Zipursky, Lambe, Kapur, & Mikulis, 1998). There is also evidence that people with schizophrenia display abnormal neural processing while trying to suppress inappropriate responses (Kiehl, Smith, Hare, & Liddle, 2000). Similarly, Pfefferbaum and colleagues (1988) found evidence that the sulci (the wrinkles in the brain) were wider in the brains of schizophrenic patients. Enlargement of the ventricles of the brain and widening of the sulci indicate the absence of brain tissue. Indeed, other research shows that

schizophrenic patients have less cortical gray matter than persons with normal psychological functioning (Mitelman et al., 2003; Lim et al., 1998; Suddath et al., 1990). The study by Suddath and colleagues (1990) is particularly interesting because their participants were identical twin pairs. The investigators examined MRI scans of MZ twins discordant for schizophrenia and found that, in almost every case, the twin with schizophrenia had larger lateral and third ventricles. In addition, the hippocampus was smaller in the schizophrenic twin, and the total volume of the gray matter in the left temporal lobe was reduced. **Figure 17·3** shows a set of MRI scans from a pair of twins. As you can see, the lateral ventricles are larger in the brain of the twin with schizophrenia. Still other research has shown a progressive loss of gray matter during adolescence among people who develop schizophrenia during childhood (Rapoport et al., 1999). Interestingly, some brain abnormalities that had previously been associated only with chronic alcoholism have also been noted in patients with schizophrenia (Deshmukh, Rosenbloom, Pfefferbaum, & Sullivan, 2002). It appears that the abnormalities exist in people with schizophrenia, even if they do not abuse alcohol. Thus, the evidence is coming together to

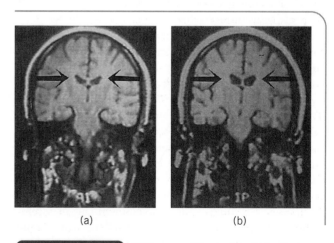

(a)   (b)

FIGURE 17·3 MRI scans of the brains of identical twins discordant for schizophrenia. (a) Normal twin. (b) Twin with schizophrenia. Arrows point to the lateral ventricles.
(Courtesy of D. R. Weinberger, National Institute of Mental Health, Saint Elizabeth's Hospital, Washington, DC.)

suggest the existence of some kind of neurological disease process.

Several studies have indicated that the cause of brain damage in schizophrenia may be a viral infection. No direct evidence for virally induced schizophrenia exists, but there are similarities between schizophrenia and known viral disorders. Stevens (1988), for example, notes interesting similarities between schizophrenia and *multiple sclerosis,* a neurological disorder (see Chapter 4). Multiple sclerosis appears to be an autoimmune disease—triggered by a virus—in which the patient's own immune system attacks the myelin sheaths that cover most axons in the central nervous system. Both multiple sclerosis and schizophrenia are more prevalent and also more severe in people who spent their childhood in latitudes far from the equator. Both diseases are more common in people with low socioeconomic status who live in crowded, deprived conditions. Both diseases are characterized by one of three general courses: (1) attacks followed by remissions, many of which produce no residual deficits; (2) recurrent attacks with only partial remissions, causing an increasingly major deficit; or (3) an insidious onset with a steady and relentless progression, leading to permanent and severe deficits. These similarities suggest that schizophrenia, like multiple sclerosis, could be a virally induced autoimmune disease.

A second possible neurological cause of schizophrenia is interference with normal prenatal brain development. Several studies show that people born during the winter months are more likely to develop schizophrenia later in life (Davies et al., 2003; Torrey et al., 1997). Torrey, Torrey, and Peterson (1977) suggested that the causal factor could be seasonal variations in nutritional factors or, more likely, variations in toxins or infectious agents in air, water, or food. Several diseases known to be caused by viruses, such as measles, influenza, and chicken pox, show a similar *seasonality effect.* The seasonality effect is seen most strongly in poor, urban locations, where people are at greater risk for viral infections (Machon, Mednick, & Schulsinger, 1983).

A seasonally related virus could affect either a pregnant woman or a newborn. Two pieces of evidence suggest that the damage is done prenatally. First, brain development is more susceptible to disruption prenatally. Second, a study of the offspring of women who were pregnant during a 1957 epidemic of type A2 influenza in Finland showed an elevated incidence of schizophrenia (Mednick, Machon, & Huttunen, 1990), but only among offspring of women who were in the second trimester of their pregnancies during the epidemic. Presumably, the viral infection produced toxins that interfered with the brain development of some of the fetuses, resulting in the later development of schizophrenia. Keep in mind, however, that influenza is just one of many potential causes of schizophrenia; a large-scale study conducted in Denmark revealed that prenatal exposure to influenza could account for only 1.4 percent of the 9462 cases of schizophrenia that were examined (Takei et al., 1996). More recently, Brown and colleagues (2004), us-

ing a U.S. sample, showed a sevenfold increase for schizophrenia when influenza exposure occurred in the first trimester.

Birth trauma is another possible neurological cause of schizophrenia. Schwarzkopf and colleagues (1989) found that if a person with schizophrenia does not have relatives with a schizophrenic disorder—that is, if there is no evidence that the disease is a result of heredity—he or she is more likely to have had a history of neurological complications at or around the time of childbirth. Thus, brain damage not related to heredity may also be a cause of schizophrenia.

Cognitive and Environmental Causes—The Family and Expressed Emotion

The personality and communicative abilities of either or both parents appear to play an influential role in the development of schizophrenic symptoms in their children. Several studies have shown that children reared by parents who are dominating, overprotective, rigid, and insensitive to the needs of others are more likely to develop schizophrenia (Roff & Knight, 1995). In many cases, a parent may be verbally accepting of the child yet in other ways reject him or her, which establishes a conflict for the child called a **double bind.** For example, a mother may encourage her son to become emotionally dependent on her yet continually reject him when he tries to hug her or sit on her lap or play with her (see Bateson, 1973; Laing & Esterson, 1964).

Children reared in families racked with discord also seem to be at greater risk of developing schizophrenia. For example, in a study of 14 schizophrenic individuals, Lidz, Fleck, and Cornelison (1965) found that each of these individuals came from a family that underwent either chronic discord in which the integrity of the parents' marriage was perpetually threatened or marital problems in which the bizarre behavior of one family member was tolerated by the other members. Children in families in which parents treat them with hostility or in which parents present confusing communication to them are at risk for developing schizophrenia (Goldstein & Strachan, 1987). Further research showed that excitableness in a child has a strong relationship with positive symptoms of adult-onset schizophrenia (Roff & Knight, 1995). However, researchers are still attempting to determine whether marital discord, family hostility, and confusing communications are causes or effects of schizophrenia.

In addition to exploring family-related causes of schizophrenia, researchers also have identified a family-related variable that affects the likelihood that a person with schizophrenia will recover from it. Brown and his colleagues (Brown, 1985; Brown, Bone, Dalison, & Wing, 1966) labeled this variable **expressed emotion**—expressions of criticism and hostility and emotional overinvolvement by family members toward the patient. Brown and colleagues found that if a patient was living in a family environment in which the level of expressed emotion was low, she or he was more likely to recover, whereas patients in families in which it was high were more likely to continue to exhibit schizophrenic symptoms.

This finding is consistent across hundreds of studies conducted in many different cultures (Jenkins & Karno, 1992). Studies from North America, England, Denmark, Italy, France, Spain, Germany, Taiwan, India, Egypt, and Australia all indicate that despite differences in the ways that people of different cultures perceive mental illness and express themselves, expressed emotion does not seem to be a culture-bound phenomenon. Two elements of expressed emotion in the families of schizophrenic patients appear to be common to all cultures; namely, critical comments and emotional overinvolvement. Jenkins and Karno (1992) also found that expressed emotion tends to be higher in many more industrialized than nonindustrialized cultures—and that people in nonindustrialized countries are more supportive of family members with schizophrenia than are people in industrialized countries. These findings may reflect the relatively greater access to jobs that a schizophrenic person has in nonindustrialized countries, as well as the greater proportion of extended families, in which more individuals can participate in the care of the schizophrenic family member.

Interim Summary

Schizophrenia

Schizophrenia is a serious form of psychopathology that occurs in every culture. It radically transforms the lives of those who suffer from it and places a heavy burden on their families. The main positive symptoms of schizophrenia include thought disorders; delusions of persecution, grandeur, and control; and hallucinations. The main negative symptoms include withdrawal, apathy, and poverty of speech. The DSM-IV-TR classifies several subtypes of schizophrenia, including paranoid, disorganized, catatonic, undifferentiated, and residual. But the distinctions between reactive and process schizophrenia and between positive and negative symptoms also seem to be important.

People who develop chronic (process) schizophrenia in their late teens through their early 30s appear to be different from other people even as children, which suggests that the disorder takes root early in life. The diathesis–stress model accurately describes the course of schizophrenia: Some people seem to inherit a genetic predisposition for the disorder, which is expressed when environmental stressors outweigh these individuals' attempts to cope with them. Positive symptoms of schizophrenia can be produced in normal people or made worse in schizophrenics by drugs that stimulate dopamine synapses (cocaine and amphetamines) and can be reduced or eliminated by drugs that block dopamine receptors (antipsychotic drugs). These findings have led to the dopamine hypothesis, which states that schizophrenia is the result of abnormal activity in neural pathways containing dopamine.

More recent studies indicate that schizophrenia can best be conceived of as two different disorders. The positive symptoms are produced by overactivity of dopamine neurons and can be treated with antipsychotic drugs. The negative symptoms may be caused by brain damage. Researchers have found direct evidence of brain damage by inspecting scans of living patients' brains.

Researchers have suggested three possible causes of the brain damage—and the corresponding negative symptoms—that accompany schizophrenia: a virus that triggers an autoimmune disease, which causes brain damage later in life; a virus that damages the brain early in life; and birth trauma. Heredity presumably interacts with the first two factors—many people may be exposed to the virus, but the virus will cause brain damage only in people with a genetic sensitivity.

Research suggests that several factors in the early family environment may contribute to the later expression of schizophrenia. The level of expressed emotion in families is a factor in individuals' recovery from schizophrenia.

QUESTIONS TO CONSIDER

1. Imagine that you are a clinical psychologist. A client of yours complains of hearing voices. You suspect that this individual may be schizophrenic, but you wish to gather more information before you make your diagnosis. What sorts of information about this person do you need before you can make your diagnosis? How would you gather it?
2. Suppose that a friend of yours, who acts a little strange at times, is diagnosed as schizophrenic. Your friend knows that the diagnosis is incorrect, but nobody believes him because his strange behavior makes the diagnosis seem believable. What would your friend have to say or do to convince you that he is normal?

Mood Disorders

Everyone experiences moods varying from sadness to happiness to elation. We're excited when our team wins a big game, saddened to learn that a friend's long-term relationship has gone sour, thrilled at a higher-than-expected raise at work, and devastated by the death of a loved one. Such is the emotional range that colors life's experiences. Some people, though, experience more dramatic changes than these. Significant shifts or disturbances in mood that adversely affect normal perception, thought, and behavior are called **mood disorders**. They may be characterized by a deep, foreboding depression or by a combination of depression and **mania**, which is defined by the DSM-IV-TR as the abnormal and persistent elevation of an expansive or irritable mood.

Description

In contrast to schizophrenia, in which the principal symptom is disordered thought, the mood disorders are primarily disorders of emotion. The most severe mood disorders are the bipolar disorders and major depressive disorder. **Bipolar I disorder** is characterized by episodes of mania by itself or in a mix with anxiety, usually accompanied by episodes of major depression. **Bipolar II disorder** is marked by major depressive episodes that are accompanied by periods of less severe mania, known as *hypomanic episodes*. **Major depressive disorder** involves persistent, severe feelings of sadness and worthlessness accompanied by changes in appetite, sleeping, and other behavior. The lifetime prevalence for major depressive disorder is about 16 percent (Nestler et al., 2002).

A less severe form of depression is called *dysthymic disorder* (pronounced "dis-thigh-mik"). The term comes from the Greek words *dus*, "bad," and *thymos*, "spirit." The primary difference between this disorder and major depressive disorder is its relatively lower severity. Similarly, *cyclothymic disorder* resembles bipolar II disorder but is less severe.

Mania   A person in the grip of mania (the Greek word for "madness") shows expansive, irritable behavior that may be wildly out of place in the situation in which it occurs. During manic episodes people appear elated and are self-confident; however, any contradiction or interference tends to make them suddenly angry. Their speech (and, presumably, their thinking) becomes very rapid. They tend to flit from topic to topic and often are full of grandiose plans. Although their thoughts are not as disorganized as those of people with schizophrenia, they tend to be restless and hyperactive, often pacing ceaselessly. They may have delusions and hallucinations that fit their exuberant mood. Davison and Neale (1990) recorded a typical interaction between a therapist and a manic client:

> *Therapist:* Well, you seem pretty happy today.
>
> *Client:* Happy! Happy! You certainly are a master of understatement, you rogue! (Shouting, literally jumping out of seat.) Why I'm ecstatic. I'm leaving for the West Coast today, on my daughter's bicycle. Only 3100 miles. That's nothing, you know. I could probably walk, but I want to get there by next week. And along the way I plan to contact a lot of people about investing in my fish equipment. I'll get to know more people that way—you know, Doc, "know" in the biblical sense (leering at the therapist seductively). Oh, God, how good it feels. It's almost like a nonstop orgasm. (Davison & Neale, 1990, p. 222)

The usual response that manic speech and behavior evoke is sympathetic amusement. In fact, when an experienced clinician finds that he or she is amused by the patient's talk and antics, the clinician begins to suspect mania. Because very few patients exhibit mania only, the DSM-IV-TR classifies all cases in which mania occurs as bipolar disorders. These patients usually experience alternating periods

▲ *The symptoms of major depression include apathy, feelings of worthlessness, social withdrawal, changes in sleeping and eating patterns, and lethargy or agitation.*

of mania and depression. Each may last from a few days to a few weeks, sometimes with several days of relatively normal behavior in between. Many therapists have observed that there often is something contrived about the patient's elevated mood during the manic phase, as though the patient may be manufacturing happiness in order to ward off an episode of major depression.

Depression   People with depression have feelings of extreme sadness and usually are full of self-directed guilt, but not because of any particular incident. Depressed people cannot always state why they are depressed. Aaron Beck (1967), a leading figure in the treatment of mood disorders, identified five major symptoms of depression: (1) a sad and apathetic mood; (2) feelings of worthlessness and hopelessness; (3) a desire to withdraw from other people; (4) sleeplessness and loss of appetite and sexual desire; and (5) a change in activity level, either to lethargy or to agitation. Most people who are labeled "depressed" actually have *dysthymic disorder*, the less-extreme form of depression described as being "down in the dumps" much of the day and for the majority of days over a period of at least two years. Major depressive disorder also must be distinguished from grief, such as the sorrow caused by the death of a loved one. People who are grieving feel sad and depressed but do not fear losing their minds or have thoughts of self-harm. In contrast, many people who suffer from major depressive disorder or from the depressive episodes of bipolar disorders commit suicide. In fact, the mortality rate (including suicide) among people with mood disorders is two to three times greater than that of the general population (Fogarty, Russell, Newman, & Bland, 1994).

People with severe depression often have delusions, especially the belief that their brains or internal organs are rotting away. Sometimes they believe that they are being punished for unspeakable and unforgivable sins, as in the following statement, reported by Coleman (1976):

My brain is being eaten away. . . . If I had any willpower I would kill myself. . . . I don't deserve to live. . . . I have ruined everything . . . and it's all my fault. . . . I have been unfaithful to my wife and now I am being punished . . . my health is ruined . . . there's no use going on . . . (sigh). . . . I have ruined everything . . . my family . . . and now myself. . . . I bring misfortune to everyone. . . . I am a moral leper . . . a serpent in the Garden of Eden. (Coleman, 1976, p. 346)

Possible Causes

The possible causes of mood disorders are many and various. Let's look at four categories of potential causes: faulty cognition, heredity, brain biochemistry, and sleep/wake cycles.

Cognitive Causes Faulty cognition seems to play a role in depression; clearly, people with mood disorders don't have the same outlook on life as others. Depressed people are generally negative about themselves and, as such, can be challenging to be around. Specifically, they are likely to say things like: "Nobody likes me," "I'm not good at anything," or "What's the point in even trying—I'll just screw up anyway." Thus, the depressed individual gets caught in a vicious circle: Negative statements strain interpersonal relationships, causing others to withdraw or to withhold social support; this in turn reinforces the depressed individual's negative statements (Klerman & Weissman, 1986; Weissman, Markowitz, & Klerman, 2000).

The changes in affect seen in depression may be not primary but secondary to changes in cognition (Beck, 1967, 1991). According to this view the primary disturbance is a distortion of the person's view of reality. For example, a depressed person may see a scratch on the surface of his or her car and conclude that the car is ruined. A person whose recipe fails may see the failure as proof of his or her basic incompetence. A person may see a nasty form letter from a creditor as a serious personal condemnation. According to Beck, whose work I mentioned earlier, depressed people's thinking is characterized by self-blame (things that go wrong are always their fault), overemphasis on the negative aspects of life (even small problems are blown out of proportion), and failure to anticipate positive change (a pessimistic attitude prevails). This kind of thinking involves negative thoughts about the self, about the world, and about the future, which Beck collectively referred to as the *cognitive triad*. In short, depressed people see no hope for future improvement. Because they blame their present miserable situation on their inadequacies and see these inadequacies as permanent characteristics, they have no reason to believe things will be different in the future.

Whereas psychoanalytic theory emphasizes the role of the unconscious in the emergence of mental disorders, Beck emphasizes the role of a person's judgment in contributing to his or her own emotional state. Beck's theory has been useful in alerting therapists to the importance of considering the thought processes, as well as the feelings, of a patient with a severe mood disorder. Of course, if we observe an association between faulty cognition and depression, we cannot necessarily conclude that the faulty cognition causes the depression; in fact, the reverse could be true. In any event, Beck's method of treatment, based on his theory, has proved to be effective in many cases (as we shall see in Chapter 18).

Attributional style (Abramson, Metalsky, & Alloy, 1989; Abramson, Seligman, & Teasdale, 1978) may be another causal factor in depression. According to this view, it is not merely experiencing negative events that causes people to become depressed. More important are the attributions people make about why those events occur. People are most likely to become depressed if they attribute negative events and experiences to their own shortcomings and believe that their lives are never going to get any better. A person's attributional style, then, serves as a predisposition or diathesis for depression. In other words, people prone to depression tend to have hopeless outlooks—"I am not good at anything I try to do, and it will never get any better. I am always going to be a lousy person."

The attributional style model suggests that depression is most likely to occur when people with pessimistic attributional styles encounter significant or frequent life stressors (Abramson, Alloy, & Metalsky, 1995). Such individuals then generalize their pessimistic attributions to otherwise moderate stressors, and eventually a deep sense of hopelessness and despair sets in. The diathesis–stress model of depression has been supported by research on both adults (e.g., Johnson et al., 2001; Metalsky, Joiner, Hardin, & Abramson, 1993) and adolescents (e.g., Abela & Sullivan, 2003; Joiner, 2000). The evidence indicates that the combination of a hopeless outlook *plus* negative life events is predictive of depression. When both components coincide, people appear to suffer a double dose of hopelessness. Not only do they perceive negative outcomes as being their own fault, but they also perceive positive outcomes as due to circumstance or to luck. In addition, they apply pessimistic attributions to a wide range of events and experiences and apply positive attributions only to a very narrow range of events and experiences, if any.

Genetic Causes Like schizophrenia, the mood disorders appear to have a genetic component. People who have first-degree relatives with a serious mood disorder are 10 times more likely to develop these disorders than are people without afflicted relatives (Rosenthal, 1970). First-degree relatives of people suffering from the bipolar disorders are 7 percent more likely than the rest of the population to suffer from the disorder (Sadovnick et al., 1994). Furthermore, the concordance rate for the bipolar disorders is 60 percent for monozygotic twins, compared with 15 percent for dizygotic twins (Kendler et al., 1993). For major depression the MZ/DZ figures are 40 percent and 11 percent, respectively (Allen, 1976). Thus, a case can be made that heritable factors predispose people to develop these disorders.

Physiological Causes—Biochemical Factors The effectiveness of certain drug therapies for mood disorders suggests to some researchers that biochemical factors may play a role in the development and course of mood disorders. Although there is a certain logic to this argument, we will see that the issue remains unsettled.

The evidence clearly shows that at least two neurotransmitters, norepinephrine and serotonin, are related to depression. People with major depression have lower levels of these neurotransmitters than do people without the disorder. It is also the case that drug therapies that increase the amount of these substances in the synapses, or make the substances available for longer periods of time, have beneficial effects on depression.

Other drugs, including *reserpine*, which is used to treat high blood pressure, can *cause* episodes of depression. Reserpine lowers blood pressure by blocking the release of norepinephrine in muscles in the walls of blood vessels, thus causing the muscles to relax. However, because the drug also blocks the release of norepinephrine and serotonin in the brain, a common side effect is depression. The existence of this side effect strengthens the argument that biochemical factors in the brain play an important role in depression.

Several studies have found evidence of biochemical abnormalities in the brains of people with mood disorders. Taking samples of neurotransmitters directly from the living brain is not possible. But when neurotransmitters are released at the synapse, a small amount is broken down by enzymes in the brain, and some of the breakdown products accumulate in the cerebrospinal fluid or pass into the bloodstream and collect in the urine. This makes it possible to analyze cerebrospinal fluid and urine for these substances.

For example, one study found that the level of a compound called 5HIAA in the cerebrospinal fluid of depressed people who had attempted suicide was significantly lower than in control participants (Träskmann, Asberg, Bertilsson, & Sjöstrand, 1981). The lower level of this compound, which is produced when serotonin is broken down, implies lower activity in serotonin-secreting neurons in the brains of depressed individuals. In fact, 20 percent of the people with levels below the median subsequently committed suicide, whereas none of the participants with levels above the median did so. Taube and colleagues (1978) obtained evidence for decreased activity of neurons that secrete norepinephrine in patients with mood disorders; in these patients they found low levels of a compound (MHPG) that appears in the urine when the neurotransmitter is broken down. Thus, the decreased activity of serotonin- and norepinephrine-secreting neurons appears to be related to depression. Additionally, researchers have found evidence of a genetic association between major depression and suicide (Lemonde et al., 2003). Certain genotypes containing the homozygous G[-1019] allele were found twice as often in depressed patients in comparison to a control group, and four times more often in suicide victims.

Although the brain biochemistry of patients with mood disorders appears to be abnormal, we cannot be certain that a biochemical imbalance is the first event in a sequence that leads to depression. Environmental stimuli may cause the depression, which may then lead to biochemical changes in the brain. For example, investigators found that the brain levels of norepinephrine were lower in dogs that were presented with inescapable electrical shocks and developed *learned helplessness* (Miller, Rosellini, & Seligman, 1977; see Chapter 13). The dogs did not inherit low norepinephrine levels; they acquired them as a result of their laboratory experience. In sum, research findings so far suggest that a tendency to develop serious mood disorders is heritable and that low levels of norepinephrine and serotonin are associated with these disorders. However, the cause-and-effect relations have yet to be worked out.

Physiological Causes—Relation to Sleep Cycles A characteristic symptom of mood disorders is sleep disturbance. Typically, people with a severe mood disorder have little difficulty falling asleep, but they awaken early and are unable to get back to sleep again. (In contrast, people with dysthymic disorder are more likely to have trouble falling asleep and getting out of bed the next day.) Kupfer (1976) reported that depressed patients tend to enter REM sleep sooner than normal people do and spend more time in this state during the last half of sleep. Noting this fact, Vogel, Vogel, McAbee, and Thurmond (1980) deprived depressed patients of REM sleep by awakening them whenever the EEG showed signs that they were entering this stage. Remarkably, the deprivation decreased their depression. These findings are supported by the observation that treatments that alleviate depression in humans, such as electroconvulsive therapy and antidepressant drugs (see Chapter 18), profoundly reduce REM sleep in cats (Moreau, Scherschlicht, Jenck, & Martin, 1995; Scherschlicht et al., 1982).

Total sleep deprivation also has an antidepressant effect. However, the effects are quite different. REM sleep deprivation requires several weeks in order to reduce depression and produces relatively long-lasting effects. Total sleep deprivation produces immediate effects—but the effects are short-lived (Wu & Bunney, 1990). **Figure 17•4** shows the mood rating of a depressed patient who stayed awake one night. As you can see, the depression was lifted by the sleep deprivation but returned the next day, after a normal night's sleep.

We still do not know why some depressed people profit from total sleep deprivation whereas others do not. A study by Reinink, Bouhuys, Wirz-Justice, and van den Hoofdakker (1990) found it possible to predict a person's responsiveness to sleep deprivation on the basis of his or her circadian pattern of mood. Most people feel better at a particular time of day—generally, either the morning or the evening. Depressed people also show fluctuations in mood. Reinink and his colleagues found that the depressed people who were most likely

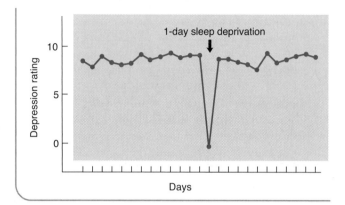

FIGURE 17·4 Sleep deprivation and depression. A single night's total sleep deprivation dramatically changes the depression rating of a depressed patient.

(From Wu, J. C., & Bunney, W. E. (1990). The biological basis of an antidepressant response to sleep deprivation and relapse: Review and hypothesis. *American Journal of Psychiatry, 147,* 14–21. Reprinted with permission from the *American Journal of Psychiatry,* copyright 1990. American Psychiatric Assciation.)

to show an improvement in mood after a night of total sleep deprivation were those who felt worst in the morning and best in the evening.

Ehlers, Frank, and Kupfer (1988) proposed an intriguing hypothesis that integrates behavioral and biological evidence concerning the relation between sleep cycles and depression. They suggest that depression is triggered environmentally through loss of *social zeitgebers.* A **zeitgeber** (from the German word for "time giver") is a stimulus that synchronizes daily biological rhythms, which are controlled by an internal biological clock located in the hypothalamus. The most important zeitgeber is light; each morning, our biological clocks are synchronized ("reset to the time zero") by daylight. As discussed in Chapter 9, these clocks control sleep and waking cycles, cycles of hormone secretion and body temperature, and many other physiological systems that fluctuate each day.

Ehlers and her colleagues (1988) assert that in humans social interactions, as well as light, may serve as zeitgebers. For example, people tend to synchronize their daily rhythms to those of their spouses. After the loss of a spouse, people's daily schedules are usually disrupted, and many widows and widowers become depressed. Flaherty and colleagues (1987) studied recently widowed people and found that the most depressed individuals were those with the greatest reduction in social contacts and regular daily activities. Ehlers, Frank, and Kupfer (1988) suggest that some people may be more susceptible to depression in the face of these changes. This susceptibility represents the genetic contribution to vulnerability to mood disorders. Almost everyone becomes depressed, at least for a period of time, after the loss of a

loved one. Other events that change a person's daily routine, such as the birth of an infant or the loss of a job, also can precipitate a period of depression. Perhaps people who "spontaneously" become depressed are in fact reacting to minor changes in their daily routine that disrupt their biological rhythms.

A similar phenomenon involves people who become depressed during the winter season, when days are short and nights are long. The symptoms of this form of depression, called **seasonal affective disorder**, are slightly different from those of major depressive disorder. Both conditions involve lethargy and sleep disturbances, but seasonal depression also includes a craving for carbohydrates and an accompanying weight gain. (As you will recall, people with major depressive disorder tend to lose their appetites.)

Seasonal affective disorder can be treated by exposure to natural or artificial light (Dalgleish, Rosen, & Marks, 1996; Lamberg, 1998; Lee & Chan, 1999; McColl & Veitch, 2001). People with seasonal affective disorder may require a stronger-than-normal zeitgeber in order to synchronize their biological clocks with the day–night cycle. Interestingly, it appears that there may be a genetic link between alcoholism and seasonal affective disorder (McGrath & Yahia, 1993). Some people who abuse alcohol tend to drink more in the fall and winter months. Family and molecular genetics studies suggest the link between alcoholism and seasonal affective disorder may be genetic (Sher, 2004). Several investigators have noticed that the symptoms of seasonal affective disorder resemble the behavioral characteristics of hibernation: carbohydrate craving, overeating and weight gain, oversleeping, and lethargy (Neuhaus & Rosenthal, 1997; Rosenthal, 2000, Rosenthal et al., 1986). Animals that hibernate do so during the winter. Their behavior is triggered by a combination of short day length and cooler temperatures. Thus, some of the brain mechanisms involved in hibernation may also be responsible for the mood changes associated with the time of year. For example, Zvolsky, Jansky, Vyskocilova, and Grof (1981) found that imipramine, an antidepressant drug, suppressed hibernation in hamsters.

Interim Summary

Mood Disorders

The serious mood disorders are primarily disorders of emotion, although delusions are also present. Bipolar I disorder consists of alternating periods of mania and depression, whereas major depressive disorder consists of depression alone. Bipolar II disorder is marked by major depressive episodes and hypomania. Beck has noted that although depression involves emotional reactions, it may be, at least in part, based on faulty cognition. A negative attributional style is also correlated with depression.

Heritability studies strongly suggest a biological component in mood disorders. This possibility receives support from the finding that biological treatments for depression, including electroconvulsive shock, antidepressant drugs, and REM sleep deprivation, can reduce symptoms, while reserpine, a hypertension drug that blocks the release of norepinephrine and serotonin, can cause depression. These findings, along with evidence from biochemical analysis of the breakdown products of norepinephrine and serotonin in depressed patients, suggest that depression results from deficiencies in the availability of these neurotransmitters. However, the fact that environmental stressors can also affect the availability of neurotransmitters warns us to be careful in inferring cause and effect.

Evidence also suggests that the primary physiological disorder in depression may manifest itself in abnormal sleep/waking rhythms. Studies have shown that REM sleep deprivation alleviates the symptoms of depression. In addition, total sleep deprivation temporarily reduces the symptoms of depression, particularly in people who tend to feel less depressed at the end of the day. An important environmental trigger of depression may be disruption of a person's daily routine and social contacts. A specific form of depression, seasonal affective disorder, can be treated by exposure to bright light, which synchronizes the biological clock with the day–night cycle.

QUESTIONS TO CONSIDER

1. Suppose that you have a friend whose mother has been diagnosed with major depressive disorder. Your friend is concerned about her mother and also worries that she herself may become depressed, because she has heard that this disorder is genetic. Knowing that you are taking a course in psychology, she asks you to tell her more about major depressive disorder and about the likelihood that she too will develop it. What do you tell her?

2. Medical students often diagnose themselves as having the diseases and disorders they are studying. In fact, what happens is that their studies simply make them more sensitive to slight deviations from their normal level of physical health. While reading the section on mood disorders, did something similar happen to you—did you become more sensitive to your mood and to deviations from your normal mood? Can you trace these deviations to specific events? If so, what were they?

Suggestions for Further Reading

Arieti, S. (2000). *The Parnas: A scene from the Holocaust.* Philadelphia: Paul Dry Books.

A noted psychiatrist offers a respectful and instructive Freudian analysis of the agoraphobia displayed by Giuseppe Pardo, the Parnas of Pisa, including the remission of symptoms during Pardo's fateful encounter with Nazi soldiers near the end of World War II.

Butcher, J. N., Mineka, S., & Hooley, J. M. (2007). *Abnormal psychology and modern life* (13th ed.). Boston: Allyn and Bacon.

This upper-division undergraduate textbook provides a systematic overview of the categories of mental illness and their treatment.

Cleckley, H. (1988). *The mask of sanity* (5th ed.). Augusta, GA: Emily S. Cleckley.

This is a classic reference on antisocial personality disorder that includes several in-depth case studies.

Nasar, S. (1998). *A beautiful mind.* New York: Simon & Schuster.

A best-selling biography of the Nobel economist, John Nash, that follows his brilliant career and the personal and family devastation wrought by paranoid schizophrenia.

North, C. N. (2003). *Welcome, silence: My triumph over schizophrenia.* Lima, OH: Academic Renewal Press.

A psychiatrist offers a first-person window on her own struggle with schizophrenia and treatment.

Spitzer, R. L., Gibbon, M., Skodol, M., Williams, J. B. W., & First, M. B. (2002). *DSM-IV-TR casebook:: A learning companion to the diagnostic and statistical manual of mental disorders, Fourth edition, Text revision.* Washington, DC: American Psychiatric Association.

An excellent source of case studies that parallel the diagnostic categories found in the DSM-IV-TR.

Vonnegut, M. (1975). *The Eden express: A personal account of schizophrenia.* New York: Praeger.

An autobiographical narrative of what it is to become schizophrenic and to receive treatment with anti-psychotic medication.

Key Terms

actuarial judgments (p. 551)

agoraphobia (p. 555)

anticipatory anxiety (p. 554)

antisocial personality disorder (p. 563)

anxiety (p. 553)

bipolar I disorder (p. 574)

bipolar II disorder (p. 574)

catatonic schizophrenia (p. 569)

clinical judgments (p. 551)

compulsion (p. 556)

conversion disorder (p. 559)

culture-bound syndromes (p. 561)

Diagnostic and Statistical Manual of Mental Disorders, Fourth Edition, Text Revision (p. 548)

diathesis–stress model (p. 548)

disorganized schizophrenia (p. 569)

dissociative amnesia (p. 560)

dissociative disorders (p. 560)

dissociative fugue (p. 560)

dissociative identity disorder (p. 560)

dopamine hypothesis (p. 571)

double bind (p. 572)

expressed emotion (p. 572)

hallucination (p. 569)

hypochondriasis (p. 558)

major depressive disorder (p. 574)

mania (p. 573)

mood disorder (p. 573)

negative symptom (p. 569)

obsession (p. 556)

obsessive-compulsive disorder (p. 556)

panic (p. 554)

panic disorder (p. 554)

paranoid schizophrenia (p. 569)

phobic disorder (p. 555)

positive symptom (p. 568)

process schizophrenia (p. 569)

reactive schizophrenia (p. 569)

residual schizophrenia (p. 569)

schizophrenia (p. 568)

seasonal affective disorder (p. 577)

social phobia (p. 555)

somatization disorder (p. 558)

somatoform disorder (p. 558)

specific phobia (p. 555)

substance-related disorders (p. 566)

thought disorder (p. 568)

Tourette's syndrome (p. 558)

undifferentiated schizophrenia (p. 569)

zeitgeber (p. 577)

18

THE TREATMENT OF MENTAL DISORDERS

Mental Disorders and Psychotherapy

Early Treatment of Mental Disorders • The Development of Psychotherapy

In past centuries people with mental disorders were greatly misunderstood and treated inhumanely. Today, numerous forms of treatment are available for the many types of psychological problems. Therapists often use different methods or combine two or more methods to treat different problems.

Insight Therapies

Psychoanalysis and Modern Psychodynamic Approaches • Humanistic Therapies • Evaluation of Insight Therapies

Insight therapies are based on the idea that people can best solve their psychological problems by talking about them with a specially trained therapist. Psychoanalytic and psychodynamic therapies attempt to get people to discover the unconscious and conscious forces that may be at the root of their problems. Humanistic therapies focus more on the contribution of current thinking and emotions to maladaptive behavior. Gestalt therapy aims to teach people to confront their feelings as they are presently experienced, placing little emphasis on past experiences. An important limitation to all insight therapies is that they are mainly relevant to mild mental disorders and not to more serious disorders, such as schizophrenia.

Behavior Therapies, Cognitive Therapies, and Cognitive–Behavioral Therapies

Therapies Based on Classical Conditioning • Therapies Based on Operant Conditioning • Maintaining Behavioral Change • Cognitive Therapies and Cognitive–Behavioral Therapies • Evaluation of Behavior, Cognitive, and Cognitive–Behavioral Therapies

Therapies derived from the basic principles of classical and operant conditioning are effective in treating several disorders, including anxiety disorders and phobias. Cognitive–behavioral therapy is also effective in changing behavior, but in this case the emphasis is on changing faulty cognitions as well as environmental conditions. Despite their effectiveness, behavior and cognitive–behavioral therapies are limited by ethical considerations.

Group Therapies and Community Psychology

Family Therapy and Couples Therapy • Community Psychology • *Biology and Culture: Cultural Belief Systems and Indigenous Healing Therapies*

Group therapies, including family and couples therapies, provide the opportunity for the therapist to observe people's interactions with one another and to suggest more adaptive responses. Community psychology stresses public education, social change, and prevention of psychological problems as strategies for fostering more effective behavior; it also provides important support services to people who might otherwise be institutionalized for their problems. Therapists sometimes work in consultation with indigenous healers or at least seek to inform themselves about indigenous healing practices in an effort to better understand clients whose cultural background includes such practices.

Biological Therapies

Drug Therapy • Electroconvulsive Therapy • Psychosurgery • Evaluation of Biological Treatments • *Evaluating Scientific Issues: Assessing the Effectiveness of Therapy*

Certain classes of drugs have been found to be highly effective in treating the symptoms of schizophrenia, depression, bipolar disorder, and anxiety-related disorders. Clinicians often can treat severe depression—as a last resort—by passing electrical current through the brain and inducing a seizure. Psychosurgery is no longer a common treatment, although one form of it is sometimes used to treat people with severe obsessive-compulsive disorder. For several reasons it is difficult to assess the effectiveness of therapies. The existing evidence, which includes meta-analyses, has identified factors that influence therapeutic outcome and, in general, provides a positive conclusion.

The Relationship between Client and Therapist
Ethical Issues • Selecting a Therapist

Because the therapeutic relationship can be exploited and abused, a detailed set of ethical standards has evolved to guide therapists in their practices. When selecting a therapist, a person should look for someone who is licensed to practice therapy, knowledgeable about mental disorders, ethical, and supportive.

Geoff had been the founder of a successful company at an early age. He had dropped out of college to start the company; but later he had put a sizable amount of the company's fortunes into a film, and unrealistic planning and bad judgment had caused the company to fold. Although his professional life was now in shambles, Geoff still believed that he could do no wrong. He was bursting with ideas and energy and felt nearly indestructible. He usually slept only about three or four hours a night, and he said that he thought he could have jumped off the Empire State Building because he believed he would have landed on his feet and walked away. Geoff decided to see a psychologist, who told him that he might be suffering from bipolar I disorder, a serious psychological condition. Geoff brushed off this information. He felt tired sometimes, but he never felt really down. He thought the psychologist couldn't possibly be right.

Geoff decided that he needed a fresh start and moved to a new city. Once there, he did not sleep for five days. Several friends recommended that he seek professional help. He checked into a hospital, was diagnosed with bipolar I disorder, and was immediately prescribed lithium. One physician recommended that Geoff also see a psychotherapist. Geoff was skeptical and thought that the lithium alone would solve his problems. Eventually he grudgingly decided to try psychotherapy, mainly to keep the doctors off his back, but he often missed appointments and had decided before his first session that it would not be of any use to him. At some point, he just stopped going.

Geoff was confident that the prescribed drugs were helping him, but he hated their side effects. He had developed shakes due to the lithium and started taking other pills to control the tremors. Geoff also needed medication to sleep; altogether, he was taking 17 pills every night before bed. Besides being uncomfortable with this large amount of medication, he felt that he was generally less aware of himself, others, and life in general, and that he was often in a "ghost state." To add to his problems, he was still having trouble focusing on one thing at a time. Even while taking medication, Geoff said he was always trying to do 80 things at once. He was interested in going back to college, but the idea of sitting through a lecture or studying for an exam seemed impossible.

Geoff decided to give psychotherapy one more try and met a therapist with whom he ended up working for several years. Today, with the therapist's help, Geoff has gained an understanding of the decisions he makes while in a manic state. The lithium provides him with enough focus to understand what his therapist is telling him. Even with medication, Geoff can still feel manic states coming on. But through psychotherapy he has gradually learned to recognize the signs and can channel them in a positive way for the most part. As Geoff sees it, there is no way he could have gained from psychotherapy without medication, but medication alone would not have allowed him to get his life fully back on track.

Recently Geoff switched to a new medication with fewer side effects. The new drug has been effective and has allowed him to stop taking several other drugs that combat the side effects of lithium. Geoff also has learned a variety of relaxation techniques and no longer needs sedatives in order to sleep. He attributes his success to a combination of medication and psychotherapy.

This chapter begins with an overview of psychotherapy, then describes four basic approaches to the treatment of mental disorders: insight therapies; behavior, cognitive, and cognitive–behavioral therapies; group therapies (including therapies for families and couples and outreach programs that serve the community); and biological treatments. Therapy is a complex process, and its outcome depends to a large extent on the relationship that the client and therapist are able to form. The final section of the chapter addresses ethical issues involved in the practice of therapy and the many considerations individuals should take into account when selecting a therapist.

Mental Disorders and Psychotherapy

Today, most societies view mental disorders as illnesses, much the same as physical diseases like cancer. Today, psychologists agree that the client or patient with a mental disorder should be treated humanely: The person needs help, and the emergence of techniques to provide such help has become a hallmark of psychology. However, this enlightened view has not always characterized humankind's treatment of people with mental disorders and other psychological problems.

Early Treatment of Mental Disorders

Sometimes mental disorders are thought of as products of relatively modern times. In truth, mental disorders have existed from antiquity. For most of that time, people with these disorders have been regarded with awe or fear. Some persons whom we now would probably classify as paranoid schizophrenic may have been regarded as prophets or seers, instruments through whom gods or spirits were speaking (see Jaynes, 1976). More often, people with paranoid schizophrenia were considered to be possessed by devils or evil spirits and were made to suffer accordingly. The earliest known attempts to treat mental disorders involved drilling holes in a living person's skull, a process known as **trephining.** Presumably, the opening was made to release evil spirits from inside the victim's head. In prehistoric times this procedure was performed with a sharp-edged stone; later civilizations, such as the Egyptians, refined the practice with more sophisticated instruments. Signs of healing at the edges of the holes in prehistoric skulls indicate that some people survived trephining. (See **Figure 18•1.**)

Many other painful and degrading practices were directed at people's presumed possession by evil spirits. If they were considered to be unwilling hosts, they were subjected to curses or insults designed to drive the demons away. If this approach had no effect, *exorcism* sought to make the person's body an unsuitable place for devils to reside in. Other rituals included beatings, starving, near drowning, and the drinking of foul-tasting concoctions. The delusional schemes of people with psychotic disorders often caused others to consider them guilty of evil deeds and grossly unworthy. In societies that accepted the notion that there were witches and devils, these people often were ready to imagine themselves as evil. Some confessed to unspeakable acts of "sorcery" and accepted their persecution and punishment as deserved.

As late as the eighteenth century, the idea that devils and spirits were responsible for peculiar behaviors in certain people remained popular in Britain and its colonies and in Europe. Fortunately, a few people believed that such extreme behaviors reflected diseases and should be treated medically and with compassion. Johann Wier, a sixteenth-century German physician, was among the first to challenge practices intended to combat witchcraft. He argued that most people who were being tortured and burned for practicing witchcraft in fact suffered from mental illness. The church condemned his writings as heretical and banned them. Wier's ideas reemerged only in the nineteenth century.

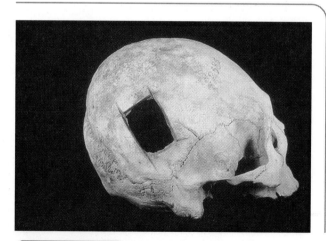

FIGURE 18•1 Among the earliest biological approaches to the treatment of mental disorders was the ancient practice of trephining, in which a hole was made in the skull to allow evil spirits to escape the person's head. (Photo © Loren McIntyre/Woodfin Camp & Associates.)

Eventually, the deep cultural belief in witchcraft and demonology waned. The clergy, the medical authorities, and the general public began to regard people with mental disorders as ill. Torture and severe persecution came to an end. However, the lives of mentally ill people did not necessarily become better. Undoubtedly, many people with mental disorders were regarded as strange but harmless and managed to maintain a marginal existence in society. Others were sheltered by their families. Often, however, people with mental disorders were consigned to "asylums" established for the care of the mentally ill. Most of these mental institutions were extraordinarily inhumane. Patients often were kept in chains and wallowed in their own excrement. Those who displayed bizarre catatonic postures or who had dramatic delusions were sometimes exhibited to the public for a fee. Many of the treatments designed to cure mental patients were only a little better than the tortures that had previously been used to drive out evil spirits. Patients were tied up, doused in cold water, bled, made to vomit, spun violently in a rotating chair, and subjected to other terrible treatments. (See **Figure 18•2**.)

Reform began as mistreatment of the mentally ill became a cause of humanitarians. Philippe Pinel (1745–1826) was a French physician who in 1793 was appointed director of La Bicêtre, a mental hospital in Paris. Pinel believed that most mental patients would respond favorably to kind treatment. As an experiment he removed the chains from some of the patients, took them out of the dungeons, and allowed them to walk about the hospital grounds. The experiment was a re-

markable success. Orderliness and general calm replaced the previous noise, stench, and pervasive aura of despair. Many patients were eventually discharged. Pinel's success at La Bicêtre was repeated when he was given charge of the larger Salpêtrière Hospital. Pinel's achievements encouraged similar reforms elsewhere. In the United States, Dorothea Dix (1802–1887) led the campaign for humane treatment of mental patients. She raised millions of dollars for the construction of mental hospitals and spurred the reform of many mental health facilities. Until well into the twentieth century, however, large mental hospitals were little more than warehouses for the mentally ill, who received little or no treatment but were merely provided with the necessities of life. Today there is much greater emphasis on treatment. The discovery of antipsychotic drugs and improvements in therapy have spared many people who otherwise would have spent their lives in institutions.

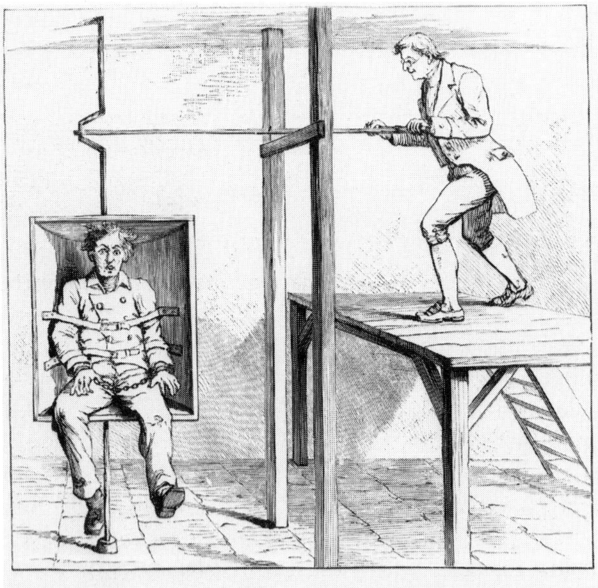

The Development of Psychotherapy

The modern approach to therapy can be traced to Franz Anton Mesmer (1734–1815), an Austrian physician who practiced in Paris in the late eighteenth and early nineteenth centuries. He devised a theory of "magnetic fluxes," according to which he attempted to effect cures by manipulating iron rods and bottles of chemicals. In reality, he hypnotized his patients and thereby alleviated some of their symptoms. As a result, hypnosis was first known as *mesmerism* (see Wegner, 2002).

Jean Martin Charcot (1825–1893), a French neurologist, began to study the therapeutic uses of hypnosis when one of his students hypnotized a woman and induced her to display the symptoms of a conversion reaction (then called *hysteria*) (see Chapters 14 and 17). Charcot examined her and concluded that she was indeed a hysterical patient. The student then woke the woman, and her symptoms promptly vanished. Charcot had previously believed that hysteria had an organic basis, but this experience changed his opinion. He began to investigate the psychological causes of hysteria and to use hypnosis in his treatment.

Before Sigmund Freud began private practice, he studied with Charcot in Paris. There he observed the effects of hypnosis on hysteria. Freud's association with Charcot, and later with Josef Breuer, started him on his life's study of the determinants of personality and the origins of mental illness. (These topics were discussed in Chapters 14 and 17.) Freud created the practice of psychoanalysis. The therapeutic methods he developed still influence many psychologists and psychiatrists; other psychologists devised therapies based on their own theoretical views of maladaptive behavior and its causes.

Although all therapists have in common a strong commitment to helping people solve their problems—whether the difficulties of coping with everyday stressors or more severe psychological disorders such as schizophrenia or depression—therapists may favor one kind of therapy or another based on their theoretical orientation. For example, therapists who believe that behavior is strongly influenced by environmental contingencies and people's perceptions of them are

THE DOCTOR THINKS THAT "NO WELL-REGULATED INSTITUTION SHOULD BE UNPROVIDED WITH THE CIRCULATING SWING." 1818.

FIGURE 18•2 This illustration of a device used in an early 19th-century mental hospital exemplifies the extremes of treatment to which mental patients were subjected.

(Illustration © Bettmann/CORBIS)

TABLE 18·1   Basic Assumptions, Goals, and Methods Involved in Major Categories of Therapies

Type of Therapy	Basic Assumptions	Primary Goals	Typical Methods of Analysis or Intervention
Psychoanalysis	Behavior is motivated by intrapsychic conflict and biological urges.	To discover the sources of conflict and resolve them through insight.	Free association; dream analysis; interpretation of transference, resistance, memory, and manner of speech.
Psychodynamic therapy	Behavior is motivated by both unconscious forces and interpersonal experiences.	To understand and improve interpersonal skills.	Interpretation of transference and modification of clients' inappropriate schemas for interpersonal relationships.
Humanistic therapies: Client-centered therapy and Gestalt therapy	People are inherently good and have innate worth.	To promote personal growth and self-actualization and to enhance clients' awareness of bodily sensations and feelings.	Reduction of incongruence through reflection, empathy, unconditional positive regard, and techniques designed to enhance personal awareness and feelings of self-worth.
Behavior and cognitive–behavioral therapies	Behavior is largely influenced by environmental contingencies, people's perception of them, or a combination of both.	To change maladaptive behavior and thinking patterns.	Manipulation of environmental variables, restructuring of thinking patterns, and correction of faulty thinking or irrational beliefs.
Family/couples therapy	Problems in relationships entail everybody involved in those relationships.	To discover how social interactions influence problems of individual behavior.	Analysis of patterns of families'/ couples' interactions and of how those involved reinforce maladaptive and adaptive thinking and behaving.

likely to use cognitive–behavioral approaches to treating their clients' problems. Therapists who believe that behavior is strongly influenced by biological factors are likely to use a combination of drug therapy and psychotherapy in treating their clients' problems, as was the case with Geoff in the opening vignette.

Most therapists today, however, adopt a more general, eclectic approach. With the **eclectic approach** the therapist uses whatever methods he or she feels will work best for a particular client at a particular time. The therapist is not strongly wedded to a certain theoretical orientation. Instead, she or he seeks the particular form of therapy that will best solve the client's problems. This often means *combining* aspects of several different treatment approaches according to the client's specific problem and personal circumstances. For example, Acierno, Hersen, and Van Hasselt (1993) have shown that combinations of behavior and cognitive–behavioral therapies are more effective in treating panic disorder than is either one alone. **Table 18·1** lists the assumptions, primary goals, and methods involved in each of the traditional forms of therapy that we will consider in the rest of this chapter.

There are a large number of reasons people may seek therapy. Some people need help in adjusting to everyday problems at home, work, or school. Others face more serious problems, such as the death of a loved one, their own approaching death, or difficulties in getting along with other people. Still others enter therapy, or are placed in therapy by mental health agencies, for very serious psychological problems such as schizophrenia, major depression, or drug abuse.

People who hit a low point in their lives may feel that their own efforts are insufficient and that family and friends cannot provide the help they need to solve their problems. Therapy is not just for people suffering from major psychological disorders. In fact, almost anyone can benefit from seeing a therapist at particularly difficult times.

Interim Summary

Mental Disorders and Psychotherapy

At different times, people suffering from emotional or behavioral problems were believed to be possessed by demons or were accused of being witches. They were often subjected to unspeakable torture, including trephining, in which a small hole was punctured in the skull of the afflicted person to allow demonic spirits to escape. Even when not being physically harmed, mental patients in sixteenth- and seventeenth-century asylums encountered abject humiliation. Philippe Pinel, a French physician, is often credited with changing the asylum environment in the late eighteenth century.

Modern therapy involves a wide array of treatment options—from psychoanalysis to drug treatment. In many cases, a person seeking therapy may find that the therapist uses an eclectic approach—borrowing methods from different treatments and blending them in a way that will work best in treating the client's problem. Certainly, such options would not be available were it not for the modern view that people should have the chance to improve their level of functioning. People seeking therapy are perhaps even more diverse than those providing therapy. Although people seek therapy for many reasons, the one element they share is that they are at a low point in life and that alternative solutions, such as trying to solve the problem alone or with the help of friends and family, have not been satisfactory.

1. What is your reaction to people with mental disorders? If you have known someone who has been diagnosed with a mental disorder, what was your initial feeling about that person when you first learned about it?
2. Would you seek the help of a therapist if you had a psychological problem you could not solve yourself? If so, describe what you might imagine therapy to be like and how it might help you. If not, describe the reasons why you would not seek help.

Insight Therapies

In the opening vignette, Geoff combined drug therapy and a form of insight therapy. Practitioners of *insight therapy* assume that people are essentially normal but learn maladaptive thought patterns and emotions, which are revealed in maladaptive behaviors. In other words, insight therapies view such behaviors as symptomatic of deeper, underlying psychological problems. Thus, once a patient understands the causes of his or her problems, the problems—and the maladaptive behaviors—will cease. Insight equals cure. In this section we will take a close look at major insight therapies: psychoanalysis, client-centered therapies, and Gestalt therapy.

The insight therapies emphasize talk between the therapist and the client as a means of uncovering the reasons for the client's problems. Insight into these reasons presumably helps the client work through the problems. Some insight therapies, such as psychoanalysis, probe for the causes in the client's past, often in childhood. Others, such as client-centered and Gestalt therapies, emphasize the present; they attempt to get the client to see the effects of his or her maladaptive thoughts and emotions and to find more adaptive ways of living.

Psychoanalysis and Modern Psychodynamic Approaches

~und Freud is credited with developing **psychoanalysis,** a ˙ therapy aimed at providing the client with insight r her unconscious motivations and impulses. Recall

from Chapter 14 that Freud's theory of personality suggests that unconscious conflicts based on the competing demands of the id (representing biological urges), the superego (representing the moral dictates of society), and the ego (representing perceived reality) often lead to anxiety. The source of these conflicts, according to Freud, can usually be traced to inadequately censored sexual and aggressive urges or stunted completion of one or more of the psychosexual stages of development.

In the early stages of therapy, the nature of the client's problem is difficult to identify because the analyst and the client are unaware of the underlying conflicts. The repression of these conflicts is seldom complete, though, and they frequently intrude into consciousness in subtle ways. By encouraging the client to talk, the analyst tries to bring these conflicts into view. The obscurity of the conflicts requires that the analyst interpret them in order to expose their true meaning and gradually weave together a more complete picture of the client's unconscious.

The purpose of psychoanalysis is to create a setting in which clues about the origins of intrapsychic conflicts are most likely to be revealed by the client. These clues are thought to be revealed in clients' dreams, health problems, memories (or failures of memory), manner of speech, and cognitive and emotional reactions. By confronting these clues, the client may gain insight into the conflict and the problems it has produced.

One of the main goals of the psychoanalyst is to *interpret* the clues about the origins of intrapsychic conflict that are provided by the client. Although clients also may provide their own interpretations of these phenomena, Freud argued that people are biased observers of their own problems; thus, their interpretations cannot be accurate. Instead, accurate interpretation is best accomplished through therapy with a specially trained therapist. Those who currently practice psychoanalysis (or one of its variants) still emphasize interpretation as the principal means of uncovering the root causes of their clients' problems (e.g., Busch, 2003b; LaFarge, 2000).

While the psychoanalyst's primary role is interpretation, the client's main job is to provide the psychoanalyst with something to interpret: descriptions of his or her fears, anxieties, thoughts, or repressed memories. This is not an easy task for the client, because she or he may unconsciously invoke one or more defense mechanisms—which, as you will recall from Chapter 14, prevent anxiety-provoking memories and ideas from reaching conscious awareness.

Freud (1933) felt that the "veil of amnesia" imposed by defense mechanisms lifts the moment that insight is achieved. It is then that the client begins to understand the actual nature of his or her problems. For some clients insight is a sudden rush of profound understanding—sort of an "Aha, so that's what was causing the problem!" experience. For other clients, perhaps the majority who undergo long-term therapy, there may be a feeling of quiet accomplishment after a long struggle. Successful treatment depends not only on the psychoanalyst's interpretations but also on the client's capacity to understand

and integrate what he or she has learned in therapy (Busch, 2003a). In the case of Geoff in the opening vignette, psychodynamic therapy would have been less effective if he had not first taken medication that enhanced this capacity.

Psychoanalytic Techniques Freud abandoned the use of hypnosis in favor of other methods. One of his techniques was **free association,** in which the client is encouraged to speak freely. Freud achieved this goal in two ways. First, he encouraged the client to report any thoughts or images that came to mind, without worrying about their meaning. Second, Freud attempted to minimize any authoritative influence over the client's disclosures by eliminating eye contact. He usually sat in a chair at the head of a couch on which the client reclined.

Freud also believed that dreams offered crucial clues, and these were among the topics clients were encouraged to discuss. *Dream interpretation,* the evaluation of the underlying meaning of dream content, is a hallmark of psychoanalysis (Freud, 1900). But, according to Freud, even dream content is subject to censoring, so the analyst must be able to distinguish between dreams' *manifest* and *latent* contents. Recall from Chapter 9 that the manifest content of a dream is the actual images and events that occur within the dream as reported by the client; latent content is the hidden meaning or significance of the dream as interpreted by the psychoanalyst. The manifest content masks the latent content because the latent content is anxiety provoking and causes the person psychological discomfort. Thus, the analyst must be especially skilled in recognizing the symbolic nature of dreams, for things are not always as they appear. For example, the client may relate a dream about being chased by a growling, vicious dog. The dog may symbolize an angry parent or spouse. The idea of a parent's or spouse's being angry and upset may be so painful to the client that it has been disguised within the dream.

Insight is not achieved quickly, nor do clients always find it easy to disclose private aspects of their personal lives. In fact, there is something of a paradox in the achievement of insight, for the painful or threatening knowledge resulting from insight is precisely what led to its repression in the first place. For example, a client may have to confront the reality of being abused as a child, or of being unloved, or of feeling peculiar, inferior, or out of place. Although the client wishes to be cured, he or she may not look forward to the anxiety and apprehension that result from recalling painful memories. The client often becomes defensive at some point during therapy, unconsciously attempting to halt further insight by censoring his or her true feelings, a process Freud called **resistance.**

A psychoanalyst recognizes resistance when a client tries to change the topic, begins to miss appointments for therapy, or suddenly forgets what he or she was about to say. The skilled therapist who encounters such diversions will redirect the discussion to the sensitive topics while minimizing the pain of rediscovery.

Over a period of months or even years of therapy sessions that may occur several times a week, clients in psychoanalysis

▲ *Freud refined his practice of psychoanalysis in this office, where he asked his clients to recline on the couch (right) and to tell him about their childhood experiences, their dreams, and their anxieties. To encourage the client's openness, Freud sat at his desk, out of the client's sight. Freud's goal was to discover his clients' unconscious motivations for the problems they were experiencing.*

gradually become less inhibited, and the discussion begins to drift away from recent events to the more distant temporal shores of early childhood. As clients relive aspects of childhood, they may begin to project powerful attitudes and emotions onto the therapist, a process called **transference.** Clients may come to love or hate the therapist with the same emotional intensity they originally experienced toward parents or siblings in childhood.

At one point Freud thought of transference as a distraction from the real issues and thus an impediment to therapy. He soon decided, however, that the experience of transference was essential to the success of his approach (Connolly, Crits-Christoph, Barber, & Luborsky, 2000). Whereas free association uncovers many of the relevant events and facts of clients' lives, transference allows them to relive significant early experiences. By becoming a substitute for the actual people in a client's life, the therapist becomes the means for illuminating the conflicts of the unconscious.

Freud likewise reasoned that the analyst could just as easily project his or her emotions onto the client, a process he called **countertransference.** Unlike transference, Freud believed countertransference to be unhealthy and undesirable. To be effective, the analyst had to remain emotionally detached and objective in appraising clients' disclosures. For this reason, he argued that the analyst, in order to understand his or her own unconscious conflicts, should undergo analysis with another therapist as part of training.

Although Freud was not the first to talk about the unconscious mind (Ellenberger, 1981), he was the first to develop a significant theory of abnormal behavior (described in Chapter 14). He also developed an equally influential therapy designed to provide the client with insight into the unconscious motives that underlie behavior. Psychoanalytic theory remains a force among contemporary therapeutic practices even a century after its founding, although the therapy based on Freud's ideas has undergone substantial modification.

Contemporary Psychodynamic Therapy

Psychoanalytic therapy today is often referred to as *psychodynamic therapy* to reflect differences between more recent psychoanalytic approaches and Freud's original psychoanalysis. For example, although psychodynamic therapies still focus on achieving insight into the unconscious, they tend to place less emphasis on psychosexual development and more emphasis on social and interpersonal experiences. Contemporary analysts also are more likely to address concerns and issues in the client's present life than to examine childhood experiences exclusively.

Psychodynamic therapists also view the ego as playing a more active role in influencing a person's thoughts and actions. Instead of viewing the ego as functioning merely to mediate between the demands of the id and superego, they believe it is a proactive component in a person's overall psychological functioning. In other words, compared to Freud, psychodynamic therapists see the ego as having more control over the unconscious. Thus, people receiving psychodynamic therapy today are seen as being less constrained by the mind's unconscious forces than Freud had asserted.

In addition, whereas Freud considered analysis extremely involved and demanding, often requiring years to complete, psychodynamic analysts now generally feel that much can be gained by shortening the process and by lessening the client's dependence on the analyst (Binder, 1998; Travis, Bliwise, Binder, & Horne-Moyer, 2001). One form of modern psychodynamic therapy, for example, is *brief psychodynamic therapy*, which takes about 10 to 25 sessions to complete (Messer, 2001). The goal of the therapist in brief psychodynamic therapy is to understand and improve the client's interpersonal skills through interpretation of transference processes. This therapy is based on Freud's belief that our early experiences with others influence the dynamics of our current relationships. Brief psychodynamic therapy focuses on the schemas that a client has for interpersonal relationships and attempts to modify those that are errant or that otherwise prevent the client from developing fulfilling relationships with others.

All forms of psychodynamic therapy share an interest in unconscious processes. An important corollary is this: Behavior is seldom important by itself. Rather, it is important only to the extent that it serves as a manifestation of the real, underlying conflict.

Humanistic Therapies

In strong contrast to psychoanalysis, which may be considered to offer a darker view of humankind, the aim of another insight therapy, **humanistic therapy,** is to provide the client with a greater understanding of his or her unique potential for personal growth and self-actualization. Humanistic therapies proceed from the assumption that people are inherently good and have innate worth. Psychological problems represent an impediment hampering a person's potential for personal growth. Humanistic therapies aim at overcoming this impediment, at retrieving the potential anew. The two major forms of humanistic therapy are client-centered therapy and Gestalt therapy.

Client-Centered Therapy

Carl Rogers (1902–1987) developed the first humanistic therapy in the 1940s, creating a major alternative to psychoanalysis. Rogers found the formalism of psychoanalysis too confining and its emphasis on intrapsychic conflict too pessimistic (Tobin, 1991). His discontent led him to develop his own theory of personality, abnormal behavior, and therapy. His **client-centered therapy** is so named because of the respect given the client during therapy: The client decides what to talk about without direction or judgment from the therapist. In this way, ultimate responsibility for resolving the client's problems rests squarely on him or her. The central focus of the therapy is on the client and not solely on a method or theory.

Rogers believed that the cause of many psychological problems can be traced to the disparity between people's perceptions of what they currently are (their *real selves*) and what they would like to be according to the ideals of their culture (their *ideal selves*). Rogers called this discrepancy between the real and the ideal self **incongruence**. The goal of client-centered therapy is to reduce incongruence by fostering experiences that will make attainment of the ideal self more likely.

Because the client, not the therapist, directs the course of therapy, the therapist strives to make the client's perceptions, thoughts, and feelings more noticeable to the client. The therapist frequently accomplishes this through *reflection;* that is, by sensitively rephrasing or mirroring the client's statements. For example:

> *Client:* I get so frustrated at my parents. They just don't understand how I feel. They don't know what it's like to be me.
>
> *Therapist:* You seem to be saying that the things that are important to you aren't very important to your parents. You'd like them now and then to see things from your perspective.

By reflecting the concerns of the client, the therapist demonstrates *empathy,* or the ability to perceive the world from another's viewpoint. The establishment of empathy is key in the therapist's effort to help the client deal with the incongruence between his or her real and ideal selves.

For Rogers (1951, p. 20), the "worth and significance of the individual" is a basic ground rule of therapy. The therapist enacts this principle in therapy through **unconditional positive regard:** The therapist asserts that the client's worth as a human being is not dependent on anything he or she thinks, does, or feels. By unconditionally accepting and approving of the client as a person, the therapist aims to help the client understand that she or he is worthwhile and important.

▲ *Carl Rogers (top right) taught that clients can best achieve personal growth through the experience of unconditional positive regard.*

Unconditional acceptance of the *person* does not necessarily mean that the therapist approves of his or her *behavior,* however. A client-centered therapist may condemn behavior if, for instance, a client has harmed another person. The key is that the therapist has an abiding belief in the basic value and humanity of the client. According to Rogers, although clients' behavior may be regrettable and unacceptable, clients' nature is invariably good. Once clients begin to feel valued in the therapeutic context, a self-healing process can begin. For example, clients usually have difficulty at first expressing feelings verbally. The therapist tries to understand those feelings and to help clients put them into words. Through this process, clients learn to understand what their feelings mean and to resolve incongruence. Consider the following example:

Alice: I was thinking about this business of standards. I somehow developed a sort of knack, I guess, of—well—habit—of trying to make people feel at ease around me, or to make things go along smoothly. . . .

Counselor: In other words, what you did was always in the direction of trying to keep things smooth and to make other people feel better and to smooth the situation.

A: Yes. I think that's what it was. Now the reason why I did it probably was—I mean, not that I was a good little Samaritan going around making other people happy, but that was probably the role that felt easiest for me to play. I'd been doing it around the home so much. I just didn't stand up for my own convictions, until I don't know whether I have any convictions to stand up for.

C: You feel that for a long time you've been playing the role of kind of smoothing out the frictions or differences or what not. . . .

A: M-hum.

C: Rather than having any opinion or reaction of your own in the situation. Is that it?

A: That's it. Or that I haven't been really honestly being myself, or actually knowing what my real self is, and that I've been just playing a sort of false role. Whatever role

no one else was playing, and that needed to be played at the time, I'd try to fill it in. (Rogers, 1951, pp. 152–153)

As this example illustrates, in Rogers's view the therapist should not manipulate events but should create conditions under which the client can achieve his or her own insights and make decisions independently.

Gestalt Therapy The development of client-centered therapy owed much to Rogers's disenchantment with psychoanalysis. For much the same reason, Fritz Perls (1893–1970), though trained in Freudian techniques, disengaged himself from psychoanalysis and founded **Gestalt therapy** (Perls, 1969). This form of therapy emphasizes the unity of mind and body by training the client to "get in touch" with bodily sensations and emotions long hidden from awareness. (Recall from Chapters 1 and 7 that the emphasis on the unity of perception was a hallmark of Gestalt psychology.) Gestalt therapy places exclusive emphasis on present experience and not on the past. Moreover, the Gestalt therapist may be quite confrontational, challenging the client to deal honestly with his or her emotions.

Like Freud, Perls believed that dreams are a rich source of information and that the client must be able to understand their symbolism. In Gestalt therapy the therapist will often ask the client to adopt the perspective of a person or even an object that appeared in a dream and to do so in an empathetic manner.

Another tool of Gestalt therapists is the *empty chair technique,* in which clients imagine talking to someone they imagine sitting in the chair beside them. This technique derives from Perls's belief that memories, fears, and feelings of guilt affect people's ongoing relationships with others. For example, the therapist may ask a woman to say the things she always wanted to say to her deceased father but didn't while he was alive. The empty chair technique allows her to experience in the here and now the feelings and perceptions she might have suppressed while her father was alive. It also allows her, perhaps for the first time, to express these feelings and to gain insight into how these feelings currently influence her perceptions of herself and her world. The Gestalt therapist also encourages clients to gain a better understanding of their feelings by talking to themselves (that is, to different parts of their personalities) and even to inanimate objects. Any attempt by a client to avoid the reality of his or her situation is challenged by the therapist, who constantly attempts to keep the client's attention focused on present problems and tries to guide the client toward an honest confrontation with them. Perls (1967, p. 331) argued, "In the safe emergency of the therapeutic situation, the neurotic discovers that the world does not fall to pieces if he or she gets angry, sexy, joyous, mournful."

Evaluation of Insight Therapies

As Chapter 17 pointed out, the processes proposed by psychoanalytic theory have not been subjected to rigorous empirical scrutiny until relatively recently (e.g., Baumeister, Dale, & Sommer, 1998; Charman, 2004; Solms, 2004). Evaluating the effectiveness of psychoanalysis has long been difficult because only a small proportion of people with mental disorders qualify for this method of treatment. To participate, a client must be intelligent, articulate, motivated enough, and well-off enough to spend three or more hours a week working hard to uncover unconscious conflicts. These qualifications rule out many people with active psychoses, as well as people who lack the financial resources and/or the time to devote to such a long-term project.

Rogers stimulated considerable research on the effectiveness of client-centered therapy. He recorded therapeutic sessions so that his techniques could be evaluated. One researcher (Truax, 1966) obtained permission from Rogers and his clients to record therapy sessions and classified the clients' statements into eight categories. For example, one category included references to improved mental health, such as "I'm feeling better lately" or "I don't feel as depressed as I used to." After each of the clients' statements, Truax noted Rogers's reaction to see whether he gave a positive response. Typical positive responses were "Oh, really? Tell me more" or "Uh-huh. That's nice" or just a friendly "Mm." Truax found that, of the eight categories of client statements, only those that indicated progress were regularly followed by positive responses from Rogers. Not surprisingly, during their therapy, the clients made more and more statements indicating progress.

Truax's study implicates social reinforcement in humanistic therapy. Rogers was an effective and conscientious therapist, but he had not intended to single out and reinforce his clients' realistic expressions of progress in therapy. (Obviously, he did not uncritically reinforce exaggerated or unrealistic positive statements.) Of course, this finding does not discredit client-centered therapy. Rogers simply adopted a very effective strategy for altering a person's behavior. He originally referred to his therapy as *nondirective;* however, when he realized that he was reinforcing positive statements, he stopped doing so.

As with most insight therapies, neither client-centered therapy nor Gestalt therapy is suitable for people with serious mental disorders. Instead, these approaches are most effective for people who are motivated enough to want to change and who are intelligent enough to be able to gain insight into their problems. Humanistic therapies are much more affordable and less time-consuming than traditional psychoanalysis. Most people would probably enjoy and benefit from talking about their problems with a person as sympathetic as Carl Rogers or as direct and honest as Fritz Perls. Rogers's insights into the dynamics of the client–therapist relationship have had a major impact on therapy (Hill & Nakayama, 2000).

Interim Summary

Insight Therapies

Insight therapies are based primarily on conversation between therapist and client. The oldest form of insight therapy, psychoanalysis, was devised by Freud. Psychoanalysis attempts to discover the forces that are warring in the client's unconscious and to resolve these inner conflicts by bringing them to consciousness and also revealing the defenses that have been established against them. Insight becomes the primary source of healing.

Unlike the psychoanalytic approach, which regards human behavior as motivated by intrapsychic conflict and biological urges, humanistic therapy emphasizes conscious, deliberate mental processes. Carl Rogers's client-centered therapy is based on the premise that people are inherently good and that their problems result from faulty perceptions. Instead of evaluating themselves in terms of their own self-concepts, people tend to judge themselves by other people's standards. Client-centered therapy rectifies this tendency by providing an environment of unconditional positive regard in which clients can find their own way to good mental health. Fritz Perls's Gestalt therapy focuses on convincing clients that they must deal honestly with their present feelings in order to understand and resolve them. The goal of this approach is to help clients confront their fears and guilt and put their emotions in proper perspective.

It is difficult to determine whether psychoanalysis is effective, because of the relatively narrow range of people that may benefit by undergoing such therapy. The people who seem most likely to benefit are those who are intelligent and able to articulate their problems. Humanistic therapies have a broader range of applicability. However, insight therapies generally are not effective with persons with serious mental disorders, such as schizophrenia.

QUESTIONS TO CONSIDER

1. If you had a psychological problem, which kind of insight therapy—psychodynamic or humanistic—would you choose? What factors would influence your choice?
2. Suppose that you were able to interview Freud, Rogers, and Perls. What sorts of questions would you ask each of them? Why would their answers to those questions be of interest to you?

Behavior Therapies, Cognitive Therapies, and Cognitive–Behavioral Therapies

Insight therapies are based on the assumption that understanding leads to behavioral change: Once people gain insight into the causes of their maladaptive behavior, they will adopt more successful behavior. In reality, however, insight is *not* always followed by behavioral change. That is where behavior and cognitive–behavioral therapies come in.

The fundamental assumption made by behavior therapists is that people *learn* maladaptive or self-defeating behavior in the same way that they learn adaptive behavior. According to the behavioral view, undesirable behavior, such as nail biting or alcohol abuse, *is* the problem, not just a symptom or a reflection of the problem. The methods that behavior therapists use to induce behavioral change are extensions of classical and operant conditioning principles. Related approaches blend behavior therapies with attention to the elimination of maladaptive thoughts and feelings and are known as cognitive or cognitive–behavioral therapies.

Therapies Based on Classical Conditioning

Remember from Chapter 5 that in classical conditioning a previously neutral stimulus (ultimately the CS) comes to elicit a new response that may be similar to the response that another stimulus (the US) naturally elicits. This occurs because the CS reliably predicts the US. According to Joseph Wolpe (1958), one of the founders of behavior therapy, neutral stimuli are conditioned by coincidence to elicit many of our everyday fears and anxieties. Consider an example: Suppose that you are involved in a car accident, and although you are not seriously hurt, you are upset for some time afterwards. When you get into a car for the first time after the accident, a sudden feeling of terror comes over you. You begin to perspire and breathe heavily, you feel that you are about to pass out, and it's all you can do to get out of the car without screaming. Your anxiety in response to getting into a car may be due to classical conditioning—the pain and fear associated with the accident (the USs) are now associated with cars (the CSs).

Systematic Desensitization The behavior therapy technique developed by Wolpe has been especially successful in eliminating fears and phobias. This technique, called **systematic desensitization,** is designed to remove the unpleasant emotional

TABLE 18•2	Sample Fear Hierarchy for Phobia of Spiders

1. Abbie [neighbor] tells you she saw one in her garage.
2. Abbie sees you, crosses the street, says there's a tiny one across the street.
3. Betty [at work] says there's one downstairs.
4. Friends downstairs say they saw one outside their apartment and disposed of it.
5. Carrie [daughter] returns from camp; says the restrooms were inhabited by spiders.
6. You see a small, dark spot out of the corner of your eye; you have a closer look; it isn't a spider.
7. You are with your husband. You see a tiny spider on a thread outside, but you can't see it very clearly.
8. You are alone. You see a tiny spider on a thread outside, but you can't see it very clearly.
9. You are reading the paper, and you see a cartoonist's caricature of a spider (with a human-like face and smile).
10. You are reading an article about the Brown Recluse.
11. You see a clear photograph of a spider's web in the newspaper.
12. You see a spider's web on the stairs at work.
13. You suddenly see a loose tomato-top in your salad.
14. You open a kitchen cabinet and suddenly see a large spider.

Source: From Geoffrey L. Thorpe and Sheryl L. Olson, *Behavior Therapy: Concepts, Procedures, and Applications,* 2/e. Published by Allyn and Bacon, Boston, MA. Copyright © 1997 by Pearson Education. Reprinted by permission of the publisher.

▲ *People who are treated with systematic desensitization for their phobias often show remarkable, positive changes in their behavior; for example, this person has overcome an intense fear of snakes.*

response produced by the feared object or situation and replace it with an incompatible response—relaxation.

The first step is for the client and therapist to construct a *hierarchy* of fear-eliciting stimuli. **Table 18•2** presents a hierarchy constructed with a person who suffered from arachnophobia, an intense fear of spiders (Thorpe & Olson, 1990). The situations provoking the least amount of fear are at the top. Next, the client is trained to achieve complete relaxation. The essential task is to learn to respond quickly to the instruction to feel profoundly relaxed by entering a condition sometimes referred to as *deep-muscle relaxation*.

Finally, the fear-eliciting stimuli are paired with the instruction that produces the learned relaxation response. For example, a person with a fear of spiders is instructed to relax and then to imagine hearing from a neighbor that she saw a spider in her garage (the least fearsome event in the hierarchy). If the client reports no anxiety, he or she is instructed to move to the next, slightly more threatening, item in the hierarchy and to imagine hearing a neighbor say that there is a tiny spider across the street; and so on. Whenever the client begins feeling anxious, he or she signals to the therapist with some predetermined gesture—say, by raising a finger. The therapist instructs the client to relax and, if necessary, describes a less threatening scene. The client is not permitted to feel severe anxiety at any time. Gradually, over a series of sessions (the average is 11), the client is able to get through the entire list, vicariously experiencing even the most feared encounters while remaining in a relaxed state.

Scientific evaluations of systematic desensitization have been positive. Numerous experiments have found that all elements of the procedure are necessary for its success. For example, a person will not overcome a phobia merely by participating in relaxation training or by constructing hierarchies of fear-producing stimuli. Only *pairings* of the anxiety-producing stimuli with instructions to relax will reduce the fear. One early testimonial came from a study by Johnson and Sechrest (1968), which attempted to reduce a strong fear of taking examinations in a group of university students. Students who underwent systematic desensitization received significantly higher grades on their final examination in a psychology course than did students who were also taking the course but who received either no treatment or relaxation training alone.

Whereas practitioners of systematic desensitization are careful not to permit their clients to become too anxious, practitioners of a procedure called **implosion therapy** attempt to rid their clients of their fears by arousing those very fears at an intense level until the clients' responses diminish through *extinction;* that is, the clients learn that nothing bad happens when they are directly exposed to the fear-eliciting stimuli. The therapist describes, as graphically as possible, the most frightening possible encounters with the object of a client's phobia. The client tries to imagine the encounter and to experience intense fear. In some cases the client actually encounters the object of his or her fear, in which case the treatment is called *flooding.* Of course, the client is protected from any adverse physical effects of the encounter, so there are no dangerous consequences. Eventually the fear response begins to subside, and the client learns that even the worst imaginable encounter can become tolerable. In other words, the client's long-entrenched *avoidance responses* have become extinguished.

Aversion Therapy   Some people are attracted by stimuli that most of us ignore, and such individuals may engage in maladaptive behavior as a result of this attraction. Sexual attraction to children is a striking example. A behavior therapy technique known as **aversion therapy** is sometimes effective in changing these behaviors. In aversion therapy the therapist seeks to induce a negative reaction to an originally attractive stimulus by pairing that stimulus with an aversive stimulus. Aversion therapy attempts to establish an unpleasant response (such as a feeling of fear or disgust) to the object that produces the undesired behavior. For example, a therapist may show pictures of children to a man who is sexually attracted to children, then administer painful electric shocks when a special apparatus detects an erectile response. Aversive therapy also has been used to treat fetishes (such as sexual attraction to women's shoes), drinking, smoking, transvestism, exhibitionism, and overeating. Sometimes emetics, or drugs that cause nausea, are paired with the ingestion of alcohol in

the treatment of problem drinking (recall the discussion of taste aversion in Chapter 5). Aversion therapy has been shown to be moderately effective in some applications, such as reducing craving among cocaine abusers (Bordnick et al., 2004). Nevertheless, the treatment is disturbing to many people because it can be characterized as punitive (Howard, Elkins, Rimmele, & Smith, 1991). B. F. Skinner (1988) himself was opposed to aversion therapy for this reason. Because the method raises serious ethical questions and can involve significant pain, the client's participation must be voluntary.

Therapies Based on Operant Conditioning

Behavior modification, a general term for behavior therapy based on operant conditioning principles, involves altering maladaptive behavior by rearranging the contingencies between behavior and its consequences. Desirable behavior can be encouraged through either positive or negative reinforcement (see Chapter 5), and undesirable behavior can be reduced through either extinction or punishment.

In the early years of behavior modification, therapists applied this approach chiefly to clients with schizophrenia and people with mental retardation (Ayllon & Azrin, 1968; Neisworth & Madle, 1982). Since the early 1960s, however, practitioners have extended the use of operant principles to a wide array of behaviors and circumstances—for example, for weight management; compliance with medical regimens; and treatment of anorexia nervosa, bed-wetting, and smoking (Kazdin, 1994). Behavior modification techniques can be found in many different settings, including hospitals, schools, day-care centers, businesses, and the home (Kazdin, 2001).

Reinforcement of Adaptive Behaviors   Therapists often use behavioral techniques to alter the behavior of emotionally disturbed people and people with mental retardation, for whom communication is difficult. Reinforcement, as described in Chapter 5, can be a powerful method of behavioral change. If the therapist has established a cordial relationship with the client, he or she can use ordinary social reinforcers such as signs of approval (friendly smiles and nods of the head) to encourage positive behavioral change. As we saw in the section on client-centered therapy, even nonbehavioral therapists use reinforcement—deliberately or inadvertently—to produce positive behavioral change.

Token Economies   The behavior therapeutic approach has been used successfully on a large scale in mental institutions. For example, therapists may ask resident patients to do chores that engage them actively with their environment. In some instances therapists also will target other specific behaviors—such as helping patients who have more severe problems—as desirable. To promote these *target behaviors,* therapists use **token economies.** In a token economy a list of tasks is compiled, and patients receive plastic tokens, such as poker chips, as rewards for performing the tasks. Later they can exchange these tokens for snacks, other desired items, or various privi-

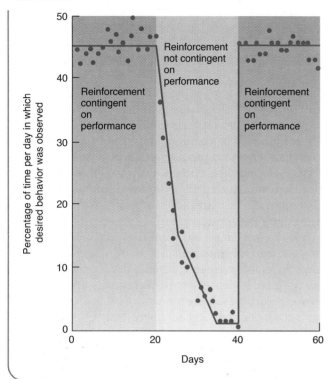

FIGURE 18•3   The effectiveness of a token economy. A token economy system of reinforcement is designed to promote patients' performance of specified chores.

(From Teodoro Ayllon and Nathan Azrin, *The Token Economy: A Motivational System for Therapy and Rehabilitation,* © 1968, pp. 249–250, 252. Reprinted by permission.)

leges. The tokens become conditioned reinforcers for desirable behaviors. **Figure 18•3** shows the strong effects of the contingencies of a pay scale used in a token economy established by Ayllon and Azrin (1968). The amount of time patients spent performing the desirable behaviors was high when reinforcement contingencies were imposed and low when they were not.

The implementation of a token economy can be difficult. Although it is based on a simple principle, the arrangement requires the cooperation of everyone involved. A mental institution includes patients, caretakers, housekeeping staff, and professional staff. If a token economy is to be effective, all staff members who deal with the patients must learn how the system works; ideally, they should also understand and agree with its underlying principles. A token economy can easily be sabotaged by a few people who believe that the system is foolish, unethical, or in some way threatening to themselves. If these obstacles can be overcome, token economies may work very well.

Modeling   Humans (and many other animals) are able to learn without directly experiencing an event. Chapter 5 pointed out that people can imitate the behavior of other people, watching what they do and, if the conditions are appropriate,

performing the same behavior (Bandura, 1986). This capability provides the basis for the behavioral technique of *modeling*. Behavior therapists have found that clients may make much better progress when they have access to a model who provides samples of successful behaviors to imitate. Bandura (1971) described a modeling session with people who had a phobic response to snakes:

> The therapist himself performed the fearless behavior at each step and gradually led subjects into touching, stroking, and then holding the snake's body with gloved and bare hands while the experimenter held the snake securely by head and tail. If a subject was unable to touch the snake following ample demonstration, she was asked to place her hand on the experimenter's and to move her hand down gradually until it touched the snake's body. After subjects no longer felt any apprehension about touching the snake under these secure conditions, anxieties about contact with the snake's head area and entwining tail were extinguished. The therapist again performed the tasks fearlessly, and then he and the subject performed the responses jointly; as subjects became less fearful, the experimenter gradually reduced his participation and control over the snake, until eventually subjects were able to hold the snake in their laps without assistance, to let the snake loose in the room and retrieve it, and to let it crawl freely over their bodies. Progress through the graded approach tasks was paced according to the subjects' apprehensiveness. When they reported being able to perform one activity with little or no fear, they were eased into a more difficult interaction. (p. 680)

This treatment eliminated fear of snakes in 92 percent of the people who participated. Modeling is successful for several reasons. People learn to make new responses by imitating those of the therapist; and, as they do so, their behavior is reinforced. When they observe a confident person approaching and touching a feared object without showing any signs of emotional distress, they may experience vicarious extinction of their own emotional responses. In fact, Bandura (1971, p. 684) reports that "having successfully overcome a phobia that had plagued them for most of their lives, people reported increased confidence that they could cope effectively with other fear-provoking events," including encounters with other people.

Behavior therapists have used modeling to establish new behaviors as well as to eliminate fears. For example, therapists may demonstrate examples of useful, appropriate social exchanges for clients whose maladaptive behaviors usually prevent such interactions. Also, as we shall see in a later section, modeling is an important aspect of group therapy. And sex therapists may employ specially prepared films or videotapes showing explicit sexual activity to help clients overcome inhibitions that hamper sexual relations with their partners.

Assertiveness Therapy   Assertiveness therapy is a procedure for helping clients to develop coping skills in interpersonal situations in which the clients may feel anxiety or be unable to function as effectively as they would like.

Therapists often use assertiveness training to help clients who feel frustrated at not being able to speak up, especially in situations in which others are trying to take advantage of them or to otherwise compromise their values or moral standards.

The first step in assertiveness therapy is to identify the variables that are causing the client to feel distressed. For instance, suppose that a female client's boss is making harassing remarks or gestures, but she is afraid to speak up for fear of losing her job. Once the variables in the situation are identified, the client practices assertive behaviors in the context of therapy, and the therapist reinforces them. For example, the client may practice confronting her boss with her feelings and requesting that he treat her more respectfully. The client also may learn various styles of assertiveness. Thus, rather than confronting her boss directly, the client learns to approach him tactfully. For example, if her boss makes a rude remark to her, she may ask, "Are you feeling okay today? Has something made you upset?" With this response the client has carefully centered the situation on the boss in an unthreatening way.

Extinction of Maladaptive Behaviors

In Chapter 5 you learned that extinction is the process by which behavior is eliminated through the removal of the previously available reinforcers. For example, extinction might be used to eliminate a child's tantrums. If such behaviors have been reinforced in the past—that is, if parents or caretakers have paid attention or even given in to the child's wishes—the extinction procedure may include ignoring the child's undesirable behavior.

There are two potential problems with using extinction. One is the *extinction burst:* When a reinforcer that has previously followed a behavior is no longer forthcoming, that behavior will often intensify temporarily. You can imagine, for example, how a child whose tantrums usually meet with social attention will likely increase his or her efforts to obtain these reinforcers during the early stages of extinction. Fortunately, however, the extinction burst is temporary. If the extinction procedure is sustained, undesirable behavior usually decreases.

▲ *A treatment strategy that is often effective in reducing tantrums in children is extinction—simply ignoring the behavior.*

The other problem with using extinction is that it is not always possible to eliminate the reinforcer that maintains undesirable behavior. For example, aggressive behavior in the classroom may be reinforced by the child's peer group, making the teacher's attempts to extinguish aggression only minimally effective. The use of extinction is also problematic when the client has direct control of the reinforcer, as in thumb sucking.

Punishment of Maladaptive Behaviors

In general, punishment is less effective than positive reinforcement. For one thing, the person whose behavior is being punished may learn to fear or dislike the person who administers the punishment. If this person is the therapist, the effect will probably interfere with other aspects of therapy, because of the fact that the therapist–client relationship is a major factor in therapeutic outcome. Second, there is a tendency on the client's part to *overgeneralize*—to avoid performing a whole class of responses related to the response that is specifically being punished. For example, after being punished for lying, a child may not tell her father any more lies; but she also may stop sharing her secrets with him. Unfortunately, it is usually easier to punish a response than it is to figure out how to reinforce other responses that will replace the undesirable behavior. Also, punishing someone else's action may be especially reinforcing when we are angry.

In some therapeutic situations, especially those in which the undesirable response is clearly harmful to the client, punishment is the most effective technique for eliminating an undesirable behavior. Cowart and Whaley (1971) reported the case of an emotionally disturbed child who persisted in self-mutilation. He banged his head against the floor until it was a swollen mass of cuts and bruises. As a result, he had to be restrained in his crib at the hospital where he was a patient. However, the consequences of such confinement for a child's development are serious. After conventional techniques had failed, the therapist attached a pair of wires to the child's leg and placed him in a room with a padded floor. The child immediately began to batter his head against the floor, and the therapist administered an electrical shock through the wires. The shock, which was certainly less damaging than the blows to the head, stopped the child short. He seemed more startled than anything else. He started banging his head against the floor again and received another shock. After a few repetitions of this sequence, the boy stopped his self-mutilative behavior and could safely be let out of his crib.

The use of aversive methods raises ethical issues, however, particularly when individuals are so severely impaired that they are unable to give informed consent to a particular therapeutic procedure. Carr and Lovaas (1983) state that aversive methods involving stimuli such as electric shock should be used only as a last resort. Punishers should be used only when patients' behavior poses a serious threat to their own well-being and after therapists have unsuccessfully tried other methods—specifically, reinforcing desirable behaviors, extinguishing the maladaptive behaviors, temporarily removing the patient from the environment that reinforces the maladaptive behaviors (a method called *time out*), and arranging for the patient to perform responses that are incompatible with the maladaptive behaviors.

Sometimes the punishing stimulus may only be imagined. In a method called **covert sensitization,** instead of receiving an actual punishing stimulus after performing actual undesirable behavior, clients imagine that they are performing the behavior and then imagine receiving an aversive stimulus. For example, Thorpe and Olson (1990) describe the case of "Frank," a man in his late twenties with a variety of social problems, including exhibitionism. He would drive far from his home town and expose his genitals to unsuspecting strangers. Although he derived sexual pleasure from this practice, he was disturbed by it and wanted desperately to stop.

The therapist used a variety of methods to help Frank improve his social skills and reduce his anxiety. In addition, the therapist used covert sensitization to eliminate the exhibitionism. The therapist encouraged Frank to imagine vivid scenes such as the following:

> He was driving around in his car, looking for a suitable victim. A woman, walking alone, appeared. Frank stopped the car and got out. He began to loosen his clothing. He was feeling strongly aroused sexually. Suddenly a police car pulled up, its lights flashing and its siren wailing. The officers looked on Frank with contempt as they handcuffed him. At the same time one of Frank's workmates arrived on the scene. This workmate was the biggest gossip at the factory. News of Frank's arrest would soon be all over town. He would obviously lose his job. His crime would be reported in the local newspaper. Frank felt physically sick with shame. He thought ahead to the prospect of a long jail sentence in protective custody as a sex offender. (Thorpe & Olson, 1990, p. 17)

Frank was able to imagine scenes such as this, and doing so made him feel very uncomfortable. Over several weeks the frequency of his exhibitionistic episodes declined.

Maintaining Behavioral Change

One of the problems with behavior therapy is that behavior learned under one set of conditions may fail to occur in different environments; that is, behavioral change may not generalize to other situations. This problem is especially evident in the treatment of alcohol addiction. Addicts may abstain from drinking in a treatment facility but go on a binge as soon as they get out.

Behavior therapists have designed specific methods to ensure that positive behavioral change generalizes to situations outside the clinic or the therapist's office. As we saw in Chapter 5, intermittent reinforcement increases resistance to extinction. Thus, it is more effective to reinforce desirable responses intermittently than it is to reinforce every desirable response the client makes.

Another useful technique that helps maintain behavioral change is the practice of *self-observation,* in which the client

is taught to recognize when his or her behavior is appropriate. For example, Drabman, Spitalnik, and O'Leary (1973) rewarded a group of disruptive boys from the same classroom for performing desirable behaviors—for example, for participating in classroom activities such as reading. The reinforcement was effective; the frequency of the boys' disruptive behaviors declined, and their academic activity increased. To make the change as permanent as possible, the researchers also reinforced the boys' behavior when their own ratings of their behaviors agreed with those of their teacher. In other words, the boys were trained to evaluate their behaviors in terms of those that should be reinforced and those that should not be. The hope was that the successful self-evaluations would become conditioned reinforcers, because they would be paired with positive reinforcement. Thus, self-evaluations would continue to reinforce the boys' behavior even after the period of training was over. Judging from the strong results, the procedure succeeded.

Therapists also frequently ask family members and friends of the client to become participants in the process of behavior therapy. These "adjunct therapists" are taught to encourage and reward desirable behaviors and to discourage or ignore undesirable ones. By these means, a client does not shuttle back and forth between two different types of environments—one type in which the therapist selectively reinforces desirable behaviors and another in which reinforcement is haphazard or even inappropriate. For example, a person with behavioral problems may receive attention from the family only when he or she acts up. Clearly, for optimal results family members need to make an effort to ignore such outbursts and to reinforce instances of desirable behavior instead.

Cognitive Therapies and Cognitive–Behavioral Therapies

The first attempts to develop therapies based on altering or manipulating cognitive processes emerged during the 1970s. Some of these attempts were undertaken by behavior therapists who suspected that maladaptive behavior—or, for that matter, adaptive behavior—might not be due to environmental variables alone. These psychologists began to explore how their clients' perceptions, thoughts, feelings, expectations, and self-statements might interact with environmental factors in the development and maintenance of maladaptive behavior (Beck, 1991). They then developed methods designed to change the maladaptive patterns of cognition that, in their view, underlay the maladaptive patterns of behavior. Attempts to change these patterns of cognition are referred to as **cognitive restructuring.**

Rational–Emotive Therapy   Interestingly, the first form of cognitive restructuring, a kind of forerunner called rational–emotive therapy, was developed back in the 1950s by Albert Ellis, a clinical psychologist. **Rational–emotive therapy** is based on the belief that psychological problems are caused by the ways in which people think about upsetting events and situations (Ellis, 2003). In contrast to cognitive–behavioral therapy (described below), rational–emotive therapy did not grow out of the tradition of behavior therapy. For many years Ellis was regarded as outside the mainstream of psychotherapy, but now his methods are practiced by many therapists. Ellis asserts that psychological problems are the result of faulty cognitions; therapy is therefore aimed at changing people's thinking and specifically their beliefs. Rational–emotive therapy is highly directive and confrontational. The therapist tells his or her clients what they are doing wrong and how they should change.

According to Ellis and his followers, emotions are the products of cognition. A *significant activating event* (A) is followed by a *highly charged emotional consequence* (C), but it is not correct to say that A has caused C. Rather, C is a result of the *person's belief system* (B). Therefore, inappropriate emotions (such as depression, guilt, and anxiety) can be abolished only if a change occurs in the person's belief system. It is the task of the rational–emotive therapist to dispute the person's beliefs and to convince him or her that they are inappropriate and should be changed. Ellis tries to show his clients that irrational beliefs are impossible to satisfy, that they make little logical sense, and that adhering to them creates needless anxiety, self-blame, and self-doubt. The following are examples of the kinds of ideas that Ellis (1973) believes to be irrational:

> The idea that it is a necessity for an adult to be loved or approved by virtually every significant person in the community.
>
> The idea that one should be thoroughly competent, adequate, and goal-oriented in all possible respects if one is to consider oneself as having worth.
>
> The idea that human unhappiness is externally caused and that people have little or no ability to control their lives.
>
> The idea that one's past is an all-important determinant of one's present behavior.
>
> The idea that there is invariably a right, precise, and perfect solution to human problems and that it is catastrophic if this perfect solution is not found. (pp. 152–153)

The excerpt below, taken from a therapy session with one of Ellis's own clients—a 23-year-old woman who felt guilty about her relationship with her parents—shows how Ellis challenges clients to examine their irrational beliefs (Ellis, 1989).

Client: The basic problem is that I am worried about my family. I'm worried about money. And I never seem to be able to relax.

Ellis: Why are you so worried about your family? Let's go into that, first of all. What's to be concerned about? They have certain demands that you don't want to adhere to.

C: I was brought up to think that I mustn't be selfish.

E: Oh, we'll have to knock that out of your head!

C: I think that that is one of my basic problems.

E: That's right, you were brought up to be Florence Nightingale.

C: Yes, I was brought up in a family of would-be Florence Nightingales, now that I realize the whole pattern of my family history. . . . My father became really alcoholic sometime when I was away in college. My mother developed breast cancer, and she had a breast removed. Nobody is healthy.

E: How is your father now?

C: Well, he's doing much better. . . . He spends quite a bit of money every week on pills. And if he misses a day of pills, he is absolutely unlivable. My mother feels that I shouldn't have left home—that my place is with them. There are nagging doubts about what I should—

E: That's a *belief.* Why do you have to keep believing that—at your age? . . . Your parents indoctrinated you with this nonsense, because it is *their* belief. But why do you still have to believe that one should not be self-interested, that one should be self-sacrificial? Who needs that philosophy? All it's gotten you, so far, is guilt. And that's all it ever *will* get you. (pp. 234–235)

Although rational–emotive therapy is directive in ways that client-centered therapy is not, there are some similarities in the two approaches. Just as Rogers emphasized unconditional positive regard, so Ellis and his followers attempt to engender a feeling of full self-acceptance in their clients. They teach that self-blame is the core of emotional disturbance and that people can learn to stop continuously rating their own personal worth and measuring themselves against impossible standards. They emphasize that people will be happier if they can learn to see failures as unfortunate events, not as disastrous ones that confirm their lack of worth. However, unlike a Rogerian therapist, a rational–emotive therapist will vigorously argue with his or her client, attacking beliefs that the therapist regards as foolish and illogical. This approach also differs from the client-centered approach in that the therapist does not need to be especially empathetic to be an effective teacher and guide.

Many therapists who adopt an eclectic approach use some of the techniques of rational–emotive therapy with some of their clients. Ellis's advocacy of rationality and his eschewal of superstition provide a common-sense approach to living. However, many psychotherapists disagree with Ellis's deemphasis of empathy in the relationship between therapist and client.

Cognitive–Behavioral Therapy for Depression The focus of **cognitive–behavioral therapy** is on changing the client's maladaptive perceptions, thoughts, feelings, and beliefs in order to change the client's behavior. This form of therapy is widely practiced today and has been shown to be effective in treating many kinds of mental disorders (Hollon, Thase, & Markowitz, 2002; McClanahan & Antonuccio, 2002; Turkington, Dudley, Warman, & Beck, 2004). Like behavior therapists—and unlike most insight therapists—cognitive–behavioral therapists are not particularly interested in events that occurred in the client's childhood. They are interested in the here and now and in altering the client's behavior so that it becomes more functional. Although they employ many methods used by behavior therapists, they believe that when behaviors change, they do so because of changes in cognitive processes.

Aaron Beck (1967, 1997) has developed a therapy for depression that shares with Ellis's therapy an emphasis on the client's perceptions, beliefs, and interpretations (Beck, 1967, 1997; Clark, Beck, & Alford, 1999). Beck's therapy, however, focuses more on faulty logic than on the beliefs themselves. Negative beliefs are seen as conclusions reached by faulty logic. A depressed person concludes that he or she is "deprived, frustrated, humiliated, rejected or punished ('a loser,' in the vernacular)" (Beck, Rush, Shaw, & Emery, 1979, p. 120). As already noted in Chapter 17, Beck views the cognitions of the depressed individual in terms of a *cognitive triad*: a negative view of the self ("I am worthless"), of the outside world ("The world makes impossible demands on me"), and of the future ("Things are never going to get better").

Even when confronted with evidence that contradicts their negative beliefs, depressed individuals often illogically interpret good news as bad news (Lewinsohn, Mischel, Chaplin, & Barton, 1980). For example, children who exhibit symptoms of depression tend to underestimate their abilities (McGrath & Repetti, 2002). A depressed student who receives an A on an exam may attribute the high grade to an easy, unchallenging exam rather than to his or her own mastery of the material. The fact that few others in the class received A's does little to convince the student that he or she deserves congratulations for having done well. The depressed student goes on believing, against contrary evidence, that the good grade was not really deserved.

Once the client recognizes such faulty logic for what it is, therapy can explore means for correcting the distortions. Consider the following example from an actual therapy session.

> A woman who complained of severe headaches and other somatic disturbances was found to be very depressed. When asked about the cognitions that seemed to make her unhappy, she said, "My family doesn't appreciate me"; "Nobody appreciates me, they take me for granted"; "I am worthless." As an example, she stated that her adolescent children no longer wanted to do things with her. Although this particular statement could very well have been accurate, the therapist decided to determine whether it was true. He pursued the "evidence" for the statement in the following interchange:
>
> *Patient:* My son doesn't like to go to the theater or to the movies with me anymore.
>
> *Therapist:* How do you know he doesn't want to go with you?
>
> *P:* Teenagers don't actually like to do things with their parents.
>
> *T:* Have you actually asked him to go with you?
>
> *P:* No, as a matter of fact, he did ask me a few times if

> I wanted him to take me . . . but I didn't think he really wanted to go.
>
> *T:* How about testing it out by asking him to give you a straight answer?
>
> *P:* I guess so.
>
> *T:* The important thing is not whether or not he goes with you but whether you are deciding for him what he thinks instead of letting him tell you.
>
> *P:* I guess you are right but he does seem to be inconsiderate. For example, he is always late for dinner.
>
> *T:* How often has that happened?
>
> *P:* Oh, once or twice . . . I guess that's really not all that often.
>
> *T:* Is he coming late for dinner due to his being inconsiderate?
>
> *P:* Well, come to think of it, he did say that he had been working late those two nights. Also, he has been considerate in a lot of other ways. (Beck, Rush, Shaw, & Emery, 1979, pp. 155–156)

Actually, as the patient later found, her son was willing to go to the movies with her.

As this example shows, cognitive–behavioral therapists do not accept clients' inferences and conclusions at face value. Instead, they discuss how clients' conclusions result from faulty logic so that clients can understand their thinking from another perspective and perhaps can change their behavior as a result. The role of cognitive change as a necessary antecedent of behavioral change can be clearly seen.

Exposure therapy, another form of cognitive–behavioral therapy, is specifically directed to the anxiety disorders, especially post-traumatic stress disorder (Follette, Ruzek, & Abueg, 2001). It has some of the features of implosion therapy, which we encountered previously as an example of behavior therapy. As in implosion therapy, the therapist encourages the client to confront the anxiety-eliciting situations that she or he would ordinarily avoid and to remain there. Rather than merely extinguishing anxiety, however, exposure therapy encourages the client to think and feel differently and thus to behave in different ways that reduce the anxiety and make it more manageable.

Evaluation of Behavior, Cognitive, and Cognitive–Behavioral Therapies

Critics of behavior therapy have cited its focus on the symptoms of psychological problems to the exclusion of root causes. Psychoanalysts even argue that treatment of the symptoms alone is dangerous. In their view, the removal of one symptom of an intrapsychic conflict will simply produce another, perhaps more serious, symptom through a process called *symptom substitution.*

There is little evidence that symptom substitution occurs. It is true that many people's behavioral problems are caused by conditions that existed in the past, and often these problems become self-perpetuating. Yet behavior therapy can, in many cases, eliminate the problem without delving into the past. For example, for one reason or another, a child may begin wetting the bed at night (a condition known as *nocturnal enuresis*). This irritates the parents, who must change the bed sheets and the child's pajamas. The child develops feelings of guilt and insecurity and wets the bed more often. Instead of analyzing bed-wetting in terms of underlying family conflict, a behavior therapist might recommend the installation of a device in the child's bed that rings a bell when he or she begins to urinate. The bell awakens the child, who goes to the bathroom to urinate and soon ceases to wet the bed. The elimination of bed-wetting causes rapid improvement in the child's self-esteem and puts the parents at ease. Symptom substitution does not appear to occur (Blacher & Baker, 1987).

On the other hand, there are some situations in which behavior therapy should not be used. For example, a person who is involuntarily confined to an institution should not be subjected to aversive techniques unless he or she clearly agrees to participate or unless the benefits far outweigh the discomfort. The decision to use aversive techniques must not rest only with people who are directly in charge of the patients, lest the procedures eventually be used merely for the sake of convenience. The decision is best left to a committee that includes people who serve as advocates for patients.

In a review of research evaluating the effectiveness of rational–emotive therapy, Solomon and Haaga (1995) concluded that the method has been shown to reduce general anxiety, test anxiety, and unassertiveness. Rational–emotive therapy has appeal and potential usefulness for those who can enjoy and profit from intellectual exchanges, including argumentation. The people who are likely to benefit most from this form of therapy are those who are self-demanding and who feel guilty for not living up to their own standards of perfection. People with serious anxiety disorders or with severe thought disorders such as schizophrenia, however, are unlikely to respond to the intellectual analysis of their problems that rational–emotive therapy includes.

Cognitive–behavioral therapists place a great deal of importance on clients' perceptions, thoughts, feelings, and beliefs but do not rely on cognitions alone. They, like their behavior-therapeutic colleagues, insist that it is not enough to have their clients introspect and analyze their thought patterns. Instead, therapists must help clients change their behavior. Moreover, just as cognitive changes can lead to behavioral changes, so can behavioral changes lead to cognitive changes. For example, when a client observes that he or she is now engaging in fewer maladaptive behaviors and behaving more adaptively, the client's self-perceptions and self-esteem may very well improve.

There are significant differences between cognitive–behavioral therapists and insight therapists. Unlike insight therapists, cognitive–behavioral therapists concern themselves with conscious, not unconscious, processes. They are also interested more in the present determinants of the client's thoughts and behaviors than in his or her past history. They use rigorous empirical methods to evaluate the effectiveness of their techniques.

Cognitive and cognitive–behavioral therapies are highly popular. Dobson and Khatri (2000) note several social influences that work in favor of these approaches to therapy. Prominent among these influences is the larger society's emphasis on efficiency. Cognitive and cognitive–behavioral therapies are attractive because they are relatively brief and affordable (Dobson & Khatri, 2000). In addition, the effectiveness of cognitive and cognitive–behavioral approaches has been strongly supported by research. For example, behavior therapy may produce as much change in brain metabolic activity as some drug therapies (Goldapple et al., 2004). Interestingly, not everyone's brain metabolic activity responds the same way to cognitive therapy. Mayberg (2003) analyzed PET scans of people suffering from depression who had undergone a variety of therapies. She identified biological markers that showed a strong correlation between a client's unique metabolic activity and therapeutic effectiveness. Future research incorporating the use of neuroimaging techniques may allow therapists to predict which clients will respond best to a particular form of therapy.

Interim Summary

Behavior Therapies, Cognitive Therapies, and Cognitive–Behavioral Therapies

Behavior therapists use the principles of classical and operant conditioning to modify behavior—to eliminate extreme fears and other maladaptive behaviors and replace them with more adaptive ones. Systematic desensitization uses classical conditioning procedures to condition relaxation to stimuli that previously produced fear. In contrast, implosion therapy attempts to extinguish fear and avoidance responses. Aversion therapy attempts to condition an unpleasant response to a stimulus with which the client is preoccupied, such as the object of a fetish.

Operant conditioning involves reinforcement, extinction, or punishment of particular behaviors in particular situations. The most formal reinforcement systems are token economies, which set up contingencies of reinforcement in institutional environments. In such arrangements the reward is made obvious to the patients. Modeling can be an important adjunct to operant conditioning; therapists who use this technique provide specific examples of desirable behaviors.

Not all instances of reinforcement and punishment are overt; they also can be vicarious. With the guidance of therapists, people can imagine their own behavior followed by novel forms of reinforcement or punishment. Although some people view behavior therapy as the simple application of the principles of conditioning, therapists must be well trained and sensitive if the techniques are to be effective. The major problem with behavior therapy is clients' tendency not to generalize behavior acquired in the therapeutic situation to situations in the outside world. Techniques to promote generalization include the use of intermittent reinforcement and the recruitment of family and friends as adjunct therapists.

Unlike cognitive–behavioral therapies, the earlier rational–emotive therapy (a form of cognitive restructuring) did not spring from the tradition of behavior therapies. Instead, it focused on modifying clients' maladaptive perceptions, thoughts, feelings, and beliefs. In rational–emotive therapy the therapist directly confronts the client, calling specific attention to irrationality and error. In this respect the therapy contrasts strongly with those provided by humanistic therapists.

Cognitive–behavioral therapies attempt to change behavior by altering the client's cognitive processes. For example, Beck has developed a therapy to help depressed clients target errors of thinking and feeling that perpetuate self-defeating behaviors and replace them with more desirable behaviors. It is also the case that behavioral change can produce changes in cognition as well. Thus, the causal relation between cognition and behavior can be considered bidirectional.

Critics have accused behavior therapists and cognitive–behavioral therapists of doing nothing more than treating the symptoms of a disorder and ignoring its basic causes. However, there is no evidence to support the idea that symptom substitution occurs in people who undergo these forms of therapy.

The use of behavior therapies and cognitive–behavioral therapies may raise ethical concerns, particularly when aversive stimuli are used. If aversive techniques are the best solution, the client's participation must be voluntary, or patient advocates must participate in the decision to use this form of therapy.

QUESTIONS TO CONSIDER

1. Think of the stimulus—either the thing or the situation—that you fear most. Based on what you have learned about systematic desensitization, create a hierarchy of your fears. Then identify ways to relax as you imagine the least fearful stimuli. How well can you maintain relaxation as you progress through the hierarchy?
2. Now, using the same hierarchy of fears, instead of trying to relax, try to alter your cognitions. What cognitive aspects of your fear are irrational? How might you change these faulty cognitions to reduce your fear?

Group Therapies and Community Psychology

So far, we have been considering individual forms of psychotherapy, those in which a single client meets with a therapist. But in many cases clients meet as a group, either because therapy is more effective that way or because it is more convenient or economical. **Group psychotherapy,** in which two or more clients meet simultaneously with a therapist to discuss problems, became common during the Second World War. The stresses of combat produced psychological problems in many military personnel, and the demand for therapists greatly exceeded the supply. What began as an economic necessity became an institution once the effectiveness of group treatment was recognized.

Because most psychological problems involve interactions with other people, treating these problems in a group setting may be worthwhile. Group therapy provides four advantages that are not found in individual therapy:

1. The group setting permits the therapist to observe and interpret actual interactions without having to rely on clients' descriptions, which may be selective or faulty.
2. A group can bring social pressure to bear on the behaviors of its members. If a person receives similar comments about his or her behavior from all the members of a group, the message is often more convincing than if a psychotherapist delivers the same comments in a private session.
3. The process of understanding the causes of maladaptive behavior in other people often helps a person gain insight into his or her own problems.
4. Knowing that other people have similar problems can bring comfort and relief to an individual. People discover that they are not alone.

The structure of group therapy sessions can vary widely. Some sessions are almost like lectures: The therapist presents information about a problem common to all members of the group, then invites discussion. For example, in a case involving a person with severe mental or physical illness, the therapist may explain to family members the nature, treatment, and possible outcomes of the disorder. Then the therapist answers questions and allows those present to share their feelings about what the illness has done to their family. Most types of group psychotherapy involve interactions among the participants.

Family Therapy and Couples Therapy

Very often dealing solely with the problems of individual clients is not enough to produce a successful outcome. Family therapy and couples therapy have become important techniques, because the structure of a client's family or marriage is a crucial part of the client's experience. In other words, helping an unhappy person frequently means also restructuring his or her relationships with other family members (Cox & Paley, 2003; Lefley, 2002). In many cases a family therapist meets with all members of a client's family and analyzes the way in which individuals interact. The therapist attempts to get family members to talk to one another instead of addressing their comments and questions only to him or her. As much as possible, the family therapist tries to collect data about family interactions—how individuals sit in relation to one another, who interrupts whom, who looks

▲ *Family therapy approaches individuals' mental disorders from the perspective that the structure of relationships within the family is part of the individual's problem and that restructuring those relationships will help all concerned to become happier.*

at whom before speaking—in order to infer the nature of relationships within the family. For example, there may be barriers between certain family members; perhaps a father is unable to communicate with one of his children. Or two (or more) family members may be so dependent on each other that they cannot function independently; they constantly seek each other's approval and, in their overdependence, make each other miserable.

For example, consider the approach developed by Salvador Minuchin (1974), **structural family therapy.** The therapist first observes a family's interactions and draws simple diagrams of the relationships he or she infers from their behaviors. He or she then identifies the counterproductive relationships and attempts to help the family restructure their dynamics in more adaptive ways.

For example, the therapist might diagram a family structure with father (F) on one side and mother (M) on the other side, allied with son (S) but estranged from daughter (D), as illustrated in the left panel of **Figure 18•4.**

The therapist would then attempt to restructure the family as shown in the right panel of the figure. That is, husband (H) and wife (W) would replace mother and father, and the new arrangement would emphasize their primary emotional relationship as spouses. The healthiest family interactions stem from an effectively functioning *marital subsystem* consisting of a husband and wife. A marriage that is completely child-oriented is always dysfunctional (Foley, 1979), and alliances between one parent and one or more children are almost always detrimental to the family.

After describing the family system, the therapist attempts to help the family restructure it by replacing maladaptive interactions with more effective ones. He or she suggests that perhaps all members of the family must change if the client is to make real improvement. The therapist gets family members to "actualize" their patterns of interaction—to act out

their everyday relationships—so that the maladaptive interactions will show themselves. Restructuring techniques include forming temporary alliances between the therapist and one or more of the family members; increasing tension in order to trigger changes in unstable structures; assigning explicit tasks and homework to family members (for example, assigning certain individuals to interact with certain other individuals); and providing support, training, and guidance. Sometimes the therapist visits the family at home. For example, if a child in a family refuses to eat, the therapist will visit during mealtime in order to see the problem acted out as explicitly as possible.

Behavior therapists also have applied their methods of analysis and treatment to families. This approach focuses on the social environment provided by the family and on the ways in which family members reinforce or punish one another's behaviors. The strategy is to identify both the maladaptive behaviors of individual members and the ways in which these behaviors are inadvertently reinforced by the rest of the family. Then the therapist helps the family members find ways to increase positive exchanges and to reinforce each other's desirable behaviors. A careful analysis of the social dynamics of a family often reveals that changes need to be made not by the individual who exhibits the most maladaptive behaviors but by the other members of the family.

All couples will find that they disagree at one time or another on important issues. Disagreements often lead to conflicts. For example, a couple may have to decide whether to

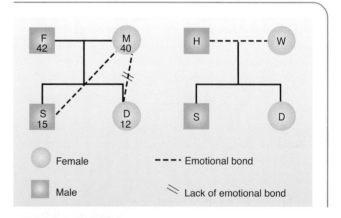

FIGURE 18•4 Genograms offer family therapists a way of visualizing psychological relationships between family members across generations. This pair of genograms includes two generations: a man aged 42 and woman aged 40 and their two children, a son aged 15 and a daughter aged 12. The genogram on the left depicts the man and woman as father (F) and mother (M), with a close emotional bond between mother and son (S) and the lack of a bond between mother and daughter (D). The therapist encourages the situation depicted in the genogram on the right, where the man and woman relate to one another as husband (H) and wife (W) without the uneven emotional bonds that existed previously between mother and children.

move in order to accommodate the career of one of the partners, how to spend their money, or how to allocate household chores. The couple's ability to resolve conflict is one of the most important factors affecting the quality and durability of their relationship.

When dealing with families and couples, therapists have learned that changes in the nature of the relations can have unforeseen consequences—and that they must be alert to these consequences. For example, LoPiccolo and Friedman (1985) describe the treatment of a couple with a sexual problem. At first, the problem appeared to belong to the man:

> A couple with a marriage of twenty years' duration sought treatment for the male's problem of total inability to have an erection. This had been a problem for over nineteen of their twenty years of marriage. Successful intercourse had only taken place in the first few months of the marriage. . . . [The wife] reported that she greatly enjoyed sex and was extremely frustrated by her husband's inability to have an erection.

The therapists used techniques developed by Masters and Johnson (1970) to treat the man's impotence, which succeeded splendidly. Within 10 weeks the couple was able to have sexual intercourse regularly, and both had orgasms. However, even though the problem appeared to have been cured, and despite the physical gratification they received from their sexual relations, they soon stopped. In follow-up investigation, the therapists discovered that

> . . . the husband had a great need to remain distant and aloof from his wife. He had great fears of being overwhelmed and controlled by her, and found closeness to be very uncomfortable. . . . For him, the inability to have an erection served to keep his wife distant from him, and to maintain his need for privacy, separateness, and autonomy in the relationship. (LoPiccolo & Friedman, 1985, p. 465)

The therapists also found that the wife had reasons to avoid sexual contact. For one thing, she apparently had never resolved the antisex sentiment imparted to her as a child by her family. In addition,

> . . . over the nineteen years of her husband being unable to attain an erection, she had come to have a very powerful position in the relationship. She very often reminded her husband that he owed her a lot because of her sexual frustration. Thus, she was essentially able to win all arguments with him, and to get him to do anything that she wanted. (LoPiccolo & Friedman, 1985, p. 465)

The therapists encouraged the couple to address these issues and helped them to resolve the problems. Eventually the couple were able to alter the structure of their marriage and resumed a more satisfying sexual relationship.

This case illustrates the fact that a couple is not simply two individuals. Long-standing problems bring adjustments and adaptations, some of which may not be healthy. Even if the original problems are successfully resolved, other patterns of behavior may persist and cause problems of their own.

The task of the family or couples therapist is formidable, as was recognized by Freud (1912), who stated, "When it comes to the treatment of relationships I must confess myself utterly at a loss and I have altogether little faith in any individual therapy of them." Of course, therapists today enjoy the benefit of many decades of research, theory, and practice not available to Freud.

Community Psychology

A quite different approach to therapy involves actively seeking out people with problems or even attempting to prevent problems before they begin. Therapists who participate in prevention are practicing **community psychology,** a form of education and treatment whose goal is to address psychological problems through assessment and intervention in the sociocultural contexts in which problems develop. Practitioners of community psychology deal with individuals and groups, establish educational programs, and design programs whose goal is to promote mental health by changing the environment.

Several different kinds of community treatment programs have been developed. One is the *community mental health center,* a facility designed to supplement the care provided by mental institutions. Instead of confining patients to an institution, community mental health centers provide outpatient care within the community. A popular form of care in the United States is called *assertive community treatment,* or ACT, which was developed in the 1970s by Stein and Test (Stein & Santos, 1998; Test & Stein, 2000). In ACT programs a multidisciplinary team responds to the needs of severely mentally ill patients. Typically, a psychiatric nurse, psychiatrist, and social worker develop a comprehensive care plan for the patient. Under this system care includes not only therapy but also assistance in the everyday demands of living (e.g., finding the patient a suitable place to live, finding the patient a job if the patient is able, arranging for transportation, and ensuring that the patient's basic physical needs are met). Important goals of ACT are ensuring patients' ability to live independently or with minimal supervision and reducing admissions to inpatient mental institutions. A recent review of the research literature showed that ACT is effective in meeting these goals (Phillips et al., 2001).

A related type of community treatment facility is the *halfway house,* a transitional setting in which patients discharged from mental institutions receive outpatient care as they gradually are reintegrated into the community. Using the halfway house as their base, patients may spend more time with their families and friends, take on part-time jobs, or return to school. Allowing previously institutionalized patients to return to their communities for treatment is called **deinstitutionalization.** For the most part, community psychologists consider it an important advance. Deinstitutionalization has dramatically reduced the number of persons confined to mental institutions in North America and Europe (Lesage et al., 2000).

Preventive Psychology Increasingly, community psychologists are stressing strategies aimed at preventing the development of psychological problems (Rappaport & Seidman, 2000). This emphasis on modifying the sociocultural variables predictive of psychological distress is called **preventive psychology.** As an analogy, think of individual therapy for psychological problems as similar to rescuing people who have fallen into a river (Rappaport, 1977). Each person rescued is a life saved. But a more effective solution would be to go upstream and correct the problem that is causing people to fall into the river in the first place.

For example, consider a long-term follow-up study conducted by Gillham, Reivich, Jaycox, and Seligman (1995). In the study researchers taught cognitive and social skills to a large group of 10- to 12-year-old children who were at risk for depression. For example, the children learned to identify negative and pessimistic beliefs and to replace them with more realistic and optimistic thoughts. The children also learned to focus on accomplishing their goals, to make decisions by considering the pluses and minuses of their options, and to think about ways that certain kinds of problems might be solved.

The researchers compared the levels of depression among children who received this training to the levels in another group of similarly aged children who also were at risk for depression but did not receive any prevention training. The results showed that the researchers' prevention program was successful—children who received the cognitive and social skills training were, on average, less depressed than were children who did not receive any training, even two years after the training. The researchers suggested that all children entering puberty are likely to benefit from the "psychological immunization against depression" that is provided by cognitive and social skills training.

Community psychologists distinguish between two kinds of prevention: primary and secondary. *Primary prevention* is any effort to eliminate the conditions responsible for psychological problems and simultaneously to bring about conditions that contribute to adaptive behavior. For example, providing children with educational materials concerning the dangers of taking drugs, while at the same time encouraging healthy recreation and exercise, represents an attempt to prevent the children from experimenting with drugs. *Secondary prevention,* on the other hand, consists of prompt identification of problems and immediate intervention to minimize the further development of these problems. Suicide hotlines, staffed 24 hours a day by trained volunteers, are examples of secondary prevention measures.

Community mental health centers provide individual and group therapy and counseling to members of the communities in which they are located. They offer immediate, accessible outpatient care for people who might otherwise find it difficult to get help. These centers are generally staffed by psychologists, psychiatrists, social workers, and nurses. But they often also employ the services of paraprofessionals who have roots in the community. A *paraprofessional* usually has not received the same level of training as mental health professionals but is able to provide at least some components of the care that professionals provide. The use of paraprofessionals has many advantages. People from culturally deprived backgrounds frequently have difficulty relating to—and communicating with—therapists. However, paraprofessionals with the same social and ethnic backgrounds may be able to gain the trust and confidence of clients and thus enable them to benefit from the professional help that is available. Also, the paraprofessionals may be able to provide practical advice and to serve as role models for clients.

Biology and Culture

Cultural Belief Systems and Indigenous Healing Therapies

Suppose that you are a clinical psychologist working in a community mental health center located in the heart of a large urban area. One of your new clients is a young man, an immigrant from Jamaica, who is depressed. He blames his lethargy and unhappiness on *obeah*—sorcery. Quite literally, this young man believes that someone has put a hex, or curse, on him (Wedenoja, 1995). The problem you face, of course, is how to treat this individual—what sort of therapy would be most effective?

This is the question you must answer with all of your clients, of course. However, this case poses a special problem, because you know from your initial contacts that you and your client have widely different cultural belief systems about the cause of mental disorders. Your training represents a Western point of view, but this man knows little, if anything, about Western psychology or psychotherapy. His only experiences stem from his native culture, and he wholeheartedly accepts and believes them.

If you treat your new client using one of the therapies discussed in this chapter, you are apt to make little progress in helping him. A better choice might be to choose to *cotreat* him with a traditional Jamaican healer who is experienced in removing hexes. Many psychologists and psychiatrists whose clientele include persons with strong beliefs based on the customs and folklore of a particular culture have found such cotreatment effective. For example, consider the following case involving a man treated at the New Horizons Community Mental Health Center in Miami, Florida (Lefley, 1984, 1994):

> A Haitian man diagnosed with schizophrenia failed to respond to ten days of inpatient therapy and drug therapy. He believed that he was cursed. The Health Center staff contacted a *houngan*—a voodoo priest— who performed an exorcism ritual on him. The man quickly calmed down, the medication soon reduced his symptoms, and he was released shortly thereafter.

The use of non-Western, culture-specific approaches to psychological (and medical) problems is called **indigenous**

▲ *People in many non-Western cultures seek indigenous healing approaches to their psychological problems.*

healing (or sometimes *ethnopsychiatry* or *ethnomedicine*). Indigenous healing therapies are quite common in many countries and within specific subcultures in North America; for example, among Native Americans and people of Asian, Latino, West Indian, and Western African descent (Aponte, Rivers, & Wohl, 1995). Indigenous healing therapies are specific to each of these cultures, which have different belief systems and methods of treatment for specific problems. However, all such approaches seem to have two elements in common:

1. The people involved believe that the psychological problem is caused by factors external to the individual, such as a hex; by conduct that is considered immoral relative to cultural standards for behavior; or by bad luck.

2. The problem is treated by ritual, often including special incantations, herbal medicine, and references to spiritual forces and agents. Generally these rituals involve calling on spiritual forces to remove the curse, to supplant the forces causing the problem, or to replace bad luck with good luck.

By understanding the belief systems of their non-Western clients and by incorporating aspects of these belief systems into their treatment plans, therapists often produce successful results, as in the example of the Haitian man given above. In fact, in some universities, clinical psychologists and psychiatrists in training receive specific instruction regarding the cultural belief systems and indigenous healing therapies they are likely to encounter in their work with clients (Zatrick & Lu, 1991). Such training appears to sensitize these clinicians to the aspects of their clients' belief systems that are likely to impede therapy, and thus puts them in a better position to understand the nature of their clients' problems.

Have you thought any more about how you might treat your young Jamaican client who had been hexed? Consider how a similar case was handled by the New Horizons Community Mental Health Center:

> An African-American woman of Bahamian ancestry came to the center complaining of depression caused by a hex placed on her by her boyfriend's

lover. She reported that the hex had caused problems for her at work and with her children. While undergoing counseling at the mental health center, she also sought out an *obeahman* because her boyfriend's girlfriend had used one to place the hex on her. The *obeahman* "cleansed her with special perfumes, oils, and herbs, and gave her special tasks that would align her with the benign forces of the universe. To finalize the therapeutic intervention, the healer took [her] to a cemetery at midnight, lowered her into an unfilled grave, and sprinkled her with grave dirt." Soon thereafter she got a raise at work, her children's behavior improved, and she broke off the relationship with her boyfriend. She continued, though, with the counseling sessions at the mental health center. (Lefley, 1994, p. 186)

We do not yet know the scientific explanation of why some people appear to be "cured" by indigenous healing—or by a mixture of indigenous healing and formal therapy—but not to be helped by formal therapy alone. As you have learned, one of the most important qualities of successful therapists is their ability to form a warm and empathetic relationship with their clients. Perhaps the familiar techniques of indigenous healing enable clients to feel more comfortable and open with their professional therapists and to establish a trusting relationship.

Interim Summary

Group Therapies and Community Psychology

Group psychotherapy was developed in response to the belief that certain problems can be treated more efficiently and more effectively in group settings. Practitioners of family therapy, couples therapy, and group behavior therapy observe people's interactions with others and attempt to help them learn how to establish more effective patterns of behavior. Treatment of groups, including families and couples, permits the therapist to observe clients' social behaviors. It may also apply social pressure to help convince clients of the necessity for behavioral change. It permits clients to learn from the mistakes of others and to observe that other people have similar problems, which is often reassuring.

In community psychology psychologists attempt to reach out to a community to establish readily available treatment facilities or to provide crisis intervention and so to keep problems from becoming worse. Community psychology also provides educational programs and promotes social changes that may prevent problems from occurring in the first place.

Indigenous healing therapies are based on belief systems regarding the causes and cures of psychological problems specific to a given culture. Although indigenous healing therapies often involve the use of culture-specific incantations and rituals, they can be effective in reducing the symptoms of psychological problems in people who believe in them. For this reason many psychologists and psychiatrists use a blend of formal therapy and indigenous healing therapy to treat immigrants from certain cultures. This method appears to be more effective than using only formal therapy, because indigenous healing lets the therapist make contact with the individual's cultural belief system and may promote a trusting relationship between therapist and client.

QUESTIONS TO CONSIDER

1. How effective might group therapy be in helping you cope with your problems, anxieties, or fears? Would you feel comfortable telling strangers about these sorts of things? Why/why not? In what ways might you benefit from hearing others discuss their problems and worries?

2. It is common practice for people to visit their physicians once a year for a checkup. It is also routine for people to visit their dentists twice a year to have their teeth cleaned and examined for cavities and other problems. Why don't people take the same preventive approach to their mental health? Suppose you were a clinical psychologist. How might you set up an annual preventive exam? For example, what would the exam consist of? What kinds of problems would you look for?

Biological Therapies

Therapies provided by psychologists target maladaptive thoughts and behaviors, but biological therapies—sometimes called biomedical therapies—target abnormal neural and other physiological functions. For that reason, biological therapies for mental disorders are traditionally carried out by psychiatrists or other physicians (who have medical degrees) rather than psychologists. As we saw in Chapter 17, an important method of treating the symptoms of schizophrenia and mood disorders is medication. Besides drug therapy, there are two other forms of biological therapy: electroconvulsive therapy and psychosurgery.

Drug Therapy

Drug therapy, often called **pharmacotherapy,** is the treatment of psychological problems with chemical agents and is the most widely used form of biomedical therapy. Although abuses have occurred, drug therapy created a revolution in the treatment of mental disorders and is a highly active area of medical and psychological research today. **Table 18•3** lists some of the drugs most commonly used to improve psychological functioning, their generic names, and their more recognizable trade names. As shown in the table, there are four general classes of drugs for the treatment of mental disorders: antipsychotic drugs, antidepressant drugs, antimanic drugs, and antianxiety drugs.

TABLE 18•3 Drugs Commonly Used to Treat Mental Disorders

General Class of Drugs	Subclass of Drugs	Generic Name	Trade Name
Antipsychotic	Phenothiazines	Chlorpromazine	Thorazine
		Thioridazine	Mellaril
		Fluphenazine	Modecate
		Trifluoperazine	Stelazine
		Perphenazine	Trilafon
	Butyrophenones	Haloperidol	Haldol
	Atypical	Clozapine	Clozaril
		Risperidone	Risperdal
Antidepressant	Tricyclics	Imipramine	Tofranil
	Monoamine oxidase inhibitors (MAOIs)	Phenelzine	Nardil
	Selective serotonin reuptake inhibitors (SSRIs)	Paroxetine	Paxil
		Fluoxetine	Prozac
		Sertraline	Zoloft
Antimanic/mood-stabilizing	Lithium salts	Lithium carbonate	Eskalith
Antianxiety	Benzodiazepines	Chlordiazepoxide	Librium
		Diazepam	Valium
		Lorazepam	Ativan
		Alprazolam	Xanax

Antipsychotic Drugs In the early 1950s, physicians working at two hospitals in France found that a new drug called *chlorpromazine* (belonging to the phenothiazine subclass of drugs) dramatically reduced the positive symptoms of schizophrenic disorders (see Chapter 17) (Lehmann & Ban, 1997; Shen & Giesler, 1998). The introduction of chlorpromazine (with the trade name Thorazine) and other **antipsychotic drugs** has had a profound effect on the treatment of schizophrenia.

There is still no cure for schizophrenia, however. The majority of antipsychotic drugs simply reduce the severity of its most prominent positive symptoms—delusions and hallucinations—apparently by blocking dopamine receptors in the brain. Presumably, the overactivity of dopamine synapses is responsible for those symptoms. Although dopamine-secreting neurons are located in several parts of the brain, most researchers believe that those involved in the symptoms of schizophrenia are located in the cerebral cortex and in parts of the limbic system near the front of the brain.

A different system of dopamine-secreting neurons in the brain is involved in the control of movement. Occasionally this system of neurons degenerates, mostly in older people, producing Parkinson's disease. Symptoms of this disorder include tremors, muscular rigidity, loss of balance, difficulty in initiating movement, and impaired breathing that makes speech indistinct. In severe cases the person is bedridden.

The major problem with most antipsychotic drugs, the phenothiazines, is that they do not discriminate between these two systems of dopamine-secreting neurons. The drugs interfere with the activity of both the circuits involved in the symptoms of schizophrenia and the circuits involved in the control of movements. Consequently, when a person with schizophrenia begins to take an antipsychotic drug, he or she sometimes exhibits a movement disorder. Fortunately, the symptoms are usually temporary and soon disappear. After taking the antipsychotic drug for several years, however, some people develop a different and more serious movement disorder known as **tardive dyskinesia** (*tardive* means "late-developing"; *dyskinesia* refers to a disturbance in movement). This often irreversible and untreatable syndrome is characterized by continual involuntary lip smacking, grimacing, and drooling (Cummings & Wirshing, 1989). Severely affected people have difficulty with talking and occasionally with breathing. The risk of developing this syndrome increases with age, dose, and duration of use (Hughes, & Pierattini, 1992; Tarsy Baldessarini, & Tarazi, 2002). For example, approximately 20 percent of older people who take antipsychotic drugs develop tardive dyskinesia. The physician can temporarily alleviate the symptoms by *increasing* the dose of the antipsychotic drug, but doing so only serves to increase and perpetuate the person's dependence on the medication (Baldessarini & Tarsy, 1980).

A more recently developed antipsychotic drug overcomes three of the important drawbacks of the typical formulations. Earlier I mentioned that most antipsychotics reduce the severity of positive symptoms of schizophrenia, such as thought disorders and hallucinations. A more recent antischizophrenia drug called *clozapine* (Clozaril) also is effective for negative symptoms, such as social withdrawal and flattened emotionality. For this reason clozapine is referred to as an "atypical" medication. This development is a major advance for the welfare and quality of life of people who have schizophrenia. Like all drugs, conventional antipsychotics don't work for everyone. For reasons that are not well understood, clozapine helps many people who receive no substantial benefit from the other antipsychotics (Bondolfi et al., 1998; Carpenter et al., 1995). Finally, clozapine appears to carry dramatically lower risks of tardive dyskinesia (e.g., Kane, 2001); there is even some indication that switching to clozapine may reduce the symptoms of tardive dyskinesia resulting from other drug treatments (e.g., Chakos et al., 2001). This may make clozapine sound like a wonder drug, and in many respects this medication may deserve the honor. But there are downsides. Clozapine is much more expensive than other antipsychotics —and it can produce serious adverse side effects (Conley & Kelly, 2001). About 2 percent of people taking clozapine suffer an inhibition of white blood cell production, which can be fatal. For this reason, only patients with normal white cell counts can take clozapine, and they must have blood tests weekly for the first six months of therapy and then every two weeks afterwards.

Antidepressant and Antimanic/Mood-Stabilizing Drugs

Antidepressant drugs are a class of drugs used to treat the symptoms of major depression. **Antimanic/mood-stabilizing drugs** are used to treat the symptoms of the bipolar disorders, which involve both depression and manic phases.

The earliest antidepressant drugs were derived from the family of chemicals known as *tricyclics;* the term refers to their "three-ring" chemical structure (Lickey & Gordon, 1991). Because their chemical structure is similar to that of antipsychotic drugs, researchers first tested tricyclics in the belief that they might provide an effective treatment for schizophrenia. Although their use as antipsychotics was quickly dismissed, researchers observed that these drugs did tend to elevate mood— a finding that suggested their potential as antidepressants.

The biology of depression is still not well understood, but the most widely accepted theory is that depression may result from a deficiency of the catecholamine neurotransmitters, norepinephrine and serotonin. Each of these neurotransmitters may be involved in different types of depression, although researchers are not sure how. Tricyclics seem to slow down the reuptake of these neurotransmitters by presynaptic axons. Of course, these drugs do not work for all depressed people; even so, about 60 to 80 percent of those whose depression has brought despair to their lives gradually return to normal after having been placed on tricyclics for two to six weeks (Hughes & Pierattini, 1992; Potter, Manji, & Rudorfer, 2001). Unfortunately, tricyclics have many side effects, including dizziness, sweating, weight gain, constipation, increased pulse, poor concentration, and dry mouth.

Another subclass of antidepressants is the *monoamine oxidase inhibitors* (MAOIs), which take one to three weeks to begin alleviating depression. MAOIs prevent enzymes in the synaptic gap from destroying dopamine, norepinephrine, and serotonin that have been released by presynaptic neurons. These drugs too can have many side effects, including high blood pressure (which can be fatal after the ingestion of certain foods—including wines, milk products, coffee, and chocolate); hyperthermia (high body temperature); blurred vision; erectile dysfunction; insomnia; and nausea. Nevertheless, MAOIs also have proved to be more effective than tricyclics in treating atypical depressions such as those involving hypersomnia (too much sleep) or mood swings (Hughes & Pierattini, 1992).

A relatively new subclass of drugs (with trade names such as Prozac, Paxil, and Zoloft) has had a major impact on pharmacotherapy for depression. Prozac, the original entry in this field, and its successors inhibit the reuptake of serotonin, leaving more of that neurotransmitter in the synaptic cleft to stimulate postsynaptic receptors. These drugs, collectively called *selective serotonin reuptake inhibitors* (or SSRIs), can have negative side effects, but to a lesser degree than do tricyclics and the MAOIs. Moreover, because they have fewer side effects, SSRIs often can be taken in larger dosages, which can produce more substantial reduction of the depressive symptoms.

Among the antimanic/mood-stabilizing drugs, *lithium carbonate* is most effective in the treatment of bipolar disorders (Schou, 2001). Manic symptoms usually decrease as soon as the blood level of lithium reaches a sufficiently high level. In bipolar I disorder (see Chapter 17), once the manic phase is eliminated, the depressed phase does not return. People with bipolar I disorder have remained free of their symptoms for years as long as they have continued taking lithium carbonate. Some people require lithium in combination with other drugs for maximum effectiveness (Grof, 2003). People who have untreated bipolar disorders have a mortality rate two to three times that of the normal population (see Ahrens et al., 1995), reflecting a higher risk of suicide and cardiovascular disease. Ahrens and colleagues (1995) report that continued treatment with lithium after symptoms have subsided reduces patients' mortality rate to that of the general population.

Lithium produces side effects, such as a fine motor tremor or excessive urine production; but in general the benefits far outweigh the adverse symptoms. However, an overdose of lithium is toxic, which means that patients' blood level of lithium must be monitored regularly.

The major difficulty clinicians face in treating bipolar I disorder is that people with this disorder often miss their "high." When medication is effective, the mania subsides along with the depression. But most people enjoy at least the initial phase of their manic periods, and some believe that they are more creative at that time. In addition, many say that they resent having to depend on a chemical crutch. As a consequence, they may stop their medication. Doing this endangers their lives, because the risk of death by suicide is particularly high during the depressive phase of bipolar I disorder.

Antianxiety Drugs Antianxiety drugs are used in the treatment of generalized anxiety, phobias, obsessions, compulsions, panic attacks, and other anxiety-related problems (see Chapter 17). The popularity of antianxiety drugs, or minor tranquilizers as they are sometimes called, is indicated by the large numbers of prescriptions that are filled in the United States, Canada, and Europe. The most popular, most effective, and most abused of these drugs are the *benzodiazepines,* often known by trade names such as Librium, Valium, and Xanax (Julien, 2000). Benzodiazepines appear to work by activating what is called the *benzodiazepine receptor,* which, in turn, produces activity in receptors sensitive to *gamma-aminobutyric acid* (GABA), an inhibitory neurotransmitter. More specifically, benzodiazepines appear to enhance the attachment of GABA molecules to the postsynaptic neuron by reconfiguring the shape of GABA receptors, thereby producing more neural activity.

Before the benzodiazepines were synthesized in the early 1960s, the major effective antianxiety drugs had been the barbiturates. The immediate success of Valium and Librium was due in part to the erroneous belief that they had a lower risk for abuse than barbiturates and were safer in cases of overdose (Lickey & Gordon, 1983). But although the benzodiazepines are the safest of the antianxiety drugs, we now know that these medications can produce physical tolerance and withdrawal symptoms when removed. Some individuals find it very difficult to stop using benzodiazepines because of the withdrawal syndrome and thus show addiction to the drugs. Taken in low dosages and for short periods, though, these drugs can be effective temporary means of reducing anxiety without involving a high risk of physical dependence.

Besides being effective in treating depression, tricyclic antidepressant drugs have been also used successfully to treat several anxiety disorders, including panic disorder and agoraphobia (Klein, 1996), and can reduce the severity of obsessive-compulsive disorder. These drugs appear to reduce the incidence of panic attacks, including those that accompany severe agoraphobia. However, antidepressant drugs do not reduce the anticipatory anxiety that a person feels between panic attacks.

Although drugs are useful in alleviating the symptoms of certain anxiety disorders, they do not cure any of these conditions, possibly because the disorders are at least partly heritable, as we saw in Chapter 17. The most effective and long-lasting treatment for anxiety is cognitive–behavioral therapy. The drugs may be especially useful in reducing symptoms so that patients can participate effectively in therapy, but they do not provide a long-term solution.

Electroconvulsive Therapy

In **electroconvulsive therapy (ECT)** a clinician attaches a pair of electrodes to a person's head and then passes a brief surge of electrical current through them. The jolt produces a seizure—a storm of electrical activity in the brain that renders the person unconscious. The seizure is believed to cause the brain to release higher than normal amounts of GABA, which decreases brain activity. This effect can benefit some patients with major depression and extreme manic disorders.

In a seizure, whether spontaneous or caused by ECT, the wild firing of neurons that control movement produces convulsions—muscular rigidity and trembling, followed by rhythmic movements of the head, trunk, and limbs. After a few minutes the person falls into a deep sleep. Today, patients undergoing ECT are anesthetized and temporarily paralyzed before the current is turned on. This procedure eliminates the convulsions but not the seizure, which is what causes the therapeutic effect.

Electroconvulsive therapy has a bad reputation among many clinicians, because in the past it has been used in misguided attempts to treat disorders such as schizophrenia (on which ECT has no useful effects), and because people have received excessive numbers of ECT treatments—sometimes hundreds. Nevertheless, it appears to be a helpful treatment as a last resort for some patients with serious depressive and manic disorders that have not yielded to other therapies, and it is accepted as appropriate practice by the American Psychiatric Association. No one knows for certain, however, why ECT is effective for some patients.

A case report by Fink (1976) illustrates the response of a depressed patient to ECT. A 44-year-old widow had been hospitalized for three months for severe depression. A course of three ECT treatments per week was prescribed for her by her therapist's supervisor. Unknown to her therapist (a trainee), the first 12 treatments were subthreshold; that is, the intensity of the electrical current was too low to produce seizures. (These treatments could be regarded as placebo treatments.) Although both the woman and her therapist expected that she would show some improvement, none was seen. In the next 14 treatments, the current was at a level sufficient to produce seizures. After five seizures, both the woman and the therapist noticed an improvement. The woman began to complain less about various physical symptoms, to participate in hospital activities, and to make more positive statements about her mood. She became easier to talk with, and the therapist's notes of their conversations grew more numerous. The fact that these responses occurred only after several seizures and not in the course of the subthreshold treatments suggests that improvement stemmed from the biological treatment and not simply from the therapist's or the woman's expectations.

Some people with severe depression do not respond to antidepressant drugs, but a substantial percentage of these people improve after a few sessions of ECT. Because antidepressant medications are generally slow acting, taking 10 days to two weeks for their therapeutic effects to begin, clinicians sometimes treat severe cases of depression with a brief course of ECT to reduce the symptoms right away. These patients then go on a maintenance dose of an antidepressant drug. Because a person with major depressive disorder runs a 15 percent chance of dying by suicide, the use of ECT may be justified in such cases (Prudic & Sackeim, 1999).

ECT treatments are not without problems. They clearly cause short-term memory loss (e.g., Lisanby et al., 2000). Although the evidence is inconclusive, there are concerns about the potential for permanent memory loss. Nowadays ECT usually is administered only to the right hemisphere, in order to minimize negative effects on memory. For many years there were concerns that ECT might cause permanent brain damage. There is no convincing evidence thus far that this is the case (e.g., Obergriesser, Ende, Braus, & Henn, 2003; Zachrisson et al., 2000). In fact, some researchers argue that the refinement of the procedure over the past several decades has led to techniques that can be effective with minimal adverse effects (Persad, 2001). Nevertheless, for some people there are intrapersonal consequences—patients may feel ashamed and humiliated that they need what is perceived as a radical treatment (Johnstone, 1999).

Psychosurgery

The third category of biological treatments for mental disorders is even more controversial than ECT. **Psychosurgery** is the treatment of a mental disorder using brain surgery in cases in which obvious organic damage is absent (see Jasper, 1995, for a historical account). In contrast, brain surgery to remove a tumor or diseased neural tissue or to repair a damaged blood vessel is not referred to as psychosurgery, and there is no controversy about such procedures.

You may recall from Chapter 13 that prefrontal lobotomies were found to have serious side effects, such as apathy and severe blunting of emotions, intellectual impairments, and deficits in judgment and planning ability. Nevertheless, the procedure was once used for a variety of conditions, most of which were not improved by the surgery. Tens of thousands of prefrontal lobotomies were performed worldwide from the 1930s through the 1950s. A simple procedure, called "icepick" prefrontal lobotomy by its critics and *leukotomy* by its proponents, even was performed on an outpatient basis. The development of antipsychotic drugs and increasing attention to the serious side effects of prefrontal lobotomy led to a sharp decline in the use of this procedure during the 1950s. Today the procedure is no longer performed (Valenstein, 1986).

A few surgeons have continued to refine the technique of psychosurgery, however, and these physicians now perform a procedure called a **cingulotomy.** This operation involves cutting the cingulum bundle, a small band of nerve fibers that connects the prefrontal cortex with parts of the limbic system (Ballantine, Bouckoms, Thomas, & Giriunas, 1987). Cingulotomies have been shown to be effective in helping some people who have severe obsessive-compulsive disorder (Jenike, 2000). Baer and his colleagues (1995) conducted a long-term follow-up study of 18 people who underwent cingulotomy for severe obsessive-compulsive disorder. For each of these people, other forms of therapy—drug therapy and behavior therapy—had been unsuccessful. After their surgeries, however, the patients in Baer and colleagues' study showed marked improvements in their functioning, decreased symptoms of depression and anxiety, and few negative side effects.

Psychosurgery is typically prescribed only as a last resort and never for a patient who cannot consent to treatment. The effects of psychosurgery are permanent; there is no way to reverse a brain lesion.

Evaluation of Biological Treatments

There can be no doubt that drug therapy is the preferred biological treatment for mental disorders. Drug therapy, though, represents a treatment option; it is not a cure. Usually the drugs are effective only to the extent that the people for whom they are prescribed actually use them. In some cases people forget to take their drugs, only to have their symptoms return. In other cases people take their drugs, get better, and stop taking the drugs because they feel that they are no longer "sick." In this case, too, the symptoms soon return. For some people, this cycle repeats itself over and over.

Thus, while drug therapy is an effective treatment option, it is not a panacea. But no actual cures for mental illness are on the horizon. Until cures are found, research will continue on the development of new and more effective drugs and on finding ways to encourage people to follow their prescription regimens more closely. As explained in the discussion of ECT and psychosurgery, these forms of treatment help some patients with severe disorders but remain controversial and have only limited applications.

Evaluating Scientific Issues

Assessing the Effectiveness of Therapy

Evaluation of therapies and therapists is a very important issue. The need for accurate evaluation has received much attention because of the human suffering and other high costs imposed by mental and emotional disorders. Still, almost everyone involved agrees that too little is known about the efficacy (or lack thereof) of therapeutic methods, in part because therapeutic effectiveness is difficult to study.

● **Why Is Therapy Difficult to Evaluate?**
Several factors make it extremely difficult to evaluate the effectiveness of a particular form of psychotherapy or an individual therapist. One factor is the problem of the *measurement* of outcome. Measuring a person's recovery from dysfunction is challenging, as there are no easily applied, commonly agreed-on criteria for mental health. Therefore, making valid before-and-after measurements is extremely difficult. Most studies rely on ratings by the clients or the therapists to determine whether a therapy has succeeded. These two measures obviously will be correlated, because therapists primarily base their ratings on what their clients say to them. Few studies include interviews with friends or family members to obtain independent evaluations of the clients' condition—and those that do generally find a weak correlation between these ratings and those of clients and therapists (Sloane et al., 1975).

Ethics also sometimes prevent clinicians from using a purely scientific method of evaluation, because of the fact that the scientific method would require that experimental and control groups be constituted in equivalent ways. For example, leaving a person who appeared to be suicidal untreated so as to make comparisons with similar people who received therapy would present risks that therapists consider unacceptable.

Self-selection—the fact that clients choose whether to enter therapy, what type of therapy to engage in, and how long to stay in therapy—makes it nearly impossible to establish either a stable sample population or a control group. That is, certain kinds of people are more likely than others to enter a particular therapy and stick with it, which produces a biased sample. Lack of a stable sample and lack of a control group make it difficult to compare the effectiveness of various kinds of therapies. Many patients change therapists or leave therapy altogether. What conclusions can we draw about the effectiveness of a therapy by looking only at the progress made by the clients who remain with it?

Yet another problem with scientific evaluation of therapy is the question of an appropriate *control group*. You may recall from Chapter 2 that the effects of therapeutic drugs must be determined through comparison with the effects of *placebos* (innocuous pills that have no known effects on people's thoughts and behavior). Researchers use placebos in order to be sure that any improvement has not occurred merely because the patient *thinks* that a pill has done some good. Placebo effects also can occur in psychotherapy: People know that they are being treated, and they may get better because they *believe* that the treatment should lead to improvement. Most researchers who evaluate psychotherapeutic techniques do not employ control groups to rule out these placebo effects. To do so, an investigator would have to design "mock therapy" sessions during which the therapist would do nothing therapeutic but would convince patients that therapy was taking place; obviously, this goal is not easily achieved.

A further complication arises from the fact that symptoms may disappear spontaneously even without therapy—a phenomenon known as the *spontaneous remission of symptoms*. Accurately estimating rates of spontaneous remission is notoriously difficult.

● **What Evidence Is There?**
In a pioneering paper on therapeutic evaluation, Hans Eysenck (1952) examined 19 studies assessing the effectiveness of psychotherapy. He reported that of the people who remained in psychoanalysis as long as their therapists thought they should, 66 percent showed improvement. Similarly, 64 percent of patients treated eclectically showed an improvement. However, 72 percent of patients who were treated only custodially (receiving no therapy) in institutions showed improvement. In other words, people got better just as fast by themselves as they did in therapy.

Subsequent studies were not much more optimistic. Some investigators, including Eysenck, concluded that it is unethical to charge a person for psychotherapy, because there is little scientific evidence that it is effective. Others said that the problems involved in performing scientific research are so great that we must abandon the attempt to evaluate therapies: Validation of the effectiveness of therapy must rely on the therapist's clinical judgment. Many forms of therapy have never been evaluated objectively, because their practitioners are convinced that their methods work and deem objective confirmation unnecessary (Dawes, 1994).

Figure 18•5 summarizes Smith, Glass, and Miller's (1980) well-known meta-analysis of 475 studies comparing the outcome effectiveness of psychodynamic, Gestalt, client-centered, systematic desensitization, behavior modification, and cognitive–behavioral therapies. A **meta-analysis** is a statistical procedure for estimating the magnitude of experimental effects reported by published studies. Relative to no therapy, each of these therapies was shown to be superior in helping people with their problems. Behavior therapies and cognitive–behavioral therapies tended to exceed others in effectiveness, although these differences were often small. More recent research has confirmed these results, indicating that most people tend to improve with respect to the symptoms that brought them to therapy (e.g., Okiishi, Lambert, Nielsen, & Ogles, 2003). Likewise, another meta-analysis confirmed that different forms of therapy seem to be about equally effective (Wampold, Minami, Baskin, & Callen, 2002; Wampold et al., 1997). Keep in mind that these data reflect hundreds of studies and thousands of clients. No conclusions can be drawn about the effectiveness of a particular therapy for any *one* client.

Each year, the editors of the popular magazine *Consumer Reports* send a large-scale survey—concerning consumer satisfaction with a tremendous range of goods and services—to their subscribers. The 1994 survey included 26 questions about treatment for mental disorders. About 7000 readers responded to this portion of the survey, 2900 of whom had seen mental health professionals for help in coping with stress or emotional problems during the previous three years. The majority (59 percent) of these people had consulted either a psychologist or a psychiatrist; the remainder had consulted a social worker, a marriage counselor, or another mental health professional.

In general the results from this survey showed that people benefited substantially from therapy (*Consumer Reports*, 1995). People who had undergone long-term treatment improved more than those who had undergone short-term treatment. In addition, all forms of therapy were found to be effective in helping people feel better, regardless of the disorders from which they were suffering.

● **What Factors Influence Outcome?**

A study by Luborsky and colleagues (1971) investigated the factors that influence the outcome of therapy, independent of the particular method used. They examined both patient variables and therapist variables. The important *patient variables* were the patient's psychological health at the beginning of the therapy, adequacy of personality, motivation for change, level of intelligence, level of anxiety (more anxious patients tended to do better), level of education, and socioeconomic status. Some of the variables seem to be self-confirming: If you are in fairly good psychological shape to begin with, you have a better chance of improving. In addition, if you are well educated and have adequate social and financial resources, your condition will probably improve. Anxiety probably is a positive predictor because anxiety provides a strong motivation to improve.

Several *therapist variables* were significant: The number of years the therapist had been practicing, the degree of similarity between the personalities of therapist and client, and the ability of the therapist to communicate empathy to the client all tended to have beneficial effects. The finding that the more experienced therapists had more success with their clients is encouraging; it suggests that therapists learn something from their years of experience, which in turn implies that *there is something to learn*. The *therapeutic alliance*, the relationship between therapist and client, also is important. Although the exact factors that contribute to a positive relationship between therapist and client differ across psychotherapies, it is clear that a positive alliance contributes to good outcomes (Kopta, Lueger, Saunders, & Howard, 1999). According to Bordin (1994) two important underlying factors are shared goals for the therapy between client and therapist and a firm bond between the two parties. Beyond these factors, it is possible that

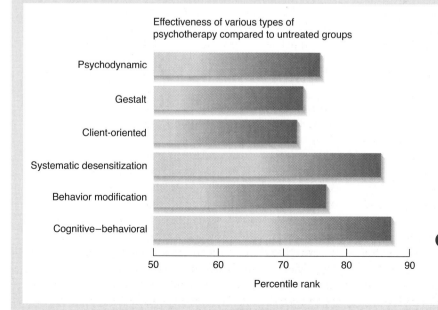

Effectiveness of various types of psychotherapy compared to untreated groups

FIGURE 18•5 Effectiveness of psychotherapy. Smith, Glass, and Miller's (1980) meta-analysis compared the relative effectiveness of different therapies.

other variables that contribute to good interpersonal relationships in everyday life also promote positive alliances in therapy. Consistent with this possibility, several studies have suggested that a therapist's ability to form understanding, warm, and empathetic relationships is one of the most important elements in effective therapy. For example, Strupp and Hadley (1979) enlisted a group of college professors on the basis of their reputations as warm, trustworthy, empathetic individuals. The professors (from departments of English, history, mathematics, and philosophy) were asked to hold weekly sessions in which they counseled students with moderate depression or anxiety. Another group of students with the same types of problems were assigned to professional therapists, both psychologists and psychiatrists; a third group received no treatment at all. Both experimental groups did significantly better than the control group. These results suggest that empathy and an effort to understand are by themselves important ingredients in the therapeutic alliance, at least for treatment of mild anxiety or depression.

● What Should We Conclude?

This chapter has tried to convey the ingenuity of clinicians in their efforts to help people with psychological problems. The magnitude of the task is formidable. One encouraging outcome of the evaluative research is that it indicates that psychotherapy is effective: Experienced and empathetic therapists are likely to help their clients get better. Another encouraging outcome is the general success achieved by behavior therapies and cognitive–behavioral therapies, even though the goals of these approaches are often circumscribed. Finally, although clinical psychologists are not responsible for the development and use of the biological therapies, they can take heart from several studies showing that psychotherapy significantly improves the mental health of clients who are also receiving drug therapy.

Interim Summary

Biological Therapies

Biological therapies for mental disorders include drugs, electroconvulsive therapy, and psychosurgery. Research has shown that treatment of the positive symptoms of schizophrenia with antipsychotic drugs, of major depression with antidepressant drugs, and of bipolar disorders with lithium carbonate are the most effective ways to alleviate the symptoms of these disorders. Atypical drugs show promise for treating the negative symptoms of schizophrenia as well. The benzodiazepines replaced barbiturates as the most effective drugs for the treatment of anxiety disorders. Though safer, they may still produce physical tolerance and withdrawal symptoms. Tricyclic antidepressant drugs can also alleviate severe anxiety that occurs during panic attacks and agoraphobia and can reduce the severity of obsessive-compulsive

disorder. Although electroconvulsive therapy can be an effective treatment for depression, there are important risks; thus, this treatment is reserved for cases in which rapid relief from severe symptoms is critical. The most controversial treatment, psychosurgery, is rarely performed today. One accepted method, cingulotomy, is a treatment for disabling compulsions that cannot be reduced by more conventional means.

Given the immense costs of problems associated with mental disorders, it is imperative to evaluate the effectiveness of therapeutic methods. Effectiveness is difficult to assess, however. Outcomes of psychotherapy are difficult to measure objectively; ethical considerations make it hard to establish control groups for some types of disorders; and self-selection and failures to complete therapy make it impossible to compare randomly selected groups of patients. However, what research there is suggests that many forms of therapy are effective. The *Consumer Reports* study found that people do indeed benefit from therapy. And the most important characteristic of a good psychotherapist appears to be the ability to form a warm, understanding alliance with a client.

QUESTIONS TO CONSIDER

1. Suppose that you have a friend who is about to begin drug therapy for a mental disorder. Suppose further that you are able to accompany your friend to one of his or her pretreatment sessions with a psychiatrist (given that, at present, only physicians, not clinical psychologists, can prescribe drugs). What questions will you ask the psychiatrist about the particular kind of drug therapy he or she is recommending for your friend? Will your questions differ depending on the kind of problem your friend is experiencing? Why or why not?

2. Suppose that your friend has now been treated for depression with tricyclics, but the treatment has failed—your friend is still extremely depressed. The psychiatrist now recommends ECT. What is your response? What sort of advice can you offer your friend and your friend's family about the psychiatrist's recommendation?

The Relationship between Client and Therapist

The special relationship that may develop between the therapist and the client is duplicated in few other places in society. With the possible exception of clergy in some religious traditions, few people earn their living by listening to others describe the deeply intimate details of their lives. Unfortunately, the same characteristics that give the therapeutic relationship its potential for healing may also lead to abuses. For this reason, psychologists have developed a set of ethical standards to guide their professional activities, and legislatures and courts have provided other regulations concerning the practice of therapy. In addition, the process of choosing a therapist requires special care.

Ethical Issues

The ethical standards for psychologists were originally defined by the American Psychological Association in 1953 as *Ethical Standards of Psychologists* (American Psychological Association, 1953). In 2002 the same organization published its most recent updated version, *Ethical Principles of Psychologists and Code of Conduct* (American Psychological Association, 2002). One of the ethical standards is specific to therapy and clearly states that sexual intimacies with clients are unethical. A therapist who suggests such intimacy to a client or who allows himself or herself to be approached sexually by a client is unquestionably violating this standard. Nonetheless, the problem of sexual relations between therapist and client, although rare, remains an issue in psychotherapy (Pope, 2000).

Another ethical standard refers to *privacy and confidentiality* and states that any information obtained about the client during therapy is confidential. This confidentiality extends to members of the client's family. The only conditions under which confidentiality may be breached are those mandated or permitted by law.

Selecting a Therapist

Chances are good that at some time you or a close friend will become worried, anxious, or depressed. In most cases people get through these times in their lives by talking with sympathetic friends, relatives, teachers, or members of the clergy. But sometimes problems persist, and the person in distress thinks about seeking professional help. How can you tell that you need to consult a therapist, and how do you go about finding a good one?

In general, if you have a problem that makes you unhappy and that persists for several months, you should seriously consider getting professional advice. If the problem is severely disruptive, you should not wait but should look for help immediately. For example, if you experience acute panic attacks, find yourself contemplating suicide, or hear voices that you know are not there, do not wait to see whether the problems go away. You might also think about consulting a professional for specific problems, such as unhealthy habits like smoking, or for specific fears, such as fear of flying. You do not have to be "mentally ill" to seek psychological help.

If you are a student at a college or university, the best place to turn to is the counseling service there. If you are not sure what mental health services are available on campus, someone in the psychology department will certainly be able to inform you. In larger universities the psychology department may operate its own clinic. If you are not a student, you should ask your physician or call your community mental health department and ask for advice. Or call the psychology department at a local college or university; someone there will help you locate sources of professional help in the community.

Table 18•4 describes some of the more common types of therapists, the training and degree credentials for each type, and the kinds of responsibilities each type of therapist assumes. As you can see, the training and the professional duties of different types of therapists vary considerably. In addition, therapists often conduct therapy from particular theoretical orientations, as you have learned in this chapter. However, research suggests that the orientation of the therapist may not be of particular consequence in the choice of a therapist, given that each orientation has both its advantages and limitations (Smith & Glass, 1977).

But be careful. Not listed in Table 18.4, because he or she is not a legitimate practitioner, is the *charlatan*, or quack, who pretends to have expert knowledge—in this case, the treatment of psychological disorders—but does not. Some charlatans may attempt to treat their clients' problems through psychic healing, astrology, palm reading, or other unscientific approaches. Other charlatans may use respectable-sounding titles such as "psychotherapist" but may be untrained and lack either knowledge of mental disorders or therapeutic skills.

TABLE 18•4 Types of Therapists, Their Degree Credentials, and Their Training and Professional Responsibilities

Title	Degree	Training Background and Professional Duties
Clinical psychologist	Ph.D. or Psy.D.	Graduate training in research, diagnosis, and therapy plus one-year clinical internship. Conducts assessment and therapy; may teach in a university setting and conduct clinical research.
Counseling psychologist	Ph.D., Psy.D. or Ed.D.	Graduate training in counseling. Conducts educational, vocational, and personal counseling.
Psychoanalyst	M.D.	Medical training plus specialized training in psychoanalysis. Conducts psychoanalytic therapy.
Psychiatrist	M.D.	Medical training plus psychiatric residency. Conducts diagnosis and biomedical therapy and psychotherapy.
Social Worker	M.S.W.	Graduate work in counseling and community psychology. Conducts psychotherapy; helps patients return to community.
Psychiatric Nurse	Nursing Diploma	Completion of approved psychiatric nursing program. Provides a variety of mental health services, usually as a member of a multidisciplinary team.

Here are three reasonable questions to answer when you feel the need to seek help from a therapist:

1. Is the therapist licensed to practice therapy in the state in which he or she is practicing?

2. What kind of formal training has the therapist received? From what academic institution(s) does the therapist hold advanced degrees? Did the therapist fulfill an internship during which he or she learned therapeutic techniques under the supervision of licensed practitioners?

3. What kind of reputation does the therapist have? Is he or she known for practicing therapy using one or more of the unscientific approaches mentioned above?

If a therapist is not licensed to practice, has little or no formal training in therapy, and/or is known to practice therapy using unscientific approaches, then you should avoid consulting with this person for therapy of any sort.

You should also talk with the therapist before commiting yourself to a course of therapy. Do you like the therapist as a person? Do you find the therapist sympathetic? If not, look elsewhere. Do not be impressed by an authoritative manner or glib assurances that the therapist knows best what you need. Look for someone who asks good questions about your problems and needs and who helps you formulate a specific and realistic set of goals. Find out whether the therapist specializes in your type of problem. For example, if you want to overcome a specific fear or break a specific habit, you may not want to embark on a series of sessions in which you are expected to talk about the history of your relations with other family members. On the other hand, if your problem is with family relations, then a family therapist may be the best person to consult. If you are unaware of what your problem is specifically, but you know you are hurting, the therapist's ability to help you identify your problem and to suggest a possible course of therapy may be a useful indicator of whether to continue to consult with her or him or to go elsewhere.

What about fees? Research indicates that the amount of money a person pays has no relation to the therapeutic benefits he or she receives. Ask the therapist about how much the services will cost. Find out whether your health plan will cover the fees. Do some comparison shopping. And be aware that therapists often will adjust their fees according to the ability of the client to pay.

How long should therapy continue? In some cases a therapist will suggest a fixed number of sessions. In other cases the arrangement will be open-ended. But how do you decide when to quit in those cases when the duration is indefinite? Here are some guidelines: If you do not make progress within what you consider a reasonable amount of time, find someone else. If the therapist seems to be trying to exploit you—for example, by suggesting that sexual relations with him or her would benefit you—run, do not walk, away. That person is violating ethical guidelines and undoubtedly is not someone who should be entrusted with your problems. If you find that therapy becomes the most important part of your life, or if you have become so dependent on your therapist that you feel unable to make deci-

sions for yourself, you should consider quitting. If your therapist seems to want you to stay on even though your original problems have been solved, it may be time to end the relationship.

Always remember that the therapist is someone *you* consult for professional advice and help. You do not owe the therapist anything other than frankness and a good-faith attempt to follow his or her advice. If you do not like the person or the advice, do not worry about hurting the therapist's feelings—look for someone else. Most people who consult therapists are glad that they did; they usually find experienced, empathetic people they can trust who really do help them with their problems.

Interim Summary

The Relationship between Client and Therapist

To enhance and protect the therapist–client relationship, the American Psychological Association has developed a set of ethical standards to guide the practice of therapy. Legislatures and courts have provided additional regulations.

Most of us experience a time in life when we are plagued by a persistent personal problem that makes us unhappy. In this situation, seeking professional help is usually a good idea. Counseling services, mental health centers, psychologists, and psychiatrists can generally be found in almost any city or town.

Finding a therapist who is right for you requires that you do some homework. As a rule, a good therapist will be licensed to practice therapy, will have specific training in the treatment of psychological problems and mental disorders, and will have a good reputation for being an empathetic and supportive therapist. If the therapist you choose turns out to be unsuitable for your needs, do not hesitate to look for a different therapist. The majority of people who seek therapy benefit by it and stand by their decision to seek it.

QUESTIONS TO CONSIDER

1. Suppose that you have been asked by your psychology teacher to give a class presentation on the topic of ethical issues in psychotherapy. During the presentation one of your fellow students asks you to provide some examples of the different ways in which a therapist could breach the confidentiality standard. What is your response?

2. Sometimes people shy away from seeking therapy because of the stigma they think will be attached to them if they do seek it. After reading this chapter, what suggestions do you have that might encourage these people to seek therapy?

3. Other than the fee paid to a therapist, what is the difference between a therapist and a friend? After all, doesn't a friend serve some of the same functions as a therapist—being a confidant, problem solver, and source of empathy, warmth, and support? What more does a therapist provide?

Suggestions for Further Reading

Aponte, J. F., & Wohl, J. (2000). *Psychological interventions and cultural diversity* (2nd ed.). Boston, MA: Allyn and Bacon.

This upper-division textbook addresses general issues faced by practitioners who deal with diverse ethnic populations as well as specific types of interventions used for specific problems.

Butcher, J. N., Mineka, S., & Hooley, J. M. (2007). *Abnormal psychology and modern life* (12th ed.). New York: Allyn and Bacon.

This very readable upper-division textbook provides a comprehensive introduction to the causes and treatment of psychological disorders.

Freud, S. (1952). *On dreams.* New York: W. W. Norton.

Freud wrote this short version of his famous book, *The Interpretation of Dreams*, in order to make his theory more accessible to the reading public. It provides a concise introduction to the psychoanalysis of dreams (focusing on one of Freud's own dreams) and to psychoanalytic theory more generally.

Kazdin, A. E. (2001). *Behavior modification in applied settings.* Pacific Grove, CA: Brooks/Cole.

A highly respected therapist provides an authoritative guide to the principles of behavior modification and their use across a wide range of applications.

Thorpe, G. L., & Olson, S. L. (1997). *Behavior therapy: Concepts, procedures, and applications* (2nd ed.). Boston, MA: Allyn and Bacon.

The authors describe various forms of behavior therapy drawn from classical and operant conditioning, social learning theory, and cognitive–behavioral theory, as well as considering research methods and behavior assessment. They also describe residential and community treatment applications.

Rogers, C. R. (1951). *Client-centered therapy.* New York: Houghton Mifflin.

The founder of the humanistic movement in psychology describes the major features of his renowned therapy and shares samples of its application.

Corsini, R., & Wedding, D. (2004). *Case studies in psychotherapy* (4th ed.). Belmont, CA: Wadsworth/Thomson.

This collection of case studies ranges across cognitive–behavioral, humanistic, and psychoanalytic therapies. Each case study focuses on the client's problem and the treatment approach that was used.

Key Terms

antianxiety drugs (p. 606)

antidepressant drugs (p. 605)

antimanic/mood-stabilizing drugs (p. 605)

antipsychotic drugs (p. 605)

aversion therapy (p. 592)

behavior modification (p. 592)

cingulotomy (p. 607)

client-centered therapy (p. 588)

cognitive–behavioral therapy (p. 596)

cognitive restructuring (p. 595)

community psychology (p. 601)

countertransference (p. 587)

covert sensitization (p. 595)

deinstitutionalization (p. 601)

eclectic approach (p. 585)

electroconvulsive therapy (ECT) (p. 606)

free association (p. 587)

Gestalt therapy (p. 589)

group psychotherapy (p. 599)

humanistic therapy (p. 588)

implosion therapy (p. 592)

incongruence (p. 588)

indigenous healing (p. 602)

meta-analysis (p. 609)

pharmacotherapy (p. 604)

preventive psychology (p. 602)

psychoanalysis (p. 586)

psychosurgery (p. 607)

rational–emotive therapy (p. 595)

resistance (p. 587)

structural family therapy (p. 600)

systematic desensitization (p. 591)

tardive dyskinesia (p. 605)

token economy (p. 592)

transference (p. 587)

trephining (p. 583)

unconditional positive regard (p. 588)

Glossary

absolute threshold The minimum intensity of a stimulus that can be detected.

accommodation The process of altering the thickness of the lens in order to focus images of near or distant objects on the retina. Also, in Piaget's theory of cognitive development, the process by which existing schemas are modified or changed by new experiences.

acetylcholine (ACh) A neurotransmitter found in the brain, spinal cord, and parts of the peripheral nervous system; responsible for muscular contraction.

achromatopsia The inability to discriminate colors; caused by damage to the visual association cortex.

acquisition An increase in the environmental guidance of behavior as the result of either a classical or an operant conditioning procedure.

action potential A brief electrochemical event that is carried by an axon from the soma of the neuron to its terminal buttons; causes the release of a neurotransmitter.

activational effect Effect of a hormone on a physiological system after the system has already developed; can affect the brain and other structures. An example is facilitation of sexual arousal and performance by sex hormones.

activation–synthesis theory A physiological theory of dreaming that explains dreaming as the creation by the brain of a story or experience. The story is synthesized in response to activation of the cortex by mechanisms in the pons and is the brain's interpretation of that activity.

actor–observer effect Our tendency to attribute our own behavior to situational factors but others' behavior to dispositional factors.

actual developmental level In Vygotsky's theory, the stage of cognitive development reached by a child, as demonstrated by the child's ability to solve problems on his or her own.

actuarial judgments Diagnoses of mental disorders or predictions of future behavior based on statistical analyses of outcome data.

adaptive significance The degree of effectiveness of behavior in adjusting to environmental conditions.

aerobic exercise Physical activity that expends considerable energy, increases blood flow and respiration, and thereby stimulates and strengthens the heart and lungs and increases the body's efficient use of oxygen.

affix A sound or group of letters that is added to the beginning of a word (prefix) or to its end (suffix) to alter its grammatical function.

agoraphobia A mental disorder characterized by fear of and avoidance of being in places where escape may be difficult; this disorder often is accompanied by panic attacks.

agrammatism A language disturbance; difficulty in the production and comprehension of grammatical features, such as proper use of function words, word endings, and word order. Often seen in cases of Broca's aphasia.

alcoholism An addiction to ethanol, the psychoactive agent in alcoholic beverages.

algorithm A procedure that consists of a series of steps that, if followed, will solve a specific type of problem.

alleles Alternative forms of the same gene for a trait.

all-or-none law Principle stating that once an action potential is triggered in an axon, it is propagated, without getting smaller, to the end of the axon.

alpha activity Rhythmical, medium-frequency electroencephalogram activity, usually indicating a state of quiet relaxation.

altruism Actions that benefit another person at a cost to the individual who executes the action.

Alzheimer's disease A fatal degenerative disease in which neurons of the brain progressively die, causing loss of memory and deterioration of other cognitive processes.

amygdala A part of the limbic system of the brain located deep in the temporal lobe; damage causes changes in emotional and aggressive behavior.

anal stage The second of Freud's psychosexual stages, during which the primary erogenous zone is the anus because of the pleasure derived from vacating a full bowel.

analytic intelligence In Sternberg's triarchic theory, the cognitive mechanisms people use to plan and execute tasks; includes metacomponents, performance components, and knowledge acquisition components.

analytic processing system The basis of deliberate, abstract, and higher order reasoning.

anandamide The most important endogenous cannabinoid.

anatomical coding A means by which the nervous system represents information; different sensory modalities are coded by the activity of different neurons whose signals originate in the sense organs of the body.

androgens The primary class of sex hormones in males. The most important androgen is testosterone.

animism The belief that all animals and all moving objects possess spirits providing their motive force.

anorexia nervosa Eating disorder characterized by severe weight loss due to reduced food intake, sometimes to the point of starvation.

anterograde amnesia A disorder caused by brain damage that disrupts a person's ability to form new long-term memories of events that occur after the time of the brain damage.

antianxiety drugs Drugs used to treat anxiety-related disorders, including benzodiazepines as well as some tricyclic antidepressants.

antibodies Proteins in the immune system that recognize antigens and help kill invading microorganisms.

anticipatory anxiety A fear of having a panic attack; may lead to the development of a phobia.

antidepressant drugs Drugs used to treat depression, including tricyclics, monoamine oxidase inhibitors, and SSRIs.

antigens The unique proteins found on the surface of bacteria; these proteins enable the immune system to recognize the bacteria as foreign substances.

antimanic mood-stabilizing drugs Drugs used to treat the bipolar disorders, such as lithium carbonate.

antipsychotic drugs Drugs used to treat schizophrenic disorders.

antisocial personality disorder A disorder characterized by a failure to conform to standards of decency; repeated lying and stealing; a failure to sustain lasting, loving relationships; low tolerance of boredom; and a complete lack of guilt.

anxiety A sense of apprehension or doom that is accompanied by many physiological reactions, such as accelerated heart rate, sweaty palms, and tightness in the stomach.

appeasement gesture Stereotyped gesture made by a submissive animal in response to a threat gesture by a dominant animal; tends to avert an attack.

archetypes Universal thought forms and patterns that Jung believed resided in the collective unconscious.

artificial intelligence A field of cognitive science in which researchers design computer programs to simulate human cognitive abilities; this endeavor may help cognitive psychologists understand the mechanisms that underlie these abilities.

artificial selection A procedure in which humans deliberately breed animals to produce offspring that possess specified characteristics.

assimilation In Piaget's theory, the process by which new information about the world is incorporated into existing schemas.

attachment A social and emotional bond between infant and caregiver that spans both time and space.

attitude An evaluation of a person, place, or thing.

attribution The process by which people infer the causes of their own and other people's behavior.

auditory hair cell The sensory neuron of the auditory system; located on the basilar membrane.

autoimmune diseases Diseases such as rheumatoid arthritis, diabetes, lupus, and multiple sclerosis, in which the immune system attacks and destroys some of the body's own tissue.

automatic processing Forming memories of events and experiences with little or no attention or effort.

autonomic nervous system (ANS) The portion of the peripheral nervous system that controls the functions of the glands and internal organs.

autosomes The 22 pairs of chromosomes that are not sex chromosomes.

availability heuristic A general rule for judging the likelihood or importance of an event by the ease with which examples of that event are recalled.

aversion therapy A form of behavior therapy in which the client is trained to respond negatively to an originally attractive stimulus that has been paired with an aversive stimulus.

avoidant attachment As observed in the Strange Situation test, a kind of attachment in which infants avoid or ignore their mothers and often do not cuddle when held.

axon A long, thin part of a neuron attached to the soma; divides into a few or many branches, ending in terminal buttons.

B lymphocytes White blood cells that develop in bone marrow and release immunoglobulins to defend the body against antigens.

Balint's syndrome A syndrome caused by bilateral damage to the parietal cortex; includes difficulty in perceiving the location of objects and in reaching for objects under visual guidance.

barbiturate A drug that causes sedation; one of several derivatives of barbituric acid.

basal ganglia Groups of neurons located in the depths of the cerebral hemispheres, adjacent to the thalamus; involved in the control of movement.

base-rate fallacy The failure to consider the actual statistical likelihood that a person, place, or thing is a member of a particular category.

basic orientations Horney's sets of personality characteristics that correspond to the strategies of moving toward others, moving against others, and moving away from others.

basic rest–activity cycle (BRAC) A 90-minute cycle (in humans) of waxing and waning alertness controlled by a biological clock in the pons; during sleep, the BRAC controls cycles of REM sleep and slow-wave sleep.

basic-level concept A concept that makes essential distinctions at an everyday level.

basilar membrane One of two membranes that divide the cochlea of the inner ear into three compartments. The auditory receptor cells based in the membrane respond to its movements.

behavior analysis The branch of psychology that studies the effect of the environment on behavior—primarily, the effects of the consequences of behavior on the behavior themselves.

behavior genetics The branch of psychology that studies the role of genetics in behavior.

behavior modification Behavior therapy based on the principles of operant conditioning.

behavioral discrepancy A change in behavior evoked by an eliciting stimulus.

behaviorism A movement in psychology that asserts that the only proper subject matter for scientific study in psychology is observable behavior.

belief in a just world The belief that people get what they deserve in life; a form of the fundamental attribution error.

benzodiazepine A class of drug having anxiolytic ("tranquilizing") effects, such as Valium (diazepam).

beta activity The irregular, high-frequency electroencephalogram activity, usually indicating a state of alertness or arousal.

binding problem The question of how the brain assembles or binds multiple sources of input into a unified perception.

Binet-Simon Scale An intelligence test developed by Binet and Simon in 1905; the precursor of the Stanford-Binet Scale.

biological evolution Changes that take place in the genetic and physical characteristics of a population or group of organisms over time.

bipedalism The ability to move about the environment upright on two legs.

bipolar cell A neuron in the retina that receives information from photoreceptors and passes it on to the ganglion cells.

bipolar I disorder A mood disorder in which alternating states of depression and mania are separated by periods of relatively normal affect.

bipolar II disorder A mood disorder; marked by major depressive episodes that are accompanied by less severe mania (hypomanic episodes).

black widow spider venom A drug that stimulates the release of the neurotransmitter acetylcholine by terminal buttons.

blindsight The ability of a person who cannot perceive objects in a part of his or her visual field to reach for them accurately while remaining unaware of seeing them.

blocking design Attenuation of the acquisition of control by a stimulus that has a favorable temporal relation to a reinforcer because it is accompanied by a second stimulus that already evoked the response.

blood-brain barrier A barrier between the blood and the brain produced by the cells in the walls of the brain's capillaries; prevents some substances from passing from the blood into the brain.

bottom-up processing Perception based on successive analyses of the details of the stimuli that are present.

botulinum toxin A drug that prevents the release of the neurotransmitter acetylcholine by terminal buttons.

brain lesion Damage to a particular region of the brain.

brain stem The "stem" of the brain, including the medulla, pons, and midbrain.

brightness A perceptual dimension of color, most closely related to the intensity of radiant energy emitted by a visual stimulus.

brightness constancy Our tendency to perceive objects as having constant brightness even when we observe them under varying levels of illumination.

Broca's aphasia Severe difficulty in articulating words, especially function words, caused by brain damage that includes Broca's area, a region of the left (speech-dominated) frontal cortex.

bulimia nervosa Eating disorder characterized by gorging binges followed by self-induced vomiting or use of laxatives; often accompanied by feelings of guilt and depression.

bystander intervention The intervention of a person in a situation that appears to require his or her aid.

cancer Disease in which malignant, uncontrolled cell growth destroys surrounding tissue.

Cannon-Bard theory Theory of emotion proposing that feelings of emotion, as well as behavioral and physiological responses, are directly elicited by the environment.

case study A detailed description of an individual's behavior during the course of clinical treatment or diagnosis.

catatonic schizophrenia A type of schizophrenia characterized primarily by motor disturbances, including catatonic postures and waxy flexibility.

causal event An event that causes another event to occur.

central fissure The fissure that separates the frontal lobe from the parietal lobe.

central nervous system The brain and the spinal cord.

central traits Personality traits that organize and influence our impressions of a person more than do other traits.

cerebellum A pair of hemispheres resembling the cerebral hemispheres but much smaller and lying beneath and in back of them; controls posture and movements, especially rapid ones.

cerebral cortex The outer layer of the cerebral hemispheres of the brain, approximately 3 mm thick.

cerebral hemispheres The largest part of the brain; the two halves of the cerebrum, covered by the cerebral cortex and containing parts of the brain that evolved most recently.

cerebral ventricle One of the hollow spaces within the brain, filled with cerebrospinal fluid.

cerebrospinal fluid (CSF) The liquid in which the brain and spinal cord float; provides a shock-absorbing cushion.

change blindness Failure to detect a change when vision is interrupted by a saccade or an artificially produced obstruction.

chemosense One of the two sense modalities (gustation and olfaction) that detect the presence of particular molecules in the environment.

child-directed speech The speech of an adult directed toward a child; differs in several ways from adult-directed speech and tends to facilitate the learning of language by children.

chromosomal aberration The rearrangement of genes within chromosomes or a change in the total number of chromosomes.

chromosomes Paired rodlike structures in the nuclei of living cells; contain genes.

chunking A process by which information is simplified by rules, which make it easily remembered once the rules are learned. For example, the string of letters NBCCBSNPR is easier to remember if a person learns the rule that organizes them into smaller "chunks": NBC, CBS, and NPR.

cilium A hairlike appendage of a cell; involved in transducing the mechanical energy of sound waves. Cilia are found on the sensory receptors in the auditory and vestibular systems.

cingulotomy The surgical destruction of the cingulum bundle, a band of nerve fibers that connects the prefrontal cortex with the limbic system; helps to reduce intense anxiety and the symptoms of obsessive-compulsive disorder.

circadian rhythm A daily rhythmical change in behaviors or physiological processes.

classical procedure A procedure developed by Pavlov whereby a neutral stimulus (CS) precedes an eliciting stimulus (US) with the result that the CS comes to evoke a learned response (CR) that usually resembles the elicited response (UR).

client-centered therapy A form of psychotherapy in which the client decides what to talk about without strong direction or judgment from the therapist.

clinical judgments Diagnoses of mental disorders or predictions of future behavior based largely on experts' knowledge of symptoms and past clinical experience.

clinical neuropsychologist A psychologist who specializes in the identification and treatment of the behavioral consequences of nervous system disorders and injuries.

clinical observation Observation of the behavior of people who are undergoing diagnosis or treatment.

clinical psychology The branch of psychology devoted to the investigation and treatment of abnormal behavior and mental disorders.

cochlea A snail-shaped chamber set in bone in the inner ear, where the auditory receptor cells are found and transduction takes place.

cocktail-party phenomenon Our ability to follow a meaningful conversation while other conversations are going on around us.

cognitive appraisal Our perception of a stressful situation; occurs in two stages, primary appraisal and secondary appraisal.

cognitive–behavioral therapy A form of psychotherapy that focuses on altering clients' perceptions, thoughts, feelings, and beliefs as well as environments to produce desired changes.

cognitive dissonance theory The theory that changes in attitude can be motivated by an unpleasant state of tension caused by a disparity between our attitudes and our behavior.

cognitive neuroscience The branch of psychology that attempts to understand cognitive psychological functions by studying the brain mechanisms that are responsible for them.

cognitive psychology The branch of psychology that studies complex behavior and mental processes such as perception, attention, learning and memory, verbal behavior, concept formation, and problem solving.

cognitive reappraisal Any coping strategy in which we alter our perception of the threat posed by a stressor in order to reduce stress. Also called cognitive restructuring.

cognitive restructuring A therapeutic process that seeks to help clients replace maladaptive thoughts with more constructive ways of thinking.

collective unconscious According to Jung, the shared unconscious memories and ideas inherited from our ancestors over the course of human evolution.

color mixing The perception of a mixture of two or more lights of different wavelengths seen together as light of an intermediate wavelength.

community psychologist A psychologist who works for the well being of individuals in the social system, attempting to improve the system rather than treating people as problems.

community psychology A form of treatment and education whose goal is to address psychological problems through assessment and intervention in the sociocultural contexts in which problems develop.

companionate love Love that is characterized by a deep, enduring affection and caring for another person, accompanied by a strong desire to maintain the relationship.

comparative psychology The branch of psychology that studies the behavior of a variety of organisms in an attempt to understand the adaptive and functional significance of behaviors and their relation to evolution.

competition A struggle for resources (food, mates, territory) with others who share the same environment (ecological niche).

compliance Engaging in a particular behavior at another person's request.

compulsion An irresistible impulse to repeat some action over and over even though it serves no useful purpose.

concept A category of objects or events that share certain attributes.

concordance research Research that studies the degree of similarity of traits between twins. Twins are said to be concordant for a trait if they express the same trait. They are said to be discordant if they express different traits.

concurrent schedule Reinforcement schedules in which reinforcers are available for responding on two or more alternative operants.

conditioned reinforcer A stimulus that functions as a reinforcing stimulus because it has been paired with an unconditioned eliciting stimulus; often referred to as a *secondary reinforcer*

conditioned emotional response (CER) A decrease in an operant response when a stimulus is presented that has been paired with an aversive eliciting stimulus. Also known as *conditioned suppression.*

conditioned response (CR) In classical conditioning, the response evoked by the CS after the institution of a classical-conditioning procedure.

conditioned stimulus (CS) In classical conditioning, a stimulus that, because of its repeated occurrence prior to an unconditioned stimulus, evokes a conditional response (CR).

conditioning Change in the environmental guidance of behavior produced by either a classical or an operant procedure; a learned change in behavior.

conditions of worth Conditions that others place on us for receiving their positive regard.

conduction aphasia An inability to remember words that are heard, although they usually can be understood and responded to appropriately. This disability is caused by damage to Wernicke's and Broca's areas.

cone A photoreceptor that is responsible for acute daytime vision and for color perception.

confidentiality Privacy of participants and nondisclosure of their participation in a research project.

confirmation bias A tendency to seek evidence that might confirm a hypothesis rather than evidence that might disconfirm it.

conformity Adoption of the attitudes and behaviors that characterize a particular group of people.

confounding of variables Inadvertent simultaneous manipulation of more than one variable. The results of an experiment in which variables are confounded permit no valid conclusions about cause and effect.

conjugate movement The cooperative movement of the eyes, which ensures that the image of an object falls on identical portions of both retinas.

conscience The internalization of the rules and restrictions of society; it determines which behaviors are permissible and punishes wrongdoing with feelings of guilt.

consciousness The awareness of complex mental processes such as perception, thinking, and remembering.

consensus The extent to which a person's behavior is what most people would do; can be a basis for others' attributions about the person's motives.

conservation The fact that specific properties of objects (for example, volume, mass, length, or number) remain the same despite apparent changes in the shape or arrangement of those objects.

consistency The extent to which a person generally behaves in the same way toward another person, an event, or a stimulus; can be the basis for others' attributions about the person's motives.

consolidation The process by which information in short-term memory is transferred to long-term memory, presumably because of physical changes that occur in neurons in the brain.

consumer psychologist A psychologist who helps organizations that manufacture products or that buy products or services.

content word A noun, verb, adjective, or adverb that conveys meaning.

contextual discrimination A discrimination in which the stimulus that guides responding depends on the value of another stimulus, the stimulus context; this creates a four-term contingency of context–discriminative stimulus–response–reinforcer.

contingency A sequential temporal relation between two events; for example, between a stimulus and a reinforcer in a classical procedure or between a response and a reinforcer in an operant procedure. A contingency is merely a temporal relation, but reliable temporal relations are often causal relations.

contralateral Residing in the side of the body opposite the reference point.

control group A comparison group used in an experiment, the members of which are exposed to the naturally occurring or zero value of the independent variable.

conventional level Kohlberg's second level of moral development, in which people realize that a society has instituted moral rules to maintain order and to serve the best interests of members of the society.

convergence In depth perception, the result of conjugate eye movements whereby the fixation point for each eye is identical; feedback from these movements provides information about the distance of visual objects from the viewer.

conversion disorder A somatoform disorder involving the actual loss of bodily function, such as blindness, paralysis, and numbness, due to excessive anxiety.

coping strategy A plan of action that a person follows to reduce the experience of stress, either in anticipation of encountering a stressor or in response to its occurrence.

cornea The transparent tissue covering the front of the eye.

coronary heart disease (CHD) The narrowing of blood vessels that supply oxygen and nutrients to the heart.

corpus callosum A large bundle of axons ("white matter") that connects the cortex of the two cerebral hemispheres.

correctional mechanism Mechanism that restores the system variable to the set point in a regulatory process.

correlation coefficient A measurement of the degree to which two variables are related.

correlational study The examination of relations between two or more measurements of behav-

ior or other characteristics of people or other animals.

counterbalancing Systematically varying of conditions in an experiment, such as the order of presentation of stimuli, so that different participants encounter the conditions in different orders; prevents confounding of independent variables with time-dependent processes such as habituation or fatigue.

countertransference Process in which a psychoanalyst projects his or her emotions onto a client.

covert sensitization A form of behavior therapy in which a client imagines the aversive consequences of his or her inappropriate behavior.

cranial nerve A bundle of nerve fibers attached to the base of the brain; conveys sensory information from the face and head and carries messages to muscles and glands.

creative intelligence In Sternberg's triarchic theory, the ability to deal effectively with novel situations and to solve problems automatically that have been encountered previously.

criterion An independent measure of the variable a test is designed to measure.

critical period A specific time in development during which certain experiences must occur for normal development to take place.

cross-cultural psychology The branch of psychology that studies the effects of culture on behavior.

cross-sectional study. A study of development in which individuals of different ages are compared at the same time.

crystallized intelligence According to Cattell, intellectual abilities that have developed through exposure to information-rich contexts, especially schools; expressed in general knowledge and skills.

CT scanner A device that uses a special X-ray machine and a computer to produce images of the brain that appear as slices taken parallel to the top of the skull.

cultural evolution The transmission over generations of cultural practices in response to environmental changes.

culture The sum of socially transmitted knowledge, customs, and behavior patterns common to a particular group of people.

culture-bound syndromes Highly unusual mental disorders that are similar to nonpsychotic mental disorders (such as phobias) but are specific to only one or a few cultures.

cumulative record Graphical presentation of data in which every response moves the curve upward as time passes.

curare A drug that binds with and blocks acetylcholine receptors, preventing this neurotransmitter from exerting its effects.

dark adaptation The process by which the eye becomes capable of distinguishing dimly illuminated objects after going from bright light to a dark setting.

dead reckoning Navigation by means of internal stimuli that are used to estimate position.

debriefing Full disclosure to research participants of the nature and purpose of a research project after its completion.

deductive reasoning The mental process by which people arrive at specific conclusions from general principles or rules.

deep processing Analysis of the complex characteristics of a stimulus, such as its meaning or its relationship to other stimuli.

deep structure The essential meaning of a sentence, without regard to the grammatical features (surface structure) of the sentence that are needed to express it in words.

defense mechanisms Mental systems that become active whenever unconscious instinctual drives of the id come into conflict with internalized prohibitions of the superego.

deferred imitation In Piaget's theory, a child's ability to imitate the actions he or she has observed others perform. Piaget believed deferred imitation results from the child's increasing ability to form mental representations of behavior performed by others.

deinstitutionalization The process of returning previously institutionalized patients to their communities for treatment of psychological problems and mental disorders.

delta activity Rhythmical electroencephalogram activity with a frequency of less than 3.5 Hz, indicating deep (slow-wave) sleep.

dendrite A treelike part of a neuron on which other neurons form synapses.

dendritic spine A small budlike protuberance on the surface of a neuron's dendrite.

denial A defense mechanism in which a person negates or dismisses the reality of an unpleasant truth.

dependent variable The variable measured in an experiment and hypothesized to be affected by the independent variable.

deprivation Reduction of an organism's contact with a stimulus below the level that the organism would choose; for example, reduced contact with food in food deprivation.

descriptive statistics Mathematical procedures for organizing collections of data.

detector Mechanism that signals when the system variable deviates from its set point in a regulatory process.

deuteranopia A form of hereditary anomalous color vision caused by defective "green" cones in the retina.

developmental psychology The branch of psychology that studies the changes in behavioral, perceptual, and cognitive capacities of organisms as a function of age and experience.

deviation IQ A procedure for computing the IQ; compares a child's score with those received by other children of the same chronological age.

Diagnostic and Statistical Manual of Mental Disorders, Fourth Edition, Text Revision A widely used manual for classifying psychological disorders; known as the DSM-IV-TR.

diathesis–stress model A causal account of mental disorders suggesting that these disorders develop when a person possesses a predisposition for a disorder and encounters stressors that exceed his or her abilities to cope with them.

dichotic listening A task that requires a person to listen to one of two different messages being presented simultaneously, one to each ear, through headphones.

difference threshold An alternative name for just-noticeable difference (jnd).

differential conditioning procedure Any conditioning procedure in which reinforcers change when the environment changes. Differential conditioning can occur with either a classical or an operant procedure.

diffusion of responsibility A factor in the failure of bystander intervention, stating the fact that when several bystanders are present, no one person assumes responsibility for helping.

direct dyslexia A reading disorder caused by brain damage in which people can read words aloud without understanding them.

discrimination Differential treatment of people based on their membership in a particular group.

discriminative stimulus In operant conditioning, the stimulus in whose presence the operant is reinforced.

disorganized schizophrenia A type of schizophrenia characterized primarily by disturbances of thought and a flattened or silly affect.

disoriented attachment As observed in the Strange Situation test, a kind of attachment in which infants behave in confused and contradictory ways toward their mothers.

display rule Culturally determined rule that prescribes modes of emotional expression and the environmental conditions under which particular emotions are expressed.

dispositional factors An individual's traits, needs, and intentions, which can affect his or her behavior.

dissociative amnesia A dissociative disorder characterized by the inability to remember important events or personal information.

dissociative disorders A class of disorders in which anxiety is reduced by a sudden disruption in consciousness, which in turn produces changes in memory or in the person's sense of identity.

dissociative fugue Amnesia with no apparent physiological cause, often accompanied by adoption of a new identity and relocation to a new community.

dissociative identity disorder A rare dissociative disorder in which two or more distinct personalities exist within the same person; each personality dominates in turn. (Formerly known as *multiple personality disorder*.)

distinctive features Physical characteristics of an object that help distinguish it from other objects.

distinctiveness The extent to which a person behaves differently toward different people, events, or other stimuli; can be the basis for others' attributions about the person's motives.

divided attention The process by which we distribute awareness among different stimuli or tasks so that we can respond to them or perform them simultaneously.

DNA (deoxyribonucleic acid) Genetic material whose molecules resemble twisted ladders. Strands of sugar and phosphates are connected by rungs consisting of nucleotide molecules of adenine, thymine, guanine, and cytosine.

doctrine of specific nerve energies Johannes Müller's observation that different nerve fibers convey specific information from one part of the body to the brain or from the brain to one part of the body.

dominant gene An allele that causes a trait to be exhibited even when only that one allele is present; that is, even in heterozygous cells.

dopamine (DA) A monoamine neurotransmitter involved in control of brain mechanisms of movement and reinforcement; a neuromodulator that is liberated widely in the frontal lobes and midbrain; plays an important role in learning.

dopamine hypothesis The hypothesis that the positive symptoms of schizophrenia are caused by overactivity of synapses in the brain that use dopamine.

dorsal stream The flow of information from the primary visual cortex to the visual association area in the parietal lobe; used to form the perception of an object's location in three-dimensional space (the "where" system).

double bind The conflict caused for a child when he or she is given inconsistent messages or cues from a parent.

double-blind study An experiment in which neither the participants nor the researchers know the value of the independent variable.

Down syndrome A genetic disorder caused by a chromosomal aberration that results from an extra 21st chromosome. People having Down syndrome show impairments in physical, psychomotor, and cognitive development.

drive A hypothetical emotional state caused by a physiological need; motivates an organism's behavior.

drive-reduction theory Hypothesis that responses are reinforced if they reduce a drive produced by a physiological need.

dualism The philosophical belief that reality consists of mind and matter.

echoic memory A form of sensory memory for sounds that have just been perceived.

eclectic approach An approach to therapy in which the therapist uses whatever method he or she feels will work best for a particular client at a particular time.

effortful processing Practicing or rehearsing information through either shallow or deep processing.

ego The general manager of personality, making decisions balancing the pleasures that will be pursued at the id's demand against the person's safety requirements and the moral dictates of the superego.

egocentrism Self-centeredness; Piaget proposes that preoperational children can see the world only from their own perspective.

ego-ideal The internalization of what a person would like to be—his or her goals and ambitions.

elaboration likelihood model A model that explains the effectiveness of persuasive messages in terms of two routes to persuasion. The central route requires a person to think critically about an argument, whereas the peripheral route entails merely the association of the argument with something positive.

elaborative rehearsal Processing information on a meaningful level, such as forming associations, attending to the meaning of the material, thinking about it, and so on.

electroconvulsive therapy (ECT) Treatment for severe depression that involves passing small amounts of electric current through the brain to produce seizures.

electroencephalogram (EEG) A record of electrical activity in the brain, obtained by placing electrodes on the scalp.

elevation A monocular cue for depth perception; objects nearer the horizon are seen as farther from the viewer.

embryonic stage The second stage of prenatal development, beginning two weeks and ending about eight weeks after conception, during which the heart begins to beat, the brain starts to function, and most of the major body structures begin to form.

emotion Relatively brief experience and display of a feeling in response to environmental events with motivational significance or in response to memories of such events.

emotional stability The tendency to be relaxed and at peace with oneself.

emotion-focused coping Any coping behavior that aims to reduce stress by changing our own emotional reaction to a stressor.

empiricism The philosophical view that all knowledge is obtained through the senses.

encephalization Increases in brain size.

encoding The process by which sensory information is converted into a form that can be used by the brain's memory system.

encoding specificity The principle that how we encode information determines our ability to retrieve it later.

endocrine gland A gland that secretes a hormone.

endogenous cannabinoid A neuromodulator whose action is mimicked by THC and other drugs present in marijuana.

endogenous opioid A neuromodulator whose action is mimicked by a natural or synthetic opiate such as opium, morphine, or heroin.

engineering psychologist A psychologist who studies the ways that people and machines work together and helps design machines that are safer and easier to operate.

enzymes Proteins that regulate bodily (somatic) cells and the processes that occur within those cells.

episodic memory A type of long-term memory that serves as a record of life experiences.

escape or withdrawal response A response that terminates or reduces a learner's contact with an aversive stimulus; the aversive stimulus may be either conditioned or unconditioned.

estrous cycle Ovulatory cycle in mammals other than primates; the sequence of physical and hormonal changes that accompany the ripening and disintegration of ova.

ethnocentrism The idea that our own cultural, racial, national, or religious group is superior to or more deserving than others.

evolutionary psychology The branch of psychology that explains behavior in terms of adaptive advantages that specific behaviors provided during the evolution of a species. Evolutionary psychologists use natural selection as a guiding principle.

exemplar A memory of a particular example of an object or an event that is used as the basis for a natural concept.

expectancy The belief that a certain consequence will follow a certain action.

experiential processing system The basis of rapid, mostly unconscious, and heuristic reasoning.

experiment A study in which the researcher changes the value of an independent variable and observes whether this manipulation affects the value of a dependent variable. Only experiments can confirm the existence of cause-and-effect relations among variables.

experimental ablation The removal or destruction of a portion of the brain of an experimental animal for the purpose of studying the functions of that region.

experimental group The group of participants in an experiment that is exposed to a particular value of the independent variable, which has been manipulated by the researcher.

explicit memory Memory that can be described verbally and of which a person is therefore aware.

expressed emotion Expressions of criticism and hostility and emotional overinvolvement by family members toward a person with schizophrenia.

extinction A decrease in the environmental guidance of learned behavior when the behavior is no longer followed by a reinforcer.

extinction-induced aggression Aggression toward another organism when responding is extinguished.

extroversion The tendency to seek the company of other people, to engage in conversation and other social behaviors with them, and to be spontaneous.

factor analysis A statistical procedure that identifies the factors that groups of data, such as test scores, have in common.

false consensus The mistaken belief that our own attitude on a topic is representative of a general consensus.

fetal alcohol syndrome A disorder that adversely affects an offspring's brain development and is caused by the mother's alcohol intake during pregnancy.

fetal stage The third and final stage of prenatal development, which lasts for about seven months, beginning with the appearance of bone tissue and ending with birth.

fight-or-flight response Physiological reactions that help ready us to fight or to flee a dangerous situation.

figure A visual stimulus that is perceived as an object.

five-factor model A theory stating that personality is composed of five primary dimensions: neuroticism, extroversion, openness, agreeableness, and conscientiousness. This theory was developed using factor analyses of ratings of the words people use to describe personality characteristics.

fixation A brief interval between saccadic eye movements during which the eye does not move; the brain accesses visual information during this time. Also, in Freudian theory, the continued attachment of psychic energy to an erogenous zone due to incomplete passage through one of the psychosexual stages.

flashbulb memories Memories established by events that are highly surprising and personally of consequence.

fluid intelligence According to Cattell, intellectual abilities that operate in relatively culture-free informational contexts and involve the detection of relationships or patterns, for example.

forensic psychologist A psychologist who studies human behavior as it may relate to the legal system and to matters involving criminal justice.

formal concept A category of objects or events defined by a list of common essential characteristics, much as in a dictionary definition.

fovea A small pit near the center of the retina containing densely packed cones; responsible for the most acute and detailed vision.

free association A method of Freudian analysis in which an individual is asked to relax, clear his or her mind of current thoughts, and then report all thoughts, images, perceptions, and feelings that come to mind, without censoring possibly embarrassing or socially unacceptable thoughts or ideas.

free nerve ending A dendrite of somatosensory neurons.

frontal lobe The front portion of the cerebral cortex, including Broca's speech area and the motor cortex; damage impairs movement, planning, and flexibility in behavioral strategies.

frustration An emotional response produced when a formerly reinforced response is extinguished.

function word A preposition, article, or other word that conveys little of the meaning of a sentence but is important in specifying its grammatical structure.

functional MRI (fMRI) A modification of the MRI procedure that permits the measurement of regional metabolism in the brain.

functionalism An approach to understanding species' behaviors and other processes in terms of their biological significance; this approach stresses the usefulness of such processes with respect to survival and reproductive success.

fundamental attribution error Our tendency to overestimate the significance of dispositional factors and to underestimate the significance of situational factors in explaining other people's behavior.

fundamental frequency The lowest, and usually most intense, frequency of a complex sound; most often perceived as the sound's basic pitch.

g factor According to Spearman, a factor that is common to performance on all intellectual tasks; includes apprehension of experience, eduction of relations, and eduction of correlates.

GABA Gamma-amino butyric acid, the most important inhibitory neurotransmitter in the brain.

ganglion cell A neuron in the retina that receives information from photoreceptors by means of bipolar cells and whose axon joins with those from other ganglion cells to form the optic nerve.

gender identity A person's private sense of being male or female.

gender role Cultural expectations about the ways in which a male or a female should think and behave.

gender stereotypes Beliefs about differences in the behaviors, abilities, and personality traits of males and females.

general adaptation syndrome The model proposed by Selye to describe the body's adaptation to chronic exposure to severe stressors. The body passes through a sequence of three physiological stages: alarm, resistance, and exhaustion.

generalize To extend the results obtained from a sample to the population from which the sample was taken.

genes Small units of DNA that synthesize structural proteins and proteins that regulate the synthesis of other proteins.

genetic engineering The new scientific discipline that manipulates genetic sequences to alter an organism's genome.

genetic marker A biochemically detectable change produced in a genetically inactive portion of a chromosome to serve as a marker for genes that are nearby on the chromosome.

genetics The study of the hereditary structures of organisms (genes) and how they influence physical and behavioral characteristics.

genital stage The final of Freud's psychosexual stages (from puberty through adolescence). During this stage the adolescent develops adult sexual desires.

genome The total set of genetic material of an organism.

genotype The genetic makeup of an organism.

germ cells The reproductive cells, a collective term for the sperm and ovum taken together.

Gestalt psychology A movement in psychology that emphasized that cognitive processes could be understood by studying their organization, not their elements.

Gestalt therapy A form of therapy that emphasizes the unity of mind and body by teaching the client to "get in touch" with unconscious bodily sensations and emotions.

glia Cells of the central nervous system that provide support for neurons and supply them with some essential chemicals.

glucocorticoid A hormone, such as cortisol, that influences the metabolism of glucose, the main energy source of the body.

glucostatic hypothesis The hypothesis that hunger is caused by a low level of glucose in the blood; glucose levels are assumed to be monitored by specialized sensory neurons called glucostats.

glutamate The most important excitatory neurotransmitter in the brain and spinal cord.

glycogen Insoluble carbohydrate synthesized from glucose and stored in the liver; can be converted back to glucose.

gray matter The portions of the central nervous system that are abundant in cell bodies of neurons rather than axons. The color appears gray relative to white matter.

ground A visual stimulus that is perceived as a background against which objects are seen.

group Two or more individuals who generally have common interests and goals.

group polarization The tendency for the initial position of a group to become more extreme during the discussion preceding a decision.

group psychotherapy Therapy in which two or more clients meet simultaneously with a therapist, discussing problems within a supportive and constructive environment.

groupthink Group members' tendency to avoid dissent in the attempt to achieve consensus in the course of decision making.

gustation The sense of taste.

habituation A decrease in an organism responding to a stimulus when that stimulus is repeatedly presented without an important consequence.

hallucination A perceptual experience that occurs in the absence of external stimulation of the corresponding sensory organ; often accompanies schizophrenia.

harmonic A component of a complex tone; one of a series of tones whose frequencies are multiples of the fundamental frequency. In music theory, also known as an overtone.

haze A monocular cue for depth perception; objects that are less distinct in their outline and texture are perceived as farther from the viewer.

health psychologist A psychologist who works to promote behavior and lifestyles that improve and maintain health and prevent illness.

health psychology The branch of psychology involved in the promotion and maintenance of sound health practices.

heredity The sum of the traits and tendencies an organism inherits from its parents and their ancestors.

heritability A statistical measure of the degree to which the variability of a particular trait in a population results from the genetic variability within the population.

hertz (Hz) The primary measure of the frequency of vibration of sound waves; cycles per second.

heuristic A general rule that guides decision making.

hippocampus A part of the limbic system of the brain, located in the temporal lobe; plays important roles in episodic memory and spatial memory.

homeostasis The process by which important physiological characteristics (such as body temperature and blood pressure) are regulated so that they remain at their optimum level.

hormone A chemical substance secreted by an endocrine gland that has physiological effects on target cells in other organs.

hue A perceptual dimension of color, most closely related to the wavelength of a pure light.

humanistic approach An approach to the study of personality that emphasizes the positive, fulfilling aspects of life.

humanistic psychology An approach to the study of human behavior that emphasizes experience, choice and creativity, self-realization, and positive growth.

humanistic therapy A form of psychotherapy focusing on the client's unique potential for personal growth and self-actualization.

Huntington's disease A genetic disorder caused by a dominant lethal gene that causes slow but progressive mental and physical deterioration; sometimes called *Huntington's chorea.*

hypochondriasis A somatoform disorder involving persistent and excessive worry about developing a serious illness. People with this disorder often misinterpret the significance of normal physical aches and pains.

hypothalamus A region of the brain located just above the pituitary gland; controls the autonomic nervous system and many behaviors related to regulation and survival, such as eating, drinking, fighting, shivering, and sweating.

hypothesis A statement, usually designed to be tested by an experiment, that tentatively expresses a cause-and-effect relationship between two or more events.

iconic memory A form of sensory memory that holds a brief visual image of a scene that has just been perceived; also known as visible persistence.

id The unconscious reservoir of libido, the psychic energy that fuels instincts and psychic processes.

illusion of out-group homogeneity A belief that members of out-groups are highly similar to one another.

illusory correlation An apparent correlation between two distinctive elements that does not actually exist.

imitation Observational learning in which the behavior of the observer is similar to the behavior of the person observed.

immune system A network of organs and cells that protects the body from invading bacteria, viruses, and other foreign substances.

immunoglobulins Disease-fighting antibodies that are released by B lymphocytes.

implicit memory Memory that cannot be described verbally and of which a person is therefore not aware.

implosion therapy A form of behavior therapy that attempts to rid people of fears by arousing the fears intensely until clients' responses diminish through extinction; they learn that nothing bad happens.

impression formation The integration of information about another person's traits into a coherent sense of who the person is.

inattentional blindness Failure to perceive an event when attention is diverted elsewhere.

inclusive fitness The reproductive success of those with whom an individual shares common genes.

incongruence In Rogers's theory, a discrepancy between a client's perceptions of her or his real and ideal selves.

independent variable The variable that is manipulated in an experiment as a means of determining cause-and-effect relations.

indigenous healing Non-Western, culture-specific approaches to the treatment of psychological and medical problems.

inductive reasoning The mental process by which people infer general principles or rules from specific information.

inferential statistics Mathematical and logical procedures for determining whether relations or differences between samples are statistically significant.

inflection A change in the form of a word (usually by addition of a suffix) to denote a grammatical feature such as tense or number.

information processing A model used by cognitive psychologists to explain the workings of the brain; according to this model, information received through the senses is processed by systems of neurons in the brain.

informed consent A person's agreement to participate in an experiment after the person has received information about the nature of the research and any possible risks and benefits.

inhibition of return A reduced tendency to perceive a target when the target's presentation is consistent with a noninformative cue. Usually, inhibition of return is tested with respect to spatial location and is present when the target is presented several hundred milliseconds after the cue.

instructional control The guidance of behavior by previously established discriminative stimuli, especially verbal stimuli; also known as *rule-governed behavior.*

intelligence A person's ability to learn and remember information, to recognize concepts and their relations, and to apply the information and recognition by behaving in an adaptive way.

intelligence quotient (IQ) A simplified single measure of general intelligence; by definition, the ratio of a person's mental age to his or her chronological age.

intermittent reinforcement A pattern of reinforcement in which the reinforcer does not occur after every CS (in the case of classical conditioning) or after every response (in operant conditioning); also called *partial reinforcement.*

interneuron A neuron located entirely within the central nervous system.

interpersonal attraction People's tendency to approach each other and to evaluate each other positively.

interposition A monocular cue for depth perception; an object that partially blocks another object is perceived as closer.

interrater reliability The degree to which two or more independent observers agree in their ratings of an organism's behavior.

interval schedules Reinforcement schedules in which reinforcers are dependent on a response after a designated period of time has elapsed.

intraspecific aggression An attack by an animal on another member of its species.

introspection Literally, "looking within" in an attempt to describe memories, perceptions, cognitive processes, or motivations.

introversion The tendency to avoid the company of other people, to be inhibited and cautious; shyness.

ion A positively or negatively charged particle; produced when many substances dissolve in water.

ion channel A special protein molecule located in the membrane of a cell; controls the entry or exit of particular ions.

ion transporter A special protein molecule located in the membrane of a cell; actively transports ions into or out of the cell.

ipsilateral Residing in the same side of the body as the reference point.

iris The pigmented muscle of the eye that controls the size of the pupil.

isolation aphasia A language disorder in which a person cannot comprehend speech or produce meaningful speech but is able to repeat speech and to learn new sequences of words; caused by brain damage to the left temporal/parietal cortex that spares Wernicke's area.

James-Lange theory Theory of emotion proposing that behavioral and physiological responses are directly elicited by situations; feelings of emotions are produced by feedback from these behavioral and physiological responses.

just-noticeable difference (jnd) The smallest difference between two similar stimuli that can be distinguished. Also called *difference threshold.*

kin selection A type of selection that favors altruistic acts directed toward individuals who share some of the altruist's genes, such as parents, siblings, grandparents, or grandchildren.

knockout mutation An experimentally induced genetic sequence that is inserted into a gene to inactivate its expression.

language universal A characteristic feature found in all natural languages.

latency period In Freudian theory, the period between the phallic stage and the genital stage, during which sexual urges are submerged.

latent content The hidden message of a dream, produced by the unconscious.

latent learning Facilitation of later learning after the learner has previously been exposed to the relation between stimuli, even in the absence of reinforcers.

law of closure A Gestalt law of perceptual organization; elements missing from the outline of a figure are "filled in" by the visual system.

law of common fate A Gestalt law of perceptual organization; elements that move together give rise to the perception of a particular figure.

law of effect Edward Thorndike's statement that stimuli that occur as a consequence of a response can increase or decrease the likelihood of an organism's making that response again.

law of good continuation A Gestalt law of perceptual organization; given two or more possible interpretations of the elements that form the outline of a figure, the brain will adopt the simplest interpretation will be preferred.

law of proximity A Gestalt law of perceptual organization; elements located closest to one another are perceived as belonging to the same figure.

law of similarity A Gestalt law of perceptual organization; similar elements are perceived as belonging to the same figure.

leakage Emotion that is expressed despite attempts to mask the emotion.

learned helplessness Reduced ability to learn a solvable avoidance task after exposure to an inescapable aversive stimulus; thought to play a role in depression.

learning An adaptive process in which the tendency to perform a particular behavior is changed by experience.

lens The transparent structure situated behind the iris of the eye; helps focus an image on the retina.

libido An insistent, instinctual force that is unresponsive to the demands of reality; the primary source of motivation.

lifestyle The aggregate behavior of a person; the way in which a person leads his or her life.

liking A feeling of personal regard, intimacy, and esteem toward another person.

limbic cortex The cerebral cortex located around the edge of the cerebral hemispheres where they join with the brain stem; part of the limbic system.

limbic system A set of interconnected structures of the brain important in emotional and species-typical behavior; includes the amygdala, hippocampus, and limbic cortex.

linear perspective A monocular cue for depth perception; the arrangement of lines drawn in two dimensions such that parallel lines receding from the viewer are seen to converge at a point on the horizon.

linguistic relativity The hypothesis that the language a person speaks influences his or her thoughts and perceptions.

locus of control An individual's beliefs that the consequences of his or her actions are controlled by internal, person variables or by external, environmental variables.

longitudinal study. A study of development in which observations of the same individuals are compared at different times of their lives.

long-term memory Memory in which information is represented on a permanent or near-permanent basis.

long-term potentiation An increase in synaptic efficacy when a presynaptic neuron is strongly activated.

loving A combination of liking and a deep sense of attachment to, intimacy with, and caring for another person.

LSD Lysergic acid diethylamide; a hallucinogenic drug that blocks a category of serotonin receptors.

magnetic resonance imaging (MRI) A technique using a device that employs the interaction between radio waves and a strong magnetic field to produce images of slices of the interior of the body.

magnetoencephalography (MEG) A method of brain study that measures the changes in magnetic fields that accompany action potentials in the cerebral cortex.

maintenance rehearsal Rote repetition of information; repeating a given item over and over again.

major depressive disorder Persistent and severe feelings of sadness and worthlessness accompanied by changes in appetite, sleeping, and other behavior.

mania Abnormal and persistent elevation of an expansive or irritable mood.

manifest content The apparent story line of a dream.

manipulation Setting the values of an independent variable in an experiment to see whether the value of another variable is affected.

masking Attempt to hide the expression of an emotion.

matching Systematically selecting participants in groups in an experiment or (more often) a correlational study to ensure that the mean values of important participant variables of the groups are similar.

matching relation In concurrent reinforcement schedules, the equal relation between the proportion of responses to a given alternative and the proportion of reinforcers received for those responses.

materialism A philosophical belief that reality can be known only through an understanding of the physical world, of which the mind is a part.

maturation Any relatively stable change in thought, behavior, or physical growth that is due to the aging process and not to experience.

mean A measure of central tendency; the sum of a group of values divided by their number; the arithmetical average.

means–ends analysis A general heuristical method of problem solving that involves looking for differences between the current state and the goal state and seeking ways to reduce the differences.

measure of central tendency A statistical measure used to characterize the value of items in a sample of numbers.

measure of variability A statistic that describes the degree to which scores in a set of numbers differ from one another.

median A measure of central tendency; the midpoint of a group of values arranged numerically.

medulla The part of the brain stem closest to the spinal cord; controls vital functions such as heart rate and blood pressure.

meiosis The process of cell division by which new sperm and ova are formed. The 23 pairs of chromosomes within a bodily (somatic) cell are randomly separated to form new sperm and ova germ cells, each of which contains 23 unpaired chromosomes.

memory The cognitive processes of encoding, storing, and retrieving information.

mendelian trait A trait showing a classical dominant, recessive, or sex-linked pattern of inheritance. Mendelian traits are discretely expressed and are controlled by a single gene.

meninges The three-layered set of membranes that enclose the brain and spinal cord.

mental age A measure of a person's intellectual development; the average level of intellectual development that could be expected in a child of a particular age.

mental model A cognitive representation of a possibility that a person can use to solve deductive problems.

mental retardation Cognitive development that is substantially below normal; often caused by some form of brain damage or abnormal brain development. Also known as *cognitive disability* or *intellectual disability*.

mere exposure effect The tendency to form a positive attitude toward a person, place, or thing based solely on repeated exposure to that stimulus.

meta-analysis A statistical procedure by which the results of many studies are combined to estimate the magnitude of a particular effect.

method of loci A mnemonic system in which items to be remembered are mentally associated with specific physical locations or landmarks.

microelectrode A thin electrode made of wire or glass that can measure the electrical activity of a single neuron.

midbrain The part of the brain stem just anterior to the pons; involved in control of fighting and sexual behavior and in decreased sensitivity to pain during these behaviors.

Minnesota Multiphasic Personality Inventory (MMPI) An objective test originally designed to distinguish individuals with psychological problems from normal individuals. The MMPI has since become popular as a means of attempting to identify personality characteristics of people in many everyday settings.

mnemonic system A special technique or strategy consciously employed in an attempt to improve memory.

model In science, a relatively simple system that works on known principles and is able to do at least some of the things that a more complex system can do.

modulation Attempt to exaggerate or minimize the expression of an emotion.

molecular genetics The branch of genetics that studies genes at the level of DNA, then relates that information to the structure and function of the organism.

monoamine A category of neurotransmitters that includes dopamine, norepinephrine, and serotonin.

monogamy The mating of one female with one male.

mood disorder A disorder characterized by significant shifts or disturbances in mood that adversely affect normal perception, thought, and behavior. Mood disorders may be characterized by deep, foreboding depression or may involve a combination of depression and mania.

moral realism The first stage of Piaget's model of moral development, which includes egocentrism and blind adherence to rules.

morality of cooperation The second stage of Piaget's model of moral development, which involves the recognition of rules as social conventions.

morpheme The minimum unit of meaning in a language, such as /p/ + /in/ to form *pin*.

motion parallax A monocular cue for depth perception; as we pass by a scene, objects closer to us appear to move farther than those more distant.

motivation A group of phenomena that affect the nature, strength, or persistence of an individual's behavior.

motor association cortex The regions of the cerebral cortex that control the primary motor cortex; involved in planning and executing behaviors.

motor neuron A neuron whose terminal buttons form synapses with muscle fibers; when an action potential travels down a motor neuron's axon, the associated muscle fibers will twitch.

muscle spindle A muscle fiber that functions as a stretch receptor; arranged parallel to the muscle fibers responsible for contraction of the muscle, it detects muscle length.

mutations Alterations in the DNA code within a single gene. Mutations can occur either spontaneously or as a result of experimental intervention.

myelin sheath The insulating material that encases most large axons.

naloxone A drug that binds with and blocks opioid receptors, preventing opiate drugs or endogenous opioids from exerting their effects.

narrative A mnemonic system in which items to be remembered are linked together by a story.

natural concept A category formed from a person's perceptions of and interactions with things in the world; based on exemplars.

natural selection The process whereby physical and behavioral differences among organisms cause different rates of reproductive success. Within a given population, some organisms will survive and reproduce more than will other organisms.

naturalistic observation Observation of the behavior of people or other animals in their natural environments.

negative afterimage The image seen after a portion of the retina is exposed to an intense visual stimulus; a negative afterimage consists of colors complementary to those of the original stimulus.

negative feedback Process whereby some mechanism reduces or terminates an action; regulatory systems are characterized by negative feedback loops.

negative punishment The process by which the frequency or strength of a response decreases when the response is followed by the termination of an appetitive stimulus. *Time-out* and *response-cost* procedures involve negative punishment.

negative reinforcement The process by which the frequency or strength of a response increases when the response is reliably followed by the termination of an aversive stimulus.

negative symptom A symptom of schizophrenia that consists of the absence of normal behaviors; negative symptoms include flattened emotion, poverty of speech, lack of initiative and persistence, and social withdrawal.

neostigmine A drug that enhances the effects of the neurotransmitter acetylcholine by blocking the enzyme that destroys it.

nerve A bundle of nerve fibers that transmit information between the central nervous system and the body's sense organs, muscles, and glands.

neural network A model of the nervous system based on interconnected networks of units that have some of the properties of neurons.

neuromodulator A substance secreted in the brain that modulates the activity of neurons that contain the appropriate receptors.

neuron A nerve cell; consists of a cell body with dendrites and an axon whose branches end in terminal buttons that synapse with muscle fibers, gland cells, or other neurons.

neuroticism The tendency to be anxious, worried, and full of guilt.

Neuroticism, Extroversion, and Openness Personality Inventory (NEO-PI-R) The instrument used to measure the elements described in the five-factor model (neuroticism, extroversion, openness, agreeableness, and conscientiousness).

neurotransmitter A chemical released by the terminal buttons that causes the postsynaptic neuron to be excited or inhibited.

neurotransmitter receptor A special protein molecule located in the membrane of a postsynaptic neuron that responds to molecules of a neurotransmitter.

nicotine A drug that binds with and stimulates acetylcholine receptors, mimicking the effects of this neurotransmitter.

nominal fallacy The false belief that we have explained the causes of a phenomenon by identifying and naming it; for example, believing that we have explained lazy behavior by attributing it to "laziness."

nonmendelian trait A trait that does not show the inheritance pattern described by Mendel. Nonmendelian traits show continuous variation in the phenotype and are usually polygenic.

non-REM sleep Sleep in stages 1 through 4, characterized by an absence of rapid eye movements.

norepinephrine (NE) A monoamine neurotransmitter involved in alertness and vigilance and control of REM sleep.

norms Data obtained from large numbers of individuals that permit the score of any one individual to be assessed relative to the scores of his or her peers.

object permanence In Piaget's theory, the idea that objects do not cease existing when they are out of sight.

objective personality tests Tests for measuring personality that can be scored objectively, such as a multiple-choice or true/false test.

object-relations theory The theory that personality is the reflection of relationships that the individual establishes with others as an infant.

observational learning Learning that takes place when we see the kinds of consequences others (called models) experience as a result of their behavior.

obsession An involuntary recurring thought, idea, or image accompanied by anxiety or distress.

obsessive-compulsive disorder Recurrent, unwanted thoughts or ideas and compelling urges to engage in repetitive ritual-like behavior, often abbreviated as OCD.

occipital lobe The rearmost portion of the cerebral cortex; contains the primary visual cortex.

olfaction The sense of smell.

olfactory bulbs Stalklike structures located at the base of the brain and containing neural circuits that perform the first analysis of olfactory information.

olfactory mucosa The mucous membrane lining the top of the nasal sinuses; contains the cilia of the olfactory receptor cells.

operant chamber A test environment in which an animal's behavior can be observed, manipulated, and automatically recorded during an operant conditioning procedure.

operant procedure A conditioning procedure in which the eliciting stimulus follows a response. Appetitive elicitors function as reinforcers; aversive elicitors function as punishers.

operation In Piaget's theory, a logical or mathematical rule that transforms an object or concept into something else.

operational definition Definition of a variable in terms of the operations the researcher performs to measure or manipulate it.

opponent process The representation of colors by the rate of firing of two types of neurons: red/green and yellow/blue.

optic disk The circular region of the retina where the axons of the ganglion cells exit the eye and form the optic nerve.

optimal-level theory Hypothesis that organisms are motivated to maintain their drives at some desired level.

oral stage The first of Freud's psychosexual stages, during which the mouth is the major erogenous zone because it appeases the hunger drive.

orbitofrontal cortex Region of the prefrontal cortex that plays an important role in recognition of situations that produce emotional responses and in translating such recognition into appropriate emotions and behavior.

organizational effect Effect of a hormone, usually during prenatal development, that produces permanent changes in the subsequent development of the organism; for example, the masculinization of the developing male brain by testosterone.

organizational psychologist A psychologist who works to increase the efficiency and effectiveness of organizations.

orienting response Any response that facilitates detecting a stimulus, as when an animal turns toward the source of a sound or a visual stimulus.

ossicles The three bones of the middle ear (the hammer, anvil, and stirrup) that transmit acoustical vibrations from the eardrum to the membrane behind the oval window of the cochlea.

oval window An opening in the bone surrounding the cochlea. The stirrup presses against a membrane behind the oval window and transmits sound waves into the fluid within the cochlea.

overextension The use of a word to denote a larger class of items than is appropriate; for example, referring to the moon as a ball.

overjustification effect The undermining of intrinsic motivation by the application of extrinsic rewards to intrinsically motivated behavior.

Pacinian corpuscle A specialized somatosensory nerve ending that detects mechanical stimuli, especially vibrations.

panic A feeling of extreme fear mixed with hopelessness or helplessness.

panic disorder Unpredictable attacks of acute anxiety that are accompanied by high levels of physiological arousal and that last from a few seconds to a few hours.

papilla A small bump on the tongue that contains a group of taste buds.

parallel processor A computing device that can perform several operations simultaneously.

paranoid schizophrenia A type of schizophrenia in which the person suffers from delusions of persecution, grandeur, or control.

parasympathetic branch The portion of the autonomic nervous system that activates functions that occur during a relaxed state.

parental investment The resources (including time, physical effort, and risks to life) that a parent expends in procreation and the feeding, nurturing, and protection of offspring.

parietal lobe The region of the cerebral cortex behind the frontal lobe and above the temporal lobe; contains the somatosensory cortex; is involved in spatial perception and memory.

Parkinson's disease A neurological disorder characterized by tremors, rigidity of the limbs, poor balance, and difficulty in initiating movements; caused by degeneration of a system of dopamine-secreting neurons.

passionate love An emotional, intense desire for sexual union with another person; also called romantic love.

peg-word method A mnemonic system in which items to be remembered are associated with a set of mental pegs already in memory, such as key words of a rhyme.

peptide A category of neurotransmitters and neuromodulators that consist of two or more amino acids, linked by peptide bonds.

perception The brain's use of information provided by sensory systems to produce a response.

period of concrete operations The third period in Piaget's theory of cognitive development, lasting from age 7 to 11, during which children come to understand the conservation principle and other concepts, such as categorization.

period of formal operations The fourth period in Piaget's theory of cognitive development, from age 11 onward, during which individuals first become capable of more formal kinds of abstract thinking and hypothetical reasoning.

peripheral nervous system The cranial and spinal nerves; that part of the nervous system peripheral to the brain and spinal cord.

person variables Individual differences in cognition, which, according to Mischel, include competencies, encoding strategies and personal constructs, expectancies, subjective values, and self-regulatory systems and plans.

personality A particular pattern of behavior and thinking prevailing across time and situations that differentiates one person from another.

personality psychology The branch of psychology that attempts to categorize and understand the causes of individual differences in patterns of behavior.

personality trait An enduring personal characteristic that reveals itself in a particular pattern of behavior in a variety of situations.

personality types Different categories into which personality characteristics can be assigned based on factors such as developmental experiences or physical characteristics.

phallic stage The third of Freud's psychosexual stages during which the primary erogenous zone is the genital area and pleasure derives from both direct genital stimulation and general physical contact.

phantom limb Sensations that appear to originate in a limb that has been amputated.

pharmacotherapy The treatment of psychological problems with chemical agents.

phenotype The appearance and behavior of an individual organism; the outward expression of the genotype.

phenylketonuria (PKU) A genetic disorder caused by a particular pair of homozygous recessive genes and characterized by the inability to break down phenylalanine, an amino acid found in many high-protein foods. The resulting high blood levels of phenylalanine cause mental retardation.

pheromones Chemical signals, usually detected by smell or taste, that regulate reproductive and social behaviors between animals.

phi phenomenon The perception of movement caused by the turning on and off of two or more lights, one at a time, in sequence; often used on theater marquees; responsible for the apparent movement of images in movies and television.

phobia Unreasonable fear of specific objects or situations, such as insects, animals, or enclosed spaces, produced by stimulus-reinforcer pairings.

phobic disorder An unrealistic, excessive fear of a specific class of stimuli that interferes with normal activities. Phobic disorders include agoraphobia, social phobia, and specific phobia.

phoneme The minimum unit of sound in a language, such as /p/.

phonetic reading Reading by decoding the phonetic structure of letter strings; reading by "sounding out."

phonological dyslexia A reading disorder in which people can read familiar words but have difficulty reading unfamiliar words or pronounceable nonwords because they cannot sound out words.

phonological short-term memory Short-term memory for verbal information.

photopigment A complex molecule found in photoreceptors; when struck by light, it splits apart and stimulates the membrane of the photoreceptor in which it resides.

photoreceptor A receptive cell for vision in the retina; a rod or a cone.

physiological psychology The branch of psychology that studies the physiological basis of behavior.

pituitary gland An endocrine gland attached to the hypothalamus at the base of the brain.

placebo An inert substance that cannot be distinguished in appearance from a real medication; used as the control substance in a single-blind or double-blind experiment.

pleasure principle The rule that the id obeys: Obtain immediate gratification, whatever form it may take.

polyandry The mating of one female with more than one male.

polygraph An instrument that records changes in physiological processes such as brain activity, heart rate, and breathing.

polygynandry The mating of several females with several males.

polygyny The mating of one male with more than one female.

pons The part of the brain stem just anterior to the medulla; involved in control of sleep.

positive symptom A symptom of schizophrenia, including thought disorder, delusions, or hallucinations.

positron emission tomography (PET) The use of a device that reveals the localization of a radioactive tracer in a human brain.

postconventional level Kohlberg's third and final level of moral development, in which people come to understand that moral rules include principles that apply across all situations and societies.

posthypnotic amnesia A failure to remember what occurred during hypnosis; induced by suggestions made during hypnosis.

posthypnotic suggestibility The tendency of a person to perform a behavior suggested by a hypnotist some time after the person has left the hypnotic state.

postsynaptic neuron A neuron with which the terminal buttons of another neuron form synapses and that is excited or inhibited by that neuron.

post-traumatic stress disorder (PTSD) An anxiety disorder in which the individual has feelings of social withdrawal accompanied by atypically low levels of emotion; caused by prolonged exposure to a stressor, such as war or a natural catastrophe.

practical intelligence In Sternberg's triarchic theory, intelligence that reflects the behaviors that were subject to natural selection: adaptation (initially fitting self to environment by developing useful skills and behaviors); selection (finding an appropriate niche in the environment); and shaping (changing the environment).

preconventional level Kohlberg's first level of moral development, which bases moral behavior on external sanctions such as authority and punishment.

prefrontal cortex The anterior part of the frontal lobe; contains the motor association cortex.

prejudice A preconceived opinion or bias; especially, a negative attitude toward a group of people who are defined by their racial, ethnic, or religious heritage or by their gender, occupation, sexual orientation, level of education, place of residence, or membership in a particular group.

prenatal period The approximately nine months between conception and birth. This period is divided into three developmental stages: the zygotic, the embryonic, and the fetal.

preoperational period The second period in Piaget's theory of cognitive development, lasting from two years of age to seven, and representing a transitional period between symbolic and logical thought. During this stage, children become increasingly capable of speaking meaningful sentences.

preoptic area A region at the base of the brain just in front of the hypothalamus; contains neurons that appear to control the occurrence of slow-wave sleep.

presynaptic neuron A neuron whose terminal buttons form synapses with and excite or inhibit another neuron.

preventive psychology Strategies that attempt to prevent the development of psychological problems by altering the sociocultural variables predictive of psychological distress.

primacy effect The tendency to remember initial information. In the memorization of a list of words, the primacy effect is evidenced by better recall of the words early in the list.

primary appraisal The first stage of cognitive appraisal, during which we evaluate the seriousness a threat (stressor).

primary auditory cortex The region of the cerebral cortex that receives information directly from the auditory system; located in the temporal lobes.

primary motor cortex The region of the cerebral cortex that directly controls the movements of the body; located in the posterior part of the frontal lobes.

primary somatosensory cortex The region of the cerebral cortex that receives information directly from the somatosensory system (touch, pressure, vibration, pain, and temperature); located in the front part of the parietal lobes.

primary visual cortex The region of the cerebral cortex that receives information directly from the visual system; located in the occipital lobes.

proactive interference Interference in recall that occurs when previously learned information disrupts our ability to remember newer information.

problem-focused coping Any coping behavior that aims to reduce stress by reducing or eliminating a stressor.

process schizophrenia According to Bleuler, a chronic form of schizophrenia characterized by a gradual onset and a poor prognosis.

progressive relaxation technique A stress-reduction method in which a person learns to (1) recognize body signals that indicate the presence of stress; (2) use those signals as a cue to begin relaxing; and (3) relax groups of muscles, beginning with those in the head and neck and proceeding to those in the arms and legs.

projection A defense mechanism in which a person attributes his or her own unacceptable thoughts or impulses to someone else.

projective tests Unstructured personality measures in which a person is shown a series of ambiguous stimuli, such as pictures, inkblots, or incomplete drawings. The person is asked to describe what he or she "sees" in each stimulus or to create stories that reflect the theme of the drawing or picture.

prosody The use of changes in intonation and emphasis to convey meaning in speech besides that specified by the particular words.

prosopagnosia A form of visual agnosia characterized by difficulty in the recognition of people's faces; may be accompanied by difficulty in recognizing other complex objects; caused by damage to the visual association cortex.

protanopia A form of hereditary anomalous color vision caused by defective "red" cones in the retina.

prototype A hypothetical idealized pattern that resides in the nervous system and is used to perceive objects or shapes by a process of comparison; recognition can occur even when an exact match cannot be found.

protoword A unique string of phonemes that an infant invents and uses as a word.

proximate causes Environmental events and conditions that shape behavior in the present environment.

psychoanalysis A form of psychotherapy aimed at providing the client with insight into his or her unconscious motivations and impulses; first developed by Sigmund Freud.

psychodynamic Characterized by conflict among instincts, reason, and conscience; describes the mental processes envisioned in Freudian theory.

psycholinguistics A branch of psychology devoted to the study of verbal behavior and related cognitive abilities.

psychology The scientific study of the causes of behavior; also, the application of the findings of psychological research to the solution of problems.

psychometrics The study of individual differences in psychological characteristics, pioneered by Galton in his laboratories at the South Kensington Museum in London.

psychoneuroimmunology Study of the interactions between the immune system and behavior as mediated by the nervous system.

psychophysics A branch of psychology that measures the quantitative relation between physical stimuli and perceptual experience.

psychosurgery Brain surgery used in an effort to relieve the symptoms of psychological disorders in the absence of obvious organic damage.

psychoticism The tendency to be aggressive, egocentric, and antisocial.

puberty The period during which people's reproductive systems mature, marking the beginning of the transition from childhood to adulthood.

punisher An aversive eliciting stimulus that decreases the strength of an operant that precedes it. Punishers may either be unconditioned or conditioned (resulting from experience). Also known as *punishing stimulus.*

punishment The process by which the frequency or strength of a response decreases when the response is followed by an aversive stimulus. (See also *negative punishment.*)

pure word deafness The ability to hear, to speak, and (usually) to write without being able to comprehend the meaning of speech; caused by bilateral temporal lobe damage.

pursuit movement The movement made by the eyes that keeps the image of a moving object projected onto the fovea.

random assignment Procedure in which each participant has an equally likely chance of being assigned to any of the conditions or groups of an experiment.

range The difference between the highest score and the lowest score of a sample.

rapid eye movement (REM) sleep A period of sleep during which dreaming, rapid eye movements, and muscular paralysis occur and the EEG shows beta activity.

ratio IQ A formula for computing the intelligence quotient: mental age divided by chronological age, multiplied by 100.

ratio schedules Reinforcement schedules in which reinforcers are dependent on a designated number of responses.

rational-emotive therapy A form of psychotherapy based on the belief that psychological problems are caused not by distressing experiences themselves but by how people think about those experiences.

rationalization A defense mechanism that justifies an unacceptable action with a more acceptable, but false, excuse.

reaction formation A defense mechanism in which a person behaves in a way that is the opposite of how he or she really feels, because the true feelings produce anxiety.

reactive schizophrenia According to Bleuler, a form of schizophrenia characterized by rapid onset and brief duration, perhaps triggered by stressful life situations.

reality principle The tendency to satisfy the id's demands realistically, which almost always involves compromising the demands of the id and superego.

receiver operating characteristic curve (ROC curve) A graph of hits and false alarms of participants under different motivational conditions; indicates people's ability to detect a particular stimulus.

recency effect The tendency to recall later information. In the memorization of a list of words, the recency effect is evidenced by better recall of the last words in the list.

receptive field That portion of the visual field in which the presentation of visual stimuli will produce an alteration in the firing rate of a particular neuron.

receptor cell A neuron that directly responds to a physical stimulus, such as light, vibrations, or aromatic molecules; also called: *sensory receptor.*

recessive gene An allele that causes a trait to be expressed only when two of the same alleles are present; that is, only in homozygous cells.

reciprocal altruism Altruism in which an individual acts to benefit another if it is likely that the other will return the favor at some later time.

reciprocal determinism The idea that behavior, environment, and person variables interact to determine personality.

reflex An automatic response to a stimulus, such as the blink reflex to the sudden unexpected approach of an object toward the eyes.

reinforcement The process by which an increase in the frequency of a response occurs when the response is reliably followed by an appetitive (positive reinforced) stimulus or terminates an aversive (negative reinforced) stimulus.

reinforcing stimulus An eliciting stimulus that functions to strengthen responding in either a classical procedure or an operant procedure. Often called simply a *reinforcer.*

reliability The repeatability of a measurement; the likelihood that if the measurement were made again it would yield the same value.

replication Repetition of an experiment or observational study in an effort to see whether previous results will be obtained; ensures that incorrect conclusions are weeded out.

representativeness heuristic A general rule for classifying a person, place, or thing into the category to which it appears to be the most similar.

repression A defense mechanism responsible for actively keeping potentially threatening or anxiety-provoking memories from being consciously discovered.

reproductive strategies Different systems of mating and rearing offspring. These include monogamy, polygyny, polyandry, and polygynandry.

reproductive success The number of viable offspring an individual produces relative to the number of viable offspring produced by other members of the same species.

residual schizophrenia A type of schizophrenia that may follow an episode of one of the other types and is marked by negative symptoms but not by any prominent positive symptom.

resistance A development during psychoanalysis in which the client becomes defensive, unconsciously attempting to halt further insight by censoring his or her emotions.

resistant attachment A kind of attachment in which infants show mixed reactions to their mothers. In the Strange Situation test, when mothers return after being absent, such infants may approach their mothers but at the same time may continue to cry or even push their mothers away.

response chaining A procedure in which a learner is taught a complex sequence of responses through reinforcement of an increasingly long series of responses; a type of shaping.

resting potential The membrane potential of a neuron when it is not producing an action potential.

retina The tissue layer that is the inside surface of the eye and contains the photoreceptors and associated neurons.

retinal disparity The fact that objects located at different distances from the observer will fall on different locations on the two retinas; provides a binocular cue for depth perception.

retrieval The active processes of locating and using stored information.

retrieval cues Contextual variables, including physical objects, or verbal stimuli, that improve the ability to recall information from memory.

retroactive interference Interference in recall that occurs when recently learned information disrupts our ability to remember older information.

retrograde amnesia Loss of the ability to retrieve memories of the past, particularly memories of episodic or autobiographical events.

reuptake The process by which a terminal button retrieves the molecules of a neurotransmitter that it has just released; terminates the effect of the neurotransmitter on the receptors of the postsynaptic neuron.

rhodopsin The photopigment that rods contain.

rod A photoreceptor that is very sensitive to light but cannot detect color.

Rorschach Inkblot Test A projective test in which a person is shown a series of symmetrical inkblots and asked to describe what he or she thinks they represent.

round window An opening in the bone surrounding the cochlea. Movements of the membrane behind this opening induce movements of the basilar membrane.

***s* factor** According to Spearman, a factor of intelligence that is specific to a particular intellectual task.

saccadic movement The rapid movement made by the eyes in scanning a visual scene.

sample A selection of elements representative of a larger population—for example, a group of participants selected to participate in an experiment.

saturation A perceptual dimension of color, most closely associated with the purity of a color.

scaffolding The matching of a mentor's efforts to a child's developmental level.

scatterplot A graph of items that have two values; one value is plotted against the horizontal axis and the other against the vertical axis.

schedule of reinforcement Reinforcement procedure that specifies the conditions necessary for reinforcement.

schema A mental framework or body of knowledge that organizes and synthesizes information about a person, place, or thing.

schizophrenia A serious mental disorder characterized by thought disturbances, hallucinations, anxiety, emotional withdrawal, and delusions.

school psychologist A psychologist who deals with the behavioral problems of students at school.

scientific method A set of rules that governs the collection and analysis of data gained through observational studies or experiments.

sclera The tough outer layer of the eye; the "white" of the eye.

script A person's knowledge about the characteristics typical of a particular type of event or situation; assists the comprehension of speech.

seasonal affective disorder A mood disorder characterized by depression, lethargy, sleep disturbances, and craving for carbohydrates. This disorder generally occurs during the winter, when the days are short. This disorder can be treated with exposure to bright lights.

secondary appraisal The second stage of cognitive appraisal, during which we evaluate the resources we have available to deal with a threat (stressor).

secure attachment A kind of attachment in which infants use their mothers as a base for exploring a new environment. In the Strange Situation test, securely attached infants will venture out from their mothers to explore, but will return periodically.

segregation analysis A correlational procedure for studying genetic influences on behavior; involves identifying specific regions of chromosomes and correlating those regions with a behavior.

selectionism Theory that explains complex outcomes as the cumulative products of simple processes; first proposed by Darwin.

selective attention The process that controls our awareness of, and readiness to respond to, particular categories of stimuli or stimuli in a particular location to the exclusion of others.

self A person's distinct individuality.

self-actualization The realization of our true intellectual and emotional potential.

self-concept Our knowledge, feelings, and beliefs about ourself.

self-control Behavior that produces a larger, long-term reward when people are faced with the choice between it and a smaller, short-term reward; also the tendency to be kind, considerate, and obedient of laws and rules.

self-efficacy People's beliefs about how well or badly they will perform tasks.

self-fulfilling prophecy An expectation that causes a person to act in a manner consistent with the expectation; the person's actions then cause the expectation to come true. Often seen in cases of stereotyping.

self-perception theory The theory that we come to understand our attitudes and emotions by observing our own behavior and the circumstances under which it occurs.

self-schema The cognitive representation of the self-concept.

self-serving bias Our tendency to attribute our accomplishments and successes to dispositional factors and our failures and mistakes to situational factors.

semantic memory A type of long-term memory that contains data, facts, and other information, including vocabulary.

semantic priming The facilitating effect of a word on the recognition of words having related meanings that are presented subsequently.

semantics The meanings and the study of the meanings of words.

semicircular canal One of a set of three organs in the inner ear that respond to rotational movements of the head.

sensation The detection of the elementary properties of a stimulus.

sensitive period. A period of time during which certain experiences have more of an effect on development than they would have if they occurred at another time.

sensorimotor period The first period in Piaget's theory of cognitive development, lasting from birth to two years, and marked by an orderly progression of increasingly complex cognitive development from reflexes to object permanence to deferred imitation and rudimentary symbolic thinking.

sensory association cortex The regions of cerebral cortex that receive information from the primary sensory areas.

sensory learning A process by which an environment–environment relation is acquired, such as between a light and a tone that occur together.

sensory memory Memory in which representations of the physical features of a stimulus are stored for very brief durations.

sensory neuron A neuron that detects changes in the external or internal environment and sends information about these changes to the central nervous system.

separation anxiety A set of fearful responses, such as crying, arousal, and clinging to the caregiver, that an infant exhibits when its caregiver attempts to leave the infant.

serotonin A monoamine neurotransmitter involved in the regulation of mood; in the control of eating, sleep, and arousal; and in the regulation of pain.

serum cholesterol A fatlike compound found in the blood. One form (LDL) promotes the formation of atherosclerotic plaques. Another form (HDL) may protect against coronary heart disease.

set point Optimum value of the system variable in a regulatory process. The set point for human body temperature is 98.6° F (37°C).

sex chromosomes The chromosomes that contain genes that regulate the development of male or female sex characteristics.

sexual selection Selection for traits that are preferentially expressed in the two sexes, including body size and sex-linked patterns of behavior.

shading A monocular cue for depth perception; the apparent light source determines whether the surface of an object is perceived as concave or convex.

shadowing The act of continuously repeating verbal material as soon as it is heard.

shallow processing Analysis of the superficial characteristics of a stimulus, such as its size or shape.

shape constancy Our tendency to perceive objects as having a constant shape regardless of their rotation or their distance from us.

shaping A procedure in which successively closer approximations to the target behavior are reinforced; commonly used in the teaching or the acquisition of complex behavior.

short-term memory An immediate memory for stimuli that have just been perceived. It is limited in terms of both capacity (7 ± 2 chunks of information) and duration (less than 20 seconds).

signal detection theory A mathematical theory of the detection of stimuli which involves discriminating a signal from the noise in which it is embedded and which takes into account participants' willingness to report detecting the signal—their *response bias*.

simulation Attempt to express an emotion that a person does not actually feel.

single-blind study An experiment in which the researcher knows the value of the independent variable but participants do not.

situational factors Physical and social stimuli that are found in an individual's environment and that can affect his or her behavior.

situationism The view that the behaviors defining a certain personality are determined solely by the current situation rather than by any persevering traits.

size A monocular cue for depth perception based on the retinal size of an object.

size constancy Our tendency to perceive objects as having a constant size, even when they are rotated or their distance from us changes.

slow-wave sleep Sleep other than REM sleep, characterized by regular, slow waves on the electroencephalogram.

social cognition The processes involved in perceiving, thinking about, and acting on social information.

social cognitive theory The idea that both consequences of behavior and an individual's beliefs about those consequences determine personality.

social facilitation The enhancement of task performance caused by the mere presence of others.

social loafing The tendency of individuals to put forth decreased effort when performing a task together with other people.

social norms Informal rules defining the expected and appropriate behavior in specific situations.

social phobia A mental disorder characterized by an excessive and irrational fear of situations in which the person is observed by others.

social psychology The branch of psychology devoted to the study of the effects people have on one another's behavior.

sociobiology The study of the genetic bases of social behavior.

soma A cell body; the largest part of a neuron (plural: somata).

somatization disorder A somatoform disorder, occurring almost exclusively among women, that involves complaints of wide-ranging physical ailments for which there is no apparent biological cause.

somatoform disorder A class of mental disorders involving bodily or physical problems for which there is no physiological basis.

somatosenses Bodily sensations; sensitivity to such stimuli as touch, pain, and temperature.

species-typical behavior A behavior seen in all or most members of a species, such as nest building, special food-getting behaviors, or reproductive behaviors.

specific phobia A mental disorder characterized by an excessive and irrational fear of specific things, such as snakes, darkness, or heights.

spinal cord A long, thin collection of nerve cells attached to the base of the brain and running the length of the spinal column.

spinal nerve A bundle of nerve fibers attached to the spinal cord; conveys sensory information from the body and carries messages to muscles and glands.

split-brain operation A surgical procedure that severs the corpus callosum, thus abolishing the direct connections between the cortex of the two cerebral hemispheres.

spontaneous recovery An increase in an environment–behavior relation with the passage of time after extinction.

standard deviation A statistic that expresses the variability of a measurement; square root of the average of the squared deviations from the mean.

Stanford-Binet Scale An intelligence test that consists of various tasks grouped according to mental age; provides the standard measure of the IQ.

statistical significance The likelihood that an observed relation or difference between two variables really exists rather than being due to chance factors.

stem cells Undifferentiated cells that can divide and produce any one of a variety of differentiated cells.

stereotaxic apparatus A device used to insert an electrode into a particular part of the brain for the purpose of recording electrical activity, stimulating the brain electrically, or producing localized damage.

stereotype An overgeneralized and thus potentially false schema describing the characteristics of a particular group.

stimulus discrimination A process whereby the environmental guidance of behavior is restricted to the environment in which the behavior was reinforced. Stimulus discrimination is produced by differential conditioning.

stimulus generalization The process by which a response occurs during a stimulus that is similar to the stimulus in whose presence the response was reinforced.

storage The process of maintaining information in memory.

Strange Situation A test of attachment in which an infant is exposed to different stimuli that may cause distress.

stranger anxiety The wariness and fearful responses, such as crying and clinging to their caregivers, that infants exhibit in the presence of strangers.

stress A pattern of physiological, behavioral, emotional, and cognitive responses to stimuli (real or imagined) that are perceived as endangering our well-being.

stress inoculation training The stress management program developed by Meichenbaum to help people develop coping skills that increase their resistance to the negative effects of stress.

stressors Stimuli that are perceived as endangering our well-being.

striving for superiority Our motivation to achieve our full potential. Adler argued that striving for superiority is born from our need to compensate for our inferiority.

structural family therapy A form of family therapy in which the therapist infers the maladaptive relationships among family members from their behavior and attempts to help the family restructure these relationships for more desirable interactions.

structuralism The system of experimental psychology that began with Wilhelm Wundt; it emphasized introspective analysis of sensation and perception.

sublimation A defense mechanism that involves redirecting pleasure-seeking or aggressive instincts toward socially acceptable goals.

subliminal perception The perception of a stimulus, as indicated by a change in behavior, at a stimulus intensity insufficient to produce a conscious sensation.

subordinate concept A more specific concept that falls within a basic-level concept.

substance-related disorders Mental disorders that are characterized by addiction to drugs or alcohol or by abuse of drugs or alcohol.

subvocal articulation An unvoiced speech utterance.

successful intelligence According to Sternberg, the ability to effectively analyze and manage personal strengths and weaknesses; in Sternberg's scheme successful intelligence draws on analytic, creative, and practical intelligence.

superego The repository of an individual's moral values, divided into the conscience—the internalization of society's rules and regulations—and the ego-ideal—the internalization of the individual's goals.

superordinate concept A general or overarching concept that includes basic-level concepts.

superstitious behavior Behavior that is acquired after being paired with a reinforcer; the relation to the reinforcer is coincidental, not causal.

surface dyslexia A reading disorder in which people can read words phonetically but have difficulty reading irregularly spelled words by the whole-word method.

surface structure The grammatical features of a sentence; its words and syntax.

survey study A study of people's responses to standardized questions.

syllogism A logical construction that contains a major premise, a minor premise, and a conclusion. The major and minor premises are assumed to be true, and the truth of the conclusion is to be evaluated by deductive reasoning.

sympathetic branch The portion of the autonomic nervous system that activates functions that accompany arousal and expenditure of energy.

synapse The junction between the terminal button of one neuron and the membrane of a muscle fiber, a gland, or another neuron.

synaptic cleft A fluid-filled gap between the presynaptic and postsynaptic membranes; the terminal button releases a neurotransmitter into this space.

syntactical rule A grammatical rule of a particular language for combining words to form phrases, clauses, and sentences.

system variable The variable controlled in a regulatory process; for example, temperature in a heating system.

systematic desensitization A form of behavior therapy in which the client is trained to relax in the presence of increasingly fearsome stimuli.

T lymphocytes White blood cells that develop in the thymus gland and produce antibodies, which defend the body against fungi, viruses, and multicellular parasites.

tachistoscope A device that can present visual stimuli for controlled (usually very brief) durations of time.

tardive dyskinesia A serious movement disorder that can occur when a person has been treated with antipsychotic drugs for an extended period.

target cell A cell whose physiological processes are affected by a particular hormone; contains special receptors that respond to the presence of the hormone.

targeted mutation A mutated gene (also called a "knockout gene") produced in the laboratory and inserted into the chromosomes of mice; abolishes the normal effects of the gene.

taste aversion A learned aversion to the smell or taste of a novel food after ingestion of that food has been followed by nausea or other strong gastric responses. Unlike most conditioned responses, taste aversions can be acquired even when there is a long interval between smelling and tasting the food (CS) and the gastric consequences of ingesting it (UR).

taste bud A small organ found in papillae that contains a group of gustatory receptor cells.

tectorial membrane A membrane located above the basilar membrane; serves as a shelf against which the cilia of the auditory hair cells move.

temperament An individual's pattern of behaviors and emotional reactions.

template A hypothetical pattern that is stored in the nervous system and is used to perceive objects or shapes by a process of comparison.

temporal coding A means by which the nervous system represents information; different stimuli are coded by the temporal pattern of neural activity, of neurons such as rate of firing.

temporal contiguity A close relation between two events in time.

temporal lobe The portion of the cerebral cortex below the frontal and parietal lobes; contains the auditory cortex.

teratogens Substances, agents, and events that can cause birth defects.

terminal button The rounded swelling at the end of the axon of a neuron; releases a neurotransmitter.

texture A monocular cue for depth perception; the relative fineness of detail present in the surfaces of objects or the ground or floor.

thalamus A region of the brain near the center of the cerebral hemispheres. All sensory information except that of olfaction is sent to the thalamus and then relayed to the cerebral cortex.

Thematic Apperception Test (TAT) A projective test in which a person is shown a series of ambiguous pictures that involve people. The person is asked to make up a story about what the people are doing or thinking. The person's responses are believed to reflect aspects of his or her personality.

theory A set of statements designed to explain a set of phenomena; more encompassing than a hypothesis.

theory of mind Expectations concerning how experience affects mental states, especially those of another.

theta activity Electroencephalogram activity of 3.5 to 7.5 Hz; occurs during the transition between sleep and wakefulness.

thought disorder A pattern of disorganized, illogical, and irrational thought that often accompanies schizophrenia.

threat gesture Stereotyped gesture that signifies that one animal is likely to attack another.

threshold The point at which a stimulus, or a change in the intensity of a stimulus, can just be detected.

timbre A perceptual dimension of sound determined by its complexity; representable by a mathematical analysis of the sound wave.

tip-of-the-tongue phenomenon An occasional problem with retrieval of information that we are sure we know but cannot immediately remember.

token economy A form of behavior therapy often used in mental institutions; target behaviors are reinforced with tokens that are exchangeable for desirable goods or special privileges.

tolerance Decreased sensitivity to a drug resulting from its continued use.

top-down processing Perception based on information provided by the context in which a particular stimulus is encountered.

Tourette's syndrome A neurological disorder characterized by tics and involuntary utterances, some of which may involve obscenities and the repetition of others' utterances.

transcranial magnetic stimulation (TMS) Direct stimulation of the cerebral cortex induced by magnetic fields generated outside the skull.

transduction The conversion of physical stimuli into changes in the activity of receptor cells of sensory organs.

transference Process in which a client begins to project powerful attitudes and emotions onto a psychoanalyst.

trephining A surgical procedure in which a hole is made in the skull of a living person.

trichromatic theory The theory that color vision is accomplished by three types of photoreceptors, each of which is maximally sensitive to a different wavelength of light.

tritanopia A form of hereditary anomalous color vision caused by a lack of "blue" cones in the retina.

two-point discrimination threshold The minimum distance between the touch applied to small points on the skin that can be detected as separate stimuli.

type A behavior pattern A behavior pattern characterized by impatience, high levels of competitiveness and hostility, and an intense disposition; supposedly associated with an increased risk of CHD.

type B behavior pattern A behavior pattern characterized by patience, relatively low levels of competitiveness and hostility, and an easygoing disposition; supposedly associated with a decreased risk of CHD.

type C personality A behavior pattern marked by cooperativeness, lack of assertiveness, patience, suppression of negative emotions, and acceptance of external authority; supposedly associated with an increased likelihood of cancer.

ultimate causes Evolutionary conditions that slowly shaped the behavior of a species in past environments.

unconditional positive regard In Rogers's approach, the therapist's assertion that a client's worth as a human being is not dependent on

anything that he or she thinks, does, or feels; love and acceptance of an individual with no strings attached.

unconditioned reinforcer An eliciting stimulus that evokes behavior because of natural selection, such as the elicitation of salivation by food, and that increases the strength of a CR in the classical procedure and the strength of an operant [if it is an appetitive elicitor]; also known as a *primary reinforcer.*

unconditioned response (UR) In classical conditioning, a response, such as salivation, that is elicited by an unconditioned stimulus. The UR may also be a learned response if it was acquired before the classical conditioning procedure under study.

unconditioned stimulus (US) In classical conditioning, a stimulus, such as food, that naturally elicits a reflexive response, such as salivation.

unconscious The inaccessible part of the mind.

underextension The use of a word to denote a smaller class of items than is appropriate; for example, referring only to one particular animal as a dog.

undifferentiated schizophrenia A type of schizophrenia characterized by fragments of the symptoms of different types of schizophrenia.

validity The degree to which the operational definition of a variable accurately reflects the variable it is designed to measure or manipulate.

variable Anything capable of assuming any of several values.

variation The differences among individuals of any given species in their genetic, biological (size, strength, physiology), and psychological (intelligence, sociability, behavior) characteristics.

ventral stream The flow of information from the primary visual cortex to the visual association area in the lower temporal lobe; used to form the perception of an object's shape, color, and orientation (the "what" system).

ventriloquism effect The apparent shift in location of a sound from its auditory source to its perceived visual location.

vertebra One of the bones that encase the spinal cord and constitute the vertebral column (plural: vertebrae).

vestibular apparatus The receptive organs of the inner ear that contribute to balance and perception of head movement.

vestibular sac One of a set of two receptor organs in each inner ear that detect changes in the tilt of the head.

visual agnosia The inability of a person who is not blind to recognize the identity or use of an object by means of vision; usually caused by damage to the brain.

voice-onset time The delay between the initial sound of a consonant (such as the puffing sound of the phoneme /p/) and the onset of vibration of the vocal cords.

wavelength The distance between adjacent waves of radiant energy; in vision, most closely associated with the perceptual dimension of hue.

Weber fraction The ratio between a just-noticeable difference and the magnitude of a stimulus; reasonably constant over the middle range of most stimulus intensities.

Wechsler Adult Intelligence Scale (WAIS) An intelligence test for adults devised by David Wechsler; contains subtests divided into verbal and performance categories.

Wechsler Intelligence Scale for Children (WISC) An intelligence test for children devised by David Wechsler; similar in form to the Wechsler Adult Intelligence Scale.

Wernicke's aphasia A disorder caused by damage to the left temporal and parietal cortex, including Wernicke's area; characterized by deficits in the recognition of speech and by the production of fluent but essentially meaningless speech.

Wernicke's area A region of the auditory association cortex located in the upper part of the left temporal lobe; involved in the recognition of spoken words.

white matter The portions of the central nervous system that are abundant in axons rather than cell bodies of neurons. The color derives from the presence of the axons' myelin sheaths.

whole-word reading Reading by recognizing a word as a whole; "sight reading."

withdrawal symptom An effect produced by discontinuance of use of a drug after a period of continued use; generally opposite to the drug's primary effects.

working memory Memory for new information and information retrieved from long-term memory; used in this text as another name for short-term memory.

zeitgeber Any stimulus, such as light, that synchronizes daily biological rhythms.

zone of proximal development In Vygotsky's theory, the increased potential for problem-solving and conceptual ability that exists for a child if expert mentoring and guidance are available.

zygotic stage The first stage of prenatal development, during which the zygote divides many times and the internal organs begin to form.

References

Abela, J., & Sullivan, C. (2003). A test of Beck's cognitive diathesis-stress theory of depression in early adolescents. *Journal of Early Adolescence, 23(4),* 384–404.

Abma, J. C., Martinez, G. M., Mosher, W. D., & Dawson, B. S. (2004). Teenagers in the United States: Sexual activity, contraception use, and child bearing, 2002. National Center for Health Statistics. *Vital Health Stat 23*(24).

Abramson, L. Y., Alloy, L. B., & Metalsky, G. I. (1995). Hopelessness depression. In Buchanan, G. M. & Seligman, M. E. P. (Eds.), *Explanatory style* (pp. 113–134). Hillsdale, NJ: Lawrence Erlbaum Associates, Inc.

Abramson, L. Y., Metalsky, G. I., & Alloy, L. B. (1989). Hopelessness depression: A theory-based subtype. *Psychological Review, 96,* 358–372.

Abramson, L. Y., Seligman, M. E. P., & Teasdale, J. D. (1978). Learned helplessness in humans: Critique and reformulation. *Journal of Abnormal Psychology, 87,* 49–74.

Acierno, R. E., Hersen, M., & Van Hasselt, V. B. (1993). Interventions for panic disorder: A critical review of the literature. *Clinical Psychology Review, 18,* 561–578.

Adair, J. G. (1984). The Hawthorne effect: A reconsideration of the methodological artifact. *Journal of Applied Psychology, 69,* 334–345.

Adair, J. G. (2001). Ethics of psychological research: New policies; continuing issues; new concerns. *Canadian Psychology, 42,* 25–37.

Adair, J. G., Paivio, A., & Ritchie, P. (1996). Psychology in Canada. *Annual Review of Psychology, 47,* 341–370.

Adair-Bischoff, C. E., & Sauve, R. S. (1998). Environmental tobacco smoke and middle ear disease in preschool-age children. *Archives of Pediatrics and Adolescent Medicine, 152,* 127–133.

Adamec, R. E., & Stark-Adamec, C. (1986). Limbic hyperfunction, limbic epilepsy, and interictal behavior: Models and methods of detection. In B. K. Doane & K. E. Livingston (Eds.), *The limbic system.* New York: Raven Press.

Adey, W. R., Bors, E., & Porter, R. W. (1968). EEG sleep patterns after high cervical lesions in man. *Archives of Neurology, 19,* 377–383.

Adler, A. (1939). *Social interest: A challenge to mankind.* New York: Putnam.

Aharon, I., Etcoff, N., Ariely, D., Chabris, C. F., O'Connor, E., & Breiter, H. C. (2001). Beautiful faces have variable reward value: fMRI and behavioral evidence. *Neuron, 32,* 537–551.

Ahrens, B., Grof, P., Moller, H.-J., Muller-Oerlinghaussen, B., & Wolf, T. (1995). Extended survival of patients on long-term lithium treatment. *Canadian Journal of Psychiatry, 40,* 241–246.

Aiello, L., & Wheeler, P. (1995). The expensive-tissue hypothesis. *Current Anthropology, 36,* 199–221.

Aiken, L. R. (2001). *Dying, death, and bereavement* (4th ed.). Mahway, NJ: Lawrence Erlbaum Associates, Inc.

Ainslie, G. (1975). Species reward: A behavioral theory of impulsiveness and impulse control. *Psychological Bulletin, 82,* 463–496.

Ainsworth, M. D. S. (1973). The development of infant–mother attachment. In B. M. Caldwell & H. R. Ricciuti (Eds.), *Review of Child Development Research, Vol. 3.* Chicago: University of Chicago Press.

Ainsworth, M. D. S., Blehar, M. C., Waters, E., & Wall, S. (1978). *Patterns of attachment.* Hillsdale, NJ: Lawrence Erlbaum Associates.

Ainsworth, M. D. S., & Bowlby, J. (1991). An ethological approach to personality development. *American Psychologist, 46,* 333–341.

Alais, D., Blake, R., & Lee, S.-H. (1998). Visual features that vary together over time group together over space. *Nature Neuroscience, 1,* 160–164.

Albright, L., Kenny, D. A., & Malloy, T. E. (1988). Consensus in personality judgments at zero acquaintance. *Journal of Personality and Social Psychology, 55,* 387–395.

Al-Issa, I. (1995). Culture and mental illness in an international perspective. In I. Al-Issa (Ed.), *Handbook of culture and mental illness: An international perspective.* Madison, CT: International Universities Press, 1995.

Allan, L. G., Siegel, S., Kulatunga-Moruzi, C., Eissenberg, T., & Chapman, A. (1997). Isoluminance and contingent color after-effects. *Perception & Psychophysics, 59,* 1327–1334.

Allen, M. G. (1976). Twin studies of affective illness. *Archives of General Psychiatry, 33,* 1476–1478.

Allik, J., & McCrae, R. R. (2002). A five-factor theory perspective. In R. R. McCrae & J. Allik (Eds.), *The five-factor model of personality across cultures.* International and cultural psychology series. New York: Kluwer Academic/Plenum Publishers.

Allik, J., & McCrae, R. R. (2004). Toward a geography of personality traits: Patterns of profiles across 36 cultures. *Journal of Cross-Cultural Psychology, 35(1),* 13–28.

Allport, G. W. (1968). The historical background of modern social psychology. In G. Lindzey & E. Aronson (Eds.), *The handbook of social psychology, Vol. 1.* Reading, MA: Addison-Wesley.

Allport, G. W., & Odbert, H. S. (1936). Trait-names: A psycholexical study. *Psychological Monographs, 47* (1, Whole No. 211).

Allyon, T., Haughton, E., & Hughes, H. B. (1965). Interpretation of symptoms: Fact or fiction? *Behavior Research and Therapy, 3,* 1–7.

Aloise-Young, P. A., Graham, J. W., & Hansen, W. B. (1994). *Journal of Applied Psychology, 79,* 281–287.

Alsobrook, J. P., & Pauls, D. L. (1997). The genetics of Tourette syndrome. *Neurologic Clinics, 15,* 381–393.

American Psychological Association. (1953). *Ethical standards of psychologists.* Washington, DC: American Psychological Association.

American Psychological Association. (2002). Ethical principles of psychologists and code of conduct. *American Psychologist, 57,* 1060–1073.

Amsel, A. (1962). Frustrative nonreward in partial reinforcement and discrimination learning: Some recent history and a theoretical extension. *Psychological Review, 69,* 306–328.

Anderson, B., & Ley, R. (2001). Dyspnea during panic attacks: An Internet survey of incidences of changes in breathing. *Behavior Modification, 25(4),* 546–554.

Anderson, C. S., Feigin, V., Bennett, D., Lin, R., Hankey, G., & Jamrozik, K. (2004). Active and passive smoking and the risk of subarachnoid hemorrhage: An international population-based case-control study. *Stroke, 35(3),* 633–637.

Anderson, D. R., & Collins, P. A. (1988). *The impact on children's education: Television's influence on cognitive development.* Washington, DC: U.S. Department of Education.

Anderson, D. R., & Field, D. (1983). Children's attention to television: Implications for production. In M. Meyer (Ed.), *Children and the formal features of television.* Munich: Saur.

Anderson, D. R., Field, D., Collins, P., Lorch, E., & Nathan, J. (1985). Estimates of young children's time with television: A methodological comparison of parent reports with time-lapse video home observation. *Child Development, 56,* 1345–1357.

Anderson, D. R., & Lorch, E. (1983). Looking at television: Action or reaction? In J. Bryant & D. R. Anderson (Eds.), *Children's understanding of television: Research on attention and comprehension.* New York: Academic Press.

Anderson, R. H., Fleming, D. E., Rhees, R. W., & Kinghorn, E. (1986). Relationships between sexual activity, plasma testosterone, and the volume of the sexually dimorphic nucleus of the preoptic area in prenatally stressed and non-stressed rats. *Brain Research, 370,* 1–10.

Anderson, S. W., Bechara, A., Damasio, H., Tranel, D., & Damasio, A. R. (1999). Impairment of social and moral behavior related to early damage in human prefrontal cortex. *Nature Neuroscience, 2,* 1032–1037.

Angrist, B. J., Rotrosen, J., & Gershon, S. (1980). Positive and negative symptoms in schizophrenia—Differential response to amphetamine and neuroleptics. *Psychopharmacology, 72,* 17–19.

Aponte, J., Rivers, R., & Wohl, J. (Eds.). (1995). *Psychological interventions and cultural diversity.* Boston: Allyn & Bacon.

Araneda, R. C., Kini, A. D., & Firestein, S. (2000). The molecular receptive range of an odorant receptor. *Nature Neuroscience, 3,* 1248–1255.

Archer, S. L., & Waterman, A. S. (1990). Varieties of identity diffusions and foreclosures: An exploration of subcategories of the identity status. *Journal of Adolescent Research, 5,* 96–111.

Arenberg, D. (1973). Cognition and aging: Verbal learning, memory, and problem solving. In C. Eisdorfer & M. P. Lawton (Eds.), *The psychology of adult development and aging.* Washington, DC: American Psychological Association.

Arieti, S. (2000). *The Parnas: A scene from the Holocaust.* Philadelphia: Paul Dry Books.

Ariyasu, H., Takaya, K., Tagami, T., Ogawa, Y., Hosoda, K., Akamizu, T., Suda, M., Koh, T., Natsui, K., Toyooka, S., Shirakami, G., Usui, T., Shimatsu, A., Doi, K., Hosoda, H., Kojima, M., Kangawa, K., & Nakao, K. (2001). Stomach is a major source of circulating ghrelin, and feeding state determines plasma ghrelin-like immunoreactivity levels in humans. *Journal of Clinical Endocrinology and Metabolism, 86,* 4753–4758.

Armfield, F. (1994). Preventing post-traumatic stress disorder resulting from military operations. *Military Medicine, 159,* 739–746.

Armstrong, G. B., & Chung, L. (2000). Background television and reading memory in context: Assessing TV interference and facilitative context effects on encoding versus retrieval processes. *Communication Research, 27,* 327–352.

Arnett, J. (1995). The young and the reckless: Adolescent reckless behavior. *Current Directions in Psychological Science, 4,* 67–71.

Arrindell, W. A. (2003). Cultural abnormal psychology. *Behaviour Research Therapy, 41,* 749–753.

Asch, S. E. (1946). Forming impressions of personality. *Journal of Abnormal and Social Psychology, 41,* 258–290.

Asch, S. E. (1951). Effects of group pressure upon the modification and distortion of judgment. In H. Guetzkow (Ed.), *Groups, leadership, and men.* Pittsburgh: Carnegie.

Asch, S. E. (1952). *Social psychology.* New York: Prentice-Hall.

Asch, S. E. (1955). Opinions and social pressure. *Scientific American, 193,* 31–35.

Ashford, J. W., Schmitt, F. A., & Kumar, V. (1996). Diagnosis of Alzheimer's disease. *Psychiatric Annals, 26,* 262–268.

Assanand, S., Pinel, J. P. J., & Lehman, D. R. (1998). Personal theories of hunger and eating. *Journal of Applied Social Psychology, 28,* 998–1015.

Astley, S. J., Clarren, S. K., Little, R. E., Sampson, P. D., & Daling, J. R. (1992). Analysis of facial shape in children gestationally exposed to marijuana, alcohol, or cocaine. *Pediatrics, 89,* 67–77.

Atkinson, R. C., & Shiffrin, R. M. (1968). Human memory: A proposed system and its control processes. In K. W. Spence & J. T. Spence (Eds.), *The psychology of learning and motivation: Advances in research and theory, Vol. 2.* New York: Academic Press.

Avison, W. R., & Cairney, J. (2003). Social structure, stress, and personal control. In S. H. Zarit, L. I. Pearlin, et al. (Eds.), *Personal control in social and life course contexts: Societal impact on aging.* New York: Springer Publishing Co.

Avraham, K. B. (1997). Deafness: Sounds from the cochlea. *Nature, 390,* 559–560.

Ayllon, T., & Azrin, N. H. (1968). *The token economy: A motivational system for therapy and rehabilitation.* New York: Appleton-Century-Crofts.

Azrin, N. H., Hutchison, R. R., & Hake, D. F. (1966). Extinction-induced aggression. *Journal of the Experimental Analysis of Behavior, 9,* 191–204.

Badcock, C. (1991). *Evolution and individual behavior: An introduction to human sociobiology.* Cambridge, MA: Blackwell.

Baddeley, A. D. (1982). Domains of recollection. *Psychological Review, 89,* 708–729.

Baddeley, A. D. (1993). Working memory and conscious awareness. In A. F. Collins, S. E. Cathercole, M. A. Conway, & P. E. Morris (Eds.), *Theories of memory.* Hillsdale, NJ: Erlbaum.

Baddeley, A. (2000). The episodic buffer: A new component of working memory? *Trends in Cognitive Sciences, 4,* 417–423.

Baer, D. M., Peterson, R. F., & Sherman, J. A. (1967). Development of imitation by reinforcing behavioral similarity to a model. *Journal of the Experimental Analysis of Behavior, 10,* 405–418.

Baer, L., Rauch, S. L., Ballantine, H. T., Jr., Martuza, R., Cosgrove, R., Cassem, E., Giriunas, I., Manzo, P. A., Dimino, C., & Jenike, M. A. (1995). Cingulotomy for intractable obsessive-compulsive disorder: Prospective long-term follow-up of 18 patients. *Archives of General Psychiatry, 52,* 384–392.

Bahrick, H. P. (1983). The cognitive map of a city—50 years of learning and memory. In G. Bower (Ed.), *The psychology of learning and memory.* New York: Academic Press.

Bahrick, H. P. (1984a). Semantic memory content in permastore: Fifty years of memory for Spanish learned in school. *Journal of Experimental Psychology: General, 113,* 12–29.

Bahrick, H. P. (1984b). Long-term memories: How durable, and how enduring? *Physiological Psychology, 12,* 53–58.

Bailey, C. H., Kandel, E. R., & Si, K. (2004). The persistence of long-term memory: A molecular approach to self-sustaining changes in learning-induced synaptic growth. *Neuron, 44,* 49–57.

Bailey, J. M., & Pillard, R. C. (1991) A genetic study of male sexual orientation. *Archives of General Psychiatry, 48,* 1089–1096.

Bailey, J. M., Pillard, R. C., Neale, M. C., & Agyei, Y. (1993). Heritable factors influence sexual orientation in women. *Archives of General Psychiatry, 50,* 217–223.

Bain, J. (1987). Hormones and sexual aggression in the male. *Integrative Psychiatry, 5,* 82–89.

Baizer, J. S., Underleider, L. G., & Desimone, R. (1991). Organization of visual input to inferior temporal and posterior parietal cortex in macaques. *Journal of Neuroscience, 11,* 168–190.

Baldessarini, R. J., & Tarsy, D. (1980). Dopamine and the pathophysiology of dyskinesias induced by antipsychotic drugs. *Annual Review of Neuroscience, 3,* 23–41.

Baldwin, J. M. (1892). The psychological laboratory in the University of Toronto. *Science, 19,* 143–144.

Ball, K., & Sekuler, R. (1982). A specific and enduring improvement in visual motion discrimination. *Science, 218,* 697–698.

Ballantine, H. T., Bouckoms, A. J., Thomas, E. K., & Giriunas, I. E. (1987). Treatment of psychiatric illness by stereotactic cingulotomy. *Biological Psychiatry, 22,* 807–819.

Baltes, P., & Schaie, K. (1974, October). Aging and IQ: The myth of the twilight years. *Psychology Today,* 35–38.

Bandura, A. (1971). Psychotherapy based upon modeling principles. In A. E. Bergin & S. L. Garfield (Eds.), *Handbook of psychotherapy and behavior change.* New York: John Wiley & Sons.

Bandura, A. (1978). The self system in reciprocal determinism. *American Psychologist, 33,* 344–358.

Bandura, A. (1982). Self-efficacy mechanism in human agency. *American Psychologist, 37,* 122–147.

Bandura, A. (1986). *Social foundations of thought and action: A social-cognitive theory.* Englewood Cliffs, NJ: Prentice-Hall.

Bandura, A. (1995). Exercise of personal and collective efficacy in changing societies. In A. Bandura (Ed.), *Self-efficacy in changing societies.* New York: Cambridge University Press.

Bandura, A. (1997). *Self-efficacy: The exercise of control.* New York: W. H. Freeman & Co., Publishers.

Bandura, A. (2002). Social cognitive theory in cultural context. *Applied Psychology, 51(2),* 269–290.

Bandura, A., & Locke, E. A. (2003). Negative self-efficacy and goal effects revisited. *Journal of Applied Psychology, 88(1),* 87–99.

Banks, M. S., Aslin, R. N., & Letson, R. D. (1975). Sensitive period for the development of human binocular vision. *Science, 190,* 675–677.

Barab, S. A., & Plucker, J. A. (2002). Smart people or smart contexts? Cognition, ability and talent development in an age of situated approaches to knowing and learning. *Educational Psychologist, 37,* 165–182.

Barash, D. (1982). *Sociobiology and behavior.* London: Hodder and Stoughton.

Barber, J. G., Bolitho, F., & Bertrand, L. D. (1999). The predictors of adolescent smoking. *Journal of Social Service Research, 26,* 51–66.

Barber, T. X. (1975). Responding to "hypnotic" suggestions: An introspective report. *American Journal of Clinical Hypnosis, 18,* 6–22.

Barclay, C. D., Cutting, J. E., & Kozlowski, L. T. (1978). Temporal and spatial factors in gait perception that influence gender recognition. *Perception and Psychophysics, 23,* 145–152.

Bard, K. A., Coles, C. D., Plaatzman, K. A., & Lynch, M. E. (2000). The effects of prenatal drug exposure, term status, and caregiving on arousal and arousal modulation in 8-week-old infants. *Developmental Psychobiology, 36,* 194–212.

Barlassina, C. D., & Taglietti, M. V. (2003). Genetics of human arterial hypertension. *Journal of Nephrology, 16,* 609–615.

Barnas, M. V., Pollina, J., & Cummings, E. M. (1991). Life-span attachment: Relations between attachment and socioemotional functioning in women. *Genetic, Social, and General Psychology Monographs, 89,* 177–202.

Barnes, M. L., & Sternberg, R. J. (1997). A hierarchical model of love and its prediction of satisfaction in close relationships. In R. J. Sternberg & M. Hojjat (Eds.), *Satisfaction in close relationships* (pp. 79–101). New York: The Guilford Press.

Bar-On, R. (1997). *BarOn Emotional Quotient Inventory: Technical manual.* Toronto: Multi-Health Systems.

Baron, R. A., & Byrne, D. (1994). *Social psychology: Understanding human interaction.* Boston: Allyn & Bacon.

Baron, R. S., Vandello, J. A., & Brunsman, B. (1996). The forgotten variable in conformity research: Impact of task importance on social influence. *Journal of Personality and Social Psychology, 71,* 915–927.

Baron-Cohen, S., Leslie, A. M., & Frith, U. (1985). Does the autistic child have a "theory of mind"? *Cognition, 21,* 37–46.

Barrick, M. R., Mount, M. K., & Judge, T. A. (2001). Personality and performance at the beginning of the new millennium: What do we know and where do we go next? *International Journal of Selection & Assessment, 9(1–2),* 9–30.

Bartlett, F. C. (1932). *Remembering: An experimental and social study.* Cambridge: Cambridge University Press.

Bartoshuk, L. M., & Beauchamp, G. K. (1994). Chemical senses. *Annual Review of Psychology, 45,* 419–449.

Basoglu, M., Salcloglle, E., & Livanou, M. (2002). Traumatic stress responses in earthquake survivors in Turkey. *Journal of Traumatic Stress, 15(4),* 269–276.

Bassili, J. N. (1993). Response latency versus certainty as indexes of the strength of voting intentions in a CATI survey. *Public Opinion Quarterly, 57,* 54–61.

Bassili, J. N. (1995). Response latency and the accessibility of voting intentions: What contributes to accessibility and how it affects vote choice. *Personality and Social Psychology Bulletin, 21,* 686–695.

Bastiaans, J. (1985). Psychological factors in the development of cancer. In E. Grundemann (Ed.), *Cancer campaign. Vol. 19: The cancer patient—Illness and recovery.* Stuttgart: Gustav Fischer Verlag.

Bateson, G. (1973). *Steps to an ecology of mind.* New York: Paladin Books.

Bauer, P. J. (2002). Long-term recall memory: Behavioral and neuro-developmental changes in the first 2 years of life. *Current Directions in Psychological Science, 11,* 137–141.

Baum, W. M. (1974). On two types of deviation from the matching law: Bias and undermatching. *Journal of the Experimental Analysis of Behavior, 22,* 231–242.

Baumeister, R. F., Dale, K., & Sommer, K. L. (1998). Freudian defense mechanisms and empirical findings in modern social psychology: Reaction formation, projection, displacement, undoing, isolation, sublimation, and denial. *Journal of Personality, 66,* 1081–1124.

Baumrind, D. (1983). Rejoinder to Lewis' reinterpretation of parental firm control effects: Are authoritative families really harmonious? *Psychological Bulletin, 94,* 132–142.

Baumrind, D. (1991). The influence of parenting style on adolescent competence and substance use. *Journal of Early Adolescence, 11,* 56–95.

Beauvois, M.-F., & Dérouesné, J. (1979). Phonological alexia: Three dissociations. *Journal of Neurology, Neurosurgery and Psychiatry, 42,* 1115–1124.

Bechara A., Tranel, D., Damasio, H., Adolphs, R., Rockland, C., & Damasio, A. R. (1995). Double dissociation of conditioning and declarative knowledge relative to the amygdala and hippocampus in humans. *Science, 269,* 1115–1118.

Beck, A. T. (1967). *Depression: Clinical, experimental and theoretical aspects.* New York: Harper and Row.

Beck, A. T. (1991). Cognitive therapy: A thirty-year retrospective. *American Psychologist, 46,* 368–375.

Beck, A. T. (1997). The past and future of cognitive therapy. *Journal of Psychotherapy Practice and Research, 6,* 276–284.

Beck, A. T., Rush, A. J., Shaw, B. F., & Emery, G. (1979). *Cognitive therapy of depression.* New York: Guilford Press.

Begg, I. M., Needham, D. R., & Bookbinder, M. (1993). Do backward messages unconsciously affect listeners? No. *Canadian Journal of Experimental Psychology, 47,* 1–14.

Begleiter, H., & Kissin, B. (1995). *The genetics of alcoholism.* New York: Oxford University Press.

Behrend, D. A., Rosengren, K. S., & Perlmutter, M. (1992). The relation between private speech and parental interactive style. In R. M. Diaz & L. E. Berk (Eds.), *Private speech: From social interaction to self-regulation* (pp. 85–100). Hillsdale, NJ: Lawrence Erlbaum Associates, Inc.

Belin, P., Zatorre, R. J., & Ahad, P. (2002). Human temporal-lobe response to vocal sounds. *Cognitive Brain Research, 13,* 17–26.

Bell, A. P., & Weinberg, M. S. (1978). *Homosexualities: A study of diversity among men and women.* New York: Simon & Schuster.

Bell, A. P., Weinberg, M. S., & Hammersmith, S. K. (1981). *Sexual preference: Its development in men and women.* Bloomington: Indiana University Press.

Bell, S. T., Kuriloff, P. J., & Lottes, I. (1994). Understanding attributions of blame in stranger rape and date rape situations: An examination of gender, race, identification, and students' social perceptions of rape victims. *Journal of Applied Social Psychology, 24,* 1719–1734.

Bellugi, U., & Klima, E. S. (1972, June). The roots of language in the sign talk of the deaf. *Psychology Today,* 61–76.

Belmore, S. M. (1987). Determinants of attention during impression formation. *Journal of Experimental Psychology: Learning, Memory, and Cognition, 13,* 480–489.

Belsky, J., & Cassidy, J. (1994). Attachment and close relationships: An individual-difference perspective. *Psychological Inquiry, 5,* 27–30.

Belsky, J., & Fearon, R. M. P. (2002). Early attachment security, subsequent maternal sensitivity, and later child development: Does continuity in development depend on continuity of caregiving? *Attachment and Human Development, 4,* 361–387.

Bem, D. J. (1972). Self-perception theory. In L. Berkowitz (Ed.), *Advances in experimental social psychology, Vol. 6.* New York: Academic Press.

Benninger, M. S. (1999). The impact of cigarette smoking and environmental tobacco smoke on nasal and sinus disease: A review of the literature. *American Journal of Rhinology, 13,* 435–438.

Berenbaum, S. A., & Snyder, E. (1995). Early hormonal influences on childhood sex-typed activity and playmate preferences: Implications for the development of sexual orientation. *Developmental Psychology, 31,* 31–42.

Berk, L. E. (2002). *Infants, children, and adolescents* (4th ed.). Boston, MA: Allyn & Bacon.

Berkeley, I. S. N., Dawson, M. R. W., Medler, D. A., Schopflocher, D. P., & Hornsby, L. (1995). Density plots of hidden value unit activations reveal interpretable bands. *Connection Science, 7,* 167–186.

Berlin, B., & Kay, P. (1969). *Basic color terms: Their universality and evolution.* Berkeley: University of California Press.

Berlyne, D. E. (1966). Motivational problems raised by exploratory and epistemic behavior. In S. Koch (Ed.), *Psychology: A study of a science, Vol. 5.* New York: McGraw-Hill.

Bernstein, I. L. (1991). Aversion conditioning in response to cancer and cancer treatment. *Clinical Psychology Review, 11,* 183–191.

Bernstein, L. J., & Robertson, L. C. (1998). Illusory conjunctions of color and motion with shape following bilateral parietal lesions. *Psychological Science, 9,* 167–175.

Bernstein, W. M., Stephenson, B. O., Snyder, M. L., & Wicklund, R. A. (1983). Causal ambiguity and heterosexual affiliation. *Journal of Experimental Social Psychology, 19,* 78–92.

Berry, J. W. (1984). Towards a universal psychology of cognitive competence. In P. S. Fry (Ed.), *Changing conceptions of intelligence and intellectual functioning.* Amsterdam: North-Holland.

Berry, J. W. (2001). A psychology of immigration. *Journal of Social Issues, 57,* 615–631.

Berry, J. W. (2003). Origins of cross-cultural similarities and differences in human behavior: An ecocultural perspective. In A. Toomela (Ed.), *Cultural guidance in the development of the human mind: Advances in child development within culturally structured environments.* Westport, CT: Ablex Publishing.

Berry, J. W., Poortinga, Y. H., Segall, M. H., & Dasen, P. R. (1992). *Cross-cultural psychology: Research and applications.* Cambridge, UK: Cambridge University Press.

Berry, J. W., Poortinga, Y. H., Segall, M. H., & Dasen, P. R. (2002). *Cross-cultural psychology: Research and applications* (2nd ed.). New York: Cambridge University Press.

Bertone, E. R., Snyder, L. A., & Moore, A. S. (2003). Environmental and lifestyle risk factors for oral squamous cell carcinoma in domestic cats. *Journal of Veterinary Internal Medicine, 17(4),* 557–562.

Berwick, D. M. (2003). Disseminating innovations in health care. *Journal of the American Medical Association, 289,* 1969–1975.

Biber, B., & Alkin, T. (1999). Panic disorder subtypes: Differential responses to CO-sub-2 challenge. *American Journal of Psychiatry, 156,* 739–744.

Bickel, W. K., & Vuchinich, R. E. (Eds.). (2000). *Reframing health behavior change with behavioral economics.* Mahwah, NJ: Lawrence Erlbaum Associates.

Bickham, D. S., Wright, J. C., & Huston, A. C. (2001). Attention, comprehension, and the educational influences of television. In D. G. Singer & J. L. Singer (Eds.), *Handbook of children and the media.* Thousand Oaks, CA: Sage Publications.

Biederman, I. (1995). Visual object recognition. In S. F. Kosslyn & D. N. Osherson (Eds.), *An invitation to cognitive science* (2nd ed.): Vol. 2. *Visual Cognition* (pp. 121–165). Cambridge, MA: MIT Press.

Biernat, M., & Wortman, C. B. (1991). Sharing of home responsibilities between professionally employed women and their husbands. *Journal of Personality and Social Psychology, 60,* 844–860.

Biglan, A., & Severson, H. H. (2003). The prevention of tobacco use. In A. Biglan, M. C. Wang, et al. (Eds.), *Preventing youth problems: Issues in children's and families' lives.* New York: Kluwer Academic/Plenum Publishers.

Binder, J. (1998). The therapeutic alliance in the relational models of time-limited dynamic psychotherapy. In J. D. Safran & J. C. Muran (Eds.), *The therapeutic alliance in brief psychotherapy.* Washington, DC: American Psychological Association.

Binder, J. R., Frost, J. A., Hammeke, T. A., Cox, R. W., Rao, S. M., & Prieto, T. (1997). Human brain language areas identified by functional magnetic resonance imaging. *Journal of Neuroscience, 17,* 353–362.

Binder, J. R., Liebenthal, E., Possing, E. T., Medler, D. A., & Ward, B. D. (2004). Neural correlates of sensory and decision processes in auditory object identification. *Nature Neuroscience, 7,* 295–301.

Binet, A., & Henri, V. (1896). La psychologie individuelle. *Année Psychologique, 2,* 411–465.

Birch, H. G. (1945). The relation of previous experience to insightful problem-solving. *Journal of Comparative Psychology, 38,* 367–383.

Birren, J. E., & Morrison, D. F. (1961). Analysis of the WISC subtests in relation to age and education. *Journal of Gerontology, 16,* 363–369.

Bishop, G. D. (1991a). Lay disease representations and responses to victims of disease. *Basic and Applied Social Psychology, 12,* 115–132.

Bishop, G. D. (1991b). Understanding the understanding of illness. In J. A. Skelton & R. T. Croyle, *Mental representation in health and illness.* New York: Springer-Verlag.

Bishop, G. D. (1994). *Health psychology: Integrating mind and body.* Boston: Allyn & Bacon.

Blacher, J., & Baker, B. L. (1987). Dry-bed training for nocturnal enuresis in three children with multiple problems. *Journal of Clinical Child Psychology, 16(3),* 240–244.

Blaxton, T. A. (1989). Investigating dissociations among memory measures: Support for a transfer appropriate processing framework. *Journal of Experimental Psychology: Learning, Memory, and Cognition, 15,* 657–668.

Bleuler, E. (1950). *Dementia praecox: or, the group of schizophrenias. Monograph series on schizophrenia.* New York: International Universities Press.

Bliss, E. L. (1986). *Multiple personality, allied disorders, and hypnosis.* New York: Oxford University Press.

Bliss, T. V., & Lomø, T. (1973). Long-lasting potentiation of synaptic transmission in the dentate area of the anaesthetized rabbit following stimulation of the perforant path. *Journal of Physiology, 232,* 331–356.

Bloom, L. (1970). *Language development: Form and function in emerging grammars.* Cambridge, MA: MIT Press.

Blough, D. S. (1966). The reinforcement of least-frequent interresponse times. *Journal of the Experimental Analysis of Behavior, 9,* 581–591.

Blum, K., Noble, E. P., Sheridan, P. J., Montgomery, A., & Ritchie, T. (1990). Allelic association of human dopamine D2 receptor gene in alcoholism. *Journal of the American Medical Association, 263,* 2055–2060.

Bodenhausen, G. V., Macrae, C. N., & Hugenberg, K. (2003). Social cognition. In T. Millon & M. Lerner (Eds.), *Handbook of psychology: Personality and social psychology, Vol. 5.* New York: John Wiley & Sons, Inc.

Boe, L. J., Heim, J. L., Abry, C., & Badin, P. L. (2004). Neandertal vocal tract: Which potential for vowel acoustics. *Interaction studies: Social Behavior & Communication in Biological and Social Systems, 5,* 409–429.

Boehnke, S. E., & Phillips, D. P. (1999). Azimuthal tuning of human perceptual channels for sound location. *Journal of the Acoustical Society of America, 106,* 1948–1955.

Bohannan, P. (1995). *How culture works.* New York: The Free Press.

Bohannon, J. N. (1993). Theoretical approaches to language acquisition. In J. B. Gleason (Ed.), *The development of language.* New York: Macmillan.

Bohannon, J. N., & Stanowicz, L. (1988). The issue of negative evidence: Adult responses to children's language errors. *Developmental Psychology, 24,* 684–689.

Bohman, M., Cloninger, C. R., von Knorring, A. L., & Sigvardsson, S. (1984). An adoption study of somatoform disorders. III. Cross-fostering analysis and genetic relationship to alcoholism and criminality. *Archives of General Psychiatry, 41,* 872–878.

Bondolfi, G., Dufour, H., Patris, M., May, J. P., Billeter, U., Eap, C. B., & Baumann, P. (1998). Risperidone versus Clozapine in treatment-resistant chronic schizophrenia: A randomized double-blind study. *American Journal of Psychiatry, 155,* 499–504.

Bonvillian, J., Nelson, K. E., & Charrow, V. (1976). Languages and language-related skills in deaf and hearing children. *Sign Language Studies, 12,* 211–250.

Boone, T. L., Lefkowitz, E. S., Romo, L., Corona, R., Sigman, M., & Au, T. K. (2003). Mothers' and adolescents' perceptions of AIDS vulnerability. *International Journal of Behavioral Development, 27,* 347–354.

Bordin, E. S. (1994). Theory and research on the therapeutic working alliance: New directions. In A. O. Horvath & L. S. Greenberg (Eds.), *The working alliance: Theory, research, and practice.* New York: John Wiley & Sons.

Bordnick, P. S., Elkins, R. L., Orr, T. E., Walters, P., & Thyer, B. A. (2004). Evaluating the relative effectiveness of three aversion therapies designed to reduce craving among cocaine abusers. *Behavioral Interventions, 19,* 1–24.

Borgida, E., & Nisbett, R. E. (1977). The differential viewpoint of abstract vs. concrete information on decisions. *Journal of Applied Social Psychology, 7,* 258–271.

Bornstein, M. H., & Arterberry, M. E. (2003). Recognition, discrimination and categorization of smiling by 5-month-old infants. *Developmental Science, 6,* 585–599.

Borysenko, J. Z. (1982). Behavioural-physiological factors in the development and management of cancer. *General Hospital Psychiatry, 3,* 69–74.

Bosarge, L. (1989). Educating college students about sexually transmitted diseases, AIDS, and safe-sex practices. Unpublished master's thesis, Auburn University.

Botwinick, J., & Storandt, M. (1974). *Memory, related functions and age.* Springfield, IL: Charles C. Thomas.

Bouchard, T. J., Jr. (1997). The genetics of personality. In K. Blum & E. P. Noble (Eds.), *The handbook of psychiatric genetics.* Boca Raton, FL: CRC Press Inc.

Bouchard, T. J., Jr., & Hur, Y.-M. (1998). Genetic and environmental influences on the continuous scales of the Myers-Briggs Type Indicator: An analysis based on twins reared apart. *Journal of Personality, 66,* 135–149.

Bouchard, T. J., & McGue, M. (1981). Familial studies of intelligence: A review. *Science, 212,* 1055–1059.

Bouchard, T. J., & Propping, P. (Eds.). (1993). *Twins as a tool of behavior genetics.* Chichester, UK: Wiley.

Bouton, M. E., Mineka, S., & Barlow, D. H. (2001). A modern learning theory perspective on the etiology of panic disorder. *Psychological Review, 108,* 4–32.

Bower, G. H. (1970). Analysis of a mnemonic device. *American Scientist, 58,* 496–510.

Bower, G. H., & Clark, M. C. (1969). Narrative stories as mediators for serial learning. *Psychonomic Science, 14,* 181–182.

Bower, M. (1991). *Classification of disciplinary events and choices as a function of childhood history.* Unpublished manuscript. University of Iowa, Iowa City, IA.

Bowers, K. S., & Davidson, T. M. (1991). A neodissociative critique of Spanos's social-psychological model of hypnosis. In S. J. Lynn & J. W. Rhue (Eds.), *Theories of hypnosis: Current models and perspectives* (pp. 105–143). New York: Guilford Press.

Bowlby, J. (1969). *Attachment and loss. Vol. 1: Attachment.* New York: Basic Books.

Bowlby, J. (1973). *Attachment and loss. Vol. 2.* New York: Basic Books.

Bowlby, J. (1982). Attachment and loss: Retrospect and prospect. *American Journal of Orthopsychiatry, 52,* 664–678.

Bowlby, J. (1988). *A secure base: Parent-child attachment and healthy human development.* New York: Basic Books, Inc.

Boynton, R. M. (1979). *Human color vision.* New York: Holt, Rinehart, and Winston.

Boysen, S. T., & Himes, G. T. (1999). Current issues and emerging theories in animal cognition. *Annual Review of Psychology, 50,* 683–705.

Bradley, C. L., & Marcia, J. E. (1998). Generativity-stagnation: A five-category model. *Journal of Personality, 66,* 39–64.

Brady, J. P., & Lind, D. L. (1961). Experimental analysis of hysterical blindness. *Archives of General Psychiatry, 4,* 331–359.

Brainerd, C. J. (2003). Jean Piaget, learning research, and American education. In B. J. Zimmerman (Ed.), *Educational psychology: A century of contributions.* Mahwah, NJ: Lawrence Erlbaum Associates.

Bransford, J. D., & Johnson, M. K. (1972). Contextual prerequisites for understanding: Some investigations of comprehension and recall. *Journal of Verbal Learning and Verbal Behavior, 11,* 717–726.

Brass, M., & Heyes, C. (2005). Imitation: Is cognitive neuroscience solving the correspondence problem? *Trends in Cognitive Sciences, 9,* 489–495.

Brauer, M., Judd, C. M., & Gliner, M. D. (1995). The effects of repeated expressions on attitude polarization during group discussion. *Journal of Personality and Social Psychology, 68,* 1014–1029.

Bray, S. R., & Born, H. A. (2004). Transition to university and vigorous physical activity: Implications for health and psychological well-being. *Journal of American College Health, 52(4),* 181–188.

Brehm, S. S. (1992). *Intimate relationships* (2nd ed.). New York: McGraw-Hill.

Brennan, P., Buffler, P. A., Reynolds, P., Wu, W. H., Wichmann, H. E., Agudo, A., Pershagen, G., et al. (2004). Secondhand smoke exposure in adulthood and risk of lung cancer among never smokers: A pooled analysis of two large studies. *International Journal of Cancer, 109(1),* 125–131.

Brewin, C. R., Andrews, B., & Valentine, J. D. (2000). Meta-analysis of risk factors for post-traumatic stress disorder in trauma-exposed adults. *Journal of Consulting and Clinical Psychology, 68,* 748–766.

Brickner, R. M. (1936). *The intellectual functions of the frontal lobe: A study based upon observations of a man after partial frontal lobectomy.* New York: Macmillan.

Briggs, S. R. (1988). Shyness: Introversion or neuroticism? *Journal of Research in Personality, 22,* 290–307.

Broadbent, D. E. (1958). *Perception and communication.* London: Pergamon Press.

Broberg, A. G., Wessels, H., Lamb, M. E., & Hwang, C. P. (1997). Effects of day care on the development of cognitive abilities in 8-year-olds: A longitudinal study. *Developmental Psychology, 33,* 62–69.

Brooks-Gunn, J. (1988). Antecedents and consequences of variations in girls' maturational timing. *Journal of Adolescent Health Care, 9,* 365–373.

Brooks-Gunn, J. (1989). Pubertal processes and the early adolescent transition. In W. Damon (Ed.), *Child development today and tomorrow.* San Francisco: Jossey-Bass.

Broverman, I. K., Vogel, S. R., Broverman, D. M., Clarkson, F. E., & Rosenkrantz, P. S. (1994). Sex-role stereotypes: A current appraisal. In B. Puka (Ed.), *Caring voices and women's moral frames: Gilligan's view.* New York: Garland Publishing.

Brown, A. S. (1991). A review of the tip-of-the-tongue experience. *Psychological Bulletin, 109,* 204–223.

Brown, A. S., Begg, M. D., Gravenstein, S., Schaefer, C. A., Wyatt, R. J., Bresnahan, M., Bagulas, V. P., & Susser, E. S. (2004). Serological evidence of prenatal influenza in the etiology of schizophrenia. *Archives of General Psychiatry, 61,* 771–780.

Brown, G. W. (1985). The discovery of expressed emotion: Induction or deduction? In J. Leff & C. Vaughn (Eds.), *Expressed emotion in families.* New York: Guilford Press.

Brown, G. W., Bone, M., Dalison, B., & Wing, J. K. (1966). *Schizophrenia and social care.* London: Oxford University Press.

Brown, J. D. (1991). Staying fit and staying well: Physical fitness as a moderator of life stress. *Personality Processes and Individual Differences, 60,* 455–461.

Brown, J. D., & Rogers, R. (1991). Self-serving attributions: The role of physiological arousal. *Personality and Social Psychology Bulletin, 17,* 501–506.

Brown, P. L., & Jenkins, H. M. (1968). Autoshaping of the pigeon's keypeck. *Journal of the Experimental Analysis of Behavior, 11,* 1–8.

Brown, R. (1973). *A first language: The early stages.* Cambridge, MA: Harvard University Press.

Brown, R., & Bellugi, U. (1964). Three processes in the child's acquisition of syntax. *Harvard Education Review, 34,* 133–151.

Brown, R., & Fraser, C. (1964). The acquisition of syntax. In U. Bellugi & R. Brown (Eds.), The acquisition of language. *Monographs of the Society for Research in Child Development, 29,* 43–79.

Brown, R., & Hanlon, C. (1970). Derivational complexity and order of acquisition in child speech. In J. R. Hayes (Ed.), *Cognition and the development of language.* New York: John Wiley & Sons.

Brown, R., & McNeill, D. (1966). The "tip-of-the-tongue" phenomenon. *Journal of Verbal Learning and Verbal Behavior, 5,* 325–337.

Brown, R. D., & Bassili, J. N. (2002). Spontaneous trait associations and the case of the superstitious banana. *Journal of Experimental Social Psychology, 38,* 87–92.

Brown, R. W., & Kulik, J. (1977). Flashbulb memories. *Cognition, 5,* 73–99.

Brownell, K. D., Greenwood, M. R. C., Stellar, E., & Shrager, E. E. (1986). The effects of repeated cycles of weight loss and regain in rats. *Physiology and Behavior, 38,* 459–464.

Browner, W. S., Westenhouse, J., & Tice, J. A. (1991). What if Americans ate less fat? A quantitative estimate of the effect on mortality. *Journal of the American Medical Association, 265,* 3285–3291.

Bruner, J. S., Goodnow, J. J., & Austin, G. A. (1956). *A study of thinking.* New York: Wiley.

Buck, K. J. (1998). Recent progress toward the identification of genes related to risk for alcoholism. *Mammalian Genome, 9,* 927–928.

Buck, L., & Axel, R. (1991). A novel multigene family may encode odorant receptors: A molecular basis for odor recognition. *Cell, 65,* 175–187.

Bureau of Labor Statistics. (2004). November 2004 national cross-industry estimates of employment and mean annual wage for SOC major occupational groups. Retrieved March 9, 2006, http://www.bls.gov/oes/home.htm

Burger, J. M., & Hemans, L. T. (1988). Desire for control and the use of attribution processes. *Journal of Personality, 56,* 531–546.

Burian, S. E., Liguori, A., & Robinson, J. H. (2002). Effects of alcohol on risk-taking during simulated driving. *Human Psychopharmacology, 17(3),* 141–150.

Burt, C. D. B., Kemp, S., & Conway, M. (2001). What happens if you retest autobiographical memory 10 years on? *Memory & Cognition, 29,* 127–136.

Busch, F. (2003a). Back to the future. *Psychoanalytic Quarterly, 72(1),* 201–215.

Busch, F. (2003b). Telling stories. *Journal of the American Psychoanalytic Association, 51(1),* 25–42.

Bushara, K. O., Hanakawa, T., Immisch, I., Toma, K., Kansaku, K., & Hallett, M. (2003). Neural correlates of cross-modal binding. *Nature Neuroscience, 6,* 190–195.

Bushman, B. J., & Huesmann, L. R. (2001). Effects of televised violence on aggression. In D. G. Singer & J. L. Singer (Eds.), *Handbook of children and the media.* Thousand Oaks, CA: Sage Publications.

Buskist, W., & Miller, H. L. (1986). Interaction between rules and contingencies in the control of human fixed-interval performance. *Psychological Record, 36,* 109–116.

Buss, A. H. (1995). *Personality: Temperament, social behavior, and the self.* Boston: Allyn & Bacon.

Buss, D. M. (1989). Sex differences in human mate preferences: Evolutionary hypotheses tested in 37 cultures. *Behavioral and Brain Sciences, 12,* 1–49.

Buss, D. M. (1990). International preferences in selecting mates: A study of 37 societies. *Journal of Cross-cultural Psychology, 21,* 5–47.

Buss, D. M. (1992). Mate preferences mechanisms: Consequences for partner choice and intrasexual competition. In J. H. Barkow, L. Cosmides, & J. Tooby (Eds.), *The adapted mind: Evolutionary psychology and the generation of culture.* New York: Oxford University Press.

Buss, D. M. (1995). Psychological sex differences: Origins through natural selection. *American Psychologist, 50,* 164–168.

Butcher, J. N., Ben-Porath, Y. S., Shondrick, D. D., Stafford, K. P., McNulty, J. L., Graham, J. R., Stein, L. A. R., et al. (2000). Cultural and subcultural factors in MMPI-2 interpretation. In J. N. Butcher (Ed.), *Basic sources on the MMPI-2.* Minneapolis: University of Minnesota Press.

Buxbaum, L. J., Glosser, G., & Coslett, H. B. (1999). Impaired face and word recognition without object agnosia. *Neuropsychologia, 37(1),* 41–50.

Byrne, D. (1997). An overview (and underview) of research and theory on the attraction paradigm. *Journal of Social & Personal Relationships, 14,* 417–431.

Cacioppo, J. T., Petty, R. E., & Crites, S. L. (1993). Attitude change. In V. S. Ramachandran (Ed.), *Encyclopedia of human behavior.* San Diego: Academic Press.

Calkins, M. W. (1892). Experimental psychology at Wellesley College. *American Journal of Psychology, 5,* 464–471.

Cambronne, D., Shih, J., & Harri, K. (1999). Innovative stress management for financial service organizations. In J. Oher (Ed.), *The employee assistance handbook.* New York: John Wiley & Sons, Inc.

Campbell, D. T. (1974). Evolutionary epistemology. In P. A. Schlipp (Ed.), *The philosophy of Karl Popper* (Vol. 14-1, pp. 413–463). LaSalle, IL: Open Court Publishing.

Campbell, D. T. (1976). On the conflicts between biological and social evolution and between psychology and moral tradition. *American Psychologist, 30,* 1103–1126.

Campbell, J. D., Trapness, P. D., Heine, S. J., Katz, I. M., Lavalee, L. F., & Lehman, D. R. (1996). Self-concept clarity: Measurement, personality correlates and cultural boundaries. *Journal of Personality and Social Psychology, 70,* 141–156.

Campfield, L. A., Smith, F. J., Guisez, Y., Devos, R., & Burn, P. (1995). Recombinant mouse OB protein: Evidence for a peripheral signal linking adiposity and central neural networks. *Science, 269,* 546–549.

Canadian Psychological Association. (2000). *Canadian code of ethics for psychologists* (3rd ed.). Ottawa: Canadian Psychological Association.

Cannon, W. B. (1929). *Bodily changes in pain, hunger, fear, and rage: An account of recent re-searches into the function of emotional excitement.* New York: Appleton-Century-Crofts.

Cannon, W. B. (1953). *Bodily changes in pain, hunger, fear and rage: An account of recent re-searches into the function of emotional excitement* (2nd ed.). Boston: Charles T. Branford.

Cannon, W. B. (1927). The James-Lange theory of emotions: a critical examination and an alternative theory. Reprinted in *American Journal of Psychology,* 1987, *100,* 567–586.

Cannon, W. B., & Washburn, A. L. (1912). An explanation of hunger. *American Journal of Physiology, 29,* 444–454.

Capaldi, E. J., Haas, A. I., Miller, R. M., & Martins, A. (2005). How transitions from nonrewarded to rewarded trials regulate responding in Pavlovian and instrumental learning following extensive acquisition training. *Learning and Motivation, 36,* 279–296.

Caplan, D., Alpert, N., & Waters, G. (1999). PET studies of syntactic processing with auditory sentence presentation. *NeuroImage, 9,* 343–351.

Carlson, E. A. (1998). A prospective longitudinal study of attachment disorganization/disorientation. *Child Development, 69,* 1107–1128.

Carlson, N. R. (1995). *Foundations of physiological psychology* (3rd ed.). Boston: Allyn & Bacon.

Carlston, D. E., & Skowronski, J. J. (1994). Savings in the relearning of trait information as evidence for spontaneous inference generation. *Journal of Personality & Social Psychology, 66,* 840–856.

Carpendale, J. I. M. (2000). Kohlberg and Piaget on stages and moral reasoning. *Developmental Review, 20,* 181–205.

Carpenter, P. A., & Just, M. A. (1983). What your eyes do while your mind is reading. In K. Rayner (Ed.), *Eye movements in reading: Perceptual and language processes.* New York: Academic Press.

Carpenter, P. A., Miyake, A., & Just, M. A. (1995). Language comprehension: Sentence and discourse processing. *Annual Review of Psychology, 46,* 91–120.

Carpenter, W. T., Conley, R. R., Buchanan, R. W., Breier, A., & Tamminga, C. A. (1995). Patient response and resource management: Another view of clozapine treatment of schizophrenia. *American Journal of Psychiatry, 152,* 827–832.

Carr, E. G., & Lovaas, O. J. (1983). Contingent electric shock as a treatment for severe behavior problems. In S. Axelrod & J. Apsche (Eds.), *The effect of punishment on human behavior.* New York: Academic Press.

Carroll, J. B. (1993). *Human cognitive abilities: A survey of factor-analytic studies.* New York: Cambridge University Press.

Carroll, S. B. (2003). Genetics and the making of *Homo sapiens. Nature, 422,* 849–857.

Carson, R. C., Butcher, J. N., & Mineka, S. (2000). *Abnormal psychology and modern life* (11th ed.). Boston: Allyn & Bacon.

Case, R. (1992). *The mind's staircase.* Hillsdale, NJ: Erlbaum.

Case, R. (1998). The development of central conceptual structures. In D. Kuhn & R. Siegler (Eds.), *Handbook of child psychology: Vol. 2. Cognition, perception, and language* (5th ed.). New York: Wiley.

Catania, A. C. (1971). Reinforcement schedules: The role of responses preceding the one that produces the reinforcer. *Journal of the Experimental Analysis of Behavior, 15,* 271–287.

Catania, A. C., Mathews, B. A., & Shimoff, E. (1982). Instructed versus shaped human verbal behavior: Interactions with nonverbal responding. *Journal of the Experimental Analysis of Behavior, 38,* 233–248.

Cath, D. C., Spinhoven, P., van de Wetering, B. J. M., Hoogduin, C. A. H., Landman, A. D., van Woerkom, T. C. A. M., Roos, R. A. C., & Rooijmans, H. G. M. (2000). The relationship between types and severity of repetitive behaviors in Gilles de la Tourette's disorder and obsessive-compulsive disorder. *Journal of Clinical Psychology, 61,* 505–513.

Cattell, R. A. (1963). Theory of fluid and crystallized intelligence: A critical experiment. *Journal of Educational Psychology, 54,* 1–22.

Cavanaugh, J. C. (1990). *Adult development and aging.* Belmont, CA: Wadsworth.

Centers for Disease Control. (1995). Update: Trends in fetal alcohol syndrome—United States, 1979–1993. *Morbidity and Mortality Weekly Reports, 44,* 249–251.

Centers for Disease Control. (1997). Alcohol consumption among pregnant and childbearing-aged women—United States, 1991–1995. *Morbidity and Mortality Weekly Reports, 46,* 346–350.

Centers for Disease Control. (2002). Alcohol use among women of childbearing age—United States, 1991–1999. *Morbidity and Mortality Weekly Reports, 51,* 273–276.

Centers for Disease Control and Prevention. (2004). *HIV/AIDS surveillance report, 2003 (Vol. 15).* Atlanta: U.S. Department of Health and Human Services.

Centers for Disease Control and Prevention. (2005). Annual smoking-attributable mortality, years of potential life lost, and productivity losses—United States, 1997–2001. *Morbidity and Mortality Weekly Report, 54,* 625–628.

Chaiken, S. (1979). Communicator's physical attractiveness and persuasion. *Journal of Personality and Social Psychology, 37,* 1387–1397.

Chakos, M., Lieberman, J., Hoffman, E., Bradford, D., & Sheitman, B. (2001). Effectiveness of second-generation antipsychotics in patients with treatment-resistant schizophrenia: A review and meta-analysis of randomized trials. *American Journal of Psychiatry, 158(4),* 518–526.

Chapin, F. S. (1938). Design for social experiments. *American Sociological Review, 3,* 786–800.

Chapman, K. L., Leonard, L. B., & Mervis, C. B. (1986). The effect of feedback on young children's inappropriate word usage. *Journal of Child Language, 13,* 101–117.

Charman, D. P. (2004). Effective psychotherapy and effective psychotherapists. In D. P. Charman (Ed.), *Core processes in brief psychodynamic psychotherapy: Advancing effective practice.* Mahwah, NJ: Lawrence Erlbaum Associates.

Chasdi, E. H. (1994). *Culture and human development: The selected papers of John Whiting*. New York: Cambridge University Press.

Chassin, L., Presson, C. C., Rose, J. S., & Sherman, S. J. (1998). Maternal socialization of adolescent smoking: Intergenerational transmission of smoking-related beliefs. *Psychology of Addictive Behaviors, 12*, 206–216.

Chassin, L., Presson, C. C., Sherman, S. J., & Edwards, D. A. (1990). The natural history of cigarette smoking: Predicting young-adult smoking outcomes from adolescent patterns. *Health Psychology, 9*, 710–716.

Chassin, L., Presson, C. C., Sherman, S. J., & Kim, K. (2003). Historical changes in cigarette smoking and smoking-related beliefs after 2 decades in a midwestern community. *Health Psychology, 22(4)*, 647–653.

Chaudhari, N., Landin, A. M., & Roper, S. D. (2000). A metabotropic glutamate receptor variant functions as a taste receptor. *Nature Neuroscience, 3*, 113–119.

Cheesman, J., & Merikle, P. M. (1986). Distinguishing conscious from unconscious perceptual processes. *Canadian Journal of Psychology, 40*, 343–367.

Cheesman, M. F. (1997). Speech perception by elderly listeners: Basic knowledge and implications for audiology. *Journal of Speech-Language Pathology and Audiology, 21*, 104–110.

Chemelli, R. M., Willie, J. T., Sinton, C. M., Elmquist, J. K., Scammell, T. E., Lee, C., Richardson, J. A., Williams, S. C., Xiong, Y., Kisanuki, Y., Fitch, T. E., Nakazato, M., Hammer, R. E., Saper, C. B., & Yanagisawa, M. (1999). Narcolepsy in orexin knockout mice: Molecular genetics of sleep regulation. *Cell, 98*, 437–451.

Cheng, P. N., & Holyoak, K. J. (1985). Pragmatic reasoning schemas. *Cognitive Psychology, 17*, 391–416.

Cheour, M., Ceponiene, R., Lehtokoski, A., Luuk, A., Allik, J., Alho, K., & Näätänen, R. (1998). Development of language-specific phoneme representations in the infant brain. *Nature Neuroscience, 1*, 351–353.

Cheour, M., Martynova, O., Näätänen, R., Erkkola, R., Sillanpää, M., Kero, P., Raz, A., Kaipio, M. L., Hiltunen, J., Aaltonen, O., Savela, J., & Hämäläinen, H. (2002). Speech sounds learned by sleeping newborns. *Nature, 415*, 599–600.

Cherry, E. C. (1953). Some experiments on the recognition of speech, with one and with two ears. *Journal of the Acoustical Society of America, 25*, 975–979.

Chomsky, N. (1957). *Syntactic structure*. The Hague: Mouton Publishers.

Chomsky, N. (1965). *Aspects of the theory of syntax*. Cambridge, MA: MIT Press.

Chu, S., & Downes, J. J. (2000). Odour-evoked autobiographical memories: Psychological investigations of Proustian phenomena. *Chemical Senses, 25*, 111–116.

Chun, M. M., & Phelps, E. A. (1999). Memory deficits for implicit contextual information in amnesic subjects with hippocampal damage. *Nature Neuroscience, 2*, 844–847.

Chung, K. C., Kowalski, C. P., Kim, H. M., & Buchman, S. R. (2000). Maternal cigarette smoking during pregnancy and the risk of having a child with cleft lip/palate. *Plastic and Reconstructive Surgery, 105*, 485–491.

Cialdini, R. B. (1993). *Influence: Science and practice* (3rd ed.). New York: HarperCollins.

Cialdini, R. B. (2000). *Influence: Science and practice* (4th ed.). Boston: Allyn & Bacon.

Cialdini, R. B., & Goldstein, N. J. (2004). Social influence: Compliance and conformity. *Annual Review of Psychology, 55*, 591–621.

Clark, D. A., Beck, A. T., & Alford, B. A. (1999). *Scientific foundations of cognitive theory and therapy of depression*. New York: John Wiley & Sons, Inc.

Clark, F. C. (1958). The effect of deprivation and frequency of reinforcement on variable-interval responding. *Journal of the Experimental Analysis of Behavior, 1*, 221–228.

Clarke-Stewart, A. (1978). And Daddy makes three: The father's impact on mother and young child. *Child Development, 49*, 466–479.

Cleckley, H. (1976). *The mask of sanity*. St. Louis: C. V. Mosby.

Cloninger, C. R. (1987). Neurogenetic adaptive mechanisms in alcoholism. *Science, 236*, 410–416.

Cloninger, C. R., Bohman, M., Sigvardsson, S., & von Knorring, A. L. (1985). Psychopathology in adopted-out children of alcoholics. The Stockholm Adoption Study. *Recent Developments in Alcoholism, 7*, 235.

Cobb, S., & Rose, R. M. (1973). Hypertension, peptic ulcer, and diabetes in air traffic controllers. *Journal of the American Medical Association, 224*, 489–492.

Cohen, L. A. (1987). Diet and cancer. *Scientific American, 102*, 42–48.

Cohen, M., Brom, D., & Dasberg, H. (2001). Child survivors of the Holocaust: Symptoms and coping after fifty years. *Israel Journal of Psychiatry & Related Sciences, 38(1)*, 3–12.

Cohen, M. E., Robins, E., Purtell, J. J., Altmann, M. W., & Reid, D. E. (1953). Excessive surgery in hysteria: Study of surgical procedures in 50 women with hysteria and 190 controls. *Journal of the American Medical Association, 151*, 977–986.

Cohen, S., Doyle, W. J., & Skoner, D. P. (1999). Psychological stress, cytokine production, and severity of upper respiratory illness. *Psychosomatic Medicine, 61*, 175–180.

Cohen, S., & Hamrick, N. (2003). Stable individual differences in physiological response to stressors: Implications for stress-elicited changes in immune related health. *Brain, Behavior, & Immunity, 17(6)*, 407–414.

Coleman, J. C. (1976). *Abnormal psychology and modern life* (5th ed.). Glenview, IL: Scott, Foresman.

Collins, A. M., & Quillian, M. R. (1969). Retrieval time from semantic memory. *Journal of Verbal Learning and Verbal Behavior, 8*, 240–248.

Condry, J., & Condry, S. (1976). Sex differences: A study of the eye of the beholder. *Child Development, 47*, 812–819.

Conley, R. R., & Kelly, D. L. (2001). Management of treatment resistance in schizophrenia. *Society of Biological Psychiatry, 50*, 898–911.

Conner, R. L., & Levine, S. (1969). Hormonal influences on aggressive behaviour. In S. Garattine & E. B. Sigg (Eds.), *Aggressive behaviour*. New York: John Wiley & Sons.

Connolly, M. B., Crits-Christoph, P., Barber, J. P., & Luborsky, L. (2000). Transference patterns in the therapeutic relationship in supportive-expressive psychotherapy for depression. *Psychotherapy Research, 10(3)*, 356–372.

Conrad, R. (1964). Acoustic confusions in immediate memory. *British Journal of Psychology, 55*, 75–83.

Conrad, R. (1970). Short-term memory processes in the deaf. *British Journal of Psychology, 61*, 179–195.

Consumer Reports. (1995, November). Mental health: Does therapy help? 734–739.

Coons, P. M. (2000). Dissociative fugue. In B. J. Sadock & V. A. Sadock (Eds.), *Kaplan and Sadock's comprehensive textbook of psychiatry* (7th ed., vol. 1, pp. 1549–1552). New York: Lippincott, Williams, & Wilkins.

Cooper, K. (1985). Running without risk. *Runner's World, 20*, 61–64.

Cooper, K. H. (1968). *Aerobics*. New York: Evans and Company.

Cooper, M. L., Frone, M. R., Russell, M., & Mudar, P. (1995). Drinking to regulate positive and negative emotions: A motivational model of alcohol use. *Journal of Personality & Social Psychology, 69(5)*, 990–1005.

Cooper, M. L., Russell, M., & George, W. H. (1988). Coping, expectancies, and alcohol abuse: A test of social learning foundations. *Journal of Abnormal Psychology, 97*, 218–230.

Cooper, R. M., & Zubek, J. P. (1958). Effects of enriched and restricted early environments on the learning ability of bright and dull rats. *Canadian Journal of Psychology, 12*, 159–164.

Coover, G. D., Murison, R., & Jellestad, F. K. (1992). Subtotal lesions of the amygdala: The rostral central nucleus in passive avoidance and ulceration. *Physiology and Behavior, 51*, 795–803.

Corbetta, M., Miezin, F. M., Doobmeyer, S., Shulman, G. L., & Petersen, S. E. (1991). Selective and divided attention during visual discriminations of shape, color, and speed: Functional anatomy by positron emission tomography. *Journal of Neuroscience, 11*, 2383–2402.

Coren, S., & Hakstian, A. R. (1988). Color vision screening without the use of technical equipment: Scale development and cross-validation. *Perception and Psychophysics, 43*, 115–120.

Corkin, S. (2002). What's new with the amnesic patient H. M.? *Nature Reviews Neuroscience, 3*, 153–160.

Corkin, S., Sullivan, E. V., Twitchell, T. E., & Grove, E. (1981). The amnesic patient H. M.: Clinical observations and test performance 28 years after operation. *Society for Neuroscience Abstracts, 7*, 235.

Corteen, R., & Williams, T. (1986). Television and reading skills. In T. M. Williams (Ed.), *The impact of television: A natural experiment in three communities*. New York: Academic Press.

Coryell, W. (1980). A blind family history study of Briquet's syndrome: Further validation of the diagnosis. *Archives of General Psychiatry, 37,* 1266–1269.

Cosmides, L. (1989). The logical of social exchange: Has natural selection shaped how humans reason? Studies with the Wason selection task. *Cognition, 31,* 187–276.

Cossu, G., Ledent, C., Fattore, L., Imperato, A., Böhme, G. A., Parmentier, M., & Fratta, W. (2001). Cannabinoid CB$_1$ receptor knockout mice fail to self-administer morphine but not other drugs of abuse. *Behavioural Brain Research, 118,* 61–65.

Costa, P. T., & McCrae, R. R. (1980). Still stable after all these years: Personality as a key to some issues in adulthood and old age. In P. B. Baltes (Ed.), *Life-span development and behavior.* New York: Academic Press.

Costa, P. T., Jr., & McCrae, R. R. (1998a). Trait theories of personality. In D. F. Barone & M. Hersen (Eds.), *Advanced personality.* New York: Plenum Press.

Costa, P. T., Jr., & McCrae, R. R. (1998b). The Revised NEO Personality Inventory (NEO-P-R). In S. R. Briggs, J. M. Cheek, & E. M. Donahue (Eds.), *Handbook of adult personality inventories.* New York: Plenum.

Council on Scientific Affairs (1985). Scientific status of refreshing recollection by the use of hypnosis: A council report. *Journal of the American Medical Association, 253,* 1918–1923.

Covington, C. Y., Nordstrom-Klee, B., Ager, J., Sokol, R., & Delaney-Black, V. (2002). Birth to age 7 growth of children prenatally exposed to drugs: A prospective cohort study. *Neurotoxicology and Teratology, 24,* 489–496.

Cowart, J., & Whaley, D. (1971). Punishment of self-mutilation behavior. Unpublished manuscript cited by Whaley, D. L., & Malott, R. W. *Elementary principles of behavior.* New York: Appleton-Century-Crofts.

Cowley, D. S., Dager, S. R., & Dunner, D. L. (1995). The lactate infusion challenge. In G. M. Asnis & H. M. van Praag (Eds.), *Panic disorder: Clinical, biological, and treatment aspects.* New York: John Wiley & Sons.

Cox, M. J., & Paley, B. (2003). Understanding families as systems. *Current Directions in Psychological Science, 12(5),* 193–196.

Craik, F. I. M., & Lockhart, R. S. (1972). Levels of processing: A framework for memory research. *Journal of Verbal Learning and Verbal Behavior, 11,* 671–684.

Craik, F. I. M., & Tulving, E. (1975). Depth of processing and the retention of words in episodic memory. *Journal of Experimental Psychology: General, 104,* 268–294.

Cramer, P. (2003). Personality change in later adulthood is predicted by defense mechanism use in early adulthood. *Journal of Research in Personality, 37,* 76–104.

Cromwell, P. F., Marks, A., Olson, J. N., & Avery, D. W. (1991). Group effects on decision-making by burglars. *Psychological Reports, 69,* 579–588.

Crosby, F. J. (1991). *Juggling: The unexpected advantages of balancing career and home for women and their families.* New York: The Free Press.

Crowe, R. R., Noyes, R., Pauls, D. L., & Slymen, D. (1983). A family study of panic disorder. *Archives of General Psychiatry, 40,* 1065–1069.

Croyle, R. T., & Cooper, J. (1983). Dissonance arousal: Physical evidence. *Journal of Personality and Social Psychology, 45,* 782–791.

Cruts, M., & Van Broeckhoven, C. (1996). Molecular genetic analysis of Alzheimer's disease. In C. N. Stefanis and H. Hippius (Eds.), *Neuropsychiatry in old age: An update.* Ashland, OH: Hogrefe & Huber Publishers.

Cummings, J. L., & Wirshing, W. C. (1989). Recognition and differential diagnosis of tardive dyskinesia. *International Journal of Psychiatry in Medicine, 19,* 133–144.

Cunningham, J. A., Wild, T. C., Bondy, S. J., & Lin, E. (2001). Impact of normative feedback on problem drinkers: A small-area population study. *Journal of Studies on Alcohol, 62(2),* 228–233.

Dabbs, J. M., Carr, T. S., Frady, R. L., & Riad, J. K. (1995). Testosterone, crime, and misbehavior among 692 male prison inmates. *Personality and Individual Differences, 18,* 627–633.

Dabbs, J. M., Frady, R. L., Carr, T. S., & Besch, N. F. (1987). Saliva testosterone and criminal violence in young adult prison inmates. *Psychosomatic Medicine, 49,* 174–182.

Dabbs, J. M., & Hargrove, M. F. (1997). Age, testosterone, and behavior among female prison inmates. *Psychosomatic Medicine, 59,* 477–480.

Dabbs, J. M., Ruback, J. M., Frady, R. L., & Hopper, C. H. (1988). Saliva testosterone and criminal violence among women. *Personality and Individual Differences, 9,* 269–275.

Dale, P. S. (1976). *Language development: Structure and function* (2nd ed.). New York: Holt, Rinehart, and Winston.

Dalgleish, T., Rosen, K., & Marks, M. (1996). Rhythm and blues: The theory and treatment of seasonal affective disorder. *British Journal of Clinical Psychology, 35,* 163–182.

Dalton, P., Doolittle, N., Nagata, H., & Breslin, P. A. S. (2000). The merging of the senses: Integration of subthreshold taste and smell. *Nature Neuroscience, 3,* 431–432.

Daly, M., & Wilson, M. I. (1999). Human evolutionary psychology and animal behaviour. *Animal Behaviour, 57,* 509–519.

Damasio, A. R., Tranel, D., & Damasio, H. (1990). Face agnosia and the neural substrates of memory. *Annual Review of Neuroscience, 13,* 89–109.

Damasio, H. (1989). Neuroimaging contributions to the understanding of aphasia. In F. Boller & J. Grafman (Eds.), *Handbook of neuropsychology, Vol. 2.* Amsterdam: Elsevier.

Damon, W., & Hart, D. (1992). Self-understanding and its role in social and moral development. In M. H. Bornstein & M. E. Lamb (Eds.), *Developmental psychology: An advanced textbook.* Hillsdale, NJ: Erlbaum.

Dana, R. H. (Ed.). (2000). *Handbook of cross-cultural and multicultural personality assessment.* Mahwah, NJ: Lawrence Erlbaum Associates.

Daniel, M. H. (1997). Intelligence testing: Status and trends. *American Psychologist, 52,* 1038–1045.

Daniels, P., & Weingarten, K. (1982). *Sooner or later: The timing of parenthood in adult lives.* New York: Norton.

Darley, J. M., & Latané, B. (1968). Bystander intervention in emergencies: Diffusion of responsibility. *Journal of Personality and Social Psychology, 8,* 377–383.

Darou, W. G. (1992). Native Canadians and intelligence testing. *Canadian Journal of Counselling, 26,* 96–99.

Darwin, C. (1859). *On the origin of species by means of natural selection.* London: Murray.

Darwin, C. (1872/1965). *The expression of the emotions in man and animals.* Chicago: University of Chicago Press.

Darwin, C. J., Turvey, M. T., & Crowder, R. G. (1972). An auditory analogue of the Sperling partial report procedure: Evidence for brief auditory storage. *Cognitive Psychology, 3,* 255–267.

Darwin, F. (1888/1950). *Charles Darwin's autobiography.* New York: Henry Schuman.

Dasgupta, N., & Greenwald, A. G., (2001). On the malleability of automatic attitudes: Combating automatic prejudice with images of admired and disliked individuals. *Journal of Personality and Social Psychology, 81,* 800–814.

Dashiell, J. F. (1935). Experimental studies of the influence of social situations on the behavior of individual human adults. In C. Murcheson (Ed.), *A handbook of social psychology.* Worcester, MA: Clark University Press.

Davies, G., Welham, J., Chant, D., Torrey, E. F., & McGrath, J. (2003). A systematic review and meta-analysis of northern hemisphere season of birth studies in schizophrenia. *Schizophrenia Bulletin, 29(3),* 587–593.

Davis, J. D., & Campbell, C. S. (1973). Peripheral control of meal size in the rat: Effect of sham feeding on meal size and drinking rats. *Journal of Comparative and Physiological Psychology, 83,* 379–387.

Davis, M. (1992). The role of the amygdala in fear-potentiated startle: Implications for animal models of anxiety. *Trends in Pharmacological Sciences, 13,* 35–41.

Davison, G. C., & Neale, J. M. (1990). *Abnormal psychology* (5th ed.). New York: John Wiley & Sons.

Dawda, D., & Hart, S. D. (2000). Assessing emotional intelligence: Reliability and validity of the Bar-On Emotional Quotient Inventory (EQ-i) in university students. *Personality and Individual Differences, 28,* 797–812.

Dawes, R. M. (1994). *House of cards: Psychology and psychotherapy built on myth.* New York: The Free Press.

Dawes, R. M., Faust, D., & Meehl, P. E. (2002). Clinical versus actuarial judgment. In T. Gilovich (Ed.), *Heuristics and biases: The psychology of intuitive judgment.* New York: Cambridge University Press.

Dawkins, R. (1996). *Climbing Mount Improbable.* New York: W. W. Norton.

Deaux, K. (1985). Sex and gender. *Annual Review of Psychology, 36,* 49–81.

Deaux, K. (1999). An overview of research on gender: Four themes from 3 decades. In W. B.

Swann, Jr., & J. H. Langlois (Eds.), *Sexism and stereotypes in modern society: The gender science of Janet Taylor Spence*. Washington, DC: American Psychological Association.

DeCasper, A. J., & Fifer, W. P. (1980). Of human bonding: Newborns prefer their mothers' voices. *Science, 208,* 1175–1176.

DeCasper, A. J., & Spence, M. (1986). Prenatal maternal speech influences newborns' perception of speech sounds. *Infant Behavior and Development, 9,* 133–150.

Deci, E. L., & Ryan, R. M. (1987). The support of autonomy and the control of behavior. *Journal of Personality and Social Psychology, 53,* 1024–1037.

De Gennaro, L., Ferrara, M., & Bertini, M. (2000). The spontaneous K-complex during stage 2 sleep: Is it the "forerunner" of delta waves? *Neuroscience Letters, 291,* 41–43.

deGroot, A. D. (1965). *Thought and choice in chess.* The Hague: Mouton Publishers.

Dehaene, S. (July 5, 2003). Natural born readers. *New Scientist,* 30–33.

Dekaban, A. (1970). *Neurology of early childhood.* Baltimore: Williams & Wilkins.

Dellas, M., & Jernigan, L. P. (1990). Affective personality characteristics associated with undergraduate ego identity formation. *Journal of Adolescent Research, 5,* 306–324.

DeLongis, A., Folkman, S., & Lazarus, R. S. (1988). The impact of daily stress on health and mood: Psychological and social resources as mediators. *Journal of Personality and Social Psychology, 54,* 486–495.

Dement, W. C. (1974). *Some must watch while some must sleep.* San Francisco: W. H. Freeman.

DeNeve, K. M., & Cooper, H. (1998). The happy personality: A meta-analysis of 137 personality traits and subjective well-being. *Psychological Bulletin, 124,* 197–229.

Dennett, D. C. (1995). *Darwin's dangerous idea: Evolution and the meanings of life.* New York: Simon & Schuster.

Dennis, W. (1973). *Children of the creche.* New York: Appleton-Century-Crofts.

DePaulo, B. M. (1994). Spotting lies: Can humans learn to do better? *Current Directions in Psychological Science, 3,* 83–86.

DePue, R. A., Luciane, M., Arbisi, P., Collins, P., & Leon, A. (1994). Dopamine and the structure of personality: Relation of agonist-induced dopamine activity and positive emotionality. *Journal of Personality and Social Psychology, 67,* 485–498.

DePue, R. A., & Monroe, S. M. (1986). Conceptualization and measurement of human disorder in life-stress research: The problem of chronic disturbance. *Psychological Bulletin, 99,* 36–51.

Dérousné, J., & Beauvois, M.-F. (1979). Phonological processing in reading: Data from alexia. *Journal of Neurology, Neurosurgery, and Psychiatry, 42,* 1125–1132.

Deshmukh, A., Rosenbloom, M. J., Pfefferbaum, A., & Sullivan, E. V. (2002). Clinical signs of cerebellar dysfunction in schizophrenia, alcoholism, and their comorbidity. *Schizophrenia Research, 57(2–3),* 281–291.

Desimone, R., & Duncan, J. (1995). Neural mechanisms of selective visual attention. *Annual Review of Neuroscience, 18,* 193–222.

Deutsch, J. A., & Gonzalez, M. F. (1980). Gastric nutrient content signals satiety. *Behavioral Neural Biology, 30,* 113–116.

Deutsch, J. A., Young, W. G., & Kalogeris, T. J. (1978). The stomach signals satiety. *Science, 201,* 165–167.

Devane, W. A., Hanus, L., Breuer, A., Pertwee, R. G., Stevenson, L. A., Griffin, G., Gibson, D., Mandelbaum, A., Etinger, A., & Mechoulam, R. (1992). Isolation and structure of a brain constituent that binds to the cannabinoid receptor. *Science, 258,* 1946–1949.

deVilliers, J. G., & deVilliers, P. A. (1978). *Language acquisition.* Cambridge, MA: Harvard University Press.

DeWit, D. J., Adlaf, E. M., Offord, D. R., & Ogborne, A. C. (2000). Age at first alcohol use: A risk factor for the development of alcohol disorders. *American Journal of Psychiatry, 157(5),* 745–750.

Diagnostic and Statistical Manual of Mental Disorders (4th edition, Text Revision). (2000). American Psychiatric Association.

Diamond, J. (1997). *Guns, germs, and steel: The fates of human societies.* New York: W. W. Norton.

Dion, K. E., Berscheid, E., & Walster, E. (1972). What is beautiful is good. *Journal of Personality and Social Psychology, 24,* 285–290.

Dion, K. L. (1986). Stereotyping based on physical attractiveness: Issues and conceptual perspectives. In C. P. Herman, M. P. Zanna, & E. T. Higgins (Eds.), *Physical appearance, stigma, and social behavior: The Ontario symposium.* Hillsdale, NJ: Lawrence Erlbaum Press.

Dion, K. L. (2003). Prejudice, racism, and discrimination. In T. Millon & M. J. Lerner (Eds.), *Handbook of psychology: Personality and social psychology, Vol. 5.* New York: John Wiley & Sons, Inc.

Dixon, P., Gordon, R. D., Leung, A., & Di Lollo, V. (1997). Attentional components of partial report. *Journal of Experimental Psychology, 23,* 1253–1271.

Dobson, K. S., & Khatri, N. (2000). Cognitive therapy: Looking backward, looking forward. *Journal of Clinical Psychology, 56,* 907–923.

Dobzhansky, T. (1937). *Genetics and the origin of species.* New York: Columbia University Press.

Dodwell, P. C., & Humphrey, G. K. (1990). A function theory of the McCollough effect. *Psychological Review, 97,* 78–89.

Doetsch, F., & Hen, R. (2005). Young and excitable: The function of new neurons in the adult mammalian brain. *Current Opinion in Neuroscience, 15,* 121–128.

Dolan, R. J. (1999). On the neurology of morals. *Nature Neuroscience, 2,* 927–928.

Donald, M. (1993). *Origins of the modern mind: Three stages in the evolution of culture and cognition.* Cambridge, MA: Harvard University Press.

Donahoe, J. W. (1997). Selection networks: Simulation of plasticity through reinforcement learning. In J. W. Donahoe & V. P. Dorsel (Eds.), *Neural-network models of cognition: Biobehavioral foundations.* Amsterdam: Elsevier Science Press.

Donahoe, J. W. (1999). Edward L. Thorndike: The selectionist connectionist. *Journal of the Experimental Analysis of Behavior, 72,* 451–454.

Donahoe, J. W. (2003). Selectionism. In K. A. Lattal & P. N. Chase (Eds.), *Behavior theory and philosophy* (pp. 103–128). New York: Kluwer Academic/Plenum Publishers.

Donahoe, J. W., Burgos, J. E., & Palmer, D. C. (1993). Selectionist approach to reinforcement. *Journal of the Experimental Analysis of Behavior, 60,* 17–40.

Donahoe, J. W., Crowley, M. A., Millard, W. J., & Stickney, K. A. (1982). A unified principle of reinforcement. *Quantitative models of behavior* (Vol. 2, pp. 493–521). Cambridge, MA: Ballinger.

Donahoe, J. W., & Palmer, D. C. (1994). *Learning and complex behavior.* Boston: Allyn & Bacon. (Reprinted Richmond, MA: Ledgetop Publishing, 2005 at http://www.LCB-online.org)

Donahoe, J. W., & Vegas, R. (2004). Pavlovian conditioning: The CS-UR relation. *Journal of Experimental Psychology: Animal Behavior Processes, 30,* 17–33.

Donahoe, J. W., & Wessells, M. G. (1980). *Learning, language, and memory.* New York: Harper & Row.

Donenberg, G. R., & Hoffman, L. W. (1988). Gender differences in moral development. *Sex Roles, 18,* 701–717.

Dong, C.-J., Swindale, N. V., & Cynader, M. S. (1999). A contingent aftereffect in the auditory system. *Nature Neuroscience, 2,* 863–865.

Donnan, G. A., Darbey, D. G., & Saling, M. M. (1997). Identification of brain region for coordinating speech articulation. *Nature, 349,* 221–222.

Dooling, D. J., & Lachman, R. (1971). Effects of comprehension on retention of prose. *Journal of Experimental Psychology, 88,* 216–222.

Doty, R. L. (2001). Olfaction. *Annual Review of Psychology, 52,* 423–452.

Dowling, J. E., & Boycott, B. B. (1966). *Proceedings of the Royal Society* (London), Series B, *166,* 80–111.

Doyon, J., LaForce, R., Jr., Bouchard, G., Gaudreau, D., Roy, J., Poirier, M., Bedard, P. J., Bedard, F., & Bouchard, J.-P. (1998). Role of the striatum, cerebellum and frontal lobes in the automatization of a repeated visuomotor sequence of movements. *Neuropsychologia, 36,* 625–641.

Drabman, R. S., Spitalnik, R., & O'Leary, K. D. (1973). Teaching self-control to disruptive children. *Journal of Abnormal Psychology, 82,* 10–16.

Dreyfus, S. E., & Dreyfus, H. L. (2000). *Mind over machine.* New York: Free Press.

Dronkers, N. F. (1996). A new brain region for coordinating speech articulation. *Lancet, 384,* 159–161.

Druckman, D., & Bjork, R. A. (1991). *In the mind's eye: Enhancing human performance.* Washington, DC: National Academy Press.

Dunbar, R. (2004). From spears to speech: Could throwing spears have laid the foundations for language acquisition? *Nature, 427,* 783.

Dunbar, R. I. M. (1993). Coevolution of neocortical size, group size and language in humans. *Behavioral and Brain Sciences, 16,* 681–735.

Dunn, J., Bretherton, I., & Munn, P. (1987). Conversations about feeling states between mothers and their young children. *Developmental Psychology, 23,* 132–139.

Dutton, D. G., & Aron, A. P. (1974). Some evidence for heightened sexual attraction under conditions of high anxiety. *Journal of Personality and Social Psychology, 30,* 510–517.

Duva, C. A., Floresco, S. B., Wunderlich, G. R., Lao, T. L., Pinel, J. P. J., & Phillips, A. G. (1997). Disruption of spatial but not object-recognition memory by neurotoxic lesions of the dorsal hippocampus in rats. *Behavioral Neuroscience, 111,* 1184–1196.

Eagly, A. H., Ashmore, R., Makhijani, M., & Longo, L. (1991). What is beautiful is good, but . . . : A meta-analytic review of research on the physical attractiveness stereotype. *Psychological Bulletin, 110,* 109–128.

Eagly, A. H., & Chaiken, S. (1998). Attitude structure and function. In D. T. Gilbert & S. T. Fiske (Eds.), *The handbook of social psychology, Vol. 1.* (4th ed.). New York: McGraw-Hill.

Eagly, A. H., & Karau, S. J. (1991). Gender and the emergence of leaders: A meta-analysis. *Journal of Personality and Social Psychology, 60,* 685–710.

Eagly, A. H., & Steffen, V. J. (1986). Gender and aggressive behavior: A meta-analytic review of the social psychological literature. *Psychological Bulletin, 100,* 309–330.

Eagly, A. H., & Wood, W. (1999). The origins of sex differences in human behavior: Evolved dispositions versus social roles. *American Psychologist, 54,* 408–423.

Eddy, N. B., Halbach, H., Isbell, H., & Seevers, M. H. (1965). Drug dependence: Its significance and characteristics. *Bulletin of the World Health Organization, 32,* 721–733.

Edison Media Research and Mitofsky International. (2005). *Evaluation of Edison/Mitofsky Election System 2004.* Retrieved July 5, 2005, http://electionarchive.org/ucvAnalysis/US/Exit_Polls_2004_Mitofsky-Edison.pdf

Ehlers, C. L., Frank, E., & Kupfer, D. J. (1988). Social zeitgebers and biological rhythms. *Archives of General Psychiatry, 45,* 948–952.

Ehrlich, P., & Feldman, M. (2003). Genes and cultures: What creates our behavioral phenome? *Current Anthropology, 44(1),* 87–107.

Eibl-Eiesfeldt, I. (1980). Evolution of destructive aggression. *Aggressive Behavior, 131,* 27–144.

Eichenbaum, H. (1999). Conscious awareness, memory and the hippocampus. *Nature Neuroscience, 2,* 775–776.

Eichenbaum, H., Stewart, C., & Morris, R. G. M. (1990). Hippocampal representation in spatial learning. *Journal of Neuroscience, 10,* 331–339.

Eikelboom, R., & Stewart, J. (1982). Conditioning of drug-induced physiological responses. *Psychological Review, 89,* 507–528.

Eimas, P. D., Siqueland, E. R., Jusczyk, P., & Vigorito, J. (1971). Speech perception in infants. *Science, 171,* 303–306.

Eisenberg, N., Fabes, R. A., Schaller, M., Miller, P., Carlo, G., Poulin, R., Shea, C., & Shell, R. (1991). Personality and socialization: Correlates of vicarious emotional responding. *Journal of Personality and Social Psychology, 61,* 459–470.

Ekman, P. (1980). *The face of man: Expressions of universal emotions in a New Guinea village.* New York: Garland STPM Press.

Ekman, P., & Friesen, W. V. (1969). Nonverbal leakage and clues to deception. *Psychiatry, 32,* 88–105.

Ekman, P., & Friesen, W. V. (1974). Detecting deception from body or face. *Journal of Personality and Social Psychology, 29,* 288–298.

Ekman, P., & Friesen, W. V. (1975). *Unmasking the face.* Englewood Cliffs, NJ: Prentice-Hall.

Ekman, P., Friesen, W. V., & Ellsworth, P. (1972). *Emotion in the human face: Guidelines for research and a review of findings.* New York: Pergamon Press.

Ekman, P., & O'Sullivan, M. (1991). Who can catch a liar? *American Psychologist, 46,* 913–920.

Ekman, P., O'Sullivan, M., & Frank, M. G. (1999). A few can catch a liar. *Psychological Science, 10,* 263–266.

Elbert, T., Pantev, C., Wienbruch, C., Rockstroh, B., & Taub, E. (1995). Increased cortical representation of the fingers of the left hand in string players. *Science, 270,* 305–307.

Elder, G. H. (1969). Appearance and education in marriage mobility. *American Sociological Review, 34,* 519–533.

Eldredge, N. (1998). *Life in the balance: Humanity and the biodiversity crisis.* Princeton, NH: Princeton University Press.

Eldredge, N., & Gould, S. J. (1972). Punctuated equilibria: An alternative to phyletic gradualism. In T. J. M. Schopf (Ed.), *Paleobiology.* San Francisco: Freeman.

Ellenberger, H. F. (1972). The story of "Anna O": A critical review with new data. *Journal of the History of the Behavioral Sciences, 8,* 267–279.

Ellenberger, H. F. (1981). *The discovery of the unconscious.* New York: Basic Books.

Ellis, A. (1973). Rational-emotive therapy. In R. Corsini (Ed.), *Current psychotherapies.* Itasca, IL: Peacock.

Ellis, A. (1989). A twenty-three-year-old woman guilty about not following her parents' rules. In D. Wedding & R. J. Corsini (Eds.), *Case studies in psychotherapy.* Itasca, IL: Peacock.

Ellis, A. (2003). Early theories and practices in rational emotive behavior therapy and how they have been augmented and revised during the last three decades. *Journal of Rational-Emotive & Cognitive Behavior Therapy, 21(3–4),* 219–243.

Elms, A. C. (1995). Obedience in retrospect. *Journal of Social Issues, 51,* 21–32.

Enard, W., Przeworski, M., Fisher, S. E., Lai, C. S., Wiebe, V., Kitano, T., Monaco, A. P., & Pääbo, S. (2002). Molecular evolution of FOXP2, a gene involved in speech and language. *Nature, 418,* 869–872.

Engberg, L. A., Hansen, G., Welker, R. L., & Thomas, D. R. (1972). Acquisition of key-pecking via autoshaping as a function of prior experience: 'Learned laziness?,' *Science, 178,* 1002–1004.

Engel, L. (1962). Darwin and the *Beagle.* In L. Engel (Ed.), *The voyage of the* Beagle. Garden City, NY: Doubleday.

Enns, J. T., & Rensink, R. A. (1991). Preattentive recovery of three-dimensional orientation from line drawings. *Psychological Review, 98,* 335–352.

Entwisle, D. (1972). To dispel fantasies about fantasy-based measures of achievement motivation. *Psychological Bulletin, 77,* 377–391.

Enzle, M. E., & Ross, J. M. (1978). Increasing and decreasing intrinsic interest with contingent rewards: A test of cognitive evaluation theory. *Journal of Experimental Social Psychology, 14,* 588–597.

Enzle, M. E., & Schopflocher, D. (1978). Instigation of attribution processes by attribution questions. *Personality and Social Psychology Bulletin, 4,* 595–599.

Epling, W. F., & Pierce, W. D. (1991). *Solving the anorexia problem: A scientific approach.* Toronto: Hogrefe and Huber Publishers.

Epstein, R. (1985). The spontaneous interconnection of three repertoires. *The Psychological Record, 35,* 131–141.

Epstein, R. (1987). The spontaneous interconnection of four repertoires of behavior in a pigeon (*Columba livia*). *Journal of Comparative Psychology, 101,* 197–201.

Epstein, R., Kirshnit, C., Lanza, R. P., & Rubin, L. (1984). Insight in the pigeon: Antecedents and determinants of an intelligent performance. *Nature, 308,* 61–62.

Epstein, S. (1979). The stability of behavior. I. On predicting most of the people much of the time. *Journal of Personality and Social Psychology, 37,* 1097–1126.

Epstein, S. P. (1986). Does aggregation produce spuriously high estimates of behavior stability? *Journal of Personality and Social Psychology, 50,* 1199–1210.

Epstein, W. (1961). The influence of syntactical structure on learning. *American Journal of Psychology, 74,* 80–85.

Eron, L. D. (1950). A normative study of the thematic apperception test. *Psychological Monographs, 64,* Whole No. 315.

Erting, C. J., Johnson, R. C., Smith, D. L., & Snider, B. D. (1989). *The Deaf way: Perspectives from the international conference on Deaf culture.* Washington, DC: Gallaudet University Press.

Eskandar, E. N., & Assad, J. A. (1999). Dissociation of visual, motor, and predictive signals in parietal cortex during visual guidance. *Nature Neuroscience, 2,* 88–93.

Eslinger, P. J., & Damasio, A. R. (1985). Severe disturbance of higher cognition after bilateral frontal lobe ablation: Patient EVR. *Neurology, 35,* 1731–1741.

Esterling, B. A., Kiecolt-Glaser, J. K., Bodnar, J. D., & Glaser, R. (1994). Chronic stress, social support, and persistent alterations in the natural killer cell response to cytokines in older adults. *Health Psychology, 13,* 291–298.

Estes, W. K., & Skinner, B. F. (1941). Some quantitative properties of anxiety. *Journal of Experimental Psychology, 29,* 390–400.

Evans, D. A., Funkenstein, H. H., Albert, M. S., Scherr, P. A., Cook, N. R., Chown, M. J., Herbert, L. E., Hennekens, C. H., & Taylor, J. O. (1989). Prevalence of Alzheimer's disease in a community population of older persons. *JAMA, 262,* 2551–2556.

Eysenck, H. (1998). *Dimensions of personality.* New Brunswick, NJ: Transaction Publishers.

Eysenck, H. J. (1939). Primary mental abilities. *British Journal of Educational Psychology, 9,* 270–285.

Eysenck, H. J. (1952). The effects of psychotherapy: An evaluation. *Journal of Consulting Psychology, 16,* 319–324.

Eysenck, H. J. (1970). *The structure of human personality* (3rd ed.). London: Methuen.

Eysenck, H. J. (1988). Personality, stress and cancer: Prediction and prophylaxis. *British Journal of Medical Psychology, 61,* 57–75.

Eysenck, H. J. (1994). Cancer, personality, and stress: Prediction and prevention. *Advances in Behaviour Research and Therapy, 16,* 167–215.

Eysenck, H. J., & Eysenck, M. W. (1985). *Personality and individual differences: A natural science approach.* New York: Plenum Press, 1985.

Fabes, R. A., Eisenberg, N., Smith, M. C., & Murphy, B. C. (1996). Getting angry at peers: Associations with liking of provocateur. *Child Development, 67,* 942–956.

Fadda, F., Mosca, E., Colombo, G., & Gessa, G. L. (1990). Alcohol-preferring rats: Genetic sensitivity to alcohol-induced stimulation of dopamine metabolism. *Physiology and Behavior, 47,* 727–729.

Fagan, J. R., III, & Singer, L. T. (1979). The role of simple feature differences in infants' recognition of faces. *Infant Behavior and Development, 2,* 39–45.

Fagot, B. I., & Hagan, R. I. (1991). Observations of parent reactions to sex-stereotyped behaviors: Age and sex differences. *Child Development, 62,* 617–628.

Fazio, R. H., & Roskos-Ewoldsen, D. R. (1994). Acting as we feel: When and how attitudes guide behavior. In S. Shavitt & T. C. Brock (Eds.), *Persuasion: Psychological insights and perspectives.* Boston: Allyn & Bacon.

Feather, N. T., & McKee, I. R. (1993). Global self-esteem and attitudes toward the high achiever for Australian and Japanese students. *Social Psychology Quarterly, 56,* 65–76.

Feeney, J. A., & Noller, P. (1991). Attachment style and verbal descriptions of romantic partners. *Journal of Social and Personal Relationships, 8,* 187–215.

Fegley, D., Kathuria, S., Mercier, R., Li, C., Goutopoulos, A., Makriyannis, A., & Piomelli, D. (2004). Anandamide transport is independent of fatty-acid amide hydrolase activity and is blocked by the hydrolysis-resistant inhibitor. *Proceedings of the National Academy of Science, USA, 101,* 8756–8761.

Feigenbaum, S. L., Masi, A. T., & Kaplan, S. B. (1979). Prognosis in rheumatoid arthritis: A longitudinal study of newly diagnosed younger adult patients. *American Journal of Medicine, 66,* 377–384.

Feingold, A. (1992). Good-looking people are not what we think. *Psychological Bulletin, 111,* 304–341.

Feingold, A. (1993). Cognitive gender differences: A developmental perspective. *Sex Roles, 29,* 91–112.

Feist, G. J., & Barron, F. X. (2003). Predicting creativity from early to late adulthood: Intellect, potential, and personality. *Journal of Research in Personality, 37,* 62–88.

Feldman, R. D. (1982). *Whatever happened to the quiz kids?* Chicago: Chicago Review Press.

Ferguson, G. A. (1982). Psychology at McGill. In M. J. Wright & C. R. Myers (Eds.), *History of academic psychology in Canada* (pp. 33–67). Toronto: Hogrefe.

Ferster, C. A., & Skinner, B. F. (1957). *Schedules of reinforcement.* New York: Appleton-Century.

Festinger, L. (1957). *A theory of cognitive dissonance.* Stanford: Stanford University Press.

Festinger, L., & Carlsmith, J. M. (1959). Cognitive consequences of forced compliance. *Journal of Abnormal and Social Psychology, 58,* 203–210.

Festinger, L., Schachter, S., & Back, K. (1959). *Social pressures in informal groups: A study of a housing community.* New York: Harper & Row.

Feynman, R. P. (1985). *Surely you're joking, Mr. Feynman!* New York: Bantam Books.

Feynman, R. P. (2001). *What do you care what other people think? Further adventures of a curious character.* New York: W. W. Norton.

Field, T. M. (1994). Infant day care facilitates later social behavior and school performance. In H. Goelman & E. V. Jacobs (Eds.), *Children's play in child care settings. SUNY series, children's play in society.* Albany, NY: State University of New York Press.

Fiez, J. A., Balota, D. A., Raichle, M. E., & Petersen, S. E. (1999). Effects of lexicality, frequency, and spelling-to-sound consistency on the functional anatomy of reading. *Neuron, 24,* 205–218.

Fink, M. (1976). Presidential address: Brain function, verbal behavior, and psychotherapy. In R. L. Spitzer & D. F. Klein, *Evaluation of psychological therapies: Psychotherapies, behavior therapies, drug therapies, and their interactions.* Baltimore: Johns Hopkins University Press.

Fisch, S., & Truglio, R. T. (Eds.). (2001). *"G" is for growing: Thirty years of research on children and Sesame Street.* Mahwah, NJ: Lawrence Erlbaum Associates.

Fisher, J. D., & Fisher, W. A. (1992). Changing AIDS-risk behavior. *Psychological Bulletin, 111,* 455–474.

Fisher, J. D., & Fisher, W. A. (2000). Theoretical approaches to individual-level change in HIV risk behavior. In J. L. Peterson & R. J. DiClemente (Eds.), *Handbook of HIV prevention: AIDS prevention and mental health.* New York: Kluwer Academic Publishers.

Fisher, N. J., Rourke, B. P., & Bieliauskas, L. A. (1999). Neuropsychological subgroups of patients with Alzheimer's Disease: An examination of the first ten years of CERAD data. *Journal of Clinical and Experimental Neuropsychology, 21,* 488–518.

Fiske, S. T. (1993). Social cognition and social perception. *Annual Review of Psychology, 44,* 155–194.

Fiske, S. T., & Taylor, S. E. (1991). *Social cognition* (2nd ed.). New York: McGraw-Hill.

Flaherty, C. F. (1982). Incentive contrast: A review of behavioral changes following shifts in reward. *Animal Learning & Behavior, 10,* 409–440.

Flaherty, J., Frank, E., Hoskinson, K., Richman, J., & Kupfer, D. (1987). Social zeitgebers and bereavement. Paper presented at the 140th Annual Meeting of the American Psychiatric Association, Chicago.

Flanagan, O. (1992). *Consciousness reconsidered.* Cambridge, MA: Bradford Books.

Flannery, R. B., Jr. (1999). Psychological trauma and posttraumatic stress disorder: A review. *International Journal of Emergency Mental Health, 1,* 135–140.

Flavell, J. H. (1992). Perspectives on perspective taking. In H. Beilin & P. B. Pufall (Eds.), *Piaget's theory: Prospects and possibilities.* Hillsdale, NJ: Lawrence Erlbaum Associates.

Flavell, J. H., Everett, B. H., Croft, K., & Flavell, E. R. (1981). Young children's knowledge about visual perception: Further evidence for the level 1–level 2 distinction. *Developmental Psychology, 17,* 99–103.

Flay, B. R., Koepke, D., Thomson, S. J., Santi, S., Best, J. A., & Brown, K. S. (1989). Six-year follow-up of the first Waterloo school smoking prevention trial. *American Journal of Public Health, 79,* 1371–1376.

Flay, B. R., Ryan, K. B., Best, J. A., Brown, K. S., Kersell, M. W., d'Avernas, J. R., & Zanna, M. P. (1985). Are social-psychological smoking prevention programs effective? The Waterloo Study. *Journal of Behavioral Medicine, 8,* 37–59.

Flexser, A. J., & Tulving, E. (1978). Retrieval independence in recognition and recall. *Psychological Review, 85,* 153–171.

Floyd, R. L., Rimer, B. K., Giovino, G. A., Mullen, P. D., & Sullivan, S. E. (1993). A review of smoking in pregnancy: Effects on pregnancy outcomes and cessation efforts. *Annual Review of Public Health, 14,* 379–411.

Fogarty, F., Russell, J. M., Newman, S. C., & Bland, R. C. (1994). Mania. *Acta Psychiatrica Scandinavica, 89(376, Suppl),* 16–23.

Foley, V. D. (1979). Family therapy. In R. J. Corsini (Ed.), *Current psychotherapies* (2nd ed.). Itasca, IL: R. E. Peacock.

Folkman, S., & Lazarus, R. S. (1991). Coping and emotion. In A. Monat & R. S. Lazarus (Eds.), *Stress and coping: An anthology.* New York: Columbia University Press.

Follette, V. M., Ruzek, J. I., & Abueg, F. R. (Eds.) (2001). *Cognitive-behavioral therapies for trauma.* New York: Guilford Press.

Fouts, R. S. (1983). Chimpanzee language and elephant tails: A theoretical synthesis. In J. de Luce & H. T. Wilder (Eds.), *Language in primates: Perspectives and implications.* New York: Springer-Verlag.

Fouts, R. S., Hirsch, A., & Fouts, D. (1983). Cultural transmission of a human language in a chimpanzee mother/infant relationship. In H. E. Fitzgerald, J. A. Mullins, & P. Page (Eds.), *Psychological perspectives: Child nurturance series, Vol. III.* New York: Plenum Press.

Fox, E., Lester, V., Russo, R., Bowles, R. J., Pichler, A., & Dutton, K. (2000). Facial expressions of emotion: Are angry faces detected more efficiently? *Cognition and Emotion, 14*, 61–92.

Franco, P., Groswasser, J., Hassid, S., Lanquart, J. P., Scaillet, S., & Kahn, A. (2000). Prenatal exposure to cigarette smoking is associated with a decrease in arousal in infants. *Journal of Pediatrics, 135*, 34–38.

Frank, S. L., Pirsch, L. A., & Wright, V. C. (1990). Late adolescents' perceptions of their relationships with their parents: Relationships among deidealization, autonomy, relatedness, and insecurity and implications for adolescent adjustment and ego identity status. *Journal of Youth and Adolescence, 19*, 571–588.

Freedman, J. L. (2002). *Media violence and its effect on aggression: Assessing the scientific evidence.* Toronto: University of Toronto Press.

Freedman, J. L., & Fraser, S. C. (1966). Compliance without pressure: The foot-in-the-door technique. *Journal of Personality and Social Psychology, 4*, 195–203.

Freud, S. (1900). *The interpretation of dreams.* London: George Allen and Unwin Ltd.

Freud, S. (1912). *Recommendations for physicians on the psychoanalytic method of treatment* (J. Riviere, Trans.), Zentralblatt, Bd. II. Reprinted in Sammlung, Vierte Folge.

Freud, S. (1933). *New introductory lectures on psychoanalysis* (J. Strachey, Trans.). New York: Norton.

Frey, U. (1997). Cellular mechanisms of long-term potentiation: Late maintenance. In J. E. Donahoe & V. P. Dorsel, (Eds.), *Neural-network models of cognition: Biobehavioral foundations* (pp. 105–128). Amsterdam: Elsevier Science Press.

Frey, U., & Morris, R. G. (1998). Weak before strong: dissociating synaptic tagging and plasticity-factor accounts of late-LTP. *Neuropharmacology, 37*, 545–552.

Friderun, A. S., & Cummins, J. M. (1996). Misconceptions about mitochondria and mammalian fertilization: Implications for theories on human evolution. *Proceedings of the National Academy of Science, 93*, 13859–13863.

Friedman, H. S., & Rosenman, R. F. (1974). *Type A behavior and your heart.* New York: Knopf.

Friedman, M., & Rosenman, R. H. (1959). Association of specific overt behavior patterns with blood and cardiovascular findings—Blood cholesterol level, blood clotting time, incidence of arcus senilis, and clinical coronary artery disease. *JAMA, 162*, 1286–1296.

Friesen, W. V. (1972). Cultural differences in facial expression in a social situation: An experimental test of the concept of display rules. Doctoral dissertation, University of California, San Francisco.

Fromkin, V. (1973). *Speech errors as linguistic evidence.* The Hague: Mouton Publishers.

Fulton, J. F. (1949). *Functional localization in relation to frontal lobotomy.* New York: Oxford University Press.

Furnham, A. (1992). Just world beliefs in twelve societies. *The Journal of Social Psychology, 133*, 317–329.

Furrow, D., & Nelson, K. (1986). A further look at the motherese hypothesis: A reply to Gleitman, Newport & Gleitman. *Journal of Child Language, 13*, 163–176.

Furrow, D., Nelson, K., & Benedict, H. (1979). Mothers' speech to children and syntactic development: Some simple relationships. *Journal of Child Language, 6*, 423–442.

Fuster, J. M. (1995). *Memory in the cerebral cortex: An empirical approach to neural networks in the human and nonhuman primate.* Cambridge, MA: MIT Press.

Gabrieli, J. D. E., Cohen, N. J., & Corkin, S. (1988). The impaired learning of semantic knowledge following bilateral medial temporal-lobe resection. *Brain and Cognition, 7*, 157–177.

Galaburda, A., & Kemper, T. L. (1979). Observations cited by Geschwind, N. Specializations of the human brain. *Scientific American, 241*, 180–199.

Galaburda, A. M. (1993). Neurology of developmental dyslexia. *Current Opinion in Neurobiology, 3*, 237–242.

Galaburda, A. M., Menard, M. T., & Rosen, G. D. (1994). Evidence for aberrant auditory anatomy in developmental dyslexia. *Proceedings of the National Academy of Sciences, 91*, 8010–8013.

Galaburda, A. M., Sherman, G. F., Rosen, G. D., Aboitiz, F., & Geschwind, N. (1985). Developmental dyslexia: Four consecutive patients with cortical anomalies. *Annals of Neurology, 18*, 222–233.

Galton, F. (1869). *Hereditary genius: An inquiry into its laws and consequences.* Cleveland, OH: World Publishing.

Galvani, A. P., & Slatkin, M. (2003). Evaluating plague and smallpox as historical selective pressures for the CCR5-delta32 HIV-resistance allele. *Proceedings of the National Academy of Science, 100*, 15276–15279.

Ganel, T., & Goodale, M. A. (2003). Visual control of action but not perception requires analytical processing of object shape. *Nature, 426*, 664–667.

Ganong, W. F. (1980). Phonetic categorization in auditory word perception. *Journal of Experimental Psychology: Human Perception and Performance, 6*, 110–125.

Garcia, J., & Koelling, R. A. (1966). Relation of cue to consequence in avoidance learning. *Psychonomic Science, 4*, 123–124.

Gardner, H. (1983). *Frames of mind.* New York: Basic Books.

Gardner, H. (1993). *Multiple intelligences: The theory in practice.* New York, NY: Basic Books.

Gardner, H. (1999). *Intelligence reframed: Multiple intelligences for the 21st century.* New York: Basic Books.

Gardner, R. A., & Gardner, B. T. (1969). Teaching sign language to a chimpanzee. *Science, 165*, 664–672.

Gardner, R. A., & Gardner, B. T. (1975). Early signs of language in child and chimpanzee. *Science, 187*, 752–753.

Gardner, R. A., & Gardner, B. T. (1978). Comparative psychology and language acquisition. *Annals of the New York Academy of Sciences, 309*, 37–76.

Garnets, L., & Kimmel, D. (1991). Lesbian and gay male dimensions in the psychological study of human diversity. In J. D. Goodchilds (Ed.), *Psychological perspectives on human diversity in America.* Washington, DC: American Psychological Association.

Garrett, V., Brantley, P., Jones, G., & McKnight, G. (1991). The relation between daily stress and Crohn's disease. *Journal of Behavioral Medicine, 34*, 187–196.

Gazzaniga, M. S. (1970). *The bisected brain.* New York: Appleton-Century-Crofts.

Gazzaniga, M. S., & LeDoux, J. E. (1978). *The integrated mind.* New York: Plenum Press.

Geary, D. C. (1995). Reflections of evolution of culture in children's cognition: Implications for mathematical development and instruction. *American Psychologist, 50*, 24–37.

Geiselman, R. E., Fisher, R. P., Firstenberg, I., Hutton, L. A., Sullivan, S., Avetissian, L., & Prosk, A. (1984). Enhancement of eyewitness memory: An empirical evaluation of the cognitive interview. *Journal of Police Science and Administration, 12*, 74–80.

Gelman, R. (1972). Logical capacity of very young children: Number invariance rules. *Child Development, 43*, 75–90.

The Genome Sequencing Consortium. (2001). Initial sequencing and analysis of the human genome. *Nature, 409*, 860–921.

Gerlernter, J., Goldman, D., & Risch, N. (1993). The A1 allele at the D2 dopamine gene and alcoholism. *Journal of the American Medical Association, 269*, 1673–1677.

Geschwind, N., Quadfasel, F. A., & Segarra, J. M. (1968). Isolation of the speech area. *Neuropsychologia, 6*, 327–340.

Giaschi, D., & Regan, D. (1997). Development of motion-defined figure-ground segregation in preschool and older children, using a letter-identification task. *Optometry and Vision Science, 74*, 761–767.

Gibbs, C. M., Latham, S. B., & Gormezano, I. (1978). Classical schedule and resistance to extinction. *Animal Learning & Behavior, 6*, 209–215.

Gibson, E. J., & Walk, R. R. (1960). The "visual cliff." *Scientific American, 202*, 2–9.

Gil, T. E. (1989). Psychological etiology to cancer: Truth or myth? *Israel Journal of Psychiatry and Related Sciences, 26*, 164–185.

Gillham, J. E., Reivich, K. J., Jaycox, L. H., & Seligman, M. E. P. (1995). Prevention of depressive symptoms in schoolchildren: Two-year follow-up. *Psychological Science, 6*, 343–351.

Gilligan, C. F. (1982). *In a different voice.* Cambridge, MA: Harvard University Press.

Gilovich, T. (1990). Differential construal and the false consensus effect. *Journal of Personality and Social Psychology, 59*, 623–634.

Gironell, A., de la Calzada, M. D., Sagales, T., & Barraquer-Bordas, L. (1995). Absence of REM sleep and altered non-REM sleep caused by a haematoma in the pontine tegmentum. *Journal of Neurology, Neurosurgery and Psychiatry, 59,* 195–196.

Gladwin, T. (1970). *East is a big bird.* Cambridge, MA: Harvard University Press.

Glaser, R., Rice, J., Sheridan, J., Post, A., Fertel, R., Stout, J., Speicher, C. E., Kotur, M., & Kiecolt-Glaser, J. K. (1987). Stress-related immune suppression: Health implications. *Brain, Behavior, and Immunity, 1,* 7–20.

Gleicher, G., & Petty, R. E. (1992). Expectations of reassurance influence the nature of fear-stimulated attitude change. *Journal of Experimental Social Psychology, 28,* 86–100.

Glenberg, A. M., Meyer, M., & Lindem, K. (1987). Mental models contribute to foregrounding during text comprehension. *Journal of Memory and Language, 26,* 69–83.

Glowatzki, E., & Fuchs, P. A. (2002). Transmitter release at the hair cell ribbon synapse. *Nature Neuroscience, 5,* 147–154.

Gluck, M. A., & Bower, G. H. (1988). Evaluating an adaptive network model of human learning. *Journal of Memory and Language, 27,* 166–195.

Gluck, M. A., & Myers, C. E. (1997). Psychobiological models of hippocampal function in learning and memory. *Annual Review of Psychology, 48,* 481–514.

Godden, D. R., & Baddeley, A. D. (1975). Context-dependent memory in two natural environments: On land and under water. *British Journal of Psychology, 66,* 325–331.

Goldapple, K., Segal, Z., Garson, C., Lau, M., Bieling, P., Kennedy, S., & Mayberg, H. (2004). Modulation of cortical-limbic pathways in major depression. *Archives of General Psychiatry, 61,* 34–41.

Goldberg, L. R. (1968). Simple models or simple processes? Some research on clinical judgments. *American Psychologist, 23,* 483–496.

Goldin-Meadow, S., & Feldman, H. (1977). The development of language-like communication without a language model. *Science, 197,* 401–403.

Goldman-Rakic, P. S. (1996). Memory: Recoding experience in cells and circuits—diversity in memory research. *Proceedings of the National Academy of Science, 93,* 13435–13437.

Goldsmith, H. H., Buss, K. A., & Lemery, K. S. (1997). Toddler and childhood temperament: Expanded content, stronger genetic evidence, new evidence for the importance of environment. *Developmental Psychology, 33,* 891–905.

Goldstein, M. J., & Strachan, A. M. (1987). The family and schizophrenia. In T. Jacob (Ed.), *Family interaction and psychopathology: Theories, methods, and findings.* New York: Plenum.

Goldstone, R. L., Medink, D. L., & Gentner, D. (1991). Relational similarity and the nonindependence of features in similarity judgments. *Cognitive Psychology, 23,* 222–262.

Golomb, M., Fava, M., Abraham, M., & Rosenbaum, J. F. (1995). Gender differences in personality disorders. *American Journal of Psychiatry, 152,* 579–582.

Gomez, L. (1997). *An introduction to object relations.* New York: New York University Press.

Goodale, M. A., & Humphrey, G. K. (1998). The objects of action and perception. *Cognition, 67,* 181–207.

Goodale, M. A., & Milner, A. D. (2004). *Sight unseen.* Oxford, UK: Oxford University Press.

Goodglass, H. (1976). Agrammatism. In H. Whitaker & H. A. Whitaker (Eds.), *Studies in neurolinguistics.* New York: Academic Press.

Goodwin, D. W., & Guze, S. B. (1996). *Psychiatric diagnosis* (5th ed.). New York: Oxford University Press.

Goodwin, K. A., Meissner, C. A., & Ericsson, K. A. (2001). Toward a model of false recall: Experimental manipulation of encoding context and the collection of verbal reports. *Memory & Cognition, 29,* 806–819.

Gortmaker, S. L., Kagan, J., Caspi, A., & Silva, A. (1997). Daylength during pregnancy and shyness in children: Results from northern and southern hemispheres. *Developmental Psychobiology, 31,* 107–114.

Gottesman, I. I. (1991). *Schizophrenia genesis: The origins of madness.* New York: Freeman.

Gottesman, I. I., & Bertelsen, A. (1989). Confirming unexpressed genotypes for schizophrenia. *Archives of General Psychiatry, 46,* 867–872.

Gottesman, I. I., & Erlenmeyer-Kimling, L. (2001). Family and twin strategies as a head start in defining prodromes and endophenotypes for hypothetical early-interventions in schizophrenia. *Schizophrenia Research, 51(1),* 93–102.

Gottesman, I. I., & Moldin, S. O. (1998). Genotypes, genes, genesis, and pathogenesis in schizophrenia. In M. F. Lenzenweger & R. H. Dworkin (Eds.), *Origins and development of schizophrenia: Advances in experimental psychopathology.* Washington, DC: American Psychological Association.

Gottesman, I. I., & Reilly, J. L. (2003). Strengthening the evidence for genetic factors in schizophrenia (without abetting genetic discrimination). In M. F. Lenzenweger & J. M. Hooley (Eds.), *Principles of experimental psychopathology: Essays in honor of Brendan A. Maher.* Washington, DC: American Psychological Association.

Gottesman, I. I., & Shields, J. (1982). *Schizophrenia: The epigenetic puzzle.* Cambridge: Cambridge University Press.

Gottfredson, L. S. (2004). Life, death, and intelligence. *Journal of Cognitive Education and Psychology, 4,* 1, 23–46.

Gottfries, C. G. (1985). Alzheimer's disease and senile dementia: Biochemical characteristics and aspects of treatment. *Psychopharmacology, 86,* 27–41.

Gould, E., Beylin, A., Tanapat, P., Reeves, A., & Shors, T. J. (1999). Learning enhances adult neurogenesis in the hippocampal formation. *Nature Neuroscience, 2,* 260–265.

Gould, S. J. (1977). *Ever since Darwin: Reflections in natural history.* New York: Norton.

Graham, J. R. (1990). *MMPI-2: Assessing personality and psychopathology.* New York: Oxford University Press.

Graham, S. A., Baker, R. K., & Poulin-Dubois, D. (1998). Infants' expectations about object label reference. *Canadian Journal of Experimental Psychology, 52,* 103–112.

Grant, B. S., & Wiseman, L. L. (2002). Recent history of melanism in American peppered moths. *Journal of Heredity, 93,* 86–90.

Grant, P. R., & Grant, B. R. (2002). Unpredictable evolution in a 30-year study of Darwin's finches. *Science, 296,* 707–711.

Gray, J. A. (1991). The neuropsychology of temperament. In J. Strelau & A. Angleitner (Eds.), *Explorations of temperament: International perspectives on theory and measurement.* London, UK: Plenum Press.

Green, D. M., & Swets, J. A. (1974). *Signal detection theory and psychophysics.* New York: Krieger.

Greenberg, J. R., & Mitchell, S. A. (1983). *Object relations in psychoanalytic theory.* Cambridge, MA: Harvard University Press.

Greenough, W. T., Cohen, N. J., & Juraska, J. M. (1999). New neurons in old brains: Learning to survive? *Nature Neuroscience, 2,* 203–205.

Greenough, W. T., & Volkmar, F. R. (1973). Pattern of dendritic branching in occipital cortex of rats reared in complex environments. *Experimental Neurology, 40,* 491–504.

Greenwald, A. G., McGhee, D. E., & Schwartz, J. L. K. (1998). Measuring individual differences in implicit cognition: The implicit association test. *Journal of Personality and Social Psychology, 74(6),* 1464–1480.

Greenwald, A. G., Nosek, B. A., & Banaji, M. R. (2003). Understanding and using the Implicit Association Test: I. An improved scoring algorithm. *Journal of Personality and Social Psychology, 85(2),* 197–216.

Greenwald, A. G., Pratkanis, A. R., Leippe, M. R., & Baumgardner, M. H. (1986). Under what conditions does theory obstruct research progress? *Psychological Review, 93,* 216–229.

Greenwald, D. F. (1990). An external construct validity study of Rorschach personality variables. *Journal of Personality Assessment, 55,* 768–780.

Greenwald, D. F. (1999). Relationships between the Rorschach and the NEO-Five Factor Inventory. *Psychological Reports, 85(2),* 519–527.

Grice, G. R. (1948). The relation of secondary reinforcement to delayed reward in visual discrimination learning. *Journal of Experimental Psychology, 38,* 1–16.

Griggs, R. A., & Cox, J. R. (1982). The elusive thematic-materials effect in Wason's selection task. *British Journal of Psychology, 73,* 407–420.

Grof, P. (2003). Selecting effective long-term treatment for biopolar patients: Monotherapy and combinations. *Journal of Clinical Psychiatry, 64 (Suppl 5),* 53–61.

Grön, G., Wunderlich, A. P., Spitzer, M., Tomczak, R., & Riepe, M. W. (2000). Brain activation during human navigation: Gender-different neural networks as substrate of performance. *Nature Neuroscience, 3,* 404–408.

Grossarth-Maticek, R., Bastiaans, J., & Kanazir, D. T. (1985). Psychosocial factors as strong predictors of mortality from cancer, ischaemic heart disease and stroke: The Yugoslav prospective study. *Journal of Psychosomatic Research, 29,* 167–176.

Grossarth-Maticek, R., & Eysenck, H. J. (1990). Personality, stress and disease: Description and validation of a new inventory. *Psychological Reports, 66,* 355–373.

Grossarth-Maticek, R., & Eysenck, H. J. (1995). Self-regulation and mortality from cancer, coronary heart disease, and other cases: A prospective study. *Personality and Individual Differences, 19,* 781–795.

Guerin, B. (1992). Social behavior as a discriminative stimulus and consequence in social anthropology. *The Behavior Analyst, 15,* 31–41.

Guerin, B. (1995). Generalized social consequences, ritually reinforced behaviors, and the difficulties of analyzing social contingencies in the real world. *Experimental Analysis of Human Behavior Bulletin, 13,* 11–14.

Guilmette, T. J., Faust, D., Hart, K., & Arkes, H. R. (1990). A national survey of psychologists who offer neuropsychological services. *Archives of Clinical Neuropsychology, 5,* 373–392.

Guimond, S., & Dube, L. (1989). La representation des causes de l'inferiorité économique desquébécois francophones. *Canadian Journal of Behavioural Science, 21,* 28–39.

Guze, S. B., Wolfgram, E. D., McKinney, J. K., & Cantwell, D. P. (1967). Psychiatric illness in the families of convicted criminals: A study of 519 first-degree relatives. *Disorders of the Nervous System, 28,* 651–659.

Gzowski, P. (1981). *The game of our lives.* Toronto: McClelland & Stewart, Inc.

Habbick, B. F., Nanson, J. L., Snyder, R. E., Cassey, R. E., & Schulman, A. L. (1996). Foetal alcohol syndrome in Saskatchewan: Unchanged incidence in a 20-year period. *Canadian Journal of Public Health, 87,* 204–207.

Haberlandt, K. (1994). *Cognitive psychology.* Boston: Allyn & Bacon.

Hackshaw, A. K., Law, M. R., & Wald, N. J. (1997). The accumulated evidence on lung cancer and environmental tobacco smoke. *British Medical Journal, 315,* 980–988.

Haddock, G., Zanna, M. P., & Esses, V. M. (1994). The (limited) role of trait-laden stereotypes in predicting attitudes toward native peoples. *British Journal of Social Psychology, 33,* 83–106.

Hadjikhani, N., Liu, A. K., Dale, A. M., Cavanagh, P., & Tootell, R. B. H. (1998). Retinotopy and color sensitivity in human visual cortical area V8. *Nature Neuroscience, 1,* 235–241.

Hadjistavropoulos, T., & Genest, M. (1994). The underestimation of the role of physical attractiveness in dating preferences: Ignorance or taboo? *Canadian Journal of Behavioural Science, 26,* 298–318.

Hadjistavropoulos, T., Malloy, D. C., Sharpe, D., Green, S. M., & Fuchs-Lacelle, S. (2002). The relative importance of the ethical principles adopted by the American Psychological Association. *Canadian Psychology, 43,* 254–259.

Haenny, P. E., Maunsell, J. H., & Schiller, P. H. (1988). State dependent activity in monkey visual cortex. II. Retinal and extraretinal factors in V4. *Experimental Brain Research, 69,* 245–259.

Hafer, C. L. (2000a). Do innocent victims threaten the belief in a just world? Evidence from a modified Stroop Task. *Journal of Personality and Social Psychology, 79,* 165–173.

Hafer, C. L. (2000b). Investment in long-term goals and commitment to just means drive the need to believe in a just world. *Personality and Social Psychology Bulletin, 26,* 1059–1073.

Hafer, C. L. (2002). Why we reject innocent victims. In M. Ross & D. T. Miller (Eds.), *The justice motive in everyday life.* New York: Cambridge University Press.

Hagan, F. E. (1982). *Research methods in criminal justice and criminology.* New York: Macmillan.

Haggard, P., Clark, S., & Kalogeras, J. (2002). Voluntary action and conscious awareness. *Nature Neuroscience, 5,* 382–385.

Haggard, P., & Eimer, M. (1999). On the relation between brain potentials and the awareness of voluntary movements. *Experimental Brain Research, 126,* 128–133.

Haier, R. J., Jung, R. E., Yeo, R. A., Head, K., & Alkire, M. T. (2004). Structural brain variation and general intelligence. *NeuroImage, 23*(1), 425–433.

Haier, R. J., White, N. S., & Alkire, M. T. (2003). Individual differences in general intelligence correlate with brain function during nonreasoning tasks. *Intelligence, 31,* 5, 429–441.

Halaas, J. L., Gajiwala, K. S., Maffei, M., & Cohen, S. L. (1995). Weight-reducing effects of the plasma protein encoded by the obese gene. *Science, 269,* 543–546.

Hall, C. S., & Nordby, V. J. (1973). *A primer of Jungian psychology.* New York: New American Library.

Halliday, M. A. K. (1975). *Learning how to mean: Explorations in the development of language.* London: Edward Arnold.

Halmi, K. (1996). Eating disorders: Anorexia nervosa, bulimia nervosa, and obesity. In R. E. Hales & S. C. Yudofsky (Eds.), *The American Psychiatric Press Synopsis of Psychiatry.* Washington, DC: American Psychiatric Association.

Hamilton, W. D. (1964).The genetical evolution of social behaviour: I and II. *Journal of Theoretical Biology, 7,* 1–52.

Hamilton, W. D. (1970). Selfish and spiteful behavior in an evolutionary model. *Nature, 228,* 1218–1220.

Hansen, C. H., & Hansen, R. D. (1988). Finding the face in the crowd: An anger superiority effect. *Journal of Personality and Social Psychology, 54,* 917–924.

Hanson, H. M. (1959). Effects of discrimination training on stimulus generalization. *Journal of Experimental Psychology, 58,* 321–334.

Hare, R. D. (1965). Temporal gradient of fear arousal in psychopaths. *Journal of Abnormal Psychology, 70,* 442–445.

Hare, R. D. (1998). *Without conscience: The disturbing world of the psychopaths among us.* New York: Guilford Press.

Hare, R. D. (1999). Psychopathy as a risk factor for violence. *Psychiatric Quarterly, 70,* 181–197.

Hare, R. D., McPherson, L. M., & Forth, A. E. (1988). Male psychopaths and their criminal

careers. *Journal of Consulting and Clinical Psychology, 56,* 710–714.

Harkins, S. G., & Petty, R. E. (1982). Effects of task difficulty and task uniqueness on social loafing. *Journal of Personality and Social Psychology, 43,* 1214–1229.

Harlow, H. (1974). *Learning to love.* New York: J. Aronson.

Harpur, T. J., Hart, S. D., & Hare, R. D. (2002). Personality of the psychopath. In P. T. Costa, Jr., & T. A. Widiger (Eds.), *Personality disorders and the five-factor model of personality* (2nd ed.). Washington, DC: American Psychological Association.

Harris, M. (1991). *Cultural anthropology* (3rd ed.). New York: HarperCollins.

Hartshorne, H., & May, M. A. (1928). *Studies in deceit.* New York: Macmillan.

Harwood, R. L., Miller, J. G., & Irizarry, N. L. (1995). *Culture and attachment: Perceptions of the child in context.* New York: Guilford.

Hatfield, E. (1988). Passionate and compassionate love. In R. J. Sternberg & M. L. Barnes (Eds.), *The psychology of love.* New Haven, CT: Yale University Press.

Hatfield, E., & Rapson, R. L. (1993). *Love, sex, and intimacy: Their psychology, biology, and history.* New York: HarperCollins.

Hayes, C. (1952). *The ape in our house.* London: Gollancz.

Hayes, S. C., & Barnes-Holmes, D. (Eds.) (2001). *Relational frame theory.* New York: Kluwer Academic/Plenum Publishers.

Hazelwood, J. D., & Olson, J. M. (1986). Covariation information, causal questioning, and interpersonal behavior. *Journal of Experimental Social Psychology, 22,* 276–291.

He, J., Vupputuri, S., Allen, K., Prerost, M. R., Hughes, J., & Whelton, P. K. (1999). Passive smoking and the risk of coronary heart disease—a meta-analysis of epidemiologic studies. *New England Journal of Medicine, 340,* 920–926.

Healy, A. F., & McNamara, D. S. (1996). Verbal learning and memory: Does the Modal Model still work? *Annual Review of Psychology, 47,* 143–172.

Heath, A. C., Meyer, J. M., & Martin, N. G. (1990). Inheritance of alcohol consumption patterns in the Australian twin survey, 1981. In C. R. Cloninger & H. Begleite (Eds.), *Genetics and biology of alcoholism.* Plainview, NY: Cold Spring Harbor Laboratory Press.

Hebb, D. O. (1949). *The organization of behavior.* New York: Wiley-Interscience.

Hebb, D. O. (1955). Drives and the C. N. S. (conceptual nervous system). *Psychological Review, 62,* 243–254.

Hebb, D. O. (1966). *A textbook of psychology.* Philadelphia, PA: W.B. Saunders Company.

Hebb, D. O. (1980). *Essay on mind.* Hillsdale, NJ: Erlbaum.

Hebb, D. O., Lambert, W. E., & Tucker, G. R. A. (1973). DMZ in the language war. *Psychology Today,* 55–62.

Heider, E. R. (1971). "Focal" color areas and the development of color names. *Developmental Psychology, 4,* 447–455.

Heider, F. (1958). *The psychology of interpersonal relations.* New York: John Wiley & Sons.

Heine, S. J. (2001). Self as cultural product: An examination of East Asian and North American selves. *Journal of Personality, 69,* 881–906.

Heine, S. J., Kitayama, S., Lehman, D. R., Takata, T., Ide, E., Leung, C., & Matsumoto, H. (2001). Divergent consequences of success and failure in Japan and North America: An investigation of self-improving motivations and malleable selves. *Journal of Personality and Social Psychology, 81,* 599–615.

Heinrichs, R. W. (2003). Historical origins of schizophrenia: Two early madmen and their illness. *Journal of the History of the Behavioral Sciences, 39(4),* 349–363.

Helms, J. E. (1992). Why is there no study of cultural equivalence in standardized cognitive ability testing? *American Psychologist, 47,* 1083–1101.

Helms, J. E. (1997). The triple quandary of race, culture, and social classes in standardized cognitive ability testing. In D. P. Fanagan, J. L. Genshaft, et al. (Eds.), *Contemporary intellectual assessment: Theories, tests, and issues* (pp. 517–532). New York: Guilford Press.

Helzer, J. E., & Canino, G. J. (1992). *Alcoholism in North America, Europe, and Asia.* New York: Oxford University Press.

Henderlong, J., & Lepper, M. R. (2002). The effects of praise on children's intrinsic motivation: A review and synthesis. *Psychological Bulletin, 128,* 774–795.

Henderson, N. D. (1982). Human behavior genetics. *Annual Review of Psychology, 33,* 403–440.

Herdt, G. (2001). Stigma and the ethnographic study of HIV: Problems and prospects. *AIDS & Behavior, 5(2),* 141–149.

Herdt, G., & Lindenbaum, S. (Eds.). (1992). *Social analyses in the time of AIDS.* Newbury Park, CA: Sage.

Herek, G. M., Capitanio, J. P., & Widaman, K. F. (2003). Stigma, social risk, and health policy: Public attitudes toward HIV surveillance policies and the social construction of illness. *Health Psychology, 22,* 533–540.

Herrnstein, R. J. (1961). Relative and absolute strength of response as a function of frequency of reinforcement. *Journal of the Experimental Analysis of Behavior, 4,* 267–272.

Herrnstein, R. J. (1970). On the law of effect. *Journal of the Experimental Analysis of Behavior, 13,* 243–266.

Herrnstein, R. J., & Murray, C. (1994). *The bell curve.* New York: Free Press.

Hettema, J. M., Neale, M. C., & Kendler, K. S. (2001). A review and meta-analysis of the genetic epidemiology of anxiety disorders. *American Journal of Psychiatry, 158,* 1568–1578.

Heyman, G. D., & Giles, J. W. (2004). Valence effects in reasoning about evaluative traits. *Merrill-Palmer Quarterly, 50,* 86–109.

Heywood, C., & Cowey, A. (1998). With color in mind. *Nature Neuroscience, 1,* 171–173.

Higgins, S. T., Budney, A. J., & Bickel, W. K. (1994). Applying behavioral concepts and principles to the treatment of cocaine dependence. *Drug and Alcohol Dependence, 7,* 19–38.

Hilgard, E. R. (1991). A neodissociation interpretation of hypnosis. In S. J. Lynn & J. W. Rhue (Eds.), *Theories of hypnosis: Current models and perspectives* (pp. 324–361). New York: Guilford Press.

Hill, C. E., & Nakayama, E. Y. (2000). Client-centered therapy: Where has it been and where is it going? A comment on Hathaway (1948). *Journal of Clinical Psychology, 56,* 861–875.

Hilton, D. J., & Slugoski, B. R. (1986). Knowledge-based causal attributions: The abnormal conditions focus model. *Psychological Review, 93,* 75–88.

Hinton, G. E., & Shallice, T. (1991). Lesioning an attractor network: Investigations of acquired dyslexia. *Psychological Review, 98,* 74–95.

Hirschman, R. S., Leventhal, H., & Glynn, K. (1984). The development of smoking behavior: Conceptualization and supportive cross-sectional survey data. *Journal of Applied Social Psychology, 14,* 184–206.

Hobson, J. A., & Pace-Schott, E. F. (2002). The cognitive neuroscience of sleep: Neuronal systems, consciousness and learning. *Nature Reviews: Neuroscience, 3,* 679–693.

Hoff, T. L. (1992). Psychology in Canada one hundred years ago: James Mark Baldwin at the University of Toronto. *Canadian Psychology, 33,* 683–694.

Hoffman, P. (1997). The endorphin hypothesis. In W. P. Morgan (Ed.), *Physical activity and mental health* (pp. 163–177). Washington, DC: Taylor & Francis.

Hofling, C. K. (1963). *Textbook of psychiatry for medical practice.* Philadelphia: J. B. Lippincott.

Hohman, G. W. (1966). Some effects of spinal cord lesions on experienced emotional feelings. *Psychophysiology, 3,* 143–156.

Hollenbeck, A. R. (1978). Television viewing patterns of families with young infants. *Journal of Social Psychology, 105,* 259–264.

Hollis, K. L. (1982). Pavlovian conditioning of signal-centered action patterns and autonomic behavior: A biological analysis of function. *Advances in the Study of Behavior, 12,* 1–64.

Hollis, K. L. (1997). Contemporary research on Pavlovian conditioning: A "new" functional analysis. *American Psychologist, 52,* 956–965.

Hollon, S. D., Thase, M. E., & Markowitz, J. C. (2002). Treatment and prevention of depression. *Psychological Science in the Public Interest, 3(2),* 39–77.

Holmes, T. H., & Rahe, R. H. (1967). The social readjustment rating scale. *Journal of Psychosomatic Research, 11,* 213, 218.

Holyoak, K. J. (1990). Problem solving. In D. N. Osherson & E. E. Smith (Eds.), *An invitation to cognitive science. Vol. 3: Thinking.* Cambridge, MA: MIT Press.

Holyoak, K. J., & Spellman, B. A. (1993). Thinking. *Annual Review of Psychology, 44,* 265–315.

Horn, J. L. (1982). The theory of fluid and crystallized intelligence in relation to concepts of cognitive psychology and aging in adulthood. In F. I. M. Craik & S. Trehub (Eds.), *Aging and cognitive processes.* New York: Plenum Press.

Horn, J. L. (1994). Theory of fluid and crystallized intelligence. In R. J. Sternberg (Ed.), *Encyclopedia of human intelligence.* New York: Macmillan.

Horn, J. L. (2002). Selections of evidence, misleading assumptions, and oversimplifications: The political message of *The Bell Curve.* In J. M. Fish (Ed.), *Race and intelligence: Separating science from myth.* Mahwah, NJ: Lawrence Erlbaum Associates.

Horn, J. L., & Cattell, R. B. (1966). Refinement and test of the theory of fluid and crystallized ability intelligences. *Journal of Educational Psychology, 57,* 253–270.

Horne, J. A. (1978). A review of the biological effects of total sleep deprivation in man. *Biological Psychology, 7,* 55–102.

Horne, J. A., & Minard, A. (1985). Sleep and sleepiness following a behaviourally "active" day. *Ergonomics, 28,* 567–575.

Horne, J. A., & Petit, A. N. (1985). High incentive effects on vigilance performance during 72 hours of total sleep deprivation. *Acta Psychologica, 58,* 123–139.

Horney, K. (1950). *Neurosis and human growth.* New York: Norton.

Hough, L. M., & Oswald, F. L. (2000). Personnel selection: Looking toward the future—Remembering the past. *Annual Review of Psychology, 51,* 631–664.

Hovland, C. I., & Weiss, W. (1951). The influence of source credibility on communication effectiveness. *Public Opinion Quarterly, 15,* 635–650.

Howard, J. H., Cunningham, D. A., & Rechnitzer, P. A. (1976). Health patterns associated with type A behavior: A managerial population. *Journal of Human Stress, 2,* 24–31.

Howard, M. O., Elkins, R. L., Rimmele, C., & Smith, J. W. Chemical aversion treatment of alcohol dependence. (1991). *Drug and Alcohol Dependence, 29,* 107–143.

Howard, R. W. (1995). *Learning and memory: Major ideas, principles, issues, and applications.* Westport, CT: Praeger.

Hoyenga, K. B., & Hoyenga, K. T. (1993). *Gender-related differences: Origins and outcomes.* Boston: Allyn & Bacon.

Hubel, D. H., & Wiesel, T. N. (1977). Functional architecture of macaque monkey visual cortex. *Proceedings of the Royal Society of London, Series B, 198,* 1–59.

Hubel, D. H., & Wiesel, T. N. (1979). Brain mechanisms of vision. *Scientific American, 241,* 150–162.

Huesmann, L. R., Moise-Titus, J., Podolski, C.-L., & Eron, L. D. (2003). Longitudinal relations between children's exposure to TV violence and their aggressive and violent behavior in young adulthood: 1977–1992. *Developmental Psychology, 39,* 201–221.

Hughes, J. R., & Pierattini, R. (1992). An introduction to pharmacotherapy. In J. Grabowski & G. R. Vandenbos (Eds.), *Psychopharmacology: Basic mechanisms and applied interventions: Master lectures in psychology.* Washington, DC: American Psychological Association.

Hulit, L. M., & Howard, M. R. (1993). *Born to talk: An introduction to speech and language development.* New York: Merrill/Macmillan.

Hull, C. L. (1943). *Principles of behavior.* New York: Appleton-Century-Crofts.

Humphrey, G. K., Herbert, A. M., Hazlewood, S., & Stewart, J. A. D. (1998). The indirect McCollough effect: An examination of an associative account. *Perception & Psychophysics, 60*, 1188–1196.

Humphrey, N. K. (2003). *The inner eye: Social intelligence in evolution.* Oxford, UK: Oxford University Press.

Hunt, E. (1985). Verbal ability. In R. J. Sternberg (Ed.), *Human abilities: An information-processing approach.* New York: W. H. Freeman.

Huston, A. C. (1983). Sex-typing. In E. M. Hetherington (Ed.), *Handbook of child psychology: Vol. 4. Socialization, personality, and social development.* New York: Wiley.

Huston, A. C., Watkins, B. A., & Kunkel, D. (1989). Public policy and children's television. *American Psychologist, 44*, 424–433.

Huston, A. C., & Wright, J. C. (1998). Mass media and children's development. In W. Damon (Ed.), *Handbook of child psychology* (Vol. 4). New York: Wiley.

Huston, A. C., Wright, J. C., Rice, M. L., Kerkman, D., & St. Peters, M. (1990). Development of television viewing patterns in early childhood: A longitudinal investigation. *Developmental Psychology, 26*, 409–420.

Ikonomidou, C. (2000). Ethanol-induced apoptotic neurodegeneration and fetal alcohol syndrome. *Science, 287*, 1056–1060.

Inglefinger, F. J. (1944). The late effects of total and subtotal gastrectomy. *New England Journal of Medicine, 231*, 321–327.

Irvine, J., Garner, D. M., Craig, H. M., & Logan, A. G. (1991). Prevalence of type A behavior in untreated hypertensive individuals. *Hypertension, 18*, 72–78.

Isenberg, D. J. (1986). Group polarization: A critical review and meta-analysis. *Psychological Bulletin, 50*, 1141–1151.

Iversen, L. (2003) Cannabis and the brain. *Brain, 126*, 1252–1270.

Izard, C. E. (1971). *The face of emotion.* New York: Appleton-Century-Crofts.

Jacklin, C. N., & Maccoby, E. E. (1983). Issues of gender differentiation in normal development. In M. D. Levine, W. B. Carey, A. C. Crocker, & R. T. Gross (Eds.), *Developmental-behavioral pediatrics.* Philadelphia: Saunders.

Jackson, D. N., Ashton, M. E., & Tomes, J. L. (1996). The six-factor model of personality: Facets from the Big Five. *Personality and Individual Differences, 21*, 391–402.

Jackson, D. N., Paunonen, S. V., Fraboni, M., & Goffin, R. D. (1996). A Five-Factor versus Six-Factor model of personality structure. *Personality and Individual Differences, 20*, 33–45.

Jackson, D. N., & Tremblay, P. F. (2002). The six-factor personality questionnaire. In B. de Raad (Ed.), *Big five assessment.* Ashland, OH: Hogrefe & Huber Publishers.

Jacobsen, C. F., Wolf, J. B., & Jackson, T. A. (1935). An experimental analysis of the functions of the frontal association areas in primates. *Journal of Nervous and Mental Disease, 82*, 1–14.

Jacobson, J. W., & Mulick, J. A. (1996). *Manual on diagnosis and professional practice in mental re-*

tardation. Washington, DC: American Psychological Association.

Jaffe, J. H. (1985). Drug addiction and drug abuse. In L. S. Goodman & A. Gilman (Eds.), *The pharmacological basis of therapeutics, Vol. 7.* New York: Macmillan.

James, W. (1884). What is an emotion? *Mind, 9*, 188–205.

James, W. (1890). *Principles of psychology.* New York: Henry Holt.

James, W. (1893). *The principles of psychology: Vol. 1.* New York: Holt.

James, W. P. T., & Trayhurn, P. (1981). Thermogenesis and obesity. *British Medical Bulletin, 37*, 43–48.

Jang, K. L., Livesley, W. J., Angleitner, A., Riemann, R., & Vernon, P. (2002). Genetic and environmental influences on the covariance of facets defining the domains of the five-factor model of personality. *Personality & Individual Differences, 33(1)*, 83–101.

Jang, K. L., Livesley, W. J., & Vernon, P. A. (1996). Heritability of the Big Five personality dimensions and their facets: A twin study. *Journal of Personality, 64*, 577–591.

Janis, I. L. (1972). *Victims of groupthink.* Boston: Houghton Mifflin.

Janis, I. L. (1982). *Groupthink: Psychological studies of policy decisions and fiascoes.* Boston: Houghton Mifflin.

Janzen, L. A., Nanson, J. L., & Block, G. W. (1995). Neuropsychological evaluation of preschoolers with fetal alcohol syndrome. *Neurotoxicology & Teratology, 17*, 273–279.

Jasper, H. H. (1995). A historical perspective: The rise and fall of prefrontal lobotomy. In H. H. Jasper & S. Riggio (Eds.), *Epilepsy and the functional anatomy of the frontal lobe.* New York: Raven Press.

Javal, E. (1879). Essai sur la physiologie de la lecture. *Annales D'Oculistique, 82*, 242–253.

Jaynes, J. (1970). The problem of animate motion in the seventeenth century. *Journal of the History of Ideas, 6*, 219–234.

Jaynes, J, (1976). *The origin of consciousness in the breakdown of the bicameral mind.* Boston: Houghton Mifflin.

Jaynes, J. (1978). *The origin of consciousness in the breakdown of the bicameral mind.* New York: Basic Books.

Jeffcoate, W. J., Lincoln, N. B., Selby, C., & Herbert, M. (1986). Correlations between anxiety and serum prolactin in humans. *Journal of Psychosomatic Research, 30*, 217–222.

Jenike, M. S. (2000). Neurological treatment of obsessive-compulsive disorder. In W. K. Goodman, M. V. Rudorfer, & J. D. Maser (Eds.), *Obsessive-compulsive disorder: Contemporary issues in treatment.* Personality and clinical psychology series. Mahwah, NJ: Lawrence Erlbaum Associates.

Jenkins, H. M., Barrera, F. J., Ireland, C., & Woodside, B. (1978). Signal-centered action patterns of dogs in appetitive classical conditioning. *Learning and Motivation, 9*, 272–296.

Jenkins, J. G., & Dallenbach, K. M. (1924). Obliviscence during sleep and waking. *American Journal of Psychology, 35*, 605–612.

Jenkins, J. H., & Karno, M. (1992). The meaning of expressed emotion: Theoretical issues raised by cross-cultural research. *American Journal of Psychiatry, 149*, 9–21.

Jensen, A. R. (1985). The nature of the black-white difference on various psychometric tests: Spearman's hypothesis. *Behavioral and Brain Sciences, 8*, 193–263.

Jensen, T., Genefke, I., & Hyldebrandt, N. (1982). Cerebral atrophy in young torture victims. *New England Journal of Medicine, 307*, 1341.

Johansson, G. (1973). Visual perception of biological motion and a model for its analysis. *Perception and Psychophysics, 14*, 201–211.

Johnson, J. G., Alloy, L. B., Panzarella, C., Metalsky, G. I., Rabkin, J. G., Williams, J. B. W., & Abramson, L. Y. (2001). Hopelessness as a mediator of the association between social support and depressive symptoms: Findings of a study of men with HIV. *Journal of Consulting & Clinical Psychology, 69(6)*, 1056–1060.

Johnson, J. G., Cohen, P., Smailes, E. M., Kasen, S., & Brook, J. S. (2002). Television viewing and aggressive behavior during adolescence and adulthood. *Science, 295*, 2468–2471.

Johnson, J. H., Butcher, J. N., Null, C., & Johnson, K. N. (1984). Replicated item level factor analysis of the full MMPI. *Journal of Personality and Social Psychology, 47*, 105–114.

Johnson, J. S., & Newport, E. L. (1989). Critical period effects in second language learning: The influence of maturational state on the acquisition of English as a second language. *Cognitive Psychology, 21*, 60–99.

Johnson, S. B., & Sechrest, L. (1968). Comparison of desensitization and progressive relaxation in treating test anxiety. *Journal of Consulting and Clinical Psychology, 32*, 280–286.

Johnson-Laird, P. N. (1985). Deductive reasoning ability. In R. J. Sternberg (Ed.), *Human abilities: An information-processing approach.* New York: W. H. Freeman.

Johnson-Laird, P. N. (1995). Deductive reasoning and the brain. In G. M. S. Gazzaniga et al. (Eds.), *The cognitive neurosciences* (pp. 999–1008). Cambridge, MA: MIT Press.

Johnson-Laird, P. N. (1999). Deductive reasoning. *Annual Review of Psychology, 50*, 109–135.

Johnson-Laird, P. N. (2001). Mental models and deduction. *Trends in Cognitive Sciences, 5*, 434–442.

Johnson-Laird, P. N., Byrne, R. M. J., & Schaeken, W. (1992). Propositional reasoning by model. *Psychological Review, 99*, 418–439.

Johnston, W. A., & Dark, V. J. (1986). Selective attention. *Annual Review of Psychology, 37*, 43–76.

Johnstone, L. (1999). Adverse psychological effects of ECT. *Journal of Mental Health, 8*, 69–85.

Joiner, T. E., Jr. (2000). A test of the hopelessness theory of depression in youth psychiatric inpatients. *Journal of Clinical Child Psychology, 29*, 167–176.

Jonçich, G. (1968). *The sane positivist: A biography of Edward L. Thorndike.* Middleton, CT: Wesleyan University Press.

Jones, D. C. (1991). Friendship satisfaction and gender: An examination of sex differences in contributors to friendship satisfaction. *Journal of Social and Personal Relationships, 8*, 167–185.

Jones, E. E. (1990). *Interpersonal perception.* New York: W. H. Freeman.

Jones, E. E., & Harris, V. A. (1967). The attribution of attitudes. *Journal of Experimental Social Psychology, 3*, 1–24.

Jones, E. E., & Nisbett, R. E. (1971). The actor and observer: Divergent perceptions of the causes of behavior. In E. E. Jones, D. E. Kamouse, H. H. Kelley, R. E. Nisbett, S. Valins, & B. Weiner (Eds.), *Attribution: Perceiving the causes of behavior.* Morristown, NJ: General Learning Press.

Jones, M. C., & Bayley, N. (1950). Physical maturing among boys as related to behavior. *Journal of Educational Psychology, 41*, 129–184.

Julesz, B. (1965). Texture and visual perception. *Scientific American, 212*, 38–48.

Jusczyk, P. W., & Hohne, E. A. (1997). Infants' memory for spoken words. *Science, 277*, 1984–1986.

Just, M. A., & Carpenter, P. A. (1987). *The psychology of reading and language comprehension.* Boston: Allyn & Bacon.

Just, M. A., Carpenter, P. A., & Wu, R. (1983). *Eye fixations in the reading of Chinese technical text* (Technical Report). Pittsburgh: Carnegie-Mellon University.

Justice, A. (1985). Review of the effects of stress on cancer in laboratory animals: Importance of time of stress application and type of tumor. *Psychological Bulletin, 98*, 108–138.

Kaernbach, C. (2004). The memory of noise. *Experimental Psychology, 51*, 240–248.

Kagan, J., Kearsley, R. B., & Zelazo, P. R. (1978). *Infancy: Its place in human development.* Cambridge, MA: Harvard University Press.

Kagan, J., Reznick, J. S., & Snidman, N. (1988). Biological bases of childhood shyness. *Science, 240*, 167–171.

Kahneman, D. (2003). A perspective on judgment and choice: Mapping bounded rationality. *American Psychologist, 58*, 697–720.

Kail, R., & Hall, L. K. (2001). Distinguishing short-term memory from working memory. *Memory & Cognition, 29*, 1–9.

Kail R. V. (2001). *Children and their development.* Upper Saddle River, NJ: Prentice Hall.

Kalish, R. A. (1976). Death and dying in a social context. In R. H. Binstock & E. Shanas (Eds.), *Handbook of aging and the social sciences.* New York: Van Nostrand Reinhold.

Kamin, L. J. (1969). Predictability, surprise, attention, and conditioning. In B. A. Campbell & R. M. Church (Eds.), *Punishment and aversive behavior* (pp. 279–296). New York: Appleton-Century-Crofts.

Kandel, E. R., & Spencer, W. A. (1968) Cellular neurophysiological approaches in the study of learning. *Physiological Review, 48*, 65–134.

Kane, J. M. (2001). Long-term therapeutic management in schizophrenia. In A. Breier, P. V. Tran, & J. M. Herrera (Eds.), *Current issues in the psychopharmacology of schizophrenia.* Philadelphia, PA: Lippincott Williams & Wilkins Publishers.

Kaplan, E. L., & Kaplan, G. A. (1970). The prelinguistic child. In J. Eliot (Ed.), *Human development and cognitive processes.* New York: Holt, Rinehart and Winston.

Kaplan, R. M. (2000). Two pathways to prevention. *American Psychologist, 55*, 382–396.

Kapp, B. S., Gallagher, M., Applegate, C. D., & Frysinger, R. C. (1982). The amygdala central nucleus: Contributions to conditioned cardiovascular responding during aversive Pavlovian conditioning in the rabbit. In C. D. Woody (Ed.), *Conditioning: Representation of involved neural functions.* New York: Plenum Press.

Karau, S. J., & Hart, J. W. (1998). Group cohesiveness and social loafing: Effects of a social interaction manipulation on individual motivation within groups. *Group Dynamics, 2*, 185–191.

Karbe, H., Herholz, K., Szelies, B., Pawlik, G., Wienhard, K., et al. (1989). Regional metabolic correlates of token test results in cortical and subcortical left hemispheric infarction. *Neurology, 39*, 1083–1088.

Karbe, H., Szelies, B., Herholz, K., & Heiss, W. D. (1990). Impairment of language is related to left parieto-temporal glucose metabolism in aphasic stroke patients. *Journal of Neurology, 237*, 19–23.

Karniol, R., & Ross, M. (1977). The effect of performance-relevant and performance-irrelevant rewards on children's intrinsic motivation. *Child Development, 48*, 482–487.

Katz, D. (1935). *The world of colour.* London: Kegan Paul, Trench, Trubner.

Kausler, D. H. (1994). *Learning and memory in normal aging.* New York: Academic Press.

Kay, P. (1975). Synchronic variability and diachronic changes in basic color terms. *Language in Society, 4*, 257–270.

Kazdin, A. E. (1994). *Behavior modification in applied settings.* Pacific Grove, CA: Brooks/Cole.

Kazdin, A. E. (2001). *Behavior modification in applied settings* (6th ed.). Belmont, CA: Wadsworth/Thomson Learning.

Keating, D. (2004). Cognitive and brain development. (2004). In R. M. Lerner & L. Steinberg (Eds.), *Handbook of adolescent psychology* (2nd ed.) (pp. 45–84). Hoboken, NJ: John Wiley and Sons.

Kebbell, M. R., & Wagstaff, G. F. (1998). Hypnotic interviewing: The best way to interview eyewitnesses? *Behavioral Sciences and the Law, 16*, 115–129.

Kehoe, E. J. (1988). A layered network model of associative learning: Learning to learn and configuration. *Psychological Review, 95*, 411–433.

Keller, S. E., Weiss, J. M., Schleifer, S. J., Miller, N. E., & Stein, M. (1983). Stress-induced suppression of immunity in adrenalectomized rats. *Science, 221*, 1301–1304.

Kelley, H. H. (1950). The warm-cold variable in first impressions of persons. *Journal of Personality, 18*, 431–439.

Kelley, H. H. (1967). Attribution theory in social psychology. In D. Levine (Ed.), *Nebraska symposium on motivation, Vol. 15.* Lincoln: University of Nebraska Press.

Kelley, K., & Byrne, D. (1992). *Exploring human sexuality.* Englewood Cliffs, NJ: Prentice Hall.

Kelly, J. F., & Hake, D. F. (1970). An extinction-induced increase in an aggressive response with humans. *Journal of the Experimental Analysis of Behavior, 14*, 153–164.

Kelly, S. J., Day, N., & Streissguth, A. P. (2000). Effects of prenatal alcohol exposure on social behavior in humans and other species. *Neurotoxicology and Teratology, 22*, 143–149.

Kendler, K. S., Pedersen, N., Johnson, L., Neale, M. C., & Mathe, A. A. (1993). A pilot Swedish twin study of affective illness, including hospital- and population-ascertained subsamples. *Archives of General Psychiatry, 50(9)*, 699–700.

Kendler, K. S., Prescott, C. A., Neale, M. C., & Pedersen, N. L. (1997). Temperance board registration for alcohol abuse in a national sample of Swedish male twins, born 1902 to 1949. *Archives of General Psychiatry, 54*, 178–184.

Kennedy, H. J., Evans, M. G., Crawford, A. C., & Fettiplace, R. (2003). Fast adaptation of mechanoelectrical transducer channels in mammalian cochlear hair cells. *Nature Neuroscience, 6*, 832–836.

Kenrick, D. T., Groth, G., Trost, M. R., & Sadalla, E. K. (1993). Integrating evolutionary and social exchange perspectives on relationships: Effects of gender, self-appraisal, and involvement level in mate selection. *Journal of Personality and Social Psychology, 64*, 951–969.

Kenrick, D. T., Li, N. P., & Butner, J. (2003). Dynamical evolutionary psychology: Individual decision rules and emergent social norms. *Psychological Review, 110*, 3–28.

Kenrick, D. T., Neuberg, S. L., Zierk, K. L., & Krones, J. M. (1994). Evolution and social cognition: Contrast effects as a function of sex, dominance, and physical attractiveness. *Personality and Social Psychology Bulletin, 20*, 210–217.

Kertesz, A. (1981). Anatomy of jargon. In J. Brown (Ed.), *Jargonaphasia.* New York: Academic Press.

Kessler, R. C., McGonagle, K. A., Zhao, S., Nelson, C., Hughes, M., Eshleman, S., Wittchen, H., & Kendler, K. (1994). Lifetime and 12-month prevalence of DSM-III-R psychiatric disorders in the United States. *Archives of General Psychiatry, 51*, 8–19.

Keyes, D. (1981). *The minds of Billy Milligan.* New York: Bantam.

Keyes, J. B. (1995). Stress inoculation training for staff working with persons with mental retardation: A model program. In L. R. Murphy, J. J. Hurrell, Jr., S. L. Sauter, & G. P. Keita (Eds.), *Job stress interventions.* Washington, DC: American Psychological Association.

Khachaturian, Z. S., & Blass, J. P. (1992). *Alzheimer's disease: New treatment strategies.* New York: Dekker.

Kheriaty, E., Kleinknecht, R. A., & Hyman, I. E. (1999). Recall and validation of phobia origins as a function of a structured interview versus the Phobia Origins Questionnaire. *Behavior Modification, 23*, 61–78.

Kiang, N. Y.-S. (1965). *Discharge patterns of single nerve fibers in the cat's auditory nerve.* Cambridge, MA: MIT Press.

Kiehl, K. A., Smith, A. M., Hare, R. D., & Liddle, P. F. (2000). An event-related potential investigation of response inhibition in schizophrenia and psychopathy. *Biological Psychiatry, 48(3),* 210–221.

Kihlstrom, J. F. (1998). Dissociations and dissociation theory in hypnosis: Comment on Kirsch and Lynn (1998). *Psychological Bulletin, 123,* 186–191.

Kilgour, A. R., Jakobson, L. S., & Cuddy, L. L. (2000). Music training and rate of presentation as mediators of text and song recall. *Memory & Cognition, 28,* 700–710.

Kimura, D. (1999). *Sex and cognition.* Cambridge, MA: The MIT Press.

Kirasic, K. C. (1991). Spatial cognition and behavior in young and elderly adults: Implications for learning new environments. *Psychology and Aging, 6,* 10–18.

Kirasic, K. C., & Bernicki, M. R. (1990). Acquisition of spatial knowledge under conditions of temporospatial discontinuity in young and elderly adults. *Psychological Research, 52,* 76–79.

Kirchengast, S., & Hartmann, B. (2003). Nicotine consumption before and during pregnancy affects not only newborn size but also birth modus. *Journal of Biosocial Science, 35,* 175–188.

Kirsch, I., & Lynn, S. J. (1998). Dissociation theories of hypnosis. *Psychological Bulletin, 123,* 100–115.

Kisilevsky, B. S., Hains, S. M. J., Lee, K., Xie, X., Huang, H., Ye, H. H., Zhang, K., & Wang, Z. (2003). Effects of experience on fetal voice recognition. *Psychological Science, 14,* 220–224.

Kissen, D. M. (1963). Personality characteristics in males conducive to lung cancer. *British Journal of Medical Psychology, 36,* 27–36.

Kitagawa, N., & Ichihara, S. (2002). Hearing visual motion in depth. *Nature, 416,* 172–174.

Kitayama, S., Markus, H. R., & Kurakawa, M. (2000). Culture, emotion, and well-being: Good feelings in Japan and the United States. *Cognition and Emotion, 14,* 93–124.

Klaczynski, P. A. (2004). A dual-process model of adolescent development: Implications for decision making, reasoning, and identity. In R. V. Kail (Ed.), *Advances in Child Development and Behavior (Volume 32).* Amsterdam: Elsevier.

Klein, D. A., & Walsh, B. T. (2004). Eating disorders: clinical features and pathophysiology: Special issue—Reviews on ingestive science. *Physiology & Behavior, 81,* 359–374.

Klein, D. F. (1996). Panic disorder and agoraphobia: Hypothesis hothouse. *Journal of Clinical Psychiatry, 57,* 21–27.

Klein, R. M. (1999). The Hebb legacy. *Canadian Journal of Psychology, 53,* 1–3.

Kleinknecht, R. A., Dinnel, D. L., Kleinknecht, E. E., Hiruma, N., & Harada, N. (1997). Cultural factors in social anxiety: A comparison of social phobia symptoms and Taijin Kyofusho. *Journal of Anxiety Disorders, 11,* 157–177.

Kleitman, N. (1961). The nature of dreaming. In G. E. W. Wolstenholme & M. O'Connor (Eds.), *The nature of sleep.* London: J. & A. Churchill.

Kleitman, N. (1982). Basic rest-activity cycle—22 years later. *Sleep, 5,* 311–317.

Klerman, G. L., & Weissman, M. M. (1986). The interpersonal approach to understanding depression. In T. Millon & G. L. Klerman (Eds.), *Contemporary directions in psychopathology: Toward the DMS-IV.* New York: Guilford Press.

Knierim, J. J., McNaughton, B. L., & Poe, G. R. (2000). Three-dimensional spatial selectivity of hippocampal neurons during space flight. *Nature Neuroscience, 3,* 211–212.

Knowles, J. A., Kaufmann, C. A., & Rieder, R. O. (1999). Genetics. In R. E. Hales, S. C. Yudofsky, & J. A. Talbot (Eds.), *Textbook of psychiatry.* Washington, DC: American Psychiatric Press.

Knowlton, B. J., Ramus, S., & Squire, L. R. (1991). Normal acquisition of an artificial grammar by amnesic patients. *Society for Neuroscience Abstracts, 17,* 4.

Knox, R. E., & Inkster, J. A. (1968). Postdecision dissonance at post time. *Journal of Personality and Social Psychology, 8,* 310–323.

Kobasa, S. C. (1979). Stress life events, personality, and health: An inquiry into hardiness. *Journal of Personality and Social Psychology, 42,* 168–177.

Kobasa, S. C. O., Maddi, S. R., Puccetti, M. C., & Zola, M. A. (1994). Effectiveness of hardiness, exercise and social support as resources against illness. In A. Steptoe & J. Wardle (Eds.), *Psychosocial processes and health: A reader.* New York: Cambridge University Press.

Koch, C., & Crick, F. (2001). The zombie within. *Nature, 411,* 893.

Koch, J. L. A. (1889). *Leitfaden der psychiatrie* (2nd ed.). Ravensburg, Austria: Dorn.

Köhler, W. (1927/1973). *The mentality of apes* (2nd ed.). New York: Liveright.

Koichi, O. (1987). Superstitious behavior in humans. *Journal of the Experimental Analysis of Behavior, 47,* 261–271.

Kojima, M., Hosoda, H., Date, Y., Nakazato, M., Matsuo, H., & Kangawa, K. (1999). Ghrelin is a growth-hormone-releasing acylated peptide from stomach. *Nature, 402,* 656–660.

Kolata, G. (1998, May 27). Scientists see a mysterious similarity in a pair of deadly plagues. *New York Times,* p. 1.

Kolb, B., Gibb, R., & Robinson, T. E. (2003). Brain plasticity and behavior. *Current Directions in Psychological Science, 12,* 1–5.

Kolb, B., & Stewart, J. (1995). Changes in the neonatal gonadal hormonal environment prevent behavioral sparing and alter cortical morphogenesis after early female frontal cortex lesions in male and female rats. *Behavioral Neuroscience, 109,* 285–294.

Kolb, B., & Wishaw, I. Q. (1998). Brain plasticity and behavior. *Annual Review of Psychology, 49,* 43–64.

Kopta, S. M., Lueger, R. J., Saunders, S. M., & Howard, K. I. (1999). Individual psychotherapy outcome and process research: Challenges leading to greater turmoil or a positive transition. *Annual Review of Psychology, 50,* 441–469.

Korol, M., Kramer, T. L., Grace, M. C., & Green, B. L. (2002). Dam break: Long-term follow-up of children exposed to the Buffalo Creek disaster. In A. M. La Greca, W. K. Silverman, et al. (Eds.), *Helping children cope with disasters and terrorism.* Washington, DC: American Psychological Association.

Kosslyn, S. M. (1973). Scanning visual images: Some structural implications. *Perception and Psychophysics, 14,* 90–94.

Kosslyn, S. M. (1975). Evidence for analogue representation. Paper presented at the Conference on Theoretical Issues in Natural Language Processing, Massachusetts Institute of Technology, Cambridge, MA, July 1975.

Kozlowski, L. T., & Cutting, J. E. (1977). Recognizing the sex of a walker from a dynamic point-light display. *Perception and Psychophysics, 21,* 575–580.

Kozulin, A., & Falik, L. (1995). Dynamic cognitive assessment of the child. *Current Directions in Psychological Science, 4,* 192–196.

Kramer, F. M., Jeffery, R. W., Forster, J. L., & Snell, M. K. (1989). Long-term follow-up of behavioral treatment for obesity: Patterns of weight regain among men and women. *International Journal of Obesity, 13,* 123–136.

Kramer, U., Lemmen, C. H., Behrendt, H., Link, E., Schafer, T., Gostomzyk, J., Scherer, G., & Ring, J. (2004). The effect of environmental tobacco smoke on eczema and allergic sensitization in children. *British Journal of Dermatology, 150(1),* 111–118.

Kraut, R. E., & Johnston, R. (1979). Social and emotional messages of smiling: An ethological approach. *Journal of Personality and Social Psychology, 37,* 1539–1553.

Krebs, D. L., & Denton, K. (1997). Social illusions and self-deception: The evolution of biases in person perception. In J. A. Simpson & D. T. Kenrick (Eds.), *Evolutionary social psychology.* Mahway, NJ: Lawrence Erlbaum Associates, Publishers.

Kriechman, A. M. (1987). Siblings with somatoform disorders in childhood and adolescence. *Journal of the American Academy of Child and Adolescent Psychiatry, 26,* 226–231.

Kroger, W. S., & Doucé, R. G. (1979). Hypnosis in criminal investigation. *International Journal of Clinical and Experimental Hypnosis, 27,* 358–374.

Krueger, R. F., Markon, D. E., & Bouchard, T. J., Jr. (2003). The extended genotype: The heritability of personality accounts for the heritability of recalled family environments in twins reared apart. *Journal of Personality, 71(5),* 809–833.

Krueger, T. H. (1976). *Visual imagery in problem solving and scientific creativity.* Derby, CT: Seal Press.

Krull, D. L., Loy, M. H.-M., Lin, J., Wang, C.-F., Chen, S., & Zhao, X. (1999). The fundamental fundamental attribution error: Correspondence bias in individualist and collectivist cultures. *Personality and Social Psychology Bulletin, 25,* 1208–1219.

Krull, D. S., & Erickson, D. J. (1995). Inferential hopscotch: How people draw social inferences from behavior. *Current Directions in Psychological Science, 4,* 35–38.

Kubitz, K. A., & Landers, D. M. (1993). The effects of aerobic exercise on cardiovascular responses to mental stress: An examination of underlying mechanisms. *Journal of Sport and Exercise Physiology, 15,* 326–337.

Kübler-Ross, E. (1969). *On death and dying.* New York: Macmillan.

Kübler-Ross, E. (1981). *Living with death and dying.* New York: Macmillan.

Kuhl, P. K., Williams, K. A., Lacerda, F., Stevens, K. N., & Lindblom, B. (1992). Linguistic experience alters phonetic perception in infants by 6 months of age. *Science, 255,* 606–608.

Kunda, Z. (1990). The case for motivated reasoning. *Psychological Bulletin, 108,* 480–498.

Kunda, Z. (1999). *Social cognition: Making sense of people.* Cambridge, MA: The MIT Press.

Kunda, Z., & Oleson, K. (1997). When exceptions prove the rule: How extremity of deviance determines deviants' impact on stereotypes. *Journal of Personality and Social Psychology, 72,* 965–979.

Kunda, Z., & Sinclair, L. (1999). Motivated reasoning with stereotypes: Activation, application, and inhibition. *Psychological Inquiry, 10,* 12–22.

Kupfer, D. J. (1976). REM latency: A psychobiologic marker for primary depressive disease. *Biological Psychiatry, 11,* 159–174.

LaFarge, L. (2000). Interpretation and containment. *International Journal of Psycho-Analysis, 81,* 67–84.

Lai, C. S. L., Fisher, S. E., Hurst, J. A., Vargha-Khadem, F., & Monaco, A. P. (2001). A forkhead-domain gene is mutated in a severe speech and language disorder. *Nature, 413,* 519–523.

Laing, R. D., & Esterson, A. (1964). *Sanity, madness, and the family.* Harmondworth, England: Pelican.

Lakoff, G., & Turner, M. (1989). *More than cool reason: The power of poetic metaphor.* Chicago: University of Chicago Press.

Lamberg, L. (1998). Dawn's early light to twilight's last gleaming . . . *Journal of the American Medical Association, 280,* 1556–1558.

Lamerson, C. D., & Kelloway, E. K. (1996). Towards a model of peacekeeping stress: Traumatic and contextual influences. *Canadian Psychology, 37,* 195–204.

Lane, S. M., Mather, M., Villa, D., & Morita, S. K. (2001). How events are reviewed matters: Effects of varied focus on eyewitness suggestibility. *Memory & Cognition, 29,* 940–947.

Lange, C. G. (1887). *Über Gemüthsbewegungen.* Leipzig, East Germany: T. Thomas.

Langer, E. J., & Abelson, R. P. (1974). A patient by any other name . . . : Clinician group difference in labeling bias. *Journal of Consulting and Clinical Psychology, 42,* 4–9.

Langer, E. J., Bashner, R. S., & Chanowitz, B. (1985). Decreasing prejudice by increasing discrimination. *Journal of Personality and Social Psychology, 49,* 113–120.

Langhans, W. (1996). Role of the liver in the metabolic control of eating: What we know and what we do not know. *Neuroscience and Biobehavioral Reviews, 20,* 145–153.

Langhans, W., Grossman, F., & Geary, N. (2001). Intrameal hepatic-portal infusion of glucose reduces spontaneous meal size in rats. *Physiology & Behavior, 73,* 499–507.

Langlois, J. H., & Downs, A. C. (1980). Mothers, fathers, and peers as socialization agents of sex-typed play behaviors in young children. *Child Development, 51,* 1237–1247.

LaPiere, R. T. (1934). Attitudes and actions. *Social Forces, 13,* 230–237.

Latané, B., & Darley, J. M. (1970). *The unresponsive bystander: Why doesn't he help?* New York: Appleton-Century-Crofts.

Laurence, J. R., & Perry, C. (1983). Hypnotically created memory among highly hypnotizable subjects. *Science, 222,* 523–524.

Laurence, J. R., & Perry, C. (1988). *Hypnosis, will, and memory: A psycho-legal history.* New York: Guilford Press.

Lavie, P., Pratt, H., Scharf, B., Peled, R., & Brown, J. (1984). Localized pontine lesion: Nearly total absence of REM sleep. *Neurology, 34,* 1118–1120.

Lazarus, A. A. (1971). *Behavior therapy and beyond.* New York: McGraw-Hill.

Lazarus, R. S. (2000). Toward better research on stress and coping. *American Psychologist, 55(6),* 665–673.

Lazarus, R. S., & Folkman, S. (1984). *Stress, appraisal, and coping.* New York: Springer.

Leckman, J. F., Pauls, D. L., Zhang, H., Rosario-Campos, M. C., Katsovich, L., Kidd, K. K., Pakstis, A. J., Alsobrook, J. P., et al. (2003). Obsessive-compulsive symptom dimensions in affected sibling pairs diagnosed with Gilles de la Tourette syndrome. *American Journal of Medical Genetics, 116B,* 60–68.

LeDoux, J. E. (1992). Brain mechanisms of emotion and emotional learning. *Current Opinion in Neurobiology, 2,* 191–197.

LeDoux, J. E. (1995). Emotion: Clues from the brain. *Annual Review of Psychology, 46,* 209–235.

Lee, D. W., Smith, G. T., Tramontin, A. D., Soma, K. K., Brenowitz, E. A., & Clayton, N. S. (2001). Hippocampal volume does not change seasonally in a non foodstoring songbird. *Neuroreport, 12,* 1925–1928.

Lee, T. M. C., & Chan, C. C. H. (1999). Dose-response relationship of phototherapy for seasonal affective disorder: A meta-analysis. *Acta Psychiatrica Scandinavica, 99,* 315–323.

Leech, S., & Witte, K. L. (1971). Paired-associate learning in elderly adults as related to pacing and incentive conditions. *Developmental Psychology, 5,* 180.

Leeser, J., & O'Donohue, W. (1999). What is a delusion? Epistemological dimensions. *Journal of Abnormal Psychology, 108,* 687–694.

Lefcourt, H. M. (1966). Internal versus external control of reinforcement: A review. *Psychological Bulletin, 65,* 206–220.

Lefcourt, H. M. (1992). Durability and impact of the locus of control construct. *Psychological Bulletin, 112,* 411–414.

Lefcourt, H. M., & Davidson-Katz, K. (1991). Locus of control and health. In C. R. Snyder & D. R. Forsyth (Eds.), *Handbook of social and clinical psychology: The health perspective.* Elmsford, NY: Pergamon Press, Inc.

Lefley, H. P. (1984). Delivering mental health services across cultures. In P. B. Pedersen, N. Sartorius, & A. Marsella (Eds.), *Mental health services: The cross-culture perspective.* Beverly Hills, CA: Sage.

Lefley, H. P. (1994). Mental health treatment and service delivery in cross-cultural perspective. In L. L. Adler & U. P. Gielen (Eds.), *Cross-cultural topics in psychology.* Westport, CT: Praeger.

Lefley, H. P. (2002). Helping families cope with mental illness: Future international directions. In H. P. Lefley & D. L. Johnson (Eds.), *Family interventions in mental illness: International perspectives.* Westport, CT: Praeger.

Leger, D. W. (1991). *Biological foundations of behavior.* New York: HarperCollins.

Lehman, D. R., Chiu, C.-Y., & Schaller, M. (2004). Psychology and culture. *Annual Review of Psychology, 55,* 689–714.

Lehmann, H. E., & Ban, T. A. (1997). The history of the psychopharmacology of schizophrenia. *Canadian Journal of Psychiatry, 42,* 152–162.

Leli, D. A., & Filskov, S. B. (1984). Clinical detection of intellectual deterioration associated with brain damage. *Journal of Clinical Psychology, 40,* 1435–1441.

Lemonde, S., Turecki, G., Bakish, D., Lisheng, D., Hrdina, P. D., Brown, C. D., Sequeira, A., et al. (2003). Impaired repression at a 5-hydroxytryptamine 1A receptor gene polymorphism associated with major depression and suicide. *The Journal of Neuroscience, 23(25),* 8788–8799.

Lennenberg, E. (1967). *Biological foundations of language.* New York: Wiley.

Leon, G. R. (1977). *Case histories of deviant behavior* (2nd ed.). Boston: Allyn and Bacon.

Lepper, M. R., Greene, D., & Nisbett, R. E. (1973). Undermining children's intrinsic interest with extrinsic reward: A test of the "overjustification" hypothesis. *Journal of Personality and Social Psychology, 28,* 129–137.

Lerner, M. J. (1980). *The belief in a just world.* New York: Plenum Press.

Lesage, A. D., Morissette, R., Fortier, L., Reinharz, D., & Contandriopoulos, A. (2000). 1. Downsizing psychiatric hospitals: Needs for care and services of current and discharged long-stay inpatients. *Canadian Journal of Psychiatry, 45,* 526–531.

LeShan, L. L., & Worthington, R. E. (1956). Personality as a factor in the pathogenesis of cancer: A review of literature. *British Journal of Medical Psychology, 29,* 49–56.

LeVay, S. (1991). A difference in hypothalamic structure between heterosexual and homosexual men. *Science, 253,* 1034–1037.

Levinson, D. J., Darrow, C. N., Klein, E. B., Levinson, M. H., & McKee, B. (1978). *The seasons of a man's life.* New York: Alfred A. Knopf.

Lewicki, M. S. (2002). Efficient coding of natural sounds. *Nature Neuroscience, 5,* 356–363.

Lewinsohn, P. M., Mischel, W., Chaplin, W., & Barton, R. (1980). Social competence and depression: The role of illusory self-perceptions. *Journal of Abnormal Psychology, 89,* 194–202.

Lewis, M., Alessandri, S. M., & Sullivan, M. W. (1990). Violation of expectancy, loss of control, and anger expressions in young infants. *Developmental Psychology, 26,* 745–751.

Lewis, M., Young, G., Brooks, J., & Michalson, L. (1975). The beginning of friendship. In M. Lewis & L. A. Rosenblum (Eds.), *Friendship and peer relations*. New York: John Wiley & Sons.

Ley, R. (2003). Respiratory psychophysiology and the modification of breathing behavior. *Behavior Modification, 27(5),* 603–606.

Li, J. S., Peat, J. K., Xuan, W., & Berry, G. (1999). Meta-analysis on the association between environmental tobacco smoke (ETS) exposure and the prevalence of lower respiratory tract infection in early childhood. *Pediatric Pulmonology, 27,* 5–13.

Li, N. P., Bailey, J. M., Kenrick, D. T., & Linsenmeier, J. A. (2002). The necessities and luxuries of mate preferences: Testing the trade-offs. *Journal of Personality and Social Psychology, 82,* 947–955.

Liberman, A. M. (1996). *Speech: A special code.* Cambridge, MA: MIT Press.

Libet, B. (2002). The timing of mental events: Libet's experimental findings and their implications. *Consciousness and Cognition, 11,* 291–299.

Lickey, M. E., & Gordon, B. (1983). *Drugs for mental illness.* New York: Freeman.

Lidz, T., Fleck, S., & Cornelison, A. R. (1965). *Schizophrenia and the family.* New York: International Universities Press.

Lieberman, P. (1992). On Neanderthal speech and Neanderthal extinction. *Current Anthropology, 33,* 409–410.

Lim, K. O., Adalsteinsson, E., Spielman, D., Sullivan, E. V., Rosenbloom, M. J., & Pfefferbaum, A. Proton magnetic resonance of cortical gray matter and white matter in schizophrenia. (1998). *Archives of General Psychiatry, 55,* 346–352.

Lindemann, B. (2000). A taste for umami. *Nature Neuroscience, 3,* 99–100.

Lindemann, B. (2001). Receptors and transduction in taste. *Nature, 413,* 219–225.

Lindsay, D. S. (1996). Contextualizing and clarifying criticisms of memory work in psychotherapy. In K. Pezdek & W. P. Banks (Eds.), *The recovered memory/false memory debate.* San Diego: Academic Press.

Lindsay, D. S. (1999). Recovered-memory experiences. In S. Taub (Ed.), *Recovered memories of child sexual abuse: Psychological, social, and legal perspectives on a contemporary mental health controversy.* American series in behavioral science and law. Springfield, IL: Charles C. Thomas Publishers.

Linsky, A. S., Bachman, R., & Straus, M. A. (1995). *Stress, culture, and aggression.* New Haven, CT: Yale University Press.

Linville, P. W., Fischer, G. W., & Salovey, P. (1989). Perceived distributions of the characteristics of in-group and out-group members: Empirical evidence and a computer simulation. *Journal of Personality and Social Psychology, 157,* 165–188.

Lipsitz, A., Brake, G., Vincent, E. J., & Winters, M. (1993). Another round for the brewers: Television ads and children's alcohol expectancies. *Journal of Applied Social Psychology, 23,* 439–450.

Lisanby, S. H., Maddox, J. H., Prudic, J., Devanand, D. P., & Sackeim, H. A. (2000). The effects of electroconvulsive therapy on memory of auto-biographical and public events. *Archives of General Psychiatry, 57,* 581–590.

Livesley, W. J., Jang, K. L., & Vernon, P. A. (2003). Genetic basis of personality structure. In T. Millon & M. J. Lerner (Eds.), *Handbook of psychology: Personality and social psychology, Vol. 5.* New York: John Wiley & Sons, Inc.

Locke, J. L. (1993). *The child's path to spoken language.* Cambridge, MA: Harvard University Press.

Loehlin, J. C. (1992). *Genes and environment in personality development.* London: Sage Publications.

Loehlin, J. C., McCrae, R. R., Costa, P. T., & John, O. P. (1998). Heritabilities of common and measure-specific components of the Big Five personality factors. *Journal of Research in Personality, 32,* 431–453.

Loehlin, J. C., & Nichols, R. C. (1976). *Heredity, environment, and personality.* Austin: University of Texas Press.

Loftus, E. F. (1979). *Eyewitness testimony.* Cambridge, MA: Harvard University Press.

Loftus, E. F., & Palmer, J. C. (1974). Reconstruction of automobile destruction: An example of the interaction between language and memory. *Journal of Verbal Learning and Verbal Behavior, 13,* 585–589.

LoLordo, V. M., & Droungas, A. (1989). Selective associations and adaptive specializations: Taste aversions and phobias. In S. B. Klein & R. R. Mowrer (Eds.), *Contemporary learning theories: Instrumental conditioning theory and the impact of biological constraints on learning* (pp. 145–179). Hillsdale, NJ: Lawrence Erlbaum Associates.

Lombardo, R., & Carreno, L. (1987). Relationship of type A behavior pattern in smokers to carbon monoxide exposure and smoking topography. *Health Psychology, 6,* 445–452.

Lonner, W. J., & Adamopoulos, J. (1997). Culture as antecedent to behavior. In J. W. Berry, Y. H. Poortinga, & J. Pandey (Eds.), *Handbook of cross-cultural psychology: Vol. 1. Theory and method* (pp. 43–83). Boston: Allyn and Bacon.

Loomis, W. F. (1967). Skin pigment regulation of vitamin-D biosynthesis in man. *Science, 157,* 501–506.

Lopez, S. R., & Guarnaccia, P. J. J. (2000). Cultural psychopathology: Uncovering the social world of mental illness. *Annual Review of Psychology, 51,* 571–598.

LoPiccolo, J., & Friedman, J. M. (1985). Sex therapy: An integrated model. In S. J. Lynn & J. P. Garskee (Eds.), *Contemporary psychotherapies: Models and methods.* New York: Merrill.

Lorenz, K. (1966). *On aggression.* New York: Harcourt Brace Jovanovich.

Lotto, R. B., & Purves, D. (1999). The effects of color on brightness. *Nature Neuroscience, 2,* 1010–1014.

Louth, S. M., Williamson, S., Alpert, M., Pouget, E. R., & Hare, R. D. (1998). Acoustic distinctions in the speech of male psychopaths. *Journal of Psycholinguistic Research, 27(3),* 375–384.

Luborsky, L., Chandler, M., Auerbach, A. H., Cohen, J., & Bachrach, H. M. (1971). Factors influencing the outcome of psychotherapy: A review of quantitative research. *Psychological Bulletin, 75,* 145–185.

Luck, S., Chelazzi, L., Hillyard, S., & Desimone, R. (1993). Effects of spatial attention on responses of V4 neurons in the macaque. *Society for Neuroscience Abstracts, 69,* 27.

Lumeng, L., Murphy, J. M., McBride, W. J., & Li, T. (1995). Genetic influences on alcohol preferences in animals. In H. Begleiter & B. Kissin (Eds.), *The genetics of alcoholism.* New York: Oxford University Press.

Lumia, A. R. (1972). The relationships among testosterone, conditioned aggression, and dominance in male pigeons. *Hormones and Behavior, 13,* 277–286.

Lundy, A. C. (1985). The reliability of the Thematic Apperception Test. *Journal of Personality Assessment, 49,* 141–145.

Lundy, A. C. (1988). Instructional set and thematic apperception test validity. *Journal of Personality Assessment, 52,* 309–320.

Luo, Y., & Baillargeon, R. (2005). When the ordinary seems unexpected: Evidence for incremental physical knowledge in young infants. *Cognition, 95,* 297–328.

Lupfer, M. B., Clark, L. F., & Hutcherson, H. W. (1990). Impact of context on spontaneous trait and situational attributions. *Journal of Personality and Social Psychology, 58,* 239–249.

Luria, A. R. (1973). Towards the mechanisms of naming disturbance. *Neuropsychologia, 11,* 417–421.

Luria, A. R. (1977). On quasi-aphasic speech disturbances in lesions of the deep structures of the brain. *Brain and Language, 4,* 432–459.

Lykken, D. T. (1988). The case against polygraph testing. In A. Gale (Ed.), *The polygraph test: Lies, truth and science.* London: Sage Publications.

Lykken, D. T. (1998). *A tremor in the blood: Uses and abuses of the lie detector.* New York: Plenum Press.

Lynn, R. (1978). Ethnic and racial differences in intelligence: International comparisons. In *Human variation: The biopsychology of age, race and sex.* New York: Academic Press.

Lytton, H., & Romney, D. M. (1991). Parents' sex-related differential socialization of boys and girls: A meta-analysis. *Psychological Bulletin, 109,* 267–296.

Lytton, W. W., & Brust, J. C. M. (1989). Direct dyslexia: Preserved oral reading of real words in Wernicke's aphasia. *Brain, 112,* 583–594.

Maccoby, E. E. (1980). *Social development: Psychological growth and the parent-child relationship.* New York: Harcourt Brace Jovanovich.

MacDonald, T., Zanna, M., & Fong, G. T. (1998). Alcohol and intentions to engage in risky health-related behaviors: Experimental evidence for a causal relationship. In J. G. Adair & D. Belanger (Eds.), *Advances in psychological science (Vol. 1).* Hove, UK: Psychology Press/Erlbaum (UK) Taylor and Francis.

MacDonald, T. K., MacDonald, G., Zanna, M. P., & Fong, G. T. (2000). Alcohol, sexual arousal, and intentions to use condoms in young men: Applying alcohol myopia theory to risky sexual behavior. *Health Psychology, 19(3),* 290–298.

MacDonald, T. K., Zanna, M. P., & Fong, G. T. (1995). Decision making in altered states: Effects of alcohol on attitudes toward drinking and driving. *Journal of Personality and Social Psychology, 68,* 973–985.

Machon, R. A., Mednick, S. A., & Schulsinger, F. (1983) Seasonality, birth complications and schizophrenia in a high risk sample. *British Journal of Psychiatry, 151:*122–124.

Machon, R. A., Mednick, S. A., & Schulsinger, F. (1983). The interaction of seasonality, place of birth, genetic risk and subsequent schizophrenia in a high risk sample. *British Journal of Psychiatry, 143,* 383–388.

MacMillan, H. L., Fleming, J. E., Streiner, D. L., Lin, E., Boyle, M. H., Jamieson, E., Duku, E. K., et al. (2001). Childhood abuse and lifetime psychopathology in a community sample. *American Journal of Psychiatry, 158(11),* 1878–1883.

Macrae, C. N., Milne, A. B., & Bodenhausen, G. V. (1994). Stereotypes as energy-saving devices: A peek inside the cognitive toolbox. *Journal of Personality and Social Psychology, 66,* 37–47.

Madon, S., Smith, A., Jussim, L., Russell, D. W., Eccles, J., Palumbo, P., & Walkiewicz, M. (2001). Am I as you see me or do you see me as I am? Self-fulfilling prophecies and self-verification. *Personality & Social Psychology Bulletin, 27,* 1214–1224.

Maffei, M., Halaas, J., Ravussin, E., Pratley, R. E., Lee, G. H., Zhang, Y., Fei, H., Kim, S., Lallone, R., & Ranganathan, S. (1995). Leptin levels in human and rodent: Measurement of plasma leptin and ob RNA in obese and weight-reduced subjects. *Nature Medicine, 11,* 1155–1161.

Magee, W. J., Eaton, W. W., Wittchen, H.-U., McGonagle, K. A., & Kessler, R. C. (1996). Agoraphobia, simple phobia, and social phobia in the National Cormorbidity Survey. *Archives of General Psychiatry, 53,* 159–168.

Magnus, H. (1880). Untersuchungen über den Farbensinn der Naturvölker. *Physiologische Abhandlungen, Ser. 2, no. 7.*

Maguire, E. A., Gadian, D. G., Johnsrude, I. S., Good, C. D., Ashburner, J., Frackowiak, R. S. J., & Frith, C. D. (2000). Navigation-related structural change in the hippocampi of taxi drivers. *Proceedings of the National Academy of Sciences of the United States, 97,* 4398–4403.

Maier, S. F., & Seligman, M. E. (1976). Learned helplessness: Theory and evidence. *Journal of Experimental Psychology: General, 105,* 3–46.

Main, M., & Solomon, J. (1990). Procedures for identifying infants as disorganized/disoriented during the Ainsworth Strange Situation. In M. T. Greenberg, D. Cicchetti, & M. Cummings (Eds.), *Attachment in the pre-school years: Theory, research, and intervention.* Chicago: University of Chicago Press.

Malpass, R. S., & Devine, P. G. (1981). Guided memory in eyewitness identification. *Journal of Applied Psychology, 66,* 343–350.

Manson, S. M., & Kleinman, A. (1998). DSM-IV, culture and mood disorders: A critical reflection on recent progress. *Transcultural Psychiatry, 35,* 377–386.

Manuck, S. B., Kaplan, J. R., & Clarkson, T. B. (1983). Behaviorally-induced heart rate reactivity and atherosclerosis in cynomolgous monkeys. *Psychosomatic Medicine, 45,* 95–108.

Manuck, S. B., Kaplan, J. R., & Matthews, K. A. (1986). Behavioral antecedents of coronary heart disease and atherosclerosis. *Arteriosclerosis, 6,* 1–14.

Marcia, J. E. (1980). Identity in adolescence. In J. Adelson (Ed.), *Handbook of adolescent psychology.* New York: Wiley.

Marcia, J. E. (1994). The empirical study of ego identity. In H. A. Bosma & T. L. G. Graafsma (Eds.), *Identity and development: An interdisciplinary approach (Vol. 172).* Thousand Oaks, CA: Sage Publications, Inc.

Margolin, D. I., Friedrich, F. J., & Carlson, N. R. (1985). Visual agnosia–optic aphasia: Continuum or dichotomy? Paper presented at the meeting of the International Neuropsychology Society.

Markus, H. (1977). Self-schemata and processing information about the self. *Journal of Personality and Social Psychology, 35,* 63–78.

Markus, H. R., & Kitayama, S. (1991). Culture and the self: Implications for cognition, emotion, and motivation. *Psychological Review, 98,* 224–253.

Markus, H. R., & Kitayama, S. (2003). Culture, self, and the reality of the social. *Psychological Inquiry, 14,* 277–283.

Markus, H. R., & Nurius, P. (1986). Possible selves. *American Psychologist, 41,* 954–969.

Marshall, J. C., & Newcombe, F. (1973). Patterns of paralexia: A psycholinguistic approach. *Journal of Psycholinguistic Research, 2,* 175–199.

Marshall, R. D., Spitzwer, R., & Liebowitz, M. R. (1999). Review and critique of the new DSM-IV diagnosis of acute stress disorder. *American Journal of Psychiatry, 156(11),* 1677–1685.

Marshark, M., Richman, C. L., Yuille, J. C., & Hunt, R. R. (1987). The role of imagery in memory: On shared and distinctive information. *Psychological Bulletin, 102,* 28–41.

Martens, R. (1969). Palmar sweating and the presence of an audience. *Journal of Experimental Social Psychology, 5,* 371–374.

Masling, J. (1960). The influence of situational and interpersonal variables in projective testing. *Psychological Bulletin, 57,* 65–85.

Masling, J. (1998). Interpersonal and actuarial dimensions of projective testing. In L. Handler & M. J. Hilsenroth (Eds.), *Teaching and learning personality assessment.* The LEA series in personality and clinical psychology. Mahwah, NJ: Lawrence Erlbaum Associates.

Maslow, A. H. (1964). *Religions, values, and peak-experiences.* New York: Viking Press.

Maslow, A. H. (1970). *Motivation and personality* (2nd ed.). New York: Harper & Row.

Masters, W. H., & Johnson, V. E. (1970). *Human sexual inadequacy.* Boston: Little, Brown.

Matsumoto, D. (2003). Cross-cultural research. In S. F. Davis (Ed.), *Handbook of research methods in experimental psychology.* Malden, MA: Blackwell Publishers.

Maurer, D., & Maurer, C. (1988). *The world of the newborn.* New York: Basic Books.

Mawson, A. R. (1974). Anorexia nervosa and the regulation of intake: A review. *Psychological Medicine, 4,* 289–308.

Mayberg, H. (2003). Modulating dysfunctional limbic-cortical circuits in depression: Towards development of brain-based algorithms for diagnosis and optimized treatment. *British Medical Bulletin, 65,* 193–207.

Mayer, J. (1955). Regulation of energy intake and the body weight: The glucostatic theory and the lipostatic hypothesis. *Annals of the New York Academy of Science, 63,* 15–43.

Mayer, J. D., & Salovey, P. (1993). The intelligence of emotional intelligence. *Intelligence, 17,* 433–442.

Mayerovitch, J. I., du Fort, G. G., Kakuma, R., Bland, R. C., Newman, S. C., & Pinard, G. (2003). Treatment seeking for obsessive-compulsive disorder: Role of obsessive-compulsive disorder symptoms and comorbid psychiatric diagnoses. *Comprehensive Psychiatry, 44(2),* 162–168.

Mayes, L. C., Cicchetti, D., Acharyya, S., & Zhang, H. (2003). Developmental trajectories of cocaine-and-other-drug-exposed and non-cocaine-exposed children. *Journal of Developmental and Behavioral Pediatrics, 24,* 323–335.

Mayr, E. (1974). Behavior programs and evolutionary strategies. *American Scientist, 34,* 650–659.

Mayr, E. (2000). Darwin's influence on modern thought. *Scientific American, 283(1),* 79–83.

Mayr, E. (2001). *What evolution is.* New York: Basic Books.

McAlister, A., Perry, C., Killen, L. A., Slinkard, L. A., & Maccoby, N. (1980). Pilot study of smoking, alcohol, and drug abuse prevention. *American Journal of Public Health, 70,* 719–721.

McArthur, L. (1972). The how and what of why: Some determinants and consequences of causal attribution. *Journal of Personality and Social Psychology, 22,* 171–193.

McCann, I. L., & Holmes, D. S. (1984). Influence of aerobic exercise on depression. *Journal of Personality and Social Psychology, 46,* 1142–1147.

McCarthy, R. A., & Warrington, E. K. (1990). *Cognitive neuropsychology: A clinical introduction.* San Diego: Academic Press.

McClanahan, T. M., & Antonuccio, D. O. (2002). Cognitive-behavioral treatment of panic attacks. *Clinical Case Studies, 1(3),* 211–223.

McClearn, G. E. (1963). The inheritance of behavior. In L. J. Postman (Ed.), *Psychology in the making* (pp. 144–252). New York: Knopf.

McClearn, G. E., Johansson, B., Berg, S., Pedersen, N. L., Ahern, F., Petrill, S. A., & Plomin, R. (1997). Substantial genetic influence on cognitive abilities in twins 80 or more years old. *Science, 276,* 1560–1563.

McClelland, J. L., & Rumelhart, D. E. (1981). An interactive activation model of context effects in letter perception: Part 1. An account of basic findings. *Psychological Review, 88,* 375–407.

McColl, S. L., & Veitch, J. A. (2001). Full-spectrum fluorescent lighting: A review of its effects on physiology and health. *Psychological Medicine, 31(6),* 949–964.

McCormick, P. A., Klein, R. M., & Johnston, S. (1998). Splitting versus sharing focal attention: Comment on Castiello and Umiltà (1992). *Journal of Experimental Psychology: Human Perception and Performance, 24,* 350–357.

McCrae, R. R., & Costa, P. T. (1997). Personality trait structure as a human universal. *American Psychologist, 52,* 509–516.

McCrae, R. R., & Costa, P. T., Jr. (1999). A five-factor theory of personality. In L. A. Pervin and O. P. John (Eds.), *Handbook of personality: Theory and research* (2nd ed.). New York: The Guilford Press.

McCrae, R. R., & Costa, P. T., Jr. (2004). A contemplated revision of the NEO Five-Factor Inventory. *Personality & Individual Differences, 36(3),* 587–596.

McCrae, R. R., Costa, P. T., & Busch, C. M. (1986). Evaluating comprehensiveness in personality systems: The California Q-Set and the five-factor model. *Journal of Personality, 54,* 430–446.

McCrae, R. R., Costa, P. T., Jr., Del Pilar, G. H., Rolland, J. P., & Parker, W. D. (1998). Cross-cultural assessment of the five-factor model: The revised NEO personality inventory. *Journal of Cross-Cultural Psychology, 29,* 171–188.

McCrae, R. R., Costa, P. T., Jr., Ostendorf, F., Angleitner, A., Hrebickova, M., Avia, M. D., Sanz, J., Sanchez-Bernardos, M. L., Kusdil, M. E., Woodfield, R., Saunders, P. R., & Smith, P. B. (2000). Nature over nurture: Temperament, personality, and life span development. *Journal of Personality and Social Psychology, 78,* 173–186.

McCullough, C. (1965). Adaptation of edge-detections in the human visual system. *Science, 149,* 1115–1116.

McFarland, C., & Miller, D. T. (1990). Judgments of self-other similarity: Just like others only more so. *Personality and Social Psychology Bulletin, 16,* 475–484.

McGinty, D. J., & Sterman, M. B. (1968). Sleep suppression after basal forebrain lesions in the cat. *Science, 160,* 1253–1255.

McGrath, E. P., & Repetti, R. L. (2002). A longitudinal study of children's depressive symptoms, self-perceptions, and cognitive distortions about the self. *Journal of Abnormal Psychology, 111(1),* 77–87.

McGrath, Y. E., & Yahia, M. (1993). Preliminary data on seasonally related alcohol dependence. *Journal of Clinical Psychiatry, 54(7),* 260–262.

McGregor, I., Newby-Clark, I. R., & Zanna, M. P. (1999). "Remembering" dissonance: Simultaneous accessibility of inconsistent cognitive elements moderates epistemic discomfort. In E. Harmon-Jones & J. Mills (Eds.), *Cognitive dissonance: Progress on a pivotal theory in social psychology.* Washington, DC: American Psychological Association.

McGue, M., Pickens, R. W., & Svikis, D. S. (1992). Sex and age effects on the inheritance of alcohol problems: A twin study. *Journal of Abnormal Psychology, 101,* 3–17.

McIlvane, W. J., & Dube, W. V (2003). Stimulus control topography coherence theory: Foundations and extensions. *Behavior Analyst, 26,* 195–213.

McKay, D. C. (1973). Aspects of the theory of comprehension, memory and attention. *Quarterly Journal of Experimental Psychology, 25,* 22–40.

McKim, W. A. (1991). *Drugs and behavior: An introduction to behavior pharmacology* (2nd ed.). Englewood Cliffs, NJ: Prentice-Hall.

McNamara, D. S., & Scott, J. L. (2001). Working memory capacity and strategy use. *Memory & Cognition, 29,* 10–17.

McNeal, J. (1990). Children as customers. *American Demographics, 12(9),* 36–39.

McNeill, D. (1970). *The acquisition of language: The study of developmental psycholinguistics.* New York: Harper & Row.

Mead, C. A. (1989). *Analog VLSI and neural systems.* New York: Addison Wesley.

Meadows, S. (1996). *Parenting behaviour and children's cognitive development.* East Sussex, UK: Psychology Press.

Mednick, S. A., Gabrielli, W. F., & Hutchings, B. (1983). Genetic influences in criminal behavior: Some evidence from an adoption cohort. In K. T. VanDusen & S. A. Mednick (Eds.), *Prospective studies of crime and delinquency.* Hingham, MA: Martinus Nyhoff.

Mednick, S. A., Machon, R. A., & Huttunen, M. O. (1990). An update on the Helsinki influenza project. *Archives of General Psychiatry, 47,* 292.

Meehl, P. E. (1954). *Clinical versus statistical prediction.* Minneapolis: University of Minnesota Press.

Meehl, P. E. (1986). Causes and effects of my disturbing little book. *Journal of Personality Assessment, 50,* 370–375.

Meichenbaum, D. (1985). *Stress inoculation training.* New York: Pergamon Press.

Meichenbaum, D. (1993). Changing conceptions of cognitive behavior modification: Retrospect and prospect. *Journal of Consulting and Clinical Psychology, 61,* 202–204.

Meichenbaum, D. (1995). Disasters, stress, and cognition. In S. E. Hobfoll & M. W. deVries (Eds.), *Extreme stress and communities: Impact and intervention.* Dordrecht, Netherlands: Kluwer Academic Publishers.

Meichenbaum, D. H. (1977). *Cognitive-behavior modification: An integrative approach.* New York: Plenum Press.

Meindl, J. R., & Lerner, M. J. (1985). Exacerbation of extreme responses to an out-group. *Journal of Personality and Social Psychology, 47,* 71–84.

Melzack, R. (1992). Phantom limbs. *Scientific American, 266(4),* 120–126.

Menn, L., & Stoel-Gammon, C. (1993). Phonological development: Learning sounds and sound patterns. In J. B. Gleason (Ed.), *The development of language.* New York: Macmillan.

Mentkowski, T. (1983). Why I am what I am. *The Florida School Herald, 82,* 1–2, 5, 12. Cited by Schein, J. D. (1989). *At home among strangers.* Washington, DC: Gallaudet University Press.

Merckelbach, H., & Muris, P. (1997). The etiology of childhood *spider phobia. Behaviour Research & Therapy, 35,* 1031–1034.

Merikle, P. M. (1988). Subliminal auditory messages: An evaluation. *Psychology and Marketing, 5,* 355–372.

Merton, R. (1948). The self-fulfilling prophecy. *Antioch Review, 8,* 193–210.

Mervis, C. B., & Rosch, E. (1981). Categorization of natural objects. *Annual Review of Psychology, 32,* 89–116.

Messer, S. B. (2001). What makes brief psychodynamic therapy time efficient. *Clinical Psychology: Science and Practice, 8(1),* 5–22.

Metalsky, G. I., Joiner, T. E., Jr., Hardin, T. S., & Abramson, L. Y. (1993). Depressive reactions to failure in a naturalistic setting: A test of the hopelessness and self-esteem theories of depression. *Journal of Abnormal Psychology, 102,* 101–109.

Metter, E. J. (1991). Brain-behavior relationships in aphasia studied by positron emission tomography. *Annals of the New York Academy of Sciences, 620,* 153–164.

Metter, E. J., Hanson, W. R., Jackson, C. A., Kempler, D., Van Lancker, D., Mazziotta, J. C., & Phelps, M. E. (1990). Tempero-parietal cortex in aphasia: Evidence from positron emission tomography. *Archives of Neurology, 47,* 1235–1238.

Meyer, R. G., & Osborne, Y. V. (1982). *Case studies in abnormal behavior.* Boston: Allyn & Bacon.

Meyer-Bahlburg, H. R. L., Ehrhardt, A. A., Rosen, L. R., Gruen, R. S., Veridiano, N. P., Vann, F. H., & Neuwalder, H. F. (1995). Prenatal estrogens and the development of homosexual orientation. *Developmental Psychology, 31,* 12–21.

Meyers, L., Dixen, J., Morrissette, D., Carmichael, M., & Davidson, J. (1990). Effects of estrogen, androgen, and progestin on sexual psychophysiology and behavior in post-menopausal women. *Journal of Clinical Endocrinology and Metabolism, 70,* 1124–1131.

Miles, H. L. (1983). Apes and language: The search for communicative competence. In J. de Luce & H. T. Wilder (Eds.), *Language in primates: Perspectives and implications.* New York: Springer-Verlag.

Milgram, S. (1963). Behavioral study of obedience. *Journal of Abnormal and Social Psychology, 67,* 371–378.

Milgram, S. (1974). *Obedience to authority.* New York: Harper & Row.

Miller, A. M., & Harwood, R. L. (2002). The cultural organization of parenting: Change and stability of behavior patterns during feeding and social play across the first year of life. *Parenting: Science and Practice, 2,* 241–272.

Miller, D. T., & Ross, M. (1975). Self-serving biases in the attribution of causality: Fact or fiction? *Psychological Bulletin, 82,* 213–225.

Miller, G. A. (1956). The magical number seven plus or minus two: Some limits on our capacity for processing information. *Psychological Review, 63,* 81–97.

Miller, G. A. (1987). *Spontaneous apprentices: Children and language.* New York: Seabury Press.

Miller, G. A., Galanter, E., & Pribram, K. (1960). *Plans and the structure of behavior.* New York: Holt, Rinehart, and Winston.

Miller, J. L., & Eimas, P. D. (1995). Speech perception: From signal to word. *Annual Review of Psychology, 46,* 467–492.

Miller, M. A., & Rahe, R. H. (1997). Life changes scaling for the 1990s. *Journal of Psychosomatic Research, 43,* 279–292.

Miller, N. E. (1977). Forward in J. Olds. *Drives and reinforcements: Behavioral studies of hypothalamic functions.* New York: Raven Press.

Miller, N. E. (1983). Behavioral medicine: Symbiosis between laboratory and clinic. *Annual Review of Psychology, 34,* 1–31.

Miller, R. J., Hennessy, R. T., & Leibowitz, H. W. (1973). The effect of hypnotic ablation of the background on the magnitude of the Ponzo perspective illusion. *International Journal of Clinical and Experimental Hypnosis, 21,* 180–191.

Miller, W. R., Rosellini, R. A., & Seligman, M. E. P. (1977). Learned helplessness and depression. In J. D. Maser & M. E. P. Seligman (Eds.), *Psychopathology: Experimental models.* San Francisco: W. H. Freeman.

Miller-Jones, D. (1989). Culture and testing. *American Psychologist, 44,* 360–366.

Milner, A. D., & Goodale, M. A. (1996). *The visual brain in action.* Oxford, UK: Oxford University Press.

Milner, B. (1970). Memory and the temporal regions of the brain. In K. H. Pribram & D. E. Broadbent (Eds.), *Biology of memory.* New York: Academic Press.

Mineka, S., & Zinbarg, R. (2006). A contemporary learning theory perspective on the etiology of anxiety disorders: It's not what you thought it was. *American Psychologist, 61,* 10–26.

Minuchin, S. (1974). *Families and family therapy.* Cambridge, MA: Harvard University Press.

Mischel, W. (1968). *Personality and assessment.* New York: John Wiley & Sons.

Mischel, W. (1976). *Introduction to personality* (2nd ed.). New York: Holt, Rinehart and Winston.

Mischel, W. (1977). The interaction of person and situation. In D. Magnusson & N. S. Endler (Eds.), *Personality at the crossroads: Current issues in interactional psychology.* Hillsdale, NJ: Lawrence Erlbaum Associates.

Mischel, W. (1979). On the interface of cognition and personality: Beyond the person-situation debate. *American Psychologist, 34,* 740–754.

Mischel, W. (1990). Personality dispositions revisited and revised: A view after three decades. In L. Pervin (Ed.), *Handbook of personality: Theory and research.* New York: Guilford Press.

Mischel, W. (2003). Challenging the traditional personality psychology paradigm. In R. J. Sternberg (Ed.), *Psychologists defying the crowd: Stories of those who battled the establishment and won.* Washington, DC: American Psychological Association.

Mischel, W., Cantor, N., & Feldman, S. (1996). Principles of self-regulation: The nature of willpower and self-control. In E. T. Higgins & A. W. Kruglanski (Eds.), *Social psychology: Handbook of basic principles.* New York: Guilford Press.

Mischel, W., & Shoda, Y. (1995). A cognitive-affective system theory of personality: Reconceptualizing situations, dispositions, dynamics, and invariance in personality. *Psychological Review, 102,* 246–268.

Mischel, W., & Shoda, Y. (1998). Reconciling processing dynamics and personality dispositions. *Annual Review of Psychology, 49,* 229–258.

Misovich, S. J., Fisher, J. D., & Fisher, W. A. (1996). The perceived AIDS-preventative utility of knowing one's partner well: A public health dictum and individuals' risky sexual behavior. *The Canadian Journal of Human Sexuality, 5,* 83–90.

Mistry, J., & Rogoff, B. (1994). Remembering in a cultural context. In W. J. Lonner & R. Malpass (Eds.), *Psychology and culture.* Boston: Allyn & Bacon.

Mitchell, J. T. (1999). Essential factors for effective psychological response to disasters and other crises. *International Journal of Emergency Mental Health, 1,* 51–58.

Mitelman, S. A., Shihabuddin, L., Brickman, A. M., Hazlett, A. E., & Buchsbaum, M. S. (2003). MRI assessment of gray and white matter distribution in Brodmann's areas of the cortex in patients with schizophrenia with good and poor outcomes. *American Journal of Psychiatry, 160(12),* 2154–2168.

Mithen, S. (1996). *The prehistory of the mind: The cognitive origins of art and science.* London: Thames and Hudson.

Miyamoto, Y., & Kitayama, S. (2002). Cultural variation in correspondence bias: The critical role of attitude diagnosticity of socially constrained behavior. *Journal of Personality & Social Psychology, 83,* 1239–1248.

Moessinger, P. (2000). Piaget: From biology to sociology. *New ideas in psychology, 18,* 171–176.

Mogg, K., & Bradley, B. P. (2003). Selective processing of nonverbal information in anxiety: Attentional biases for threat. In P. Philippot (Ed.), *Nonverbal behavior in clinical settings.* Series in affective science. London, UK: Oxford University Press.

Mogg, K., Bradley, B. P., Williams, R., & Matthews, A. (1993). Subliminal processing of emotional information in anxiety and depression. *Journal of Abnormal Psychology, 102,* 304–311.

Mogg, K., Philippot, P., & Bradley, B. P. (2004). Selective attention to angry faces in clinical social phobia. *Journal of Abnormal Psychology, 113(1),* 160–165.

Mollon, J. D. (1989). "Tho' she kneel'd in that place where they grew . . .": The uses and origins of primate colour vision. *Journal of Experimental Biology, 146,* 21–38.

Monahan, J. L., Murphy, S. T., & Zajonc, R. B. (2000). Subliminal mere exposure: Specific, general, and diffuse effects. *Psychological Science, 11,* 462–466.

Money, J., Schwartz, M., & Lewis, V. G. (1984). Adult erotosexual status and fetal hormonal masculinization and demasculinization: 46,XX congenital virilizing adrenal hyperplasia and 46,XY androgen-insensitivity syndrome compared. *Psychoneuroendocrinology, 9,* 405–414.

Monroe, S. M., & Hadjiyannakis, K. (2002). The social environment and depression: Focusing on severe life stress. In I. H. Gotlib & C. L. Hammen (Eds.), *Handbook of depression.* New York: Guilford Press.

Montemayor, R. (1974). Children's performance in a game and their attraction to it as a function of sex-typed labels. *Child Development, 45,* 152–156.

Moody, K. (1980). *Growing up on television: The TV effect.* New York: Time Books.

Moray, N. (1959). Attention in dichotic listening: Affective cues and the influence of instructions. *Quarterly Journal of Experimental Psychology, 11,* 56–60.

Moreau, J. L., Scherschlicht, R., Jenck, F., & Martin, J. R. (1995). Chronic mild stress-induced anhedonia model of depression: Sleep abnormalities and curative effects of electroshock treatment. *Behavioural Pharmacology, 6(7),* 682–687.

Morris, B. J., & Sloutsky, V. (2002). Children's solutions of logical versus empirical problems: What's missing and what develops? *Cognitive Development, 16,* 907–928.

Morris, R. G. M., Garrud, P., Rawlins, J. N. P., & O'Keefe, J. (1982). Place navigation impaired in rats with hippocampal lesions. *Nature, 297,* 681–683.

Morris, T. A. (1980). "Type C" for cancer? Low trait anxiety in the pathogenesis of breast cancer. *Cancer Detection and Prevention, 3,* 102.

Morton, J. (1979). Word recognition. In *Psycholinguistics 2: Structures and processes.* Cambridge, MA: MIT Press.

Moscovitch, M. (1995). Recovered consciousness: A hypothesis concerning modularity and episodic memory. *Journal of Clinical and Experimental Neuropsychology, 17,* 276–290.

Moynihan, J. A. (2003). Mechanisms of stress-induced modulation of immunity. *Brain, Behavior, & Immunity, 17,* S11–S16.

Mullen, R. (2003). Delusions: The continuum versus category debate. *Australian & New Zealand Journal of Psychiatry, 37(5),* 505–511.

Muller, U., & Carpendale, J. I. M. (2000). The role of social interaction in Piaget's theory: Language for social cooperation and social cooperation for language. *New Ideas in Psychology, 18,* 139–156.

Murphy, J. (1976). Psychiatric labeling in cross-cultural perspective: Similar kinds of disturbed behavior appear to be labeled abnormal in diverse cultures. *Science, 191,* 1019–1028.

Murphy, S. T., Monahan, J. L., & Zajonc, R. B. (1995). Additivity of nonconscious affect: Affective priming with optimal and suboptimal exposure. *Journal of Personality and Social Psychology, 64,* 589–602.

Murray, C. (2005 September). The inequality taboo. *Commentary, 120(2),* 13–22.

Murray, D. M., Pirie, P., Leupker, R. V., & Pallonen, U. (1989). Five- and six-year follow-up results from four seventh-grade smoking prevention strategies. *Journal of Behavioral Medicine, 12,* 207–218.

Musso, M., Moro, A., Glauche, V., Rijntjes, M., Reichenbach, J., Büchel, C., & Weiller, C. (2003). Broca's area and the language instinct. *Nature Neuroscience, 6,* 774–781.

Myers, D. G., & Bishop, G. D. (1970). Discussion effects on racial attitudes. *Science, 169,* 778–789.

Myerson, J., Rank, M. R., Raines, F. Q., & Schnitzler, M. A. (1998). Race and general cognitive ability: The myth of diminishing returns to education. *Psychological Sciences, 9,* 139–142.

Naeser, M. A., Palumbo, C. L., Helm-Estabrooks, N., Stiassny-Eder, D., & Albert, M. L. (1989). Severe nonfluency in aphasia: Role of the medial subcallosal fasciculus and other white matter pathways in recovery of spontaneous speech. *Brain, 112,* 1–38.

Nafe, J. P., & Wagoner, K. S. (1941). The nature of pressure adaptation. *Journal of General Psychology, 25,* 323–351.

Nairne, J. S. (2002). Remembering over the short-term: The case against the standard model. *Annual Review of Psychology, 53,* 53–81.

Nakazawa, K., Sun, L. D., Rondi-Reig, L., Wilson, M. A., & Tanegawa, S. (2003). Hippocampal CA3 NMDA receptors are crucial for memory acquisition of one-time experience. *Neuron, 24,* 147–148.

Nanson, J. L., & Hiscock, M. (1990). Attention deficits in children exposed to alcohol prenatally. *Alcoholism, Clinical & Experimental Research, 14,* 656–661.

Nardi, A. E., Lopes, F. L., Valenca, A. M., et al. (2004). Psychopathological description of hyperventilation-induced panic attacks: A comparison with spontaneous panic attacks. *Psychopathology, 37(1),* 29–35.

Nardi, A. E., Valenca, A. M., Nascimento, I., Zin, W. A., & Versani, M. (2002). Carbon dioxide test as an additional clinical measure of treatment response in panic disorder. *Arquivos de Neuro-Psiquiatria, 60(2),* 358–361.

Nasar, S. (1998). *A beautiful mind.* New York: Simon and Schuster.

National Center for Health Statistics. (2004). Health, United States, 2004, with chartbook on trends in the health of Americans. Hyattsville, Maryland.

National Heart, Lung, and Blood Institute. (2004). *Morbidity and mortality: 2004 chart book on cardiovascular, lung, and blood diseases.* Washington, DC: National Institutes of Health.

National Institute of Child Health and Human Development. (1997). The effects of infant child care on infant–mother attachment security: Results of the NICHD study of early child care. *Child Development, 68,* 860–879.

Neisser, U. (1964). Visual search. *Scientific American, 210,* 94–102.

Neisser, U. (1969). Selective reading: A method for the study of visual attention. Paper presented at the 19th International Congress of Psychology, London.

Neisser, U., & Becklen, R. (1975). Selective looking: Attending to visually significant events. *Cognitive Psychology, 7,* 480–494.

Neisser, U., Boodoo, G., Bouchard, Jr., T. J., Boykin, A. W., Brody, N., Ceci, S. J., Halpern, D. R., Loehlin, J. C., Perloff, R., Sternberg, R. J., & Urbina, S. (1996). Intelligence: Knowns and unknowns. *American Psychologist, 51,* 77–101.

Neisworth, J. T., & Madle, R. A. (1982). Retardation. In A. S. Bellack, M. Hersen, & A. E. Kazdin, (Eds.), *International handbook of behavior modification and therapy.* New York: Plenum Press.

Neitz, J., He, J. C., & Shevell, S. K. (1999). Trichromatic color vision with only two spectrally distinct photopigments. *Nature Neuroscience, 2,* 884–888.

Nelson, G., Chandrashekar, J., Hoon, M. A., Feng, L., Zhao, G., Ryba, N. J. P., & Zuker, C. S. (2002). An amino-acid taste receptor. *Nature, 416,* 199–202.

Nesdadt, G., Samuels, J., Riddle, M., Bienvenu, J., Liang, K., LaBuda, M., Walkup, J., Grados, M., & Hoen-Saric, R. (2000). A family study of obsessive-compulsive disorder. *Archives of General Psychiatry, 57,* 358–363.

Nestler, E. J., Barrot, M., DiLeone, R. J., Eisch, A. I., Gold, S. J., & Monteggia, L. M. (2002). Neurobiology of depression. *Neuron, 34,* 13–25.

Neuhaus, I. M., & Rosenthal, N. E. (1997). Light therapy as a treatment modality for affective disorders. In A. Honig & H. M. van Praag (Eds.), *Depression: Neurobiological, psychopathological and therapeutic advances.* Wiley series on clinical and neurobiological advances in psychiatry. New York: John Wiley & Sons, Inc.

Neumarker, K. J. (1997). Mortality and sudden death in anorexia nervosa. *International Journal of Eating Disorders, 21,* 205–212.

Nevin, J. A., & Grace, R. C. (2000). Behavioral momentum and the Law of Effect. *Behavioral and Brain Sciences, 23,* 73–130.

Nevin, J. A., & Grace, R. C. (2005). Resistance to extinction in the steady state and in transition. *Journal of Experimental Psychology: Animal Behavior Processes, 31,* 199–212.

Newcomer, R. R., & Perna, F. M. (2003). Features of posttraumatic distress among adolescent athletes. *Journal of Athletic Training, 38(2),* 163–166.

Newell, A., & Simon, H. A. (1972). *Human problem solving.* Englewood Cliffs, NJ: Prentice-Hall.

Newport, E. L. (1975). Motherese: The speech of mothers to young children. San Diego: University of California, Center for Human Information Processing.

Newport, E. L., Gleitman, H. R., & Gleitman, L. (1977). Mother, I'd rather do it myself: Some effects and noneffects of maternal speech style. In C. E. Snow & C. A. Ferguson (Eds.), *Talking to children: Language input and acquisition.* Cambridge, UK: Cambridge University Press.

NICHD Early Child Care Research Network. (2003). Does quality of child care affect child outcomes at age 4-1/2? *Developmental Psychology, 39,* 451–469.

Nichols, T. R., Graber, J. A., Brooks-Gunn, J., & Botvin, J. I. (2004). Maternal influences on smoking initiation among urban adolescent girls. *Journal of Research on Adolescence, 14(1),* 73–97.

Nicoladis, E. (2003). What compound nouns mean to preschool children. *Brain and Language, 84,* 38–49.

Nicolas, A., Petit, D., Rompre, S., & Montplaisir, J. (2001). Sleep spindles characteristics in healthy subjects of different age groups. *Clinical Neurophysiology, 112,* 521–527.

Nielsen, A. C. (1990). *Annual Nielsen report on television: 1990.* New York: Nielsen Media Research.

Nielsen, L. L., & Sarason, I. G. (1981). Emotion, personality, and selective attention. *Journal of Personality and Social Psychology, 41,* 945–960.

Nisbett, R. E., & Schachter, S. (1966). Cognitive manipulation of pain. *Journal of Experimental Social Psychology, 2,* 227–236.

Nisbett, R. E., & Wilson, T. D. (1977). Telling more than we can know: Verbal reports on mental processes. *Psychological Review, 84,* 231–259.

Norman, P., Bennett, P., Smith, C., & Murphy, S. (1998). Health locus of control and health behaviour. *Journal of Health Psychology, 3,* 171–180.

Norman, W. T. (1963). Toward an adequate taxonomy of personality attributes: Replicated factor structure in peer nomination personality ratings. *Journal of Abnormal and Social Psychology, 66,* 574–583.

Norwich, K. H., & Wong, W. (1997). Unification of psychophysical phenomena: The complete form of Fechner's Law. *Perception and Psychophysics, 59,* 929–940.

Novin, D., VanderWeele, D.A., & Rezek, M. (1973) Infusion of 2-deoxy-D-glucose into the hepatic-portal system causes eating: evidence for peripheral glucoreceptors. *Science, 181,* 858–860.

Obergriesser, T., Ende, G., Braus, D. F., & Henn, F. A. (2003). Long-term follow-up of magnetic resonance-detectable choline signal changes in the hippocampus of patients treated with electroconvulsive therapy. *Journal of Clinical Psychiatry, 64(7),* 775–780.

O'Brien, M., Peyton, V., Mistry, R., Hruda, L., Jacobs, A., Caldera, Y., Huston, A., & Roy, C. (2000). Gender-role cognition in three-year-old boys and girls. *Sex Roles, 42,* 1007–1025.

O'Donnell, C., & Pratt, J. (1996). Inhibition of return along the path of attention. *Canadian Journal of Experimental Psychology, 50,* 386–392.

Ogden, C. L., Carroll, M. D., & Flegal, K. M. (2003). Epidemiologic trends in overweight and obesity. *Endocrinology and Metabolism Clinic of North America, 32,* 741–760.

Öhman, A., Fredrikson, M., Hugdahl, K., & Rimmo, P-A. (1976). The premise of equipotentiality in human classical *conditioning*: Conditioned electrodermal responses to potentially phobic stimuli. *Journal of Experimental Psychology: General, 105,* 313–337.

Öhman, A., & Soares, J. J. (1994). "Unconscious anxiety": Phobic responses to masked stimuli. *Journal of Abnormal Psychology, 103,* 231–240.

Öhman, A., & Soares, J. J. (1998). Emotional conditioning to masked stimuli: Expectancies for aversive outcomes following nonrecognized fear-relevant stimuli. *Journal of Experimental Psychology: General, 127,* 69–82.

Okagaki, L., & Sternberg, R. J. (1993). Putting the distance into students' hands: Practical intelligence for school. In R. R. Cocking & K. A. Renninger (Eds.), *The development and meaning of psychological distance.* Hillsdale, NJ: Erlbaum Associates.

Okiishi, J., Lambert, M. J., Nielsen, S. L., & Ogles, B. M. (2003). Waiting for supershrink: An empirical analysis of therapist effects. *Clinical Psychology & Psychotherapy, 10(6),* 361–373.

Oldenburg, D. (1990). Hidden messages. *The Washington Post*, April 3.

Olds, J. (1956). Pleasure centers of the brain. *Scientific American*, 107–108.

Olds, J., & Milner, B. (1954). Positive reinforcement produced by electrical stimulation of septal areas and other regions of rat brains. *Journal of Comparative and Physiological Psychology, 47*, 419–427.

Oliver, D. L., Beckius, G. E., Bishop, D. C., Loftus, W. C., & Batra, R. (2003). Topography of inter-aural temporal disparity coding in projections of medial superior olive to inferior colliculus. *Journal of Neuroscience, 23*, 7438–7449.

Olney, J. W., Wozniak, D. F., Farber, N. B., Jevtovic-Todorovic, V., Bittigau, P., & Ikonomidou, C. (2002). The enigma of fetal alcohol neurotoxicity. *Annals of Medicine, 34*, 109–119.

Olson, J. M., Roese, N. J., & Zanna, M. P. (1996). Expectancies. In E. T. Higgins & A. W. Kruglanski (Eds.), *Social psychology: Handbook of basic principles*. New York: Guilford Press.

O'Neill, D. K. (1996). Two-year-old children's sensitivity to a parent's knowledge state when making requests. *Child Development, 67*, 659–677.

O'Regan, J. K., Rensink, R. A., & Clark, J. J. (1999). Change-blindness as a result of "mudsplashes." *Nature, 398*, 34.

Orne, M. T. (1959). The nature of hypnosis: Artifact and essence. *Journal of Abnormal and Social Psychology, 58*, 277–299.

Orne, M. T., Whitehouse, W. G., Dinges, D. F., & Orne, E. C. (1988). Reconstructing memory through hypnosis. In H. M. Pettinati (Ed.), *Hypnosis and memory*. New York: Guilford Press.

Orvis, B. R., Kelley, H. H., & Butler, D. (1976). Attributional conflict in young couples. In J. H. Harvey, W. J. Ickes, & R. F. Kidd (Eds.), *New directions in attribution research, Vol. 1*. Hillsdale, NJ: Erlbaum.

Osborne, K. A., Robichon, A., Burgess, E., Butland, S., Shaw, R. A., Coulthard, A., Pereira, H. S., Greenspan, R. H., & Sokolowski, M. B. (1997). Natural behavior polymorphism due to a cGMP-Dependent protein kinase of Drosophia. *Science, 277*, 834–836.

Ostrom, T. M., & Sedikides, C. (1992). Out-group homogeneity effects in natural and minimal groups. *Psychological Bulletin, 112*, 536–552.

Overmier, J. B. (1998). Learned helplessness: State or stasis of the art? In M. Sabourin, F. Craik, & M. Robert (Eds.), *Advances in psychological science: Biological and cognitive aspects* (Vol. 2, pp. 301–315). Hove, England: Psychology Press/Erlbaum.

Overmier, J. B., & Seligman, M. E. P. (1967). Effects of inescapable shock upon subsequent escape and avoidance responding. *Journal of Comparative and Physiological Psychology, 63*, 28–33.

Owens, R. E. (1992). *Language development: An introduction*. New York: Merrill/Macmillan.

Paffenbarger, R. S., Hyde, J. T., Wing, A. L., & Hsieh, C. C. (1986). Physical activity, all-cause mortality, and longevity of college alumni. *New England Journal of Medicine, 314*, 605–612.

Paikoff, R. L., & Brooks-Gunn, J. (1991). Do parent-child relationships change during puberty? *Psychological Bulletin, 110*, 47–66.

Palmer, D. C. (2004). Data in Search of a Principle: A Review of Relational Frame Theory: A Post-Skinnerian Account of Human Language and Cognition. *Journal of the Experimental Analysis of Behavior, 81*, 189–204.

Palmer, D. C., & Donahoe, J. W. (1992). Essentialism and selectionism in cognitive science and behavior analysis. *American Psychologist, 47*, 1344–1358.

Palmer, S. E. (1975). The effects of contextual scenes on the identification of objects. *Memory and Cognition, 3*, 519–526.

Park, B. (1986). A method for studying the development of impressions in real people. *Journal of Personality and Social Psychology, 51*, 907–917.

Park, B., & Rothbart, M. (1982). Perception of out-group homogeneity and levels of social categorization: Memory for the subordinate attributes of in-group and out-group members. *Journal of Personality and Social Psychology, 42*, 1051–1068.

Parke, R. D. (2000). Father involvement: A developmental psychological perspective. *Marriage and Family Review, 29*, 43–58.

Parke, R. D., & Tinsley, B. R. (1981). The father's role in infancy: Determinants of involvement in caregiving and play. In M. E. Lamb (Ed.), *The role of the father in child development*. New York: John Wiley & Sons.

Parkin, A. J., Blunden, J., Rees, J. E., & Hunkin, N. M. (1991). Wernicke-Korsakoff syndrome of nonalcoholic origin. *Brain and Cognition, 15*, 69–82.

Parsian, A., & Cloninger, C. R. (1995). Genetic components of alcoholism and subtypes of alcoholism. In B. Tabakoff & P. L. Hoffman (Eds.), *Biological aspects of alcoholism: WHO expert series on biological psychiatry, Vol. 4*. Seattle, WA: Hogrefe & Huber.

Pato, M. T., Pato, C. N., & Pauls, D. L. (2002). Recent findings in the genetics of OCD. *Journal of Clinical Psychiatry, 63(6)*, 30–33.

Patterson, F. G., & Linden, E. (1981). *The education of Koko*. New York: Holt, Rinehart and Winston.

Patton, J., Stinard, T., & Routh, D. (1983). Where do children study? *Journal of Educational Research, 76*, 280–286.

Paulesu, E., Frith, U., Snowling, M., Gallagher, A., Morton, J., Frackowiak, R. S. J., & Frith, C. D. (1996). Is developmental dyslexia a disconnection syndrome? *Brain, 119*, 143–157.

Paulesu, E., McCrory, E., Fazio, F., Menoncello, L., Brunswick, N., Cappa, S. F., Cotelli, M., Cossu, G., Corte, F., Lorusso, M., Pesenti, S., Gallagher, A., Perani, D., Price, C., Frith, C. D., & Frith, U. (2000). A cultural effect on brain function. *Nature Neuroscience, 3*, 91–96.

Paulhus, D. L., Lysy, D. C., & Yik, M. S. M. (1998). Self-report measures of intelligence: Are they useful as proxy IQ tests? *Journal of Personality, 66*, 525–554.

Pauls, D. L., & Alsobrook, J. P. (1999). The inheritance of obsessive-compulsive disorder. *Child and Adolescent Psychiatric Clinics of North America, 8*, 481–496.

Pauls, D. L., & Leckman, J. F. (1986). The inheritance of Gilles de la Tourette's syndrome and associated behaviors. *New England Journal of Medicine, 315*, 993–997.

Paunonen, S. V. (2003). Big Five factors of personality and replicated predictions of behavior. *Journal of Personality & Social Psychology, 84(2)*, 411–422.

Pavlov, I. P. (1927). *Conditioned reflexes*. Oxford, UK: Oxford University Press.

Pearce, J. M., & Bouton, M. E. (2001). Theories of associative learning in animals. *Annual Review of Psychology, 52*, 111–139.

Pease, D. M., Gleason, J. B., & Pan, B. A. (1993). Learning the meaning of words: Semantic development and beyond. In J. B. Gleason (Ed.), *The development of language*. New York: Macmillan.

Pederson, D. R., Gleason, K. E., Moran, G., & Bento, S. (1998). Maternal attachment representations, maternal sensitivity, and the infant-mother attachment relationship. *Developmental Psychology, 34*, 925–933.

Pederson, D. R., & Moran, G. (1996). Expressions of the attachment relationship outside the strange situation. *Child Development, 67*, 915–927.

Pelkovitz, D., & Kaplan, S. (1996). Posttraumatic stress disorder in children and adolescents. *Child and Adolescent Psychiatric Clinics of North America, 5*, 449–469.

Pelleymounter, M. A., Cullen, M. J., Baker, M. B., Hecht, R., Winters, D., Boone, T., & Collins, E. (1997). Effects of the obese gene product on body weight regulation in ob/ob mice. *Science, 269*, 540–543.

People v. Kempinski. No. W80CF 352 (Circuit Court, 12th District, Will County, Illinois, October 21, 1980).

Perlman, D., & Oskamp, S. (1971). The effects of picture content and exposure frequency on evaluations of Negroes and whites. *Journal of Experimental Social Psychology, 7*, 503–514.

Perlmutter, M., & Hall, E. (1992). *Adult development and aging* (2nd ed.). New York: John Wiley & Sons.

Perls, F. S. (1967). Group vs. individual therapy. *ETC: A Review of General Semantics, 34*, 306–312.

Perls, F. S. (1969). *Gestalt therapy verbatim*. Lafayette, CA: Real People Press.

Persad, E. (2001). Electroconvulsive therapy: The controversy and the evidence. *Canadian Journal of Psychiatry, 46(8)*, 702–703.

Persky, H., Lief, H. I., Strauss, D., Miller, W. R., & O'Brien, C. P. (1978). Plasma testosterone level and sexual behavior of couples. *Archives of Sexual Behavior, 7*, 157–173.

Pervin, L. A. (1975). *Personality: Theory, assessment, and research*. New York: John Wiley & Sons.

Peskin, J. (1982). Measuring household production for the GNP. *Family Economics Review, 3*, 16–25.

Peters, R. K., Cady, L. D., Bischoff, D. P., Bernstein, L., & Pile, M. C. (1983). Physical fitness and subsequent myocardial infarction in healthy workers. *JAMA, 249*, 3052–3056.

Petersen, S. E., Fox, P. T., Posner, M. I., Mintin, M., & Raichle, M. E. (1988). Positron emission tomographic studies of the cortical anatomy of single-word processing. *Nature, 331,* 585–589.

Petersen, S. E., Fox, P. T., Snyder, A. Z., & Raichle, M. E. (1990). Activation of extrastriate and frontal cortical areas by visual words and word-like stimuli. *Science, 249,* 1041–1044.

Peterson, L. R., & Peterson, M. J. (1959). Short-term retention of individual verbal items. *Journal of Experimental Psychology, 58,* 193–198.

Peterson, R. (1985). Pubertal development as a cause of disturbance: Myths, realities, and unanswered questions. *Genetic, Social, and General Psychology Monographs, 111,* 205–232.

Petitto, L. A., Zatorre, R. J., Gauna, K., Nikelski, E. J., Dostie, D., & Evans, A. C. (2000). Speech-like cerebral activity in profoundly deaf people processing signed languages: Implications for the neural basis of human language. *Proceedings of the National Academy of Sciences, USA, 97,* 13 961–13 966.

Petty, R. E., & Wegener, D. T. (1999). The elaboration likelihood model: Current status and controversies. In S. Chaiken & Y. Trope (Eds.), *Dual-process theories in social psychology.* New York: Guilford Press.

Petty, R. E., Wegener, D. T., & Fabrigar, L. R. (1997). Attitude change: Multiple roles for persuasion variables. In D. Gilbert, S. Fiske, & G. Lindzey (Eds.), *Handbook of social psychology* (4th ed.). New York: McGraw-Hill.

Petty, R. E., Wheeler, S. C., & Tormala, Z. L. (2003). Persuasion and attitude change. In T. Millon & M. J. Lerner (Eds.), *Handbook of psychology: Personality and social psychology, Vol. 5.* New York: John Wiley & Sons, Inc.

Pfefferbaum, A., Zipursky, R. B., Lim, K. O., Zatz, L. M., Stahl, S. M., & Jernigan, T. L. (1988). Computed tomographic evidence for generalized sulcal and ventricular enlargement in schizophrenia. *Archives of General Psychiatry, 45,* 633–640.

Phares, E. J. (1979). *Clinical psychology: Concepts, methods, and profession.* Homewood, IL: Dorsey Press.

Phillips, S. D., Burns, B. J., Edgar, E. R., Mueser, K. T., Linkins, K. W., Rosenheck, R. A., Drake, R. E., & McDonel Herr, E. C. (2001). Moving assertive community treatment into standard practice. *Psychiatric Services, 52(6),* 771–779.

Piaget, J. (1952). *The origins of intelligence in children.* (M. Cook, Trans.). New York: International Universities Press.

Piaget, J. (1972). Intellectual evolution from adolescence to adulthood. *Human Development, 15,* 1–12.

Picariello, M. L., Greenberg, D. N., & Pillemer, D. B. (1990). Children's sex-related stereotyping of colors. *Child Development, 61,* 1453–1460.

Pichora-Fuller, M. K., & Schneider, B. A. (1998). Masking-level differences in older adults: The effect of the level of the masking noise. *Perception & Psychophysics, 60,* 1197–1205.

Pickens, R. W., Svikis, D. S., McGue, M., Lykken, D. T., Heston, L. L., & Clayton, P. J. (1991). Heterogeneity in the inheritance of alcoholism: A study of male and female twins. *Archives of General Psychiatry, 48,* 19–28.

Pierce, J. P., Choi, W. S., Gilpin, E. A., Farkas, A. J., & Berry, C. C. (1998). Tobacco industry promotion of cigarettes and adolescent smoking. *Journal of the American Medical Association, 279,* 511–515.

Pierce, J. P., & Gilpin, E. A. (1995). A historical analysis of tobacco marketing and the uptake of smoking by youth in the United States: 1890–1977. *Health Psychology, 14,* 500–508.

Pierce, W. D., & Epling, W. F. (1997). Activity anorexia: The interplay of culture, behavior, and biology. In P. Lamal (Ed.), *Cultural contingencies: Behavior analytic perspectives on cultural practices.* Westport, CT: Prager Publishers/ Greenwood Publishing Group, Inc.

Pika, S., Liebal, K., & Tomasello, M. (2003). Gestural communication in young gorillas (*Gorilla gorilla*): Gestural repertoire, learning, and use. *American Journal of Primatology, 60,* 95–111.

Pilleri, G. (1979). The blind Indus dolphin, *Platanista indi. Endeavours, 3,* 48–56.

Pilon, D. J., & Friedman, A. (1998). Grouping and detecting vertices in 2-D, 3-D, and quasi-3-D objects. *Canadian Journal of Experimental Psychology, 52,* 114–126.

Pinel, J. P. J., Assanand, S., & Lehman, D. R. (2000). Hunger, eating, and ill health. *American Psychologist, 55,* 1105–1116.

Pinhas, L., Toner, B. B., Ali, A., Garfinkel, P. E., & Stuckless, N. (1999). The effects of the ideal of female beauty on mood and body satisfaction. *Eating Disorders, 25,* 223–226.

Pinker, S. (1990). Language acquisition. In D. N. Osherson & H. Lasnik (Eds.), *An invitation to cognitive science. Vol. 1: Language.* Cambridge, MA: MIT Press.

Pinker, S. (1994). *The language instinct.* New York: William Morrow.

Pinker, S. (1997). *How the mind works.* New York: Norton.

Pinker, S. (1999). *Words and rules: The ingredients of language.* New York: Basic Books.

Pinker, S. (2001). Talk of genetics and vice versa. *Nature, 413,* 465–466.

Pittenger, C., & Kandel, E. R. (2003). In search of general mechanisms of long-lasting plasticity: *Aplysia* and the hippocampus. *Philosophical Transaction of the Royal Society of London: Biological Sciences, 358,* 757–763.

Pitts, M., & Phillips, K. (1998). *The psychology of health: An introduction* (2nd ed.). London, UK, and New York: Routledge.

Plagens, P., Miller, M., Foote, D., & Yoffe, E. (1991, April 1). Violence in our culture. *Newsweek,* 46–52.

Platt, J. R. (1973). Percentile reinforcement: Paradigms for experimental analysis of response shaping. In G. H. Bower (Ed.), *The psychology of learning and motivation: Advances in research and theory.* Oxford, England: Academic Press.

Plomin, R. (1990). *Nature and nurture: An introduction to behavioral genetics.* Pacific Grove, CA: Brooks/Cole.

Plomin, R., & Asbury, K. (2001). Nature and nurture in the family. *Marriage & Family Review, 33(2–3),* 273–281.

Plomin, R., & Bergeman, C. S. (1991). The nature of nurture: Genetic influence on "environmental" measures. *Behavioral and Brain Sciences, 14,* 373–427.

Poduslo, S. E., & Yin, X. (2001). A new locus on chromosome 19 linked with late-onset Alzheimer's disease. *Neuroreport, 12,* 3759–3761.

Poggio, G. F., & Poggio, T. (1984). The analysis of stereopsis. *Annual Review of Neuroscience, 7,* 379–412.

Polka, L., & Werker, J. (1994). Developmental changes in perception of nonnative vowel contrasts. *Journal of Experimental Psychology: Human Perception and Performance, 20,* 421–435.

Pomerleau, O. F. (1992). Smoking treatment comes of age. *Psychopharmacology and Substance Abuse Newsletter, 24,* 3.

Poole, M. E., Langan-Fox, J., & Omodei, M. (1991). Sex differences in perceived career success. *Genetic, Social and General Psychology Monographs, 117,* 155–174.

Pope, K. S. (2000). Therapists' sexual feelings and behaviors: Research, trends, and quandaries. In L. T. Szuchman & F. Muscarella (Eds.), *Psychological perspectives on human sexuality.* New York: John Wiley & Sons, Inc.

Porter, R. H., Makin, J. W., Davis, L. B., & Christensen, K. M. (1992). Breast-fed infants respond to olfactory cues from their own mother and unfamiliar lactating females. *Infant Behavior and Development, 15,* 85–93.

Porter, R. H., & Winberg, J. (1999). Unique salience of maternal breast odors for newborn infants. *Neuroscience and Biobehavioral Reviews, 23,* 439–449.

Posner, M. I., Snyder, C. R. R., & Davidson, B. J. (1980). Attention and the detection of signals. *Journal of Experimental Psychology: General, 109,* 160–174.

Potter, S. M., Zelazo, P. R., Stack, D. M., & Papageorgiou, A. N. (2000). Adverse effects of fetal cocaine exposure on neonatal auditory information processing. *Pediatrics, 105,* E40.

Potter, W. Z., Manji, H. K., & Rudorfer, M. V. (2001). Tricyclics and tetracyclics. In A. F. Schatzberg & C. B. Nemeroff (Eds.), *Essentials of clinical psychopharmacology.* Washington, DC: American Psychiatric Association.

Poulin-Dubois, D., Graham, S., & Sippola, L. (1995). Early lexical development: The contribution of parental labelling and infants' categorization abilities. *Journal of Child Language, 22,* 325–343.

Powell, K. E., Thompson, P. D., Caspersen, C. J., & Kendrick, J. S. (1987). Physical activity and the incidence of coronary heart disease. *Annual Review of Public Health, 8,* 253–287.

Pratkanis, A. R., Eskenazi, J., & Greenwald, A. G. (1990). What you expect is what you believe, but not necessarily what you get: On the effectiveness of subliminal self-help audiotapes. Paper presented at the annual convention of the Western Psychological Association, Los Angeles, 1990. (Cited by Druckman & Bjork.)

Premack, D. (1959). Toward empirical behavioral laws: I. Positive reinforcement. *Psychological Review, 66,* 219–233.

Premack, D. (1976). Language and intelligence in ape and man. *American Scientist, 64,* 674–683.

Prescott, C. A., & Kendler, K. S. (1999). Age at first drink and risk for alcoholism: A noncausal association. *Alcoholism: Clinical & Experimental Research, 23(1),* 101–107.

Pressman, J. D. (1998). *Last resort: Psychosurgery and the limits of medicine.* New York: Cambridge University Press.

Prichard, J. C. (1835). *A treatise on insanity and other disorders affecting the mind.* London: Sherwood, Gilbert, and Piper.

Propping, P., Kruger, J., & Janah, A. (1980). Effect of alcohol on genetically determined variants of the normal electroencephalogram. *Psychiatry Research, 2,* 85–98.

Propping, P., Kruger, J., & Mark, N. (1981). Genetic disposition to alcoholism: An EEG study in alcoholics and their relatives. *Human Genetics, 59,* 51–59.

Prudic, J., & Sackeim, H. A. (1999). Electroconvulsive therapy and suicide risk. *Journal of Clinical Psychiatry, 60,* 104–110.

Pulcino, T., Galea, S., Ahern, J., Resnick, H., Foley, M., & Vlahov, D. (2003). Posttraumatic stress in women after the September 11 terrorist attacks in New York City. *Journal of Women's Health, 12(8),* 809–820.

Rachlin, H. (1970). *Modern behaviorism.* New York: Freeman.

Rahe, R. H., & Arthur, R. J. (1978). Life changes and illness reports. In K. E. Gunderson & R. H. Rahe (Eds.), *Life stress and illness.* Springfield, IL: Thomas.

Rainville, P., Duncan, G. H., Price, D. D., Carrier, B., & Bushnell, M. C. (1997). Pain affect encoded in human anterior cingulate but not somatosensory cortex. *Science, 277,* 968–971.

Rajecki, D. J. (1990). *Attitudes* (2nd ed.). Sunderland, MA: Sinauer Associates.

Ramey, C. (1994). Abecedarian project. In R. J. Sternberg (Ed.), *Encyclopedia of human intelligence.* New York: Macmillan.

Rampon, C., Tang, Y.-P., Goodhouse, J., Shimizu, E., Kyin, M., & Tsien, J. Z. (2000). Enrichment induces structural changes and recovery from nonspatial memory deficits in CA1 NMDAR1-knockout mice. *Nature Neuroscience, 3,* 238–244.

Rapoport, J. L., Giedd, J. N., Blumenthal, J., Hamburger, S., Jeffries, N., Fernandez, T., Nicolson, R., Bedwell, J., Lenane, M., Zijdenbos, A., Paus, T., & Evans, A. (1999). Progressive cortical change during adolescence in childhood-onset schizophrenia: A Longitudinal MRI study. *Archives of General Psychiatry, 56,* 649–654.

Rappaport, J. (1977). *Community psychology: Values, research and action.* New York: Holt, Rinehart and Winston.

Rappaport, J., & Seidman, E. (2000). *Handbook of community psychology.* New York: Kluwer Academic/Plenum Publishers.

Rayner, K., & Pollatsek, A. (1989). *The psychology of reading.* Englewood Cliffs, NJ: Prentice-Hall.

Rayner, K., Sereno, S. C., & Raney, G. E. (1996). Eye movement control in reading: A comparison of two types of models. *Journal of Experimental Psychology: Human Perception and Performance, 22,* 1188–1200.

Réale, D., McAdam, A. G., Boutin, S., & Berteaux, D. (2003). Genetic and plastic responses of a northern mammal to climate change. *Proceedings of the Royal Society of London, 270,* 591–596.

Reber, A. S. (1992). The cognitive unconscious: An evolutionary perspective. *Consciousness and Cognition, 1,* 93–133.

Recanzone, G. H., Makhamra, S. D. D. R., & Guard, D. C. (1998). Comparison of relative and absolute sound localization ability in humans. *Journal of the Acoustical Society of America, 103,* 1085–1097.

Rees, G. (2001). Seeing is not perceiving. *Nature Neuroscience, 4,* 678–680.

Rees, G., Friston, K., & Koch, C. (2000). A direct quantitative relationship between the functional properties of human and macaque V5. *Nature Neuroscience, 3,* 716–723.

Rees, G., Kreiman, G., & Koch, C. (2002). Neural correlates of consciousness in humans. *Nature Reviews: Neuroscience, 3,* 261–270.

Regier, D. A., Boyd, J. H., Burke, J. D., Rae, D. S., Myers, J. K., Kramer, M., Ropins, L. N., George, L. K., Karno, M., & Locke, B. Z. (1988). One-month prevalence of mental disorders in the United States. *Archives of General Psychiatry, 45,* 977–986.

Reichle, E. D., Pollatsek, A., Fisher, D. L., & Rayner, K. (1998). Toward a model of eye movement control in reading. *Psychological Review, 105,* 125–157.

Reingold, E. M., Charness, N., Pomplun, M., & Stampe, D. M. (2001). Visual span in expert chess players: Evidence from eye movements. *Psychological Science, 12,* 48–55.

Reinink, E., Bouhuys, N., Wirz-Justice, A., & van den Hoofdakker, R. (1990). Prediction of the antidepressant response to total sleep deprivation by diurnal variation of mood. *Psychiatry Research, 32,* 113–124.

Reinke, B. J., Holmes, D. S., & Harris, R. L. (1985). The timing of psychosocial changes in women's lives: The years 25 to 45. *Journal of Personality and Social Psychology, 48,* 1353–1364.

Reiser, M., & Nielsen, M. (1980). Investigative hypnosis: A developing specialty. *American Journal of Clinical Hypnosis, 23,* 75–83.

Rescorla, R. A., & Wagner, A. R. (1972). A theory of Pavlovian conditioning: Variations in the effectiveness of reinforcement and nonreinforcement. In A. H. Black & W. F. Prokasy (Eds.), *Classical conditioning II* (pp. 64–99). New York: Appleton-Century-Crofts.

Rest, J. R. (1979). *Development in judging moral issues.* Minneapolis: University of Minnesota Press.

Review Panel. (1981). Coronary-prone behavior and coronary heart disease: A critical review. *Circulation, 673,* 1199–1215.

Reynolds, A. G., & Flagg, P. W. (1983). *Cognitive psychology* (2nd ed.). Boston: Little, Brown.

Rhee, S. H., Hewitt, J. K., Young, S. E., Corely, R. P., Crowley, T. J., & Stallings, M. C. (2003). Genetic and environmental influences on substance initiation, use, and problem use in adolescents. *Archives of General Psychology, 60(12),* 1256–1264.

Rheingold, A. A., Acierno, R., & Resnick, H. S. (2004). Trauma, posttraumatic stress disorder, and health risk behaviors. In P. P. Schnurr & B. L. Green (Eds.), *Trauma and health: Physical health consequences of exposure to extreme stress.* Washington, DC: American Psychological Association.

Rice, M. L., Huston, A. C., Truglio, R., & Wright, J. (1990). Words from "Sesame Street": Learning vocabulary while viewing. *Developmental Psychology, 26,* 421–428.

Richards, R. J. (1987). *Darwin and the emergence of evolutionary theories of mind and behavior.* Chicago: University of Chicago Press.

Rief, J. S., Bruns, C., & Lower, K. S. (1998). Cancer of the nasal cavity and paranasal sinuses and exposure to environmental tobacco smoke in pet dogs. *American Journal of Epidemiology, 147(5),* 488–492.

Riesenhuber, M., & Poggio, T. (1999). Hierarchical models of object recognition in cortex. *Nature Neuroscience, 2,* 1019–1025.

Riggs, L. A., Ratliff, F., Cornsweet, J. C., & Cornsweet, T. N. (1953). The disappearance of steadily fixated visual test objects. *Journal of the Optical Society of America, 43,* 495–501.

Rips, L. J., Shoben, E. J., & Smith, E. E. (1973). Semantic distance and the verification of semantic relations. *Journal of Verbal Learning and Verbal Behavior, 12,* 1–20.

Rischer, C. E., & Easton, T. A. (1992). *Focus on human biology.* New York: HarperCollins.

Ritter, S., Dinh, T.T., & Zhang, Y. (2000). Localization of hindbrain glucoreceptive sites controlling food intake and blood glucose. *Brain Research, 856,* 37–47.

Roberson, D., Daviews, I., & Davidoff, J. (2000). Color categories are not universal: Replications and new evidence from a Stone-Age culture. *Journal of Experimental Psychology: General, 129,* 369–398.

Robins, R. W., & Beer, J. S. (2001). Positive illusions about the self: Short-term benefits and long-term costs. *Journal of Personality and Social Psychology, 80,* 340–352.

Rodin, J., Schank, D., & Striegel-Moore, R. (1989). Psychological features of obesity. *Medical Clinics of North America, 73,* 47–66.

Roediger, H. L. (1990). Implicit memory: Retention without remembering. *American Psychologist, 45,* 1043–1056.

Roediger, H. L., III, & McDermott, K. B. (1995). Creating false memories: Remembering words not presented in lists. *Journal of Experimental Psychology: Learning, Memory, and Cognition, 21,* 803–814.

Roff, J. D., & Knight, R. (1981). Family characteristics, childhood symptoms, and adult outcome in schizophrenia. *Journal of Abnormal Psychology, 90,* 510–520.

Roff, J. D., & Knight, R. A. (1995). Childhood antecedents of stable positive symptoms in schizophrenia. *Psychological Reports, 77(1),* 319–323.

Rogers, C. R. (1961). *On becoming a person.* Boston: Houghton Mifflin.

Rogers, C. T. (1951). *Client-centered therapy.* Boston: Houghton Mifflin.

Rogers, M. P., Trentham, D. E., McCune, W. J., Ginsberg, B. I., Rennke, H. G., Reike, P., & David, J. R. (1980). Effect of psychological stress on the induction of arthritis in rats. *Arthritis and Rheumatology, 23,* 1337–1342.

Rogoff, B. (1990). *Apprenticeship in thinking: Cognitive development in social context.* New York: Oxford University Press.

Rogoff, B., & Chavajay, P. (1995). What's become of research on the cultural basis of cognitive development. *American Psychologist, 50,* 859–877.

Rogoff, B., & Waddell, K. J. (1982). Memory for information organized in a scene by children from two cultures. *Child Development, 53,* 1224–1228.

Rohling, M. L., Langhinrichsen-Rohling, J., & Miller, L. S. (2003). Actuarial assessment of malingering: Rohling's interpretive method. In R. D. Franklin (Ed.), *Prediction in forensic and neuropsychology: Sound statistical practices.* Mahwah, NJ: Lawrence Erlbaum Associates.

Rollins, B. C., & Feldman, H. (1970). Marital satisfaction over the life cycle. *Journal of Marriage and the Family, 32,* 20–28.

Roodenrys, S., Hulme, C., Lethbridge, A., Hinton, M., & Nimmo, L. M. (2002). Word-frequency and phonological-neighborhood effects on verbal short-term memory. *Journal of Experimental Psychology: Learning, Memory, and Cognition, 28,* 1019–1034.

Rosch, E. (1973). On the internal structure of perceptual and semantic categories. In R. E. Moore (Ed.), *Cognitive development and the acquisition of language.* New York: Academic Press.

Rosch, E. (1999). Reclaiming concepts. *Journal of Consciousness Studies, 6,* 61–77.

Rosch, E. (2002). Principles of categorization. In D. J. Levitin (Ed.), *Foundations of cognitive psychology: Core readings.* Cambridge, MA: MIT Press.

Rosch, E. H. (1975). Cognitive representations of semantic categories. *Journal of Experimental Psychology: General, 104,* 192–233.

Rosch, E. H., Mervis, C. B., Gray, W. D., Johnson, D. M., & Boyes-Braem, P. (1976). Basic objects in natural categories. *Cognitive Psychology, 8,* 382–439.

Rose, G. A., & Williams, R. T. (1961). Metabolic studies of large and small eaters. *British Journal of Nutrition, 15,* 1–9.

Rose, R. J. (1995). Genes and human behavior. *Annual Review of Psychology, 46,* 625–654.

Rosenbaum, D. A. (2002). Motor control. In H. Pashler & S. Yantis (Eds.), *Steven's handbook of experimental psychology* (3rd ed.): *Vol. 1. Sensation and perception* (pp. 315–339). New York: Wiley.

Rosenbaum, R. S., Priselac, S., Kohler, S., Black, S. E., Gao, F., Nadel, L., & Moscovitch, M. (2000). Remote spatial memory in an amnesic person with extensive bilateral hippocampal lesions. *Nature Neuroscience, 3,* 1044–1048.

Rosenfarb, I. S., Bellack, A. S., Aziz, N., Kratz, M., & Sayers, S. (2004). Race, family interactions, and patient stabilization in schizophrenia. *Journal of Abnormal Psychology, 113(1),* 109–115.

Rosenhan, D. L. (1973). On being sane in insane places. *Science, 179,* 250–258.

Rosenman, R. H., Brand, R. J., Jenkins, C. D., Friedman, M., Straus, R., & Wurm, M. (1975). Coronary heart disease in the Western Collaborative Group Study: Final follow-up experience of 8-1/2 years. *JAMA, 233,* 872–877.

Rosenman, R. H., Brand, R. J., Jenkins, C. D., Friedman, M., Straus, R., & Wurm, M. (1994). Coronary heart disease in the Western Collaborative Group Study: Final follow-up experience of 8-1/2 years. In A. Steptoe & J. Wardle (Eds.), *Psychosocial processes and health: A reader.* New York: Cambridge University Press.

Rosenthal, D. (1970). *Genetic theory and abnormal behavior.* New York: McGraw-Hill.

Rosenthal, N. E. (2000). A patient who changed my practice: Herb Kern, the first light therapy patient. *International Journal of Psychiatry in Clinical Practice, 4,* 339–341.

Rosenthal, N. E., Genhart, M., Jacobson, F. M., Skwerer, R. G., & Wehr, T. A. (1986). Disturbances of appetite and weight regulation in seasonal affective disorder. *Annals of the New York Academy of Sciences, 499,* 216–230.

Rosenthal, R. (1985). From unconscious experimenter bias to teacher expectancy effects. In J. B. Dusek, V. C. Hall, & W. J. Meyer (Eds.), *Teacher expectancies.* Hillsdale, NJ: Lawrence Erlbaum Press.

Rosenzweig, M. R., & Bennett, E. L. (1996). Psychobiology of plasticity: Effects of training and experience on brain and behavior. *Behavioural Brain Research, 78,* 57–65.

Roskos-Ewoldsen, D. R., & Fazio, R. H. (1992). The accessibility of source likability as a determinant of persuasion. *Personality and Social Psychology Bulletin, 18,* 19–25.

Rosmand, R. (2005). Role of stress in the pathogenesis of the metabolic syndrome. *Psychoneuroendocrinology, 30,* 1–10.

Ross, C., Miller, S. D., Bjornson, L., & Reagor, P. (1991). Abuse histories in 102 cases of multiple personality disorder. *Canadian Journal of Psychiatry, 36,* 97–101.

Ross, C. A. (1997). *Dissociative identity disorder: Diagnosis, clinical features, and treatment of multiple personality* (2nd ed.). New York: John Wiley & Sons, Inc.

Ross, G., Nelson, K., Wetstone, H., & Tanouye, E. (1986). Acquisition and generalization of novel object concepts by young language learners. *Journal of Child Language, 13,* 67–83.

Ross, J., & Ma-Wyatt, A. (2004). Saccades actively maintain perceptual continuity. *Nature Neuroscience, 7,* 65–69.

Ross, L. (1977). The intuitive psychologist and his shortcomings: Distortions in the attribution process. In L. Berkowitz (Ed.), *Advances in experimental social psychology. Vol. 10.* New York: Academic Press.

Rosser, R. (1994). *Cognitive development: Psychological and biological perspectives.* Boston: Allyn & Bacon.

Roth, E. M., & Mervis, C. B. (1983). Fuzzy set theory and class inclusion relations in semantic categories. *Journal of Verbal Learning and Verbal Behavior, 22,* 509–525.

Roth, G., & Dicke, U. (2005). Evolution of brain and intelligence. *Trends in Cognitive Sciences, 9,* 250–257.

Rothkopf, E. Z. (1971). Incidental memory for location of information in text. *Journal of Verbal Learning and Verbal Behavior, 10,* 608–613.

Rotter, J. B. (1966). Generalized expectancies for internal versus external control of reinforcement. *Psychological Monographs, 80(1, Whole No. 609).*

Rotter, J. B. (1990). Internal versus external control of reinforcement: A case history of a variable. *American Psychologist, 45,* 489–493.

Rovee-Collier, C. (1999). The development of infant memory. *Current Directions in Psychological Science, 8,* 80–85.

Rovee-Collier, C. K., & Gekowski, M. J. (1979). The economics of infancy: A review of conjugate reinforcement. In H. W. Reese & L. P. Litsitt (Eds.), *Advances in Child Development* (Vol. 13, pp. 195–225). New York: Academic Press.

Rudy, J. (1991). Elemental and configural associations, the hippocampus and development. *Developmental Psychobiology, 24,* 221–236.

Rumelhart, D. E., McClelland, J. L., & the PDP Research Group. (1986). *Parallel distributed processing: Explorations in the microstructure of cognition.* Cambridge, MA: MIT Press.

Ruscher, J. B. (1998). Prejudice and stereotyping in everyday communication. *Advances in Experimental Social Psychology, 30,* 241–307.

Rushing, W. A. (1995). *The AIDS epidemic: Social dimensions of an infectious disease.* Boulder, CO: Westview Press.

Rutherford, A., & Endler, N. S. (1999). Predicting approach-avoidance: The roles of coping styles, state anxiety, and situational appraisal. *Anxiety, Stress & Coping: An International Journal, 12,* 63–84.

Ruvolo, A., & Markus, H. (1992). Possible selves and performance: The power of self-relevant imagery. *Social Cognition, 9,* 95–124.

Ruzgis, P., & Grigorenko, E. L. (1994). Cultural meaning systems, intelligence, and personality. In R. J. Sternberg & P. Ruzgis (Eds.), *Personality and intelligence* (pp. 248–270). New York: Cambridge University Press.

Ryan, R. M., & Deci, E. L. (2000). Self-determination theory and the facilitation of intrinsic motivation, social development, and well-being. *American Psychologist, 55,* 68–78.

Ryan, R. M., & Deci, E. L. (2002). Overview of self-determination theory: An organismic-dialectical perspective. In E. L. Deci & R. M. Ryan (Eds.), *Handbook of self-determination research.* Rochester, NY: University of Rochester Press.

Ryback, R. S., & Lewis, O. F. (1971). Effects of prolonged bed rest on EEG sleep patterns in young, healthy volunteers. *Electroencephalography and Clinical Neurophysiology, 31,* 395–399.

Rymer, R. (1992). A silent childhood. *The New Yorker* (April 23), pp. 41–81.

Sachs, J. S. (1967). Recognition memory for syntactic and semantic aspects of connected discourse. *Perception and Psychophysics, 2,* 437–442.

Sachs, O. (1989). *Seeing voices: A journey into the world of the deaf.* Berkeley, CA: University of California Press.

Sacks, O. W. (1995). *An anthropologist on Mars: Seven paradoxical tales.* New York: Alfred A. Knopf.

Sadato, N., Pascualleone, A., Grafman, J., Ibanez, V., Deiber, M. P., Dold, G., & Hallett, M. (1996). Activation of the primary visual cortex by Braille reading in blind subjects. *Nature, 380,* 526–528.

Sadovnick, A. D., Remick, R. A., Lam, R. W., Zis, A. P., Yee, I. M. L., & Baird, P. A. (1994). Morbidity risks for mood disorders in 3,942 first degree relatives of 671 index cases with single depression, recurrent depression, bipolar I or bipolar II. *American Journal of Medical Genetics, 54,* 132–140.

Saegert, S. C., Swap, W., & Zajonc, R. B. (1973). Exposure, context, and interpersonal attraction. *Journal of Personality and Social Psychology, 25,* 234–242.

Saffran, E. M., Marin, O. S. M., & Yeni-Komshian, G. H. (1976). An analysis of speech perception in word deafness. *Brain and Language, 3,* 209–228.

Saffran, E. M., Schwartz, M. F., & Marin, O. S. M. (1980). Evidence from aphasia: Isolating the components of a production model. In B. Butterworth (Ed.), *Language production.* London: Academic Press.

Sakai, F., Meyer, J. S., Karacan, I., Derman, S., & Yamamoto, M. (1979). Normal human sleep: Regional cerebral haemodynamics. *Annals of Neurology, 7,* 471–478.

Salapatek, P. (1975). Pattern perception in early infancy. In L. B. Cohen & P. Salapatek (Eds.), *Infant perception: From sensation to cognition, Vol. 1.* New York: Academic Press.

Salmon, U. J., & Geist, S. H. (1943). Effect of androgens upon libido in women. *Journal of Clinical Endocrinology and Metabolism, 172,* 374–377.

Salovey, P., & Mayer, J. D. (1989–1990). Emotional intelligence. *Imagination, Cognition and Personality, 9,* 185–211.

Salthouse, T. A. (1984). Effects of age and skill in typing. *Journal of Gerontology, 113,* 345–371.

Salthouse, T. A. (1988). Cognitive aspects of motor functioning. In J. A. Joseph (Ed.), *Central determinants of age-related declines in motor function.* New York: New York Academy of Sciences.

Sande, G. N., Goethals, G. R., & Radloff, C. E. (1988). Perceiving one's own traits and others': The multifaceted self. *Journal of Personality and Social Psychology, 54,* 13–20.

Sanders, L. D., Newport, E. L., & Neville, H. J. (2002). Segmenting nonsense: An event-related potential index of perceived onsets in continuous speech. *Nature Neuroscience, 5,* 700–703.

Sandrini, G., Milanov, I., Malaguti, S., Nigrelli, M. P., Moglia, A., & Nappi, G. (2000). Effects of hypnosis on diffuse noxious inhibitory controls. *Physiology & Behavior, 69,* 295–300.

Santana, M.- A., & Dancy, B. L. (2000). The stigma of being named "AIDS carriers" on Haitian-American women. *Health Care for Women International, 21,* 161–171.

Santed, M. A., Sandin, B., Chorot, P., Olmedo, M., & García-Campayo, J. (2003). The role of negative and positive affectivity on perceived stress-subjective health relationships. *Acta Neuropsychiatrica, 15(4),* 199–216.

Santos, M. D., Leve, C., & Pratkanis, A. R. (1994). Hey buddy, can you spare seventeen cents? Mindful persuasion and the pique technique. *Journal of Applied Social Psychology, 24,* 755–764.

Sapolsky, R. M. (1996). Why stress is bad for your brain. *Science, 273,* 749–775.

Sarason, B. R., & Sarason, I. G. (1999). *Abnormal psychology: The problem of maladaptive behavior* (10th ed.). Upper Saddle River, NJ: Prentice-Hall Inc.

Savage-Rumbaugh, E. S. (1990). Language acquisition in a nonhuman species: Implications for the innateness debate. *Development Psychobiology, 23,* 599–620.

Savage-Rumbaugh, E. S., Murphy, J., Sevcik, R. A., Brakke, K. E., Williams, S. L., & Rumbaugh, D. M. (1993). Language comprehension in ape and child. *Monographs of the Society for Research in Child Development, 58,* 1–254.

Savage-Rumbaugh, E. S., Shanker, S., & Taylor, T. J. (1998). *Apes, language, and the human mind.* New York: Oxford University Press.

Saxena, S., & Rauch, S. L. (2000). Functional neuroimaging and the neuroanatomy of obsessive-compulsive disorder. *Pediatric Clinics of North America, 23,* 563–586.

Scarr, S., & Weinberg, R. A. (1976). IQ performance of black children adopted by white families. *American Psychologist, 31,* 726–739.

Scarr, S., & Weinberg, R. A. (1978). The influence of "family background" on intellectual attainment. *American Sociological Review, 43,* 674–692.

Schacter, D. L. (2001). *The seven sins of memory.* Boston: Houghton Mifflin.

Schacter, D. L., & Dodson, C. S. (2002). Misattribution, false recognition and the sins of memory. In A. Baddeley, M. Conway, & J. Aggleton (Eds.), *Episodic memory: New directions in research* (pp. 71–85). New York: Oxford University Press.

Schachter, S. (1964). The interaction of cognitive and physiological determinants of emotional state. In P. H. Liederman & D. Shapiro (Eds.), *Psychobiological approaches to social behavior.* Stanford, CA: Stanford University Press.

Schachter, S. (1982). Recidivism and self-cure of smoking and obesity. *American Psychologist, 37,* 436–444.

Schachter, S., & Singer, J. E. (1962). Cognitive, social and physiological determinants of emotional state. *Psychological Review, 69,* 379–399.

Schaie, K. W. (1990). Intellectual development in adulthood. In J. E. Birren & K. W. Schaie (Eds.), *Handbook of the psychology of aging* (3rd ed.). San Diego: Academic Press.

Schaie, K. W. (1996). *Intellectual development in adulthood: The Seattle Longitudinal Study.* Cambridge: Cambridge University Press.

Schaie, K. W., & Strother, C. R. (1968). A cross-sequential study of age changes in cognitive behavior. *Psychological Bulletin, 70,* 661–684.

Schanberg, S. M., & Field, T. M. (1987). Sensory deprivation stress and supplemental stimulation in the rat pup and preterm human neonate. *Child Development, 58,* 1431–1447.

Schank, R., & Abelson, R. P. (1977). *Scripts, plans, goals, and understanding.* Hillsdale, NJ: Lawrence Erlbaum Associates.

Schein, J. D. (1989). *At home among strangers.* Washington, DC: Gallaudet University Press.

Scherschlicht, R., Polc, P., Schneeberger, J., Steiner, M., & Haefely, W. (1982). Selective suppression of rapid eye movement sleep (REMS) in cats by typical and atypical antidepressants. In E. Costa & G. Racagni (Eds.), *Typical and atypical antidepressants: Molecular mechanisms.* New York: Raven Press.

Schiffman, H. R. (1996). *Sensation and perception: An integrated approach.* New York: Wiley.

Schleifer, S. J., Keller, S. E., Camerino, M., Thornton, J. C., & Stein, M. (1983). Suppression of lymphocyte stimulation following bereavement. *Journal of the American Medical Association, 15,* 374–377.

Schleifer, S. J., Keller, S. E., & Stein, M. (1985). Stress effects on immunity. *Psychiatric Journal of the University of Ottawa, 10(3),* 125–131.

Schmauk, F. J. (1970). Punishment, arousal, and avoidance learning in sociopaths. *Journal of Abnormal Psychology, 122,* 509–522.

Schmitt, D. P., & Buss, D. M. (1996). Strategic self-promotion and competitor derogation: Sex and context effects on the perceived effectiveness of mate attraction tactics. *Journal of Personality and Social Psychology, 70,* 1185–1204.

Schmolck, H., Buffalo, E. A., & Squire, L. R. (2000). Memory distortions develop over time: Recollections of the O. J. Simpson trial verdict after 15 and 32 months. *Psychological Science, 11,* 39–45.

Schneider, B. (1997). Psychoacoustics and aging: Implications for everyday listening. *Journal of Speech-Language Pathology and Audiology, 21,* 111–124.

Schou, M. (2001). Lithium treatment at 52. *Journal of Affective Disorders, 67(1–3),* 21–32.

Schultz, W. (2001). Reward signaling by dopamine neurons. *The Neuroscientist, 7,* 293–302.

Schuster, M. A., Collins, R., Cunningham, W. E., Morton, S. C., Zierler, S., Wong, M., Tu, W., & Kanouse, D. E. (2005). Perceived discrimination in clinical care in a nationally representative sample of HIV-infected adults receiving health care. *Journal of General Internal Medicine, 20,* 807–813.

Schwab, J. (1995). The Sandalu bachelor ritual among the Laiapu Enga (Papua, New Guinea). *Anthropos, 90,* 27–47.

Schwartz, M. F., Marin, O. S. M., & Saffran, E. M. (1979). Dissociations of language function in dementia: A case study. *Brain and Language, 7,* 277–306.

Schwartz, M. F., Saffran, E. M., & Marin, O. S. M. (1980). The word order problem in agrammatism. I. Comprehension. *Brain and Language, 10,* 249–262.

Schwarzkopf, S. B., Nasrallah, H. A., Olson, S. C., Coffman, J. A., & McLaughlin, J. A. (1989). Perinatal complications and genetic loading in schizophrenia: Preliminary findings. *Psychiatry Research, 27,* 233–239.

Scialfa, C. T., & Joffe, K. M. (1998). Response times and eye movements in feature and conjunctive search as a function of target eccentricity. *Perception & Psychophysics, 60,* 1067–1082.

Scoboria, A., Mazzoni, G., Kirsch, I., & Milling, L. S. (2002). Immediate and persisting effects of misleading questions and hypnosis on memory reports. *Journal of Experimental Psychology: Applied, 8,* 26–32.

Scott, S. K., Blank, C. C., Rosen, S., & Wise, R. J. S. (2000). Identification of a pathway for intelligible speech in the left temporal lobe. *Brain, 123,* 2400–2406.

Scoville, W. B., & Milner, B. (1957). Loss of recent memory after bilateral hippocampal lesions. *Journal of Neurology, Neurosurgery and Psychiatry, 20,* 11–21.

Scribner, S. (1977). Modes of thinking and ways of speaking: Culture and logic reconsidered. In P. N. Johnson-Laird & P. C. Wason (Eds.), *Thinking: Readings in cognitive science.* Cambridge, UK: Cambridge University Press.

Searles, L. V. (1949). The organization of hereditary maze brightness and maze dullness. *Genetic Psychology Monographs, 39,* 279–375.

Sears, D. (1983). The person-positivity bias. *Journal of Personality and Social Psychology, 44 (2),* 233–250.

Segall, M. H., Campbell, D. T., & Herskovits, M. J. (1966). *The influence of culture on visual perception.* Indianapolis, IN: Bobbs-Merrill.

Segall, M. H., Dasen, P. R., Berry, J. W., & Poortinga, Y. H. (1999). *Human behavior in global perspective: An introduction to cross-cultural psychology* (2nd ed.). Boston: Allyn & Bacon.

Seligman, M. E. P. (1971). Phobias and preparedness. *Behavior Therapy, 2,* 307–320.

Seligman, M. E. P. (1975). *Helplessness.* San Francisco: W. H. Freeman.

Seligman, M. E. P., & Nolen-Hoeksema, S. (1987). Explanatory style and depression. In D. Magnusson & A. Oehman (Eds.), *Psychopathology: An interactional perspective. Personality, psychopathology, and psychotherapy.* Orlando, FL: Academic Press.

Seligman, M. E. P., & Schulman, P. (1986). Explanatory style as a predictor of productivity and quitting among life insurance sales agents. *Journal of Personality and Social Psychology, 50,* 832–838.

Selkoe, D. J. (1989). Biochemistry of altered brain proteins in Alzheimer's disease. *Annual Review of Neuroscience, 12,* 463–490.

Selye, H. (1956/1976). *The stress of life.* New York: McGraw-Hill.

Selye, H. (1991). History and present status of the stress concept. In A. Monat & R. S. Lazarus (Eds.), *Stress and coping.* New York: Columbia University Press.

Selye, H. (1993). History of the stress concept. In L. Goldberger & S. Breznitz (Eds.), *Handbook of stress: Theoretical and clinical aspects* (2nd ed.). New York: Free Press.

Shakin, E. J., & Holland, J. (1988). Depression and pancreatic cancer. *Journal of Pain and Symptom Management, 3,* 194–198.

Sharpe, D., Adair, J. G., & Roese, N. J. (1992). Twenty years of deception research: A decline in subjects' trust? *Personality and Social Psychology Bulletin, 18,* 585–590.

Shavit, Y., Depaulis, A., Martin, F. C., Terman, G. W., Pechnick, R. N., Zane, C. J., Gale, R. P., & Liebeskind, J. C. (1986). Involvement of brain opiate receptors in the immune-suppressive effect of morphine. *Proceedings of the National Academy of Sciences, USA, 83,* 7114–7117.

Shavit, Y., Lewis, J. W., Terman, G. W., Gale, R. P., & Liebeskind, J. C. (1984). Opioid peptides mediate the suppressive effect of stress on natural killer cell cytotoxicity. *Science, 223,* 188–190.

Sheffield, F. D., Wulff, J. J., & Backer, R. (1951). Reward value of copulation without sex drive reduction. *Journal of Comparative and Physiological Psychology, 44,* 3–8.

Shellenberg, G. D. (1997). Molecular genetics of Alzheimer's disease. In K. Blum & E. P. Nobel (Eds.), *Handbook of psychiatric genetics.* Boca Raton, FL: CRC Press.

Shen, W. W., & Giesler, M. C. (1998). The discoverers of the therapeutic effect of chlorpromazine in psychiatry: Qui etaient les vrais premiers practiciens? (letter). *Canadian Journal of Psychiatry, 43,* 423–424.

Sher, L. (2004). Etiology, pathogenesis, and treatment of seasonal and non-seasonal mood disorders: Possible role of circadian rhythm abnormalities related to developmental alcohol exposure. *Medical Hypotheses, 62(5),* 797–801.

Sherif, M. (1936). *The psychology of social norms.* New York: Harper.

Sherif, M., Harvey, O. J., White, B. J., Hood, W. E., & Sherif, C. W. (1961). *Intergroup conflict and cooperation: The robbers cave experiment.* Norman, OK: Institute of Group Relations.

Sherry, D. F., Jacobs, L. F., & Gaulin, S. J. C. (1992). Spatial memory and adaptive specialization of the hippocampus. *Trends in Neuroscience, 15,* 298–303.

Sherry, D. F., & Schacter, D. L. (1987). The evolution of multiple memory systems. *Psychological Review, 94,* 439–454.

Shettleworth, S. (1972). Constraints on learning. In D. S. Lehrman, R. A. Hinde, & E. Shaw (Eds.), *Advances in the study of behavior. Vol. 4.* New York: Academic Press.

Shibley Hyde, J., & Plant, E. A. (1995). Magnitude of psychological gender differences: Another side to the story. *American Psychologist, 50,* 159–161.

Shifren, J. L., Braunstein, G. D., Simon, J. A., Casson, P. R., Buster, J. E., Redmond, G. P., Burki. R. E., Ginsburg, E. S., Rosen, R. C., Leiblum, S. R., Caramelli, K. E., & Mazer, N. A. (2000). Transdermal testosterone treatment in women with impaired sexual function after oophorectomy. *New England Journal of Medicine, 343,* 682–688.

Shimp, C. P. (1969). Optimal behavior in free-operant environments. *Psychological Review, 76,* 97–112.

Shotland, R. L., & Heinold, W. D. (1985). Bystander response to arterial bleeding: Helping skills, the decision-making process, and differentiating the helping response. *Journal of Personality and Social Psychology, 49,* 347–356.

Sidman, M. (1994). *Equivalence relations and behavior: A research story.* Boston: Authors; Cooperative Publishers.

Sidman, M., Rauzin, R., Lazar, R., Cunningham, S., Tailby, W., & Carrigan, P. (1982). A search for symmetry in the conditional discriminations of rhesus monkeys, baboons, and children. *Journal of the Experimental Analysis of Behavior, 37,* 23–44.

Simons, D. J. (2000). Current approaches to change blindness. *Visual Cognition, 7,* 1–15.

Simons, D. J., & Chabris, C. F. (1999). Gorillas in our midst: Sustained inattentional blindness for dynamic events. *Perception, 28,* 1059–1074.

Simons, D. J., & Levin, D. T. (1998). Failure to detect changes to people in a real-world interaction. *Psychonomic Bulletin and Review, 5,* 644–649.

Simons, R. C. (1996). *Boo! Culture, experience, and the startle reflex.* New York: Oxford University Press.

Simons, R. C., & Hughes, C. C. (1993). Culture-bound syndromes. In A. C. Gaw (Ed.), *Culture, ethnicity, and mental illness.* Washington, DC: American Psychiatric Press.

Singer, D. G. (1993). Creativity of children in a television world. In G. L. Berry & J. K. Asamen (Eds.), *Children and television: Images in a changing sociocultural world.* Newbury Park, CA: Sage Publications, Inc.

Singer, D. G., & Singer, J. L. (1990). *The house of make-believe.* Cambridge, MA: Harvard University Press.

Singer, L. T., Arendt, R., Minnes, S., Farkas, K., Salvator, A., Kirchner, H. L., & Kliegman, R. (2002). Cognitive and motor outcomes of cocaine-exposed infants. *Journal of the American Medical Association, 287,* 1952–1960.

Singer, M., & Ritchot, K. F. M. (1996). The role of working memory capacity and knowledge access in text inference processing. *Memory & Cognition, 24,* 733–743.

Singh, R., Onglato, M. L. U., Sriram, N., & Tay, A. B. G. (1997). The warm-cold variable in impression formation: Evidence for a positive-negative asymmetry. *British Journal of Social Psychology, 36,* 457–477.

Singh, R., & Teoh, J. B. P. (2000). Attitudes and attraction: A test of two hypotheses for the similarity-dissimilarity asymmetry. *British Journal of Social Psychology, 38,* 427–443.

Sinha, P. (2002). Recognizing complex patterns. *Nature Neuroscience, 5,* 1093-1097.

Sirevaag, A. M., Black, J. E., Shafron, D., & Greenough, W. T. (1988). Direct evidence that complex experience increases capillary branching and surface area in visual cortex of young rats. *Developmental Brain Research, 43,* 299–304.

Sivacek, J., & Crano, W. D. (1982). Vested interest as a moderator of attitude-behavior consistency. *Journal of Personality and Social Psychology, 43,* 210–221.

Skinner, B. F. (1937). Two types of conditioned reflex: A reply to Konorski and Miller. *Journal of General Psychology, 16,* 272–279.

Skinner, B. F. (1938). *Behavior of organisms.* New York: Appleton-Century-Crofts.

Skinner, B. F. (1948). "Superstition" in the pigeon. *Journal of Experimental Psychology, 38,* 168–172.

Skinner, B. F. (1953). *Science and human behavior.* New York: Macmillan.

Skinner, B. F. (1966). The ontogeny and phylogeny of behavior. *Science, 153,* 1203–1213.

Skinner, B. F. (1971). *Beyond freedom and dignity.* New York: Vantage.

Skinner, B. F. (1981). Selection by consequences. *Science, 213,* 501–504.

Skinner, B. F. (1984). An operant analysis of problem solving. *Behavioral and Brain Sciences, 7,* 583–613.

Skinner, B. F. (1986). The evolution of verbal behavior. *Journal of the Experimental Analysis of Behavior, 45,* 115–122.

Skinner, B. F. (1988, June). Skinner joins aversives debate. *American Psychological Association APA Monitor,* 22.

Skowronski, J. J., & Carlston, D. E. (1989). Negativity and extremity biases in impression formation. *Psychological Bulletin, 105,* 131–142.

Slaughter, V., & Repacholi, B. (2003). Individual differences in Theory of Mind: What are we investigating? In B. Repacholi & V. Slaughter (Eds.), *Individual differences in Theory of Mind: Implications for typical and atypical development.* New York: Psychology Press.

Sloane, R. B., Staples, F. R., Cristol, A. H., Yorkston, N. J., & Whipple, K. (1975). *Psychoanalysis versus behavior therapy.* Cambridge, MA: Harvard University Press.

Smith, C., & Lapp, L. (1991). Increased number of REMs following an intensive learning. *Sleep, 14,* 325–330.

Smith, G. P., & Gibbs, J. (1992). Role of CCK in satiety and appetite control. *Clinical Neuropharmacology,* 15 Suppl 1 Pt A, 476.

Smith, M. C., Coleman, S. P., & Gormezano, I. (1969). Classical conditioning of the rabbit's nictitating membrane response at backward, simultaneous, and forward CS-US intervals. *Journal of Comparative and Physiological Psychology, 69,* 226–231.

Smith, M. L., & Glass, G. V. (1977). Meta-analysis of psychotherapy outcome studies. *American Psychologist, 32,* 752–760.

Smith, M. L., Glass, G. V., & Miller, T. I. (1980). *Benefits of psychotherapy.* Baltimore: Johns Hopkins University Press.

Smulders, T. V., Sasson, A. D., & DeVoogd, T. J. (1995). Seasonal variation in hippocampal volume in a food-storing bird, the black-capped chickadee. *Journal of Neurobiology, 27,* 15–25.

Sneed, C. D., McCrae, R. R., & Funder, D. C. (1998). Lay conceptions of the five-factor model and its indicators. *Personality and Social Psychology Bulletin, 24,* 115–126.

Snow, C. E. (1977). Mothers' speech research: From input to interaction. In C. E. Snow & C. Ferguson (Eds.), *Talking to children: Language input and acquisition.* Cambridge: Cambridge University Press.

Snow, C. E. (1986). Conversations with children. In P. Fletcher & M. Garman (Eds.), *Language acquisition* (2nd ed.). Cambridge: Cambridge University Press.

Snow, C. E., Arlman-Rupp, A., Hassing, Y., Jobse, J., Joosten, J., & Vorster, J. (1976). Mothers' speech in three social classes. *Journal of Psycholinguistic Research, 5,* 1–20.

Snow, M. E., Jacklin, C. N., & Maccoby, E. E. (1983). Sex-of-child differences in father-child interaction at one year of age. *Child Development, 54,* 227–232.

Snow, W. G., & Weinstock, J. (1990). Sex differences among non-brain-damaged adults on the Wechsler Adult Intelligence Scales: A review of the literature. *Journal of Clinical and Experimental Neuropsychology, 12,* 873–886.

Snyder, L. (1999). This way up: Illusions and internal models in the vestibular system. *Nature Neuroscience, 2,* 396–398.

Snyder, M., Tanke, E. D., & Berscheid, E. (1977). Social perception and interpersonal behavior: On the self-fulfilling nature of social stereotypes. *Journal of Personality and Social Psychology, 35,* 656–666.

Snyder, S. H. (1974). *Madness and the brain.* New York: McGraw-Hill.

Soares, J. J., & Öhman, A. (1993). Backward masking and skin conductance responses after conditioning to nonfeared but fear-relevant stimuli in fearful subjects. *Psychophysiology, 30,* 460–466.

Sober, E. (1984). *The nature of selection: Evolutionary theory in philosophical focus.* Cambridge, MA: MIT Press.

Sobesky, W. E. (1983). The effects of situational factors on moral judgments. *Child Development, 54,* 575–584.

Solkoff, N., & Matuszak, D. (1975). Tactile stimulation and behavioral development among low-birthweight infants. *Child Psychiatry and Human Development, 6,* 33–37.

Solkoff, N., Yaffe, S., Weintraub, D., & Blase, B. (1969). Effects of handling on the subsequent development of premature infants. *Developmental Psychology, 4,* 765–768.

Solms, M. (May 2004). Freud returns. *Scientific American,* 82–88.

Solomon, A., & Haaga, D. A. F. (1995). Rational emotive behavior therapy research: What we know and what we need to know. *Journal of Rational-Emotive & Cognitive Behavior Therapy, 13(3),* 179–191.

Solomon, G. F. (1987). Psychoneuroimmunology: Interactions between central nervous system and immune system. *Journal of Neuroscience Research, 18,* 1–9.

Sowell, E. R., Thompson, P. M., Holmes, C. J., Jernigan, T. L., & Toga, A. W. (1999). *In vivo* evidence for post-adolescent brain maturation in frontal and striatal regions. *Nature Neuroscience, 2,* 859–861.

Spanos, N. P. (1991). A sociocognitive approach to hypnosis. In S. J. Lynn and J. W. Rhue (Eds.), *Theories of hypnosis: Current models and perspectives* (pp. 324–361). New York: Guilford Press.

Spanos, N. P. (1996). *Multiple identities & false memories: A sociocognitive perspective.* Washington, DC: American Psychological Association.

Spanos, N. P., & Chaves, J. F. (1991). History and historiography of hypnosis. In S. J. Lynn & J. W. Rhue (Eds.), *Theories of hypnosis: Current models and perspectives.* (pp. 43–78). New York: Guilford Press.

Spanos, N. P., Weekes, J. R., & Bertrand, L. D. (1985). Multiple personality: A social psychological perspective. *Journal of Abnormal Psychology, 94,* 362–376.

Spence, K. W. (1956). *Behavior theory and conditioning.* New Haven: Yale University Press.

Spear, N. E., & Riccio, D. C. (1994). *Memory: Phenomena and principles.* Boston: Allyn & Bacon.

Spearman, C. (1927). *The abilities of man.* London: Macmillan.

Spears, R., & Haslam, S. A. (1997). Stereotyping and the burden of cognitive load. In R. Spears (Ed.), *The social psychology of stereotyping and group life.* Oxford, UK: Blackwell Publishers, Inc.

Sperling, G. A. (1960). The information available in brief visual presentation. *Psychological Monographs, 74 (no. 498).*

Sperry, R. W. (1966). Brain bisection and consciousness. In J. Eccles (Ed.), *Brain and conscious experience.* New York: Springer-Verlag.

Spiegel, D., Bloom, J. R., Kraemer, H. C., & Gottheil, E. (1989). Effect of psychosocial treatment on survival of patients with metastatic breast cancer. *Lancet, 2,* 888–891.

Spiegel, D., Bloom, J., & Yalom, I. D. (1981). Group support for patients with metastatic breast cancer. *Archives of General Psychiatry, 38,* 527–533.

Spirduso, W. W., & MacRae, P. G. (1990). Motor performance and aging. In J. E. Birren & K. W. Schaie (Eds.), *Handbook of the psychology of aging* (3rd ed.). San Diego: Academic Press.

Squire, L. R. (1987). *Memory and brain.* New York: Oxford.

Squire, L.R. (1992). Memory and the hippocampus: A synthesis from findings with rats, monkeys, and humans. *Psychological Review, 99,* 195–231.

Staddon, J. E. R., & Hinson, J. M. (1983). Optimization: A result or a mechanism. *Science, 221,* 976–977.

Staddon, J. E. R., & Simmelhag, V. L. (1981). The "superstition" experiment: A reexamination of its implications for principle of adaptive behavior. *Psychological Review, 78,* 3–43.

Stager, C. L., & Werker, J. F. (1997). Infants listen for more phonetic detail in speech perception than in word-learning tasks. *Nature, 388,* 381–382.

Standing, L. (1973). Learning 10,000 pictures. *Quarterly Journal of Experimental Psychology, 25,* 207–222.

Starzyk, K. B., & Quinsey, V. L. (2001). The relationship between testosterone and aggression: A meta-analysis. *Aggression and Violent Behavior, 16,* 579–599.

Stasser, G. (1991). Pooling of unshared information during group discussion. In S. Worchel, W. Wood, & J. Simpson (Eds.), *Group process and productivity.* Beverly Hills, CA: Sage.

Steele, C. M., & Josephs, R. A. (1990). Alcohol myopia: Its prized and dangerous effects. *American Psychologist, 45,* 921–933.

Steen, S. N., Oppliger, R. A., & Brownell, K. D. (1988). Metabolic effects of repeated weight loss and regain in adolescent wrestlers. *Journal of the American Medical Association, 260,* 47–50.

Steenland, K. (1999). Risk assessment for heart disease and workplace ETS exposure among non-smokers. *Environmental Health Perspectives, 107(6),* 859–863.

Steenland, K., Thun, M., Lally, C., & Heath, C., Jr. (1997). Environmental tobacco smoke and coronary heart disease in the American Cancer Society CPS-II cohort. *Circulation, 94,* 622–628.

Steiger, H., Lehoux, P. M., & Gauvin, L. (1999). Impulsivity, dietary control and the urge to binge in bulimic syndromes. *Eating Disorders, 26,* 261–274.

Stein, L. I., & Santos, A. B. (1998). *Assertive community treatment of persons with severe mental illness.* New York: W. W. Norton & Co., Inc.

Stein, M. B., Millar, T. W., Larsen, D. K., & Kryger, M. H. (1995). Irregular breathing during sleep in patients with panic disorder. *American Journal of Psychiatry, 152,* 1168–1173.

Steinhauer, K., Alter, K., & Friederici, A. D. (1999). Brain potentials indicate immediate use of prosidic cues in natural speech processing. *Nature Neuroscience, 2,* 191–196.

Steinhausen, H., & Spohr, H. (1998). Long-term outcome of children with fetal alcohol syndrome: Psychopathology, behavior, and intelligence. *Alcoholism, Clinical and Experimental Research, 22,* 334–338.

Sterman, M. B., & Clemente, C. D. (1962a). Forebrain inhibitory mechanisms: Cortical synchronization induced by basal forebrain stimulation. *Experimental Neurology, 6,* 91–102.

Sterman, M. B., & Clemente, C. D. (1962b). Forebrain inhibitory mechanisms: Sleep patterns induced by basal forebrain stimulation in the behaving cat. *Experimental Neurology, 6,* 103–117.

Stern, K., & McClintock, M. K. (1998). Regulation of ovulation by human pheromones. *Nature, 392,* 177–179.

Stern, M., & Karraker, K. H. (1989). Sex stereotyping of infants: A review of gender labeling studies. *Sex Roles, 20,* 501–522.

Stern, W. (1914). *The psychological methods of testing intelligence.* Baltimore: Warwick and York.

Sternberg, R. J. (1988a). *The triarchic mind: A new theory of human intelligence.* New York, NY: Viking.

Sternberg, R. J. (1988b). Triangulating love. In R. J. Sternberg & M. L. Barnes (Eds.), *The psychology of love.* New Haven, CT: Yale University Press.

Sternberg, R. J. (1995). For whom the bell curve tolls: A review of *The bell curve. Psychological Science, 6,* 257–261.

Sternberg, R. J. (1996). *Successful intelligence.* New York, NY: Simon Schuster.

Sternberg, R. J. (1997). The triarchic theory of intelligence. In D. P. Fanagan, J. L. Genshaft, P. L. Harrison, et al. (Eds.), *Contemporary intellectual assessment: Theories, tests, and issues* (pp. 92–104). New York: Guilford Press.

Sternberg, R. J. (1999). A theory of successful intelligence. *Review of General Psychology, 3,* 292–316.

Sternberg, R. J. (2002). Beyond g: The theory of successful intelligence. In R. J. Sternberg & E. L. Grigorenko (Eds.), *The general factor of intelligence: How general is it?* Mahwah, NJ: Lawrence Erlbaum Associates.

Sternberg, R. J. (2003a). Construct validity of the theory of special intelligence. In R. J. Sternberg & J. Lautrey (Eds.), *Models of intelligence: International perspectives.* Washington, DC: American Psychological Association.

Sternberg, R. J. (2003b). *Wisdom, intelligence, and creativity synthesized.* New York: Cambridge University Press.

Sternberg, R. J., Conway, B. E., Ketron, J. L., & Bernstein, M. (1981). People's conceptions of intelligence. *Journal of Personality and Social Psychology, 41,* 37–55.

Sternberg, R. J., & Grigorenko, E. L. (1999). Myths in psychology and education regarding the gene-environment debate. *Teachers College Record, 100,* 536–553.

Sternberg, R. J., & Grigorenko, E. L. (2001). Ability testing across cultures. In L. A. Suzuki & J. G. Ponterotto (Eds.), *Handbook of multicultural assessment: Clinical, psychological, and educational applications* (2nd ed.). San Francisco: Jossey-Bass.

Sternberg, R. J., & Kaufman, J. C. (1998). Human abilities. *Annual Review of Psychology, 49,* 479–502.

Sternberg, R. J., & Lubart, T. I. (1996). Investing in creativity. *American Psychologist, 51,* 677–688.

Sternberger, L. G., & Burns, G. L. (1990). Obsessions and compulsions: Psychometric properties of the Padua inventory with an American college population. *Behavior Research and Therapy, 28,* 341–345.

Stevens, J. R. (1988). Schizophrenia and multiple sclerosis. *Schizophrenia Bulletin, 14,* 231–241.

Stevens, S. S. (1975). *Psychophysics: Introduction to its perceptual, neural, and social prospects.* New York: Wiley.

Stewart, J. (2004). Pathways to relapse: Factors controlling the reinitiation of drug seeking after abstinence. In R. A. Bevins & M. T. Bardo, (Eds.), *Motivational factors in the etiology of drug abuse* (Vol. 50, pp. 197–234). Nebraska Symposium on Motivation. Lincoln, NE: University of Nebraska Press.

Stewart, S. H., Mitchell, T. L., Wright, K. D., & Loba, P. (2004). The relations of PTSD symptoms to alcohol use and coping drinking in volunteers who responded to the Swissair Flight 111 airline disaster. *Journal of Anxiety Disorders, 18(1),* 51–68.

Stich, S. P. (1990). Rationality. In D. N. Osherson & E. E. Smith (Eds.), *An invitation to cognitive science. Vol. 3: Thinking.* Cambridge, MA: MIT Press.

Stine, E. L., & Bohannon, J. N. (1983). Imitations, interactions, and language acquisition. *Journal of Child Language, 10,* 589–603.

Stokoe, W. C. (1983). Apes who sign and critics who don't. In J. de Luce & H. T. Wilder (Eds.), *Language in primates: Perspectives and implications.* New York: Springer-Verlag.

Stone, A. A., Marco, C. A., Cruise, C. E., Cox, D. S., & Neale, J. M. (1996). Are stress-induced immunological changes mediated by mood? A closer look at how both desirable and undesirable daily events influence sIgA antibody. *International Journal of Behavioral Medicine, 3,* 1–13.

Stone, A. A., Reed, B. R., & Neale, J. M. (1987). Changes in daily event frequency precede episodes of physical symptoms. *Journal of Human Stress, 13,* 70–74.

Strachan, T., & Read, A. P. (1999). *Human molecular genetics.* New York: Wiley.

Strait, D. S., Grine, F. E., & Moniz, M. A. (1997). A reappraisal of early hominid phylogeny. *Journal of Human Evolution, 32,* 17–82.

Streissguth, A. P. (2001). Recent advances in fetal alcohol syndrome and alcohol use in pregnancy. In D. P. Agarwal & H. K. Seitz (Eds.), *Alcohol in health and disease.* New York: Marcel Dekker, Inc.

Strupp, H. H., & Hadley, S. W. (1979). Specific vs. nonspecific factors in psychotherapy. *Archives of General Psychiatry, 36,* 1125–1136.

Stuart, T. D., & Garrison, M. E. B. (2002). The influence of daily hassles and role balance on health status: A study of mothers of grade school children. *Women & Health, 36(3),* 1–10.

Sturgis, E. T. (1993). Obsessive-compulsive disorders. In P. B. Sutker & H. E. Adams (Eds.), *Comprehensive handbook of psychopathology* (2nd ed.). New York: Plenum Press.

Substance Abuse and Mental Health Services Administration. (2005). *Results from the 2004 National Survey on Drug Use and Health: National findings.* (Office of Applied Studies, NSDUH Series H-28, DHHS Publication No. SMA 05-4062). Rockville, Maryland.

Suddath, R. L., Christison, G. W., Torrey, E. F., Casanova, M. F., & Weinberger, D. R. (1990). Anatomical abnormalities in the brains of monozygotic twins discordant for schizophrenia. *New England Journal of Medicine, 322,* 789–794.

Sullivan, E. V., Lim, K. O., Mathalon, D., Marsh, L., Beal, D. M., Harris, D., Hoff, A. L., Faustman, W. O., & Pfefferbaum, A. (1998). A profile of cortical gray matter volume deficits characteristic of schizophrenia. *Cerebral Cortex, 8,* 117–124.

Sullivan, M. W., & Lewis, M. (2003). Contextual determinants of anger and other negative expressions in young infants. *Developmental Psychology, 39,* 693–705.

Sullivan, R. M., Taborsky-Barba, S., Mendoza, R., Itano, A., Leon, M., Cotman, C. W., Payne, T. F., & Lott, I. (1991). Olfactory classical conditioning in neonates. *Pediatrics, 87,* 511–518.

Sun, H., & Frost, B. J. (1998). Computation of different optical variables of looming objects in pigeon nucleus rotundus neurons. *Nature Neuroscience, 1,* 296–303.

Sun, J., & Perona, P. (1998). Where is the sun? *Nature Neuroscience, 1,* 183–184.

Suzuki, D. T., Griffiths, A. J. F., Miller, J. H., & Lewontin, R. C. (1989). *An introduction to genetic analysis* (4th ed.). New York: Freeman.

Suzuki, K., Takei, N., Iwata, Y., Sekine, Y., Toyoda, T., Nakamura, K., Minabe, Y., et al. (2004). Do olfactory reference syndrome and Jiko-shu-kyofu (a subtype of Taijin-kyofu) share a common entity? *Acta Psychiatrica Scandinavica, 109(2),* 150–155.

Swaab, D. F., & Hofman, M. A. (1990). An enlarged suprachiasmatic nucleus in homosexual men. *Brain Research, 537,* 141–148.

Swanson, L. W. (1982). The projections of the ventral tegmental area and adjacent regions: a combined fluorescent retrograde tracer and immunofluorescence study in the rat. *Brain Research Bulletin, 9,* 321–353.

Sweet, W. H. (1986). Participant in "Brain Stimulation in Behaving Subjects." *Neurosciences Research Program Workshop,* December.

Swedo, S. S., Rapaport, J. L., & Cheslow, D. L. (1989). High prevalence of obsessive-compulsive symptoms in patients with Sydenham's chorea. *American Journal of Psychiatry, 146,* 246–249.

Szasz, T. S. (1960). The myth of mental illness. *American Psychologist, 15,* 113–118.

Szasz, T. (2002). Parity for mental illness, disparity for mental patients. *Ideas on Liberty, 52,* 33–34.

Szymusiak, R., & McGinty, D. (1986). Sleep-related neuronal discharge in the basal forebrain of cats. *Brain Research, 370,* 82–92.

Takei, N., Mortensen, P. B., Klaening, U., Murray, R. M., Sham, P. C., O'Callaghan, E., & Munk, J. P. (1996). Relationship between in utero exposure to influenza epidemics and risk of schizophrenia in Denmark. *Biological Psychiatry, 40,* 817–824.

Tanenhaus, M. K. (1988). *Psycholinguistics: An overview.* Cambridge: Cambridge University Press.

Tang, Y.-P., Shimizu, E., Dube, G. R., Rampon, C., Kerchner, G. A., Zhuo, M., Lium G., & Tsien, J. Z. (1999). Genetic enhancement of learning and memory in mice. *Nature, 401,* 63–69.

Taras, H. L., Sallis, J. F., Patterson, T. L., Nader, P. R., & Nelson, J. A. (1989). Television's influence on children's diet and physical activity. *Journal of Developmental and Behavioral Pediatrics, 10,* 176–180.

Tarsy, D., Baldessarini, R. J., & Tarazi, F. I. (2002). Effects of newer antipsychotics on extrapyramidal function. *CNS Drugs, 16(1),* 23–45.

Tattersall, I. (1997, April) Out of Africa again . . . and again? *Scientific American, 276,* 60–67.

Tattersall, I. (2000, January). Once we were not alone. *Scientific American, 282,* 56–62.

Taube, S. L., Kirstein, L. S., Sweeney, D. R., Heninger, G. R., & Maas, J. W. (1978). Urinary 3-methoxy-4-hydroxyphenyleneglycol and psychiatric diagnosis. *American Journal of Psychiatry, 135,* 78–82.

Tavris, C., & Sadd, S. (1977). *The Redbook report on female sexuality.* New York: Delacorte Press.

Taylor, T. L., & Klein, R. M. (1998). Inhibition of return to color: A replication and nonextension of Law, Pratt, and Abrams (1995). *Perception and Psychophysics, 60,* 1452–1456.

Tehan, G., Hendry, L., & Kocinski, D. (2001). Word length and phonological similarity effects in simple, complex, and delayed serial recall tasks: Implications for working memory. *Memory, 9,* 333–348.

Temoshok, L. (1987). Personality, coping style, emotion and cancer: Towards an integrative model. *Cancer Surveys, 6,* 545–567.

Temoshok, L., Heller, B. W., Sagebiel, R. W., Blois, M. S., Sweet, D. M., DiClemente, R. J., & Gold, M. L. (1985). The relationship of psychosocial factors to prognostic indicators in cutaneous malignant melanoma. *Journal of Psychosomatic Research, 29,* 139–153.

Terrace, H. S., Petitto, L. A., Sanders, R. J., & Bever, T. G. (1979). Can an ape create a sentence? *Science, 206,* 891–902.

Terry, R. D., & Davies, P. (1980). Dementia of the Alzheimer type. *Annual Review of Neuroscience, 3,* 77–96.

Test, M. A., & Stein, L. I. (2000). Practical guidelines for the community treatment of markedly impaired patients. *Community Mental Health Journal, 36,* 47–60.

Thelen, E., & Corbetta, D. (2002). Microdevelopment and dynamic systems: Applications to infant motor development. In N. Granott & J. Parziale (Eds.), *Microdevelopment: Transition processes in development and learning.* Cambridge studies in cognitive perceptual development. New York: Cambridge University Press.

Thibadeau, R., Just, M. A., & Carpenter, P. A. (1982). A model of the time course and content of reading. *Cognitive Science, 6,* 157–203.

Thomas, D. R., & Thomas, D. H. (1974). Stimulus labeling, adaptation level, and the central tendency shift. *Journal of Experimental Psychology, 103,* 896–899.

Thomas, R. M. (1996). *Comparing theories of child development* (4th Ed.). Pacific Grove, CA: Brooks/Cole.

Thompson, M. S., Judd, C. M., & Park, B. (2000). The consequences of communicating social stereotypes. *Journal of Experimental Social Psychology, 36,* 567–599.

Thompson, S. C., Kent, D. R., Thomas, C., & Vrungos, S. (1999). Real and illusory control over exposure to HIV in college students and gay men. *Journal of Applied Social Psychology, 29,* 1128–1150.

Thorndike, E. L. (1898). Animal intelligence: An experimental study of the associative processes in animals. *Psychological Review Monograph Supplement, 2,* (Whole No. 8).

Thorndike, E. L. (1903). *Elements of psychology.* New York: A. G. Seiler.

Thorndike, E. L. (1905). *The elements of psychology.* New York: Seiler.

Thorpe, G. L., & Olson, S. L. (1990). *Behavior therapy: Concepts, procedures, and applications.* Boston: Allyn & Bacon.

Thurstone, L. L. (1938). *Primary mental abilities.* Chicago: University of Chicago Press.

Timberlake, W., & Allison, J. (1974). Response deprivation: An empirical approach to instrumental performance. *Psychological Review, 81,* 146–164.

Timberlake, W., & Lucas, G. A. (1985). The basis of superstitious behavior: Chance contingency, stimulus substitution, or appetitive behavior? *Journal of the Experimental Analysis of Behavior, 44,* 279–299.

Tobin, S. A. (1991). A comparison of psychoanalytic self-psychology and Carl Rogers's person-centered therapy. *Journal of Humanistic Psychology, 31,* 9–33.

Tolman, E. C., & Honzik, C. H. (1930). Introduction and removal of reward, and maze performance in rats. *University of California Publications in Psychology, 4,* 257–275.

Tomasello, M., & Farrar, J. (1986). Joint attention and early language. *Child Development, 57,* 1454–1463.

Tooby, J., & Cosmides, L. (1989). Evolutionary psychology and the generation of culture, Part I: Theoretical considerations. *Ethology and Sociobiology, 10,* 39–49.

Tooby, J., & Cosmides, L. (1990). On the universality of human nature and the uniqueness of the individual: The role of genetics and adaptation. *Journal of Personality, 58,* 17–67.

Tootell, R. B., Reppas, J. B., Dale, A. M., & Look, R. B. (1995). Visual motion after-effect in human cortical area MT revealed by functional magnetic resonance imaging. *Nature, 375,* 139–141.

Tordoff, M. G., & Friedman, M. I. (1988). Hepatic control of feeding: Effect of glucose, fructose, and mannitol infusion. *American Journal of Physiology, 254,* 969–976.

Torgerson, S. (1983). Genetic factors in anxiety disorders. *Archives of General Psychiatry, 40,* 1085–1089.

Torrey, E., Fuller, E., Miller, J., Rawlings, R., & Yolken, R. H. (1997). Seasonality of births in schizophrenia and bipolar disorder: A review of the literature. *Schizophrenia Research, 28,* 1–38.

Torrey, E. F., Torrey, B. B., & Peterson, M. R. (1977). Seasonality of schizophrenic births in the United States. *Archives of General Psychiatry, 34,* 1065–1070.

Tosteson, A. N., Weinstein, M. C., Hunink, M. G., Mittleman, M. A., Williams, L. W., Goldman, P. A., & Goldman, L. (1997). Cost-effectiveness of population-wide educational approaches to reduce serum cholesterol levels. *Circulation, 95,* 24–30.

Träskmann, L., Åsberg, M., Bertilsson, L., & Sjöstrand, L. (1981). Monoamine metabolites on CSF and suicidal behavior. *Archives of General Psychiatry, 38,* 631–636.

Travis, L. A., Bliwise, N. G., Binder, J. L., & Horne-Moyer, H. L. (2001). Changes in clients' attachment styles over the course of time-limited dynamic psychotherapy. *Psychotherapy: Theory, Research, Practice, Training, 38(2),* 149–159.

Trehub, S. E., & Thorpe, L. A. (1989). Infants' perception of rhythm: Categorization of auditory sequences by temporal structure. *Canadian Journal of Psychology, 43,* 217–229.

Treisman, A. M. (1960). Contextual cues in selective listening. *Quarterly Journal of Experimental Psychology, 12,* 242–248.

Tremblay, S., Shiller, D. M., & Ostry, D. J. (2003). Somatosensory basis of speech production. *Nature, 423,* 866–869.

Triplett, N. (1897). The dynamogenic factors in pacemaking and competition. *American Journal of Psychology, 9,* 507–533.

Trivers, R. L. (1971). The biology of reciprocal altruism. *Quarterly Review of Biology, 46,* 35–57.

Trivers, R. L. (1972). Parental investment and sexual selection. In B. Campbell (Ed.), *Sexual selection and the descent of man.* Chicago: Aldine.

Tronick, E., Als, H., Adamson, L., Wise, S., & Brazelton, T. B. (1978). The infant's response to entrapment between contradictory messages in face-to-face interaction. *Journal of the American Academy of Child Psychiatry, 17,* 1–13.

Truax, C. B. (1966). Reinforcement and nonreinforcement in Rogerian psychotherapy. *Journal of Abnormal Psychology, 71,* 1–9.

Trussell, L. O. (2002). Transmission at the hair cell synapse. *Nature Neuroscience, 5,* 85–86.

Tryon, R. C. (1940). Genetic differences in maze-learning ability in rats. *Yearbook of the National Society for the Study of Education, 39,* 111–119.

Tulving, E. (1972). Episodic and semantic memory. In E. Tulving & W. Donaldson (Eds.), *Organization of memory.* New York: Academic Press.

Tulving, E. (2002). Episodic memory: From mind to brain. *Annual Review of Psychology, 53,* 1–25.

Tulving, E., & Schacter, D. L. (1990). Priming and human memory systems. *Science, 247,* 301–306.

Tupes, E. C., & Christal, R. E. (1961). Recurrent personality factors based on trait ratings. *USAF ASD Technical Report,* 61–97.

Turkington, D., Dudley, R., Warman, D. M., & Beck, A. T. (2004). Cognitive-behavioral therapy for schizophrenia: A review. *Journal of Psychiatric Practice, 10(1),* 5–16.

Turner, A. M., & Greenough, W. T. (1985). Differential rearing effects on rat visual cortex synapses. I. Synaptic and neuronal density and synapses per neuron. *Brain Research, 329,* 195–203.

Turner, S. M., Beidel, D. C., Stanley, M. A., & Heiser, N. (2001). Obsessive-compulsive disorder. In P. B. Sutker & H. E. Adams (Eds.), *Comprehensive handbook of psychopathology* (3rd ed.). New York: Kluwer Academic/Plenum Publishers.

Tversky, A., & Kahneman, D. (1974). Judgment under uncertainty: Heuristics and biases. *Science, 185,* 1124–1131.

Tversky, A., & Kahneman, D. (1982). Judgment under uncertainty: Heuristics and biases. In D. Kahneman, P. Slovic, & A. Tversky (Eds.), *Judgment under uncertainty.* New York: Cambridge University Press.

Tyrell, J. B., & Baxter, J. D. (1981). Glucocorticoid therapy. In P. Felig, J. D. Baxter, A. E. Broadus, & L. A. Frohman (Eds.), *Endocrinology and metabolism.* New York: McGraw-Hill.

Ullman, L. P., & Krasner, L. (1969). *Psychological approach to abnormal behavior.* Englewood Cliffs, NJ: Prentice-Hall.

Ungerleider, L. G., & Mishkin, M. (1982). Two cortical visual systems. In D. J. Ingle, M. A. Goodale, & R. J. W. Mansfield (Eds.), *Analysis of visual behavior.* Cambridge, MA: MIT Press.

United States Department of Labor. Bureau of Labor Statistics. (2005). *November 2004 national occupation and wage estimates.* Retrieved November, 2005. http://www.bls.gov/oes/oes_data.htm

United States Department of Labor (2005). *Employment characteristics of families summary.* Released June 9, 2005. Available at http://www.bls.gov/news.release/famee.nr0.htm. Downloaded 26 July 2005.

Uno, H., Tarara, R., Else, J. G., Suleman, M. A., & Sapolsky, R. M. (1989). Hippocampal damage associated with prolonged and fatal stress in primates. *The Journal of Neuroscience, 9,* 1705–1711.

Uyeda, L., Tyler, I., Pinzon, J., & Birmingham, C. L. (2002). Identification of patients with eating disorders: The signs and symptoms of anorexia nervosa and bulimia nervosa. *Eating & Weight Disorders, 7,* 116–123.

Vaillant, G. E. (2002). The study of adult development. In E. Phelps, F. F. Furstenberg, Jr., et al. (Eds.), *Looking at lives: American longitudinal studies of the twentieth century.* New York: Russell Sage Foundation.

Vaillant, G. E., & Milofsky, E. S. (1982). The etiology of alcoholism. *American Psychologist, 37,* 494–503.

Valenstein, E. S. (1986). *Great and desperate cures: The rise and decline of psychosurgery and other radical treatments for mental illness.* New York: Basic Books.

Vallerand, R. J., & Ratelle, C. F. (2002). Intrinsic and extrinsic motivation: A hierarchical model. In E. L. Deci & R. M. Ryan (Eds.), *Handbook of self-determination research.* Rochester, NY: University of Rochester Press.

Vallerand, R. J., & Reid, G. (1984). On the causal effects of perceived competence on intrinsic motivation: A test of cognitive evaluation theory. *Journal of Sport Psychology, 6,* 94–102.

Van Goozen, S. H., Wiegant, V. M., Endert, E., Helmond, F. A., & Van de Poll, N. E. (1997). Psychoendocrinological assessment of the menstrual cycle: the relationship between hormones, sexuality, and mood. *Archives of Sexual Behavior, 26,* 359–382.

Vecera, S. P., & Farah, M. J. (1994). Does visual attention select objects or locations? *Journal of Experimental Psychology, 123,* 146–160.

Vernon, P. A., Jang, K. L., Harris, J. A., & McCarthy, J. M. (1997). Environmental predictors of personality differences: A twin and sibling study. *Journal of Personality and Social Psychology, 72,* 177–183.

Vernon, P. E. (1979). *Intelligence: Heredity and environment.* San Francisco: W. H. Freeman.

Vitaliano, P. P., Zhang, J. P., & Scanlan, J. M. (2003). Is caregiving hazardous to one's physical health? A meta-analysis. *Psychological Bulletin, 129(6),* 946–972.

Vogel, G. W., Vogel, F., McAbee, R. S., & Thurmond, A. G. (1980). Improvement of depression by REM sleep deprivation. *Archives of General Psychiatry, 37,* 247–253.

Vollrath, M. (2000). Personality and hassles among university students: A three-year longitudinal study. *European Journal of Personality, 14,* 199–215.

Vom Saal, W., & Jenkins, H. H. (1970). Blocking the development of stimulus control. *Learning & Motivation, 1,* 52–64.

Voyat, G. (1998). In tribute to Piaget: A look at his scientific impact in the United States. In R. W. Reiber & K. Salzinger (Eds.), *Psychology: Theoretical-historical perspectives* (2nd ed.). Washington, DC: American Psychological Association.

Vroomen, J., Bertelson, P., & de Gelder, B. (2001). The ventriloquist effect does not depend on the direction of automatic visual attention. *Perception & Psychophysics, 63,* 651–659.

Vygotsky, L. S. (1934/1987). Thinking and speech. In R. W. Rieber & A. S. Carton (Eds.), *The collected works of L. S. Vygotsky: Vol. 1. Problems of general psychology* (N. Minick, Trans.). New York: Plenum.

Wade, C., & Tavris, C. (1994). The longest war: Gender and culture. In W. J. Lonner & R. Malpass (Eds.), *Psychology and culture.* Boston: Allyn & Bacon.

Wagner, R. K., & Sternberg, R. J. (1983). Executive control of reading. Cited by Sternberg, R. J. (1985). *Beyond IQ: A triarchic theory of human intelligence.* Cambridge: Cambridge University Press.

Wahlsten, D. (1997). The malleability of intelligence is not constrained by heritability. In B. Devlin, S. E. Fienberg, D. P. Resnick, & K. Roeder (Eds.), *Intelligence, genes, and success.* New York: Copernicus.

Wahlsten, D. (1999). Single gene influences on brain and behavior. *Annual Review of Psychology, 50,* 599–624.

Wakelin, A., & Long, K. M. (2003). Effects of victim gender and sexuality on attributions of blame to rape victims. *Sex Roles, 49,* 477–487.

Walker, E., & Lewine, R. J. (1990). Prediction of adult-onset schizophrenia from childhood home movies of the patients. *American Journal of Psychiatry, 147,* 1052–1056.

Walker, L., de Vries, B., & Trevethan, S. D. (1994). Moral stages and moral orientations in real-life and hypothetical dilemmas. In B. Puka (Ed.), *Caring voices and women's moral frames: Gilligan's view.* New York: Garland Publishing, Inc.

Walker, L. J. (1989). A longitudinal study of moral reasoning. *Child Development, 60,* 157–166.

Wallace, S. T., & Alden, L. E. (1997). Social phobia and positive social events: The price of success. *Journal of Abnormal Psychology, 106,* 416–424.

Wallace, W. T. (1994). Memory for music: Effect of melody on recall of text. *Journal of Experimental Psychology: Learning, Memory, and Cognition, 20,* 1471–1485.

Wallston, K. A., Wallston, B. S., & DeVellis, R. (1978). Development of multidimensional health locus of control (MHLC) scales. *Health Education Monographs, 6,* 160–170.

Walster, E., Aronson, V., Abrahams, D., & Rottman, L. (1966). Importance of physical attractiveness in dating behavior. *Journal of Personality and Social Psychology, 4,* 508–516.

Walster, E., & Berscheid, E. (1971, June). Adrenaline makes the heart grow fonder. *Psychology Today,* pp. 47–62.

Wampold, B. E., Minami, T., Baskin, T. W., & Callen, S. (2002). A meta-(re)analysis of the effects of cognitive therapy versus "other therapies" for depression. *Journal of Affective Disorders, 69(2–3),* 159–165.

Wampold, B. E., Mondin, G. W., Moody, M., Stich, F., Benson, K., & Ahn, H. (1997). A meta-analysis of outcome studies comparing bonafide psychothempies: Empirically, "all must have prizes." *Psychological Bulletin, 122,* 203–215.

Ward, I. (1972). Prenatal stress feminizes and demasculinizes the behavior of males. *Science, 175,* 82–84.

Washburn, M. F. (1922). Introspection as an objective method. *Psychological Review, 29,* 89–112.

Wason, P. (1968). Reasoning about a rule. *Quarterly Journal of Experimental Psychology, 20,* 273–281.

Wason, P. C., & Johnson-Laird, P. N. (1972). *Psychology of reasoning: Structure and content.* Cambridge, MA: Harvard University Press.

Waters, E., Merrick, S., Treboux, D., Crowell, J., & Albersheim, L. (2000). Attachment security in infancy and early adulthood: A twenty-year longitudinal study. *Child Development, 71,* 684–689.

Watkins, C. E., Campbell, V. L., Nieberding, R., & Hallmark, R. (1995). Contemporary practice of psychological assessment by clinical psychologists. *Professional Psychological Research and Practice, 26,* 54–60.

Watkins, C. E., Jr. (2000). Some final thoughts about using tests and assessment procedures in counseling. In C. E. Watkins, Jr. & V. L. Campbell (Eds.), *Testing and assessment in counseling practice* (2nd ed.). Contemporary topics in vocational psychology. Mahwah, NJ: Lawrence Erlbaum Associates.

Watson, J. B. (1930). *Behaviorism* (rev. ed.). New York: W. W. Norton.

Watson, J. D. (1968). *The double helix: A personal account of the discovery of the structure of DNA.* New York: Atheneum.

Watson, J. S., & Ramey, C. T. (1972). Reactions to responsive contingent stimulation in early infancy. *Merrill-Palmer Quarterly, 18,* 219–227.

Watt, A., & Honey, R. C. (1997). Combining CSs associated with the same or different USs. *Quarterly Journal of Experimental Psychology, 50B,* 350–367.

Webster, D. M., Richter, L., & Kruglanski, A. W. (1996). On leaping to conclusions when feeling tired: Mental fatigue effects on impressional primacy. *Journal of Experimental Social Psychology, 32,* 181–195.

Wedenoja, W. (1995). Social and cultural psychiatry of Jamaicans, at home and abroad. In I. Al-Issa (Ed.), *Handbook of culture and mental illness: An international perspective.* Madison, CT: International Universities Press.

Wegner, D. M. (2002). *The illusion of conscious will.* Cambridge, MA: MIT Press.

Wegner, D. M. (2003). The mind's best trick: How we experience conscious will. *Trends in Cognitive Sciences, 7,* 65–69.

Weidner, G., Sexton, G., McLellarn, R., Connor, S. L., & Matarazzo, J. D. (1987). The role of type A behavior and hostility in an elevation of plasma lipids in adult women and men. *Psychosomatic Medicine, 49,* 136–145.

Weigel, R. H., Vernon, D. T. A., & Tognacci, L. N. (1974). Specificity of the attitude as a determinant of attitude-behavior congruence. *Journal of Personality and Social Psychology, 30,* 724–728.

Weinberg, R. A., Scarr, S., & Waltdman, I. D. (1992). The Minnesota Transracial Adoption Study: A follow-up of IQ test performance at adolescence. *Intelligence, 16,* 117–135.

Weinstein, C. S., Fucetola, R., & Mollica, R. (2001). Neuropsychological issues in the assessment of refugees and victims of mass violence. *Neuropsychology Review, 11(3),* 131–141.

Weir, W. (1984). Another look at subliminal "facts." *Advertising Age, 55,* 46.

Weisner, T. S., & Wilson-Mitchell, J. E. (1990). Nonconventional family lifestyles and sex typing in six-year-olds. *Child Development, 61,* 1915–1933.

Weissman, M. M., Markowitz, J. C., & Klerman, G. L. (2000). *Comprehensive guide to interpersonal psychotherapy.* New York: Basic Books.

Weissman, M. M., Warner, V., Wickramaratne, P. J., & Kandel, D. B. (1999). Maternal smoking during pregnancy and psychopathology in offspring followed to adulthood. *Journal of the American Academy of Child and Adolescent Psychiatry, 38,* 892–899.

Weltzin, T. E., Hsu, L. K. G., Pollice, C., & Kaye, W. H. (1991). Feeding patterns in bulimia nervosa. *Biological Psychiatry, 30,* 1093–1110.

Wen, J. Y. M., Kumar, N., Morrison, G., Rambaldini, G., Runciman, S., Rousseau, J., & van der Kooy, D. (1997). Mutations that prevent associative learning in *C. elegans. Behavioral Neuroscience, 111,* 354–368.

Werker, J. F., Pegg, J. E., & McLeod, P. J. (1994). A cross-language investigation of infant preference for infant-directed communication. *Infant Behavior and Development, 17,* 323–333.

Werker, J. F., & Tees, R. C. (1999). Influences on infant speech processing: Toward a new synthesis. *Annual Review of Psychology, 50,* 509–535.

West-Eberhard, M. J. (2005). The maintenance of sex as a developmental trap due to sexual selection. *Quarterly Review of Biology, 80,* 47–53.

Westen, D. (1998). The scientific legacy of Sigmund Freud: Toward a psychodynamically informed psychological science. *Psychological Bulletin, 124,* 333–371.

Wheeler, L., & Kim, Y. (1997). What is beautiful is culturally good: The physical attractiveness stereotype has different content in collectivist cultures. *Personality and Social Psychology Bulletin, 23,* 795–800.

Whishaw, I. Q. (2000). Loss of the innate cortical engram for action patterns used in skilled reaching and the development of behavioral compensation following motor cortex lesions in the rat. *Neuropharmacology, 39,* 788–805.

Whishaw, I. Q., & Wallace, D. G. (2003). On the origins of autobiographical memory. *Behavioural Brain Research, 138,* 113–119.

White, A., Horner, V., & de Waal, F. B. (2005). Conformity to cultural norms of tool use in chimpanzees. *Nature, 437,* 737–740.

White, G. L. (1980). Physical attractiveness and courtship progress. *Journal of Personality and Social Psychology, 39,* 660–668.

White, L., & Edwards, J. N. (1990). Emptying the nest and parental well-being: An analysis of national panel data. *American Sociological Review, 55,* 235–242.

Whitehead, R. G., Rowland, M. G. M., Hutton, M., Prentice, A. M., Müller, E., & Paul, A. (1978). Factors influencing lactation performance in rural Gambian mothers. *Lancet, 2,* 178–181.

Whorf, B. L. (1956). Science and linguistics. In J. B. Carroll (Ed.), *Language, thought and reality: Selected writings of Benjamin Lee Whorf.* Cambridge, MA: MIT Press.

Widiger, T. A., & Sankis, L. M. (2000). Adult psychopathology: Issues and controversies. *Annual Review of Psychology, 51,* 377–404.

Wiehe, S. E., Garrison, M . M., Christakis, D. A., Ebel, B. E., & Rivara, F. P. (2005). A systematic review of school-based smoking prevention trials with long-term follow-up. *Journal of Adolescent Health, 36,* 162–169.

Wiggins, J. S., & Pincus, A. L. (2002). Personality structure and the structure of personality disorders. In P. T. Costa, Jr., & T. A. Widiger (Eds.), *Personality disorders and the five-factor model of personality* (2nd ed.). Washington, DC: American Psychological Association.

Wiggins, J. S., & Trapnell, P. D. (1997). Personality structure: The return of the Big Five. In R. Hogan, J. A. Johnson, & S. Briggs (Eds.), *Handbook of personality psychology.* San Diego: Academic Press.

Williams, D. R. (1968). The structure of response rate. *Journal of the Experimental Analysis of Behavior, 11,* 251–258.

Williams, K., Harkins, S., & Latané, B. (1981). Identifiability as a deterrent to social loafing: Two cheering experiments. *Journal of Personality and Social Psychology, 40,* 303–311.

Williams, T. M., & Boyes, M. C. (1986). Television-viewing patterns and use of other media. In T. M. Williams (Ed.), *The impact of television: A natural experiment in three communities.* Orlando, FL: Academic Press.

Williamson, S., Harpur, T. J., & Hare, R. D. (1991). Abnormal processing of affective words by psychopaths. *Psychophysiology, 28,* 260–273.

Wilson, E. O. (1975). *Sociobiology: The new synthesis.* Cambridge, MA: Harvard University Press.

Wilson, R. S., Mendes de Leon, C. F., Barnes, L. L., Schneider, J. A., Bienias, J. L., Evans, D. A., & Bennett, D. A. (2002). Participation in cognitively stimulating activities and risk of incident Alzheimer Disease. *Journal of the American Medical Association, 287,* 742–748.

Wilson, T. D., & Gilbert, D. T. (2003). Affective forecasting. In M. P. Zanna (Ed.), *Advances in experimental social psychology* (Vol. 35, pp. 345–411). San Diego: Academic Press.

Winkler, I., & Cowan, N. (2005). From sensory to long-term memory evidence from auditory memory reactivation studies. *Experimental Psychology, 52,* 3–20.

Winn, M. (2002). *The plug-in drug: Television, computers, and family life.* New York: Penguin.

Wise, E. A., Price, D. D., Myers, C. D., Heft, M. W., & Robinson, M. E. (2002). Gender role expectations of pain: Relationship to experimental pain perception. *Pain, 96(3),* 335–342.

Woerner, P. L., & Guze, S. B. (1968). A family and marital study of hysteria. *British Journal of Psychiatry, 114,* 161–168.

Wolpe, J. (1958). *Psychotherapy by reciprocal inhibition.* Stanford, CA: Stanford University Press.

Wood, D. L., Sheps, S. G., Elveback, L. R., & Schirder, A. (1984). Cold pressor test as a predictor of hypertension. *Hypertension, 6,* 301–306.

Wood, R. M., & Gustafson, G. E. (2001). Infant crying and adults' anticipated caregiving responses: Acoustic and contextual influences. *Child Development, 72,* 1287–1300.

Wood, W. (2000). Attitude change: Persuasion and social influence. *Annual Review of Psychology, 51,* 539–570.

Wood, W., & Eagly, A. H. (2002). A cross-cultural analysis of the behavior of women and men: Implications for the origins of sex differences. *Psychological Bulletin, 128,* 699–727.

Woodall, K. L., & Matthews, K. A. (1993). Changes in and stability of hostile characteristics: Results from a 4-year longitudinal study of children. *Journal of Personality and Social Psychology, 63,* 491–499.

Woods, S. C., Seeley, R. J., Porte, D., Jr., & Schwartz, M. W. (1998). Signals that regulate food intake and energy homeostasis. *Sciences, 280,* 1378–1383.

Woodworth, R. S., & Schlosberg, H. (1954). *Experimental psychology.* New York: Holt, Rinehart and Winston.

Woody, E., & Sadler, P. (1998). On reintegrating dissociated theories: Comment on Kirsch and Lynn (1998). *Psychological Bulletin, 123,* 192–197.

Worchel, F. F., Aaron, L. L., & Yates, D. F. (1990). Gender bias on the Thematic Apperception Test. *Journal of Personality Assessment, 55,* 593–602.

World Health Organization. (2003). *The World Health Report 2003—Shaping the future.* Retrieved April 23, 2004, http://www.who.int/en/.

Wu, H., Wang, J., Cacioppo, J. T., Glaser, R., Kiecold-Glaser, J. K., & Malarkey, W. B. (1999). Chronic stress associated with spousal caregiving of patients with Alzheimer's dementia is associated with down regulation of B-lymphocyte CH mRNA. *Journals of Gerontology Series A–Biological Sciences & Medical Sciences, 54A(4),* M212–M215.

Wu, J. C., & Bunney, W. E. (1990). The biological basis of an antidepressant response to sleep deprivation and relapse: Review and hypothesis. *American Journal of Psychiatry, 147,* 14–21.

Wyer, R. R., Jr., & Srull, T. K. (Eds.). (1994). *Handbook of social cognition* (2nd ed.). Hillsdale, NJ: Erlbaum.

Yalch, R. F. (1991). Memory in a jingle jungle: Music as a mnemonic device in communicating advertising slogans. *Journal of Applied Psychology, 76,* 268–275.

Yarmey, A. D. (2003). Eyewitness identification: Guidelines and recommendations for identification procedures in the United States and in Canada. *Canadian Psychology, 44,* 181–189.

Yates, W. R., Perry, P., & Murray, S. (1992). Aggression and hostility in anabolic steroid users. *Biological Psychiatry, 31,* 1232–1234.

Yi, H., Williams, G. D., & Smothers, B. A. (2004*). Surveillance Report #69: Trends in alcohol-related fatal traffic crashes, United States, 1977–2002.* Bethesda, MD: National Institute on Alcohol Abuse and Alcoholism, Division of Epidemiology and Prevention Research.

Young, A., Stokes, M., & Crowe, M. (1984). Size and strength of the quadriceps muscles of old and young women. *European Journal of Clinical Investigation, 14,* 282–287.

Young, M. C. (1998). *The Guinness book of world records.* New York: Bantam Books.

Youniss, J., & Smollar, J. (1985). *Adolescent relations with mothers, fathers, and friends.* Chicago: University of Chicago Press.

Zachrisson, O. C. G., Balldin, J., Ekman, R., Naesh, O., Rosengren, L., Agren, H., & Blennow, K. (2000). No evident neuronal damage after electroconvulsive therapy. *Psychiatry Research, 96,* 157–165.

Zajonc, R. B. (1965). Social facilitation. *Science, 149,* 269–274.

Zajonc, R. B. (1968). Attitudinal effects of mere exposure. *Journal of Personality and Social Psychology, Monograph Supplement, 9,* 1–27.

Zanna, M. P., & Rempel, J. K. (1988). Attitudes: A new look at an old concept. In D. Bar-Tal & A. W. Kruglanski (Eds.), *The social psychology of knowledge.* Cambridge, UK: Cambridge University Press.

Zaslow, M. J. (1991). Variation in child care quality and its implications for children. *Journal of Social Issues, 47,* 125–138.

Zatorre, R. J., Bouffard, M., Ahad, P., & Belin, P. (2002). Where is "where" in the human auditory cortex? *Nature Neuroscience, 5,* 905–909.

Zatrick, D. F., & Lu, F. G. (1991). The ethnic/minority focus unit as a training site in transcultural psychiatry. *Academic Psychiatry, 15,* 218–225.

Zhong, L. J., Goldberg, M. S., Parent, M. E., & Hanley, J. A. (2000). Exposure to environmental tobacco smoke and the risk of lung cancer: A meta-analysis. *Lung Cancer, 27,* 3–18.

Zhu, S., Melcer, T., Sun, J., Rosbrook, B., & Pierce, J. P. (2000). Smoking cessation with and without assistance: A population-based analysis. *Ameri-can Journal of Preventive Medicine, 18(4),* 305–311.

Zihl, J., von Cramon, D., Mai, N., & Schmid, C. (1991). Disturbance of movement vision after bilateral posterior brain damage: Further evidence and follow-up observations. *Brain, 114,* 2235–2252.

Zipursky, R. B., Lambe, E. K., Kapur, S., & Mikulis, D. J. (1998). Cerebral gray matter volume deficits in first episode psychosis. *Archives of General Psychiatry, 55,* 540–546.

Zola, D. (1984). Redundancy and word perception during reading. *Perception and Psychophysics, 36,* 277–284.

Zuckerman, B., & Brown, E. R. (1993). Maternal substance abuse and infant development. In C. H. Zeanah, Jr. (Ed.), *Handbook of infant mental health.* New York: Guilford Press.

Zuckerman, M. (1991). *Psychobiology of personality.* Cambridge: Cambridge University Press.

Zurif, E. G. (1990). Language and the brain. In D. N. Osherson & H. Lasnik (Eds.), *Language: An invitation to cognitive science. Vol. 1.* Cambridge, MA: MIT Press.

Zvolsky, P., Jansky, L., Vyskocilova, J., & Grof, P. (1981). Effects of psychotropic drugs on hamster hibernation: Pilot study. *Progress in Neuropsychopharmacology, 5,* 599–602.

Photo Credits

Page ii, Pablo Picasso, "Three Musicians," Fountainebleu, Summer 1921. Oil on canvas, 6'7" x 7'3 3/4". Mrs. Simon Guggenheim Fund (55.1949). Photograph © The Museum of Modern Art/Licensed by Scala/Art Resource, NY. © 2007 Estate of Pablo Picasso/Artists Rights Society, ARS, New York.

Chapter 1

Page 2, © Diana Ong/SuperStock; p. 4, Courtesy of Deborah Wearing; p. 5 top, © Alfredo Estrella/AFP/Getty Images; p. 5 bottom, © SW Productions/Photodisc/Getty Images; p. 10, © Kurt Scholz/SuperStock; p. 11, © Mary Evans Picture Library/The Image Works; pp. 13, 14, 15, National Library of Medicine; p. 17 left, The Ferdinand Hamburger, Jr. Archives of the Johns Hopkins University; p. 17 right, Archives of the History of American Psychology-The University of Akron; p. 18, © Bettmann/CORBIS; p. 19 both, Archives of the History of American Psychology-The University of Akron; p. 21, McGill University, PR000387/McGill University Archives.

Chapter 2

Page 24, © Diana Ong/SuperStock; p. 26, © Michael Rosenfeld/Getty Images; p. 29 top left, Copyright © 2005 by the American Psychological Association. Reprinted with permission; p. 29 bottom left, © Charles Votaw; p. 29 right, Courtesy NASA/JPL-Caltech; p. 30, © Michael Nichols/National Geographic Image Collection; p. 31, © Spencer Grant/PhotoEdit; p. 40, © David Young Wolff/PhotoEdit; p. 41, © Alexander Klimchuk/ITAR-TASS/Landov; p. 44, © Jonathan Selig/Getty Images; p. 45 left, © Anders Ryman/CORBIS; p. 45 right, Center for International Earth Science Information Network (CIESIN), Columbia University; and Centro Internacional de Agricultura Tropical (CIAT). 2005. Gridded Population of the World Version 3 (GPWv3): Population Density Grids. Palisades, NY: Socioeconomic Data and Applications Center (SEDAC), Columbia University. Available at http://sedac.ciesin.columbia.edu/gpw. (2006); p. 51, © Kevin Fleming/CORBIS.

Chapter 3

Page 54, © Diana Ong/SuperStock; p. 56, © Bettmann/CORBIS; p. 58, © North Wind Picture Archives; p. 65 left, © John Reader/Photo Researchers, Inc.; p. 65 middle, © Hartmut Schwarzbach/Peter Arnold, Inc.; p. 65 right, © Thomas Pflaum/VISUM/The Image Works; p. 67 top, © CNRI/SPL/Photo Researchers, Inc.; p. 67 bottom, © David Phillips/Photo Researchers, Inc.; p. 70 both, © Breck P. Kent/Animals Animals/Earth Scenes; p. 72, © Will & Deni McIntyre/Photo Researchers, Inc.; p. 73, © Peter Cade/Getty Images; p. 76, © David Madison/Getty Images.

Chapter 4

Page 82, © Diana Ong/SuperStock; p. 97, © C. Allan Morgan/Peter Arnold, Inc.; p. 98 left, © Rick Gomez/CORBIS; p. 98 right, © Jack Fields/Photo Researchers, Inc.; p. 100, © Science Photo Library/Photo Researchers, Inc.

Chapter 5

Page 122, © Diana Ong/SuperStock; p. 128, © Andersen Ross/Getty Images; p. 134, © Dion Ogust/The Image Works; p. 136, © Bob Daemmrich/The Image Works; p. 137, © Monika Graff/The Image Works; p. 140, © Jess Stock/Getty Images; p. 142, © Bob Daemmrich/The Image Works; p. 143, © Chris Gardner/CP Photo Archive; p. 144, © L. Kolvoord/The Image Works.

Chapter 6

Page 154, © Diana Ong/SuperStock; p. 156, © AP/Wide World Photos; p. 157, © Digital Vision/Getty Images; p. 161, © Getty Images; p. 170 right, © Gary Yeowell/Getty Images; p. 176, © Joe Sohm/The Image Works; p. 183, © Michael Newman/PhotoEdit; p. 184, © Omikron/Photo Researchers, Inc.; p. 189, © AP/Wide World Photos.

Chapter 7

Page 192, © Diana Ong/SuperStock; p. 194, © Stockbyte/Getty Images; p. 203 left, © Colin Hawkins/Getty Images; p. 203 right, © Bill Foley/Landov; p. 216, © Kurt Scholz/SuperStock; p. 219, © CORBIS SYGMA; p. 222, M.C. Escher "Convex and Concave," 1955. Lithograph. © 2006 The M.C. Escher Company BV-the Netherlands. All rights reserved. www.mcescher.com. Photo © Art Resource, NY.

Chapter 8

Page 226, © Diana Ong/SuperStock; p. 230, © Chad Ehlers/Getty Images; p. 233, © Andersen Ross/Photodisc/Getty Images; p. 236, © AP/Wide World Photos; p. 237, © Steve Prezant/CORBIS; p. 240 left, © Mary Kate Denny/PhotoEdit; p. 240 right, © David Young-Wolff/PhotoEdit; p. 243, © First Image/The Image Works; p. 245 left, © Syracuse Newspapers/Jennifer Grimes/The Image Works; p. 245 right, © Ryan McVay/Getty Images; p. 252, © Jeff Greenberg/The Image Works; p. 253 left, © John Eastcott/Yva Momatiuk/Woodfin Camp & Associates; p. 253 top right, © Betty Press/Woodfin Camp & Associates; p. 253 bottom right, © Mark S. Wexler/Woodfin Camp & Associates; p. 255, © AP/Wide World Photos; p. 259, © Bob Daemmrich/PhotoEdit.

Chapter 9

Page 262, © Diana Ong/SuperStock; p. 265, © S. Lousada/Petit Format/Photo Researchers, Inc.; p. 270, © Erik de Castro/Reuters/CORBIS; p. 280, © AP/Wide World Photos; p. 282, © Adam Woolfitt/Woodfin Camp & Associates; p. 283, © Chris Noble; p. 287, Marc Chagall, "Winter Night in Vitebsk," 1948. Oil on canvas. © 2007 Artists Rights Society (ARS) New York/ADGP, Paris. Photo © SuperStock; p. 288, © Photodisc/Getty Images.

Chapter 10

Page 292, © Diana Ong/SuperStock; p. 294, © AP/Wide World Photos; p. 295, © Scott T. Smith/CORBIS; p. 302, © Own Franken/CORBIS; p. 305, © D. E. Cox/Getty Images; p. 306, © Nancy Sheehan Photography; p. 311, © Dorothy Littell Greco/The Image Works; p. 319, Courtesy of CNN.

Chapter 11

Page 322, © Diana Ong/SuperStock; p. 325, © Nicholas DeVore/Getty Images; p. 328, © Nigel Dickinson/Peter Arnold, Inc.; p. 337, © James Shaffer/PhotoEdit; p. 339, © George Steinmetz; p. 341, © EyeWire, Inc.; p. 350, © AP/Wide World Photos; p. 353, © Steve Mason/Photodisc/Getty Images.

Chapter 12

Page 356, © Diana Ong/SuperStock; p. 358, © Mark Richards/PhotoEdit; p. 360, © Neil Harding/Getty Images; p. 366, © The Copyright Group/SuperStock; p. 367, Steve Gordon © Dorling Kindersley; p. 371, © Will Hart; p. 375, © Michael Newman/PhotoEdit; p. 377, © Stockbyte; p. 381, © Robert Harbison; p. 383 left, © David Young-Wolff/PhotoEdit; p. 383 right, © Syracuse Newspapers/Gary Walts/The Image Works; p. 388, © Spencer Grant/PhotoEdit; p. 393, © Jeff Greenberg/PhotoEdit; p. 395, © Richard Hutchings/PhotoEdit; p. 397, © Ariel Skelley/CORBIS.

Chapter 13

Page 400, © Diana Ong/SuperStock; p. 409, © Anders Ryman/CORBIS; p. 420, © Mark C. Burnett/Photo Researchers, Inc.; p. 422 top, © Tom Walker/Stock Boston; p. 431, © Wayne Eastep/Getty Images; p. 434, © Peter Kramer/Getty Images.

Chapter 14

Page 436, © Diana Ong/SuperStock; p. 438 both, © D. Gorton; p. 441, © Michael Newman/PhotoEdit; p. 444, © Myrleen Ferguson Cate/PhotoEdit; p. 449, © Mark Richards/PhotoEdit; p. 451, © Soren Hald/Getty Images; p. 457, © Jim Arbogast/Photodisc/Getty Images; p. 458, © Nancy Sheehan/PhotoEdit; p. 462, © Philippe Halsman/Magnum Photos; p. 463, © SW Productions/Brand X Pictures/Jupiterimages; p. 468, © Erik Lesser/Reuters/Landov; p. 469, © Pete Saloutos/CORBIS.

Chapter 15

Page 472, © Diana Ong/SuperStock; p. 474, © Don Mason/CORBIS; p. 475, © Digital Vision/Getty Images; p. 477, © Keren Su/Getty Images; p. 480, © AP/Wide World Photos; p. 481, © Gary Conner/PhotoEdit; p. 484, © Alex Wong/Getty Images; p. 489, © Scott Houston/CORBIS; p. 492, © Peter M. Fisher/CORBIS; p. 494, © AP/Wide World Photos; p. 497 both, Copyright 1965 by Stanley Milgram. From the film *Obedience*, distributed by Penn State Media Sales. Courtesy of Alexandra Milgram; p. 501, © Patrick Molnar/Getty Images; p. 503, © Ken Chernus/Getty Images.

Chapter 16

Page 508, © Diana Ong/SuperStock; p. 511, © Robert Frerck/Woodfin Camp & Associates; p. 512, © G. Baden/zefa/CORBIS; p. 521, © Allen Russell/Index Stock Imagery; p. 523, © AP/Wide World Photos; p. 525, © Rick Wilking/Reuters/Landov; p. 529, © AP/Wide World Photos; p. 530, © Andrejs Liepins/Photo Researchers, Inc.; p. 537, © Eye Wire Inc.; p. 538, © Jena Cumbo/Getty Images; p. 539, © Ken Karp/Pearson Education/PH College.

Chapter 17

Page 542, © Diana Ong/SuperStock; p. 545, © Jed Jacobsohn/Getty Images; p. 547, © Betty Press/Woodfin Camp & Associates; p. 548, © Larry Dale Gordon/Getty Images; p. 551, © Nancy Sheehan/PhotoEdit; p. 553, © Bill Horsman/Stock Boston; p. 556, © Arlene Collins/The Image Works; p. 561, © John Eastcott/Yva Momatiuk/Woodfin Camp & Associates, Inc.; p. 563, © Phil Snell/CP Photo Archive; p. 574, © Zave Smith/CORBIS.

Chapter 18

Page 580, © Diana Ong/SuperStock; p. 587, © AP/Wide World Photos; p. 589, © Michael Rougier/Life Magazine/Getty Images; p. 591, © Jerry Howard/Stock Boston; p. 594, © Michael Newman/PhotoEdit; p. 600, © Frank Pedrick/The Image Works; p. 603, © Bruce Hands/Getty Images.

Name Index

Subject Index